FEMINIST PERSPECTIVES ON LAW
LAW'S ENGAGEMENT WITH THE
FEMALE BODY

AUSTRALIA
LBC Information Services
Sydney

CANADA and USA
Carswell
Toronto ● Ontario

NEW ZEALAND
Brooker's
Auckland

SINGAPORE and MALAYSIA
Thomson Information (S.E. Asia)
Singapore

FEMINIST PERSPECTIVES ON LAW
LAW'S ENGAGEMENT WITH THE FEMALE BODY

JO BRIDGEMAN
AND
SUSAN MILLNS

LONDON
SWEET & MAXWELL
1998

Published in 1998 by
Sweet & Maxwell of
100 Avenue Road, London NW3 3PF
Typeset by Wyvern 21 Ltd.
Printed in Great Britain by Clays Ltd, St. Ives plc

No natural forests were destroyed to make this product;
only farmed timber was used and replanted

British Library Cataloguing in Publication Data

A CIP catalogue record for this book
is available from the British Library

ISBN 0421–597–50X

ACKNOWLEDGMENTS

For their willingness to discuss issues arising from this project, our thanks go to Bernard Jackson, Anne Morris, Sue Nott and Sally Sheldon. We would also like to thank Rachel Chapman for her invaluable research assistance and for commenting upon the whole of the text.

Grateful acknowledgment is made to the following authors and publishers for permission to quote from their works:

All England Law Reports. Reproduced with permission of Butterworths.

Allen, H., "Rendering them harmless: the Professional Portrayal of Women Charged with Serious Violent Crimes" in P. Carlen & A. Worral (eds), *Gender, Crime and Justice* (1987). Reproduced with permission of Oxford University Press.

Arney, W. R., "Power and Profession of Obstetrics" (University of Chicago Press, 1982).

Arthur, S. L., "The Norplant Prescription: Birth Control, Women Control or Crime Control" Originally published in (1992) 40 U.C.L.A. L. Rev. Copyright 1992, The Regents of the University of California. All Rights Reserved.

Atoki, M., "Should Female Circumcision Continue to be Banned? (1995) 3 *Feminist Legal Studies*. Reproduced with permission of Deborah Charles Publications.

Barton, L. J., "The Story of Marital Rape" (1992) 108 L.Q.R. 260. Sweet & Maxwell Ltd.

Bell, C., "Casde Note: Planned Parenthood of Southeastern Pennsylvania *et al.* v. Robert Casey *et al.*" (1993) 1 *Feminist Legal Studies*. Reproduced with permission of Deborah Charles Publications.

Beveridge, F. & Mullally, S. "International Human Rights and Body Politics" in J. Bridgeman & S. Millns (eds), *Law and Body Politics: Regulating the Female Body* (Dartmouth Press, Ashgate Publishing Group, 1995).

Bibbings, L., "Female Circumcision: Mutilation or Modification?" in J. Bridgeman & S. Millns (eds), *Law and Body Politics: Regulating the Female Body* (Dartmouth Press, Ashgate Publishing Group, 1995).

Bordo, S., *Unbearable Weight: Feminism, Western Culture and the Body* (University of California Press, 1993).

Bottomley, A., "What is Happening in the Family? A Feminist Critique of Conciliation" in J. Brophy & C. Smart (eds), *Women in Law: Exploration in Law, Family and Sexuality* (Routledge, 1984).

Brazier, M. & Bridge, C., "Coercion and Caring: Analysing Adolescent Autonomy" (1996) 16 *Legal Studies* 84. Butterworths.

Bridgeman, J., "Old Enough to Know Best?" (1993) *Legal Studies* 69. Butterworths.

British Medical Journal for (1984) 287 B.M.J. 64.

Clarke, L., "Abortion: A Rights Issue?" in R. Lee & D. Morgan *Birthrights: Law and Ethics at the Beginning of Life* (Routledge, 1989).

Conaghan, J., "Equity rushes in where tort fears to tread: the Court of Appeal Decision in *Burris v. Azadini*" (1996) 4(2) *Feminist Legal Studies*. Reproduced with permission of Deborah Charles Publications.

Conaghan, J., "Gendered Harms and the Law of Tort: Remedying (Sexual) harassment" (1996) O.J.L.S. 407. Reproduced with permission of Oxford University Press.

Croall, H., *Target Women: women's victimisation and white collar crime* (University of Wales Press).

Cunningham, R. L., "Legislating on Human Fertilization and Embryology in the United Kingdom" (1991) 12 Stat. L.R. 214.

Daly, M., *Gyn/Ecology: The Metaethics of Radical Feminism* (The Women's Press, 1991).

Davis, K., *Reshaping the Female Body: The Dilemma of Cosmetic Surgery* (Routledge, 1995).

de Gama, K., "Commentary on *Re S*" [1993] *Journal of Social Welfare and Family Law* 147. Routledge.

Diduck, A., "Legislating Ideologies of Motherhood" *Social and Legal Studies*, Vol. 2, 461. Reproduced by permission of Sage Publications Ltd and the Author.

Dine, J. & Watt, B., "Sexual Harassment: Moving Away from Discrimination" (1995) 58 M.L.R. 58. Blackwell Publishing.

Docherty, C., "Female Offenders" in McLeans & Burrows (eds), *The Legal Relevance of Gender*. Macmillan Press Ltd.

Douglas, G., *Law, Fertility and Reproduction* (Sweet & Maxwell, 1991).

Douglas, G., "The Intention to be a Parent and the Making of Mothers" (1994) 57 M.L.R. 636. Blackwell Publishers.

Douglas, G., Hebenton, B. & Thomas, T., "The Right to Found a Family" (1992) *New Law Journal* 537. Butterworths.

Downer, C., "Through the Speculum" in R. Arditti, R. Duelli & S. Minden (eds), *Test-Tube Women—What Future for Motherhood?* (Pandora Press, 1984).

Duncan, S., "Disrupting the Surface Order and Innocence: Towards a Theory of Sexuality and the Law" (1994) 2 *Feminist Legal Studies* 3. Reproduced with permission of Deborah Charles Publications.

Duncan, S., "Law as Literature: Deconstructing the Legal Text" (1994) 5(1) *Law and Critique*. Reproduced with permission of Deborah Charles Publications.

Duncan, S., "Law's Sexual Disciple: Visibility, Violence and Consent" (1995) 22 *Journal of Law and Society*. Blackwell Publishers.

Easton, "Pornography as incitement to racial hatred" (1995) 3 *Feminist Legal Studies* 89. Reproduced with permission of Deborah Charles Publications.

Edwards, "Battered Women Who Kill" (1990) *New Law Journal* 1380. Butterworths.

Eekelar, J. M. & Dingwall, R. W., "Some Legal Issues in Obstetric Practice", *Journal of Social Welfare Law*. Blackwell Publishing.

Family Court Reporter, *South West Hertfordshire Health Authority v. KB* (1994) 2 F.C.R. 1051. Reproduced with permission of Butterworths.

"Feminist Discourse, Moral Values and the Law—A Conversation" (1985) 34 *Buffalo Law Review* 11.

Ferguson, P., "Liability for Pharmaceutical Products: A Critique of the 'Learned Intermediary' Rule" (1992) 12 O.J.L.S. 59. Reproduced with permission of Oxford University Press.

Flynn, L., "Interpretation and Disputed Accounts in Sexual Harassment Cases: *Stewart v. Cleveland Guest (Engineering) Ltd*" (1996) 4 *Feminist Legal Studies*. Reproduced with permission of Deborah Charles Publications.

Fox, M., "Legal Responses to Battered Women Who Kill" in J. Bridgeman & S. Millns, *Law and Body Politics: Regulating the Female Body* (Dartmouth Press, Ashgate Publishing Group, 1995).

Freeman, M.D.A., "Sterlising the mentally handicapped" in M.D.A. Freeman (ed.), *Medicine, Ethics and the Law* (Sweet & Maxwell, 1988).

Freeman, M.D.A., "After Warnock—Whither the Law" [1986] *Current Legal Problems* 33.

Frug, M. J., "A Postmodern Feminist Legal Manifesto (An Unfinished Draft)" (1992) 105 *Harvard Law Review* 1045.

Gibson, S., "The Discourse of Sex/War: Thoughts on Catherine MacKinnon's 1993 Oxford Amnesty Lecture" (1993) 1 *Feminist Legal Studies*. Deborah Charles Publications.

Gibson, S., "The Structure of the Veil" (1989) 52 M.L.R. 420. Blackwell Publishers.

Gilligan, C., *In a Different Voice: Psychological Theory and Women's Development* (Harvard University Press, 1982).

Gorea, G., "Sex Discrimination: A Question of Gyncide" in *Gyn/Ecology: The Metaethics of Radical Feminism* (The Womens Press, 1991).

Grubb, A., (1994) Med. L. Rev. 208.

Gunning, "Arrogant Perception, World-travelling and Multi-cultural feminism: The case of female genital Services" (1991–92) 23 *Columbian Human Rights Law Review* 189.

Harding, L. M., "The Debate on Surrogate Motherhood: The Current Situation, Some Arguments and Issues; Questions Facing Law and Policy" (1984) *Journal of Social Welfare and Family Law* 37.

Harpwood, V., *Legal Issues in Obstetrics* (Dartmouth Press, Ashgate Publishing Group, 1986).

Heidensohn, F., *Women and Crime* (Routledge, 1985).

HMSO for various crown and parliamentary copyright material.

Hewson, B., "Sexual Harassment at the Bar: A Recent Problem?" (1985) *New Law Journal* 1514. Butterworths.

Hogan, B., "Mrs Payne's Punishment" (1980) *Criminal Law Review* 400. Sweet & Maxwell Ltd.

Howe, A., "The Problem of Privatized Injuries: Feminist Strategies for Litigation" in M. A. Fineman and N. S. Thomadsen (eds), *At the Boundaries of Law: Feminism and the Power of Law* (Routledge, 1991).

Incorporated Council of Law reporting for England and Wales for various extracts from The Law Reports.

The Independent, "Woman who Killed Baby is Freed", News Item: September 1, 1995. The Independent Newspaper Publishing Plc.

Jackson, E., "The Problem with Pornography: A Critical Survey of the Current

Debate" (1995) 3 *Feminist Legal Studies*. Reproduced with permission of Deborah Charles Publications.

Johnson, D. E., "The Creation of Fetal Rights: Conflicts with Women's Constitutional Rights to Liberty, Privacy and Equal Protection" *The Yale Law Journal*, Vol. 95. Reprinted by permission of the Yale Journal Co. and Fred B. Rothman Co.

Jordans for various extracts from the Family Law Reports.

Kappeler, "The International Slave Trade in Women, or, Procurers, Pimps and Prostitutes" (1990) *Law & Critique* 219. Reproduced with permission of Deborah Charles Publications.

Kelly, J., "Nevada Vice" (1993) *New Law Journal* 948. Butterworths.

Kennedy, I., *Treat Me Right: Essays in Medical Law and Ethics* (Clarendon Press, 1992). Reproduced with permission of Oxford University Press.

Keywood, K., "Sterilising the Woman with Learning Disabilities—Possibilities for a Feminist Ethic of Decision-making" in Feminist Legal Research Unit (University of Liverpool, *Women's Access to Health Care: Law, Society and Culture* (Working Paper No. 4) (1996).

Keywood, K., "Sterilising the Woman with Learning Difficulties—In Her Best Interests" in J. Bridgeman & S. Millns (eds), *Law and Body Politics: Regulating the Female Body* (Dartmouth Press, Ashgate Publishing Group, 1995).

Kingdom, E., "Body Politics and Rights" in J. Bridgeman and S. Millns, *Law and Body Politics: Regulating the Female Body* (Dartmouth Press, Ashgate Publishing Group, 1995).

Kingdom, E., *What's Wrong With Rights? Problems for Feminist Politics of Law* (Edinburgh University Press, 1991).

Lacey, N., "Theory into Practice? Pornography and the public/private Dichotomy" in A. Bottomley & J. Conaghan (eds), *Feminist Theory and Legal Strategy* (Blackwell Publishers).

Lees, S., *Ruling Passions: Sexual Violence, Reputation and the Law* (Open University Press, 1997).

Leeson, J. & Gray, J., *Women and Medicine* (Tavistock Publications, 1978).

Leng, R., "Imprisonment for Prostitutes" (1992) *New Law Journal* 270. Butterworths.

Lewis, J. & Cannell, F., "The Politics of Motherhood in the 1980s: Warnock, Gillick and Feminists" (1986) 13 *Journal of Law and Society*. Blackwell Publishers.

Leonard, A., "Remedies for Sexual Harassment" (1991) *New Law Journal* 1514. Butterworths.

Loenen, T., "Comparative Legal Feminist Scholarship and the Importance of a Contextual Approach to Concepts and Strategies: The Case of the Equality Debate" (1995) 3 *Feminist Legal Studies* 71. Reproduced with permission of Deborah Charles Publications.

Mackay, I. & Bradshaw, J., "Skirting Around Sexual Harassment" (1995) *New Law Journal* 338. Butterworths.

MacKinnon, C. A., "Difference and Dominance: On Sex Discrimination" in *Feminism Unmodified: Discourses on Life and Law* (Harvard University Press, 1987).

MacKinnon, C. A., "Feminism, Marxism, Method and the State: An Agenda for Theory" (1981–1982) 7 *Signs* 515.

MacKinnon, C. A.; "Feminism, Marxism, Method and the State: Toward Feminist Jurisprudence" (1983) 8 *Signs* 635.

MacKinnon, C. A., "Privacy v. Equality: beyond Roe v. Wade" in *Feminism Unmodified: Discourses on Life and Law* (Harvard University Press, 1987).

MacKinnon, C. A., *Toward a Feminist Theory of State* (Harvard University Press, 1989).

MacKinnon, C. A., "Francis Biddle's Sister: Pornography, Civil Rights and Speech" in *Feminism Unmodified: Discourses on Life and Law* (Harvard University Press, 1987).

McColgan, A., "Common Law and the Relevance of Sexual History Evidence" (1996) 16 O.J.L.S. 275. Reproduced with permission of Oxford University Press.

McColgan, A., "In Defence of Battered Women Who Kill" (1993) O.J.L.S. 508. Reproduced with permission of Oxford University Press.

McKNorrie, K., *Family Planning Practice and the Law* (Dartmouth Press, Ashgate Publishing Group, 1991).

Mahood, L., *The Magdelenes: Prostitutes in the Nineteenth Century* (Routledge, 1990).

Majury, D., "Strategizing in Equality" in M. A. Fineman & N. S. Thomasden (eds), *At the Boundaries of Law: Feminism and Legal Theory* (Routledge, 1991).

Mason, J. K., *Medico-Legal Aspects of Reproduction and Parenthood* (Dartmouth Press, Ashgate Publishing Group, 1990).

Masson, J., "Re W: appealing from the golden cage" (1993) 5 *Journal of Child Law*. Tolley Publications.

Medical Law Review, Commentary on Attorney-General's Reference (No. 3 of 1994) (1995) Med. L. Rev. 302.

Medical Law Review, Johnson v. Calvert (Commentary) (1994) Med. L. Rev. 239. Reproduced with permission of Oxford University Press.

Millns, S., "Making 'social judgments that go beyond the purely medical': The Reproductive Revolution and Access to Fertility Treatment Services" in J. Bridgeman & S. Millns (eds), *Law and Body Politics: Regulating the Female Body* (Dartmouth Press, Ashgate Publishing Group, 1995).

Minson, J. P., "Social Theory and Legal Argument: Catherine MacKinnon on Sexual Harassment" (1991) 19 *International Journal of the Sociology of Law 355.*

Moody, S., "Images of Women: Sentencing in Sexual Assault Cases in Scotland" in J. Bridgeman & Millns (eds), *Law and Body Politics: Regulating the Female Body* (Dartmouth Press, Ashgate Publishing Group, 1995).

Morgan, D. & Lee, R., *Blackstone's Guide to the Human Fertilisation and Embryology Act 1990* (Blackstone Press Ltd, 1991).

Morgan, D., "Making Motherhood Male: Surrogacy and the Moral Economy of Women" (1985) 12 *Journal of Law and Society* 219. Blackwell Publishers.

Morgan, D., "Who to Be or Not to Be: The Surrogacy Story" (1986) 49 M.L.R. 358. Blackwell Publishers.

Morgan, K., "Gender, Rites and Rights: The Bio-politics of Beauty and Fertility" in Summer, L. W. & Boyle, J., *Philosphical Perspectives in Bioethics* (University of Toronto Press).

Morris, A. E. & Nott, S. M., *Working Women and the Law: Equality and Discrimination in Theory and Practice* (Routledge, 1991).

Morris, A. & Wilczyski, A., "Rocking the Cradle: Mothers Who Kill their Children" in H. Birch (ed), *Moving Targets: Women, Murder and Representation* (Basic Books, Virago Press).

Mossman, M. J., "Feminism and Legal Method: The Differences it Makes" in M. A. Fineman & N. S. Thomasden (eds), *At the Boundaries of Law: Feminism and Legal Theory* (Routledge, 1991).

Nicolson, D., "Telling Tales: gender Discrimation, gender Construction and Battered Women Who Kill" (1953) 3 *Feminist Legal Studies.* Reproduced with permission of Deborah Charles Publications.

Nicholson, D. & Sanghvi, R., "Battered Women and Provocation: The Implications of *R. v. Ahluwalia*" (1993) *Criminal Law Review* 728. Sweet & Maxwell Ltd.

Nicholson, D. & Sanghvi, R., "More Justice for Battered Women" (1995) *New Law Journal* 1122. Butterworths.

Noonan, S., "Battered Women Syndrome: Shifting the Parameters of Criminal Defences or (Re)inscribing the familiar?" in A. Bottomley & J. Conaghan (eds), *Feminist Perspectives on the Foundational Subjects of Law* (Cavendish Publishing Ltd, 1996).

O'Donovan, K., "Defences for Battered Women Who Kill" (1991) 18 *Journal of Law and Society* 219. Blackwell Publishers.

O'Donovan, K., "Law's Knowledge: The Judge, The Expert, the Battered Woman and her Syndrome" (1993) 20 *Journal of Law and Society*. Blackwell Publishers.

O'Donovan, K., "The Medicalisation of Infanticide" (1984) *Criminal Law Review* 259. Sweet & Maxwell Ltd.

Orbach, S., *Hunger-Strike: The Anorectic's Struggle as a Metaphor for our Age* (Penguin, 1993).

Palmer, S., "Critical Perspectives on Women's Rights: The European Convention on Human Rights and Fundamental Freedoms" in A. Bottomley (ed.), *Feminist Perspectives on the Foundational Subjects of Law* (Cavendish Publishing, 1996).

Pollock, S., "Refusing to take Women Seriously: 'Side Effects' and the Politics of Contraception" in R. Arditti, R. Duelli & S. Minden (eds), *Test-Tube Women—What Future for Motherhood?* (Pandora Press, 1984).

Pollock, S., "Sex and the Contraceptive Act" in H. Homans (ed.), *The Sexual Politics of Reproduction* (Gower Press, Ashgate Publishing Group, 1985).

Radford, L., "Pleading for Time: Justice for Battered Women Who Kill" in H. Burch (ed.), *Moving Targets: Women, Murder and Representation* (Basic Books, Virago Press).

Rakusen, J., "Depro-Provera: The Extent of the Problem. A Case Study in the Politics of birth control" in H. Robertson (ed.), *Women, Health and Reproduction* (Routledge & Kegan Paul, 1981).

Roach Anelu, S. L., "Critiquing the Law: Themes and·Dilemmas in Anglo-American Feminist Legal Theory" (1992) 19 *Journal of Law and Society* 423. Blackwell Publishers.

Roberts, S., "Warnock and Surrogate Motherhood: Sentiment or Argument?" in P. Bryne (ed.), *Rights and Wrongs in Medicine* (King Edward's Hospital Fund for London, 1986). Reproduced with permission of Oxford University Press.

Rubenstein, M., "Pin-ups and Sexual Harassment" (September/October 1994) 57 *Equal Opportunities Review* 24.

Sandland, R., "Between 'Truth' and 'Difference': Poststructuralism, Law and the

Power of Feminism" (1995) 3 *Feminist Legal Studies*. Reproduced with permission of Deborah Charles Publications.

Schneider, E. M. "The Dialectics of Rights and Politics: Perspectives from the Women's Movement' in M. A. Fineman & N. S. Thomasden (eds), *At the Boundaries of Law: Feminism and Legal Theory* (Routledge, 1991).

Sheldon, S., "Subject Only to the Attitude of the Surgeon Concerned: The Judicial Protection of Medical Discretion" (1996) *Social & Legal Studies* 95. Reprinted by permission of Sage Publications Ltd and the Author.

Sheldon, S., "The Law of Abortion and the Politics of Medicalisation" in J. Bridgeman & S. Millns (eds), *Law and Body Politics: Regulating the Female Body* (Dartmouth Press, Ashgate Publishing Group, 1995).

Sheldon, S., "Who is the Mother to Make Judgment?: The Constructions of Woman in English Abortion Law" (1993) 1 *Feminist Legal Studies* 3. Reproduced with permission of Deborah Charles Publications.

Slack, T., "Female Circumcision: A Critical Appraisal" (1988) 10 *Human Rights Quarterly* 437. Reproduced with permission of the Johns Hopkins University Press.

Sloman, S., "Surrogacy Arrrangements Act 1985" (1985) 135 *New Law Journal* 978. Butterworths.

Smart, C., "Disruptive Bodies and Unruly Sex: The Regulation of Reproduction and Sexuality in the Nineteenth Century" in C. Smart (ed.) *Regulating Womanhood: Historical Essays on Marriage, Motherhood and Sexuality* (Routledge, 1992).

Smart, C., *Feminism and the Power of the Law* (Routledge, 1989).

Smart, C., "Law's Power, the Sexed Body and Feminist Discourse" (1990) 17(2) *Journal of Law and Society* 194. Blackwell Publishers.

Smart, C. & Brophy, J., "Locating Law: A Discussion of the Place of Law in Feminist Politics" in J. Brophy & C. Smart (eds), *Women in Law: Exploration in Law, Family and Sexuality* (Routledge, 1984).

Smith, P., "On Equality: Justice, Discrimination and Equal Treatment" in P. Smith (ed.), *Feminist Jurisprudence* (1993). Reproduced with permission of Oxford University Press.

Sohrab, J. A., "Avoiding the 'Exquisite Trap': A Critical Look at the Equal Treatment/ Special Treatment Debate in law" (1993) 1 *Feminist Legal Studies*. Reproduced with permission of Deborah Charles Publications.

Stewart, Dobbin & Gatowski, "Definition of Rape: Victim, Police and Prosecutors" (1996) 4 *Feminist Legal Studies* 160. Reproduced with permission of Deborah Charles Publications.

Tong, R., *Feminist Thought: A Comprehensive Introduction* (Unwin Hyam, 1989).

Walsh, V., "Contraception: The Growth of a Technology" in The Brighton Women and Science Group, *Alice Through the Microscope* (Virago Press, Ashgate Publishing Group, 1980).

Wells, C., "Battered Woman Syndrome and Defences to Homicide: Where Now?" (1994) 14 *Legal Studies* 266. Butterworths.

Wells, C., "Domestic Violence and Self-Defence" (1990) *New Law Journal* 127. Butterworths.

Wells, C., "Patients, Consent and Criminal Law" *Journal of Social Welfare and Family Law* 65. Routledge.

Widdet, C. & Thompson, M., "Justifying Treatment and Other Stories" (1997) 1 *Feminist Legal Studies*. Reproduced with permission of Deborah Charles Publications.

Wilczynski, *Child-Killing by Parents: Social, Legal and Gender Issues* (University of Wales Press).

While every care has been taken to establish and acknowledge copyright, and copyright owners, the publishers tender their apologies for any accidental infringement. They would be pleased to come to a suitable arrangement with the rightful owners in each case.

CONTENTS

SECTION ONE
THEMES IN FEMINIST LEGAL THOUGHT

SECTION FOUR
OFFENSIVE BODIES

TABLE OF CASES

TABLE OF STATUTES

TABLE OF STATUTORY INSTRUMENTS

GENERAL INTRODUCTION

As the title of this book indicates, its purpose is to offer its readers the opportunity to familiarise themselves with a collection of materials thereby facilitating a discussion of feminist perspectives upon law. The format is intended to introduce readers to a number of texts, comprising legal cases, other primary legal sources and a range of non-legal materials.[1] These texts are interwoven with explanation and commentary with the aim of guiding the reader through the legal issues addressed in the book and highlighting recurring themes and differing perspectives.

1. Why feminist perspectives?

The use of the term "feminist perspectives" in the title is to indicate our own perspectives as authors, and also those perspectives expressed in some of the extracts used. Other extracts are not particularly "feminist" and are included to provide balance, or to illustrate reaction to, or further explanation of, a particular feminist position.

The term "perspectives" (in the plural) is used to indicate to the reader that not all feminists think alike. It cannot be said that feminist perspectives on law have developed in a clear-cut fashion so that there exists a definite and identifiable "feminist" angle on any particular issue at any one time. Much of the subject matter covered in this book has generated substantial debate amongst feminists themselves. This reader is designed to uncover some of these divergences of opinion, as well as those between feminists and non-feminists. What will become apparent, however, is that what many of the extracts do have in common is a critical approach to law, taken from a standpoint which is woman-centred.

The feminist perspectives which we offer are upon "law". Again, it is possible to attribute to this word a whole host of meanings. Firstly, our perspectives gaze upon both statute law and common law. These are primarily those of England and Wales, although we do, occasionally, make reference to the laws of other jurisdictions where this may particularly inform the debate and we refer to the influence of international and European laws (those of the European Union and the European Convention on Human Rights) where appropriate. Beyond positive law we also offer perspectives on aspects of legal theory and law reform proposals, and on techniques of regulation, legal

---

[1] For reasons of space, these extracts have been reproduced largely without their original footnotes.

procedures, and other methods of constraint and control which may have an effect on the way in which women are perceived and processed through the legal system. In addition, we refer to techniques of legal interpretation and legal method which may influence the way in which women's experiences are transposed into the legal order.

Nonetheless, this book is not just intended to be of relevance to those with a legal background. We hope that it will provide perspectives to engage the interest of those involved in other disciplines, notably social and political sciences. It is not our intention to perpetuate the myth of law's inaccessibility to all but the legally initiated. In this respect we would like to think that the collection will be of interest to a wide range of readers and sufficiently accessible to those with or without experience in law.

2. Why law's engagement with the female body?

In terms of legal substance, we make no attempt to provide a feminist critique of all aspects of law. We are selective, for reasons of space, interest and expertise. We do not cover the general principles of contract law, tort law, property law or criminal law for example.[2] Instead our collection confines itself to aspects of what may be loosely termed "body politics", that is areas where law interacts with the body, and for our purposes we are looking at legal interaction with the *female* body. Hence, we consider legal regulation of the body in, *inter alia*, areas of reproduction, sexuality, body imagery and female criminality. It will, nevertheless, become apparent that areas of body politics do indeed interrelate with, and fall into, the various traditionally-defined areas of law. So, for example, we do consider contract law in so far as it determines disputes arising out of surrogacy arrangements. We look at tort law in so far as it concerns the provision of information about contraception, the sterilisation of women with learning difficulties and the freedom to consent to cosmetic surgery, and we raise issues of criminal law, to the extent that the termination of a pregnancy and female circumcision are criminal offences and in as much as it is the criminal law which provides the defences available to women who kill.

Equally, we do not wish to suggest that the areas of law and body politics which we have chosen to explore are exclusive. Body politics reaches areas of employment law,[3] European Union law[4] and international law[5] which are excluded from this volume. What we hope to achieve is, nevertheless, a syn-

---

[2] For an overview of feminist perspectives on the core, or foundational, law subjects see A. Bottomley (ed.), *Feminist Perspectives on the Foundational Subjects of Law* (Cavendish: London, 1996).

[3] In the area of pregnancy at work, for example, see A. E. Morris & S. M. Nott, "The Law's Engagement with Pregnancy" in J. Bridgeman & S. Millns (eds), *Law and Body Politics: Regulating the Female Body* (Dartmouth: Aldershot, 1995), pp. 53–78.

[4] L. Flynn, "The Body Politic(s) of E.C. Law" in T. K. Hervey & D. O'Keeffe (eds), *Sex Equality Law in the European Union* (John Wiley: Chichester, 1996), pp. 301–320.

[5] F. Beveridge & S. Mullally, "International Human Rights and Body Politics" in J. Bridgeman & S. Millns (eds), *Law and Body Politics: Regulating the Female Body* (Dartmouth: Aldershot, 1995), pp. 240–272.

thesis of some of the more obvious ways in which the female body and the law engage. Following from this we hope to enable the reader to develop skills of analysis which may be applied to subjects excluded from this study.

Through the areas we have chosen to consider, questions are explored about the role of the law in regulating both the corporeal, or physical, bodies of women and also the meanings attributed to the female body in law. On the first count the physical body is introduced as a site of legal regulation through, for example, legal provisions governing the use of infertility treatment services to bring about a pregnancy, the termination of a pregnancy, the legality of a surgeon cutting into the body for cosmetic purposes or in the performance of genital surgery. These areas of bodily regulation should not be underestimated. Calliope Farsides has pointed out the extent to which the processes of the female body, such as menstruation, pregnancy, childbirth and menopause, "all demand an acknowledgement by the woman of her functioning as a physical body."[6] She observes how these bodily processes are frequently talked about by women as if they happen to them, rather than being part of them. However, she suggests, "women are trying to establish ownership of their own bodies, and control over their bodily functions; first by creating their own metaphors and placing their own meaning and interpretation on bodily experiences, and then by seeking to exert control over the reality of their bodily experiences and the processes of production in which they are engaged."[7] The issue of female autonomy and control over the body is one which runs in various guises throughout this collection.

The significance of the body need not, however, be viewed solely through its corporeality. Discourses within dominant culture, including legal discourse, influence our feelings and our reactions to the body contributing to the formation of beliefs about appropriate roles for the body, its appropriate appearance and its behaviour.[8] This text seeks also, therefore, to explore the politics of the body and the role of the law in the government of the body.[9] Carol Smart has considered the interaction between law and the body by highlighting the interest which legal discourse has shown in bodies or body parts as falling within its jurisdiction and hence as appropriate sites for legal regulation:

C. SMART
Feminism and the Power of Law[10]

". . . [L]aw, both in its jurisprudential mode and applied mode, has been deeply interested in things corporal. For example, the criminal law on rape is most concerned about

[6] C. Farsides, "Body Ownership" in S. McVeigh & S. Wheeler (eds), *Law, Health & Medical Regulation* (Aldershot: Dartmouth, 1992), p. 35.
[7] C. Farsides, *ibid.*, p. 37.
[8] Jacobs, Keller-Fox & Shuttleworth (eds), *Politics: Women and the Discourses of Science* (London: Routledge, 1990), p. 4.
[9] See further S. Bordo, *Unbearable Weight: Feminism, Western Culture, and The Body* (Berkeley: University of California Press, 1993); T. Murphy, "Feminism on Flesh" (1997) 8 *Law and Critique* 37.
[10] (London: Routledge, 1989), pp. 92–93.

exact degrees of penile penetration, whether ejaculation took place, which bodily orifices were penetrated, and to what effect. The civil law on marriage is still interested
in whether marital intercourse takes place, and whether the child of a woman is also
the child of her husband. Violent crimes are categorized by the degree of harm caused
to bodies, and bits of bodies — from semen to hair — constitute the very basis of
forensic evidence in criminal trials. The application of some parts of the law depends
on a detailed appraisal of the body, and draw heavily on medical knowledge to establish legal issues. But even in an abstract sense law gives consideration to bodies, for
example in defining the act of rape as penile penetration of the vagina, law gives
consideration to all other sexual acts which are excluded from this definition. It gives
primacy to this specific act, calling others merely indecent assault. So law is not concerned with bodies just because its rules are applied in the context of criminal or civil
trials. It is concerned with bodies because it has defined them as specific sites of activity
over which the law should have jurisdiction."

Smart points out that the tendency is for legal discourse to treat women as if
they were their bodies and nothing else. Explanations for the behaviour of
women are therefore located within the processes of the female body.[11]
Another thread of this book is to investigate, through an examination of the
legal meanings attributed to the female body, the ways in which law contributes to this tendency.

3. Why now?

A further explanation (justification) for the publication of this reader may be
found in its appearance as the twentieth century draws to a close and the
opportunity it therefore offers for an assessment of some of the changes, and
resistances to change, which have affected the lives of women over the past
century. While the book is very much grounded in recent legal developments,
these developments can often be understood more fully via an appreciation of
their origins and historical evolution. Our understanding of the position of
women in western society at the end of the twentieth century, and the role of
the law in perpetuating the subordination of women or as a tool of emancipation, is enhanced if these issues are addressed in the context of the legal disabilities to which women have historically been exposed.

It has been argued that:

> "[i]n the period in which Western culture was established, and still has its
> roots, it was beyond argument that women and men should normally have
> specific, and, frequently exclusive, roles, even if there have always been the
> occasional exceptions. However, such a theory of separate roles has fre-
> quently led . . . to the deliberate subordination of one group to another. It is
> hard to see any innate inferiority in the domestic role, but in all societies
> throughout history it has been so treated."[12]

---

[11] C. Smart, *Feminism and the Power of Law, ibid.*, p. 96.
[12] O. F. Robinson, "The Historical Background" in S. McLean & N. Burrows (eds), *The Legal
Relevance of Gender* (London: Macmillan Press, 1988), pp. 40–41.

The confinement of women to the domestic sphere and the designation of the role assigned to women as inferior is culturally and historically specific. However, it is undeniably the case that within western democracies the separation of the sexes into separate spheres of public and private, the presumption that, women should undertake primary responsibility for domestic and caring arrangements located in the private sphere and the lack of value accorded to these responsibilities compared with the activities of men in the public sphere, has led to the relative absence of women's physical bodies in public life.

Yet women's bodies are now emerging into the public gaze and are receiving unprecedented exposure in popular culture. Female bodies recently under popular scrutiny in the headlines include that of a woman pregnant with eight foetuses who refused selective termination[13]; that of a woman made subject to a court declaration that it was lawful for doctors to perform a Caesarian upon her without her consent (on the grounds that the pain of labour and drugs given to relieve that pain had rendered her incompetent to make decisions about the management of birth)[14]; that of an anorexic woman whose refusal to consent to food and treatment was respected as a consequence of which she died[15]; those of women who have suffered violent abuse from their partners and subsequently killed their abuser[16]; and that of a rape victim questioned in court by the man accused of perpetrating the crime.[17]

Feminists and others have succeeded in raising the visibility of women's bodies in many ways. It is hoped that this book will continue this trend in exposing the law as a site of struggle over the body and in mapping the female body into law.

4. Contents

The book is divided into four main sections. In section one we introduce the key themes which underpin many of the substantive issues of the book. These include debates about the public and the private, equality and difference, dominance and subordination, rights and strategies, power and truth. In introducing these themes we offer a range of extracts from feminist legal scholarship outlining a variety of feminist perspectives on law. We consider how these perspectives inter-relate as they draw upon or develop out of each other, changing as the limitations of existing theoretical arguments are understood.

In the second section, on "Reproductive Bodies", we consider the role of women in reproduction and the interaction of the law with women as they seek to facilitate or prevent conception, and to take control of their pregnancies and the circumstances surrounding childbirth. Despite the number of

---

[13] C. Garner, "Octuplet Woman 'happy' to give birth", *The Independent*, August 11, 1996.
[14] C. Dyer, "Mother vs Big Brother", *The Guardian*, December 19, 1996.
[15] S. Weale, "Anorexic woman dies as mental health act ties doctors' hands", *The Guardian*, January 4, 1996.
[16] See, for example, Heather Mills' interview with Sara Thornton: H. Mills, "A tortured soul in search of peace", *The Independent*, June 3, 1996.
[17] P. Toynbee, "A cruel spectator sport that women dread", *The Independent*, August 23, 1996.

women at the end of this century who are choosing not to have children, motherhood continues to be viewed as one of, if not the, principal role(s) for women. In this section we will examine legal collusion with this view and address the legal position of women when they seek, accept or reject motherhood.

In section three, on "Sexual Bodies", the law's engagement with the bodies of women when represented or treated as a sex object is analysed. We examine the violation of women's bodies through an assessment of the law of rape and sexual harassment. We then go on to consider the objectification of women's bodies through the laws regulating images of women, covering laws on obscenity (and their relationship with the regulation of pornography) through to the control of images of women in popular culture, the implications of disordered eating, the resort to cosmetic surgery in pursuit of the ideal body and the prohibition upon female genital surgeries.

The final section, on "Offensive Bodies", considers the legal response to female criminality and the criminalisation of women whose conduct is considered offensive because their behaviour departs from that normally expected of their sex. Through legal explanations (and hence determination and treatment) of women who offend, we hope to show ways in which female criminals are marginalised, while popular constructions of what it means to be female are reinforced.

SECTION ONE

THEMES IN FEMINIST LEGAL THOUGHT

INTRODUCTION

"Feminist legal theory does not constitute a unified body of knowledge or a set of universal concerns or perspectives, but is shaped by different political agendas and institutional frameworks occurring within particular societies. Diversity in feminist thought stems from complex cultural, class, race, national, sexual and other differences."[1]

Feminism has been influenced and inspired by a diverse range of ideas: liberal; socialist; radical; humanist; psychoanalytic; and critical theory as well as by issues such as the green and peace movements.[2] As Joni Lovenduski and Vicky Randall explain, this myriad of theoretical perspectives and practical concerns which informs feminism has both strengthened and divided the feminist movement. Lovenduski and Randall chart British feminist movements from 1979, explaining the focus of different theories, the divisions which arose between feminist perspectives, and the difficulty in reconciling differences between women (of class, race, ethnic origin, nationality, religion and culture) with a desire to assert unity amongst feminists. However, feminism does not pose a single set of problems. Instead it raises a diverse range of concerns arising out of the different experiences of women's lives.

E. M. Schneider
"The Dialectics of Rights and Politics: Perspectives from the Women's Movement"[3]

"Feminist theory is characterized by an emphasis on dialectical process and the interrelationship of theory and practice. Feminist theory emphasises the value of direct and personal experience as the place that theory should begin, as embodied in the phrase 'the personal is political'. This phrase reflects the view that the realm of personal

[1] S. L. Roach, "Critiquing the Law: Themes and Dilemmas in Anglo-American Feminist Legal Theory" (1992) 19 *Journal of Law and Society* 423.
[2] J. Lovenduski & V. Randall, "Difference, Identity and Equality" in *Contemporary Feminist Politics* (Oxford: Oxford University Press, 1993), p. 57.
[3] In M. A. Fineman & N. S. Thomadsen (eds), *At the Boundaries of Law, Feminism and Legal Theory* (New York: Routledge, 1991), p. 301, pp. 304–305.

experience, the 'private' which has always been trivialized, is an appropriate and important subject of public inquiry, and that the 'private' and 'public' worlds are inextricably linked. The notion of consciousness-raising as feminist method flows from this insight. This method is a form of praxis because it transcends the theory and practice dichotomy. Consciousness-raising groups start with personal and concrete experience, integrate this experience into theory, and then, in effect, reshape theory based upon experience and experience based upon theory. Theory expresses and grows out of experience but it also relates back to that experience for further refinement, validation, or modification.

The fact that this process begins with the self, and then connects to the larger world of women, is important. For feminists, theory is not 'out there', but rather is based on the concrete, daily, and 'trivial' experiences of individuals, and so emerges from the shared experience of women talking. Because feminist theory grows out of direct experience and consciousness actively asserting itself, feminist theory emphasizes context and the importance of identifying experience and claiming it for one's own.

Feminist theory involves a particular methodology, but it also has a substantive viewpoint and political orientation. Recognizing the links between individual change and social change means understanding the importance of political *activity*, not just theory. Theory emerges from practice and practice then informs and reshapes theory. At the same time, because of its dialectical cast, feminist theory encompasses a notion of process that encourages a grounded and reflective appreciation of this interrelationship — its possibilities and limits, visions and defeats."

In this explanation of the feminist method of consciousness-raising, which draws upon personal experience and relates that experience to theory, Elizabeth Schneider emphasises the centrality of women's experiences to feminism. Consciousness-raising provides women with the opportunity to talk to each other about their lives and to identify common ground, which then forms the focus of their campaigns.[4] Consciousness-raising as a feminist method has been described by Catharine MacKinnon as "the collective critical reconstitution of the meaning of women's social experience, as women live through it."[5] To analyse issues from a feminist perspective is necessarily to participate in a dynamic process. The concerns faced by women are culturally and historically specific and understandings as to possible solutions and appropriate means of change are in a constant process of re-assessment and modification. But more fundamentally, the experiences of women differ. One major and valid criticism of twentieth century western feminism has been its domination by the concerns of vocal white middle-class women which may not be, indeed have not been, the primary concerns of women whose background and experiences are different. There is no one feminist perspective, no single standpoint and no unified vision.

In this section we identify some of the recurring themes in feminist legal scholarship which have played a central role in the dialogue occurring within

---

[4]   O. Banks, *Faces of Feminism* (Oxford: Blackwell, 1981), Chap. 12, "Radical Feminism".

[5]   C. A. MacKinnon, "Feminism, Marxism, Method, and the State: An Agenda for Theory" (1981–82) 7 *Signs* 515 at 543. The importance of consciousness-raising in affirming women's experiences as shared experiences and their knowledge as valid is emphasised in C. A. MacKinnon, *Toward a Feminist Theory of The State* (Cambridge MA: Harvard University Press, 1989).

feminist discourse. The themes raise questions about the ways in which law has been, and continues to be, employed in maintaining women's subordinated position within societal structures and institutions. While engaging with these debates, we are also concerned, as feminist lawyers, to investigate the potential of law as a tool for change.

CHAPTER 1

ARE WOMEN "PERSONS" TOO?

The issues of concern to feminism derive from the real experiences of women's lives. Whilst there is much debate within feminist legal scholarship upon the focus of feminism's challenge to the oppression or subordination of women, and upon the role which the law may usefully play in improving the conditions of the lives of women, there are a number of themes which re-occur. Focusing upon the themes in feminist legal theory enables the debates to be considered without presenting feminist approaches to the law as neatly pigeon-holed into rigid categories based on political or other affiliations.

A consideration of the themes in feminist legal theory, as with the substantive issues considered in the chapters which follow, has to be grounded in the reality of women's lived experience. We take as our starting point the position of women at the end of the nineteenth century who were, in legal terms, and in public life, "non-persons". These women were faced with legal disabilities which, today, seem almost inconceivable. The legal rights which were available equally to all men were denied to women. Recognition as a juridical person was, therefore, a necessary first step before women could claim entitlement to legal rights.[1]

1.1 The quest for legal personality

Challenge was made to the legal categorisation of women as non-persons through a series of cases in which women sought recognition as legal persons and equal entitlement to participate alongside men in the public sphere, that is to vote in local and national elections, to participate in government, to receive education and to gain admission to the professions.[2] The question which the courts were repeatedly asked to consider was whether women who had the qualifications required by legislation to participate in various aspects of public life could do so unless Parliament had expressly excluded them, or whether they were excluded and could only be permitted to participate if

---

[1] The same argument about legal non-personhood is still alive today with regard to the status of the foetus which is not recognised as having legal personality. See A. Diduck, "Legislating Ideologies of Motherhood" (1993) 2 *Social & Legal Studies* 461 at 476.

[2] For a full discussion of these cases see A. Sachs & J. H. Wilson, *Sexism and the Law: A Study of Male Beliefs and Legal Bias in Britain and the United States* (Oxford: Martin Robertson: 1978), pp. 22–66.

expressly allowed to do so by legislation.[3] In short, where legislation permitted a "man" or "persons" with specified qualifications to hold office or in some way participate in public life, were women with those qualifications entitled to do the same?

In *Chorlton v. Lings*[4] Mary Abbott claimed that, following the extension of the franchise by the Representation of the People Act 1867, she was entitled to be included on the electoral register. The court held that Parliament had intended to alter the qualifications upon which someone became eligible to vote, but not the "description of persons who were to vote". Bovill C.J. said that "man" as used in the 1867 Act "was intentionally used, in order to designate expressly the male sex; and it amounts to an express enactment and provision that every man, as distinguished from women, possessing the qualification, is to have the franchise".[5] The election of Lady Sandhurst to the London County Council was successfully challenged by another candidate who was granted a declaration to the effect that her election was void and that he had thereby been elected because, although women were entitled to vote in county council elections, they were not entitled to sit as councillors.[6] The claimant in *Bebb v. Law Society* had been refused permission to sit the Law Society preliminary examination on the grounds that she would not be able to practice as a solicitor.[7] Despite the relevant legislation referring to "person", the court held that when the legislation was passed women were not entitled to practice as solicitors and the legislation did not remove that disability.

One of the most famous cases to come before the courts was that of Sophia Jex-Blake and her female colleagues of the University of Edinburgh. These women sought a court order to the effect that, having been registered as medical students, they should be able to complete their degrees and, if they passed their examinations, to graduate.[8] By a majority of seven to five, their claim was rejected. While professing to decide the case on "strict legal grounds",[9] Lord Neaves, one of the majority, gave his reasons for dismissing the claim in the following terms:

Jex-Blake v. Senatus of Edinburgh University
(1873) 11 M. 784 at 790–795, *per* Lord Neaves

". . . I think I may say that the whole of the consulted Judges have arrived at the conclusion that the purpose contemplated in founding these Universities [of Scotland] was the education of young men. That view seems to be confirmed by a general refer-

---

[3] A. Sachs & J. H. Wilson, *ibid.*, p. 5.
[4] *Chorlton v. Lings* (1868) L.R. 4 C.P. 374.
[5] *Ibid.*, at 387.
[6] *Beresford-Hope v. Lady Sandhurst* (1889) 23 Q.B.D. 79.
[7] *Bebb v. Law Society* [1914] 1 Ch. 286.
[8] *Jex-Blake v. Senatus of Edinburgh University* (1873) 11 M. 784. For further explanation of this case see A. Sachs & J. H. Wilson, *supra*, n. 2 at pp. 17–22.
[9] *Ibid.*, *per* Lord Neaves at 795.

ence to the charters of the Universities, to the history of the country, to the state of public feeling upon such subjects; and I agree with the majority of the consulted Judges that the long usage which has followed, and which all of our brethren admit to be an important element, is here a conclusive consideration. From the year 1411 to about the year 1860, a period of 450 years, there is no instance produceable of a woman having been educated at any Scottish University. I need not dwell on the legal importance of that fact, which is so well demonstrated and enforced in some of the opinions we have received; and I do not think that any satisfactory or even plausible answer has been made to it.

The attempt at an answer consists in this, that the resort to an University is merely optional — what is called in law *res merae facultatis*, a mere privilege — which the party entitled to it may enforce or not as he pleases, and which cannot be lost *non utendo*; and the case is put of an abstinence from University study by Roman Catholics, Jews, Indians, or negroes. It is asked, 'Can it be said that the University could not, by vote and resolution, have admitted these persons?' In my view of the matter no vote or resolution would be needed for such persons; they would be admitted as a matter of course, because no legal principle could be assigned for excluding them. The general law does not make any distinction of religion in matters of right, and, where the national will does so, it operates by imposing a test upon admission. Where there is no test there is no foundation for a plea of exclusion. As little, and perhaps even less, can it be said that there is any ground for excluding students in respect of the colour of their skin. But the material element of consideration here is, that the law does recognise the difference of sex as an established and well-known element, leading sometimes to the exemption and sometimes to the absolute exclusion, of women from a variety of duties, privileges, and powers . . .

In this state of the law — there being an undoubted category by which females, in consequence of their sex, are excluded from certain functions competent to males — it becomes a question depending upon the general evidence, and upon the actings of parties, whether the privileges, honours, and functions connected with University education were designed for men alone, as they have been so enjoyed, or were designed for young men and women indiscriminately.

This seems to me to be the first and great question in the case. I am inclined to think that it is the only question, but it is certainly the leading question, and it is put forward as such by the pursuers in their first declaratory conclusion — namely, that it should be declared 'that the pursuers are entitled to attend the classes of any of the professors of the University of Edinburgh, and to receive instruction from the professors in said University, upon making due payment of all fees exigible from students at the University for said instruction.' This is a very clear proposition, and one which, if decided in the pursuers' favour, would be conclusive of the whole cause. It is very plain what is its meaning, and what would be its effect. The Universities were undoubtedly instituted for the education of male students. Were they also and equally instituted for the education of females? If so, every female presenting herself as a student at the door of the College is entitled to be admitted to any class on the usual terms. If there is not this equality, have male students a preference, and to what extent and effect, and on what clause or rule of law does that preference rest? It seems to me impossible to take any middle course in this matter as to abstract right, or to draw a distinction at all between male and female students, except by declaring that, while males have a right to a University education, females have none . . .

This leads me to the consideration that very weighty reasons may have operated on the national mind in constituting and continuing the Universities as exclusive schools for the academical education of young men. It is not necessary that we should adopt all the views of our ancestors in this respect. It is enough if we see that such views existed and were entertained with an earnestness that acted forcibly on the national will, which, after all, is the great foundation of all laws and public institutions. It is a belief, widely entertained, that there is a great difference in the mental constitution of the two sexes, just as there is in their physical conformation. The powers and suscept-ibilities of women are as noble as those of men; but they are thought to be different, and, in particular, it is considered that they have not the same power of intense labour as men are endowed with. If this be so, it must form a serious objection to uniting them under the same course of academical study. I confess that, to some extent, I share in this view, and should regret to see our young females subjected to the severe and incessant work which my own observation and experience have taught me to consider as indispensable to any high attainment in learning. A disregard of such an inequality would be fatal to any scheme of public instruction, for, as it is certain that the general mass of an army cannot move more rapidly than its weakest and slowest portion, so a general course of study must be toned and tempered down to suit the average of all the classes of students for whom it is intended; and that average will always be lowered by the existence of any considerable numbers who cannot keep pace with the rest.

Add to this the special acquirements and accomplishments at which women must aim, but from which men may easily remain exempt. Much time must, or ought to be, given by women to the acquisition of a knowledge of household affairs and family duties, as well as to those ornamental parts of education which tend so much to social refinement and domestic happiness; and the study necessary for mastering these must always form a serious distraction from severer pursuits, while there is little doubt that, in public estimation, the want of these feminine arts and attractions in a woman would be ill supplied by such branches of knowledge as a University could bestow.

In all this I assume that regard is to be had to the average powers of the female mind, and not to the different position of remarkable and exceptional women; and, in reference to this subject it may be noticed that we are apt to get a false view of the question by comparing extraordinary women with ordinary men, whereas the true rule is, to compare together the ordinary run of both sexes, and then, if we please, to compare the rarer examples of superior excellence among men and women — the Agnesis, the Lady Jane Greys, the Martineaus, and the Somervilles, with the Galileos, the Bentleys, the Adam Smiths, and the Isaac Newtons.

There is no reason why a false delicacy should prevent us from considering the effect which in the public mind must always have been given to the special element of sex in this question . . .

The period of life attained by the youth who are there educated, say from sixteen to twenty-two, is the most of all susceptible of the more tender feelings of our nature; and, without the slightest suggestion of anything in the least degree culpable, how is it possible to feel secure that, with a number of young men and women assembled together at a University, there shall not occur hasty attachments and premature en-tanglements, that may exercise a blighting influence on all their future life? What effect it might exercise upon their [sic] immediate studies it would be hazardous to conjecture. It might, in some cases, produce a strange emulation; it might in others lead to total idleness among these mixed schoolfellows . . .

I am satisfied that the non-attendance of women at the Universities in times past, which is an indisputable fact, was not a mere accident, or a mere arbitrary abstinence from the enforcement of a legal privilege, but arose from a consciousness, shared by them with the whole community, that the Universities were not instituted for them, though women would undoubtedly receive indirectly the benefits the Universities were calculated to confer, in making better men of their fathers, their brothers, their husbands, and their sons.

I have dwelt thus long on a point virtually conceded by all the consulted Judges because I think the condition of matters prior to the late regulations is of the utmost importance, and because the strength and solidity of the considerations which determined the old practice and constitution of the Universities enable us better to decide whether these could be, and have been, effectually changed in the case of the University of Edinburgh.

The argument here in favour of the ladies' claims arises out of the power given by the late Act of Parliament (21st and 22d Vict. 1858). The University Courts there established have this power conferred on them, *videlicet*, 'to effect improvements in the internal arrangements of the University, after due communication with the Senatus Academicus and with the sanction of the Chancellor;' and on 10th November 1869, the University Court of Edinburgh made a regulation that 'women shall be admitted to the study of medicine in the University.'

It is upon this and other relative regulations that the interlocutor under review must now be considered as exclusively based. This view of their case does not seem to be satisfactory to the pursuers, who complain of it as evading their just legal demands, and leaving their position to rest on a very precarious and slippery foundation. I do not wonder at this feeling, and I confess that, if the pursuers' claims were to be held as entirely dependent on the regulations of the University Court I should consider this state of things as a great calamity to all concerned. If the admission of women to the study of medicine is to be held a mere matter of regulation it is of course liable to be changed, modified, or repealed from time to time, as the enacting body may think proper. This is inherent in the nature of such regulations, and the consequence would be that no reliance could be placed on the continuance of the privilege or permission thus given, which might be suddenly withdrawn or curtailed, to the great disappointment and injury of those interested. There could be no fixity of tenure in such circumstances. No class in the community, no individual woman, could trust to medicine as an available professional opening, and no justice could be done to a system thus imperfectly introduced. In the meantime, the question, involving, as it does, important interests and exciting considerations, would remain a subject of keen and bitter contention, and make the University Court a permanent battle-field between the partisans of the opposing factions. How far this would conduce to the interests of science, and to the peace or prosperity of our Universities, it is not difficult to conjecture.

But apart from these views I consider that the regulations in question, admitting women to the study of medicine in the University of Edinburgh, are wholly illegal, and palpably beyond the statutory power conferred upon the University Courts. Those Courts are empowered to effect improvements in the internal arrangements of the University, but the proposal to confer on women a right of admission to the study of medicine, not previously possessed by them, appears to me to be not an internal regulation, but an external innovation, and that, too, of the most serious kind. I cannot consider it to be mere matter of arrangement whether one-half of the population has or has not a right of admission to the University. To admit those who, in consequence of their sex, had no legal claim to University study, and to declare that they now should have such a claim, appears to me to be an essential and fundamental alteration, or rather subversion, of the established consuetudinary constitution of the University, which it is wholly beyond the power of a University Court to effect.

I do not suppose it can be maintained that the University Court can make any change they please. I should think even that if the University Court here had enjoined a system of mixed classes of medical study, some of our brethren who are favourable to the interlocutor under review would hold such a regulation as incompatible with "the law and constitution of the University." Nor do I suppose the objection to it would be removed by the adoption of the Pentonville Prison partition, which has been suggested. Or, suppose that the University Court had enacted that any professor who refused to have separate classes for the sexes should be bound to devote his single class to the exclusive instruction of women, so as to enable them in some degree to make up their leeway, as in competition with their male friends, I take it that any such innovation would be disregarded by a Court of law as utterly null, just as much as if a regulation had been made by which the wholesale admission of women was accompanied with the total exclusion of men.

Considering, as I do, that these regulations are beyond the powers of the University Court that passed them — that is to say, in the sense which the pursuers have put upon them — I consider it quite unnecessary, in order to set them aside, that a reduction of them should be brought. The University Court has no authority over the University or over the Senatus Academicus, except within the province which the statute has assigned to it. Beyond those limits it has no standing, and its dealings and declarations are mere waste paper.

I ought, at the same time, to advert to the view that these regulations do not import, in any practical form, what they are said to infer; and in that aspect they are liable to the observation that they do not at all support the conclusion sought to be deduced from them. Accordingly, the declarator which the Lord Ordinary has pronounced comes, on the face of it, to be a mere *brutum fulmen*, that can have no effect and can lead to no result.

Women, it is said, are admitted to the study of medicine, but that is only if they find classes that they can attend; they are only to be taught in separate classes, and professors are permitted to have separate classes; but none of the professors are enjoined to have such classes, and it cannot be said that any professor is bound to have them, while, as to graduation, nothing whatever is said. This then, is a decree which is wholly unenforceable, and can establish no legal or available right. It is not the business of a Court of law to pronounce declarators that lead to nothing, and this Court has always refused to do so.

It is clear that the pursuers themselves see the case in this very light, and hence it is that with strict logical propriety they rested their action upon the first of their conclusions, namely, that they are entitled to attend the classes of any of the professors upon payment of students' fees. Had they made out that proposition they would have had a plain and enforceable right, because any professor refusing to receive them would then have been guilty of a breach of duty. But as that general right seems now universally given up, and the regulations alone relied upon by the Lord Ordinary, and those Judges who agree with him, there seems no solid ground left on which the action or decree can stand . . .

I may take this opportunity of saying that I consider the attempt of the pursuers to explain the absence of females from our Universities, by the condition of women in Scotland, and the course of our natural history generally, to be wholly unsuccessful. Though naturally and willingly keeping aloof from public life, the condition of Scottish women in the 15th and 16th centuries was anything but slavish or degraded, nor were they considered as very timid or submissive. The evidence of Don Pedro d'Ayala, who was the Spanish Ambassador at the Court of James IV., is conclusive on this subject, and it is acknowledged that he was a keen and correct observer, as his character of that noble but unhappy monarch too plainly shews. The Scottish women, he tells us, 'are courteous in the extreme,' and, he adds, 'they are really honest, though very bold.' 'They are absolute mistresses of their houses, and even of their husbands in all things concerning the administration of their property, income, or expenditure.' Such women' could not easily have been stopped from asserting a legal right intended for them, but they were doubtless aware that their proper place was at home, learning to rule their husbands, and bring up their children, with those happy domestic results of which Scotland has so much reason to be proud.

In deciding this case, as I am bound to do, upon strict legal grounds, I do not take up the time of the Court in saying much as to the personal feelings which it is calculated to excite. I will say this, however, that I have felt great sympathy with these ladies, both as to the object they had in view and as to the position in which they have been placed. I think that, from very natural motives and with the best intentions, but with unfortunate results, their friends have led them to form expectations which could never be realised in the way contemplated. Again, I think it very natural for those ladies who feel a vocation in that direction to wish to make themselves useful, and to earn an honourable independence, and I have no doubt there are departments of medical or surgical practice in which women may be fitly and successfully employed. There was an important branch of surgical practice in which their sex was long exclusively engaged, and which continued indeed to be their appanage from the time when Moses was found in the ark of bulrushes down till the beginning of the sixteenth century; for in 1522 a doctor was burnt alive in Hamburg for personating a woman in an obstetric case. That branch of practice in women's hands may now be looked upon with some contempt, but this I think a great mistake, and it might probably with great advantage be associated with other branches of domestic practice, for which women would be well adapted. This might surely be done without any material change in the constitution of the Universities. The rules of the London University, with its advanced notions, throw some light on this subject, for they refuse to accord to women the honour of graduation. In fact, any grievance of the pursuers arises out of the Medical Act of 1858. It is for the Legislature to determine the matter; but, if it was thought right, that Act might be amended by opening a somewhat wider door for medical qualification. The case certainly affords no ground for subverting the constitution of our Universities, or affecting the dignity and weight which belong to the highest honour attending the medical profession. The national object here is, and ought to be, to accomplish and adorn the character of a British physician, not only with all medical and physiological science, but also with the highest philosophy, intellectual and moral, and with all the resources of literature and learning which can aid him in his high functions. Any change that would incur the risk of lowering the standard that now exists, and which we have seen exemplified in so many of our great physicians and professors, is infinitely to be deprecated, and such a danger, I think, would be incurred by the revolution in the medical teaching of our Universities that has here been attempted to be brought about; while at the same time it would otherwise affect, and, in my opinion, deteriorate our Universities in a way unknown to any period of their history."

It was not until the passage of the Sex Disqualification Removal Act 1919 that the exclusion of women from exercising public functions or holding public office on the grounds of sex or by virtue of marriage was removed. Section 1 of the Sex Disqualification Act 1919 provides:

"A person shall not be disqualified by sex or marriage from the exercise of any public function, or from being appointed to or holding any civil or judicial office or post, or from entering or assuming or carrying on any civil profession or vocation, or from admission to any incorporated society . . ."

Section 3 enabled universities to make provision to admit women, stating that nothing in university statutes or charters would be taken to exclude women. This statutory provision was followed by a Privy Council decision, hearing an appeal from the Supreme Court of Canada, which considered the question of whether women were eligible for appointment to the Canadian Senate. This required the Privy Council to decide whether "qualified persons" included women:

Edwards v. Att.-Gen. of Canada
[1930] A.C. 124 at 128 and 134, *per* Lord Sankey L.C.

"The exclusion of women from all public offices is a relic of days more barbarous than ours, but it must be remembered that the necessity of the times often forced on man customs which in later years were not necessary . . .

The word [person] is ambiguous and in its original meaning would undoubtedly embrace members of either sex. On the other hand, supposing in an Act of Parliament several centuries ago it had been enacted that any person should be entitled to be elected to a particular office it would have been understood that the word only referred to males, but the cause of this was not because the word 'person' could not include females but because at common law a woman was incapable of serving a public office. The fact that no woman had served or has claimed to serve such an office is not of great weight when it is remembered that custom would have prevented the claim being made or the point being contested.

Customs are apt to develop into traditions which are stronger than law and remain unchallenged long after the reason for them has disappeared."

In comparison with the earlier cases in which the courts held that the terms "man" and "persons" excluded women unless specifically provided otherwise, Lord Sankey L.C. held that Parliament would have expressly excluded women if that had been its intention.

The judiciary, throughout the cases in which it was maintained that women were excluded from public responsibilities, repeatedly denied that it believed women were less able than men:

"We have been asked to hold, what I for one quite assent to, that, in point of intelligence and education and competency women . . . are at least equal to a great many, and probably, far better than many, of the candidates . . . but that is really not for us to consider."[10]

The judiciary explained its reluctance to admit women to the public sphere

---

[10]   *Bebb v. Law Society, supra,* n. 7 at 294.

not in terms of a belief in women's inferiority but out of respect for the nature of women who should be protected from the demands of the public world. As Bovill C.J. said in *Chorlton v. Lings*:

Chorlton v. Lings
(1868) L.R. 4 C.P. 374 at 388, *per* Bovill C.J.

"[T]he Act of 1867 does 'expressly' in every sense exclude persons under a legal incapacity, and women are under a legal incapacity to vote at elections. What was the cause of it, it is not necessary to go into: but, admitting that fickleness of judgment and liability to influence have sometimes been suggested as the ground of exclusion, I must protest against its being supposed to arise in this country from any underrating of the sex either in point of intellect or worth. That would be quite inconsistent with one of the glories of our civilisation, — the respect and honour in which women are held. This is not a mere fancy of my own, but will be found in Selden, de Synedriis Beterum Ebraeorum, in the discussion of the origin of the exclusion of women from judicial and like public functions, where the author gives preference to this reason, that the exemption was founded upon motives of decorum, and was a privilege of the sex . . ."

This same conception of the female role was likewise employed in the Canadian case *Re French*,[11] in which a direction of the court was sought on the question whether women could be admitted to the New Brunswick Bar. As Mary Jane Mossman explains, the judicial conception of the nature of women originated in the dominant social thinking of the time:

M. J. Mossman
"Feminism and Legal Method: The Difference it Makes"[12]

". . . Relying on the decision of the United States Supreme Court in *Bradwell v. Illinois* in 1873 (83 U.S. (16 Wall) 130), Mr Justice Barker adopted as his own the 'separate spheres' doctrine enunciated there:

> '. . . the civil law, as well as nature herself, has always recognized a wide difference in the respective spheres and destinies of man and woman. Man is, or should be, woman's protector and defender. The natural and proper timidity and delicacy which belongs to the female sex evidently unfits it for many of the occupations of civil life. The constitution of the family organization, which is founded in the divine ordinance as well as in the nature of things, indicates the domestic sphere as that which properly belongs to the domain and functions of womanhood (p.365).'

---

[11] *Re French* (1905) 37 N.B.R. 359.
[12] In M. A. Fineman & N. S. Thomadsen (eds), *At the Boundaries of Law: Feminism and Legal Theory* (New York: Routledge, 1991), p. 283, pp. 287–288.

The language of the *Bradwell* decision expressed very clearly an unqualified acceptance of the idea of difference between men and women, a difference which was social as well as biological. From the perspective of legal method, however, it is significant that no evidence was offered for his assertions about the 'timidity and delicacy' of women in general; no authorities were cited for the existence of 'divine law'; and no studies were referred to in support of the conclusion that the domestic sphere belonged 'properly' to women (and vice versa). The court merely cited the existence of divine and natural law in general terms.

The legal reasoning used by Mr Justice Barker does not seem consistent at all with the recognized principles of legal method: the reliance on relevant and persuasive evidence to determine facts, the use of legal precedents to provide a framework for analysis, and a rational conclusion supported by both evidence and legal principles. Yet, if Barker J.'s ideas are not the product of legal method, what is their source?

The answer, of course, is that the ideas he expressed were those prevailing in the cultural and professional milieu in which he lived . . .

. . . What is significant here is the court's uncritical acceptance of ideas from the mainstream of intellectual life, as if they were factual rather than conceptual. Moreover, in accepting these ideas and making them an essential part of his decision, Barker J. provided an explicit and very significant reinforcement of the idea of gender-based difference. In this way, the particular decision denying French's claim to practice law had an impact well beyond the instant case. Thereafter, in the law, as well as in other intellectual traditions, there was a recognized and 'legitimate' difference between women and men."

Mary Jane Mossman explains that the idea of women as delicate, unstable by nature and as suited to a function within the domestic sphere whilst unsuited to the demands of the public realm, originated in religious, scientific and philosophical thought. But through judicial acceptance, however, the idea gained legal authority.[13] As a consequence of the industrial revolution, the home was no longer the focus of the economic unit that it had been. Whereas production had centred on the home, a place in which everyone contributed their labour, the industrial revolution took labour out of the home and into factories. This had a greater impact upon middle-class women who became confined to the home, than upon working-class women who were employed in the factories. The judicial conception of sex roles was built upon the separate spheres for men and women, seeing them as arising out of natural and complementary differences.[14] Albie Sachs and Joan Hoff Wilson argue that

---

[13]   Mary Jane Mossman examines the "Persons" cases in Canada to analyse the strategies for feminism and the ways in which legal method may hinder women's equality claims in law. She argues that legal method sets the boundaries of inquiry through acceptance by the judiciary that it is simply applying the law and that questions of morals or politics are irrelevant. Furthermore, Mossman argues, judges are selective in their choice of relevant facts and precedents and the interpretation which they give to statutes. These points lead Mossman to the conclusion that it may be overly optimistic to expect the court to make decisions leading to significant change for women. Bringing cases to court does, however and at least, highlight the issues involved (M. J. Mossman, "Feminism and Legal Method: The Difference it Makes" in M. A. Fineman & N. S. Thomadsen (eds), *ibid.*, p. 283).

[14]   R. Tong, *Feminist Thought: A Comprehensive Introduction* (London: Unwin Hyman, 1989), p. 13.

this conception of women, as delicate and principally ornamental, ignored the reality of the lives of working-class women who engaged in long hours of hot, heavy and dirty labour. Neither did the accepted judicial portrayal of women accurately reflect the reality of the lives of middle and upper-class women. The view of women as fragile, docile and decorative conferred status upon middle-class men whose wives' public inactivity was an indicator of their social standing. The reality was that middle and upper-class men depended upon the labours of their wives in running the home, giving orders to servants, dealing with deliveries and organising entertainment. Both the hard work of women in the home and the display of their inactivity were essential to a husband's career.

A. SACHS & J. H. WILSON
Sexism and the Law: A Study of Male Beliefs and Legal Bias in Britain and the United States[15]

"THE MYTH OF MALE PROTECTIVENESS"

The male monopoly cases reveal the existence of [. . .] the myth of male protectiveness. Women were variously described as refined, delicate and pure, quite as worthy and noble as men, but different. One judge said he shared the widely held view that women were intellectually inferior to men, and in particular were incapable of severe and incessant work, while another judge expressly left open the question of whether women were fickle in judgment and liable to influence. But the general view of those who spoke of the unfitness of women for public life was that their incapacity should be seen as an exemption flowing from respect rather than a disability based on inferiority. Men and women were different but complementary, rather than separate but equal . . .

The most striking aspect of the judicial and other pronouncements on female delicacy is that what was asserted as incontrovertible fact was in reality nothing more than fallacious abstraction. Very few of the women whom the judges knew, whether they were litigants, or cleaners of the courtroom, or servants in the home, actually corresponded in any way to the judicial representation. At the time when the judges were speaking, more than a million unmarried women alone were employed in industry, while a further three quarters of a million were in domestic service. The judges had only to read the *Edinburgh Review* to discover a 'horrifying' analysis by an anonymous feminist of the nature, pay and conditions of women's work. For the great majority of Victorian women, as for the great majority of Victorian men, life was characterised by drudgery and poverty rather than by refinement and decorum. Applying the judges' criteria, then, most women were simply not women . . .

Underlying all the judgments, it is possible to discern the central theme of domesticity. In the minds of the judges, the graciousness of an accomplished hostess would be totally undermined by the combative intellectuality thought appropriate to a professional person. Middle-class men did not share the objection of many of the members of the nobility to work, in fact they prided themselves on their industriousness, nor

[15] (Oxford: Martin Robertson, 1978), pp. 53–63.

did they object to women working, since they employed women to clean and cook in their homes, as well as to milk and reap on their farms and spin in their factories. What they did object to with a vehemence indicative of a special interest, was to their own wives working. Women of the middle class were expected to run households in which the menfolk could eat, be clothed, entertain and sleep in comfort. Secondly, they were to produce sons for business, the professions, the military and the church and daughters for good marriages. Thirdly, they were to display in their households a graciousness, refinement and sentiment, lacking in the hard world of business, which would mark off the reputation of their families and maintain the esteem of their class. It was this third requirement that distinguished the middle-class woman from her working-class cousin. Working-class women were also required to look after the home and reproduce sons and daughters, but they were expected not to attempt graces above their station. A degree of spending that would indicate taste and refinement in a middle-class woman, would be castigated as reckless and profligate if gone in for by a working-class woman. In terms of male ideology, the model working-class wife was pious and thrifty, qualities which were not inconsistent with work outside the home, while the prototype middle-class wife, on the other hand, was ornamental and decorous, attributes which were incompatible with outside employment . . .

The extraordinary emphasis on proper dress, decorum and etiquette for Victorian ladies was tied to attempts by the industrialists to surpass the gentry not only in economic and political power, but in manners and self-esteem as well. Leisure for women became a mark of status just when the dignity of labour was being contrasted with the indolence of the aristocracy and the laziness of the poor. It has been said that by the mid-nineteenth century the wife's idleness was the most sensitive indicator of social standing, because through her the income of the husband was translated into symbols of respectability. In these terms the inanity of female existence in prosperous Victorian homes could become comprehensible if seen as the wife's contribution to the social esteem of the whole family. The courts gave express recognition to this principle when they defined 'pin money' as an allowance made by a husband to his wife for the purchase of dresses and ornaments 'in order that his dignity in society may be maintained' . . .

At the same time, the increasingly manifold and increasingly useless accomplishments of the townsman's wife were symbols of his increasingly high social status.

Yet the emphasis on the elaborate clothing, cultivated speech and social refinement of the urban ladies should not be taken as proof that the role of the middle-class wife was purely ornamental or symbolical. In addition to being required to display social delicacy, she had to manage what was in effect a large economic and political enterprise, namely the household. She had to hire and fire servants, bargain with tradesmen, control children and attend to the multitudinous needs of her husband. Whether regarded (as by Mill, Engels and Veblen) as a head servant, or else as a manager, her tasks were detailed and multifarious, requiring what today would be called great skills in home economics, personnel management and interpersonal relations. As Mill told Members of Parliament, women whose chief daily business was the laying out of money so as to produce the greatest results with the smallest means, could give lessons to his hearers who contrived to produce such singularly poor results with such vast means.

The vaunted complementarity of the sexes, invariably expressed in semi-mystical terms, had practical roots in a division of labour in respect of which the husband supervised minions at work and the wife supervised minions at home. Different attributes were required for the performance of their respective tasks, and these attributes were given exaggerated reflection in the culture of the times. It is suggested, then, that the main reason why Victorian men resisted the entry of middle-class women into public life and the professions was their interest in ensuring that their wives remained housekeepers. Mill certainly hinted as much, adding that it was a reason that men were ashamed to advance because of its manifest injustice . . .

Although the issue of women in the professions presented itself to the men as a projected assault on all that was decent and proper in society, underlying their sense of spiritual shock was a fear that the satisfactory ordering of their own material lives would be shattered. These men had a direct, material stake in keeping their wives at home running their households, attending to their comforts and providing the ambience necessary for the furtherance of their careers. This fitted in with the ethic which said that sentiment should be kept out of business, where it was inconvenient for trade, and kept in the home, where it was useful for domesticity; sentiment was feminised, and women were sentimentalised over. Charitable activity confined to suitable hours was one form of work that was not incompatible with the kind of service that middle-class men sought from their wives, and it also became possible for the many women who were not going to marry, to enter newly established public service occupations such as teaching and nursing, provided they did so subject to the tutelage of men."

Similar arguments about the nature of women were presented at the time to justify the refusal to extend the vote to women. Such arguments included the fact that the female sex, being of a delicate nature, should not be exposed to the masculine concerns of public life; women's duties lay in the domestic sphere, tending their home and raising their family; intellectually, women were viewed as incapable of grappling with political issues; and, anyway, the interests of women were sufficiently represented by their husbands or male relatives.[16]

The challenge made, through law, to the social position of women was directed against the denial that women were legal persons entitled to legal rights. It was necessary also to challenge the view of womanhood upon which this denial rested, a view which set women up as being by nature only suited to the tasks of tending for husband, children and home, complementing the role their male relatives played in the public sphere. The capacity for rational thought valued in liberal societies was developed by men through education and their participation in the public sphere. Women, by comparison, entertaining themselves with poetry, music and literature came to be seen as dominated not by rational thought but by their emotions. Many of the themes which have dominated feminist legal theory are apparent in this perception of the nature and appropriate role of women.

From this there arise a series of important questions. To what extent has

---

[16] T. D. Fergus, "Women and the Parliamentary Franchise in Great Britain" in S. McLean & N. Burrows (eds), *The Legal Relevance of Gender: Some Aspects of Sex-Based Discrimination* (London: Macmillan, 1988), p. 80. For further consideration of the suffrage campaign see O. Banks, "Votes for Women" in *Faces of Feminism* (Oxford: Blackwell, 1981). Women at the turn of the century have been variously described as "angels in the home" or "doll's house women". For personalised accounts of women's emergence out of the "doll's house", see A. Holdsworth, *Out of the Doll's House: The Story of Women in the Twentieth Century* (London: BBC Books, 1988).

the law perpetuated the division between public and private spheres and failed to afford protection to women in the private sphere? Having secured recognition as legal persons, might equality best be obtained by focusing upon the ways in which women resemble men, or does it require acknowledgement of their differences? If removal of legal discrimination has not secured equality for women, is this because women are not considered to be equal to men but subordinated to them? Does equipping women, as individuals, with equal rights to be used in adversarial battles against the conflicting rights of others still allow for recognition to be given to women's relationships and ties with others? Rather than simply operating as a tool to discriminate against women or subordinate women, does the law construct an "ideal Woman" against whom all "real life" women are judged? It is in investigating these intriguing questions that the themes discussed in the remainder of this first section emerge.

1.2   Public and private: situating women

The division of society into two spheres, the public world of men and the private realm of women, was considered an appropriate division suited to the particular characteristics of male and female.[17] The public/private divide refers not only to the distinction between the world of finance, education, government and the professions and that of the domestic sphere, but also to the scope of legal regulation and the distinction between those areas of life into which the law should and should not intrude. The public sphere refers principally to the area in which relations between the individual and the State are played out, an area in which legal regulation is viewed as appropriate. There is also a further layer of relations occurring within the public sphere which concern arrangements between private individuals and in which State intervention is more restricted. For instance, in the realm of employment, the State, while expected to intervene to a certain extent by passing legislation on, for example, health and safety and unfair dismissal, is not expected to fetter the pursuit of individual satisfaction by limiting employers' and employees' choice. Beyond this public realm lies the domestic sphere, the site of the family, reproduction and sexuality which has traditionally appeared to be beyond the scope of legal regulation.[18]

Katherine O'Donovan argues that the boundaries between public and private are continually shifting so that a private issue may become a matter of public concern and hence the object of legal regulation. She emphasises that not only does the law identify the boundary between the two spheres, it determines the content of each.[19] Zillah Eisenstein argues that "[a]lthough the meaning of 'public' and 'private' changes in concrete ways, the assignment of public space to men and private space to women is continuous in Western

---

[17]   Z. R. Eisenstein, *The Radical Future of Liberal Feminism* (London: Longman, 1981), p. 5.
[18]   K. O'Donovan, *Sexual Divisions in Law* (London: Weidenfeld and Nicolson, 1985), p. 3.
[19]   K. O'Donovan, *ibid.*, p. 3.

history."[20] The organisation, based upon a division between the sexes, of men into the public realm and women into the private is, she argues, consistent throughout western liberal democracies.[21] Not only was the private realm beyond State interference, it was to be protected from interference by the State.[22] Feminists have highlighted the harm done to women within the private sphere. Given the role of the law in defining the boundary between public and private, feminists have identified how the law has been instrumental in failing to provide women with protection against harm. The privacy of the family meant, for example, that women were subjected to batterings labelled "domestic violence", or that a husband could have sex with "his" wife without her consent and it was of no legal consequence. The division into public and private meant a lack of legal protection afforded to women in those areas designated as private. Despite the view that the law should have no place within the domestic sphere it does impact upon it through, for example, criminal laws and tax laws. Further, as Katherine O'Donovan states, where the law does not regulate, other mechanisms of control might exist. She suggests that the absence of legal regulation leaves men in control, due to their greater economic power.[23]

The focus of liberal feminism upon the legal demarcation of the private realm, and the legal failure to acknowledge the harm perpetrated there upon women, has resulted in a shifting of the boundaries between private and public so that issues previously considered to be private have been moved into the public domain. Examples of this shift may be found in the Abortion Act 1967, which legalises, in certain circumstances, the termination of a pregnancy by a registered medical practitioner; in legislation imposing upon the Secretary of State a duty to make provision for the giving of advice about, and supply of, contraception; and in the Domestic Violence and Matrimonial Proceedings Act 1976 which marks an acknowledgement that it may be necessary for the protection of family members to allow State intervention in the family unit.

The limitation of legal reform is, however, apparent from these examples. The availability of abortion and contraception, and the recognition of violence within the private sphere, are not sufficient in themselves to ensure the equality of women with men. Contraception has to be safe, effective and acceptable; abortion services free and non-judgmental; and violence within the home has to be treated as a serious crime by law enforcement agencies.[24] An issue may be unregulated by the law either because the law fails to recognise the particular wrong as a harm or because the law privatises the issue. Surgical operations performed for cosmetic reasons are one instance of the failure of the law to recognise that certain acts performed upon the bodies of women may

---

[20] Z. R. Eisenstein, *supra*, n. 17 at p. 22.

[21] Z. R. Eisenstein, *ibid.*

[22] Z. R. Eisenstein, *ibid.*, p. 25.

[23] K. O'Donovan, *supra*, n. 18 at p. 8.

[24] For consideration of contraception and abortion see Chap. 5. The effects of the inadequate legal response to violence against women are considered in relation to women who eventually kill their abusive partner in Chap. 11.1.

generate harm.[25] On the second count, the Surrogacy Arrangements Act 1985, for example, which makes it a criminal offence to arrange or negotiate a surrogacy arrangement on a commercial basis (whilst permitting informal arrangements), can be considered to have privatised surrogacy.[26]

The enactment of legislation addressing issues within the private domain may be perceived as part of the increasing encroachment of law into everyday life. Past experience may provide some foundation for scepticism about the protection which the law can offer women and force acknowledgement that the law does not work to the benefit of women for much of the time. Whilst the formulation and application of the law may be open to criticism, legislative change does at least amount to an acknowledgement that a problem exists which deserves to be taken seriously. It formally recognises that women, like men, are equally deserving of respect.

---

[25] See below, Chap. 10.2.
[26] See below, Chap. 4.2.

CHAPTER 2

ARE RIGHTS RIGHT FOR WOMEN?

Having secured recognition as legal persons, women pursued legal reform seeking rights to equal treatment with men, and seeking to remedy the legally-sanctioned discrimination against women. By amending existing laws and passing new laws, it was hoped that the sexist nature and discriminatory effect of laws could be remedied and that, through legal reform, women might attain equal rights and, hence, equal treatment in law. Whilst granting "rights" does not necessarily confer anything concrete, claims of rights have powerful rhetorical force and have had some successes in securing equality of opportunity for women. Claims to rights may be important individually, collectively and publicly:

> "The women's rights movement has had an important affirming and individualising effect on women's consciousness. The articulation of women's rights provides a sense of self and distinction for individual women, while at the same time giving women an important sense of collective identity. Through this articulation, women's voices and concerns are heard in a public forum and afforded a legal vehicle for expression. But rights claims do not only define women's individual and collective experience, they also actively shape public discourse. Claims of equal rights and reproductive choice, for example, empowered women."[1]

The powerful rhetoric of rights, and the empowerment achieved through identification of a right, means that, despite the limited success of claims to rights in areas such as abortion,[2] feminists are presented with a dilemma about whether it is appropriate to continue with a strategy based upon rights:

C. SMART
Feminism and the Power of Law[3]

"We are, therefore, faced with a dilemma. Historically rights have been almost an intrinsic part of feminist claims. Now rights constitute a political language through

---

[1] E. M. Schneider, "The Dialectics of Rights and Politics: Perspectives from the Women's Movement" in M. A. Fineman & N. S. Thomasden (eds), *At the Boundaries of Law, Feminism and Legal Theory* (New York: Routledge, 1991) p. 301, pp. 312–313.
[2] See below, Chap. 5.3.
[3] (London: Routledge, 1989), pp. 143–144.

which certain interests can be advanced. To couch a claim in terms of rights is a major step towards a recognition of a social wrong. Hence, Catharine MacKinnon (1987) has argued that transposing the notion of sexual harassment into a matter of employment rights, and pornography into a matter of civil rights, has put these issues onto a visible public agenda. To claim that an issue is a matter of rights is to give the claim legitimacy.

It is also the case that to pose an issue in terms of rights is to make the claim 'popular'. This is not to say that everyone agrees, but it makes the claim accessible, it means that it can be brought under the umbrella of trade union debates, parliamentary consideration, media reportage, and so on. It enters into a linguistic currency to which everyone has access. Moreover, whilst the extension of rights is associated with the foundations of democracy and freedom, the claim to rights is always already loaded. It is almost as hard to be against rights as it is to be against virtue.

Rights also have another appeal. They are depicted as a protection of the weak against the strong, or the individual against the state. No matter how (in)effective they are in achieving such protections, there is little doubt that a reduction in rights is equated with a loss of power or protection. Hence the (now) regular challenge to women's abortion rights in the U.K. is regarded as an attempt to reduce women's autonomy and ability to determine their own reproductive careers. A change to the existing legislation which reduced women's access to abortion would be a real diminution of women's rights even in a context where we know that not all women have access to abortion or adequate contraceptive methods.

We cannot deny that rights do amount to legal and political power resources. However, the value of such resources seems to be ascertainable more in terms of losses if such rights diminish, than in terms of gains if such rights are sustained. This is not as paradoxical as it may seem. The denial of rights in a given area like abortion will have the definite consequence of forcing women to go through with pregnancies which are unwanted. The provision of abortion rights does not however, guarantee that any woman who wants an abortion can have one. The law may concede a right, but if the state refuses to fund abortions or abortion clinics, it is an empty right.

The dilemma that needs to be faced is whether to continue the feminist tradition of couching claims in terms of rights."

The rights debate is pertinent to specific feminist political campaigns and raises further questions regarding the usefulness and consequences for women of a formal declaration or Bill of Rights.[4] The United Kingdom is a signatory to the European Convention on Human Rights and Fundamental Freedoms without yet having incorporated it into domestic law.[5] This has meant that British feminists are not forced to express their claims in terms of rights in the way that their sisters in other jurisdictions have been. For example, in Canada, the Charter of Fundamental Rights and Freedoms (1982) and in the United States, the Constitution (1798) together with its First Amendment have forced

---

[4] For a consideration of the arguments concerning feminist advocacy of a U.K. Bill of Rights see E. Kingdom, "Formal Declarations of Rights" in *What's Wrong With Rights? Problems for Feminist Politics of Law* (Edinburgh: Edinburgh University Press, 1991).

[5] The Convention does, however, take effect in international law. See Lord Lester of Herne Hill, "European Human Rights and the British Constitution" in J. Jowell & D. Oliver (eds), *The Changing Constitution* (Oxford: Clarendon Press, 3rd ed., 1994), p. 33.

North American feminists to engage with rights discourse.[6] In surveying the recent debates on the possible incorporation of the European Convention on Human Rights and Fundamental Freedoms into U.K. domestic law, Stephanie Palmer considers the limitations of rights discourse in dealing with the claims, of women:

S. PALMER
"Critical Perspectives on Women's Rights: The European Convention on Human Rights and Fundamental Freedoms"[7]

"The feminist critique of rights has several related aspects. One facet of this critique is that rights are inherently individualistic and competitive and women's experience is not easily translated into this narrowly accepted language of rights. Rights rhetoric can simplify complex power relations but it fails to overcome existing structural inequalities which are woven into women's daily lives. A perverse but consistent result of rights-based strategies is the reinforcement of the most privileged groups in society. Nicola Lacey observes a link between rights claims and ascribing formal equality.

'In a world in which white, male and middle-class people both have more effective access to legal forums and meet a more sympathetic response when they get there, the ascription of formally equal rights will in effect entrench the competitively asserted rights of these privileged people.'

Feminists have also convincingly illustrated that the ostensibly universal category of 'individual' suggested by liberal theorists is constructed on the basis of male attributes. The liberal legal world ignores the gender inequalities which are built into the very definition of the system. Men and women cannot compete if the gender neutral rules are established to suit the apparent interests and needs of a man's world. Consistent with many other international human rights documents, the European Convention embodies the classical liberal position of the individual and there is an assumption that human rights discourse is gender-neutral.

Another facet of the critique of rights rests on their inapplicability in the private sphere. The public world of state, market, politics and men is perceived as superior to the private realm of women and the family. In the USA and Canada, the public/private dichotomy has been at the centre of the argument concerning the ineffectiveness of rights. The argument is that rights discourse takes for granted that there is or should be a division between the public world, that enforces rights, and a private world of family life in which individuals pursue their diverse goals, relatively free from state interference. The limitation of rights usage to the public sphere is a special disadvantage to women and children who may face oppression in the hidden private sphere.

On a more pragmatic level, many feminists fear that by diverting attention away from political reform and into legal disputes, rights-based strategies will limit aspira-

---

[6]   See the extract below taken from E. Kingdom, "Body Politics and Rights" in J. Bridgeman & S. Millns (eds), *Law and Body Politics: Regulating the Female Body* (Aldershot: Dartmouth, 1995), p. 1.

[7]   In A. Bottomley (ed.), *Feminist Perspectives on the Foundational Subjects of Law* (London: Cavendish, 1996), p. 223, pp. 225–226.

tions by merely reframing debates within the dominant discourse and increasing reliance upon a predominantly male judiciary. Thus, this emphasis on rights will inevitably be at the expense of other aspects of women's situation. As the legal system is skewed in favour of those whose interests are already protected in the law (the prevalent norms are based on male attributes), then rights discourse iś unlikely to change the structural inequalities of power. Moreover, the discourse may not allow women to address the fundamental issues underlying inequality, questions of the feminisation of poverty, inequality in earnings, and the organisation of child care. A primary concern, then, is that rights may be appropriated by the powerful and women's concerns will continue to be marginalised."

Stephanie Palmer weighs the problems of rights discourse against its benefits. Benefits include the fact that claims formulated in terms of rights have, in the past, resulted in legislation aimed at eradicating discrimination against women[8]; the acceptability of rights discourse has enabled marginalised perspectives to be introduced into debate; and that rights discourse enables a claim to be made forcefully and empowers individuals. As Carol Smart suggests, giving by way of example the right to reproductive choice, identification of a rights claim enables an issue which was previously considered private to be brought into the public realm.[9] Stephanie Palmer concludes that women cannot give up on the law and suggests that women should welcome the potential of a document such as the European Convention specifying formal rights:

> "[T]he introduction of the European Convention into domestic law may provide an opportunity to unsettle existing discourses. A space may be created which would allow women's perspectives and experiences to enter into the law. There could be openings to ask previously unasked questions and to reframe debates. The introduction of a formal declaration of rights will not solve political and social conflicts within a society but it can heighten awareness of the conflicts. It has the potential to mobilise movements, to influence political debate, and, perhaps, to bring about social change."[10]

Traditional declarations of rights have focused upon civil and political rights, such as the right to life, the right to freedom of expression, the right to bodily integrity and the right to a fair trial, rather than upon social and economic rights such as the right to housing, adequate food and a minimum standard of living. Social and economic rights often implicate the private sphere and, therefore, may have more resonance with women's concerns. Yet, whilst being expressed in gender neutral terms, the specific harms suffered by women are frequently not considered to amount to an infringement of their civil and political rights.

---

[8]   For example, the Equal Pay Act 1970 and the Sex Discrimination Act 1975.
[9]   C. Smart, *Feminism and the Power of Law*, *supra*, n. 3 at p. 146.
[10] S. Palmer, "Critical Perspectives on Women's Rights: The European Convention on Human Rights and Fundamental Freedoms" in A. Bottomley (ed.), *supra*, n. 7 at p. 242.

S. PALMER
"Critical Perspectives on Women's Rights: The European Convention on Human Rights and Fundamental Freedoms"[11]

". . . [T]he participation of women in political life and formal equality in the eyes of the law has not led to social justice or real equality between men and women. Those matters of concern to women, in the field of civil and political rights, are often defined in law in such a way that women's voice is not heard. For example, the law of pornography is perceived within a framework of freedom of expression versus morality, even though it clearly affects the status and dignity of women and may even contribute to violence against women. The law on abortion is regulated by the criminal law and controlled as a medical matter, rather than as an issue of women's right to choose. Thus the right to terminate a pregnancy could easily be qualified by the competing interests of the State in the welfare of foetal life. Domestic violence against women is not a central part of the civil and political rights agenda. It is only very recently that the criminal law has protected women against martial rape. The priority of traditional rights is the protection of men and women within the public sphere. It provides a system of rights that the individual can assert against the state. But where the harms against women are distinctive, their needs are rarely addressed.

It is hardly surprising that some feminists should be sceptical about the difference that more rights would make to their everyday lives. They point to legislation such as the Sex Discrimination Act 1975 which has failed to deliver the promised equality between men and women. Some feminists suggest that a rights-based strategy is misguided in a liberal legal world antipathetic to feminist ideals. Feminists, such as the sociologist Carol Smart, have even concluded that the use of rights discourse to achieve equality has been counterproductive; it has led to false hopes and perhaps even been detrimental to women's claims. Understandably, experience of the limitations of rights-based discrimination statutes has led to doubts about the wisdom of exploiting law as the most critical strategy in achieving equality."

This masking of the harms inflicted upon women occurs within the context of the public/private divide discussed in the first chapter. By failing to recognise harm inflicted upon women as infringing their legal rights, the law has identified a private sphere immune from legal interference:

F. BEVERIDGE & S. MULLALLY
"International Human Rights and Body Politics"[12]

"The exclusion of women's accounts of their experiences from legal discourse has been facilitated by the public/private dichotomy of liberal theory and practice. Criticisms of the public/private divide have been central to feminist critiques of the liberal State. Carol Pateman has argued that the 'dichotomy between the public and the private . . . is, ultimately, what the feminist movement is all about.' Contemporary liberalism expresses its commitment to liberty by sharply separating the public power of the State

---

[11] In A. Bottomley (ed.), *ibid.*, pp. 224–225.
[12] In J. Bridgeman & S. Millns (eds), *Law and Body Politics: Regulating the Female Body* (Aldershot: Dartmouth, 1995), p. 240, pp. 248–251.

from the private relationships of civil society, and by setting strict limits on the State's ability to intervene in private life. However, as Pateman notes, this division between private and public spheres is constructed as a division within the world of men. Civil society is conceptualised by liberal theory in abstraction from domestic life, and so the latter remains 'forgotten' in theoretical discussion. The domestic sphere is thus rendered invisible within liberal theory and practice.

Failure to apply concepts of rights and justice to the domestic sphere reflects the lingering influence of pre-liberal ideas about the 'naturalness' of the traditional family. The traditional family is seen as a bastion of civilisation and a precondition for social stability and so remains immune to judicial reform. The idea of the domestic sphere as constituting a separate sphere to which the concept of justice is not appropriate is accepted also by Rawls. He suggests that the concept of an independent self distinct from its values and ends may not be appropriate when considering one's 'personal affairs' or family ties. This leads one to Sandel's conclusion:

> 'As the independent self finds its limits in those aims and attachments from which it cannot stand apart, so justice finds its limits in those forms of community that engage the identity as well as the interests of the participants.'

For these reasons and others, the domestic sphere has not been subjected to the same tests of justice as the public sphere. Rights discourse has generally failed to transcend this notion of 'separate spheres of justice' and has instead concerned itself with problems arising within the 'public' rather than the domestic sphere.

Difficulties in articulating harms suffered by women within this conceptual framework have been exacerbated by the legal recognition of a right to privacy. The right to privacy is a derivation of the classical liberal values of freedom and autonomy. It separates the personal or the intimate from the public sphere, where the 'public' includes both State and civil society. It serves to remove a sphere of action from the regulation or control of the State . . .

Rights serve to draw a distinction between public and private fields. Rights can render certain matters private, either through silence (the failure of law to specifically recognise particular claims), or through the invocation of a 'privatising' right (privacy, autonomy, freedom). Thus some claims are protected at the expense of others, by rendering some of the claims involved invisible to law. To leave the body in a 'private' or 'intimate' sphere, beyond legal control, is therefore to replicate the 'invisibility' of women and women's bodies in dominant discourses of rights. Gender neutral rights discourses fail to take account of the deeply gendered nature of society: they are predicated on a public/private divide which is not gender neutral.

The dichotomies between public and private and between the State and civil society are reproduced in international law through traditional doctrines of State responsibility and a focus within international human rights law on direct State violations of individual rights. Harms suffered by women at the hands of private individuals or within the family have been placed outside of the conceptual framework of international human rights. Feminists have argued that a failing of international human rights norms is that by not recognising the gendered consequences of their application they render invisible particular problems suffered by women:

> 'The differences in the nature and the level of threats to the enjoyment of their rights to life and to bodily integrity that women and men face justify the conclusion that women and men do not enjoy these rights on an equal

basis, which is the promise held out to women by the major human rights instruments.'

Where the particular problems faced by women have been addressed in the substance of human rights instruments, the instruments (and related enforcement mechanisms) have generally been located on the periphery of the international human rights process."

Rights discourse is inherently individualistic. The presentation of rights as possessed by individuals forces those individuals into an adversarial process in which one right is pitted in opposition to another in order to determine which presents the strongest claim.

F. BEVERIDGE & S. MULLALLY
"International Human Rights and Body Politics"[13]

"Rights discourse has also been criticised by feminists because of what is perceived as the inherent indeterminacy of rights claims. Unresolved normative conflicts abound within theories of rights and determinate criteria for resolving such conflicts are often not available. Resorting to rights strategies, it is argued, raises the spectre of provoking competing and often conflicting rights claims which potentially limit a woman's autonomy and control over her body to an even greater extent. Rights may produce counter claims to other rights including, *inter alia*, foetal rights, children's rights and men's rights to decide whether or not a biological offspring is born."

Elizabeth Kingdom focuses upon the dilemma arising from the experience of feminists who presented claims in terms of rights and have now become wary of how much this can achieve because "[a]ppeals to rights, however attractive at first sight, frequently conceal inadequate theories of law in relation to women's social position."[14] She suggests an alternative discourse to rights, one of "capabilities, capacities and competencies".[15] In a later piece, Elizabeth Kingdom suggests that it is not necessary to always resort to rights discourse or to reject it completely. There may be circumstances when rights discourse is an appropriate strategy:

E. KINGDOM
"Body Politics and Rights"[16]

"There are at least three strategic reasons which provide grounds for deciding to adopt rights discourse. The first, which I call the ineluctability of rights discourse, is where

[13] F. Beveridge & S. Mullally, *ibid.*, p. 247.
[14] E. Kingdom, *What's Wrong With Rights? Problems for Feminist Politics of Law*, *supra*, n. 4 at p. 1.
[15] E. Kingdom, "Birthrights: Equal or Special?", *ibid.*, p. 130.
[16] In J. Bridgeman & S. Millns (eds), *supra*, n. 12 at p. 1, pp. 10–17.

the legal-political context in question is so firmly defined in terms of rights discourse that for any intervention to be successful it too must be cast in those terms. The second, which I call the re-assertion of rights discourse, is where the limitations of rights discourse are judged to be less important than its political effectiveness. The third, which I call the conversion strategy, is where feminists can devise ways to convert conventionally conceived 'women's rights' into rights which genuinely improve women's position.

1. The ineluctability of rights discourse
The absence in the U.K. of a formal bill of rights and a written constitution presents U.K. feminists with different possibilities of involvement in legal-political issues from those experienced by feminists in Canada and in the U.S. The existence of the Canadian Charter of Rights and Freedoms and of the American Constitution can be seen as requiring feminist interventions in legal politics at the level of the State to formulate their strategies in terms of the prevailing rights discourse. As we shall see, feminists are by no means agreed on the progressive nature of this type of rights discourse. Similarly, Hilary Charlesworth, noting this disagreement, observes that in Australia 'the politics of federalism and legalism have produced a culture wary of rights discourse.'

It is arguable, then, that the experiences of feminists involved in American and Canadian constitutional politics cannot easily be translated to the U.K. On the other hand, U.K. feminists cannot afford to postpone assessment of the best ways to intervene in legal politics of this sort. Debates on the desirability of a U.K. bill of rights are intensifying, as are demands for the incorporation of the European Convention on Human Rights into British Law. More generally, at a time when the balance of power between European Community law and that of its Member States is far from static, the potential of the European Social Charter could become more of a feminist issue if the U.K. government is forced into greater European involvement, or indeed seeks it out . . .

2. The re-assertion of rights discourse
From the early 1980s, representatives of the Critical Legal Studies movement (henceforth CLS) have sustained a critique of rights discourse which is conveniently summarised into four main points by Mark Tushnet:

'(i) Once one identifies what counts as a right in a specific setting, it invariably turns out that the right is unstable; significant but relatively small changes in the social setting can make it difficult to sustain the claim that a right remains implicated.
(ii) The claim that a right is implicated in some settings produces no determinate consequences.
(iii) The concept of rights falsely converts into an empty abstraction (reifies) real experiences that we ought to value for their own sake.
(iv) The use of rights in contemporary discourse impedes advances by progressive social forces.'

. . . The criticism levelled against CLS work is that, far from impeding progressive politics, rights discourse is an essential strategy of particular importance both for feminist politics in general and for feminist bodyright strategy as it involves poor women and women of colour . . .

[A] vital weakness of the CLS position is that it neglects the motivational power of rights discourse.

'For the historically disempowered, the conferring of rights is symbolic of all the denied aspects of their humanity: rights imply a respect that places one in the referential range of self and others, that elevates one's status from human body to social being.'

... Feminists ... need only to remember that legal outcomes are produced by a variety of conditions, some of which may be formally legal, others emanating from feminist politics, others again a function of the personalities and particular circumstances of the parties involved.

Support for this position can be found in the work of Frances Olsen, Martha Minow and Didi Herman. At first sight, Olsen's work on the dilemma between rights-oriented and non-rights strategies is like Schneider's: a formulaic approach according to which feminists must decide either to use rights discourse or not to do so. In fact, Olsen emphasises the immensely complex ways in which rights discourse can both restrict feminist thinking and support campaigns for important social reforms. Consonant with this observation, Martha Minow argues for using rights discourse as a tool of communal dialogue in which conflict is made audible and unavoidable; she knows the limitations of rights discourse but sees its potential too: 'rights rhetoric bears traditional meanings, but it is capable of carrying new meanings.'

Didi Herman also recognises this potential. In the context of the emergence of new social movements, she analyses the wins and losses associated with the appeal to rights in the campaigns and struggles for legal equality waged by Canadian lesbians and gays. Her view is that the 'lesbian and gay rights problematic' cannot be restricted to an abstract debate about the pros and cons of rights discourse: '[m]ore often than not, rights claims are neither radical rearticulations nor dangerous and diversionary.' Herman is correct to expose the artificiality of an all-or-nothing approach to the use of rights discourse, not least since that limited view precludes what I shall now discuss, the conversion strategy.

3. The conversion strategy

... [C]ritical examination of rights discourse otherwise fixed at the level of indignant rhetoric can produce a reconceptualisation which gives directions for clearly identifiable bodyright strategy, ... To formulate a conversion strategy like this is inevitably a complex task, requiring attention to very different types of documents and analyses ...

First, the conversion strategy demands familiarity with exploitable shifts in rights discourse. Nedjati analyses the changing jurisprudence of the concept and scope of individual human rights in the European Commission. He notes that the Commission is taking a more liberal approach by its willingness to take into account the economic and social conditions of the High Contracting Party involved in the case in question. For example, in a case brought against compulsory sex education in Denmark, the Commission ruled that, given the social development of Denmark, it could reasonably be held that compulsory sex education could help to combat unwanted pregnancies and should not therefore be banned ...

As well as demanding familiarity with variations in rights discourse, the conversion strategy is aided by scrutiny of different feminist approaches to bodyright strategy. A useful source is Hellum's work on new reproductive technology, the variety of positions advanced by feminists and the corresponding slogans they have adopted. Her discussion brings to mind the feminist critique of the legal subject as having a right over its body discussed in *Right Over Body*. She cites rights-based positions, such as the demand of the Norwegian Association of Childless Persons that childlessness be seen as a disease entitling women, including lesbian and single women, to statutory rectification. Hellum suggests that this position is not merely optimistic. It underestimates the extent to which reproductive technology treats women's bodies as fertility machines. In contrast, FINRAGE (Feminist International Network Against Reproductive and Genetic Engineering) adopted the slogan 'we are our bodies, we are our eggs' to deny the dichotomy between body and soul [sic] and that between fertility and body. These dramatically opposed positions surely make it otiose to observe that unity among feminists over whether to adopt a rights-orientated strategy, over the choice of feminist slogans, indeed over bodyright strategy in general, is not to be expected.

To underline this point, Outshoorn provides an informative description of the different slogans adopted by the women's liberation movement in different countries to express its demand for women to be the moral judges over abortion and to take responsibility for their decision.

> 'In a country with a strong natural rights tradition, such as the United Kingdom or the United States, abortion was defined as a woman's right. In the Federal Republic of Germany and in the Netherlands the demand was phrased in terms of control over one's body enshrined in the German feminist slogan 'Dein Körper gehört dich' [Your body belongs to you] or the Dutch 'Baas in eigen buik' [Boss of your belly].'

As noted previously, despite feminist critiques of the notion of the legal subject and the ease with which law assimilates it into its preferred category of ownership, the feminists whom Outshoorn describes here have clearly decided to play the legal game and deploy the discourse of right over body. As she observes, however, the result has been that the resolution of the opposition between pro-choice and anti-abortion movements is inevitably moved into the parliamentary arena, leading to extended and frequently acrimonious political hostilities."

The debate about the utility of resorting to rights claims revolves around two considerations. One is the appropriateness of seeking "equal" rights for women as opposed to asserting women's "difference". The second is the possibility for women to approximate the status of the autonomous individual who is the usual subject of legal rights. It is to these issues that we now turn.

2.1 Equality and its limitations

2.1.i *Equality and difference*
Should women strive to assert their equality to, or difference from, men? Hence, might equality be achieved through claims for equal rights with men or should the law be encouraged to acknowledge difference? Given that we live in a society constructed by men and in which men currently hold privileged positions, which option represents the most attractive proposition for feminists?

Before being able to respond to these questions it is necessary to ascertain what "equality" means. In this respect it is appropriate to make a distinction between equal treatment, equal opportunities and equal consequences. Failure to provide maternity provision in the workplace means that men and women are treated equally. But because women usually undertake the role of primary carer for their children, it may be that employment opportunities available to men and women differ as a result and that women suffer discrimination. Legislation passed in an attempt to achieve equality for women, such as the Equal Pay Act 1970 and the Sex Discrimination Act 1975, presents formal equality for women. It does not necessarily (and invariably does not materially) translate into substantive equality, given the position of women in society. A major criticism of this legislation is how ineffective it has been in achieving equality of outcome for women in the public sphere of the work-place.[17]

Patricia Smith refers to three distinct conceptualisations of equality: material equality, moral equality and the Aristotelean notion that like cases should be treated alike and unlike cases differently in proportion to their differences. She explains how, given that within liberal thought women are not considered to be the same as men, different treatment is justified.

P. SMITH
"On Equality: Justice, Discrimination, and Equal Treatment"[18]

"Are men and women equal? What does it mean to say that they are or are not? It may help to consider what it means to say that any two things are equal. Sometimes when we say that two things are equal, we mean that they are the same, identical, or interchangeable. Let us call this *material* or *factual* equality. Often courts have referred to equality in this way, but it is a very restricted notion of equality, and it does not actually apply well to human beings, as no two human beings are ever identical. Nevertheless, when courts determine the equality of classes of persons, they are deciding whether those classes are materially the same. This often translates into assumptions (or deliberations) about whether they would function in the same way in certain specified circumstances. This analysis has always caused problems for women because traditional worldviews have always delegated different roles and functions to men and women, as though the roles were defined by nature. That is, men and women have been viewed as materially different — different in their factual character.

Often when we say that two things are equal, we mean that they are of comparable value, that they are worth the same. We mean something like that when we refer to human beings as being equal. When we say that 'all men are created equal,' we mean that morally speaking, they are of equal worth. Let us call that *moral* equality. Every human life, we say, has the same intrinsic value, but what that amounts to in practical terms has always been a difficult matter, especially when races, sexes, and nationalities have been viewed as materially different.

People frequently claim that they are entitled to equality: to equal opportunities, equal treatment, equal protection of the law, or perhaps even an equal distribution of material goods. These sorts of claims to equality are much like claims to justice. Equal

[17] A. E. Morris & S. M. Nott, *Working Women and the Law: Equality and Discrimination in Theory and Practice* (London: Routledge, 1991).
[18] In P. Smith (ed.), *Feminist Jurisprudence* (Oxford: Oxford University Press, 1993), p. 17, pp. 17–20.

treatment and just treatment may be the same thing. We know that equality and justice are closely connected, but what the connection is has always generated considerable controversy. The old Aristotelian notion of procedural justice enjoins us to treat like cases alike and unlike cases differently in proportion to their differences. According to this formula (which is certainly one of the most widely accepted propositions in the history of philosophy and law), the puzzle of equality has three pieces.

First, we must identify like cases. Are men and women (or Christians and Jews, blacks and whites, rich and poor, or educated and illiterate) relevantly similar or different? This is the question on which most of history has focused. Second, once we have identified who is alike or equal, what does it mean to treat these equals alike? What is equal opportunity, equal treatment, or equal protection of the law? Third, if people can be different but still equal, what does it mean to treat different cases in proportion to their differences? This last question has hardly been discussed at all in traditional legal and philosophical discourse, but it is central to recent feminist discussions of equality.

Consider the first set of issues. We must be able to recognize which cases are alike, and that is not as easy as it might seem. In fact, no two cases, situations, or individuals (except mathematical abstractions) are exactly alike in every respect. So we must decide which features are relevant to our considerations, and those relevant features will then determine whether the cases are equal. For example, some features of men and women are similar, and others are not. We must decide which features are relevant to the case in question and whether those features are similar. Thus, determinations of equality require judgment; they are not self-evident . . .

It is this presumption (the presumption of *in*equality) that began to change in the seventeenth century, with movements for the recognition of universal or human rights and democratic, constitutional government. In philosophy, Hobbes presumed the natural equality of all men, as did Locke, Rousseau, Kant, and most major thinkers in the Western tradition from that time on (a striking exception being Nietzsche). Even those thinkers, however, did not presume the moral or material equality of men and women.

Still, we should keep in mind that the presumption of equality was true in theory or in rhetoric more than in fact and that it did not mean that all men were to be treated equally. Instead, it meant that unequal treatment had to be justified. That is, it did not deny inequality altogether; it merely shifted the burden of proof. So even though the English law spoke bravely of the rights of all Englishmen, English workers who did not own property were denied the right to vote, because property ownership was considered a relevant difference. Even though the American revolutionaries declared all men to be created equal, their Constitution recognized slavery as a legitimate practice, because blacks were considered relevantly different. Even in the twentieth century, illiteracy was considered a relevant ground for denying basic rights, such as the right to vote. Certain races, nationalities, and classes have always been denied equal rights. And women have always been, and still are, denied equal rights on the ground that they are different and therefore not equal. We may say that all men are created equal, but we do not act as though it were true. Furthermore, we did not even say that women are equal to men until very recently, and even now the claim is highly controversial.

So determining which cases are alike, who are moral equals, and what counts as a relevant difference are difficult matters that have progressed very slowly through human history. Nevertheless, addressing these questions is absolutely crucial to understanding the nature of equality. The traditional view is that unless we can determine which cases are alike, our answers to the other two issues will be futile ... [M]any feminists now believe that this position is mistaken, or at least overdrawn.

The second set of issues requires us to figure out what it means to treat like cases alike. In many cases this is a relatively easy task (especially given the way in which the first issue has been handled). Once it has been determined that two cases are alike, they must be treated the same. For example, if two groups, say landowners and non-landowners, are deemed political equals, then they should have the same political rights: the same right to vote, the same right to a fair trial, the same right to free speech, and so forth. Similarly, if two legal cases are found to be alike, then they must have the same determination according to the same rule of law. Thus, it appears that the difficult question is the first one — which cases are alike. Once that is determined, it is usually not difficult to decide how to treat them alike ...

The [final] set of issues asks what it means to treat different cases differently in proportion to their differences.

One interesting thing about this last set of issues is that it has hardly been discussed at all. Philosophers have had little to say about what it means to treat different cases in proportion to their differences. And in law, a determination of difference in the courts has always led to deference to legislative action of any sort. This has always been a particular problem for women.

For example, because women were considered different, they could be banned from universities, libraries, businesses, and professions. It was simply up to the legislatures (which, of course, were composed entirely of men) to deal with such matters as they saw fit. If they felt that it was inappropriate or disruptive for any woman to attend a university or enter a library or a business establishment, they could bar women from the premises. If they felt that it was indecent or 'unladylike' for any woman to practice law, or carpentry, or bartending, or medicine, they could deny all women a license to practice, simply on the ground that they are women. Such action in the United States would violate the constitutional rights of men, but because women were considered different, they had no constitutional rights to equal protection of the law. It did no good to appeal to the courts. The courts, assuming that this was not an equal protection issue and thus not a constitutional issue, deferred to the legislatures. Women had few rights of their own, and certainly no right to be treated as equal to men. This view was seldom challenged until the 1970s.

What this shows is that despite the egalitarian movements of the seventeenth and eighteenth centuries and the ever-widening presumption that 'all men are created equal,' the ancient presumption of inequality was maintained between men and women until well into the twentieth century. Although women gained the right to vote in 1920, their progress toward equality was otherwise sharply limited. Until the 1970s the courts maintained the idea that separate spheres of endeavor for men and women were natural and good. Women should inhabit the private domain of home and family into which the law ought not intrude. Only men should inhabit the public sphere of politics and market. This assumption made women dependent on men and subject to their authority. Thus, hierarchal institutions of patriarchy were maintained as though decreed by nature."

Patricia Smith argues that men and women are not in fact the same. This is not only because no two people are alike, but also because men and women have separate roles which have historically been ascribed to them. The claim to moral equality also confronts problems given that these ascribed material differences are overladen with distinct and opposing values. The Aristotelean notion that like cases should be treated alike and unlike cases in accordance with their differences, means that treating women differently could be justified because women are different from men. Smith explains that women started by arguing that they were the same as men and therefore should be treated like men in law, in politics and in economic activities. She points out three shortcomings of this approach:

    (i)   The standard of comparison is the male norm. Similar treatment is only justified if women are the same as men in respect of the quality under consideration;

    (ii) Women are starting from an unequal position (because they have in the past been excluded), and are not competing on the same basis (because social norms require women to be also primarily responsible for running the home);

    (iii) Where the male is the norm, it may be impossible for equal treatment to be attained in those areas of women's lives, such as pregnancy, which are not experienced by men. In such cases, claims that women are the same as men work to the detriment of women. In the example of provision for pregnant women in the workplace, a woman is clearly in a different situation from that in which a man could find himself. To claim that the similarity is with men who are temporarily disabled is to compare a normal process with an illness. To recognise the difference is to perpetuate discrimination against women because of their capacity for childbearing.[19]

The content of equality, criticised above for taking as its standard of comparison a male norm, may depend upon the values of the particular society in which equality is sought:

T. LOENEN
"Comparative Legal Feminist Scholarship and the Importance of a Contextual Approach to Concepts and Strategies: The Case of the Equality Debate"[20]

"[D]oes equality in itself say anything about the *content* of the treatment of likes/ unlikes? Does it answer the critique of both U.S. and European feminists, that the dominant standard of treatment is geared to a male model of living and working? The Aristotelian definition of equality does not seem to give any clues in this respect. It is completely silent as to which treatment is due. But this is only so if one treats the definition as a mere abstract, semantic device, and not as a concept that is embedded in a specific legal culture. I do not think it is possible, or meaningful, to isolate a

---

[19]   P. Smith, "On Equality: Justice, Discrimination, and Equal Treatment" in P. Smith (ed.), *ibid.*, p. 21.
[20]   (1995) 3 *Feminist Legal Studies* 71 at 85.

concept in this way. So I do not agree with Westen that the concept of equality is 'empty'. I do acknowledge, however, that the content of equality (or rather, the content of the *treatment* which should be equal) will depend on the overall values, principles and aspirations prevalent in a given society. We cannot escape our historic boundaries and think beyond them. In that sense equality will always be contextually defined' and thus contingent. But that is not the same as 'empty'. These values, principles and aspirations must be our point of reference for interpreting equality and giving it content."

Julia Sohrab considers how in the United Kingdom, because of the male comparitor and the failure to acknowledge the responsibilities of women in the private sphere, equal treatment claims may do no more than assist women who start from a privileged position to put themselves in the same position as middle-class (privileged) men. Equal treatment does not, therefore, necessarily translate into equality of outcome for all women and, furthermore, those women who do achieve equality are required to fit into the public structure that was determined without their participation, and to assimilate into existing practices. Sohrab further argues that equality may amount to nothing more than a procedure so that, despite formal equality, equality of outcome is not achieved:

J. A. Sohrab
**"Avoiding the 'Exquisite Trap': A Critical look at the Equal Treatment/
Special Treatment Debate in Law"[21]**

"[T]here are many criticisms to be made of equal treatment as a way of achieving substantive equality.

While appearing to be a neutral standard, equal treatment as interpreted by the courts tends to apply the 'male norm'. Because equal treatment implies a comparison with men, women have been granted equality insofar as they are perceived to be the *same* as men. Some courts have held for instance that there can be no discrimination on grounds of pregnancy because there is no male equivalent. In the words of the judge in *Bliss* 'any inequality between the sexes in this area is not created by legislation but *by nature*' (emphasis added). Here a relevant 'difference' supported unequal treatment, no matter how categorical, disadvantageous or cumulative it was. This type of reasoning forces one to find a 'sex-neutral category' to compare with, such as men with a temporary disability. This not only reinforces, but crucially does not challenge the 'naturalness' of the 'difference'; no argument is in sight about differences being socially constructed. It just reinforces the idea of women as 'victims' of their hormones. Even after the judgment of the European Court of Justice (ECJ) in *Dekker* this issue has not been definitively resolved. The ECJ held that discrimination on the grounds of pregnancy has to be direct discrimination on the grounds of sex, but in the U.K. in the *Webb* case the court persisted in applying a comparative approach and maintaining

---

[21] (1993) 1 *Feminist Legal Studies* 141 at 146–152. It should be noted that the decision of the Court of Appeal in the *Webb* case, referred to in this extract, was overturned by the House of Lords following referral of the case to the European Court of Justice (*Webb v. EMO (U.K.) Ltd* [1994] I.R.L.R. 482; *Webb v. EMO (U.K.) Ltd (No. 2)* [1995] 1 W.L.R. 1454).

that dismissing a pregnant woman for reasons arising out of her pregnancy would be direct discrimination only if a male employee would have received more favourable treatment.

Even in circumstances where women are compared to men, comparison with the 'male model' will not necessarily bring women substantive equality with men. The male model does not take into account the roles and activities of women in the 'private sphere' nor the segregated nature of the labour market. As Wildman has put it: 'if people have been treated differently in society they will appear in dissimilar positions when they are compared'. MacKinnon has argued that equal treatment or gender neut-rality only means that while a few women gain access to the preconditions necessary to assert equality on male terms, the majority of women lose the guarantees of their 'traditional' roles. Equal treatment feminists appear to ignore the structural barriers that gendered social relations create. That is, if pregnancy and motherhood are barriers into the workplace, then demanding gender-neutral parental leave laws seems to ring hollow. Equal treatment feminists are also criticised for aspiring to the model of the conditions and norms typically found among middle-class white men. Their priority, it is argued, is to get greater access to the workplace, to challenge the 'stereotypical assumptions' that generally impede or structure women's employment differently to men's, but this cannot help the women who do conform to these stereotypical assump-tions.

Therefore one is left wondering whether anti-discrimination legislation can offer more than merely access to male-defined resources (in the broadest sense) for a few relatively privileged women. The male model appears to place us in 'Wollstonecraft's dilemma': either we must become like men or accept subordination and dependency.

Giving women the same rights as men also tends to freeze the status quo: its logic allows no challenge to the general practices in any area. The rights that men have are not necessarily ideal, such as being able to do nightwork or working in hazardous and unsafe employment. Moreover men may not have all the rights that feminists want. Thus as Gibson has put it: ' "equal rights" can be no more than a demand for access to the structure. If it is the structure which is the problem, equal rights to it are not an exciting prospect'. An approach which is not frozen into the status quo would for instance be to challenge the employment market, which is structured in stereotypically male terms; workers with family responsibilities who need a 'family wage' but who do not participate primarily in childrearing or caring work. Indeed writers such as Dowd and Joan Williams squarely locate the challenge for feminists as being to the *structure* of the workplace. Accepting the male model prevents us from looking at these struc-tures and seeing that to decrease inequality in employment there must be a recognition that workers of both sexes have home lives and personal needs as well as work com-mitments.

While the 'male model' is a very useful analytical tool, it is important to look critic-ally at it. Feminist literature tends to accept that behind this model will always be a real man, and so the model will always work to the disadvantage of women. Thus a crucial question is whether equal treatment or the male model really are 'male'. Indeed it is the case that equal treatment while proclaimed to be a gender-neutral standard more often than not conceals male gendered life patterns. But where the model applied is a male one, rather than a gender neutral one, this is a political decision on the part of the courts, and does not mean that equal treatment is inherently male. Where the model applied is male, it is focused this way because of interest-oriented legislation and interpretation by the courts, the administration of which is not free from contradiction. Moreover, when the male model is biased towards men we need to be aware of what men are envisaged; this man will not necessarily correspond to real men but rather to the 'prototype' who is conceived as independent, unconnected to others, abstracted from messy realities. Not all men will fit this prototype, although more may fit it than women . . .

It has been forcefully argued that equal treatment is 'empty' because it offers no criteria for determining which differences are relevant and what counts as legitimate. This criticism can for instance be aimed at constitutional guarantees of equality for all: here where equal treatment does not refer to specific goals, it may become 'procedural', that is concerned with rules of conduct 'irrespective of the end being pursued' . . .

But equal treatment is not inherently empty, and the interpretation of equality which mainly privileges the male standard is a political decision. Where there are goals and there is judicial or political will, equality provisions can be used effectively . . . But interpretation of course depends on the criteria used, and even where there are criteria for interpreting equality, these may simply not be feminist criteria, or they may be too vague formulations of a goal, such as 'equal opportunity in the workplace'. If feminist political strength were greater this could possibly influence the criteria used by the courts."

Susie Gibson, in the article from which Julia Sohrab quotes, expands upon the unattractive character of "equal rights" when contextualised within what is a problematic structure:

S. Gibson
"The Structure of the Veil"[22]

"In the context of law, then, we can pose the equality issues as follows. First we cannot, in any meaningful way, argue that the legal *structure* is 'equal' because any system (legal or otherwise) must consolidate certain prior decisions as to social priorities. In the context of, say, property law, the decision must be made as to whether this or that relationship is sufficiently important to bind third parties. That decision having been made, a *hierarchy* of priorities has been established. Secondly, 'equal rights' can be no more than a demand for access to the structure. If it is the structure which is the problem, equal rights to it are not an exciting prospect. This is the limitation of 'formal equality,' and an element in the explanation of so called 'substantive inequality.' Thirdly, 'like treatment' contains a 'due process' aspect which I have not discussed here, but which may arise as an issue in certain circumstances. Fourthly, any 'equality of outcome' may only, in this hierarchised structure, express the pre-determined priorities of the system. 'Equality of outcome' cannot alter what those priorities are and does not alter the methods of management (competition or whatever) of resources. This is the limitation upon attempting to 'equalise' substantive 'inequality,' and an element in the explanation of why 'legal equality' is an ultimately limited objective, albeit perhaps the only feasible one for feminist lawyers."

The perspectives of feminist lawyers pursuing the object of "legal equality" may be widened by Elizabeth Kingdom's identification of four alternative

---

[22]   (1989) 52 *Modern Law Review* 420 at 439.

responses to the limitations of the equal treatment position. The four alternatives are:

  (i)   to maintain the focus upon equality;
  (ii) to focus campaigns upon non-legal strategies;
  (iii) to focus upon the difference between the law and its effects to identify scope for change;
  (iv) to combine equal rights with special rights:

E. KINGDOM
What's Wrong With Rights? Problems for Feminist Politics of Law[23]

"The first response is that, no matter how deep the scepticism and disillusion with equality legislation, the equal rights strategy must be sustained. The moral principle of gender equality, so it could be argued, has been badly served, whether by poorly drafted legislation, whether by that enacted legislation's weakness in comparison with other areas of law, whether through the sexism of the judiciary, or through lack of political will on the part of employers and unions. What is needed, on this argument, is continued pressure for legislative reform, better funding of agencies such as the EOC to improve enforcement, and constant publicity for the potential of the laws in making society more just.

The second response is from those feminists who have opted for analyses and strategies which they see as more radical. These feminists . . . are not concerned 'to achieve formal legal equality. This is primarily because much of the work has been done, but it is also because there is now little faith that formal equality will provide substantive equality'. Such feminists prefer to put their political energies into struggles outside the sphere of the law, for example in setting up rape crisis centres, rather than engaging directly with what they see as bastions of male power and privilege.

The third response is the one from Smart and Brophy[24] . . . They acknowledge the discrepancy between formal legal equality and substantive equality, but what distinguishes their position from the second is that they resist the notion of law as a unified bastion of male power and privilege. On the other hand, they insist that the law must not be 'read' as gender-neutral and that 'it is important to distinguish between the law and the *effects* of law and legal processes in order to identify the contradictions which allow space for change'.

These three responses all emphasise the gap between formal equality and substantive equality and they propose remedies through a variety of legal or extra-legal strategies. In contrast, and this is the fourth response, supporters of the special rights strategy see the problem of equality as a problem with the prevailing analyses of the moral principle of gender equality. The remedy, it is argued, lies in the redefinition of that moral principle in terms of a combination of equal rights and special rights, a combination which must find expression in legislation."

Focusing upon special rights or women's difference, however, may be little

---

[23]   (Edinburgh: Edinburgh University Press, 1991), p. 120.
[24]   C. Smart & J. Brophy, *Women in Law: Explorations in Law, Family and Sexuality* (London: Routledge and Kegan Paul, 1985), p. 15.

more than the other side of the equality coin, involving the identification of situations and circumstances in which women are distinct from men, which under the Aristolean principle, would justify their different treatment. This is not without its own difficulties and may be just as restrictive of women's choices as the traditional equality doctrine in leading to a paternalistic approach to women's difference.

A. E. MORRIS & S. M. NOTT
Working Women and the Law: Equality and Discrimination in Theory and Practice[25]

"The term 'paternalism' is one which is well known to lawyers since it is central to a debate which originated in the nineteenth century and still continues today: that is, when can the law legitimately be used to restrict the liberty of the individual? John Stuart Mill in his essay *On Liberty* was categorical in his belief that paternalism was not a legitimate basis for legal intervention. Apart from some minor concessions — to protect the very young, for example — he was adamant that the desire to act in others' best interests might simply present an excuse for those in power to have society reflect their values and hence exercise a form of tyranny. Mill wrote:

> 'the sole end for which mankind are warranted, individually or collectively, in interfering with the liberty of action of any of their number is self-protection. That the only purpose for which power can be rightfully exercised over any member of a civilised community, against his will, is to prevent harm to others. His own good, either physical or moral, is not a sufficient warrant. He cannot rightfully be compelled to do or forbear because it will be better for him to do so, because it will make him happier, because, in the opinions of others, to do so would be wise or even right.'

Over the years jurists have returned to this debate, particularly when faced with a practical dilemma which has moral overtones such as the law's treatment of homosexuality or prostitution. Though the question is raised most frequently in relation to sexual morality, the issue of when the freedom of the individual can legitimately be curbed is central to law and legal systems. Even if one accepts John Stuart Mill's premise that the law should be used only to prevent behaviour likely to cause harm to others, one can argue endlessly over what exactly that might mean. Undoubtedly it would include physical harm, but does it extend to financial or emotional harm? For example, does an individual have the right to indulge in a habit such as smoking, drinking or drug taking when its consequences might be to cause physical harm to that individual and emotional upheaval to his or her family? Apart from seeking to clarify what exactly is included in the term 'harm', some commentators have disagreed with the fundamental premise put forward by Mill. Jurists such as Stephen and Devlin have argued that society is justified in using the law to underpin those values which are seen as essential to the well-being of that society. The question of whether the individual harms anyone but himself or herself by their conduct is immaterial if the

[25] (London: Routledge, 1991), pp. 31–33, 35.

integrity of society is threatened. Others have suggested that, in certain circumstances, it is proper to protect the individual from self-inflicted harm.

In an essay entitled 'Paternalism', Gerald Dworkin gives various instances in which paternalistic legislation appears justified. The first of these is where it is a 'kind of insurance policy which we take out against making decisions which are far-reaching, potentially dangerous and irreversible'. In these circumstances the individual consents to the state acting on his or her behalf on the basis that at some future date the individual may disregard or not truly appreciate the long-term damage he or she might do to themselves. The second instance involves decisions that might be reached 'under extreme psychological and sociological pressures'. Once more Dworkin emphasises that without those pressures the individual might make a reasoned choice. As it is, the individual is not able to do so, and without legal intervention might arrive at a decision which is not capable of being reversed. The third situation which might warrant legal intervention 'involves dangers which are either not sufficiently understood or appreciated correctly by the persons involved'. On this basis an individual might be prepared to run a considerable risk, particularly if its immediate result is some kind of pleasure or benefit, at the same time disregarding or being ignorant of what might be a very real danger.

From the situations described by Dworkin it would appear that they all have one element in common, namely the potential inability of the individual to make an informed choice. As others have pointed out, John Stuart Mill's thesis of individual choice rests on the premise that, whatever the situation, the individual can and does make not only an autonomous, but also a rational choice regarding their own personal well-being. In reality this may be far from the truth:

> 'Mill endows the average individual with 'too much of the psychology of a middle-aged man whose desires are relatively fixed, not liable to be artificially stimulated by external influences; who knows what he wants and what gives him satisfaction or happiness; and who pursues these things when he can'.'

In theory, therefore, there appears to be a good deal of strength in the argument that some measure of paternalism is an essential quality of any modern legal system. The problem is of course where to draw the line beyond which the 'nanny' state will not interfere. As Dworkin himself admits, there are a great many everyday human activities which carry with them a considerable risk. They include cigarette smoking and driving. Since it is not practicable totally to forbid such activities an effort is made to warn individuals of and protect them from the dangers involved. The strength of these warnings is perhaps tempered by potential losses in revenue and appeals to the rights of the individual.

An analysis of paternalism is directly relevant to the laws affecting working women because it appears to be the guiding force which once inspired much of their treatment. The legislation which banned women and children from the mines and regulated their hours of work is commonly described as 'protective' legislation, implying that there was a paternalistic motive behind the legislation . . .

Paternalism demonstrates that, once a particular case or group of individuals is defined as vulnerable, it legitimises the use of law to protect those individuals. The judgement that the group or class is vulnerable is open to challenge and may change as the years pass. What the paternalistic approach does *not* insist upon is that the group singled out for protection in law should, as a consequence, be accorded inferior treatment. If, for example, it is decided that a woman is vulnerable because of her potential to bear children, that may be a reason for protecting her from hazards at work. The decision might be taken to protect her by excluding her completely from the workplace. Alternatively, work practices could be modified to eliminate, in so far as it is possible, potential dangers. In principle, both approaches are paternalistic, but the former results in the woman being treated in an inferior fashion, the latter as deserving of special consideration. The logic of paternalism is to use the law to protect, and it is not inevitable that the desire to protect must put the individual at a disadvantage. It is essential to appreciate this fact and that, in the past, paternalism has often been used in a negative and not a positive fashion."

2.1.ii *Equality strategies*

Feminists have been versatile in their responses to the challenges of the equality/difference debate. Diana Majury suggests considering "women's specificities" rather than women's differences as a way of avoiding the male as the norm for comparison.

D. MAJURY
"Strategizing in Equality"[26]

"The equality debate among feminist legal thinkers in the United States is polarized between those who describe themselves as equal treatment proponents and those who support some level of legal recognition of women's specificity. I refer here to women's specificity even though I think the term 'specificities' is more appropriate. I use the singular rather than the plural here because most of the writers who wish to affirm at least some of women's 'differences' from men seem to treat women as an undifferentiated group and to ignore differences among women. This assumption — that all women are the same — is one of my major concerns with this approach to equality.

I refer to the women who acknowledge, at least to a limited extent, women's specificity in their approach to equality, as women's difference advocates, rather than women's specificity advocates, because I think it is a more accurate characterisation of their position. However, I have problems with the use of the term difference in the context of equality. Difference is used to refer to women's difference from men, with a clear, implicit acceptance of men as the norm and women as the deviators therefrom. While attempting to affirm and accommodate women's specific attributes, there is within the language of the theory a subtle devaluing of those attributes. The term 'women's specificities' reflects an attempt to circumvent the acceptance of the male norm implicit in the term women's difference. It is an indication of the thoroughness of male domination of our language that we cannot find a term that avoids any implication of male as the norm.

[W]omen's difference advocates propose models of equality that affirmatively provide for at least some differences between women and men. Ann Scales (1981), for example, argues for what she describes as an 'incorporationist approach.' Pursuant to Scales's approach women are recognized as having rights different from men only with respect to those aspects of childbearing and childrearing which are completely unique to women, that is pregnancy and breastfeeding. Following a similar approach, Sylvia Law (1984) proposes an equality model which would distinguish between laws draw-

---

[26] In M. A. Fineman & N. S. Thomadsen (eds), *supra*, n. 1 at p. 320, pp. 321–323.

ing explicit sex-based distinctions and those governing reproductive biology. According to Law, sex-based distinctions are based on culturally imposed stereotypes and are therefore appropriately dealt with through a comparative equal treatment analysis. Distinctions relating to reproduction, however, are based on 'real differences' and therefore require an impact analysis. This distinction between a comparative equal treatment analysis and an impact analysis can be understood by looking at the issue of maternity leave. A refusal specifically to provide maternity leave would constitute equal treatment pursuant to a comparative equal treatment analysis — women and men are being treated in the same way and therefore equally. However, an impact analysis would characterize the refusal to provide maternity leave as discrimination against women because the impact of not providing maternity leave places women at a significant disadvantage in their participation in the paid labor force.

The maternity leave issue similarly provides a useful vehicle through which to examine the contrast between an equal treatment approach and a differences approach, as well as to highlight the limitations shared by both sides of the debate. The equal treatment model would require that maternity be dealt with in exactly the same manner as any other disability which renders a worker temporarily unable to work. On the other hand, difference advocates support some form of maternity leave, separate and distinct from any disability benefits which may be available to the woman worker.

Despite their apparent dissimilarity, the equal treatment model and the women's difference models share a common understanding of equality, an understanding that severely limits the ability of each to address the very real inequalities that women experience. For both sides of the debate, equality means treating people the same. Equal treatment advocates allow no deviation from identical treatment; women's difference advocates justify limited deviation in the name of 'real' difference. Only when the same treatment is seen, for physiological reasons, as not possible for women and men do these feminists argue that we need to expand our understanding of equality to incorporate women's differences. Difference advocates presumably would not support, for example, women-only professional associations because such associations would not be seen to be reproductively or physiologically based.

Those who wish to 'accommodate' women's difference are in search of a clear definition or principle according to which one would be able to determine the appropriate deviations from the norm of identical treatment. They seek an equality formula which can be applied to any situation with consistent and foreseeable results. A variety of different formulae have been proposed. For equal treatment advocates, the equality formula is self-evident — identical treatment in *all* circumstances. Any formulaic approach to equality, whether based on an equal treatment or a differences model, denies the complexity, variety, and compound nature of the problems of inequality that women experience. In the name of clarity, consistency and ease of application, an equality formula collapses women's inequalities into a male-defined standard and reduces those inequalities to biologically-based differences."

Majury argues that equality has frequently been focused upon at the expense of investigation of the specific problem in the context of which argument arises. Rather than taking one model of equality as a starting point and attempting to apply it to all the inequalities of women's lives, she argues that it would be preferable to start with the particular problem and consider from that point which equality model, if any, can be employed to address the problem.

D. MAJURY
"Strategizing in Equality"[27]

"*Equality as Strategy*

To pursue equality as a strategy, I have had to turn away from definitions of equality, legal models, and frameworks. Instead I have begun to look at the specific needs and problems that women experience and the inequalities that women suffer in order to develop ways of addressing these issues in an equality context. The strategy is to argue from the particularized inequality as the means to get it recognized as such — heard, seen and felt as inequality. In this undertaking, none of the existing equality models are of any help. As abstract constructs, these models do not and cannot address the realities of women's lives. An equality framework does not assist one in identifying problems nor in figuring out how to respond to them. In fact, the imposition of an equality model can tend to obscure or distort the realities of women's lives and the inequalities as they are experienced by women. It seems to me, for example, a distortion to characterize the problem of women losing their jobs because of pregnancy as a problem with disability benefits. This is not to downplay the seriousness of inadequate disability benefits nor to say that the solution to the absence of maternity benefits might not be improved disability benefits. But the problem is not the rules regarding disability benefits, it is an unwillingness to accommodate pregnancy within the paid labor force. Once the problem is identified and the desired solution determined, an equality-based approach might be helpful as a tool to work toward the desired result. However, an 'equality' analysis, as such, provides no insight into the problem.

My concern when a lot of time and energy are spent talking and theorizing about equality is that 'equality' becomes vested with a life and meaning of its own, divorced from the particularized experiences of inequality it is intended to address. Equality then becomes a formulaic solution to be imposed on situations of inequality with little or no consideration for the particularities of that situation. In this process, people tend to become wedded to their own equality formula, thereby losing their ability to respond to changing circumstances. The 'equality debates' flow from these rigidly-held positions. Given the ability of our male-dominated systems (legal, political and social) to co-opt, appropriate, misinterpret and subvert feminist challenges, it is dangerous for feminists to become too attached to any particular approach or strategy. We then lose our ability to recognize a strategy's limitations in a male-dominated system and we are unwilling to change course when our strategy has been overtaken or subverted.

An equality strategy involves two very separate undertakings. First, one has to isolate the problem, the specific inequality to be addressed and determine the desired solution. Second, one has to devise an appropriate way to achieve that solution. Many equality theorists seem to have collapsed these two undertakings into one and in so doing have lost sight of the original problem. Isolating the problem is usually a fairly clear task, although the problem itself is often complex. Determining the desired solution is usually more difficult. The various equality models really do not assist in developing solutions; the answers must necessarily flow from the specifics of the situation itself.

The second undertaking in the equality as strategy approach is to identify the method(s) that can be employed toward the desired solution. The legal process is, of course, only one possible method: it can be rejected as inappropriate in the circum-

[27]   D. Majury, *ibid.*, pp. 331–333.

stances; it can be adopted as the exclusive strategy or as the strategy of first instance; or it can be used in conjunction with other methods. Having decided to use the legal system, reliance upon an equality guarantee is only one of a number of possible legal approaches. In making the choice for or against using an equality guarantee, it is inappropriate to allow pre-existing equality formulae to foreclose or constrain one's decision. It is, however, important, in assessing equality as a strategy, to consider the prominence of such equality formulae and their acceptance by decision makers. One must be prepared to argue against the application of an equality formula where such a formula would operate to women's detriment. It would be a mistake, however, to reject equality arguments altogether. Given the current ambiguity about the legal meaning of equality, it would be short sighted, at this time, to concede equality to the equal treatment proponents or to those who argue for a limited acknowledgement of women's difference. These approaches are too easily turned against women.

In this undertaking, it is critically important that feminists not evaluate strategies and desired results in terms of their impact on a particular model of equality. This is not to say that the potential effect of a particular strategy should not be part of the evaluation process. The rigidity and inflexibility inherent in a formulaic approach to equality are probably more harsh and limiting for the most vulnerable groups in our society: women of color, women with disabilities, lesbians. We need to retain a flexible approach to equality in order to be able to respond to multiple inequalities. An assessment of the anticipated 'costs' of a particular strategy, and upon whom the burden of those costs might principally fall, is a critical part of the evaluation of any strategy (Fineman, 1983). Strategies and results need to be evaluated in terms of their effect upon women and other disadvantaged groups, not in relation to some abstract theory of equality. Solutions should not be adjusted to fit a narrow concept of equality. Reliance upon an equality guarantee should not be rejected as a strategy simply because the desired solution does not seem to fit into an accepted model of equality.

Feminist equality discussions would be better focused on specific issues rather than on the abstract polar notions of 'equal treatment' and so-called 'special treatment'. I have had numerous conversations with feminist equality litigators in which their response to a proposed solution or strategy has been 'Oh no, we can't argue that, it conflicts with our approach to equality' or 'that's special treatment, not equality' or 'we have to argue X because that's what is 'equal'.' These attitudes reflect an inappropriate privileging of equality over the very real needs of the women who are suffering the very real inequality. In contrast, equality strategy seeks to expand the meanings and understandings of equality to address the inequalities to which women are subjected. Given the prominence and lip-service currently paid to equality discourse in Canadian legal forums, women would be foolish to abandon 'equality' to those who seek to use it against women. Rather, we should use the indeterminacy of equality to argue on women's behalf in a variety of different circumstances.

The equality project, as I have outlined it, requires that the identification of the problem and the determination of the solution be seen as distinct and separate from implementation. Notions of equality should not dictate the solution. The role of legal advocates should be to create and develop implementation strategies, that is, to determine how to pursue the desired solution most effectively."

The important point which Majury makes is that the law and equality discourse must not come to dominate in the search for a way to deal with the subordination of women. Rather they are tools to be used by women where appropriate, or alternatively left aside where inapplicable, depending on what the situations demands.[28] Hence the decision to focus upon equality or difference in law, indeed, the decision to invoke legal mechanisms at all, is to be undertaken strategically.

Julia Sohrab also argues that the dichotomised equal/special treatment debate and the equality principle itself have been of too great concern to feminists. They are a diversionary red-herring. Whilst the pursuit of equality is a valuable strategy in some situations, it is not in all. It is not possible to formulate an equal or a special rights model which can be employed in relation to every issue, nor will either equal or special treatment present an appropriate strategy for use in all circumstances. Sohrab emphasises that the starting point must be the problem that is being addressed. The problem must be approached in a flexible manner, with various strategies in mind from which the most appropriate can then be selected:

J. A. SOHRAB
"Avoiding the 'Exquisite Trap': A Critical look at the Equal Treatment/ Special Treatment Debate in Law"[29]

"[B]oth equal and special treatment have their limitations. While each approach to law represents a useful strategy, approach or claim in the struggle for substantive gender equality, neither tactic can guarantee that it will not ultimately have serious and damaging side-effects for women. Protection or protective legislation offers some amelioration for women at the bottom of the hierarchy but in the end serves to confirm their position of labour market inferiority, while equality or equal opportunities offers some improvement for women at the top of the hierarchy, but also confirms women's inferior position in the labour market, because many women enter this market on different terms than men. The debate in fact is rather abstract, with participants trying to propose one ideal model of equality that will always benefit women, without ever operating to their detriment. Special treatment advocates struggle to define a principle which could determine the appropriate deviations from the norm of identical treatment. This 'quest' clearly places too great a strain on the concept, and indeed on feminists to formulate it but also fundamentally ignores the differences in interest between women. The continued use of the equal/special distinction makes it easier to treat all complex cases in this rarefied way, but the distinction would not easily lend itself to give guidance in, for instance, producing draft legislation or engaging in analysis of the social effects of legislation. The terms 'equality' and difference are not concrete descriptions of some empirical reality, but are rather part of a political contest about the resolution of some social problems. It is in this sense that arguing over different abstract models of equality is a costly distraction; an approach is needed that can be flexible and operate through more than one strategy, and which will expose, rather than obscure, fundamental social problems.

The perceived necessity of making a choice between equal or special treatment is a false choice. In some areas equal rights are necessary, while in others it is gender-specific rights that are necessary, for instance in pregnancy. Neither approach is, nor

---

[28] D. Majury, *ibid.*, p. 336.
[29] J. A. Sohrab, *supra*, n. 21 at 158–162.

should be, the exclusive 'answer' or strategy or claim, and arguing over substantive equality by opposing equal with special and vice-versa is at best redundant and at worst a costly distraction. In tackling work and family issues moreover gender is not the only factor; we must not ignore other powerful constraints such as class, race and post-industrial capitalism. The male standard may in fact hide a liberal capitalist economic standard, and so whichever strategy feminists pursue, if capitalist concerns dominate the policy process then capitalist needs are likely to win out. Thus discrimination on the grounds of sex need not be the only paradigm within which we argue or justify the resolution of the issues or orient our public policy . . .

So, feminists should debate the meanings attached to the concepts equal treatment and special treatment *only* in terms of specific social problems to be addressed. It is crucial to see the limitations of these concepts in thinking and talking about social problems. We should campaign for far-reaching social changes, otherwise we will continue asking for 'palliatives which will prove inadequate' . . .

Feminist strategies must involve a calculation of specific issues, tactics and possible outcomes, and there is no single principle which can determine this. There are however several relevant considerations. Strategies should not depend on abstract model building to fit all cases. Engaging with equality in law, if at all, should be as a means rather than as an end. It is also crucial to keep in mind the differences between women, and to recognise that different groups of women may have quite different interests. Another aspect of a more flexible strategy is the acceptance that feminist answers to a given problem can change once conditions change. Bacchi argues that for good political reasons feminists must sometimes adopt strategies which achieve limited goals. It is also important to recognise those problems for which 'equality' may not be the most effective rhetoric or strategy to use, as for example, Catharine MacKinnon's attempts to pose pornography and abortion as issues of 'sex discrimination'."

Herma Hill Kay considers two models of equality. She suggests that "an assimilationist model of equality" is useful when the court is considering cases where men and women have characteristics which can be compared. However, she points out, there are cases which arise because of differences between the sexes, when there is no point of comparison. The alternative model which she seeks to develop in such cases (pregnancy, for example), is "episodic analysis".[30] This approach to equality differs from those approaches which acknowledge sexual difference, constructing difference as either irrelevant or as meaning that men and women's differences should be equally valued. Kay's approach suggests that differences, specifically reproductive differences, are only legally relevant when reproduction itself is at issue.[31] She argues that acknowledgement of differences has focused upon *sex* rather than reproductive behaviour, and that difference should only be relevant when the reproductive function of women is being exercised, *i.e.* during the time that a woman is pregnant. So where a woman chooses never to become a mother, and a man never a father, the sex difference becomes irrelevant:

[30] H. H. Kay, "Equality and Difference: The Case of Pregnancy" in P. Smith (ed.), *Feminist Jurisprudence* (Oxford: Oxford University Press, 1993), p. 27.
[31] H. H. Kay, *ibid.*, p. 36.

"The relevance of this episodic analysis of biological reproductive sex differences for a theoretical model of equality between women and men is that it recognizes that those differences exist but regards them as inconsequential except during the specific occasions on which they are utilised."[32]

Kay argues that, during pregnancy, women (who are usually like men) become unlike men and the concept of equality demands that they are, during pregnancy, treated differently. In short, in order to ensure equality of opportunity, the difference of being pregnant has to be acknowledged so that women are not disadvantaged as a consequence of their reproductive capabilities.

The scope of the equality/special treatment debate (like that of the rights debate) is further limited by the traditional spheres to which it has been wedded. Kate Harrison points out that equality laws, together with the areas in which feminists have sought equality, have been concentrated within the public world on issues such as employment and education.[33] Whilst this has meant some important legal changes, equality laws have not, as Harrison explains, extended into other areas of women's lives. She cites, by way of example, the private sphere of the family, in which disadvantageous and hurtful treatment of women is not viewed as a form of discrimination.[34]

"Also outside the scope of equality laws are the kinds of harm uniquely or most commonly suffered by women at the hands of men; for example, rape, domestic violence, sexual harassment — more controversial examples are sexual exploitation through prostitution and pornography and enforced medical treatment. Unless these forms of disadvantage are seen as discrimination against women then outlawing discrimination will not, of itself, guarantee progress for women."[35]

2.2 Autonomous individuals, care and connection

The focus, principally within liberal feminism, upon securing for women recognition as legal persons entitled to equal rights with men which can be asserted against the legal rights of others, has been questioned above for its failure to adequately tackle discrimination against women. This focus is also

---

[32] H. H. Kay, *ibid.*, p. 37.
[33] The Sex Discrimination Act 1975, for example, applies to discrimination in employment, education and housing matters and in the provision of goods, facilities and services.
[34] K. Harrison, "Women's rights" (1993) 143 New L.J. 621. Gillian More levels a similar criticism at the case law of the European Court of Justice which she argues applies the Aristolean concept of equality to the treatment of men and women as workers, perpetuating in an extreme fashion the public/private divide and doing very little to remedy discrimination against women: "The community's formula for sex equality is, it is argued, abstract, narrow and rigid: it is conceptually incapable of eradicating all but the most superficial inequalities faced by women. It helps only those women workers who are already well-assimilated to men: it reinforces inequalities based on gender differences; it restricts the use of positive action; and it masks the fact that many of women's inequalities at work are intimately related to their role in the family." (G. C. More, "Equal Treatment of the Sexes in European Community Law: What does 'Equal' mean?" (1993) 1 *Feminist Legal Studies* 45 at 64).
[35] K. Harrison, *ibid.*, at 621.

challenged by other feminists for its failure to acknowledge relationships and co-operative, collective values.[36] Fiona Beveridge and Siobhan Mullally discuss this criticism of rights discourse, that is, that it proceeds from the assumption of an individual asserting rights against the competing and conflicting rights of others, and in doing so fails to acknowledge the social, economic and cultural context and also the individual's relationships with and responsibilities towards, other people.

F. BEVERIDGE & S. MULLALLY
"International Human Rights and Body Politics"[37]

"One body of criticism relates to the *form* of rights discourse epitomised by the perpetual opposition of 'rights' to corresponding duties, freedoms, powers and privileges. Essentially rights are portrayed as the property of individuals (or occasionally groups), property which under the law serves within the context of identified relationships to privilege the bearer in some way against interference from other individuals or legal entities. In rights discourse it is necessary to accord priority to conflicting rights, powers and privileges: hence the task facing claimants of a right is twofold — first, they must identify themselves as within the category recognised as being in possession of the claimed right, and secondly, they must establish that in the particular context their claimed right or privilege should be accorded priority over the conflicting claims. A number of critics have argued that the assumption upon which this rights discourse is predicated of a society of free-willed individuals, motivated by self-interest, perpetually seeking prioritisation of their own claims (rather than accommodation, negotiation or some other form of compromise) is false, either because it misrepresents the way in which individuals operate generally, or because it misrepresents the way in which women in particular operate (*i.e.* that it is inherently sexist) . . .

This concept of the self as essentially separate from and antagonistic towards others conflicts with competing cultural conceptions of the self as 'essentially connected' to others and as embedded in existing social practices and roles. Rawls summarises the liberal view of the self by saying that 'the self is prior to the ends which are affirmed by it', that is, the self is prior to its socially given roles and relationships, and is free only if it is capable of holding these features of its social situation at a distance and judging them according to the dictates of reason. A number of feminist writers, reiterating the criticisms voiced by communitarians, believe that this is a false view of the self. It ignores the fact that the self is 'embedded' or 'situated' in social practices and that we cannot always stand back and opt out of those roles and relationships . . .

The individualistic concept of the self on which rights discourse is based has led to problems for feminists particularly in relation to body politics; its underlying logic seems to lead them to conclusions which are unpalatable. The self is abstracted not only from its social, economic and cultural context but also from the physical body of the subject herself. This seems to invite recognition of the right of the subject herself to do what she wants with her body — a position which can then be interpreted variously to include the 'right to choose' in relation to abortion, the right to consent

---

[36]   D. L. Rhode, "Feminist Perspectives on Legal Ideology" in J. Mitchell & A. Oakley (eds), *What is Feminism?* (Oxford: Blackwell, 1986), p. 151.
[37]   In J. Bridgeman & S. Millns (eds), *supra*, n. 6 at p. 240, pp. 241–242, 244.

to a wide range of non-essential 'medical' practices (cosmetic surgery, body alteration, fertility treatments) as well as sporting and sexual practices (from boxing to sadism). The view of the subject as an abstract disembodied 'self' does little to assist in drawing lines between such practices and seems to lead to conclusions unacceptable to many feminists."

The work of psychologist Carol Gilligan offers one feminist perspective upon the abstract individualism of rights discourse and the role of the isolated individual in decision-making.[38] This perspective identifies women's "different voice" in articulating moral choices.

C. GILLIGAN
In a Different Voice: Psychological Theory and Women's Development[39]

"The shift in imagery that creates the problem in interpreting women's development is elucidated by the moral judgments of two eleven-year-old children, a boy and a girl, who see, in the same dilemma, two very different moral problems. While current theory brightly illuminates the line and the logic of the boy's thought, it casts scant light on that of the girl. The choice of a girl whose moral judgments elude existing categories of developmental assessment is meant to highlight the issue of interpretation rather than to exemplify sex differences *per se*. Adding a new line of interpretation, based on the imagery of the girl's thought, makes it possible not only to see development where previously development was not discerned but also to consider differences in the understanding of relationships without scaling these differences from better to worse.

The two children were in the same sixth-grade class at school and were participants in the rights and responsibilities study, designed to explore different conceptions of morality and self. The sample selected for this study was chosen to focus the variables of gender and age while maximizing developmental potential by holding constant, at a high level, the factors of intelligence, education, and social class that have been associated with moral development, at least as measured by existing scales. The two children in question, Amy and Jake, were both bright and articulate and, at least in their eleven-year-old aspirations, resisted easy categories of sex-role stereotyping, since Amy aspired to become a scientist while Jake preferred English to math. Yet their moral judgments seem initially to confirm familiar notions about differences between the sexes, suggesting that the edge girls have on moral development during the early school years gives way at puberty with the ascendance of formal logical thought in boys.

The dilemma that these eleven-year-olds were asked to resolve was one in the series devised by Kohlberg to measure moral development in adolescence by presenting a conflict between moral norms and exploring the logic of its resolution. In this particular dilemma, a man named Heinz considers whether or not to steal a drug which he cannot afford to buy in order to save the life of his wife. In the standard format of Kohlberg's interviewing procedure, the description of the dilemma itself — Heinz's

---

[38] C. Gilligan, *In a Different Voice: Psychological Theory and Women's Development* (Cambridge MA: Harvard University Press, 1982).
[39] C. Gilligan, *ibid.*, pp. 25–29, 31.

predicament, the wife's disease, the druggist's refusal to lower his price — is followed by the question, 'Should Heinz steal the drug?' The reasons for and against stealing are then explored through a series of questions that vary and extend the parameters of the dilemma in a way designed to reveal the underlying structure of moral thought.

Jake, at eleven, is clear from the outset that Heinz should steal the drug. Constructing the dilemma, as Kohlberg did, as a conflict between the values of property and life, he discerns the logical priority of life and uses that logic to justify his choice:

> 'For one thing, a human life is worth more than money, and if the druggist only makes $1,000, he is still going to live, but if Heinz doesn't steal the drug, his wife is going to die. (*Why is life worth more than money?*) Because the druggist can get a thousand dollars later from rich people with cancer, but Heinz can't get his wife again. (*Why not?*) Because people are all different and so you couldn't get Heinz's wife again.'

Asked whether Heinz should steal the drug if he does not love his wife, Jake replies that he should, saying that not only is there 'a difference between hating and killing,' but also, if Heinz were caught, 'the judge would probably think it was the right thing to do.' Asked about the fact that, in stealing, Heinz would be breaking the law, he says that 'the laws have mistakes, and you can't go writing up a law for everything that you can imagine.'

Thus, while taking the law into account and recognizing its function in maintaining social order (the judge, Jake says, 'should give Heinz the lightest possible sentence'), he also sees the law as man-made and therefore subject to error and change. Yet his judgment that Heinz should steal the drug, like his view of the law as having mistakes, rests on the assumption of agreement, a societal consensus around moral values that allows one to know and expect others to recognize what is 'the right thing to do.'

Fascinated by the power of logic, this eleven-year-old boy locates truth in math, which, he says, is 'the only thing that is totally logical.' Considering the moral dilemma to be 'sort of like a math problem with humans,' he sets it up as an equation and proceeds to work out the solution. Since his solution is rationally derived, he assumes that anyone following reason would arrive at the same conclusion and thus that a judge would also consider stealing to be the right thing for Heinz to do. Yet he is also aware of the limits of logic. Asked whether there is a right answer to moral problems, Jake replies that 'there can only be right and wrong in judgment,' since the parameters of action are variable and complex. Illustrating how actions undertaken with the best of intentions can eventuate in the most disastrous of consequences, he says, 'like if you give an old lady your seat on the trolley, if you are in a trolley crash and that seat goes through the window, it might be that reason that the old lady dies.' . . .

In contrast, Amy's response to the dilemma conveys a very different impression, an image of development stunted by a failure of logic, an inability to think for herself. Asked if Heinz should steal the drug, she replies in a way that seems evasive and unsure:

> 'Well, I don't think so. I think there might be other ways besides stealing it, like if he could borrow the money or make a loan or something, but he really shouldn't steal the drug — but his wife shouldn't die either.'

Asked why he should not steal the drug, she considers neither property nor law but rather the effect that theft could have on the relationship between Heinz and his wife:

'If he stole the drug, he might save his wife then, but if he did, he might have to go to jail, and then his wife might get sicker again, and he couldn't get more of the drug, and it might not be good. So, they should really just talk it out and find some other way to make the money.'

Seeing in the dilemma not a math problem with humans but a narrative of relationships that extends over time, Amy envisions the wife's continuing need for her husband and the husband's continuing concern for his wife and seeks to respond to the druggist's need in a way that would sustain rather than sever connection. Just as she ties the wife's survival to the preservation of relationships, so she considers the value of the wife's life in a context of relationships, saying that it would be wrong to let her die because, 'if she died, it hurts a lot of people and it hurts her.' Since Amy's moral judgment is grounded in the belief that, 'if somebody has something that would keep somebody alive, then it's not right not to give it to them,' she considers the problem in the dilemma to arise not from the druggist's assertion of rights but from his failure of response.

As the interviewer proceeds with the series of questions that follow from Kohlberg's construction of the dilemma, Amy's answers remain essentially unchanged, the various probes serving neither to elucidate nor to modify her initial response. Whether or not Heinz loves his wife, he still shouldn't steal or let her die; if it were a stranger dying instead, Amy says that 'if the stranger didn't have anybody near or anyone she knew,' then Heinz should try to save her life, but he should not steal the drug. But as the interviewer conveys through the repetition of questions that the answers she gave were not heard or not right, Amy's confidence begins to diminish, and her replies become more constrained and unsure. Asked again why Heinz should not steal the drug, she simply repeats, 'Because it's not right.' Asked again to explain why, she states again that theft would not be a good solution, adding lamely, 'if he took it, he might not know how to give it to his wife, and so his wife might still die.' Failing to see the dilemma as a self-contained problem in moral logic, she does not discern the internal structure of its resolution; as she constructs the problem differently herself, Kohlberg's conception completely evades her.

Instead, seeing a world comprised of relationships rather than of people standing alone, a world that coheres through human connection rather than through systems of rules, she finds the puzzle in the dilemma to lie in the failure of the druggist to respond to the wife. Saying that 'it is not right for someone to die when their life could be saved,' she assumes that if the druggist were to see the consequences of his refusal to lower his price, he would realize that 'he should just give it to the wife and then have the husband pay back the money later.' Thus she considers the solution to the dilemma to lie in making the wife's condition more salient to the druggist or, that failing, in appealing to others who are in a position to help . . .

Thus in Heinz's dilemma these two children see two very different moral problems — Jake a conflict between life and property that can be resolved by logical deduction, Amy a fracture of human relationship that must be mended with its own thread. Asking different questions that arise from different conceptions of the moral domain, the children arrive at answers that fundamentally diverge, and the arrangement of these answers as successive stages on a scale of increasing moral maturity calibrated by the logic of the boy's response misses the different truth revealed in the judgment of the girl. To the question, 'What does he see that she does not?' Kohlberg's theory provides a ready response, manifest in the scoring of Jake's judgments a full stage higher than Amy's in moral maturity; to the question, 'What does she see that he does not?' Kohlberg's theory has nothing to say. Since most of her responses fall through the sieve of Kohlberg's scoring system, her responses appear from his perspective to lie outside the moral domain."

Thus Gilligan found that boys and girls reason differently. Whilst boys tend to reason in terms of autonomy, individualised justice and rights (adopting an "ethic of justice"), girls tend to focus upon relationships and sustaining those relationships (adopting an "ethic of care"). From this position Gilligan identifies different modes of moral reasoning: a masculine mode based upon competing rights which are prioritised in order to achieve justice, and a feminine mode which is contextual, narrative and focused upon relationships and responsibilities. Challenging the view that men have a more developed sense of morality, Carol Gilligan argues that their mode is simply "different" from the feminine mode. Through listening to women considering whether to terminate a pregnancy, Gilligan identified three moral perspectives articulated by the feminine voice:

C. GILLIGAN
In a Different Voice: Psychological Theory and Women's Development[40]

"Women's constructions of the abortion dilemma in particular reveal the existence of a distinct moral language whose evolution traces a sequence of development. This is the language of selfishness and responsibility, which defines the moral problem as one of obligation to exercise care and avoid hurt. The inflicting of hurt is considered selfish and immoral in its reflection of unconcern, while the expression of care is seen as the fulfillment of moral responsibility. The reiterative use by the women of the words *selfish* and *responsible* in talking about moral conflict and choice, given the underlying moral orientation that this language reflects, sets the women apart from the men whom Kohlberg studied and points toward a different understanding of moral development.

The three moral perspectives revealed by the abortion decision study denote a sequence in the development of the ethic of care. These different views of care and the transitions between them emerged from an analysis of the ways in which the women used moral language — words such as *should, ought, better, right, good*, and *bad*, by the changes and shifts that appeared in their thinking, and by the way in which they reflected on and judged their thought. In this sequence, an initial focus on caring for the self in order to ensure survival is followed by a transitional phase in which this judgment is criticised as selfish. The criticism signals a new understanding of the connection between self and others which is articulated by the concept of responsibility. The elaboration of this concept of responsibility and its fusion with a maternal morality that seeks to ensure care for the dependent and unequal characterizes the second perspective. At this point, the good is equated with caring for others. However, when only others are legitimized as the recipients of the woman's care, the exclusion of herself gives rise to problems in relationships, creating a disequilibrium that initiates the second transition. The equation of conformity with care, in its conventional defini-

---

[40] C. Gilligan, *ibid.*, pp. 73–74.

tion, and the illogic of the inequality between other and self, lead to a reconsideration of relationships in an effort to sort out the confusion between self-sacrifice and care inherent in the conventions of feminine goodness. The third perspective focuses on the dynamics of relationships and dissipates the tension between selfishness and responsibility through a new understanding of the interconnection between other and self. Care becomes the self-chosen principle of a judgment that remains psychological in its concern with relationships and response but becomes universal in its condemnation of exploitation and hurt. Thus a progressively more adequate understanding of the psychology of human relationships — an increasing differentiation of self and other and a growing comprehension of the dynamics of social interaction — informs the development of an ethic of care. This ethic, which reflects a cumulative knowledge of human relationships, evolves around a central insight, that self and other are interdependent. The different ways of thinking about this connection or the different modes of its apprehension mark the three perspectives and their transitional phases. In this sequence, the fact of interconnection informs the central, recurring recognition that just as the incidence of violence is in the end destructive to all, so the activity of care enhances both others and self."

Having considered the various responses to the Heinz dilemma and to the decision to abort, four key differences emerge between the male and female modes of reasoning. These are summarised by Rosemary Tong:

R. TONG
Feminist Thought: A Comprehensive Introduction[41]

"First, women tended to stress the moral agent's continuing relationships to others, whereas men tend to stress the agent's formal, abstract rights. Thus, the typical woman is prepared to forsake some of her rights if she can thereby cement a faltering, but extremely meaningful, human relationship. Second, when making a moral decision, women espouse a somewhat more consequentialist point of view, calculating the effects of the moral agent's action on all who will be touched by it, whereas men espouse a somewhat more nonconsequentialist point of view, according to which principles must be upheld even if some people get hurt in the process. Third, women are usually more willing to accept excuses for a moral agent's behaviour, whereas men generally label behaviour as morally inexcusable just because it is morally unjustifiable ... Finally, women usually interpret a moral choice within the context of the historical circumstances that produced it, whereas men usually abstract that choice from its particularities and analyze it as if it represented some universal type of moral choice."

As a result of the identification of these four differences, Gilligan was able to develop an alternative scale of moral development to that traditionally used by psychologists. This is again neatly summarised by Rosemary Tong:

[41] (London: Unwin Hyam, 1989), pp. 162–163.

R. TONG
Feminist Thought: A Comprehensive Introduction[42]

"Because Gilligan believed that women's style of moral reasoning diverges in several important ways from that of men, she rejected Kohlberg's scale of moral development as a universal standard upon which to evaluate both men's and women's moral progress. Kohlberg's scale consists of six stages through which a person must pass if he or she is to become a fully functioning moral agent. Stage one is 'the punishment and obedience orientation.' To avoid the 'stick' of punishment and/or receive the 'carrot' of a reward, the child does as he or she is told. Stage two is 'the instrumental relativist orientation.' Based on a limited principle of reciprocity — 'you scratch my back and I'll scratch yours' — the child does what satisfies his or her own needs and occasionally the needs of others. Stage three is 'the interpersonal concordance or 'good boy-nice girl' orientation.' The adolescent conforms to prevailing mores because he or she seeks the approbation of other people. Stage four is 'the 'law and order' orientation.' The adolescent begins to do his or her duty, show respect for authority, and maintain the given social order for its own sake. Stage five is 'the social-contract legalistic orientation.' The adult adopts an essentially utilitarian moral point of view according to which individuals are permitted to do as they please, provided that they refrain from harming people in the process. Stage six is 'the universal ethical principle orientation.' The adult adopts an essentially Kantian moral point of view that provides a moral perspective 'universal' enough to serve as a critique of any conventional morality, including that of the United States. The adult is no longer ruled by self-interest, the opinion of others, or the force of legal convention, but by self-legislated and self-imposed universal principles, such as those of justice, reciprocity, and respect for the dignity of human beings as individual persons.

Gilligan took exception to Kohlberg's sixfold scale not because it reflects an immoral or amoral position, but because girls and women tested on it rarely get past stage three. She feared that people would interpret this curious result as somehow confirming Freud's sense that women are less moral than men, but it also occurred to Gilligan that women's low scores on Kohlberg's test had little to do with any deficiency in women's ability to reason morally and much to do with the construction of Kohlberg's scale.

Gilligan's reflections ultimately led her to develop an alternative to Kohlberg's scale that, in her opinion, more adequately represents women's approach to moral reasoning. For Kohlberg, the moral self is an individual legislating absolute laws for everyone without exception. In contrast, for Gilligan, the moral self is an individual working with other individuals to identify mutually agreeable solutions to thorny human relations problems. Whereas Gilligan described Kohlberg's 'male' moral point of view as an ethics of justice, she described her 'female' moral point of view as an ethics of care. Gilligan believed that woman's moral development takes her from an egocentric, or selfish, position to an overly altruistic, or self-sacrificial, position and, finally, to a self-with-others position in which her interests count as much as anyone else's.

At level one, the least-developed level of moral sensibility, a woman's care is directed completely inward. She feels scared and vulnerable, in need of affection and approval. For example, the women in Gilligan's abortion study who felt alone in the world,

---

[42]   R. Tong, *ibid.*, pp. 164–165.

helpless, and uncared for saw a baby as someone who would care for them, who would give them some love. However, as they struggled through their abortion decisions, many came to describe as 'selfish' the decision to bring a child into the world without having the material and psychological resources to care for him or her. In Gilligan's estimation, for a woman to come to this kind of conclusion is to reach level two of moral development.

At level two, a woman shifts from self-centeredness to other-directedness. She becomes the stereotypical nurturant woman, who subjugates her wants and needs to those of other people's and who claims that all she wants to do is what the other person wants. This is the kind of woman who, in Gilligan's study, would have her lover, husband, parents, or church tell her whether to have an abortion. According to Gilligan, a woman can suppress her wants and needs in the interest of sustaining a relationship only so long before she starts feeling resentful. Thus, to develop as a moral person, a woman must take steps to avoid this destructive boiling point. She must, insisted Gilligan, push beyond level two to level three of moral development, where she will learn how to care for herself as well as others.

At level three, the decision to abort, for example, becomes a complex choice the woman must make about how best to care for the fetus, herself, and anyone likely to be affected by her decision. One of the women in Gilligan's study explained her decision to have an abortion as just such a choice: 'I would not be doing myself or the child or the world any kind of favor having this child. I don't need to pay off my imaginary debts to the world through this child, and I don't think that it is right to bring a child into the world and use it for that purpose.' Thus, in Gilligan's view, a woman attains full moral stature when she stops vacillating between egoism and altruism, recognising instead the falseness of this polarity and the depth of her connection to others and of their connection to her."

Several debates follow from Carol Gilligan's work. First, Gilligan has been criticised for making generalisations based upon sex.[43] She disputes this, arguing that she has identified two different modes of moral reasoning, and that, whilst the ethic of care had been identified through listening to women, and the ethic of justice through analysing male modes of reasoning, this is not an absolute distinction. Secondly, the methodology of Gilligan's work has been criticised for failing to consider the context in which the women in her study considering a termination made their decision, and for not obtaining men's attitudes to abortion. Further, identification of women with an ethic of care may have negative consequences for women. It may be that women emphasise caring because it is a role for which they have traditionally been valued. Focusing upon relationships and responsibilities merely perpetuates the subordination of women in this respect. Catharine MacKinnon, for example, argues that a woman's "different voice" is a consequence of her subordination.

[43] R. Tong, *ibid.*, pp. 166–167.

"Feminist Discourse, Moral Values and the Law — A Conversation"[44]

"*MacKinnon*: *Why* do women become these people, more than men, who represent *these* values? This is really very important. For me, the answer is clear: the answer is the subordination of women. That does not mean that I throw out those values. Those are nice values; everyone should have them. I'm not saying that taking these values seriously would not transform discourse, which would be a good thing under any circumstance of gender. She also has found the voice of the victim — yes, women are a victimized group. The articulation of the voice of the victim is crucial because laws about victimization typically are made by people with power, and come from the perspective with power. I think the interjection of that perspective has important possibilities.

What bothers me is identifying women with it. I'm not saying that Carol does this expressly in her book. But I am troubled by the possibility of women identifying with what is a positively valued feminine stereotype. It is 'the feminine'. It is actually called 'the feminine' in the middle chapter of the book. Given existing male dominance, those values amount to a set-up to be shafted. I am particularly worried about the legal impact of this. Take what Carrie said. If Jake and Amy converse, what happens? Well, we heard if Jake does not listen to Amy, he wins. There is something gendered about that. What happens if Amy doesn't listen to Jake? She loses. You see what I mean? The reason I put it out like that is because I think the power issues are crucial and unignorable. If it is male dominance which has created people in these images, then *recognizing that* really matters for the applications. So I think the explanation part is crucial on its own, but also for the applications. Power is socially constructed such that if Jake simply chooses not to listen to Amy, he wins; but if Amy simply chooses not to listen to Jake, she loses. In other words, Jake still wins because that is the system. And I am trying to work out how to change that system, not just how to make people be more fully human within it.

Gilligan: Your definition of power is his definition.

MacKinnon: That is because the society *is* that way, it operates on his definition, and I am trying to change it.

Gilligan: To have her definition come in?

MacKinnon: That would be part of it, but more to have a definition that she would articulate that she cannot now, because his foot is on her throat.

Gilligan: She's saying it.

MacKinnon: I know, but she is articulating the feminine. And you are calling it hers. That's what I find infuriating.

Gilligan: No, I am saying she is articulating a set of values which are very positive.

MacKinnon: Right, and I am saying they are feminine. And calling them hers is infuriating to me because we have never had the power to develop what ours really would be."

Deborah Rhode explains the obvious implications for the law of Carol Gilligan's identification of a "different voice" given the basis of western legal systems, premised upon "hierarchies and abstract rules and principles" which accord "inadequate emphasis to responsibilities arising from concrete relation-

[44]   I. Marcus & P. G. Spiegelman (moderators), E. C. DuBois, M. C. Dunlap, C. J. Gilligan, C. A. MacKinnon & C. J. Menkel-Meadow (conversants): (1985) 34 *Buffalo Law Review* 11 at 74–75.

ships. In tones that both echo and influence other relational feminists, she [Gilligan] advocates an ethic of responsibility as well as rights, an ethic which is more attentive to care, co-operation, and context in the resolution of human problems."[45] Deborah Rhode continues to explain that the importance of Gilligan's work for feminist jurisprudence is in demonstrating the need to recognise values, and of acknowledging the limitations of the traditional rights-orientated approach in attaining this recognition.

To focus upon reasoning based upon relationships rather than determinations of justice based upon abstract reasoning has implications for the whole nature of the legal system as presently constructed around the rights of isolated autonomous individuals. Carol Gilligan suggests that the ethic of care should be incorporated, or assimilated, into the legal system as it is currently constituted. For example, Carrie Menkel-Meadow has explored whether mediation as a form of dispute resolution is more fitting to female values of care and connectedness than the adversarial nature of our current legal system. She suggests that this may not be without problems. For example, mediation may be seen as a suitable method of dispute resolution in those areas in which women traditionally work, such as family or child law, but incorporation of an ethic of care within this area will not affect the legal system as a whole. There are further doubts about the use of mediation in determining custody or financial settlement upon divorce where, given the inequality between men and women, a different form of resolution may still result in women being disadvantaged.[46] Anne Bottomley exposes the problematic usage of conciliation in family law:

A. BOTTOMLEY
"What is happening to family law? A feminist critique of conciliation"[47]

"Crucial structural changes are developing in family law in which the practice of something called conciliation plays a central role . . . [I]n the present social structure these changes are likely to be detrimental to women. This detrimental effect operates at a number of levels. Firstly, at the level of the effect on individual women in pursuing their own cases and secondly, at a broader level, in a seeming 'privatisation' of family law. This, in fact, cloaks a continuing intervention and supervision of families by courts and related agencies which is rendered benevolent by images of caring and the welfare of children.

. . . [I]n the present social situation the development of conciliation, both as an alternative to the legal process and as a development within it, is one which, while seemingly attractive, is highly problematic. But I must add two caveats. Firstly, the development of conciliation is here to stay . . . [But i]t will not be in the interests of

---

[45]   D. L. Rhode, *Justice & Gender* (Cambridge MA: Harvard University Press, 1989), p. 308.
[46]   See C. Menkel-Meadow, "Portia in a Different Voice: Speculating on Women's Lawyering Process" (1987) 1 *Berkeley Women's Law Journal* 39, cited in S. L. Roach Anleu, "Critiquing the Law: Themes and Dilemmas in Anglo-American Feminist Legal Theory" (1992) 19 *Journal of Law and Society* 423 at 425.
[47]   In J. Brophy & C. Smart (eds), *supra*, n. 24 at p. 162, pp. 163–164.

women in its present form, or forms, and I do not believe that it could ever be entirely satisfactory for women within the present social structure. Secondly, I am crucially aware of the many problems of the legal system, from the professional domination of lawyers and the sexism of judges through to the reality of alienation and repression which characterise bourgeois law. However, as with many feminists, my attitude towards the use of law is necessarily ambivalent. In the present situation the use of lawyers, arguments around rules and the procedural safeguards of formal justice may well serve women's interests better than regulation through a more informal, welfarist approach which seems to emphasise party control and choice. Ironically, many of us who have spent time exposing the problems of the legal system must now necessarily argue its benefits in the face of changes which threaten, on the one hand, a new pattern of professional domination and, on the other, an emphasis on private arrangements."

However, acknowledging connections and relationships may have implications beyond legal procedure touching also upon substantive civil and criminal laws. Robyn Martin considers the masculinity inherent within the very concept of the reasonable man used in the law of tort, and challenges:

> "the neutrality, and validity of any test held up as a standard of behaviour to which all members of society must conform. The reasonable man test is based on an assumption, that there can be one ideal, one truth, one and only one appropriate behaviour in any given situation. If it were to be recognized that there were possible pluralities of behaviour, different but equally valid responses to given stimuli, then some alternative way of identifying behaviour for the purpose of signalling liability in negligence would need to be considered."[48]

Martin considers the positivistic notion of law as a science based upon the values of neutrality, autonomy and rationality and argues instead that "[a]n alternative model of justice and fairness might be based not on rights and duties but on responsibilities and the reduction of conflict in society."[49] She argues that behind the supposedly neutral test of the reasonable man lie the moral values of the judiciary deciding the case and also its idea of what behaviour is considered to be appropriate, given the judges' own experiences of life. To introduce the gender neutral reasonable person would not result in any change to the standards and values which the law of tort maintains. Martin suggests that, rather than the current focus upon rights — the right to act in a way that causes harm as long as it is reasonable — the focus should be upon responsibilities arising out of particular relationships or as a consequence of participating in certain activities. Focusing upon responsibility rather than rights looks to the cause of the harm, an approach which could bring about productive changes within the legal system.

In a similar vein, Robin West draws comparisons between liberal theory, critical theory, cultural feminism and liberal feminism to explore how to

---

[48] R. Martin, "A Feminist View of the Reasonable Man: An Alternative Approach to Liability in Negligence for Personal Injury" (1994) 23 *Anglo-American Law Review* 334 at 342.
[49] R. Martin, *ibid.*, at 334. The reasonable man of criminal law is considered in Chap. 11.

develop a new "reconstructive feminist theory".[50] She explains that, according to liberal theory the individual is a separate autonomous individual who may form relationships but who values his freedom from others. Women, West argues, are connected to other life through their potential or actual experi-, ences of pregnancy, heterosexual intercourse, menstruation and breast feeding. This connection means that women have different priorities, feelings and emotions from men. Women, she argues, are raised by women, carry, give birth to and care for infants. There is a continuity for the female whilst the male develops his sense of identity through the experience of difference from his primary carer. West argues that cultural feminism celebrates this material connection to others:

> "[W]omen are ultimately more 'connected' — psychically, emotionally, and morally — to other human beings because women, as children were raised by women and women raise children because women, uniquely, are physically and materially 'connected' to those human beings when the human beings are fetuses and then infants. Women are more empathic to the lives of others because women are physically tied to the lives of others in a way which men are not. Women's moral voice is one of responsibility, duty and care for those who are first physically attached, then physically dependent, and then emotionally interdependent. Women think in terms of the needs of others rather than the rights of others because women materially, and then physically, and then psychically, provide for the needs of others. Lastly, women fear separation from the other rather than annihilation by him, and 'count' it as a harm, because women experience the 'separating' pain of childbirth and more deeply feel the pain of maturation and departure of adult children."[51]

In comparison, West suggests, radical feminism[52] sees the connection of women as oppressive, invasive and destructive:

> "According to cultural feminist accounts of women's subjectivity, women value intimacy, develop a capacity for nuturance, and an ethic of care for the 'other' with which we are connected, just as we learn to dread and fear separation from the other. Radical feminists tell a very different story. According to radical feminism, women's connection with the 'other' is above all else invasive and intrusive: women's potential for material 'connection' invites invasion into the physical integrity of our bodies, and intrusion into the existential integrity of our lives."[53]

For example, West argues that Shulamith Firestone[54] sees the experience of pregnancy (wanted or unwanted) for women not as an experience to be valued for the intimacy or the connection to the developing foetus which it provides,

---

[50] R. West, "Jurisprudence and Gender" (1988) 55 *University of Chicago Law Review* 1.
[51] R. West, *ibid.*, at 21.
[52] Radical feminism is discussed below in Chap. 3.
[53] R. West, *supra*, n. 50 at 15
[54] S. Firestone, *The Dialectic of Sex* (New York: Bantam Books, 1970). Firestone's work is discussed below in the introduction to Section 2.

but as "an assault on the physical integrity and privacy of the body."[55] Likewise West argues that, for radical feminists, sex, whether consensual or rape, "blurs the physical boundaries between self and other, and that blurring of boundaries between self and other constitutes a profound invasion of the self's physical integrity."[56]

West states that that women both value intimacy and fear intrusion. Hence, a first step in devising a feminist theory of law is to challenge the present construction of what amounts to legal harm. It is argued that, where harm is recognised as such by men, the law affords protection to women. But the law does not intervene to protect women against harm as understood by women:

R. West
"Jurisprudence and Gender"[57]

"III.   Feminist Jurisprudence

By the claim that modern jurisprudence is 'masculine,' I mean two things. First, I mean that the values, the dangers, and what I have called the 'fundamental contradiction' that characterize women's lives are not reflected at any level whatsoever in contracts, torts, constitutional law, or any other field of legal doctrine. The values that flow from women's material potential for physical connection are not recognized as values by the Rule of Law, and the dangers attendant to that state are not recognized as dangers by the Rule of Law.

First, the Rule of Law does not value intimacy — its official value is autonomy. The material consequence of this theoretical undervaluation of women's values in the material world is that women are economically *impoverished*. The value women place on intimacy reflects our existential and material circumstance; women will act on that value whether it is compensated or not. But it is not. Nurturant, intimate labor is neither valued by liberal legalism nor compensated by the market economy. It is not compensated in the home and it is not compensated in the workplace — wherever intimacy is, there is no compensation. Similarly, separation of the individual from his or her family, community, or children is not understood to be a harm, and we are not protected against it. The Rule of Law generally and legal doctrine in its particularity are coherent reactions to the existential dilemma that follows from the liberal's description of the male experience of material separation from the other: the Rule of Law acknowledges the danger of annihilation and the Rule of Law protects the value of autonomy. Just as assuredly, the Rule of Law is *not* a coherent reaction to the existential dilemma that follows from the material state of being connected to others, and the values and dangers attendant to that condition. It neither recognizes nor values intimacy, and neither recognizes nor protects against separation.

Nor does the Rule of Law recognize, in any way whatsoever, muted or unmuted, occasionally or persistently, overtly or covertly, the contradiction which characterizes women's, but not men's lives: while we value the intimacy we find so natural, we are

---

[55]   R. West, *supra*, n. 50 at 29.
[56]   R. West, *ibid.*, at 32.
[57]   (1988) 55 *University of Chicago Law Review* 1 at 58–61.

endangered by the invasion and dread the intrusion in our lives which intimacy entails, and we long for individuation and independence. Neither sexual nor fetal invasion of the self by the other is recognized as a harm worth bothering with. Sexual invasion through rape is understood to be a harm, and is criminalized as such, only when it involves some other harm: today, when it is accompanied by violence that appears in a form men understand (meaning a plausible threat of annihilation); in earlier times, when it was understood as theft of another man's property. But marital rape, date rape, acquaintance rape, simple rape, unaggravated rape, or as Susan Estrich wants to say 'real rape' are either not criminalized, or if they are, they are not punished — to do so would force a recognition of the concrete, experiential harm to identity formation that sexual invasion accomplishes.

Similarly, fetal invasion is not understood to be harmful, and therefore the claim that I ought to be able to protect myself against it is heard as nonsensical. The argument that the right to abortion mirrors the right of self defense falls on deaf ears for a reason: the analogy is indeed flawed. The right of self defense is the right to protect the body's security against annihilation liberally understood, not invasion. But the danger an unwanted fetus poses is not to the body's security at all, but rather to the body's integrity. Similarly, the woman's fear is not that the she will die, but that she will cease to be or never become a self. The danger of unwanted pregnancy is the danger of invasion by the other, not of annihilation by the other. In sum, the Rule of Law does not recognize the danger of invasion, nor does it recognize the individual's need for, much less entitlement to, individuation and independence from the intrusion which heterosexual penetration and fetal invasion entails. The material consequence of this lack of recognition in the real world is that women are *objectified* — regarded as creatures who can't be harmed.

The second thing I mean to imply by the phrase 'masculine jurisprudence' is that both liberal and critical legal theory, which is about the relation between law and life, is about men and not women. The reason for this lack of parallelism, of course, is hardly benign neglect. Rather, the distinctive values women hold, the distinctive dangers from which we suffer, and the distinctive contradictions that characterize our inner lives are not reflected in legal theory because legal theory (whatever else it's about) is about actual, real life, enacted, legislated, adjudicated law, and women have, from law's inception, lacked the power to make law protect, value, or seriously regard our experience. Jurisprudence is 'masculine' because jurisprudence is about the relationship between human beings and the laws we actually have, and the laws we actually have are 'masculine' both in terms of their intended beneficiary and in authorship. Women are absent from jurisprudence because women *as human beings* are absent from the law's protection: jurisprudence does not recognize us because law does not protect us. The implication for this should be obvious. We will not have a genuinely ungendered jurisprudence (a jurisprudence 'unmodified' so to speak) until we have legal doctrine that takes women's lives as seriously as it takes men's. We don't have such legal doctrine. The virtual abolition of patriarchy is the necessary political condition for the creation of non-masculine feminist jurisprudence.

It does not follow, however, that there is no such thing as feminist legal theory. Rather, I believe what is now inaccurately called 'feminist jurisprudence' consists of two discrete projects. The first project is the unmasking and critiquing of the patriarchy behind purportedly ungendered law and theory, or, put differently, the uncovering of what we might call 'patriarchal jurisprudence' from under the protective covering of 'jurisprudence.' The primary purpose of the critique of patriarchal jurisprudence is to show that jurisprudence and legal doctrine protect and define men, not women. Its second purpose is to show how women — that is, people who value intimacy, fear separation, dread invasion, and crave individuation — have fared under a legal system which fails to value intimacy, fails to protect against separation, refuses to define invasion as a harm, and refuses to acknowledge the aspirations of women for individuation and physical privacy.

The second project in which feminist legal theorists engage might be called 'reconstructive jurisprudence.' The last twenty years have seen a substantial amount of feminist law reform, primarily in the areas of rape, sexual harassment, reproductive freedom, and pregnancy rights in the workplace. For strategic reasons, these reforms have often been won by characterizing women's injuries as analogous to, if not identical with, injuries men suffer (sexual harassment as a form of 'discrimination;' rape as a crime of 'violence'), or by characterizing women's longing as analogous to, if not identical with, men's official values (reproductive freedom — which ought to be grounded in a right to individuation — conceived instead as a 'right to privacy,' which is derivative of the autonomy right). This misconceptualization may have once been a necessary price, but it is a high price, and, as these victories accumulate, an increasingly unnecessary one. Reconstructive feminist jurisprudence should set itself the task of rearticulating these new rights in such a way as to reveal, rather than conceal their origin in women's distinctive existential and material state of being."

West advocates a "reconstructive feminist jurisprudence" or theory of law whose goal should be "to provide descriptions of the 'human being' underlying feminist legal reforms that will be true to the conditions of women's lives."[58] This demands that law recognise the experiences of women. Of course, life experiences can be widely different between women. However, women's experiences, particularly those connected to their bodies and sexuality, are recognised by other feminists too as being crucial to the task of developing a feminist legal theory freed from masculine interpretations of women's situation. It is to the construction of a feminist jurisprudence, grounded in female (sexual) experience(s) that we turn in the following chapter.

---

[58]   R. West, *ibid.*, at 70.

CHAPTER 3

FEMINIST JURISPRUDENCE: TOWARD AND BEYOND

3.1 Sexuality and dominance

The failure to secure equality with men by giving women access to the public world and legal rights, has been explained by locating the subordination of women in the understanding that women are not considered to be equal with men but are valued less than them. Further, that it is primarily as a result of male attempts to control the female body and of the construction of female sexuality to serve male needs that women are oppressed.[1] Sexuality is understood as fundamental to the formation of identity. As female sexuality is constructed in male terms, women are unable to identify their own wants and needs. Drawing upon Marxism, Catharine MacKinnon argues that women are alienated as a consequence of the construction of their sexuality in male terms: "[s]exuality is to feminism what work is to marxism: that which is most one's own yet most taken away."[2] Rosemary Tong explains the position:

R. TONG
Feminist Thought: A Comprehensive Introduction[3]

"[S]ocially constructed sexual roles make it exceedingly difficult for a woman to identify and develop her own sexual desires and needs. As many radical feminists see it, sexuality is the crucial issue in feminism because 'aggression and the "need" to dominate form a routine part of what is accepted as [normal] male sexuality.' Male violence against women is normalized and legitimized in sexual practices through the assumption that when it comes to sex, men are by nature aggressive and dominant, whereas women are by nature passive and submissive.

Because male dominance and female submission are the norm in something as fundamental as sexuality, they become the norm in other contexts as well. As most radical

---

[1]   R. Tong, *Feminist Thought: A Comprehensive Introduction* (London: Unwin Hyam, 1989), p. 72. See specifically the work of Catharine MacKinnon, notably "Feminism, Marxism, Method, and the State: An Agenda for Theory" (1981–82) 7 *Signs* 515; "Feminism, Marxism, Method, and the State: Toward Feminist Jurisprudence" (1983) 8 Signs 635; *Feminism Unmodified: Discourses on Life and Law* (Cambridge MA: Harvard University Press, 1987); *Toward a Feminist Theory of the State* (Cambridge MA: Harvard University Press, 1989).
[2]   C. A. MacKinnon, "Feminism, Marxism, Method, and the State: An Agenda for Theory" (1981–82) 7 *Signs* 515.
[3]   (London: Unwin Hyam, 1989), p. 110.

feminists see it, women will never be men's full political, economic, and social equals until heterosexual relations are entirely egalitarian — a state of affairs not likely to be achieved so long as women's sexuality is interpreted in terms of men's sexuality . . .

MacKinnon worked with traditional Marxist arguments, using them to make analogies between the oppression of workers and the oppression of women. Work is important in Marxist theory, because through work people shape not only their material environment but also their personal identities. Thus, to deprive people of the products of their work is to separate them from what literally constitutes their identity. Analogously, sexuality is important in feminist theory because woman's personal identity is very bound up with her sexuality . . . [W]omen will always remain subordinate to men unless sexuality is reconceived and reconstructed."

Catharine MacKinnon, in applying her analysis to law, argues that laws are gendered, while being presented as neutral and objective. Their purported application to everyone in a universal, abstract fashion amounts to nothing more than the application of a male perspective:

C. A. MacKinnon
Toward a Feminist Theory of the State[4]

"If objectivity is the epistemological stance of which women's sexual objectification is the social process, its imposition the paradigm of power in the male form, then the state appears most relentless in imposing the male point of view when it comes closest to achieving its highest formal criterion of distanced aperspectivity. When it is most ruthlessly neutral, it is most male; when it is most sex blind, it is most blind to the sex of the standard being applied. When it most closely conforms to precedent, to 'facts', to legislative intent, it most closely enforces socially male norms and most thoroughly precludes questioning their content as having a point of view at all."

Furthermore, laws are gendered in substantive terms because they are formulated from a male standpoint. This is an example of "radical feminism", that is "feminism unmodified" by any other discourse. It represents not simply an application of existing principles of political philosophy to women, but a political philosophy derived from the experiences of women.

C. A. MacKinnon
"Feminism, Marxism, Method, and the State: Toward Feminist Jurisprudence"[5]

"Feminism has been widely thought to contain tendencies of liberal feminism, radical feminism, and socialist feminism. But just as socialist feminism has often amounted to marxism applied to women, liberal feminism has often amounted to liberalism applied to women. Radical feminism is feminism. Radical feminism — after this, feminism

[4] (Cambridge MA: Harvard University Press, 1989), p. 248.
[5] (1983) 8 *Signs* 635 at 639–640.

unmodified — is methodologically post-marxist. It moves to resolve the marxist-feminist problematic on the level of method. Because its method emerges from the concrete conditions of all women as a sex, it dissolves the individualist, naturalist, idealist, moralist structure of liberalism, the politics of which science is the epistemology. Where liberal feminism sees sexism primarily as an illusion or myth to be dispelled, an inaccuracy to be corrected, true feminism sees the male point of view as fundamental to the male power to create the world in its own image, the image of its desires, not just as its delusory end product. Feminism distinctively as such comprehends that what counts as truth is produced in the interest of those with power to shape reality, and that this process is as pervasive as it is necessary as it is changeable."

"Consciousness-raising" is the method by which a feminist jurisprudence can be developed, as male power is revealed by shared accounts. MacKinnon explains what this method means:

C. A. MacKinnon
"Feminism, Marxism, Method, and the State: An Agenda for Theory"[6]

"The substantive principle governing the authentic politics of women's personal lives is pervasive powerlessness to men, expressed and reconstituted daily *as* sexuality. To say that the personal is political means that gender as a division of power is discoverable and verifiable through women's intimate experience of sexual objectification, which is definitive of and synonymous with women's lives as gender female. Thus, to feminism, the personal is epistemologically the political, and its epistemology is its politics. Feminism, on this level, is the theory of women's point of view. It is the theory of Judy Grahn's 'common woman' speaking Adrienne Rich's 'common language'. Consciousness raising is its quintessential expression. Feminism does not appropriate an existing method—such as scientific method—and apply it to a different sphere of society to reveal its pre-existing political aspect. Consciousness raising not only comes to know different things as politics; it necessarily comes to know them in a different way. Women's experience of politics, of life as sex object, gives rise to its own method of appropriating that reality: feminist method. As its own kind of social analysis, within yet outside the male paradigm just as women's lives are, it has a distinctive theory of the *relation* between method and truth, the individual and her social surroundings, the presence and place of the natural and spiritual in culture and society, and social being and causality itself.

Having been objectified as sexual beings while stigmatized as ruled by subjective passions, women reject the distinction between knowing subject and known object — the division between subjective and objective postures — as the means to comprehend social life. Disaffected from objectivity, having been its prey, but excluded from its world through relegation to subjective inwardness, women's interest lies in overthrowing the distinction itself. Proceeding connotatively and analytically at the same time, consciousness raising is at once common sense expression and critical articulation of concepts. Taking situated feelings and common detail (common here meaning both ordinary and shared) as the matter of political analysis, it explores the terrain that is most damaged, most contaminated, yet therefore most women's own, most intimately known, most open to reclamation. The process can be described as a collective 'sym-

---

[6]   (1981–82) 7 *Signs* 515 at 535–537.

pathetic internal experience of the gradual construction of [the] system according to its inner necessity,' as a strategy for deconstructing it.

Through consciousness raising, women grasp the collective reality of women's condition from within the perspective of that experience, not from outside it. The claim that a sexual politics exists and is socially fundamental is grounded in the claim of feminism *to* women's perspective, not from it. Its claim to women's perspective *is* its claim to truth. In its account of itself, women's point of view contains a duality analogous to that of the marxist proletariat: determined by the reality the theory explodes, it thereby claims special access to that reality. Feminism does not see its view as subjective, partial, or undetermined but as a critique of the purported generality, disinterestedness, and universality of prior accounts. These have not been half right but have invoked the wrong whole. Feminism not only challenges masculine partiality but questions the universality imperative itself. Aperspectivity is revealed as a strategy of male hegemony."

The problem is, however, that consciousness-raising assumes that a commonality of concerns and perspectives will be articulated and fails to acknowledge the differences between women:

S. L. ROACH ANLEU
**"Critiquing the Law: Themes and Dilemmas in Anglo-American Feminist
Legal Theory"**[7]

"MacKinnon's concern is not just to identify male dominance and propose a feminist theory, but to engage in practical action and the transformation of power relations through a feminist method, namely consciousness raising. She suggests that consciousness raising enables women to view the shared reality of their condition from within the perspective of their own experience. This methodology permits a critique of the purported generality, disinterestedness, and universality of prior accounts. The collective speaking of women's experience uncovers and analyses male dominance. MacKinnon claims that 'the feminist theory of knowledge begins with the theory of the point of view of *all* women on social life' (emphasis added). All women either will or will not be hit in particular ways by the reality of gender, the totality of which will then comprise the meaning of gender as a social category.

She seems to suggest that, despite diverse experiences, a coherent women's perspective will emerge through consciousness raising, and the totality of these experiences enables women to transcend ideological distortion and enunciate the truth about the world. MacKinnon assumes that women's experiences and accounts will be complementary not conflicting; that the feminist critique of knowledge and male power is an amalgam of all women's partial views. However, taking experience as the level of analysis raises several interpretive questions. How can accounts or experiences be evaluated? How can we say that some women's experiences are more real or more accurate than others? Who determines the criteria? Some women have access to male power; is their experience less valid than those who do not have access to power? MacKinnon argues that to show that an observation or experience is not the same for all women proves only that it is not biological, not that it is not gendered. To say that

[7]   (1992) 19 *Journal of Law and Society* 423 at 429–430.

all experiences are gendered is as true for men as for women. If all accounts are equally as valid, then can the same be said of men's accounts? Moreover, how does consciousness raising cast off the male point of view which has been imposed? Given these problems, claims that women will produce an accurate depiction of reality either because they are women or because they are oppressed appear highly implausible.

The notion of the maleness of law, that law reflects and perpetuates male dominance which is 'metaphysically nearly perfect' begs the further question of how MacKinnon (and other proponents of the viewpoint that law is patriarchal) can explain her own knowledge base. How has she been able to transcend the hegemonic strictures of male dominance? If the so-called female attributes result from oppression, cannot the same be said of MacKinnon's own critique? She is extremely critical of feminists and others who disagree with her views on pornography and defines them not as feminists, thereby reducing feminism to her own viewpoint. Dissenting voices or perspectives are excluded. On one level, MacKinnon claims there is a distinctive women's perspective that is privileged, yet, when she confronts women's accounts which differ from her own, she denies them, thereby undermining her notion of a women's standpoint."

The "male" reference point of radical feminism does not refer to a biological male. It refers to gender, not sex, a social rather than physical construct. Although the "male" perspective may be the point of view of the majority of biological males, it is not the point of view of all males and can be a perspective held by some biological females.[8] The power relations between males and females are not biologically determined, but socially constructed. The oppression of women is not a consequence of biology but a consequence of constructions in western society at this particular historical moment. As Emily Jackson comments on the work of Catharine MacKinnon, "this argument is dangerously defeatist: if cultural forces have determined gender, and we are all inescapably gendered, we cannot speak out about sex inequality without affirming our cultural identity as gendered women."[9] Taken to its logical conclusion this argument may mean that women are not able to speak as women about the reality of their oppression.

Catharine MacKinnon grounds her approach by emphasising male power over women, that is the dominance of men and the subordination of women:

C. A. MacKinnon
"Feminism, Marxism, Method, and the State: Toward Feminist Jurisprudence"[10]

"Feminism has no theory of the state. It has a theory of power: sexuality is gendered as gender is sexualized. Male and female are created through the erotization of dominance and submission. The man/woman difference and the dominance/submission

---

[8]   C. A. MacKinnon, "Feminism, Marxism, Method, and the State: Toward Feminist Jurisprudence" (1983) 8 *Signs* 635 at 636.

[9]   E. Jackson, "Catharine MacKinnon and Feminist Jurisprudence: A Critical Appraisal" (1992) 19 *Journal of Law and Society* 195 at 198.

[10]   (1983) 8 *Signs* 635 at 635–639.

dynamic define each other. This is the social meaning of sex and the distinctively feminist account of gender inequality. Sexual objectification, the central process within this dynamic, is at once epistemological and political. The feminist theory of knowledge is inextricable from the feminist critique of power because the male point of view forces itself upon the world as its way of apprehending it.

The perspective from the male standpoint enforces woman's definition, encircles her body, circumlocutes her speech, and describes her life. The male perspective is systemic and hegemonic. The content of the signification "woman" is the content of women's lives. Each sex has its role, but their stakes and power are not equal. If the sexes are unequal, and perspective participates in situation, there is no ungendered reality or ungendered perspective. And they are connected. In this context, objectivity — the nonsituated, universal standpoint, whether claimed or aspired to — is a denial of the existence or potency of sex inequality that tacitly participates in constructing reality from the dominant point of view. Objectivity, as the epistemological stance of which objectification is the social process, creates the reality it apprehends by defining as knowledge the reality it creates through its way of apprehending it. Sexual metaphors for knowing are no coincidence. The solipsism of this approach does not undercut its sincerity, but it is interest that precedes method.

Feminism criticizes this male totality without an account of our capacity to do so or to imagine or realize a more whole truth. Feminism affirms women's point of view by revealing, criticizing, and explaining its impossibility. This is not a dialectical paradox. It is a methodological expression of women's situation, in which the struggle for consciousness is a struggle for world: for a sexuality, a history, a culture, a community, a form of power, an experience of the sacred. If women had consciousness or world, sex inequality would be harmless, or all women would be feminist. Yet we have something of both, or there would be no such thing as feminism. Why can women know that this — life as we have known it — is not all, not enough, not ours, not just? Now, why don't all women?

The practice of a politics of all women in the face of its theoretical impossibility is creating a new process of theorizing and a new form of theory. Although feminism emerges from women's particular experience, it is not subjective or partial, for no interior ground and few if any aspects of life are free of male power. Nor is feminism objective, abstract, or universal. It claims no external ground or unsexed sphere of generalization or abstraction beyond male power, nor transcendence of the specificity of each of its manifestations. How is it possible to have an engaged truth that does not simply reiterate its determinations? *Dis*-engaged truth only reiterates *its* determinations. Choice of method is choice of determinants — a choice which, for women as such, has been unavailable because of the subordination of women. Feminism does not begin with the premise that it is unpremised. It does not aspire to persuade an unpremised audience because there is no such audience. Its project is to uncover and claim as valid the experience of women, the major content of which is the devalidation of women's experience.

This defines our task not only because male dominance is perhaps the most pervasive and tenacious system of power in history, but because it is metaphysically nearly perfect. Its point of view is the standard for point-of-viewlessness, its particularity the meaning of universality. Its force is exercised as consent, its authority as participation, its supremacy as the paradigm of order, its control as the definition of legitimacy. Feminism claims the voice of women's silence, the sexuality of our eroticized desexualization, the fullness of 'lack,' the centrality of our marginality and exclusion, the public nature of privacy, the presence of our absence. This approach is more complex than transgression, more transformative than transvaluation, deeper than mirror-imaged resistance, more affirmative than the negation of our negativity. It is neither materialist nor idealist; it is feminist. Neither the transcendence of liberalism nor the determination of materialism works for us. Idealism is too unreal; women's inequality is enforced, so it cannot simply be thought out of existence, certainly not by us. Materialism is too real; women's inequality has never not existed, so women's equality never has. That is, the equality of women to men will not be scientifically provable until it is no longer necessary to do so. Women's situation offers no outside to stand on or gaze at, no inside to escape to, too much urgency to wait, no place else to go, and nothing to use but the twisted tools that have been shoved down our throats. If feminism is revolutionary, this is why."

The result of this arrangement is the pure objectification of women:

> "[o]bjectivity is the methodological stance of which objectification is the social process. Sexual objectification is the primary process of the subjection of women. It unites act with word, construction with expression, perception with enforcement, myth with reality. Man fucks woman; subject verb object."[11]

From this perspective, MacKinnon offers a stinging critique of the sameness/difference debate which she views as masking hierarchy and the reality of male dominance and as failing to explain why the male standard is that by which sameness or difference is measured.

C. A. MacKinnon
"Difference and Dominance: On Sex Discrimination"[12]

"In reality, which this approach is not long on because it is liberal idealism talking to itself, virtually every quality that distinguishes men from women is already affirmatively compensated in this society. Men's physiology defines most sports, their needs define auto and health insurance coverage, their socially designed biographies define workplace expectations and successful career patterns, their perspectives and concerns define quality in scholarship, their experiences and obsessions define merit, their objectification of life defines art, their military service defines citizenship, their presence defines family, their inability to get along with each other — their wars and rulerships — defines history, their image defines god, and their genitals define sex. For each of their differences from women, what amounts to an affirmative action plan is in effect, otherwise known as the structure and values of American society. But whenever women are, by this standard, 'different' from men and insist on not having it held against us, whenever a difference is used to keep us second class and we refuse to smile about it, equality law has a paradigm trauma and it's crisis time for the doctrine.

What this doctrine has apparently meant by sex inequality is not what happens to

---

[11] C. A. MacKinnon, notably "Feminism, Marxism, Method, and the State: An Agenda for Theory", *supra*, n. 2 at 541.
[12] In *Feminism Unmodified: Discourses on Life and Law* (Cambridge MA: Harvard University Press, 1987), pp. 36–37.

us. The law of sex discrimination that has resulted seems to be looking only for those ways women are kept down that have *not* wrapped themselves up as a difference — whether original, imposed, or imagined. Start with original: what to do about the fact that women actually have an ability men still lack, gestating children in utero. Pregnancy therefore is a difference. Difference doctrine says it is sex discrimination to give women what we need, because only women need it. It is not sex discrimination not to give women what we need because then only women will not get what we need . . .

I will also concede that there are many differences between women and men. I mean, can you imagine elevating one half of a population and denigrating the other half and producing a population in which everyone is the same? What the sameness standard fails to notice is that men's differences from women are equal to women's differences from men. There is an *equality* there. Yet the sexes are not socially equal. The difference approach misses the fact that hierarchy of power produces real as well as fantasied differences, differences that are also inequalities. What is missing in the difference approach is what Aristotle missed in his empiricist notion that equality means treating likes alike and unlikes unlike, and nobody has questioned it since. Why should you have to be the same as a man to get what a man gets simply because he is one? Why does maleness provide an original entitlement, not questioned on the basis of *its* gender, so that it is women — women who want to make a case of unequal treatment in a world men have made in their image (this is really the part Aristotle missed) — who have to show in effect that they are men in every relevant respect, unfortunately mistaken for women on the basis of an accident of birth?"

Needless to say, not all feminists are convinced by MacKinnon's account of male dominance.

S. L. ROACH ANLEU
"Critiquing the Law: Themes and Dilemmas in Anglo-American Feminist Legal Theory"[13]

"Even though MacKinnon rejects objectivity and positivism she provides a simple causal model of women's subordination. She accepts that race and class do mediate gender relations and claims she is not advancing a theory of biological imperatives, but maintains that male (and female) is a social and political concept, not a biological attribute. Not all men adopt a male viewpoint or have male power equally, but most do, especially with regard to women. To the extent that they cannot create the world from their point of view, they find themselves unmanned, castrated, literally or figuratively. By the same token, women frequently adopt the male standpoint and 'pass'. She argues that men are as they are because they have power, and therefore their domination is not biological; however, she never questions the origin of that power. It is impossible to disentangle male and power in her theory which means that real males have power, and power is exercised by real males — a tautology. This argument veers toward accepting a fundamental nature or essence by viewing women as universally subordinated by men. While seeking to capture the variety of women's experiences, MacKinnon's conception of women collapses into the very stereotype she seeks to critique; she portrays women as passive, submissive, dominated, and victims of rape,

[13]   (1992) 19 *Journal of Law and Society* 423 at 430–431.

sexual harassment, pornography, or, more generally, sexuality as defined by male domination."

MacKinnon argues that acknowledging the hierarchy in which male has power over female, a hierarchy which is entrenched in law, and the consequent relationship of dominance and submission as opposed to sameness and difference, leads to recognition of many issues as sexual equality issues which are not otherwise appreciated as such. Differences, in her view, are not causes of inequality between men and women but the consequence of domination by men. Differences follow from inequality. Focusing upon difference serves to hide the power relationship between the genders. Focusing upon inequality reveals the domination by men of women.

C. A. MacKinnon
Toward a Feminist Theory of the State[14]

"Inequality on the basis of sex, women share. It is women's collective condition. The first task of a movement for social change is to face one's situation and name it. The failure to face and criticize the reality of women's condition, a failure of idealism and denial, is a failure of feminism in its liberal forms. The failure to move beyond criticism, a failure of determinism and radical paralysis, is a failure of feminism in its left forms. Feminism on its own terms has begun to give voice to and describe the collective condition of women as such, so largely comprised as it is of all women's particularities. It has begun to uncover the laws of motion of a system that keeps women in a condition of imposed inferiority. It has located the dynamic of the social definition of gender in the sexuality of dominance and subordination, the sexuality of inequality: sex as inequality and inequality as sex. As sexual inequality is gendered as man and women, gender inequality is sexualized as dominance and subordination. The social power of men over women extends through laws that purport to protect women as part of the community, like the rape law; laws that ignore women's survival stake in the issue, like the obscenity law, or obscure it, like the abortion law; and laws that announce their intent to remedy that inequality but do not, like the sex equality law. This law derives its authority from reproducing women's social inequality to men in legal inequality, in a seamless web of life and law.

Feminist method adopts the point of view of women's inequality to men. Grasping women's reality from the inside, developing its specificities, facing the intractability and pervasiveness of male power, relentlessly criticizing women's condition as it identifies with all women, it has created strategies for change, beginning with consciousness raising. On the level of the state, legal guarantees of equality in liberal regimes provide an opening. Sex inequality is the true name for women's social condition. It is also, in words anyway, illegal sometimes. In some liberal states, the belief that women already essentially have sex equality extends to the level of law. From a perspective that understands that women do *not* have sex equality, this law means that, once equality is meaningfully defined, the law cannot be applied without changing society. To make

[14]   (Cambridge MA: Harvard University Press, 1989), pp. 241–245.

sex equality meaningful in law requires identifying the real issues, and establishing that sex inequality, once established, matters.

Sex equality in law has not been meaningfully defined for women, but has been defined and limited from the male point of view to correspond with the existing social reality of sex inequality. An alternative approach to this mainstream view threads through existing law. It is the reason sex equality law exists at all. In this approach, inequality is a matter not of sameness and difference, but of dominance and subordination. Inequality is about power, its definition, and its maldistribution. Inequality at root is grasped as a question of hierarchy, which — as power succeeds in constructing social perception and social reality — derivatively becomes categorical distinctions, differences. Where mainstream equality law is abstract, this approach is concrete; where mainstream equality law is falsely universal, this approach remains specific. The goal is not to make legal categories that trace and trap the status quo, but to confront by law the inequalities in women's condition in order to change them.

This alternate approach centers on the most sex-differential abuses of women as a gender, abuses that sex equality law in its sameness/difference obsession cannot confront. It is based on the reality that feminism, beginning with consciousness raising, has most distinctively uncovered, a reality about which little systematic was known before 1970: the reality of sexual abuse. It combines women's sex-based destitution and enforced dependency and permanent relegation to disrespected and starvation-level work — the lived meaning of class for women — with the massive amount of sexual abuse of girls apparently endemic to the patriarchal family, the pervasive rape and attempted rape about which nothing is done, the systematic battery of women in homes, and prostitution — the fundamental condition of women — of which the pornography industry is an arm. Keeping the reality of gender in view makes it impossible to see gender as a difference, unless this subordinated condition of women is that difference. This reality has called for a new conception of the problem of sex inequality, hence a new legal conception of it, both doctrinally and jurisprudentially.

Experiences of sexual abuse have been virtually excluded from the mainstream doctrine of sex equality because they happen almost exclusively to women and because they are experienced as sex. Sexual abuse has not been seen to raise sex *equality* issues because these events happen specifically and almost exclusively to women as women. Sexuality is socially organized to require sex inequality for excitement and satisfaction. The least extreme expression of gender inequality and the prerequisite for all of it, is dehumanization and objectification. The most extreme is violence. Because sexual objectification and sexual violence are almost uniquely done to women, they have been systematically treated as the sex difference, when they represent the socially situated subjection of women to men. The whole point of women's social relegation to inferiority as a gender is that this is not generally done to men. The systematic relegation of an entire people to a condition of inferiority is attributed to them, made a feature of theirs, and read out of equality demands and equality law, when it is termed a 'difference.' This condition is ignored entirely, with all the women who are determined by it, when only features women share with the privileged group are allowed to substantiate equality claims.

It follows that seeing sex equality questions as matters of reasonable or unreasonable classification of relevant social characteristics expresses male dominance in law. If the shift in perspective from gender as difference to gender as dominance is followed, gender changes from a distinction that is ontological and presumptively valid to a detriment that is epistemological and presumptively suspect. The given becomes the contingent. In this light, liberalism, purporting to discover gender, has discovered male and female in the mirror of nature; the left has discovered masculine and feminine in the mirror of society. The approach from the standpoint of the subordination of women to men, by contrast, criticizes and claims the specific situation of women's enforced inferiority and devaluation, pointing a way out of the infinity of reflections in law-and-society's hall of mirrors where sex equality law remains otherwise trapped.

Equality understood substantively rather than abstractly, defined on women's own terms and in terms of women's concrete experience, is what women in society most need and most do not have. Equality is also what society holds that women have already, and therefore guarantees women by positive law. The law of equality, statutory and constitutional, therefore provides a peculiar jurisprudential opportunity, a crack in the wall between law and society. Law does not usually guarantee rights to things that do not exist. This may be why equality issues have occasioned so many jurisprudential disputes about what law is and what it can and should do. Every demand from women's point of view looks substantive, just as ever demand from women's point of view requires change. Can women, demanding actual equality through law, be part of changing the state's relation to women and women's relation to men?

The first step is to claim women's concrete reality. Women's inequality occurs in a context of unequal pay, allocation to disrespected work, demeaned physical characteristics, targeting for rape, domestic battery, sexual abuse as children, and systematic sexual harassment. Women are daily dehumanized, used in denigrating entertainment, denied reproductive control, and forced by the conditions of their lives into prostitution. These abuses occur in a legal context historically characterized by disenfranchisement, preclusion from property ownership, exclusion from public life, and lack of recognition of sex-specific injuries. Sex inequality is thus a social and political institution.

The next step is to recognize that male forms of power over women are affirmatively embodied as individual rights in law. When men lose power, they feel they lose rights. Often they are not wrong. Examples include the defense of mistaken belief in consent in the rape law, which legally determines whether or not a rape occurred from the rapists' perspective; freedom of speech, which gives pimps rights to torture, exploit, use, and sell women to men through pictures and words, and gives consumers rights to buy them; the law of privacy, which defines the home and sex as presumptively consensual and protects the use of pornography in the home; the law of child custody, which purports gender neutrality while applying a standard of adequacy of parenting based on male-controlled resources and male-defined norms, sometimes taking children away from women but more generally controlling women through the threat and fear of loss of their children. Real sex equality under law would qualify or eliminate these powers of men, hence men's current 'rights' to use, access, possess, and traffic women and children."

Reconceptualising inequalities as predicated upon power inequities has extensive implications for law reform. It is apparent that, because of the power imbalance between males and females, simply recognising women's differences within law will not eradicate oppression. Catharine MacKinnon gives a number of examples of reframing equality issues in terms of dominance. One is sexual assault. Its victims are primarily female, the perpetrators primarily male. Although the State does provide criminal laws against sexual violence, they are ineffective either through failure to enforce them or because of the way in which women who seek to rely upon them are treated within the legal system. Sexual assault is, in Catharine MacKinnon's analysis, an (in)equality issue. So too is reproductive control whereby, "women are socially disadvantaged in controlling sexual access to their bodies through social learning, lack of information, social pressure, custom, poverty and enforced economic dependence, sexual force, and ineffective enforcement of laws against sexual assault".[15] Consequently, and because contraceptive technology is not safe, acceptable and effective, women do not have control over their reproductive lives. They are sexually unequal. Pornography, which portrays a universal image of what women are and what women want from sex, thereby encouraging male sexual violence against women, is likewise an issue of sex inequality.

The practicalities of reframing differences as inequalities are considered by Ann Scales:

A. C. SCALES
"The Emergence of Feminist Jurisprudence: An Essay"[16]

"Coping with Equality
The problem of inequality of the sexes stands in complex relation to the problem of survival. Inequality in the sexual division of labor ensures replication of the model of aggression. Pathological aggression accounts for inequality. If these connections are ever to be unpacked, if we are serious about survival, we need a radically more serious approach to equality. Law must embrace a version of equality that focuses on the real issues — domination, disadvantage and disempowerment — instead of on the interminable and diseased issue of differences between the sexes. I endorse the definition of equality proposed by Professor MacKinnon in 1979: The test in any challenge should be 'whether the policy or practice in question integrally contributes to the maintenance of an underclass or a deprived position because of gender status.' MacKinnon contrasts this to the 'differences approach,' calling it the 'inequality approach.' I would call the former 'thinking like a lawyer;' the latter, 'thinking like a person.'

That is not to say that the proposed standard will be easy to implement. It will require us to bring the very best of our humanness to bear. That is a scary proposition. No data yet exist to reassure us on the standard's reliability, and by its own terms, results cannot be predicted without the compilation of records very different from those underlying previously decided cases. The critics appropriately worry, for example, that classifications designed to address the real problems of women (such as pregnancy legislation) will serve to reinforce stereotypes about women's place. The problem for feminist legal scholars, I think, is that we are unsure how to measure what about stereotyping is at issue in a given case. The notion of stereotyping connotes oversimplification, inattention to individual characteristics, lack of seriousness, and invariance. We use the concept of stereotyping without difficulty when the challenged practice is based upon an untrue generalization. All of the connotations of stereotyping

---

[15] C. A. MacKinnon, *supra*, n. 4 at p. 246.
[16] In P. Smith (ed.), *Feminist Jurisprudence* (Oxford: Oxford University Press, 1993), p. 94, pp. 101–104.

are clearly implicated in negative ways. In such cases, both the differences approach and the inequality approach would prohibit the classification.

The inequality approach focuses upon two other sources of feminist discomfort: first, the need for a reliable approach to generalizations which are largely true (either because of biology or because of highly successful socialization) and, second, the need to distinguish between beneficial and burdensome legislation.

Only the inequality approach attempts to reckon with true generalizations. Indeed, in that view, different treatment based upon unique physical characteristics would be 'among the *first* to trigger suspicion and scrutiny.' In the past, biological differences have been used to show that classifications are not sex based. Thereby, the reasons for having antidiscrimination laws have been seen as the reasons to allow discrimination. The inequality approach unravels the tautology. It makes no sense to say that equality is guaranteed only when the sexes are already equal. The issue is not freedom to be treated without regard to sex; the issue is freedom from systematic subordination because of sex.

The inequality approach would also reach stereotypes which, though not biologically based, have largely made themselves true through a history of inequality. Consider the situation in *Phillips v. Martin Marietta Corp.*, where the company hired males with preschool-aged children but would not hire women in that category. As a variation, suppose the trial court had found that women with small children did in fact have greater responsibilities and therefore were, as a group, less well suited for the jobs in question. Such a finding would correspond to the facts of allocation of child-raising responsibility. The only challenge that will work in this scenario is one from an 'exceptional' woman candidate for employment — a woman with preschool-aged children whose job performance will not be impaired by her obligations to them. The policy will be deemed irrational as applied to her.

Compare the inequality approach, which is triggered not by irrationality but by disadvantage. In our scenario, the inequality approach is superior because it reaches the worse injustice: The fact that women who fit the stereotype are precluded from advancement in our economic system. A challenge adjudicated by that standard would succeed on behalf of the unexceptional as well as the exceptional. Employers (and other employees who have carried a disproportionately lower burden in child rearing) would then essentially have to compensate for the benefits they have derived from women's double burden. Such payment should include damages, and court-ordered advancement, day care, parents' leave, and reallocation of workers' hours and rewards. This redistribution of historical burdens and benefits may seem a sweeping remedy, but it is the only one which addresses the reality.

With respect to our second problem, the discernment of genuinely beneficial classifications, suppose that the same company offered a hiring preference for women with school-aged children and provided some relief from the double burden. The offer undoubtedly 'reinforces a stereotype,' but what shall we make of the fact that the stereotype is in large part — if only contingently and temporarily — true? But true only because women carry a disproportionate burden of the child-caring responsibility in our society. Especially when women can elect to receive the benefits (as opposed to risking stigmatization by them), what is the objection to such a plan? Disadvantage has a way of replicating and reinforcing itself. To oppose the scheme is to be reduced to relying upon a groundswell of exceptional behaviors within the disadvantaged group itself. Historically, however, disadvantaged groups have been forced to rely upon surrogates to better themselves. That has not required that the groups thus assisted conform for all time to the surrogates' perceptions of them (or even to their own perceptions of themselves).

Beneficial classifications, therefore, seem necessary to the ultimate undoing of stubborn stereotypes. It is true that in our history, stereotypical differences, both real and imagined, have served primarily as convenient, 'natural' justifications for imposition of burdens. It does not follow, however, that we cannot use differences progressively. Injustice does not flow directly from recognizing differences; injustice results when those differences are transformed into social and economic deprivation. Our task, then, is to exercise our capacity for discernment in more precise ways. Allegedly beneficial classifications, even when they invoke a stereotype, must be measured against what is objectionable in stereotyping. Beneficial classifications, such as the employment preference in our example, will survive under the inequality approach if they do not have those characteristics. Insofar as the employment preference oversimplifies, it is an oversimplification in the service of a profound complexity, as is any well-drafted policy. The preference provides to individuals the opportunity to demonstrate their capacities when the stereotype is set aside. It evinces laudable seriousness toward the problem, especially insofar as the stereotyper takes upon itself some of the burden of the past discrimination. Last, and perhaps most important, it is not invariant. By definition it points to the stereotype for the purpose of undoing it, as an example of how revised present arrangements can relieve centuries of disadvantage. When allegedly beneficial classifications do not have this form or when once beneficial schemes cease to have it, the inequality approach would prohibit them.

Admittedly, the inequality approach would sometimes require that different standards be used for men and women. If that were not so, however, the approach would not be working. Its emphasis is upon enforced inferiority, not sex-differentiated treatment. When the aim is to discover the reality of domination, the standard to be applied depends upon the context. The inequality approach requires an investigation which must delve as deeply as circumstances demand into whether the challenged policy or practice exploits gender status. To worry in the abstract about which standard should be applied at what time is to replicate the fallacy of the differences approach.

In short, the inequality approach means that we have to think more broadly about what we want 'equality' to mean. The traditional bases for differentiation between the sexes are socially created categories, given meaning only by assigned biases. We create the relevant comparisons and are free to do so *de novo* in light of social realities. Thus, in the preferential hiring situation, we would say that the right at stake, rather than the right to be treated without regard to sex, is the right not to have one's existence bifurcated because of sex. In the pregnancy situation, it is the right to have one's total health needs taken as seriously as are those of the other sex.

Logic is no obstacle to the implementation of the inequality approach. The obstacles are, rather, perception and commitment. When the fact of judicial manipulation has been so salient in the past, why should we now expect those responsible for implementing the law to be able to see, in any given situation, how women have been disadvantaged? Accustomed as judges are to looking for similarities and differences, they cannot or will not make the assessments of deprivation and disempowerment . . .

The proposed inequality standard will not take root overnight. Developments in feminist theory take decades to manifest themselves in law. But it will happen; the difficulty of the process must not stop us from demanding that change or from continuing the tradition that makes it possible."

As these examples show, radical feminism has two substantive foci. It is not limited to an analysis of how men have constructed female sexuality in a way which emphasises male fulfilment and controls women through sexual violence. A further focus is how men have controlled women's bodies in reproduction.[17] Taking the latter issue first, one may cite the work of Shulamith Firestone who, in *The Dialectic of Sex*, locates the subordination of women to men in the biological function of reproduction.[18] She argues that women should resort to technologies, such as abortion, contraception or sterilisation, in order to cast aside their role as reproducers. Having freed themselves in this fashion, Firestone envisages a society in which parenting would be undertaken by any suitable adult irrespective of sex. Following from this the family, as both a biological and an economic unit, would no longer be sustainable. She considers that technology offers women freedom from reproduction and men freedom from production which could lead to a breakdown of the distinctions in society which have enabled the oppression of women. Given the extent to which the law participates in the regulation of methods of control and facilitation of reproduction, the arguments of Shulamith Firestone have obvious legal implications. This is even more so with the development of new reproductive technologies adding methods such as *in vitro* fertilisation and gamete intra-fallopian transfer to techniques such as artificial insemination by donor and surrogacy. Firestone's work has, however, been criticised for advocating a means of removing from women the very thing over which women have power — their necessary and unique role in reproduction.[19] Further, it is argued that it is not female biology which is the source of women's oppression, but male control over female biology.

The second focus of radical feminism is upon sex and sexuality as pivotal to male power over women. Given the understanding of the appropriation of female sexuality to meet the needs of men, radical feminists have provided a critique of laws on rape, incest, prostitution, sexual assault, pornography and abortion. Catharine MacKinnon considers that the State, through its laws, maintains the power of men over women's sexuality and hence ensures the subordination of women to men. This she argues is the case even in the examples of laws which, at first sight, seem to prohibit harms against women. For example, the laws against rape, she suggests, merely prevent sexual violence against a "woman who is not yours", the laws on obscenity ensure the eroticisation of pornographic material, and abortion facilitates the avoidance of male responsibility for sexual intercourse.[20]

---

[17] In addition to these two major themes of radical feminism, Rosemary Tong, in *Feminist Thought: A Comprehensive Introduction, supra*, n. 1 at p. 72, acknowledges also radical feminism's celebration of female culture, stating that "[d]uring the last twenty years, radical feminists have, in a variety of ways, been creating and celebrating women's religion, science, art, poetry, literature, song, dance, cuisine, horticulture."

[18] S. Firestone, *The Dialectic of Sex* (New York: Bantam Books, 1970). The discussion here is based upon the analysis of Firestone's work by Rosemary Tong, *ibid.*, pp. 72–76.

[19] See further Chap. 4 in which the argument that reproductive technologies have enabled the extension of male/medical control over women, rather than, as Shulamith Firestone suggests, the liberty of women, is explored.

[20] C. A. MacKinnon, *supra*, n. 8 at 644.

MacKinnon argues that rape is portrayed as a crime of violence and yet for both its victims and perpetrators it is "about" sex:

> "When a woman has been raped, and it is sex that she cannot experience without connecting it to that, it was her sexuality that was violated. . . . Rape is defined by distinction from intercourse, not nonviolence, intercourse."[21]

However, the act of rape, the crime of rape, is defined in terms of what men perceive to be violating, that is penetration of the vagina by the penis without consent.[22] It is argued that, because pornography provides the universal understanding that sex is what women are for and that sex is what women want, certain types of women (wives, prostitutes and women who have had sexual relationships before) are not rapable. Popular understanding has it that women like to be violated, that is they take pleasure from violence, and women who say "no" do not always mean "no". From this perspective what constitutes rape to a woman may not seem like rape to a man, appearing instead as just another act of sexual intercourse.

Likewise, MacKinnon argues that sexual harassment is not an abuse of power, it is an abuse of sexuality. However, the law has been defined from the male perspective. Consequently, normal sexual initiation only becomes illegal when it amounts to an abuse of power, such as when it occurs between employer and employee or between teacher and student.[23]

From these concrete examples, MacKinnon argues that the law is constructed from a male standpoint, based upon masculinist assumptions about female behaviour. Despite the claim that the law is gender neutral, despite the claim to objectivity, Catharine MacKinnon exposes the law as constructed from a male point of view. Having identified the problem, she advocates that "[j]ustice will require change, not reflection — a new jurisprudence, a new relation between life and law."[24] It is upon debate of the construction of a new (feminist) jurisprudence that we concentrate in the remainder of this chapter.

3.2 Feminist jurisprudence and beyond

The attraction of a feminist jurisprudence is outlined by Carol Smart in her book *Feminism and the Power of Law*:

C. SMART
Feminism and the Power of Law[25]

"The idea of a feminist jurisprudence is tantalizing in that it appears to hold out the promise of a fully integrated theoretical framework and political practice which will

---

[21] C. A. MacKinnon, "Sex and Violence: A Perspective (1981)" in *Feminism Unmodified: Discourses on Life and Law, supra,* n. 12 at p. 88.
[22] C. A. MacKinnon, *ibid.,* p. 87. See Chap. 7 below for further discussion.
[23] C. A. MacKinnon, *ibid.,* p. 90. See Chap. 8 below for further discussion.
[24] C. A. MacKinnon, *supra,* n. 8 at 658.
[25] (London: Routledge, 1989), pp. 66–67.

be transformative, unlike the partial or liberal measures of the past which have merely ameliorated or mollified women's oppression (*e.g.* equal pay legislation). It promises a general theory of law which has practical applications. Because it appears to offer the combination of theory and practice, and because it will be grounded in women's experience, the ideal of a feminist jurisprudence appears to be a way out of the impasse of liberal feminist theories of law reform. Thus not only does it imply a better understanding of law, but it also seeks to tackle philosophical issues, such as the idea of feminist justice and feminist legal method, as well as procedural issues, such as how law should be administered and in which forums ... Not withstanding that the term 'feminist jurisprudence' does not always imply the totality of a general theory, the need for a new direction has been clearly expressed in feminist writing."

3.2.i   *Articulating feminist jurisprudence*

Two authors, Robin West and Catharine MacKinnon, have already been noted above as having identified the need for a "feminist jurisprudence". To recap, West argues patriarchy must end before a feminist jurisprudence can be envisioned, stating:

"[w]e will not have a genuinely ungendered jurisprudence (a jurisprudence 'unmodified' so to speak) until we have legal doctrine that takes women's lives as seriously as it takes men's. We don't have such legal doctrine. The virtual abolition of patriarchy is the necessary political condition for the creation of non-masculine feminist jurisprudence."[26]

MacKinnon's "new jurisprudence, a new relationship between life and law"[27] comprises a legal system based upon female perspective and experience:

C. A. MacKinnon
"Toward Feminist Jurisprudence"[28]

"Law, in liberal jurisprudence, objectifies social life. The legal process reflects itself in its own image, makes be there what it puts there, while presenting itself as passive and neutral in the process. To undo this, it will be necessary to grasp the dignity of women without blinking at the indignity of women's condition, to envision the possibility of equality without minimizing the grip of inequality, to reject the fear that has become so much of women's sexuality and the corresponding denial that has become so much of women's politics, and to demand civil parity without pretending that the demand is neutral or that civil equality already exists ...

Abstract rights authoritize the male experience of the world. Substantive rights for women would not. Their authority would be the currently unthinkable: nondominant authority, the authority of excluded truth, the voice of silence. It would stand against both the liberal and left views of law. The liberal view that law is society's text, its rational mind, expresses the male view in the normative mode; the traditional left view

---

[26]   R. West, "Jurisprudence and Gender" (1988) 55 *University of Chicago Law Review* 1 at 60.
[27]   C. A. MacKinnon, "Toward Feminist Jurisprudence" in *Toward a Feminist Theory of the State, supra,* n. 4 at p. 249.
[28]   C. A. MacKinnon, *ibid.,* pp. 248–249.

that the state, and with it the law, is superstructural or ephiphenomenal, expresses it in the empirical mode. A feminist jurisprudence, stigmatized as particularized and protectionist in male eyes of both traditions, is accountable to women's concrete conditions and to changing them. Both the liberal and the left view rationalize male power by presuming that it does not exist, that equality between the sexes (room for marginal corrections conceded) is society's basic norm and fundamental description. Only feminist jurisprudence sees that male power does exist and sex equality does not, because only feminism grasps the extent to which antifeminism is misogyny and both are as normative as they are empirical. Masculinity then appears as a specific position, not just the way things are, its judgments and partialities revealed in process and procedure, adjudication and legislation."

For those who may find this approach, as MacKinnon says, "particularized and protectionist", some might even say sexist, MacKinnon defends her vision as follows:

C. A. MacKinnon
"Toward Feminist Jurisprudence"[29]

"To the extent feminist law embodies women's point of view, it will be said that its law is not neutral. But existing law is not neutral. It will be said that it undermines the legitimacy of the legal system. But the legitimacy of existing law is based on force at women's expense. Women have never consented to its rule — suggesting that the system's legitimacy needs repair that women are in a position to provide. It will be said that feminist law is special pleading for a particular group and one cannot start that or where will it end. But existing law is already special pleading for a particular group, where it has ended. The question is not where it will stop, but whether it will start for any group but the dominant one. It will be said that feminist law cannot win and will not work. But this is premature. Its possibilities cannot be assessed in the abstract but must engage the world."

Criticism of MacKinnon's approach is not, however, aimed simply at its apparent sexism. Carol Smart has argued that the quest for a feminist jurisprudence may ultimately be futile. One of the problems she identifies with this quest is the way in which it constitutes an exercise in "grand theorizing" which ignores the individual aspects and concrete realities of women's lives:

C. Smart
Feminism and the Power of Law[30]

"The overarching problem that I find with the quest for a feminist jurisprudence which takes the form of constructing a general theory of law, is the question of whether it is worth the effort of merely replacing one abstraction about law with another. Both

---

[29]   C. A. MacKinnon, *ibid.*, p. 249.
[30]   C. Smart, *supra*, n. 25 at pp. 68–69.

feminists and Marxists have been critical of the notion of an 'essence' of law that derives in an uncontaminated fashion from an absolute truth. Both have argued in different ways that the vision of a suprahuman and objective jurisprudence is in fact the 'appearance' of law which has been constructed and which reflects the power of law, not its purity and neutrality. Feminists have gone further in critiquing the academic practice of constructing abstract, universal theories. This critique is not merely a statement that what is universal is really male, but goes further to challenge the very practice of 'grand theory' construction. Feminist analysis increasing [*sic*] falls into the category of 'deconstruction', which challenges naturalistic, overgeneralized and abstract assumptions about the social world. Feminist work has a growing affinity with the idea of analysing the micro-politics of power, and the everyday oppressions of women which are invisible to the grand theorist. Hence the search for this kind of feminist jurisprudence, whilst understandable, runs counter to these insights . . .

The idea of a feminist jurisprudence also seems to imply that law can remain a discrete area of activity, detached and somehow superior to 'society'. Although many of the feminists who write in this area are careful to avoid this positivistic assumption about law, the very terminology of jurisprudence has the effect of turning the debate into an exclusively legal one. It is as if it becomes a matter only for lawyers and this runs counter to the aim of feminism which is to include the diversity of women and women's experience."

Having considered MacKinnon's assertion that "[r]adical feminism is feminism", Smart continues:

C. SMART
Feminism and the Power of Law[31]

"this passage reveals everything that is problematic with the search for a total feminist jurisprudence. It sets up a specific feminist theory as superior to other versions, not on the basis of a set of political values, but on the basis that radical feminism is the Truth and its truth is established through the validity of its method and epistemology. This is scientific feminism; it attempts to proclaim its unique truth above all other feminisms and other systems of thought. It turns experience into objective truth because it has taken on the mantle of a positivism which assumes that there must be an ultimate standard of objectivity. The search for feminist jurisprudence seems to be vulnerable to this tendency to want to claim that its truth is better than other truths . . .

[T]he problem of attempting to construct a feminist jurisprudence is that it does not de-centre law. On the contrary, it may attempt to change its values and procedures, but it preserves law's place in the hierarchy of discourses which maintains that law has access to truth and justice. It encourages a 'turning to law' for solutions, it fetishizes law rather than deconstructing it. The search for a feminist jurisprudence is generated by a feminist challenge to the power of law as it is presently constituted, but it ends with a celebration of positivistic, scientific feminism which seeks to replace one hierarchy of truth with another."

For Smart, therefore, the articulation of a feminist jurisprudence does not

---

[31] C. Smart, *ibid.*, pp. 70–71, 88–89.

adequately address the differences between women's varied experiences. It also tries to universalise these experiences by turning them into an objective reality which posits itself as an absolute truth able to disqualify alternative accounts. Smart argues instead that it is towards "deconstructing" law that feminists should turn their attention. Alternatively stated:

> "[i]t is not the space now occupied by a traditional positivist or even liberal abstract jurisprudence which we should seek to fill with another abstraction called feminist jurisprudence, rather — or so it seems to me — we should seek to construct feminist discourses on laws."[32]

This new direction is addressed by Smart in terms of the deconstruction and (re)construction of feminist legal discourse, together with the articulation of the complex relationship between law, power and feminism.

3.2.ii   *Postmodern legal feminism: law, power and truth*

It is not only "grand theorizing" which Carol Smart identifies as being problematic in the search for a feminist jurisprudence. Also problematic is the fact that, in engaging with this search, feminists may be accepting the terms of a debate which has already been constructed without regard to their interests.

C. SMART
Feminism and the Power of Law[33]

"At present it seems as if feminist 'legal theory' is immobilized in the face of the failure of feminism to affect law and the failure of law to transform the quality of women's lives. Feminist scholarship has become trapped into debates about the 'usefulness' of law to the emancipation of women, or the relative merits of 'equality' versus 'difference' as strategies, or the extent to which law reflects the interest of patriarchy, or simply men. These are necessary debates but they have the overwhelming disadvantage of ceding to law the very power that law may then deploy against women's claims ... Put simply, in accepting law's terms in order to challenge law, feminism always concedes too much."

Smart's scepticism about law leads her to advocate "deconstructing the discursive power of law",[34] a project which draws upon the work of the French philosopher Michel Foucault[35]:

---

[32]   C. Smart, *ibid.*, p. 69.
[33]   C. Smart, *ibid.*, p. 5.
[34]   C. Smart, *ibid.*, p. 5.
[35]   See particularly M. Foucault, *Madness and Civilization* (London: Tavistock, 1971); *The Birth of the Clinic* (New York: Vintage Books, 1975); *The History of Sexuality*, Vol. 1 (London: Allen Lane, 1979); *Discipline and Punish* (New York: Vintage Books, 1979).

C. Smart
Feminism and the Power of Law[36]

"Concepts like truth, power, and knowledge are central to this enterprise and it is, therefore important to acknowledge their source in the work of Foucault . . . [Foucault] attempts to construct a non-economic analysis of power which better reflects the mechanisms of power in the twentieth century. The idea of power as a commodity which some people, or a class of people, may 'own' (usually because they command wealth or economic resources) is inadequate to an understanding of contemporary society. His argument is that society has become transformed such that, whilst in the past the linkage of power and judicial rights may have been valid, this is no longer the case. The transformation that Foucault identifies is the development of the disciplinary society. By this he means the growth of new knowledges (*e.g.* medicine, criminology, pedagogics, epidemiology, etc.) which came to constitute the 'modern episteme'.

These knowledges create new fields of exploration and bring with them new modes of surveillance and regulation of the population. Hence the criminal is no longer someone who breaks the law and who must be punished. He is pathologized, he needs to be subjected to close surveillance and ultimately to cure or normalization . . .

Foucault's concentration on the growth of the disciplinary society reflects his greater interest in the mechanisms of power than the 'old' question of who has power. He also rejects the tendency which is apparent in the traditional formulation of power, of treating power as if it were negative, repressive and juridical. He maintains that power is creative and technical. By this it is meant that the mechanisms of power create resistances and local struggles which operate to bring about new forms of knowledge and resistance. Hence power is productive, not simply a negative sanction which stops or restricts oppositional developments . . .

Truth/knowledge
. . . [Foucault] is not concerned with what is considered to be the usual quest of science, namely to uncover the truth, rather he is interested in discovering how certain discourses claim to speak the truth and thus can exercise power in a society that values this notion of truth. He argues that making the claim to be a science is in fact an exercise of power because, in claiming scientificity, other knowledges are accorded less status, less value . . .

Foucault does not compare the scientist's claim to truth, and hence exercise of power, with the lawyer's claim. Law does not fit into his discussion of science, knowledge, and truth because . . . he identifies it in relation to the regime of power that predates the modern episteme. Yet I wish to argue that there are very close parallels in terms of the 'claim to truth' and the effect of power that the claim concedes. I am not saying that law attempts to call itself a science, but then it does not have to. Law has its own method, its own testing ground, its own specialized language and system of results. It may be a field of knowledge that has a lower status than those regarded as 'real' sciences, none the less it sets itself apart from other discourses in the same way that science does . . .

If we accept that law, like science, makes a claim to truth and that this is indivisible from the exercise of power, we can see that law exercises power not simply in its

---

[36] C. Smart, *supra*, n. 25 at pp. 6–11.

material effects (judgements) but also in its ability to disqualify other knowledges and experiences. Non-legal knowledge is therefore suspect and/or secondary."

Hence, feminist knowledge and female experience are silenced in the face of the power of law. Feminists should resist acceding to law's claims and enhancing its power. Smart concludes that:

> "[i]t is therefore important for feminism to sustain its challenge to the power of law to define women in law's terms. Feminism has the power to challenge subjectivity and to alter women's consciousness. It also has the means to expose how law operates in all its most detailed mechanisms. In doing this it can increase the resistance to law and may effect a shift in power. Whilst it is important that feminism should recognize the power that law can exercise, it is axiomatic that feminists do not regard themselves as powerless."[37]

In a later article entitled "The Woman of Legal Discourse"[38] Carol Smart takes her analysis a stage further. Having identified the empowerment of law via its deployment, she goes on to state that:

> "[t]he move to use law for 'women' also collides with the recent and profound recognition in feminist theory deriving from other disciplines, that to invoke an unproblematic category of Woman, while presuming that this represents all women, is an exclusionary strategy".[39]

It is to Smart's assessment of the "category of Woman" that we now move. This involves revealing first how law is "gendered" and second how law operates as a "gendering strategy". On the first count, Smart reveals three phases in the identification of law as a gendered phenomenon: the first is that "law is sexist", the second that "law is male" and the third that "law is gendered."[40]

The "law is sexist" approach deals with the liberal feminist agenda of addressing the disadvantages women suffer in law through their differentiation from men. Its solution is to eradicate that differentiation. Smart comments that this insight, while important, misrepresents the problem:

> "[t]he concept of sexism implies that we can override sexual difference as if it were epiphenomenal rather than embedded in how we comprehend and negotiate the social order ... If eradicating discrimination is dependent on the eradication of differentiation, we have to be able to think of a culture without gender. Thus what seems like a relatively easy solution such as the incorporation of gender-neutral terminology into law, masks a much deeper problem. Moreover, as many feminists have argued, it is not at all certain that the desired outcome of feminism is some form of androgyny."[41]

---

[37] C. Smart, *supra*, n. 25 at p. 25.
[38] C. Smart, "The Woman of Legal Discourse" (1992) 1 *Social and Legal Studies* 29.
[39] C. Smart, *ibid.*, at 30.
[40] C. Smart, *ibid.*
[41] C. Smart, *ibid.*, at 31–32.

The "law is male" approach moves on a stage from this initial position:

"The idea that 'law is male' arises from the empirical observation that most lawmakers and lawyers are indeed male. It transcends this starting point however because of the realization that maleness or masculinity, once embedded in values and practices, need not be exhaustively anchored to the male biological referent, *i.e.* men . . . Thus, in comparison to the 'law is sexist' approach, this analysis suggests that when a man and woman stand before the law, it is not that law fails to apply objective criteria when faced with the feminine subject, but precisely that it does apply objective criteria and these criteria are masculine."[42]

This perspective too, however, is not unproblematic:

"Firstly, this approach perpetuates the idea of law as a unity rather than problematizing law and dealing with its internal contradictions. Secondly, and without necessarily being explicit, this approach presumes that any system founded on supposedly universal values and impartial decision making (but which is now revealed to be particular and partial) serves in a systematic way the interests of men as a unitary category . . .

Any argument that starts with ceding priority to the binary division of male/female or masculine/feminine walks into the trap of demoting other forms of differentiation, particularly differences within these binary opposites. Thus the third problem with this sort of approach is that divisions such as class, age, race, religion tend to become mere additives or afterthoughts."[43]

Having identified these problems, Smart moves on to the third stage in her analysis which is to take "law as gendered":

"The shift between taking 'law as male' and taking 'law as gendered' is fairly subtle, and the transition does not entail a total rejection of all the insights of the former. But while the assertion that 'law is male' effects a closure in how we think about law, the idea of it as gendered allows us to think of it in terms of processes which will work in a variety of ways and in which there is no relentless assumption that whatever it does exploits women and serves men . . . But further, the idea of 'law as gendered' does not require us to have a fixed category or empirical referent of Man and Woman. We can now allow for the more fluid notion of a gendered subject position which is not fixed by either biological psychological or social determinants to sex. Within this analysis we can turn our focus to those strategies which attempt to do the 'fixing' of gender to rigid systems of meaning rather than falling into this practice ourselves.

This means we can begin to see the way in which law insists on a specific version of gender differentiation, without having to posit our own form of differentiation as some kind of starting or finishing point. We can therefore avoid the pitfall of asserting a pre-cultural Woman against which to measure

[42] C. Smart, *ibid.*, at 32.
[43] C. Smart, *ibid.*, at 32–33.

patriarchal distortions (*i.e.* a starting point), as well as avoiding a Utopianism which envisions what women will be once we overcome patriarchy (*i.e.* the finishing point) . . .

With this approach we can deconstruct law as gendered in its vision and practices, but we can also see how law operates as a technology of gender . . . That is to say we can begin to analyse law as a process of producing fixed gender identities rather than simply as the application of law to previously gendered subjects.

The revised understanding of 'law as gendered' rather than as sexist or male has led to a modified form of enquiry. Instead of asking 'How law can transcend gender?', the more fruitful question has become, 'How does gender work in law and how does law work to produce gender?' What is important about these enquiries is that they have abandoned the goal of gender neutrality. Moreover, law is now redefined away from being that system which can impose gender neutrality towards being one of the systems (discourses) that is productive not only of gender difference, but quite specific forms of polarized difference. Law is seen as bringing into being both gendered subject positions as well as (more controversially?) subjectivities or identities to which the individual becomes tied or associated."[44]

From this analysis of "law as gendered" flows Smart's key argument that law operates as a "gendering strategy". Smart explains what this concept entails:

"Woman is no longer self-evident . . . Such a statement is, of course, an affront to common sense which knows perfectly well what women are and reacts keenly should anyone try to blur the naturally given boundaries between the two (also naturally given) sexes. Yet first we must concede a distinction between Woman and women. This is familiar to feminists who have for some centuries argued that the *idea* of Woman (sometimes the *ideal* of Woman) is far removed from real women. Moreover, feminism has typically claimed an access to real women denied those who perceive the world through patriarchal visions. So the distinction between Woman and women is not new but it has become more complex. For example, we have begun to appreciate that Woman is not simply a patriarchal ideal and that the women that feminism(s) invoke(s) are perhaps the Woman of/constructed by feminist discourse(s) rather than an unmediated reality simply brought to light. In other words, the claim to an absolute reality located in the body of women against which the excesses of patriarchy can be measured has become less tenable. Feminism does not 'represent' women . . .

So if we accept that Woman and women are not reducible to biological categories or — at the very least — that biological signs are not essences which give rise to a homogeneous category of women, we can begin to acknowledge that there are strategies by which Woman/women are brought into being . . .

There is of course, a distinction to be made between the discursive production of a type of Woman and the discursive construction of Woman. I want

---

[44]   C. Smart, *ibid.*, at 33–34.

to invoke both of these meanings because it is my argument that they work symbiotically. Put briefly the (legal) discursive construction of a *type* of Woman might refer to the female criminal, the prostitute, the unmarried mother, the infanticidal mother and so on. The discursive construction of Woman, on the other hand, invokes the idea of Woman in contradistinction to Man. This move always collapses or ignores differences within categories of Woman and Man in order to give weight to a supposedly prior differentiation — that between the sexes. Thus this prior differentiation acts as a foundationalist move on which other differentiations can be grounded. Thus the female criminal is a type who can be differentiated from other women but, at the same time, what she is is abstracted from the prior category of Woman always already opposed to Man. Thus she may be an abnormal woman because of her distance from other women, yet simultaneously she celebrates the natural difference between Woman and Man . . .

Woman therefore represents a dualism, as well as being one side of a prior binary distinction. Thus in legal discourse the prostitute is constructed as the bad woman, but at the same time she epitomizes Woman in contradistinction to Man because she is what any woman could be and because she represents a deviousness and a licentiousness arising from her (supposedly naturally given) bodily form, while the man remains innocuous."[45]

The construction of Woman in contradistinction to Man, and the production of the prototype ideal Woman are themes which re-emerge throughout this book. The volume of material which has been generated proves that feminists have responded with affirmative action to Smart's concluding request, that:

"much work needs to be done in tracing how women have resisted and negotiated constructions of gender . . . Recognizing that law is a more complex problem than might once have been thought need not, however, lead to despair since we can quite clearly see that feminist scholarship and enquiry are also much more tenacious and insightful than might once have been imagined."[46]

One particular line of insightful enquiry which has been opened up is that by Sheila Duncan who has investigated the construction of the "female Other" in relation to that of the male legal subject in the law on sexuality.[47] These constructions, Duncan argues, are premised on binary opposites and work to construct "the power of the subject and to negate the subjectivity of the constructed Other."[48]

---

[45] C. Smart, *ibid.*, at 35–36.
[46] C. Smart, *ibid.*, at 40.
[47] S. Duncan, " 'Disrupting the Surface of Order and Innocence': Towards a Theory of Sexuality and the Law" (1994) 2 *Feminist Legal Studies* 3.
[48] S. Duncan, *ibid.*, at 6.

S. DUNCAN
" 'Disrupting the Surface of Order and Innocence': Towards a Theory of Sexuality and the Law"[49]

"First, it is important to examine the concept of the male subject. It is argued that at the level of law and philosophy the subject is male. Luce Irigaray states:

> 'even when aspiring to a universal, neutral state, this subject has always written in the masculine form, as man . . . It is man who has been the subject of discourse whether in the field of theory, morality or politics.'

Irigaray goes on to argue that 'any theory of the subject has always been appropriated by the 'masculine'. She then sets out the relationship between this male subject and the female Other, stressing that the lack of subjectivity of the latter is essential to buttress and construct the subjectivity of the former:

> 'Once imagine that the woman imagines and the subject looses its fixed obsessional character . . . If there is . . . no opaque matter which in theory does not know herself, then what pedestal remains for the ex-sistence of the 'subject'?'

Cixous underscores this concept arguing that:

> 'There has to be some "Other". No master without slave'. While Irigaray goes further in arguing that woman is not only Other but is quite specifically man's Other: "his negative or mirror-image situated outside representation." '

The male subject speaks through a discourse — a concept developed by Michel Foucault and indicating a particular way of seeing and expressing (aspects of) the world. For Foucault, there are many competing discourses. There is no fundamental or unmediated meaning, there is only relative meaning within the discourse.

The intention here is to explore one discourse — the discourse which will be called the dominant male discourse which is inhabited and defined by the male speaking subject. That discourse will be explored as it informs and expresses the law of sexuality and, specifically, as it constructs the male subject and the female Other within that law. The construction of the gendered Other within the discourse of the gendered subject extends beyond Foucauldian notions to look at structural issues suggested particularly by the work of Irigaray. In her complex analysis of the gendering of discourse, Irigaray argues that in imaginary and symbolic terms, language can be seen as a territory, a house or a home:

> 'men continually seek, construct, create for themselves houses everywhere.
> That house of language which for man even constitutes a substitute for his home in a body . . . woman is used to construct it but (as a result?) it is not available to her.'

---

[49] S. Duncan, *ibid.*, at 7–12.

For Irigaray,

> 'the "subject of philosophy" is narcissistic, closed to the encounter with the Other, while the Other (woman) has not yet acceded to subjectivity.'

This study is concerned to analyse how the dominant male discourse constructs the subject and the Other within one specific text — the law — a text which at the symbolic level is part of the 'home' of the male subject.

For Foucault, each discourse contains its own explanations and understandings which generate its power. The dominant discourse is a discourse in the sense that it is a particular way of seeing the world but, it is argued that the meaning and power of this discourse is pervasive and expressed in the law of sexuality to exclude competing meanings and interpretations. While Foucault's concept of power is fluid, momentary, 'in play' it is argued that power-knowledge leaves room for gender to be not merely a site of difference but also a site of power. In this sense, the dominant male discourse is also a site of power.

It is true that Foucault is concerned to emphasise the productive and creative aspects of power and it is argued here that the dominant male discourse as expressed in the law is productive and creative in its capacity to construct the power of the male subject.

Further, for Foucault, there are three levels of analysis of power:

> 'We must distinguish the relationships of power as strategic games between liberties — strategic games that result in the fact that some people try to determine the conduct of others — and the states of domination, which are what we ordinarily call power. And between the two, between the games of power and the states of domination, you have governmental technologies ... The analysis of these techniques is necessary, because it is often through this kind of technique that states of domination are established and maintain themselves. In my analysis of power, there are three levels: the strategic relationships, the techniques of government and levels of domination.'

This study is concerned to analyse power at all three levels: first, in the 'strategic relationships' between the male subject and the female Other in relation to the rape, incest and prostitution encounters, secondly, in relation to 'techniques of government' — the way in which the law is played out in respect of that construction in those aspects of the text and, thirdly, the way in which those techniques maintain 'levels of domination.'

Binary Opposites: the Role of Reason, Consent and the Logic of Desire
It is important to explore this discourse which is inhabited and defined by the male speaking subject. It is necessary to analyse how this discourse sustains and underwrites gender power in the text of the law.

Derrida's concept of *différence* allows notions of 'male' and 'female' as expressed in the law to be theorised in terms of his critique of binary oppositions. At the root of this binary opposition between for example, man/woman, culture/nature is the value given to the first term at the expense of the second.

For the purposes of an analysis of the law of sexuality, one of the most powerful of these 'opposites' is that of reason and emotion. Reason is attached to the male pole and emotion to the female. Reason is valued and emotion derided. The male is constructed as objective and logical and the female as emotional and subjective. This dichotomy is fundamental to a deconstruction of the law of sexuality.

As Lloyd argues, reason (like law) does not simply reflect but also consititutes the terms and context of sexual difference. An analysis of the law of sexuality will unearth a series of paradoxes around the notion of reason, particularly as it informs the concept of consent. That analysis will consider how and to what extent reason and consent underpin the power of the dominant male discourse by legitimating sexual violence.

It is possible to explore within the law, the ambivalent relationship between reason and sexuality. It is argued by Foucault that:

> 'The West has managed not only, or not so much, to annex sex to a field of rationality ... but to bring us almost entirely — our bodies our minds, our individuality, our history — under the sway of a logic of concupiscence and desire.'

It is important to see how that logic is played out in the law of sexuality.

It is necessary to go beyond a critique of reason which does not recognise the gendered nature of that concept and the implication for gender power of that which is repressed by the elevation of reason. It will be seen that the logic of desire as expressed in the law of sexuality can leave feminists seeking the application of 'reason' in opposition to the use of its shadow: the will to power — the determination to control, to manipulate through a facilitating notion of consent in the law of sexuality.

While the law of sexuality is focused at its surface on two purposes: first, dealing with a sub-group of men, namely sexual offenders and secondly, containing male sexuality, beneath that surface of innocence, it provides sustenance for a discourse predicated on a series of notions which do not proscribe sexual violence but, rather, sustain it.

In theorising what lies beneath that surface by analysing the construction of the male subject and the female Other through the text of the law, it is possible to see at one level of generality the male subject confronting the female Other but concretely, the individual male confronts the individual female and the power relations immanent in that relationship are inherent in the rape, incest or prostitution encounter. Such power relations are reflected in and constituted by the law which pertains to each.

It will be argued that the construction of the female as Other is achieved by the denial of subjectivity to the individual female victim of the rape and incest encounter. A denial which powerfully constructs consent against her and which develops a series of mythologies about her. Roland Barthes defines mythology saying that it is generated from history —

> 'It cannot possibly evolve from the nature of things.
>   It points out and it notifies; it makes us understand something and it imposes it on us.'

In shifting the subject from the static to the eternal plane, the myth constructs its own 'truth' and denies the truth of the individual woman as it facilitates her creation as Other. Her truth is silenced. She is excluded.

It is possible to read from the law the beginnings of an alternative discourse. The discourse of the female Other. A discourse of silence and exclusion."

As Duncan states, in the above extract, she applies her analysis to laws on sexuality, specifically those on rape, prostitution and incest. While the latter is not covered in this book, consideration is given in later chapters to the construction of the female Other in the laws on rape and prostitution.[50] Duncan concludes that the dominant male discourse is able to construct the male subject in the law of sexuality. In doing so it extends the power upon which male sexuality is predicated, facilitating non-consensual access to women's bodies.

> "The dominant male discourse ... creates and extends the power which underpins the sexuality of the male subject to facilitate the non-consensual taking of women in rape and incest and the buying of them on the subject's own terms in prostitution.
>
> Further, the law constructs the female as Other not as freely consenting subject but as Other for the male subject in the space of unreason, for the logic of desire.
>
> In these constructions, lie the paradox of the law of sexuality. It exists purportedly to defend and protect the 'victims' of rape, incest and prostitution but even in so far as it does so, it reasserts, through its constructions, the power of the speaking male subject through and the exclusion of the woman as Other from, the dominant male discourse as it is expressed in and enshrined by that law."[51]

It might be thought that the dominance of the male legal subject and the denial of the subjectivity of the female Other may lead feminists to be wary of employing law to seek redress for their grievances. Carol Smart has come close to this position, arguing that it is important to "discourage a resort to law as if it holds the key to unlock women's oppression."[52] In her conclusion to *Feminism and the Power of Law* she reiterates this perspective:

> "Law cannot be ignored precisely because of its power to define, but feminism's strategy should be focused on this power rather than on constructing legal policies which only legitimate the legal forum and the form of law. This strategy does not preclude other forms of direct action or policy formation. For example, it is important to sustain an emphasis on non-legal strategies and local struggles. However, it is important to resist the temptation that law offers, namely the promise of a solution."[53]

Ralph Sandland responds to Smart's reluctance to engage with law reform. He argues that Smart's position leads her to fall into "an unwarranted nihilism which fails to recognise the strategic potential of a feminism informed by poststructuralist thought to pursue a deconstructivist agenda *within* legal arenas and discourses."[54] Sandland explains why:

---

[50] See Chaps 7 and 12 below.
[51] S. Duncan, *supra*, n. 47 at 28.
[52] C. Smart, *supra*, n. 25 at p. 5.
[53] C. Smart, *ibid.*, p. 165.
[54] R. Sandland, "Between 'Truth' and 'Difference': Poststructuralism, Law and the Power of Feminism" (1995) 3 *Feminist Legal Studies* 4 at 14.

R. SANDLAND
"Between 'Truth' and 'Difference': Poststructuralism, Law and the Power of Feminism"[55]

"Smart is of course not alone in her ambivalence to law reform, but her allegiance to poststructuralism does distance her from the mainstream of feminism, just as she distances herself from it. Many feminists have been concerned that poststructuralism may undermine the polemic force of feminism. Smart's poststructuralism carries the potential to destabilize her feminism: the former 'fractures' the latter as much as it fractures modern thought more generally. In this section I attempt to explicate this tension between poststructuralism and feminism (as a modernist discourse). My argument is that Smart, in her critique of feminist jurisprudence, fails to engage with the exact nature of the relationship between *her* continued allegiance to feminism in the face of her poststructuralism. I want to show that, necessarily, 'poststructuralist feminism' contemplates a dialogue between the 'post' discourses and modernism, or, if you prefer, between the absence of self (or Other) and a situated, value-laden interest-driven self; and that appreciating this fact (that the modern/postmodern distinction is illusory) serves to liberate the 'post' discourses from their *self*-imposed silence.

As we have seen, Smart's methodology may be described as a wholesale commitment to the deconstructive impulse. Events, debates and claims must be bracketed off in order to discover their discursive referents. 'Reality' functions as a second-level discourse where one must constantly be aware that so much is always already given. Smart's position here has resonances of Baudrillard's 'ironic detachment' and politics of 'nonparticipation of nondesire, of nonknowledge, of silence of . . . total resistance to the ultimatum of historical and political reason.' Yet by placing herself alongside this sort of approach Smart removes herself to a point from where, for all her protestations that law must be seen as 'refracted' and contradictory rather than monolithic and internally consistent, the haphazard and uneven surface of law cannot be deciphered. Smart, in her insistence that law must be deconstructed and defetishized seems to be saying that the *substance of the law* is irrelevant, or not worth bothering with. When law is engaged with on its own terms so much is always already given that such engagement can only be counter-productive. From her point of view, for example, all cases are wrongly decided, and they would still be wrongly decided if the substantive outcome [had] been different, since all cases must fall to be decided within a given (legal) framework which fails to challenge the deployment of sex(uality)/gender-as-identity, on the one hand, and which legitimizes Law on the other. Smart seems to feel that it is not enough (indeed, it is self-defeating) merely to speak with the voice of Other. One must rather speak from the *vantage point* of Other. Attempt, that is, a discourse of the non-discursive.

The popularity of this strategy owes much to Lyotard's influential attempt to define the postmodern. For Lyotard 'The postmodern is that which, in the modern, puts forward the unpresentable in presentation itself; that which denies itself the solace of good form, the consensus of a taste which would make it possible to share collectively the nostalgia for the unattainable . . . our business is not to supply reality but to invent allusions to the conceivable which cannot be presented.' Whereas modernism is posited on the rock of its own History and (although this claim is becoming harder to sustain) its own Future, postmodernism by contrast rests on shifting sands. To bring the post-

---

[55] R. Sandland, *ibid.*, at 15–19.

modern into being, one must think the unthinkable and speak the unspeakable. Hence, the postmodern cannot exist since existence would be to modernise. Or rather, it can only exist as 'allusions', as an intuition but one that remains unarticulated. Postmodernism is something like the dream that modernism forgets, knowing it has forgotten it, in the process of awakening: 'not modernism at its end but in the nascent state, and that state is constant.' And this, for Lyotard, redefines the field of conflict. Politics is rejected as being always already constituted and irredeemable: 'The language game of legitimation is not state-political but philosophical.'

Lyotard erects this (suspiciously modernist-looking) dichotomy between politics and philosophy in order to distance himself from Marxism and emphasise that power resides not in the 'State' but in the 'System'. Since the State cannot be anything but the congealment of truth, one must bracket it and its problems in order to locate its various discursive and systemic antecedents. Yet having located the System one must then refuse to acknowledge it, deny its possibility, fail to recognise the possibility of its possibility. Having located philosophy as the locus of truth-production (language and concepts) philosophy is made a vortex, at the same time as the self — its subject — is fractured. The Other appears, and it is outwith the bounds of Truth. But my concern is that to speak from the *vantage point* of Other is not to speak at all, at least not coherently.

This, it seems to me, is to offer a strategy of 'no resistance', one posited on (implicitly looking forward to) the 'end of identity' but which is unable to deal with the Here and Now, which offers no mechanism to actualize its vision. To forsake politics for philosophy in this way is not merely methodologically suspect (because it constitutes these disciplines in the process) but it also renders the 'post' discourses politically suspect on their own terms because in making this distinction these discourses — as discourses — recognise their own modernity (hence Baudrillard's irony). Faced with this choice between having to accede to modernity in giving voice to the Other, or resisting modernity through silence, both Baudrillard and Lyotard opt for the latter. My point here is that Smart's work too is an example of this tendency. For example, in her discussion of rape she refuses to react politically but *only* philosophically. She rejects the relevance of her 'visceral reaction and anger' to the legal construction of rape because reacting in terms of one's identity 'does not allow for the desexuating of women's bodies.' Women, she argues, must reject their construction as 'victims' of rape because 'victim' is an always already loaded term. Deployed in an analysis of rape the idea of woman-as-victim intersects the familiar range of cultural meanings which speaks of women's inferiority. Woman-as-victim merely 'confirms women in their discursive place' as woman-as-victim.

Yet is it the case that *all* discourse must be rejected if we are to escape the confines of Truth? Can we in fact situate ourselves outside of the power/truth/discourse nexus? As I have already argued above, Smart's claim rests on the view that through dichotomising politics and philosophy, etc, and then jettisoning the former and collapsing the latter, we can indeed do this. However, as she confesses, 'This may mean . . . moving out into unchartered territory.' And this vagueness and uncertainty, I would argue, speaks of the unresolved tension inherent in 'presenting the unpresentable' This conceptual blockage, it seems to me, is only required because of Smart's rigid allegiance to her dichotomous model of analysis — the philosophy/politics, etc, distinctions that she makes. But if we collapse the distinction(s) then does not the tension re-emerge as a space for dialogue? That is, instead of accepting this modernist dichotomy uncritically, we appreciate both the constraint that it places on us *and* its contingency. Pat Carlen has recently argued that the challenge posed by the 'post' discourses is how we are to learn to work within 'the contradiction of having to recognise (in the process of politics) but needing to deny (in the process of knowledge-production)'. So, for example, rather than refusing to enter into (the) discourse (of the victim of rape) is it not more fruitful (at least sometimes) to attempt to supplant the notion of victim with an empowering discourse, based on the concept of Survivor? — even if this does not challenge the discursive category 'Woman'?"

Sandland concludes that Smart is caught in her own trap because:

> "she fails to see that one cannot 'be' a poststructuralist. Such a claim is too 'determinate'. Smart eloquently warns of the dangers in couching claims in terms of identity, but her case is not so strong that it precludes *all* such claims. She does not tackle the central problematic in her position, which is that appeals couched in terms of (something which looks like) truth are all that are available to us in the present position."[56]

Sandland, however, is able to offer an alternative course of action based upon a strategic assessment of when it is appropriate to engage with law and to present arguments couched in language which modernity understands. Here is how:

> "We must — empirically, politically, by reference to some normative meas-ure – weigh the tactical and strategic advisability of both silence *and* the positive articulation of opposition in the specific context which has arisen. We must decide when to trade only in 'allusions' and the unsaid and when (and then how) to represent the unpresentable in a discourse which is compre-hensible to modernity. We must work within this tension of being sceptical of truth and sceptical of our scepticism; within this space opened up between 'truth' and 'difference' . . ."[57]

> "Such a jurisprudence must necessarily advocate a somewhat eclectic attitude to law reform. It must prioritize the abolition of legal restraints on sex(uality)/ gender (*i.e.* the deconstruction of the legally-sexed subject) and yet immedi-ately temper the 'purity' of this aim with an awareness of its risk factor. My point here is that Smart's concerns with the construction of identity, and the manufactured and totalizing quality of truth actually free up the possibility of thinking in this way. The heuristic power of her model excavates the cultural, geographical and temporal specificity of sex, and reveals the 'erotic popula-tions' who benefit from these particular configurations. Her work, in that it simultaneously accepts the reality of oppression on the grounds of gender, sexual orientation, race, etc., and yet dismisses these categories as contingent and fragile, is itself produced in this dialogical tension between recognition and denial. I want to suggest that this leads, not to deconstruction over reform, as Smart argues, but towards a case by case evaluation of the merits of one goal over the other. The aim should be to identify those situations in which deconstruction and reform *merge*. In the legal arena it is no longer a

---

[56] R. Sandland, *ibid.*, at 20–21.
[57] R. Sandland, *ibid.*, at 21.

case of sex-as-truth, but rather the question of how, and when, phallocentric truth can best be subverted."[58]

In this way Sandland advocates that deconstruction is possible through reform:

"[M]ost often the agenda has been to unpack or deconstruct law's claims in order to reveal law's oppressive and essentialist underpinnings. I want to start from a slightly different position, by asking: 'Why *does* law always attempt to change the subject?' Maybe part of the answer is that entering into a debate on sexuality is a dangerous strategy for law. Perhaps we would do well to appreciate that law appreciates the danger to its own legitimacy in entering into such a discourse. In other words, I want to suggest that a 'de-fetishized' understanding of law should be sensitive both to law's claim to Truth *and* to the contingency of such claims. I want further to suggest that this point is particularly pertinent when gender or sexuality is 'the' issue precisely because gender and sexuality are constructed by law as being 'beyond construction' and in this sense 'beyond law': these things are seen as 'given' and hence not 'constructed' at all. When law is called upon to adjudicate on gender or sexuality, the fallacy of this claim is implicitly acknowledged. And it seems to me that only an essentialist, monolithic reading of law could suggest that, in every instance, it is law's legitimacy (or, at least, *only* law's legitimacy) which stands to benefit from this entering into discourse."[59]

Sandland gives three examples of legal cases which substantiate his argument, one of which is particularly pertinent to the subject matter of this book and is considered in more detail in the chapter on rape. The decision in question is *R. v. R..*[60] This case put an end to the marital rape exemption which dictated that it was not unlawful for a husband to rape his wife. There was little legal justification for the decision reached by the House of Lords, it being simply acknowledged by Lord Keith that the exemption was in this day and age anachronistic. Feminists, however, have been cautious in their response to the decision because of its partiality and its failure to tackle the more deep-seated problematic construction of the law on rape and the act of rape from a male perspective. Sandland responds to this feminist pessimism in the following terms:

R. SANDLAND
"Between 'Truth' and 'Difference': Poststructuralism, Law and the Power of Feminism"[61]

"Putting the point bluntly, I feel that there is a danger in this sort of approach of understating its own political and jurisprudential purchase as a subversive force inter-

---

58 R. Sandland, *ibid.*, at 27–28.
59 R. Sandland, *ibid.*, at 28–29.
60 [1991] 4 All E.R. 481. The other two examples given by Sandland are *Cossey v. U.K.* (1990) 13 E.H.R.R. 622; and *R. v. Brown* [1993] 2 All E.R. 75.
61 R. Sandland, *supra*, n. 54 at 33–36.

rupting the 'unmodified' liberal paradigm. A more 'post' analysis would require a more contextual, less meta-theoretically informed approach that would locate *R. v. R.* as a symbolically significant juncture in one particular struggle around the meaning of sex and the invisibility of gender (woman) in legal discourse. This is not to deny that the arguments for the non-possibility of rape within marriage are amongst the weakest in the range of patriarchal justifications, and so amongst the easiest to knock down. But it is to insist that, first, the symbolic is as significant as the material when considering the construction of reality — so that it is incorrect to see a 'symbolic' victory as being '*merely* phyrric', and undermined by the material reality of (marital) rape. O'Donovan has argued that the continued existence and attraction of marriage is explicable in terms of its symbolic aspects, its 'mythic tradition', which have been relatively untouched by the materialist critique. The same is true in the present context. It is as important to deconstruct the symbolic aspects of male sexuality-as-dominance, alongside changing the practices and relations of gender. Second, the affiliation to grand theory which requires that specific events — such as *R. v. R.* — are ascriptively located within a methodology which moves from the general to the particular, and so detects no *particularities*, but merely examples of a general proposition, must likewise be rejected. 'Decentring' the law does not render this approach useless, but if we are to look for a range of meanings within the text of *R. v. R.* then we can place alongside it recognition of a significant event in the genealogy of and opposition to patriarchal power. My point here is that although Lord Keith purported to apply legal method and reasoning techniques, his decision was the product of another, different mode of reasoning, informed by a different 'truth'. In Smart's terminology, Lord Keith was, at this moment of his 'fractured' existence, a feminist. Whatever the link between the abolition of the marital rape exemption and the rules of evidence in rape trials, Lord Keith posits an autonomy residing in the body of the married woman that abruptly interrupts the discourse of the female body-as-property that was propounded by Hale and has operated normatively and covertly for much of the ensuing time-period.

This, I would argue, is a positive reconstruction of Woman by law which in the process demonstrates the open-endedness of legal discourse. It suggests a strategy which would seek to identify those points in the discourse where an appeal to 'justice' might be sufficiently compelling to persuade law to bring itself into 'disrepute'. Moreover, there is of course little cause to resist the abolition of marital rape as a legal impossibility. What this case does show us, therefore, is that poststructuralist feminism, in isolating the particular relations of power that are manifest in the exemption, must be ready to *extend* the legal control of sexuality when to do so has the effect of displacing male oppression of women with legal censure of a construction of a masculinity which has hitherto been exalted. This tactic, which would be anathema to Smart, is suggested by poststructuralism. Mary Joe Frug has argued that law constructs Woman through the juxtaposition of images which provide for the *terrorization*, the *maternalization*, and the *sexualization* of the female body. She argues that 'By deploying these images, legal discourse rationalizes, explains and renders authoritative the female body rule network.' The marital rape exemption can be seen to sit at the intersection of these three images. As such, its abolition interrupts this configuration in that it desexualizes the Wife, at the same time that it sexualizes the rapist-husband through regulating (albeit at the symbolic level) his behaviour.

The relevance of this to the present discussion is that *R. v. R.* reminds us that desexualization as a general strategy is of problematic and uncertain application because sex is not a 'thing' but a relation and so the implementation of a particular approach will impact differently upon the various actors involved. This is why, as I suggested earlier, it is impossible to be 'against' reform as an on-going strategy: because on occasion a given reform will equate with desexualization from one point of view, but not from another. The wisdom of engaging in reform then becomes a strategic and political question, resting on an analysis of power relations. So for example, decon-struction-through-reform might be feasible here, but not with regard to the category of 'rape' itself. It can (and has) been argued forcibly that the desexualization of rape as a strategy 'fails to consider the very real power differences between men and women, and that rape is in many ways a mere extension of what are culturally defined as 'normal' heterosexual relations' and that it would be improvident, having the effect of bolstering the legal non-discourse on gender, to deny 'rape' conceptually. Instead, as I suggested earlier, the better strategy might be to produce 'survivor discourse'. That is, to change the dynamics of the situation rather than attempt to deconstruct the cat-egory. It seem[s] to me that implicit in the *R. v. R.* judgment is the recognition of the socially constructed and asymmetrical notion of (male) desire, so that the sexuality of the married man can properly be brought within the ambit of legal regulation; his sexuality is not outside power/the social after all. Such ambivalence as is caused by *R. v. R.* stems from the recognition that the decision of itself does nothing to address the shameful state of the law of rape and the extra-legal impediments to combating rape in or out of marriage effectively. But the judgement in this case, if phyrric in this sense, does emphasise the possibility for infiltrating and destabilizing legal method."

Finally, it would be a missed opportunity to end this chapter without picking up on the passing reference made by Sandland to the writings of the American feminist Mary Joe Frug.[62] Frug offers a rather different perspective upon post-modern feminist thinking, but one which is also helpful for our analyses of the female body.[63] Her "postmodern feminist legal manifesto" was unfortu-nately never completed, it being partially drafted when Frug was murdered whilst out walking in 1991. It is nonetheless extremely insightful for both its definition of the relationship between postmodernism, feminism and law and for the applications and examples given of this. Frug first sets out her terms of reference:

M. J. FRUG
"A Postmodern Feminist Legal Manifesto (An Unfinished Draft)"[64]

"I am worried about the title of this article.

Postmodernism may already be passe, for some readers. Like a shooting star or last night's popovers, its genius was the surprise of its appearance. Once that initial moment has passed, there's not much value in what's left over.

For other readers, postmodernism may refer to such an elaborate and demanding genre — within linguistics, psychoanalysis, literary theory, and philosophy — that claiming an affinity to 'it' will quite properly invoke a flood of criticism regarding the omissions, misrepresentations, and mistakes that one paper will inevitably make.

---

[62] See M. J. Frug, *Postmodern Legal Feminism* (London: Routledge, 1992).
[63] M. J. Frug, "A Postmodern Feminist Legal Manifesto (An Unfinished Draft)" (1992) 105 *Harvard Law Review* 1045.
[64] M. J. Frug, *ibid.*, at 1045–1048.

The manifesto part may also be troublesome. The dictionary describes a manifesto as a statement of principles or intentions, while I have in mind a rather informal presentation; more of a discussion, say, in which the 'principles' are somewhat contradictory and the 'intentions' are loosely formulated goals that are qualified by an admission that they might not work. MacKinnon, of course, launched feminism into social theory orbit by drawing on Marxism to present her biting analysis. Referring to one word in a Karl Marx title may represent an acknowledgement of her work, an unconscious, copyKat posture; but I don't want to get carried away. I am in favor of localized disruption. I am against totalizing theory.

Sometimes the 'PM's that label my notes remind me of female troubles — of premenstrual and postmenopausal blues. Maybe I am destined to do exactly what my title prescribes; just note the discomfort and keep going.

One "Principle"

... The postmodern position locating human experience as inescapably within language suggests that feminists should not overlook the constructive function of legal language as a critical frontier for feminist reforms. To put this 'principle' more bluntly, legal discourse should be recognized as a site of political struggle over sex differences.

This is not a proposal that we try to promote a benevolent and fixed meaning for sex differences [. . .] Rather, the argument is that continuous interpretive struggles over the meaning of sex differences can have an impact on patriarchal legal power.

Another "Principle"

In their most vulgar, bootlegged versions, both radical and cultural legal feminisms depict male and female sexual identities as anatomically determined and psychologically predictable. This is inconsistent with the semiotic character of sex differences and the impact that historical specificity has on any individual identity. In postmodern jargon, this treatment of sexual identity is inconsistent with a decentered, polymorphous, contingent understanding of the subject.

Because sex differences are semiotic — that is, constituted by a system of signs that we produce and interpret — each of us inescapably produces herself within the gender meaning system, although the meaning of gender is indeterminate or undecidable. The dilemma of difference, which the liberal equality guarantee seeks to avoid through neutrality, is unavoidable.

On Style

Style is important in postmodern work. The medium *is* the message, in some cases — although by no means all. When style is salient, it is characterized by irony and by wordplay that is often dazzlingly funny, smart, and irreverent. Things aren't just what they seem.

By arguing that legal rhetoric should not be dominated by masculine pronouns or by stereotypically masculine imagery, legal feminists have conceded the significance of style. But the postmodern tone sharply contrasts with the earnestness that almost universally characterizes feminist scholarship ...

Although the flip, condenscending, and mocking tones that often characterize postmodernism may not capture the intensity and urgency that frequently motivate feminist legal scholarship, the postmodern style does not strike me as 'politically incorrect.' Indeed, the oppositional character of the style arguably coincides with the oppositional spirit of feminism. Irony, for example, is a stylistic method of acknowledging and challenging a dominant meaning, of saying something and simultaneously denying it. Figures of speech invite ideas to break out of the linear argument of a text; they challenge singular, dominant interpretations.

I confess to having considerable performance anxiety about the postmodern style myself. It may require more art, more creativity and inspiration, than I can manage. But I don't think feminist legal activists need to adopt the postmodern medium in order to exploit the postmodern message; my point about the style is simply that it doesn't require us, strategically, to dismiss postmodernism as an influence on our work."

Frug then proceeds to apply her manifesto to her specific area of interest which is the female body. Frug argues convincingly that law participates in the terrorisation, the maternalisation and the sexualisation of women's bodies.

M. J. Frug
"A Postmodern Feminist Legal Manifesto (An Unfinished Draft)"[65]

"I have chosen the relationship of law to the female body as my principal focus. I am convinced that law is more cunningly disguised but just as implicated in the production of apparently intractable sex-related traits as in those that seem more legally malleable. Since the anatomical distinctions between the sexes seem not only 'natural' but fundamental to identity, proposing and describing the role of law in the production of the meaning of the female body seems like the most convincing subject with which to defend my case. In the following sections, I will argue that legal rules — like other cultural mechanisms — encode the female body with meanings. Legal discourse then explains and rationalizes these meanings by an appeal to the 'natural' differences between the sexes, differences that the rules themselves help to produce. The formal norm of legal neutrality conceals the way in which legal rules participate in the construction of those meanings.

The proliferation of women's legal rights during the past two decades has liberated women from some of the restraining meanings of femininity. This liberation has been enhanced by the emergence of different feminisms over the past decade. These feminisms have made possible a stance of opposition toward a singular feminine identity; they have demonstrated that women stand in a multitude of places, depending on time and geographical location, on race, age, sexual preference, health, class status, religion, and other factors. Despite these significant changes, there remains a common residue of meaning that seems affixed, as if by nature, to the female body. Law participates in creating that meaning.

I will argue that there are at least three general claims that can be made about the relationship between legal rules and legal discourse and the meaning of the female body:

(1) Legal rules permit and sometimes mandate the *terrorization* of the female body.

---

[65]   M. J. Frug, *ibid.*, at 1049–1052.

This occurs by a combination of provisions that inadequately protect women against physical abuse and that encourage women to seek refuge against insecurity. One meaning of 'female body,' then, is a body that is 'in terror,' a body that has learned to scurry, to cringe, and to submit. Legal discourse supports that meaning.

(2) Legal rules permit and sometimes mandate the *maternalization* of the female body. This occurs with the use of provisions that reward women for singularly assuming responsibilities after childbirth and with those that penalize conduct — such as sexuality or labor market work — that conflicts with mothering. Maternalization also occurs through rules such as abortion restrictions that compel women to become mothers and by domestic relations rules that favor mothers over fathers as parents. Another meaning of 'female body', then, is a body that is 'for' maternity. Legal discourse supports that meaning.

(3) Legal rules permit and sometimes mandate the *sexualization* of the female body. This occurs through provisions that criminalize individual sexual conduct, such as rules against commercial sex (prostitution) or same sex practices (homosexuality) and also through rules that legitimate and support institutions such as the pornography, advertising, and entertainment industries that eroticize the female body. Sexualization also occurs, paradoxically, in the application of rules such as rape and sexual harassment laws that are designed to protect women against sex-related injuries. These rules grant or deny women protection by interrogating their sexual promiscuity. The more sexually available or desiring a woman looks, the less protection these rules are likely to give her. Another meaning of 'female body,' then, is a body that is 'for' sex with men, a body that is 'desirable' and also rapable, that wants sex and wants raping. Legal discourse supports that meaning.

These groups of legal rules and discourse constitute a system that 'constructs' or engenders the female body. The feminine figures the rules pose are naturalized within legal discourse by declaration — 'women *are* (choose one) weak, nurturing, sexy' — and by a host of linguistic strategies that link women to particular images of the female body. By deploying these images, legal discourse rationalizes, explains, and renders authoritative the female body rule network. The impact of the rule network on women's reality in turn reacts back on the discourse, reinforcing the 'truth' of these images.

Contractions of confidence in the thesis that sex differences are socially constructed have had a significant impact on women in law. Liberal jurists, for example, have been unwilling to extend the protection of the gender equality guarantee to anatomical distinctions between female and male bodies; these differences seem so basic to individual identity that law need not — or should not — be responsible for them. Feminist legal scholars have been unable to overcome this intransigence, partly because we ourselves sometimes find particular sex-related traits quite intransigent. Indeed, one way to understand the fracturing of law-related feminism into separate schools of thought over the past decade is by the sexual traits that are considered unsusceptible to legal transformation and by the criticisms these analyses have provoked within our own ranks.

The fracturing of feminist criticism has occurred partly because particular sex differences seem so powerfully fixed that feminists are as unable to resist their 'naturalization' as liberal jurists. But feminists also cling to particular sex-related differences because of a strategic desire to protect the feminist legal agenda from sabotage. Many feminist critics have argued that the condition of 'real' women makes it too early to be post-feminist. The social construction thesis is useful to feminists insofar as it informs and supports our efforts to improve the condition of women in law. If, or when, the social construction thesis seems about to deconstruct the basic category of woman, its usefulness to feminism is problematized. How can we build a political coalition to advance the position of women in law if the subject that drives our efforts is 'indeterminate,' 'incoherent,' or 'contingent?'

I think this concern is based upon a misperception of where we are in the legal struggle against sexism. I think we are in danger of being politically immobilized by a system for the production of what sex means that makes particular sex differences seem 'natural.' If my assessment is right, then describing the mechanics of this system is potentially enabling rather than disempowering; it may reveal opportunities for resisting the legal role in producing the radical asymmetry between the sexes.

I also think this concern is based on a misperception about the impact of deconstruction. Skeptics tend to think, I believe, that the legal deconstruction of 'woman' — in one paper or in many papers, say, written over the next decade — will entail the immediate destruction of 'women' as identifiable subjects who are affected by law reform projects. Despite the healthy, self-serving respect I have for the influence of legal scholarship and for the role of law as a significant cultural factor (among many) that contributes to the production of femininity, I think 'women' cannot be eliminated from our lexicon very quickly. The question this paper addresses is not whether sex differences exist — they do — or how to transcend them — we can't — but the character of their treatment in law."

By way of example, Frug investigates the treatment of sex difference in the law on prostitution, and we too will return to her perspective at this juncture.[66] But it is from this thematic point that we launch into our own consideration of the relationship between law and the female body and the treatment meted out to women as a result of their differences (both physical and socially constructed). The themes which have been discussed in the first three chapters are drawn through the sections which follow, revealing that feminist dialogue and feminist discourse are beginning to permeate law's (male) defences and to resonate in its (male) ears. Hence, law is not completely impervious to feminist legal thought (although, of course, it may appear relatively so at times). The fact that this book has been possible, in the sense of being viewed as a viable project, is testament both to the significant impact of law upon the female body and also to feminists' desire to resist, to engage with and to strategise over the legal and political meanings which are attributed to that body.

---

[66] See below, Chap. 12.

SECTION TWO

REPRODUCTIVE BODIES

INTRODUCTION

THE CONSTRUCTION OF MOTHERHOOD

This section considers the legal regulation of motherhood. Under scrutiny is the extent to which, and the ways in which, the law facilitates or prohibits the attainment of motherhood and regulates medical intervention upon the bodies of women as it seeks to assist or prevent conception. Within the last forty years, medical science has developed the oral contraceptive pill, seen the birth of the first "test-tube baby" and the development of techniques of facilitating conception such as *in vitro fertilisation* (IVF) and gamete intra-fallopian transfer (GIFT) and extended available methods of monitoring the foetus during pregnancy and birth. Medical advances in the sphere of human reproduction have both been welcomed as extending women's reproductive choice and denounced as facilitating the extension of control by others, principally the male-dominated medical profession, over the bodies of women:

> "[M]edical and scientific advances in the sphere of reproduction — so often hailed as the liberators of twentieth-century women — have, in fact, been a double-edged sword. On the one hand, they have offered women a greater technical possibility to decide if, when and under what conditions to have children; on the other, the domination of so much reproductive technology by the medical profession and by the state has enabled others to have an even greater capacity to exert control over women's lives."[1]

The limitation of women to the domestic sphere as a consequence of the industrialisation of labour has been accompanied by the delineation of motherhood as the primary female role, to the extent that women have been reduced to this one function and their suitability for alternative roles within the public realm has been denied. As Michelle Stanworth suggests, "the technical possibility of fertility control coexists with a powerful ideology of motherhood —

---

[1] M. Stanworth, "Reproductive Technologies and the Deconstruction of Motherhood" in M. Stanworth (ed.), *Reproductive Technologies: Gender, Motherhood and Medicine* (Cambridge: Polity Press, 1987), pp. 15–16.

the belief that motherhood is the natural, desired and ultimate goal of all 'normal' women, and that women who deny their 'maternal instincts' are selfish, peculiar or disturbed."[2]

Women's role in mothering has at different times been perceived to be either biologically determined (*i.e.* because women bear children they are the appropriate persons to rear them) or socially constructed (the discourses of *inter alia* science, medicine and law participating in the construction of women as mothers). The result has been the perpetuation of the confinement of women to the "private" domestic sphere of the home and of restrictions (or obstacles, such as inadequate child-care) placed upon their access to the "public" economic sphere. This extends beyond the examples considered in this section to include, for example, foetal protection policies in the context of paid employment. Michael Thomson argues:

> "... (t)he indiscriminate nature of the [foetal protection] policies constructs all women as potentially pregnant, as primarily bearers and rearers of children, first and foremost 'biological actors' ... In defining women by their generative organs as primarily breeders, women become homogenized. Foetal protection policies ignore individuality and the existence of autonomous interests beyond the traditional family group. The possibility that women may choose not to have children, or may plan when to have them is not recognized. Women may only participate in the public/economic sphere within the terms of heterosexuality and traditional views of womanhood."[3]

Liberal feminism's pursuit of the extension of choices available to women sought to free women from the constraints of domesticity. This demanded reproductive choice for women in the form of freedom from repeated unwanted pregnancies, achievable via access to contraception and abortion services. At the same time, maximisation of choice meant that developments in fertility treatments were to be welcomed as extending reproductive options.

Central to all aspects of reproductive choice is the idea of reproductive control. Women have sought to assert the liberal values of autonomy and self-determination against interventions in their bodily processes by the medical profession,[4] not only by seeking control over their bodies in the prevention and facilitation of pregnancy, but also during periods of pregnancy and childbirth. Formerly a private matter, reproduction was brought into the public domain as an issue fundamental to the liberation of women.

---

[2] M. Stanworth, *ibid.*, p. 15.
[3] M. Thomson, "Employing the Body: The Reproductive Body and Employment Exclusion" (1996) 5 *Social & Legal Studies* 243 at 259.
[4] J. Outshoorn, "Abortion Law Reform: A Woman's Right to Choose?" in M. Buckley & M. Anderson (eds), *Women, Equality and Europe* (Basingstoke: Macmillan Press, 1988), p. 206.

M. Thomson
"After *Re S*"[5]

"... The debate [surrounding reproductive freedom] had expressed the conflict between the demand for women's reproductive autonomy, and increasingly anachronistic ideas of the *natural* role of women ... Historically the control of women's participation in society has been legitimated by reference to her *natural role*. The natural role of women was seen as confined within the sphere of home and family. Female involvement outside of this sphere was construed as detrimental to the health of the woman and society ... [T]he medical profession constructed women who sought abortions as either ignorant, or evil 'rebellious women who had abandoned their maternal duties for selfish and personal ends' ... This formulation reflects the historical perception of women as existing solely within the private sphere. Freedom to make educational or reproductive choices was seen as incompatible with the ideology of 'true womanhood', and the maternal ethic of care and responsibility."

It was through reform of the law, securing for women legal rights in relation to reproduction, that reproductive choice and control were to be realised. Bearing this in mind, one of the aims of the chapters in this section is to consider the extent to which laws regulating human reproduction provide women with control mechanisms over their reproductive bodies.

Whilst also situating women's role in reproduction as fundamental to their position in society, radical feminism, rather than focusing upon taking control of reproduction and expanding reproductive choice, instead located reproduction as central to the domination of women by men. This is the position adopted by Shulamith Firestone in *The Dialectic of Sex*[6], as neatly summarised by Rosemary Tong:

R. Tong
Feminist Thought: A Comprehensive Introduction[7]

"In *The Dialectic of Sex*, Shulamith Firestone claimed that patriarchy — the systematic subordination of women — is rooted in the biological inequality of the sexes. Firestone's reflections on women's reproductive role led her to a feminist revision of the materialist theory of history offered by Marx and Engels. Although Marx and Engels correctly focused upon class struggle as the driving forces of history, said Firestone, they paid scant attention to what she termed *sex class*. Firestone proposed to make up for this oversight by developing a feminist version of historical materialism in which sex class, rather than economic class, is the central concept.

To appreciate Firestone's co-optation of Marxist method, we have only to contrast her definition of historical materialism with that of Engels. We will remember that Engels defined historical materialism as

[5] (1994) 2 Med. L. Rev. 127 at 141–142.
[6] S. Firestone, *The Dialectic of Sex* (New York: Bantam Books, 1970).
[7] (London: Unwin Hyam, 1989), pp. 72–76.

that view of the course of history which seeks the ultimate cause and great moving power of all historical events in the economic development of society, in the changes of the modes of production and exchange, in the consequent division of society into distinct classes, and in the struggles of these classes against one another.

Firestone took Engel's definition and reformulated it as follows:

Historical materialism is that view of the course of history which seeks the ultimate cause and the great moving power of all historical events in the dialectic of sex: the division of society into two distinct biological classes for procreative reproduction, and the struggles of these classes with one another; in the changes in the modes of marriage, reproduction and child care created by these struggles; in the connected development of other physically-differentiated classes [castes]; and in the first division of labor based on sex which developed into the [economic-cultural] class system.

In other words, for Firestone, the original class distinction is between men and women, and it is a *class* distinction to which orthodox Marxists have paid scant attention.

Firestone's argument is bound to trouble the orthodox Marxist, for she considered relations of reproduction rather than of production to be the driving force in history. If we want to understand why women are subordinate to men, we require a biological, not an economic, explanation. Firestone reminded us, however, that we should attribute the inequality between the sexes not to the observable, biological differences between them, but to the fact that men's and women's differing reproductive roles led 'to the first division of labor at the origins of class, as well as furnishing the paradigm of caste discrimination based on biological characteristics.'

Because Firestone believed that the roots of women's oppression are biological, she concluded that women's liberation requires a biological revolution, in much the same way that Marx concluded that the essentially economic oppression of workers required an economic revolution. Whereas the proletariat must seize the means of *production* in order to eliminate the economic class system, women must seize control of the means of *reproduction* in order to eliminate the sexual class system; and just as the ultimate goal of the communist revolution is, in a classless society, to obliterate class distinctions, the ultimate goal of the feminist revolution is, in an androgynous society, to obliterate sexual ones. As soon as the biological realities of reproduction are overcome, said Firestone, the fact that some persons have wombs and others have penises will 'no longer matter culturally.' The only valid distinction between men and women will have been vanquished.

What makes this biological revolution a real possibility is technology. When Firestone wrote *The Dialectic of Sex*, only the reproduction-controlling technologies of contraception, sterilization, and abortion were widely used. Today, eighteen years later, the reproduction-aiding techniques of artificial insemination by donor, in vitro fertilization, and embryo transfer are also quite widely used. Due to these technologies and to legal arrangements such as contracted motherhood, a woman who begets a child need not bear it, and a woman who bears a child need not rear it. Furthermore, as soon as it is possible to beget a child in vitro and bring it to term ex utero, women's role in the reproductive process will be no larger than men's. Women will donate ova to egg banks, and men will donate sperm to sperm banks. After the in vitro union of ovum and sperm, the resulting embryo will be gestated outside of the womb in an artificial placenta; and when the fetus finally reaches full term, any number of caring human beings, male or female, will be able to attend to its needs.

Firestone believed that when women and men stop playing substantially different roles in the reproductive drama, it will be possible to eliminate all sexual roles. She was convinced that these roles have been imposed upon people in order to shore up' the biological family. When technology is able to perfect 'artificial' ways for people to reproduce, the need for the biological family will disappear and, with it, the need to impose genital heterosexuality as a means of ensuring human reproduction. Lesbianism and male homosexuality will no longer be viewed as freely chosen alternatives to the norm of heterosexuality or as perversions resulting from the degrading influence of capitalist society. Instead, the categories of homosexuality and heterosexuality will be abandoned; and institutionalized sexual intercourse, in which male and female each play a well-defined role, will disappear.

The biological family's demise as a reproductive unit will also spell its demise as an economic unit. Firestone was enough of a Marxist to believe that biology's sexual division of labor has served capitalism well. The fact that women reproduce makes it easy for capitalism to confine women to the private, or domestic, realm and to send men out to labor in the public realm. Over time, the biological family has evolved into an economic unit in which women engage in unpaid productive work and in which women and children engage in the kind of consumption that bolsters the capitalist economy. However, once women no longer have to reproduce, the primary rationale for keeping them at home disappears; and with the entrance of women into the workplace, the family will no longer exist as an economic unit.

Because Firestone was unconvinced, however, that the workplace, as we know it, is a life-enhancing spot for women or for men, she saw women's entrance into it as a stopgap measure. If men and women have been at odds with each other largely because of their confining and distorting reproductive and productive roles, one way to end the war between the sexes is to eliminate both roles by developing technology that can replace them. If technology can eliminate the role of woman-the-reproducer, it can eliminate the role of man-the-producer. In godlike fashion, technology can ensure that no person need 'bear children in pain and travail' and that no person need 'toil by the sweat of the brow in order to live.'

When there are no longer distinct reproductive and productive roles for women and men, Firestone believed it will be possible to overcome all of the relations, structures, and ideas that have always divided the human community: oppressing male/oppressed female, exploiting capitalist/exploited worker, white master/black slave. Firestone envisioned an androgynous culture that will surpass not only the peak experiences of male technological culture and female aesthetic culture, but also combine them into an integrated whole. She saw this development as 'more than a marriage, rather an abolition of the cultural categories themselves, a mutual cancellation — a matter-antimatter explosion, ending with a poof! culture itself.' What Firestone called for was nothing short of a new creation. Indeed, she commented that 'if there were another word more all-embracing than *revolution* we would use it.'

Firestone wished to explode masculinity and femininity, but she was convinced that this explosion will not occur unless humans abandon patriarchal *reproduction* as well as capitalist *production*. No matter how much educational, legal, and political equality women achieve, and no matter how many women enter public industry, nothing fundamental will change for women so long as biological reproduction remains the rule rather than the exception. As Firestone saw it, biological reproduction is neither in women's best interests nor in those of the children so reproduced. The joy of giving birth — invoked so frequently in this society — is a patriarchal myth. In fact, pregnancy is 'barbaric,' and natural childbirth is 'at best necessary and tolerable,' at worst, 'like shitting a pumpkin.' Moreover, biological motherhood is the root of further evils, especially the vice of possessiveness that generates feelings of hostility and jealousy among human beings. Engels's *Origin* was incomplete not so much because he failed to account adequately for the production of surplus value, as because he failed to explain why men wish so intensely to pass *their* property on to *their* children. As Firestone saw it, the vice of possessiveness — the favoring of one child over another on account of its being the product of one's own ovum or sperm — is precisely what must be overcome if we are to put an end to divisive hierarchies.

Shulamith Firestone may welcome medical advances in methods of contraception, abortion techniques and fertility treatments as means to enable women to cast aside their traditional role in reproduction. However, criticism of Shulamith Firestone's work has focused upon the argument that it is not the female role in reproduction in itself which is the cause of female subordination, but rather it is *male* control over female reproduction which is the problem. A further purpose of the chapters in this section is to consider the extent to which Firestone's critics are right to argue that these advances in human reproductive techniques merely extend male control over the female body.

The liberal and radical perspectives on female reproduction can be criticised as treating women as a homogenous group, with advances in medicine and laws on human reproduction being perceived as having the same impact upon all women. By way of contrast, Carol Smart argues that what is understood by "Woman" is not reducible to biology or sex difference but is constructed through discourses, and as such is a constantly changing phenomenon.[8] Legal, medical, social and scientific discourses construct different types of women to which individuals become linked. As explained above in Chapter 3, Smart argues that disciplines, including law, construct an ideal of Woman as Mother, who is positioned in opposition to Man. They also construct specific *types* of women, such as the "bad" mother, who may be positioned against the ideal. Real women become tied to the constructions of these typologies and measured for their (lack of) compliance with the ideal. From this perspective, laws do not have the same impact upon all women. They have different effects depending upon the ways in which, and the extent to which, the circumstances of a particular woman depart from, or match up to, the ideal. Smart takes as her example the unmarried mother, who is popularly blamed for many of society's ills in the 1990s, tracing the development of the legal construction of this type of woman, characterised as bad and unstable, from laws on infanticide adopted in the seventeenth century.

---

[8]   C. Smart, "The Woman of Legal Discourse" (1992) 1 *Social & Legal Studies* 29.

C. Smart
"The Woman of Legal Discourse"[9]

"The unmarried mother obviously served (and still serves) to reinforce our cultural understanding of what 'proper' motherhood means. In this sense she is a *type* of woman rather than Woman. Yet she simultaneously operates in the discourse as Woman because she always invokes the proper place of Man. She is the problem (supposedly) because she does not have a man. Therefore Man is the solution, he signifies the stability, legitimacy and mastery which is not only absent in her but inverted. The unmarried mother is therefore also quintessential Woman because she represents all those values which invert the desirable characteristics of Man.

At this point it may appear that my concerns are with the symbolic. However, my interests extend beyond this because my purpose in mapping the development of the legal subject 'unmarried mother' is to throw light on the dominant regime of meaning which always already treats this woman as problematic and destabilizing. Just as Foucault has shown that categories such as the criminal or the homosexual are not pre-existing entities to be investigated and understood by science, so we can also see that the unmarried mother comes into being as a consequence of specific strategies and knowledges. While she is not a fixed or unchanging category she enters into an established web of meanings which make instability and dangerousness virtually self-evident and matters of common sense.

The significance of this for the contemporary situation is that more and more women can be fitted into this category. The Act of 1623 [making it a capital offence for an unmarried mother to kill her child] that I started with affected relatively few women. Now the category includes the never married and the divorced lone mother. (The widow is rarely included because she is thought to keep the symbolic father alive, and so is hardly a lone mother.) More recently this category has extended further to include the 'surrogate' mother and the woman seeking infertility treatment."

In this section on "reproductive bodies", the way in which the discipline of law contributes to the construction of Woman as (ideal) Mother is explored. The idealised figure is compared with the "types" of women who, because they do not fulfil the ideal, have limitations imposed upon their reproductive freedom. For example, the woman seeking to terminate her pregnancy and the woman offering to carry a child for another as a surrogate (only to give it away after birth) both challenge the basic assumption that motherhood is woman's ultimate goal and fulfilment. In turn, the law, in imposing limits upon the availability of abortion,[10] and in establishing who is the mother of the child born following a surrogacy arrangement,[11] operates to uphold and reinforce the social construction of Woman as Mother. Further, the law reinforces the ideal of Woman as Mother in contradistinction to *types* of mothers through limitations placed upon the reproductive freedom of women who fail to meet this ideal. For example, single motherhood is still seen as a subversive act and a direct challenge to the ideal of the nuclear family. So whilst the State,

---

[9] C. Smart, *ibid.*, at 38–39.
[10] See discussion of the Abortion Act 1967 in Chap. 5.3.
[11] See discussion of the Human Fertilisation and Embryology Act 1990, ss. 27 and 30, in Chap. 4.2.

through legal regulation, cannot prevent the creation of one parent families by divorce or conception outside of marriage (although it can, of course, pro-foundly affect those families) it can prevent the creation of one parent families through legal requirements relating to limitations upon access to fertility treatments.[12] Also, whilst some young women who, having decided that they do not wish to have any children, seek sterilisation as a contraceptive method may be denied the operation on the grounds that they may change their minds, the potential for motherhood of women with learning difficulties is removed by the practice of sterilisations lawfully performed without their consent.[13]

What emerges consistently is the role of the law in reinforcing the location of motherhood within the nuclear family. The Warnock Committee, which was established to consider the "social, ethical and legal implications" of medical and scientific developments in human fertilisation and embryology and to recommend appropriate safeguards, noted that the evidence submitted for the consideration of the Committee demonstrated a diversity of viewpoints about fertility treatments. However, the Committee identified a common belief in the need for "*some principles or other* to govern the development and use of the new techniques. There must be *some* barriers that are not to be crossed, *some* limits fixed, beyond which people must not be allowed to go."[14] The Report makes recommendations for legislation to provide a "broad framework" setting out "the minimum requirement for a tolerable society".[15] The proposals in the Warnock Report, to a large extent enacted by the Human Fertilisation and Embryology Act 1990, are consistent with much of the law regulating motherhood in that they entrench childbearing and rearing within the nuclear family. This ideal is however one which is less frequently experienced in families formed following "unassisted conception" with increasing numbers of births outside marriage, marriages ending in divorce and women choosing to raise children on their own.[16]

Jane Lewis and Fenella Cannell compare the underlying motivations behind the campaigns of Mrs Gillick (who sought to prevent her daughters being given contraceptive or abortion advice or treatment without her consent whilst they were under the age of sixteen)[17] and the conclusions of the War-nock Committee.[18] They identify two principal motivations, which are equally applicable to abortion as an issue. First, the construction of motherhood and the location of motherhood within the confines of the nuclear family; and secondly, the battle for control over reproduction between women themselves and the medical profession. Mrs Gillick, they argue, considered that sex should only occur within the boundaries of marriage and that it was the role

---

[12] See discussion of the Human Fertilisation and Embryology Act 1990, s. 13(5) in Chap. 4.1.
[13] Discussed in Chap. 5.4.
[14] *Report of the Committee of Inquiry into Human Fertilisation and Embryology*, DHSS, Cmnd. 9314 (1984), Foreword, para. 5.
[15] *Ibid.*, para. 6.
[16] See M. Stanworth, *supra*, n. 1 at pp. 23–24.
[17] Discussed in Chap. 5.1.
[18] J. Lewis & F. Cannell, "The Politics of Motherhood in the 1980s: Warnock, Gillick and Feminists" (1986) 13 *Journal of Law and Society* 321.

of the mothers of young girls (not that of the medical profession) to control their daughters' sexuality. The Warnock Committee saw the place of reproduction as located within the nuclear family so that a child should be born to two heterosexual parents who, if not married, should at least be in a stable family. Surrogacy was objectionable because it introduces another party into the creation of a child. Both the non-procreative sex of teenagers and surrogacy presented a threat to the valued position of the woman who allowed her husband sex only after marriage and provided him with the children he would support. The law was called upon by both Mrs Gillick and the Warnock Committee to entrench the nuclear family as the network surrounding the ideal Woman/Mother figure.

Alison Diduck explains that ideologies of motherhood result from the competing discourses of, amongst other things, science and feminism, so the ideologies which emerge are distinct in different cultures and at different periods in time.[19] The ideology of motherhood is further infused with factors such as race, religion and gender relations so that the "ultimate tapestry which emerges is law infused with constructs of motherhood interwoven with many different strands. The ideological significance of these dominant constructs and the law which supports them is that they then appear to be natural, normal and legitimate."[20]

One particular ideology which Alison Diduck considers is that of female self-sacrifice. The depiction of women as self-sacrificing is apparent in the legal approaches to the issues discussed in this section, particularly abortion and the medical treatment of pregnant women. In her analysis of child welfare cases in Canada, Diduck examines how the cases reveal "resistance to particular ideologies which have predominated in the application of child welfare legislation: ideologies of motherhood which construct mother in a particular way, ideologies of individualism which construct pregnancy and law in certain ways and ideologies of the modern 'rational man' which construct medicine and science in certain ways."[21]

What is important in engaging with these constructs is the way in which women resist. Michelle Stanworth emphasises that despite the strength of the ideology of motherhood, women do exercise decisions and resist pressures placed upon them. Women choose to bear and rear children and women choose not to:

> "[T]he ideology of motherhood attempts to press women in the direction of child-bearing, and . . . in this sense women's motivations are socially shaped. But 'shaped' is not the same as 'determined'; . . . The very existence of a range of sanctions and rewards designed to entice women into marriage and motherhood indicates, not that conformity is guaranteed, but that avoidance of motherhood (and autonomous motherhood) are genuine options, which efforts are made to contain."[22]

---

[19] A. Diduck, "Legislating Ideologies of Motherhood" (1993) 2 *Social & Legal Studies* 461.
[20] A. Diduck, *ibid.*, at 462.
[21] A. Diduck, *ibid.*, at 464.
[22] M. Stanworth, *supra*, n. 1 at p. 17.

As Alison Diduck's analysis reveals, where women fail to sacrifice themselves in accordance with current ideologies of motherhood, legal discourse is invoked in protection of the foetus in the language of rights. That is, steps are taken to identify the foetus as a juridical person and vest it with legal rights which can be presented against the conflicting rights of the mother. There remains a tendency for the mother to be perceived as a danger to the foetus so that legal rights are necessary to enable it to stand against her as an equal. Katherine De Gama cites Keyserlingk who "seeks to persuade us that 'unless armed with juridicial personality as the basis of *his* right to care and protection', the foetus would be 'unable to compete on a more or less equal basis with other parties with whom *his* needs and rights may be in conflict' because they would be legal persons, and '*he* [the foetus] would remain more or less at the mercy of their ethics, whims or compassion'."[23] Rather than seeing the foetus and the woman as separate right-bearing individuals, it may be that a perception of the foetus as dependent upon, and connected to, the woman's body, results in a different approach to the rights of pregnant women.[24]

Katherine De Gama compares the approaches in Britain and the U.S. to legal issues arising from reproduction, notably abortion, compulsory blood transfusions, enforced caesarians, the detention of pregnant women who threaten harm to the foetus through drug use, and the punishment of women for "harm" sustained by the foetus *in utero*.[25] She explains the focus upon the right to privacy in the U.S. and the lack of rights discourse in the U.K. Whilst acknowledging the powerful rhetoric of claims to rights which further provides "a forum for resistance" she notes how "feminism, . . . insists upon the need to redefine conceptual frameworks and agendas."[26] Feminist jurisprudence, of which she argues issues of reproductive control raising wider questions about sexuality, parenting and the family will be central, must "give . . . voice not to abstract, ungendered rights but to women's experience".[27]

Susan Bordo argues that it is necessary to reconceptualise the debate, moving away from the opposition of the right of the foetus to life and the right of the woman to choose, towards a consideration of the (varied) experiences of women which are nonetheless common in that they are all women's experiences of motherhood.[28] Bordo argues that feminists should not fear "the idea of emphasizing the experiential significance of pregnancy and birth, out of a fear of the conceptual proximity of such notions to constructions of mothering as the one true destiny for women."[29] She suggests that the domina-

---

[23] K. De Gama, "A Brave New World? Rights Discourse and the Politics of Reproductive Autonomy" in A. Bottomley & J. Conaghan (eds), *Feminist Theory and Legal Strategy* (1993) 20 *Journal of Law and Society* 114 at 116, citing E. Keyserlingk, "The Unborn Child's Right to Prenatal Care — A Comparative Perspective" [1984] *McGill Legal Studies* 79 (De Gama's italics).
[24] A. Diduck, *supra*, n. 19 at 470–472.
[25] K. De Gama, *supra*, n. 23.
[26] K. De Gama, *ibid*., at 128.
[27] K. De Gama, *ibid*.
[28] S. Bordo, *Unbearable Weight: Feminism, Western Culture and the Body* (California: University of California Press, 1993), p. 95.
[29] S. Bordo, *ibid*.

tion of the debate in terms of foetal right to life against a woman's right to choose has enabled pro-lifers to portray women as presenting a threat to the foetus which they value as nothing:

> "This image — so cruelly unrepresentative of most women's experiences — must be challenged, must be shown to be a projection of 'evil mother' archetypes, reflective of deep cultural *anxieties* about women's autonomy rather than the *realities* of its exercise."[30]

It is to the legal resolution of this aspect of body politics that we now turn. The roles and legal rights of the protagonists in the debate — women, foetuses, putative fathers and doctors — are addressed through discussion of mechanisms which facilitate motherhood (fertility treatment services and surrogacy), which prevent motherhood (contraception, abortion and sterilisation) and which accompany the propulsion towards motherhood (during pregnancy and the process of giving birth).

[30] S. Bordo, *ibid.*

CHAPTER 4

FACILITATING MOTHERHOOD

In this chapter we look at ways in which the law regulates the bodies of women who are seeking to have children and have problems with (or reject) conception via heterosexual intercourse. We consider two alternative routes to motherhood, via new reproductive technologies and surrogacy.

In following the first path we will explore the extent to which medical discretion is a factor in granting access to treatments, the legal construction of women seeking treatments and the feminist arguments supporting and opposing new reproductive technologies. We also consider several case studies which have recently arisen and which show the complexities of current regulation.[1] In the second half of this chapter we discuss legal responses to surrogacy arrangements. This discussion is conducted within the context of the ethical and social issues raised by surrogacy and feminist perspectives upon surrogacy arrangements with a view to analysing the implications for the regulation of women's bodies in this controversial area of body politics.

4.1 New reproductive technologies

4.1.i *The reproductive revolution*
Since the birth of the first "test-tube" baby, Louise Brown, in 1978, developments in what have come to be termed the "new reproductive technologies" have led to a veritable explosion of possibilities for achieving and bringing to term a pregnancy.

> "The term *new reproductive technologies* (NRTs) is recent. The NRTs include IVF[2] embryo transfer,[3] sex preselection, genetic engineering of embryos, cloning (making genetically identical individuals) and more. They

---

[1] For more in depth discussion of the legal issues raised by new reproductive technologies see I. Kennedy & A. Grubb, *Medical Law: Text with Materials* (London: Butterworths, 1994), pp. 758-819.

[2] "A 'treatment service' . . . in which a woman's egg is fertilised by mixing with sperm outside the body in a petri dish (the 'test-tube')", D. Morgan & R. Lee, *Blackstone's Guide to the Human Fertilisation and Embryology Act 1990* (London: Blackstone Press, 1991) p. xii.

[3] "[T]he process of transferring a fertilised egg in the course of IVF or gift procedures, where following development *in vitro* for two or three days, or after flushing from a woman's uterus by lavage (at five days), an early embryo is placed in the uterus of an infertile woman in order to try and achieve implantation and pregnancy", D. Morgan & R. Lee, *ibid.*, p. xi.

are new because they are relatively recent developments, based on new capabilities."[4]

The new technologies have, however, not been received uncritically by feminists. While some feminists see the technologies as extending the possibility for women in relation to reproduction and as, therefore, empowering for those who choose to use them,[5] other feminists are more sceptical about the possibilities of the new technologies seeing them as disempowering women and reducing their role in reproduction.[6]

One of the key features of the new technologies is that they permit a deconstruction of the role of reproducer and mother. The birth mother is not, where reproductive technologies are employed, necessarily the biological mother of the child nor following surrogacy does she intend to be its social mother.

G. COREA
The Mother Machine: Reproductive Technologies from Artificial Insemination to Artificial Wombs[7]

"[Reproductive technologies] are transforming the experience of motherhood and placing it under the control of men. Woman's claim to maternity is being loosened; man's claim to paternity strengthened. Moreover, these techniques are creating for women the same kind of discontinuous reproductive experience men now have . . . How will woman's claim to maternity be.loosened? . . . [I]n future there will be three kinds of mothers:

- The genetic mother who 'donates' or sells her eggs
- The surrogate or natal mother who carries the baby
- The social mother who raises the child

Under this system of dismembered motherhood, none of these three women will have a compelling claim to her child."

Whilst making women's role in reproduction "discontinuous", reproductive technologies have the potential to confound existing assumptions about parenting. By challenging expectations about continuity between genetic, gestational and social parenting, new reproductive technologies offer the potential for alternative orderings of family relationships beyond the "traditional" heterosexual marital union.

New reproductive technologies may have the potential to extend reproduct-

---

[4] P. Spallone, *Beyond Conception: The New Politics of Reproduction* (Hampshire: MacMillan Education Ltd, 1989) p. 14.
[5] Lesbians and single women, for example, may view the new technologies as enabling them to achieve a conception without the necessity of engaging in heterosexual intercourse.
[6] G. Corea *et al.* (eds), *Man-Made Women: What Future for Motherhood?* (London: Pandora Press, 1985); G. Corea, *The Mother Machine: Reproductive Technologies from Artificial Insemination to Artifical Wombs* (London: The Women's Press, 1985).
[7] G. Corea *et al.*, *ibid.*, pp. 289-290.

ive choices available to women, yet even the usage of the term "new" reproductive technologies is challenged by some feminists who see the technologies
as facilitating male/medical control over the reproductive process in a similar
way as permitted by the older technologies of abortion, contraception and
sterilisation.

R. D. Klein
"What's 'new' about the 'new' reproductive technologies?"[8]

" 'In one way — not much; in another — everything.' This might be an answer to the
question 'What's "new" about the "new" reproductive technologies?' ...

Whether 'old' or 'new', these procedures have in common that they represent an
artificial invasion of the human body — predominantly the female body. Increasingly,
more and more control is taken away from an individual's body and concentrated in
the hands of 'experts' — the rapidly — and internationally — growing brigade of
'technodocs': doctors, scientists and pharmaceutical representatives (most of them
male, white, and of Euro-American origin) who fiercely compete with one another on
this 'new frontier' of scientific discovery and monetary profits.

Such developments, however, do not take place in a vacuum. They reflect the interests, needs and wishes of the powers that be. Consequently, assessment of the 'old' as
well as the 'new' reproductive technologies must recognize them as powerful socio-
economic and political instruments of control ...

An analysis of reproductive technologies must expose the role they play in the multi-
faceted exploitation and domination of women. This holds true for the 'old' as well
as the 'new' ones but the 'new' technologies, in my view, reinforce the degradation and
oppression of women to an unprecedentedly horrifying degree. They reduce women to
living laboratories: to 'test-tube women'."

It is not only the women upon whom reproductive treatments are conferred
who are perceived as victims of the new technologies. Gena Corea examines
the eugenic considerations which, she argues, lie behind the use of reproductive technologies and their ultimate role in "gynicide", that is, the deliberate
extermination of women:

G. Corea
"Sex Determination: A Question of Gynicide"[9]

"[T]hree of the other new reproductive technologies could also be used to predetermine
the child's sex.

1. Embryo transfer. Before being implanted in a woman's womb, cells from the

---

[8] In G. Corea *et al.* (eds), *Man-Made Women: What Future for Motherhood?*, *supra*, n.6 at
pp. 64–65.
[9] In G. Corea, *The Mother Machine: Reproductive Technologies from Artificial Insemination
to Artificial Wombs*, *supra*, n.6 at pp. 200–201, 202 and 203.

embryo might be snipped off and examined under a microscope to detect its sex. If the embryo were the wrong sex, it could be discarded.

2. *In vitro fertilization* ... Steptoe and Edwards have proposed freezing human embryos for later implantation and Wood's IVF team in Australia is already doing this. This procedure would provide enough time before implantation to determine the embryo's sex.

3. *Cloning*. Cloning, or asexual reproduction, has not yet been achieved in humans. It involves taking a single cell from a person and inducing it to begin dividing so that it produces an organism genetically identical to the parent. The sex of the child would be the sex of the person who donated the body cell. Rockefeller University president Dr Joshua Lederberg, who received a Nobel Prize in 1958 for his research in the genetics of microbes, has written: 'Nuclear transplantation [cloning] is one method now verified to assure sex control, and this might be sufficient motive to assure its trial.'

Proponents of sex predetermination have offered several rationales for its use, including population control. In 1973, John Postgate proposed, as the solution to the world's alleged population problem, the distribution of a pill assuring the birth of boys. This 'manchild' pill, made freely available to all, could be used mostly in Third World countries where the desire to breed male children 'amounts to an obsession,' according to Postgate. The resulting deficiency of females (breeders) would limit the number of babies who could be born in the following generation, thereby reducing population growth. Further, couples would stop producing child after child in an attempt to get the desired number of sons.

Postgate describes how women would live in a world in which many of their kind had been eliminated. 'All sorts of taboos would be expected and it is probable that a form of purdah would become necessary. Women's right to work, even to travel alone freely, would probably be forgotten transiently. Polyandry might well become accepted in some societies; some might treat their women as queen ants, others as rewards for the most outstanding (or most determined) males.' ...

Another rationale for sex control is therapeutic. The practice will help eliminate sex-linked genetic diseases, proponents argue. In 1980, Steptoe and Edwards announced that they would pioneer experiments to help couples determine the sex of the child with a method involving timing of intercourse. Edwards explained that the aim was to combat the genetic disorders that produce hemophilia and some forms of muscular dystrophy. This therapeutic rationale is intrinsic to many of the new reproductive technologies, ethicist Dr Raymond noted, adding: 'For it focuses the discussion off the social and feminist dimensions of the issue onto the more personal, curative and supposedly benevolent aspects of the technology.'

Sex control will be a boon to mental, as well as physical, health some argue. 'The direct psychological effects of being able to control the sex of child in line with preferences would seem to be considerable, and almost wholly positive,' researcher Edward Pohlman concluded. 'The conception of children of an undesired sex is often undesirable from a mental health standpoint.' Many psychotherapists, he explained, believe that the birth of a 'wrong sex' child may lead to sex role confusion, which may lead to homosexuality or to psychological problems ...

Sex predetermination, besides contributing to mental health, is also alleged to provide an expansion of options and increased freedom. Researchers Saul Rosenzweig and Stuart Adelman, noting that 'fetal sex determination in the first trimester in pregnancy with selective abortion may soon be widely practiced,' refer to sex predetermination as 'this new step in human sexual autonomy.' They further observe: 'Parents may soon be able to engage in total family planning, *i.e.*, control of family size, spacing between children, sex of offspring, and male-female sequence.'

Social scientists do not stand alone in defending sex predetermination. Dr Clifford Grobstein, embryologist, justifies it in terms of increased individual freedom and con-' trol over reproduction. 'In general terms, the rationale is to utilize expanding options and capability to make beneficial choices in terms of purpose rather than of accident or chance,' he writes.

Dr Ronald Ericsson, who has developed one method for obtaining male offspring, also has benevolent reasons for his work. He 'says his intention is not to promote boy babies but to prevent the tragedy of unwanted children' . . .

We have masses of people in the studies saying that they do not care for one type of human being (female), that they 'prefer' another type (male), and this is being treated as perfectly acceptable. We must question the use of the word 'preference' in this context. We are not talking about preferences for vacation sites — the seashore rather than the mountains. We are talking about human beings and whether ones with certain biological features will be allowed to come into existence."

Beyond the eugenics issue, some feminists have also highlighted further dangers to women of the introduction of new reproductive technologies. Not only do the technologies, some of which involve invasive and painful intrusions upon the body of the woman, offer very low success rates (in terms of a successful pregnancy and birth of a live child), but research into new reproductive technologies may occur at the expense of research into other areas of women's health, particularly because it may lead to a lack of investigation into infertility (one of the main reasons for resorting to the new technologies) and its causes:

P. Spallone
Beyond Conception: The New Politics of Reproduction[10]

"IVF does not cure infertility. IVF does not heal women's blocked tubes or the subfertility in men. It does nothing to answer the question of infertility from 'unknown causes'. In fact, IVF carries a risk of causing fertility problems in women, many of whom have no fertility problem in the first place. IVF is highly invasive biochemically and surgically; the powerful drugs and manipulation of internal organs are known causes of reproductive system damage.

IVF is a 'technical fix' in that it bypasses the *causes* of fertility problems. IVF is not going to change the fertility problems of women, if anything it is going to make them worse. Most importantly, this is not the way it has to be. Many of the causes of infertility are known *and preventable*. Some of the most obvious preventable causes come from cervical cancer, from reproductive tract infections which have not been diagnosed and treated properly, from doctor-prescribed contraceptives and sloppy abdominal surgery, and from lack of information given to women on known and probable causes."

---

[10] P. Spallone, *supra*, n. 4 at pp. 70–71.

G. Douglas
"Assisted Reproduction and the Welfare of the Child"[11]

"[I]t is highly likely that assisted reproduction treatment to relieve *infertility* will be *low* on that list [of priorities]. Infertility is problematical as a health issue. It is not life-threatening, although it may be deeply distressing and demoralising. It may never even be diagnosed unless a person reaches a point in life when he or she wishes to have a child. It may be hard to justify expending large amounts of money on treating it, which might otherwise be used to alleviate severely debilitating illnesses, . . . Furthermore, the success rates for assisted reproduction treatment have been disappointing, and yet treatments such as IVF are very expensive. (There was a range, for large centres, of live birth rates from 2.1 to 22.9 per cent per IVF treatment cycle in 1990, with the average being 14.2 per cent. A treatment cycle of IVF can easily cost over £2,000 in the private sector). It is therefore not surprising that assisted reproduction (and infertility treatment as a whole) does not receive a high priority in the NHS. Where treatment *is* offered, it can be rationed, by GPs who may decline to refer a patient to a specialist, or by waiting list at the clinic. Treatments may not be offered at all. For example, the Lancet reported in 1991 that North East Thames Region had decided to delete five conditions from the NHS treatment list. These were varicose veins, lumps and bumps, wisdom teeth, tatoos — and infertility. Other London Health Authorities have followed suit. For those who experience severe psychological pain because of their inability to conceive, it is no doubt distressing to have one's condition associated with 'lumps and bumps' and tatoos. It is accordingly also unsurprising that the private sector of medicine has developed a large number of clinics to fill the gap for those with the money to afford it."

Gillian Douglas considers the alternatives available to infertile couples and suggests that, in the light of the limitations of these alternatives, the new reproductive technologies do have something to offer women.

G. Douglas
Law, Fertility and Reproduction[12]

"It would be wrong to assume that treatment for infertility always involves the use of the new reproductive technologies. Rather, they are a last resort, and there are other procedures which are much more commonly attempted, such as drug treatment, or surgery. It is also sometimes argued that the new techniques are not 'cures' for infertility, but merely circumvent it. This view seems to invite the response, 'so what?' The fact that a condition is not cured does not inevitably mean that a treatment to avoid its consequences should not be given. A much weightier argument is that a better use of resources would be to seek to prevent infertility in the first place, for example through the development of safer contraceptives, better screening and diagnosis of pelvic inflammatory disease or the better control of environmental pollution. There is a relative dearth of research into the causes of infertility, yet no shortage of funds for the development of the high tech new treatments.

[11] [1993] *Current Legal Problems* 53 at 59–60.
[12] (London: Sweet & Maxwell, 1991), pp. 106–107.

It may also be argued that childless couples should seek to adopt the many children waiting·in care, or the millions who suffer deprivation in the third world, rather than resort to expensive infertility treatment, and that they are selfish in only wanting to adopt healthy, white babies, rather than handicapped, black or older children. But there is no reason why infertile couples should be expected to fulfil the needs of such children, rather than anyone else. These children may have special needs which not all infertile (or fertile) people could adequately meet. To expect them to be taken on, for lack of anything else, by infertile couples, is to devalue both the children and the childless. The question of entitlement to infertility treatment is a separate matter.

Finally, it may be suggested that instead of helping couples to have children, we should promote attitudes which accept childlessness and enable women (especially) to fulfil themselves in other ways than parenthood. But while we may accept that there should be a genuine choice for women as to whether they become mothers, it is patronising to assume that women are presently incapable of deliberately choosing whether to have children — except when they deliberately choose *not* to do so."

Douglas' up-beat perspective on the potential of the new technologies is echoed by other critiques of the sceptical views of writers such as Corea and Klein. Gena Corea's abhorrence of "dismembered motherhood" (in the extract cited above) is described somewhat differently in a thought-provoking essay by Michelle Stanworth in which Stanworth challenges the feminist critique of new reproductive technologies.

M. STANWORTH
"Reproductive Technologies and the Deconstruction of Motherhood[13]

"[I]t is suggested that men's alienation from reproduction — men's sense of disconnection from their seed during the process of conception, pregnancy and birth — has underpinned through the ages a relentless male desire to master nature, and to construct social institutions and cultural patterns that will not only subdue the waywardness of women but also give men an illusion of procreative continuity and power. New reproductive technologies are the vehicle that will turn men's illusions of reproductive power into a reality. By manipulating eggs and embryos, scientists will determine the sort of children who are born — will make themselves the fathers of humankind. By removing eggs and embryos from women and implanting them in others medical practitioners will gain unprecendented control over motherhood itself. Motherhood as a unified biological process will be effectively deconstructed: in place of 'mother', there will be ovarian mothers who supply eggs, uterine mothers who give birth to children and, presumably, social mothers who raise them. Through the eventual development of artificial wombs, the capacity will arise to make biological motherhood redundant. Whether or not women are eliminated, or merely reduced to the level of 'reproductive prostitutes', the object and the effect of the emergent technologies is to deconstruct motherhood and to destroy the claim to reproduction that is the foundation of women's identity.

The problem with this analysis is not that it is too radical, as some have claimed;

---

[13] In M. Stanworth (ed.), *Reproductive Technologies: Gender, Motherhood and Medicine* (Cambridge: Polity Press, 1987), pp. 16–18.

rather, in seeking to protect women from the dangers of new technologies, it gives too much away. There is a tendency to echo the very views of scientific and medical practice, of women and of motherhood, which feminists have been seeking to transform. This analysis entails, in the first instance, an inflated view of science and medicine, the mirror image of that which scientists and medical practitioners often try themselves to promote ... Any understanding of the constraints within which science and medicine operate, and of the way these can be shaped for the greater protection of women and men, is effectively erased.

Also integral to this approach is a view of women that comes uncomfortably close to that espoused by some members of the medical professions. Infertile women are too easily 'blinded by science' ...; they are manipulated into 'full and total support of any technique which will produce those desired children' ...; the choices they make and even their motivations to choose are controlled by men ...

Finally this approach tends to suggest that anything 'less' than a natural process, from conception through to birth, represents the degradation of motherhood itself. The motherhood that men are attempting to usurp becomes a motherhood that is biologically defined, and to which all women are assumed to have the same relationship. While it is the case that the lives of all women are shaped by their biological selves, and by their assumed or actual capacity to bear children, our bodies do not impose upon us a common experience of reproduction; on the contrary, our bodies stand as powerful reminders of the differentiating effects of age, health, disability, strength and fertility history."

To reject the use of new reproductive technologies as some feminists would advocate is to remove one possible means for women who wish (a real wish whether or not that wish is socially constructed) to bear a child. Rather than turning our backs on the new reproductive technologies for fear of becoming "test-tube" women, a more appropriate question must be to ask how the regulation of these technologies extends reproductive options for those women who need to, or choose to, resort to them.

4.1.ii *Legal regulation of new reproductive technologies*

The Human Fertilisation and Embryology Act 1990 was introduced to deal with aspects of research upon embryos and with new reproductive technologies.[14] The Act was passed following the Warnock Report on Human Fertilisation and Embryology published in 1984 which had investigated the implications of developments in the field of human assisted reproduction.[15] The Act was a necessity given the enormity of scientific progress in these areas and the consequent lack of legal regulation dealing with the situations raised by new technological developments.

4.1.ii.a Determining mothers and fathers.

One of the questions raised by the use of new reproductive technologies is that of who are legally the mother

---

[14] The 1990 Act also amended the law on abortion (see Chap. 5.3 below).

[15] *Report of the Committee of Inquiry into Human Fertilisation and Embryology*, Cmnd. 9314 (1984).

and father of any resulting child. The 1990 Act has answered these questions in a way which shores up the traditional nuclear family, seeking to ensure that, for the most part, children born via reproductive technologies are not fatherless, but also aims to ensure a ready supply of sperm donors who are not deterred by the prospect of facing, at some point in the future, legal responsibility for any resulting child.

The Human Fertilisation and Embryology Act 1990 provides:

Meaning of "mother"

27.—(1) The woman who is carrying or has carried a child as a result of the placing in her of an embryo or of sperm and eggs, and no other woman, is to be treated as the mother of the child. . .

Meaning of "father"

28.—(1) This section applies in the case of a child who is being or has been carried by a woman as the result of the placing in her of an embryo or of sperm and eggs or her artificial insemination.

(2) If —

    (a)   at the time of the placing in her of the embryo or the sperm and eggs or of her insemination, the woman was a party to a marriage, and

    (b)   the creation of the embryo carried by her was not brought about with the sperm of the other party to the marriage, then, subject to subsection (5) below,[16] the other party to the marriage shall be treated as the father of the child unless it is shown that he did not consent to the placing in her of the embryo or the sperm and eggs or to her insemination (as the case may be).

(3) If no man is treated, by virtue of subsection (2) above, as the father of the child but —

    (a)   the embryo or the sperm and eggs were placed in the woman, or she was artificially inseminated, in the course of treatment services, provided for her and a man together by a person to whom a licence applies, and

    (b)   the creation of the embryo carried by her was not brought about with the sperm of that man, then, subject to subsection (5) below, that man shall be treated as the father of the child.

Giving effect to the common law presumption that the mother of the child is the woman who gives birth to it and to the intention of the woman seeking

---

[16] Subs. 5 reads: "Subsections (2) and (3) above do not apply —

    (a)   in relation to England and Wales and Northern Ireland, to any child who, by virtue of the rules of common law, is treated as the legitimate child of the parties to a marriage,

    (b)   in relation to Scotland, to any child who, by virtue of any enactment or other rule of law, is treated as the child of the parties to a marriage, or

    (c)   to any child to the extent that the child is treated by virtue of adoption as not being the child of any person other than the adopter or adopters."

access to fertility treatment services (with the exception of the surrogate mother discussed below) to bear a child to care for as social parent, the birth mother is deemed the legal mother of the child. The question of who is the legal father is more complicated:

D. MORGAN & R. LEE
Blackstone's Guide to the Human Fertilisation and Embryology Act 1990[17]

"Section 28 defines 'father' for the purposes of the Act. It is a complex and difficult provision, but one of great significance creating, as it does, a new class of child, the (legally) 'fatherless child' . . .

It proceeds by providing a saving in certain circumstances for any child treated as the legitimate child of the parties to a marriage or of any person, whether by virtue of statute or common law. So, where a woman is married, section 28(2) provides that if she becomes pregnant following embryo transfer, or GIFT or ZIFT, or following artificial insemination, her husband is to be treated as the father of any resulting child. However, if he can show that he did not consent to the treatment service, he is not to be treated as father under section 28(2), although he will remain the child's presumed father by virtue of section 28(5). This saves the common law presumption of paternity that a child is the child of a marriage, unless the husband shows otherwise. It will also deal with the husband who changes his mind about accepting his wife's child as his own. Section 28(2) provides that the lack of consent must be shown to have been at the time of the treatment of his wife, and not at some later time. Thus, a man who has not consented to his wife's treatment (and there is no requirement in the Act that it be sought, although it is almost invariable practice) may later accept that the child is his. As section 28(2) is drafted, his lack of consent at the time of treatment would have been enough for him later to disown the child. The common law presumption will operate to secure the continuing link between the child and its presumed father. The man could, if he so wished, then seek to rebut the common law presumption. This he would have to do by way of blood tests, or any other method of DNA testing. The scheme of section 28(2) extends that introduced by the Family Law Reform Act, section 27 for artificial insemination to the other treatments here discussed, and, by saving the common law presumption, refines the earlier provision, which had made the question of the husband's consent conclusive as to paternity.

Section 28(3) applies in a similar way to an unmarried woman who seeks infertility treatment together with a man who is not the sperm donor. That man, and no other person, is to be treated as the father of the child subject to the section 28(5) presumptions. There was disquiet and confusion throughout the Parliamentary debates about access to treatment of what are sometimes called 'unconventional' families, despite the evidence that the 'conventional' family of the advertisements of the 1940s and 1950s has disappeared. Section 13(5) provides that before a woman is provided with treatment services regard is to be paid to the welfare of the child, including the need of that child for a father. It is thought that this will act as a major 'screening' device in respect of access to treatment services, although many clinics already refuse to provide assistance to single women, and only six or seven are known to accept single or lesbian women. But in truth, that section is an odd provision. *Ex hypothesi*, the child has a

---

[17]   D. Morgan & R. Lee, *supra*, n. 2 at pp. 154–156.

father; the section is not making special provision for parthenogenesis. What the section means to provide for, of course, is that the woman seeking treatment should have a man. That is rather different. Given this, it is extraordinary that, as we shall see, section 28 goes on to create categories of 'legally fatherless' children and to prevent some children from ever discovering their genetic origins. However, as we have seen, the policy behind the legislation is actively to discourage treatment for those infertile people who live outside the umbrella of the nuclear family. This was made crystal clear in one contribution to the debate by Lord Chancellor Mackay:

'. . . if it is to remain possible for unmarried couples to receive the benefit of treatment to bring a child into being, both should have imposed upon them the responsibility for the child. I was most concerned that this proposal [to amend the Bill] should not be seen as encouraging unmarried people to use infertility treatments thus undermining marriage or leading to children having unsuitable fathers because of the difficulty in distinguishing partners to stable relationships from more transitory ones' (House of Lords, Official Report, March 20, 1990, col. 1209–10).

Where a married woman seeks treatment services together with a man other than her husband, her husband will nonetheless be treated as, or be presumed to be the father, unless he can defeat both the statutory provision and the common law presumption.

Where a man is by virtue of section 28(2) or 28(3) treated as a child's father, section 28(4) provides that no other man is to be so regarded. Section 28(6)(a) provides that where a donor's gametes are used in accordance with the consents required under Schedule 3, paragraph 5, then the donor is not to be treated as the father of the child. An attempt to ensure that the birth certificate of a child born following treatment services should have this fact endorsed upon it was defeated in the House of Commons.

Section 28(6) is intended to provide 'protection' to a donor whose sperm is used in accordance with his consent to establish a pregnancy to which a married woman's husband has not consented. Two conclusions seem to follow. First, that a child born in such circumstances will be one of the new legally 'fatherless children'. Secondly, where sperm is used outwith the effective consents given under Schedule 3, paragraph 5, a donor may not be protected by section 28(6)(a), and may indeed be treated as the father of a child produced without his consent."

Women seeking access to fertility treatment services are pursuing the goal which is understood to be the ultimate fulfilment for women — motherhood. However, the legal response is to seek to ensure that children of the reproductive revolution are born into traditional two-parent family structures through limitations imposed upon those who may be judged suitable to receive fertility treatment services. In the interests of the child who may be born as a result, some women, those who do not measure up to the ideal, may be denied access to fertility treatment services.

4.1.ii.b Access to treatment services. While infertility may be the reason for some couples to have recourse to new reproductive technologies, this may not be the sole reason. Lesbians and single women may, for example, desire to conceive via an alternative route to heterosexual intercourse. This raises the

question of which women are considered suitable for access to the new reproductive technologies, or to phrase the question negatively, which women are
considered unsuitable for motherhood. Annexed to this first issue is the further
question of the extent to which autonomous motherhood, in this context the
exercise of a woman's choice to become a parent, is recognised and assisted
in the law governing access to the new reproductive technologies.

Michelle Stanworth states that:

> "a belief in maternal instinct coexists with obstacles to autonomous mother-
> hood — obstacles, that is, to motherhood for women who are not in a stable
> relationship to a man. According to ideologies of motherhood, all women
> *want* children; but single women, lesbian women (and disabled women) are
> often expected to forgo mothering 'in the interest of the child'."[18]

Women do not have the legal right to demand that they receive treatment
services. In this sense they do not have a right to reproduce.[19] Gillian Douglas,
Bill Hebenton and Terry Thomas consider whether limitations imposed upon
access to fertility treatment services may be a breach of the European Convention on Human Rights and Fundamental Freedoms:

G. DOUGLAS, B. HEBENTON & T. THOMAS
"The right to found a family"[20]

"It has been argued that there are many human rights principles involved in a decision
to refuse infertility treatment. Indeed the National Council for Civil Liberties in a
briefing paper suggested that 'a law which, either specifically or in practice, has the
effect of restricting the access of certain categories of women to have a child . . . may
well be in breach of the European Convention on Human Rights' under Art. 8, which
guarantees the right to respect for private and family life, Art. 12, which gives a right
to marry and found a family, and Art. 14, which prohibits discrimination.

However, the Health Minister Virginia Bottomley has stated:

> 'Our legal advice is that it is unlikely that the European Court of Human
> Rights would consider that Art. 8 would impose a positive duty on the Gov-
> ernment to ensure that single women had the same rights of access to treat-
> ment as married women. I am also advised that Art. 14 would not be
> breached if Art. 8 was not and that Art. 12 has no application in the case of
> single women who want to have children by means of AID or IVF.'

There are other principles which have been cited in this arena: for example, Arts 16,
25 and 27 of the Universal Declaration of Human Rights, together with Art. 26 of the

---

[18] M. Stanworth, *supra*, n. 13 at p. 15.
[19] Although see the discussion below in Chap. 5.4 on the sterilisation of women with learning
disabilities, particularly the discussion of *Re D (A Minor) (Wardship: Sterilisation)* [1976] 1 All
E.R. 326 in which Heilbron J. stated that "[t]he type of operation proposed is one which involves
the deprivation of a basic human right, namely the right of a woman to reproduce".
[20] (1992) 142 New L.J. 537 at 537–538.

International Covenant on Civil and Political Rights. Only the European Convention has an effective enforcement machinery, and since the European Commission and Court tend to be fairly conservative and to seek a consensus among signatory states before finding in favour of 'new' social arrangements which challenge state laws, the government's advice is probably sound at present.

There is a distinct lack of consensus among Council of Europe states as to the desirable approach to be taken to assisted reproduction techniques, and a state which restricts access is therefore unlikely to be found in breach of the Convention."

The decision to treat a woman is one subject to the individual policies which are in place at each treatment centre and which operate under the guidance of Ethics Committees. How do they decide which women to take or reject?

Obviously resources are a factor. The NHS does not provide treatment services on demand. Some authorities are more likely to provide treatment than others. For example, in 1994 a thirty-seven year-old woman was refused leave to seek judicial review of Sheffield Health Authority's decision to deny her IVF treatment on the grounds of her age. The application of an age criterion was found to be lawful because a lack of resources meant that treatment should be limited to those whom it would most benefit.[21]

This raises the issue of the nature of what is provided by the new reproductive technologies. Are they "treatments" (to which all those who suffer from the disease of infertility may lay claim) or are they "services" (which may not necessarily be provided to all who request them, but may nevertheless be requested by those who suffer no illness or infertility but do not wish to conceive via heterosexual intercourse). The language of the new reproductive technologies is ambivalent, with both terms being deployed.

S. MILLNS
"Making 'social judgments that go beyond the purely medical': The Reproductive Revolution and Access to Fertility Treatment Services"[22]

"If the 'treatment' aspect of reproductive treatment services is stressed, this implies that infertility is a disease and all those patients who find themselves suffering from it might expect to be treated. The clinical discretion of the medical practitioner would be called for in deciding on a medical basis, and given limited resources, which of those suffering from the disease had the best chance of receiving successful treatment. On the other hand, if viewed as a 'service', screening clients on the basis of social as well as medical criteria may be more justifiable, as clients would not be in a position to expect access to the service simply because of their infertility. Ultimately, medical criteria might be dispensed with altogether and clients granted access simply on the basis of having sufficient financial resources to purchase the service.

Some feminists have resisted the description of new reproductive technologies as treatments. They argue that control over women, perpetuated through use of the tech-

---

[21] *The Times*, October 18, 1994; *The Independent*, October 18, 1994.
[22] In J. Bridgeman & S. Millns (eds), *Law and Body Politics: Regulating the Female Body* (Aldershot: Dartmouth, 1995), p. 90.

nologies, is disguised by the rhetoric of therapy and the cure of disease and illness. Corea argues the language exists to describe reproductive technologies in terms of therapy, but not in terms of 'social control or political rule'. So talk of treatment obscures the reality of who is performing or offering that treatment. The implications of using the language of treatment and service is illustrated in a somewhat macabre fashion by the Code of Practice adopted by the Human Fertilisation and Embryology Authority. The Code describes the woman seeking treatment services as a 'client'. The point at which the client becomes a 'patient' is when treatment without consent is contemplated, that is 'where the procedure is necessary to save the patient's life, cannot be postponed, and she is unconscious and cannot indicate her wishes.' The patient receiving medical treatment in this scenario, unconscious and oblivious, is clearly subject to medical, if not social and political, control."

The issue of financial resources aside, the Human Fertilisation and Embryology Act 1990 sets out the criteria relevant to a consideration of who should be permitted access to fertility treatment services in terms which echo the earlier Warnock Report.

The Warnock Report states that:

> "some individuals will have a more compelling case for treatment than others. In the circumstances, medical practitioners will, clearly, use their clinical judgment as to the priority of the individual case bearing in mind such considerations as the patient's age, the duration of infertility and the likelihood that treatment will be successful."[23]

This sentiment was given effect in section 13(5) of the Human Fertilisation and Embryology Act 1990 which provides that:

> "[a] woman shall not be provided with treatment services unless account has been taken of the welfare of any child who may be born as a result of the treatment (including the need of that child for a father), and of any other child who may be affected by the birth)."

This sub-section is amplified by the *Code of Practice* issued by the Human Fertilisation and Embryology Authority:

> "[I]n deciding whether or not to offer treatment, centres should take account both of the wishes and needs of the people seeking treatment and of the needs of any children who may be involved. Neither consideration is paramount over the other, and the subject should be approached with great care and sensitivity. Centres should avoid adopting any policy or criteria which may appear arbitrary or discriminatory."[24]

---

[23] *Report of the Committee of Inquiry into Human Fertilisation and Embryology, supra*, n.15 at para. 2.12.
[24] Human Fertilisation and Embryology Authority, *Code of Practice* (December 1995), para. 3.3.

The Code further expands upon the criteria which treatment providers should consider:

(a) The commitment of the person seeking treatment and that of her husband or partner (if any) to have a child.
(b) Their age and medical history and the medical history of their families.
(c) The needs of any child who may be born, and the meeting of those needs by the prospective parent(s).
(d) Any risk of harm to the child such as that resulting from inherited disorders, problems during pregnancy or from neglect or abuse.
(e) The effect on any existing children in the family.[25]

Unusually in the sphere of access to medical treatment, section 13(5) makes the social situation of the woman seeking access to services a relevant consideration. The section makes it clear that the focal point of decision-making is the welfare of the child and, in particular, the need of the child for a father.

4.1.ii.b.(1) *The welfare of the child.* The clinical decision-maker may decide that a woman's life-style is such that she would be unsuitable for motherhood because the welfare of any child who may be born as a result may be at risk.

The question of access to fertility treatment services was dealt with in the case of *Ex parte Harriott*.[26] Harriott, a former prostitute, subsequently married, sought *in vitro* fertilisation treatment services. Her request for treatment, (prior to the introduction of the Human Fertilisation and Embryology Act 1990), was refused and the consultant decided her name should be taken off the waiting list following the discovery that she had been deemed unsuitable for adoption, due to convictions for soliciting and running a brothel and due to her poor understanding of the role of a foster-parent. Harriott unsuccessfully sought judicial review to quash the advice given by the Infertility Service Ethical Committee at the hospital which had considered her case at one of its meetings and the decision of the medical team to refuse treatment.

R. v. Ethical Committee of St Mary's Hospital (Manchester), ex parte Harriott
[1988] 1 F.L.R. 512 at 518–519, *per* Schiemann J.

"In my judgement, the [Ethical] committee's function was to provide a forum for discussion amongst professionals. It is essentially an informal body. If the committee in a particular case refused to give advice or does not have a majority view as to what advice should be given, then I do not consider that the courts can compel it to give advice or to embark upon a particular investigation.

Mr Bell, for the committee, submitted that judicial review does not lie to review any

---

[25] *Ibid.*, para. 3.17.
[26] *R. v. Ethical Committee of St Mary's Hospital (Manchester), ex p. Harriott* [1988] 1 F.L.R. 512. This case was decided prior to the introduction of the Human Fertilisation and Embryology Act 1990. It provides, nevertheless, a telling account of judicial acceptance of medical determinations of suitability of women seeking fertility treatment services.

advice given by the committee. As at present advised, I would be doubtful about accepting that submission in its full breadth. If the committee had advised, for instance, that the IVF unit should in principle refuse all such treatment to anyone who was a Jew or coloured, then I think the courts might well grant a declaration that such a policy was illegal: ... But I do not need to consider that situation in this case. Here the complaint is that the committee's advice was that the consultant must make up her own mind as to whether the treatment should be given. That advice was, in my judgment, unobjectionable."

This judgment might be taken to indicate that a refusal to treat on the grounds of religion or ethnicity would be unlawful. As seen above in the example of Sheffield Health Authority's refusal to treat a thirty-seven year-old woman, the same cannot necessarily be said of the refusal to treat on the ground of the age of the woman seeking treatment.

S. MILLNS

"Making 'social judgments that go beyond the purely medical': The Reproductive Revolution and Access to Fertility Treatment Services"[27]

"The issue of child welfare is one which may be a factor in the making of a medical assessment of the woman requesting treatment services, where her body is so constituted as to raise questions about her being physically fit to carry and raise a child. Of those deemed bodily unfit for access to treatment services, the most obvious example is the older woman. On 25 December 1993 a fifty-nine year-old British woman gave birth to twins after having been refused access to treatment services in the United Kingdom and subsequently obtaining them in Italy. In cases such as this, concern is expressed on two grounds. The first is that the physical implications of child-bearing cannot be borne so well by older women. Such implications include the increased possibility of multiple births through the use of fertility drugs, high blood pressure, the pains of childbirth or, alternatively, the increased need for a caesarian, and the difficulty of producing breast milk. The second ground is that older women are unable to cope with the stress of rearing a child. The older woman is, therefore, deemed literally physically unfit for child-bearing and child-rearing.

Under the Human Fertilisation and Embryology Authority's Code of Practice no upper age limit is set for receiving treatment services. There is merely an upper age limit imposed for the donation of semen (age fifty-five) and for the donation of eggs (age thirty-five). Some consultants have expressed the view that the matter is one between the woman and her doctor and that every case must be considered individually. Such individual consideration should involve a distinction being drawn between child-bearing and child-rearing. A woman who wants to receive treatment services because her menopause has been unusually early, may be physically incapable of bearing a child, but is not thereby incapable of rearing one. Similarly an older woman, with a wealth of life-experience and time to devote to bringing up a child, is not necessarily incapable of doing so simply because of her age.

The case of the physically unfit mother is revealing of the absence of discussion of an unfit aged father. While it appears that it is only the woman's attributes which are

---

[27] In J. Bridgeman & S. Millns (eds), *supra*, n. 22 at pp. 91–93.

being put under the spot-light, questions might legitimately be asked about men fathering children at a late stage in life. While virile older men are congratulated for still having it in them, a woman's 'shrivelled old uterus', as one male doctor describes it, is seen as past it and incapable of fulfilling any further useful function. Just because it is biologically possible for older men to father children, this is irrelevant in terms of their suitability for child-rearing. If one aim of restricting access to treatment services is to provide a child with two parents until that child's middle-age, then, all things being equal, more emphasis should be placed on the age of the father.

A woman's physical signs of ageing may have less to do with the refusal to allow her access to reproductive technologies, than the fact that by doing so she is being reprimanded for her failure to bear children earlier in life. Where a woman has decided to postpone having children while pursuing a successful career, some might argue that she should be prepared to live with the consequences of her decision. It was reported that the fifty-nine year-old woman, cited above, had a successful career and was a millionaire business woman. Had she really wanted to be a mother, why was she not prepared to sacrifice her career for this? This question, of course, presupposes that there exists a real possibility of choice for women to pursue a successful career or to choose to start a family, and says nothing about the circumstances which make it extremely difficult for women, and not men, to do both.

There is, further, something which appears subversive about the pregnancy of an older woman. Her pregnancy serves as a reminder of her sexuality, something which is widely ignored or dismissed as nonexistent. This is not unlike the lack of discussion of the sexuality of women with disabilities whose sexual needs often go unrecognised. In the field of reproductive technologies it is quite probable that under the auspices of s.13(5), and the making of a clinical judgment, a woman with a physical disability might similarly be refused access to treatment services on the basis that to do so would not be in the interests of any resulting child."

4.1.ii.b.(2) *The need for a father.* A further criterion to be considered in the decision to offer fertility treatment services is, according to section 13(5), "the need of th[e] child for a father". To what extent is it necessary, therefore, that a woman be in a position to provide a father-figure in order to gain access to treatment services? The Warnock Report had stated that "we are not prepared to recommend that access to treatment should be based exclusively on the legal status of marriage."[28] Nor does the 1990 Act make it a specific requirement that a woman is married in order to be granted access to treatment services. However, this does not constitute a green-light for autonomous motherhood. Warnock expands the point:

> "To judge from the evidence many believe that the interests of the child dictate that it should be born into a home where there is a loving, stable, heterosexual relationship and that, therefore, the deliberate creation of a child for a woman who is not a partner in such a relationship is morally wrong . . .
>
> [W]e believe that as a general rule it is better for children to be born into a two-parent family, with both father and mother, although we recognise

---

[28] *Report of the Committee of Inquiry into Human Fertilisation and Embryology, supra,* n. 15 at para. 2.5.

that it is impossible to predict with any certainty how lasting such a relationship will be."[29]

The members of the Committee here acknowledge that the heterosexual two-
parent family is not necessarily stable, but still prefer this unit to a stable
same-sex couple, or single parent. There is an implicit assumption that children born into non-conventional families suffer prejudice or disadvantage.
This view is challenged by Susan Golombok and John Rust:

S. GOLOMBOK & J. RUST
"The Warnock Report and single women: what about the children?"[30]

"Following the publication of the Warnock Report, the influence of parents on the
social, emotional and pyschosexual development of their children has become a topic
of renewed interest. The Warnock Committee decided not to sanction AID and IVF
for single heterosexual women, or for lesbian women. Implicit in this decision was
their concern about the harmful effects on children of growing up in a fatherless
family. But how much do we really know about children who are raised in such households?

CHILDREN IN FATHERLESS FAMILIES
SOCIAL AND EMOTIONAL DEVELOPMENT

The studies of the social and emotional development of children in fatherless families
have been plagued by methodological problems, and it is difficult to evaluate them as
a whole because they are all so different. However, it is clear that children in these
families are more likely to have emotional and behavioural problems. But this is not,
as is often assumed, because of the absence of a father — it is a direct consequence of
the poverty and isolation that these families have to endure. Also, children whose
mothers had previously been married to, or cohabited with, their father would probably have experienced a period of turmoil at home while the parents were separating,
a situation which is also well known to cause emotional problems in children. So it is
the family discord which precedes separation, and the economic hardship and lack of
support which follows, which are to blame, and not simply the fact that the children
are being raised in a fatherless family . . .

CHILDREN IN LESBIAN FAMILIES

Lesbian families differ from conventional nuclear families not only in the absence of a
father in the home, but also in the mother's sexual orientation. Several studies have
now been carried out to examine empirically the development of children in lesbian

---

[29]   *Report of the Committee of Inquiry into Human Fertilisation and Embryology, ibid.*, paras
2.9 and 2.11.
[30]   (1986) 12 *Journal of Medical Ethics* 182 at 182–185.

families. They all compare children in lesbian families with children in one-parent heterosexual families so that all the children are reared by women, and the two groups of families differ only in the sexual orientation of the mother. The results of these investigations are remarkably similar despite differing measuring techniques, geographical areas and sampling methods. The British study compared 37 children in lesbian families and 38 children in heterosexual one-parent families, all aged between 5 and 17 years.

SOCIAL AND EMOTIONAL DEVELOPMENT

... The expectation that a mother's lesbianism would, in itself, increase the likelihood of pyschiatric disorder in her children arises largely from the assumptions that the children would be teased, ostracised or disapproved of by their peers, and that they would be adversely affected by this. In fact, we found no differences between the two groups of children in the incidence of psychiatric disorder as measured by standard psychiatric interviews and questionnaires. If anything, there was a tendency towards more behavioural and emotional problems among the children in the heterosexual families. Neither was there any difference in the quality of the children's relationships with their friends.

[The article concludes]

Single women who have AID or IVF might generally be expected to be more motivated towards motherhood than those who have not needed or wanted to go to such extremes in order to give birth. Certainly, from this sign of commitment, and from the empirical evidence reviewed here, we would not forsee special problems for children brought up in such families. The Warnock Report says nothing about the many children who are born into non-loving and unstable heterosexual relationships ... Given the extent to which children are abused within the traditional system, surely the double standards which have so far permeated the debate about eligibility for AID and IVF should be recognised?"

The Human Fertilisation and Embryology Act 1990, while not adopting the Warnock recommendation in identical terms, does specify that the need of a child for a father is one factor which should weigh in the balance when deciding whether to treat a woman. On this basis it would appear that single women and women in non-heterosexual relationships may be denied access to fertility treatment services on the grounds of their lack of relationship to a man.

An amendment had been introduced into the House of Lords which would have made it a criminal offence to provide treatment to unmarried couples. The requirement that the Human Fertilisation and Embryology Authority draw up a *Code of Practice* on issues including access to treatment services leaves the treatment team with discretion, within the parameters of the *Code*, to determine who should be given treatment.

R. L. CUNNINGHAM
"Legislating on Human Fertilization and Embryology in the United Kingdom"[31]

"An important development in policy emerged in the White Paper; it argued that the new Authority should have a duty to draw up a code of practice which would be laid before Parliament:

'The code of practice might include guidelines for screening of donors, obtaining consent from patients and donors, use of stored gametes and embryos; counselling and appropriate training for medical and nursing staff.'

Although perhaps implicit in the Warnock recommendations this was a new concept. As the following example shows it was to prove effective as a way of dealing with parliamentary concerns about these and other issues in the course of debates on the bill.

Groups which sought to uphold family values argued that the licensed treatments involving donation should be restricted by law so as to prevent artificial insemination by donor, for example, being made available to single women or lesbian couples. An amendment moved by Lady Saltoun which would have confined such treatments to married couples and which was regarded by the government as a conscience issue was defeated at Lords Committee by only one vote. The government's response was to require the code of practice to give guidance about the importance, when such treatments were being considered, of the welfare of the child which might result and of any existing children. This requirement was later strengthened by an amendment moved at the Report stage in the Commons to define the welfare of the child as including the need of the child for a father. Without the flexibility of a statutory code of practice, to be drawn up by the new Authority, approved by Ministers and made available to Parliament, the government might well have faced a row about civil rights. The provision about a code of practice proved an uncovenanted benefit."

In relation to the provision of treatment to single women the Human Fertilisation and Embryology Authority's *Code of Practice* provides:

HUMAN FERTILISATION AND EMBRYOLOGY AUTHORITY
Code of Practice (1995)[32]

"Further factors will require consideration in the following cases:
   (a) where the child will have no legal father. Centres are required to have regard to the child's need for a father and should pay particular attention to the prospective mother's ability to meet the child's needs throughout his or her childhood. Where appropriate, centres should consider particularly whether there is anyone else within the prospective mother's family and social circle willing and able to share the responsibility for meeting those needs, and for bringing up, maintaining and caring for the child."

[31] (1991) 12 Stat.L.R. 214 at 223–224.
[32] Para. 3.19.

A further issue has arisen in the context of fatherless families, that of "posthhumous pregnancies", achieved using sperm taken from a donor who has subsequently died.[33] What is the position of a woman seeking to use the sperm of her dead husband in order to have their child? Anyone donating gametes or receiving treatment must be given the opportunity to receive counselling and must be provided with relevant information to enable them to be in a position to, as required, give their written consent to, *inter alia*, what is to happen to stored sperm or embryos in the event of their death.[34] The 1990 Act does not prohibit consent to the use of stored sperm or embryos after death but discourages such use by providing that a resulting child is legally fatherless.[35]

An unanticipated issue arose in relation to the use of sperm taken without consent with the express purpose of using it to conceive a child. Diane Blood and her husband had been actively trying to have a child since 1994. Mr Blood became seriously ill in 1995 and Mrs Blood asked for sperm to be taken from him as he lay dying in hospital in a coma. He had given no written consent to his sperm being used by his wife subsequent to his death. Mrs Blood applied for judicial review of the decision of the Human Fertilisation and Embryology Authority not to give over to her the sperm in order for her to be artifically inseminated.

Sir Stephen Brown P. in the Family Division of the High Court dismissed the application finding that the taking of Mr Blood's sperm was a unilateral act undertaken at Mrs Blood's request. The couple had not therefore been receiving treatment services together. Furthermore, the Authority had acted within the limits of discretion in its refusal to allow the sperm to be exported for use in another country and this did not constitute a violation of European Union law on the freedom to obtain medical services in another Member State

---

[33]   The very use of the phrase "posthumous pregnancy" is not without interest to the construction of the situation of the woman seeking treatment. As Michael Thomson suggests in his analysis of the "monstrous feminine" subject constructed by the Human Fertilisation and Embryology Act "[t]he title is misleading but informative — suggesting a pregnant cadaver, a monstrous act of procreation" (M. Thomson, "Legislating for the Monstrous: Access to Reproductive Services and the Monstrous Feminine" in Feminist Legal Research Unit, University of Liverpool (ed.), *Women's Access to Health Care: Law, Society and Culture (Working Paper No. 4)* (Liverpool: University of Liverpool, 1996), p. 134.

[34]   Sched. 3, para. 2(2) provides:
"A consent to the storage of any gametes or any embryo must —
   (a) . . .
   (b) state what is to be done with the gametes or embryo if the person who gave consent dies or is unable because of incapacity to vary the terms of the consent or to revoke it, . . ."

The Guardian reported on February 25, 1997 that, in a "first case of its kind" a widow whose husband had died of cancer had conceived twins following fertility treatment using sperm taken from her husband prior to his treatment. Her husband had given written consent to the use of his sperm in the event of his death. She gave birth to a child (one foetus had died *in utero*) in August 1997 (*The Times*, August 30, 1997).

[35]   Human Fertilisation and Embryology Act 1990, s.28(6): "Where —
   (a) . . .
   (b) the sperm of a man, or any embryo the creation of which was brought about with his sperm, was used after his death, he is not to be treated as the father of the child."

because the relevant Articles of the Treaty of Rome (Arts 59 and 60) could not be used to circumvent national law, particularly in a matter such as this concerning ethical and social policy considerations. In dismissing Mrs Blood's application, Sir Stephen Brown P. indulges in an intimate narrative account of the life of Mrs Blood, leaving no doubt as to his sympathy with this widow and his interpretation of her as a suitable mother figure, were it not for the legal difficulty created by the absence of her partner's consent:

R. v. Human Fertilisation and Embryology Authority, ex parte Blood
[1996] 3 W.L.R. 1176 at 1178, 1190–1191, *per* Sir Stephen Brown P.

"The applicant is a widow now aged 30 years. She was married to her husband Stephen in 1991. They had been courting for nine years before that. They lived a happy married life and greatly wished to have a family. They had married according to the rites of the Anglican Church using the traditional service contained in the 1662 Book of Common Prayer. The applicant had her own business. She had set up her own company in advertising and public relations dealing particularly with matters concerning nursery products. They lived a normal sex life. Towards the end of 1994 they began actively trying to start a family. On 26 February, 1995 tragedy unexpectedly struck . . .

[Having given the legal reasons for dismissing the application the judge continues:]

The powers of the court on an application for judicial review are limited and are not always fully appreciated. It is not for the court to make the decision on the fundamental matter in question. Parliament has entrusted that responsibility to the authority. The authority must act within the powers given to it by Parliament. The duty of this court is to see whether the authority has acted properly within the scope of that discretion. It cannot assist the applicant for the court to express the view that it might itself have made a different decision if it had had the authority to do so. I have found this to be a most anxious and moving case. My heart goes out to this applicant who wishes to preserve an essential part of her late beloved husband. The refusal to permit her so to do is for her in the nature of a double bereavement. Nevertheless for the reasons of law that I have endeavoured to explain I am unable to accede to this application for relief by way of judicial review and I must therefore dismiss the application."

Following this judgment the Human Fertilisation and Embryology Authority reconsidered its refusal to allow Mrs Blood to take her husband's sperm abroad, but upon reconsideration it reached the same decision.[36] Mrs Blood then appealed against the judgment of the High Court. This time she was successful. While indicating that the act of taking Mr Blood's sperm had itself been unlawful (clarifying the legal position so that the situation would never arise again), the Court of Appeal willingly accepted Mrs Blood's claim that the decision of the Authority had not been taken following adequate consid-

---

[36] *The Times*, November 22, 1996.

eration of European Union law, notably Mrs Blood's right to receive treatment in another Member State.

R. v. Human Fertilisation and Embryology Authority, ex parte Blood
[1997] 2 W.L.R. 806 at 820–822, *per* Lord Woolf, CA

"It is now therefore necessary to turn to the actual decision of the authority in this case. In giving its reasons for its latest decision, the members of the authority clearly attached importance to the briefing paper prepared for their use. This is made clear by the fact that at the end of the paper there is set out the submissions which Mr Pannick advanced before Sir Stephen Brown P. to justify the decision of the authority to refuse to make an exception in the case of Mrs Blood. Those reasons follow very closely the four reasons given by the authority when it reached its further decision. It is therefore significant that the background paper, HFEA (96)(39), although it makes reference to Lord Lester's argument on E.C. law contains only a short paragraph which deals with this subject. This records, at para. 16, that the President "found that Community law did not assist that applicant noting that Parliament had specifically considered the issues of public policy underlying the need for written consent." This is hardly a satisfactory summary of the position in relation to article 59.

Parliament did not place any express restriction on the authority's discretion. Parliament by the Act of 1990 had left issues of public policy as to export to be determined by the authority. It is the authority's decision that therefore has to be capable of being justified in relation to article 59. In coming to its decision the authority was required to take into account that to refuse permission to export would impede the treatment of Mrs Blood in Belgium and to ask whether in the circumstances this was justified. The material which was placed before the authority in order to assist them to perform this task is known. Unfortunately it makes no mention of this requirement.

Turning next to consider the reasons given by the authority bearing this in mind, the position appears to be: (1) the first reason given by the authority is a correct statement that in this case there has not been compliance with the Act of 1990 in relation to storage or use in the United Kingdom. This is the starting point for the subsequent reasoning which is the essence for the explanation why the authority was not prepared to exercise its undoubted discretion to permit export in Mrs Blood's favour. It was a permissible and proper starting point: in giving a particular direction, the authority is using delegated powers, which should be used to serve and promote the objects of the legislation, which clearly attach great importance to consent, the quality of that consent, and the certainty of it. The authority must balance that against Mrs Blood's cross-border rights as a Community citizen. (2) The second reason, by referring to the fact that Mrs Blood has no prior connection with any country to which she wishes to export the sperm, ignores the fact that she has the right to receive treatment in Belgium and that Parliament has placed no restriction on the authority's discretion to permit this. It therefore tends to confirm that the authority was unaware of the extent of those cross-border rights. (3) The third reason given by the authority, is based on the desirability of the consent being in clear and formal terms. This is unexceptional. However it does not acknowlege that the evidence that Mrs Blood puts forward that her husband would have given his consent in writing if he had had the opportunity to do so is compelling. (4) The fourth reason given by the authority that

Mr Blood had not considered or given his consent to the export of his sperm is a consideration to which the authority was entitled to have regard.

Parliament had delegated to the authority the responsibility for making decisions in this difficult and delicate area, and the court should be slow to interfere with its decisions. However the reasons given by the authority, while not deeply flawed, confirm that the authority did not take into account two important considerations. The first being the effect of article 59. The second being that there should be, after this judgment has been given, no further cases where sperm is preserved without consent. The authority is not to be criticised for this because in relation to the law it was dependent upon the guidance it received. However the fact remains that having not received the appropriate guidance the authority did not take into account two matters which Mrs Blood is entitled to have taken into account.

From the argument before us and those reasons it is reasonably clear that it was a concern of the authority that if they gave Mrs Blood consent to export, this would create an undesirable precedent which could result in the flouting of the Act. While as already indicated this can, in the appropriate case, be a legitimate reason for impeding the provision of services in another member state it is a consideration which can not have any application here. The fact that storage cannot lawfully take place without written consent, from a practical point of view means that there should be no fresh cases. No licensee can lawfully do what was done here namely preserve sperm in this country without written consent. If the authority had appreciated this, it could well have influenced its decision and, in particular, overcome its reluctance to identify Mr Blood's wishes on the basis of Mrs Blood's evidence and the material which she can produce to support that evidence. It would be understandable for the authority not to wish to engage upon an inquiry of this nature where there can be other cases where the evidence is not so credible since it could lead to invidious comparisons. However the position is different if this case will not create an undesirable precedent.

If the authority had taken into account that Mrs Blood was entitled to receive treatment in Belgium unless there is some good reason why she should not be allowed to receive that treatment the authority may well have taken the view that as the Act did not prohibit this they should have given their consent. The authority could well conclude that as this is a problem which will not recur there is not any good reason for them not to give their consent. If treated in Belgium, Mrs Blood is proposing to use a clinic which in general terms adopts the same standards as this country. The one difference being that they do not insist upon the formal requirements as to written consent which are required in this country. The need for formal requirements is not obvious in this situation.

Apart from the effect of E.C. law the authority's view of the law was correct. It is not possible to say even taking into account E.C. law that the authority are bound to come to a decision in Mrs Blood's favour. What can be said is that the legal position having received further clarification the case for their doing so is much stronger than it was when they last considered the matter. The second decision cannot stand because it is by no means clear that the authority would have come to the same decision if it had taken into account these two additional considerations. The appeal must therefore be allowed. As to what relief should be granted in the light of this judgment can be determined after we have had the opportunity of hearing submissions of counsel.

In this case there is no need to make a reference to the European Court. The principles to be applied are clear. Any difficulty relates to their application.

If the authority is to reconsider their decision it will have to direct itself correctly as to the law, that is the law including European Law. This will involve starting from the premise that to refuse to allow the export of the sperm is contrary to article 59 unless there are appropriate reasons to justify this. The onus is therefore on the authority to provide reasons which meet the standards set by European law. In deciding whether it can be justified the authority are entitled to take into account the public interest. The authority will also have to take account the nature of the present case; again a matter of which it was not aware when it came to its recent decision.

It is unnecessary to consider whether the present reasons would have passed the scrutiny to which they could be subject under European law since the underlying decision is flawed. It will, however, be apparent from what has been stated that this is unlikely."

Mrs Blood hailed this resolution of the legal arguments as "a victory for common sense and justice".[37] One cannot, however, but speculate upon the impact that Mrs Blood's traditional marital history, family-planning strategy and occupation involving "nursery products", had on the ultimate decision. Had she been unmarried at the time of her partner's death, had she not been already engaged in trying to start a family, had she been involved in selling products of a less traditionally "feminine" nature would she have been equally successful in her claim?

Following the quashing of its decision by the Court of Appeal, the Human Fertilisation and Embryology Authority reconsidered its position. This time it took into account the fact that there would be no precedent set by the Blood case (given that sperm should never again be taken without consent) and that E.U. law permitted Mrs Blood to receive medical treatment in another Member State subject only to exceptions based upon public policy (which were insufficiently made out in this case). The Authority's decision to allow Mrs Blood to export her husband's sperm brought her one step closer to the resolution of her "agonising situation".[38] Only technology can do the rest.

4.2 Surrogacy

4.2.i *Legal, social and ethical issues*

A surrogacy arrangement occurs when one woman (the surrogate) agrees to bear a child for another and to give up the baby to that other (the commissioning parent) when it is born. Susan Downie suggests that prior to the development of the contraceptive pill and the provision of legal abortion women who gave up their babies for adoption because of their social circumstances were "surrogate" mothers.[39] This view suggests that a surrogate mother is a woman who continues a pregnancy intending to give up the child after birth. The commonly accepted (and narrower) definition of a surrogate mother is that given legal force in the Surrogacy Arrangements Act 1985 of a woman

---

[37]   *The Times*, February 7, 1997.
[38]   [1997] 2 W.L.R. 806 at 822, *per* Lord Woolf, CA. See *The Times*, February 28, 1997.
[39]   S. Downie, "Surrogate Mothers", *Baby Making: The Technology and Ethics* (London: Bodley Head, 1988), p. 113.

who enters into an agreement prior to conception to carry a child who upon birth is handed over to a specific individual or couple.

The practice of surrogacy presents a challenge to dominant norms surrounding parenthood and particularly, motherhood. Traditional norms within western democracies presuppose that the same woman conceives, carries, gives birth to, and cares for the child, so that "mother" means genetic, gestational and social mother. As with the use of new reproductive technologies, in a surrogacy arrangement these roles can be divided amongst two or even three women.[40]

Surrogacy arrangements are believed to have a long history (the Biblical examples of Sarah, Abraham and Hagar (Genesis 16, 1–6) and Jacob, Rachel and Leah (Genesis 30, 1–24) are often cited). In addition to "partial surrogacy" whereby the surrogate conceives following sexual intercourse with the commissioning male or through the use of low-tech artificial insemination, the development of fertility treatments, specifically *in vitro* fertilisation, presents the possibility of "full surrogacy" where the surrogate is implanted with the embryo of the commissioning couple.[41] A more value-laden description for "full" surrogacy, arising from the lack of genetic relationship between the woman and the foetus she is carrying, is "womb-leasing". As surrogacy involves other people, beyond a heterosexual couple, in the creation of a child, some sectors of society respond to surrogacy with uncertainty if not active disapproval. However, as with fertility treatments, surrogacy is also a response to societal pressures upon couples to produce a child that is genetically related to (at least one of) them.[42] At the core of the dilemma relating to surrogacy is that whilst the aim of an arrangement is the creation of a child (possibly for a heterosexual couple and possibly genetically related to one of the commissioning parties), it represents a distortion of the "normal" family relationship and challenges dominant constructions of motherhood.

The Warnock Committee, considering surrogacy within the remit of its Report on human fertilisation and embryology, saw many social and moral problems with surrogacy. This may be explained by the concentration of the Committee on "convenience surrogacy", which it viewed as insidious, and commercial surrogacy which it feared would result in the exploitation of the parties involved.[43] The Report recommended that it should be a criminal offence to operate either a profit or non-profit making surrogacy agency or

---

[40]   Likewise, the social father may not be the genetic father.

[41]   Section 36(2) of the Human Fertilisation and Embryology Act 1990, amended s. 1(6) of the Surrogacy Arrangements Act 1985 to make it clear that the definition of "surrogate mother" also covers pregnancies resulting from the placing in the surrogate of an egg in the process of fertilisation or of sperm and eggs.

[42]   This pressure may result in the subsequent concealment of the circumstances of the birth of the child from neighbours, family, medical professionals providing ante-natal care, and even from the child itself. A person born following a surrogacy arrangement and subject to a parental order is, however, entitled to obtain details of their birth upon reaching the age of 18 (section 51 of the Adoption Act 1976, as amended by The Parental Orders (Human Fertilisation and Embryology) Regulations 1994 (S.I. 1994 No. 2767)). See "Commentary: The Parental Orders (Human Fertilisation and Embryology) Regulations 1994 (S.I. 1994 No. 2767)" (1995) 3 Med.L.Rev. 204.

[43]   *Report of the Committee of Inquiry into Human Fertilisation and Embryology, supra*, n. 15.

for professionals to participate in bringing about a surrogacy pregnancy.[44] Envisaging that private arrangements would still exist, the Report recommended that legislation should make it clear that such arrangements were unenforceable.[45] Michael Freeman explains that the Warnock Committee's condemnation of "convenience surrogacy" and objection to commercial surrogacy was based upon the moral objection to the use by individuals of others as a means to an end. This suggests that the law should protect against the harm which may be done to another by surrogacy. He explains that, at the same time, the Warnock Committee considered that it would be a greater wrong for the law to intrude into the private lives of individuals which would occur if all surrogacy were criminalised. Hence, the majority recommended that it should be a criminal offence for agencies (both profit making and non-profit making) to participate in the formation of a surrogacy arrangement, leaving scope for private, unenforceable arrangements:

M.D.A. FREEMAN
"After Warnock — Whither the Law?"[46]

"The Warnock Committee's condemnation of surrogacy is not easy to understand. A surrogacy arrangement may be readily justified on utilitarian grounds: the maximisation of pleasure over pain is incontrovertible . . . But when it comes to surrogacy the committee, so firmly wedded to autonomy on artificial insemination, *in vitro* fertilisation and egg and embryo donation, adopts a paternalistic stance. A woman should not be allowed to use her uterus for financial profit and treat it as an incubator for someone else's child. It is, the report notes, 'the moral and social objections to surrogacy' that 'weighed heavily' with the committee. From the evidence submitted to the committee 'it seems . . . that the weight of public opinion is against the practice.' The committee appears to endorse Lord Devlin's philosophy on the legal enforcement of morals. Devlin argued that there is a public morality which provides the cement of any human society, and that the law, especially the criminal law, must regard it as its primary function to maintain this public morality. He further argued that whether in fact in a particular case the law should be brought into play by specific criminal sanctions should depend on the state of public feeling.

It would be surprising if Mary Warnock herself would wish to be associated with the Devlinite position on law and morality and, in publications and lectures since the publication of the report, she has endeavoured to distance herself from this philosophy. In the Introduction to *A Question of Life*, she attacks Devlin's consensus view of morality as a 'myth.' She distinguishes, following Hart, two levels of morality, the 'primary' and the 'critical.' At the first level, the question is whether a certain practice is morally right or wrong; at the second, whether the infringement of liberty as a result of legal intervention would itself be morally right or wrong. In her Introduction (to the book, not the Report) she applies this analysis to surrogacy. Before I examine what

---

[44]   *Report of the Committee of Inquiry into Human Fertilisation and Embryology, ibid.,* para. 8.17.
[45]   *Report of the Committee of Inquiry into Human Fertilisation and Embryology, ibid.*
[46]   [1986] *Current Legal Problems* 33 at 35–37.

she says there, it may be useful to return to the Report and examine the inquiry's view of surrogacy, as it is set out in the Report.

The Committee first deals with surrogacy 'for convenience alone.' In other words, instead of considering whether if surrogacy could be justified for the infertile it could also be defended in the case of fertile women who did not want a pregnancy to interfere with a career or some such similar reason, the committee reversed the process and started with, what most would agree, is the least meritorious case. *Sub silentio* a consequentialist argument is being adduced: look what surrogacy might lead to! The committee does not, however, put the case against on the 'slippery slope' argument. It says surrogacy for the fertile is 'totally ethically unacceptable.' It does not tell us whose ethics have imposed this judgment. It offers no appreciation at all of why some women might find the use of surrogates convenient. It gives the following reason: 'That people should treat others as a means to their own ends, however desirable the consequences, must always be liable to moral objection.' If this argument had been applied consistently, and note the word 'always' is used, no embryo experimentation could be allowed unless embryos were not 'others,' and artificial insemination by a donor, egg donation and embryo donation would have to be rejected. So also, though it is outside the scope of the report, would blood transfusions. It is the spectre of surrogacy for convenience that led the committee into an argument which belies much of the rest of the report.

The committee's report is concerned with the 'serious risk of commercial exploitation.' Mary Warnock, in her Introduction, tells us that the Inquiry agreed unanimously that they disapproved of the practice. She tells us that this was 'largely because of possible consequences for the child.' (In the report surrogacy is said to be 'potentially damaging' to the child, and also 'degrading.') This disposes of the first level of morality. She then tells us that the committee also agreed that surrogacy could not be prevented by law 'because of the intrusiveness of any law that would be enforceable.' 'The Inquiry therefore concentrated,' we are told, 'on how surrogacy for commercial purposes might be checked . . .' There was, apparently, unanimous agreement that 'it would be morally wrong to envisage a law which would intrusively curtail human freedom, and which would in addition be impossible to enforce.' Warnock continues: 'The Inquiry, then, while unanimously answering the first-order question negatively, holding that surrogacy was wrong, nevertheless held that legislation should not be invoked to prevent it. We did, however, by a majority recommend that the commercial use of surrogacy arrangements, as a way of making money for an agency, could and should be made a criminal offence. For not only was the wrongness of surrogacy compounded by its being exploited for money, but also a law against agencies would not be intrusive into the private lives of those who were actually engaged in setting up a family.' "

The Warnock Report considered the following arguments against surrogacy:

(i)   A surrogacy arrangement involves (at least) three people in the procreation of a child. The Committee believed that it was supported by public opinion in its view of procreation as appropriate within a marital relationship which was a "loving partnership" between two people.[47] Reproduction should, in the Committee's view, only occur within the confines of the nuclear family, so that a child should only be born to two heterosexual parents. The privacy

---

[47]   *Report of the Committee of Inquiry into Human Fertilisation and Embryology, supra*, n. 15 at para. 8.10.

of the family should be assured both from the intrusion of additional parties into the process of procreation and from the involvement of the medical profession which would be necessitated in surrogacy arrangements following assisted reproduction. Consequently, surrogacy is, in its view, both unnatural and unacceptable.[48] The Report claimed that "the weight of public opinion' is against the practice",[49] suggesting that this view was widely held within society, without providing evidence for this assertion.

(ii) Surrogacy involves a woman using her body for financial gain to gestate a child for another couple, an act which the Committee considered to be contrary to "human dignity".[50]

(iii) The surrogate mother becomes pregnant in order to carry a child whom she will, after birth, give away. This "distorts" the relationship between mother and child.[51]

(iv) Breaking the bond which has developed between mother and foetus during the pregnancy may prove to be damaging to the child who will, in any event, be degraded as a consequence of being "bought for money".[52]

The Committee acknowledged the contrary arguments in favour of legal surrogacy arrangements:

(i)   Given the present limitations of medicine, surrogacy may offer the only way in which a man whose partner is infertile can have a child who is genetically related to him.[53]

(ii) Respecting a woman's freedom to use her body as she chooses, surrogacy should not be prohibited.[54]

The Government's response to the Warnock Report and also to the public and media reaction to the birth of Baby Cotton to a surrogate mother was the Surrogacy Arrangements Act 1985. This legislation follows broadly, without going as far as, the recommendations of the Warnock Report in that it criminalises those participating in commercial (but not non-commercial)

---

[48] These beliefs are identified by Jane Lewis and Fenella Cannell in "The Politics of Motherhood in the 1980's: Warnock, Gillick and Feminists" (1986) 13 *Journal of Law and Society* 321 as the basis of the Gillick campaign (concerning the provision of contraceptives to girls under the age of sixteen, discussed below) as well as the Warnock Report.
[49] *Report of the Committee of Inquiry into Human Fertilisation and Embryology, supra*, n. 15 at para. 8.10.
[50] *Report of the Committee of Inquiry into Human Fertilisation and Embryology, ibid.*, para. 8.10.
[51] *Report of the Committee of Inquiry into Human Fertilisation and Embryology, ibid.*, para. 8.11.
[52] *Report of the Committee of Inquiry into Human Fertilisation and Embryology, ibid.*, paras 8.11 and 8.12.
[53] *Report of the Committee of Inquiry into Human Fertilisation and Embryology, ibid.*, para. 8.13.
[54] *Report of the Committee of Inquiry into Human Fertilisation and Embryology, ibid.*, para. 8.14. An interesting comparison with the views of Warnock are the attitudes of those organising commercial arrangements in the U.S. (see G. Corea, "Surrogate Motherhood: Happy Breeder Woman" in G. Corea, *supra*, n. 6, and of women who have had a "surrogate" pregnancy (S. Downie, *supra*, n. 39 at pp. 119–129).

arrangements other than the surrogate mother or commissioning couple to "avoid children being born to mothers subject to the taint of criminality".[55]

Surrogacy Arrangements Act 1985, ss. 1 and 2
(c. 49)

Meaning of "surrogate mother", "surrogacy arrangement" and other terms

1.—(1)   The following provisions shall have effect for the interpretation of this Act.

(2)   "Surrogate mother" means a woman who carries a child in pursuance of an arrangement —

   (a) made before she began to carry the child, and
   (b) made with a view to any child carried in pursuance of it being handed over to, and parental responsibility being met (so far as practicable) by, another person or other persons.

(3)   An arrangement is a surrogacy arrangement if, were a woman to whom the arrangement relates to carry a child in pursuance of it, she would be a surrogate mother.

(4)   In determining whether an arrangement is made with such a view as is mentioned in subsection (2) above regard may be had to the circumstances as a whole (and, in particular, where there is a promise or understanding that any payment will or may be made to the woman or for her benefit in respect of the carrying of any child in pursuance of the arrangement, to that promise or understanding).

(5)   An arrangement may be regarded as made with such a view though subject to conditions relating to the handing over of any child.

(6)   A woman who carries a child is to be treated for the purposes of subsection (2)(a) above as beginning to carry it at the time of the insemination or of the placing in her of an embryo, of an egg in the process of fertilisation or of sperm and eggs, as the case may be, that results in her carrying the child.

(7)   "Body of persons" means a body of persons corporate or unincorporate.

(8)   "Payment" means payment in money or money's worth.

(9)   This Act applies to arrangements whether or not they are lawful.

Negotiating surrogacy arrangements on a commercial basis, etc.

2.—(1)   No person shall on a commercial basis do any of the following acts in the United Kingdom, that is —

   (a) initiate or take part in any negotiations with a view to the making of a surrogacy arrangement,
   (b) offer or agree to negotiate the making of a surrogacy arrangement, or
   (c) compile any information with a view to its use in making, or negotiating the making of, surrogacy arrangements;

and no person shall in the United Kingdom knowingly cause another to do any of those acts on a commercial basis.

---

[55]   *Report of the Committee of Inquiry into Human Fertilisation and Embryology, ibid.*, para. 8.19. On January 19, 1997, however, it was reported that a surrogate mother had been arrested on suspicion of deception after allegedly taking £4,000 from a childless couple and refusing to hand over the baby (*The Observer*, January 19, 1997). She was later released and no charges were brought (*The Guardian*, July 26, 1997).

(2) A person who contravenes subsection (1) above is guilty of an offence; but it is not a contravention of that subsection —

(a) for a woman, with a view to becoming a surrogate mother herself, to do any act mentioned in that subsection or to cause such an act to be done, or

(b) for any person, with a view to a surrogate mother carrying a child for him, to do such an act or to cause such an act to be done.

(3) For the purposes of this section, a person does an act on a commercial basis (subject to subsection (4) below) if —

(a) any payment is at any time received by himself or another in respect of it, or

(b) he does it with a view to any payment being received by himself or another in respect of making, or negotiating or facilitating the making of, any surrogacy arrangement.

In this subsection "payment" does not include payment to or for the benefit of a surrogate mother or prospective surrogate mother.

(4) In proceedings against a person for an offence under subsection (1) above, he is not to be treated as doing an act on a commercial basis by reason of any payment received by another in respect of the act if it is proved that —

(a) in a case where the payment was received before he did the act, he did not do the act knowing or having reasonable cause to suspect that any payment had been received in respect of the act; and

(b) in any other case, he did not do the act with a view to any payment being received in respect of it.

(5) Where —

(a) a person acting on behalf of a body of persons takes any part in negotiating or facilitating the making of a surrogacy arrangement in the United Kingdom, and

(b) negotiating or facilitating the making of surrogacy arrangements is an activity of the body,

then, if the body at any time receives any payment made by or on behalf of —

(i) a woman who carries a child in pursuance of the arrangement,

(ii) the person or persons for whom she carries it, or

(iii) any person connected with the woman or with that person or those persons, the body is guilty of an offence.

For the purposes of this subsection, a payment received by a person connected with a body is to be treated as received by the body.

(6) In proceedings against a body for an offence under subsection (5) above, it is a defence to prove that the payment concerned was not made in respect of the arrangement mentioned in paragraph (a) of that subsection.

(7) A person who in the United Kingdom takes part in the management or control —

(a) of any body of persons, or

(b) of any of the activities of any body of persons,

is guilty of an offence if the activity described in subsection (8) below is an activity of the body concerned.

(8) The activity referred to in subsection (7) above is negotiating or facilitating the making of surrogacy arrangements in the United Kingdom, being —

(a) arrangements the making of which is negotiated or facilitated on a commercial basis, or

(b) arrangements in the case of which payments are received (or treated for the

purposes of subsection (5) above as received) by the body concerned in contravention of subsection (5) above.

(9)   In proceedings against a person for an offence under subsection (7) above, it is
a defence to prove that he neither knew nor had reasonable cause to suspect that the
activity described in subsection (8) above was an activity of the body concerned; and
for the purposes of such proceedings any arrangement falling within subsection (8)(b)
above shall be disregarded if it is proved that the payment concerned was not made in
respect of the arrangement.

Section 3 makes it is a criminal offence to advertise in relation to a surrogacy
arrangement:

Surrogacy Arrangements Act 1985, s. 3
(c. 49)

Advertisements about surrogacy
3.—(1)   This section applies to any advertisement containing an indication
(however expressed) —

   (a)   that any person is or may be willing to enter into a surrogacy arrangement
          or to negotiate or facilitate the making of a surrogacy arrangement, or
   (b)   that any person is looking for a woman willing to become a surrogate mother
          or for persons wanting a woman to carry a child as a surrogate mother.

(2)   Where a newspaper or periodical containing an advertisement to which this
section applies is published in the United Kingdom, any proprietor, editor or publisher
of the newspaper or periodical is guilty of an offence.

(3)   Where an advertisement to which this section applies is conveyed by means of
a telecommunication system so as to be seen or heard (or both) in the United Kingdom,
any person who in the United Kingdom causes it to be so conveyed knowing it to
contain such an indication as is mentioned in subsection (1) above is guilty of an
offence.

(4)   A person who publishes or causes to be published in the United Kingdom an
advertisement to which this section applies (not being an advertisement contained in
a newspaper or periodical or conveyed by means of a telecommunication system) is
guilty of an offence.

(5)   A person who distributes or causes to be distributed in the United Kingdom an
advertisement to which this section applies (not being an advertisement contained in
a newspaper or periodical published outside the United Kingdom or an advertisement
conveyed by means of a telecommunication system) knowing it to contain such an
indication as is mentioned in subsection (1) above is guilty of an offence.

(6)   In this section "telecommunication system" has the same meaning as in the
Telecommunications Act 1984.

The offences in section 3 may extend to the surrogate or commissioning parents who, unlike under section 2, are not specifically excluded. It is not, however, entirely clear what amounts to advertising. For example, is a local newspaper which runs a story about a couple who are looking for a surrogate
running an advertisement? This may be an effective way of highlighting the
plight of infertile couples and result in offers from women to bear a child for

them. Presumably if the newspaper does not take part in negotiating an agreement for payment (or engage in any of the other acts prohibited by s.2) and covers a story as opposed to publishing an advertisement, no offence is committed. To make it entirely clear that surrogacy arrangements are not enforceable by or against any of the parties involved, section 1A was inserted into the 1985 Act by the Human Fertilisation and Embryology Act 1990 to that effect.

The hastily enacted 1985 Act has been widely criticised.[56] That is not to say, however, that arrangements made privately amongst people known to each other will never be successful (indeed, it is more probably the case that they are successful and simply do not receive publicity).[57] The position now is that while commercial agreements are illegal, arrangements facilitated by charitable organisations such as COTS (Childlessness Overcome Through Surrogacy), or agreements reached between family and friends, are permitted. It is for the parties themselves to negotiate the terms of their agreement, terms which are legally unenforceable. Professionals approached by parties wishing to enter a surrogacy arrangement cannot provide advice for a fee:

S. SLOMAN
"Surrogacy Arrangements Act 1985"[58]

"The question of professional involvement in surrogacy is now in a complex and confused state. If surrogacy is to be permitted then the law should ensure that the parties directly involved are not exploited and that legal, medical and other necessary facilities are available. In seeking to stop third parties profiteering the draftsman has failed to deal satisfactorily with the position of those who would provide such services for a fee.

During the Bill's passage through Parliament there was particular concern expressed over the possible effects on the legal profession. It is the inclusion of the words 'negotiations' and 'negotiate' in section 2(1)(a) and (b) which cause most difficulty. Mr Kenneth Clarke, then Minister for Health, sought to reassure members of the House of Commons. In his opinion a solicitor can give a client general legal advice about surrogacy and is permitted to give such advice to both sides. If the parties have already reached agreement then a solicitor can produce a document setting out that agreement in legal language. However, it would be unwise for a solicitor to go further than this. In particular he must avoid any action which could be construed as 'taking part in negotiations', section 2(1)(a) or 'offering or agreeing to negotiate', section 2(1)(b). Therefore, according to the Minister, a solicitor will be committing an offence if he either contacts the other party's legal advisor on his client's behalf, or drafts an agree-

---

[56] See M. D. A. Freeman, "After Warnock — Whither the Law?" [1986] *Current Legal Problems* 33; E. Blyth, "Section 30 — The Acceptable Face of Surrogacy?" [1993] *Journal of Social Welfare and Family Law* 248.
[57] Unless the interest arises for other reasons, as in the case of Edith Jones who was implanted with an embryo created from the gametes of her daughter and son-in-law and gave birth to a girl. The media interest was not in the possibilities for successful informal surrogacy arrangements, but that Edith Jones had given birth to her granddaughter (*The Times*, December 8, 1996).
[58] (1985) 135 New L.J. 978 at 979–980.

ment for the parties or having been consulted by all parties intervenes in the 'interchange about terms', and takes a fee. Perhaps of greater concern is Ms Jo Richardson's suggestion (which was not challenged by the Minister) that if a solicitor is instructed by all the parties to produce a document embodying the terms of their agreement, and he perceives that the terms are unfavourable to one side, he cannot point this out without contravening section 2(1)(a). This places the solicitor in an impossible position, for he has a duty to explain the desirability of a particular course of action and yet may be guilty of an offence if he does so. If there is a clear conflict of interest then a solicitor is required to insist that both sides are separately represented. In the case of surrogacy it is suggested that even where the agreement appears satisfactory a solicitor should not produce a document for the parties unless they have obtained or been encouraged to obtain separate legal advice. There is an important distinction between surrogacy and other situations in family law where the parties instruct a solicitor having already reached agreement (for example where a couple have settled the distribution of the matrimonial assets on divorce, or the question of custody of their children). In the latter situation the parties' decision is subject to scrutiny by the court and is not binding until approved, however, the court has no duty to oversee surrogacy agreements and the protection given at the time of adoption may come too late . . .

. . . Parliament should have ensured that the existing services are readily available. It is unfortunate that the amendment proposed by Ms Jo Richardson was not accepted. It would have excluded from section 2:

'A payment to a non-profit making organisation . . . or to a qualified solicitor or barrister or registered medical practitioner who advises, counsels or assists persons making . . . a surrogacy arrangement in the course of his normal professional practice'.

Although some counselling facilities are provided by the NHS, local authorities and voluntary organisations, there is a danger that the uncertainty surrounding section 2 may lead to 'amateurish or exploitive do-it-yourself arrangements'."

Parties entering into a surrogacy arrangement will need not only legal advice but also medical screening, psychological advice and counselling. The difficulties faced by parties to a surrogacy arrangement were noted by Latey J. in *Re Adoption Application*:

> "Other than those outlawed by the Surrogacy Arrangements Act 1985, surrogacy arrangements are not against the law as it stands. But those contemplating taking this path should have their eyes open to the kind of pitfalls, obstacles and anxiety that they are likely to meet. Mr and Mrs A, a devoted and very nice couple, encountered many of them. So too did Mr and Mrs B. And they found themselves caught in a tangled web of family and social embarrassment and deception, including the deception of doctors and others, from whom they could not escape . . . One cannot sit in these courts and hear all the multitude of professionals and others without knowing well the depth of longing in couples, devoted to each other, who cannot have a child through no fault of their own. But before they go down the path of surrogacy they should know and know fully what it may entail. It is not a primrose path."[59]

The 1985 Act effects a compromise position. While accepting that surrogacy

---

[59] *Re Adoption Application* [1987] 3 W.L.R. 31 at 37, *per* Latey J.

arrangements will continue to be made, whatever the legal position, it prohibits commercial surrogacy and renders the establishment of surrogacy arrangements difficult by making it a criminal offence to advertise. In short, the law criminalises commercial arrangements but makes it clear that private arrangements are "not the law's business".[60] Derek Morgan compares the underlying philosophy of the Surrogacy Arrangements Act 1985 with the approach taken to prostitution by the Wolfenden Committee.[61] Whilst the law prohibits the public face of both surrogacy and prostitution, both are permitted as private arrangements:

D. MORGAN
"Who to Be or Not to Be: The Surrogacy Story"[62]

"It is possible, I think, to detect in the approach of the legislature to the Surrogacy Act a resonance of the philosophy which informed the *Wolfenden Report on Homosexual Offences and Prostitution*. In the same way that Wolfenden observed that 'the possible consequences of clearing the streets are less harmful than the constant public parading of the prostitute's wares,' the surrogacy debate in the United Kingdom has proceeded on the basis that, with appropriate censorship, some aspects of the practice will be rendered suitable for private consumption. As Wolfenden legitimated the approach of the ensuing Street Offences Act 1959 in appearing to tackle the visible manifestations of prostitution while ignoring its underlying causes, so the Surrogacy Act has attempted to remove the offending pages of the surrogacy story from the public folio to leave a privately-printed text which can be safely passed around 'within the family.' But, as Katherine O'Donovan reminds us, 'the whole fabric of personal life is printed with colours from elsewhere.'

The Wolfenden strategy was the precursor for the Hart-Devlin debate which the surrogacy story recaptures. What has changed, however, is the emergence of a new understanding of the boundaries constructed between personal and public life; the personal is political and the political personal. This, one of the major contributions of feminist thought and jurisprudence, has signalled the need and encouraged the demand for new ways of thinking and new ways of thinking about thinking. Even a partial and fragmentary understanding of surrogacy, ... which ignores the implications of this new dynamic, will not capture the full complexities which surrogacy exposes. What Stuart Hall has identified as the key interpellative structure of the Wolfenden regime, the respectable man, has as its counterpart in the Warnock Report and the ensuing surrogacy debates 'decent and family-loving people.' There is an irony in the way in which the so-called 'permissive' legislative response to prostitution according to the program loaded by the Wolfenden Report is paralleled by the essentially 'proscriptive' responses to what Andrea Dworkin had called 'reproductive prostitution.' The common denominator to both equations of social welfare is the concern to get it out of sight; off the streets of shame and out of the highways of commerce. That surrogacy has not yet been exhaustively proscribed, however, recalls Wolfenden's view

---

[60] To use the often cited terminology of the Wolfenden *Report on Homosexual Offences and Prostitution*, Cmnd. 247 (1957), para. 257.
[61] *Ibid.*
[62] (1986) 49 *Modern Law Review* 358 at 366–368.

of the role of law: that there is a sphere of civil life which is 'in brief and crude terms, not the law's business.' . . .

[B]ehind these decisions to regulate the practice of surrogacy, to prohibit it or to condone it as long as it remains relatively invisible, lies a theory about law itself and its proper role or limitations: '. . . legal non-intervention does not rule out other forms of social control. Theories about the limits of law may contain views about the suitability of other agencies to regulate activities labelled private.' "

As with prostitution, by permitting surrogacy arrangements as long as they are kept out of the public domain, the law fails to provide adequate protection for those who enter into such arrangements.

One issue which will be of importance to parties who enter into a private surrogacy arrangement is who, in law, are the mother and father of the child and therefore have rights and responsibilities in respect of that child. The legal presumption *mater est quam gestatio demonstrat* (the mother of the child is the one who gives birth to it) means that if the pregnancy follows sexual intercourse or artificial insemination without licensed medical assistance, the surrogate is the legal mother. The Human Fertilisation and Embryology Act 1990, s. 27 makes it clear that this is also the case for pregnancies resulting from licensed assisted conception.[63] The surrogate will be the legal mother of the child, whether or not she wants to be. If the pregnancy follows sexual intercourse the commissioning man will be the genetic father. If the surrogate is married it will be necessary to rebut the presumption *pater est quem nuptiae demonstrant*, that the child is that of the man who is party to the marriage. If the surrogate is married and is impregnated following licensed assisted conception, by virtue of section 28 of the Human Fertilisation and Embryology Act 1990 it is her husband who is the legal father of the child if he consented to the treatment. If the surrogate is not married the child is legally fatherless. However, the intention of the parties, at least at the point they entered into the agreement, is for the commissioning couple, not the surrogate or her husband, to be the social parents with parental rights and responsibilities.

As Gillian Douglas explains,[64] prompted by the concern of MPs at the facts of *Re W (Minors)*,[65] section 30 was inserted late in the passage of the Human Fertilisation and Embryology Bill (and seemingly contradicts ss. 27 and 28) enabling, in certain conditions, the commissioning couple to obtain a parental order. In *Re W* the commissioning couple were forced to adopt "their" child born following a "full" surrogacy arrangement. The commissioning father could have established paternity by rebutting the legal presumption that the husband of the surrogate was the legal father. However, there was uncertainty as to who was the legal mother given the presumption in law that the mother

---

[63]   Section 27 is discussed in Chap. 4.1. This section is principally aimed at ensuring that women who undergo fertility treatment (and thus may not be genetically related to the resulting child) attain the status of legal mother of the child. It also applies where a surrogate pregnancy results from fertility treatment.

[64]   G. Douglas, "The Human Fertilisation and Embryology Act 1990" (1991) 21 *Family Law* 110.

[65]   *Re W (Minors)* [1991] F.C.R. 419.

of the child is she who gives birth to it. The surrogate had carried and given birth to the child, but it was genetically the child of the commissioning mother.

Section 30,[66] which was brought into force by the Human Fertilisation and Embryology Act (Commencement No. 5) Order 1994, requires a number of conditions to be fulfilled before a court will make a parental order:

Human Fertilisation and Embryology Act 1990, s. 30(1)–(7)
(c. 37)

Parental orders in favour of gamete donors

30.—(1)   The court may make an order providing for a child to be treated in law as the child of the parties to a marriage (referred to in this section as "the husband" and "the wife") if —

    (a)   the child has been carried by a woman other than the wife as the result of the placing in her of an embryo or sperm and eggs or her artificial insemination,

    (b)   the gametes of the husband or the wife, or both, were used to bring about the creation of the embryo, and

    (c)   the conditions in subsections (2) to (7) below are satisfied.

(2)   The husband and the wife must apply for the order within six months of the birth of the child or, in the case of a child born before the coming into force of this Act, within six months of such coming into force.

(3)   At the time of the application and of the making of the order —

    (a)   the child's home must be with the husband and the wife, and

    (b)   the husband or the wife, or both of them, must be domiciled in a part of the United Kingdom or in the Channel Islands or the Isle of Man.

(4)   At the time of the making of the order both the husband and the wife must have attained the age of eighteen.

(5)   The court must be satisfied that both the father of the child (including a person who is the father by virtue of section 28 of this Act), where he is not the husband, and the woman who carried the child have freely, and with full understanding of what is involved, agreed unconditionally to the making of the order.

(6)   Subsection (5) above does not require the agreement of a person who cannot be found or is incapable of giving agreement and the agreement of the woman who carried the child is ineffective for the purposes of that subsection if given by her less than six weeks after the child's birth.

(7)   The court must be satisfied that no money or other benefit (other than for expenses reasonably incurred) has been given or received by the husband or the wife for or in consideration of —

    (a)   the making of the order,

    (b)   any agreement required by subsection (5) above,

    (c)   the handing over of the child to the husband and the wife, or

    (d)   the making of any arrangements with a view to the making of the order, unless authorised by the court.

---

[66] Discussed by Eric Blyth in "Section 30 — The Acceptable Face of Surrogacy?", *supra*, n. 56.

The effect of a parental order is to extinguish the parental rights and responsibilities of the surrogate and her husband or partner and to vest them for all purposes in the commissioning couple. A section 30 order enables the court to give legal effect to the intention of the parties, if they are all willing to go through with the arrangement after the birth of the child. No order will be made if the surrogate does not agree "unconditionally" (s. 30(5)), an agreement which she cannot give until six weeks after the birth (s. 30(6)). If she no longer wishes to give up the child, she cannot be forced to do so. Section 30 perpetuates the apparent preference shown in custody cases (discussed below) for the wishes of the surrogate as her dissent is sufficient to prevent an order being made to the commissioning couple. Despite her description as a surrogate, she is believed to have bonded with the child prior to its birth and as such is perceived as the natural mother who cannot be forced to go through with an agreement made prior to conception to give up her child. Subsequently, the Parental Orders (Human Fertilisation and Embryology) Regulations 1994, applying provisions of the Adoption Act 1976 to section 30 cases, make it clear that the primary consideration of the court is the welfare of the child.[67]

In those cases where one or more of the conditions set out in section 30 does not apply (for example, the child is not genetically related to one or both of the commissioning couple (s. 30(1)); the commissioning couple are not married (s. 30(1)); the arrangement was made with a single male or homosexual couple; or the child is not already living with them (s. 30(3)(a))), the commissioning couple may seek to adopt the child or seek to have it made a ward of court. In such cases the primary question is the welfare of the child, that is, what is in the best interests of the child?

In *Re P (Minors) (Wardship: Surrogacy)*,[68] the surrogate mother changed her mind about handing over to the commissioning couple twins born following artificial insemination with the sperm of the commisioning male. Both she and the father approached the local authority who applied to the court to have the children made wards of court. In this case and in *A v. C*,[69] in which the surrogate likewise found that she could not give up the baby, the court placed decisive importance upon the bonding between mother and child when weighing up the facts to determine what was in the best interests of the babies. Sir John Arnold P makes repeated reference to the surrogate as "their mother":

Re P (Minors) (Wardship: Surrogacy)
[1987] 2 F.L.R. 421 at 424, 425–6, 427, *per* Sir John Arnold P.

"These children have been, up to their present age of approximately 5 months, with, quite consistently, their mother and in those circumstances there must necessarily have

---

[67] See "Commentary: The Parental Orders (Human Fertilisation and Embryology) Regulations 1994 (S.I. 1994 No. 2767)", *supra*, n. 42.
[68] *Re P (Minors) (Wardship: Surrogacy)* [1987] 2 F.L.R. 421.
[69] *A v. C* [1985] F.L.R. 453. Custody of the child had been awarded to the surrogate at first instance. The Court of Appeal considered her appeal against access awarded to the commissioning

been some bonding of those children with their mother and that is undoubtedly coupled with the fact that she is their mother, a matter which weighs predominantly in the balance in favour of leaving the children with their mother, but there are other factors which weigh in the opposite balance and which, as is said by Mr B through his counsel, outweigh the advantages of leaving the children with their mother and it is that balancing exercise which the court is required to perform . . .

What then are the factors which the court should take into account? I have already mentioned on the side of Mrs P the matters which weigh heavily in the balance are the fact of her maternity, that she bore the children and carried them for the term of their gestation and that ever since she has conferred upon them the maternal care which they have enjoyed and has done so successfully. The key social worker in the case who has given evidence testifies to the satisfactory nature of the care which Mrs P has conferred upon the children and this assessment is specifically accepted by Mr B as being an accurate one. I start, therefore, from the position that these babies have bonded with their mother in a state of domestic care by her of a satisfactory nature and I now turn to the factors which are said to outweigh those advantages, so as to guide the court upon the proper exercise of the balancing function to the conclusion that the children ought to be taken away from Mrs P, and passed over, under suitable arrangements, to Mr and Mrs B. They are principally as follows. It is said, and said quite correctly, that the shape of the B family is the better shape of a family in which these children might be brought up, because it contains a father as well as a mother and that is undoubtedly true. Next, it is said that the material circumstances of the B family are such that they exhibit a far larger degree of affluence than can be demonstrated by Mrs P. That, also, is undoubtedly true. Then it is said that the intellectual quality of the environment of the B's home and the stimulus which would be afforded to these babies, if they were to grow up in that home, would be greater than the corresponding features in the home of Mrs P. That is not a matter which has been extensively investigated, but I suspect that that is probably true. Certainly, the combined effect of the lack of affluence on the part of Mrs P and some lack of resilience to the disadvantages which that implies has been testified in the correspondence to the extent that I find Mrs P saying that shortage of resources leads to her sitting at home with little E and overeating, because she has no ability from a financial point of view to undertake anything more resourceful than that. Then it is said that the religious comfort and support which the B's derive from their Church is greater than anything of that sort available to Mrs P. How far that is true, I simply do not know. I do know that the B's are practising Christians and do derive advantages from that circumstance, but nobody asked Mrs P about this and I am not disposed to assume that she lacks that sort of comfort and support in the absence of any investigation by way of cross-examination to lay the foundations for such a conclusion. Then it is said, and there is something in this, that the problems which might arise from the circumstance that these children who are, of course, congenitally derived from the semen of Mr B and bear traces of Mr B's Asiatic origin would be more easily understood and discussed and reconciled in the household of Mr and Mrs B, a household with an Asiatic ethnic background than they would be if they arose in relation to these children while they were situated in the home of Mrs P, which is in an English village and which has no non-English connections. Obviously that is expressed contingently as a factor, although there is no means by which the court can measure the likelihood or otherwise of the contingency which has regard to racial discrimination. The situation in which

male. The Court concluded that, in the best interests of the child, all links with the commissioning male should be completely severed.

Mrs P lives is not, as it seems to me, likely to breed that sort of intolerance. She lives in a smallish country community, large in terms of a village but small in terms of a town where there is very little penetration by immigrant citizens which does not seem to me to be a community in which racial discrimination is very likely, but it is a factor which contingently at least may have some importance ...

As regards the other factors, they are, in the aggregate, weighty, but I do not think, having given my very best effort to the evaluation of the case dispassionately on both sides, that they ought to be taken to outweigh the advantages to these children of preserving the link with the mother to whom they are bonded and who has, as is amply testified, exercised over them a satisfactory level of maternal care, and accordingly it is, I think, the duty of the court to award the care and control of these babies to their mother."

The outcome of the case seems to follow from a view that bonding is a mystical and inevitable feature of the mother/child relationship. It cannot, however, be inevitable, unless there was something "abnormal" about the surrogate in *Re C*,[70] who left the baby in hospital a matter of hours after she was born. The "best interests" of the child leave the court to determine custody on a case by case basis. If the surrogate is prepared to go through with the agreement, the best interests of the child would, it seems, tilt the balance in favour of the commissioning couple. *Re C* is the legal judgment of the case of Baby Cotton.[71] In this case, the surrogate and commissioning couple were willing to go through with the agreement, but the local authority, uncertain about the position arising from surrogacy, obtained a place of safety order. The father issued wardship proceedings and, after making inquiries, the local authority supported the application. As the surrogate did not want the baby, the court had to decide between putting the child into the care of the commissioning couple or that of foster parents. The judge gave the commissioning couple care and control, and allowed them to take the baby out of the jurisdiction on the undertaking that they return her should the court so order.

Re C
[1985] F.L.R. 846 at 848, *per* Latey J.

"So, what is best for this baby? Her natural mother does not ask for her. Should she go into Mr and Mrs A's care and be brought up by them? Or should some other arrangement be made for her, such as long-term fostering with or without adoption as an end?

The factors can be briefly stated. Mr A is the baby's father and he wants her, as does his wife. The baby's mother does not want her. Mr and Mrs A are a couple in their 30s. They are devoted to each other. They are both professional people, highly qualified. They have a very nice home in the country and another in a town. Materially

---

[70]   *Re C* [1985] F.L.R. 846.
[71]   K. Cotton & D. Winn, *Baby Cotton: For Love and Money*, (London: Dorling Kindersley Publishers, 1985).

they can give the baby a very good upbringing. But, far more importantly, they are both excellently equipped to meet the baby's emotional needs. They are most warm, caring, sensible people, as well as highly intelligent. When the time comes to answer the child's questions, they will be able to do so with professional advice if they feel they need it. Looking at this child's well-being, physical and emotional, who better to' have her care? No one."

What is notable from this short extract is how again, despite the fact that she conceived the baby with the intention of giving her to the commissioning couple, the judge talks of the surrogate mother as the "natural mother" and the "baby's mother". This is of course consistent with the legal presumption at common law and the position following the 1990 Act but not with the intention of the parties nor the terminology used to describe her, the "surrogate". As Michelle Stanworth argues, the description of the gestational mother as "surrogate" denies the essential role she has in the creation of the child:

> "it is the involvement of a pregnant and birthing woman which makes the process of reproduction possible. And it is precisely the significance of her pregnancy which the terms of the discussion deny."[72]

De Cruz suggests that these surrogacy cases are consistent with the judicial consideration of cases on the determination of custody awards following divorce in terms of the way in which the parties, especially the surrogate, are described.[73] He suggests that the judgments in *A v. C* and *Re P* are consistent in the way that "maternal preference" and "preservation of the status quo" (where the child has remained with its mother since birth) feature as determining factors. The majority of the Supreme Court of California in *Johnson v. Calvert*[74] took a different approach to determining custody after surrogacy from that taken by the English courts. In that case the parties had entered into a contractual agreement following which an embryo created from the gametes of the commissioning couple, Mark and Crispina Calvert, had been implanted in the surrogate, Anna Johnson. Six months into the pregnancy, as a result of a deterioration in the relationship between the parties, both sought a declaration as to their parental rights. The majority of the Supreme Court dismissed the appeal from the Court of Appeal which had affirmed the decision of the trial court that the Calverts were the child's parents, that Anna Johnson had no parental rights and that the contract was enforceable:

[72] M. Stanworth, *supra*, n. 13 at p. 26.
[73] S. P. de Cruz, "Surrogacy, Adoption and Custody" (1988) 18 *Family Law* 100 at 105.
[74] *Johnson v. Calvert* (1993) 5 Cal. 4th 84.

Johnson v. Calvert
"Commentary" (1994) 2 Med. L. Rev. 239 at 240–241

"*Held*, . . .

1. Crispina Calvert was the child's 'natural mother' under California law.

(a)   The only Californian statute defining parental rights is the Uniform Parentage Act 1975, which was enacted to eliminate the legal distinction between legitimate and illegitimate children and to replace it with the concept of parentage. The legislation was never intended to govern surrogacy disputes, yet it facially applies to any parentage determination, including the rare case in which a child's maternity is in issue.

(b)   The Uniform Parentage Act recognises both genetic motherhood (as established by the results of blood tests) and gestational motherhood (as established by proof of having given birth to the child) as ways of establishing that a woman is a child's 'natural mother'. In the instant case, Crispina Calvert was the genetic mother and Anna Johnson the gestational mother, and each therefore had equal rights under the Uniform Parentage Act to be considered the child's natural mother.

(c)   For each child, however, California law accords the legal rights and responsibilities of parenthood to only one 'natural mother'. This is despite advances in reproductive technology which make it possible, as in the instant case, for the female biological role in reproduction to be divided between two women. It was therefore necessary for the court to make a choice between these two women.

(d)   *Per Panelli J. (Lucas C.J., Mosk, Baxter, George and Arabian JJ. concurring)*: When one woman is the genetic mother of a child and a different woman is its gestational mother, the issue of who is the child's 'natural mother' at law is to be resolved by enquiring into the parties' intentions as manifested in the surrogacy agreement. The woman who intended to procreate the child — she who intended to bring about the birth of a child whom she intended to raise as her own — is the natural mother under California law.

(i)   In the instant case, that woman was the genetic mother, Crispina Calvert. The parties' aim was to bring the Calverts' child into the world, not for the Calverts to donate their zygotes to Anna Johnson. Crispina Calvert from the outset and at all times intended to parent the child and raise it as her own. Although the gestational function performed by Anna Johnson was necessary to bring about the child's birth, she would not have been given the opportunity to do this had she, prior to implantation of the zygote, manifested her own intent to be the child's mother. There was no reason why Anna Johnson's late change of heart should vitiate the determination that Crispina Calvert was the child's natural mother.

(ii)   The instant case should be compared with a true 'egg donation' situation, where a woman gestates and gives birth to a child formed from the ovum of another woman with the intent to raise the child as her own. In such a case, the gestational mother and not the genetic mother would be the natural mother of the child under California law.

(e)   *Per Kennard J. (dissenting)*: It was inappropriate for the majority to rely on the 'intent' of the genetic mother as determinative of parental rights over a child born of a gestational surrogacy arrangement. A better way of resolving the issue is to ask which solution would be in the 'best interests' of the child.

(i)   The approach of the majority devalued the role of the gestational mother, who has, like the genetic mother, a substantial claim to be the natural mother of the child. The role of a woman who agrees to carry a fetus to term for the genetic mother is more than that of mere employment to perform a specified biological function. A pregnant woman's commitment to the fetus which she intends to carry to term is not just physical, it is also psychological and emotional. This commitment involves an assumption of parental responsibility no less than the genetic mother's intent to raise the child involves an assumption of parental responsibility. The gestational mother is a conscious agent of creation no less than the genetic mother.

(ii)   The majority's reliance on intent was also unsatisfactory because it constituted an endorsement of unregulated gestational surrogacy. It would permit enforcement of gestational surrogacy agreements without requiring any of the protections necessary to minimise the possibility of overreaching or abuse by a party with economic advantage.

(iii)   In examining the problems arising out of gestational surrogacy, a court is deciding the fate of a child. The analytic framework chosen by the majority — based on the concept of 'intent' — is inadequate to this task, because that framework is grounded in principles of tort, intellectual property and commercial contract law. The court should instead look to family law, in particular to child welfare law, and adopt the 'best interests of the child' test to determine who can best assume the social and legal responsibilities of motherhood for a child born of a gestational surrogacy arrangement. The intent of the genetic mother to procreate a child is certainly relevant to the question of the child's best interests; but it should not alone decide the matter."

The court held that under the California Civil Code incorporating the Uniform Parentage Act 1975, both the surrogate and the commissioning mother had presented evidence which could support a finding that either was the child's "natural mother" (the former by giving birth the latter by a blood test). The American Civil Liberties Union, acting as amicus, argued that the child had two legal mothers. This argument, which would have further challenged traditional norms regarding parenting, and which the description of the gestational mother as surrogate seeks to deny, was rejected by the court. It therefore had to choose between two legal claims. The majority held that the commissioning mother was the mother because the commissioning parents had had the intention to create a child which they could bring up. In the minority, Kennard J. rejected the reliance placed by the majority upon intention as inapplicable to the case under consideration. Whereas the concept of intention was used appropriately in the areas of "tort, intellectual property and commercial contract law", it was not appropriate to "family law". It failed, in his opinion, to reflect the psychological and emotional contribution of the surrogate which, like the intent of the commissioning couple, demonstrated an assumption of parental responsibility. Kennard J. preferred to determine the issue by the employment of the "best interests" test. Gillian Douglas explains that, despite increasing acknowledgement in English Law of social parenting, the approach taken by the majority of the Supreme Court will not be adopted by our courts, not only because of a distaste for surrogacy but also because of a continuing sense of importance in having children who are genetically related to ourselves. Vesting parental responsibility in accordance with intention to parent may have far-reaching consequences in terms of parenting because it challenges the present view of parenting as occurring within (and only within) a unit based upon two parents, one of whom is male and the other female. It might also erode the expectation that a woman will be the primary carer because of her ability to bear a child and the consequent limitation of women to this role:

G. Douglas
"The Intention to be a Parent and the Making of Mothers"[75]

"Intention is not usually recognised as being of significance in determining issues in Family Law. However, the trend in the law relating to parental status in both this country and others throughout this century has been to grant greater recognition to the *social* rather than the biological aspects of parenthood. Unlike biological parenthood which can occur without being planned and intended, social parenthood is an act of will (albeit that it may be done for a variety of reasons, ranging from the altruistic desire to provide a home for a needy child, to a grudging acceptance of a *felt* obligation to, say, a relative's child left orphaned by a car crash). The law provides a variety of means of accommodating the intention to assume social parenthood. For example, the law of adoption enables people not genetically related to a child to become her legal parents in order that they may act as her social parents. Adoption cannot take place without the prospective parents *applying* for an adoption order, *i.e.* manifesting their intention and desire to acquire parental status. An unmarried father who seeks to play a full role in his child's life must manifest that intention by either making an agreement with the child's mother, or by persuading a court that he has a contribution to make to the child justifying a parental responsibility order under section 4 of the Children Act 1989. Indeed, calls for such fathers to be granted automatic parental responsibility are based in part at least upon the view that weight should be given to their *desire* to act as social parents. The Human Fertilisation and Embryology Act 1990 enables those who wish to become social parents, but are unable to provide their own genetic material to do so, to acquire parental status if they procreate through assisted reproduction using donated gametes.

The Implications of Intention as the Determining Factor in Parentage

The California Court's reliance on intention may therefore be seen to be as much a recognition of its already established importance in forging a legal relationship between parent and child as an instance of breaking new ground. Nonetheless, it has potentially interesting consequences for our attitudes to parenthood and family formation in general. For instance, it has been argued that using intention in this way is a means of avoiding gender-based stereotypes and biologically-determined differences when determining issues of parenthood. While men and women cannot physically play the same role in the procreation of children, both can have the intention to become a parent. Giving weight to intention, rather than to biological roles, therefore provides a means to treat claims to parenthood equally, regardless of gender difference. On the other hand, it could be argued that focusing upon intention is very much a *male* approach to parenthood because it fits far more closely to men's experience of procreation than to that of most women. Just as the commissioning mother was unable to

---

[75]   (1994) 57 *Modern Law Review* 636 at 638–9, 640–641.

carry and give birth to her own child, so too was her husband; for men, *all* women who carry children are surrogates. Relying upon their intention to produce and raise a child is a very convenient way for men to assert their parentage over children . . .

If the intention to have and rear a child were to be the main criterion for legal parenthood, anyone who had this intention could seek out gamete donors and a surrogate and claim the 'product' of these people's labours when the child was born. This would render irrelevant the assumption that to be the parents of a particular child presupposes a relationship (sexual or not) of not more than two persons of different sex. There would be no reason why more than two people could not be recognised as 'parents,' nor why they should be of different sex . . .

Why, then, not take the more straightforward route of the California court and accept that the intention to act as parent should be the key indicator for parental status? The short answer is because of the disapproval of surrogacy as a form of assisted reproduction. English law views the gestational mother as the legal mother because this will produce the right result in terms of parentage for all cases except for surrogacy. Reliance on intent would also destroy the prohibitions on private adoption placements which underpin our adoption law. But underlying these restrictions is a deeper assumption. We still require, or at least prefer, some sort of biological link to a child, be it genetic *or* gestational, because we view children as in some way the physical recreations of their parents. We still refuse to face up to the reality of our acceptance of the importance of social parenthood — to an idea of parenthood as departing from the traditional, pseudo-biological model of two people of the opposite sex creating and rearing their offspring."

In his commentary on this case, Andrew Grubb makes the point that determining the issue on the basis of the intention of the parties amounts to making surrogacy contracts enforceable, as the intention of the parties upon entering into the arrangement will always be for parental rights and responsibilities to be vested in the commissioning couple.[76] This is contrary to the approach in the Surrogacy Arrangements Act 1985 and section 30. Whilst the intent test would result in parental responsibility always being invested in the commissioning couple, with the best interests test this is not a foregone conclusion:

Johnson v. Calvert
"Commentary" (1994) 2 Med. L. Rev. 239 at 243–244

"Commentary . . .
The Supreme Court did this because it considered that the child, on the face of it, had two mothers — a genetic and a gestational mother. The law could only, however, recognise one woman as the child's mother and so a choice had to be made. No doubt this makes sense and accords with conventional reproductive practice. It is particularly important if parentage is seen as determining (or is crucially linked to) the issue of who should care for the child and be responsible for the child's upbringing. The Supreme Court, of course, made this link — English law would [. . .] be much more circumspect about the linkage in 'gestational' surrogacy cases.

---

[76] (1994) 2 Med. L. Rev. 239 at 243.

The approach of the court is, however, not without its difficulties. First, it results *in effect* to an enforcement of the surrogate contract since it is the contract which will reflect the *parties'* intentions prior to the pregnancy being established. By definition the parties' intentions will be that the commissioning couple should bring up the child — that, after all, is what the whole exercise is about. The majority, therefore, do not allow for changes of mind and essentially stamp a contractual model upon the relationship between the surrogate and commissioning couple . . .

A second problem with the majority's approach is the linkage between legal parentage and the upbringing of the child. To do this determines *a priori* the issue of a child's 'best interests' on the basis of parental status. As a rule of thumb, of course, parents should be seen as the appropriate carers for their children. Any other rule would not comport with the broadly liberal political philosophies of America or England. But, such a rule is only a prima facie rule: there may be any number of situations where the rule is demonstrated not to provide the correct solution for a particular child. Indeed, given the context of surrogacy it could be argued that blindly to apply the rule is always dangerous. Each case must be considered individually to determine what is 'best' for the child. Of course, in practice the courts will most likely follow the intention of the parties where there is no disagreement but that is not the kind of case with which we, or the Supreme Court, are concerned. Where the parties no longer agree and a 'tug of war' occurs over the child's future why should the *original* intention of the parties (now in the past), determine the future upbringing of the child? . . .

[T]he 1990 Act only determines the *status* question of parentage and hence who will prima facie have 'parental responsibility' for any child under section 2 of the Children Act 1989. Neither the 1990 Act nor the Children Act provides any *a priori* rule of who will ultimately be *allocated* the care and upbringing of the child. If the issue arises before a court, parentage, while relevant, will always be subject to the 'welfare principle' in section 1 of the Children Act and hence an evaluation of the child's 'best interests'. It is difficult to see how the original 'intention of the parties' can have a significant impact on this issue.

Can it really be the case that a surrogate's decision to renege on an arrangement which is legally unenforceable and teeters on the brink of being contrary to public policy should count against her when determining the child's 'best interests'? Arguably, the contrary is the case. It may show a real commitment to the child's well-being and care which may be born of her experiences of pregnancy and birth. The relative circumstances of the surrogate and commissioning couple will be relevant though this tends to reinforce social stereotypes that material well-being (usually the commissioning couple's privilege) is important (see *In the Matter of Baby M* (1988) 537 A.2d 1227 (N.J. Sup.Ct.)). However, a surrogate who has demonstrated her ability to care for the child after its birth may yet be able to persuade a court that the child's 'best interests' lie with her as its social mother (see *e.g. Re P (Minors) (Wardship: Surrogacy)* [1987] 2 F.L.R. 421 (Arnold P.)). In *Johnson*, of course, the commissioning couple already had custody of the child and not the surrogate."

It may be the case that because of the circumstances, neither party wishes to care for the child born following a surrogacy arrangement. This was initially the position in the Michigan case of Stiver and Mallahoff. The child was born with microcephaly, (an abnormally small head which indicates mental difficulties). At first both the commissioning father and the surrogate mother rejected the child and the father initiated a claim against Judy Stiver for breach of contract (the surrogacy contract having prohibited her from engaging in sexual intercourse after (but not before) insemination). Blood tests established that Judy Stiver's husband was the baby's father whereupon the couple took care of it. Both Alexander Mallahoff and Judy Stiver initiated claims against the gynaecologists who had told her that she was not pregnant when she was inseminated.[77]

Surrogacy presents a challenge to dominant understandings about motherhood and the possibility of extending the parenting of children beyond the heterosexual couple. This potential was recognised in a note by Jonathan Montgomery discussing *Re C* and *A v. C*:

J. MONTGOMERY
"Constructing a Family — After a Surrogate Birth"[78]

"The two cases [*Re C* and *A v. C*] take a further decision to retain the existing conceptual tools of family law. Parenthood could have been defined more widely, so as to leave the children with more than two parents. However, the courts chose to uphold the model of the nuclear family as the most appropriate for child care ... If the courts approach the legal questions which follow a surrogate birth in this way it is difficult to argue that surrogacy undermines the family unit. But there is more than one understanding of the family available. Historically the law has built a paradigm of the family on a permanent relationship between one man and one woman to the exclusion of all other. This paradigm has an ontological unity derived from its religious origins and in the modern context has been reworked as a biological structure. The concept of family which the courts have used to determine parenthood in [surrogacy cases] is different. It is based on an understanding of the family as a social unit whose function is bringing up children. If this is the criterion the way is open for single parents, short-term relationships, even homosexual ones to claim the right to parenthood if scientific evidence can be adduced that their care of children is as good as any other."

It is interesting to compare the attitudes of Sir John Arnold P. and Ormrod L.J. in *Re P* and *A v. C* respectively to the nature of a surrogacy agreement and hence to the parties, particularly the women, who enter into such agreements.[78a]

Re P (Minors) (Wardship: Surrogacy)
[1987] 2 F.L.R. 421 at 424–425, *per* Sir John Arnold P.

"First of all, I should say something about the circumstance that there is here an underlying agreement. There was, as I have indicated, an agreement between the

---

[77] S. Downie, *supra*, n. 39 at p. 133.

[78] (1986) 49 *Modern Law Review* 635 at 641.

[78a] Eric Blyth suggests that the difference in judicial attitudes towards surrogacy identifiable in *A v. C* (1978) in comparison with *Re C* (1985), *Re Adoption Application* (1987) and *Re P* (1987) is due to a "shift in opinion over time". Over the course of the decade, he suggests, the "distaste for surrogacy [which] was clear" in the first case had tempered so that "subsequent judgements convey an altogether less antagonistic approach". E. Blyth, *supra*, n. 56 at 257.

mother and Mr B, not, I think, at all an agreement of which one of the terms was that care and control in a wardship context should be given to Mr B; the agreement foresaw an adoption by Mr B and Mrs B, but whatever the exact nature of the agreement was, the wardship jurisdiction is not one which is, or is ever, regulated by contract. It is a jurisdiction in which, as I have already indicated, the court's duty is to decide the case, taking into account as the first and paramount consideration, the welfare of the child or children concerned and if that consideration leads the court to override any agreement that there may be in the matter, then that the court is fully entitled to do. It is, therefore, not of great importance in this case to rule upon the validity, or otherwise, of the agreement which was made. One possible view about that matter is that there is, or may in certain circumstances be, an element concerning the surrogacy agreement which is repellent to proper ideas about the procreation of children, so as to make any such agreement one which should be rejected by the law as being contrary to public policy. It is not necessary in this case, for the reasons which I have indicated, to come to any conclusion upon that point. The existence of the agreement is relevant to this extent, that plainly one of the factors which has to be taken into account in determining where the welfare of the children lies, is the factor of the character of the rival custodians who were put forward for consideration and it might be that the willingess of those persons to enter into a surrogacy agreement would reflect upon their moral outlook so adversely as to disqualify them as potential custodians at all, but I do not think that that factor enters into the present case.

Mrs B's history was that she had had a pregnancy, which was unsuccessful, in that she did not carry the child to full term and was left with a uterine infection, a state of ill-health which was regarded by the adoption agency to which the B's applied to find a child to adopt, as disqualificatory of their selection as adoptive parents, so that at the stage at which the transaction between Mr B and Mrs P took place, which was in the late part of 1985, the position of the B's was that they dearly wanted a child, as Mr B expressed it in the witness-box, to complement their already strong marriage and Mrs P freely offered herself in the role of a surrogate mother and approached them for that purpose and I can see nothing shameful in Mr B in those circumstances entering into the arrangement which he did enter into and nothing in the fact that he was willing to enter into such an arrangement to show him in a character so disreputable as to disqualify him as a custodian for children. Nor does it seem to me that anything could be said of a significant nature against Mrs P because of her willingess to enter into such an arrangement. There is no doubt that she had a genuine conviction that by so doing she could help and confer a benefit on someone in the position of Mr and Mrs B who wanted, but were unable to have, a child and this was a part of her motivation and there is nothing in any way ignoble about that. The rest of it was a desire to confer security, principally upon her little boy E, who was then some seven years-old and without any very substantial support from his father, Mrs P and the boy otherwise subsisting on social security payments. She wanted the boy to have more advantages in life than were likely to stem from those circumstances and it was that which provided the incentive for that part of her motivation which involved financial ambitions and again there seems to me nothing ignoble about that, so that although there was this arrangement, or agreement, call it what one will, it does not seem to me in the circumstances of this case to have any decisive effect upon the outcome."

In this case the agreement is portrayed as one which everybody concerned entered into with the best of motives. In *A v. C*, the Court of Appeal removed from the commissioning (and genetic) father rights of access which had been given at first instance following the refusal of the surrogate to hand over the baby. In contrast with Sir John Arnold P.'s view of the agreement in *Re P* Ormrod L.J. in *A v. C* described the arrangement as, "a sordid commercial bargain" the primary instigator of which was the commissioning father who then involved his weak willed wife (for whom there was a degree of sympathy given her infertility) in the unpleasant arrangement:

A v. C
[1985] F.L.R. 453 at 454, *per* Ormrod L.J.

"The father, who is in a position to know very well how to behave, found himself in a position of some difficulty, because he was living, unfortunately for him, with a lady who, through no fault of her own, could not have any more children. He appears to have become obsessed with the idea that it was essential to his future happiness that he should be able to be the father of a child himself and have the pleasure and the privilege of bringing that child up as his own child. It is a state of mind which is very easy to understand and sympathize with. It is very unfortunate for both men and women when they find themselves in a situation where they are unable to have that very natural satisfaction.

The only difference between this father and the others is that the others try to accept it, whereas this father embarked upon the most extraordinarily naive plan to achieve his object — simply to find a woman who was prepared to be artificially impregnated with his semen to produce a baby which would then be handed over to him and the lady with whom he was living (and to whom he is now married) for adoption. It is a simple, logical, but totally inhuman proceeding, and shows, in my view, very grave defects in his character and, indeed, in the characters of all three participants, because the lady with whom he was living was definitely involved in the plan, no doubt now to her great regret. One can feel very sorry for her in that she must feel that it was her fault in a sense that the father was in the position in which he was, so that she felt obliged to help him and take part in this most extraordinary and irresponsible arrangement. It is unnecessary to make any more comment on the irresponsibility shown by all three of the adults in this case, which is perhaps only rivalled by the irresponsibility of the person who performed the insemination on the mother. Having said that, so far as the background is concerned, I do not propose to say any more about it."

In pursuit of his own ends, the father exploited a woman who was less in a position to know "how to behave". This woman, once pregnant, was naturally unable to keep to the agreement she had made:

A v. C
[1985] F.L.R. 453 at 455, *per* Ormrod L.J.

"I do not think that it will be useful to travel over this sad and miserable story any more. It is enough to say that the mother, at a fairly early stage in the pregnancy, began, quite naturally, to feel grave doubts about the course which she had embarked upon and by the time the child was born she had plainly made up her mind that she could not possibly go on with such a bizarre and unnatural arrangement and she forewent the substantial sum of money which she was to be paid in the event of her handing over the baby.

The judge has described the mother's situation and her background and the father's. It is quite apparent that there is a wide gulf socially and culturally between them and that the future contains nothing at all except bitterness for their future relationship. We are dealing here with two people who have never had any sort of relationship together at all, not even a relationship amounting to one single isolated act of intercourse taking place casually on some occasion and never to be repeated. Here we have nothing but the clinical fact that the father has contributed the necessary male sperm to the conception of this child. That is the sum total of his contribution to this child."

Cumming-Bruce L.J. agreed. He perceived the relationship to be exploitative of the surrogate, taking advantage of her position and her emotions:

A v. C
[1985] F.L.R. 453 at 459, *per* Cumming-Bruce L.J.

". . . What happened was that a girl aged 19, who manifestly at the time was already involved in considerable troubles, was procured by a man and a woman years older than herself to take part in a kind of baby-farming operation of a wholly distasteful and lamentable kind. The fact that the motives of the promotors, as seen through their spectacles, were fine motives designed to satisfy the father's eagerness for parenthood, is neither here nor there. The arrangement which they persuaded this girl of 19 to take part in was a guilty bargain which should never have been made and, before the baby was born, the mother was having second thoughts. After the baby was born, that operation of nature which is familiar in the case of a good many mothers came to life with the baby, and the mother from that moment was determined not to part from her little boy. She was faced with a terribly upset father because she tried to back out of the arrangement."

Thus motherhood is presented as the primary female objective, a classic illustration of Michelle Stanworth's point that motherhood is "the natural, desired and ultimate goal of all 'normal' women," so that "women who deny their maternal instincts are selfish, peculiar or disturbed."[79] In this view the woman who permits a surrogate to bear a child on her behalf is deserving of our pity for the lengths to which she will go to attain the status of mother but also deserving of our condemnation for asking another woman to bear a child and then relinquish it. She takes her pursuit of this ideal to such extremes that she is asking the impossible of another woman. The commissioning mother in *A v. C* was, like her husband, "unstable, unreliable, unsuitable and obsessive",[80]

---

[79] M. Stanworth, *supra*, n. 13 at p. 15.
[80] *A v. C, supra*, n. 69 at 456.

deserving of our pity because of both her infertility and her lack of will in refusing to get involved. That she could ask another woman to deny her maternal instincts and give up to her the child she had carried was demonstrative of the lengths to which she would go for her own selfish needs. The woman who agrees to bear a child for another is portrayed as weak, manipulated and naive about the strengths of her natural maternal feeling. It can be no surprise when she finds herself unable to keep to the bargain she foolishly made. The surrogate in *A v. C*, whilst irresponsible for entering into such an agreement, is portrayed as having made a mistake for which she should not be required to pay for the rest of her life. Breaking ties with the commissioning father would enable her to "marry and have a family" providing for this child "a reasonably normal life". It was inevitable because of the "close physical bond between mother and child which tends to get closer from the time of birth onwards for some considerable time" that she would not be able to give up her child.[81] The legal construction of Woman, the ideal Mother, is apparent in these cases, bonding with her child at or before birth she will forgo the promise of money and subject herself to further financial hardship to be mother to her own.

4.2.ii *Surrogate motherhood: paid work or prostitution?*
The approach taken to the regulation of surrogacy in the Surrogacy Arrangements Act 1985 suggests that the principal objections to surrogacy are the payment of a woman to bear a child and the consequences for this child who is, on one view, paid for. Prior to the 1985 Act surrogacy arrangements may have operated within the free market, women offering their services to fulfil a demand and receiving remuneration for their work. Rather than regulating the practice of surrogacy in the public realm, as a legitimate form of employment providing protection to parties entering into an agreement, the Surrogacy Arrangements Act 1985 limits surrogacy to the unregulated private sphere. In so doing the Act prevents the value of women's work in reproduction being acknowledged:

D. MORGAN
"Making Motherhood Male: Surrogacy and the Moral Economy of Women"[82]

"The concept of the market defines an important aspect of a 'public' sphere of social existence, and it contrasts with the 'private' realm of domesticity and personal relations, in which family life is seen as a matrix of purely private arrangements, construed as the result of individual freedom and choice. The public realm is associated with conceptions of individuality, purposive action and rationality. The echoes of this distinction are audible in the voices of men and women, who speak of different truths,

---

[81] *Ibid*, at 457.
[82] (1985) 12 *Journal of Law and Society* 219 at 230–232.

'[men] of the role of separation as it defines and empowers the self, [women] of the ongoing process of attachment that creates and sustains the human community.' The realms of the public and the privated exist in a relationship of mutual presupposition and exclusion and the nature of each is determined by what it excludes. The market is male and the home is where the women are; 'what has happened has not been a simple exclusion of women, but a constitution of femininity through that exclusion ... Femininity has been constructed through exclusion, as a necessary "complement" to maleness.'

Poole argues that the triad of characteristics which identify a market economy, the individual, the social division of labour and private ownership, and the social relations which they constitute, presuppose a sphere of social life in which the individuals who participate in the market are themselves produced and reproduced. To make sense of the apparent sacrifice of self-interest involved in order to produce, nurture and care for other self-interested individuals requires the assumption of goods of a quite different kind to those involved in ordinary market transactions. 'To comprehend the social processes here, we need also to suppose that there are human relationships ... which are conceptually distinct from the contractual and voluntary engagements for mutual benefit typical of the market.' I suggest that it is the 'ethic of responsibility,' identified by Carol Gilligan, which activates these engagements and lies at the centre of women's moral concern, and that it is men's fear of the abandonment of this ethic which has motivated the present responses to surrogacy. Legal, medical and more generally social ideology have figured women at the core of personal, domestic life. Whereas with the emergence of capitalism, women became increasingly involved in wage labour and the production of goods for exchange, the consequence of the split of material production between its socialised forms and private labour performed predominantly by women within the home, was that this homework was denied social recognition and hence value. The bourgeois class then used the theory that women's moral influence would temper the savagery of capitalist competition to assuage its guilt and soothe its tensions. It is the need to underline and confirm these distinctions which has informed the canonical parliamentary handling of the Surrogacy Bill, an example of what Lesley Doyal has called the 'subterranean and more subtle aspects of the social control of women.'

The methodology has its precursors. On one view, surrogate mothers might be thought to be confounding the domestic imagery in which they are swaddled, symbolically casting off some forms of social control by taking their singular reproductive function into the market place. The Surrogacy Bill, like the Contagious Diseases legislation of the nineteenth century, is then used to legitimate control over them. This is consistent with the sexual stereotype through which the law views women, confining their proper sphere of sexuality to bearing their husband's children. This, of course, has a dual aspect, that of bearing children, and that of bearing nobody's children but their husband's. As soon as the reproductive facility can be asserted as a strength as well as a means of enforcing weakness, then the law is on hand to turn the world the right way up again. As Lesley Doyal has argued, the development of reproductive technology has, for women, been a contradictory process. While technically it has increased the capacity of women to control their own bodies, it has also increased the capacity of others — especially male medical technocrats — to exercise control over women's lives. The notion that reproduction belongs to women takes on a new dynamic with the ability to reproduce without the need of patriarchal genetics. This, I think, is part of the most fundamental threat to male hegemony and the construction of patriarchy which the reproduction revolution represents. It suggests that men, in their bodily incarnation, are dispensable, for procreation as well as recreation.

Whereas scientific and technical housecraft and child-rearing were used to 'fill the vacuum left by the removal of paid employment once the munitions demands of the' second world war were satisfied or over' there is now a significant reversal. Surrogacy presages a technological moral panic which heralds forth the resurrection of magic and mystique. The 'incongruity of market notions and babies' is remarked because it might fracture the special relationship of women with babies, mediated through their bodies. It is this which enables men to avoid equal responsibility for childcare, ensure differential employment opportunities and to reproduce patterns of income inequality which ensure that women remain a form of 'economic pariah,' not just on individual men but in the ideology of family life and the moral economy of women. Motherhood thus presents a very real dilemma to women who do not wish to become dependent on men but who cannot earn enough to work and pay for child care alone. This 'coincides with the material manifestation of women's inferior economic position, but it also coincides with the resurrection of the significance of marriage,' such that motherhood 'entails economic dependency or poverty' for the vast majority of women.

Surrogacy, bringing as it does, market notions towards reproduction, requires the recognition of the capitalist value of women's work. This would force a revaluation of the care and concern for others, an overriding commitment to relationships and responsibilities, with which women's moral strength has been characterized:

> 'Women's place in man's life cycle has been that of nurturer, caretaker and helpmate, the weaver of those networks of responsibility on which she in turn relies. But while women have thus taken care of men, men have, in their theories of psychological development, as in their economic arrangements, tended to assume or devalue that care.'"

Derek Morgan suggests that the Surrogacy Arrangements Act 1985 continues the social control of women, reinforcing the understanding that a woman should bear her husband's child and only his child, and that she should not receive, nor expect, payment for it. He suggests that men, individually and collectively, have a lot to lose from surrogacy. Tying women to motherhood keeps women out of the public realm and in the home where they undertake work. This work is necessary to enable men to function adequately in the public sphere, but is ultimately devalued by them. Derek Morgan notes how male control over reproduction may be extended by medical developments in human reproduction and the legal regulation of those developments. In this analysis, surrogacy extends male control over women beyond that exercised within the marital relationship. Fertility treatments and surrogacy mean that parts of other women's bodies can be used in the creation of a child, in the way that parts of the bodies of prostitutes are used for sex and then discarded. Andrea Dworkin, in *Right-wing Women*, identifies a "brothel" model and a "farming" model to portray the alternatives for women under patriarchy:

A. Dworkin
Right-wing Women[83]

"There are two models that essentially describe how women are socially controlled and sexually used: the brothel model and the farming model.

The brothel model relates to prostitution, narrowly defined; women collected together for the purposes of sex with men; women whose function is explicitly non-reproductive, almost anti-reproductive; sex animals in heat or pretending, showing themselves for sex, prancing around or posed for sex.

The farming model relates to motherhood, women as a class planted with the male seed and harvested; women used for the fruit they bear, like trees; women who run the gamut from prized cows to mangy dogs, from highbred horses to sad beasts of burden . . .

In the brothel model, the woman is acknowledged to be for sex without reference to reproduction . . . [T]he women are held to a strictly sexual standard of behaviour and accountability; they sell themselves for sex, not to make babies. They do what men want them to do for money that men pay them and that then they usually turn over to a man. Women are defined strictly with reference to sex and they are defined unfailingly without reference to personality or individuality or human potential; they are used without reference to anything but sex orifices and sex class and sex scenes. In the brothel model, several women belong to one man or in some cases are supervised by an older woman who is herself accountable to a rich man or men. The job of the women is to bring in — to a man or to a house — a certain amount of money by servicing a certain number of men. They sell parts of their bodies — vagina, rectum, mouth; and they also sell acts — what they say and what they do . . .

Before the advent of any reproductive technologies, the farming model used to be very distinct from the brothel model. Even though the woman was not human — the land — or was less than human — a cow — farming had the symbolic overtones of old-fashioned agrarian romance; plowing the land was loving it, feeding the cow was tending it. In the farming model, the woman was owned privately; she was the home-stead, not a public thoroughfare. One farmer worked her. The land was valued because it produced a valuable crop; and in keeping with the mystique of the model itself, sometimes the land was real pretty, special, richly endowed; a man could love it . . .

[However, b]oth the farming model and the brothel model dispose of women as women: they are paradigms for the mass use of a whole class; in both there is no humanity for women. The brothel model has been efficient. It uses the women in it until they are used up . . . The farming model has always been relatively inefficient. It is sloppier. Picking a woman who lives in the home with the man on a continuing basis is harder. Picking a woman who can and will have children is harder. There is more leeway for her attitudes to interfere. She has ways of saying no or subverting male sexual and reproductive intentions. The brothel model simply requires that the women under it be women: it does not matter who they are or what they are like or where they come from or what they think; they get worn down fast by being used the same way and being reduced to the same common denominator; nothing is necessary except that they be female. The farming model requires the constant application of force (explicit or implicit, usually a nice combination), incentive, reward; and a lot of plain luck with respect to fertility and reproductive vigor."

---

[83] (London: The Women's Press, 1983), pp. 174–186.

Dworkin explains how motherhood now approximates prostitution. Juliette Zipper and Selma Sevenhuijsen summarise the argument thus:

J. ZIPPER & S. SEVENHUIJSEN
"Surrogacy: Feminist Notions of Motherhood Reconsidered"[84]

"Because the traditional 'model' of mothering (labelled by Dworkin 'the farming model') does not work any more for the system of male domination, patriarchy extends 'the brothel model' to biological reproduction. In this model, parts of the body (for example, eggs) can be sold and women can be used, tortured and thrown away; the impulse to use women in this way is presented as the essence of maleness. Applying the brothel model to biological reproduction brings advantages for patriarchy, because it disposes of women as women, who as a result of feminism have become a threat to the stable continuation of male supremacy."

This is particularly so in the case of surrogacy. Hence, Andrea Dworkin criticises the defence of surrogacy in terms of the freedom of women to use their bodies as they choose. She argues that this freedom is so rigorously defended because it enables males to obtain the products of reproduction without the responsibilities:

A. DWORKIN
Right-wing Women[85]

"Women can sell reproductive capacities the same way old-time prostitutes sold sexual ones but without the stigma of whoring because there is no penile intrusion . . . does the state have a right to interfere with this exercise of individual female will (in selling use of the womb)? if a woman wants to sell the use of her womb in an explicit commercial transaction, what right has the state to deny her this proper exercise of femininity in the marketplace? Again, the state has constructed the social, economic, and political situation in which the sale of some sexual or reproductive capacity is necessary to the survival of women; and yet the selling is seen to be an act of individual will — the only kind of assertion of individual will in women that is vigorously defended as a matter of course by most of those who pontificate on female freedom. The state denies women a host of other possibilities, from education to jobs to equal rights before the law to sexual self-determination in marriage; but it is state intrusion into her selling of sex or a sex-class — specific capacity that provokes a defense of her will, her right, her individual self — defined strictly in terms of the will to sell what is appropriate for females to sell."

This raises the question whether surrogacy can be defended as the right of women as self-determining, autonomous individuals to use their bodies as they choose or, given the existing inequalities in power between men and

---

[84] In M. Stanworth (ed.), *supra*, n. 13 at pp. 124–125.
[85] A. Dworkin, *supra*, n. 83 at p. 182.

women, whether the decision to act as a surrogate can ever be a free choice. Susan Ince offered herself as a potential surrogate in North America in order to investigate the safeguards, pressures and protections in this unregulated industry:

S. INCE
"Inside the Surrogate Industry"[86]

"The language and process encountered in my experience within a surrogate company is consistent with the reproductive prostitution model described by Dworkin. The surrogate is paid for 'giving the man what his wife can't'. She 'loves being pregnant', and is valued solely and temporarily for her reproductive capacity. After she 'enters the fold' she is removed from standard legal protections and is subject to a variety of abuses. She is generally considered to be mercenary, collecting large unearned fees for her services, but the terms of the system are in reality such that she may lose more permanent opportunities for employment, and may end up injured or dead with no compensation at all. Even the glowing descriptions of the surrogates sound remarkably like a happy hooker with a heart of gold."

If surrogacy is like prostitution in that they both involve the exploitation of a woman who uses her body for financial gain, should the law be used to prevent women from participating in either activity?[87] The comparisons which Derek Morgan has made between prostitution and surrogacy were noted at the beginning of this section. He suggests that the approach taken by the law to both (forms of labour?) is such as to ensure that they occur out of the public view, thereby exposing the parties involved to the dangers of unregulated activity. Shelley Roberts considers surrogacy as a form of employment. Rather than drawing a comparison with prostitution (or other forms of female employment) she suggests that the nature of the work (undertaken for 24 hours a day, which cannot be terminated, and with limitations imposed as to diet, alcohol consumption and activity) means that slavery is a more appropriate comparison:

S. ROBERTS
"Warnock and Surrogate Motherhood: Sentiment or Argument?"[88]

"It has been suggested by some feminists that the advent of paid surrogacy has at last given recognition to the important work done by mothers and has legitimised

---

[86] In R. Arditti, R. Duelli Klein & S. Minden (eds), *Test-Tube Women. What future for motherhood?* (London: Pandora Press, 1984), p. 115.

[87] Although not discussing the prostitution analogy, Michael Freeman in "Is surrogacy exploitative?" in S. A. M. McLean (ed.), *Legal Issues in Human Reproduction* (Aldershot: Gower, 1989) concludes that surrogacy neither exploits nor dehumanises women.

[88] In P. Byrne (ed.), *Rights and Wrongs in Medicine* (King Edward's Hospital Fund for London) (Oxford: Oxford University Press, 1986), pp. 89–90.

childbearing as an occupation. Certainly, the receipt of payment for tasks of hardship and risk is not prima facie deemed so exploitative as to render it illegal. Our country permits (even conscripts) young men to act as fighter pilots in wartime. Society recruits and the law allows miners, construction workers and trawlermen to work in occupations which may drain them of their vitality. There are specific provisions for 'danger pay' in numerous forms of employment. In at least some of these cases, the employees may have taken the jobs as a matter of last resort, unable to find work elsewhere.

To the argument that there is a social benefit attached to many high-risk occupations, childless couples would certainly argue that surrogates perform an equally noble service. Furthermore, even the 'profession' of prostitution, which many would consider both dangerous and of dubious social value, is permitted to continue, albeit under restricted conditions. Thus, if surrogacy can be classified as employment and the risks have been accepted by the women involved, it seems on one argument that the practice may not be deemed exploitative in general, or at least no more so than others permitted by law.

But is surrogate motherhood really a form of employment? Some of its features would suggest that it is not. Unlike most jobs, it does not prevent the surrogate from holding other positions contemporaneously. There are no specific tasks to perform (aside from the crucial 'passive' presence of the surrogate at the time of insemination and delivery). Furthermore, the requirements imposed upon a surrogate as a consequence of the agreement all relate to aspects of life ordinarily considered to be outside the ambit of employer — employee relations, and, if part of a contract, many might even be illegal. The surrogate is 'on duty' 24 hours a day, every day. There is no possibility of terminating the employment (without incurring criminal, or at least moral sanctions by having an abortion). The commissioning couple seeks to assert control not over work, but over aspects of personal life such as diet, medical care, sexual relations, the ingestion of alcohol and tobacco and even psychological attitude (not forming a bond with the child is one of the covenants included in some surrogacy agreements). Thus, such an agreement does not seem to be employment, as we know it, but rather something akin to slavery."

Lorraine M. Harding notes the comparison frequently made between prostitution and surrogacy and suggests that an alternative comparison, and one which does not carry the same moral overtones as prostitution, is that a surrogacy agreement is a gift relationship. This enables the decision to act as a surrogate to be seen either as prompted by altruism or as a reciprocal benefit rather than as the exploitation of the economically and morally impoverished:

L. M. HARDING
"The Debate on Surrogate Motherhood: The Current Situation, Some Arguments and Issues; Questions Facing Law and Policy"[89]

"Surrogacy has been compared with prostitution for obvious reasons. Both appear to be an arrangement in which a woman 'sells her body' in a way deemed more intimate and somehow more morally problematic than, say, the selling of muscle power as

---

[89]   [1984] *Journal of Social Welfare and Family Law* 37 at 59–60.

labour in return for a wage. Questions centre partly on what the sexual and reproductive organs are thought to be *for*, and whether exchanging their use for money is compatible with their assumed purpose. If the Christian view, for example, is that the use of the sexual and reproductive parts of the body is essentially an adjunct to marriage, and must be confined to marriage, then it is easy to see why the Church might reject surrogate motherhood. From a feminist perspective, an objection might be that both prostitution and surrogacy depend on women trading specifically female aspects of their biology, and the danger is that women's sexual and reproductive abilities will be emphasised to the detriment of their other abilities and potentialities. It may reasonably be argued that women turn to both prostitution and surrogate motherhood when other means of earning a livelihood are denied them, because of their lack of skills and qualifications, and because labour markets and other social systems are structured in such a way as to prevent them selling their labour in other ways in order to earn a reasonable living. (It seems clear, for example, that part of Kim Cotton's motivation was that she needed to earn some extra money but was tied to the house with small children and lacked qualifications and marketable skills.) But the use of prostitution and surrogacy as means of earning money may also serve to reinforce women's disadvantage in other economic activities, and to reinforce the view of women as having primarily a sexual and reproductive function in relation to society as a whole. There may then be clear pressures on women to engage in these arrangements in order to support themselves. For example, if prostitute, surrogate mother, or for that matter striptease artist, became simply another job which women could and should do as an alternative to being supported by the state, a woman who was 'signing on' as available for work could be threatened with loss of benefit if she did not apply for, or keep, such a job.

Even in situations less extreme than this there is a fear that women — in particular poor women — may be exploited by paid surrogacy arrangements in a way similar to, though probably more severe than, exploitation by paid arrangements for sex. Pregnancy and birth, like sexual intercourse, carry certain physical and emotional risks. It may be held that no woman should undertake such risks as a result of economic pressure. It may also be speculated that if women had genuine economic security, both prostitution and surrogate motherhood would 'wither away' because no woman would volunteer for these tasks. This however raises the next question, which is the *non*-economic motivation to become a surrogate mother.

An alternative view of surrogate motherhood is to see it, not as a form of prostitution, in the sense of a commercial exploitation of female biology, but as a 'gift relationship' between the surrogate and the commissioning couple. Titmuss used the term 'gift relationship' in relation to the donation of blood made, not in exchange for money, but as a free gift so that unknown others — strangers — in need might be helped. Examining the stated motivations of blood donors, however, Titmuss found that pure altruism, simply the desire to help others, was not the only element; a sense of actual or anticipated reciprocity was also present in some responses — some voluntary donors had themselves received transfusions, or their relatives had, or the donors thought that they or their relatives might need blood in the future. Some donors responded to appeals; some became aware of the need through the war or witnessing accidents; and a small number saw blood donation as an expression of gratitude for good health. A parallel here might be a surrogate who feels a sense of gratitude for her own children.

The most obvious analogy with blood donation in the reproductive field might be the donation of semen, although in fact this is usually paid for. There may be an element of reciprocity here where the fertile husbands of wives who have been treated for infertility agree to be donors. But the 'donation' of nine months of pregnancy followed by the rigours of birth and recovery afterwards would seem to be a rather different order of gift from both blood donation and semen donation — and one unlikely to involve reciprocity. In which case a woman who 'gives' these experiences for no material gain, as Mary Stewart did, might well be admired for her generosity and altruism. Surrogate mothers have spoken of their view of surrogacy as a gift — of love or of life. And it might be argued that even a payment of £6,500, as was made to Kim Cotton, is something of an underpayment for nine months 'work,' given the hazards, discomforts and pain. The element of gift or altruism may be argued to remain. (Nevertheless it should be remembered that both Kim Cotton and 'Kirsty Stevens' made much money from publishing their stories.)

The concepts of prostitution and gift relationship carry very contrasting moral overtones, and yet may be used to describe the same process or arrangement. The appropriateness of either concept depends on the analysis made of the various elements in the surrogacy situation, in particular: exploitation (not forgetting that the commissioning couple as well as the surrogate may be exploited); the economic position of women and its effects on their search for suitable remunerated work; the motivation for undertaking surrogacy; and the social contexts deemed desirable for the activities of sex and reproduction."

Is organ donation a more appropriate comparison than prostitution? Shelley Roberts compares surrogacy with the donation of renewable bodily fluids such as blood or sperm and with organs which cannot be donated because it would result in bringing life to an end such as the heart or liver. She suggests that the use of the womb for the period of a pregnancy — what she considers to be the lease of the womb for nine months — fits into the category of donation that is only acceptable if taken gratuitously such as the donation of a kidney.[90]

S. ROBERTS
"Warnock and Surrogate Motherhood: Sentiment or Argument?"[91]

"[I]f we find it completely acceptable to think of a woman offering her physical and mental strength to serve as a nurse in the care of a newborn baby, why not simply extend the idea backward in time and allow for what can be called pre-natal nannies?

The answer may lie in the nature of what surrogacy involves. It is a complete, albeit temporary, disposal of part of one's body. It is arguable that there ought to be a distinction made between body material that can be sold, tissue that can only be donated and organs that may not even be given away. The law is clear as regards the last group. There are certain organs without which a person cannot survive, such as the heart and liver. Their removal cannot be rendered permissible by consent and would be considered a crime. Were it technically possible, we would also baulk at the donation of hands or feet, even though these are not indispensable to life.

The first category would arguably comprise renewable material, such as blood and sperm, as regards which the extraction process is relatively harmless and painless. This

---

[90]   The Human Organ Transplants Act 1989 makes it a criminal offence to give or receive payment for an organ for transplant.

[91]   In P. Byrne (ed.), *supra*, n. 88 at pp. 90–91.

leaves the intermediate group, where donation is allowed, but commercialisation is arguably contrary to public policy. In this category might be found such body tissue as kidneys, skin and bone marrow.

Can the sale of a womb, or rather its nine-month lease, be categorised within one of these headings? As regards the matter of nine months, it seems to make little difference to distinguish between permanent and temporary dispositions of tissue. We would disallow the lease of a heart on the same grounds that we forbid its outright sale or donation. Similarly, we would probably allow a kidney to be borrowed temporarily, but question the commercial lending of the organ for reward, were such a procedure medically feasible. If the functioning capacities of these organs could be borrowed without actual removal from the body, it is suggested that this would make no difference to the analysis.

What, then, of surrogacy? Surrogate motherhood contemplates the temporary borrowing of a womb's physiological capabilities, such that they cannot be used by the woman in whose body the womb is situated, but it does not involve the removal of the organ. Such a disposition of the womb would not be so severe as to result in death or serious impairment, provided all went well. Thus, borrowing a womb does not fall into the third category, which would make it always unlawful. The first category of tissue use, however, seems equally inappropriate, as surrogacy could certainly not be characterised as a harmless or painless procedure. Thus, it seems that the intermediate position is indicated. Society will permit a gratuitous donation, but ought to condemn the sale, lease, or other exchange of the womb for money."

The comparison with organ donation assumes the use of the womb in the development of the foetus as the employment of a body part without affecting the mind of the pregnant woman. It sees the womb as an incubator ignoring the connection between the woman and the developing foetus and the active role the woman plays during pregnancy.[92]

Whether the comparison looks to employment or the donation of organs, the question arises as to whether or not the law should provide for or prevent the payment of surrogates. As a form of labour or the donation of the use of her body, should a woman not be adequately recompensed for carrying a child for another? The Surrogacy Arrangements Act 1985 does not rule out payment of the surrogate mother. However, section 30(7) of the Human Fertilisation and Embryology Act 1990 may limit payment. Before making a parental order the court must be satisfied that no money has changed hands other than expenses reasonably incurred, unless authorised by the court. This leaves open the question of what would be covered by "expenses", and whether the court will be willing to authorise

---

[92]   G. Corea, "Surrogate Motherhood: Happy Breeder Woman", *supra*, n. 54. The comparison with organ donation was accepted by the Court of Appeal of Paris in *Procureur Général v. Madame X* which permitted the adoption of a child following a surrogacy arrangement (in French Law organ donations are legal if they are not performed in exchange for money). The *Cour de Cassation* quashing the decision of the Court of Appeal of Paris rejected this comparison (Cass. Ass. Plénière May 31, 1991 J.417). For a discussion of surrogacy in French Law see E. Steiner, "Surrogacy Agreements in French Law" (1992) 41 *International and Comparative Law Quarterly* 866. Surrogacy arrangements have since been criminalised in France by Law no. 94–653 of July 29, 1994.

payment beyond reasonable expenses. In *Re Q (Parental Order)*,[93] Johnson J. authorised payment of £8,280, £3,280 to cover clothes, medical expenses and child care provision (expenses) and £5,000 to cover loss of earnings. Authorising the payment of these sums retrospectively he looked to the reasoning of Latey J. in *Re Adoption Application*.[94] This reasoning would, in any event, be applicable in cases where adoption rather than a parental order is sought. It is an offence contrary to section 57 of the Adoption Act 1976 to give or receive payment in relation to the adoption of a child, the grant of consent to adoption, or handing over a child with a view to adoption, unless payment is authorised by the court.

In *Re Adoption Application*, Latey J. considered whether the offence of "payment or reward ... for adoption" had been committed contrary to section 50 of the Adoption Act 1958 (section 57 of the 1976 Act not then being in force). The parties wanted to abide by the arrangement whereby conception had taken place by sexual intercourse and the commissioning couple had agreed to pay the surrogate £10,000 to compensate her for loss of earnings, expenses and "emotional and physical factors". She accepted £5,000 before the birth and handed the baby over but turned down the balance because she had made money from the book she wrote of her experiences.[95] The commissioning couple sought to acquire parental rights by adoption. Latey J. held that the payments were not to procure her consent to adoption but were expenses to recompense for her time and inconvenience. Even if they amounted to illegal payments he had the power to ratify them retrospectively. Presumably, Latey J. interpreted the provisions and the facts in this way in order to uphold an arrangement which had worked and to enable the child to remain with parents who had provided a loving, caring and stimulating environment for the child almost since birth. The discussion of the facts of this case in the judgment of Latey J. are set out in full below as the attitude which is revealed in his narrative is indicative of the approach he takes to the question of payment (it also serves as a further comparison with the cases of *Re P* and *A v. C* set out above):

Re Adoption Application
[1987] 3 W.L.R. 31 at 31–38, *per* Latey J.

"Mr and Mrs A apply to adopt a little child, now aged 2 years and 4 months. The child's mother (whom I shall call 'the mother') is Mrs B. The child was conceived as a result of a surrogacy arrangement, as it is described, between Mr and Mrs A and Mrs B and her husband, Mr B. As a result of that arrangement Mr A and Mrs B had sexual intercourse on a few occasions and in due course the child was conceived. It was

[93] *Re Q (Parental Order)* (1996) 4 Med. L. Rev. 207.
[94] *Re Adoption Application, supra,* n. 59.
[95] K. Stevens, *Surrogate Mother: One Woman's Story* (London: Century, 1985).

in no sense a love affair. It was physical congress with the sole purpose of procreating a child. As soon as there was conception intercourse ceased.

What led up to this arrangement was this: Mr and Mrs A are a devoted couple. To complete and fulfil their union they dearly wanted a child. For medical reasons Mrs A was and is unable to have a baby. They did everything they could with medical help and advice, including surgery, to overcome this but to no avail. They then tried to adopt a child both in this country and abroad, again to no avail. As to this country, the principal reason given was their ages. This is surprising. At that time Mr A was barely 40, and Mrs A in her mid-30s, well within the normal age of parenthood, I would have thought. Another and subsidiary reason may have been that it was their second marriage, each having been divorced. But there is no doubt that their marriage is solid and stable, especially now that they have the baby, or toddler as it now is.

Then they heard a radio programme, and Mrs A saw a television programme, about surrogacy. They saw it as their last chance.

In the meanwhile, Mr and Mrs B had two children of their own. They decided at that time to have no more (though recently they have had a third child). Mrs B is one who enjoys pregnancy despite sickness and backache. She too heard, saw and read about surrogacy. She was deeply and genuinely moved about the plight of childless couples. There is no question about her sincerity about this. After much thought she decided to embark on this path. She discussed it with her husband, who was not, at first, enthusiastic but acquiesced and later supported her.

She put an advertisement in a magazine. Mr and Mrs A saw it and answered it. They met and the arrangement was made. Finance entered into it and this aspect of it is at the heart of whether an adoption order can be made in this case and, if it can be, whether it should be made. This is because of the terms of certain statutory enactments which I will come to shortly.

The mother, Mrs B, was in full-time employment. She and her husband's joint income enabled them and their children to live in comfort. If she became pregnant it would mean giving up her job and earnings. It would mean incurring other expenses. She had responses from other couples — one couple in particular who offered a very large sum of money. This was not what she wanted.

She agreed with Mr and Mrs A to act as a surrogate mother because as she says:

> 'I wanted to help a childless couple. My own children are very precious to me and I sympathised greatly with any couple who were unable to have children of their own, so much so that I was willing to have another pregnancy in order to give someone else that joy.'

She wanted a couple with whom she could be friendly, empathise, have a rapport. She and Mr and Mrs A found each other and she declined the others, including the couple offering the very large sum.

The two couples agreed a global sum of £10,000. The mother says:

> 'The money represented only my loss of earnings, expenses in connection with the pregnancy, and emotional and physical factors. I emphasise that I did not go into the arrangements for commercial reasons, nor did I accept the money to hand [the child] over. I would have done that in any event. In fact, overall, I was marginally worse off. This does not bother me since my motive was not financial.'

In his report the child's *guardian ad litem* says:

> 'The mother does *not* appear to have been primarily motivated in entering
> into the arrangements by financial considerations. She appears to have felt
> strongly that through a surrogacy arrangement she could offer an important
> service to a childless couple and to have regarded the money mainly as the
> equivalent of compensation for the loss of earnings while pregnant . . . Her
> interest in surrogacy the mother attributes to a particular pleasure she has in
> having babies and a great sympathy for women who are unable to experience
> the joy of having and caring for a baby. The public discussions and debates
> she heard about this subject struck a special chord for her, thus her initiative
> in advertising herself.'

I have heard the mother speak about this in her evidence. I am left in no doubt that it
is the plain, unvarnished truth.

Mr and Mrs A paid £1,000 when she was some months pregnant, and £4,000
shortly after the baby was born. The balance of £5,000 was due some months later,
but the mother refused to accept it. This was because she and a professional writer as
co-author wrote a book: 'Surrogate Mother. One Woman's Story,' from which she
made money. That book has been put in as part of the material in this case. It was
written pseudonymously and with care to conceal the identity of the child and those
connected with the child. I have tried to do the same in this judgment. In the interest
of the child nothing must be published which might point to the child's identity with
serious consequences to the child later in life, if it were publicly known. Mr and Mrs
A's close circle know the facts. They accept and love the child. Mr and Mrs A are very
intelligent people who adore the child. They have already worked out what and when
they are going to tell the child, and done so admirably, as it seems to me. But for any
public publicity to happen about this child as it grows up would certainly damage its
emotional development and might be disastrous.

If the word 'commercial' has any bearing on what has to be decided in this case and
if it connotes a profit or financial reward element there was nothing commercial in
what happened. There was no written contract or agreement; no lawyers were consulted until after the baby was born. The arrangement was one of trust which was
fully honoured on both sides.

The rest of the history can be told briefly. The child was born in hospital with Mrs
A present at the birth and Mr A joining them almost immediately. Two days later the
mother and child went to Mr and Mrs A's home. The four of them spent a week
together. The mother went back to her own home. Mr and Mrs A and the child have
been together since. The child has thrived. The three of them have been and are
supremely happy. The mother and Mr and Mrs A have kept in contact. The mother
and Mr B have had a third child. They are closer than they ever have been.

Leaving aside questions of morality and ethics it is now a happy story, though all
four of them went through many anxious, distressing and embarrassing moments,
which I will mention briefly later.

The questions are whether in law an adoption order is permissible; and, if it is,
whether it is a correct exercise of the discretion to make it.

I am indebted to counsel for their most helpful arguments. Counsel for Mr and Mrs
A and for the child's *guardian ad litem*, who strongly supports the application for
adoption, while properly advancing their clients' cases, were careful to apprise me of
anything I should know which pointed in the opposite direction.

On my invitation the Attorney-General instructed counsel, Mr Holman, to appear as *amicus curiae*. Mr Holman stressed that there was no public policy formulated regarding surrogacy arrangements other than as was enshrined in the Surrogacy Arrangements Act 1985 which illegalises commercial surrogacy agencies and negotiations and advertisements; and save in so far as it may already be enshrined in the Adoption Act 1958 and Children Act 1975.

The Surrogacy Arrangements Act 1985 had not been enacted when the arrangement in the instant case was entered into and carried out. Otherwise, as Mr Holman said, there is no public policy in existence. There is active consideration and consultation with the public being carried out by the government and its advisers. A consultation paper entitled 'Legislation on Human Infertility Services and Embryo Research' was presented to Parliament in December 1986 which includes, among several other topics, the wider implications of surrogacy. It needs no saying that there is no more difficult and sensitive subject. Presumably when the consultations and considerations are complete, policies will be formulated and put before Parliament. It is there, in my opinion, that questions of morality and ethics should be weighed. There is no requirement in the instant case for the court to weigh them, which it is not equipped to do and should not attempt. I agree fully about this with counsel for the Attorney-General who also has the benefit of advice from a senior member of the legal staff of the Department of Health and Social Security.

Whether or not an adoption order can and, if it can, should be made, falls to be considered in the light of the relevant provisions of the Adoption Act 1958 and the Children Act 1975. As I had hoped he would, Mr Holman advanced the arguments against the making of an order. Counsel for the applicants and the child's *guardian ad litem* put the arguments in favour.

Section 50(1) of the Adoption Act 1958, as amended, enacts:

> 'Subject to the provisions of this section, it shall not be lawful to make or give to any person any payment or reward for or in consideration of — (a) the adoption by that person of a child; (b) the grant by that person of any agreement or consent required in connection with the adoption of a child; (c) the transfer by that person of the actual custody of a child with a view to the adoption of the child; or (d) the making by that person of any arrangements for the adoption of a child.'

Subsection (2) sets out the penalties for any contravention. Subsection (3) enacts (omitting words immaterial to the present case):

> 'This section does not apply . . . to any payment or reward authorised by the court to which an application for an adoption order in respect of a child is made.'

Next there is section 22(5) of the Children Act 1975, which enacts:

> 'The court shall not make an adoption order in relation to a child unless it is satisfied that the applicants have not, as respects the child, contravened section 50 of the 1958 Act (prohibition of certain payments in relation to adoption).'

Then there is section 57(2) of the Adoption Act 1958 (interpretation section) which enacts:

> 'For the purposes of this Act, a person shall be deemed to make arrangements for the adoption of a child or to take part in arrangements for the placing of a child in the actual custody of another person, if (as the case may be) — (a) he enters into or makes any agreement or arrangement for, or for facilitating, the adoption of the child by any other person, whether the adoption is effected, or is intended to be effected, in pursuance of an adoption order or otherwise; or (b) he enters into or makes any agreement or arrangement for, or facilitates, the placing of the child in the actual custody of that other person; or if he initiates or takes part in any negotiations of which the purpose or effect is the conclusion of any agreement or the making of any arrangement therefor, or if he causes another to do so.'

Lastly, there is section 3 of the Children Act 1975, which provides:

> 'In reaching any decision relating to the adoption of a child, a court or adoption agency shall have regard to all the circumstances, first consideration being given to the need to safeguard and promote the welfare of the child throughout his childhood; and shall so far as practicable ascertain the wishes and feelings of the child regarding the decision and give due consideration to them, having regard to his age and understanding.'

The first question, therefore, is whether in the present case there has been 'any payment or reward' within the meaning of section 50 of the Adoption Act 1958 — 'for adoption,' to put it conveniently albeit imprecisely. This is a question of fact to be decided on the evidence. Mr and Mrs A and Mrs B have all given evidence. All are transparently honest. They did not make notes. They did not take legal advice. Not surprisingly, their recollection of the precise sequence of events and what was discussed and when is not clear. What does come out strongly is that what was wanted was a baby and that Mr and Mrs A should have it from birth to care for and bring up. And that it was upon this that they were all concentrating. It was only after the payments had been made and the baby was born that any of them began to turn their minds in any real sense to adoption and the legalities.

In my judgment there was no payment or reward within the meaning of section 50(1) of the Adoption Act 1958. But if I am mistaken about this and the payments do rank as payments or rewards within the meaning of the section, is that the end of the matter? Is there an absolute prohibition against adoption regardless of the adverse effects on this child and its family.

. Much of the argument has been directed towards this question. It turns on the interpretation to be given to section 50(3) which provides, as I have said, that the prohibition shall not apply 'to any payment or reward authorised by the court . . .' Can such authorisation be given only in advance of the making of a proposed payment or giving of a reward? Or can it be given for a payment or reward already made or given?

In his role as *amicus curiae*, Mr Holman advanced the arguments in favour of the former interpretation. If that is the correct view the results, as he acknowledges, would be draconian indeed. It would mean, for example, that any payment, however modest and however innocently made, would bar an adoption and do so however much the welfare of the child cried aloud for adoption with all the security and legal rights and status it carried with it: and that, be it said, within the framework of legislation whose first concern is promoting the welfare of the children concerned.

I do not believe that Parliament ever intended to produce such a result (nor, anticipating, has it done so in my judgment). The result it intended to produce is wise and humane. It produced a balance by setting its face against trafficking in children, on the one hand, but recognising that there may be transactions which are venial and should not prohibit adoption, on the other hand.

Nor in my judgment does the language of the section compel the draconian interpretation. What does 'authorise' mean in this context? Counsel have been unable to find any reported cases on the point, perhaps because none is necessary. In the *Shorter Oxford English Dictionary* 'authorise' is described variously as: '(1) To set up or acknowledge as authoritative . . . (2) To give legal force to . . . (3) To give formal approval to; to sanction, countenance . . .; to justify . . .'

To my mind, in plain language, there is nothing in 'authorise' or its synonyms to suggest that authorisation can only be given prospectively. On the contrary, it can equally well be given retroactively. Mr Baker, the Deputy Official Solicitor, has been in court during the argument and with his wide experience he informed me through Mr Holman that authorisation is much more likely to be called for for something which has happened than for something which is in future contemplation. For these reasons the correct interpretation is the second one, with the result that Parliament has produced the result it intended to.

It follows that in each case the court has a discretion whether or not to authorise any payment or reward which has already been made or may be contemplated in the future. In exercising that discretion the court would no doubt balance all the circumstances of the case with the welfare of the child as first consideration against what Mr Levy well described as the degree of taint of the transaction for which authorisation is asked. If the matter were to reach that stage, Mr Holman, with evident pleasure and relief, submitted that authorisation be given and an adoption order made.

The evidence and the full and balanced reports are all one way. As I have said this little child is thriving and it and its family are supremely happy. It is all accurately and clearly summarised in the *guardian ad litem's* report and I cannot do better than quote from it:

'Mr and Mrs A appear both to be sensible, warm and open people. Their relationship with the child is loving and appears a very normal parent/child relationship. . . . Both the doctor and health visitor are entirely happy with the care the As give the child and are entirely happy with the child's physical, social and emotional development . . . In all respects the care the child receives from Mr and Mrs A appears excellent. The child has lived with Mr and Mrs A since two days after birth. [The child] has known no other home or parents . . . It is also most desirable that Mr and Mrs A feel fully responsible for the child now and into the future. Anything other than adoption will leave them with some fear that at some future date their care of the child may be interfered with or even [the child] be removed from them. Such a fear, given the existing background anxieties could, in my view, have a corrosive effect on their feelings of commitment to the child. If the parents feel less than fully secure in their rights, duties and responsibilities to the child then this insecurity will communicate itself to the child affecting, in turn, its feelings of security with them which would be to its detriment.'

I agree unreservedly with every word of that. If I am mistaken in my finding that the payments did not fall within the prohibited ambit, I should without hesitation exercise discretion by authorising them and making the adoption order.

For all these reasons the adoption order is made. For the sake of completeness I should add that the mother consents, and at a preliminary hearing I declared paternity, and approved the placement with a view to adoption.

This being the first case of its kind to come to court in this country I was invited by counsel to make some further remarks and it may be helpful to do so. Other than those outlawed by the Surrogacy Arrangements Act 1985, surrogacy arrangements are not against the law as it stands. But those contemplating taking this path should have their eyes open to the kind of pitfalls, obstacles and anxiety that they are likely to meet. Mr and Mrs A, a devoted and very nice couple, encountered many of them. So too did Mr and Mrs B. And they found themselves caught in a tangled web of family and social embarrassment and deception, including the deception of doctors and others, from which they could not escape. There was not, I stress, any illegality. They went to all lengths within their power and knowledge to avoid any illegality. To give just one example, Mrs B declined medical and other financial benefits to which in the ordinary course she would have been entitled and which she could have had and no one the wiser. I shall not go into more detail in this case. It is enough to say that all the way through they have had to find ways to get over obstacles, and they have had to resort to all manner of shifts and stratagems. The expense has been heavy. And there have been these proceedings. These people have had three years of unremitting anxiety and many moments of distress, though I know that it has all been worthwhile for them in the end.

Last and very far from least there is that fact that in other cases it might well not end up happily. In the nature of things those who undertake the role of surrogate mother are those with very strong maternal instincts. The likelihood must be there that when the baby arrives the mother cannot bear to part with it. The trauma and turmoil then for all needs no describing.

One cannot sit in these courts and hear all the multitude of professionals and others without knowing well the depth of longing in couples, devoted to each other, who cannot have a child through no fault of their own. But before they go down the path of surrogacy they should know and know fully what it may entail. It is not a primrose path.''

One purpose in drawing analogies with female employment/prostitution or organ donation is to make comparisons with the legal regulation of those activities and thereby question whether an alternative means of regulating surrogacy would be more acceptable than that presently found in the Surrogacy Arrangements Act 1985. Shelley Roberts criticises Warnock and the subsequent legislation for the superficial approach taken to surrogacy, arguing that it fails to identify what is considered to be objectionable about surrogacy and then to respond appropriately. Instead it takes a "prostitution" type approach, viewing surrogacy as permissible as long as it is carried out in a way which allows society not to confront it, that is as long as it occurs off the streets and out of sight.[96] She argues that different legal responses are appropriate depending upon the exact objection to the practice.

4.2.iii *Alternative Models of Regulation*

The present system allows surrogacy arrangements, for which money can be paid but provides no safeguards against exploitation of either the surrogate or the commissioning couple, no medical screening and no means of assuring anonymity. Giving the agreement the status of an enforceable contract may seem the obvious solution to clarify the rights and obligations of the parties, but, as Michael Freeman argues, the courts are unlikely to enforce a contract which makes a mother hand over a baby, states circumstances in which she should or should not seek an abortion, or that she should not smoke, drink or eat certain foods whilst pregnant. Should the surrogate mother change her mind and no longer feel in a position to hand over the baby, the courts are not likely to order specific performance which would be the remedy sought by the commissioning couple who want a baby, not damages.[97]

A number of different models of state regulation have been considered in the context of surrogacy:

V. PAYNE
"The Regulation of Surrogate Motherhood"[98]

"It has been suggested by B. M. Dickens in *Genetics and the Law* (1986, 3rd ed., Plenum Press), that there are three broad conceptual approaches which may be used in the regulation of surrogate motherhood. Firstly, 'the static approach' which centres upon biological parenthood as the determining factor, with regard being had to the status and role of the family within society. The static approach may also centre upon family stability as the central issue. Thus, in either of these forms the traditional roles of parenthood are maintained. It is in this sense 'static' since there is no envisaged change of these traditional roles.

Secondly, the 'private ordering approach', which recognizes the sanctity of contracts. The main determining factor would be that of public policy, enabling individuals to enter into agreements which reflect individual preference and bargaining power: the state would not intervene in the private arrangement of individuals . . .

Thirdly, the 'state regulation approach'. This may be considered as two approaches, the punitive approach and the inducement approach. The punitive approach is the opposite to the laissez-faire standpoint of the private ordering approach, as it envisages strict state control by the use of sanctions. The inducement approach would encourage the use of other practices by attaching advantages to these, that is by attaching legal approval either expressedly or impliedly."

It has been suggested that the approach taken by the Surrogacy Arrangements

---

[96] S. Roberts, "Warnock and Surrogate Motherhood: Sentiment or Argument?" in P. Byrne (ed.), *supra*, n. 88 at p. 103.
[97] M. D. A. Freeman, *supra*, n. 46 at 43–44.
[98] (1987) 17 *Family Law* 178.

Act 1985 combines "elements of the 'prohibitory' State Regulation model with facets of Private Ordering".[99] Veronica Payne argues for a "combination of strict state control of the state regulation approach and the private ordering approach. In other words, the ability to enter into such arrangements but within clearly defined boundaries — a kind of limited paternalism".[1] David Macphee and Kathy Forest advocate regulation of surrogacy following the findings of their study of the psychological effects of surrogacy upon both "commissioning mothers" and "surrogate mothers" in two programme centres. They argue that a regulatory model would ensure appropriate screening of prospective surrogates (including medical examination, legal advice and counselling on both the psychological and the social implications), enable the surrogate to choose the commissioning couple as well as they her (facilitating "mutuality of choice") informed consent procedures and support and educational facilities.[2]

By way of comparison with the approach taken by the Surrogacy Arrangements Act 1985 are the proposals of the Ontario Law Reform Commission in their *Report on Artificial Reproduction and Related Matters* (1985) recommending[3]:

- that the suitability of all the parties would be evaluated by the court in advance of conception;
- after the birth there would be provision for the testing of the infant to confirm that it was the child of the commissioning male;
- the surrogate who refused to give up the child could be compelled by the court to do so;
- all payments to the surrogate would have to receive prior court approval;
- the parties should agree on:
    (i) arrangements for the future of the child if one of the commissioning couple died or they no longer lived together;
    (ii) the right of the surrogate to further information about the child or contact with it;
    (iii) restrictions on the activities of the surrogate prior to and after conception;
    (iv) prenatal diagnostic screening.
- the commissioning couple would be registered as the child's legal parents.

---

[99] D. Morgan, "Who to be or Not to Be: The Surrogacy Story", *supra*, n. 62 at 364.

[1] V. Payne, "The Regulation of Surrogate Motherhood" (1987) 17 *Family Law* 178 at 180. M. D. A. Freeman, *supra*, n. 46, prefers the regulatory approach. He argues that surrogacy will continue to be practised because it fulfils the needs of those wishing to parent a child and the regulatory approach is the most appropriate way of ensuring that the interests of all those involved are considered. It "would necessitate the establishment of standards and the monitoring of practices" (p. 46).

[2] D. Macphee & K. Forest, "Surrogacy: Programme Comparisons and Policy Implications" [1990] *International Journal of Law and the Family* 308.

[3] A "private ordering approach", D. Morgan, *supra*, n. 62.

The Surrogacy Arrangements Act 1985 prohibits commercial arrangements but takes a *laisser faire* approach to private agreements. It fails to provide in advance any answers to questions which might arise from disputes surrounding surrogacy and ensures that any agreement reached by the parties prior to conception is not enforceable. Any disputes will be dealt with by the normal, adversarial processes of the courts. A minority of the Warnock Committee dissented from the conclusions of the majority recommending that the licensing authority (which the Report recommended be set up to license fertility treatment services) should be empowered to license non-profit making agencies to facilitate surrogacy arrangements for infertile couples referred to them by gynaecologists as a matter of last resort.[4] Acknowledging that couples faced with no other option will enter into surrogacy arrangements, they considered that some of the pitfalls which would result from such arrangements could be avoided given that the agencies could match the commissioning couple with a suitable surrogate mother and provide counselling so that all the parties at least considered the social, legal and personal difficulties of such an arrangement.[5] The dissenting parties considered that public opinion had not reached a fully formed view on surrogacy which had (in 1984) only recently received publicity. The minority were of the view that legislation prohibiting surrogacy completely should not be too hastily enacted, but that first an assessment should be made of the demand and whether a regulated agency could provide suitable services, that, "the door be left slightly ajar so that surrogacy can be more effectively assessed".[6]

---

[4]   *Report of the Committee of Inquiry into Human Fertilisation and Embryology, supra*, n. 15, Expression of Dissent, para. 1.
[5]   *Report of the Committee of Inquiry into Human Fertilisation and Embryology, ibid.*, Expression of Dissent, para. 5.
[6]   *Report of the Committee of Inquiry into Human Fertilisation and Embryology, ibid.*, Expression of Dissent, para. 9. The independent review of surrogacy announced by the new Labour Government to examine, in particular, the payment of surrogates and whether an independent body should regulate surrogacy arrangements may yet provide an effective assessment of surrogacy (*The Times*, June 12,1997).

CHAPTER 5

PREVENTING MOTHERHOOD

5.1 Contraception

This chapter considers the laws governing methods of preventing conception. In practical terms, this includes barrier methods such as the contraceptive sheath (condom and femidom), the diaphragm, the cap and the contraceptive sponge, and non-barrier methods such as the oral contraceptive (combined/progestogen-only pill), injectable methods (Depo-Provera) and contraceptive implants. As all these methods act, primarily, to prevent conception, the legal issues which arise in relation to their use are the same. Consequently, no differentiation is made between the methods of preventing conception unless it is necessary to do so.

Abortion and, more recently, fertility treatments, have been the focus for feminist analyses of reproduction and for consideration of the extent to which the law sanctions medical interventions and intrusions upon the female body. Contraception, in comparison, has received very little feminist analysis. This chapter considers the development of State provision of contraception and the reasons for the resistance to public supply of contraception. The legalisation of abortion and State provision of contraception have, in the opinion of many, contributed much to the liberation of women by giving us control over our reproductive lives and freeing us from domesticity. In *Gillick v. West Norfolk and Wisbech Area Health Authority*[1] (discussed further below), Lord Scarman suggested, that the contraceptive pill, "unknown to our fathers but of immense consequence to society", had "introduced a new independence, and offers new options, for women".[2] This chapter examines the extent to which this can be considered to be true.

5.1.i *State provision of contraception*

The Secretary of State is under a *duty*, by virtue of section 5(1)(b) of the National Health Service Act 1977 "to arrange, to such extent as he considers necessary to meet all reasonable requirements in England and Wales, for the giving of advice on contraception, the medical examination of those seeking advice on contraception, the treatment of such persons and the supply of contraceptive substances and appliances." Methods of preventing conception

---

[1] *Gillick v. West Norfolk and Wisbech Area Health Authority* [1986] 1 A.C. 112.
[2] *Ibid.*, at 176D.

have been employed for centuries, and private birth control clinics providing methods of contraception were set up in England in the early twentieth-century.[3] Opponents of State provision of contraception argued that contraception was associated with prostitution, that use of contraception presented a threat to the family (by facilitating a change in the role of women) and put forward religious objections. Vivien Walsh, in her description of the development towards State provision of contraception, explains that one reason for the resistance was the preservation of moral values:

V. WALSH
"Contraception: The Growth of a Technology"[4]

"Opposition to birth control
Until recently most countries, or at least those that favoured a growth in the birth rate, had pro-natalist laws and policies. The power and prosperity of states has historically been associated by their rulers with large numbers, especially of workers, potential consumers and, when necessary, potential members of the armed forces. Governments have attempted to encourage population growth through, for example, welfare benefits, tax allowances and a minimum age for marriage, as well as prohibition of birth control.

In Britain, a government publication (1954) stated that 'the state played practically no part in the great spread during the twentieth century of the knowledge and use of birth control methods'. In America, 'open association with contraception and its positive promotion was an activity which our government shunned like the plague', and in fact 'all attempts to frustrate the process of parenthood have been discouraged by government and the courts'.

In the United States, where the Pill was first developed and marketed, the Federal Comstock Laws (named after the senator who introduced them in the 1870s) and various individual state laws banned the sale, display, advertising and even the use of contraceptives. Contradictory regulations were adopted by several states. For example, Nebraska forbade the sale of contraceptives but set quality standards for those sold; Mississippi both prohibited contraceptives and offered birth control supplies through the state's own health services.

Many of the research programmes financed by the American birth control movement in the 1930s had to be undertaken in Britain as a result of the legal situation. During this period, Margaret Sanger and her colleagues were continuously involved in legal battles. Although they managed to obtain several favourable court decisions, the continued existence of the laws provided an excuse which was used by the medical profession and the government to avoid taking any action about birth control. After the Second World War the legislation was less stringently applied. Pincus and his co-workers carried out their research on the Pill in Massachusetts, where anti-birth control legislation was not amended until 1966. But the laws were still activated from time to time to harass those who ran birth control clinics.

In the U.K. there was never direct legal prohibition of birth control, although laws

---

[3] A. Leathard, *The Fight for Family Planning: The Development of Family Planning Services in Britain 1921-1974* (London: Macmillan, 1980).
[4] In The Brighton Women & Science Group, *Alice Through the Microscope* (London: Virago, 1980), pp. 187–189.

concerning pornography (*e.g.* The Obscene Publications Act, 1857), for example, had from time to time up to the Second World War been interpreted to include contraceptive information. Neither the state nor the medical profession was, however, anxious to promote or sponsor birth control. In 1930 a 'permissive' memorandum (*i.e.*, not circulated, but supplied on request to local authorities) was issued, which was the outcome of years of pressure by the birth control movement. This gave local authorities the power, if they wished, to provide contraceptive advice to married women in their maternity and child welfare clinics, 'in cases where a further pregnancy would be detrimental to health'. Thirty-six authorities did take advantage of those provisions, but such was the lack of knowledge among their medical staff that they were often obliged to refer their clients to the voluntary clinics.

By 1949 the Royal Commission on Population was recommending that advice on contraception should be available 'to all married persons who wanted it', and that it should be a 'duty of the National Health Service'. The recommendation was not taken up either by the government or the medical profession (although GPs began to prescribe the Pill when it was introduced), and in the 1960s the Family Planning Association (FPA) was still calling for birth control advice to be provided by the NHS. It was 1974 before free contraceptive supplies and advice were available and unmarried women were officially accepted as clients by all the clinics. During 1976, 446 FPA clinics came under the administration of the health authorities. Recent cutbacks in public expenditure, however, have already begun to threaten this service.

British and American policies seem to have been a reflection more of a desire to 'safeguard' public morals than to increase population size; in other countries, restrictions on contraception were more explicitly part of population policy. France introduced the 'Code de la Famille' in 1940 in response to an absolute decline in population during the depression, by which marriage and childrearing were encouraged by various welfare and tax benefits, while contraception and abortion were restricted.

The most extreme example of state intervention on population matters took place under fascism in Germany. The racially (and socially) 'inferior' were sterilised and/or sent to the gas chambers. Aryan women were prevented from working or from using contraceptives (as well as being denied many other rights) and subjected to intensive propaganda in order to force them to breed as rapidly as possible.

On the other hand, Sweden has adopted a generally pro-natalist policy, which has taken the form of encouraging wanted children, by providing welfare benefits, nurseries and paid maternity leave, while making birth control freely available to those who want to enjoy sex but not to have children."

As mentioned above a further objection was that contraception would result in a breakdown in the family. However, in a changing society (and changing moral climate), arguments that birth control would help to maintain the patriarchal family were persuasive:

S. POLLOCK
"Sex and the Contraceptive Act"[5]

"In Britain, the provision of contraceptive and abortion facilities has been firmly rooted in family planning. Concern to protect the patriarchal family structure has

---

[5] In H. Homans (ed.), *The Sexual Politics of Reproduction* (Aldershot: Gower Press, 1985), p. 66.

been pivotal to decisions about making birth control facilities available to women. Widespread provision of contraceptives for women was resisted on the grounds that freedom from fear of pregnancy would lead to promiscuity. This, in turn, would lead to the disruption and destruction of family life. Historically, the 'social grounds' in the fight for women's rights to contraceptives, abortion and sterilisation have had to be argued in terms of family stability in order to gain approval from both the medical profession and legislators. Arguments about overburdened and unwed mothers' needs to limit births gained a sympathetic ear, while debates about women's rights did not. Not surprisingly, proponents of birth control provision have usually stated their case in terms of the health and welfare of the family unit.

In the attempt to maintain the patriarchal family structure as the stable unit of society, fears of condoning women's 'promiscuity' have had to be weighed against the evidence of pregnancy and childbirth outside of marriage. The rising illegitimacy rates and illegal abortion figures of the 1960s were used to argue that the provision of birth control facilities was unavoidable if heterosexual family life were to be preserved. Both contraceptive and abortion facilities came about on this basis: the lesser of two evils.

Sex education, too, found approval in the face of teenage pregnancy; even so, the emphasis has been much more upon the morals of family life and the mechanics of reproduction than it has upon practical sexual matters or contraception.

Family planning is the form which population control takes. In the promotion of small families and the prevention of motherhood outside marriage, a reduction in the quantity of births is achieved, while the patriarchal family as the basic unit of social organisation is maintained. The international emphasis upon family planning supports family-based social orders, whilst diffusing the selective ways in which population control may be applied to various racial, national and economic groups."

The perceived need to control population growth in the Third World was also material in bringing about a change in moral attitudes towards the use of contraception in Britain.

V. Walsh
"Contraception: The Growth of a Technology"[6]

"Encouragement of birth control
What was it that stimulated the rapid change in prevailing attitudes, particularly official attitudes, at the time the Pill was becoming a practical possibility? It seems to have been above all a fear of a world 'population explosion'. This fear acted as the vital catalyst in the complex but quite sudden change of public, medical and government attitudes to birth control.

Sudden alarm at world population growth, however, was a political response rather than the reasoned analysis of demographic trends and their underlying social causes. A prevailing fear of overpopulation in the 1950s seems to have replaced a recent enough fear of underpopulation (in the 1930s) among demographers and economists just as rapidly and emotively as among politicians and journalists. The doubtful validity of new 'consensus' opinion about the population explosion does not alter the fact that the strength of prevailing attitudes had a marked influence on government

---

[6]   In The Brighton Women & Science Group, *supra*, n. 4 at pp. 189–191.

policy — and the plans of the pharmaceutical companies. (Company policy was also influenced by financial incentives) ... For example, population growth is widely believed to be the cause of starvation in the Third World, although it has been shown [. . .] that food production is now increasing at one and three-quarters times the rate of the population. Starvation is a social, not a technical, problem, requiring redistribution of resources; but it is population control that is posed as the solution in official policy.

Demands from political leaders in the West for measures to limit reproduction in the poverty-stricken countries of the Third World made it impossible to sustain generalised moral or social objections to contraception at home. Sooner or later, under the pressure of social and economic changes, [. . .] contraception would have become acceptable. But the widespread fear of the 'population bomb' suddenly advanced its legitimisation.

As experience was soon to show in 1960, the better off, well educated, mainly white, women in the United States and the West generally were the drug industry's prime market for an oral contraceptive. It did not matter, given the new climate of opinion, that concern about rapid population growth in the underdeveloped countries had little to do with the desire of the more affluent social strata of the West to plan their children to suit their new life-styles. Most of the drug companies and scientists who have commented on the motivation of their development work cite the 'population explosion' as the main impulse.

In governmental and public anxiety, the scientists had found an acceptable reason for doing their research, and the drug companies for investing in a potentially profitable innovation. Gregory Pincus, who played a key role in the development of the Pill, cites it as one of the reasons he began research in 1950. Marrian and Nelson, who were both working on the biochemistry of reproduction, state that this gave an important impetus to research. *Science Newsletter*, reporting early findings by Pincus and others, used the sensational headline: 'the explosive increase in world population could be squelched by a tiny pill'. This is not at all untypical of the popular and semi-technical reporting of that period.

Governments themselves, however, were still relatively slow to respond to demands for action on the population question, though they themselves contributed to the general alarm.

Shortly after the Second World War, proposals that the U.S. Government adopt a definite population policy at home — or get the United Nations to adopt such a policy abroad — had very little support. It was in the second half of the 1950s, the time when the Pill was going through clinical tests before being marketed, that policies began to change. In 1959 the recommendations of the controversial Draper Report — that the United States should support U.N. schemes for birth control in under-developed countries — were accepted. In that same year, however, Eisenhower said of birth control: 'I cannot imagine anything more emphatically a subject that is not a proper political or governmental activity, or function or responsibility.' Six years later Eisenhower and Truman became co-chairmen of the honorary sponsors of Planned Parenthood — World Population; and Johnson became the first president to report federal support for population control.

Public attitudes and official thinking were at last brought more or less into line with the widespread and fairly long-established practice of contraception.

Prejudice, taboo, policies and laws had retarded innovation in birth control and the spread of such techniques that did exist. Fear of the 'population explosion' and the consequent change in laws and policies in turn served to promote or speed up the use of birth control and innovation in technique."

Middle-class, educated, white women were already using contraception. The fear of society being populated by an increasing proportion of the poor, and the employment of the stereotypes of "overburdened and unwed mothers", were material in the decision that the State should provide means to prevent conception. Contraception removes the threat of pregnancy enabling women to be sexually active for their own pleasure and has therefore been associated with promiscuous women of low morals. Before pharmaceutical companies would manufacture contraceptives and doctors prescribe them, it was necessary to challenge the stereotype of the sort of woman who used them.

C. Smart
"Disruptive Bodies and Unruly Sex: The Regulation of Reproduction and Sexuality in the Nineteenth Century"[7]

"Infanticide and abortion were seen as the means deployed by poor working-class women to regulate reproduction and pressures upon them to conform were less concerned with the value of the lost offspring than with a struggle over who should control unruly populations. The practice of birth control was seen as a different kind of threat, at least initially, because the decline in the birth rate from the 1880s was regarded as problematic for the quality of the population. It was feared that the poor were overproducing and the higher classes were failing to replace themselves. This fear was set not only in an eugenicist context but also an imperialist one in which there was a fear that the white races would be overrun by those of 'lesser value'. Foucault refers to the construction of the Malthusian couple as part of the deployment of power *vis à vis* populations. More accurate might be a focus on the mother or potential mother as a key actor in the struggle over this form of regulation. The point is that men/fathers were rarely invoked in nineteenth-century debates over birth control. They may have been called upon to lessen the sufferings of their wives, and in practice methods of contraception such as withdrawal, rhythm and the condom required their active co-operation. Yet the issue was a woman's issue. It was women, rather than men, who were to be denied the knowledge of the various methods and it was women rather than men who were constructed as 'unnatural' or a threat to the moral order if they engaged in such practices.

McLaren has pointed to the competing interests involved in the struggle over birth control in the nineteenth century and, following his analysis, it is by no means clear that all women were in favour of birth control. Equally important, the medical profession at this time was not interested in supporting birth control, and the mainstream of the profession disassociated itself from the movement in the early stages. Indeed, the public face of the profession presented contraceptive methods and devices as injurious to health.

The main obstacle to the spread of knowledge of contraception was, however, the fear of unleashing female sexuality and the fear that marriage would be undermined by the subversion of its main purpose (*i.e.* biological reproduction). Birth-control methods, therefore, had to be rendered dangerous by the detractors, whilst the pro-

---

[7] In C. Smart (ed.), *Regulating Womanhood: Historical Essays on Marriage, Motherhood and Sexuality* (London: Routledge, 1992), pp. 19–22.

moters aimed to 'domesticate' them, that is to make them safe, pro-family and familiar. The struggle to redefine birth control was particularly hard for Victorian women who, in promoting contraception, became associated with all the immoral values attached to the practice itself . . .

The trials of Annie Besant in 1877 and 1878 capture this process. The first trial was a prosecution for obscene libel brought against her and Charles Bradlaugh for republishing an American pamphlet by a Dr Knowlton, entitled *Fruits of Philosophy; or, the Private Companion of Young Married Couples* at the price of 6 pence. The trial was a showpiece rather than a run-of-the-mill prosecution. Besant and Bradlaugh had republished the pamphlet precisely to challenge the informal censorship that was operating in relation to the dissemination of this kind of knowledge. But it was also a show trial in as much as both defended themselves in person and were able to put before the court, and hence the public, articulate arguments on sexuality, marriage and contraceptive practices.

What is particularly interesting about Besant's speech is the sources of knowledge she draws upon. She used Malthus, Darwin and social statistics to mount a case against traditional Christian morality. Her argument was pro-marriage and pro-sex but it was based on an idea of ordination by Nature rather than God. Moreover, for her what was ordained by Nature was discoverable through scientific method. She stated:

> 'I can show you from Mr Darwin — that what Knowlton says about health is shown to be true by the fact that married women live longer than unmarried women, and this is a point you get right through every census table that you can take up. You will find there that marriage has a distinctly lengthening effect on human life; you will find that bachelorhood or spinsterhood distinctly shortens life; and it is only reasonable it should be so, gentlemen, because those who despise the natural instincts of nature can scarcely be surprised if nature revenges herself by shortening the life which they do not know how to use. I will put it to you . . . that unmarried women . . . suffer from a number of diseases, special to the reproductive organs, that married women, as a rule, do not suffer from, because they have not thwarted nature in the fashion that those who lead a celibate life must do.'

Besant went on to argue that marriage was not only naturally ordained, but that early marriage, coupled with contraceptive practices to reduce the size of families, would solve problems of immorality and prostitution and the exploitation of young working-class women.

What is revealing about Besant's speech is the extent to which she accepts a particular notion of Woman as constructed in scientific discourses and attempts to use this version as if it were a form of emancipatory knowledge. Unfortunately for her, it was precisely the espousal of such views which one year later lost her the custody of her eight-year-old daughter to her estranged husband. Whilst the judge in the obscene libel case had obviously been impressed by Mrs Besant's intelligence and loquacity, the judge in the custody case found her an unfit mother precisely because of this sign of unorthodoxy.

Although Besant was ultimately acquitted (on a technicality) on the charge of obscene libel, and she later published her own work on birth control, the movement did not become widely influential until after the trial of Marie Stopes in the 1920s. She had attempted to harness theories about women's nature to a pro-woman cause, but these theories were not free-floating evident truths but discourses which made the intelligent, speaking woman (*i.e.* Besant herself) an oxymoron. Once moved to the arena of a custody battle in which she was judged in terms of mothering, the self-same intelligent articulateness quickly disqualified her. Mothers could not be free thinkers; mothers follow their maternal instincts."

Just as popular discourse has constructed an image of ideal womanhood and the perfect mother, it has been demonstrated above that legal discourse is productive of Woman.[8] It is suggested that legal discourse constructs an idea of the Woman to whom the law will apply who can be viewed in opposition to the Man of Legal Discourse. The Woman of Legal Discourse is not, however, a unitary concept. Different laws are constitutive of different constructs of women. Nevertheless, legal, medical and social discourses have tended to construct the ideal mother as heterosexual, white, middle-class and economically dependent upon her husband. Women's capacity for reproduction almost becomes a moral and natural duty to reproduce so that motherhood ceases to be one of many roles for women, but becomes elevated to women's primary and natural identity. Contraception prevents a woman becoming a mother. But it is not utilised in a uniform fashion with uniform consequences for women. Women who do not live up to the ideal mother may find that methods of contraception are made readily available to them and that, while these methods are effective in preventing pregnancy, they may also pose risks to their health. Young, white, middle-class women who do not wish ever to have children may find that they are denied their chosen method of preventing motherhood, namely sterilisation, whilst women with learning difficulties are sterilised in their "best interests".[9]

Section 1 of the National Health Service (Family Planning) Act 1967 empowered local health authorities in England and Wales, with the approval of the Minister of Health, to make provision for the giving of advice on contraception, for the medical examination of people seeking advice on contraception for the purpose of determining what advice to give, and the supply of contraceptive substances and contraceptive appliances. This was repealed by section 4 of the National Health Service Reorganisation Act 1973 which replaced the *power* of local health authorities to provide for such advice and treatment with a *duty* upon the Secretary of State to do so. Section 4 was replaced in like terms by section 5(1)(b) of the National Health Service Act 1977, which is currently in force. Despite the lengthy history of the use of means of preventing conception and the efforts of campaigners such as Marie Stopes for the widespread provision of contraception,[10] it is only in recent years that local health authorities have had the *power* to provide contraception, and even more recently, that the Secretary of State has had a *duty* to do so. State provision of contraception was the inevitable corollary of the Abortion Act 1967. The State had accepted the need to provide (in the limited

---

[8]   C. Smart, "The Woman of Legal Discourse" (1992) 1 *Social & Legal Studies* 29. See Section One above for discussion of this argument.
[9]   Considered in Chap. 5.4.
[10] See A. Leathard, *supra*, n.3.

circumstances considered in Chapter 5.3), lawful terminations of pregnancies, it had also to provide services which would assist women to avoid unwanted pregnancies.[11] As with abortion, a change in attitudes resulting from the increased acceptability of the use of contraception amongst the medical profession was instrumental in bringing about State provision.

One question which follows from the State provision of contraception is whether men and women have the right to control their reproductive capacity in order to avoid conception or childbirth. In the previous chapter the right to control reproductive capacity was considered in terms of access to fertility treatments to alleviate childlessness. In the United States, the right to privacy has been held to include the right to abortion,[12] the right to use contraception,[13] and the right to procreate.[14] These rights are not absolute but can be qualified by a compelling State interest. Further, whilst they protect individuals from State interference, they do not positively ensure that individuals are able to exercise these rights. The right to use contraception may amount to little if the user cannot afford to pay for contraceptive services and devices. The claim for reproductive freedom to use contraception derives from the right not to have one's body interfered with against one's will and the right to do with one's body as one wishes. In the U.K., women might have the right to control their reproductive lives through the use of contraception but this right depends upon obtaining access to contraception and successful negotiation with the medical profession. The ability to control reproductive capacity cannot be considered in isolation from the construct of the ideal mother. Women who do not fit the construct of the ideal woman are denied the exercise of this ability. This is blatantly the case when women with learning difficulties are sterilised. However, lack of choice extends to other women, such as those who are coerced into using contraception. Hence, for some women contraception is available to enable them to plan their family, yet other women, who do not live up to the ideal mother, may find that the methods of contraception which are made available to them are those which take from them control of their reproductive lives.

5.1.ii *Contraception and eligibility*

5.1.ii.a The age of the contraceptive patient and the criminal liability of doctors. The National Health Service Act 1977 does not refer to the age of the patient to whom the Secretary of State has a duty to provide contraceptive advice and treatment. For females the age of consent to (hetero)sexual intercourse is 16 and therefore, the presumption may be that a girl under the age of 16 cannot lawfully be provided with contraceptive advice and treatment.

---

[11] G. Douglas, *Law, Fertility and Reproduction* (London: Sweet & Maxwell, 1991), p. 43; A. Leathard, *ibid.*, p. 133.

[12] *Roe v. Wade* (1973) 410 U.S. 113.

[13] *Griswold v. Connecticut* (1965) 318 U.S. 479.

[14] *Eisenstadt v. Baird* (1972) 405 U.S. 438.

A girl under the age of 16 does not herself commit any offence by having (hetero)sexual intercourse, whilst her partner commits a serious criminal offence contrary to section 5 or section 6 of the Sexual Offences Act 1956 (depending upon the age of the girl).[15]

The question of the criminal liability of doctors, that is, whether a doctor who gave a girl under the age of 16 contraceptive advice and treatment would be an accessory to an offence contrary to section 5 or section 6, came before the courts in *Gillick v. West Norfolk and Wisbech Area Health Authority*.[16] The facts of *Gillick* are set out in the judgment of Lord Fraser.

Gillick v. West Norfolk and Wisbech AHA
[1986] 1 A.C. 112, HL, at 162–165, *per* Lord Fraser

"My Lords, the main question in this appeal is whether a doctor can lawfully prescribe contraception for a girl under 16 years of age, without the consent of her parents. The second appellant, the Department of Health and Social Security ('the DHSS') maintains that a doctor can do so. The respondent, Mrs Gillick, maintains that he cannot. The first appellant, West Norfolk and Wisbech Area Health Authority, was not represented when the appeal reached this House, but in the Court of Appeal they were represented by the same counsel as the DHSS.

In December 1980, the DHSS issued guidance on family planning services for young people, which was a revised version of earlier guidance on the same subject, and which stated, or implied, that, at least in certain cases which were described as "exceptional," a doctor could lawfully prescribe contraception for a girl under 16 without her parents' consent. Mrs Gillick, who is the mother of five daughters under the age of 16, objected to the guidance and she instituted the proceedings which have led to this appeal, and in which she claims a declaration against both appellants that the advice given in the guidance was unlawful ...

The advice, the lawfulness of which is in dispute, is a revised version of part of a comprehensive Memorandum of Guidance on the family planning service which had

---

[15] Section 5 of the Sexual Offences Act 1956 states:
"It is a felony for a man to have unlawful intercourse with a girl under the age of thirteen."
Section 6 provides:
"(1) It is an offence, subject to the exceptions mentioned in this section, for a man to have unlawful sexual intercourse with a girl under the age of sixteen ...
(2) Where a marriage is invalid under section two of the Marriage Act, 1949, or section one of the Age of Marriage Act, 1929, (the wife being a girl under the age of sixteen), the invalidity does not make the husband guilty of an offence under this section because he has sexual intercourse with her, if he believes her to be his wife and has reasonable cause for the belief.
(3) A man is not guilty of an offence under this section because he has unlawful sexual intercourse with a girl under the age of sixteen, if he is under the age of twenty four and has not previously been charged with a like offence, and he believes her to be of the age of sixteen or over and has reasonable cause for the belief. In this subsection 'a like offence' means an offence under this section or an attempt to commit one, or an offence under paragraph (1) of section five of the Criminal Law Amendment Act, 1885."
[16] [1984] Q.B. 581; [1985] 2 W.L.R. 413, CA; [1986] 1 A.C. 112, HL. The question whether the doctor would commit an offence contrary to section 28 of the Sexual Offences Act 1956, which makes it an offence for, *inter alia*, anyone who has "care" of the girl to cause or encourage another to have unlawful sexual intercourse with her, was rejected by both the High Court and Court of Appeal. The House of Lords focused upon the liability of the doctor as an accessory.

been issued to health authorities in May 1974 under cover of a circular (HSC(I.S.) 32) from the DHSS The Memorandum of Guidance was divided into a number of sections, one of which was section G which was headed 'The Young.' The revised section G, which contains the disputed advice, is as follows:

'Clinic sessions should be available for people of all ages, but it may be helpful to make separate, less formal arrangements for young people. The staff should be experienced in dealing with young people and their problems. There is widespread concern about counselling and treatment for children under 16. Special care is needed not to undermine parental responsibility and family stability. The department would therefore hope that in any case where a doctor or other professional worker is approached by a person under the age of 16 for advice in these matters, the doctor, or other professional, will always seek to persuade the child to involve the parent or guardian (or other person in loco parentis) at the earliest stage of consultation, and will proceed from the assumption that it would be most unusual to provide advice about contraception without parental consent.

It is, however, widely accepted that consultations between doctors and patients are confidential; and the department recognises the importance which doctors and patients attach to this principle. It is a principle which applies also to the other professions concerned. To abandon this principle for children under 16 might cause some not to seek professional advice at all. They could then be exposed to the immediate risks of pregnancy and of sexually-transmitted diseases, as well as other long-term physical, psychological and emotional consequences which are equally a threat to stable family life. This would apply particularly to young people whose parents are, for example, unconcerned, entirely unresponsive, or grossly disturbed. Some of these young people are away from their parents and in the care of local authorities or voluntary organisations standing in loco parentis.

The department realises that in such exceptional cases the nature of any counselling must be a matter for the doctor or other professional worker concerned and that the decision whether or not to prescribe contraception must be for the clinical judgment of a doctor.'

That advice emphasised, more strongly than section G in its original form had done, that the cases in which a doctor could properly advise a girl under 16 years of age about contraception without parental consent would be most unusual. If the advice had been contained in a legal document there might well have been room for argument as to its exact effect, but, in my view, it is perfectly clear that it would convey to any doctor or other person who read it that the decision whether or not to prescribe contraception for a girl under 16 was in the last resort a matter for the clinical judgment of a doctor, even if the girl's parents had not been informed that she had consulted the doctor, and even if they had expressed disapproval of contraception being prescribed for her. Mrs Gillick objected to the guidance, in its amended form, and after some correspondence with the area health authority, she wrote to the acting area administrator on 3rd March, 1981 a letter which included this paragraph:

'I formally forbid any medical staff employed by Norfolk AHA to give any contraceptive or abortion advice or treatment whatsoever to my four daughters whilst they are under 16 years without my consent.'

Mrs Gillick's youngest (fifth) daughter has been born since that letter was sent. The acting administrator replied on 9th March, 1981 acknowledging the letter and stating that the AHA held to the view 'that treatment prescribed by a doctor is a matter for that doctor's clinical judgment taking into account all the factors of the case.'

On 5th August, 1982 Mrs Gillick began these proceedings against the area health authority and the DHSS, in which she seeks the following declarations (as amended before the master):

> '(i) A declaration against the [area health authority] and the [DHSS] that on a true construction of the said notice and in the events which have happened, including and in particular the publication and the circulation of the said notice, the said notice has no authority in law and gives advice which is unlawful and wrong, and which adversely affects or which may adversely affect the welfare of the plaintiff's said children, and/or the rights of the plaintiff as parent and custodian of the said children, and/or the ability of the plaintiff properly and effectively to discharge her duties as such parent and custodian; (ii) a declaration against the [area health authority] that no doctor or other professional person employed by the [area health authority] either in the Family Planning Service or otherwise may give any contraceptive and/or abortion advice and/or treatment to any child of the plaintiff below the age of 16 without the prior knowledge and consent of the said child's parent or guardian.'

Woolf J. [1984] Q.B. 581 refused to grant the declarations sought by Mrs Gillick and dismissed the action. The Court of Appeal (Eveleigh, Fox and Parker L.JJ.), allowed the appeal and granted the declarations. Against that decision the DHSS now appeals."

The majority of the House of Lords held that the doctor would not be aiding and abetting an offence contrary to section 5 or section 6 of the Sexual Offences Act 1956. The case was a civil law case and, although the most authoritative decision to date upon the criminal liability of a doctor, would not be binding should a criminal case be brought in the future.[17] The dissenting view of Lord Brandon was that as it was an unlawful act for a man to have sexual intercourse with a girl under the age of 16, it necessarily amounted to a criminal offence and was contrary to public policy for any person, doctor, teacher, social worker or parent, to promote, encourage or facilitate such an act. If His Lordship were correct, teenagers under the age of 16 would not, lawfully, be able to obtain information about contraception relevant to their own circumstances from any source.

5.1.ii.b Age of the contraceptive patient and consent. A consultation in

---

[17]   See further I. H. Dennis, "The Mental Element for Accessories", in P. Smith (ed.), *Essays in Honour of J. C. Smith* (London: Butterworths, 1987). The relevance of this case for the provision of information by teachers is considered by J. Bridgeman in "Don't Tell the Children: the department's guidance on the provision of information about contraception to individual pupils" in N. Harris (ed.), *Children, Sex Education and the Law* (London: NCB, 1996). For a consideration of whether a doctor owes a duty of confidentiality to a patient under the age of 16, enabling young girls to seek the advice of their doctor in the knowledge that their parents will not be told, see J. Montgomery, "Confidentiality and the Immature Minor" (1987) 17 *Family Law* 107.

which a woman seeks contraceptive advice and treatment will almost inevitably require the doctor to have some physical contact with the patient; for example, taking blood pressure before prescribing the pill, fitting a diaphragm or cap or the administration of an injection. A doctor must obtain the consent of a competent adult patient to the physical contact involved. A competent adult patient must be informed as to the broad nature of the procedure before a valid consent can be given.[18] A doctor who does not obtain the consent of a competent adult patient to the physical contact involved in the consultation will be liable for both criminal and civil battery.[19] The issue of whether a girl under the age of 16 can be given contraceptive advice and treatment cannot be determined simply by considering the age of consent to sexual intercourse or the criminal liability of the doctor. *In Gillick v. West Norfolk and Wisbech AHA* the court further considered whether a girl *below the age of 16* had the (legal) capacity to give her consent to contraceptive advice and treatment. The nine judges who considered the case throughout its progress in the courts were divided (5:4 in favour of the final outcome), the House of Lords deciding by a majority (3:2) that a girl under the age of 16 who had sufficient understanding and intelligence to comprehend the nature and implications of the proposed treatment can consent to contraceptive advice and treatment. It is insightful to compare the approaches taken by Lord Scarman and Lord Fraser (both in the majority):

Gillick v. West Norfolk and Wisbech AHA
[1986] 1 A.C. 112, HL, at 182–183, 185–186, 188–189, *per* Lord Scarman

"The law has . . . to be found by a search in the judge-made law for the true principle. The legal difficulty is that in our search we find ourselves in a field of medical practice where parental right and a doctor's duty may point us in different directions. This is not surprising. Three features have emerged in today's society which were not known to our predecessors: (1) contraception as a subject for medical advice and treatment; (2) the increasing independence of young people; and (3) the changed status of woman. In times past contraception was rarely a matter for the doctor: but with the development of the contraceptive pill for women it has become part and parcel of every-day medical practice, as is made clear by the department's *Handbook of Contraceptive Practice* (1984 revision), particularly para. 1.2. Family planning services are now available under statutory powers to all without any express limitation as to age or marital status. Young people, once they have attained the age of 16, are capable of consenting to contraceptive treatment, since it is medical treatment: and, however extensive be parental right in the care and upbringing of children, it cannot prevail so as to nullify the 16-year old's capacity to consent which is now conferred by statute. Furthermore, women have obtained by the availability of the pill a choice of life-style with a degree of independence and of opportunity undreamed of until this generation and greater, I would add, than any law of equal opportunity could by itself effect.

[18]   *Chatterton v. Gerson* [1981] Q.B. 432.
[19]   See I. Kennedy & A. Grubb, *Medical Law: Text and Materials* (London: Butterworths, 1989), pp. 171–229.

The law ignores these developments at its peril. The House's task, therefore, as the supreme court in a legal system largely based on rules of law evolved over the years by the judicial process, is to search the overfull and cluttered shelves of the law reports for a principle, or set of principles recognised by the judges over the years but stripped of the detail which, however appropriate in their day, would, if applied today, lay the judges open to a justified criticism for failing to keep the law abreast of the society in which they live and work.

It is, of course, a judicial commonplace to proclaim the adaptability and flexibility of the judge-made common law. But this is more frequently proclaimed than acted upon. The mark of the great judge from Coke through Mansfield to our day has been the capacity and the will to search out principle, to discard the detail appropriate (perhaps) to earlier times, and to apply principle in such a way as to satisfy the needs of their own time. If judge-made law is to survive as a living and relevant body of law, we must make the effort, however inadequately, to follow the lead of the great masters of the judicial art . . .

Although statute has intervened in respect of a child's capacity to consent to medical treatment from the age of 16 onwards, neither statute nor the case law has ruled on the extent and duration of parental right in respect of children under the age of 16. More specifically, there is no rule yet applied to contraceptive treatment, which has special problems of its own and is a late-comer in medical practice. It is open, therefore, to the House to formulate a rule. The Court of Appeal favoured a fixed age limit of 16, basing themselves on a view of the statute law which I do not share and upon their view of the effect of the older case law which . . . I cannot accept. They sought to justify the limit by the public interest in the law being certain. Certainty is always an advantage in the law, and in some branches of the law it is a necessity. But it brings with it an inflexibility and a rigidity which in some branches of the law can obstruct justice, impede the law's development, and stamp upon the law the mark of obsolescence where what is needed is the capacity for development. The law relating to parent and child is concerned with the problems of the growth and maturity of the human personality. If the law should impose upon the process of 'growing up' fixed limits where nature knows only a continuous process, the price would be artificiality and a lack of realism in an area where the law must be sensitive to human development and social change. If certainty be thought desirable, it is better that the rigid demarcations necessary to achieve it should be laid down by legislation after a full consideration of all the relevant factors than by the courts confined as they are by the forensic process to the evidence adduced by the parties and to whatever may properly fall within the judicial notice of judges. Unless and until Parliament should think fit to intervene, the courts should establish a principle flexible enough to enable justice to be achieved by its application to the particular circumstances proved by the evidence placed before them.

The underlying principle of the law was exposed by Blackstone and can be seen to have been acknowledged in the case law. It is that parental right yields to the child's right to make his own decisions when he reaches a sufficient understanding and intelligence to be capable of making up his own mind on the matter requiring decision . . .

I would hold that as a matter of law the parental right to determine whether or not their minor child below the age of 16 will have medical treatment terminates if and when the child achieves a sufficient understanding and intelligence to enable him or her to understand fully what is proposed. It will be a question of fact whether a child seeking advice has sufficient understanding of what is involved to give a consent valid in law. Until the child achieves the capacity to consent, the parental right to make the decision continues save only in exceptional circumstances. Emergency, parental neglect, abandonment of the child, or inability to find the parent are examples of exceptional situations justifying the doctor proceeding to treat the child without parental knowledge and consent: but there will arise, no doubt, other exceptional situations in which it will be reasonable for the doctor to proceed without the parent's consent.

When applying these conclusions to contraceptive advice and treatment it has to be borne in mind that there is much that has to be understood by a girl under the age of 16 if she is to have legal capacity to consent to such treatment. It is not enough that she should understand the nature of the advice which is being given: she must also have a sufficient maturity to understand what is involved. There are moral and family questions, especially her relationship with her parents; long-term problems associated with the emotional impact of pregnancy and its termination; and there are the risks to health of sexual intercourse at her age, risks which contraception may diminish but cannot eliminate. It follows that a doctor will have to satisfy himself that she is able to appraise these factors before he can safely proceed upon the basis that she has at law capacity to consent to contraceptive treatment. And it further follows that ordinarily the proper course will be for him, as the guidance lays down, first to seek to persuade the girl to bring her parents into consultation, and if she refuses, not to prescribe contraceptive treatment unless he is satisfied that her circumstances are such that he ought to proceed without parental knowledge and consent."

Gillick v. West Norfolk and Wisbech AHA
[1986] 1 A.C. 112, HL at 166–169, 174, *per* Lord Fraser

"*1. The legal capacity of a girl under 16 to consent to contraceptive advice, examination and treatment*
There are some indications in statutory provisions to which we were referred that a girl under 16 years of age in England and Wales does not have the capacity to give valid consent to contraceptive advice and treatment. If she does not have the capacity, then any physical examination or touching of her body without her parents' consent would be an assault by the examiner. One of those provisions is section 8 of the Family Law Reform Act 1969 which is in the following terms:

> '(1) The consent of a minor who has attained the age of 16 years to any surgical, medical or dental treatment which, in the absence of consent, would constitute a trespass to his person, shall be as effective as it would be if he were of full age; and where a minor has by virtue of this section given an effective consent to any treatment it shall not be necessary to obtain any consent for it from his parent or guardian. (2) In this section 'surgical, medical or dental treatment' includes ... (3) Nothing in this section shall be construed as making ineffective any consent which would have been effective if this section had not been enacted.'

The contention on behalf of Mrs Gillick was that section 8(1) shows that, apart from the subsection, the consent of a minor to such treatment would not be effective. But I do not accept that contention because subsection (3) leaves open the question whether consent by a minor under the age of 16 would have been effective if the section had not been enacted. That question is not answered by the section, and subsection (1) is, in my opinion, merely for the avoidance of doubt.

Another statutory provision which was referred to in this connection is the National Health Service (General Medical and Pharmaceutical Services) Regulations 1974 (S.I. 1974 No. 160) as amended by the National Health Service (General Medical and Pharmaceutical Services) Amendment Regulations 1975 (S.I. 1975 No. 719). These regulations prescribe the mechanism by which the relationship of doctor and patient under the National Health Service is created. Contraceptive services, along with maternity medical services, are treated as somewhat apart from other medical services in respect that only a doctor who specially offers to provide contraceptive or maternity medical services is obliged to provide them: see the definition of 'medical card' and 'treatment' in regulation 2(1), regulations 6(1)(a) and 14(2)(a) and Schedule 1, paragraph 13. But nothing turns on this fact. Two points in those regulations have a bearing on the present question although, in my opinion, only an indirect bearing. The first is that by regulation 14 any 'woman' may apply to a doctor to be accepted by him for the provision of contraceptive services. The word 'woman' is not defined so as to exclude a girl under 16 or under any other age. But regulation 32 provides as follows:

'An application to a doctor for inclusion on his list . . . may be made, either — (a) on behalf of any person under 16 years of age, by the mother, or in her absence, the father, or in the absence of both parents the guardian or other adult person who has the care of the child; or (b) on behalf of *any other person who is incapable* of making such an application by a relative or other adult person who has the care of such person; . . .' (Emphasis added).

The words in paragraph (b) which I have emphasised are said, by counsel for Mrs Gillick, to imply that a person under 16 years of age is incapable of applying to a doctor for services and therefore give some support to the argument on behalf of Mrs Gillick. But I do not regard the implication as a strong one because the provision is merely that an application 'may' be made by the mother or other parent or guardian and it applies to the doctor's list for the provision of all ordinary medical services as well as to his list for the provision of contraceptive services. I do not believe that a person aged 15, who may be living away from home, is incapable of applying on his own behalf for inclusion in the list of a doctor for medical services of an ordinary kind not connected with contraception . . .

Reference was also made to section 48 of the Education Act 1944 which deals with medical inspection and treatment of pupils at state school. Section 48(3) which imposes on the local education authority a duty to provide for medical and dental inspection of pupils was repealed and superseded by the National Health Service Reorganisation Act 1973, section 3 and Schedule 5. The Act of 1973 in turn was replaced by the National Health Service Act 1977, s. 5(1)(a). Section 48(4) of the Education Act 1944 which has not been repealed imposes a duty on the local education authority to arrange for encouraging pupils to take advantage of any medical treatment provided under section 48 but it includes a proviso in the following terms:

'Provided that if the parent of any pupil gives to the authority notice that he objects to the pupil availing himself of any medical treatment provided under this section, the pupil shall not be encouraged . . . so to do.'

I do not regard that provision as throwing light on the present question. It does not prohibit a child under the stipulated age from availing himself of medical treatment or an education authority from providing it for him. If the child, without encouragement from the education authority, 'wishes to avail himself of medical treatment' the section imposes no obstacle in his way. Accordingly, in my opinion, the proviso gives no support to the contention from Mrs Gillick, but on the contrary points in the opposite direction.

The statutory provisions to which I have referred do not differentiate so far as the capacity of a minor under 16 is concerned between contraceptive advice and treatment and other forms of medical advice and treatment. It would, therefore, appear that, if the inference which Mrs Gillick's advisers seek to draw from the provisions is justified, a minor under the age of 16 has no capacity to authorise any kind of medical advice or treatment or examination of his own body. That seems to me so surprising that I cannot accept it in the absence of clear provisions to that effect. It seems to me verging on the absurd to suggest that a girl or a boy aged 15 could not effectively consent, for example, to have a medical examination of some trivial injury to his body or even to have a broken arm set. Of course the consent of the parents should normally be asked, but they may not be immediately available. Provided the patient, whether a boy or a girl, is capable of understanding what is proposed, and of expressing his or her own wishes, I see no good reason for holding that he or she lacks the capacity to express them validly and effectively and to authorise the medical man to make the examination or give the treatment which he advises. After all, a minor under the age of 16 can, within certain limits, enter into a contract. He or she can also sue and be sued, and can give evidence on oath. Moreover, a girl under 16 can give sufficiently effective consent to sexual intercourse to lead to the legal result that the man involved does not commit the crime of rape — see *R. v. Howard* [1966] 1 W.L.R. 13 at 15 when Lord Parker C.J. said:

'in the case of a girl under 16, the prosecution, in order to prove rape, must prove either that she physically resisted, or if she did not, that her understanding and knowledge were such that she was not in a position to decide whether to consent or resist ... there are many girls under 16 who know full well what it is all about and can properly consent.'

Accordingly, I am not disposed to hold now, for the first time, that a girl aged less than 16 lacks the power to give valid consent to contraceptive advice or treatment, merely on account of her age ...

On this part of the case accordingly I conclude that there is no statutory provision which compels me to hold that a girl under the age of 16 lacks the legal capacity to consent to contraceptive advice, examination and treatment provided that she has sufficient understanding and intelligence to know what they involve ...

[T]here may well be cases, and I think there will be some cases, where the girl refuses either to tell the parents herself or to permit the doctor to do so and in such cases, the doctor will, in my opinion, be justified in proceeding without the parents' consent or even knowledge provided he is satisfied on the following matters: (1) that the girl (although under 16 years of age) will understand his advice; (2) that he cannot persuade her to inform her parents or to allow him to inform the parents that she is seeking contraceptive advice; (3) that she is very likely to begin or to continue having sexual intercourse with or without contraceptive treatment; (4) that unless she receives contraceptive advice or treatment her physical or mental health or both are likely to suffer; (5) that her best interests require him to give her contraceptive advice, treatment or both without the parental consent."

For both judges whether a girl under the age of sixteen could give a valid consent to contraceptive advice and treatment depended upon her understanding. Lord Scarman emphasises that the doctor must be satisfied that the girl possesses sufficient understanding and intelligence to enable her to understand the broad nature of the advice and the wider social consequences of her proposed actions. Lord Fraser suggests that a girl under the age of sixteen has sufficient capacity to give a valid consent if, *inter alia*, she will understand his advice and that, unless the doctor provides the advice requested, her physical or mental health or both are likely to suffer. This will be a very difficult test for doctors to apply and requires far more of teenagers before they can give a valid consent than is required of adults.[20]

5.1.ii.c   Age, the contraceptive patient and popular morality. Evident within the judgments in *Gillick* is the view of contraception as essentially a medical matter. However, on this medical matter views are very much influenced by personal morals. Lord Fraser in the House of Lords referred to the development of legislation providing for contraception from the National Health Service (Family Planning) Act 1967 to the National Health Service Act 1977 and then continued:

> "These, and other, provisions show that Parliament regarded 'advice' and 'treatment' on contraception and the supply of appliances for contraception as essentially medical matters. So they are, but they may also raise moral and social questions on which many people feel deeply, and in that respect they differ from ordinary medical advice and treatment."[21]

Lord Templeman's was one of the minority judgments in the case. His views upon the traditional values of the patriarchal family, heterosexual marriage and motherhood are clear from the following extract:

Gillick v. West Norfolk and Wisbech AHA
[1986] I A.C. 112, HL at 202–203, *per* Lord Templeman

"The doctor who provides contraceptive facilities without the knowledge of the parent deprives the parent of the opportunity to protect the girl from sexual intercourse by persuading and helping her to avoid sexual intercourse or by the exercise of parental power which may prevent sexual intercourse. The parent might be able to bring pressure on a male participant to desist from the commission of the offence of sexual intercourse with a girl under 16. The parent might be able and willing to exercise parental power by removing the family or the girl to a different neighbourhood and environment and away from the danger of sexual intercourse.

The second objection is that a parent will sooner or later find out the truth, probably

---

[20]   The decision in *Gillick* has been widely criticised. See M. Jones, "Consent to Medical Treatment by Minors after Gillick" (1986) 2 *Professional Negligence* 41; J. Eekelaar, "The Eclipse of Parental Rights" (1986) 102 *Law Quarterly Review* 4.
[21]   [1986] 1 A.C. 112 at 166.

sooner, and may do so in circumstances which bring about a complete rupture of good relations between members of the family and between the family and the doctor. It is inevitable that when the parent discovers that the girl is practising sexual intercourse, the girl will in self justification and in an attempt to reassure the parent reveal that she is relying on contraceptive facilities provided by the doctor in order to avoid pregnancy. The girl and the doctor will be the loser by this revelation.

The third and main objection advanced on behalf of the respondent parent, Mrs Gillick, in this appeal is that the secret provision of contraceptive facilities for a girl under 16 will, it is said, encourage participation by the girl in sexual intercourse and this practice offends basic principles of morality and religion which ought not to be sabotaged in stealth by kind permission of the National Health Service. The interests of a girl under 16 require her to be protected against sexual intercourse. Such a girl is not sufficiently mature to be allowed to decide to flout the accepted rules of society. The pornographic press and the lascivious film may falsely pretend that sexual intercourse is a form of entertainment available to females on request and to males on demand but the regular, frequent or casual practice of sexual intercourse by a girl or a boy under the age of 16 cannot be beneficial to anybody and may cause harm to character and personality. Before a girl under 16 is supplied with contraceptive facilities, the parent who knows most about the girl and ought to have the most influence with the girl is entitled to exercise parental rights of control, supervision, guidance and advice in order that the girl may, if possible, avoid sexual intercourse until she is older. Contraception should only be considered if and when the combined efforts of parent and doctor fail to prevent the girl from participating in sexual intercourse and there remains only the possibility of protecting the girl against pregnancy resulting from sexual intercourse.

These arguments have provoked great controversy which is not legal in character. Some doctors approve and some doctors disapprove of the idea that a doctor may decide to provide contraception for a girl under 16 without the knowledge of the parent. Some parents agree and some parents disagree with the proposition that the decision must depend on the judgment of the doctor. Those who favour doctor power assert that the failure to provide confidential contraceptive treatment will lead to an increase in pregnancies amongst girls under 16. As a general proposition, this assertion is not supported by evidence in this case, is not susceptible to proof and in my opinion is of doubtful validity. Availability of confidential contraceptive treatment may increase the demand for such treatment. Contraceptive treatment for females usually requires daily discipline in order to be effective and girls under 16 frequently lack that discipline. The total number of pregnancies amongst girls of under 16 may, therefore, be increased and not decreased by the availability of contraceptive treatment. But there is no doubt that an individual girl who is denied the opportunity of confidential contraceptive treatment may invite or succumb to sexual intercourse and thereby become pregnant. Those who favour parental power assert that the availability of confidential contraceptive treatment will increase sexual activity by girls under 16. This argument is also not supported by evidence in the present case, and is not susceptible to proof. But it is clear that contraception removes or gives an illusion of removing the possibility of pregnancy and therefore removes restraint on sexual intercourse. Some girls would come under pressure if contraceptive facilities were known to be available and some girls under 16 are susceptible to male domination.

Parliament could decide whether it is better to have more contraception with the possibility of fewer pregnancies and less disease or whether it is better to have less contraception with the possibility of reduced sexual activity by girls under 16. Parliament could ensure that the doctor prevailed over the parent by reducing the age of consent or by expressly authorising a doctor to provide contraceptive facilities for any girl without informing the parent, provided the doctor considered that his actions were for the benefit of the girl. Parliament could, on the other hand, ensure that the parent prevailed over the doctor by forbidding contraceptive treatment for a girl under 16 save by or on the recommendation of the girl's general medical practitioner and with the consent of the parent who has registered the girl as a patient of that general practitioner. Some girls, it is said, might pretend to be over 16 but a doctor in doubt could always require confirmation from the girl's registered medical practitioner."

In July 1992, the Conservative Government published its Health Strategy in the White Paper, *The Health of the Nation: A Strategy for Health in England*,[22] with one of its stated objectives being to reduce the rate of conceptions in the under-sixteens to 4.8 per 1,000 thirteen to fifteen year-olds by the year 2000. Kaye Wellings in *Sexual Behaviour in Britain: The National Survey of Sexual Attitudes & Lifestyles*[23] suggests that at least 20 per cent of sixteen years-olds are sexually active, and in some areas this percentage may be significantly higher. The dilemma expressed by Lord Templeman is whether denying teenagers information about and access to contraception will discourage them from engaging in sexual intercourse or whether these services should be available to teenagers to protect them from the unwanted consequences of intercourse. Lord Templeman's views are based upon a construction of teenage girls as irresponsible, exploitable and vulnerable. Jane Lewis and Fenella Cannell argue that the Gillick campaign has to be understood within the context of the "politicisation" of the family in the 1980s. They argue that Mrs Gillick's case was founded upon the presumption that sex and reproduction were to be limited to within the traditional family following marriage. The family and hence the mother, was more suited than the medical profession to preventing teenage sexual activity. Allowing doctors to provide teenage girls with contraception permitted them to intrude into the family and to undermine the traditional power of mothers within the home:

J. LEWIS & F. CANNELL
"The Politics of Motherhood in the 1980s: Warnock, Gillick and Feminists"[24]

"THE GILLICK CASE

1. Parents Versus Doctors
Mrs Gillick's philosophy, as opposed to the details of her political campaign, have to be pieced together, for she has been careful to confine her arguments to a narrow range

---

[22] *The Health of the Nation: A Strategy for Health in England*, Cmnd. 1986 (1992).
[23] K. Wellings *et al.*, *Sexual Behaviour in Britain: The National Survey of Sexual Attitudes & Lifestyles* (Harmondsworth: Penguin, 1994).
[24] (1986) 13 *Journal of Law and Society* 321 at 326–329.

of issues. At the core of her thinking is the belief that biological parents have the natural right to control children. She argues that being a parent is hard work and that parents' rights over their children should not be usurped by professionals or the State. There are three strands to Mrs Gillick's attack on the medical profession. First, she maintained that the provision of contraceptives to under sixteen year-olds involved a social not a clinical judgment, and that parents were the proper people to make social judgments affecting their children . . .

Second, Mrs Gillick argued that doctors were encouraging illicit sex by prescribing for under sixteen year-olds . . .

Finally, both Mrs Gillick and many of her supporters charged the medical profession with a vested interest in promoting birth control, bordering on commercial graft. This did not form part of Mrs Gillick's legal case, but shows the depth of her anti-professional feeling. She claimed that medical practice in birth control clinics was 'not so much about medical ethics, but more of good business practice' . . .

In the courts, Mrs Gillick asked for a declaration, first, that the advice in the D.H.S.S. Circular was unlawful because it amounted to advising doctors to commit the offence of causing or encouraging illicit sexual intercourse with girls under sixteen years of age, and, second, that a doctor could not give birth control advice and treatment to any child under sixteen without the parents' consent, because to do so would be inconsistent with the parents' rights . . . The Court of Appeal, . . . agreed with Mrs Gillick. Lord Justice Parker suggested that 'talk of clinical judgment is . . . misplaced', for he could 'see nothing particularly clinical in a decision to fit an intra-uterine device in a Roman Catholic girl aged 13 . . .'. He took the position that it was 'clearly established that a parent or guardian has, as such, a parcel of rights in relation to children in his [*sic*] custody . . . [which] can be neither abandoned nor transferred'. His judgment that parents had the right to complete control over their children was supported by Lord Justice Eveleigh, who felt that it was impossible to say that a parent with 'Mrs Gillick's attitude is not acting in the best interests of the child'. Nevertheless he chose to base his judgment on an appeal to child welfare (which he derived from parental rights), rather than parental rights *per se*. The House of Lords decision confirmed the legal commentary that followed the judgment by the Court of Appeal, much of which rejected such a view of complete parental control as too broad . . .

Two of the Law Lords followed the Court of Appeal in supporting Mrs Gillick, and, in so doing, followed Lord Justice Parker in their assessment of parental rights. It seems clear that they did so for pragmatic reasons. Having decided that the outcome they wished to avoid was premature sexual activity on the part of the teenage girls, their 'hunch' told them that this was best accomplished by assuring Mrs Gillick that she had full right to control her children. Lord Templeman held that without the parent the doctor would not be able to form a view, 'clinical or otherwise', and Lord Brandon maintained that to permit birth control treatment for under sixteen year-olds 'must involve promoting, encouraging or facilitating the having of sexual intercourse between the girl and the man'. Lords Fraser, Scarman and Bridge preferred to work from guiding principles in respect to child welfare. As Lord Fraser put it: 'parental rights to control a child do not exist for the benefit of the parent', and in the words of Lord Scarman: 'parental rights are derived from parental duty and exist only so long as they are needed for the protection of the person and property of the child'. Thus a majority of the Law Lords derived parental rights from parental duties and the 'dwindling right' of a parent to control the child. Lord Fraser held that it was absurd to suggest that a boy or girl could not consent to examination for a broken bone at fifteen years of age, and pointed out that the courts had already held it possible for an under age girl to 'give sufficiently effective consent to sexual intercourse' to prevent a man being convicted of rape. Thus as long as the child understood the issues involved she or he (the courts never acknowledged that they were talking only about female children) should be treated autonomously.

2. *The Control of Female Sexuality by the Good Mother*

The debate in the courts was phrased in terms of parental rights versus those of the medical profession, but the subject of the debate was in fact the control of female sexuality and the role of mothers. In the case of the dissenting Law Lords, the concern about teenage sexuality was made quite explicit. In Lord Templeman's memorable phrase: 'There are many things which a girl under 16 needs to practice, but sex is not one of them'. He went on to argue that the birth control pill only gave the illusion of removing the possibility of pregnancy because under sixteen year-olds were too ill-disciplined to take it regularly, and yet in providing such an illusory protection it simultaneously removed restraint on sexual intercourse.

The dissentient Law Lords were, in common with many other supporters of Mrs Gillick, concerned above all to stop teenage sex. Like Lord Devlin, they believed they were deciding whether it was parents or doctors who were to be given the power to determine whether minors were 'to be provided with the means of sexual promiscuity'. In view of the words he chose to frame the issue, it is not surprising that Lord Devlin went on to declare that the battle 'may be socially the most important to come before the courts this decade'. Intertwined with the firm belief that sex and reproduction belong inside marriage was the idea that 'the good mother' would stop teenage sex. Almost all shades of opinion harbour doubts as to the capacity, physical and emotional, of young teenagers for motherhood. The medical profession favoured preventing teenage pregnancy, intervening to prescribe contraceptives according to informally agreed criteria. According to a poll in one medical journal, ninety per cent were ready to give contraceptives to a girl who said she had a steady boyfriend, thereby signalling her maturity. The same rationale has been found to apply to doctors deciding whether a young woman 'merits' an abortion. Feminists strongly object to such criteria, seeing them as part and parcel of the medical construction of, and control over, women's 'contraceptive career'.

In the formulation of the pro-Gillick lobby, 'good mothers' are best relied on to prevent the creation of a following generation of 'bad mothers'. The firm emphasis of Mrs Gillick herself and of a substantial number of her supporters is on the right of mothers to control their daughter's sexuality in the name of protection."

Lewis and Cannell argue that the focus of Mrs Gillick's campaign was upon the need to protect young girls from sexual exploitation and to protect values of "traditional" morality. At the same time, it was about the role of the mother within the family:

> "The determination to uphold parental rights over (girl) children derives from the desire to exalt family power over professional power and to curb female sexuality. Furthermore, the campaign for parental rights has been presented in terms of a defence of women's power within the family."[25]

[25] J. Lewis & F. Cannell, "The Politics of Motherhood in the 1980's: Warnock, Gillick and Feminists", *ibid.*, at 331.

5.1.iii   *Effective contraception and women's health*

5.1.iii.a   Health risks. The duty imposed upon the Secretary of State to arrange for the provision of advice, treatment and supply of contraceptives may have been imposed because contraception is perceived to be a medical matter (a view accepted in *Gillick*) and, therefore, one which has a valid call upon the resources of the National Health Service. Contraception is provided to women to enable us to regulate our fertility, not, as with the majority of drugs or medical devices, to treat a disease or illness. Nevertheless, women who use contraceptives expose themselves to health risks. Contraception is, in this respect, a mixed blessing for women. It has, to some extent, removed the fear of an unwanted pregnancy but at the cost of new potential risks to health. Scarlett Pollock suggests that the methods of contraception available and used ensure effectiveness and male pleasure at the expense of creating risks to women's health. This, she argues, is a consequence of the power inequalities between men and women. The silencing of women and the failure to acknowledge women's sexual needs mean that male priorities dominate.[26] As with any area of medical treatment a woman must consent to the touching involved in the medical consultation and make a decision as to which form of contraception to use based upon information regarding the costs and benefits of the various methods available:

G. DOUGLAS
Law, Fertility and Reproduction[27]

"The method of contraception used by a person depends on a number of factors. The most important is the choice or preference of the user. But it may be misleading to assume that the choice is a particularly informed one. Thomas, for example, has argued that the medical literature presents doctors with a picture of a woman as having a 'contraceptive career,' with different contraceptive needs applying to different stages of the reproductive lifecycle. Thus, in the sexually active period before childbirth, the need to prevent pregnancy is considered paramount, so that the pill or IUD is thought appropriate. Then comes a period of childbearing when pregnancies are spaced. Avoidance of pregnancy is regarded as less important here, so that a less reliable method, such as the diaphragm, may be suggested. When childbearing is complete, sterilisation may be discussed (and Thomas notes that, at this point, potential health risks from the pill or IUD may be stressed for the first time). Thomas concludes that such an approach is based on the assumptions that birth should take place within marriage, that births should be spaced and limited, and that childbearing should not be delayed too long because of health risks for both mother and foetus. On this analysis, woman's 'choice' in contraception becomes that of the doctor, and little attention is paid to those women who want a different 'career,' such as early sterilisation.

In law, choice becomes a matter of consent — has the person consented to be treated

---

[26]   S. Pollock, "Sex and the Contraceptive Act" in H. Homans (ed.), *supra.*, n. 5.
[27]   G. Douglas, *supra.*, n. 11 at pp. 49–50, 61–65.

by a particular method? In particular, if a medical examination or procedure is to be carried out, a lack of consent to this may make the act an unlawful battery. Furthermore, before consent can be given, information may be required so that the person can weigh up which method she should opt for . . .

(i)   Choosing to have contraceptive treatment at all

It is clear that if a doctor decided, for example, to sterilise a woman during a caesarean operation, or inserted an IUD post-partum without telling her, a battery would be committed. A patient may sign a consent form before undergoing an operation, whereby he or she authorises the surgeon to carry out any further measures which are deemed immediately necessary to the patient's life or health. In fact, such consent is probably not required where the patient's condition as revealed during the operation is such that further treatment is needed and it is unreasonable to postpone it. But in *Devi v. West Midlands Area Health Authority*, the plaintiff was undergoing a minor gynaecological operation, when the surgeon discovered that her womb was ruptured. He sterilised her at once, and she recovered damages since she had not expressly consented to the operation and it was not *immediately* necessary.

The onus is on the plaintiff to prove lack of consent, and in *Chatterton v. Gerson*, Bristow J. held that, although consent must be 'real,' once a patient is informed in broad terms of the nature of what is going to be done, and consents, that consent is real. Any claim against the doctor in such a situation should then be in negligence rather than battery, which should be reserved for cases where the doctor proceeds without any consent.

(ii)   Choosing a particular method

If the patient appears to have consented, then she would have to argue that the doctor was negligent in explaining to her the risks of the proposed treatment. This is of particular importance in the sphere of contraception. There is a variety of methods to choose from, offering different degrees of safety in terms of side-effects and effectiveness in terms of avoidance of conception.

Safety. Doubts about the safety of female contraceptives, and criticism of the cavalier attitude taken to women's fears and concerns about side-effects, are increasing. For example, it was recently claimed that the pill would eventually be seen as a health supplement taken by most women, and offering protection against ovarian and uterine cancer. Yet it was later reported that three million pill-users under 35 are to be warned for the first time of a slightly increased risk of developing breast cancer. Professor Clair Chilvers, a leading researcher into the pill, was quoted as saying:

> 'At the moment, *we do not know* what the risks are for women after the menopause, because women who have had prolonged early use of the pill are only about 40 years old now, *so we will not know* for another 10–15 years.'

While it may be true to say that for most women, use of the pill is safer than undergoing pregnancy or childbirth, how are they expected to assess this sort of warning? It appears that only when several hundreds of thousands more women have run the risk for another decade will we be in a position to judge, which is small comfort for women today.

It has also been alleged that new contraceptive techniques have been tested on third-world or poor women first; for example, the contraceptive pill was first tested in Puerto Rico, and the controversial injectable hormone contraceptive Depo-Provera is alleged to have been tried extensively on poorer women. In fact, it is clear that *all* women who wish to use contraceptives have been used as guinea-pigs, as evidenced by the litigation arising from use of the Dalkon Shield IUD involving nearly 200,000 women around the world. This has been associated with around 20 deaths due to contraction of pelvic inflammatory disease, and the risk of maternal death from perforation, spontaneous abortion, ectopic pregnancy and septic complications of pregnancy is also higher with the IUD. Other types of contraception are much safer; while female sterilisation carries a small risk of death, so does any operation involving general anaesthetic; vasectomy is not associated with a meaningful risk of death. Barrier methods are not regarded as carrying this type of risk.

Lesser side-effects, if they may be called that, range from a higher risk of stroke for some women on the pill; pelvic inflammatory disease caused by the IUD leading to infertility; severe disturbance of the menstrual cycle, including prolonged heavy bleeding and delayed return of fertility with Depo-Provera; to greater risk of gall-stones from the pill, and vaginal irritation from spermicides used in conjunction with the condom, cap or diaphragm or on their own. Generally, 'the risk to the user of controlling fertility is least when a simple method of contraception, such as the condom, is linked with back-up legal abortion in the case of unwanted pregnancy.' Unfortunately, such an approach is not generally advocated, either because abortion is seen as problematical, or possibly, as Pollock argues, because contraceptives are developed with men's sexual enjoyment, rather than women's health, as the prime concern, so that male unwillingness to use a condom is given greater weight than women's need for a safe and effective contraceptive.

Effectiveness. The effectiveness of a contraceptive depends in part upon the acceptability of the method, and the motivation for using it. It has been found, for example, that effectiveness in use improves as couples reach the number of children desired to complete their family. In ranking order of use effectiveness of the main methods, sterilisation is almost completely effective, injectables are next most effective, followed by oral contraceptives, IUDs, condoms and diaphragms, and *coitus interruptus*. The problem for women is that the more reliable methods take control over the reproductive decision away from the woman. Sterilisation is usually irreversible; injectables are frequently much longer-lasting in effect than the woman might want; IUDs should be removed by skilled personnel (thus, in China, women can be prevented from seeking to become pregnant without official approval by being denied the opportunity to have the IUD removed). The reliability of barrier methods may not be stressed by medical professionals precisely because they do not require medical skill in their prescription.

The final conundrum is that, where the man takes the contraceptive precaution, such as using a condom or perhaps in the future, taking a male pill, the woman must trust him. While this is equally true for a man whose partner is the contraceptive user, the consequences for him of an unwanted pregnancy are never as drastic as they are for the woman. Even if a fully reliable and safe male contraceptive were developed, many women might still be reluctant to leave things entirely to the man.

(iii) Information required to make a choice

How much information is the doctor required to give to enable the person to choose between all these? In *Sidaway v. Board of Governors of the Bethlem Royal Hospital*, the House of Lords adopted the *Bolam* test . . . It was open to question whether this test, originally framed in relation to a doctor's duties in respect of diagnosis and treatment, should apply to disclosure of information, but in *Sidaway*, their lordships (apart from Lord Scarman) did regard it as a basic starting-point, though they differed in their views of precisely how far it should apply.

Although the case concerned surgery, and may be of most significance in relation to major interventions, it is of general application, and has been held to apply to advice about choice of contraceptive methods. In *Gold v. Haringey Health Authority*, at first instance, Schiemann J. had held that it only applied to therapeutic and not contraceptive situations, but the Court of Appeal rejected the distinction ... While I would argue that they were correct to do so, they should also have recognised that the decision to use contraception depends upon social as well as medical factors, for which *Bolam* is an inadequate test.

Yet the same line was taken by the Court of Appeal in *Blyth v. Bloomsbury Area Health Authority*, a case involving Depo-Provera. The plaintiff knew what this was, but was not informed of all the risks attaching to the injection. The court considered that 'there was no obligation on the hospital to give the patient all the information available to the hospital.' Astonishingly, this is apparently so, even in response to a general request for information. Thus, even if a patient asks, a doctor can still withhold information, unless, presumably, a direct and specific question is put to him or her — failure to provide an accurate answer would surely then amount to fraud and negative the consent of the patient.

Where a failure to warn is established, it seems that liability will still only follow if the plaintiff can show that she would not have proceeded with the treatment or would have taken steps to minimise the risk had she been aware of it — the problem of causation. In *Thake v. Maurice* causation was made out, because the plaintiff showed that she would have been alert to the possibility of pregnancy resulting from her husband's failed vasectomy, and would have been able to seek an abortion in time. But if the plaintiff would have proceeded with the treatment anyway, or would have refused to have an abortion, she will not have established that her loss was due to the failure to warn."

As Gillian Douglas mentions, contraceptive appliances, such as IUDs,[28] and drugs, such as the oral contraceptive pill, have been associated with a number of "health scares", often following from their initial introduction as a method (it being only through use by large numbers of women that unexpected side-effects become apparent). For example, initial use of the oral contraceptive pill was followed by concerns about a link between the pill and thrombosis, identified as resulting from high levels of oestrogen.[29] In 1995, there were further concerns, this time surrounding "new generation" pills, precipitated by the announcement of the Committee on Safety of Medicines (CSM), on October 18, 1995, that the preliminary results of three studies indicated that seven brands of pill — those containing the synthetic hormones gestodene or desogestrel in combination with oestrogen — carried an increased risk of thrombosis.

[28] See P. R. Ferguson, *Drug Injuries and the Pursuit of Compensation* (London: Sweet & Maxwell, 1996), pp. 7–8. Effective contraception may be provided without consideration of the consequences, whereby women have used methods of contraception to time childbearing only to find they are infertile as a consequence of contraceptive use (see L. Doyal, "Infertility — a Life Sentence? Women and the National Health Service" in M. Stanworth (ed.), *Reproductive Technologies: Gender, Motherhood and Medicine* (Cambridge: Polity Press, 1987), p. 185).
[29] A. Leathard, *supra*, n. 3 at p. 112.

5.1.iii.b Side-effects. As a consequence of the way the judiciary and the legislature have dealt with contraception issues, effective control of how and when women use contraception has been given to the medical profession. Viewed as a medical matter, the choices available to women are constrained by the personal opinions of the medical practitioner. Research undertaken by Scarlett Pollock reveals that women found doctors dismissed as irrelevant recognised side-effects of concern to women because they were not life-threatening. The side-effects of contraception may be dismissed as "subjective" discounting women's experiences and problems identified by women because they are not classed as medical problems.

S. POLLOCK
"Refusing to take Women Seriously: 'Side Effects' and the Politics of Contraception"[30]

"Side Effects
Few women received from their doctors any information about side effects and health risks. Some were given advice about which contraceptive method to use; others were simply prescribed a particular brand of the pill or fitted with a specific sort of coil. Health risks were dismissed as negligible while side effects were demeaned as unimportant. The link between symptoms, possible side effects and the early indication of damage to women's health was rarely made. Women were discouraged from experimenting with contraception by their doctors, and advised to be content with what they had. Especially in view of the reliability of the pill and the coil, women were told that they were or ought to be 'happy on it' and that 'it would be silly to change' unless serious side effects were recognised.

Here lies the catch. Whether or not the symptoms women experience are interpreted as side effects; whether or not they are seen as serious; and who has the power to decide if they are and what should be done about them — determine the extent to which women are able to be flexible and to find the most suitable contraceptive method for them. As long as symptoms are not recognised to be possible side effects nor regarded as serious, there appears to be no problem — except for the woman. In her doctor's eyes, she is 'happy' or should be.

Women's symptoms are commonly dismissed by doctors who show little interest in women's problems with contraception. Yet women do not have the luxury of being able to dismiss their doctors so easily. Medical control over the availability of birth control makes women acutely aware of the significance of their doctor's attitudes. Women are forced to be concerned about their doctor's opinions about contraception, abortion, sexuality and proper womanhood in order to obtain or change their contraceptives to those distributed by medics.

When medics cast suspicion upon the reliability of the statements made by patients, they protect their own views from challenge or change. Their legitimacy as the proper decision-makers in contraceptive or other health matters is reinforced. This form of legitimization is frequently used by dominant social groups to safeguard their position.

---

[30] In R. Arditti, R. Duelli Klein & S. Minden (eds), *Test-Tube Women: What Future for Motherhood?* (London: Pandora Press, 1984), pp. 141-151.

The medical prerogative to reference an individual's physical or mental state as unhealthy is a powerful means of bringing that person's rationality or reliability into doubt. Whether people are portrayed as weakened, diseased, over-anxious, sickly, hysterical, pathological or neurotic, the result is the same — they appear to be incapable and unreliable.

These adjectives are applied most often to women. And they are applied regardless of any individual woman's state of health or illness. Medicine as a profession has played a central role in defining women to be intellectually incapable, lacking in physical stamina, periodically polluting, sexually dangerous and emotionally unfit solely on the grounds of being female and not male. It was not surprising that the women I talked to had encountered all of these attitudes over several years of using contraception. Medical dominance, accentuated by male dominant perceptions of women, resulted in frequent conflicts between women and their doctors. Convincing her doctor that she is a rational and responsible human being, and not 'another neurotic female', is not always an easy task for a woman.

Is it related?

'Come back if you have any problems' was the extent of the advice most women received when first prescribed the pill or fitted with the coil. The first problem they had was trying to work out what sort of problem was likely to be considered a problem associated with the contraceptive. When symptoms occurred which women thought might be related, and these were reported to their doctors, more often than not women found their complaints were dismissed or invalidated. Yet the advice remained the same:

> 'I've complained before of what I thought might be side effects of the pill and they very much pooh-poohed it, saying: "You're getting neurotic about it, hearing a lot of stories, whereas in fact it doesn't do this." Every time I go to the family planning clinic they say: "Oh it's nothing, it's nothing." When I told them I'd been on it (the pill) for six years and wanted to know whether I should take a break off it, they said: "Well, it's a mild one so it doesn't particularly matter. As soon as you have any side effects, then it's time to start thinking about coming off it." '

How could the woman in this example find such advice reassuring when she had over several years been reporting symptoms which included cramps, migraine, depression, loss of sex drive and vaginal thrush (yeast)? How was it even possible for her to follow the advice she was given? As each time she asked about a symptom she thought might be a side effect, it was dismissed as nothing or treated in isolation, she was unable to work out whether her symptoms indicated that it was time to start thinking about coming off it . . .

Doctors of the women I spoke with seemed to have very definite opinions about the side effects and risks involved in using contraceptives — so definite that what the women said about their reactions often made very little difference. In some cases women were left wondering whether they hadn't really imagined it all; neither their symptoms nor their questions appeared to make any impression upon their doctor . . .

The experience of having their symptoms and questions invalidated was combined with the general atmosphere of medics being too busy and having more important things to do than turn their attention to women who were complaining of nothing. So, women grew less inclined to discuss their symptoms with doctors. Over time, many doubts were raised in the women's minds about the general level of medical expertise. Indeed, cynicism increased with experience of consulting doctors.

Medical control over distribution of many birth control measures meant that women had to continue to negotiate with their doctors even if they would rather not. Learning how to negotiate included assessing which symptoms their doctors were likely to consider as possible side effects. One criterion emerged as particularly significant: could the symptom be measured independently by the doctor? That is, if the medic did not have to rely upon the woman's word for evidence but was able to use measures such as bacterial cultures, weight scales or blood pressure levels, it seemed more likely that it would be recognised as a side effect. Less tangible symptoms, including mood changes, headaches, reduced sex drive, cramps, and other pains and discomforts, were less likely to be said by doctors to be related to the contraceptive method. Instead, being female and/or being unfeminine were implied to be the source of the women's symptoms.

In practice, 'other reasons' for symptoms were associated by doctors with patriarchal ideas about the 'normal' characteristics of females or 'abnormal' and unladylike behaviour. Women inferred from their doctor's approach that it was nothing unusual for women to experience, or think they experienced, untoward symptoms. Vaginal discharge and discomfort, for example, were treated as natural despite the insistence of the women involved that this was not so . . .

This is a very serious problem for women. It can and frequently does result in the failure to quickly assess and deal with symptoms which may indicate or develop into serious health problems. It forces women to live with unnecessary discomfort and pain. The invalidation of our experience precludes the possibility of finding further evidence about side effects, their relation to health risks and the effects of using contraceptives over many years. The acknowledged ignorance about long-term effects of contraceptives such as the pill, the coil, and Depo-Provera; the high proportion of women worldwide who use them; and the length of time over which women have and will continue to use them make it urgent that this problem be confronted.

Is it serious?
Who decides what is serious and for whom? How are women to decide whether symptoms are serious enough to warrant changing contraceptive methods? When does a symptom indicate a risk to the woman's health rather than simply a discomfort to put up with? Questions such as these are continually part of women's experiences and dilemmas of contraception. Medical ignorance of these issues is not helped by the dismissal of the questions as unimportant; by the dismissal of women as unimportant; by the dismissal of contraception as a social issue — except when it comes to sharing medical powers over birth control; nor by the dismissal as insignificant health risks which do not appear to be fatal.

The women I talked with had a great deal of difficulty trying to find out from their doctors whether their symptoms were something to be concerned about, and what should be done about them. Medical assumptions about contraceptive technology as low-risk-few-side-effects overrode what women reported as their experience. Hence, women found it hard to have a decent conversation with their doctors about what was happening to them . . .

Women found that their doctors did not consider their symptoms, even where they were recognised to be side effects as serious because they did not seem to present life-threatening hazards. Thus for the majority of women little attention was paid to their symptoms:

'They seem to think that if something isn't really, really serious — if it isn't going to kill you — then it isn't an important side effect, when it is! Somehow they maintain such a distance and say: "Oh, yes, well, you do get a certain amount of side effects when you're on the pill. Just keep on it and if it's still there in another few months . . ." I just thought: "Well God Almighty there I am having to sleep with my legs on top of a pillow they're so sore when they're lying flat — there's something wrong." '

This disregard for women's pain and discomfort was sometimes compounded by moralistic or punitive sexual attitudes:

'So I went to the doctor and the first thing she said was: "Are you on the pill?" and I said "Yes." "Oh, well, that's why then. If you go on the pill you expect to get these things. I'm not going to treat you. There's nothing wrong with you." '

The relationship between symptoms which were seen as 'merely' side effects and those which indicate life-threatening illnesses was rarely discussed. Side effects and health risks seemed to be regarded in medical 'knowledge' as two entirely separate issues. Side effects were taken to be common but insignificant while health risks were significant but uncommon. The potential for discovering the relation between them was thus completely missed . . .

It is obviously too late to recognise symptoms as serious only when they begin to threaten a woman's health and perhaps her life. As so many women are affected by the contraceptives available in adverse ways, we need a much clearer understanding of side effects and their relation to women's health. The only way to obtain more information is to take women seriously, to take our symptoms seriously, and to share and accumulate this evidence. When symptoms can be recognised as having a possible relation to contraception, women are in a better position to weigh up whether or not this is something to be concerned about. Changes can be noted, discussed and assessed regularly. The experience of other women is essential in judging our own symptoms. Too many women have suffered side effects and damage to their health as a result of women's symptoms not being taken seriously. We must learn from this experience before almost an entire generation of women pay the consequences in terms of our health."

Whether a doctor has been negligent in failing to acknowledge symptoms is judged by the *Bolam* standard. McNair J. in *Bolam v. Friern Hospital Management Committee*,[31] stated:

"The test is the standard of the ordinary skilled man exercising and professing to have that special skill. A man need not possess the highest expert skill at the risk of being found negligent . . . [I]t is sufficient if he exercises the ordinary skill of an ordinary competent man exercising that particular art . . . A doctor is not guilty of negligence if he acted in accordance with a practice accepted as proper by a responsible body of medical men skilled in that particular art . . . Putting it the other way round, a doctor is not negligent, if he is acting in accordance with such a practice, merely because there is a body of opinion that takes a contrary view."

---

[31]　*Bolam v. Friern Hospital Management Committee* [1957] 2 All E.R. 118.

If a doctor fails to acknowledge the side-effects which a woman, to whom the doctor has prescribed contraceptives, describes, and the woman suffers harm, the doctor would not be found negligent as long as "he acted in accordance with a practice accepted as proper by a responsible body of medical men skilled in that particular art".

5.1.iii.c Information about the risks. Not only must patients be informed of the broad nature of the contraceptive treatment, but doctors are under a duty to provide information to enable patients to decide whether to consent to a proposed course of contraceptive treatment. The House of Lords in *Sidaway v. Board of Governors of Bethlam Royal Hospital*[32] held that the appropriate test as to the amount of information which a doctor was under a duty to provide patients was to be decided on the basis of the test in *Bolam v. Friern Hospital Management Committee* (see above).[33] If the doctor fails to "act in accordance with a practice rightly accepted as proper by a body of responsible and skilled medical opinion" in providing information as to the consequences of the treatment, the risks and side-effects, and of alternatives, the doctor may be liable in negligence for any harm suffered by the patient. However, if it is not common practice or if there is a substantial body of medical practice which would not inform women of the side-effects of the method of contraception, a doctor will not be negligent for failing to do so. The only question then is whether a court would find the practice itself unreasonable. However, to succeed in an action in negligence the patient will also have to prove that harm was a result of the treatment consented to, and that consent would not have been given if fully informed. The trial judge in *Gold v. Haringey Health Authority*[34] drew a distinction between the advice which a doctor was under a duty to provide "in a therapeutic context and advice or warning in a contraceptive context". Schiemann J. held that, in providing information about contraception, the doctor owes a higher duty than in the therapeutic context. The claim in this case was that the plaintiff had not been warned that the sterilisation operation (contraception) might not succeed, that had she been informed her husband would have had a vasectomy, and consequently, she would not have become pregnant. Schiemann J. held that *Bolam* did not apply in a contraceptive context and applied his own judgement as to what the plaintiff should have been told. The Court of Appeal,[35] rejected the distinction, and held that the *Bolam* test applied in both therapeutic and non-therapeutic contexts. A doctor providing advice as to contraception must comply with a competent body of professional opinion. The Court of Appeal in *Blyth v. Bloomsbury Health Authority*[36] considered an appeal by the defendant health

---

[32] *Sidaway v. Board of Governors of Bethlam Royal Hospital* [1985] 1 A.C. 871.
[33] *Supra*, n. 31. For discussions of the ratio in *Sidaway* see H. Teff, "Consent to Medical Procedures: Paternalism, Self-Determination or Therapeutic Alliance?" (1985) 101 *Law Quarterly Review* 431; and M. Brazier, "Patient Autonomy and Consent to Treatment: the role of the law?" (1987) 7 *Legal Studies* 169.
[34] *Gold v. Haringey Health Authority* [1986] 1 F.L.R. 125.
[35] [1988] 1 Q.B. 481.
[36] *Blyth v. Bloomsbury Health Authority* (1989) 5 *Professional Negligence* 167.

authority against the finding by the trial judge that it had been negligent in insufficiently informing and advising the plaintiff about the possible side-effects of Depo-Provera, administered following a rubella injection after the birth of her first child. Where the woman asks a specific question a doctor is required to fulfil the test set out in *Sidaway*. Jonathan Montgomery suggests that these cases mark out the issue as solely within the field of medical "expertise" giving doctors "the power to control where power lies and the law legitimates power under the guise of expert knowledge."[37] Denying to women information about methods of contraception is an effective means of limiting women's control over reproductive matters.

The methods of contraception available, with the exception of barrier methods, ensure that women have to frequently consult their doctor. Women depend on medicine and doctors to attain some control over their own fertility.[38] We also depend upon the doctor to provide us with information about available methods of contraception. How fully women are informed about the risks and side-effects of methods of contraception depends upon the doctor having the time to provide the information and the ability to communicate it in a manner which is comprehensible to the women seeking advice. The cases suggest that inherent within the test in *Sidaway* is an acknowledgement that information which the doctor considers may lead the patient to make an unbalanced judgment, and refuse her consent to the method of contraception which the doctor considers is in her best interests, may be withheld. The judgments suggest that this is based upon the doctor's knowledge of the individual patient. But, in addition to individual patient knowledge, it has to be asked whether doctors make use of institutionalised cultural and social stereotypes of race, ethnicity and social class to deny women information. Given the trade off between effectiveness and risks to health some doctors may act upon beliefs surrounding class, ethnicity and race to deny certain women information upon which to make the decision as to which contraceptive method to choose. In doing so they may make the assumption that women are not capable of adequately assessing their situation because of their lack of medical training, their prejudices, their personality, or perhaps even their lifestyle (which clearly amounts to a breach of the doctor's duty of care). This said, do those in charge of giving out contraception largely dictate the contraceptives that women will "choose", since their own prejudices govern the information put across as well as the contraceptives available?[39] Differences between women may lead doctors to act upon beliefs about types of women, providing differing amounts of information about the available methods of contraception, thus denying some women the right to make an informed choice between effectiveness and risks. As noted by Gillian Douglas above, Hilary Thomas's

[37] J. Montgomery, "Power/Knowledge/Consent: Medical Decisionmaking" (1988) 51 *Modern Law Review* 245 at 247.
[38] H. Roberts, *The Patient Patients: Women and their Doctors* (London:, Pandora Press, 1985), p. 3.
[39] P. Foster, *Women and the Health Care Industry: An Unhealthy Relationship?* (Buckingham: OUP, 1995), pp. 15–18.

study of medical literature on contraception led her to identify a medical construction of the "contraceptive career":

> "Different types of patient and of the situation of the patient have been devised. This has led to the identification of different stages in lifecycle — the reproductive lifecycle — and of the contraceptive needs which are thought to be associated with each stage. These stages are: a sexually active period before childbearing, including perhaps before marriage; a period of childbearing during which pregnancies are spaced; and the period of fertile years after the desired number of children have been born."[40]

The real needs of women are ignored as each individual is matched with the method of contraception considered to be appropriate to her stage in the contraceptive career.

If, as Lord Fraser states in *Gillick*, "contraception and the supply of appliances for contraception [are] essentially medical matters", there seems to be little evidence of concern for women's health in the "medical matter" of contraception provision.

5.1.iii.d *Manufacturer's legal duties.* In addition to the duty imposed upon the medical profession to provide information to women seeking their advice about and supplies of contraceptives, the manufacturer of contraceptive drugs and appliances is under a duty at both common law and under the Consumer Protection Act 1987 with regard to the provision of information to the user of their "products".[41] The duty imposed at common law is to provide adequate information about how to use the product and warnings of risks and side-effects. The duty is also a continuing duty so that if research reveals information after the product has been put into circulation, the manufacturer must have a system in place to either recall the product or to convey that information to users.

In addition to the common law, the Consumer Protection Act 1987 imposes upon the manufacturer strict liability for unsafe products.[42] Under section 2, liability for harm caused wholly or partly by a defect in the product is placed upon the following people:

2.–(1)   Subject to the following provisions of this Part, where any damage is caused

---

[40]   H. Thomas, "The Medical Construction of the Contraceptive Career" in H. Homans (ed.), *supra*, n. 5 at p. 61.

[41]   For a full discussion see P. R. Ferguson, *supra*, n. 28.

[42]   This legislation was the result of a thorough consideration of laws on product liability throughout Europe in the light of the harm caused by Thalidomide to the foetuses of women who took the drug whilst pregnant and uncertainty as to whether they were able to recover compensation under the common law. See Royal Commission on Civil Liability and Compensation for Personal Injury, Cmnd. 7054 (1978); *Liability for Defective Products*, Law Com. No. 82 (London: HMSO, 1977); and the E.C. Directive on Product Liability (Council Directive of July 25, 1985 (85/374/EEC)).

wholly or partly by a defect in a product, every person to whom subsection (2) below applies shall be liable for the damage.

(2)   This subsection applies to —

- (a)   the producer of the product;
- (b)   any person who, by putting his name on the product or using a trade mark or other distinguishing mark in relation to the product, has held himself out to be the producer of the product;
- (c)   any person who has imported the product into a member State from a place outside the member States in order, in the course of any business of his, to supply it to another.

The Act imposes strict liability upon the producer, "own brander" or importer of the product into the E.C.[43] Liability under the Act is strict but not absolute. Therefore, liability is incurred only where products are "defective", as set out in section 3:

3.—(1)   Subject to the following provisions of this section, there is a defect in a product for the purposes of this Part if the safety of the product is not such as persons generally are entitled to expect; and for those purposes "safety", in relation to a product, shall include safety with respect to products comprised in that product and safety in the context of risks of damage to property, as well as in the context of risks of death or personal injury.

(2)   In determining for the purposes of subsection (1) above what persons generally are entitled to expect in relation to a product all the circumstances shall be taken into account, including —

- (a)   the manner in which, and purposes for which, the product has been marketed, its get-up, the use of any mark in relation to the product and any instructions for, or warnings with respect to, doing or refraining from doing anything with or in relation to the product;
- (b)   what might reasonably be expected to be done with or in relation to the product; and
- (c)   the time when the product was supplied by its producer to another;

and nothing in this section shall require a defect to be inferred from the fact alone that the safety of a product which is supplied after that time is greater than the safety of the product in question.

Whether a product is "defective" or not is defined in terms of consumer expectations. This necessitates consideration of what people are generally entitled to expect which depends entirely upon the circumstances of the case. The risks have to be weighed against the benefits and the costs of not using the contraceptive, that is, a higher risk of unwanted pregnancy. The possible risks and side-effects of methods of contraception such as the contraceptive pill, injectable contraceptives and the IUD are known but accepted by many women who use them. Formulating the concept of "defect" in terms of "consumer expectations" means that a product, which causes harm of the kind

---

[43]   Liability is only imposed upon a supplier, such as a pharmacist, in limited circumstances, when the supplier, if asked within a reasonable period after which the damage occurs, is unable to identify the manufacturer, own brander or importer who supplied the product to him (s.2(3)).

which it is known, and expected, to cause, is not "defective". For example, if a woman suffers pelvic inflammatory disease as a result of an infection due to the insertion of an IUD which leaves her infertile (a known risk of this method of contraception), that product would not be considered "defective".[44]

However, section 3(2)(a) provides that in determining whether a product is "defective" consideration will be given to information, specifically instructions and warnings, provided with the product. A product, such as the oral contraceptive pill, IUD or diaphragm may be defective because the information provided with the product did not give an adequate warning of risks or side-effects. This may be, for example, because the warning is expressed in language which is comprehensible only to the medically qualified or is presented in very small writing. Following the deaths of a number of young women linked to the oral contraceptive pill, it has been suggested that the warning provided of the risk of thrombosis on leaflets provided with the pills is inadequate and that it should be clearly marked on the packet itself.[45] In February 1997, *The Sunday Times* reported plans to initiate a class action against the manufacturers of five of the "new generation" pills which were the subject of the announcement by the CSM in October 1995 warning of the early results of three studies which suggested an increased risk of thrombosis amongst users of these pills. It is alleged that the failure to provide adequate warning of the increased risks of these pills resulted in women suffering harmful and, in some cases, fatal side-effects.[46]

5.1.iv *Contraception and reproduction*
At the beginning of this chapter fears of population growth in the developing world were discussed in the context of their instrumentality in enabling women to obtain contraception in the West. Population controllers still see a need to limit population in the developing world, and frequently, because of less strict or even non-existent drug regulation, methods of contraception which are not permitted in the West are administered. Third World women have been used as guinea pigs in the development of contraception, as in the "testing" of the oral contraceptive pill on the women of Puerto Rico. Contraceptives not licensed for use in the West, because of uncertainty surrounding their safety, have been distributed in the developing world. Hazell Croall notes how Depo-Provera was used in U.S. sponsored population control programmes in the developing world after it had been banned in the U.S. and that, following the identification of the harm caused by the Dalkon Shield IUD, it was sold in the developing world at vastly discounted prices.[47] Contra-

---

[44] For further consideration of the concept of defectiveness see A. Stoppa, "The concept of defectiveness in the Consumer Protection Act 1987: a critical analysis" (1992) 12 *Legal Studies* 210.
[45] L. Lightfoot, "Families to sue on Pill Deaths", *The Sunday Times*, February 26, 1995.
[46] N. Pope, *The Sunday Times*, February 2, 1997.
[47] H. Croall, "Target Women: Women's Victimization and White Collar Crime" in R. E. Dobash, R. P. Dobash & L. Noakes (eds), *Gender and Crime* (Cardiff: University of Wales Press, 1995), pp. 227, 234, 240.

ception, where it prevents pregnancy, will offer women a means by which to avoid the risks to health presented by childbearing. Yet, are the risks of pregnancy and childbirth merely replaced by the risks of unmonitored contraception? As Jill Rakusen shows in her discussion of the administration of Depo-Provera, discrimination in the provision of contraception is not limited to its distribution in the developing world.

J. RAKUSEN
"Depo-Provera: The Extent of the Problem. A Case Study in the Politics of Birth Control"[48]

"The 'advantage' of DP is that, by virtue of its being injectable, control need not lie in the woman's hands. It has therefore been considered particularly useful, especially in population control programmes in the Third World, and for women anywhere who 'aren't sufficiently motivated to take a pill every day; cannot or *will not* use the Pill or IUD, and choose not to use condom, foam or diaphragm'; who are 'unable or unwilling' to use alternatives; who are 'illiterate, unreliable or irresponsible'. 1978 estimates are that between three and five million women in roughly seventy countries are using DP. The potential for the abuse of such a drug is obviously enormous.

Without doubt, the biggest potential abuse is in the Third World, where some population control programmes appear to be geared to reducing birth rates with little regard for the people at whom these programmes are directed.

Reports indicate that nearly half the mothers in Africa who are using birth control currently use DP. Thousands more use it in Asia and Latin America. Aggressive policies of distributors like the International Planned Parenthood Federation (IPPF) and of Upjohn, the manufacturers, contribute to wide 'acceptance' of the drug . . . [I]t is undoubtedly the case that contraceptives are big business with an enormous potential market, and there is particular potential for aggressive marketing techniques in the Third World.

In a deposition to the U.S. Securities and Exchange Commission unearthed by Minkin, the manufacturers of DP admitted paying $2,710,000 in bribes to 'employees of foreign governments and to their intermediaries for the purpose of obtaining sales to government agencies'. Bribes to hospital employees raised this total to $4,098,000, and a further $147,579 was paid out 'in connection with other foreign governmental actions related to the company's business'. Upjohn's deposition specifically notes that the above figures exclude 'small amounts which were paid to minor government employees to expedite governmental services'.

The speed with which DP can be given is unashamedly regarded by population controllers as one of DP's big bonuses ('cost effectiveness' being the prime motive). This, together with DP's 'beauty' as a method of contraception that women can't control for themselves, leads to family planning workers favouring DP and its like above other methods, particularly if they are being paid incentives for 'recruits' to their programmes. In turn it leads to screening and follow-up being either cursory or non-existent.

Adequate monitoring and follow-up are uncommon for another reason, the rationale being that if they were carried out (involving, for example, pelvic examinations and cervical smears), few women would 'accept' the method. This desire to 'protect'

---

[48] In H. Roberts (ed.), *Women, Health and Reproduction* (London: Routledge & Kegan Paul, 1981), pp. 77–83.

women from having knowledge about, and feeling comfortable with, their own bodies is a particularly ironic aspect of the DP saga. It should also be evident that if proper screening and follow-up were practised, far fewer women would end up on DP, since speed would be lost and it would no longer be possible to treat them as if on a conveyor belt.

Given concerns for cost effectiveness, the introduction of DP has meant that other methods which are more time-consuming to fit, and dispense, start to lose favour. An open letter from an observer in Africa makes this point:

> 'Everyone in FP [Family Planning] seems to think that because the diaphragm requires careful fitting and inserting and needs washing and storage it is not feasible for most situations here. Most clinic workers up-country are not trained in its use; even if they were, they might well be daunted by the need to give time-consuming individual instruction. And they can't afford to provide jellies, foams, creams.'

This last point illustrates how only those contraceptives which are valuable in terms of population control, as opposed to valuable as far as women's health is concerned, are considered appropriate for distribution abroad at subsidised rates.

I should add that some western medical schools today no longer teach students how to fit the diaphragm — together with the sheath, the safest method of birth control. As Dr Robert Hatcher of Emory University and Grady Memorial Hospital, Atlanta testified at the U.S. Select Committee on Population, some doctors 'discourage diaphragms because of the time it takes to fit them properly'. As for sheaths, there is a fear in the Indian sub-continent that western rejects are commonly dumped there — which could go some way towards explaining Asian men's so-called aversion to sheaths. As one former field-worker told me, 'Out of twenty I blew up, ten were defective.'

Another reason for the undisguised pleasure with which population controllers regard DP is that, in some under-developed countries, injections are considered by many of the indigenous population as the best form of medicine. The population controllers build on this by fostering the belief that because DP is an injectable, it must be good.

Many abuses relating to DP centre on the question of choice and informed consent. Indeed, for a variety of reasons, few women are offered anything but a travesty of choice. I have already shown how the distributors manipulate the choices available. Depo-Provera is also associated with clear-cut coercion, as are programmes involving other 'desirable' methods such as sterilisation and IUDs ... Again, it is black and minority group women who are particularly at risk from this kind of abuse.

Apart from examples of consent being sought under duress, cases have been reported where consent has not been sought at all. Examples from Scotland reported to me by social workers include a young girl who was given DP under the guise of a glucose injection; and a short-stay patient in a mental hospital who was informed after having been given an injection that this was for contraception. Mental patients are particularly vulnerable to this kind of abuse: it is, after all, almost as easy to give them the Pill without their knowledge, for they're often given six or seven pills a day anyway. Informed social workers suspect that DP as well as the Pill is not uncommonly given to unsuspecting women, *e.g.* to girls with little 'wrong' with them other than the label 'promiscuous'. In one working-class mental hospital in Scotland, it is fairly common knowledge among staff that DP is used in this way, 'especially by those psychiatrists who like zapping people with Modecate', as one of them put it to me. The case of a black 14-year-old from London serves as a final example of how DP can be given without the knowledge of the woman concerned: she had decided on the Pill, having changed her mind from the IUD, only to find that she had been given DP without her knowledge while she was under a general anaesthetic having an abortion. She only found out about this 'by accident' when she asked for her Pill prescription.

I have already illustrated some of the factors at work which impinge on the question of choice for women in the Third World. The above example opens up the question of the vulnerability of their black sisters in the West. There are considerable grounds for the widespread belief that black and Asian women are being singled out in a racist way as prime targets for DP. Of those women who *are* asked for their consent, it is doubtful whether many of them are given even cursory details on which to base their decision.

Leeds is one of several places in Britain where DP is given to many Asian women at the same time as routine post-delivery rubella injections; examples have come to light of both black and white women — but mainly black — being told that they *must* have the DP injection with that for rubella (DP is never essential, and certainly not in these circumstances). Furthermore, there are no grounds for the apparently prevalent belief that Asian women are more in need of rubella injections than their white sisters.

Many health and social workers have expressed concern about what appears to be a racist approach to contraception among their colleagues, and the Campaign Against Depo-Provera is collecting information on this issue in an attempt to find out the extent of the problem.

There are many case histories of Asian women suffering side-effects from DP (such as uncontrollable bleeding) which they had not been warned about (and although an Urdu leaflet on DP was produced in Rochdale, a town with a high immigrant population, it omitted to discuss such problems as heavy bleeding). In some cases doctors had not considered the symptoms important enough to warrant investigation, or had failed to grasp that symptoms such as dizziness, headaches, or even loss of periods, might in fact be side-effects of the drug. Sometimes, women had even been given another drug to counteract what their doctors had failed to recognise as side-effects from the first drug.

Because DP does not require any action on the woman's part, some doctors seem to feel that they do not need to explain anything. Certainly, as a community health worker reports, they often find 'explaining' difficult, sometimes believing that 'these women' don't understand anything anyway. Another worker reports:

> 'The women are treated not as human beings but as objects. Nurses and doctors point at them and talk about them as though they had no feelings. Their preferences are never sought. In addition there is the language problem . . . no hospital in this area employs interpreters.'

Often women try to avoid going to the doctor or family planning clinic because the experience is so unpleasant. Their English teachers may sometimes accompany them, but, as one Leeds teacher illustrates, this is not necessarily much help:

> 'They treated N. very badly, like an idiot; never explained anything. The nurse constantly talked to me, not to N. She told me: "These people have a low threshold of pain and can't be trusted to take pills regularly." That's presumably why they got her on the injections. She's been on them for nearly

three years now, with very bad headaches and back pain. She won't go to the clinic any more because they have been *so* unpleasant and rude, so she's stopped getting the injections.'

Research by Wendy Savage suggests that large numbers of women in Britain, probably the vast majority, are inadequately informed about DP. Similarly, a study of 150 women interviewed by the U.S. Institute for the Study of Medical Ethics reveals that few women had been warned of its possible dangers. With all this evidence, the following statement by the then Health Minister for England and Wales, Roland Moyle, is interesting: 'I would expect a doctor prescribing any contraceptive to discuss fully with the patient the possible short- and long-term side effects.' "

5.1.iv.a Enforced contraception and "unfit" mothers. Norplant is a method of birth control which involves the implantation of six matchstick-size capsules beneath the skin of a woman's upper arm. The capsules slowly release a synthetic hormone that can prevent conception for up to five years. Norplant was approved for use as a contraceptive in the U.S. by the Food and Drug Administration in 1990. It was heralded as "the most effective contraceptive ever made available"[49] but was soon the focus of controversy. Stacey Arthur identifies the three major controversies within the social and legal fields in the U.S. as being the use of Norplant in limiting the growth of poor and minority populations, the provision of incentives to drug users and women on welfare to use the implant and the employment of Norplant as a probation condition (it has since caused controversy in the U.K. because of allegations of unacceptable side-effects and the inability of doctors to remove the device).[50]

Tamar Lewis in "Implanted birth control device renews debate over forced contraception", quotes Dr Georges Annas, Director of the Programme on Law, Medicine and Ethics at Boston University School of Medicine:

> "A lot of people have given up on social policy, on taking care of poor women, and there is an increasing undercurrent that since we don't really know what to do about crack addicts, people with AIDS[,] and child abusers, we should stop them from having kids."[51]

Bills were introduced in States such as Kansas and Louisiana, which would have provided financial incentives (an initial sum when implanted and a monthly incentive) for women receiving welfare to use Norplant. A debate arose as to the use of Norplant as a means of social control and coercion:

> "On December 12, 1990, The Philadelphia Inquirer published an editorial

---

[49] *Newsday*, December 15, 1990, quoted by S. L. Arthur, "The Norplant Prescription: Birth Control, Woman Control, or Crime Control?" (1992) 40 U.C.L.A. L. Rev. 1 at 4.

[50] L. Jenkins, "Women sue over birth control implant", *The Times*, August 19, 1995; L. Hunt, "Mother sues over 'lost' implants", *The Independent*, May 20, 1995.

[51] T. Lewis, "Implanted birth control device renews debate over forced contraception", *New York Times*, January 10, 1991, quoted in M. T. Flannery, "Norplant: the New Scarlet Letter?" (1992) 8 *Journal of Contemporary Health Law and Policy* 201 at 208.

that ignited a national controversy over the appropriate use of Norplant. The editorial suggested that in order to curb the growing poverty among welfare recipients, mothers on welfare should be offered incentives to use Norplant. However, so many readers found the editorial racially tainted that the paper renounced the column and published an apology ... The developers of Norplant, including Dr Sheldon Segal, anticipated and feared such coercive use of the drug by government ... Dr Segal states that '[a]ny coercive purpose ... is a gross misuse of the method,' and that the line between incentive and coercion becomes gray especially 'when you single out a welfare mother, wave a $500 bill in front of her face and say that the government is going to induce you not to have children'."[52]

After noting the way in which the contraceptive implant, Norplant, has been employed as a means of social control in the U.S. Peggy Foster speculates:

"Since Norplant is only just becoming available for use in Britain, we clearly do not have any evidence of it being used in a coercive or overtly controlling way in relation to British women. However, given the tide of moral panic generated in the early 1990s against single young mothers living on benefit and calls for welfare benefits to be restricted to women with just one child, it may well not be long before some right-wing politician suggests that single mothers on income support should agree to Norplant as a condition of receiving further benefits."[53]

Coercing women on welfare to use Norplant in an effort to reduce the number of children born to women relying upon income from the State shows the sanctions imposed upon mothers whose lives do not match the construction of ideal motherhood. The same is true of court-ordered contraception.

S. L. ARTHUR
"The Norplant Prescription: Birth Control, Women Control or Crime Control?"[54]

"In December of 1990, the Federal Drug Administration approved Norplant for use as a contraceptive in the United States. The device was no sooner heralded as 'the most effective contraceptive ever made available,' than it became the focus of bitter controversy across the country.

Weeks after the FDA's approval, the Philadelphia Inquirer printed an editorial in which it suggested that Norplant could be a useful tool for 'reducing the underclass,' linking the need for population control to black women on welfare. A 'storm of well-deserved criticism' prompted the Inquirer to publish an apology for its 'misguided' statements. After Norplant's originator, Dr Sheldon Segal, read about the Inquirer controversy, he expressed outrage that a device intended to enhance reproductive freedom might be used coercively to restrict it.

[52] M. T. Flannery, *ibid*, at 208.
[53] P. Foster, *supra*. n. 39 at p. 23.
[54] (1992) 40 U.C.L.A. L. Rev. 1 at 4–6.

Similar concerns about coercion were soon raised in the Kansas legislature when one of its members proposed a bill authorizing the state to offer five hundred dollars and a free annual checkup to any welfare mother who would agree to use Norplant. Several months later, when Governor Pete Wilson of California took steps to make Norplant easily available to teens and female drug abusers, he drew fire from Conservative Republicans and the ultra-conservative Focus on the Family. At that time, the governor stated that he had not yet decided whether drug abusers should be required to use the contraceptive implant.

But no one can claim more responsibility for Norplant's notoriety than Tulare County, California, Superior Court Judge Howard Broadman. In one case that rocked the legal community, inspired passionate editorials, and generated stacks of hate mail and fan letters for the judge, Broadman ordered the defendant convicted of child abuse in *People v. Johnson* to use Norplant for three years as a condition of her probation. Darlene Johnson, who has been represented by the American Civil Liberties Union, appealed the order and drew amicus curiae support from prominent medical and women's rights organisations. The previous year in the case of *People v. Zaring*, Judge Broadman had conditioned the probation of another female offender on her willingness to practice contraception. Linda Zaring, a drug addict with five children, had been convicted of use and possession of narcotics, but had not been charged with or convicted of child abuse.

Critics of Judge Broadman depict him as an overzealous kook, but the controversial birth control orders in *Johnson* and *Zaring* cannot be dismissed as the anomalous expressions of one maverick jurist. In November of 1990, a Florida trial judge ordered the young female defendant in *State v. Wilder* to use birth control during probation after she suffocated her newborn daughter. And in April of 1991, a trial judge in Indiana ordered the defendant in *State v. Carlton* to use Norplant after she allowed her boyfriend to kill her six-month old son. In fact, *Johnson, Zaring, Wilder,* and *Carlton* are only four of at least twenty cases since 1966 in which trial courts in ten different states have ordered criminal defendants to be sterilized, to practice contraception, or otherwise to limit pro-creative conduct.

The many controversies surrounding Norplant have captured the public's attention and have inspired debate on the broader question of whether judicially-mandated contraception by any method is appropriate. Very little has been written in support of mandatory contraception as a condition of probation. Opponents have been more prolific in their condemnation of the practice, arguing that such conditions are beyond the statutory authority of the courts, violate the right to privacy, constitute thinly-disguised unauthorised eugenic sterilization, and discriminate against women in violation of equal protection."

Michael Flannery argues that, in cases where the courts find prospective abuse or neglect, parental rights can be terminated by offering Norplant as a means of sentence reduction or a condition of probation as long as the defendant voluntarily waives the collateral rights surrounding its effect.[55] He argues that as long as it is voluntarily and not mandatorily imposed it will provide a valid means of solving problems, especially in cases where the woman continues to abuse substances during gestation and is consequently unable to care for herself and her addicted child. In contrast, James H. Taylor argues that imposing

[55]   M. T. Flannery, *supra*, n. 51.

a Norplant condition upon probation is not reasonably related to the goals of probation of rehabilitating the offender or protecting society against future harm and thus is invalid.[56] In addition, he argues it infringes the right to procreate which, given that there is an alternative probation condition (no-custody), is not outweighed by the need for Norplant. Would a Norplant condition be a legitimate condition of probation in the U.K. which lacks a bill of constitutional rights? Will the requirement of consent ensure that Norplant is not used by the State as in the U.S. experience? In order for consent to be valid, it must be given voluntarily.[57] A woman who had consented to the administration of a contraceptive as a condition of probation would not have given her consent freely.

5.2   Contragestion

This section will consider methods of birth control or family planning which act to prevent implantation rather than inhibit conception. Interceptive methods prevent implantation of a fertilised ovum and therefore raise different legal issues to those discussed above. Methods of contragestion include the Intra-Uterine Device (IUD), menstrual extraction, and the post-coital or morning-after pill.

K. McKNorrie

Family Planning Practice and the Law[58]

"The IUD (intra-uterine device)

This is the longest established contragestive, and probably the most commonly used in the world. According to Potts and Diggory:

> 'More or less any foreign body placed in the uterus prevents pregnancy in the majority of cases and intrauterine contraceptive devices (IUDs) have a lengthy history . . . It is surprising, after so many years of use, that it is still not known for certain how IUDs work in human beings. Almost certainly they produce no systemic hormonal effects . . . The insertion of an IUD post-coitally appears to prevent pregnancy and there is strong empirical evidence that at least one of the actions of the IUD must occur after fertilization.'

The most likely explanation of how the IUD works is that its presence increases the level of white blood cells in the uterus, which then attack the fertilized egg as a foreign body. However it works, the result is that the fertilized egg, as happens naturally to a large percentage of fertilized eggs, fails to implant and is lost in the next menstrual flow or is absorbed into the woman's body through phagocystosis. The IUD will also dislodge any embryos that were implanted before its insertion.

---

[56]   J. H. Taylor, "Court-ordered Contraception: Norplant as a Probation Condition in Child Abuse" (1992) 44 *Florida Law Review* 379.
[57]   *Leigh v. Gladstone* (1909) 26 T.L.R. 139; *Freeman v. Home Office (No. 2)* [1984] Q.B. 524.
[58]   (Aldershot: Dartmouth, 1991), p. 52.

Menstrual Extraction

Menstrual extraction is a post-coital procedure whereby the uterine contents are sucked out at around the time the woman would expect to begin menstruating. This may be done for genuinely therapeutic reasons, such as, for example, to assist a woman who suffers from dysmenorrhoea: or it may be done for birth control reasons, — that is, to extract any fertilized or implanted egg that may have been brought into existence by an episode of unprotected intercourse.

Post-coital Pills

High doses of certain contraceptive pills taken very shortly after unprotected intercourse (within 72 hours) have high efficiency rates in preventing pregnancy. These will act in the main after fertilization: 'the altered hormonal environment probably upsets the sequence of events necessary for implantation'. The intention is invariably to render the uterus inhospitable to implantation — that is, to prevent implantation rather than fertilization."

Methods of contragestion are on the borderline between contraception and abortion. This is explicitly acknowledged by Carol Downer, who, with Lorraine Rothman, developed the technique of menstrual extraction in the 1970's:

> "We chose this term deliberately to blur the distinction between removing a menstrual period and terminating a pregnancy. In our society, abortion is used solely as a means to control women's reproduction, but to a woman faced with the possibility of terminating a pregnancy, the important thing is to have her period on time."[59]

Blurring the distinction between abortion and contraception raises important issues about whether methods of contragestion can be employed without the restraints of the Abortion Act 1967 (discussed in Chapter 5.3 below). Both abortion and contraception have to be considered within a framework which recognises the complexity of women's needs in the sphere of reproduction. In the last section it was emphasised how the constructed Woman of Legal Discourse can be compared with real women and how the legal construction can have a direct impact upon women's lives. In this section the particular question under examination is the extent to which the control of women's reproductive lives in the area of contragestion is located, by legislation, and judicial interpretation of that legislation, firmly in the hands of the medical profession which is deemed most able to articulate and respond to women's needs.

5.2.i   *The legality of contragestion*

Does contragestion amount to abortion? The law on abortion is discussed more fully below. However, the legality of methods of contragestion have also

---

[59]   C. Downer, "Through the Speculum", in R. Arditti, R. Duelli Klein & S. Minden (eds), *supra*, n. 30 at p. 422.

to be considered in light of the offences of "procuring a miscarriage" contrary
to sections 58 and 59 of the Offences Against the Person Act 1861:

> **58.**—Every woman, being with child, who, with intent to procure her own
> miscarriage, shall unlawfully administer to herself any poison or other nox-
> ious thing, or shall unlawfully use any instrument or other means whatsoever
> with the like intent and whosoever, with intent to procure the miscarriage of
> any woman, whether she be or not with child, shall unlawfully administer to
> her or cause to be taken by her any poison or other noxious thing, or shall
> unlawfully use any instrument or other means whatsoever with the like
> intent, shall be guilty of an offence, and being convicted thereof shall be liable
> to imprisonment.

> **59.**—Whosoever shall unlawfully supply or procure any poison or other
> noxious thing, or any instrument or thing whatsoever, knowing that the same
> is intended to be unlawfully used or employed with intent to procure the
> miscarriage of any woman, whether she be or not be with child, shall be
> guilty of an offence, and being convicted thereof shall be liable to imprison-
> ment for a term not exceeding five years.

In an article written in 1974, Victor Tunkel expressed the view that techniques
which operate after the moment of *fertilisation*, being acts done "with intent
to procure a miscarriage" in contravention of section 58 of the Offences
Against the Person Act 1861, meant that a registered medical practitioner had
to comply with the Abortion Act 1967, which permits abortion in certain
circumstances, in order for the technique to be lawful.[60] Ian Kennedy disputes
this interpretation of the law:

I. KENNEDY
Treat Me Right: Essays in Medical Law and Ethics[61]

"When is a woman 'pregnant', or 'with child', so that a 'miscarriage' cannot be procured except under the circumstances envisaged by the Abortion Act. One view is that
expressed informally by the DHSS ... that a woman is not pregnant until a fertilized
egg has been implanted in her womb ... [O]n this basis, the DHSS intimated that
postcoital birth control was not unlawful as practised now by PAS, and could properly
be regarded as contraception if performed within 72 hours of intercourse. The choice
of 72 hours as the time-limit seems somewhat odd if implantation is taken as the
moment at which a woman becomes pregnant. Certainly it cannot be justified on this
basis on any rational, scientific grounds, since implantation may well take longer than
72 hours. Perhaps it reflects an abundance of caution, or is chosen as reflecting an
average period of time during which the fertilized egg is in the fallopian tube before
descending.

---

[60] See V. Tunkel, "Modern Anti-pregnancy Techniques and the Criminal Law" [1974] Crim.
L.R. 461.
[61] (Oxford: Clarendon Press, 1992), pp. 34–36.

LEGITIMATE AND SERIOUS DIFFERENCES OF VIEW

There is, of course, another view as to when a woman can be said to be pregnant. In correspondence with the Minister of Health, which was made public in the autumn of 1981, Father McGuire, Chairman of the Sheffield branch of Life, argued that human life begins at fertilization. This means, he maintained, that postcoital birth control is a form of abortion, because a woman is 'with child' in that she has conceived. As I have indicated, the Minister, through his officials in the DHSS, rejected this view in a spirited exchange which is excellently reported in the *Sunday Times* of 27 September 1981. I too am unpersuaded by the argument of Life, though I readily concede that this is not an area where there are certainties, and that there is room for legitimate and seriously held differences.

I would reject the view taken by Life principally from the point of view of the language and spirit of the law. But it is fair to say that there is also a perfectly respectable philosophical argument which I will mention briefly before I turn to the law. On a philosophical level some may argue that biological life may not be owed any duty as a human life until some point is reached in its development. This was the view taken in the well-known Report of the British Council of Churches in 1962. The point at which biological life is owed a duty of protection as human life, is, the Report concluded, the point of implantation of the fertilized egg in the womb. 'A woman cannot abort', says the Report, 'until the fertilized egg has nidated and thus become attached to her body.' Therefore, the British Council of Churches found 'nothing objectionable' in the use of techniques to prevent implantation. This view was expressed, of course, in the context of the pill and the IUD; but it is equally applicable to postcoital birth control. It suggests that ethically good arguments exist to justify the practice. As I have said, however, those who begin from different premisses will remain unconvinced. My own position is somewhere in between. It is that an early embryo is owed a duty of protection, but that this duty is not absolute. It may have to give way to the claims of another (the mother) for good reason.

THE LEGALITY OF ANY PROCEDURES AIMED AT PREVENTING IMPLANTATION

Let me now turn to my reasons for regarding the view taken by Life as being wrong in law. Remember that, in interpreting what the law may be, I am really attempting to predict what a court would decide if called upon to resolve the dispute, by interpreting the words of the Offences Against the Person Act and the Abortion Act. I am not here concerned with what the law ought to be, with what a court ought to decide, but rather with what the law is, with what a court is likely to decide. The first point is linguistic. In the ordinary use of language, we do not think of a fertilized egg as a 'child'. Nor would we think of a woman as 'pregnant' until implantation has taken place. As the officials in the DHSS argued, you cannot procure a miscarriage until you have a carriage, and you would not ordinarily use the notion of 'carrying' a child until it was implanted in the womb. This argument finds favour with Professor Williams who, after noting, as I have said, that the language of the Acts is unspecific, suggests that there is no reason why a court should not decide that 'the word "miscarriage" in the section on abortion means the miscarriage of an implanted blastocyst.' Thus, on the basis of the language used, it would, in my view, be extremely unlikely that a court would find that the present procedure, performed within 72 hours, was an abortion, with all that this implies. I am fortified in this view by a second point. The use of IUDs as a regular form of contraception has become so widespread that its lawfulness cannot seriously be disputed. If the law allows the use of IUDs as contraception in ordinary circumstances, then, to be consistent, it must allow the use of IUDs and the other procedures in the context of postcoital birth control, because the effect is the same in all cases, the prevention of a fertilized egg being implanted in the womb. Thus, for reasons based on ordinary use of language and on consistency and established acceptance of IUDs, any procedure of postcoital birth control aimed at preventing implantation, certainly in the first 72 hours after intercourse and probably (as I will suggest) during the whole of the period of time known to be required for implantation, is not an abortion as a matter of law. It follows that the present procedure does not, in my view, offend against the law; nor is it an unethical procedure. I have already admitted, however, that others may (and do) not agree. It is to be regretted, therefore, that we do not have in this country well-established methods for clarifying the law by asking the courts to issue declaratory judgments. And while there remain those who argue that the law forbids postcoital birth control, it behoves all those who favour and promote it to observe a proper caution both in what they do and in what they say. Just to mention one, apparently trivial example, Ms Grahame, in the paper to which I referred earlier, speaks at one point of distances travelled by those seeking help, and says that, 'despite this 61.7 per cent were treated within 48 hours of exposure to pregnancy'. 'Exposure to the risk of pregnancy' may be a preferable expression in the context."

The Attorney-General expressed his view in a written parliamentary answer on May 10, 1983. Four cases in which the morning-after pill had been prescribed had been referred to his office and the office of the Director of Public Prosecutions.

(1983) 42 PARLIAMENTARY DEBATES, H.C. 236
Written Answers: May 10, 1983

"ATTORNEY-GENERAL

"Morning After" Pill

Dr Hampson asked the Attorney-General how many complaints have been received, either by himself or by the Director of Public Prosecutions, which relate to the supply of what is commonly called the 'morning after' pill; and whether he proposes to institute criminal proceedings in connection with any of the complaints.

The Attorney-General: One complaint has been made direct to my Department and three to the Director of Public Prosecutions. Each complaint alleges that the supply and administration of such post-coital medications contravenes sections 58 and 59 of the Offences against the Persons Act 1861 and that a woman using such medication may commit an offence under section 58 of the Act.

Such pills are intended to be taken by women following unprotected intercourse to inhibit implantation in the womb of any fertilised ovum. The sole question for resolution therefore is whether the prevention of implantation constitutes the procuring of a miscarriage within the meaning of sections 58 or 59 of the Offences against the Persons Act 1861. The principles relating to interpretation of statutes require that the words of a statute be given the meaning which they bore at the time the statute was passed.

Further, since the words were used in a general statute, they are prima facie presumed to be used in their popular, ordinary or natural sense.

In this context it is important to bear in mind that a failure to implant is something which may occur in the manner described above or quite spontaneously. Indeed in a significant proportion of cases the fertilised ovum is lost either prior to implantation or at the next menstruation. It is clear that, used in its ordinary sense, the word 'miscarriage' is not apt to describe a failure to implant — whether spontaneous or not. Likewise, the phrase 'procure a miscarriage' cannot be construed to include the prevention of implantation. Whatever the state of medical knowledge in the 19th century, the ordinary use of the word 'miscarriage' related to interference at a stage of pre-natal development later than implantation.

In the light of the above I have come to the conclusion that this form of post-coital treatment does not constitute a criminal offence within either sections 58 or 59 of the Offences against the Persons Act 1861. No proceedings are to be instituted."

The Attorney-General stated that the rules of statutory interpretation required the words in the 1861 Act to be given the meaning which they would have had at the time the Act was passed. Further, there was a presumption that the meaning was that given to them in their "popular, ordinary, or natural sense". In his view, "miscarriage" did not, in either of these senses, mean a failure to implant or prevention of implantation.[62] The opinion of the Attorney-General may have assured medical practitioners that they committed no offence by prescribing the morning-after pill without complying with the terms of the Abortion Act 1967. Similarly, performing menstrual extraction or inserting an IUD to prevent implantation of a fertilised ovum would not constitute a criminal act. His opinion was not, however, uncontroversial.

(1984) 287 *British Medical Journal* 64

"But even if the Attorney-General is right to say that 'miscarriage' must refer to a stage of fetal development after implantation, it would seem to be unlawful to use the postcoital pill at some point after implantation has taken place. And how can the time of implantation itself be ascertained?

Mr Ian Kennedy, the 1980 Reith lecturer and reader in law at King's College, London, suggests that the courts will judge postcoital birth control to be contraception rather than abortion up to the point at which implantation must have happened; according to him, the consensus of informed medical scientific opinion agrees that the maximum period before implantation is from seven to 10 days, up to which point postcoital methods will be legal. He therefore views as overcautious the opinion by the Department of Health and Social Security that postcoital birth control is ethically and legally unobjectionable within 72 hours of intercourse.

Mr Kennedy asserts that a miscarriage cannot be procured 'until you have a carriage,' which, he says, does not happen until implantation. Furthermore, section 58 of the Act speaks of 'a woman with child'; but a fertilised egg 'is not a child.'

These are contentious premises on which to found a legal argument. But even if they

---

[62] Consistent with this view the Human Fertilisation and Embryology Act 1990, s. 2(3), provides that a woman is not to be treated as carrying a child until the embryo has implanted.

are accepted section 58 may still catch the doctor who supplies the drug. The supplier must 'cause to be taken' by the woman, 'whether she be or be not with child,' 'any poison or other noxious thing,' 'with intent to procure (her) miscarriage.' There will be no difficulty in classing the drug as a noxious thing if it is capable of causing a miscarriage. If the drug is prescribed, the prescribing doctor will have caused it to be taken. The question of whether implantation has or has not taken place is irrelevant even on Mr Kennedy's view of the status of a fertilised egg, since the section applies whether or not the woman be with child, so the only remaining element for the prosecution to prove is the intent to procure a miscarriage. That would depend very much on when the drug was prescribed. If the prescription and supply of the drug were given at a time when on balance it was more likely than not that implantation had taken place, the necessary intent might not be difficult to establish. There is no obvious reason why the courts should hold back from finding the necessary intent until implantation has definitely rather than probably taken place.

If Mr Kennedy and the Attorney-General are wrong and 'miscarriage' is a term apt to be applied before implantation a prosecution under section 58 and section 59 will the more readily succeed. It has been argued that 'carriage' is a term as applicable in the case of a woman carrying an unimplanted embryo as it is when implantation has taken place; and Professor Glanville Williams, who has contended recently that the term 'miscarriage' historically only applied at a much later stage, took a different view in 1958, when he made the unequivocal statement that '. . . English law . . . regard(s) any interference with pregnancy, however early it may take place, as criminal, unless for therapeutic reasons. The foetus is a human life to be protected by the criminal law from the moment when the ovum is fertilised.'

But whatever the animation of an unimplanted blastocyst, the law is a living thing: *tempora mutantur, et lex mutatur in illis*. Attitudes and practices change and develop, and the law will reflect this. For years now intra-uterine devices have been used without legal difficulty, though their prescription offends against Glanville Williams's earlier statement of the law, and Mr Kennedy is probably right when he says that the courts will take the same view as he does.

None the less a test case may yet be brought by 'Life' or some other branch of the anti-abortion lobby; for the Attorney-General's opinion, though respectfully described by *The Times* as a 'ruling,' has no legal force. Nevertheless if a doctor were to be convicted for prescribing the postcoital pill the sentence for the commission of an act which the Attorney-General had publicly stated not to be a crime would surely be a nominal one.

To be safe, however, doctors should follow the DHSS guidelines and prescribe within 72 hours of intercourse taking place, or at least before there is a probability of implantation. Even for two or three days after the first 72 hours, the legal risk should be slight."

It has been argued that the Attorney-General's statement, for which he gave no authority, is misconceived on the basis that the word "miscarriage" in both medical and popular usage refers to the termination of pregnancy at any point after conception, not only after implantation.[63]

Estimates vary as to the period of time from fertilisation of the ovum to its implantation in the uterus, it being thought to occur at between four and ten

---

[63]   See I. J. Keown, "Miscarriage: A Medico-legal Analysis" [1984] Crim.L.R. 604.

days. The *Family Medical Encyclopedia*[64] suggests that implantation occurs at four to five days after conception, whilst the estimate in Kennedy and Grubb's *Medical Law: Text and Materials* is five to ten days.[65] Ian Kennedy suggests that the present time limit, within which the morning-after pill is prescribed, of 72 hours, is conservative. The term "emergency contraception" is now preferred to "morning-after" as it more accurately conveys that contragestive methods may legally be administered within a few days of unprotected intercourse.[66]

I. KENNEDY
Treat Me Right: Essays in Medical Law and Ethics[67]

"ISSUES ARISING FROM THE USE OF POST-COITAL CONTRACEPTION

Having considered the present 72-hour practice, I want now to move on to examine some other issues which arise, or could arise, from the use of post-coital birth control. Perhaps it ought to be said at the outset that it is clear that the need it serves is a very real one. Ms Grahame reports that in the first nine months of offering the service, 554 women were seen, of whom 516 were treated. Eighty per cent of the women were over 24 years of age. They were often conscientious family-planners whose lives had become disrupted or who had been advised against using the pill and whose alternative precautions had failed. Against this background, the need is felt to extend the service to women who fall outside the 72-hour limit which, at present, PAS feels obliged to observe. The question is whether it is lawful to extend the time-limit within which either a combination of hormones is given or an IUD is fitted. If the aims of this symposium are to make this form of birth control more widely known to GPs and to maximize its benefits, this question has to be both raised and answered. Hormones can undoubtedly be effective after far more than three days have elapsed since intercourse; so, equally, can IUDs.

In answering this question it is important to notice the background against which the answer is given. The courts are undoubtedly conservative in their interpretation of the Abortion Act, which is the relevant law. This was clearly illustrated in the recent case brought by the Royal College of Nursing. Lord Wilberforce in the House of Lords went out of his way, albeit in dissent, to indicate that the Abortion Act is to be strictly construed. 'In my opinion', he wrote, 'this Act should be construed with caution . . . the Act is not one for 'purposive' or 'liberal' or 'equitable' construction.' With this caution in mind, I still hold to my view that postcoital birth control is lawful as contraception, rather than abortion, up to the maximum period before implantation, whatever the official view of the DHSS may be. The question is then one of what this maximum time period may be. My answer is that it is that time period which the consensus of informed medical scientific opinion states is the maximum time after intercourse before implantation takes place. This may be anywhere between 7 and 10 days. This is a matter of expert opinion, and, I repeat, depends on what constitutes the consensus of informed opinion.

---

[64] *Family Medical Encyclopaedia* (London: Hamlyn Publishing Group Ltd, 1984), p. 279.
[65] I. Kennedy & A Grubb, *supra*, n. 19 at p. 557.
[66] F. C. Reader, "Emergency contraception" (1991) 93 *British Medical Journal* 801.
[67] I. Kennedy, *supra*, n. 61 at pp. 36–38.

The crime under section 58 consists, however, of doing certain acts 'with intent to procure the miscarriage' of a woman. Is not a doctor who thinks that a fertilized egg may be implanted and gives the pill 'just in case' guilty of the crime since, by the doctrine of conditional intent, he intends to procure a miscarriage? The response must be that up to the maximum time for implantation, he is entitled to believe that there is no implantation and can justify his prescription of the pill as being done with the intention of preventing carriage rather than procuring miscarriage.

If, however, the number of days after intercourse is greater than this agreed maximum time-limit, it follows that prescribing hormones or fitting an IUD is unlawful, unless done in accordance with the provisions of the Abortion Act, because the woman would be deemed pregnant by our definition. As Williams put it, 'Even dating the prohibition of abortion from implantation would not establish the legality of the gel and prostaglandin preparations now being developed [nor the late insertion of the IUD, I would add], which expel the fetus at an early stage after implantation.' This, I submit, is the present reality against which those who wish to think of the future and do what they can to develop post-coital birth control, must plan. It is best regarded as an emergency treatment, but its widest possible use may be encouraged, provided the appropriate time constraints are adhered to. To those who would advocate that its use be extended beyond the period of 7 to 10 days which, I have suggested, may be the maximum, the reply must be that the law as it is written at present forbids this as a form of contraception rather than abortion. The only way to change this state of affairs is, of course, to get the legislation changed. Quite frankly, the recent history of public and Parliamentary debates on abortion persuades me that this is a very remote possibility. This must be accepted as a social fact, a legitimate expression of public will. Given the vigilance with which certain groups scrutinize decisions about abortion and contraception, everyone working in this field is well advised to accept this or risk prosecution."

Thus, in the opinion of the Attorney-General, the morning-after pill prescribed to prevent implantation, (presently up to 72 hours after unprotected intercourse) does not "procure a miscarriage" and therefore, no offence contrary to sections 58 and 59 of the Offences Against the Person Act 1861 is committed. However, if the morning-after pill is prescribed after the point at which medical evidence establishes that implantation is likely to occur, it operates so as "to procure a miscarriage" and an offence may be committed if the act is done "with intent" (see below 5.2.ii.c) and, therefore, any medical practitioner who prescribed the morning-after pill would commit a criminal offence unless the requirements of the Abortion Act 1967 were complied with.

The legality of IUDs fitted after unprotected intercourse (presently up to five days) was discussed in the case of *R. v. Dhingra.*[68] In this case the trial judge followed the reasoning of the Attorney-General and held that an offence contrary to section 58 is only committed if the procedure operates after implantation. A medical practitioner had fitted his secretary with an IUD 11 days after intercourse and was charged with an offence contrary to section 58. He was acquitted as the judge withdrew the case from the jury on the grounds that the woman could not have been pregnant at the time. Wright J.

---

[68]   January 25, 1991 (unrep.).

said "[i]t is highly unlikely any ovum became implanted and only at the completion of implantation does the embryo become a fetus. At this stage she can be regarded as pregnant".[69]

The legality of menstrual extraction, like that of the IUD, rests upon whether the procedure is carried out at a point before which implantation is likely to occur, or whether it is carried out after implantation. Menstrual extraction has been advocated as a means of taking control of menstruation and as a method of safe and easy abortion that can be performed by women upon each other. As such it raises questions beyond whether a registered medical practitioner has to comply with the Abortion Act 1967.

5.2.ii *Reproductive control*

Menstrual extraction has been advocated by Rebecca Chalker and Carol Downer in *A Woman's Book of Choices*[70] as a process which women (who are not registered medical practitioners) can perform upon one another as a means of self discovery and empowerment. Reproductive control was at the very essence of the development of this technique; that is control by women of their reproductive lives, presenting a challenge to the control more usually exercised by the medical profession.[71] The women's health movement in the 1970s focused upon women obtaining information about the female body and upon providing support for each other in obtaining medical services, or by providing services for each other through self-help groups and women's clinics:

J. LEESON & J. GRAY
Women and Medicine[72]

"The birth of the women and health movement took place in 1973 as a result of imported enthusiasm from the USA in the form of Carol Downer, one of the most experienced women from the American self-help movement. She came to Britain in October 1973 and visited several towns and cities, including Manchester and London. She gave talks accompanied by slides of self-examination, showing how to insert a speculum into the vagina, and how a woman can then see her cervix for herself with a mirror. There were various slides of the cervix (the mouth of the womb) showing healthy and unhealthy ones as well as pregnant and non-pregnant ones. She then demonstrated on herself how to insert a speculum and the women present at the meetings were invited to have a look at their own cervices with a mirror and torch. She talked about her experiences in America, including her court case. (She had been cleared of the charge of practising medicine without a licence. This followed her inserting yoghurt into a woman's vagina, a well-known treatment for thrush).

---

[69] Quoted in J. K. Mason & R. A. McCall Smith, *Law and Medical Ethics* (London: Butterworths, 1994), p. 111.
[70] R. Chalker & C. Downer, *A Woman's Book of Choices* (New York: Four Walls Eight Windows, 1992).
[71] For an analysis of the context in which reproductive control has to be considered, see R. P. Petchesky, *Abortion and Women's Choice* (London: Verso, 1986). There has been recent debate as to whether emergency oral contraception should be made available over the counter (A. Glasier, "Emergency contraception: time for de-regulation?" (1993) 100 *British Journal of Obstetrics and Gynaecology* 611).
[72] (London: Tavistock Publications Ltd, 1978), pp. 194–198.

She told the gathered women of the invention of the Del-EM by Lorraine Rothman, which incorporates the Karman plastic cannula (tube), attached to a syringe and an airtight bottle. She explained how this device is used in self-help clinics for 'menstrual extraction' — the process of sucking out a woman's menstrual blood and womb lining at the time her period is due. Carol Downer in a *Nova* article by Carolyn Faulder, in August 1973, is quoted as saying:

> 'We are totally unconcerned with the question of whether or not a certain menstrual extraction would be classified as an abortion. We simply want to control our own bodies, to regulate our reproduction at whatever point we are in our reproduction cycle, or to relieve menstrual cramps, or to ensure a menstrual period will not spoil a vacation.'

As a result of the enthusiasm felt by many women in London, Leeds, and Manchester, women and health groups were set up using the book *Our Bodies, Ourselves* as a guide, and armed with the specula obtained from Carol Downer.

The first things that had to be discussed were attitudes to the NHS. In Manchester there were several meetings devoted to this question, where women also began self-examination. The Manchester group included several women working in the NHS, who felt that they did not want to develop into an alternative medicine group outside the NHS. They believed that, although the service had many faults, the main emphasis should still be on putting pressure on the NHS to change for the better. At the same time it should be defended against attacks from those wishing to erode the principle, 'paid out of taxation and free at the time of use'.

How did they plan to pressurize the NHS? The first step was to educate themselves by reading about their own bodies and discussing the information, and by examining themselves and getting rid of fears and taboos. Then it would be possible to begin to challenge medical mystification. The next was to support each other, for example, by discussing their problems before going to doctors, or by accompanying one another; they would challenge injustices, and fight for women patients' rights through all the legitimate channels of the NHS. To do this it was necessary to learn how the NHS works, both in theory and in practice. Finally, if the legitimate channels failed to acknowledge the wrongs, the failure would have to be publicly exposed.

Somehow, out of all these different strands emerged a fluctuating but continuing group, which has engaged in a wide range of activities. Self-examination progressed, and records were kept of observations. Herbal medicines, yoga, and massage were studied and used. The relationship between diet and health was discussed. Some were already vegetarians, and others decided to join them.

Instances of injustice experienced by patients were taken up, and support was given to women having problems with their doctors. Some of the group went to an STD clinic (still known as the VD clinic) and wrote an article criticizing the way they were handled, others went to a family planning clinic and wrote about that, suggesting improvements. Many aspects of women's health have been discussed and regular articles written for the *Manchester Women's Paper*. Leaflets were produced on various illnesses, suggesting what women should do about them, and these were given out from market stalls. A play was written and performed for various women's organizations. Free pregnancy tests were carried out. Some women gave talks in schools on sex education, and on women and health generally . . .

Women and health groups have also been functioning in London, Leamington Spa, Birmingham, Glasgow, Swansea, Leeds, Sheffield, Bristol, Cambridge, and York. In the main, their activities have been similar to those of the Manchester group, but some groups have also been involved in menstrual extraction.

Menstrual extraction has raised certain problems. The first relates to its legality. Some legal advisers have expressed the opinion that since pregnancy cannot be tested at the time the period is due (you have to wait until two weeks after this), you cannot be performing an abortion since you don't know whether or not you are pregnant; the provisions of the Abortion Act therefore do not apply. It could also be argued that menstrual extraction is no more a method of abortion than the intra-uterine contraceptive device. Others stress that under the Offences Against the Person Act, it is illegal to use an instrument with the intention of performing an abortion whether the woman is pregnant or not. Because of this confusion and because this issue has not yet been tested in law, menstrual extraction is being carried out shrouded in secrecy. This means that only those women known and trusted are given menstrual extractions by women's groups, and that every one of these menstrual extractions carried a potential legal risk.

The second problem which has been debated extensively is that in performing menstrual extractions secretly, women's groups can only communicate to limited numbers of women how abortion is 'demystified' by this procedure. Not only that, but women's groups are effectively giving an alternative but highly restricted service, rather than using their energy and time to put pressure on the NHS to provide a service generally. Some members of women and health groups argue that they should give priority to making the NHS ensure the ready availability of abortion in all regions, and to putting pressure on various Area Health Authorities to provide out-patient abortion facilities as part of widely available well-woman clinics.

Perhaps priority should also be given to pressing for proper sex education in schools about menstruation, for doctors to be more sympathetic and understanding of menstrual disorders, and to persuading general practitioners to perform menstrual extraction. However by doing menstrual extractions themselves, at least women and health groups can show that it is technically possible, and that it can be done by groups of lay women on each other gently and efficiently."

Whilst there were divisions within the women's health movement, principally on the question of whether the health care with which women were being provided in the NHS could be improved, or whether it was necessary to provide women with alternative health care,[73] the impetus for the movement was the imbalance in power relations between men and women or, more specifically, between women and the male-dominated medical profession.

C. DOWNER
"Through the Speculum"[74]

"The underlying principle of all of the work of the Feminist Women's Health Centers is the strategy of undermining the patriarchal structure of society and male dominance by challenging the social control of women's sexuality and reproduction. The institutions of marriage and the laws which regulate divorce, abortion, prostitution, birth

[73] J. Leeson & J. Gray, *ibid.*, p. 199.
[74] In R. Arditti, R. Duelli Klein & S. Minden (eds), *supra.*, n. 30 at p. 421.

control and homosexuality isolate women from each other and brutally repress their sexuality and reproductive rights. The FWHCs have worked in national coalitions to support the women's movement's impressive campaigns against these laws.

As we progressed in our understanding of the patriarchy, we saw that in addition to laws which maintain the patriarchal family, all institutions of a sexist society function to reinforce women's inferior status, but the male-dominated medical institutions have the special role of enforcing women's sexual and reproductive compliance. Further, we realized that the external oppressive controls and exploitation of women's sexuality has a subjective expression — intense shame — which deprives us of the strength and vigor to assert our most basic rights."

Gaining and sharing knowledge about women's bodies was not only empowering for women but it enabled the dominance of female reproduction by the medical profession to be challenged and, by the provision of services by and for women, that dominance to be eroded.[75]

A woman who performs menstrual extraction upon another is subject to the laws governing the procuring of a miscarriage, so that failure to comply with these laws will mean that a criminal offence is committed. Sections 58 and 59 of the Offences Against the Person Act 1861 provide that the procurement of a miscarriage can be carried out by two offenders; the woman herself and any other person involved in the procedure.

5.2.ii.a The Woman as principal offender. Menstrual extraction has been labelled "DIY abortion" or "self-abortion". However, these terms may be misleading. Given what is involved in carrying out menstrual extraction, it is practically impossible for a woman to carry out the procedure upon herself. It is necessary for other women, having received training in the technique, to carry out an extraction.[76] If a woman cannot perform menstrual extraction upon herself she cannot commit the offence contrary to section 58 as a principal. However, a woman upon whom menstrual extraction is performed may be charged with aiding and abetting others to procure a miscarriage[77] or with conspiracy. The question of conspiracy to commit an offence contrary to section 58 of the Offences Against the Person Act 1861 is discussed in the case of *R. v. Whitchurch*.[78]

R. v. Whitchurch
(1890) 24 Q.B.D. 420 at 420–421, *per* Wills J.

"At the assizes for the county of Northampton on November 28, 1889, Thomas William Whitchurch, John Howe, and Elizabeth Cross were indicted in the following

---

[75] C. Downer, *ibid*. Books such as Boston Women's Health Book Collective, *The New Our Bodies, Ourselves: A Health Book By and For Women* (Boston Women's Health Book Collective) (English ed., A. Phillips & J. Rakusen (eds)), (Harmondsworth: Penguin, 1989) were written to disseminate information more extensively amongst women.
[76] Explained in R. Chalker, & C. Downer, supra., n. 70.
[77] *R. v. Sockett* (1908) 24 T.L.R. 893.
[78] (1890) 24 Q.B.D. 420.

terms: — The jurors, &c., present that Thomas William Whitchurch, John Howe, and Elizabeth Cross, believing that the said Elizabeth Cross was then pregnant and that in due course of nature she would be delivered of a child begotten by the said John Howe, and wickedly intending and contriving to conceal such pregnancy and to prevent such her delivery in due course of nature, on June 1, 1889, did amongst themselves unlawfully, knowingly, and wickedly conspire, combine, confederate, and agree together feloniously and unlawfully to procure the miscarriage of the said Elizabeth Cross by unlawfully administering to and causing to be taken by her certain noxious things, and by unlawfully using certain instruments and other means, with intent to procure the miscarriage of the said Elizabeth Cross. The indictment then set out a number of acts done in pursuance of the conspiracy, but it is unnecessary for the purposes of this case to set out more of the indictment than I have already given. The evidence established that the prisoners all believed that Elizabeth Cross was pregnant, and that for the purpose of procuring abortion Whitchurch and Howe, with her consent and by her procurement, both administered to her noxious drugs and used, or caused to be used, upon her, instruments; but there was no evidence that she was in fact pregnant, and for the purposes of the present case it must be taken that she was not in fact pregnant. Mr Hammond Chambers then objected that for a woman not being pregnant to do, or cause to be done, acts upon herself for the purpose of procuring abortion was no offence either at common law or by statute, and therefore she could not be convicted of conspiracy with other persons that they should do upon her and she should suffer the same acts. I was of opinion that, whether or not it was no offence for a woman not pregnant to do acts to herself intending thereby to procure an abortion which was actually impossible, it would none the less be criminal in her to conspire to commit a felony (which the administration of drugs and the use of instruments would have been in her as well as in the men if she had been pregnant — see 24 & 25 Vict. c. 100, s. 58), because the commission of the felony was rendered impossible by circumstances unknown to her. I was further of opinion that for the woman to conspire with the men to have certain things done to her, the doing of which constituted a felony on the part of the men, was criminal, although the object to be attained, if effected by herself alone and without the help of the men, might not have been criminal, and I directed the jury, if they believed the evidence, to convict the prisoners. The jury convicted all the prisoners. The men had been previously convicted of the felony of administering drugs and using instruments for the purpose of procuring the miscarriage of the female prisoner. The question for the Court was whether the conviction against the woman could be sustained.

Conviction affirmed."

5.2.ii.b Other offenders.

5.2.ii.b Other offenders. As menstrual extraction is carried out at or about the day the woman's period is due there may be no medical evidence that the woman is pregnant. The offence contrary to section 58 of the 1861 Act makes a distinction between women as principals and other offenders in its requirement of *actual* pregnancy. If the woman is herself charged with the offence it is necessary to show that she was pregnant. However, where liability falls upon others performing menstrual extraction, with the pregnant woman as conspirator, it is not necessary to prove that the woman was actually pregnant.[79]

---

[79] See V. Tunkel, *supra*, n. 60 at 462.

5.2.ii.c Intent. The offence contrary to section 58 requires an intention to procure a miscarriage plus any act, effective or otherwise, carried out to further that intention. In criminal law, where the purpose or aim of an act is to bring about a certain consequence, that act is done with intention. Further, a jury may infer that an act is intentional where the defendant foresaw that the consequence which resulted from the defendant's voluntary act was virtually certain to result from that act.

Whether one who performs menstrual extraction upon another acts "with intent" to procure a miscarriage depends upon whether the woman who aims to bring about a period foresees as virtually certain that the act may remove an ovum which has implanted. If menstrual extraction is performed on a woman at a point prior to which any fertilised ovum would be implanted there can be no intent to procure a miscarriage. If menstrual extraction is performed at a point at which it is foreseen as virtually certain that any ovum, if fertilised, could have implanted, there is intent to procure a miscarriage. Even if this is not the purpose of the act, it is the virtually certain consequence and therefore gives rise to liability.

The extent to which menstrual extraction can be lawfully performed, therefore, depends upon the point at which medical evidence establishes that implantation is likely to occur. Variations in the menstrual cycles of individual women mean that it is very difficult to determine exactly when a fertilised ovum becomes implanted and therefore, the time during which menstrual extraction is lawful.

The *mens rea* of the offence contrary to section 58 has been explained in the context of menstrual extraction because this technique has been advocated as a means of reproductive control which women can perform upon each other. As far as medical practitioners are concerned, current medical practice is to prescribe the morning-after pill only up to 72 hours after unprotected intercourse, and to fit an IUD up to five days after unprotected intercourse, so that such practices cannot be interpreted as done "with intent to procure a miscarriage". To this extent, medical practice has been determined by the boundaries of the law.

Some commentators, due to their interpretation of the intent required by section 58 of the Offences Against the Person Act 1861, have expressed doubts as to whether menstrual extraction can be lawfully performed at all, even by doctors seeking to comply with the Abortion Act 1967.

J. K. Mason

Medico-Legal Aspects of Reproduction and Parenthood[80]

"The legal position in respect of very early terminations of a prophylactic nature remains to be considered. The procedure of menstrual extraction or menstrual regulation has been mentioned above . . ., from which it will be seen that it must be illegal

---

[80] (Aldershot: Dartmouth, 1990), p. 122.

unless it is performed within the terms of the Abortion Act 1967 and the Abortion Regulations 1968. Even then, the legality is suspect firstly because, as the Director of Public Prosecutions pointed out, it is impossible to hold a prognostic opinion as to the effect of a pregnancy in good faith if one is uncertain as to whether a pregnancy exists. Secondly, the Abortion Act refers to 'a termination of pregnancy' not to a termination of 'possible pregnancy' and there is no prospective way of being certain that a pregnancy exists at the time menstrual extractions are usually performed. The extracter might, therefore, still be guilty of intending to procure the miscarriage of a woman 'whether or not she be with child'. This legal lacuna was considered by the Lane Committee, who recommended that the Act should be amended so as to include as not being unlawful 'acts done with intent to terminate a pregnancy if such exists' — but no action has been taken.

There are thus very good reasons for supposing that the Director of Public Prosecutions was right in doubting the legality of the procedure but his opinion was later refuted by the Attorney General and the Solicitor General. The powers of such officers are, however, subject to political fluctuations and their interpretation of the law was, at least, suspect — nothing which has happened in the last decade has helped to resolve the doubts. This situation has to be regarded as most unsatisfactory. As things stand, menstrual extraction, which does little more than ensure what is the natural end point of some 40 per cent of implantations, has to be regarded as being unlawful when, given precisely the same risks to health or family conditions, a second trimester termination, with all its attendant physical and psychological trauma, could be perfectly legal. It seems unlikely that the drafters of the Abortion Act would have supported such a development and it is surprising that doctors who act with the best interests of patients and society at heart should still remain in jeopardy."

The Abortion Act 1967 was introduced, according to Lord Wilberforce in *Royal College of Nursing v. DHSS* "to prevent existing methods being carried out by unqualified persons and to insist that they should be carried out by doctors."[81] Lord Diplock and Lord Keith, in the same case, took the view that the Act aimed to ensure that abortion is carried out safely, with all proper skill and in hygienic conditions. Sally Sheldon examines the shift in the focus of the abortion debate from a political one to a medical one.[82] She suggests that support of the medical profession was vital to the decriminalisation of abortion, but a consequence of decriminalisation has been the entrenchment of the law on abortion in a medical model of control which leaves women dependent upon the goodwill of the medical profession.

A final issue for determination is whether the performance of menstrual extraction by one medically unqualified woman upon another is contrary to the laws governing the practice of medicine. The law does not forbid in general terms the practice of medicine or surgery by unqualified persons, but provides for the registration of persons who possess certain medical qualifications. A person who practices medicine or surgery without being registered is disadvantaged compared with a registered practitioner. The basis of these laws

---

[81] *Royal College of Nursing v. DHSS* [1981] 2 W.L.R. 279 at 293.
[82] S. Sheldon, "The Law of Abortion and the Politics of Medicalisation" in J. Bridgeman & S. Millns (eds), *Law and Body Politics: Regulating the Female Body* (Aldershot: Dartmouth, 1995); S. Sheldon, *Beyond Control: Medical Power and Abortion Law* (London: Pluto Press, 1997).

is that it is expedient for those seeking medical help to be able to distinguish between the qualified and unqualified practitioner.[83] Women who perform menstrual extraction on one another do nothing to contravene these laws.

The practice of menstrual extraction, as advocated by Carol Downer and Rebecca Chalker, is aimed at providing women with the means to greater control over our reproductive lives. The legislation, and the interpretation given to the legislation by the judiciary, puts decisions about control of reproduction into the province of the medical profession. Women, having had "unprotected" sex have to explain themselves to medical practitioners in order to obtain from them the means of preventing pregnancy. The uncertainty which exists surrounding the legality of the practice of menstrual extraction, discourages the employment of self-help methods and means that control over female reproduction lies primarily with the medical profession.

5.3 Abortion

This section considers the legality of terminating a pregnancy which has progressed beyond the hazy period of implantation and the legal constructions placed upon the protagonists in the decision to abort. The debate surrounding abortion is frequently presented within a moral or ethical framework and is often steeped in the language of rights — that is the right of a foetus to life and the conflicting right of a woman to choose an abortion. The two positions inherent in this conflict are summed up by Morgan and Lee in their discussion of the passage of abortion provisions in the Human Fertilisation and Embryology Act 1990 which amended the Abortion Act 1967.

D. MORGAN & R. G. LEE
Blackstone's Guide to the Human Fertilisation and Embryology Act 1990[84]

"ARGUMENTS FOR CHANGE: PRO-BIRTH

[. . .] For many of those who were anti-abortion, or who wanted to seek a reduction in the scope and availability of abortion, the fundamental starting point was conception itself, in the same way as it had been in the debates over embryo research. Life begins at conception, and no one but God has the authority to end it. There were some prepared to accept that rape, incest and related incidents might disclose grounds for termination:

> 'The pro-life group readily concedes that there are certain tragic circumstances in which an abortion is justified (House of Commons, Official Report, April 24, 1990, col. 216).'

However, the main force of their arguments relied upon conception as the beginning

---

[83] (1992) 30 *Halsbury's Laws of England* (4th ed.), para. 2.
[84] (London: Blackstone Press, 1991), pp. 38–40.

of life or variations upon that approach. Why, they asked, if embryo experiments were banned from 14 days onwards, was abortion allowed up to 18, 20, or 28 weeks? If it is proper to defend the life of an unborn child when damaged in the womb by a drug such as Thalidomide, why is it so illogical to defend it against being aborted? Free and easy abortion is in the interests of men because it removes for them the problem of pregnancy; the operation involves the consumption of scarce NHS resources compounded by the incidence of women coming from outside the U.K. for late abortions. They charged that since the 1967 Act there had been a general decline in respect for the sanctity of life. Additionally, some abortions were carried out on some foetuses who were able, or who were capable of being helped, to sustain life, as in the 'Carlisle baby' case, in which it was reported that an aborted foetus 'lived' in a kidney dish for 3 hours; and that recently a doctor at King's College Hospital London had aborted a foetus in a twinned pregnancy at $27\frac{1}{2}$ weeks for a mild form of handicap.

Seeking to lower time limits, this lobby argued that legislation should work for the future and anticipate further technological development which will enable even less mature foetuses to be kept alive. They asked at what point, if at all, the rights of the unborn child prevailed over those of the woman. And they asked why a prostaglandin injection is given to kill a child if in terminating the pregnancy it has already been deemed to be incapable of life. Abortions were said to be sought on trivial grounds, such as a hare lip or facial deformity . . .

As the unborn child at 18 weeks is complete in organs and sensitive to touch and sound, the foetus can feel pain and the sensory neurones are more sensitive than those of an adult or a newborn. David Alton MP argued that abortion is always the greater of two evils; the argument of choice cannot be accepted as it amounts to choosing to take another's life; 'I believe that that is a modern heresy,' he said (House of Commons, Official Report 24 April 1990, col. 223). This was allied with an appeal that as we are each 'God's handiwork' and that there is a unique plan for each of us in our lives, that uniqueness entails that we cannot be seen as expendable raw material. Finally, the pro-birth proponents argued that back street abortions had been on the decline before the 1967 Act and late abortions were conducted solely for profit; in 1984 over 60 per cent of late abortions were performed by just 11 private clinics.

ARGUMENTS FOR CONTINUITY: PRO-CHOICE

Those who argued in favour of retention or even extension of the current provision pointed out that since Sweden had introduced abortion on demand up to 18 weeks, 95 per cent of all terminations had been carried out before 13 weeks of pregnancy. In addition, they argued for a retention of the upper time limits because of a fear of a return by women to back street abortions, and the time delay in obtaining medical diagnoses. They asserted the woman's right to choose, and emphasised the need to respect her judgment about the disability of any resulting child — her child. Very immature births, it was said, gave rise to brain and other damage which meant the consumption of very high technological resources in the NHS; this striving to keep alive foetuses which had been aborted (as an amendment moved by Baroness Cox to the Commons' amendment would have provided . . .) would have been repugnant and self-defeating. The four-week 'grace period' in calculating correctly the date of the last menstrual period, meant in fact that an 18-week limit would reduce the availability of abortions after 14 weeks (the 1984 RCOG survey suggested that only 3 per cent of its members would favour an 18-week limit); and that arguments designed to cut time limits were in fact disguised arguments to do away with all abortions. They pointed to the disappearance of sex education and contraceptive advice services, and the reduc-tion of local authority resources in family planning services (in April 1990 it was reported that a third of authorities were cutting such services) and reports of four week delays in confirming pregnancy testing, which all led to fears about the provision of safe, effective, compassionate abortion services. Prohibiting abortions in the late period — between 24 and 28 weeks — would deny to a very small but important number of women and young girls (23 in 1988) abortions which they desperately need. These would include: cases where late detection of severe foetal abnormality makes any late abortion especially distressing; young women who become pregnant without realising or knowing it and who are frightened and unsupported; women in the meno-pause with irregular periods who became pregnant without realising it; and those who suffer because of the irregularity of NHS provision."

The law on abortion is, however, not specifically concerned with protecting the right of a woman to choose an abortion or the right of a foetus to life. It is rather more concerned with achieving a compromise between diverse and conflicting interests. To this extent British women may seek lawful termina-tion of their pregnancy in certain circumstances. In England and Wales the number of abortions performed in 1995 was 154,298.[85] Women requiring terminations come from all walks of life, all social classes and very diverse backgrounds. However, popular perceptions of the woman requiring an abor-tion are focused on particular categories of women who are seen perhaps as selfish and uncaring, or alternatively immature and irresponsible. It is evident that the construction of the "Woman of Legal Discourse" described by Carol Smart can be carried through an analysis of the legal discourse on abortion which has constructed its female subject to match the populist perception of women seen as needing or deserving an abortion. Sally Sheldon, in a discus-sion of the parliamentary debates leading to the enactment of the Abortion Act 1967, looks at perceptions of the typical woman seeking a termination which, she argues, underpin the ideology of that Act.

S. SHELDON

" 'Who is the Mother to Make the Judgment?': The Constructions of
Woman in English Abortion Law"[86]

"The Constructions of Woman Employed in Parliament
'From my reading of the Parliamentary debates which preceded the passing of the

---

[85] Office for National Statistics, *Population and Health Monitor*, AB 96/6, October 29, 1996. This marks an increase from the 1969 figure of 54,819, with the number of terminations having peaked in 1990 at 186,912 (The Birth Control Trust, *Abortion Review*, Winter 1993, No.50). The situation in Northern Ireland is different. The 1967 Abortion Act does not extend to North-ern Ireland, where the legal position is still governed by the 1861 Offences Against The Person Act and the decision in *R. v. Bourne* [1939] 1 K.B. 687. The lack of legal clarity in Northern Ireland may in fact constitute a violation of international law, more particularly the European Convention on Human Rights, because of its uncertainty. This has led to calls for legislative intervention (S. Lee, "Abortion Law in Northern Ireland — The Twilight Zone", *Report of the Standing Advisory Commission on Human Rights* (1992–93) 317–326).
[86] (1993) 1 *Feminist Legal Studies* 3 at 5–13.

Abortion Act of 1967, two major constructions of the 'type' of woman who would want an abortion emerge. Both accounts reflect this Woman as marginal and deviant, standing against a wider norm of women who do not need/desire abortion. These constructions reflect strategies used by the proponents and opponents of increasing access to abortion, and on a broader level, reflect images of women that were/are predominant in other social discourses. Both typifications are extreme — they are predicated partially on stereotypes, and partially on real and concrete examples which continually recur within the debates as leitmotivs to become generalized as representing the reality of the woman who seeks abortion.

The structure adopted within this section is to identify two major constructions of Woman used within the debates, which may be broadly (though not always consistently) identified with the reformer/opponent split. Thus, I would argue, whilst the reformers represent the woman who would seek to terminate a pregnancy as an emotionally weak, unstable (even suicidal) victim of her desperate social circumstances, the conservatives view her as a selfish, irrational child. Such a schema is inevitably a simplification and imposes a unity and coherence which is doubtless lacking, but nonetheless it is useful in understanding and highlighting the kinds of constructions used in the debates.

(a) Woman as a Minor

This construction is typically adopted by opponents of abortion (although normally in their accounts the central place would be ceded to the foetus). It represents Woman as a minor in terms of immaturity or underdevelopment with regard to matters of responsibility, morality, and even to her very femininity or 'womanliness'. Her decision to abort is trivialised and denied rational grounding, being perceived as mere selfishness: she will abort, 'according to her wishes or whims,' for example, in order to avoid the inconvenience of having to postpone a holiday. She is immoral for being sexually active for reasons other than procreation; she is irresponsible for not having used contraception, and now for refusing to pay the price for her carelessness; she is unnatural and 'unwomanly' because she rejects the natural outcome of sexual intercourse for women: maternity. There is a hint that one day she will come to realise the error of her ways and want children, yet maybe will be unable to have them as a result of the abortion.

Jill Knight plays heavily on the idea of the woman as selfish and irresponsible. She reveals an image of women seeking abortion as selfish, treating '[b]abies ... like bad teeth to be jerked out just because they cause suffering ... simply because it may be inconvenient for a year or so to its mother.' She later adds that '[a] mother might want an abortion so that a planned holiday is not postponed or other arrangements interfered with.' The ability of the Woman to make a serious decision regarding abortion is trivialised. It is not expected that the Woman will make a careful decision considering all parties, but rather (like a child) she will make a snap decision for her own convenience.

The task of the law is thus perceived essentially as one of responsibilisation: if the Woman seeks to evade the consequences of her carelessness, the law should stand as a barrier. It is often stated that allowing women to take the easy way out encourages them to be irresponsible: 'People must be helped to be responsible, not encouraged to be irresponsible ... Does anyone think that the problem of the 15-year-old mother can be solved by taking the easy way out? ... here is the case of a perfectly healthy baby being sacrificed for the mothers convenience ... For goodness sake, let us bring up our daughters with love and care enough not to get pregnant and not let them degenerate into free-for-alls with the sleazy comfort of knowing, "She can always go and have it out." '

By forcing her to continue with the pregnancy then, the law will seek to ensure that the pregnant woman will be more responsible in the future. As one M.P. comments with regard to whether abortion should be allowed to a fifteen year old girl: 'one needs to think twice before one removes all the consequences of folly from people.'

The Woman who seeks abortion is also seen as morally immature, and hence undeserving of help. Simon Mahon asks who is to be given priority in terms of treatment: is it the 'feckless girl who has an unwanted pregnancy from time to time' or the 'decent married woman who is awaiting investigation or treatment for sterility?' The use of this rhetorical trick of opposing the 'girl' to the 'decent married woman,' serves to emphasise that the girl is not only feckless but is also indecent and unworthy of respect.

The Parliamentary debates often reflect an implicit assumption that it is wrong for women to make a distinction between sex and procreation, they should not indulge in sex, if pregnancy is not desired. William Deedes makes these sentiments clear in expressing his concern that: 'science and its little pill will enable so-called civilised countries to treat sex more and more as a sport and less and less as a sacrament in love,' a divine instrument of procreation. Perhaps the single most telling quotation in this instance is that of David Steel himself, defending a clause which was included in the original wording of the Bill but dropped after debate in Parliament . . . The clause sought to allow abortion to 'a pregnant woman being a defective or becoming pregnant while under the age of 16 or becoming pregnant as a result of rape.' He states: 'Most honourable Members would agree *that to have a woman continue with a pregnancy which she did not wish to conceive*, or in respect of which she was incapable of expressing her wish to conceive, *is a practice which we deplore*, but the difficulty is to find an acceptable wording which will enable termination to be carried out following sexual offences of this kind but which does not allow an open gate for the pretence of sexual offences.'

What is startling here is Steel's correlation of 'a pregnancy which she did not wish to conceive' with conception following rape. Steel fails to imagine that the vast majority of requests for abortion will be for pregnancies that the woman did not wish to conceive — thus in using this as an argument to justify abortion in cases of rape, he implicitly equates consensual intercourse with desired conception. Wanting sex equals wanting pregnancy and motherhood.

The woman who rejects maternity is seen to reject the very essence of Womanhood. Kevin McNamara provides a strong account of Woman's maternal instinct: 'How can a woman's capacity to be a mother be measured before she has a child? Fecklessness, a bad background, being a bad manager, these are nothing to do with love, that unidentifiable bond, no matter how strange or difficult the circumstances, which links a mother to her child and makes her cherish it.'

This implicit assumption of Woman as mother is further reflected in the consideration of her as having existing responsibilities to children and family, (and an apparent inability to see her outside of this role). Jill Knight informs us that: 'if it comes to a choice between the mothers life or the baby's, the mother is very much more important,' this is not however, because the woman is more important in her own right, but rather because '[s]he has ties and responsibilities to her husband and other children.'

(b) Woman as a Victim

The second construction strongly present in the parliamentary debates is that of

Woman as victim. This construction is typically that of the reforming forces, where the Woman and her social situation enjoy a far more central place. Advantage was taken of public sympathy for the situation of women at this time, given the highly restricted access to abortion. Newspapers and books had reported horror stories of back-street and self-induced abortions, and as David Steel noted in the debates, in the years preceding the introduction of the Abortion Act, an average of thirty women per year were dying at the hands of criminal abortionists.

The Woman of this construction is not 'only on the fringe, but literally, physically inadequate.' She is portrayed as distraught, out of her mind with the worry of pregnancy (possibly because she is young and unmarried, but normally because she already has too many children). She is desperate, and should the doctor not be able to help her, who knows what she will stop at (suicide is often discussed). Her husband is either absent or an alcoholic, her housing situation is intolerable. She is at the end of her tether simply trying to hold the whole situation together. As Madeleine Simms, of the Abortion Law Reform Association (ALRA), later wrote: 'It was chiefly for the worn out mother of many children with an ill or illiterate or feckless or brutal or drunken or otherwise inadequate husband that we were fighting.'

The following letter to Lord Silkin (referred to in the debates) provides a good example of the 'type' of Woman envisaged by the reformist forces: 'Dear Lord Silkin, I am married to a complete drunk who is out of work more than he is in. I have four children and now at 40 I am pregnant again; I was just beginning to get on my feet, and get some of the things we needed. I've been working for the last three years, and cannot bear the thought of that terrible struggle to make ends meet again. I've tried all other methods that I've been told about; without success, so as a last resort I appeal to you to please help me if you possibly can.'

Lord Silkin himself comments, in presenting the Bill for its second reading that: 'the vast majority of women who are concerned with this are not, as I might have expected originally, single women, but married women, of an age approaching forty or more, with a number of children, who have become pregnant again, very often unexpectedly, and who for one reason or another find themselves unable to cope with an additional child at that age ... [T]he kind of person that I really want to cater for [is] the prospective mother who really is unable to cope with having a child, or another child, whether she has too many already or whether, for physical or other reasons she cannot cope.'

The same kind of image is also drawn in the House of Commons, where one M.P. speaks of 'the mothers with large families and the burdens of large families very often with low incomes.' Another M.P. describes the illegal abortions he knows of: 'I have represented abortionists, both medical and lay. I have, therefore, met the 30s. Abortion with Higginson's syringe and a soapy solution undertaken in a kitchen by a grey-faced woman on a *distracted multi-child mother, often the wife of a drunken husband*. I have also come across the more expensive back-bedroom abortion by the hasty medical man whose patient returns to a distant town, *there to lie in terror and blood and without medical attention.*'

Even Bernard Braine, a vocal opponent of the Bill accepts the image of the Woman presented by the reformers: 'The hope of the sponsors of the Bill is to change the law that many abortions which take place at the moment illegally either in the back streets or, *self-induced by some poor unfortunate woman, driven to desperation* — shall be brought into the framework of legality.'

The Woman is portrayed as someone who is not completely in control of her actions, who will be driven to madness if relief is denied to her. David Owen states that: '[s]uch a woman is in total misery, and could be precipitated into a depression deep and lasting. What happens to that woman when she gets depressed? She is incapable of looking after those children so she retires into a shell of herself and loses all feeling, all her drive and affection.' A more extreme example is given by Lena Jeger, who speaks of the case of an 'honest young woman' with five children, recently deserted by her husband, who was refused an abortion because 'she did not seem quite depressed enough.' The woman was forced to continue the pregnancy, and her depression following the birth of her sixth baby was so extreme, that she killed the baby by throwing it on the floor. The woman was now in Holloway prison, the children in care. Lord Strange notes that 'nearly every woman in this condition [of unwanted pregnancy] would be in a state bordering on suicide.'

The woman's irrationality is sometimes conceptually linked to her pregnant condition, as David Owen states, for example: '[t]he reproductive cycle of women is intimately linked with her psyche.' This plays on notions of women as dominated by their biology, as existing through their ovaries. This image of the desperate woman is emphasized by contrasting it with the cool, impassive figure of the doctor.

The idea that maternity is the female norm is exploited rather than challenged by the reformists. Madeleine Simms argued that it was precisely the woman with a fully developed 'maternal instinct' who might require an abortion, pointing out however that most women wished to have not more than two or three children, and they were appalled if they found they were having more children than they believed they could adequately care for. Should they accidentally become pregnant, she argued, they would then seek an abortion because of their feelings of 'responsibility to their husband and family, and because of their maternal instinct towards their existing children.' In the House of Lords, Joan Vickers sums up sentiments which are often expressed or implicit in statements of other M.P.s when she notes that: 'I think that most women desire motherhood. It is natural for a woman to want to have a child . . . It is only in extreme cases that a woman wants to terminate her pregnancy.'

In defending the need for a social clause (to allow abortion where the woman's social circumstances are deemed inadequate) within the Act, Roy Jenkins argued that without the presence of such a clause 'many women who are far from anxious to escape the responsibilities of motherhood, but rather wish to discharge their existing ones more effectively, would be denied relief.' Edward Dunwoody argues, in similar vein, that in 'many cases where we have over-large families the mother is so burdened down physically and emotionally with the continual bearing of children that it becomes quite impossible for her to fulfil *her real function, her worthwhile function as a mother*, of holding together the family unit, so that all too often the family breaks apart, and it is for this reason that we have all too many problem families in many parts of the country.'

It is also argued that women should be allowed to abort handicapped foetuses, because the woman who is forced to give birth to a handicapped child will seldom allow herself to become pregnant again. This implicitly asserts that the role of the law must be to protect and entrench motherhood."

Before evaluating the role played by the other protagonists in the abortion debate, the following section sets out the development of the law on abortion and offers various perspectives indicative of the ways in which the law may, as Sheldon argues above, "protect and entrench motherhood".

5.3.i *The law on abortion*

In 1803 Lord Ellenborough's Act made abortion a statutory offence for the first time. A distinction was drawn at the stage of quickening, that is about 16–18 weeks into pregnancy, when movement could be felt by the pregnant woman and it was thought the soul of the foetus entered its body. An abortion at the post-quickening stage was a capital offence. The distinction between quick and non-quick foetuses and the capital nature of the offence were later abandoned by the Offences Against the Person Act 1837.

The current law on abortion has three sources: the Offences Against the Person Act 1861, the Infant Life (Preservation) Act 1929 and the Abortion Act 1967 as amended by section 37 of the Human Fertilisation and Embryology Act 1990. The Offences Against the Person Act 1861 makes it an offence to procure a miscarriage, more often referred to as abortion. The relevant provisions are sections 58 and 59 of the Act which are discussed above in the context of contragestion. This Act is complemented by the Infant Life (Preservation) Act 1929 which creates the offence of child destruction:

> 1.—(1) Subject as hereinafter in this subsection provided, any person who, with intent to destroy the life of a child capable of being born alive, by any wilful act causes a child to die before it has an existence independent of its mother, shall be guilty of felony, to wit, of child destruction, and shall be liable on conviction thereof on indictment to penal servitude for life:
>
> Provided that no person shall be found guilty of an offence under this section unless it is proved that the act which caused the death of the child was not done in good faith for the purpose only of preserving the life of the mother.
>
> (2) For the purposes of this Act, evidence that a woman had at any material time been pregnant for a period of twenty-eight weeks or more shall be prima facie proof that she was at that time pregnant of a child capable of being born alive.

This Act was originally introduced to cover the period of time during which the child was being born. It was alleged that some women killed their babies as they were being born and yet committed neither murder (as the child was not fully born) nor the procurement of a miscarriage. The 1929 Act introduced the offence of child destruction — that is the destruction of a foetus capable of being born alive. The proviso in section 1(2), that at 28 weeks a child is presumed to be capable of being born alive, however, extended the terms of the Act back into pregnancy. The presumption of viability at 28 weeks was also merely a rebuttable one which could be overturned by evidence to the contrary to the effect that a foetus of less than 28 weeks gestation was capable of being born alive.

The imprecise nature of the relationship between the Acts of 1861 and 1929 was discussed in the case of *R. v. Bourne*,[87] in which the judge, Macnaghten J., creatively linked the two statutes by reading into the 1861 Act the defence contained in the 1929 Act. Bourne, an eminent obstetrical surgeon, performed an abortion on a 14 year-old victim of a violent rape. He informed the authorities and was charged with unlawfully procuring the miscarriage of the girl contrary to section 58 of the Offences Against the Person Act 1861. He was found not guilty.

R. v. Bourne
[1939] 1 K.B. 687, *per* Macnaghten J. (summing-up the case to the jury)

"Members of the jury, now that you have heard all the evidence and the speeches of counsel, it becomes my duty to sum-up the case to you and to give you the necessary directions in law, and then it will be for you to consider the facts in relation to the law as laid down by me, and, after consideration, to deliver your verdict. In a trial by jury it is for the judge to give directions to the jury upon matters of law, and it is for the jury to determine the facts; the jury, and the jury alone, are the judges of the facts in the case.

The charge against Mr Bourne is made under section 58 of the Offences Against the Person Act, 1861, that he unlawfully procured the miscarriage of the girl who was the first witness in the case. It is a very grave crime, and judging by the cases that come before the Court it is a crime by no means uncommon. This is the second case at the present session of this Court where a charge has been preferred of an offence against this section, and I only mention the other case to show you how different the case now before you is from the type of case which usually comes before a criminal court. In that other case a woman without any medical skill or medical qualifications did what is alleged against Mr Bourne here; she unlawfully used an instrument for the purpose of procuring the miscarriage of a pregnant girl; she did it for money; 2*l.* 5*s.* was her fee; a pound was paid on making the appointment, and she came from a distance to a place in London to perform the operation. She used her instrument, and, within an interval of time measured not by minutes but by seconds, the victim of her malpractice was dead on the floor. That is the class of case which usually comes before the Court.

The case here is very different. A man of the highest skill, openly, in one of our great hospitals, performs the operation. Whether it was legal or illegal you will have to determine, but he performs the operation as an act of charity, without fee or reward, and unquestionably believing that he was doing the right thing, and that he ought, in the performance of his duty as a member of a profession devoted to the alleviation of human suffering, to do it. That is the case that you have to try to-day.

It is, I think, a case, of first instance, first impression. The matter has never, so far as I know, arisen before for a jury to determine in circumstances such as these, and there was, even amongst learned counsel, some doubt as to the proper direction to the jury in such a case as this.

The defendant is charged with an offence against section 58 of the Offences Against the Person Act, 1861. That section is a re-enactment of earlier statutes, the first of which was passed at the beginning of the last century in the reign of George III. (43

---

[87] [1939] 1 K.B. 687.

Geo. 3, c. 58, s. 1.) But long before then, before even Parliament came into existence, the killing of an unborn child was by the common law of England a grave crime: see Bracton, Book III. (De Corona), fol. 121. The protection which the common law afforded to human life extended to the unborn child in the womb of its mother. But, as in the case of homicide, so also in the case where an unborn child is killed, there may be justification for the act.

Nine years ago Parliament passed an Act called the Infant Life (Preservation) Act, 1929 (19 & 20 Geo. 5, c. 34). Sect. 1, sub-s. 1, of that Act provides that 'any person who, with intent to destroy the life of a child capable of being born alive, by any wilful act causes a child to die before it has an existence independent of its mother, shall be guilty of felony, to wit, of child destruction, and shall be liable on conviction thereof on indictment to penal servitude for life: Provided that no person shall be found guilty of an offence under this section unless it is proved that the act which caused the death of the child was not done in good faith for the purpose only of preserving the life of the mother.' It is true, as Mr Oliver has said, that this enactment provides for the case where a child is killed by a wilful act at the time when it is being delivered in the ordinary course of nature; but in my view the proviso that it is necessary for the Crown to prove that the act was not done in good faith for the purpose only of preserving the life of the mother is in accordance with what has always been the common law of England with regard to the killing of an unborn child. No such proviso is in fact set out in section 58 of the Offences Against the Person Act, 1861; but the words of that section are that any person who 'unlawfully' uses an instrument with intent to procure miscarriage shall be guilty of felony. In my opinion the word unlawfully is not, in that section, a meaningless word. I think it imports the meaning expressed by the proviso in s. 1, sub-s. 1, of the Infant Life (Preservation) Act, 1929, and that s. 58 of the Offences Against the Person Act, 1861, must be read as if the words making it an offence to use an instrument with intent to procure a miscarriage were qualified by a similar proviso.

In this case, therefore, my direction to you in law is this — that the burden rests on the Crown to satisfy you beyond reasonable doubt that the defendant did not procure the miscarriage of the girl in good faith for the purpose only of preserving her life. If the Crown fails to satisfy you of that, the defendant is entitled by the law of this land to a verdict of acquittal. If, on the other hand, you are satisfied that what the defendant did was not done by him in good faith for the purpose only of preserving the life of the girl, it is your duty to find him guilty. It is said, and I think said rightly, that this is a case of great importance to the public and, more especially, to the medical profession; but you will observe that it has nothing to do with the ordinary case of procuring abortion to which I have already referred. In those cases the operation is performed by a person of no skill, with no medical qualifications, and there is no pretence that it is done for the preservation of the mother's life. Cases of that sort are in no way affected by the consideration of the question which is put before you to-day.

What then is the meaning to be given to the words 'for the purpose of preserving the life of the mother.' There has been much discussion in this case as to the difference between danger to life and danger to health. It may be that you are more fortunate than I am, but I confess that I have found it difficult to understand what the discussion really meant, since life depends upon health, and it may be that health is so gravely impaired that death results. A question was asked by the learned Attorney-General in the course of his cross-examination of Mr Bourne. 'I suggest to you, Mr Bourne,' said the Attorney-General, 'that there is a perfectly clear line — there may be border-line cases — there is a clear line of distinction between danger to health and danger to life.'

The answer of Mr Bourne was: 'I cannot agree without qualifying it; I cannot say just yes or no. I can say there is a large group whose health may be damaged, but whose life almost certainly will not be sacrificed. There is another group at the other end whose life will be definitely in very great danger.' And then he adds: 'There is a large body of material between those two extremes in which it is not really possible to say how far life will be in danger, but we find, of course, that the health is depressed to such an extent that life is shortened, such as in cardiac cases, so that you may say that their life is in danger, because death might occur within measurable distance of the time of their labour.' If that view commends itself to you, you will not accept the suggestion that there is a clear line of distinction between danger to health and danger to life. Mr Oliver wanted you to give what he called a wide and liberal meaning to the words 'for the purpose of preserving the life of the mother.' I should prefer the word 'reasonable' to the words 'wide and liberal.' I think you should take a reasonable view of those words.

It is not contended that those words mean merely for the purpose of saving the mother from instant death. There are cases, we are told, where it is reasonably certain that a pregnant woman will not be able to deliver the child which is in her womb and survive. In such a case where the doctor anticipates, basing his opinion upon the experience of the profession, that the child cannot be delivered without the death of the mother, it is obvious that the sooner the operation is performed the better. The law does not require the doctor to wait until the unfortunate woman is in peril of immediate death. In such a case he is not only entitled, but it is his duty to perform the operation with a view to saving her life . . .

As I have said, I think those words ought to be construed in a reasonable sense, and, if the doctor is of opinion, on reasonable grounds and with adequate knowledge, that the probable consequence of the continuance of the pregnancy will be to make the woman a physical or mental wreck, the jury are quite entitled to take the view that the doctor who, under those circumstances and in that honest belief, operates, is operating for the purpose of preserving the life of the mother . . .

I do not think it is necessary for me to recapitulate the evidence that has been given before you as to the reasons why Mr Bourne in this case thought it right to perform the operation. You remember his evidence. The learned Attorney-General accepts his evidence as a frank statement of what actually passed through his mind. In view of the age and character of the girl and the fact that she had been raped with great violence, he thought that the operation ought to be performed. As I told you yesterday, and I tell you to-day, the question that you have got to determine is not are you satisfied that he performed the operation in good faith for the purpose of preserving the life of the girl. The question is, has the Crown proved the negative of that? If the Crown has satisfied you beyond reasonable doubt — if there is a doubt, by our law the accused person is always entitled to be acquitted — if the Crown has satisfied you beyond reasonable doubt that he did not do this act in good faith for the purpose of preserving the life of the girl, then he is guilty of the offence with which he is charged. If the Crown have failed to satisfy you of that, then by the law of England he is entitled to a verdict of acquittal.

Verdict Not Guilty"

The creativity shown by Macnaghten J. in his interpretation of the law is matched by his representation of the factual circumstances of abortion at that time. Sally Sheldon, in a comprehensive review of abortion case law, argues that:

> "[i]t was the norm in such cases to distinguish between 'respectable' qualified medical providers of abortion acting within the bounds of good medical practice and unscrupulous, unqualified backstreet abortionists, operating for profit. However, this stark division between the altruistic medical practitioner and the callous, professional abortionist seems far from representing the reality. It belies the fact that a great many of the medical practitioners were actually charging inflated fees and that at least some backstreet abortionists were motivated more by compassion than by profit. Nonetheless, Bourne's eventual acquittal rested squarely on the fact that he was a qualified doctor, a noteworthy fact given that at this time no such distinction existed in law as to the professional status of the abortionist . . . [I]n *Bourne* a permissive judicial attitude towards the performance of terminations is integrally related to the tightening of an exclusionary medical monopoly over access to abortion."[88]

The horror of prevalent backstreet abortion practices led to the introduction of a Private Member's Bill by David Steel MP which went on to become the Abortion Act 1967. This Act legalised abortion in circumstances where the risk to the life of the woman, or the risk of injury to her physical and mental health, or that of any existing children, in continuing with the pregnancy was greater than the risk of termination. It also provided for abortion where there was a substantial risk of serious foetal handicap. Section 5(1) of this Act specifically retained in force the Infant Life (Preservation) Act 1929. Therefore abortions were lawful only if performed in accordance with that Act too. This effectively meant that the presumption of foetal viability at 28 weeks was read into the 1967 Act. Terminations after that date, or on proof of viability before that date, would constitute child destruction, unless carried out in good faith to save the life of the pregnant woman. With the advancement of medical technology concern grew that foetuses were routinely viable at an earlier stage than 28 weeks. This led to the courts, in the two cases considered below, having to determine what was meant by the phrase "capable of being born alive".

A prospective father, C, sought an injunction to prevent his ex-partner from having an abortion. The foetus was between 18 and 21 weeks and a termination was authorised by two medical practitioners in accordance with the Abortion Act 1967. C contended that the foetus was capable of being born alive within section 1(1) of the Infant Life (Preservation) Act 1929 because at 18 to 21 weeks it demonstrated real and discernible signs of life. Therefore an abortion would amount to child destruction. In the High Court his application was considered and dismissed by Heilbron J.:

---

[88]   S. Sheldon, "Subject Only to the Attitude of the Surgeon Concerned: The Judicial Protection of Medical Discretion" (1996) 5 *Social & Legal Studies* 95 at 99.

C v. S
[1987] 1 All E.R. 1230, QBD, *per* Heilbron J.

"[T]he affidavits are important. They indicate very clearly the wide difference in thinking and interpretation between medical men, all of high reputation and great experience, in regard to the language used in the 1929 Act. I will now read the affidavits, so as to incorporate their explanation of certain phrases and terms into this judgment. I begin, because it was the first, with that of Mr Norris, emeritus consultant gynaecologist at St Peter's Hospital, Chertsey. He stated in para. 2 of his first affidavit that 'an unborn child of eighteen weeks gestation were it to be delivered by hysterotomy would be live born'. He then went on to refer to a definition of this expression or condition by the World Health Assembly under Art.23 of the Constitution of the World Health Organisation in 1976 (subsequent to both the Acts in this matter) as being:

> 'the complete expulsion or extraction from its Mother of a product of conception irrespective of the duration of pregnancy, which after such separation breathes or [and I emphasise the 'or' in his affidavit] shows any other evidence of life such as beating of the heart, pulsation of the umbilical cord or definite movement of voluntary muscle whether or not the umbilical cord has been cut or the placenta is attached'.

To that affidavit Professor John Richard Newton replied. He did so, in his first affirmation, on 16 February. He said:

> 'I am the Layson Tait Professor of Obstetrics and Gynaecology and Head of Department at the Birmingham University Medical School Queen Elizabeth Hospital Edgbaston Birmingham. I have been a Gynaecologist for twenty years and held my present position since 1979.'

He had been shown a copy of Mr Norris's affidavit and asked to comment on it and in regard to para. 2 he said:

> 'I believe it confusing in the circumstances to use the words 'live born' for a foetus of 18 weeks gestation. As Mr Norris says the term has been defined by Article 23 of the World Health Assembly in 1976. There is now produced . . . a copy of a report known as 'Report on Foetal Viability and Clinical Practice' which was prepared in August 1985 by a representative committee on behalf of the Royal College of Obstetricians and Gynaecologists, the British Paediatric Association, Royal College of General Practitioners, Royal College of Midwives, British Medical Association and the Department of Health and Social Security . . . I refer in particular to the twelfth page of that report in which reference is made to the recommendation of the World Health Organisation concerning perinatal statistics. The committee to which I have referred above was charged with the task of considering foetal viability and comparison is made between the World Health Organisation definition and the concept of foetal viability. As will be seen from the report the purpose behind the World Health Organisation definition was to standardise the perinatal statistics for member countries of births. The purpose behind the definition was specifically not to define independent foetal viability and the

committee go on to consider that concept and I believe that to be the important concept in these circumstances. Foetal viability means that the foetus is
capable of independent human existence separate from the mother.'

He then refers to the contents of this report of the various prestigious colleges and
associations of doctors and says:

'It will be seen that in the survey of 29 neo-natal intensive care units in the
United Kingdom during 1982 no foetus of less than 23 weeks survived after
delivery. It is my conclusion therefore that a foetus of anything below 23
weeks cannot survive independent of its mother and has therefore no viability.'

A few days later Mr Norris swore a second affidavit, in order to amplify the first. He
then suggested that the period of gestation was 2, or possibly 3, weeks more than the
18 weeks which had been mentioned. He went on to explain the expression 'live born'
which had been used in his first affidavit:

'4 . . . In case there is any ambiguity I wish to assert that in so stating I mean that
in my opinion any foetus of eighteen weeks or longer gestation is capable of being
born alive and that by 'alive' I mean showing real and discernible signs of life within
the meaning of the World Health Organisation definition set out in my original Affidavit and of the Births and Deaths Registration Act 1926 current when the Infant Life
(Preservation) Act 1929 was passed and also of the Births and Deaths Registration Act
1953 now current. Under the provisions of both these statutes such a child shall be
registered as a live birth.
    5. A child of eighteen or even twenty-one weeks gestational age although capable of
being born alive and capable of surviving for some time outside the womb is not
generally regarded by the medical profession as being viable because present paediatric
skills are insufficient to assist it to remain alive for more than a limited time.'

On the same day, 19 February, Professor Newton, having read the second affidavit of
Mr Norris, stated in a further affidavit:

'1 . . . Although he uses the expression 'live born' in [his first] affidavit he
does not mention, nor did I understand that he was specifically referring to
the words actually appearing in an Act of Parliament namely the words 'born
alive' in Section 1 Infant Life (Preservation) Act 1929. This has now been
drawn to my attention and I give my comments.
    2. The expression 'born alive' used in the Infant Life (Preservation) Act
1929 raises difficulties before the expiration of 28 weeks of gestation.
    3. Although it is difficult to generalise, for reasons which I will refer to in
paragraph 4 after 8 weeks of gestation some fetuses will exhibit some primitive fetal movement, have a primitive heart tube which contracts and the circulation has started to develop but these fetuses will be quite incapable of life
separate from the mother.
    4. Each individual fetus in each individual mother develops differently and
at different rates . . .'

He then refers to the difficulty of the medical assessment of the gestational period in any particular case, which must be approximate and which may be complicated, as indeed in this case, by irregular menstruation. However, there are some firm generalisations on development which could be made:

'In a fetus of 18–21 weeks gestation the cardiac muscle is contracting and a primitive circulation is developing, but in my opinion lung development does not occur until after 24 weeks gestation; before this time the major air passages have been formed and there is gradual development of the bronchioles but these terminate in a blind sac incapable of gas exchange prior to 24 weeks.'

He says that a fetus of 18 to 21 weeks gestation could be delivered by hysterotomy but that would not be routinely used on such a fetus, and he describes the type of operation:

'Once placental separation occurs whether the delivery has been by hysterotomy or vaginally it will not be able to respirate . . . What constitutes 'born alive' is controversial among the medical profession and often turns not only on medical knowledge but on the moral views of the person giving his opinion. I would mention that the development of each particular fetus in each particular mother is an individual process, the progress of which [at] any stage before 28 weeks can best be ascertained by an examination of the particular mother in question or at the very least detailed knowledge of that individual person.'

With that I must entirely agree, and counsel for Mr C conceded that that must be so. It is an important aspect of this case, to which I will later refer. Professor Newton continued:

'Whether or not a fetus up to 24 weeks of gestation is delivered by hysterotomy or vaginal delivery it will not be capable of surviving once the placental separation occurs. Up to 24 weeks in my opinion the lungs are incapable of sustaining life because they are not adequately developed. The development of other organs within the fetus is at an equally primitive stage incapable of sustaining life. I do not consider the indicia referred to in paragraph 3 hereof to equate with being 'alive'. I equate 'alive' with being able to sustain a separate independent existence and in my opinion [. . .] a fetus is clearly not capable of being able to do [so] until after 24 weeks of gestation.'

Finally, I draw attention to the affidavit of Professor Rivers FRCP, a reader in paediatrics at St Mary's Hospital Medical School since 1978 and having a special interest in new-born intensive care. He stated:

'2. Although a foetus of 18/21 weeks gestation displays some signs of life in the womb in my opinion such foetuses are unable to perform the function of lung respiration without which they cannot live separate from their mothers once the umbilical cord is clamped and/or the placenta is removed. Obviously therefore a foetus of such gestation cannot even be mechanically ventilated since the lungs are not sufficiently developed for lung inflation and gas exchange to occur.

3. Whether such a foetus is "born" before the umbilical cord is clamped and or the placenta is removed or whether it is to be considered "alive" after this has happened are matters which cause difficulty and controversy to such an extent that, for example, the medical profession prefer to use the words "viable" foetus rather than the very difficult expression "born alive".'

Counsel for Mr C submitted that 'being born alive' is a much more restrictive concept than viability, for that embraces not only being born alive but surviving, for however short a time, thereafter, that the 1929 Act is unconcerned with viability, but that there is no ambiguity in the words used and they cannot be extended to cover the other concept.

Therefore, if a doctor aborts an 18-week fetus, counsel argued, he is inevitably doing so on one capable of being born alive, regardless of the fact, which he accepted, that not all fetuses are either identical or in the same condition in different mothers, even though of the same period of gestation. If Mr Norris's view is correct, he continued, 'all fetuses' must necessarily include the one in this case.

Abortion itself is a very controversial subject. It has been; it still is. Many people feel genuinely and sincerely for and against its operation. It involves sociological, moral and profound religious aspects which arouse anxieties. Parliament itself has been much exercised over this subject for many years. None of these matters concern or affect my considerations or my ultimate decision. The court endeavours, to the best of its ability, to interpret the law and, as Baker P. said in *Paton v. Trustees of BPAS* [1978] 2 All E.R. 987 at 989; [1979] 1 Q.B. 276 at 278: 'My task is to apply the law free of emotion or predilection'.

Since the enactment of the 1929 Act there have undoubtedly been rapid, extensive and truly remarkable developments in medical science, not least in the field of obstetrics. Some matters have become much clearer, some have remained obscure and difficult to determine; so it is perhaps understandable that the questions when life begins, when a fetus is capable of being born alive and when a child is actually alive are all problems of complexity for even the greatest medical minds. The determination of when life ends is now also a matter of concern and dispute.

Having said that, this case, I remind myself, concerns to some extent the meaning of the phrase 'capable of being born alive'. Unless Mr Norris' unequivocal assertion that *all* fetuses of 18 weeks' gestation *are* capable of being born alive is taken at face value as credible, then in reality and in the hospital where the decisions are taken it is the doctor (one of a team and probably one not yet designated) who has to make his decision on that problem in respect of Miss S's unborn child. We do not know on what basis he will make his prognosis, for that is what is entailed, or indeed, if by now he has been nominated, whether he has made the decision and on what criteria.

That the phrase is ambiguous would seem to follow from the differing points of view as disclosed in the affidavits and the exhibits.

In the nineteenth century, on charges of murder of a very young infant who died or was killed before or not long after separation from its mother at birth, I found some, perhaps a little, assistance, for the judge, after hearing medical evidence, sometimes in agreement but often in conflict, would direct the jury on the meaning of 'born alive', not, be it noted, 'born alive and surviving', which was a necessary pre-condition for a conviction. Such directions, based on interpretation of that very phrase, prior to the 1929 Act, interpretations which one can presume would be known to the draftsmen of the Act and which might have been of some assistance, were, except for one case that has been produced (though there may of course be more), based on interpretations called from the doctors and bear a certain similarity to those in the affidavits of Professor Newton and Professor Rivers, rather than in that of Mr Norris.

In *R. v. Handley* (1874) 13 Cox C.C. 79 Brett J, a very distinguished judge, directed the jury that a child was considered to have been 'born alive' when it existed as a live child, that is to say breathing and living by reason of its breathing through its own lungs alone, without deriving any of its living or power of living by or through any connection with its mother.

In *R. v. Poulton* (1832) 5 C. & P. 329, 172 E.R. 997 even the fact of the child having breathed was said not to be conclusive proof of it having been in 'a living state' after birth. In that case three doctors had given evidence and the judge told the jury (5 C. & P. 329 at 330; 172 E.R. 997 at 998):

> '. . . if there is all this uncertainty among these medical men, perhaps you would think it too much for you to say that you are satisfied that the child was born alive.'

In *R. v. Enoch* (1833) 5 C. & P. 539; 172 E.R. 1089, and similarly in *R. v. Wright* (1841) 9 C. & P. 754; 173 E.R. 1039, the judge directed the jury that to be alive there must be, in addition to breathing, a circulation independent of the mother. The limited indicia of life which Mr Norris said was sufficient would not at any rate have accorded with those directions.

Counsel's case that Mr C was entitled to an injunction because a crime was threatened depended, it appears, partly, as counsel for Miss S submitted, on the extraordinary and dogmatic assertion with regard to the ability to be born alive of *every* 18 week fetus, without any personal knowledge or examination of any of these countless unborn children, partly on his interpretation of 'being born alive' and partly on the view adumbrated by counsel for Mr C that, if any doctor was intending to perform an abortion on an 18-week fetus, it would be perverse of him or her to assert other than that the fetus was capable of being born alive. Counsel, though not Mr Norris, submitted that no other interpretation of 'live born' than that of Mr Norris is within the words of the Act.

I disagree. Counsel for Mrs [*sic*] S pointed out that Mr Norris did not disagree with Professor Newton that an 18-week fetus cannot breathe and cannot even be mechanically ventilated. I would have thought that to say, as he has, that a child is live born or alive, even though it cannot breathe, would surprise not only doctors but many ordinary people.

The word 'viable' is, I believe from what I have heard in this case, sometimes used interchangeably and in a number of cases where others might use the words 'born alive'. In the United States of America, in the Supreme Court, in *Roe v. Wade* (1973) 410 U.S. 113 at 163 it was said:

> 'With respect to the State's important and legitimate interest in potential life, the 'compelling' point is at *viability*. This is so because the fetus then presumably has the capability of meaningful life outside the mother's womb. State regulation protective of fetal life after viability thus has both logical and biological justifications.' (*My emphasis.*)

As far as the phrase in the 1929 Act is concerned, counsel for Mr C submits, it either contains an ambiguity or the phrase is a technical one. In my view, one or both of those submissions is or are correct. That expression, in my judgment, does not have a clear and plain meaning. It *is* ambiguous. It is a phrase which is capable of different interpretations, and probably for the reason that it is also a medical concept and, as with the example of earlier days, the expertise of doctors may well be required and gratefully received to assist the court.

Even distinguished medical men have found considerable difficulties but have discovered that it is more helpful to equate that phrase with viability, possibly with the example from the parliamentary draftsman in mind.

I cannot accept counsel for the plaintiff's submission that this is not, at any rate in this court, even partly a matter of expert opinion as to the meaning of 'alive', for I have to point out that the first expert, namely Mr Norris, who produced an affidavit on that very topic was introduced by him. Professor Newton replied later.

Counsel on behalf of the Official Solicitor, acting as amicus curiae, submitted that the alleged threatened criminality raised a difficult question of interpretation and pointed out that s.5(1) of the 1967 Act itself incorporates the word 'viable' in the phrase which refers to 'protecting the life of the viable foetus', a section to which I have already referred. By that date, he argued, Parliament would no doubt be aware of the controversies over the law on abortion and it is possible that the use of that word is some indication that Parliament thought it necessary to use that particular qualifying word. I think that that is possible too, though I would not attach too much weight to the parenthesis containing that word as an aid to construction.

Perhaps it is more significant that, though the reference to a fetus of 28 weeks or more being deemed 'capable of being born alive' is referable to the burden of proof, it is probably dealing with a fetus of an age that would be known or expected to be viable in 1929.

Mr Norris, of course, does not limit his statement to a question of presumption. He goes much further and in effect make his 18 weeks an irrebuttable presumption, thus, at a stroke, as it were, reducing the 28 weeks to 18.

Council for the Official Solicitor submitted that the court should reject Mr Norris's interpretation of 'born alive' as the minimum indicia, without breathing, possibly without circulation and minus a number of indications referred to by Professor Newton.

In considering this submission, I find Mr Norris's statements as to the inevitability of every 18-week fetus being born alive unacceptable. It is not necessary for me, nor would I want, to try to decide on affidavit evidence in a somewhat limited sphere the answer, which baffles men and women with great scientific expertise, to a very profound question. I would, however, say that I am not greatly attracted to the very limited definition relied on by Mr Norris and I do not accept it as a realistic one.

I now, finally, come to consider the alleged criminality and to decide, as I am asked to do, whether or not I should grant the injunction which is sought. I note, first of all, that this is a matter of the utmost urgency and importance.

Counsel for Mr C no longer claims qua father, but it is not unimportant to point out, as Baker P. did in *Paton v. Trustees of BPAS* [1978] 2 All E.R. 987 at 990; [1979] Q.B. 276 at 279–280, that, apart from a right to apply for custody of or access to an illegitimate child, the father has no other rights whatsoever, and the equality of parental rights provision in s.1(1) of the Guardianship of Minors Act 1971 and s.1(7) of the Guardianship Act 1973 expressly does not apply to an illegitimate child; parental rights are exclusively vested in the mother.

An injunction of the nature sought is rare. Indeed, a case of this sort is rare. The Paton's case was, I understand the first to be heard in this country. Such an injunction should not issue, in any event, on evidence which is conflicting, or uncertain, as here, and, in my opinion for such an injunction to issue there must, most importantly, be strong evidence against the proposed defendant and virtual certainty that what is being complained of constitutes a defined criminal offence. Every case depends on its own facts and circumstances and none more so than this, for the graver the offence the more vital it is that, before an injunction issues to interfere with the operative procedures being prepared because of the risk to the health of Miss S, it is shown that an offence is virtually certain to be committed if no injunction issues. Moreover, the statute whose terms have to be interpreted in order to found this alleged offence is a penal one and the offence which it is said will be committed is one which attracts a penalty, as I have indicated, of life imprisonment. Such statute must be strictly construed.

I ask myself, first of all, how can an unknown, unascertained doctor, one who will be personally responsible for making the necessary clinical judgments, particularly preoperatively, be said at this stage to be about to commit a criminal offence because another doctor, namely Mr Norris, gives it as his opinion, unsupported by any other evidence or examination, that the hospital doctor will be, must be, committing this offence because, it is said, if he intends to do this operation, he must know that the fetus could be born alive, 'alive' meaning what Mr Norris says it means, and that if he nevertheless continues the termination he is not only perverse but guilty of the offence of child destruction.

On the other hand, there is before me compelling evidence that Mr Norris's opinion is not accepted by a wide body of eminent medical opinion and by many reputable doctors.

I am not satisfied that a potential crime has been proved. If a doctor were to be charged, which is difficult to envisage, any such offence would have to be proved to the standard of certainty, the burden of proof, a heavy one, would be on the prosecution to produce evidence to establish all the elements of their case, including proof of the accused's requisite men rea (because such an offence would not be provable on an objective basis) and Mr Norris's evidence as to the notional 'perverse doctor' would not avail in any attempt to prove an offence under the 1929 Act.

In my view, there is no sufficient basis for saying that there is a threatened crime and, if a case were brought, the judge would in my judgment be bound to stop the case, as I would. I have no hesitation in coming to the conclusion that counsel for Mr C has not made out his case for an injunction.

In view of my conclusion, which disposes of the matter, I have not thought it necessary to add to this already long judgment by considering another hurdle that counsel might have encountered by reason of the decisions with regard to a private individual seeking to prevent the commission of an offence by way of an injunction, following the *Gouriet* line of cases (see *Gouriet v. Union of Post Office Workers* [1977] 3 All E.R. 70; [1978] A.C. 938).

The applications are dismissed."

C appealed.

C v. S
[1987] 1 All E.R. 1230, CA, *per* Sir John Donaldson M.R.

"We have received affidavit evidence from three doctors, none of whom has examined Miss S. Their evidence is thus necessarily directed at the stage in the development of a fetus which can normally be expected to have been reached by the 18th to 21st week.

On this, as one would expect, they are in substantial agreement. At that stage the cardiac muscle is contracting and a primitive circulation is developing. Thus the fetus could be said to demonstrate real and discernible signs of life. On the other hand, the fetus, even if then delivered by hysterotomy, would be incapable ever of breathing either naturally or with the aid of a ventilator. It is not a case of the fetus requiring a stimulus or assistance. It cannot and will never be able to breathe. Where the doctors disagree is as to whether a fetus, at this stage of development, can properly be described as 'a child capable of being borne [*sic*] alive' within the meaning of the 1929 Act. That essentially depends on the interpretation of the statute and is a matter for the courts.

We have no evidence of the state of the fetus being carried by Miss S but, if it has reached the normal stage of development and so is incapable ever of breathing, it is not in our judgment 'a child capable of being born alive' within the meaning of the 1929 Act and accordingly the termination of this pregnancy would not constitute an offence under that Act."

The question of foetal viability arose again in the case of *Rance v. Mid-Downs Health Authority*,[89] this time in the context of a claim for damages in respect of a child born with disabilities. The plaintiff brought an action for damages against the Area Health Authority for its failure to ascertain that her foetus was suffering from spina bifida and its consequent failure to offer her a termination. An ultrasound scan had been carried out at about 26 weeks and the plaintiff contended that the Health Authority had been negligent in failing to discover the abnormality. The Health Authority denied negligence and argued, successfully, that even if the abnormality had been discovered by the scan, the termination of the pregnancy, which would have occurred when the foetus was 27 weeks old, would have been an offence under section 1 of the Infant Life (Preservation) Act 1929 because the foetus was capable of being born alive.

Rance v. Mid-Downs Health Authority
[1991] 1 All E.R. 801, *per* Brooke J.

"It was not in issue that an abortion in this case would have been prima facie at offence under s. 58 of the 1861 Act, but would have been prima facie rendered lawful under s. 1(1)(b) of the 1967 Act, provided that it did not involve the destruction of the life of a child 'capable of being born alive', contrary to s. 1 of the 1929 Act. The question of mixed fact and law which I have to determine is whether John would have been a child capable of being born alive at the time any hypothetical abortion might have taken place. As I have already said, part of the answer to this question involves the interpretation, for the first time in an English court, of the words 'a child capable of being born alive', in the context of an abortion carried out between 27 and 28 weeks of a pregnancy [. . .]

Would John have been at the time of a hypothetical abortion a child 'capable of being born alive' within the meaning of the 1929 Act?

[89] *Rance v. Mid-Downs Health Authority* [1991] 1 All E.R. 801.

To interpret the intention of Parliament when it enacted the 1929 Act, I must put myself in the draftsman's chair in 1929. I must identify the historical background and the mischief which the Act was enacted to remedy and I must construe the words in dispute in the context of the Act as a whole. If the natural and ordinary meaning of the words is clear, I must give effect to them, even if I find their effect goes beyond what was needed to deal with the mischief. If that meaning is ambiguous, then I must call in aid other appropriate canons of construction to help me to identify Parliament's intention. I must also consider the effect, if any, on the construction of the 1929 Act of s. 5(1) of the 1967 Act."

After considering the historical background, Brooke J. continued:

"English law has always made a distinction between the status of a foetus or child in its mother's womb and the status of a child born alive. It is manslaughter unlawfully to kill a child born alive and murder if the requisite intent is proved. Four nineteenth century cases illustrate the approach of English judges when the termination of life occurred at or near the moment of birth. In *R. v. Poulton* (1832) 5 C. & P. 329; 172 E.R. 997 there was evidence that the baby had breathed but insufficient evidence that the child had ever been fully born. The jury was told by a medical expert that it frequently happened that a child was born as far as the head was concerned but that death took place before the whole delivery was complete. Littledale J. directed the jury that they must be satisfied that the child had been born alive before they could convict and added (5 C. & P. 329 at 330; 172 E.R. 997 at 998):

> 'With respect to the birth, the being born must mean that the whole body is brought into the world; it is not sufficient that the child respires in the progress of the birth.'

In *R. v. Enoch* (1833) 5 C. & P. 539; 172 E.R. 1089 Parke J. adopted this ruling when he directed the jury that the child might breathe before it was born but its having breathed was not sufficiently life to make the killing of the child murder and that there must have been an independent circulation of the child.

In *R. v. Brain* (1834) 6 C. & P. 349; 172 E.R. 1272 Parke J. directed a jury that if a child had been wholly born, and was alive, it was not essential that it should have breathed at the time it was killed, since many children were born alive, yet did not breathe for some time after birth.

Finally, in *R. v. Handley* (1874) 13 Cox C.C. 79 Brett J. was concerned with a case in which a newly born child was found dead. The umbilical cord was separated, the internal viscera were healthy and the bowels had acted soon after birth. The bladder and stomach were empty. The general effect of the medical evidence was that the child was full born, was born alive and from the inflated condition of the lungs had lived for an hour or more. Brett J. directed the jury that a child was considered to have been born alive, *i.e.* whether it existed as a live child, that is to say, breathing and living by reason of its breathing through its own lungs alone, without deriving any of its living or power of living by or through any connection with the mother.

Parliament showed that it was aware of the common law approach to the concept of being alive in its legislation relating to the registration of births and deaths. For example, the statutory definition of the expression 'still-born', in s. 12 of the Births and Deaths Registration Act 1926, is that it:

'. . . shall apply to any child which has issued forth from its mother after the twenty-eighth week of pregnancy and which did not at any time after being completely expelled from its mother, breathe or show any other signs of life.'

In 1929, therefore, the law protected the foetus in utero when it prohibited acts done unlawfully to procure a miscarriage. It protected the child which was born as a live child, breathing and living without any connection with its mother. It provided no protection, however, to the child while it was in the process of being born and before it had been completely separated from its mother, and the extinction of the child's potential life at this intermediate stage was not an offence. This lacuna in the law was identified by Talbot J. when charging the grand jury at the Liverpool Assizes in June 1928 in these words:

'The law upon the matter is unsatisfactory and it is right that every appropriate opportunity should be taken to call public attention to it. It is a felony to procure abortion and it is murder to take the life of a child when it is fully born, but to take the life of a child while it is being born and before it is fully born is no offence whatever.'

(Cited in the *Report of the Select Committee on the Infant Life (Preservation) Bill* (H.L. Paper (1987–88) No. 50) para. 8.)

I am satisfied that this was the mischief which Parliament intended to remedy when it enacted the 1929 Act. In remedying the mischief, it adopted the concept of 'born alive', which was now well understood following the direction of Brett J. in *R. v. Handley*, and it extended the protection of the law to the child who was capable of being born alive up to the moment when it was in fact born alive and therefore qualified to receive the protection of the law of homicide. It was agreed between counsel that in the event the words used by Parliament in 1929 extended to cover not only the actual period of birth but also the period when the child capable of being born alive was still in its mother's womb.

Parliament gave effect to its new determination to protect the existence of the child capable of being born alive in s. 1(1) of the 1929 Act. In contrast, s. 1(2) of the Act was concerned with practical ways and means of giving effect to Parliament's intentions. Parliament could have chosen to resolve the difficult problem of proving in a criminal court that the child whose existence was terminated was capable of being born alive, by enacting a cut-off date, say at 28 weeks, before which there was a conclusive presumption that a child was incapable of being born alive and after which there was a rebuttable presumption that it was so capable. However, this course was not adopted. Parliament created the rebuttable presumption that a child of over 28 weeks' gestation was capable of being born alive, but it was otherwise silent on matters of evidential proof. Therefore, if the Crown succeeded in proving, to a criminal standard of proof, that a particular child of under 28 weeks' gestation had been capable of being born alive, the defendant would be convicted of an offence under the new Act if the other ingredients of the offence were proved. The difficulty was not with the concept 'capable of being born alive', but with proving to a jury's satisfaction, without the help of a statutory presumption or information derived from modern technological know-how, that the child in question had had those attributes.

In my judgment the meaning of the words 'born alive' are clear, and the meaning of the words 'capable of being born alive' are also clear. The anencephalic child (who lacks all or most of the cerebral hemispheres but is capable of using its lungs) and the spina bifida child (who possesses one or more of the adverse criteria identified by Professor Lorber) is each born alive if, after birth, it exists as a live child, that is to say breathing and living by reason of its breathing through its own lungs alone, without deriving any of its living or power of living by or through any connection with its mother. For the purposes of this judgment I do not have to consider the case of life before breathing, which was referred to in *R v Brain*. Once the foetus has reached a state of development in the womb that it is capable, if born, of possessing those attributes, it is capable of being born alive within the meaning of the 1929 Act . . .

I do not consider that the enactment of s. 5(1) of the 1967 Act ('Nothing in this Act shall affect the provisions of the Infant Life (Preservation) Act 1929 (protecting the life of the viable foetus)') changes or modifies the meaning of the 1929 Act in any way. The primary dictionary meaning of the word 'viable', which is derived from the French word 'vie', is 'capable of living'. I was also referred to *Larousse*, which shows that the primary meaning of the French word 'viable' is 'qui peut vivre'. I have allowed for the fact that the 1967 Act was derived from a private member's Bill, of which Lord Diplock commented in *Royal College of Nursing of the U.K. v. Dept of Health and Social Security* [1981] 1 All E.R. 545 at 567; [1981] A.C. 800 at 824:

> '. . . maybe for that reason, it lacks that style and consistency of draftsmanship both internal to the Act itself and in relation to other statutes which one would expect to find in legislation that had its origin in the office of parliamentary counsel.'

However, even if I was persuaded that Parliament could alter the clear meaning of an earlier Act by this rather elliptic means — and there is certainly nothing in the excerpt from *Craies on Statute Law* (7th edn, 1971) pp. 146–149 to which I was referred, to suggest that this method of 'legislative declaration' or 'parliamentary exposition' has any precedent — I do not consider that in 1967 Parliament intended to do so. In my judgment the word 'viable' was simply being used as a convenient shorthand for the words 'capable of being born alive' and I cannot discern any Parliamentary intention in 1967 to change the effect of the 1929 Act.

Counsel for the plaintiffs submitted at the beginning of his closing speech that the words 'capable of being born alive' meant 'viable', in the sense of 'capable of being born alive and surviving into old age in the normal way without intensive care or surgical intervention.' He submitted that in 1929 Parliament can only have had in mind the natural capacity given to a child to survive without artificial aids and interventions unthought of in 1929. He pointed out that any other interpretation, given the wider meaning for which he contended, introduced considerably more uncertainty. If not into old age, then what length of survival should be postulated? Why stop at 7 or 28 days? If intensive care, what degree of intensive care? The care of a specialist referral centre or a peripheral hospital? Is operative intervention to be postulated or not?

When I tested this submission in argument, he appeared to be willing to withdraw from it, and his fall-back submission was that the words entailed the concept of being alive and surviving for a reasonable period. He said that it would be for a jury to decide how long was reasonable, but he suggested that 28 days, or possibly seven days, would have been the sort of period which Parliament would have had in mind.

The posing of all these questions, and the shifting stances adopted by counsel in argument, strengthen me in my conviction that my preferred construction of the disputed words is correct. I do not believe for one moment that Parliament intended the protection it was affording to children in the course of being born to be limited to the class of healthy children originally identified by counsel and to be denied to those children whose expectation of long life was not so assured at the moment of birth. Nor do I consider, particularly in the light of the historical background to the Act, that Parliament intended the concept of 'capable of being born alive' to be left to be decided by different juries' views of what period of survival after birth should be regarded as reasonable in order to qualify the child for the protection of the Act."

Foetal viability at a stage earlier than 28 weeks is one factor which contributed to the amendment of the Abortion Act 1967 by section 37 of the Human Fertilisation and Embryology Act 1990.[90] The 1990 Act was primarily intended to legislate upon embryo research and fertility treatment services, but was also used to deal with ambiguities produced by the Abortion Act 1967 particularly in the wake of medical opinion that foetuses could be viable before 28 weeks. The amended section 1 of the Abortion Act 1967 reads:

> **1.**—(1) Subject to the provisions of this section, a person shall not be guilty of an offence under the law relating to abortion when a pregnancy is terminated by a registered medical practitioner if two registered medical practitioners are of the opinion, formed in good faith
>
> (a) that the pregnancy has not exceeded its twenty-fourth week and that the continuance of the pregnancy would involve risk, greater than if the pregnancy were terminated, of injury to the physical or mental health of the pregnant woman or any existing children of her family; or
>
> (b) that the termination is necessary to prevent grave permanent injury to the physical or mental health of the pregnant woman; or
>
> (c) that the continuance of the pregnancy would involve risk to the life of the pregnant woman, greater than if the pregnancy were terminated; or
>
> (d) that there is a substantial risk that if the child were born it would suffer from such physical or mental abnormalities as to be seriously handicapped.
>
> (2) In determining whether the continuance of a pregnancy would involve such risk of injury to health as is mentioned in paragraph (a) or (b) of subsection (1) of this section, account may be taken of the pregnant woman's actual or reasonably foreseeable environment.

The main thrust of section 37 is that it in effect breaks down into separate grounds those grounds originally grouped together in the 1967 legislation. These now become sections 1(1)(a), 1(1)(c) and 1(1)(d). Section 37 introduces a new time limit of 24 weeks for one of these grounds (s.1(1)(a)). The section also introduces one new ground for abortion (s.1(1)(b)). The relationship

---

[90]   Section 37 was the culmination of a series of attempts to amend the 1967 Abortion Act. For a detailed breakdown of legislative proposals prior to 1990 see S. Millns & S. Sheldon "Abortion" in P. Cowley (ed.), *The Conscience of Parliament: Moral Issues in British Politics* (Ilford: Frank Cass, forthcoming).

between the 1967 Act and previous legislation is also resolved. Section 37(4) replaces section 5(1) of the 1967 Act which now reads "No offence under the Infant Life (Preservation) Act 1929 shall be committed by a registered medical practitioner who terminates a pregnancy in accordance with the provisions of this Act." Effectively this allows for termination on any grounds other than section 1(1)(a) to term, whether the foetus is or is not viable. Where the terms of section 1 are not complied with, however, the risk of prosecution under both the 1861 and 1929 Acts remains. The implications of the 1990 reforms for women seeking termination of a pregnancy are varied and, as the following extract makes clear, questions of viability have not been rendered immaterial to the question of the limits placed upon the legality of abortion:

S. SHELDON
"The Law of Abortion and the Politics of Medicalisation"[91]

"Whilst the 1990 reforms entrenched a comparatively high upper time-limit into the law, however, they cannot be seen as an unmitigated victory. First, the adoption of a medical framework for political debate served to exclude broader social considerations — in this light the adoption of viability as a cut-off point is in itself problematic. Secondly, the opportunity for a move towards liberalisation of the law was missed, the medicalisation of the debates making it difficult to challenge medical control over access to abortion. Finally, the parliamentary debates also highlighted a worrying use of medical knowledges to support a construction of the foetus as a separate individual.

1. The limits of viability
The most important change made to the Abortion Act by the 1990 legislation was to insert a fixed upper time-limit of twenty-four weeks. Exceptions to this limit allow terminations until term where abortion is necessary to prevent grave permanent injury to the physical or mental health of the woman, or where continuance of the pregnancy threatens the life of the woman, or where there is a substantial risk that if the child is born it would suffer from such physical or mental abnormalities as to be seriously handicapped. The limit adopted is that recommended by the Royal College of Obstetricians and Gynaecologists — twenty-four weeks is the point when the foetus is deemed to become 'viable' or capable of sustaining independent life outside the womb. David Steel, recommending the adoption of this limit, told the House of Commons that:

'[i]t would be a great mistake for the House to set aside the opinion of established medical bodies . . . We are not entitled to cast aside all these opinions as though they did not matter, or to pluck out of the air a figure that we think might be better.'

The choice is here presented as between the acceptance of medical judgment or

[91]   In J. Bridgeman & S. Millns (eds), *supra*, n. 82 at pp. 114–119.

complete arbitrariness: it seems that there are no valid considerations other than medical ones.

Anti-choice MPs opposed this time-limit not with their traditional religious-moral arguments of foetal humanity, but rather with medical 'facts' and a reliance on scientific knowledges. In particular, they emphasised the need to 'legislate for the future' as:

> 'medical techniques are advancing so rapidly that, long before 20 years is up, we shall regard a termination within 20 weeks as ludicrous . . . By that time, medical techniques will be so good that a foetus will be viable much earlier than that.'

. . . [T]he medical framework for debate was clearly marked in press coverage. For example, on 23 April 1990, the day before the MPs voted on the proposed amendments, *The Guardian* ran an article which was described as 'an attempt to summarise the arguments'. It was entitled: 'Most doctors opt for twenty-four-week limit' and began with the words: '[t]here are few supporters for retaining the present 28-week limit, as the medical consensus is that babies are viable from twenty-four weeks, given the intensive care and technology of modern premature baby units.' Thus the perceived framework within which the issue of abortion should be decided was essentially structured by medical knowledges, broader social issues being obscured.

The adoption of viability as the cut-off point for abortions was heralded as a victory for pro-choice campaigners, as it currently ensures an upper limit which is high in comparison to other Western abortion laws. However, the effect of the 1990 debates has been to entrench in the public — and parliamentary — consciousness that abortion is permissible prior to viability, but should be forbidden after this point. This is a notion which future campaigns may find hard to dislodge. One letter to *The Times* goes so far as to argue that the destruction of the handicapped viable foetus is no longer a matter of abortion, but rather of euthanasia. Whilst the present state of medical science makes it impossible to sustain neo-natal life at much less than twenty-four weeks of gestational development for reasons of lung development, it is surely not inconceivable that this limit will be gradually pushed downwards. If this happens, pro-choice groups will face a particularly bitter struggle to try and separate out the legitimacy of abortion from the notion of viability.

More immediately, the concentration on viability as the decisive factor obscures other considerations. As McNeil writes, the adoption of viability as a dividing line shifts the focus of decision-making away from women who make complex evaluations of their particular circumstances and of the *social* sustainability of new life. Such decisions have little to do with what medical science can sustain technologically:

> 'saying that it is theoretically possible to plug a 24-week-old foetus into life support apparatuses is very different from saying that you personally will take primary responsibility for supporting — in every sense — a child through to adulthood.'

2. The entrenchment of medical control

Another cause for concern at the medicalisation of public and parliamentary debate is that this can only further serve to entrench medical control of abortion. The more abortion becomes viewed as primarily a medical phenomenon, the more it seems inevitable that it must fall into the sphere of authority of doctors who should maintain both their technical control over it *and* the power to decide who should have access to abortion services. The medical control of abortion is accepted within the 1990 debates, when even pro-choice MPs emphasise that the decision to terminate a pregnancy should be made in conjunction with a doctor. In 1990, two amendments which addressed the medical control of abortion were tabled. The first, which sought to allow abortion on request within the first twelve weeks of pregnancy, was not selected for vote. The second, which sought to allow abortions during the same period with the approval of only one doctor, was defeated by 228 to 200 votes. Thus, Parliament sees it as more acceptable to allow the abortion of handicapped foetuses until birth than it does to allow this step towards female reproductive autonomy. The failure to pass either of these proposals through Parliament is a missed opportunity as it is unlikely abortion will be put to the vote again in the near future.

3. Foetal separation

The other worrying trend, highlighted during the debates on the Human Fertilisation and Embryology Bill, is the use of medical knowledges to support the construction of the foetus as a separate individual. Whilst anti-choice supporters have long made such assertions, these have been phrased in a religious-moral rhetoric. Now such claims have been recoded in a form which exploits the prevalence of an assumption of foetal separation in medical discourse. During the 1990 parliamentary debates, the Society for the Protection of Unborn Children (SPUC) sent each MP a plastic replica of a foetus at twenty weeks of gestation. Although various MPs expressed their distaste at this strategy as 'obscene' and 'a gross act of bad taste', not one commented on what I would see as the most worrying aspect of this tactic: that the foetus is represented in total abstraction from the body of the woman that carried it. It emphasises everything that is 'babylike' about a foetus whilst hiding the essential difference from a baby — that whilst the baby is separate and can exist independently of its mother (where there is someone else to care for it), the foetus is not and cannot exist without the body of the pregnant woman which actively nourishes and supports it. Its representation as a free-floating and separate entity embodies a fundamental deceit, and one which has not been adequately contested. An anti-choice sympathiser in Parliament commented:

> '[w]hen I opened my parcel I found a legitimate and graphic piece of campaigning, because nobody disputes that that is what a 20-week old foetus looks like. If somebody had been able to produce medical evidence that this was a grotesque mock-up that was totally inaccurate and grossly misleading, it would have been the most obscene piece of campaigning that anyone could indulge in. However nobody has suggested that. When I was in the Post Office yesterday an hon. Member came in, took his parcel, opened it, and threw it in the bin. I could not help thinking that this is what happens to many foetuses.'

Worryingly, no one in the House of Commons challenged Cormack to suggest that this abstraction of the foetus from the body of the woman, this 'graphic piece of campaigning' was indeed a 'grotesque mock-up' and 'totally inaccurate and grossly misleading' and that indeed it should not only be *medical* evidence which has the authority to challenge it. The failure to note this essential deceit in SPUC's representation of the issue reflects an unconscious acceptance of the construction of abortion as revolving essentially around this free-floating foetus and what status is to be attributed to it. Once the woman is abstracted from the equation in this way then SPUC are already half-way to proving their argument and a central claim: that there is a negligible difference between a foetus in the last stages of gestational development and the newborn baby. Such an assertion is made by Anne Widdecombe:

> 'At the moment, a child in an incubator can be kept alive, loved and cherished with all the resources of medical science being devoted to saving it, while a child of identical age and identical gestation in the womb has no rights and can be destroyed. There is something wrong with the law which allows that degree of inequity between *two individuals who are exactly the same except that we can see one and we cannot see the other* . . . we must bring about a situation in which there is at least equality. At present, we have a law which states that *a child who is seen is protected but that a child at an identical stage who is not seen is not protected.*'

In this argument, Widdecombe completely obscures the presence of the woman whose body is sustaining the pregnancy. She is challenged by Emma Nicholson who notes that:

> '[t]he Hon. Member for Maidstone (Miss Widdecombe) talked of identical babies whose only difference at 20 weeks was that one was visible and the other invisible to the naked eye. That is not true because the baby invisible to the naked eye may be hideously deformed and if born and brought to life, may face a future of unimaginable suffering. It may be visible to the naked eye through modern machinery and perhaps it can be kept alive, despite its wretched existence for many years.'

Having implicitly accepted the central importance of the foetus and ignoring the occlusion of the pregnant woman, Nicholson adopts the terrain set out by Widdecombe and uses an essentially eugenicist argument to oppose her.

In practice, the medicalisation of public and parliamentary debate, the representations suggesting foetal separation and the perceived logicality of medical control are integrally related and mutually supporting. As medical knowledges become more important, the issue of the (medically determined) status of foetal life becomes increasingly central and the place of medical knowledges and the authority of medical experts becomes ever more entrenched. Moreover, developments in other areas of medicine — such as obstetrics, the management of childbirth and in utero surgery — have equally led to the construction of the foetus as a separate patient, with the doctor the person best placed to represent its interests. This conceptualisation of the medical role equally serves to reinforce a sense of the doctor as the 'foetal protector', and the right authority to take control in cases involving a request for an abortion."

5.3.ii *Balancing rights*

The evolution of the law on abortion has centred around finding a compromise in which various interests can be reconciled. Claims for recognition of the foetus as a separate identity have been central to the addition of the foetus as a party whose interests have to be balanced along with those of the woman, the putative father and the medical profession. This has resulted in all sides of the debate claiming that their particular rights should be extended, at the expense of those of other interested parties. As outlined in the first section of this book the assertion of rights claims generally, and in the case of abortion the assertion of the particular rights to choose or to life, has been questioned by feminists. Rights claims, made at the level of abstract individualism, inevitably lead to a polarisation of the interests involved. The conflict between woman and potential father, or woman and foetus has to be resolved by an adversarial battle. Perceived as a separate individual endangered by the pregnant woman, the foetus, particularly, is presented as in need of recognition as a legal person with legal rights to assert against the conflicting rights of the pregnant woman. There is little acknowledgement of the connection and relationship between the parties involved.

The following extract from *What's Wrong with Rights? Problems for Feminist Politics of Law* by Elizabeth Kingdom demonstrates some of the problems in the use of rights discourse by feminists:

E. KINGDOM
What's Wrong with Rights? Problems for Feminist Politics of Law[92]

"A woman's right to choose
Recognition of the connection between women's access to abortion and contraceptive services and their unequal economic and social status undoubtedly played a large part in attracting and informing the support for the National Abortion Campaign (NAC) of men and women in unions, in the Labour Party, and in left-wing groups. Since 1975, repeated attempts to restrict the availability of abortion by legislative means have been resisted on the grounds that, as Simms has put it: 'no true state of equality can exist for women in a society which denies them freedom and privacy in respect of fertility control'.

But it is precisely that sort of appeal to the values of freedom and privacy — an appeal which is encapsulated in the campaign slogan 'a woman's right to choose' — that has given rise to misgivings over, and in some cases outright hostility towards, some of the terms in which pro-choice campaigns have been conducted. It has been argued that slogans such as a woman's right to choose, the right to control one's own fertility, and the right to determine one's own sexuality accentuate the notion of a right as inhering in an individual, as the moral entitlement of an individual human being which is possessed independently of prevailing social conditions. Jane Marshall and others supporting the establishment of WRRC wrote that 'some of us feel we have become complacent about what 'A Woman's Right to Choose' means. 'Choice' suggests being able to pick from an ideal set of options'. In terms of political philosophy, this means that the concept of free choice is more easily situated in the ideology of liberal individualism, and the right to control one's own body is more easily placed within the ideology of the private citizen resisting the morally illegitimate encroachment of the bourgeois state into private matters, than within the ideology of solidarity and collective decision-making characteristic of much socialist and feminist thinking. Following this sort of argument, Kate Marshall states that the demand for a woman's right to choose implies that what is at issue is an individual problem, not a social one; invoking the rights of the individual is to rely on a concept of rights which is 'at the centre of bourgeois ideology' and is therefore 'a step towards the ruling class'.

---

[92]   (Edinburgh: Edinburgh University Press, 1991), pp. 54–59.

A more complex position is advanced by Greenwood and Young. It too is presented in terms of the dichotomy between reform and revolution — between, on the one hand, campaigns for reformist legislation and, on the other, struggle for the transition to a socialist society in which women achieve genuine equality. From this perspective, one might expect them to attack any slogan which appeals to what might appear to be bourgeois rights. In fact, they propose that women's right to control their own fertility be demanded as an absolute right. They suggest, furthermore, that the demand for this absolute right and for genuine freedom of choice can transcend reformism.

To develop this intriguing argument, Greenwood and Young describe the struggles leading up to the 1970 New York State legislation whereby abortion was made legal on the request of the patient, on condition that she was not more than fourteen weeks pregnant and on condition that the operation was performed by a licensed physician. They note the American feminists' complaint that 'despite the liberalization, the medical profession still monopolized the practice of abortion'. They also note, with implied sympathy, the feminists' argument that the only solution to this problem was to decriminalise abortion and to place it in the hands of self-help groups. In discussing the limits of reformism in this country, they indicate support for ALRA's campaign for abortion up to twenty-four weeks, on the grounds that achieving this demand could lead to a situation where there was effectively no time limit at all. In such a situation, they say, it would be relatively easy to call for legal acceptance of no time limits.

In making these points, Greenwood and Young clearly underestimated the tenacity of anti-abortion groups in seeking to reduce the time limits for lawful termination. But optimism is not the most interesting thing about their position. What is striking is the dilemma which their position creates. This is the dilemma that, on the one hand, law is a fundamental threat to women's abortion rights and, on the other, it is correct to campaign within the legal sphere. The dilemma is compounded by the recognition that such legal campaigns can deflect campaigners' attention from the fact that reformist measures undermine the whole basis of women's struggles.

Greenwood and Young attempt to resolve this dilemma in two ways. First, they propose that the abortion debate can be directly related to the limited alternatives open to women in prevailing social conditions and that, by linking the debate to the eleven demands of the Working Women's Charter (WWC), the debate can be 'widened in terms of general demands put forward from a socialist perspective'. Secondly, in their discussion of the inability of the Society for the Protection of Unborn Children to recognise the fundamental problems faced by all women and by the working class (a criticism which they also make, though less severely, of the pro-choice campaigners), they argue for a welding of free abortion on demand to the full range of social changes necessary for genuine freedom of choice. Only in this way, they claim, is it possible to transcend reformism.

There are at least two problems with this position. In the first place, simply widening the abortion debate in the manner suggested in no way removes the reformist label as Greenwood and Young themselves would attach it. Among other things, the WWC argues for a national minimum wage, compulsory day release for 16- to 19-year-olds in employment, free state-financed child-care facilities, and an increase in child benefits. All these measures would require legislation. But Greenwood and Young argue that legislation, even where it has been to the advantage of the labour movement, is subject to pressures which are 'undeniably shaped by ruling class interests'. Whilst they claim that they reject simplistic analyses according to which significant legislative gains are dismissed by the left as 'the direct expression of ruling class interests', their

strategy for coping with the reform/revolution dilemma presupposes precisely the separation of the interests of the working class and those of the ruling powers that is
characteristic of that dilemma. This is because, for them, legislative measures, however
wide they may be, still have to be viewed with suspicion as shaped by ruling-class
interests.

The second problem is that to appeal to a woman's right to choose as an absolute
right is indeed to transcend the reform/revolution dichotomy, but that it does so for
reasons and with effects which should make the manoeuvre unacceptable to feminists.
An absolute right is one which is possessed independently not just of prevailing social
conditions but of any social conditions whatsoever. Once a woman's right to choose
is situated in the sphere of absolutes, there is a necessary and unbridgeable gap between
it and any possible social conditions, including legal practices. It can have no purchase
on debates about whether abortion should be lawful up to twenty-four, or twenty-
eight, or any number of weeks. Greenwood and Young have replaced the notion of a
woman's right to choose as a right which is appropriately demanded only of a bourgeois state with the notion of an absolute right which can be enjoyed in no state at
all. So, when Ruth Holley writes that 'nowhere do women have the absolute right to
control their own fertility, the absolute right to decide whether or not to have children',
the statement has to be treated not as grounds for initiating a campaign, but as a
truism. This is because by definition there is nowhere 'in the real world' that absolute
rights can be enjoyed. It is merely a corollary of this general argument to point out
that absolute rights cannot be enjoyed in a socialist state.

Certainly, some of the pro-choice campaigners have argued for a shift away from
abstract moral debate, such as whether fetuses have rights. Their argument is pitched
at the level of strategy — the avoidance of debates which suit the purpose of the
anti-abortion pressure groups. Now, there is no denying that to be drawn into a process of pitching claim and counter-claim at the level of absolute rights is to risk defeat
in public debate, but the full implications of that observation need to be drawn out.
Even if that debate were won, it would indeed be a moral victory. But it would be a
moral victory which runs the risk of being only a moral victory. For to continue to
claim a woman's right to choose as an absolute right, which is possessed independently
of any prevailing or even foreseeable social conditions, is to remove the rationale for
the formulation of strategies directed to the improvement of existing social conditions.
The sphere of absolute rights by definition transcends that of social and legal rights.
Consequently, the absolute right of a woman to choose cannot be reduced to a list of
legal rights. The result is that those involved in drafting and interpreting abortion
legislation can continue to go about their work secure in the knowledge that the legal
sphere is incapable of recognising and giving substantive expression to rights which
fall outside not just the legal sphere but also any set of social conditions.

What is the force of this critique? Does it carry any clear message for the strategy
of feminist campaigns to improve women's situation in relation to abortion? These
questions invite two opposed responses. For convenience I shall call the first the rejectionist response, and the second the retentionist response. Feminists taking the rejectionist position will propose that the appeal to a woman's right to choose should be
abandoned and the slogan dropped from the campaign. On this view, feminists should
not clutter up their campaigns with abstract philosophical non-sense about rights
which can never be given any practical expression. Instead, efforts might be directed
to finding campaign slogans which can be related to 'the real world'. But, retentionist
pro-choice campaigners might reply, this response leaves out of account the undoubted
success of uniting men and women of otherwise disparate political persuasions to resist

attacks on the AA and to work for further improvements to facilitate access to abortion facilities. With all its faults, the notion of a woman's absolute right to choose should be retained as an ideological weapon, as a statement of principle the acceptance of which is crucial to the achievement of a moral climate within which feminist objectives can be achieved.

There is much to be said for the rejectionist response. The invocation of an absolute right smacks of utopianism and it is hardly conducive to the precise formulation of politically and legally realisable objectives to improve women's social position. There are, moreover, other slogans — 'free abortion on demand' and 'every child a wanted child' — which have been used in feminist campaigns to improve access to contraceptive and abortion facilities and which do not have the same absolutist connotation.

To justify retention of the slogan, however, feminists might make a number of points about the use of slogans for political purposes. The retentionist position might begin with the observation that it would be foolish to suggest that, to be successful, a campaign has to be governed by ideologically pure slogans which are a perfect match for all of the campaign's short- and long-term aims. On the contrary, when Marshall complains that even anti-abortionists signed the NAC petition for a woman's right to choose because they believed in individual choice, NAC activists might well congratulate themselves on having adopted such a politically and ideologically sophisticated slogan and on having understood the complex ways in which the climate of popular opinion could be exploited to yield support for feminist struggles. Clearly, the fact that there can be no legal recognition of a woman's right to choose is no obstacle to people *believing* in the possibility of securing absolute rights. And it would not be the first time that a campaign had the support of people who might well be hostile to it if its longer-term goals were spelled out in detail. Calculation of this sort might make it perfectly sensible to retain the slogan, with all its absolutist connotations, on the understanding that, even if the principle cannot be realised in practice, it nonetheless serves to orientate public opinion towards the reception of those more advanced objectives which pro-choice campaigners have in mind.

The difficulty with this retentionist strategy is not so much that it is vulnerable to the charge of political cynicism as that it presupposes the ability to distinguish between support for pro-choice campaigns which acknowledges the limitations of the notion of a woman's right to choose, and support which is given precisely because that right is presented as an absolute one. There is no reason to suppose that activists in pro-choice campaigns are immune to the undoubted attractions and comforts of belief in absolute rights. Indeed, as noted above, some feminist pro-choice campaigners do appeal to a woman's absolute right to choose, not just when engaged in winning over public opinion, but also when debating with other campaigners.

There are other dangers in the retentionist response. These are serious for those feminists who are not prepared to abstain from legal struggle for the pursuit of their objectives. First, if it is accepted that an absolute right can have no expression in actual or foreseeable social and legal conditions, then it is a natural, if not a logical, inference that the only social conditions compatible with that absolute right are ones in which there is no relevant legislation at all. In the case of abortion, this would mean not merely the decriminalisation of abortion but also its deregulation. There would be no regulations governing the organisation and distribution of abortion services, no controls over the technical competence of persons performing abortions, and no regulations on safety standards.

But to demand deregulation, effectively the abolition of all restrictions on the availability of abortion, makes nonsense of the demand made by almost all pro-choice campaigners, the demand for mandatory provision of abortion services under the National Health Service. It makes nonsense of that demand because it is inconceivable that mandatory provision of this kind could be achieved without legislation and hence without some forms of restriction, such as rules governing hours of work or follow-up counselling. Furthermore, if a woman's right to choose is interpreted to mean deregulation, it immediately follows that women seeking and getting abortions would have no *legal* rights, and no legal *redress*, since abortion would be unconnected with questions of legality. Few feminists would be prepared to countenance such a reactionary situation.

The second danger of the retentionist position, even where it is not associated with demands for deregulation, is that appeals to a woman's right to choose are notoriously vague in their meaning. It may well be the case that appealing to that right is a politically effective way of opening the attack on existing legislation and related medical practices, and that it is a politically effective way of resisting a particular set of proposals for reform which are not strong enough. But, for the reasons given above, an absolute right cannot be reduced to any set of concrete proposals. Simply to assert a woman's right to choose is to skate over the complex business of working out specific proposals and strategies for improving abortion and related provision. In this way, the slogan 'a woman's right to choose' can constitute an obstacle to serious engagement with the complex and detailed legal issues, . . ., which often have direct effects on the chances of achieving feminist objectives."

Having aired the scepticism voiced by some feminists about claims couched in the language of rights it is now opportune to consider the extent to which *legal* rights are granted to those involved in the abortion debate.

5.3.ii.a Foetal rights. Feminists have expressed concern about the centrality accorded to the foetus in the abortion debate. This centrality, or "fetocentrism",[93] is achieved at the expense of the woman in whose body the foetus is contained and on whose body the foetus is dependant. Petchesky forcefully argues that this construction should be resisted:

> "A feminist challenge to fetocentrism has to assert that, while some fetuses may become at some point *transplantable*, no fetus is actually viable. Fetuses are biologically dependent on a pregnant woman and will be physically and socially dependent on her after birth. This dependence provides the basis for both her moral obligation to regard the fetus with care and her moral right to decide whether to keep it."[94]

Similarly, Sally Sheldon, in the extract cited above, has noted the centrality accorded to the position of the foetus in its depiction as separate from the body of the pregnant woman in the parliamentary debates leading to the passage of the Human Fertilisation and Embryology Act 1990. To assess how far the centrality of the foetus in the abortion debate has been translated into substantive law the question may be asked, does a foetus have any legal rights?

[93] R. P. Petchesky, *Abortion and Woman's Choice* (London: Longman, 1984), p.xii.
[94] R. P. Petchesky, *ibid.*, p.xii.

It is well established in English Law that the foetus is not recognised as a legal person (and, hence, does not have legal rights). The rights of a foetus were discussed in the case of *Re F (in utero),*[95] in which the Court of Appeal had to decide whether a foetus could be made a ward of court. The defendant, a pregnant woman, had a history of mental disturbance and drug abuse. She already had one child which was a ward of court and was being cared for by foster parents. She left the flat in which she had been living and the plaintiff, the local authority, unsure of her whereabouts, was concerned for the welfare of her foetus. The local authority appealed against the decision of Hollings J. in which he had dismissed its application to make the unborn child of the defendant a ward of court.

Re F (in utero)
[1988] 2 All E.R. 193 at 194–196, *per* May L.J. at 197–199,
per Balcombe L.J.

"MAY L.J. . . . On these facts, which I have only briefly outlined, I have no doubt myself that if the court had power I would give leave to issue the necessary originating summons and make the unborn child a ward of court. As I have said, however, the sole question in this appeal is whether we have the power to do so.

The judge accepted that wardship proceedings are unlike other civil proceedings. There is no lis between the parties concerned. In wardship proceedings the court is exercising a parental jurisdiction in which the paramount consideration is the child's welfare. But in the case of an unborn child the only orders to protect him or her which the court could make would be with regard to the mother herself. Thus in the first place there would have to be an order authorising the local authority to find the mother. Then perhaps an order that she should live in a certain place and probably attend a certain hospital. All of these would be restrictive of the mother's liberty. Further, there could well be medical problems which would have to be solved: the mother might wish one course of action to be taken; it might be in the interests of the child that an alternative procedure should be followed. Until the child is actually born there must necessarily be an inherent incompatibility between any projected exercise of wardship jurisdiction and the rights and welfare of the mother.

This counsel for the local authority accepted in the course of the hearing before us. But, as I have indicated, he stressed that wardship proceedings are indeed unlike any other civil proceedings. He referred us to the dictum quoted by the judge from the judgment of Lord Esher M.R. in *R. v. Gyngall* [1893] 2 Q.B. 232 at 239:

'It [wardship] was a parental jurisdiction, a judicially administrative jurisdiction, in virtue of which the Chancery Court was put to act on behalf of the Crown, as being the guardian of all infants, in place of a parent, and as if it were the parent of the child, thus superseding the natural guardianship of the parent.'

The judge also quoted a passage from the speech of Lord Scarman in *Re E (SA) (a*

---

[95] *Re F (in utero)* [1988] 2 All E.R. 193.

minor) (wardship) [1984] 1 All E.R. 289 at 290; [1984] 1 W.L.R. 156 at 158 where he said:

> '... a court exercising jurisdiction over its ward must never lose sight of a fundamental feature of the jurisdiction that it is exercising, namely that it is exercising a wardship, not an adversarial, jurisdiction. Its duty is not limited to the dispute between the parties: on the contrary, its duty is to act in the way best suited in its judgment to serve the true interest and welfare of the ward. In exercising wardship jurisdiction, the court is a true family court. Its paramount concern is the welfare of its ward.'

In these circumstances, counsel for the local authority submitted that the court at the present time should not be averse to extending the wardship jurisdiction in a proper case. Any argument that an extension to cover the circumstances of the instant case might open the floodgates to many similar applications, counsel suggested, could and should be countered by the court going no further than being prepared to ward a viable child en ventre sa mère, that is to say a child of not less than 28 weeks. In addition, counsel submitted that the interoperation of the provisions of R.S.C. Ord. 90, r. 3(2) and *Practice Direction* [1982] 1 All E.R. 319; [1982] 1 W.L.R. 118 made it clear that the factual inability to make an unborn child a party to wardship proceedings was no reason why these should not be started.

Counsel further contended that one could distinguish the recent cases which attracted some publicity of *Paton v. Trustees of BPAS* [1978] 2 All E.R. 987; [1979] Q.B. 276 and *C v. S* [1987] 1 All E.R. 1230; [1988] Q.B. 135. The first case was concerned with a claim by a husband to restrain his wife and the trustees of a charitable organisation from causing or permitting an abortion to be carried out on the wife without the husband's consent. The claim failed on the ground, as Baker P. held, that an unborn child had no rights of his own, nor had the husband, to sue for the relief claimed. In any event, Baker P. pointed out that it would have been quite impossible to enforce any order which the court might have made had it been minded to do so. The second case involved a claim brought by a putative father of a foetus of 18 to 21 weeks en ventre sa mère for an injunction restraining the mother and the local health authority from performing an abortion on the former. The ratio of the decision both at first instance before Heilbron J. and in the Court of Appeal was that it had not been shown that the projected abortion would amount to any criminal offence and that, therefore, the plaintiff was not entitled to relief. Heilbron J. also held that the father had no *locus standi* in the proceedings, either as father or husband or as the next friend of the unborn child. Counsel submitted that these cases should be distinguished on the grounds that they were not concerned with any wardship jurisdiction and that in each there was quite clearly a lis between the parties.

Counsel accepted that there is no authority directly on the point which arises for our decision but very properly drew our attention to the dictum of Baker P. in *Paton v. Trustees of BPAS* [1978] 2 All E.R. 987 at 989; [1979] Q.B. 287 at 279:

> 'The first question is whether this plaintiff has a right at all. The foetus cannot, in English law, in my view, have any right of its own at least until it is born and has a separate existence from the mother. That permeates the whole of the civil law of this country (I except the criminal law, which is now irrelevant), and is, indeed, the basis of the decisions in those countries

where law is founded on the common law, that is to say, in America, Canada, Australia, and, I have no doubt, in others.'

Heilbron J. expressly agreed with this view in her judgment in *C v. S* and said ([1987] 1 All E.R. 1230 at 1234–1235; [1988] Q.B. 135 at 140):

'As to the position of the second plaintiff and his claim that the unborn child has the locus standi to make this application, counsel produced a wealth of authorities from far and wide, some of which he cited. His research and that of his junior was extensive, but it would serve no useful purpose, nor do I propose, to refer to most of them, for they did appear to be somewhat remote from the issue whether or not the unborn child could be a party to this motion ... The authorities, it seems to me, show that a child, after it has been born, and only then in certain circumstances based on his or her having a legal right, may be a party to an action brought with regard to such matters as the right to take, on a will or intestacy, or for damages for injuries suffered before birth. In other words, the claim crystallises on the birth, at which date, but not before, the child attains the status of a legal persona, and thereupon can then exercise that legal right. This also appears to be the law in a number of Commonwealth countries. In *Medhurst v. Medhurst* (1984) 46 O.R. (2d) 263 Reid J. held in the Ontario High Court that an unborn child was not a person and that any rights accorded to the fetus are held contingent on a legal personality being acquired by the fetus on its subsequent birth alive. Nor could its father, the husband in that case, act as the fetus's next friend. A similar decision was taken in *Dehler v. Ottawa Civic Hospital* (1979) 25 O.R. (2d) 748, quoted with approval by Reid J., and affirmed by the Ontario Court of Appeal (see (1980) 29 O.R. (2d) 677n).'

In an *obiter dictum* in the course of his judgment in the Court of Appeal in *C v. S* Sir John Donaldson M.R. said ([1987] 1 All E.R. 1230 at 1243; [1988] Q.B. 135 at 152–153):

'Let me say what I would otherwise have said ... the questions whether a putative father has any right to be heard on an application of this nature and whether a fetus is a legal person in law capable of suing do not arise, and of course we do not rule on them. But I have also to say that, if we had been in favour of Mr C on all other points, we should have had to have given very considerable thought to the words of Baker P. in *Paton v. Trustees of BPAS* [1978] 2 All E.R. 987 at 992; [1979] Q.B. 276 at 282 where he said: '... not only would it be a bold and brave judge ... who would seek to interfere with the discretion of doctors acting under the [Abortion Act 1967], but I think he would really be a foolish judge who would try to do any such thing, unless possibly, there is clear bad faith and an obvious attempt to perpetrate a criminal offence. Even then, of course, the question is whether that is a matter which should be left to the Director of Public Prosecutions and the Attorney-General.'

Finally, we were referred to a helpful passage in Lowe and White *Wards of Court* (2nd edn, 1986) p. 18, paras 2–3, where the authorities and general arguments are discussed.

Even though this is a case in which, on its facts, I would exercise the jurisdiction if I had it, in the absence of authority I am driven to the conclusion that the court does not have the jurisdiction contended for. I respectfully agree with the dictum from the judgment of Baker P. in *Paton v. Trustees of BPAS*. I also agree with the comments made by Heilbron J. in her judgment in *C v. S* which I have also quoted earlier in this judgment.

Secondly, I respectfully agree with the judge below in this case that to accept such jurisdiction and yet to apply the principle that it is the interest of the child which is to be predominant is bound to create conflict between the existing legal interests of the mother and those of the unborn child and that it is most undesirable that this should occur . . .

BALCOMBE L.J. . . . Of particular significance in the present case is that there is no recorded instance of the courts having assumed jurisdiction in wardship over an unborn child. Indeed, the whole trend of recent authority is to the contrary effect. In *Paton v. Trustees of BPAS* [1978] 2 All E.R. 987; [1979] Q.B. 276 Baker P. refused an application by a husband for an injunction to restrain his wife from having an abortion. In the course of his judgment Baker P. said ([1978] 2 All E.R. 987 at 989–990; [1979] Q.B. 276 at 279):

'The first question is whether this plaintiff has a right at all. The foetus cannot, in English law, in my view, have any right of its own at least until it is born and has a separate existence from the mother. That permeates the whole of the civil law of this country (I except the criminal law, which is now irrelevant), and is, indeed, the basis of the decisions in those countries where law is founded on the common law, that is to say, in America, Canada, Australia, and, I have no doubt, in others. For a long time there was great controversy whether after birth a child could have a right of action in respect of pre-natal injury. The Law Commission considered that and produced a working paper (Law Com. no. 47) in 1973, followed by a final report (Report on Injuries to Unborn Children, Law Com. no. 60 (Cmnd. 5709)), but it was universally accepted, and has since been accepted, that in order to have a right the foetus must be born and be a child. There was only one known possible exception which is referred to in the working paper (Law Com. no. 47, p. 3), an American case, *White v. Yup* (1969) 458 P. 2d 617, where a wrongful death of an eight month old viable foetus, stillborn as a consequence of injury, led an American court to allow a cause of action, but there can be no doubt, in my view, that in England and Wales, the foetus has no right of action, no right at all, until birth. The succession cases have been mentioned. There is no difference. From conception the child may have succession rights by what has been called a 'fictional construction' but the child must be subsequently born alive. See per Lord Russell of Killowen in *Elliot v. Joicey* [1935] A.C. 209 at 233; [1935] All E.R. Rep. 578 at 589. The husband's case must therefore depend on a right which he has himself.'

To the like effect is the judgment of Heilbron J. in *C v. S* [1987] 1 All E.R. 1230; [1988] Q.B. 135. This was another attempt by a father to prevent the mother of his unborn child having an abortion, but in this case the unborn child was named as the second plaintiff, suing by his father and next friend (the first plaintiff). On this aspect of the case the judge said ([1987] 1 All E.R. 1230 at 1234–1235; [1988] Q.B. 135 at 140):

> 'The authorities, it seems to me, show that a child, after it has been born, and only then in certain circumstances based on his or her having a legal right, may be a party to an action brought with regard to such matters as the right to take, on a will or intestacy, or for damages for injuries suffered before birth. In other words, the claim crystallises on the birth, at which date, but not before, the child attains the status of a legal persona, and thereupon can then exercise that legal right. This also appears to be the law in a number of Commonwealth countries. In *Medhurst v. Medhurst* (1984) 46 O.R. (2d) 263 Reid J. held in the Ontario High Court that an unborn child was not a person and that any rights accorded to the fetus are held contingent on a legal personality being acquired by the fetus on its subsequent birth alive. Nor could its father, the husband in that case, act as the fetus's next friend. A similar decision was taken in *Dehler v. Ottawa Civic Hospital* (1979) 25 O.R. (2d) 748, quoted with approval by Reid J., and affirmed by the Ontario Court of Appeal (see (1980) 29 O.R. (2d) 677n).'

The judge then cited with approval the last portion of the passage from the judgment of Baker P. in *Paton v. Trustees of BPAS* and continued ([1987] 1 All E.R. 1230 at 1235; [1988] Q.B. 135 at 141):

> 'In his reply, counsel's final position was summarised in this way: (1) he no longer relied on the numerous succession cases but he wished to retain some reliance on the position of the unborn child in *Thellusson v. Woodford* (1799) 4 Ves. 227; 31 E.R. 117; (2) he did not claim that a child had either a right to be born or a right to life in view of the terms of the [Abortion Act 1967]; but (3) he maintained that the unborn child had a right to be a party because it was the subject of a threatened crime, that is to say, that of child destruction. If there was no such threat, then this claim too failed. In my judgment, there is no basis for the claim that the fetus can be a party, whether or not there is any foundation for the contention with regard to the alleged threatened crime, and I would dismiss the second plaintiff from this suit and the first plaintiff in his capacity as next friend.'

That case came before this court, but the part of the appeal relating to the rights of the unborn child was dismissed by consent, without a ruling of this court (see [1987] 1 All E.R. 1230 at 1243; [1988] Q.B. 135 at 153)."

Although, as illustrated above, case law has repeatedly determined that foetal rights crystalise only on birth,[96] the case of *Re S*,[97] in which the High Court gave a declaration to the effect that it would be lawful to perform a caesarian section upon S despite her refusal of consent, indicates the willingness of the court, in one particular situation, to recognise the legal interests (if not rights) of an unborn child. As discussed below in Chapter 6, the conflictual rights

---

[96] See further *B v. Islington Area Health Authority* [1991] 1 All E.R. 825.
[97] *Re S* [1992] 3 W.L.R. 806.

model fails to acknowledge the connection between the pregnant woman and the foetus. The research undertaken by Carol Gilligan into the abortion decision (and which is referred to in Chapter 2 in the discussion of the ethic of care) demonstrated the moral reasoning of women in terms of conflicting responsibilities towards the self and others:

C. GILLIGAN
In a Different Voice: Psychological Theory and Women's Development[98]

"When birth control and abortion provide women with effective means for controlling their fertility, the dilemma of choice enters a central arena of women's lives. Then the relationships that have traditionally defined women's identities and framed their moral judgments no longer flow inevitably from their reproductive capacity but become matters of decision over which they have control. Released from the passivity and reticence of a sexuality that binds them in dependence, women can question with Freud what it is that they want and can assert their own answers to that question. However, while society may affirm publicly the woman's right to choose for herself, the exercise of such choice brings her privately into conflict with the conventions of femininity, particularly the moral equation of goodness with self-sacrifice. Although independent assertion in judgment and action is considered to be the hall-mark of adulthood, it is rather in their care and concern for others that women have both judged themselves and been judged.

The conflict between self and other thus constitutes the central moral problem for women, posing a dilemma whose resolution requires a reconciliation between femininity and adulthood. In the absence of such a reconciliation, the moral problem cannot be resolved. The 'good woman' masks assertion in evasion, denying responsibility by claiming only to meet the needs of others, while the 'bad woman' forgoes or renounces the commitments that bind her in self-deception and betrayal. It is precisely this dilemma — the conflict between compassion and autonomy, between virtue and power — which the feminine voice struggles to resolve in its effort to reclaim the self and to solve the moral problem in such a way that no one is hurt.

When a woman considers whether to continue or abort a pregnancy, she contemplates a decision that affects both self and others and engages directly the critical moral issue of hurting. Since the choice is ultimately hers and therefore one for which she is responsible, it raises precisely those questions of judgment that have been most problematic for women. Now she is asked whether she wishes to interrupt that stream of life which for centuries has immersed her in the passivity of dependence while at the same time imposing on her the responsibility for care. Thus the abortion decision brings to the core of feminine apprehension, to what Joan Didion (1972) calls 'the irreconcilable difference of it — that sense of living one's deepest life underwater, that dark involvement with blood and birth and death', the adult questions of responsibility and choice . . .

In its simplest construction, the abortion decision centers on the self. The concern is pragmatic and the issue is survival. The woman focuses on taking care of herself because she feels that she is all alone. From this perspective, *should* is undifferentiated

[98] (Massachussetts: Harvard University Press, 1982) pp. 70–71, 74–75, 76–77, 82–83, 85, 94, 105.

from *would*, and other people influence the decision only through their power to affect its consequences. Susan, an eighteen-year-old, asked what she thought when she found herself pregnant, replies: 'I really didn't think anything except that I didn't want it. (*Why was that?*) I didn't want it, I wasn't ready for it, and next year will be my last year and I want to go to school.' Asked if there is a right decision or a right way to decide about abortion, she says: 'There is no right decision. (*Why?*) I didn't want it.' For her, the question of rightness would emerge only if her own needs were in conflict; then she would have to decide which needs should take precedence. This is the dilemma of Joan, another eighteen-year-old, who sees having a baby not only as a way of increasing her freedom by providing 'the perfect chance to get married and move away from home,' but also as restricting her freedom 'to do a lot of things.' . . .

In the transition that follows this position, the concepts of selfishness and responsibility first appear. Their reference initially is to the self, in a redefinition of the self-interest that has so far served as the basis for judgment. The transitional issue is one of attachment or connection to others. The pregnancy highlights this issue not only by representing an immediate, literal connection but also by affirming, in the most concrete and physical way, the capacity to assume adult feminine roles. Although having a baby at first seems to offer respite from the loneliness of adolescence and to solve conflicts over dependence and independence, in reality the continuation of an adolescent pregnancy generally compounds these problems, increasing social isolation and precluding further steps toward independence.

To be a mother in the societal as well as the physical sense requires the assumption of parental responsibility for the care and protection of a child. However, in order to be able to care for another, one must first be able to care responsibly for oneself. The growth from childhood to adulthood, conceived as a move from selfishness to responsibility, is articulated by Josie, a seventeen-year-old, in describing her response to pregnancy:

> 'I started feeling really good about being pregnant instead of feeling really bad, because I wasn't looking at the situation realistically. I was looking at it from my own sort of selfish needs, because I was lonely. Things weren't really going good for me, so I was looking at it that I could have a baby that I could take care of or something that was part of me, and that made me feel good. But I wasn't looking at the realistic side, at the responsibility I would have to take on. I came to this decision that I was going to have an abortion because I realized how much responsibility goes with having a child. Like you have to be there; you can't be out of the house all the time, which is one thing I like to do. And I decided that I have to take on responsibility for myself and I have to work out a lot of things.'

Describing her former mode of judgment, the wish to have a baby as a way of combating loneliness and making connection, Josie now criticizes that judgment as both 'selfish' and 'unrealistic.' The contradiction between the wish for a baby and the wish for freedom to be 'out of the house all the time' — that is, between connection and independence — is resolved in terms of a new priority. As the criterion for judgment shifts, the dilemma assumes a moral dimension, and the conflict between wish and necessity is cast as a disparity between 'would' and 'should.' In this construction the 'selfishness' of willful decision is counterposed to the 'responsibility' of moral choice:

> 'What I want to do is to have the baby, but what I feel I should do, which is

what I need to do, is have an abortion right now, because sometimes what you want isn't right. Sometimes what is necessary comes before what you want, because it might not always lead to the right thing.' . . .

The transitional phase that follows this judgment is marked by a shift in concern from goodness to truth. The transition begins with reconsideration of the relationship between self and other, as the woman starts to scrutinize the logic of self-sacrifice in the service of a morality of care. In the abortion interviews this transition is announced by the reappearance of the word *selfish*. Retrieving the judgmental initiative, the woman begins to ask whether it is selfish or responsible, moral or immoral, to include her own needs within the compass of her care and concern. This question leads her to reexamine the concept of responsibility, juxtaposing the concern with what other people think with a new inner judgment.

In separating the voice of the self from the voices of others, the woman asks if it is possible to be responsible to herself as well as to others and thus to reconcile the disparity between hurt and care. The exercise of such responsibility requires a new kind of judgment, whose first demand is for honesty. To be responsible for oneself, it is first necessary to acknowledge what one is doing. The criterion for judgment thus shifts from goodness to truth when the morality of action is assessed not on the basis of its appearance in the eyes of others, but in terms of the realities of its intention and consequence . . .

Although from one point of view, paying attention to one's own needs is selfish, from a different perspective it is not only honest but fair. This is the essence of the transitional shift toward a new concept of goodness, which turns inward in acknowledging the self and in accepting responsibility for choice. Outward justification, the concern with 'good reasons,' remains critical for Janet: 'I still think abortion is wrong, and it will be unless the situation can justify what you are doing.' However, the search for justification produces a change in her thinking, 'not drastically, but a little bit.' She realizes that in continuing the pregnancy, she would punish not only herself but also her husband, toward whom she has begun to feel 'turned off and irritated.' This leads her to consider the possible consequences of self-sacrifice both for the self and for others. At the end, Janet says, 'God can punish, but He can also forgive.' What remains in question for her is whether her claim to forgiveness is compromised by a decision that not only meets the needs of others but also is 'right and best for me.' . . .

Once obligation extends to include the self as well as others, the disparity between selfishness and responsibility dissolves. Although the conflict between self and other remains, the moral problem is reconstructed in light of the realization that the occurrence of the dilemma itself precludes nonviolent resolution. The abortion decision comes to be seen as a 'serious' choice affecting both self and others: 'This is a life that I have taken, a conscious decision to terminate, and that is just very heavy, a very heavy thing.' While accepting the necessity of abortion as a highly compromised resolution, Sarah turns her attention to the pregnancy itself, which to her denotes a failure of responsibility, a failure to care for and protect both other and self . . .

The abortion study suggests that women impose a distinctive construction on moral problems, seeing moral dilemmas in terms of conflicting responsibilities. This construction was traced through a sequence of three perspectives, each perspective representing a more complex understanding of the relationship between self and other and each transition involving a critical reinterpretation of the conflict between selfishness and responsibility. The sequence of women's moral judgment proceeds from an initial concern with survival to a focus on goodness and finally to a reflective understanding of care as the most adequate guide to the resolution of conflicts in human relationships. The abortion study demonstrates the centrality of the concepts of responsibility and care in women's constructions of the moral domain, the close tie in women's thinking between conceptions of the self and of morality, and ultimately the need for an expanded developmental theory that includes, rather than rules out from consideration, the differences in the feminine voice. Such an inclusion seems essential, not only for explaining the development of women but also for understanding in both sexes the characteristics and precursors of an adult moral conception."

Carol Gilligan's study of women making the decision whether to terminate a pregnancy enabled her to identify moral maturity in the resolution of conflict between the self and others through an appreciation of interdependency and in terms of responsibility and care. By way of contrast to the connection between woman and foetus identified by Gilligan is the "unity of persons" approach. This approach, taken by the Court of Appeal in *Attorney-General's Reference (No. 3 of 1994)*,[99] in which the Court of Appeal held that where a child is born alive but dies as a consequence of injuries inflicted upon it whilst *in utero* or upon the pregnant woman, liability for murder or manslaughter may follow, is discussed in Chapter 6. The consequences of the "unity of persons" approach for medical terminations of pregnancy is examined in the following extract:

Attorney-General's Reference (No. 3 of 1994) (Commentary) (1995) 3 Med. L. Rev. 302 at 308–310

"*Abortions and Murder (and Manslaughter)*: For medical lawyers the most interesting issue arising out of the case . . . is whether the Court of Appeal's decision has any implications for *medical* abortions. The Court of Appeal thought not, but its conclusion may not stand up to analysis.

One matter is beyond dispute. The Abortion Act 1967 does not expressly or impliedly create a defence to a charge of murder or homicide. The legislative intention behind the 1967 Act is clear from its provisions which remove criminal liability for an offence under the law relating to abortion which means under the 1861 Act (ss. 1(1) and 6(1)) and, since 1990, under the Infant Life (Preservation) Act 1929 (s. 5(1)). Parliament was only concerned with offences prohibiting *in utero* deaths.

Clearly the court was right that homicide is irrelevant in the following situations. First, if the termination results in the fetus dying *in utero* and the requirements of the Abortion Act 1967 are satisfied, there can be no murder or manslaughter charge since there would be no 'live birth'. Equally, no offence would be committed under s. 58 of the Offences Against the Person Act 1861 or under the Infant Life (Preservation) Act 1929 (see, Abortion Act 1967, ss. 1(1) and 5(1) respectively). Secondly, since the doctor's liability for homicide can only arise if the child is 'born alive', there can be no liability where the child is unable to breathe or exist independently of its mother (see, *Rance*). In practice, therefore, early abortions will not create problems for the law in this context perhaps including terminations up to 20 weeks gestation (but notice 'still-

---

[99] *Attorney-General's Reference (No. 3 of 1994)* (1995) 3 Med.L.Rev. 302.

birth' is defined as death after 24 weeks of pregnancy: Births and Deaths Registration Act 1926, s. 12 (as amended by Still-Birth (Definition) Act 1992)).

But, what if there is a 'live birth'? Does the law treat differently a death caused *ex utero* following a violent assault upon the mother and one following an abortion? Perhaps, it *should* but *does* it in fact?

(a) *An Unlawful Act?*: The Court of Appeal stated that a doctor's action in terminating the pregnancy, unlike that of the violent assailant, would not be unlawful if the terms of the 1967 Act were complied with and hence could not be murder or manslaughter. This, however, is analytically problematic. Murder does not require an unlawful act. What murder requires is that *the death be caused unlawfully*: but by this the law means, merely not in circumstances where the defendant has a defence, for example, self-defence, provocation, diminished responsibility, etc. Murder may be committed by a wholly lawful act. Take the following example. If a defendant driving a car in a perfectly lawful manner, *i.e.*, within the speed limit, decides to use his car as a weapon to kill someone and he drives at them and kills them, his liability for murder does not depend upon whether his driving was inherently unlawful. Rather, it depends upon his intention and whether he caused the death. The same is true for manslaughter committed by 'gross negligence' (see, *R. v. Adamako* [1994] 3 All E.R. 79 (H.L.)) but not, of course, for unlawful act manslaughter. Hence, the Court of Appeal was wrong to assert that a doctor who carried out an abortion which leads to the death *ex utero* of the child, cannot be guilty of murder because his act is lawful. The analysis must be more sophisticated than this if the doctor's conduct is to fall outside the law of murder (or manslaughter). There are, in fact, two situations where the doctor may cause the death of the child *ex utero*.

(b) *Intending Death Ex Utero*: A doctor may carry out an abortion intending the fetus to die after birth. This may be an unlikely situation in practice but if it were to arise there is no doubt that in principle the doctor would commit murder if the child were born alive. More likely in practice would be the situation where the doctor inadvertently brought about a live birth and the child dies. Here, the doctor would commit the offence of manslaughter by gross negligence if his negligence in bringing about the live birth and subsequent death was characterised as sufficiently serious by a jury (see, *R. v. Adamako, supra*).

(c) *Intending Death in Utero*: The doctor may intend to kill the child *in utero* but, in fact, produces a live birth. Again, for the reason given in (b) immediately above, this could be manslaughter by gross negligence (see, e.g., *R. v. Senior*) but could it also amount to murder? Unlike the violent assailant on a pregnant woman, the doctor's action will be solely directed towards the unborn child. However, if the 'unity of persons' approach of the Court of Appeal is applied, the doctor's intention will *in law* (though not in fact) be directed against the woman. Of course, he does not intend to kill the mother (read to include the fetus), only to kill the fetus. That, as we know, is not a relevant intention for murder (and the principle of transferred intention).

Could it be said, however, that by intending to bring about a miscarriage, the doctor *intends serious bodily harm to the woman* (read to include the fetus)? Arguably, he does, at least to the same extent that a violent assailant would intend serious bodily harm to the woman (read to include the fetus) even if no harm is caused to the woman alone. If so, the doctor's intention to cause serious bodily harm to the mother will, under the principle of transferred intention, suffice for the offence of murder of the child once born.

Certainly, the physical (and, perhaps, also psychological) effects on a pregnant woman of a miscarriage are capable of being viewed as serious bodily harm but the courts could distinguish between miscarriages resulting from medical interventions and those from violent attacks. The courts could reach the view that properly performed medical treatment, including an abortion, is never *harm*, let alone serious harm, to a patient. If the courts were to adopt this view it would be a sure way of avoiding the potential of liability for murder in this situation by negating the doctor's *mens rea*.

The argument, of course, goes much further than the abortion context and would put all medical treatment outside the scope of the criminal law of violent offences. While the latter proposition undoubtedly represents English law, it is not based upon medical treatment falling outside the notion of harm, rather it is based upon the fact that exceptionally consent to such harm in the medical context is a defence to what would otherwise be a crime (see, *R. v. Brown* [1993] 2 All E.R. 75 (H.L.) especially *per* Lord Mustill at 109–10).

It is suggested that this is where the answer to the doctor's criminal liability really lies. If the mother's consent to the harm to her is legally valid, which it is under the 'unity of persons' approach, and would exempt the doctor from liability under ss. 18 or 20 of the Offences Against the Person Act 1861 for serious harm caused to her, then he should not be liable for the death of the child *ex utero*. His conduct ought not to give rise to any criminal liability if his action (with the relevant intention) is justified by the consent of the woman which is itself recognised on public policy grounds. This is not the same reasoning as that offered by the Court of Appeal which turns upon his conduct being lawful under the Abortion Act 1967. Here, it is proposed that the doctor's 'intention to cause serious injury' — which is a relevant (and essential) requisite of liability for murder — is justified by the circumstances and so his conduct is criminally neutral: *a fortiori* for manslaughter. (Not so, of course, if he also intends the fetus to die *ex utero* to which she cannot consent in any event.) In this one context, therefore, the 'unity of persons' approach adopted by the Court of Appeal works satisfactorily. The woman is not consenting to harm to the fetus (let alone to its death once born), which would seem to run counter to the criminal law's usual prohibition, but rather to (serious) harm to herself. However, even if that were rejected, it is suggested that the same conclusion could be reached by the court on the basis that the public policy in England underlying the Abortion Act 1967 permits a woman to consent to harm (through a termination) to a fetus if that termination falls within the grounds set out in s. 1 of the Act. Consequently, the 'unity of persons' approach, which as was suggested earlier will be problematic elsewhere in the law, is not essential to explain why a doctor is not liable for homicide."

A useful comparison of the rights accorded to the foetus can be made between Britain and the Republic of Ireland. In Ireland the foetus is accorded a certain status. Abortion is still prohibited by section 58 of the Offences Against the Person Act 1861 and in 1983 a referendum, instigated by the Pro-life Amendment Campaign, resulted in an amendment to the Irish Constitution to protect the life of the unborn. Article 40.3.3 of the Constitution provides:

'The State acknowledges the right to life of the unborn and, with due regard to the equal right to life of the mother, guarantees in its laws to respect, and, as far as practicable, by its laws to defend and vindicate that right.'

This amendment provoked a series of challenges in the courts at a national and European level which tried to define the nature of the "equal" balance between foetal and maternal rights and the scope of the constitutional provision. These challenges were based around whether the constitutional provision meant that Irish women should be denied access to information about abortion services elsewhere and whether they should be free to travel to make use of those services. In *S.P.U.C. (Ireland) v. Grogan*,[1] the Society for the Protection of Unborn Children sought to stop the dissemination of information in student handbooks about abortion clinics in Britain. A preliminary reference was made to the European Court of Justice (ECJ) to ascertain whether a restriction on the provision of information was a breach of European Community law. The case was discussed on the basis of a possible restriction in the provision of services (that is abortions) which would be contrary to the Treaty of Rome. The ECJ held that, although abortion provision was a service, there was no restriction on its provision because the link between the information provided by the students and the service provided by British clinics was not sufficiently strong. The distributor had no economic interest in the provision of the service. Leo Flynn points out the implications of this decision in the context of the primacy attached to market values in European Law and its consequent negative impact for women:

L. FLYNN
"The Body Politic(s) of E.C. Law"[2]

"This judgment reinforces . . . the primacy of the market in E.C. law, and the dominance of the masculine logic that is associated with it. It is not necessarily undesirable to be placed *outside* the market. Patricia Williams points out that while the market's precise boundaries vary over time, it is, nonetheless, constant in one feature:

> 'whether something is inside or outside the marketplace . . . has always been a way of valuing it. Where a valued object is located outside the market, it is generally understood to be too 'priceless' to be accommodated by ordinary exchange relationships; if the prize is located within the marketplace, then all objects placed outside become 'valueless'. Traditionally, the *Mona Lisa* and human life have been the sort of objects removed from the fungibility of commodification, as priceless. Thus when black people were bought and sold as slaves, they were placed beyond the bounds of humanity.'

In short, to be excluded from the market, as the Court of Justice did to the information providers in *S.P.U.C. v. Grogan*, is not to share even the limited benefits that it offers. This reminds us that it is not the market itself that is problematic. Instead, our concern should be that the market could become the only source of valuing others and the world around us. However, it may be that we should press for E.C. law to abandon the market as its primary source of legitimacy because the concept cannot endure the

---

[1]   *S.P.U.C. (Ireland) v. Grogan* [1991] E.C.R. I-4733.
[2]   In T. K. Hervey & D. O'Keeffe (eds), *Sex Equality Law in the European Union* (Chichester: John Wiley, 1996), pp. 314–316.

transformational pressures this would entail and/or because the market cannot deliver what women require of it.

In the present case, by placing the students' information distribution activities outside the scope of the market, the Court marginalised and deprecated their efforts, finding that there was no basis on which E.C. law could consider the restrictive regulations imposed on them by Ireland.

The Court excluded voluntary action, organised through a loose network and based on collective effort, from the scope of activities valued and capable of receiving protection from E.C. law. This form of organisation was devalued and undermined, notwithstanding the strong integration element that is fostered by local, low-level co-ordination between voluntary groups in different Member States. Instead, the Court implicitly favoured more orthodox and formal processes of exchange between individuals and undertakings through contracts, agency agreements, and other forms of business interaction directly constituted by law. This business mode of organisation is one that ignores the many activities by women in informal economic sectors.

The judgment therefore ignores the activities of many women, economically significant though their actions may be. It also ignores the under-representation of women amongst the ranks of autonomous decision-makers in that business world. In effect, the judgment forces women, the ultimate recipients of abortion services, to accept the overwhelming control over pregnancy termination services by men (through the medicalisation of these procedures and the commercialisation of support services). By denying a form of action that is often exploited by women and by encouraging a male-oriented mode of organization and interaction, *S.P.U.C. v. Grogan* reinforces the qualities of passivity and acquiescence read onto the female body (especially when pregnant) by a patriarchal society."

A similar question of access to information has been dealt with by the European Court of Human Rights in Strasbourg. In *Open Door Counselling, Dublin Well Woman Centre Ltd v. Ireland*,[3] a petition was brought to challenge an injunction granted in the Irish courts which restrained counselling organisations in Ireland from providing information on abortion services abroad. In this case, unlike *Grogan*, a breach of an international obligation was found. The Court held that there had been a violation of Article 10 of the European Convention on Human Rights which guarantees freedom of expression.

In *Attorney-General v. X*,[4] the competing rights of woman and foetus were discussed in the context of the right to travel from Ireland to obtain an abortion. An injunction was granted by the High Court in Ireland to restrain a 14 year-old rape victim from leaving Ireland to obtain an abortion in Britain. The girl had threatened to take her own life if forced to continue with the pregnancy. The task for the court was to weigh up the balance between the rights of the girl and those of the foetus. The decision was appealed to the Supreme Court which lifted the injunction.

---

[3]   *Open Door Counselling, Dublin Well Woman Centre Ltd v. Ireland* (1993) 15 E.H.R.R. 244.
[4]   *Attorney-General v. X* [1992] 2 C.M.L.R. 277.

Attorney-General v. X
[1992] 2 C.M.L.R. 277; Judgment of the High Court, *per* Costello J.

"[17] (2) The second issue arises from the mother's right to life acknowledged by the Eighth Amendment. It was submitted on behalf of the defendants that although the Eighth Amendment required the courts to defend and vindicate the life of the unborn, that they were, in doing so, to have regard to the equal right to life of the mother, that in doing so in this case the Court should not make the order sought because this would prejudice the mother's right to life because of the very real danger which it is said the evidence established that she would take her own life if the order was made and she was unable to procure an abortion.

[18] The situation which has arisen in this case is not one of those which may arise in the practice of medicine, namely, a situation in which surgical intervention, necessary to save the life of the unborn, may involve risk to the mother's life, or in which the surgical intervention necessary to save the life of a mother may involve risk to the life of the unborn. This is a case in which the risk to the mother's life comes from herself. What the Court is asked to do is not to make an order because if it did the mother may take her own life.

[19] I think that in a case such as this, involving a young girl in a highly distressing and deeply disturbing situation, the Court has a duty to protect her life not just from the actions of others but from actions she may herself perform.

[20] What the Court, therefore, is required to do is to assess by reference to the evidence the danger to the life of the child and the danger that exists to the life of the mother. I am quite satisfied that there is a real and imminent danger to the life of the unborn and that if the Court does not step in to protect it by means of the injunction sought its life will be terminated. The evidence also establishes that if the Court grants the injunction sought there is a risk that the defendant may take her own life. But the risk that the defendant may take her own life if an order is made is much less and is of a different order of magnitude than the certainty that the life of the unborn will be terminated if the order is not made. I am strengthened in this view by the knowledge that the young girl has the benefit of the love and care and support of devoted parents who will help her through the difficult months ahead. It seems to me, therefore, that having had regard to the rights of the mother in this case, the Court's duty to protect the life of the unborn requires it to make the order sought."

Attorney-General v. X
[1992] 2 C.M.L.R. 277; Judgment of the Supreme Court, *per* Finlay C.J.

"*Interpretation of Article 40.3.3*

[34] In the course of his judgment in MCGEE V. THE ATTORNEY GENERAL Walsh J. stated as follows:

'In this country, it falls finally upon the judges to interpret the Constitution and in doing so to determine, where necessary, the rights which are superior or antecedent to positive law or which are imprescriptible or inalienable. In the performance of this difficult duty there are certain guidelines laid down in the Constitution for the judge. The very structure and content of the Articles dealing with fundamental rights clearly indicate that justice is not subordinate to the law. In particular, the terms of section 3 of Article 40 expressly subordinate the law to justice. Both Aristotle and the Christian philosophers have regarded justice as the highest human virtue. The virtue of prudence was also esteemed by Aristotle, as by the philosophers of the Christian world. But the great additional virtue introduced by Christianity was that of charity — not the charity which consists of giving to the deserving for that is justice, but the charity which is also called mercy. According to the Preamble, the People gave themselves the Constitution to promote the common good, with due observance of prudence, justice and charity so that the dignity and freedom of the individual might be assured. The judges must, therefore, as best they can from their training and their experience interpret these rights in accordance with their ideas of prudence, justice and charity. It is but natural that from time to time the prevailing ideas of these virtues may be conditioned by the passage of time; no interpretation of the Constitution is intended to be final for all time. It is given in the light of prevailing ideas and concepts.'

[35] In the course of his judgment in THE STATE (HEALY) *v.* DONOGHUE O'Higgins C.J. stated as follows:

'The Preamble to the Constitution records that the People "seeking to promote the common good, with due observance of prudence, justice and charity, so that the dignity and freedom of the individual may be assured, true social order attained, the unity of our country restored and concord established with other nations, do hereby adopt, enact, and give to ourselves this Constitution."

In my view, this Preamble makes it clear that rights given by the Constitution must be considered in accordance with concepts of prudence, justice and charity, which may gradually change or develop as society changes and develops and which fall to be interpreted from time to time in accordance with prevailing ideas. The Preamble envisages a Constitution which can absorb or be adapted to such changes. In other words, the Constitution did not seek to impose for all time the ideas prevalent or accepted with regard to these virtues at the time of its enactment. Walsh J. expressed this view very clearly in MCGEE *v.* THE ATTORNEY GENERAL, when he said at page 319 of the Report ...'

The learned Chief Justice then quoted from that portion of the judgment of Walsh J. which I have set out above in this judgment. I not only accept the principles set out in these two judgments as correct and appropriate principles which I must follow in interpreting the provisions of this sub-article of the Constitution, but I find them particularly and peculiarly appropriate and illuminating in the interpretation of a sub-article of the Constitution which deals with the intimate human problem of the right of the unborn to life and its relationship to the right of the mother of an unborn child to her life.

[36] I accept the submission made on behalf of the Attorney-General in this case, that the doctrine of the harmonious interpretation of the Constitution involves in this case a consideration of the constitutional rights and obligations of the mother of the unborn child and the interrelation of those rights and obligations with the rights and

obligations of other people and, of course, with the right to life of the unborn child as well.

[37] Such a harmonious interpretation of the constitution carried out in accordance with concepts of prudence, justice and charity, as they have been explained in the judgment of Walsh J. in MCGEE *v.* THE ATTORNEY-GENERAL leads me to the conclusion that in vindicating and defending as far as practicable the right of the unborn to life but at the same time giving due regard to the right of the mother to life, that the Court must, amongst the matters to be so regarded, concern itself with the position of the mother within a family group, with persons on whom she is dependent, within in other instances, persons who are dependent upon her and her interaction with other citizens and members of society in the areas in which her activities occur. Having regard to that conclusion, I am satisfied that the test proposed on behalf of the Attorney General that the life of the unborn could only be terminated if it were established that an inevitable or immediate risk to the life of the mother existed, for the avoidance of which a termination of the pregnancy was necessary, insufficiently vindicates the mother's right to life.

[38] I, therefore, conclude that the proper test to be applied is that if it is established as a matter of probability that there is a real and substantial risk to the life as distinct from the health of the mother, which can only be avoided by the termination of her pregnancy, that such termination is permissible, having regard to the true interpretation of Article 40.3.3 of the Constitution.

Has the appellant by evidence satisfied this test?

[39] With regard to this issue, the findings of fact made by the learned trial Judge in the High Court are as follows:

> '[6] When the defendant learned that she was pregnant she naturally was greatly distraught and upset. Later she confided in her mother that when she learned she was pregnant she had wanted to kill herself by throwing herself downstairs. On the journey back from London she told her mother that she had wanted to throw herself under a train when she was in London, that as she had put her parents through so much trouble she would rather be dead than continue as she was. On 31 January, in the course of a long discussion with a member of the Garda Siochana, she said: "I wish it were all over; sometimes I feel like throwing myself downstairs." And in the presence of another member of the Garda Siochana, when her father commented that the "situation was worse than a death in the family" she commented: "Not if it was me".
>
> [7] On the day of her return from London the defendant's parents brought her to a very experienced clinical psychologist. He explained in his report that he had been asked to assess her emotional state, that whilst she was co-operative she was emotionally withdrawn, that he had concluded that she was in a state of shock and that she had lost touch with her feelings. She told him that she had been crying on her own, but had hidden her feelings from her parents to protect them. His opinion was that her vacant, expressionless manner indicated that she was coping with the appalling crisis she faced by a denial of her emotions. She did not seem depressed, but he said that she "coldly expressed a desire to solve matters by ending her life." In his opinion, in her withdrawn state "she was capable of such an act, not so much because she is depressed but because she could calculatingly reach the conclusion that

death is the best solution." He considered that the psychological damage to her of carrying a child would be considerable, and that the damage to her mental health would be devastating. His report was supplemented by oral testimony. He explained in the course of his consultation with the defendant she had said to him: "It is hard at 14 to go through the nine months" and that she said: "It is better to end it now than in nine months' time." The psychologist understood this to mean that by ending her life she would end the problems through which she was putting her parents with whom she has a very strong and loving relationship.'

[40] The psychologist who gave oral evidence as well as submitting a report, (which was admitted by agreement in evidence before the learned trial Judge in the High Court) stated that when he had interviewed this young girl and was anxious to have a continuing discussion with her parents who accompanied her and not having anybody available to remain with the young girl in the waiting room, his view of the risk of her committing suicide was so real, on his past experience in this field of medicine, that notwithstanding its obvious inappropriateness he requested her to remain in the room while he discussed the problem with her parents.

[41] I am satisfied that the only risk put forward in this case to the life of the mother is the risk of self-destruction. I agree with the conclusion reached by the learned trial Judge in the High Court that that was a risk which, as would be appropriate in any other form of risk to the life of the mother, must be taken into account in reconciling the right of the unborn to life and the rights of the mother to life. Such a risk to the life of a young mother, in particular, has it seems to me, a particular characteristic which is relevant to the question of whether the evidence in this case justifies a conclusion that it constitutes a real and substantial risk to life.

[42] If a physical condition emanating from a pregnancy occurs in a mother, it may be that a decision to terminate the pregnancy in order to save her life can be postponed for a significant period in order to monitor the progress of the physical condition, and that there are diagnostic warning signs which can readily be relied upon during such postponement.

[43] In my view, it is common sense that a threat of self-destruction such as is outlined in the evidence in this case, which the psychologist clearly believes to be a very real threat, cannot be monitored in that sense and that it is almost impossible to prevent self-destruction in a young girl in the situation in which this defendant is if she were to decide to carry out her threat of suicide.

[44] I am, therefore, satisfied that on the evidence before the learned trial judge, which was in no way contested, and on the findings which he has made, that the defendant appellants have satisfied the test which I have laid down as being appropriate and have established as a matter of probability that there is a real and substantial risk to life of the mother by self-destruction which can only be avoided by termination of her pregnancy.

[45] It is for this reason that, in my view, the defendants were entitled to succeed in this appeal, and the orders made in the High Court have been set aside."

Obviously there is a difference in the balance between maternal and foetal rights in the judgments of Costello J. and Finlay C.J. Both judgments serve to illustrate how, given the circumstances in which X had been impregnated, and her threat to take her own life if forced to continue with the pregnancy, the facts of this case reveal the inapplicability of the construction of the abortion debate as a conflict between maternal and foetal interests.

Following the legal uncertainty left by these cases a further referendum was held in November 1992. The Irish people were asked to approve the following amendments to Art. 40.3.3:

> 1. It shall be unlawful to terminate the life of an unborn unless such termination is necessary to save the life, as distinct from the health, of the mother where there is an illness or disorder of the mother giving rise to a real and substantial risk to her life, not being a risk of self-destruction.
>
> 2. This subsection shall not limit freedom to travel between the State and another state.
>
> 3. This subsection shall not limit freedom to obtain or make available, in the State, subject to such conditions as may be laid down by law, information relating to services lawfully available in another state.

The first provision was rejected while the second and third were accepted. Thus the Irish Constitution now provides for a right to information and a right to travel. The right of the foetus is not absolute, but the conditions under which this right can be made subject to any rights of the woman carrying the foetus remain unclear.[5]

5.3.ii.b Putative fathers' rights. British courts have had to consider whether a father can exercise any rights in the decision to terminate a pregnancy. One notorious example is that of Mr Paton who applied to the High Court for an injunction restraining his wife from causing or permitting an abortion to be carried out on her without his consent. His application did not succeed.

Paton v. Trustees of British Pregnancy Advisory Service
[1978] 2 All E.R. 987, *per* Sir George Baker P.

"The first question is whether this plaintiff has a right at all. The foetus cannot, in English law, in my view, have any right of its own at least until it is born and has a separate existence from the mother. That permeates the whole of the civil law of this country (I except the criminal law, which is now irrelevant), and is, indeed, the basis of the decisions in those countries where law is founded on the common law, that is to say, in America, Canada, Australia, and, I have no doubt, in others . . .

---

[5] For further discussion of the Irish abortion debate see C. Gearty, "The Politics of Abortion" (1992) 19 *Journal of Law and Society* 441; M. Fox & T. Murphy, "Irish Abortion: Seeking Refuge in a Jurisprudence of Doubt and Delegation" (1992) 19 *Journal of Law and Society* 454; N. Whitty, "Law and the Regulation of Reproduction in Ireland: 1922–1992" (1993) 43 *University of Toronto Law Journal* 851; R. Pearce, "Abortion and the Right to Life Under the Irish Constitution" (1993) 6 *The Journal of Social Welfare and Family Law* 386.

The husband's case must therefore depend on a right which he has himself. I would say a word about the illegitimate, usually called the putative, but I prefer myself to refer to the illegitimate, father. Although American decisions to which I have been referred concern illegitimate fathers, and statutory provisions about them, it seems to me that in this country the illegitimate father can have no rights whatsoever except those given to him by statute. That was clearly the common law. One provision which makes an inroad into this is s.14 of the Guardianship of Minors Act 1971, and s.9(1) and some other sections of that Act applicable to illegitimate children, giving the illegitimate father or mother the right to apply for the custody of or access to an illegitimate child. But the equality of parental rights provision in s.1(1) of the Guardianship Act 1973 expressly does not apply in relation to a minor who is illegitimate: see s. 1(7).

So this plaintiff must, in my opinion, bring his case, if he can, squarely within the framework of the fact that he is a husband. It is, of course, very common for spouses to seek injunctions for personal protection in the matrimonial courts during the pendency of or, indeed, after divorce actions, but the basic reason for the non-molestation injunction often granted in the family courts is to protect the other spouse or the living children, and to ensure that no undue pressure is put on one or other of the spouses during the pendency of the case and during the breaking-up of the marriage.

There was, of course, the action for restitution of conjugal rights, a proceeding which always belied its name and was abolished in 1970. It arose because in ecclesiastical law the parties could not end the consortium by agreement. In a sense the action for restitution was something of a fiction. The court ordered the spouse to return to cohabitation. If the spouse did not return then that spouse was held to be in desertion. No more could happen. The court could not compel matrimonial intercourse: *Forster v. Forster*. So matrimonial courts have never attempted the enforcement of matrimonial obligations by injunction.

The law is that the court cannot and would not seek to enforce or restrain by injunction matrimonial obligations, if they be obligations such as sexual intercourse or contraception (a non-molestation injunction given during the pendency of divorce proceedings could, of course, cover attempted intercourse). No court would ever grant an injunction to stop sterilisation or vasectomy. Personal family relationships in marriage cannot be enforced by the order of a court. An injunction in such circumstances was described by Judge Mager in *Jones v. Smith* in the District Court of Appeal of Florida as 'ludicrous'."

Not satisfied, and despite the fact the abortion had been carried out, Mr Paton went on to take his case to the European Commission of Human Rights.[6] He argued that the law on abortion in England and Wales violated Arts 2 and/or 5, 6, 8, 9 of the European Convention on Human Rights. The Commission considered relevant only Arts 2 (which provides that "Everyone's right to life shall be protected by law ...") and 8 (which guarantees the right to respect for private and family life). The Commission concluded that Art. 2 did not guarantee an absolute right to life of the foetus. The Commission recognised the physical connection between the foetus and the woman sustaining it, appreciating the consequences of vesting the foetus with an absolute right to life for the woman upon whom it depended.

[6] *Paton v. U.K.* (1981) 3 E.H.R.R. 408.

Paton v. U.K.
(1981) 3 E.H.R.R. 408

"19. The 'life' of the foetus is intimately connected with, and cannot be regarded in isolation from, the life of the pregnant woman. If Article 2 were held to cover the foetus and its protection under this Article were, in the absence of any express limitation, seen as absolute, an abortion would have to be considered as prohibited even where the continuance of the pregnancy would involve a serious risk to the life of the pregnant woman. This would mean that the 'unborn life' of the foetus would be regarded as being of a higher value than the life of the pregnant woman."

The Commission found it unnecessary to consider the right to life of the foetus at all stages of the pregnancy as this case only concerned the initial stages (the abortion having been carried out at 10 weeks) and at that stage the right to life of the foetus was limited by the need to protect the life and health of the woman. The complaint under Art. 2 was therefore inadmissible. Similarly, the complaint under Art. 8 was dismissed as the interference in the applicant's right to respect for his family life was justified under paragraph 2 of Art. 8 because it was necessary to protect the rights of another, namely the pregnant woman.

The issue of the rights of the putative father was also played out in the case of *C v. S* (outlined above).[7] C, an unmarried putative father, unsuccessfully requested an injunction on his own behalf and on behalf of the second plaintiff, the foetus. Although he conceded that as the father of the foetus he had no *locus standi*, he claimed that he had sufficient personal interest because the termination would amount to a crime concerning the life of his child. He also claimed that the foetus was a party to the proceedings since it was the subject of the imminent crime. In the High Court his claims were dismissed by Heilbron J. who relied on the decision in *Paton v. Trustees of BPAS*. In the Court of Appeal Sir John Donaldson M.R. found it unnecessary to rule on the issues satisfied that the termination was lawful if carried out in accordance with the provisions of the Abortion Act 1967.

5.3.ii.c Parents' rights. In *Re B (Wardship: Abortion)*,[8] a local authority applied for leave to have the pregnancy of a 12 year-old girl terminated. The girl herself wished to have the termination and was supported in this wish by the putative father and her grandparents by whom she been brought up. On being informed of the pregnancy the local authority had made the girl a ward of court. The girl's mother opposed the termination saying "I don't believe in abortion, it is not right to take the baby's life". It was held that termination would be in the girl's best interests as the continuation of the pregnancy involved greater risks to her mental and physical health than did the abortion.

---

[7] *C v. S* [1987] 1 All E.R. 1230.
[8] *Re B (Wardship: Abortion)* [1991] 2 F.L.R. 426.

Re B (Wardship: Abortion)
[1991] 2 F.L.R. 426, *per* Hollis J.

"If the mother's view is to prevail, it means that this girl will be forced to continue with her pregnancy against her own expressed wishes. One can easily imagine what a mental turmoil she may thus suffer. She may have to leave school for an extended period, not least to avoid adverse comment there, she may reject the baby when born, she will have to face the traumatic considerations as to what should happen to the baby after birth. There is, of course, the possibility that having felt the baby in her arms she will want to keep it, which the mother herself agrees would be impractical. There, thus, might follow a traumatic period for the ward when a decision is come to, possibly through the courts, as to whether the baby should be adopted or cared for by other members of the extended family . . .

In the end, I came to the clear conclusion that it would be in the ward's best interests to have her pregnancy terminated and that, having balanced all the risks, a continuance of the pregnancy would involve risk to the ward greater than if the pregnancy were terminated, of injury to her physical and mental health."

It is not difficult to imagine the practical implications of the applications sought by Paton, C and B's mother, some of which are addressed in the judgments in *Re F*. By way of comparison, in the United States following the decision in *Roe v. Wade*,[9] abortion has been protected under the constitutional right to privacy (see below). This decision has, however, been challenged on several occasions in the Supreme Court, notably in *Planned Parenthood of Southeastern Pennsylvania, et al. v. Robert Casey, et al.*,[10] where the Supreme Court was asked to rule on the validity of provisions in the Pennsylvania Abortion Control Act 1982 (amended in 1988 and 1989). One provision required girls under the age of 18 to obtain informed consent from a parent or judge before having an abortion. A second provided that where a wife intended to have a termination she was required to notify her husband of her intention. The court decided that the former provision was constitutional and therefore lawful while the latter was not.

C. BELL
"Case Note: *Planned Parenthood of Southeastern Pennsylvania, et al.* v. *Robert Casey, et al.*"[11]

"The position taken by O'Connor, Kennedy and Souter was both a practical and a theoretical compromise. The 'essential holding' of *Roe* that they reaffirmed, provides that while a woman has a constitutional liberty to terminate her pregnancy until viability of the foetus, it is not the almost unlimited right advocated by earlier cases, and therefore does not prohibit a State from all interference on behalf of the foetus. Rather,

---

[9] *Roe v. Wade* (1973) 410 U.S. 113.
[10] *Planned Parenthood of Southeastern Pennsylvania, et al. v. Robert Casey, et al.* (1992) 112 S. Ct. 2791.
[11] (1993) 1 *Feminist Legal Studies* 91 at 95–96.

the State can act to protect its 'important and legitimate interest in potential life' as long as this action does not 'impose an undue burden on a woman's ability to make [an abortion] decision.' 'An undue burden exists, and therefore a provision of law is invalid, if its purpose or effect is to place substantial obstacles in the path of a woman seeking an abortion before the fetus attains viability.' On analysis of the evidence the three justices found that the husband notification requirement would impose a substantial obstacle and was therefore unduly burdensome and unconstitutional. The other provisions although imposing some 'burden' on women seeking abortions were found not to impose 'undue' burdens and were therefore upheld as constitutional.

This compromise was pragmatic as it cut a middle ground between permitting abortion on demand in the earlier stages of pregnancy and outlawing abortion almost completely throughout pregnancy. The former position was essentially that protected by the earlier interpretations of *Roe*, while the latter position is that which would be implemented by many States if *Roe* was overruled.

The compromise was theoretical because the 'undue burden' standard of review for State provisions cuts middle ground between the 'strict scrutiny' standard advocated by Blackmun and Stevens and the 'rationality' standard of Rehnquist, White, Scalia and Thomas. The strict scrutiny test would invalidate legislation which is not 'both necessary and narrowly tailored to serve a compelling government interest'. Government, that is State interest in protecting the foetus is not considered to become compelling until viability and so this produces the abortion on demand position described above. The rationality test would only invalidate legislation which is not 'rationally related to a legitimate State interest.' Protection of the foetus is considered to be such an interest, and so this standard would permit almost all State legislation outlawing abortion.

Where does this compromise position leave women and legislatures? For women, abortion is still technically a constitutional right. It cannot be banned completely in any State by criminalising either the woman or the performing physician. *Casey* also leaves the abortion decision in the woman's hands — neither State nor husband can legislatively be given a veto. However, the State can go to considerable lengths to influence the woman's decision by enforced persuasion and by making the process of obtaining an abortion more cumbersome."

5.3.ii.d Women's rights: a right to choose and a right to privacy. As seen above, British abortion law provides no "right" for a woman to have a termination. If it were to do so, this would require serious consideration to be given to the question of how such a right may be constructed.

L. CLARKE
"Abortion: A Rights Issue?"[12]

"It is common to hear abortion discussed in terms of rights — of the mother, the foetus and also of the father; the law, however, recognizes none of these. The Abortion Act 1967 gives a 'right' only to doctors; to form an opinion as to whether or not abortion is justified. A woman has no 'right' to an abortion even if her circumstances are such that she falls within the terms of the Act. Similarly, where two doctors form

[12]   In R. Lee & D. Morgan, *Birthrights: Law and Ethics at the Beginnings of Life* (London: Routledge, 1989), pp. 163, 168.

the relevant opinion, she has no right *not* to have an abortion (although in practice any such abortion would amount to an assault) . . .

'A woman's right to choose' is an old slogan, but one which highlights three important issues. First, for the reasons outlined above it is essential that *women* must have the legal right to decide whether or not to have an abortion. It is for this reason that proposals for the 'medicalization' of abortion should be carefully examined; whilst it is essential that abortion be decriminalized it is not sufficient that it be seen simply as another medical procedure within the area of the individual doctor's 'clinical judgment'. Second, abortion should be a *'right'* with a corresponding duty on the state to provide safe, free abortions.

Once women have the *legal* right to abortion, it will be possible to focus attention on the morality of abortion. The foetus (and the father) can have no *legal* rights *vis-à-vis* the mother, but many have strong moral rights which vary from case to case. There is a pressing need for a morality of abortion, which confronts the notion of competing rights of mother and foetus (and perhaps father) and gives women guidance and support in making the choice.

Lastly, there must be a real *choice*. Many women feel they cannot possibly decide to bear the child they have conceived because of their economic and social circumstances. For very many women, deciding to have a child condemns them to a life on the breadline, living in sub-standard housing, existing on inadequate social security payments and unable to see any prospect of improving their situation through finding employment. State nursery provision, more council house building and adequate financial support for children would probably prevent more abortions than any reduction in the time limit, yet no Private Member's Bill advocates these measures."

One way of giving some legal effect to the right to choose is that taken by the Supreme Court in the United States in its decision in *Roe v. Wade*.[13] By virtue of the United States having a written constitution, the Court was able to support the right of a woman to choose an abortion through a constitutional notion of privacy. In a similar vein, the presence of a written constitution in the Republic of Ireland, and the consequent possibility of a potential decision similar to the *Roe v. Wade* privacy decision there, sparked the pro-life impetus for the 1983 referendum and the enshrinement of the right to life of the unborn within the constitution itself.

The protection of abortion through the right to privacy has, however, been criticised. Christine Bell points out in her comment upon the decision in *Planned Parenthood of Southeastern Pennsylvania, et al. v. Robert Casey, et al.* (above) "the State can go to considerable lengths to influence the woman's decision by enforced persuasion and by making the process of obtaining an abortion more cumbersome."[14] One such way is to deny State funding for abortion so that poorer women will find it more difficult to terminate an unwelcome pregnancy. Consequently there is no legal requirement in the United States that public funding be made available to support abortion services.[15] In the following extract Catharine MacKinnon offers a critical analysis

[13]   *Roe v. Wade, supra,* n. 9.
[14]   C. Bell, *supra,* n. 11 at 96.
[15]   *Harris v. McRae* (1980) 448 U.S. 297; *Webster v. Reproductive Health Services* (1989) 492 U.S. 490; *Rust v. Sullivan;* (1991) 111 U.S. 1759. It is not only in the United States that access to abortion can be determined by access to resources to fund a termination. In Britain, where

of the right to privacy which echoes her articulation of the theme of dominance of women by men discussed in Chapter 3 above:

C. A. MacKinnon
"Privacy v. Equality: Beyond *Roe v. Wade*"[16]

"In 1973 *Roe v. Wade* found that a statute that made criminal all abortions except those to save the life of the mother violated the constitutional right to privacy. The privacy right had been previously created as a constitutional principle in a case that decriminalized the prescription and use of contraceptives. Note that courts use the privacy rubric to connect contraception with abortion through privacy in the same way that I just did through sexuality. In *Roe* that right to privacy was found 'broad enough to encompass a woman's decision whether or not to terminate her pregnancy.' In 1977 three justices observed: 'In the abortion context, we have held that the right to privacy shields the woman from undue state intrusion in and external scrutiny of her very personal choice.'

In 1981 the Supreme Court in *Harris v. McRae* decided that this right to privacy did not mean that federal Medicaid programs had to fund medically necessary abortions. Privacy, the Court had said, was guaranteed for 'a woman's *decision* whether or not to terminate her pregnancy.' The Court then permitted the government to support one decision and not another: to fund continuing conceptions and not to fund discontinuing them. Asserting that decisional privacy was nevertheless constitutionally intact, the Court stated that 'although the government may not place obstacles in the path of a woman's exercise of her freedom of choice, it need not remove those not of its own creation.' It is apparently a very short step from that which the government has a duty *not* to intervene in to that which it has *no* duty to intervene in.

The idea of privacy, if regarded as the outer edge of the limitations on government, embodies, I think, a tension between the preclusion of public exposure or governmental intrusion, on the one hand, and autonomy in the sense of protecting personal self-action on the other. This is a tension, not just two facets of one whole right. In the liberal state this tension is resolved by demarking the threshold of the state at its permissible extent of penetration into a domain that is considered free by definition: the private sphere. It is by this move that the state secures to individuals what has been termed 'an inviolable personality' by ensuring what has been called 'autonomy or control over the intimacies of personal identity.' The state does this by centering its self-restraint on body and home, especially bedroom. By staying out of marriage and the family, prominently meaning sexuality—that is to say, heterosexuality—from contraception through pornography to the abortion decision, the law of privacy proposes to guarantee individual bodily integrity, personal exercise of moral intelligence, and freedom of intimacy. But if one asks whether *women's* rights to these values have been

---

abortion is available under the National Health Service, obtaining a funded abortion can depend greatly on the geographical location in which the abortion is sought. While in 1995 slightly more than 70 per cent of terminations were funded by the NHS, there were stark regional disparities with some Health Authorities funding less than half of terminations in their area. (Office of Population Censuses and Surveys, *1994 Abortion Statistics*, Series AB, No. 21 (London: HMSO, 1996)).

[16] In *Feminism Unmodified: Discourses on Life and Law* (Cambridge MA: Harvard University Press, 1987), pp. 96–97, 99.

guaranteed, it appears that the law of privacy works to translate traditional social values into the rhetoric of individual rights as a means of subordinating those rights to specific social imperatives. In feminist terms, I am arguing that the logic of *Roe* consummated in *Harris* translates the ideology of the private sphere into the individual woman's legal right to privacy as a means of subordinating women's collective needs to the imperatives of male supremacy.

This is my retrospective on *Roe v. Wade*. Reproduction is sexual, men control sexuality, and the state supports the interest of men as a group. *Roe* does not contradict this. So why was abortion legalized? Why were women even imagined to have such a right as privacy? It is not an accusation of bad faith to answer that the interests of men as a social group converged with the definition of justice embodied in law in what I call the male point of view. The way the male point of view constructs a social event or legal need will be the way that social event or legal need is framed by state policy. For example, to the extent that possession is the point of sex, illegal rape will be sex with a woman who is not yours unless the act makes her yours. If part of the kick of pornography involves eroticizing the putatively prohibited, illegal pornography— obscenity—will be prohibited enough to keep pornography desirable without ever making it truly illegitimate or unavailable. If, from the male standpoint, male is the implicit definition of human, maleness will be the implicit standard by which sex equality is measured in discrimination law. In parallel terms, abortion's availability frames, and is framed by, the conditions men work out among themselves to grant legitimacy to women to control the reproductive consequences of intercourse . . .

In the context of a sexual critique of gender inequality, abortion promises to women sex with men on the same reproductive terms as men have sex with women. So long as women do not control access to our sexuality, abortion facilitates women's heterosexual availability. In other words, under conditions of gender inequality, sexual liberation in this sense does not free women; it frees male sexual aggression. The availability of abortion removes the one remaining legitimized reason that women have had for refusing sex besides the headache."

5.3.iii   *The medicalisation of abortion*
It has already been noted that the relationship between law and medicine is a powerful one. This is especially so for the application of laws on abortion.[17] For a woman to obtain a termination she must gain the consent of two registered medical practitioners formed in good faith. The abortion must then be carried out also by a registered medical practitioner (Abortion Act 1967, s. 1(1)). The antiprogestin RU486, more popularly known as the "abortion pill", offers the potential to empower women and disempower doctors in the process of termination. Sally Sheldon discusses the procedure involved in the administration of RU486[18] and argues that:

---

[17]   S. Sheldon, "The Law of Abortion and the Politics of Medicalisation" in J. Bridgeman & S. Millns (eds), *Law and Body Politics: Regulating the Female Body* (Aldershot: Dartmouth, 1995) 105; S. Sheldon, "Subject Only to the Attitude of the Surgeon Concerned: The Judicial Protection of Medical Discretion" (1996) 5 *Social & Legal Studies* 95; S. Sheldon, *Beyond Control: Medical Power and Abolition Law* (London: Pluto Press, 1997).

[18]   "The basic procedure for an antiprogestin termination . . . has three stages: 1) the woman will be referred to a licensed clinic where she will be physically examined and given a pregnancy test. Her medical history will be screened for contraindications to the use of RU486/PG. If there are none, she can be given RU486. Most women will start to bleed the following day. 2) Between 36 and 48 hours later the woman must return to the clinic to receive the prostaglandins which

"[m]edical control of abortion is legitimated by the appearance of necessity to ensure safety: the promise that only the medical professional can promise health. Despite the increased level of control imposed to date, with antiprogestins it may become apparent that these two levels are out of step, and the medical monopoly may seem increasingly untenable. The role of the doctor in the medical termination changes from active to passive. He/she becomes a background figure, needed only to supervise and to intervene if anything goes wrong. It seems to me that although the basic technical and bureaucratic control of abortion is currently greater in the case of antiprogestin terminations, that this control somehow becomes emptier and more artificial in the sense that it depends much more on stringent rules and bureaucracy than on accepted medical need . . . It would seem to be just as safe for a nurse, midwife or trained lay person to administer both courses of treatment given access to specialised medical help in case of need. This means that the traditional justification for the need for medical technical control — safety — would no longer ring true here. Antiprogestins seem then to offer greater future potential for arguing for safe abortions, performed by trained law personnel with medical personnel necessary only as backup."[19]

The legally required involvement of the medical profession in carrying out terminations may have more than a passing association with the construction of this profession in legal discourse. Just as the law adopts a particular construction of the aborting woman, it also adopts a particular perception of the medical personnel carrying out the abortion—that is of a male-dominated profession which is rational, in control, and capable of decision making, in a way that the aborting woman is not.

S. Sheldon
" 'Who is the Mother to Make the Judgment?': The Constructions of Woman in English Abortion Law"[20]

"The Construction of the Doctor within the [Parliamentary] Debates
A very clear construction of the typical doctor also appears within the debates, in strong contrast to the figure of the Woman. The doctor is a male figure, always referred to as 'he.' Doctors are referred to as 'medical men', 'professional medical gentlemen' and 'professional men.' William Deedes notes that 'the medical profession comprises

---

will complete the abortion. The woman will stay at the clinic for the next 4–6 hours. Most (up to 90 per cent) abort there; a small number will abort after leaving the clinic. 3) The woman must return several days later for a medical examination to make sure the abortion is complete and to monitor if she has experienced any side effects. With an RU486/PG termination, there is a 4 per cent chance of incomplete abortion. In such cases, the woman will need to undergo a surgical termination (normally by vacuum aspiration)". (S. Sheldon, "Antiprogestin Terminations: Issues of Access and Control" in Feminist Legal Research Unit (University of Liverpool) (ed.), *Women's Access to Healthcare: Law, Society and Culture (Working Paper No.4)* (Liverpool: University of Liverpool, 1996), pp. 77–78).

19   S. Sheldon, *ibid.,* pp. 100–101.
20   (1993) 1 *Feminist Legal Studies* 3 at 13–14, 17–18.

a great diversity of men' and Jill Knight says that 'the GP is a skilled man.' The doctor is perceived as the epitome of maturity, common sense, responsibility and professionalism. He is a 'highly skilled and dedicated', 'sensitive, sympathetic' member of a 'high and proud profession', which acts 'with its own ethical and medical standards' displaying 'skill, judgment and knowledge.' Peter Mahon, M.P. reminds us that 'it would be as well if we applauded the work of some of these men [gynaecologists] to keep our homes and families and country right.'

In presenting the Bill at its Second Reading, David Steel went so far to say that he felt that given mere contact with her doctor and the ability to discuss her pregnancy with him, the woman would 'in some way be reassured and feel that she has been offered some guidance, and no abortion will take place at all.' David Owen echoes this sentiment later in the debates, noting that '[i]f we allow abortion to become lawful under certain conditions, a woman will go to her doctor and discuss with him the problems which arise . . . he may well be able to offer that support which is necessary for her to continue to full term and successfully to have a child.' . . .

The Woman of the Abortion Act is clearly treated as someone who cannot take decisions for herself, rather responsibility is handed over to the reassuringly mature and responsible (male) figure of the doctor. The legislation assumes that the doctor is far better equipped to judge what is best for the woman, even though he may never have met her before, and have no real knowledge of, nor interest in, her concrete situation. This construction is perhaps an inevitable result of the constructions of Woman used within the debates. If Woman is distraught and irrational, then she is an unsuitable party to take such an important decision. Equally, if she is selfish and self-centred, intellectually and morally immature, portrayed as only considering her own needs, and giving no weight to other factors (such as the foetus) in her snap decisions, she is again incapable of taking such an important decision. She is thus in need of the normalising control of the doctor to impose either calm and rationality or morality and consideration of others.

The power of doctors in the field of abortion is very often justified by the argument that abortion is essentially a medical matter. However, the actual decision whether or not to abort is not normally one that requires expert medical advice. Further, the doctor's decision-making power is not contained within a narrow, limited medical field. In judging whether or not abortion could be detrimental to the mental or physical health of the pregnant woman or existing children of her family, 'account may be taken of the pregnant woman's actual or reasonably foreseeable environment,' thus her whole lifestyle, home and relationships are opened up to his scrutiny, so that he may judge whether or not she is a deserving case for relief."

Having constructed the medical profession in such a way, it is not difficult to see why the judiciary is unwilling to question decisions taken on the basis of medical knowledge. This has been illustrated above in the example of the foetal viability cases of *Rance v. Mid-Downs Health Authority* and *C v. S*. A more recent example has arisen in the case of the prosecution of Reginald Dixon for the unlawful procurement of a miscarriage under section 58 of the Offences Against the Person Act 1861.[21] Writing before the trial was completed, Sally Sheldon sets out the facts and possible resolutions to the case:

[21] *The Times*, December 22, 1995.

S. SHELDON

"Subject Only to the Attitude of the Surgeon Concerned: The Judicial Protection of Medical Discretion"[22]

"In March 1993, Barbara Whiten, a 35-year-old woman, was in hospital for a hysterectomy to relieve a painful and chronic disease of the womb which she believed had left her unable to conceive. The operation was performed by a consultant gynaecologist and obstetrician, Reginald Dixon. During the operation, Mr Dixon noticed that Mrs Whiten's uterus was enlarged, one possible cause of this being pregnancy. He decided against delaying the removal of the womb so that a scan could be arranged to determine the cause of the swelling and (if due to pregnancy) to give Mrs Whiten the opportunity to decide whether she wished to go ahead with the operation. Rather, he removed ovaries and uterus and the next day informed her that she had been pregnant and that he had removed a healthy 11-week-old foetus, stating this to be 'the usual practice'. Mrs Whiten, who had been trying to conceive for some years, was horrified.

In a letter to Mr and Mrs Whiten, Mr Dixon said that he believed an emergency termination to be justified on the grounds of Mrs Whiten's age, her desire for a hysterectomy and her history of depression. In a second letter he acknowledged that with hindsight he would have been better advised to have sewn up the abdomen and arranged a pregnancy scan. Nevertheless, he contended that his decision was taken in good faith and that he had acted within the bounds of what he considers to be 'usual practice'. This latter, at least, seems to be true: in the course of their investigations of Barbara Whiten's complaint, the police uncovered two similar cases at the same hospital. In the first of these, a woman told detectives that a trainee gynaecologist acting under the supervision of Reginald Dixon ignored her concerns that she might be pregnant and removed her womb (with foetus intact) in December 1991 (see *The Observer*, March 27, 1994). In the second case, another woman went into the same hospital for an evacuation of the womb which she had been advised would enhance her subsequent chances of a successful pregnancy. She asserts that when she told the hospital that she thought that she might be pregnant, she was told that she had nothing to worry about. Following the operation, she was informed that she had been pregnant (*The Independent*, April 6, 1994).

Reginald Dixon is now to be prosecuted under s. 58 of The Offences against the Person Act, 1861. The crucial issue will be whether he can claim a defence under the Abortion Act, as s. 1 foresees the need for the consent of two doctors and Mr Dixon did not obtain the necessary second signature. Section 1(4) provides a defence for the doctor who terminates a pregnancy without such second opinion only in an emergency situation, that is when 'he is of the opinion, formed in good faith, that the termination is immediately necessary to save the life or to prevent grave permanent injury to the physical or mental health of the pregnant woman'.

Here, the legal outcome will rest upon not whether the situation *objectively* constituted an emergency, but *subjectively* whether Mr Dixon believed in good faith that it did so (there is no requirement of reasonableness). It seems that the only argument which he could attempt to ground such a defence would be one of Mrs Whiten's alleged mental instability. What would seem to me to be of crucial *ethical* significance — the presence or absence of Mrs Whiten's consent — is *legally* irrelevant to the current criminal action against Mr Dixon. The Abortion Act is not constructed in such

---

[22]   S. Sheldon, *supra.*, n. 17 at 103–106.

a way as to offer an appropriate tool for addressing Mrs Whiten's injury: where it may be useful in protecting the medical relationship from outside challenge, it appears that it is extremely limited in terms of the protection offered to women within its bounds. The only other potential criminal action, a charge of battery (where considerations of consent, or lack thereof, would take centre stage), has never been sustained against a doctor acting in good faith.

Barbara Whiten's case is bound to have significant resonances for those with an interest in the history of the medical regulation of women, standing as another landmark in a long and well-documented catalogue of medical paternalism. Mr Dixon here feels justified in taking an important decision for Mrs Whiten. Significantly, it is her mental history, in particular her depression, which forms the justification for Mr Dixon's denial of her autonomy. This recalls the construction of woman as hysterical or unstable as grounds for medical intervention, an idea which runs like a leitmotif through the history of the medical regulation of women and which has, in the past, justified such Draconian intervention as ovariectomies. Mr Dixon's only possible defence to the various charges which may be brought against him would seem to be that this was an emergency situation — an emergency because Mrs Whiten's mental instability would have rendered her incapable of facing the situation calmly and rationally and making an informed choice.

Mr Dixon may well be judicially vindicated in his contention that his actions fall within the bounds of usual — and lawful — medical practice. The fact is that English law explicitly grants the authority to doctors to take important decisions regarding female reproduction, even when it is clear that these decisions are only rarely based on strictly medical criteria. This is true not only of abortion but also elsewhere, most notably for access to infertility treatment services. Medical paternalism is not merely permitted by the law, in these cases it is actively condoned and enforced. Such paternalism may easily fall within the bounds of 'good medical practice', leaving the doctor beyond prosecution.

Mrs Whiten also has the possibility of bringing a civil action. Against an action in battery, Mr Dixon has two potential defences. First, there is the defence of tacit consent which permits the doctor to carry out further surgery without which the patient's life or health will be immediately at risk as it is reasonable to assume the patient would have consented to the operation had he or she been able. The standard form which patients sign before undergoing surgery authorizes: 'any procedure in addition to the investigation or treatment described on this form [which] will only be carried out if it is necessary and in [the patient's] best interests and can be justified for medical reasons'.

There is also a second possible defence: necessity. In emergency situations, the doctor is justified in taking any necessary action to save life and to proceed without consent 'with any procedure which it would be unreasonable, as opposed to merely inconvenient, to postpone until consent could be sought'. The crucial factor with regard to the success of both defences is whether the abortion was immediately necessary. As we saw, Mr Dixon sought to justify his contention that it was on the grounds of Mrs Whiten's mental state, her age, history of depression, and desire for a hysterectomy.

Mrs Whiten might also sue in negligence. Here, she would need to demonstrate that Mr Dixon's actions in failing to obtain her consent to the termination fell below the required standard of care, the relevant test being that he did not act 'in accordance with a practice accepted as proper by a responsible body of medical men skilled in that particular art.' In practice, this means that some of Mr Dixon's colleagues must testify that his decision was not outside the boundaries of what other medical professionals accept to be reasonable. The essential test is once again to be determined within the medical profession, and if a 'responsible body of medical men skilled in that particular art' is operating with similar standards (even if such standards seem unreasonable or unacceptable to the broader public) then Mr Dixon will not be liable. It seems that Mr Dixon will have few problems in producing expert witnesses in his defence. A spokesperson for the hospital where he works commented: 'We shall continue to give Mr Dixon our full support. He has served the hospital and community well over the last 13 years, and we and his colleagues continue to have every confidence in him'.

Similarly, the Royal College of Obstetricians and Gynaecologists told *The Independent* that 'I do not believe any gynaecologist does something which is not in the best interests of his patient. Once this case has been heard there may be things we need to look at again, and possibly tighten up, but we don't know that'."

In an afterword, appended after the trial was concluded, Sheldon is vindicated in her analysis:

S. SHELDON
"Subject Only to the Attitude of the Surgeon Concerned: The Judicial Protection of Medical Discretion"[23]

"A verdict in the trial of Reginald Dixon was eventually reached by Nottingham Crown Court on 21 December 1995 (see reports in *The Guardian*, *The Independent* and *The Times*, December 22, 1995). Dixon was acquitted of unlawful procurement of miscarriage under s. 58 of the Offences against the Person Act, 1861. It was accepted that he had acted without the necessary second signature foreseen in the Abortion Act. However, it was held that he had acted within the terms of s. 1(4) of the Act which allows a registered medical practitioner to perform a termination without complying with certain formalities (including obtaining a second signature) when the situation is an 'emergency'. The court accepted that Mr Dixon had honestly believed this to be an emergency situation in that he believed Mrs Whiten would not have been able to cope with an unwanted and unplanned pregnancy and that if she had had the baby there would have been a grave risk of permanent injury to her mental health.

The family solicitor said that the Whitens had not yet had time to consider the possibility of bringing an action in the civil courts."

It is not just the judiciary which has been persuaded by the superiority of medical over other discourses in the abortion debate. Parliament too was very much persuaded by the view of the medical profession that foetal viability occurred around 24 weeks when adopting the 1990 reforms. Hence the agreement of that time period as the appropriate limit within which terminations can be carried out on the grounds of risk of injury to physical or mental health under section 1(1)(a) of the amended Abortion Act 1967. The consequences of this situation are summed up in the following extract:

[23]   S. Sheldon, *ibid.*, at 109.

S. Sheldon
"The Law of Abortion and the Politics of Medicalisation"[24]

"[T]he recasting of abortion as a narrow technical issue, its (re)construction as essentially a matter for the expert knowledge and control of doctors and medical science has had very positive effects in paving the way for women's access to the provision of safe, legal terminations. Medicalisation has also played a central role in the apparent depoliticisation of abortion in Britain. Moreover, it seems that medical knowledges, and the protection of medical discretion, have in many instances benefited pro-choice positions ... But medicalisation also has serious shortcomings. It has entrenched a medical model of control which leaves women dependent on medical goodwill ... The law has constructed women seeking abortion as supplicants who must go cap in hand to request permission to terminate their pregnancies ... the English legal model is one of abdication of control to doctors: doctors are free to be as liberal — or as illiberal — as they choose.

For those who believe women should have the right to control their own fertility, medicalisation has thus been both the greatest strength and the greatest weakness of the British legislation. It has left access to abortion well protected against outside challenge, yet entirely dependent on medical goodwill. Moreover, the medicalisation of abortion has now become so grounded in our understanding of it that it becomes difficult even to imagine an alternative legal context."

It is not only within the abortion debate that it is difficult to see an alternative context to the medicalisation of decision-making. We now turn to the issue of preventing pregnancy via sterilisation, finding ourselves in familiar terrain as regards the imposition of medical control over women's bodies.

5.4 Sterilisation

A sterilisation operation may be performed as a method of contraception, for therapeutic reasons (such as a hysterectomy to treat menorrhagia (excessive menstruation)) or for "menstrual management". Sterilisation is a permanent, or irreversible,[25] method of contraception and, as such, is most commonly chosen by couples who have completed their families. The survey, *Sexual Behaviour in Britain*,[26] published in 1994, found that, of those surveyed who had had at least one heterosexual partner in the past year, 23.3 per cent of women and 21.4 per cent of men had relied upon male or female sterilisation to avoid pregnancy.[27] As a chosen means of contraception, we have moved away from the view of sterilisation expressed by Lord Denning in *Bravery v.*

---

[24] In J. Bridgeman & S. Millns (eds), *supra*, n. 17 at pp. 119–120.
[25] Although the use of clips and rings "has increased the ability to reverse sterilisation the operation is still difficult to do, expensive and success is not guaranteed so that the operation should still be considered irreversible" (J. Guillebaud, "Contraception" in A. McPherson (ed.), *Women's Problems in General Practice* (Oxford: Oxford University Press, 1993), p. 109).
[26] K. Wellings, J. Field, A. Johnson & J. Wadsworth, *Sexual Behaviour in Britain: The National Survey of Sexual Attitudes and Lifestyles* (Harmondworth: Penguin, 1994).
[27] In 1987, 42 per cent of women aged 35–44 relied upon either male or female sterilisation: J. Guillebaud, *supra*, n. 25.

Bravery[28] when, dissenting upon the question of whether a wife whose husband had undergone a vasectomy could obtain a divorce on the grounds of his cruelty, he stated that:

> "When it [the sterilisation operation] is done with the man's consent for a just cause, it is quite lawful; as, for instance, when it is done to prevent the transmission of an hereditary disease. But when it is done without just cause or excuse, it is unlawful, even though the man consents to it. Take a case where a sterilisation operation is done so as to enable a man to have the pleasure of sexual intercourse, without shouldering the responsibilities attaching to it. The operation then is plainly injurious to the public interest. It is degrading to the man himself. It is injurious to his wife and to any woman whom he may marry, to say nothing of the way it opens to licentiousness; and, unlike contraceptives, it allows no room for a change of mind on either side."

There is no longer any question that a sterilisation operation for contraceptive purposes can be lawfully carried out. One question to arise, however, has been whether a medical practitioner may be liable for damages when a woman conceives after she has undergone sterilisation. The Court of Appeal in *Gold v. Haringey Health Authority*[29] held that a medical practitioner must act in accordance with the practice of a competent body of professional opinion. Whilst it is now common practice to inform patients of the possibility that sterilisation may fail, it was not so at the time when Mrs Gold underwent the operation in 1979. Her claim for damages failed.[30] Where pregnancy follows after a sterilisation operation which was negligently performed, as in *Emeh v. Kensington and Chelsea and Westminster Area Health Authority*[31] or in *Allen v. Bloomsbury Health Authority*[32] (where the plaintiff was pregnant at the time of the operation and her pregnancy survived), damages will be available, including for loss of earnings and for the financial cost of bringing up the child. The damages awarded for the discomforts of pregnancy and the pain of childbirth will, however, be offset against the benefit of avoiding the physical and emotional pain of a termination. In addition the non-financial burden of bringing up a child is offset by the joy that that child brings. Sterilisation as a form of contraception which, unlike the oral contraceptive, does not expose the body to long term use of synthetic hormones, may nevertheless be denied to young women who do not wish to have children.[33] Whilst sterilis-

---

28 *Bravery v. Bravery* [1954] 1 W.L.R. 1169 at 1180.
29 *Gold v. Haringey Health Authority* [1987] 3 W.L.R. 649.
30 A. Grubb, "Contraceptive Advice and Doctors — A Law Unto Themselves?" [1988] *Cambridge Law Journal* 12; S. Lee, "A Reversible Decision on Consent to Sterilisation" (1987) 103 *Law Quarterly Review* 513; C. R. Symmons, "The problem of 'informed consent' in the 'wrongful birth' cases" (1987) 3 *Professional Negligence* 56.
31 *Emeh v. Kensington and Chelsea and Westminster Area Health Authority* [1985] Q.B. 1012.
32 *Allen v. Bloomsbury Health Authority* [1993] 1 All E.R. 651.
33 M. Stanworth, "Reproductive Technologies and the Deconstruction of Motherhood" in M. Stanworth (ed.), *Reproductive Technologies: Gender, Motherhood and Medicine* (Cambridge: Polity Press, 1987), p. 15; M. Brazier, *Medicine, Patients and the Law* (Harmondsworth: Penguin Books, 1992), p. 382; H. Draper, "Sterilization abuse: women and consent to treatment" in M.

ation may be refused to this type of woman, the courts have considered the legality of, and facilitated, the sterilisation of women with learning difficulties, who cannot themselves give a valid consent to the operation. If sterilisation is refused to young women who have the capacity to understand the nature of the operation, its risks, and the irreversibility of it as a method of contraception on the grounds that they may, in the future, change their mind, what justifications may be given for the sterilisation of young women with learning difficulties, given that it is a major operation which permanently removes the ability of a woman to have children?

In Chapter 2.5.1 above, we considered whether women who were deemed to be "unfit" for motherhood were encouraged to use effective forms of contraception thereby preventing the making of "unfit" mothers. Whilst a young professional woman who requests sterilisation because she is sure that she does not want children may be refused on the grounds that she may later change her mind, are young women with learning difficulties sterilised because they are considered unfit for motherhood? Once again this raises the question of in whose estimation are these women deemed unfit and by what criteria is fitness for motherhood judged?

The laws in the U.S. earlier this century which facilitated the sterilisation of "criminals, idiots, the feeble-minded, imbeciles, the insane, drunkards, drug fiends, epileptics, syphilitics, and moral and sexual perverts"[34] and the Nazi programme of compulsory sterilisation are held up as terrible examples of policies never pursued in England and Wales:

M.D.A. Freeman
"Sterilising the Mentally Handicapped"[35]

"Sterilisation: the Historical Context
I will start with a quotation from a reform school administrator in the United States. 'Many people' he said, 'are "put off " by what Hitler did in Germany; but, again, you have to be practical.' . . . But sterilisation for eugenic or other social control purposes neither begins nor ends in Nazi Germany. As an ideology eugenics can be traced back to 1869 and, whisper it not too loudly, to the portals of that bastion of liberalism,

---

Brazier & M. Lobjoit (eds), *Protecting the Vulnerable: Autonomy and Consent in Health Care* (London: Routledge: 1991), pp. 83–87. Sterilisation is not itself free from side-effects. In addition to the risks involved in a general anaesthetic, sterilisation has been reported to carry psychological and physical side effects as well as regret amongst those who later change their mind (J. Guillebaud, *supra*, n. 25 at p. 109.).

[34] N. Cica, "Sterilising the Intellectually Disabled: The Approach of the High Court in *Department of Health v. J.W.B. and S.M.B.*" (1993) 1 Med.L.Rev. 186 at 224. Adele Clark discusses what she terms "subtle sterilization abuses" (in comparison with "blatant sterilization abuses" which is sterilisation against the person's will, without knowledge or without informed consent) "in which a woman or man *legally consents* to sterilization, but the *social conditions* in which they do so are abusive — the conditions of their lives constrain their capacity to exercise genuine reproductive choice and autonomy" (A. Clark, "Subtle Forms of Sterilization Abuse: A Reproductive Rights Analysis" in R. Arditti, R. Duelli Klein & S. Minden (eds) *Test-Tube Women: What future for motherhood?* (London: Pandora Press, 1984), p. 189).

[35] In M. D. A. Freeman (ed.), *Medicine, Ethics and the Law* (Stevens: London, 1988), pp. 56–59.

University College London. The first attempt to pass a law mandating involuntary sterilisation was made in Michigan in 1897. It failed. But vasectomies were already being used at an Indiana state reformatory (they started in about 1890). A Dr Sharpe employed this procedure on 600 to 700 boys.

In 1907 Indiana became the first American state to pass a compulsory sterilisation statute. Similar statutes were soon enacted in Washington, California and Connecticut and, by the time the eugenics movement reached its peak in the 1920s, 28 states in the USA had passed involuntary sterilisation laws. A number of them were declared unconstitutional: some were impugned as 'cruel and unusual' punishment; others fell foul of 'due process' or 'equal protection under the law' clauses. But in 1927 the Supreme Court decided *Buck v. Bell.*

Carrie Buck was, in the language of the day, 'feeble-minded,' the daughter of a mother alleged to be feeble-minded and the mother herself, research has shown, of a daughter of above average intelligence (though in the law report she is described as an 'illegitimate feeble minded child'). Her proposed sterilisation under a Virginia statute was challenged on 'due process' and 'cruel and unusual' punishment grounds. The court's response was it was not done as a punishment, and that in fact sterilising her enabled her to be released to the community . . . Due process and equal protection arguments were also rejected. The sterilisation statute was upheld as constitutional. The only opinion was given by Justice Holmes. His judgment is not good news for the 'bad woman.' He noted that the attack was 'not upon the procedure but upon the substantive law.' However, he argued:

> 'We have seen more than once that the public welfare may call upon the best citizens for their lives. It would be strange if it could not call upon those who already sap the strength of the State to make lesser sacrifices, often not felt to be such by those concerned. In order to prevent our being swamped with incompetents, it is better for all the world if instead of waiting to execute degenerate offspring for crime or to let them starve for their imbecility, society can prevent those who are manifestly unfit from continuing their kind. The principle that sustains compulsory vaccination is broad enough to cover cutting the fallopian tubes. Three generations of imbeciles are enough.' . . .

Justice Holmes's opinion has been castigated so often that anything I might say about it is otiose. A couple of points, however, should be made if only to guide us through the thickets of the Jeanette case.[36] First, Holmes's analysis, in particular his analogies, is weak (the temptation is to describe it as 'sub-standard' whatever the implications of this might be!). His language is intemperate and value-laden. The war analogy is fatuous: the enemy who kills our soldiers is in no way comparable to the progeny of a mentally handicapped person who may require state support. The principle behind compulsory vaccination (a policy, incidentally, opposed by the very Social Darwinists who advocated eugenics) cannot encompass involuntary sterilisation, any more than it would the cutting off of the hands of habitual thieves: the quality of the intrusion is totally different. Secondly, it needs to be said that Holmes was far too readily convinced that due process had been observed. It surely behoves any judge sanctioning the deprivation of a basic human right to invoke higher standards of scrutiny than in the ordinary case.

[36] *Re B (A Minor) (Wardship: Sterilisation)* [1987] 2 W.L.R. 1213. This case is discussed in Chap. 5.4.i below.

There have been a number of significant cases in the USA since *Buck v. Bell*. There have been attempts to reverse the decision. That this has not happened is in part attributable to the fact that the line of argument has changed. Eugenics (or rather 'negative' eugenics) is out of fashion: instead, the appeal is grounded on the burden placed on society by the need to care for the handicapped. The most interesting of the recent cases is *North Carolina Association for Retarded Children v. State of North Carolina* in 1976. The statute challenged authorised both voluntary and involuntary sterilisations. There was a duty to institute sterilisation proceedings when the relevant official felt it was either in (i) the best interests of the retarded person or (ii) the public at large or (iii) where the retarded person would be likely, unless sterilised, to procreate children with a tendency to serious physical, mental or nervous disease or deficiency or would be unable to care for the child or (iv) when the next of kin or legal guardian of the retarded person 'requests' that he file the petition. The court found (iv) irrational and irreconcilable with (i), (ii) and (iii). But it thought the first three provisions made out 'a complete and sensible scheme.' The fourth, however, granted to the retarded person's next of kin or legal guardian 'the power of a tyrant.' The scheme was thus found constitutional with the exception of the fourth provision. The language and ideology of Holmes's 'incantation' was rejected. 'Medical and genetical experts,' the Court noted, 'are no longer sold on sterilization to benefit either retarded patients or the future of the Republic.' The case is also significant for containing a number of general propositions about the origins of mental retardation, about expression of sexuality, about the ability of the handicapped to use contraceptive methods. Finally, the opinion holds that in rare unusual cases it can be medically determined that involuntary sterilisation is in the best interests of either the mentally retarded persons, or the state, or both.

A lot of people have been sterilised in the USA pursuant upon the compulsory programmes depicted here. By 1964, by which time the programmes had long passed their peak, 63,678 such sterilisations had taken place. Those sterilised were mainly young women and for the large part they were poor and came from socio-economically and culturally deprived environments. Whether it was, as Gonzales indicates, a popular way of controlling reproduction, it certainly was a convenient method for controlling the reproductive urges of the populace. Given the population concerned and the imperfections of classification, the dangers of labelling with sterilisation merely an incident of stigmatisation were difficult to overcome. The evidence suggests they were not surmounted.

In the light of all this, it is somewhat surprising that forced sterilisation policies should be associated with Nazi Germany. But the reputation is deserved for no political system has pursued the policy with greater vigour or ruthlessness. The Nazi compulsory sterilisation law dates from 1933, the very outset of the Third Reich and long before the Nuremberg Laws. The 1933 law created 'hereditary health courts' made up of a district judge and his physicians to supplement, what was called, the 'Law on the Prevention of Hereditary Diseases in Future Generations.' A variety of diagnoses could lead to forced sterilisations including hereditary blindness or deafness, epilepsy, Huntingdon's disease and alcoholism. Many others designated 'anti-social,' such as Gypsies or, what were called, 'Rhineland bastards' (children conceived after the First World War by French North African occupation troups) were also sterilised. A gradual shift towards measures aimed at racial elimination is evident here, as it became all too evident later. The USA and Nazi Germany are but two of the countries in which involuntary sterilisation policies have been pursued. Most recently, under Indira Gandhi, Indian governments have used sterilisation as a method of population control;

in theory persons agreed to be sterilised (some, I seem to remember, in return for gifts of transistor radios) but in practice there is no doubt that forced sterilisation was carried out on a wide scale."

Michael Freeman continues to explain that young people, both male and female, in England and Wales are sterilised, but what we do not know is how many. Before considering the justifications which have been advanced before the courts for the sterilisation of young people without their consent, it is necessary to explain the difference in the powers of the court in respect of minors and adults who are unable, due to lack of capacity, to give or refuse their consent to medical treatment. Consent, obtained from a competent patient, to medical treatment renders lawful what would otherwise be a civil and criminal battery. The concern which has been paramount in the legal consideration of the sterilisation of women with learning difficulties has been to determine the basis upon which decisions can be made as to whether treatment should be provided to patients who lack the capacity to give or refuse their consent. It should, however, be noted that the lack of legal competence of the women whose sterilisation becomes a question for the courts is not addressed in the legal judgments in these cases, but simply assumed. Nor, as Kirsty Keywood points out, does the court ever consider that capacity to understand is related to the way in which the information is communicated. Realisation of this would require a reconsideration of the provision of information as necessary to enhance competence.[37] However, a search for a way by which to enable sterilisation operations to be lawfully performed in the absence of consent has dominated the judicial consideration of sterilisation. Lord Templeman in *Re B (A Minor) (Wardship: Sterilisation)*, said;

> "In my opinion sterilisation of a girl under 18 should only be carried out with the leave of a High Court judge. A doctor performing a sterilisation operation with the consent of the parents might still be liable in criminal, civil or professional proceedings. A court exercising the wardship jurisdiction emanating from the Crown is the only authority which is empowered to authorise such a drastic step as sterilisation after a full and informed investigation . . . No one has suggested a more satisfactory tribunal or a more satisfactory method of reaching a decision which vitally concerns an individual but also involves principles of law, ethics and medical practice."[38]

The appropriate procedure (although, it must be emphasised, no court approval is required) in the case of minors is to apply for an order under the inherent jurisdiction (or if the minor is a ward of court under wardship) of the High Court. The court can then give consent to any procedure which is in the girl's "best interests", the welfare of the minor being the paramount

---

[37]   K. Keywood, "Sterilising the Woman with Learning Disabilities — Possibilities for a Feminist Ethic of Decision-making" in Feminist Legal Research Unit (University of Liverpool) (ed.), *supra*, n. 18 at pp. 56–61.
[38]   *Re B (A Minor) (Wardship: Sterilisation)* [1987] 2 W.L.R. 1213 at 1218B-C, E.

consideration. In the case of adults (over the age of 18), the court does not have comparable jurisdiction, hence it cannot give consent. Where, however, the incompetent adult herself is not and will never be in a position to give a valid consent, the court can declare that the procedure proposed by the medical practitioners is in her best interests. Medical treatment carried out in the best interests of the adult is lawful, despite the lack of consent. The question is how to determine, in any one case, or as a matter of principle, what is in the best interests of the individual.

5.4.i *In whose best interests?*

The House of Lords first considered the sterilisation of a woman with learning difficulties in the case of *Re B (A Minor) (Wardship: Sterilisation).*[39] The facts and legal issues are set out in the judgment of Lord Oliver:

Re B (A Minor) (Wardship: Sterilisation)
[1987] 2 W.L.R. 1213 at 1218–1222, *per* Lord Oliver

"My Lords, this appeal concerns a girl of 17 who was born on 20 May, 1969 and who has been in the care of the first respondent, the Sunderland Borough Council, since 31 May, 1973 under the provisions of section 1(2)(a) of the Children and Young Persons Act 1969. Thus it is the council which, during her minority, exercises parental rights over her. On 18 June, 1986 the council applied by originating summons to the Family Division of the High Court of Justice for an order making the minor a ward of court and for leave to be given for her to undergo a sterilisation operation. Initially the sole defendant to the summons was the second respondent, the mother of the minor, but on 28 August, 1986 an order was made joining the minor herself as second defendant and the Official Solicitor was appointed as her *guardian ad litem*. It will be necessary to recount in some detail the circumstances in which the application came to be made, but purely as a matter of the procedural history it is sufficient at this stage to say that the leave sought by the council was supported by the mother but opposed by the Official Solicitor on behalf of the minor. The summons was heard by Bush J. at Newcastle on 20 January, 1987 ... Bush J. came to the firm conclusion that the only possible decision for the future welfare of the minor was that the leave sought by the council should be given and the operation carried out. The Official Solicitor appealed to the Court of Appeal which, on 16 March, 1987, unanimously dismissed the appeal. From that decision the Official Solicitor now appeals to your Lordships ...

The minor is the second of the three children of the marriage of her mother, a marriage which terminated in divorce in 1977. From a comparatively early age it became apparent that she was mentally retarded, was prone to outbursts of aggression and was epileptic. She was received into care at the age of four and was described as being then like a wild animal. After a spell in a residential nursery she was moved, in August 1975, to a residential institution managed by the council for both minor and adult persons suffering from mental handicap. She has lived there ever since and it is envisaged that she will continue to live there for the foreseeable future. That institution has an associated school at which she may stay until she is 19 but it is likely that

---

[39] *Ibid.*

thereafter she will be transferred to an adult training centre at which it will not be possible to provide the degree of supervision that she at present experiences. She suffers from what is described as a 'moderate' degree of mental handicap but has a very limited intellectual development. Her ability to understand speech is that of a six-year-old, but her ability to express herself has been described as comparable to that of a two-year-old child. No cause for her mental handicap has been established but the report of Dr Berney, a consultant psychiatrist who gave evidence before the judge, indicates that her epilepsy and the degree of her mental incapacity suggest an underlying abnormality of the brain. It is not envisaged that she will ever be capable of caring for herself in the community or reach a stage where she could return permanently to her mother's care. She is capable of finding her way round a limited locality, of dressing and bathing herself and performing simple household tasks under supervision and she has been taught to cope with menstruation; but the evidence is that she is unlikely to show an improvement in mental capacity beyond that of a six-year-old child. She has, in the past, shown evidence of extremes of mood and can become violent and aggressive, a phenomenon associated with pre-menstrual tension. Since the middle of 1986 there has been prescribed for her a drug known as danazol to help in controlling her irregular periods and relieving pre-menstrual tension, whilst her epilepsy is controlled by anti-convulsant drugs. She suffers from obesity and an earlier attempt to treat her outbursts of violence with microgynon 30 (a combined oral contraceptive) had to be abandoned because it produced a significant increase in weight. Another behavioural feature of significance is her high tolerance of pain. There is evidence that she bites her arm and that if injured she interferes with the process of healing by opening and probing the wounds.

What prompted the application to the court was the consciousness on the part of her mother and officers of the council responsible for her care that she was beginning to show recognisable signs of sexual awareness and sexual drive exemplified by provocative approaches to male members of the staff and other residents and by touching herself in the genital area. There was thus brought to their attention the obvious risk of pregnancy and the desirability of taking urgent and effective contraceptive measures . . .

[T]he risks involved in her becoming pregnant are formidable. The evidence of Dr Berney is that there is no prospect of her being capable of forming a long-term adult relationship, such as marriage, which is within the capacity of some less mentally handicapped persons. She has displayed no maternal feelings and indeed has an antipathy to small children. Such skills as she has been able to develop are limited to those necessary for caring for herself at the simplest level and there is no prospect of her being capable of raising or caring for a child of her own. If she did give birth to a child it would be essential that it be taken from her for fostering or adoption although her attitude towards children is such that this would not cause her distress. So far as her awareness of her own sexuality is concerned, she has, as has already been mentioned, been taught to manage for herself the necessary hygienic mechanics of menstruation, but it has not been possible to teach her about sexuality in any abstract form. She understands the link between pregnancy and a baby but is unaware of sexual intercourse and its relationship to pregnancy. It is not feasible to discuss contraception with her and even if there should come a time when she becomes capable of understanding the need for contraception, there is no likelihood of her being able to develop the capacity to weigh up the merits of different types of contraception or to make an informed choice in the matter. Should she become pregnant, it would be desirable that the pregnancy should be terminated, but because of her obesity and the irregularity of her periods there is an obvious danger that her condition might not be noticed until it was too late for an abortion to take place safely. On the other hand, the risks if she were permitted to go to full term are serious, for although it is Dr Berney's opinion that she would tolerate the condition of pregnancy without undue distress, the process of delivery would be likely to be traumatic and would cause her to panic. Normal delivery would be likely to require heavy sedation, which could be injurious to the child, so that it might be more appropriate to deliver her by caesarean section. If this course were adopted, however, past experience of her reaction to injuries suggests that it would be very difficult to prevent her from repeatedly opening up the wound and thus preventing the healing of the post-operative scar. It was against this background and in the light of the increasing freedom which must be allowed her as she grows older and the consequent difficulty of maintaining effective supervision that those having the care of the minor concluded that it was essential in her interests that effective contraceptive measures be taken. Almost all drugs appear to have a bad effect upon her and the view was formed, in which her mother concurred, that the only appropriate course offering complete protection was for her to undergo sterilisation by occluding the fallopian tubes, a relatively minor operation carrying a very small degree of risk to the patient, a very high degree of protection and minimal side effects. There is, however, no possibility that the minor, even if of full age, would herself have the mental capacity to consent to such an operation. Hence the application to the court.

The necessity for the course proposed has been exhaustively considered by the Official Solicitor on the minor's behalf and there have been obtained two very careful and detailed reports from Dr Berney who is a consultant in child and adolescent psychiatry, and Mr Barron, a consultant of obstetrics and gynaecology to the Newcastle Health Authority. Both agree upon the absolute necessity of taking effective contraceptive measures and the report of Mr Barron, in particular, contains a detailed consideration of the various options. It is unnecessary for present purposes to dilate upon the numerous possible courses which have been considered. Her limited intelligence effectively rules out mechanical methods whilst at the same time the way in which certain contraceptive drugs are likely to react with the anti-convulsant drugs administered for her epileptic condition severely limits the available choices. In the end it emerges as common ground that the only alternative to sterilisation which even merits consideration is the administration daily in pill form of the drug progestogen supplemented for the present, at any rate, by the danazol which she is presently taking. This involves a number of disadvantages and uncertainties. In the first place, it involves a regular and uninterrupted course which must be pursued over the whole of the minor's reproductive life of some 30 years or so. Secondly, it involves a *daily* dosage — a matter which has given great concern to those having the care of the minor. Miss Ford, the social worker most closely connected with her, was of the opinion that if the minor was in one of her violent moods there was no possible way in which the pill could be administered. Thirdly, the side effects of the drug over a long term are not yet known. Possibilities canvassed in the course of the evidence of Dr Lowry, the consultant paediatrician at Sunderland District General Hospital, were weight-gain, nausea, headaches and depression. But fourthly, and perhaps even more importantly, the effectiveness of this course is entirely speculative. The matter can perhaps best be summed up in the answer given by Mr Barron when he was asked in examination-in-chief for an assessment of the prospects of achieving a satisfactory contraceptive regime by way of pill. He said:

'It would be very speculative because you have a problem here of a girl who is obese who is still quite young, who has all kinds of problems like, for example, taking anti-convulsant therapy for epilepsy, which affect the manner of working certainly of oestrogens, all of which make her a particularly difficult person in whom to perform a normal judgment. Therefore, I think that we might find a successful modus vivendi, but it is difficult to be certain. I think it is perhaps — if you want a kind of guess, I would say that we have a 30 to 40 per cent chance of getting some formulation that would be successful. But of course it would have to be taken for a very long time.'

In answer to a further question he surmised that an experimental period of 12 to 18 months might be required.

Here then is the dilemma. The vulnerability of this young woman, her need for protection, and the potentially frightening consequences of her becoming pregnant are not in doubt. Of the two possible courses, the one proposed is safe, certain but irreversible, the other speculative, possibly damaging and requiring discipline over a period of many years from one of the most limited intellectual capacity. Equally it is not in doubt that this young woman is not capable and never will be capable herself of consenting to undergo a sterilisation operation. Can the court and should the court, in the exercise of its wardship jurisdiction, give on her behalf that consent which she is incapable of giving and which, objectively considered, it is clearly in her interests to give?"

The selection of the "facts" upon which the court justified its decision to authorise sterilisation is considered below.

Whereas the court can give consent to medical procedures performed upon minors, the wardship jurisdiction ends at the age of majority and there is no longer a comparable jurisdiction over adults. In *T v. T*,[40] Wood J. gave a declaration to the effect that it would be lawful for a termination of pregnancy and sterilisation operation to be performed upon T despite her inability to consent to the procedures. As with younger women the question was "what was in her best interests?". This was determined by what medical practice "demands". There had to be agreement (*i.e.* no two contrasting views) as to the best course.[41]

The House of Lords considered the lawfulness of the proposed sterilisation of an adult woman in *Re F (Mental Patient: Sterilisation)*,[42] the facts of which are set out in the judgment of Lord Brandon:

Re F (Mental Patient: Sterilisation)
[1989] 2 W.L.R. 1025 at 1065, *per* Lord Brandon

"F. . . was born on January 13, 1953, so that she is now 36. She suffers from serious mental disability, probably as a consequence of an acute infection of the respiratory

---

[40]   *T v. T* [1988] 1 All E.R. 613.
[41]   *Ibid.*, 621h at 625f. For comment on *T v. T* see J. Fortin, "Sterilisation, the Mentally Ill and Consent to Treatment" (1988) 51 *Modern Law Review* 634; M. J. Gunn, [1988] *Journal of Social Welfare Law* 336; J. P. A. P. O'Brien, "Mentally handicapped adults: consent and medical treatment" (1988) 4 *Professional Negligence* 152.
[42]   *Re F (Mental Patient: Sterilisation)* [1989] 2 W.L.R. 1025.

tract which she had when she was about nine months old. She has been a voluntary in-patient at Borocourt Hospital (a mental hospital under the control of the health authority) since 1967 when she was 14. Her mental disability takes the form of an arrested or incomplete development of the mind. She has the verbal capacity of a child of two and the general mental capacity of a child of four to five. She is unable to express her views in words but can indicate what she likes or dislikes, for example, people, food, clothes and matters of routine. She experiences emotions such as enjoyment, sadness and fear, but is prone to express them differently from others. She is liable to become aggressive. Her mother is her only relative and visits her regularly. There is a strong bond of affection between them. As a result of the treatment which F. has received during her time in hospital she has made significant progress. She has become less aggressive and is allowed considerable freedom of movement about the hospital grounds which are large. There is, however, no prospect of any development in her mental capacity.

The question of F. being sterilised has arisen because of a relationship which she has formed with a male patient at the same hospital, P. This relationship is of a sexual nature and probably involves sexual intercourse, or something close to it, about twice a month. The relationship is entirely voluntary on F.'s part and it is likely that she obtains pleasure from it. There is no reason to believe that F. has other than the ordinary fertility of a woman of her age. Because of her mental disability, however, she could not cope at all with pregnancy, labour or delivery, the meaning of which she would not understand. Nor could she care for a baby if she ever had one. In these circumstances, it would, from a psychiatric point of view, be disastrous for her to conceive a child. There is a serious objection to each of the ordinary methods of contraception. So far as varieties of the pill are concerned she would not be able to use them effectively and there is a risk of their causing damage to her physical health. So far as an intra-uterine device is concerned, there would be danger of infection arising, the symptoms of which she would not be able to describe so that remedial measures could not be taken in time."

The House of Lords differed in their approach compared with that taken by Wood J. in *T v. T*. Whilst agreeing that the court could declare that the proposed procedure was in the best interests of the woman, the question whether it was in her best interests was to be determined by the *Bolam* test. If a competent body of professional opinion agree that sterilisation is in her best interests, a medical practitioner who performs a sterilisation operation will not commit a criminal or civil battery.[43] Lord Brandon said that sterilisation would be in the best interests of those with learning disabilities "if, but only if, it is carried out in order either to save their lives, or to ensure improvement or prevent deterioration in their physical or mental health."[44]

The House of Lords agreed that best interests was to be determined in accordance with the *Bolam* test without placing the limitation suggested by Lord Brandon upon the circumstances when it would be in a woman's best interests. This permits doctors to perform an operation such as sterilisation upon an incompetent adult patient as long as a competent body of profes-

---

[43] For commentary upon the role of the judiciary in *Re F* see J. Shaw, "Sterilisation of Mentally Handicapped People: Judges Rule OK?" (1990) 53 *Modern Law Review* 91.
[44] *Re F (Mental Patient: Sterilisation)*, *supra*, n. 42 at 1067C-D.

sional opinion would have done the same thing. This raises the question whether a decision to permanently remove the ability of a woman to bear children should be taken by the medical profession. As a matter of practice the views of others, such as parents, siblings, social workers and carers, will be taken into consideration. But, not only is no independent review of the decision required, the doctor will be acting *lawfully* as long as a competent body of professional opinion agree that sterilisation is in the woman's best interests. With minors, the best interests of the young woman is determined not in accordance with a competent body of professional opinion but by the court weighing up the facts. Upholding the decision of the lower courts, Lord Oliver in *Re B* stated:

> "this case is not about sterilisation for social purposes; it is not about eugen-
> ics; it is not about the convenience of those whose task it is to care for the
> ward or the anxieties of her family; and it involves no general principle of
> public policy. It is about what is in the best interests of this unfortunate
> young woman and how best she can be given the protection which is essential
> to her future wellbeing so that she may lead as full a life as her intellectual
> capacity allows".[45]

As argued in the comment upon *Re B* in the journal *Family Law* "[t]he prin-
ciple of law to be applied in such cases is easy to state — it is to do whatever will best promote the minor's welfare — but much less easy to apply. The cases will always depend on the judge's assessment of the facts."[46] The best interests test considers the *facts* of the individual case, it is not concerned, as Lord Oliver states, with "general principle". Is the judiciary in the best position (and is a court a more appropriate decision-making body than the medical profession) to weigh up all the facts and assess whether sterilisation is in the best interests of a young woman? La Forest J. in the Canadian case of *Re Eve*, felt that this was not the case:

> "The irreversible and serious intrusion on the basic rights of the individual is
> simply too great to allow a court to act on the basis of possible advantages
> which, from the standpoint of the individual, are highly debatable. Judges are
> generally ill-informed about many of the factors relevant to a wise decision in
> this difficult area. They generally know little of mental illness, of techniques
> of contraception or their efficacy. And, however well presented a case may
> be, it can only partially inform."[47]

Michael Freeman compares the case of *Re B* with *Re Eve* to suggest both that the courts *can* be a suitable forum for deciding cases and that the English courts presently are not:

---

[45] *Re B (A Minor) (Wardship: Sterilisation)*, *supra*, n. 38 at 1224. For commentary upon *Re B* see M. Hinchliffe, "Re B (A Minor)" (1987) 17 *Family Law* 271; S. P. de Cruz, "Sterilisation, Wardship and Human Rights" (1988) 18 *Family Law* 6.
[46] Comment on *Re B* (1989) 19 *Family Law* 102.
[47] *Re Eve* (1986) 31 D.L.R. (4th) 1 at 32.

"The Canadian Supreme Court refused to authorise Eve's sterilisation. Its reasons for doing so are set out in one, very full, well-argued and well-documented judgment. It contains copious reference to periodical literature and, with the assistance of the Canadian Law Reform Commission, an awareness of the research results of those who have studied mental retardation. The Court was helped in its deliberations by the participation of several *amici curiae*, who presented the view of interested third parties, enabling it to benefit from the widest range of arguments. It also spent 16 months pondering its judgment. By contrast the House of Lords barely reserved judgment. There were, of course, no *amici curiae*. The speeches are thin. The only judge with Family Division experience declined to give a judgment . . ."[48]

Requiring the court to consider whether a proposed treatment is in the best interests of the individual will provide procedural protection. *Re D*[49] was only referred to court because there was disagreement amongst those caring for D about her behaviour, social abilities and future prospects. If there had not been this disagreement, D would have been sterilised (as, presumably, other young women have been). However, the extent to which the court protects the interests of the individual depends upon the presentation of *all* the facts to the court and the assumptions upon which the court proceeds when weighing up those facts. Andrew Bainham argues that a comparison of the content of "best interests" in more than one area[50] demonstrates the lack of "coherent and consistent principles". This is despite judicial comments to the effect that the best interests test is an "absolute standard and an unproblematic concept which can act as a panacea for all ills affecting children". This is not surprising, he suggests, when the judiciary are the very individuals who "get to define its content in any given situation".[51]

It is clear from the judgments which factors form the "content" of the test of whether sterilisation is in the best interests of a woman with learning difficulties. It is equally clear which assumptions about the women whose bodies are before the court influence the relative weight given to these factors. Here we examine five of these assumptions and factors: the mental age of the woman compared with her physical development and sexuality; her freedom; the unwanted consequences of intercourse; the risks of non-permanent forms of contraception; and eugenics arguments.

5.4.i.a Mental age compared with physical development and sexuality.

Consider the following statements. *Re M (A Minor) (Wardship: Sterilization), per* Bush J.:

"she has developed physically perfectly normally, but emotionally and psychologically she operates at around the age of 5 or 6 years and in some

---

[48] M.D.A. Freeman, "Sterilising the Mentally Handicapped" in M.D.A. Freeman (ed.), *supra*, n. 35 at p. 66.

[48] *Re D (A Minor) (Wardship: Sterilisation)* [1976] 1 All E.R. 326.

[50] The comparison he uses with sterilisation cases is the *Gillick* case (discussed above).

[51] A. Bainham, "Handicapped Girls and Judicial Parents" (1987) 103 *Law Quarterly Review* 334 at 339.

respects lower than that. She has normal sexual appetites and has become
sexually aware, . . ."[52]

Re P (A Minor) (Wardship: Sterilization), per Eastham J.:

"T looks a perfectly normal and reasonably attractive young lady of 17 . . .
Unfortunately, although she looks perfectly normal, her intellectual development is that of a child of 6 years of age, and that intellectual development
will never improve . . . Although her intelligence is limited to that of a child
of 6, T has the sexual libido appropriate to a girl of 17, . . ."[53]

"[S]he appears to be the possessor of normal libido (sexual drive) and when
in an unsupervised setting with a sexually active male the likelihood of intercourse is high, especially if he should be unscrupulous and ready to take
advantage of her. Theoretically, she might be 'warned off' but girls like T
are readily seduced . . ."[54]

Norma Martin identifies the construction of the woman with learning difficulties as both sexually dangerous and vulnerable in the House of Lords judgment in *Re B*:

"*Re B* illustrates the pervasiveness of two contradictory myths regarding the
sexuality of the mentally handicapped. On the one hand, they are seen as
having strong sexual inclinations but poor self-control, and therefore are a
menace to society at large. True to this view, Lord Hailsham describes Jeannette as 'a danger to others.' But on the other hand, individuals with mental
handicaps are seen as being child-like, and since children are asexual until
puberty, the mentally handicapped are also sexually 'innocent'. So Lord Hailsham also describes Jeannette as being 'vulnerable to sexual approaches,' and
the impression of childishness is reinforced by her having a mental age of five
or six, as opposed to a particular I.Q. In Jeanette's case, the second view
proved more significant. Sterilisation is justified as a protective, rather than
coercive, measure in this paternalistic judgment."[55]

It is apparent from the above that the assessment of the mental age of the
woman, which enables the court to portray her as a child-like figure in need
of protection from exploitation, ignores the experience of her years:

K. KEYWOOD
"Sterilising the Woman with Learning Difficulties — In her Best Interests?"[56]

"THE CONSTRUCTION OF LEARNING DIFFICULTY

A closer examination of the judgments in sterilisation cases reveals the emphasis placed
by the court and medical profession on the pathology of learning difficulties. The

---

52 *Re M (A Minor) (Wardship: Sterilization)* [1988] 2 F.L.R. 497 at 498B.
53 *Re P (A Minor) (Wardship: Sterilization)* [1989] 1 F.L.R. 182 at 183D, E, F.
54 *Re P (A Minor) (Wardship: Sterilization), ibid.*, 192A-B, citing the report of psychiatrist, Dr
Heller.
55 N. Martin, *Re B (A Minor)* [1987] J.S.W.L. 369 at 373.
56 In J. Bridgeman & S. Millns (eds), *supra*, n. 17 at pp. 130–132.

women who are the subject of sterilisation cases are frequently referred to in terms of their pathology, that is, what is wrong or abnormal about them. The most common example of this is the description of women in terms of their intellectual capacity, usually by reference to their mental age. To equate women with small children is to deny the years of practical experience of these women and the extent of their behavioural skills which cannot be measured by intelligence testing. By labelling persons intellectually abnormal, the medical and 'psy' professions explain the difference in treatment between 'them' and 'us' as arising from *their* abnormalities rather than *our* responses to these differences. This clinical explanation of mental handicap thus views learning difficulty as a medical problem requiring a medical (or rather a surgical) solution. It has been rightly argued that the medical profession has overstepped its authority and has not stopped at providing medical care for the mentally disabled. In focusing on the psychological abnormalities of the person with learning difficulties, it has created a way of thinking that justifies the exclusion of persons with learning difficulties from enjoyment of society on the same terms as the non-disabled. In sterilisation cases the courts have paid little attention to the behavioural skills of the woman with learning difficulties, relying essentially on medical testimony as to her mental condition and intellectual ability. As Carson rightly notes, parenting is a skill which can be measured by reference to behavioural ability rather than intelligence.

Analysis of sterilisation cases reveals that reference to the psychological disfunction of women with learning difficulties has been used as a justification to sterilise women without examining the environmental influences on learning ability, such as the conditions the women live in or the quality of care they receive. In the case of *Re B* the court took note of the fact that the seventeen year-old woman was unable to comprehend the link between intercourse and pregnancy. What was not considered, however, was the quality of sex education the woman had been given. If the link between intercourse and pregnancy had never been explained to her, or had been explained in purely clinical terms which she could not be expected to understand, it should hardly come as a surprise to hear that her understanding of the consequences of intercourse was rather vague. In the case of *Re P* the judge, prior to authorising sterilisation on a seventeen year-old woman, heard evidence that the woman's perception of sexual intercourse as painful would protect her from unwanted sexual advances. This again clearly raises concern about the quality of the sex education provided which is not questioned by the judge. The vulnerability of the woman with learning difficulties has been taken into account by the court when determining her best interests. In *Re P* the seventeen year-old woman's vulnerability to sexual exploitation was remarked upon by a psychiatrist who commented that 'girls like T are readily seduced'. This statement was not challenged by the court as suggesting that her present environment was in any way unsatisfactory. The concern that such women might be seduced, due to their trusting nature and dependence on others, ignores the extent to which their dependence has been fostered by an environment which prevents them from making choices and having those choices respected by others.

The courts' reliance on the medical explanation of learning difficulty ignores the extent to which it is a social construct. The courts are trying to answer the question, 'how should society react to the sexuality of persons with learning difficulties?' by reference to a medical ideology which has no place in the treatment of persons with learning difficulties in society. The question should be answered by analysing society's response to learning difficulty, rather than perceiving learning difficulty as the inherent cause of the problem ...

THE CONSTRUCTION OF SEXUALITY

The cultural norms which are presently attached to the sexuality of women with learning difficulties are based upon myths which deny the reality of their sexuality and justify their sterilisation. It is necessary therefore to deconstruct their sexuality and provide a more realistic account of their sexual needs: a realistic appraisal of the sexuality of women with learning difficulties would not justify non-consensual sterilisation procedures for contraceptive purposes.

The present construction of the sexuality of women with learning difficulties is based not only on myths surrounding the sexuality of mentally handicapped persons, but also on myths relating to female sexuality. In sterilisation cases, the myths are restated and compounded by the courts and it becomes apparent that women with learning difficulties are being sterilised not only on the grounds of their intellectual subnormality but also because of their gender. Despite the growing recognition of the sexual needs of persons with learning difficulties, the belief that these people have uncontrollable sexual desires, thus rendering them a threat to the rest of the population, has been accepted for many years and still persists. Citing Barr, Craft notes that: '[t]he sexual desires [in mental defectives] are exaggerated in proportion to the animal over the physic forces.' This assumption, that people with learning difficulties pose a sexual threat, has also been made in sterilisation cases. In *Re B* Lord Hailsham noted that the woman, who was showing signs of sexual awareness, would become a danger to others.

A contrasting, but equally relevant, myth pertaining to mental handicap is that people with learning difficulties are child-like and have no sexual desires. As Craft notes, this belief stems from the myth that children are asexual until puberty: '[W]hatever their actual age, individuals with mental handicaps remain forever children. Children are not sexual, therefore those who have a mental handicap cannot be sexual.' This view of the sexual immaturity of persons with learning difficulties has been compounded by some of the judges in sterilisation cases, who, as was noted earlier, constantly refer to the women about to be sterilised in terms of their mental age. In the case of *Re P* Justice Eastham noted that the seventeen year-old woman 'although she looks perfectly normal, her intellectual development is that of a child of 6 years.' This may well explain the judiciary's reluctance to acknowledge the sexual needs of people with learning difficulties, focusing rather on their vulnerability and need for protection."

Whilst presenting an image of these women as sexual beings in need of protection because of their childlike minds, the solution which the courts accept is removal of the threat of pregnancy by sterilisation (of the vulnerable).[57] If protection is required, is it not required first and foremost from unwanted sexual advances, rather than from an unwanted pregnancy?

5.4.i.b Freedom. Rather than demonstrating any concern with unwanted

---

[57] Felicity Scroggie focuses upon the difficulties of carers of handicapped children suggesting that sterilisation may seem [to carers] to be in the best interests of their child when they are faced with difficult questions about the child's sexuality, and when the parents feel themselves inadequately informed about sex education (and how to pass it on to their child) and lack financial assistance and support services (F. Scroggie, "Why do parents want their children sterilised? A broader approach to sterilisation requests" (1990) 17 *Journal of Child Law* 35).

sexual intercourse, the courts seem to forget the need of the woman for protection, and accept that sterilisation will increase her freedom. Bush J. considering the case of *Re B* in the Family Division,[58] was prepared to hold that sterilisation would be lawful, being in B's "best interests", emphasising that she should have "as much freedom as in the circumstances is possible" and that, as she was "showing a sexual awareness which will lead to the probability of sexual intercourse with someone at some stage and, therefore, the possibility of pregnancy", contraception was necessary.[59] The possibility of pregnancy arising from a possible sexual relationship at some time in the future was sufficient justification to sterilise her now. The justification was her freedom, presumably, including the freedom to enter into a sexual relationship.

Likewise, in *Re W*, the court was concerned that W, aged 20, with "severe learning difficulties, mobility and hearing problems, and suffer[ing] from severe epilepsy and a minor degree of cerebral palsy" should live in the community as much as possible.[60] This involved socialising with people of both sexes and, consequently, there was a possibility that she may in the future become pregnant with detrimental effect. Hollis J. held that, in making a declaration "on the basis of existing circumstances", the court could consider W's "foreseeable future". He was anxious to avoid waiting "until it was possibly too late".

This case may lend support to the view taken by Robert Lee and Derek Morgan who suggest that the comparison between *Re B* and *Gillick* goes beyond the provision of contraception (to those who are unable to consent themselves due to learning difficulties or immaturity) to the institution of the family and the role of the family in care in the community. This is implicit in the case of *Re B, per* Lord Oliver:

> "Although at present she is subject to effective supervision, her degree of incapacity is not such that it would be thought right that she should, effectively, be institutionalised all her life. The current approach to persons of her degree of incapacity is to allow them as much freedom as is consistent with their own safety and that of other people and although the likelihood is that she will, for the foreseeable future, continue to live at the residential institution, she visits her mother and her siblings at weekends and will, inevitably, be much less susceptible to supervision when she goes to an adult training centre."[61]

Cost-cutting in health and social provision force children to rely upon their parents and the State to rely upon the family. *Re B*, Lee and Morgan suggest, is about maintaining the impression that the family can cope with the additional responsibilities arising due to the policy of community care. Sterilising B was a necessary solution to provide her with the freedom to be cared for in

---

[58] *Re B (A Minor) (Wardship: Sterilisation)* [1987] 2 All E.R. 206.
[59] *Re B (A Minor) (Wardship: Sterilisation)*, *ibid.*
[60] *Re W (Mental Patient: Sterilisation)* (1993) 23 *Family Law* 208.
[61] *Re B (A Minor) (Wardship: Sterilisation)*, *supra*, n. 38 at 1220D.

the community.[62] Talking of children, parents and the State ignores the real relationships involved in both *Re B* and *Gillick*, that is, relationships between the State, mothers as primary carers and their daughters.

5.4.i.c Unwanted consequences. In the case of *Re M (A Minor) (Wardship: Sterilization)*, Bush J. stated:

> "[T]o go through the experience of pregnancy, possibly leading at the end to a caesarian operation, would be a traumatic experience which might harm her mental health. She . . . is unlikely ever to understand what childbirth is about, and one can only think that it would be a lonely experience for her of pain and anguish."[63]

One of the criticisms of the cases which have determined that sterilisation of an incompetent patient without her consent is not unlawful is that, with the exception of "therapeutic sterilisation", the operation is seen as the solution to the problem of possible pregnancy. This is clear from the case of *Re B* in which Lord Oliver said:

> "What prompted the application to the court was the consciousness on the part of her mother and officers of the council responsible for her care that she was beginning to show recognisable signs of sexual awareness and sexual drive exemplified by provocative approaches to male members of the staff and other residents and by touching herself in the genital area. There was thus brought to their attention the obvious risk of pregnancy and the desirability of taking urgent and effective contraceptive measures."[64]

Whilst sterilisation may remove the problem of possible pregnancy it does nothing to address other aspects of being a sexually active woman, notably sexually transmitted diseases and cervical cancer. Margaret Brazier questions the decision to authorise the sterilisation of P, focusing upon the consequences of sexual intercourse not addressed by sterilisation such as sexually transmitted disease or unwanted sexual advances. Brazier notes:

> "Pregnancy, the judge found, would be a disaster for P. No doubt that is true. But of itself that finding is manifestly insufficient to justify non-consensual sterilisation. Pregnancy is a disaster for all too many women. Yet no one suggests that all women likely to be incapable of coping with childbirth and/ or child care should be forcibly sterilised. P was to be sterilised because she is labelled as 'mentally handicapped' ".[65]

The assumption is made that demonstration of sexual interest is followed

[62] R. Lee & D. Morgan, "Sterilisation and Mental Handicap: Sapping the Strength of the State" (1988) 15 *Journal of Law and Society* 229.
[63] *Re M (A Minor) (Wardship: Sterilisation)*, *supra*, n. 52 at 498D.
[64] *Re B (A Minor) (Wardship: Sterilisation)*, *supra*, n. 38 at 1220B.
[65] M. Brazier, "Sterilisation: down the slippery slope?" (1990) 6 *Professional Negligence* 25 at 26.

shortly by sexual intercourse, without enquiring into the environment in which the woman finds herself (where she may be "exploited"), or whether she actually is sexually active, or heterosexually active. In *Re F*, it was assumed that F was in a "relationship of a sexual nature" which "probably involves sexual intercourse, or something close to it, about twice a month" from which "it is likely that she obtains pleasure".[66]

K. KEYWOOD

"Sterilising the Woman with Learning Difficulties — In her Best Interests?"[67]

"The courts' concern for the vulnerability of women with learning difficulties is well-founded, as many women run the risk of sexual exploitation. It is disappointing to note, however, that the judiciary are only concerned with preventing the physical manifestations of that exploitation (*i.e.* pregnancy), rather than putting an end to any sexual abuse that may be taking place. In the case of *Re W*, Justice Hollis commented that a twenty year-old woman could not be taught to protect herself from unwanted sexual advances and that consequently there was a risk that someone might take advantage of her. In confirming that sterilisation was in the woman's best interests, the judge did not address the woman's need to be protected from sexual abuse. Even after a sterilisation operation, the woman would still be at risk of sexual exploitation through physical and emotional abuse and sexually transmitted diseases. The only way to effectively combat such exploitation is the development of programmes which aim to foster independence and confidence. Craft outlines the situations in which abuse may take place. At no point does she state that persons with learning difficulties are inherently vulnerable due to their intellectual impairment. Instead she identifies the vulnerability as stemming from the person's environment, in the form of institutional hierarchies, unscrupulous carers and inadequate support services. The solution to the problem of vulnerability of persons with learning difficulties lies in the development of socio-sexual education programmes and the encouragement of decision-making and assertive behaviour. A surgical strategy solves nothing.

It is also unfortunate to note that the courts' somewhat misplaced concern for the woman's vulnerability seems to be at the expense of recognition of her sexual needs and desires. Morgan has rightly noted that the courts in the case of *F v. West Berkshire* failed to ascertain F's precise sexual needs and wants, commenting only that she described her physical involvement with her partner as 'nice'. In failing to ascertain whether F enjoyed penetrative heterosexual intercourse, more or less than other forms of physical contact, or more or less than contact with members of the same sex, the courts have remained indifferent to her sexuality. This may be because the courts feel that persons with learning difficulties, like children, should not be encouraged or allowed to explore their sexuality. Instead they must simply be protected from some of its consequences. The courts' perception of women with learning difficulties as asexual creatures, requiring protection from unwanted sexual advances provides them with a justification to approve sterilisation operations. Their reasoning, however, is ill-founded and ignores the reality of the experiences of women with learning difficulties."

---

[66] *Re F (Mental Patient: Sterilisation)*, *supra*, n. 42 at 1065F, *per* Lord Brandon.
[67] In J. Bridgeman & S. Millns (eds), *supra*, n. 17 at pp. 132–134.

5.4.i.d   Risks of non-permanent forms of contraception. The side-effects of non-permanent methods of contraception, readily dismissed as "subjective" when complained of by women who do not have learning difficulties, are emphasised in sterilisation cases.

Re M (A Minor) (Wardship: Sterilization), per Bush J.:

> "[A]ll the other possibilities, such as intra-uterine contraceptive device, or being injected with Depo-Provera at regular intervals, carry difficulties, risks, and side-effects . . ."[68]

Re P (A Minor) (Wardship: Sterilization), per Eastham J.:

> "Some contraceptive measures have already been put into effect, in the sense that Depo-Provera has been attempted, but abandoned because of the side-effects, which can be very pronounced when using that method of contraception. The side-effects can include vaginal bleeding (which occurred in the case of T), feeling unwell, gaining weight, headaches and breast tenderness — all relatively common complications."[69]

Suffice to say that the risks of sterilisation, an operation performed under general anesthetic, are ignored.

5.4.i.e   Eugenics. Despite protestations that the decision whether a sterilisation operation is in the best interests of a woman is decided solely in the light of her individual circumstances, do the courts in reality consider the probability that the young woman has a genetic condition which may be passed on to any child?

Re M (A Minor) (Wardship: Sterilization)
[1988] 2 F.L.R. 497 at 498–499, *per* Bush J.

"Dr Kingston had said that there was a 50 per cent risk of the mother's medical condition being passed on to any children of J; 50 per cent risk of severe mental retardation in any children that she might have. The implication there was that he was now favouring the operation on eugenic grounds, a matter which the House of Lords, in *Re B (A Minor) (Wardship: Sterilization)*, were careful to emphasize was not that [*sic*] case and should not enter into consideration in this respect.

We are the victims of the European history of operations of this kind in the way in which some countries and some regimes have misused this kind of operation for eugenic purposes. It is, therefore, right that we in this country should be particularly watchful that we do not go down that road, and that people should not be sterilized merely because they are severely handicapped or weak, or likely to give birth to children who may equally be so. Dr Goldthorp, I am satisfied, was not viewing it from a

---

[68]   *Re M (A Minor) (Wardship: Sterilization)*, *supra*, n. 52 at 499D.
[69]   *Re P (A Minor) (Wardship: Sterilization)*, *supra*, n. 53 at 183F.

eugenic point of view. The importance of his observation is not the eugenics but the fact that if J were pregnant then she would have to be monitored even more carefully than any normal, healthy adult because of this 50 per cent chance of it being passed on to any child she might bear. Tests would have to take place, which would be very uncomfortable for her and would have to be done under anaesthetic, whereby blood would be taken from the foetus by means of uterine puncture and tested in that way. So if the foetus was – and it was a 50 per cent chance – diseased, then an abortion would have to be carried out. It is that risk that one is entitled to look at, so far as the ward is concerned, and to say that this adds to the danger of her becoming pregnant."

The case of *Re M* is considered in the next extract in which Kirsty Keywood argues that sterilisation to prevent the birth of a handicapped child to a woman with learning difficulties perpetuates the devaluation of people with learning difficulties.

K. KEYWOOD
"Sterilising the Woman with Learning Difficulties – In her Best Interests?"[70]

"A[n] erroneous assumption lies in the belief that mentally handicapped persons will in turn give birth to children with learning difficulties, thus resulting in the decline of the nation's intelligence ... The view that parents with learning difficulties give birth to children with similar conditions has been discredited by studies which show that incidence of mental retardation through organic causes (*i.e.* biological accidents) among the offspring of parents with learning difficulties is equal to the rest of the population. There is some evidence to suggest, however, that parents with low IQs which cannot be explained by any organic pathology are more likely to have children with low IQs. This may be explained, however, on the grounds that persons with learning difficulties are likely to live in impoverished circumstances and it is impossible to say whether the learning difficulties of children are a result of living in poverty, or a consequence of being raised by parents with learning difficulties.

The fear of intellectual decline, though explicitly stated to have no relevance to U.K. sterilisation cases, clearly has some import on a judge's decision to approve sterilisation. The fact that a woman with learning difficulties might give birth to a handicapped child has been cited as a relevant factor in determining the woman's best interests. In the case of *Re M* Justice Bush was keen to stress that sterilisations on women with learning difficulties should not be carried out 'merely because they are severely handicapped or weak, or likely to give birth to children who may equally be so.' It is somewhat surprising to note that he then went on to authorise the sterilisation of the seventeen year-old ward on the ground that if she became pregnant, there was a fifty per cent chance of her disability being passed on to the foetus. In such an eventuality, the judge assumed that the foetus would have to be aborted. Such an assumption clearly smacks of eugenic ideology. The abortion of a foetus on the sole ground that it would be intellectually impaired if allowed to be born, adds to the myth that people with learning difficulties are less desirable members of society."

---

[70] In J. Bridgeman & S. Millns (eds), *supra*, n. 17 at pp. 133–134.

It is apparent from the above that the best interests test enables the court to present the evidence selectively to support the conclusion which it has reached. Derek Morgan seeks to redress this selectivity by revealing some of the "hidden facts" in *Re F*:

D. MORGAN
[1990] *Journal of Social Welfare Law* 204 at 210–211

"I want to suggest that there are facts about F's individual case, and about sterilisation as a method of contraception, which although known, do not form part of the public record of F's case. These 'facts' throw doubt on the wisdom of the court's examination of her case, and of the integrity of the forensic process which is supposed to serve her 'best interests.' Three such 'hidden' facts will serve to illustrate the point. First, Scott Baker J. accepts without comment the observation made by the clinician in charge of *both F and P* that P's mental illness is such that he cannot be held criminally liable for his actions, which might amount to unlawful sexual intercourse with a woman who is a defective (*sic.*) under section 7 of the Sexual Offences Act 1956. (It is arguable whether P would have a defence under s.7(2) by reason of his inability to know that F was 'a defective.'). But it is allowed to pass without comment that section 9 of the same Act creates a separate offence of procuring a woman who is a 'defective' to have sexual intercourse, as it goes unobserved that by allowing the intercourse to proceed the hospital may be aiding and abetting offences under those sections . . . The point of these arguments is not to deny that F may experience sexual pleasure, far less that people with learning difficulties do not have the same sorts of rights to experience as anyone else. It is, however, to reinforce the point that her sexual pleasure, let alone satisfaction, is assumed against the flimsiest and most contentious of backgrounds. Pregnancy is the only risk which is ever canvassed throughout the case. Abuse, sexually transmitted disease, including AIDS, perioperative death under general anaesthesia, may all be small and less significant risks than that of pregnancy (this is assumed and never assessed); not one of these risks is mentioned as a relevant criterion against which the best interests test should, or even could, be calibrated.

The last hidden fact is perhaps the most troubling. It emerged during argument in Chambers but does not form part of the public record of the case that P was having a relationship — whether sexual or not is not clear — with at least six other women in the hospital. Even where a particular partner was in contemplation, as with P, the courts did not canvass men's responsibility for contraception. As Carson so graphically puts it, 'there can be few medical contra-indications to the use of condoms'. And yet, even with such background evidence, the question does not even surface.

Against the fact of P's open philandering, which is blocked out from the judicial calendar, stands the presumption of F's promiscuity. It is in Scott Baker J.'s initial judgment that this paradox is most clearly seen. He was troubled that the effect of finding the proposed sterilisation unlawful would be to 'prevent F having a sexual relationship with P *or indeed anyone else*,' which 'would restrict the little freedom she was able to have to a point where she would *probably* feel frustrated and where the quality of her life would be impaired.' In other words, he found it inconceivable that F could find pleasure and satisfaction without a man in her life. There is, I think, an extraordinary echo here of the attitudes more commonly associated with the early twentieth century, which may make us wonder how far our thinking has really shifted in relation to people with a learning difficulty and their sexuality. As Torman wrote in 1916: 'There is no investigator who denies the fearful role played by mental deficiency in the production of vices, crime and delinquency ... Not all criminals are feeble minded, but all feeble minded are at least potential criminals. That every feeble minded woman is a potential prostitute would hardly be doubted by anyone.' Our vocabularies may be outpacing our values."

The cases discussed above are all concerned with the sterilisation of *women* with learning difficulties. There are no cases considering the sterilisation of men. In contrast to the view that the sterilisation of women with learning difficulties protects them (and society) from any unwanted pregnancy resulting from the excesses of their dangerous sexuality, Mason and McCall Smith suggest that the gender-based nature of the cases is illustrative of justice because there is no medical justification (founded in unwanted pregnancy) for the sterilisation of males.[71] The judgments reveal great deference to the medical profession and acceptance of the medical view as to what is in the best interests of the woman. Hollis J. in *Re W (A Patient)*,[72] made a declaration that the sterilisation of W would be lawful as in her best interests. Despite the fact that there was but a small risk of pregnancy her sterilisation was supported by a competent body of professional opinion and this seemed to satisfy the judge:

"Sterilisation would be, in all the circumstances, clearly in W's best interests. This was because pregnancy for W would be a tragedy; alternative contraceptive methods were regarded as unsuitable; and there was 'no practical reason' why sterilisation would be to W's detriment".[73]

Ian Kennedy says in his commentary on this case:

"[A]s Hollis J.'s judgment ... illustrates, the medical opinion in favour of sterilisation will carry the day, provided it is accepted that sterilisation is just another medical treatment. The court's involvement in decisions about sterilisation therefore can be seen to be merely symbolic. And given that the court's role is to rubber stamp the doctor's opinion, it is not clear precisely what its involvement symbolises."[74]

Alison Wertheimer criticises the medical model accepted in *Re B*, and wonders how the court can claim to be acting in the woman's best interests without attempting to discern her feelings and by looking to a surgical solution rather than seeking to educate about sexuality and personal relationships.[75] Margaret Brazier has suggested that the judiciary paid "lipservice" to the serious nature

---

[71] J. K. Mason & R. A. McCall Smith, *Law and Medical Ethics* (London: Butterworths, 1994), p. 88.
[72] *Re W (A Patient)* (1993) 1 Med.L.Rev. 234.
[73] *Re W (A Patient)*, ibid., 235.
[74] *Re W (A Patient)*, ibid., 236.
[75] A. Wertheimer, "Sterilisation: for better or worse?" (1987) 38 *Childright* 17.

of the procedure under question in *Re P* but failed to really analyse the issue of whether P was capable of giving or refusing her consent to the procedure at the time of the case or in the future. Consequently, she suggests that the judiciary seemed to be more concerned with protecting the medical profession from actions in negligence and was overly preoccupied with the others involved in the decision such as mother, carers and any child.[76]

Kirsty Keywood considers an "ethic of care" approach which takes account of relationships and the consequences for the woman within her family. The danger of this approach, she suggests, is that the woman may be sterilised in the interests of her family. Keywood, however, identifies the potential of this approach to focus upon the formation of relationships enabling the woman to develop control over her own reproductive life through, for example, education about sexual relationships and information about contraception:

K. KEYWOOD
"Sterilising the Woman with Learning Disabilities — Possibilities for a Feminist Ethic of Decision-Making"[77]

"The current judicial approach to determining the best interests of the learning-disabled woman test has served to perpetuate myths surrounding the sexuality of women with learning disabilities. Previous research suggests that these women are not sterilised to protect them from others, but to protect them from their own dangerous sexuality. Myths surrounding the sexuality of persons with learning disabilities and also myths surrounding female sexuality compound to provide very powerful justifications for confirming that sterilisation would be in the woman's best interests. In the case of *Re B*, for example, Lord Hailsham noted that the 17 year-old woman was showing signs of sexual awareness and 'would thus become a danger to others'. On the other hand the vulnerability of the learning-disabled woman is acknowledged through the constant reference to her child-like mental age. In *Re W* Hollis J. commented that a 20 year-old woman could not be taught to protect herself from unwanted sexual advances and that consequently there was a risk that someone might take advantage of her. It was not recognised, however, that the elimination of the risk of pregnancy would do nothing to eliminate the risk of sexual abuse.

At present, the best interests analysis adopted by the courts is in my view too vague and allows courts to take into account considerations that have no place in determining the fate of the learning-disabled woman. The Law Commission in their report, *Mental Incapacity*, have proposed that decisions on behalf of mentally incompetent persons should continue to be made in the patient's best interests, but that in making such a determination, regard should be had to the following:

1. The ascertainable past and present wishes and feelings of the person, and factors they would consider if able to do so;
2. the need to permit and encourage the person to participate, or to improve

---

[76] M. Brazier, *supra*, n. 65 at 27.
[77] In Feminist Legal Research Unit (University of Liverpool) (ed.), *supra*, n. 18 at pp. 61–65.

his or her ability to participate as fully as possible in anything done for and any decision affecting him or her.

3. The views of other people whom it is appropriate and practicable to consult about the person's wishes and feelings and what would be in his or her best interests;

4. Whether the purpose for which any action or decision is required can be as effectively achieved in a manner less restrictive of the person's freedom of action.

In the case of sterilisation procedures for contraceptive purposes, the Law Commission have further proposed that there should be prior court authorisation. In other words, the Law Commission have attempted to give some clarification and substance to the best interests test.

It has been suggested that Carol Gilligan's ethic of care could be used as a model for decision-making in cases where courts are considering the removal of nutrition and hydration from patients in a persistent vegetative state. It was suggested that decisions about the patient's care should be made by family members, taking into account the wants and needs of the wider family and that such decisions should not be limited to a consideration of the interest of the patient which ultimately may conflict with the interests of her wider family. My understanding of this argument is that the law in this area should recognise the importance of the patient's familial relationships, thus heralding a move away from abstract conceptions of justice and fairness and to a more consequentialist consideration of the patient's situation.

It is clear that the English courts have struggled to resolve the extent to which the interests of those caring for the learning-disabled patient should be taken into account when considering patient's best interests. I am reluctant, however, to endorse an ethic of care model for learning-disabled women whom it is proposed should be sterilised. I question whether Gilligan's ethic of care is too essentialist to fit within a legal system which is comprised of and controlled largely by men. I am also concerned that it obscures the fact that an ethic of care may be for some women a strategy for survival, rather than a celebration of female psychological development.

Notwithstanding these reservations, an ethic of care does at least emphasise the need for a model of decision-making that acknowledges the importance of relationships. Relationships are particularly important for people with learning disabilities. Those with communication difficulties are particularly reliant on the relationships they form in order to convey their wants and dislikes. Furthermore, the competence of the learning-disabled patient is dependent on the relationships she has with those who care for her. Determining the extent to which familial relationships should feature in health-care decisions taken in the best interests of the patient is rather more problematic, however. It may well be, for example, that the parents of a woman with a learning disability seek to have their daughter sterilised because they cannot effectively supervise her and protect her from sexual advances and the risk of pregnancy. Without sterilisation, the parents may feel that their daughter can no longer reside with them and will have to go into a residential unit. It may be feared that the family bond would thus become weaker without surgical intervention. Alternatively, a woman with learning disabilities who lives in a residential unit may be sterilised for fear that she would not otherwise be allowed to mix freely with male residents (and staff?) for fear that she may form sexual relationships and become pregnant. Again it might be feared that the woman's ability to form social relationships would thus be impeded were she not to be sterilised. In such situations sterilisation may therefore be perceived as the only way to maintain close family and social relationships. My concern is that the woman's reproductive freedom could be balanced against and sacrificed to her need to maintain relationships. I suggest that there are far more effective ways to assist a learning-disabled woman in taking charge of her sexuality and contraception, all of which would require the woman to engage into a deeper dialogue with her family and carers. Relationships do *not* have to be sacrificed at the expense of the woman's reproductive freedom.

Alternatively some women have not been able or encouraged to develop relationships and articulate their moral development. For them, an ethic of care based on relational decision-making could be problematic. This point was highlighted by Warnick J. in the Australian case of *L and GM Applicants and MM v. Director General, Department of Family Services and Aboriginal and Islander Affairs.* The Australian courts had previously recognised that the views of family members, particularly primary care-givers are relevant to the court's determination of the patient's best interests. Warnick J. concluded that the best interests of the child is the perspective from which all other facets and values must be viewed. In this case the parents' views about the desirability of having their daughter sterilised were not deemed relevant to the determination of the best interests of their daughter. The girl had no concept of her parents' wishes and had no feelings about whether those wishes were met or not. It could not therefore be said that the parents' views in this case were relevant. For these reasons, an ethic of care in Gilligan's terms would be problematic for women with learning disabilities."

The cases do not specify the factors that are relevant to a determination of best interests. The practice note issued by the Official Solicitor sought to be more explicit in setting out the appropriate factors, emphasising that the judge should be satisfied that the sterilisation was in the best interests of the woman and not of those caring for her or of public convenience. The factors to be considered by the judge should include: the incapacity of the patient now and in the foreseeable future; the need for contraception (including whether the woman is physically capable of procreation and is likely to engage in sexual activity presenting the possibility of pregnancy now or in the near future); the fact that pregnancy and birth may cause the patient trauma or psychological damage greater than the sterilisation operation; whether or not the patient is capable of caring for a child with a reasonable amount of help; whether there is any alternative less invasive method which could be successfully used; and whether all contraceptive methods have, despite supervision, education and training proved unworkable or inapplicable.[78] The *Practice Note*, however, has no legal force.

In its review of the provision of medical treatment to mentally incapacitated adults (referred to by Kirsty Keywood in the above extract), the Law Commission stressed the need to focus upon the individual, stating that "[n]o statutory guidance could offer an exhaustive account of what is in a person's best interests, the intention being that the individual person and his or her individual circumstances should always determine the result."[79] The Law Commission

---

[78] *Practice Note* [1993] 3 All E.R. 222.
[79] Law Commission Report No. 231, *Mental Incapacity* (London: HMSO, 1995), para. 3.26. Simon Lee draws upon the questions asked by MacDonald J. in the Supreme Court of Prince

emphasised that "[d]ecisions taken on behalf of a person lacking capacity require a careful, focused consideration of that person *as an individual*".[80] As noted by Keywood, the Commission recommended a checklist of factors to be taken into account. While this list should not be applied too rigidly it does at least make it clear that best interests are not to be determined by medical considerations alone.[81]

5.4.ii   *The right to reproduce*

In *Re D (A Minor) (Wardship: Sterilisation)*,[82] the first occasion upon which a court was asked to consent to the sterilisation of a young woman with learning difficulties, Heilbron J. considered that sterilisation amounted to "the deprivation of a basic human right, namely the right of a woman to reproduce, and therefore it would, if performed on a woman for non-therapeutic reasons and without her consent, be a violation of such right".[83] The appeal to the fundamental right to reproduce is rhetorically forceful, presenting in stark terms the infringement upon D's personal integrity which the proposed operation would have entailed. In subsequent cases the judiciary has been dismissive of the view that women with learning difficulties have a right to reproduce which would be violated by sterilisation. In *Re B*, Bush J. distinguished *Re D*, thus, not denying the existence of a right but denying that depriving B of that right would have any meaning to her:

> "... by depriving her of what Heilbron J. described as 'a basic human right
> ... the right of a woman to reproduce', one is in effect depriving her of
> nothing because she will never desire the basic human right to reproduce and,
> indeed, far from it being a question of not desiring it, on the facts of this case
> it would be positively harmful to her."[84]

Lord Hailsham, in the House of Lords in the same case, denied that B possessed a right to reproduce:

> "To talk of the 'basic right' to reproduce of an individual who is not capable
> of knowing the causal connection between intercourse and childbirth, the
> nature of pregnancy, what is involved in delivery, unable to form maternal

---

Edward Island considering *Re Eve* (1981) 115 D.L.R. (3d) 283 to suggest a more detailed list of relevant considerations rather than the vagaries of the best interests test ("From D. to B. to T.: sterilising mentally handicapped teenagers" (1988) 15 *Journal of Child Law* 15).

[80]   Law Commission Report No. 231, *ibid.*, para. 3.27, emphasis in original.

[81]   The Law Commission suggests that a sterilisation operation proposed to relieve pain and discomfort caused by menstruation (para. 6.9), along with abortion (para. 6.10) would come within the category of treatments requiring certification from an independent medical practitioner. Court approval should be sought for sterilisation for contraceptive purposes, being "any treatment or procedure intended or reasonably likely to render the person permanently infertile ... unless it is to treat a disease of the reproductive organs or relieve existing detrimental effects of menstruation" (para. 6.4).

[82]   *Re D (A Minor) (Wardship: Sterilisation)*, *supra*, n. 49.

[83]   *Re D (A Minor) (Wardship: Sterilisation)*, *ibid.*, 332h.

[84]   *Re B (A Minor) (Wardship: Sterilisation)*, *supra*, n. 58 at 208g.

> instincts or to care for a child appears to me wholly to part company with reality."[85]

This assumes that human rights are extended only to those who are capable of appreciating the content of those rights. So, should humans have a right to reproduce and a right to *choose* to reproduce? Grubb and Pearl argue that the latter is consistent with Arts 2, 3, 8 and 12 of the European Convention for the Protection of Human Rights and Fundamental Freedoms and the approach taken by the House of Lords in *Re B*. This, they suggest, is part of the right to self-determination and, if the patient lacks the competence to make a decision for herself, it must be made by another.[86] In *L and GM v. MM: The Director-General, Department of Family Services and Aboriginal and Islander Affairs*, Warnick J. considered the case was concerned with "the right to personal inviolability".[87] In this case the Family Court of Australia determined that sterilisation of a 17 year-old woman for non-therapeutic reasons was not in her "best interests". As Ian Kennedy in his commentary on this case suggests, "[t]he approach taken by the Family Court (and the conclusions reached as a consequence) show yet again the divide between Commonwealth and English law. Increasingly, the English courts march alone and to a different tune."[88] The significant difference, Kennedy suggests, lies in the focus within the Commonwealth upon human rights:

> "the ultimate issue is one of human rights. The exploration of best interests becomes clearer. The best interests test translates as a close examination of the evidence supporting the arguments for and against sterilisation within a framework of respect for human rights of the incapable person and, in Warnick J.'s elegant phrase, 'the responsibility of the capable for the incapable'."[89]

In the following extract Michael Freeman considers the underlying question of *why* we lay claim to a right to reproduce, seeking out a "justifying principle" which may found this claim:

M. D. A. FREEMAN
"Sterilising the Mentally Handicapped"[90]

"Discussion of the right to reproduce raises a number of questions.

First, does the right to reproduce exist? Two published articles on the question come

---

[85]   *Re B (A Minor) (Wardship: Sterilisation), supra,* n. 38 at 1216E.

[86]   A. Grubb and D. Pearl, "Sterilisation and the Courts" (1987) 46 *Cambridge Law Journal* 439 at 447.

[87]   *L and GM v. MM: The Director-General, Department of Family Services and Aboriginal and Islander Affairs* (1995) 3 Med. L. Rev. 94.

[88]   *L and GM v. MM: The Director-General, Department of Family Services and Aboriginal and Islander Affairs, ibid.,* 95.

[89]   *L and GM v. MM: The Director-General, Department of Family Services and Aboriginal and Islander Affairs, ibid.,* 97; N. Cica, "Sterilising the Intellectually Disabled: The Approach of the High Court in *Department of Health v. J.W.B. and S.M.B*" (1993) 1 Med. L. Rev. 186, compares the approach taken in the English courts with that taken in this, the first case to be considered in the High Court of Australia.

[90]   In M. D. A. Freeman (ed.), *supra,* n. 35 at pp. 70–77.

to different conclusions. Kingdom, who tells us that 'appealing to the right to reproduce is a liability in feminist politics and an obstacle to the development of social policy,' concludes there is no right as such to reproduce. She reaches her conclusion after analysing *Re D*. 'If,' she says, 'the possibility of a right to reproduce is dependent on a judgment about the presence or absence of medical grounds for sterilisation' (as it would be if the therapeutic/non-therapeutic distinction is accepted), 'then there is no clear basis for ascribing this right to an individual.' McLean, on the other hand, believes there is a right to reproduce, though, with both its extent and exercise limited, she has to conclude it is not a 'general' right. Gillon's view is similar: he writes of a general prima facie right 'not to be stopped.' Wald, who like Kingdom and McLean quotes the United States Supreme Court in *Eisenstadt v. Baird*, asserts that the right to bear children is a 'basic civil right of man [*sic*].' Carby-Hall, in a thoughtful unpublished paper, also assumes the existence of a right to reproduce, though as we shall see, holds that Jeanette for one did not possess it.

What none of these thinkers do is attempt to answer the question *why* we have (or do not have) the right in question. Both Kingdom and McLean make the mistake of examining the positive law and drawing their conclusions (which happen to be different) from their interpretation of legal codes. This is a misleading approach. Even if they were to find the right to reproduce embodied in a legal system (or even in all legal systems), it would not follow that a normatively necessary moral requirement had been established. Whether the right to reproduce exists is independent of what Heilbron J. said in *Re D* or the House of Lords in *Re B*. It depends on moral argument.

The other thinkers, to which reference has been made, tend to assume the existence of the right in some form or other . . .

It is not . . . difficult to explain why rights are important. A society without rights would be morally impoverished. Rights are important because, as Bandman has put it, they 'enable us to stand with dignity, if necessary to demand what is our due without having to grovel, plead or beg or to express gratitude when we are given our due . . .' In Feinberg's words: 'A world with claim-rights is one [in] which all persons, as actual or potential claimants, are dignified objects of respect . . . No amount of love or compassion, or obedience to higher authority, or *noblesse oblige*, can substitute for those values. Given the social history of this century it is not surprising that we should wish to construct a right to reproduce, or that the United Nations Declaration on Human Rights should talk of 'the right to marry and found a family.'

But we still need a justifying principle. Why do we have the rights we have and do we have the right to reproduce? One common answer links rights with interests. Such a view was implicit in Bentham and Ihering and is found in such contemporary writers as Feinberg and McCloskey. Thus, Feinberg writes that 'the sort of beings who can have rights are precisely those who have (or can have) interests.' . . .

In what other ways, then, can rights be grounded? There are any number of justifications. I will consider only a few, and only briefly. There is the intuitionist answer found in thinkers ranging from Jefferson to Nozick. But it offers no argument at all and therefore is unlikely to convince those whose intuitions tell them otherwise. It certainly offers little to resolve the sterilisation dilemma.

There are purely formal answers: the argument that all persons ought to be treated alike unless there is a good reason for treating them differently, that, in other words, persons have the right to equal treatment. But what is a 'good reason' for treating persons differently? Gender and colour have now been almost universally accepted as indefensible distinctions: age and intelligence have not. The principle looks egalitarian but potentially could undermine egalitarianism. Those who support the Lords' decision in *Re B*. will find differences between Jeanette and the 'normal' woman (lesser intelligence and competence, inability to defer gratification, the ease with which she might be led astray) and those who criticise the decision as unwarranted discrimination will argue that she has more in common with 'normal' women than separates her from them (similar feelings, drives, desires and so on). Ironically, if this line of argument is pursued, it becomes relatively easy to defend discrimination by the gifted against those of ordinary intelligence . . .

I believe it is possible to argue, as Melden does, that we have the rights we do because of our status as moral agents, and that we cannot explain what it is to be a moral agent without eventual reference to our rights. But here we come up against the arguments of Neville. He has two arguments in favour of sterilising the mentally handicapped. One (he calls it the 'humble' argument) maintains that sterilisation is in their best interests. His arguments here add little to what has already been said and need no further elaboration or comment. He calls his second argument 'philosophical.' It is an attempt to defend the policy of sterilisation against the Kantian objection that it is wrong because it denies the subjects their proper place in the moral community, treating them as means only and not ends in themselves, and also against the objection that it is wrong for community representatives to carry out a policy of doing violence to particular subjects.

Neville tries to answer both of these objections. He attempts to neutralise the fears of the objectors. Far from treating persons as things, rather than as responsible agents, Neville claims, he admits somewhat paradoxically, that 'to refrain from sterilisation is to do them the violence of preventing them from participating in the moral community in one of the most important respects of which they are capable.' The characteristics of the moral community he sets out as follows: (i) membership is relative to the capacity for taking moral responsibility; (ii) most capacities for taking moral responsibility need to be developed; 'ordinary socialisation' develops most of them; (iii) a 'general moral imperative for any community is that its structures and practices foster the development of the capacities for responsible behaviour whenever possible, and avoid hindering that development.' He agrees that the idea of a moral community is 'an ideal that exists in pure form only in the imagination.' He accepts partial membership for children. But as far as the mildly mentally retarded are concerned (and it should be stressed that he is justifying involuntary sterilisation of the mildly retarded), they, unlike children, do not develop in such a way that 'emotional maturity' is achieved at the same time as 'bodily maturity.' The example he gives could come straight from *Re B.* 'For instance, the emotional and intellectual capacities to manage conventional birth control methods, to adjust to pregnancy, or to raise children do not develop by the time their physical development and their social peers among unretarded people are ready for sexual activity.'

Neville is prepared to admit mildly mentally retarded people as members of the moral community on condition that they meet certain restrictions, the only one of which he mentions is involuntary sterilisation. What kind of a 'moral' community is it that can only admit sterilised members of the class of the mildly mentally handicapped? Neville gropes for an analogy and comes up with an 'imperfect' one. 'Just as people with bad eyesight may be licensed to drive with the restriction that they wear glasses, so mildly mentally retarded people may be required to meet certain restrictions in order to be members of the moral community.' The analogy is 'imperfect,' he believes, because 'a person cannot choose to be in or out of the moral community; one is either in the position to be held responsible or one is not.' I believe it is imperfect because it is quite fatuous.

Neville does not spell out his reasons for believing the mildly mentally retarded are irresponsible. I suspect what he has in mind is the supposed inability to care for any children parented, with the burden accordingly falling on the state. But fundamental rights cannot justifiably be abrogated merely because respecting them involves the community in expense. Furthermore, the evidence on parenting competence is shaky. Can incompetence be tested objectively? 'Normal' parents may also be deficient. There is 'clear injustice' when a parent 'adjudged "normal" is sometimes able to "get away" with a number of defects in parenting capability, whereas the retarded person, simply because he or she is labelled retarded, is liable to the instigation of sterilisation procedures.' . . .

The rights we have we have simply by virtue of being human. The right to reproduce is one of these rights. Involuntary sterilisation, save where it is carried out for exclusively medical reasons, denies an aspect of humanity. Adequate moral systems must recognise these rights and must do all that is feasible to sustain moral agency. Faced with a choice of changing the world or denying the less able (those who have not achieved and who may never achieve moral agency) access to it, Neville goes for the latter solution. It will be clear that I choose the former solution. If this prioritises the civil liberties of all, including the mentally handicapped, in the name of equal liberty for all at the cost of the general welfare, so be it. But the general welfare should not suffer for it is 'a public good . . . that [society] is infused with a sense of respect for human beings.' A good criterion for judging a society is the way it treats its weaker members."

Freeman concludes that the courts should focus upon the rights of women with learning difficulties rather than, as they do at present, upon their welfare, and that only in compelling circumstances should the right not to be sterilised be overridden.

Kirsty Keywood notes that the right to reproduce may ensure that women are not sterilised without their consent, but does not require any positive action ensuring that women with learning difficulties receive information about contraception and sexuality, and about how to cope with unwanted sexual advances. By comparison, the right to bodily integrity may encompass a positive duty to be provided with information, education and means of protecting oneself. Keywood considers the argument of Ian Kennedy that recognition of the harm done by the sterilisation of women with learning difficulties has to acknowledge reproductive capacity as a fundamental aspect of the identity of the woman concerned:

K. KEYWOOD
"Sterilising the Woman with Learning Disabilities — Possibilities for a Feminist Ethic of Decision-making"[91]

"An alternative/co-existing strategy may be to acknowledge the symbolic and actual harm that is done when a woman is sterilised. Ian Kennedy, in his article, *'Patients, Doctors and Human Rights'* states:

---

[91] Feminist Legal Research Unit (University of Liverpool), *supra*, n. 18 at pp. 67–68.

'Non-Consensual non-therapeutic sterilisation involves the destruction of an essential feature of a person's identity, of that which at a very basic level represents a sense of self. A woman may be mentally handicapped. She may have a mental age of four or five years. But if she is 25 she has many of the qualities of a 25 year-old. In particular, she has 25 years of experience and has seen how women and men are treated and how they react and behave. Some sense that women are different and the difference lies in the fact that they are women will have been acquired, rudimentary as it may be. Womanness is inextricably identified with reproductive capacity, although this may not be its only feature. To destroy irrevocably this reproductive capacity is, on this analysis, to destroy a fundamental, perhaps the only remaining element of a sense of self. Institutionalised and ignored, the woman is now to be sterilised.'

There is much force in Kennedy's analysis. It avoids some of the more problematic aspects of rights discourse, yet portrays the dangers involved in sterilisation programmes. Most importantly, this analysis makes clear the relationship between a woman's reproductive capacity and her sense of identity. One potential dilemma for feminists may be the reluctance with which women should continue to be identified primarily by their reproductive capacity. Whilst feminism has done much to reveal the gendered nature of medical controls over reproduction, an analysis of non-consensual sterilisation that locates female identity and feminist possibilities in reproductive capacity may be used against women to justify greater medical intervention in women's reproductive health, *e.g.* cervical screening, the performance of caesarian sections, the use of fertility treatments, etc."

Ian Kennedy concludes that women with learning difficulties should never be sterilised without their consent for non-therapeutic reasons. Kirsty Keywood's reservations are, nonetheless, hard to resist. The argument that the ability to bear children is a fundamental aspect of being a Woman (and Ian Kennedy admits that he is merely suggesting that it is *an* aspect) does not acknowledge that the ability to bear children is a fundamental aspect of the social construction of Woman. The absence of the ability to bear children (through infertility, contraception or the menopause) must not be taken to mean that the childless woman is somehow lacking in womanhood. Yet, if a presentation of sterilisation in this way were to ensure the protection of women with learning difficulties one might be prepared to accept this limitation, given its practical benefits. However, as Kirsty Keywood argues, such a formulation may effectively prevent the sterilisation of women with learning difficulties without requiring any positive action. Women with learning difficulties need education and assistance to develop the skills necessary to live with their sexuality.

Elizabeth Kingdom argues that we should avoid the appeal of the rhetoric of rights and instead focus upon the formation of concrete policies.[92] The

---

[92]   E. Kingdom, "Consent, Coercion and Consortium: The Sexual Politics of Sterilisation" in E. Kingdom, *What's Wrong with Rights? Problems for Feminist Politics of Law* (Edinburgh: Edinburgh University Press, 1991), p. 63.

danger of claiming that a woman has a right to reproduce (or the right to choose to reproduce) is the consequential generalisation of that right (following from the claim of men to equal treatment), which may work to the detriment of women.[93] Kingdom suggests that "appealing to a right such as the right to reproduce is a practice which is not only unconducive to engagement with practical policy formation but, deliberately or otherwise, diverts attention from it".[94] In sterilisation cases it would seem that not only does the judiciary resist the appeal to rights, but it ignores the issues of policy, placing paramount importance upon the assessment of the best interests made by the medical profession. Both the young woman who, in the knowledge that she does not want children, seeks, but is refused a sterilisation operation and the woman with learning difficulties who is sterilised without her consent in her best interests are measured against the ideal Woman. The law which, on the one hand fails to ensure that the former woman can obtain the operation which she seeks, and on the other assures the medical profession of the legality of the operation on the latter, at one and the same time responds to this ideal and reaffirms it. Women are not treated identically under the law, but commonly in comparison with the ideal of Woman as Mother.

5.4.iii *Therapeutic/non-therapeutic sterilisation*

La Forest J. in the Canadian Supreme Court in *Re Eve*,[95] held that sterilisation should never be authorised for non-therapeutic reasons, arguing that the "grave intrusion on a person's rights and the certain physical damage that ensues from non-therapeutic sterilization without consent, when compared to the highly questionable advantages that can result from it, have persuaded me that it can never safely be determined that such a procedure is for the benefit of that person".[96] Lord Hailsham in *Re B* commented that he considered, "the distinction they purport to draw between 'therapeutic' and 'non-therapeutic' purposes of this operation in relation to the facts of the present case above as totally meaningless".[97] However, the courts have subsequently made this distinction. In *Re E (A Minor) (Medical Treatment)*, Sir Stephen Brown P. in the Family Division of the High Court held that where the surgery was proposed for medical reasons (such as in this case relieving menorrhagia (excessive menstruation)), which would have the effect of sterilisation, there was no need to obtain consent for the proposed operation from the court, thus drawing the distinction between therapeutic and non-therapeutic sterilisation (for which judicial consent is good practice).[98] Despite the lack of clarity as to the distinction between a therapeutic or non-therapeutic operation, the Family Division has held that with adults, where two medical practitioners are satisfied that the operation is necessary for therapeutic purposes, in her

---

[93] E. Kingdom, *ibid.*, p. 72.
[94] E. Kingdom, *ibid.*, p. 84.
[95] *Re Eve, supra*, n. 47.
[96] *Re Eve, ibid.*, 32.
[97] *Re B (A Minor) (Wardship: Sterilisation), supra*, n. 38 at 1216D.
[98] *Re E (A Minor) (Medical Treatment)* [1991] 2 F.L.R. 585.

best interests and where no less intrusive means of treating the condition is available, a declaration of the court is not required.[99] This represents a further instance of one of the major themes of this section, that is the ease with which legal authority defers to medical knowledge, with the consequent triumph of medical control over female reproductive choice.

---

[99]   *Re GF (Medical Treatment)* (1992) 22 *Family Law* 63.

CHAPTER 6

PATHOLOGISING PREGNANCY

Once a private issue, the management of pregnancy and childbirth has moved into the public arena with increased monitoring of the progress of pregnancy and the development of techniques of medical intervention for use during birth:

V. Harpwood
Legal Issues in Obstetrics[1]

"Pregnancy is no longer merely a private matter between a woman, her family and the medical team who care for her. Although abortion has long been a political issue, other matters relating to pregnancy and childbirth have become political concerns, particularly since the 1970s, and are now the preoccupation of pressure groups, the press, governments, and the European Union. While health care in general in the U.K. is now subject to a new kind of regulation, pregnancy and childbirth have been especially identified as among the main targets for 'health gain' in the 1990s. The government hopes to achieve this target not only by improving the perinatal mortality rates, but by giving women more freedom, greater choice and a stronger voice in their treatment.

Numerous influences are responsible for the shift of emphasis in pregnancy from the private to the public domain. The evolution of the present trend can be traced most directly to the emerging consumer movement of the 1960s and 70s, coupled with the Women's Movement which established itself at about the same time. However, even earlier, the international recognition of basic human rights after the second World War laid the foundations for arguments advanced in support of the 'rights' of pregnant women . . .

Advances in medical technology, such as the use of ultrasound and amniocentesis, which offer much more reliable ante-natal screening and diagnosis than was previously possible, have led to greater involvement of women in decisions about their treatment and that of their unborn babies. New approaches to the training of midwives have led to more sensitive treatment of women patients during antenatal care and labour, and after miscarriage and stillbirth, and to the involvement of their partners in the processes of pregnancy and birth . . .

Perhaps the strongest inspiration for change has come from women themselves. Some of the women who experienced childbirth in the 1970s, and who had been influenced by new social, educational and political aspirations of women, identified the

---

[1]   (Aldershot: Dartmouth, 1996), pp. 29–30.

need to change attitudes towards pregnancy and childbirth. Support groups emerged to advise women about many aspects of pregnancy, childbirth and lactation. For example, the Society to Support Home Confinement was formed to resist pressure from the medical profession for hospital births for all. The Association for Improvements in Maternity Services (AIMS) was founded to examine critically the claims of the medical profession about many aspects of maternity care, and to campaign for the interests of women. These and other organisations, such as the National Childbirth Trust, provide information, education and support to women and their partners on numerous matters relating to pregnancy, birth and the postnatal period. However, many of the women who have benefited from the work of these organizations are articulate and well informed, and the people who most need information may not have been helped by what are essentially middle-class and professional groups."

As Vivienne Harpwood identifies, government policy has been to increase the participation and choice of pregnant women in decision-making during pregnancy and childbirth. Despite this focus, debates concerning the provision of services to, and decisions by, pregnant women who have decided to continue with their pregnancy are dominated by a perception of the woman and foetus in conflict. The social construction of motherhood demands that women sacrifice themselves during their pregnancy. Any decision taken by them which departs from the "norm" is perceived to present a threat to the foetus. Further, the extent to which a woman may be perceived to present a threat to her foetus seems to depend upon the extent to which she departs from the ideal of Woman as Mother who is "a white, middle class married wom[a]n of certain age[] and parity".[2] This understanding ignores the lengths to which women modify their lives to accommodate the demands made by their pregnancy and forgets that the relationship others have with the foetus can only occur through the mother who, with rare exceptions, rather than presenting a threat is the sustainor and protector of the developing foetus. The foetus is conceived of as an independent being trapped inside a potentially hostile body and unable to defend itself. Consequently, the law is often invoked to provide the developing foetus with means of protection.

6.1 Motherhood and the medical professions

The twentieth century saw the development of modern medicine and the new speciality of obstetrics, permitting professional obstetricians to take over the care of pregnancy and childbirth from midwives. William Arney describes how, whilst women have been the traditional attendants at normal births, with male midwives assisting at abnormal births, the latter came to dominate, assisted by developments in medicine which increasingly led to a view of the human body as a machine:

---

[2] H. Homans, "Discomforts in Pregnancy: Traditional Remedies and Medical Prescriptions" in H. Homans, *The Sexual Politics of Reproduction* (Aldershot: Gower, 1985), p. 139.

"All births, like all machines, carried in them the potential for pathology, the potential for breaking down. Technology that controlled and dominated the forces of birth, just as one dominated and controlled the forces of a machine, replaced midwives' attendance of birth. The boundary between normal and abnormal births became fuzzy, as did the division of labour organized around old dichotomies ... [M]en assumed control of the right to designate births normal and abnormal and rose to dominate the social organization around childbirth."[3]

After the Second World War, birth became an event to be managed:

"[E]very aspect of birth became more carefully controlled, as a structure of control I call 'monitoring' was deployed across a greatly expanded obstetrical space. Everyone — women, husbands or significant others, and obstetricians — got caught up in the monitoring's webs of power and so became more and more alienated from the event and experiences of childbirth."[4]

As the century progressed there was a trend towards the medical management of pregnancy and birth with increasing numbers of hospital births,[5] increasing use of foetal monitoring, ante-natal testing, intervention during pregnancy and invasive techniques during delivery.[6]

W. R. ARNEY
Power and the Profession of Obstetrics[7]

"[O]bstetrics literally discovered the fetus around World War II. This discovery had certain immediate political consequences, but it had more important long-term consequences for the profession as a whole. The fetus was the point of intersection of many social processes, and the profession could involve itself in those processes by following them outward from the fetus. A new language of normalcy emerged. Pregnancy and childbirth were no longer treated as discrete events with beginnings and ends, events to be terminated before pathology showed itself. Pregnancy and childbirth

---

[3] W. R. Arney, *Power and the Profession of Obstetrics* (Chicago: University of Chicago Press, 1982), p. 8.

[4] W. R. Arney, *ibid.*, p. 9.

[5] In 1927, 15 per cent of all births took place in hospital. By 1946 the rate had risen to 54 per cent and by 1964 the figure was 69.7 per cent (B. Beech, "The Politics of Maternity: Childbirth Freedom v. Obstetric Control" in S. Edwards (ed.), *Gender, Sex and the Law* (Croom Helm, 1985)). In the financial year 1988/89, 99.3 per cent of births took place in hospital (see J. Davies, "The role of the midwife in the 1990's" in T. Chard & M. Richards (eds), *Obstetrics in the 1990's — Current Controversies* (Oxford: MacKeith Press, 1992)). Reporting in 1992, the Winterton Report noted that the level of hospital births had remained fairly constant at 98 per cent over the previous ten years (*The Winterton Report*, Health Committee Second Report, House of Commons, Maternity Services, (1992) Vol. 1, para. 25).

[6] During the 1950s the caesarian rate was 2.2 per cent of all births. By 1983 it had risen in England to between 8.6 per cent and 11.5 per cent. Rates in consultant units range from 0 per cent to 25 per cent (*Changing Childbirth — Interventions in Labour in England and Wales*, Report of the Maternity Alliance, cited in B. Beech, *Who's Having Your Baby?* (London: Bedford Square Press, 1991)).

[7] *Supra*, n. 3 at pp. 94, 95 and 100.

were reconceptualized as a set of processes, an infinitely divisible series of intimately known events to be kept on their obstetrically known 'natural' courses by simple, undramatic, individualized, corrective management schemes. Pregnancy and birth were only one set of processes experienced by a woman, a system of systems within systems, and everything had to be considered in assessing a woman's trajectory through pregnancy and birth and in designing management schemes to optimize each birth. Monitoring and surveillance of every aspect of birth and every aspect of the environment surrounding birth replaced classic, dramatic interventions in pregnancy. A new order of obstetrical control appeared . . .

All of these kinds of modifications occurred around the time of the second transformation of obstetrics, just as the natural childbirth movement began to gather momentum. The profession of obstetrics had been able to gain for itself a degree of autonomy, one might even say sovereignty, over childbirth. But the sovereignty of a profession is always a contingent sovereignty, dependent in part on continuing support from the state and on the willingness of clients to remain clients, accepting the work of the profession as offered. The natural childbirth movement threatened the contingent sovereignty of obstetrics by telling women that they had alternatives to the models of pregnancy held by obstetricians and to the ways obstetricians managed pregnancy and birth. At the same time, particularly in Britain, the government threatened to amend the franchise of medicine. Both social bases of obstetrics, its franchise and its 'material,' were on the verge of being withdrawn. Also, based partly on wartime advances in technology, the tools of obstetrics improved and the profession gained greater access to the fetus . . .

[T]echnological advances are only a part of a more broad-based, penetrating 'monotoring concept.' The monitoring concept represents a change in the deployment of obstetrical power and a new mode of social control over childbirth which I will call simply 'monitoring.' Monitoring allows the profession to extend the obstetrical project out into the community and into every aspect of every woman's life. Power and control are magnified by making the object of control more visible and accessible, more 'known' through multiple monitoring schemes. After the monitoring concept was in place, obstetrics did not need to confine itself to the abnormal or potentially pathological birth; every birth became subject to its gaze. Monitoring permitted the 'lighter, more precise' intervention of a disciplinary power to replace the harsher, more dramatic interventions of a power which sought to confine the evil that pregnancy might present. Monitoring changed the focus of interest of the profession from the mother to the fetus and thereby justified a wider array of interventions while, at the same time, it allowed the profession to make the claim that births were more natural and 'physiologic.' "

An important point to be gleaned from this extract is the extent to which monitoring of pregnancy extended social control over women, as the monitoring expanded beyond the surveillance of abnormal pregnancies to all pregnancies and beyond the confines of the hospital to other aspects of women's lives. Further, the focus of monitoring was no longer the pregnant woman, but the foetus. Meanwhile, women have not been passive recipients of this "medicalisation" of pregnancy and childbirth, but have resisted the domination by medical science and the male dominated professions. For example, charities and voluntary organisations such as the National Childbirth Trust and the Association for Improvements in Maternity Services, established in

1956 and 1960 respectively, aim to provide women with information. Furthermore they undertake research into women's experiences of childbirth to encourage changes in the delivery of maternity services reflecting what women themselves want.[8]

The development of medical technology which has enabled an image of the foetus to be seen, facilitating testing of the foetus for disabilities and foetal surgery, may be welcomed by individual women. The image of their foetus may be comforting. Equally, it may be of help in enabling women to make decisions about their pregnancy.[9] At the same time, as Rosalind Petchesky argues, the technology has the potential to be used to pressurise women into making a particular decision. For example, the image of a developing foetus might be deployed in an attempt to prevent a woman from deciding to have an abortion. Further, the information provided by science has, to a certain extent, usurped the knowledge of women about their pregnant bodies and about their foetus. Whilst the information provided by the technology may be helpful, Rosalind Petchesky argues that it has to be integrated into women's experiences, not used to push them aside as irrelevant.[10] Foetal testing, for example, may provide women with information so that they can prepare for additional demands of a child with special needs or, in the light of the information given, make a decision to terminate the pregnancy. Michelle Stanworth reports a study of British consultant obstetricians, 75 per cent of whom said that amniocentesis was given subject to the requirement that the pregnant woman agree, before testing, to terminate her pregnancy should the test reveal a handicapped foetus.[11] The information provided by the advances in medical science (and it is important to remember that prenatal testing provides information, often in terms of chance, not a "cure") should not be used in this way to force decisions upon women. Many women have not, however, rejected medical science in favour of proclaiming pregnancy and childbirth as "natural" events. Rather, women have worked with the potential of medical science emphasising that scientific developments should be used appropriately. Obstetric technology has an important role in assisting, monitoring or re-assuring women experiencing problems in pregnancy or difficult labours but may not be needed by other women. This stance has meant that in recent years there has been a return, identified in *Changing Childbirth*,[12] to midwife care of normal births and the limitation of medical intervention to "abnormal" births.

[8] J. Leeson & J. Gray, *Women and Medicine* (London: Tavistock Publications, 1978), pp. 186–188.
[9] R. P. Petchesky emphasises the context in which this occurs, this being a society where visual images are important (R. P. Petchesky, "Foetal Images: the Power of Visual Culture in the Politics of Reproduction" in M. Stanworth (ed.), *Reproductive Technologies: Gender, Motherhood and Medicine* (Cambridge: Polity Press, 1987)).
[10] R. P. Petchesky, *ibid.*
[11] M. Stanworth, "Reproductive Technologies and the Deconstruction of Motherhood" in M. Stanworth, *supra*, n. 9 at p. 31.
[12] *Changing Childbirth — Interventions in Labour in England and Wales*, Report of the Maternity Alliance, cited in B. Beech, *supra*, n. 6.

V. Harpwood
Legal Issues in Obstetrics[13]

"In the past the main focus in obstetric care has been on the need to reduce levels of perinatal, neonatal and maternal mortality, which had given cause for concern for many years, and which to some extent had been accepted in previous centuries as the inevitable hazards of childbirth. In 1907 legislation was introduced to monitor the number of births and provide for some antenatal care, home visits and in-patient beds. A drive towards the provision of hospital and maternity-home deliveries followed . . .

By 1927, however, only 15 per cent of births took place in an institutional setting. This rose to 34.8 per cent by 1937 and to 53.7 per cent by 1946. Ironically, it was the middle-class women who today seek non-intervention regimes in childbirth and home deliveries who were campaigning for institutional deliveries at that time, partly because there was provision for analgesia in hospitals which could not be offered by many midwives or GPs carrying out home deliveries. They were supported by obstetricians who sought an extension to the availability of hospital deliveries on the grounds of safety. The demand for hospital deliveries increased steadily, and there were insufficient beds available to satisfy it by the 1950s, so a process of selection was instituted, based in the main upon safety factors, such as maternal age and parity. The hospital birth rate continued to rise steadily throughout the 1960s and 1970s, with isolated GP units becoming less popular. By 1992 the percentage of births in NHS hospitals with consultant units was 96.5 per cent, as against 1.4 per cent of deliveries in GP units, 0.7 per cent in non-NHS hospitals and 1.3 per cent home deliveries.

There is little doubt that clinical procedures and maternity provisions were developed with safety as a priority, and the Maternity Services Advisory Committee which was established in 1980 on the recommendation of the House of Commons Social Services Committee, made a number of proposals for making improvements in maternity care, one of which was as follows: 'As unforeseen complications can occur in every birth, every mother should be encouraged to have her baby in a maternity unit where emergency facilities are readily available.'

The received wisdom continued to be that institutional deliveries were safer, in terms of perinatal mortality, although the assumptions underlying this had been challenged by a handful of researchers in the late 1970s.

The much more recent government-funded report entitled *Where to be Born?* reaches the conclusion that there is no evidence that hospitals are the safest places to have babies:

'Lack of sufficient data means that it is not possible to conclude with any degree of confidence that babies born to low-risk women in hospitals with obstetric facilities are exposed to greater or lesser risk of death due to obstetric intervention than similar babies born elsewhere.'

It points out that those babies born at home who die soon after delivery are often premature or very small, and that such deaths frequently occur when home delivery was not planned and was 'accidental', before the woman could reach hospital. It cannot be denied that a hospital must be the safest place for those mothers and babies who require emergency treatment during or very soon after the birth. One problem

---

[13]   V. Harpwood, *supra*, n. 1 at pp. 41–44.

which has arisen is that, with the reduction over the years in home deliveries, GPs and midwives were becoming deskilled in intrapartum care and were focusing their experience more on antenatal practice and postnatal care of mothers who were being discharged from hospital earlier than in the previous decade, when a ten-day period of hospital confinement had been common. To a large extent this problem still exists, and is one reason why some GPs are now reluctant to take on responsibility for home deliveries.

In the hospital setting during the 1970s, mothers were required to accept clinical regimes in which they had little or no opportunity to state their preferences. Labour was often induced as a matter of convenience to suit the traditional 'working day', and routine enemas and pubic shaves for women in labour were very common. This approach reflected the paternalistic, 'doctor knows best' (or in some cases 'sister knows best') approach which for many years dominated medical practice. It was during the late 1970s that women's groups began to seek a new regime in maternity care which offered them more choice in the treatment they received, including the option of natural childbirth, and in 1975 the 'Domino' scheme was developed as a good working compromise. Under this scheme community midwives are responsible for the antenatal care of low-risk women, accompanying them to hospital and delivering their babies, as long as there are no complications. Women suffering no complications are allowed to return home with their babies after only a few hours.

Intimations of a change in official government attitudes towards priorities in maternity care are detectable in a House of Commons Social Services Committee Report in 1989 which states: 'We believe that maternity and obstetric services should be considered as a whole, and not exclusively in terms of their impact on mortality.'

The report of the House of Commons Health Committee on Maternity Services for the session 1991–2 adapts and expands this view with its statement:

'In some circumstances the quality of the professional help is literally vital. But it is the mother who gives birth and it is she who will have the lifelong commitment which motherhood brings. She is the most active participant in the birth process. Her interests are ultimately bound up with those of her baby. For these reasons we made the normal birth of healthy babies to healthy women the starting-point and focus of our inquiry. Getting this right is vital for our society as a whole and has a fundamental bearing on the quality of life of most women and their families.'

The Committee concluded that the time had come for a shift of emphasis in the development of policies for maternity services to give due weight to other criteria for success additional to the reduction of perinatal mortality, and that such a changed emphasis would require a change in the entire culture surrounding the provision of antenatal and obstetric care.

An important indication of the recognition now given to maternal choice is the approach taken by the Department of Health's Expert Maternity Group which produced the report entitled *Changing Childbirth* in 1993. This report opens with a chapter entitled 'Woman Centred Care', which emphasizes that maternity services should be tailored to the unique needs of each individual woman and:

'should take account of her ethnic, cultural, social and family background. The services should recognize the special characteristics of the population they are designed to serve. They should be attractive and accessible to all women, particularly those who may be least inclined to use them.'

The report promotes the involvement of women in the planning of their care throughout the antenatal period and during labour, and the provision of information to women about the available services and clinical options. There is a commitment to respect both the privacy and the autonomy of the individual woman. According to the report, the first principle of good maternity care is that:

'The woman must be the focus of maternity care. She should be able to feel that she is in control of what is happening to her and able to make decisions about her care, based on her needs, having discussed matters fully with the professionals involved.'

This approach represents a significant victory for those women's groups which for several years had been demanding that mothers should be given a greater say in the maternity care they receive. In theory at least, it is a triumph for patient autonomy over medical paternalism, and reflects similar sentiments to those expressed in the White Paper *Working for Patients*, with its declared aim of 'putting patients first'."

6.2 Legal response to the dangers of childbirth

Whilst the general trend is away from the use of technology and intervention in "normal" births,[14] the case of *Re S (An Adult: Refusal of Medical Treatment)*,[15] raised the question of the role of the law when the views of the medical practitioners on the appropriate management of birth depart from those of the pregnant woman.

Re S (An Adult: Refusal of Medical Treatment)
[1992] 3 W.L.R. 806, *per* Sir Stephen Brown P.

"This is an application by a health authority for a declaration to authorise the surgeons and staff of a hospital to carry out an emergency caesarean operation upon a patient, who I shall refer to as 'Mrs S.'

Mrs S. is 30 years of age. She is in labour with her third pregnancy. She was admitted to a London hospital on October 10, 1992 with ruptured membranes and in spontaneous labour. She has continued in labour since. She is already six days overdue beyond the expected date of birth, which was October 6, 1992, and she has now refused, on religious grounds, to submit herself to a Caesarean section operation. She is supported in this by her husband. They are described as 'Born Again Christians' and are clearly quite sincere in their beliefs.

I have heard the evidence of the surgeon, who is in charge of this patient at the hospital. He has given, succinctly and graphically, a description of the condition of

---

[14] This trend is emphasised by pressure groups, by women who are showing an increasing willingness to complain when birth has not been managed in accordance with their wishes and also by government, reflecting its view of the appropriate approach to childbirth.
[15] *Re S (An Adult: Refusal of Medical Treatment)* [1992] 3 W.L.R. 806.

this patient. Her situation is desperately serious, as is also the situation of the as yet unborn child. The child is in what is described as a position of 'transverse lie;' with the elbow projecting through the cervix and the head being on the right side. There is the gravest risk of a rupture of the uterus if the section is not carried out and the natural labour process is permitted to continue. The evidence of the surgeon is that we are concerned with 'minutes rather than hours' and that it is a 'life and death' situation. He has done his best, as have other surgeons and doctors at the hospital, to persuade the mother that the only means of saving her life, and also I emphasise the life of her unborn child, is to carry out a Caesarean section operation. The surgeon is emphatic. He says it is absolutely the case that the baby cannot be born alive if a Caesarean operation is not carried out. He has described the medical condition. I am not going to go into it in detail because of the pressure of time.

I have been assisted by Mr James Munby, appearing for the Official Solicitor as *amicus curiae*. The Official Solicitor answered the call of the court within minutes and, although this application only came to the notice of the court officials at 1.30 p.m. it has come on for hearing just before 2 p.m. and now at 2.18 p.m. I propose to make the declaration which is sought. I do so in the knowledge that the fundamental question appears to have been left open by Lord Donaldson of Lymington M.R. in *Re T. (Adult: Refusal of Consent to Treatment)* [1992] 3 W.L.R. 782, and in the knowledge that there is no English authority which is directly in point. There is, however, some American authority which suggests that if this case were being heard in the American courts the answer would be likely to be in favour of granting a declaration in these circumstances: see *Re A.C.* (1990) 573 A.2d 1235, 1240, 1246–1248, 1252.

I do not propose to say more at this stage, except that I wholly accept the evidence of the surgeon as to the desperate nature of this situation, and that I grant the declaration as sought, which will include provision for the necessary consequential treatment in addition to the Caesarean operation."

The question of law, which Sir Stephen Brown P. answered in the affirmative, was whether it was lawful to perform a caesarian section upon a competent adult woman despite her refusal to consent. Sir Stephen Brown P. looked for support for his decision to the U.S. case of Angela Carder.[16] Angela Carder had been fighting leukaemia for fourteen years and was believed to have overcome the disease when she became pregnant. Her leukaemia returned and she instructed her medical carers that they were to provide her with the treatment she required. She was twenty-six and a half weeks pregnant when the George Washington University Hospital performed a court-ordered caesarian upon her, appreciating in doing so that, whilst the operation increased the chances of the foetus surviving, it would probably hasten her death. Both Angela and the foetus died. The Court of Appeals overturned the decision of the lower court, ruling:

". . . in virtually all cases the question of what is to be done is to be decided by the patient — the pregnant woman — on behalf of herself and the fetus."[17]

---

[16] *Re AC* 573 2d 1235 (D.C.App. 1990).
[17] *Re AC, ibid.*, at 1237.

Re AC does not, as Sir Stephen Brown P. interpreted it, provide support for court-ordered treatment of pregnant women, indeed the exact opposite. The majority decision made it clear that it would have to be an "exceptional" case for the wishes of the patient to be overridden:

> "[I]t would be an extraordinary case indeed in which a court might ever be justified in overriding the patient's wishes and authorising a major surgical procedure such as a caesarean section . . . Indeed, some may doubt that there could ever be a situation extraordinary or compelling enough to justify a massive intrusion into a person's body, such as a caesarean section, against that person's will."[18]

Contrary to the tenor of *Re AC*, Sir Stephen Brown P. considered that if *Re S* were being heard in America, the court would be in favour of granting the application. His Lordship was persuaded that the circumstances in S's case were "extraordinary" enough.

As Katherine de Gama makes clear in her commentary on *Re S*,[19] the U.S. Constitution and consequent focus upon rights discourse means that the issue of reproductive control has been approached within a very different context in that jurisdiction from that prevailing in the United Kingdom[20]:

K. DE GAMA
[1993] *Journal of Social Welfare and Family Law* 147 at 148–150

"[T]hree years after Angela Cardner's death the decision was overturned. The much celebrated victory marked a turning point for American women in the struggle for reproductive autonomy. *Re AC* was the first court-ordered caesarian case to go to a fully considered appeal in the United States. Eight judges heard detailed evidence from over 100 interest groups, including health and women's rights lobbies. By a majority of seven to one the District of Columbia Court of Appeals held that pregnant women retain an almost unfettered right to determine their own health care choices, even if their decisions conflict with the medical profession's assumptions about the best interests of the foetus. Maternal rights could only be trumped by the 'most extraordinary and almost unthinkable circumstances.' The facts of Angela Cardner's case did not fall into this category. If a case as 'extraordinary' as this was unable to satisfy the test, a routine obstetrical complication such as a transverse lie surely could not.

In the United States, the legal construction of the foetus as a locus of rights is not uncommon, evidenced for example in the first instance decision in *Re AC*. The emergence of 'foetal rights,' backed by the sanction of criminal and civil penalties, is coterminous with the ascendency of the New Right as a moral and political force. The rhetoric of rights, appropriated by a coalition of anti-feminist doctors, lawyers and

---

[18] *Re AC, ibid, per* Terry J. at 1252.
[19] K. de Gama, Commentary on *Re S* [1993] *Journal of Social Welfare and Family Law* 147.
[20] The rights of pregnant women and the foetus under the U.S. Constitution are discussed by Janet Gallagher in J. Gallagher, "Prenatal Invasions & Interventions: What's Wrong with Fetal Rights?" (1987) 10 *Harvard Women's Law Journal* 9.

judges now provides the ideological underpinning for a campaign for curbs on abortion and checks on the activities of all pregnant women . . .

Curiously, notwithstanding the efforts of the foetal rights lobby, the foetus lacks full juridical status in the United States, falling somewhere between patient and person. Ironically, it is from the very case which popularly enshrines the principle that a foetus cannot be a legal person that the discourse of foetal rights has emerged. The landmark ruling of *Roe v. Wade*, which establishes a womans constitutional right to abortion remains an authority, qualified but not overruled. Implicit in the 14th amendment is a fundamental right to privacy, sufficiently wide to include the right to terminate a pregnancy in the first trimester. However, packed with the political appointments of the last two Republican administrations, the Supreme Court appears now to be engaged in an unceasing war of attrition against women's reproductive autonomy . . .

The problem for women, however, is not only the rolling back of *Roe v. Wade*, but more the context in which it is being subverted. Ironically, the very structure of a decision hailed as an affirmation of women's reproductive autonomy has opened the door to the state regulation of women's bodies and lives. As an immediate, albeit not inevitable consequence of the form in which rights are articulated, pregnant women in the United States who refuse to acquiesce to prevailing models of maternal conduct suspend constitutional rights elsewhere considered to be 'fundamental.' In establishing a right to privacy, *Roe v. Wade* was justifiably applauded as a triumph. But, what is less well remembered is that the Supreme Court asserted also that the State had 'an important and legitimate interest in protecting the potentiality of human life.' In the first, heady days of the 1970s it was assumed that the State's interest must necessarily be subordinated to a woman's right to make choices about her life and body. In the 1980s, the political landscape shifted. In later cases, the substance and the structure of the decision were distinguished. 'Parties' to a pregnancy began to emerge in the courtroom, their respective rights and interests constructed around the three distinct trimesters of pregnancy. In the first trimester, the right to privacy prevents state intervention, in the second the issue is framed in terms of maternal health, and in the third the state acquires an interest in safeguarding potential life. Foetal rights activists in the United States have subverted this shifting framework of rights in an attempt to compel the state to protect a viable foetus.

Where doctors have argued that a foetus has little chance of survival without a caesarian section or blood transfusion courts in North America have disregarded claims to freedom of religion and bodily integrity and compelled obstetrical interventions on the pregnant body. As few cases are reported, the extent of court-ordered surgical interventions remains unknown. Some studies suggest, however, that courts are willing to sanction non-consensual treatment in between 75 per cent. and 85 per cent. of cases. Certainly, some 25 non-forcible caesarians have been reported . . . In *Raleigh Fitkin-Paul Memorial Hospital v. Anderson* (1964) 201 A 2d 537 N.J., one of the first cases, decided ten years before *Roe v. Wade*, the Supreme Court of New Jersey sanctioned the administration of a blood transfusion to a Jehovah's witness in an attempt to save a 32-week foetus. The reasoning was as perfunctory and puzzling as that of the High Court in *Re S*. The court reviewed cases in which medical treatment could be compelled in order to save a *child* and cases where recovery in tort was available retrospectively for injuries sustained *in utero*. It then conflated the two only tangentially related sets of issues in a conclusion which insisted upon a *foetus's* right to legal protection. Consideration was not given to the issue of a woman's right to privacy, autonomy and bodily integrity. More recently, in *Re Jamaica Hospital* (1985) 128 Misc. 2d 1006 491 N.Y.S. 2d 898 S.C., the Supreme Court of New York refused, on similar facts, to distinguish the born and the unborn and assumed it to be entirely unproblematic to exercise a wardship jurisdiction over a foetus, despite the appalling implications for the pregnant woman with whom it remained inextricably connected. In *Jefferson v. Griffin Spalding County Hospital Authority* (1988) 274 S.E. 2d 457 Ga., an application to stay a court-ordered blood transfusion and caesarian deemed by doctors to be the only way to save a 39-week foetus was refused by the Supreme Court of Georgia. The autonomy of the pregnant woman was 'outweighed by the duty of the State to protect a living unborn human being from meeting his or her death.' As in so many cases of coercive intervention, medical opinion masquerades as incontrovertible fact. The baby was in fact delivered vaginally with few complications.

Our political and juridical traditions are very different. The courts in the United Kingdom have until now refused to exercise any kind of protective jurisdiction over a foetus. *Re S*, however, fits squarely into one of the disquietening caveats to the consent doctrine elaborated by Lord Donaldson M.R. in *Re T* [1992] N.L.J. 1125. Here, the Court of Appeal reaffirmed that, 'The law requires that an adult patient who is capable of exercising a choice must consent if medical treatment . . . is to be lawful.' However, Lord Donaldson tentatively suggested the principle would have to be reconsidered if a competent pregnant woman's healthcare decisions placed the life of a foetus in jeopardy. Such a situation, he noted, presented, 'a novel problem of considerable legal and ethical complexity.' Unfortunately, however, the reasoning in the case which provided the opportunity for the examination of the issue was pathetically cursory and confused."

As mentioned in the above extract, the High Court in *Re S* took up the exception mentioned by Lord Donaldson in *Re T (An Adult) (Consent to Medical Treatment)*,[21] that the only situation in which adults no longer possessed an absolute right to give or refuse their consent to medical treatment was "a case in which the choice may lead to the death of a viable foetus". However, in *Airedale NHS Trust v Bland*,[22] Lord Keith emphasised:

> ". . . it is unlawful, so as to constitute both a tort and the crime of battery, to administer medical treatment to an adult, who is conscious and of sound mind, without his consent: *In Re F (Mental Patient: Sterilisation)* [1990] 2 A.C. 1. Such a person is *completely* at liberty to decline treatment, even if the result of his doing so will be that he will die."[23]

It is not logical to talk of an "absolute right" to determine whether to give or refuse consent to medical treatment (including life-sustaining treatment) and then to include exceptions to that "absolute right". If the right is not an "absolute right" but a "qualified right", it must be clear exactly what the qualifications are and the principles upon which they are based. It is not clear from the judgment in *Re S* in whose interests the declaration was made that it would be lawful to perform the caesarian. If the declaration was based upon the interests of the mother, this is an unexplained exception to the "absolute

---

21   *Re T (An Adult) (Consent to Medical Treatment)* [1992] 3 W.L.R. 782.
22   *Airedale NHS Trust v Bland* [1993] 3 W.L.R. 316.
23   *Airedale NHS Trust v Bland, ibid.*, at 360H (emphasis added).

right". If the declaration was based upon the interests of the foetus, why should the "absolute right" to determine medical treatment be qualified because the woman is pregnant? Are pregnant women any different in terms of the legal rights which should be afforded to them as a consequence of the responsibilities which they have to the foetus? Derek Morgan suggests not:

> "Even if there may be a course to be set between the scylla of treating pregnant women as fetal containers and the charybdis of regarding the foetus as no more than uterine cargo, the price which we must be prepared to pay for protecting the integrity and autonomy of all competent adults is the rare, occasional risk of death or serious injury to an unborn foetus or to the woman herself."[24]

It is important to acknowledge that in the majority of cases pregnant women do follow medical advice. However, consent is considered to be of fundamental importance in the doctor/patient relationship recognising, ethically and legally, respect for the autonomy and self-determination of the individual and placing the "patient" at the centre of medical decision-making. To override the refusal of consent of a competent pregnant woman denies her the respect for autonomy enjoyed by other competent adults and facilitates invasion of her bodily integrity.

The case of *Re S* raises once more the question of foetal rights as the decision implies that the foetus had rights which took precedence over the rights of the mother, a conclusion which is contrary to previous authority.[25] To be acknowledged as a person is the first necessary step to claim legal rights which may then be posited against competing claims of other rights-bearing individuals.[26] *Re S* may cast doubts upon the established position in English law that the foetus has no legal personality until it is born and has an existence independent of its mother. The Court of Appeal confirmed in *Burton v. Islington Health Authority* and *De Martell v. Merton and Sutton Health Authority*,[27] that, where harm was inflicted upon a foetus *in utero*, it was not until birth that the damage occurred as it was nonsensical in both "law and logic" to hold that damage could be caused before existence.[28] The Court of Appeal in *Re F (in utero)*[29] concluded that the court did not have the jurisdiction to

---

[24] D. Morgan, "Whatever happened to Consent?" (1992) 142 New L.J. 1448.

[25] Impliedly vesting the foetus with rights at least at the point of birth (as in *Re S*) or after viability (as suggested by Lord Donaldson M.R. in *Re T*) returns one to the debate surrounding foetal rights considered in Chaps 5.2 and 5.3.

[26] See the discussion in Chap. 1 in relation to the recognition of women as legal persons. In the context of motherhood see further A. Diduck, "Legislating Ideologies of Motherhood" (1993) 2 *Social & Legal Studies* 461 at 476.

[27] *Burton v. Islington Health Authority* and *De Martell v. Merton and Sutton Health Authority* (1993) 1 Med. L. Rev. 103.

[28] The child "suffered damage at the moment that, in law, he achieved personality and inherited his damaged body" (*Burton v. Islington Health Authority* and *De Martell v. Merton and Sutton Health Authority, ibid.*, 104; discussed by A. Whitfield, "Common Law Duties to Unborn Children" (1993) 1 Med. L. Rev. 28).

[29] *Re F (in utero)* [1988] 2 All E.R. 193. See further the discussion of *Re F* in the context of abortion (Chap. 5.3 above).

make a foetus a ward of court. Acknowledging that in English Law the foetus did not have any legal rights, Balcombe L.J. further considered the consequences of making a foetus a ward of court which would necessarily entail exercising control over the mother as "an unborn child has . . . no existence independent of its mother". Given that to control the mother in the interests of the foetus would infringe the mother's liberty, it was for Parliament and not the courts to decide whether and in what circumstances control could be exercised, the limits of that control, and to establish safeguards:

Re F (in utero)
[1988] 2 All E.R. 193 at 199–201, *per* Balcombe L.J.

"However, these decisions only relate directly to the legal rights of the foetus: they are not decisive of the question before us, namely has the court power to protect a foetus by making it a ward of court?

The statutory provisions relating to wardship afford no assistance in answering this question as they are negative in character. Section 41 of the Supreme Court Act 1981 refers to a minor being made a ward of court and s. 1(1) of the Family Law Reform Act 1969 provides that minority ends on the attainment of the age of 18; neither Act contains anything to indicate whether it is possible for a person to be a minor before birth. The Rules of the Supreme Court are likewise silent on this point: see Ord. 90, r. 3(1) and (2).

Counsel, who appeared for the local authority before us, in the course of a persuasive argument referred us to the Infant Life (Preservation) Act 1929. Section 1(1) of that Act provides that, subject to an exception for an act done in good faith for the purpose only of preserving the life of the mother, 'any person who, with intent to destroy the life of a child capable of being born alive, by any wilful act causes a child to die before it has an existence independent of its mother' shall be guilty of a criminal offence. Section 1(2) provides that, for the purposes of the Act, 'evidence that a woman had at any material time been pregnant for a period of twenty-eight weeks or more shall be primâ facie proof that she was at that time pregnant of a child capable of being born alive'. Counsel conceded that, if the jurisdiction in wardship existed, it was likewise limited to a child capable of being born alive. Whilst I can understand the practical reasons for this concession, it does not appear to me to rest on any logical basis. If there is jurisdiction to protect a foetus by making it a ward of court, I do not see why that jurisdiction should start only at a time when the foetus is capable of being born alive. A foetus at an earlier stage of pregnancy is protected by the criminal law by ss. 58 and 59 of the Offences against the Person Act 1861, although the extent of that protection has been greatly reduced by the provisions of the Abortion Act 1967. However, I do not find these provisions of the criminal law of assistance in answering the question before us.

Counsel also sought to rely on Art. 2(1) of the European Convention for the Protection of Human Rights and Fundamental Freedoms (Rome, 4 November 1950; TS 71 (1953); Cmd. 8969): 'Everyone's right to life shall be protected by law.' However, in *Paton v. U.K.* (1980) 3 E.H.R.R. 408, on a complaint by the unsuccessful plaintiff in *Paton v. Trustees of BPAS*, the European Commission of Human Rights ruled that on its true construction Art. 2 is apt only to apply to persons already born and cannot apply to a foetus (at 413 (para. 8)). They continued (at 415 (para. 19)):

'The 'life' of the foetus is intimately connected with, and cannot be regarded in isolation from, the life of the pregnant woman. If Article 2 were held to cover the foetus and its protection under this Article were, in the absence of any express limitation, seen as absolute, an abortion would have to be considered as prohibited even where the continuance of the pregnancy would involve a serious risk to the life of the pregnant woman. This would mean that the 'unborn life' of the foetus would be regarded as being of a higher value than the life of the pregnant woman. The 'right to life' of a person already born would thus be considered as subject not only to the express limitations mentioned in paragraph 8 above but also to a further, implied limitation.'

Thus, far from assisting counsel's submission, Art. 2 of the convention, as interpreted by the European Commission, is in my judgment against him.

We were also referred to s. 1 of the Guardianship of Minors Act 1971, which (as amended) provides:

'Where in any proceedings before any court . . . (a) the legal custody or upbringing of a minor . . . is in question, the court, in deciding that question, shall regard the welfare of the minor as the first and paramount consideration . . .'

'Legal custody' is defined by s. 86 of the Children Act 1975 as 'so much of the parental rights and duties as relate to the person of the child', and this definition is incorporated by reference in the 1971 Act by s. 20(2) of that Act; see also s. 85 of the 1975 Act for a definition of 'parental rights and duties'. I do not derive any assistance from these provisions. They do not contain anything to suggest that they contemplate minority commencing before birth; in any event, the legal custody or upbringing of a minor is not in question when the subject matter of the proposed proceedings is an unborn child.

In the end it seems to me that the question is one of first principles on which there is no direct authority. However, the question has been the subject of academic discussion. Phillips 'Wardship and Abortion Prevention' (1979) 95 L.Q.R. 332 at 333 suggests that the courts should be prepared to extend jurisdiction in wardship to an unborn child. Lyon and Bennett 'Abortion — Whose Decision' (1979) 9 Fam. Law 35 at 37 suggest that, while an extension of the notion of wardship would be required to make it applicable to a foetus, that would be 'a logical and natural development'. Radevsky 'Wardship and Abortion' (1980) 130 N.L.J. 813 and Lowe 'Wardship and Abortion Prevention — Further Observations' (1980) 96 L.Q.R. 29 and 'Wardship and Abortion — A Reply' (1981) 131 N.L.J. 561 are to the opposite effect. Both these latter make the point that any such extension of the law should be left to Parliament, while Lowe stresses the point that any such extension of wardship would necessarily involve controlling the mother. In the latest edition of his work on *Wards of Court* (2nd edn, 1986) p. 18, Lowe partially resiles from his previous attitude, suggesting that 'since the court is occasionally faced with novel circumstances the door should, possibly, be left open for the future development of the jurisdiction in this respect'.

Approaching the question as one of principle, in my judgment there is no jurisdiction to make an unborn child a ward of court. Since an unborn child has, *ex hypothesi*, no existence independent of its mother, the only purpose of extending the jurisdiction to include a foetus is to enable the mother's actions to be controlled. Indeed, that is the purpose of the present application. In the articles already cited Lowe gives examples of how this might operate in practice (96 L.Q.R. 29 at 30):

> 'It would mean, for example, that the mother would be unable to leave the jurisdiction without the court's consent. The court being charged to protect the foetus' welfare would surely have to order the mother to stop smoking, imbibing alcohol and indeed any activity which might be hazardous to the child. Taking it to the extreme were the court to be faced with saving the baby's life or the mother's it would surely have to protect the baby's.'

Another possibility is that the court might be asked to order that the baby be delivered by Caesarian section: in this connection see Fortin 'Legal Protection for the Unborn Child' (1988) 51 M.L.R. 54 at 81 and the U.S. cases cited in note 16, in particular *Jefferson v. Griffin Spalding County Hospital Authority* (1981) 274 SE 2d 457. Whilst I do not accept that the priorities mentioned in the last sentence of the passage cited above are necessarily correct, it would be intolerable to place a judge in the position of having to make such a decision without any guidance as to the principles on which his decision should be based. If the law is to be extended in this manner, so as to impose control over the mother of an unborn child, where such control may be necessary for the benefit of that child, then under our system of parliamentary democracy it is for Parliament to decide whether such controls can be imposed and, if so, subject to what limitations or conditions. Thus, under the Mental Health Act 1983, to which we were also referred, there are elaborate provisions to ensure that persons suffering from mental disorder or other similar conditions are not compulsorily admitted to hospital for assessment or treatment without proper safeguards: see ss. 2, 3 and 4 of that Act. If Parliament were to think it appropriate that a pregnant woman should be subject to controls for the benefit of her unborn child, then doubtless it will stipulate the circumstances in which such controls may be applied and the safeguards appropriate for the mother's protection. In such a sensitive field, affecting as it does the liberty of the individual, it is not for the judiciary to extend the law."

Staughton L.J. concluded that the court did not have jurisdiction to ward a foetus and emphasised that the orders sought by the local authority in the interests of the foetus were directed at the pregnant woman:

Re F (in utero)
[1988] 2 All E.R. 193 at 210d–h, *per* Staughton L.J.

"It will be observed that all [the orders sought by the local authority] are orders directed at the mother, as in the nature of things they must be until the child is born.

When the wardship jurisdiction of the High Court is exercised, the rights, duties and powers of the natural parents are taken over or superseded by the orders of the court. Until a child is delivered it is not, in my judgment, possible for that to happen. The court cannot care for a child, or order that others should do so, until the child is born; only the mother can. The orders sought by the local authority are not by their nature such as the court can make in caring for the child; they are orders which seek directly to control the life of both mother and child. As was said by the European Commission of Human Rights in *Paton v. UK* (1980) 3 E.H.R.R. 408 at 415 (para.

19): 'The 'life' of the foetus is intimately connected with, and cannot be regarded in isolation from, the life of the pregnant woman.'

We were urged by counsel to extend the wardship jurisdiction; but, in my judgment, we are being asked to create a new, perhaps similar, jurisdiction to care for mother and foetus together. I can see that there may be arguments that the court should have such powers. One would hope that they would be needed very rarely, but a need may well exist. I do not think that it is for this court to create that jurisdiction. The exercise of it would, in this case, directly impinge on the liberty of the mother. Where Parliament has granted similar powers, for example in the Mental Health Act 1983, safeguards and limits have been provided; there have to be certificates of qualified doctors who have examined the patient, and such like. No doubt that was done after careful consideration of the topic, and of the circumstances in which a person's liberty should be taken away.

This court is in no position to inquire into the problem of mothers who may neglect or harm their children before birth, or to decide in what circumstances and with what safeguards there should be power to restrict the liberty of the mother in order to prevent that happening. Even if the court were entitled to extend the jurisdiction, as counsel puts it, in that way, it is not a power which the court should exercise."

The coerced, court-ordered treatment of pregnant women places limits upon the autonomous decisions of pregnant women whose rights are subordinated to the rights of the foetus. Previous authority suggests that the rights of the pregnant woman to self-determination must override the claims of the foetus of a right to life. Alison Diduck considers the feminist criticisms of rights discourse in the context of pregnancy wherein the argument for the ascription of rights to the foetus as an isolated atomistic individual is inconsistent with the experience of pregnancy and the connection between the pregnant woman and the foetus which she carries:

A. DIDUCK
"Legislating Ideologies of Motherhood"[30]

"[M]uch has been written about society's right or its responsibility to protect 'unborn children'. At the risk of oversimplifying the literature, the argument goes something like this: once a woman chooses to forego a termination of the pregnancy, she is responsible for ensuring the foetus comes to no harm, and society has an obligation to ensure that she does so. The reasoning behind this is that the foetus is thought to be a human life, a child, entitled to full recognition by and protection of the law. The problem with this picture is that women are rights-bearing entities as well, and sometimes the interests of these two legal 'persons' conflict. When such a conflict occurs, there is a *competition* for rights, and many speak at this stage of 'balancing' the interests and the rights of each.

More recently, however, the illusory nature of the mother/foetus dichotomy has been explored. Whether by celebrating women's experiences of pregnancy (including that of being one and at the same time two), or by falling back on women's recent and

---

[30] A. Diduck, *supra*, n. 26 at 463–464.

hard won recognition as rights-bearing individuals to whom some degree of personal autonomy and dignity is owed, much of the literature has been an examination of the relationship of abstract ideas to their embodiment in legislation. For example, Barbara Katz Rothman attempts to present a view of conception, gestation and birth that is woman-centred rather than as an experience which is defined by male language and male perspectives. Rather than constructing parenthood as a purely genetic relationship, she proposes a view of parenthood which values nurturing, connection and caring relationships more than genetic ties, and then constructs a model feminist policy, including legal principles, in its light.

Brettel Dawson, too, notes the ill fit of reproduction to the language of the law when she states 'there isn't a language for foetuses that recognizes their integration with women; there isn't a language for (pregnant) women which integrates their connection with the foetus'. It is clear that the competing rights analysis is not appropriate in this woman-centred world of reproduction."

In *Attorney-General Reference (No. 3 of 1994)*,[31] the Court of Appeal held that where injuries are inflicted upon a foetus *in utero* or upon a pregnant woman so that the child is born alive but subsequently dies as a result of the injuries, the accused may be guilty of murder or manslaughter. This reference confirmed that it is not murder to kill a foetus *in utero* (although it may be an offence contrary to the Offences Against the Person Act 1861, s. 58, or the Infant Life (Preservation) Act 1929 (see Chap. 5.3 above)). Considering the case in which the accused intended to kill or cause serious bodily harm to the foetus *in utero*, the problem that the accused would not have the required intent to kill a "person in being" was dealt with by seeing the woman and the foetus as a "unity". The objections to this approach are considered in the following commentary upon the case:

A. Grubb
"Commentary on *Attorney–General's Reference (No. 3 of 1994)*"[32]

"*Is the 'Unity of Persons' Approach Correct?*: It seems reasonably certain that the Court of Appeal opted for the 'unity of persons' approach believing that the only alternative was to see the unborn child as a legal person in itself *i.e.*, a 'separate persons' approach. Potentially, the latter might have startling consequences when the law was concerned with the relationship between the mother and her baby. Under the 'separate persons' approach both would be legal persons with consequent legal rights. In many situations there would be a clash of these rights which would resound through much of the law relating to abortion (which would require re-thinking) and to, for example, maternal obligations to the unborn child. The law would have to decide whose right should prevail in any given situation of conflict. The implications of this approach makes it an unattractive option for English law and, as we have seen, English law has rejected it.

By contrast, the 'unity of persons' approach makes these problems melt away since

---

[31] *Attorney–General's Reference (No 3 of 1994)* (1995) 3 Med. L. Rev. 302.
[32] *Ibid.*, 306–307.

there is only one legal person in existence. It would, for example, justify the ventilation of a comatose pregnant woman who had no hope of recovery long enough to allow the fetus to develop so as to have a fighting chance of survival once born. It is problematic to see such intervention as being in the mother's, as opposed to the fetus', best interests but under the 'unity of persons' approach this would be in the *mother's* best interests. If this approach is rejected, another explanation for the legality of this kind of intervention must be found which is by no means impossible.

Nevertheless, the Court of Appeal's adoption of the 'unity of persons' approach is itself problematic because it sees the fetus as merely a body part of the mother: it is just another organ comprised in the mother's biological entity.

First, this does not sit comfortably with most people's perception of the unborn child. It contradicts general perceptions that there is something special about an unborn child: it is not merely the flesh and blood of the mother. Indeed, of course, it is genetically distinct from the mother. Few parents who have seen an ultra scan of their unborn child would subscribe to the 'unity of persons' approach. It is not accepted by the vast majority of feminist writers who recognise that the specialness of the entity itself and the relationship it has with its mother confound the rather crude description imposed by the 'unity of persons' approach. In reality, (potential) parents, doctors and others do not behave as if the mother is merely growing a vegetable.

Secondly, the 'unity of persons' approach is outwith the law's stance in other areas. Putting it shortly, there would never be a legal entity to protect or whose interests could be considered by the law. Thus, any law which took account of the fetus would not be coherent. Legislation limiting the availability of abortion could only be justified on the basis of maternal interests, *i.e.* health. The Abortion Act 1967 plainly is not consistent with this. Equally, the law could not protect the fetus against the mother's decision, for example, to refuse medical treatment that will harm it. The decision in *Re S (Adult: Refusal of Medical Treatment)* [1992] 4 All E.R. 671 is *only* explicable on the basis of the law concedes some kind of separateness to the fetus. *Re S* must be wrong if the 'unity of persons' approach is fully embraced by English law. Of course, to reject this approach does not necessarily mean that *Re S* is correct. Even those who argue that *Re S* represents a wrong turn for English law, do not do so on the basis that the fetus is merely part of the mother. The argument is more subtle than that looking at whether the fetus' interests are sufficiently strong to override the mother's prima facie right to refuse treatment and the legal policy argument of whether the law should countenance coercive action against a competent adult. It has also been suggested that the pre-natal injury cases cannot stand with the 'unity of persons' approach. If this is correct, the English law would require re-consideration (*e.g., Burton v. Islington H.A.* [1992] 3 All E.R. 833 (C.A.) and Congenital Disabilities (Civil Liability) Act 1976, s.1).

So where does this leave the law? If neither the 'unity of persons' or the 'separateness of persons' approach makes common sense or sensible law, what should the law do? The solution lies in an approach which is now widely recognised of seeing the fetus as a *de facto* entity (though not a legal person) which has interests that the law must take account of when any decision is made, or action taken, affecting the fetus. As an approach, it has considerable support amongst leading feminist scholars. For example, Professor Catharine MacKinnon describes the status of a fetus as follows:

'More than a body part but less than a person, where it is, is largely what it is. From the standpoint of the pregnant woman, it is both me and not me. It 'is' the pregnant woman in the sense that it is in her and of her and is hers more than anyone's. It 'is not' her in the sense that she is not all that is there.'

Some have termed this *de jure* unity but *de facto* separateness as a co-existence "Not-One-But-Not-Two". Why should English law embrace this approach? There are a number of reasons. First, it is more flexible than the other two approaches and allows for a sensitive accommodation of the interests of the mother and fetus. It does not dictate, merely by its description, whose interests should prevail in mother and fetus cases. It does not, for example, mean that the mother may always have her way regardless of the effect on the fetus; neither may the claims of the fetus always trump the claims of the mother. It allows for both sets of interests to be taken into account. Secondly, it actually reflects how we popularly conceptualise the position of the pregnant woman. Thirdly, alien though all this may sound to the more rigid, and black or white, attitude of English law, it is in fact reflected in the law already. It is what much of English law concerned with the fetus is actually based on: for example, when an abortion may be carried out; that the contingent interests of a fetus may justify a pre-natal injury action in tort or inheritance by as-yet-unborn children and why the courts have genuine concerns when a pregnant woman's refusal of medical treatment may harm her fetus."

As Andrew Grubb points out, if the woman and foetus are to be perceived legally as a "unity of persons", the decision in *Re S* must be wrong as it accords some recognition to the foetus as a separate entity.

Examining the position in the U.S., Dawn Johnsen argues that foetal rights which crystallise upon live birth, such as inheritance rights or rights to sue in respect of injury inflicted pre-natally, and the extension of criminal sanctions for harm caused *in utero* to a child subsequently born alive, are based upon the connection of the foetus with its parents and the interests they have in addition to the interests of the subsequently born child. These rights she suggests are of a very different nature from those given to the "fetus *qua* fetus".[33] From court ordered treatment, to removing a child from its mother because of "prenatal abuse", or incarcerating a woman to prevent "abuse" of her foetus through, for example, the use of drugs, there is potential for control over pregnant women to be extended:

D. E. JOHNSEN
"The Creation of Fetal Rights: Conflicts with Women's Constitutional Rights to Liberty, Privacy and Equal Protection"[34]

"The creation of fetal rights that can be used to the detriment of pregnant women is a very recent phenomenon, and thus far has occurred in only a relatively small number of cases. Yet, absent an increased awareness of the costs to women's autonomy, these rights will almost certainly continue to expand. Given the fetus's complete physical

---

[33] D. E. Johnsen, "The Creation of Fetal Rights: Conflicts with Women's Constitutional Rights to Liberty, Privacy, and Equal Protection" (1986) 95 *Yale Law Journal* 599 at 604.
[34] D. E. Johnsen, *ibid.*, 605–609.

dependence on and interrelatedness with the body of the woman, virtually every act of the pregnant woman has some effect on the fetus. A woman could be held civilly or criminally liable for fetal injuries caused by accidents resulting from maternal negligence, such as automobile or household accidents. She could also be held liable for any behavior during her pregnancy having potentially adverse effects on her fetus, including failing to eat properly, using prescription, nonprescription and illegal drugs, smoking, drinking alcohol, exposing herself to infectious disease or to workplace hazards, engaging in immoderate exercise or sexual intercourse, residing at high altitudes for prolonged periods, or using a general anesthetic or drugs to induce rapid labor during delivery. If the current trend in fetal rights continues, pregnant women would live in constant fear that any accident or 'error' in judgment could be deemed 'unacceptable' and become the basis for a criminal prosecution by the state or a civil suit by a disenchanted husband or relative.

In addition to advocating expansion of criminal penalties and tort recovery, commentators have advocated a wide range of new forms of state regulation of pregnant women's behaviour. One such suggestion is that public benefits be withheld from pregnant women who refuse to submit to physical examinations or to abstain from drugs or alcohol. 'High risk' parents could be required to undergo genetic or post-conception screening. Pregnant women could be prohibited from drinking alcohol and required to submit to breathalyzer tests to ensure compliance. One commentator has even proposed allowing punitive damages against women who intentionally harm their fetuses.

Perhaps the most foreboding aspect of allowing increased state involvement in pregnant women's lives in the name of the fetus is that the state may impose direct injunctive regulation of women's actions. When expanded to cover fetuses, child custody provisions may be used as a basis for seizing custody of the fetus to control the woman's behavior. As noted by one commentator, '[t]he principal difficulty with the state taking custody of a conceived but unborn child is that the mother herself necessarily is taken into custody.' This fact forcefully demonstrates the threat to women's autonomy inherent in the creation of any fetal right that treats the fetus as an entity independent from the woman. Nevertheless, advocates of fetal rights have proposed that the state increasingly take custody of fetuses and, in some cases, civilly commit pregnant women to 'protect' their fetuses.

This threat appears particularly immediate in the area of coerced medical treatment of pregnant women. Women already have been compelled to submit to blood transfusions and cesarean sections against their will, when it was believed to be in the interest of the fetus. This phenomenon, troubling in its own right, is susceptible to even more dangerous expansion given new procedures in fetal therapy and fetal surgery. When fully developed, these procedures, which had promised to enhance women's reproductive freedom, may be used to restrict it. Some in the medical profession advocate compulsory medical treatment, including forced surgery, where it is determined by medical professionals to be in the interest of the fetus."

As discussed by Dawn Johnsen, in addition to the employment of civil law in the U.S. to control the activities of pregnant women, the criminal law has been invoked both to detain pregnant women for the period of their pregnancy and to punish women post delivery for "harming" the foetus during the course of their pregnancy.[35] English Law has not gone so far as to prosecute women for

---

[35] Discussed by M. Thomson, "After *Re S*" (1994) 2 Med.L.Rev. 127 at 137–140.

causing "harm" to the foetus by their activities whilst pregnant.[36] Possible prosecutions might include those for drugs offences when the foetus is born an addict or for child neglect when a low birth weight foetus is born to a mother who smoked, drank excessive amounts of alcohol or failed to eat a proper diet. However, in *D (A Minor) v. Berkshire C.C.,*[37] a baby, which after birth suffered drug withdrawal symptoms following from her exposure to drugs whilst *in utero*, was removed from her parents at birth and put into foster care. The House of Lords upheld the care order on the grounds that the court, in deciding whether the child's development or health was being impaired or whether the child was being ill-treated, should consider not only the present but also the past circumstances, including the treatment of the foetus *in utero*. Whilst the mother in this case was not subject to the punishment of the criminal law, she was punished by the removal of her child from her without any consideration of her ability to care for that child after birth.[38]

Women who are pregnant change their behaviour in many ways in order to ensure their own health and that of the foetus. Dawn Johnsen argues that the decisions made by a pregnant woman must be understood in the context of all the circumstances of her life. When the State exercises control over her in what are purported to be the interests of the foetus, the extent to which the interests of the foetus are integral to her decision-making are not acknowledged:

D. E. JOHNSEN
"The Creation of Fetal Rights: Conflicts with Women's Constitutional Rights to Liberty, Privacy and Equal Protection"[39]

"Allowing the state to control women's actions in the name of fetal rights, however, reflects a view of the fetus as an entity separate from the pregnant woman, with interests that are hostile to her interests. In fact, by granting rights to the fetus assertable against the pregnant woman, and thus depriving the woman of decisionmaking autonomy, the state affirmatively acts to create an adversarial relationship between the woman and the fetus. By separating the interests of the fetus from those of the pregnant woman, and then examining, often post hoc, the effect on the fetus of isolated decisions made by the woman on a daily basis during pregnancy, the state is likely to exaggerate the potential risks to the fetus and undervalue the costs of the loss of autonomy suffered by the woman.

Where the woman has chosen not to exercise her right to abort her fetus, she is likely to care deeply about the well-being of the child she will bear. It is therefore more

---

[36] J. R. Leiberman, M. Mazor, W. Chaim & A. Cohen in "The Fetal Right to Live" (1979) 53 *Obstetrics and Gynecology* 515, argue that a woman who is refusing to consent to a caesarian section in circumstances where the foetus is in distress and at risk of dying should be told that she is committing an offence contrary to the Infant Life (Preservation) Act 1929, on the basis that maternal responsibility imposes upon her a duty to act so that her refusal to act incurs liability.

[37] *D (A Minor) v. Berkshire C.C.* [1987] 1 All E.R. 20.

[38] N. Martin, Case comment [1987] *Journal of Social and Welfare Law* 183.

[39] D. E. Johnsen, *supra*, n. 33 at 613.

rational to assume that women will consider potentially harmful effects to their children resulting from their actions during pregnancy than to subject all women to state regulation of their actions during pregnancy. Furthermore, because the decisions a woman makes throughout her pregnancy depend on her individual values and preferences, complicated sets of life circumstances, and uncertain probabilities of daily risk, the woman herself is best situated to make these complex evaluations."

Dawn Johnsen notes that, whilst originally foetal rights were admitted which acknowledged the fundamental connection between the foetus and the woman carrying it (and the putative father), the foetus has since been accorded the status of a separate individual in its own right with interests which conflict with those of its mother. She argues that extending foetal rights in this way undermines the autonomy of pregnant women, extending state control over them. The High Court in *Re S* assumed that the interests and rights of two individuals were in conflict and the decision in that case seeks to protect the party perceived to be in the weaker position.[40]

Michael Thomson argues that the foetus has been ascribed rights and positioned as an adversary of the woman sustaining it, with the effect of entrenching the position of women within the private sphere. The very personhood and potential of a woman is subsumed to her potential as a foetal carrier, her most valued role, and one most frequently used to justify her categorisation as "Other" and thereby to exclude her from the public realm.[41] To this end, the decision of *Re S* is consistent with the view of motherhood as a woman's primary role and the law can be seen to participate in the limitation of women to ensure fulfilment of this role. Further, it appears that, on this construction, women cannot be trusted. The law must play a dutiful role in protecting the vulnerable foetus which is perceived to be in conflict with, as opposed to connected to, the woman upon whose body it depends for survival.

D. E. JOHNSEN
"The Creation of Fetal Rights: Conflicts with Women's Constitutional Rights to Liberty, Privacy and Equal Protection"[42]

"Granting rights to fetuses in a manner that conflicts with women's autonomy reinforces the tradition of disadvantaging women on the basis of their reproductive capability. By subjecting women's decisions and actions during pregnancy to judicial review, the state simultaneously questions women's abilities and seizes women's rights to make

---

[40] Foetal protection policies can also be understood to proceed upon a notion of Woman as a threat to the foetus, or even to potential foetuses. The law must operate to protect her and her (potential) foetus because she is considered unable to make an informed decision about the risks her employment, and the substances to which it exposes her, present to her reproductive health (see M. Thomson, "Employing the Body: The Reproductive Body and Employment Exclusion" (1996) 3 *Social and Legal Studies* 243 at 259).

[41] M. Thomson, *supra*, n. 35.

[42] D. E. Johnsen, *supra*, n. 33 at 624–625.

decisions essential to their very personhood. The rationale behind using fetal rights laws to control the actions of women during pregnancy is strikingly similar to that used in the past to exclude women from the paid labor force and to confine them to the 'private' sphere. Fetal rights could be used to restrict pregnant women's autonomy in both their personal and professional lives, in decisions ranging from nutrition to employment, in ways far surpassing any regulation of the actions of competent adult men. The state would thus define women in terms of their childbearing capacity, valuing the reproductive difference between women and men in such a way as to render it impossible for women to participate as full members of society."

As Alison Diduck identifies, the woman who refuses to undergo proffered medical treatment is seen as a "bad" mother who selfishly pursues her own wishes contrary to the construct of female self-sacrifice.[43] It is women who depart from the "norm" of the ideal mother who are most likely to be perceived as acting selfishly and in conflict with their foetus. In their study of court-ordered treatment of pregnant women, Veronica Kolder, Janet Gallagher and Michael Parsons found that 81 per cent of the women subjected to court orders were black, Asian or Hispanic, 44 per cent were not married and 24 per cent did not speak English as their first language.[44] It may be that medical professionals are better able to communicate with their white, middle-class patients so that they are able to explain the reasons for the proposed intervention following which agreement is given, or to hear and respect the reasons for the woman's refusal. It may be that women who, because of age, race, class or ethnicity depart from the ideal mother figure, are more readily perceived to be a threat to their foetus and from this assumption follows forced intervention. S may have been seen as making an irrational (if competent) decision, prioritising her own selfish whims over the life of her foetus. The assumption that she represented a threat to her viable foetus may seem, as an initial response, to be the only conclusion — after all, the medical evidence was that the foetus was in a position of transverse lie, her membranes were in danger of rupturing and her consultant explained the situation as a matter of life or death. This ignores the relationship between S and the foetus with which she had been intimately connected for the period of her pregnancy. Not only had S been told in an earlier pregnancy that she would have to have a caesarian (only going on to give birth naturally) but her belief system rejected such surgical intervention. On the facts, once the court order was made, she agreed to the caesarian believing it to be a message from God that her life was to be saved. The foetus by this stage had died. In the light of her previous experience and her religious beliefs, her decision can be understood as one made according to her understanding of what was in the best interests of herself and the foetus. Trying to understand S's decision in the light of her previous experiences demonstrates the inadequacy of the liberal position, placing paramount importance upon the autonomous decisions of isolated

---

[43]   A. Diduck, *supra*, n. 26 at 462.
[44]   V. E. B. Kolder, J. Gallagher & M. T. Parsons, "Court Ordered Obstetrical Interventions" (1987) 316 *New England Journal of Medicine* 1192 at 1195.

separate individuals, in analysing this case. Are we truly, at all times, isolated, autonomous individuals?:

C. WELLS
"Patients, Consent and Criminal Law"[45]

"The emergency for S arose while she was in full-term labour with what would have been her third child. Thus, socially situated as a mother, both actual and potential, her refusal of a Caesarian section to save the lives of both of her baby and herself, was difficult to comprehend. The decision to operate on her was made in the knowledge that she did not consent. It was not, as in *Re T*, based on the conjecture that perhaps her lack of consent was contingent. The argument here is conducted on the assumption that her lack of consent was as real and unvitiated as consent can be.

While emphasising that consent is important because of the value placed on freedom, Kennedy acknowledges that it is a 'subtle and complex concept'. Freedom, autonomy and self-determination are expressions of a noble aspiration that human beings should be able to maximise control over their own lives. None of these, however, can be regarded as absolute or unproblematic. Any expression of autonomy or self-determination which fails to recognise that individual lives are partly determined by social, economic and cultural conditions is deficient. The ideal of patient autonomy is deeply reassuring. In trying to reach an acceptable understanding of forced emergency treatment I find myself struggling to keep the two contrasts in the same picture. On the one hand the image of the surgical team bearing down on an unwilling patient with its spectre of naked self-defence in the face of coercion is offensive. On the other, there is the competing thought of the sense of despair that must affect those seeking to help, to do that which is both a natural and in this instance a professional reflex, to preserve the life of another. If this contradiction could be resolved by the invocation of a simple principle, that would render the whole thing so much easier. But it does not seem to me that it can be. Some alternative conceptions of freedom and autonomy need to be considered, in order that the singular emphasis on the right of autonomy can be put into some perspective.

Feminism, for example, not only qualifies but actually transforms ethics. While liberal political theory and its counterpart in ethics are presented as gender-neutral, feminism exposes the inaccuracy of this self-image. The picture painted by traditional philosophy of the untrammelled, self-determining subject has to be reassessed: 'If the salient features of your social experience are seeking to please, fitting in with others, being the one whom others count on . . . then it is no cause for surprise if the familiar image is irrelevant or cues feelings of inadequacy'. While adult women have to be seen as competent to make life and death decisions, it is difficult to ignore the huge contrast between male and female subjectivity. Male subjectivity is supported by a range of social institutions with the result that male selfhood is constructed partly by excluding women. Although these dominant models are descriptively inadequate for men too, the difference is that men's absence from women's groupings is seen *as* absence."

The case of *Re S* raises a wider question of the relationship between doctor and patient and the options available to the medical profession when the

[45] [1994] *Journal of Social Welfare and Family Law* 65 at 68–69.

patient makes a decision which is, in its opinion, irrational. In S's, case neither her medical carers nor the court could stand by and allow her to make a decision which they considered was presenting a danger to both S and her foetus. The training of professionals, doctors and lawyers, is geared to helping others within the limits of their professional expertise. Despite the desire to secure what they, in their medical judgment, consider to be the best treatment, it may be that court-ordered treatment has a detrimental effect upon the relationship between a pregnant woman and the medical professionals providing her care. Enforced medical intervention will not necessarily ensure that the woman receives the treatment which the professionals consider to be in the "best interests" of either herself or the foetus. Janet Gallagher suggests that the "[i]ntroduction of the physically controlling and invasive policies proposed by fetal rights advocates could be expected to aggravate existing patterns of avoidance of prenatal care".[46] She gives the example of a woman who was required by a court order to admit herself to hospital by a specified date and time. The order stated that if she did not do so she would be taken to hospital by the police where the hospital staff were authorised to carry out any necessary medical procedure. She went, with her family, into hiding and delivered her baby vaginally.[47]

J. GALLAGHER
"Pre-natal Invasions & Interventions: What's Wrong with Fetal Rights?"[48]

"Pregnancy and childbirth are profoundly significant human tasks and experiences; they are as charged as sexuality or death. It is not by happenstance that we turn to cases involving sexual intimacy or the right to die with dignity when confronted by the pregnancy and birthing conflicts. In all of these contexts, government intrusion and medical hegemony affect not only the individual's body, but the deepest core of her personal, spiritual identity.

So, we set limits on the reach of the state and of the medical profession. We defer to the decision making of those most directly involved, not out of naiveté or a belief that people invariably will act in their own or one another's best interests, but out of recognition that licensing state intervention in such intimate areas exacts unacceptable social costs.

A competent woman may choose to undergo surgery or therapy for the sake of the fetus. But we cannot exact the gift of life by state power. Until the child is brought forth from the woman's body, our relationship with it must be mediated by her. The alternative adopts a brutally coercive stance toward pregnant women, viewing them as vessels or means to an end which may be denied the bodily integrity and self-determination specific to human dignity.

The Caesarean section and other 'fetal rights' cases possess great symbolic and precedential significance, but they have less to do with the status of the fetus than with the moral and legal status of women. They reinforce deep societal stereotypes of women,

---

[46] J. Gallagher, *supra*, n. 20 at 53.
[47] J. Gallagher, *ibid.*, at 47.
[48] J. Gallagher, *ibid.*, at 57–58.

particularly of pregnant women, as somehow incompetent to make moral decisions. They also serve to legitimize a forceful, even physically violent, assertion of doctors' control over pregnancy and childbirth at a time when prospective parents are raising serious and effective challenges to the medical model of birth. Courts must be wary of serving as 'enforcers' of a medical model that would distort an intimate, important moment in the life of an individual and her family."

Further, the medical profession should be assured that, should the foetus be born alive but harmed as a consequence of the mother's refusal of medical treatment, the foetus will have no cause of action against either its mother or the medical profession. The Congenital Disabilities (Civil Liability) Act 1976 (s.4(5)) replaced the common law in respect of liability to a child born with disabilities. The 1976 Act makes the child's action dependent upon a breach of duty to its parent (although the parent need not have suffered actionable damage herself):

J. M. EEKELAAR & R. W. J. DINGWALL
"Some Legal Issues in Obstetric Practice"[49]

"If this is a correct analysis of the statutory and professional position of obstetric attendants, it would seem imperative that it be reflected in the law relevant to their common law liability. Left to itself, it seems clear that the common law would have developed in this way. In *Whitehouse v. Jordan* an infant claimed damages as a result of injuries incurred during a forceps delivery. Although that particular action failed, there was never any doubt that the obstetric attendants owed the baby a duty of professional care during delivery. In *McKay v. Essex Area Health Authority* a child was born with damage caused by her mother contracting German measles during pregnancy. The gist of the action was that the mother's doctor had been negligent in failing to diagnose the condition and, thereby, offer her an opportunity to terminate the pregnancy. As such, the action was dismissed, since the child was, essentially, claiming damages for entering life with a disability ('wrongful life') and the court held that there was no means of evaluating that damage against not being born at all. Nevertheless, it was again accepted that the doctor owed a duty of care towards the unborn child even at a time well before delivery. In this instance, however, the injury had not been the consequence of any failing on his part but was caused solely, and unavoidably, by the mother's illness. An unborn child is also, at least partly, protected by the law of homicide. Grossly negligent procedures resulting in the child's death after birth may amount to manslaughter, although it seems that this covers only acts, not omissions (such as failure by the mother to summon assistance).

These features in the English common law were, however, abruptly terminated by the Congenital Disabilities (Civil Liability) Act 1976. This Act applies to all births after July 22, 1976. (The births in *Whitehouse* and *McKay* both occurred prior to that date.) The Act sought to enlarge the circumstances in which children might bring proceedings for injuries sustained *in utero*. It did this by allowing children, who had been born alive, to claim for injuries received during their mothers' pregnancies or

---

labour if these resulted from an 'occurrence' for which the defendant was liable in tort *to the child's parent*. Thus, an act of common law negligence, like an excessive dose of x-radiation, for instance, or breach of any other common law duty to a child's mother which caused injury to that child would also incur a liability to the child. There is no need to establish an independent duty to the child. Instead of adding this remedy to the unborn child's common law rights, however, the Act states that 'in respect of any (birth after the passing of the Act) it (the Act) replaces any law in force before its passing whereby a person could be liable to a child in respect of disabilities with which it might be born.' 'Any law in force' appears to include the common law as declared in *Whitehouse* and *McKay*. If a child is to recover compensation, it is now necessary to show that the defendant was 'liable in tort' to a parent of the child, although this requirement has the modification that the parent does not have to have suffered some 'actionable injury.' Nevertheless, there must still have been some breach of legal duty towards the parent.

What difference does this make to the position of a child who has been injured by negligent delivery procedures? The answer would seem to be that unless the culpable acts or omissions can also be construed as breaching a legal duty to the mother, the child has lost its remedy. It is by no means clear that all such failures can be so construed. Inexpert manipulation of forceps, inadequate use of available monitoring equipment or a failure to make a Caesarean incision at an appropriate time all appear to be wrongs which primarily affect the child's well-being rather than the mother's and outside the scope of any duty to her. It is possible that the child's position could be saved by treating any default as a breach of duty towards the mother on the grounds that injury to the child is foreseeably likely to cause her consequential emotional distress. The child's action would then be parasitic upon her actual or potential claim.

This circuitous reasoning breaks down, however, if the attendant's default is the result of undue consideration for the mother or, particularly, if it was at her insistence by rejecting available and offered treatments. It is hard to see how the attendant could be in breach of a legal duty towards the mother when he is doing what she demands. Indeed, the Act itself compels a child's claim to be reduced by the extent to which the parent had contributed to the disability and, even, to be totally excluded if this has been done in respect to the parents' own case. If a woman, for example, refuses a Caesarean section when indicated on sound professional grounds, or rejects the application of foetal monitoring, and the child subsequently goes into distress and sustains brain damage as a result of protracted labour, the child has no claim, either against the attendant (who will have committed no tort against the mother) or against the woman herself (since the 1976 Act disallows any claim by the child against its mother for ante-natal injuries unless they were incurred while she was driving).

Moreover, the abolition of an independent duty of care towards the child makes it harder for an attendant to resist a possible claim in assault if, in the child's interests, he disregards the mother's wishes in respect of procedures involving her person. The presence of such a duty would fortify any defence to such a claim founded on the principle of necessity or of using reasonable force to prevent a crime, *viz.* negligent manslaughter of the child. Its absence may call into question the application of the law of manslaughter for grossly negligent delivery procedures."

The BMA Ethics Committee has subsequently provided a statement to the effect that it does not consider *Re S* to be good practice. However, the case remains law and, demonstrating the power of law, may be used to effect compliance with the proposals of the medical profession in individual situations.

There have been further examples of court-ordered caesarians. While these new cases do not explicitly contravene the guidelines of the Royal College of Obstericians and Gynaecologists after *Re S*, in that they do not involve competent decisions being overridden, they subvert the guidelines by deeming the pregnant woman to be incompetent. For example, Johnson J. made a declaration that it would be lawful to perform a caesarian section upon Fahima Chowdhury, despite her refusal to consent because of the pain she had suffered following a caesarian operation in a previous delivery.[50] His Lordship held that her refusal was incompetent. The patient was, at this point, three days into her labour and refusing a caesarian recommended in the light of the risk that her scar, from her previous caesarian, might rupture. In response to the strength of opinion she expressed upon her refusal (she said "I would rather die than have a caesarean again") Johnson J. said "I concluded that a patient who could speak in terms which seemed to accept the inevitability of her own death was not a patient who was able properly to weigh up the considerations."

The Court of Appeal in *Re MB*[51] reaffirmed the right of competent pregnant women to make decisions regarding the birth of their child. To be respected, it was not necessary for the refusal to be a rational refusal but it had to be a competent refusal: that is, treatment information must be taken in, retained, believed and weighed up to reach a decision.[52] MB's unborn baby was in a breech position, for which normal practice was to deliver by caesarian section. Whilst MB consented to the caesarian, she would not consent to the use of needles to take blood or for the provision of anaesthesia. The Court of Appeal affirmed the declaration of the High Court that it would be lawful to provide anaesthesia by way of injection facilitating the performance of the caesarian. It was considered that fear, in this case the fear of needles, may provide the basis of a rational refusal or may "paralyse the will and thus destroy the capacity to make a decision". Her fear, the Court concluded, rendered her temporarily incompetent. The question became whether the use of a needle to provide anaesthesia was in her best interests. Her desire for the birth of her child, the harm which she would suffer if the child were to die or be born handicapped as a consequence of her refusal against the belief that there would be no lasting effect from the forced treatment led to the conclusion that it was in her best interests. On the one hand the Court emphasised the importance placed upon self-determination inherent within the legal requirement of consent to treatment but, on the other, found that the circumstances rendered it inapplicable, facilitating the refused treatment. Given that there is no recorded case in which a court has respected the refusal of a woman to medical intervention relating to the birth of her child, the question has to be

---

[50] *Rochdale Healthcare (NHS) Trust v. C* [1997] 1 F.C.R. 274. See also J. Bale, "Woman challenges hospital's right to impose Caesarean", *The Times*, September 23, 1996.
[51] *Re MB* (1997) 27 *Family Law* 542.
[52] *Re C (Adult: Refusal of Treatment)* [1994] 1 W.L.R. 290.

asked upon what basis will the courts in the future be prepared to find labouring women incompetent?[53]

It was recognised in *Norfolk and Norwich Healthcare (NHS) Trust v. W,*[54] that should W not submit to the court-ordered caesarian the only way it could be performed would be by using force upon her. W had been in a car accident and upon arrival at hospital was in "arrested" labour. This presented a risk that the foetus would suffocate. In addition, it was feared that scars from an earlier caesarian would rupture. Both were considered to present risks to both W and the foetus. The order sought was that it would be lawful to perform a forceps delivery or, should that not be successful, a caesarian section. Johnson J. accepted medical evidence to the effect that W was not competent to give or refuse her consent, but that she was not suffering from a mental disorder for the purposes of the Mental Health Act 1983. The question, therefore, was whether the procedures could be lawfully performed at common law and whether any force necessary to perform the forceps delivery or caesarian could be used upon her.

Norfolk and Norwich Healthcare (NHS) Trust v. W
[1996] 2 F.L.R. 613, *per* Johnson J.

" 'At common law a doctor cannot lawfully operate on adult patients of sound mind, or give them any other treatment involving the application of physical force however small ('other treatment'), without their consent. If a doctor were to operate on such patients, or give them other treatment, without their consent, he would commit the actionable tort of trespass to the person. There are, however, cases where adult patients cannot give or refuse their consent to an operation or other treatment . . . In my opinion, the solution to the problem which the common law provides is that a doctor can lawfully operate on, or give other treatment to, adult patients who are incapable, for one reason or another, of consenting to his doing so, provided that the operation or other treatment concerned is in the best interests of such patients. The operation or other treatment will be in their best interests if, but only if, it is carried out in order either to save their lives, or to ensure improvement or prevent deterioration in their physical or mental health.' [*Per* Lord Brandon of Oakbrook in *Re F (Mental Patient: Sterilisation)* [1990] 2 A.C. 1 at 55; [1989] 2 F.L.R. 376 at 419.]

In the Tameside case [discussed below] Wall J. specifically left open the question whether the court has the power at common law to authorise the use of reasonable force as a necessary incident of treatment or whether the power was limited to cases which fell within section 63 of the Mental Health Act 1983 . . .

I held that in circumstances such as the present the court does have a power at common law to authorise the use of reasonable force. I reject the line of argument

---

[53] Kirkwood J. held that a phobia of needles rendered L incompetant on the basis that her fear meant that she was unable to weigh up the information in order to make a decision. He made the declaration sought that it would be lawful to provide anaesthesia by way of injection in order to carry out a caesarian section in her best interests, *Re L (Patient: Non-Consensual Treatment)*, December 13, 1996, LEXIS, Enggen; see C. Dyer, "Mother vs Big Brother", *The Guardian*, December 19, 1996.

[54] *Norfolk and Norwich Healthcare (NHS) Trust v. W* [1996] 2 F.L.R. 613.

which had been put to Wall J. in the Tameside case, preferring the submissions made to me by Mr Munby, Q.C. I seek to apply the principle enunciated by Lord Goff of Chieveley in *Re F*, namely that there must be a necessity to act and:

'. . . the action taken must be such as a reasonable person would in all the circumstances take, acting in the best interests of the assisted person.' "

Considering that the proposed procedures were in W's best interests as necessary for her physical health, Johnson J. approved of the use of reasonable force upon her in order to carry out the procedures. Johnson J., in the extract above refers to the case of *Tameside and Glossop Acute Services Trust v. CH (A Patient)*,[55] in which the use of reasonable force upon a pregnant woman detained under the Mental Health Act 1983 had been authorised. In addition to sanctioning physical restraint of the pregnant woman, *Tameside* represents a further extension of the use of the Mental Health Act 1983 to force treatment upon women.[56] CH was detained under section 3 suffering from schizophrenia. She was in the 38th week of her pregnancy and the foetus was failing to grow, suggesting that the placenta was not functioning properly. Dr G, a consultant obstetrician and gynaecologist at the hospital, sought a declaration of the court that it would be lawful to induce her labour and, if necessary, to perform a caesarian section upon her without her consent, believing that the foetus was in danger of dying. The question was whether a caesarian section was medical "treatment for her mental disorder" and thus could be carried out without her consent under section 63 of the Mental Health Act 1983.

Tameside and Glossop Acute Services Trust v. CH (A Patient)
[1996] 1 F.C.R. 753

"Can it be said that the performance of a Caesarian section, and, if required, restraint applied to her to enable it to be carried out, is treatment for the Defendant's mental disorder?
   Section 63 reads:

'The consent of a patient shall not be required for any medical treatment given to him for the mental disorder from which he is suffering, not being treatment falling within section 57 or 58 above, if the treatment is given by or under the direction of the responsible medical officer.'

The definition section of the Act, section 145(1) defines 'medical treatment' as including 'nursing, and also includes care, habilitation and rehabilitation under medical supervision'. Sections 57 and 58 refer to specified forms of treatment requiring consent and a second opinion which are not applicable to the instant case, although they

---

[55]   *Tameside and Glossop Acute Services Trust v. CH (A Patient)* [1996] 1 F.C.R. 753.
[56]   The use of the Mental Health Act 1983 in the treatment of adult anorexics is considered in Chap. 9.

emphasise the stringent restrictions surrounding certain forms of treatment imposed by the Act . . .

Is the question of inducing the Defendant's labour or causing her to be delivered of her child by Caesarian section 'entirely unconnected' with her mental disorder? At first blush, it might appear difficult to say that performance of a Caesarian section is medical treatment for the Defendant's mental disorder.

I am, however, satisfied that on the facts of this case so to hold would be 'too atomistic a view', to use Hoffmann L.J.'s phrase in . . . *B v. Croydon Health Authority* [1995] Fam. 133; [1995] 1 All ER 683 . . .

There are several strands in the evidence which, in my judgment, bring the proposed treatment within section 63 of the Act. Firstly, there is the proposition that an ancillary reason for the induction and, if necessary the birth by Caesarian section is to prevent a deterioration in the Defendant's mental state. Secondly, there is the clear evidence of Dr M that in order for the treatment of her schizophrenia to be effective, it is necessary for her to give birth to a live baby. Thirdly, the overall structure of her treatment requires her to receive strong anti-psychotic medication. The administration of that treatment has been necessarily interrupted by her pregnancy and cannot be resumed until her child is born. It is not, therefore, I think stretching language unduly to say that achievement of a successful outcome of her pregnancy is a necessary part of the overall treatment of her mental disorder . . .

I am therefore satisfied that the treatment of the Defendant's pregnancy proposed by Dr G is within the broad interpretation of section 63 of the Mental Health Act approved by the Court of Appeal in *B v. Croydon Health Authority*: it follows that since the Defendant's consent to it is not required, Dr G is entitled, should he deem it clinically necessary, to use restraint to the extent to which it may be reasonably required in order to achieve the delivery by the Defendant of a healthy baby."

These cases demonstrate the desire to ensure that the pregnant woman submits to treatment proposed by the medical profession sanctioning the use of force against her if necessary.

The importance of *Re S*, which would not stand up to scrutiny on appeal and which the BMA has said it believes is wrongly decided, is both as a precursor to these further cases and as a paradigmatic example of perceptions of pregnant women as a danger to their foetus, which as a separate entity requires the protection of the law. It suggests a failure to understand the connection between a pregnant woman and her foetus, and illustrates clearly the way in which the law contributes to the construct of the ideal self-sacrificing mother and punishes women who depart from that ideal. In a casenote to the cases *Tameside and Glossop Acute Services NHS Trust v. CH (A Patient)* and *Norfolk and Norwich Healthcare (NHS) Trust v. W*, Ceri Widdett and Michael Thomson locate these legal developments within medical discourses of the female body and mind remaining from the nineteenth century. We conclude this section on "Reproductive Bodies" with an extract from this casenote which vividly illustrates how law and medicine consort in the perpetuation of entrenched beliefs of the pregnant woman as different:

C. WIDDETT & M. THOMSON
"Justifying Treatment and Other Stories"[57]

"In *CH* the legality of a (possible) non-consensual Caesarian section was asserted through an expansive (*holistic*) interpretation of s.63. A Caesarian section was interpreted as 'medical treatment given ... for the mental illness from which [she was] suffering'. In *C* and *W* both women were judged incompetent. Neither woman had a mental disorder which would bring them within the ambit of the Mental Health Act. Indeed in the case of *C* the only health care professional to be consulted stated that *C*'s mental capacity was not in question and she was in fact fully competent. The approach taken in each of these cases is problematic not only in terms of its effect on mental health care and practice — legitimating non-consensual non-routine procedures without adequate safeguards — but also because it is suggestive of other narratives with repercussions considerably beyond mental health.

In *CH* the suggested proximity between the defendant's mental health and her pregnancy may be located within broader stories regarding female instability during pregnancy. Yet there are more specific *medical* discourses evoked here. Whilst there are evident narratives of medical power and legitimacy there are more obvious echoes of influential medical stories about women.

. . . [I]n his evidence to the Court Dr G asserted that it was in the defendant's interests to give birth to a live child. Yet the degree to which her interests were believed to be best served by a live birth varied considerably within the judgement. At first it was merely recognised that 'it cannot benefit her schizophrenia to have the added stress of a still-birth'. From this rather neutral stance, however, a live-birth shifted to becoming central to the defendant's recovery — Dr G asserting that: 'the best treatment he could give the defendant was to give her a live baby.' This position was supported by Dr M — her consultant psychiatrist. Dr M offered a bleak prognosis in the event of a still-birth. The defendant would experience a deterioration of her mental health, facing increasing paranoia and an impeded recovery. Yet the picture if she should have a live-birth differed dramatically:

> The prognosis if she delivers a healthy infant is that she can recover from her psychosis and be able to provide care and support for her child. She will then be in a stable mental condition and rational and free from psychotic symptoms . . . The best interests of the patient lie in her producing a healthy child.

Having a child is clearly constructed as curative and normalising. In *C* and *W* there is the same nexus constructed between pregnancy/reproduction and mental health. In *W*, Mr Justice Johnson concluded that:

> although she was not suffering from a mental disorder within the meaning of the statute, she lacked the mental competence to make a decision about the treatment that was proposed because she was incapable of weighing-up the considerations that were involved. She was called upon to make that decision at a time of acute emotional stress and physical pain in the ordinary course

---

[57] (1997) 5 *Feminist Legal Studies* 77 at 84–89. The case referred to in this extract as "C" is *Rochdale Healthcare (NHS) Trust v. C, supra,* n. 50.

of labour made even more difficult for her because of her own particular mental history.

... [I]n *C* the judge followed this same route and returned to the three-fold test set out in *Re C.* He concluded:

> the patient was not capable of weighing-up the information that she was given, the third element. The patient was in the throes of labour with all that is involved in terms of pain and emotional stress.

The implications of these judgments are considerable. It is possible that women in labour (and perhaps earlier) may only have the capacity to withhold consent so long as they do not. This discourse may easily be located within the psychiatric and medical discourses of the last century. There are a number of points of convergence.

For a substantial period of the nineteenth-century the female reproductive organs were considered central to any definition of Woman. The reproductive organs were: 'the *controlling* organs in the female body'. Indeed, the uterus and ovaries 'gave woman all the characteristics of body and mind'. Given the centrality of the female reproductive organs they became intimately tied to all aspects of women's health, particularly ill health. Women's bodies, as Foucault argued, were 'integrated into the sphere of medical practice, by reason of a pathology intrinsic to it; whereby it was placed in organic communication with the social body.' Typical of this medical discourse is the following extract from one of the numerous guides to women's health of this period:

> [Most] diseases will be found, on due investigation, to be in reality, no disease at all, but merely the sympathetic reaction or the symptoms of one disease, namely, a disease of the womb.

As a corollary a woman's good health — mental and physical — depended on the proper functioning of her reproductive organs. The influential anti-abortion campaigner Horatio Storer, for example, stated in 1868: 'Every married woman, until the so called turn of life, should occasionally bear a child . . . as the best means of insuring her health.' CH's health was intimately tied to bearing a (live) child. More specifically the prognosis for her mental health was polarised by the possible outcomes of her pregnancy. To an extent this poignantly mirrors the phenomenon of hysteria in the last century — a phenomenon which perhaps most clearly embodied the pathologising and integration detailed above. The cause and treatment of hysteria became (obsessively) located in the female reproductive organs.

The degree to which there remains this proximity between women's mental health and reproduction is further suggested if we turn again to the case law considered above. The case of *Re C* proves an interesting parallel. . . . [I]n this case a schizophrenic was held entitled to refuse treatment for gangrene. The gangrene was constructed as entirely unconnected with the mental disorder. It is difficult to distinguish this from the situation CH found herself in. A Caesarian section could only be seen as treatment for her mental illness under s. 63 if the nineteenth-century discourses of the hysterical uterus-centred woman are still influential. In sharp contrast to CH's treatment is Thorpe J.'s response to C's wish to refuse treatment for gangrene. Thorpe J. informed the Court: 'His rejection of amputation seemed to result from sincerely held conviction. He had a certain dignity of manner that I respect.' Even if we remain unconvinced by suggestions that politically unacceptable nineteenth-century discourses are still shaping mental health practice and law it is clear that women are afforded less respect than men in terms of self determination, bodily integrity, and autonomy.

The degree to which the psychiatric and medical discourses seem imbricated in older sociobiological narratives is also suggested in what we learn of CH from the report of the Official Solicitor's agent. CH becomes 'well orientated and clearly aware of the problems suffered by the foetus, in particular the inter-uterine growth retardation.' It is clear from the agent's report that CH understood the need to induce labour and the possibility that a deterioration in the foetus may necessitate a Caesarean section. In response to this report Dr M remained unconvinced, stating that he doubted CH's co-operation in the procedures. As Mr Justice Wall recounted: 'He thought she saw the solicitor as an ally, whereas she saw psychiatrists and obstetricians as opponents.' The agent's report becomes an object of the defendant's psychotic paranoia. Mr Justice Wall refers to it no further. This account of CH is marginalised notwithstanding the quite distinct impression we receive of her through it. There appears no tension between the two accounts of CH — she remains within the court as Drs G and M portray her.

These cases are therefore illustrative of a number of areas of concern within both mental health care and the medical management of pregnancy. The cases are suggestive of an expansionist trend in mental heath care law and practice. They also suggest an increasing judicial presence in the delivery room of a sort already witnessed in the United States. Medical professionals seem increasingly able to over-ride refusal of con- sent to non-routine operations that cannot in any real sense be understood as for the 'mental illness from which [the patient] is suffering'. Similarly a woman's capacity to withhold consent appears now to be contingent on whether or not she is pregnant. This ability to over-ride a refusal of consent is perhaps of concern most particularly because of the inadequate safeguards in this area. Concern must also arise in terms of the particular narrative which emerges regarding the nexus between women's mental health and their reproductive systems/lives. This narrative/image damages women's autonomy and bodily integrity. Its impact is considerable. It is important to note that this image is one that haunts women's everyday experience of mental health care and continues to inflect medical practice more generally."

SECTION THREE

SEXUAL BODIES

INTRODUCTION

THE CONSTRUCTION OF SEXUAL BODIES

This section is about harm and damage. In addition to the harms inflicted upon the bodies of women which are legally recognised as injuries, there are also a myriad of harms caused to women which are not presently acknowledged by the law as causing damage.[1] We propose here to conflate the two situations, in order to raise questions about the limits of legally recognised harms and to expose the absence of any rational boundaries between harm for which legal redress is available and damage which remains unacknowledged.

The section considers harm inflicted upon women's sexual bodies through acts of sexual violence (notably rape) and sexual harassment, and through images of the bodies of women as sex objects in pornography. Also considered is the harm resulting from the dissemination of sex-stereotyped images of women's role by the mass media, specifically those used in advertising, and the harm caused by legally sanctioned medical interventions upon the bodies of women suffering from anorexia, an illness which represents an extreme manifestation of the conflicts experienced by women over their bodies and their place in the world. Finally we investigate the harm caused when women resort to surgery to alter their bodies in accordance with dominant constructs of beauty. Consistent with the attitudes towards women and their appropriate role, discussed in relation to advertising images and anorexia, are attitudes towards cosmetic surgery, routinely carried out upon women in Britain, and genital surgery which, in its modern practice, arises primarily as a consequence of the traditions of peoples of different cultures living within England and Wales.

---

[1] Regina Graycar and Jenny Morgan include within their consideration of the continuum of "social injuries" to women the sterilisation of women without their consent and the provision of dangerous contraceptives. These issues are considered in this text in the section on "Reproductive Bodies" (Chaps 5.4 and 5.2 respectively). Both issues raise questions about the ways in which the fertility of those women who fail to meet the standards of the ideal mother is curtailed to prevent the creation of "unfit" mothers. These two examples show how women are not treated consistently and that legally sanctioned harms may differ according to the circumstances of the individual woman (R. Graycar & J. Morgan, *The Hidden Gender of Law* (Leichhardt NSW: The Federation Press, 1990), pp. 272–398).

The concern of this section thus extends beyond the abuse of the female body for sex and the use of female bodies in sexual images to a consideration of the pressures upon women to modify their bodies in accordance with current ideals of femininity, and hence the sexed body. This section addresses explicitly what may only be implicit in the sections on "Reproductive Bodies" and "Offensive Bodies", that the female body is sexed. Our concern is to explore the law's engagement with the sexed body where harm is inflicted either directly upon the bodies of women for sex (in rape), because of their sex (in sexual harassment and the court-ordered treatment of anorexics), in order to modify the body in accordance with dominant ideals of the female body (in cosmetic surgery and female genital surgery) or where harm is inflicted indirectly through the dissemination of images of the female body (in pornography and advertising).

A starting feminist presumption when approaching these issues (and one which of course other feminists might wish to reserve the right to rebut) is to suggest that each manifests an instance of control over women's sexual bodies. This control is not necessarily exercised through legal mechanisms, although in some cases (such as the forced treatment of anorexics) it certainly is. It might also be exercised through a display of male power over women. Catharine MacKinnon has argued that this element of power is pervasive:

C. A. MacKinnon
"Feminism, Marxism, Method, and the State: Toward Feminist Jurisprudence"[2]

"The liberal state coercively and authoritatively constitutes the social order in the interests of men as a gender, through its legitimizing norms, relation to society, and substantive policies. It achieves this through embodying and ensuring male control over women's sexuality at every level, occasionally cushioning, qualifying, or de jure prohibiting its excesses when necessary to its normalization. Substantively, the way the male point of view frames an experience is the way it is framed by state policy. To the extent possession is the point of sex, rape is sex with a woman who is not yours, unless the act is so as to make her yours. If part of the kick of pornography involves eroticizing the putatively prohibited, obscenity law will putatively prohibit pornography enough to maintain its desirability without ever making it unavailable or truly illegitimate. The same with prostitution. As male is the implicit reference for human, maleness will be the measure of equality in sex discrimination law . . . Gender, elaborated and sustained by behavioural patterns of application and administration, is maintained as a division of power."

The division of power between men and women in this perspective plays a part in determining what is defined as being harm to women. Having addressed the masculinist view inherent in traditional approaches to issues of violation of female bodies, MacKinnon advocates her approach to the prob-

---

[2]   (1983) 8 *Signs* 635 at 644.

lem which is based upon the recognition of harm grounded in women's own experiences:

C. A. MacKinnon
"Sex and Violence: a perspective"[3]

"My approach would claim our perspective; we are not attempting to be objective about it, we're attempting to represent the point of view of women. The point of view of men up to this time, called objective, has been to distinguish sharply between rape on the one hand and intercourse on the other; sexual harassment on the one hand and normal, ordinary sexual initiation on the other; pornography or obscenity on the one hand and eroticism on the other. The male point of view defines them by distinction. What women experience does not so clearly distinguish the normal, everyday things from those abuses from which they have been defined by distinction. Not just 'Now we're going to take what *you* say is rape and call it violence'; 'Now we're going to take what *you* say is sexual harassment and call it violence'; 'Now we're going to take what *you* say is pornography and call it violence.' We have a deeper critique of what has been done to women's sexuality and who controls access to it. What we are saying is that sexuality in exactly these normal forms often *does* violate us. So long as we say that those things are abuses of violence, not sex, we fail to criticize what has been made of sex, what has been done to us *through* sex, because we leave the line between rape and intercourse, sexual harassment and sex roles, pornography and eroticism, right where it is."[4]

Robin West explores the issue of the conceptualisation of harm in an article entitled "Jurisprudence and Gender".[5] She argues that both liberal and critical legal theory proceed from an understanding of human beings as first and foremost separate from each other but that "the claim that we are individuals 'first,' and the claim that what separates us is epistemologically and morally prior to what connects us — while 'trivially true' of men, are patently untrue of women. Women are not essentially, necessarily, inevitably, invariably, always, and for ever separate from other human beings: women, distinctively, are quite clearly 'connected' . . ."[6] West explains that the law only recognises as harm injuries to the essentially separate being and does not recognise as harms injuries suffered by women who are primarily connected. The lack of recognition and redress given to harms which fail to match up with male-defined expected outcomes of acts of rape and sexual harassment and of permissible pornographic images is picked up by other feminists and extended into other areas. For example, Hazel Croall considers the victimization of women by white collar crime and corporate crime. Croall argues that this is

---

[3] In C. A. MacKinnon, *Feminism Unmodified: Discourses on Life and Law* (London: Harvard University Press, 1987), pp. 86–87.

[4] The distinction between approaching the specific issue of rape as a question of sex or violence is addressed in Chap. 7 below.

[5] An extract from which is reproduced in Chap. 2 above.

[6] R. West, "Jurisprudence and Gender" (1988) 55 *University of Chicago Law Review* 1 at 2.

an issue which, like the violence inflicted upon the female body by husbands, friends or lovers in private, is rarely acknowledged. After considering the harm to women workers exposed to hazards in the workplace, low pay and sexual harassment, she considers the harm done to women as consumers:

H. Croall
"Target Women: women's victimization and white–collar crime"[7]

"Women consumers as victims

Consumers are a major group victimized by corporate or business crime . . ., mainly covered by the Trade Descriptions, Weights and Measures, Consumer Protection and Food Acts. Despite a plethora of regulations, these acts contain loopholes and ambiguities, and many unsafe or deceptive practices are inadequately regulated. It is for example often difficult to define precisely when a 'description' is 'misleading' under the Trade Descriptions Act, and many deceptive selling strategies, such as the use of deceptive packaging, lie in the grey area between legality and illegality. Analyses of consumer crime also reveal the narrow line between acceptable selling strategies and fraud, and many deceptive practices are morally unacceptable, whether or not they are criminal.

Women's health and safety is threatened by products marketed for female consumers like cosmetics and slimming products. As reproducers, women are particularly susceptible to the dangers of contraceptives and they are major consumers of drugs. The growing cosmetic surgery industry, much of it in the less well-regulated private sector, has also been the subject of recent investigation. Women consumers are also routinely deceived. Advertisements appealing to the 'cereal packet' . . . image of the family may make housewives the target of a host of frauds and rip-offs involving packaging, advertising, false descriptions and bargain offers . . .

Many have argued that the multimillion-pound slimming industry is insufficiently regulated. Products causing concern include slimming aids, 'diets', plastic pants to increase fluid loss and skin patches purporting to speed up metabolic rate. Gallstones, constipation, heart stress, infertility, depression and mood swings have all been related to 'dieting' . . ., and herbal teas sold as slimming aids have recently been associated with potentially fatal liver failure . . . In the USA the Food and Drugs Administration have found that 'cholesterol free' products contain highly saturated fats, and some 'sugar free' foods contain ingredients unsafe for allergy sufferers . . . Regulations for slimming products, however, are less stringent than those for 'drugs', as they are not subject to the same testing protocols . . .

The drug industry is itself high on the list of 'criminogenic' industries — with intense competition producing a variety of offences including inadequate or falsely reported testing procedures, deceptive advertising and the suppression of damaging information . . . Women are often adversely affected by the activities of these legal 'drug pushers' . . . For example, women suffering from anxiety were widely prescribed the tranquil-

---

[7] In R. Emerson, R. P. Dobash & L. Noaks (eds), *Gender and Crime* (Cardiff: University of Wales Press, 1995), pp. 232–237.

lizers Valium and Librium — despite the fact that these led to addiction and accidental or intentional overdoses . . .

Even more dangers are posed by the lucrative market in cosmetic surgery, as indicated by recent revelations about silicone breast implants. Rashes, allergies and arthritis have been found to occur when these leak, releasing silicone into the body. In America, a Federal Court found that Dow Corning had acted with 'fraud, malice and oppression' in failing to disclose information about the product's hazards . . . Implants have now been banned in America, where there is now a growing trade in 'explantations' — which cost more than the original surgery . . . In Britain, however, plastic surgeons, who have dismissed women's claims as 'anecdotal evidence' . . ., have been accused by one solicitor of minimizing the danger to protect the breast-enlargement market, where operations cost about £3,000 . . . Women undergoing the operation must now register with the Health Department. An alternative product, the saline implant, now undergoing tests, has been suspected of being more prone to leaking and deflation, and of fostering fungal colonies and micro-organisms . . .

Pregnant women, along with the elderly, may be particularly vulnerable to listeriosis — a form of which, 'materno-fetal listeriosis', can lead to abortion, stillbirth, or brain damage in babies born with the disease. The incidence of this disease, linked to cook-chill foods, rose between 1969 and 1988. While reported incidents have fallen since the publicity in 1989, the real rate may be three times higher than official figures, as many miscarriages are not attributed to the disease. While these concerns should, . . . have caused a major rethink by the food industry, this has not happened . . .

Women can be 'ripped off' in a variety of ways by products aimed at female consumers . . .

The slimming industry not only endangers women's health but also makes exaggerated claims about its products. The spokesperson for a recently formed anti-dieting campaign claims that 95 per cent of diets do not work — if dieting was a product, she argues, most dieters would demand their money back . . . The Consumer Association's magazine Which? has called for more prosecutions and tougher penalties for the producers of slimming pills, which, they conclude, are a waste of money and possibly dangerous . . .

Cosmetic products are also the source of much complaint on the grounds of exaggerated claims. Anti-wrinkle creams, for example, were recently investigated by the *Guardian* . . . If these work at all, they may damage skin tissues, but most cannot repair age-related skin damage. Those that appear to have some effect do so by moisturizing, and the effect is short-lived. Advertising is blamed for the large sale of these products — the author of the report argues that 'while the media continues to portray men of all ages alongside young, smooth skinned women as a vision of success, women will go on investing in pots of worthless goop'. The packaging of cosmetics can also be deceptive. Many cosmetic manufacturers use 'double-skinned' containers — giving the impression that the package contains more than it does. This can amount to a 'misleading' description, but prosecutions are rare and costly."

In the same way that not all of the harms perpetrated upon the bodies of women discussed by Hazel Croall amount to crimes, nor do all of the issues considered in Chapters 7–10 below. Failure to recognise a particular harm to women as amounting to a wrong which the State should intervene to prevent or punish contributes to the trivialisation of that harm and provides State sanction for its perpetuation. Robin West argues that the feminist project must secure recognition of women's specific injuries:

R. WEST
"Jurisprudence and Gender"[8]

"The goal of reconstructive feminist jurisprudence is to render feminist reform rational. We must change the fact that, from a mainstream point of view, arguments for feminist legal reform efforts are (or appear to be) invariably irrational. The moral questions feminist reforms pose are always incommensurable with dominant moral and legal categories. Let me put it this way: given present moral categories, women's issues are crazy issues. Arguments for reproductive freedom, for example, are a little insane: pro-choice advocates can't explain the difference between reproductive freedom and infanticide; or how this right can possibly be grounded in the Constitution; or how it is that women can claim to be 'nurturant' and at the same time show blatant disregard for the rights and feelings of fetuses. In fact, my sense, drawn from anecdotal evidence only, is that the abortion issue is increasingly used in ethics as well as constitutional law classrooms to exemplify the 'irrationality' of individual moral commitment. Rape reform efforts that aim to expand the scope of the defined harm are also perceived, I believe, as insane. Why would anyone possibly object to non-violent sex? Isn't sex always pleasurable? Feminist pornography initiatives are viewed as irrational, and the surrogate motherhood issue is no better. There's an air of irrationality around each of these issues.

That air of irrationality is partly real and partly feigned. The reason for the air of irrationality around particular, substantive feminist legal reform efforts, I believe, is that feminist legal reforms are by necessity advocated in a form that masks rather than reflects women's true subjective nature. This is hardly surprising: language, of course, constrains our descriptive options. But whether or not surprising, the damage is alarming, and we need to understand its root. Arguments for reproductive freedom, for example, are irrational because the categories in which such arguments must be cast are reflective of men's, not women's, nature. This culture thinks about harm, and violence, and therefore self defense, in a particular way, namely a Hobbesian way, and a Hobbesian conception of physical harm cannot possibly capture the gender-specific subjective harm that constitutes the experience of unwanted pregnancy. From a subjective, female point of view, an abortion is an act of self defense, (not the exercise of a 'right of privacy') but from the point of view of masculine subjectivity, an abortion can't possibly be an act of self defense: the fetus is not one of Hobbes' 'relatively equal' natural men against whom we have a right to protect ourselves. The fetus is unequal and above all else dependent. That dependency and inequality is the essence of fetushood, so to speak. Self-defense doctrine with its Hobbesian background and overlay simply doesn't apply to such dependent and unequal 'aggressors,' indeed, the notion of aggression itself does not apply to such creatures.

Rape reform efforts to criminalize simple rape are also irrational, as Susan Estrich has discovered, and for the same reason: subjectively, 'simple rapes' are harms, but from the point of view of masculine subjectivity, non-violent acts that don't threaten annihilation or frustration of projects can't possibly be 'harmful.' In both cases, we have tried to explain feminist reform efforts through the use of analogies that don't work and arguments that are strained. The result in both cases is internally inconsistent, poorly reasoned, weak, and ultimately vulnerable legal doctrine.

'Reconstructive feminist jurisprudence,' I believe, should try to explain or recon-

---

[8]   R. West, *supra*, n. 6 at 68–70.

struct the reforms necessary to the safety and improvement of women's lives in direct language that is true to our own experience and our own subjective lives. The dangers of mandatory pregnancy, for example, are invasion of the body by the fetus and the intrusion into the mother's existence following childbirth. The right to abort is the right to defend against a particular bodily and existential invasion. The harm the unwanted fetus does is not the harm of annihilation, nor anything like it: it is not an assault, or a battery, or a breached contract, or an act of negligence. A fetus is not an equal in the state of nature, and the harm a fetus can do is not in any way analogous to that harm. It is, however, a harm. The fetus is an 'other,' and it is perfectly sensible to seek a liberal sounding 'right' of protection against the harm the fetus does.

We need, though, to be more accurate in our description of the harm. Unwanted intercourse is 'harmful' because it is invasive, not because it is (necessarily) violent. For that reason alone, the harm of intercourse is descriptively incommensurate with liberal concepts of harm. But it is not incommensurate with women's lives. The goal of reconstructive feminist jurisprudence should be to provide descriptions of the 'human being' underlying feminist legal reforms that will be true to the conditions of women's lives. Our jurisprudential constructs — liberalism and critical theory — might then change as well to account for true descriptions of women's subjectivity."

Finding new vocabulary with which to describe harm is no easy task. To raise awareness of the specific harms committed towards women and to secure recognition of entitlement to legal remedy, Adrian Howe advocates the concept of "social injury":

A. HOWE
"The Problem of Privatized Injuries: Feminist Strategies for Litigation"[9]

"My starting point is women's pain — not our physical pain (although that cannot be separated out) — but rather that pain we feel, as gendered women, at an intimate, hitherto private level. The question of the centrality of women's pain to feminist legal theory was raised by Robin West when, in the process of clarifying the nature of women's legally unrecognized 'gender-specified injuries,' she called on feminist legal scholars to set about describing, phenomenologically, our gender-specific pain in order to 'communicate its magnitude' and thus insure its legal recognition. As phenomenology is neither my field nor my forte, this paper takes a different but complementary journey. Its theoretical starting point is the unlikely field of criminology. I have argued elsewhere that criminology is incapable and unworthy of reclamation. But within criminology there is one significant though neglected concept — that of 'social injury' — which scholars have begun to theorize in ways that have extended analysis of the legal regulation of harmful corporate decision-making. 'Social injury,' I believe, has a potential to be theorized in ways which may lead to the progressive development of feminist legal theory that Robin West and others have called for.

My intention then, is to seize upon the concept of 'social injury' in order to prise it out from criminology and develop it around *our* pain. I mean the pain caused by the 'hidden injuries' of all gender-orientated societies — that lived, internalized experience

---

[9] In M. A. Fineman & N. S. Thomadsen, *At the Boundaries of Law: Feminism and Legal Theory* (New York: Routledge, 1991), pp. 148–149, 153–154.

of lower gender status as personal failure; that felt sense of a lack of a 'badge of ability' which is central to the effectiveness of the ideology of equality. I will argue that this resulting self-identity is an injured one — not a privatized, personal injury, but a *social* one. Importantly, we have begun to name the injuries associated with lower gender status. Over the last two decades our once privatized injuries such as domestic violence (now criminal assault in the home), have become public issues. But while some of our injuries are thereby becoming legally cognizable, others are still dismissed in the legal culture. Moreover, we ourselves are divided over whether some of our injuries should be made actionable at all.

My argument is pitched at several different levels. First, it is offered as a contribution to the development of feminist legal strategies. The specific legal strategy advocated here is that we publicize and thus politicize those injuries — those intimate intrusions into our lives — which we want to make legally cognizable. More broadly, the paper is submitted as a contribution to the process of developing 'collectively, and within an international framework' a more adequate — because more experientially grounded — feminist theory of law. More broadly still, it is offered as a contribution to two current feminist projects — the 'deconstructive project' which identifies and deconstructs male perspectives on 'human' experience and the feminist 'reconstructive project' which, according to Sandra Harding and Merrill Hintikka, identifies 'distinctive aspects of women's experience which can provide resources for the construction of more representatively human understanding'. The distinctive aspect of women's experience which I am suggesting we focus on within legal discourse is that of our injuries: we should value them, politicize them and, when necessary, demand that they become actionable . . .

This concept of "social injury", developed in relation to women's social injuries, could, I suggest, become a valuable tool for feminist theorists and lawyers wanting to devise litigation strategies in which women's substantive differences — for example, the way we feel the pain of sex stereotypes substantively differently from men — will be taken into account by law reform. The notion of social injury, perhaps self-evidently, could be especially useful to those of us interested in extending analysis of the group-based — that is, social — nature of women's 'private' injuries within an anti-discrimination context.

The case for prioritizing the concept of social injury within feminist legal theory is a strong one. Most importantly, the concept of injury has a long and therefore legitimated history within legal discourse. Indeed, injury's strength is that it is legally cognizable: it has actionable status. Many forms of injury have been actionable, as the history of torts and contract law and the evolution of worker's compensation demonstrates. That injury has always been an actionable claim is, I suggest, of vital significance for feminist legal theorists. Consider, for example, that it has been the 'hurtfulness' of the oppression of women, the 'damage done to women' by sex stereotypes and our socialization as inferior which, according to Juliet Mitchell, has concerned feminists since the French Revolution. Consider too a recent feminist philosophical definition of oppression — oppression in its 'everyday, common-or-garden, O.E.D. sense':

> 'it refers to the condition of being oppressed, where, to oppress, means . . .
> to press *injuriously* upon or against; to subject to pressure with *hurtful* or
> overpowering effect (my emphasis).'

If we were to rename our oppressions as injuries and insist that injury has always been a legally actionable claim, we would be in a strong position to join the discussion taking place within criminology and Critical Legal Theory about 'relevant' social injuries and to insist that any new 'sophisticated' typology of preventable harms developed there includes harm to women. More broadly, we would be in a strong position to intervene progressively in the development of a new commonsense understanding of socially injurious behaviors which should become legally actionable."

By way of example, an innovative way to draw attention to social injuries caused to women as a result of pornography was devised in the United States by Catharine MacKinnon and Andrea Dworkin. This innovation is considered in more depth below in the section dealing with images of the body. But, by way of offering a taste of things to come, and also by way of contextualising this issue within the themes of the book, it is expedient to point out the impact of the public/private dichotomy in the failure to recognise social injury resulting from the availability of pornography.

N. LACEY
"Theory into Practice? Pornography and the Public/Private Dichotomy"[10]

"My concern here is not to engage in further analysis of pornography but rather to focus specifically on the contribution which the critique of the public/private dichotomy has made to feminist analyses of pornography. In the first place, pornography in liberal society has largely been constructed as a matter of private consumption, and hence as outside the ambit of political critique or action. Without any proof of the contribution of pornography to overt acts of violence, and without any overt violence or coercion in its production, pornography has been taken to be either an instance of expression or a form of sexual practice and hence within the sphere of individuals' privacy. Feminist critique has brought pornography into the sphere of the public and has insisted upon its political relevance. This is both because of the inter-dependence argument — the argument that private oppression inevitably leads to public disadvantage — and because the traditional denomination of pornography as private can itself be shown to be disingenuous. The liberal analysis which constructs pornography as a matter of private sexual preference in one breath constructs it as a matter of public rights to free expression in the next. In what might be called a 'no-lose situation' for the producers and consumers of pornography, the production of pornography is seen as a matter of public right, and hence protected, whilst its consumption is constructed as a matter of private interest, and also protected. Both public and private sides of the dichotomy are manipulated in ways which exclude anti-pornography arguments. Another twist to the conundrum comes from the ways in which the public right to pornographic expression has often been limited to the private sphere: legal regulation of pornography tends to focus on public manifestations which cause offence. This policy compromise may be functional to the meaning of pornography by in effect making pornography easily available whilst maintaining the illusion of illicitness which forms part of the power of pornography to arouse.

In many senses, then, issues of public and private suffuse the feminist analysis and critique of the traditional construction of pornography: the private consumption of

[10] In A. Bottomley & J. Conaghan (eds), *Feminist Theory and Legal Strategy* (Oxford: Blackwell Publishers, 1993), pp. 104–105.

pornography inevitably impacts on the public status of women — on women's citizenship. However, in the work of several feminist lawyers, the critique of the privatization of pornography has been developed in the form of inferences from critique to practice, and to practice in a very specific legal reformist guise ... [T]his specific attempt at reform, ... illustrates some of the theoretical problems ..., as well as some of the pitfalls of making simple inferences from theory to strategy. In response to a local grassroots movement in Minneapolis, Andrea Dworkin and Catharine MacKinnon were invited to draft an anti-pornography ordinance. The political process included lengthy hearings in which many women gave painful and appalling evidence about the effect of pornography on their lives. The hearings helped to produce a political atmosphere in which pornography was widely acknowledged to be a serious social harm with a differential impact upon women."

A "commonsense understanding" of social injury, as advocated by Adrian Howe, demands scrutiny not just of the injurious behaviour of *men* (both individually and as a group), it also demands that attention be given to the behaviour of *women* who may engage in self-harm or the harm of others. It is from this commonsense understanding that the legal understanding of harm in preventing or permitting such behaviour can be assessed.

With regard to men's violation of women's bodies (our first concern in this section) harm often appears obvious. It is physically manifested in a brutal form in instances of sexual violence and sexual harassment. Equally graphic for many feminists is the harm caused by the objectification of women's bodies through the availability of pornographic and other images of the female body (our second concern).

Not quite so straightforward, however, are the harms issuing from women's acts of body modification in pursuit of a certain body image (our third site of investigation). The examples of the law's engagement with anorexia, cosmetic surgery and female genital surgeries raise the question of the freedom of women to choose to modify their bodies. It is suggested that the prevailing social, economic and cultural conditions within which women make such choices serve to fetter their freedom of choice. Women decide to modify their bodies to attain standards of success (or survival). These standards are dictated by dominant norms regarding how the female body is meant to look and how women are expected to behave. Where success depends upon the appearance of one's sexualised body, be it a fatless body, a young wrinkleless face, or surgically altered genitals as external evidence of virginity and restrained sexuality, women have little choice.

The limits of the law are apparent in all areas of regulation of the female body. Legal definitions of rape and sexual harassment, and the lack of definition of pornography, necessitate that female sexual experiences are squeezed through a masculine interpretative sieve, before harm is legally recognised as such. With regard to body modification, the legal prohibition of harm does nothing to change the conditions in which such body modification occurs. In all cases recognition of injury requires an appreciation of, and a willingness to challenge, the social and cultural conditions in which harm to the female body occurs.

CHAPTER 7

SEXUAL VIOLENCE

"Rape is an abuse of power"[1]

- Men rape because they own (have) the law.
- They rape because they are the law.
- They rape because they make the law.
- They rape because they are the guardians of the peace, of law and order.
- They rape because they have the power, the language, the money, the knowledge, the strength, a penis, a phallus.

Men say that:
- in any case we're asking for it,
- that we are not careful enough,
- that we shouldn't follow strangers,
- but that you can't say no to your father,
- that we provoke it,
- that we are accomplices,
- that we shouldn't go out without a protector, etc.

We say to ourselves:
- what is it that dies in a woman when she has been raped?
- rape leaves you helpless, voiceless, paralyzed, frigid, traumatized,
- what woman does not live in fear of being raped?
- how many little girls are "raped" just by seeing men expose themselves in public gardens?
- why is it that rape is never punished?
- why is rape impossible to prove?
- why do they always refer a raped woman to a law that favors rapists?
- why is a woman not a "real woman" until she has been raped?

Bodily rape is merely the acting out of a daily ideological reality.
Rape is an initiation
      they say that we are becoming women,

---

[1] Anon., "Le viol est un abus de pouvoir" in *Le quotidien des femmes* (May 3, 1975) translated by Isabelle de Courtivron in E. Marks & I. de Courtivron (eds), *New French Feminisms* (Hertfordshire: Harvester Wheatsheaf, 1981), pp. 194–5.

we say that we are being forced to enter the legal system.
Rape does not exist
    they say it's natural,
    we say: it's the law.
Rape exists; it's a reality. The raping of silent girls by fathers, by brothers; the raping of isolated women by men.
    in any case it exists in women's minds as fear, as anguish.
    it exists in men's minds as a right.

7.1 "Rape myths" and the perfect rape

One way in which men can gain control of women's bodies, physically and psychologically, is through rape. In the above poem rape is identified as a site of struggle. At a physical level it encompasses a struggle for male access to the female body. At the level of meaning it comprises a struggle over the interpretation of an act which represents different things to men and women.

Our concern in this chapter is to investigate the construction of the law on rape. But before considering the legal provisions governing the criminal act of rape, it is necessary to dispel some of the popular myths about what constitutes "real rape".

M. W. STEWART, S. A. DOBBIN & S. I. GATOWSKI
"Definitions of Rape: Victims, Police and Prosecutors"[2]

"Common cultural myths and stereotypes about rape include the belief that rape is a sex act rather than an assault, that raped women are somehow less respectable, that women lie about being raped, and the belief that women are responsible for their own victimization. For example, cultural myths tell us that: 'Only bad girls get raped'; 'Women provoke rape by their physical appearance'; 'All women want to be raped'; and 'Women ask for it'. They also tell us that 'Any healthy woman can resist a rapist if she really wants to' and that 'Women "cry rape" only when they've been jilted'."

One effect of rape myths is to perpetuate stereotypical expectations of appropriate male and female sexual behaviour. As Stewart, Dobbin and Gatowski argue:

"[o]ne of the most predominant [myths] is the 'pedestal myth' which holds women to a higher standard of moral conduct. In essence, women are placed on a pedestal, women should be virtuous, they should not be sexually active nor should they tell dirty jokes or get drunk. The expectation that women should be more virtuous than men promotes a double standard and gives men a privileged position over women. 'Pedestal myths' allow others to believe that victims 'got what they deserved' because they behaved in an inappropriately provocative way. Therefore, the women are 'legitimate victims' only when the rape gives the appearance of violating traditional female

---

[2] (1996) 4 *Feminist Legal Studies* 159 at 160.

role expectations. Thus, 'pedestal myths' force the victim into the role of a fallen angel who is forced by the justice system to defend her 'heavenly qualities after her fall from grace'."[3]

In perpetuating such constructions, legal representations of rape continue the distinction between real rape (*i.e.* legal rape) and other degrees of forced intercourse which do not fulfil the legal requirements.

7.2 The legal definition of rape

The legal definition of rape has proved hugely problematic for many feminists. Critique of the definition is based largely upon the construction of the act of rape from a male perspective and its failure to consider adequately female experience of acts of sexual violence.

The Sexual Offences Act 1956, s. 1(1) (as amended by the Criminal Justice and Public Order Act 1994, s. 142) provides:

"It is an offence for a man to rape a woman or another man".[4]

Rape has a statutory definition which is contained in section 1(2) of the Sexual Offences Act 1956 (as amended by the Criminal Justice and Public Order Act 1994, s. 142)[5]:

1.—(2) A man commits rape if-
    (a) he has sexual intercourse with a person (whether vaginal or anal) who at the time of the intercourse does not consent to it; and
    (a) at the time he knows that the person does not consent to the intercourse or is reckless as to whether that person consents to it.

The two elements which comprise the legal definition demand an act and a state of mind. The act is that of sexual intercourse with a person who does not consent. The state of mind is that the man knows that the person does not consent, or is reckless as to whether she or he consents. Feminists contend that both of these elements are determined by masculine perceptions of sexual violence.

---

[3] M. W. Stewart, S. A. Dobbin & S.I. Gatowski, *ibid.*, at 161.

[4] Prior to amendment in 1994, section 1(1) read "[i]t is an offence for a man to rape a woman." Given the parameters of this book we do not propose to investigate the implications of rape performed upon male victims, although prosecutions for such a crime may yet prove interesting for feminist monitoring, particularly in so far as differences in the construction of male and female consent to sexual acts arise and for comparative legal constructs of "legitimate victims". See M. Morgan-Taylor & P. Rumney "A male perspective on rape" (1994) 144 New L.J. 1490–1493; and S. Lees, "Male rape" in S. Lees, *Ruling Passions: Sexual Violence, Reputation and the Law* (Buckingham: Open University Press, 1997), pp. 89–107.

[5] Previously the definition was contained in section 1(1) of the Sexual Offences (Amendment) Act 1976: "For the purposes of section 1 of the Sexual Offences Act 1956 (which relates to rape) a man commits rape if — (a) he has unlawful sexual intercourse with a woman who at the time of the intercourse does not consent to it; and (b) at that time he knows that she does not consent to the intercourse or he is reckless as to whether she consents to it."

7.2.i *Sexual intercourse*

The first requirement contained within the legal definition of rape is that of an act of sexual intercourse. Intercourse is defined as penetration of the vagina or anus. Ejaculation is not required.[6] Feminists have criticised this definition for its failure to acknowledge the gravity of other acts of sexual violence and abuse which do not legally constitute rape. Catharine MacKinnon argues that legal rape entails a specific form of violation because of its concentration on penetration:

> "Like heterosexuality, the crime of rape centers on penetration. The law to protect women's sexuality from forcible violation/expropriation defines the protected in male genital terms. Women do resent forced penetration. But penile invasion of the vagina may be less pivotal to women's sexuality, pleasure or violation, than it is to male sexuality."[7]

Carol Smart also identifies the "phallocentrism" inherent in legal discourse, particularly that of rape.

C. SMART
"Law's Power, the Sexed Body, and Feminist Discourse"[8]

"Phallocentrism is a term which is now familiar in feminist psychoanalytic literature and which is becoming widely adopted. It is deployed to refer to a culture which is structured to meet the needs of the masculine imperative. However, it is a term which is meant to imply far more than the surface appearance of male dominance which is all that is captured by concepts like inequality and discrimination which, in turn, are the standard (inadequate) terms used where law is concerned. The term 'phallocentrism' invokes the unconscious and raises profound questions on the part that the psyche and subjectivity play in reproducing patriarchal relations. Phallocentrism attempts to give some insight into how patriarchy is part of women's (as well as men's) unconscious, rather than a superficial system imposed from outside and kept in place by social institutions, threats, or force. It attempts to address the problem of the construction of gendered identities and subjectivities. Law must, therefore, be understood both to participate in the construction of meanings and subjectivities and to do so within the terms of a phallocentric culture . . .

The concept of phallocentrism has, of course, a particular significance for an understanding of sexuality and desire, . . . To state it briefly, within phallocentric culture sexuality is always presumed to be heterosexuality and thus heterosexuality achieves a spurious universality against which 'deviations' (which are called by special names) are judged. In turn this (hetero)sexuality is overdetermined by the prioritized activity

---

[6] Section 44 of the Sexual Offences Act 1956 provides: "Where, on the trial of any offence under this Act, it is necessary to prove sexual intercourse (whether natural or unnatural), it shall not be necessary to prove the completion of the intercourse by the emission of seed, but the intercourse shall be deemed complete upon proof of penetration only."

[7] C. A. MacKinnon, "Feminism, Marxism, Method, and the State: Toward Feminist Juisprudence" (1983) 8 *Signs* 635 at 647.

[8] (1990) 17 *Journal of Law and Society* 194 at 201–202.

of intercourse and its satisfactions become synonymous with the pleasures of the phallus."

Sheila Duncan gives a further example of the primacy of the phallus in the construction of the act of intercourse, citing the case of *R. v. Clarence*[9]:

S. DUNCAN
"Law's Sexual Discipline: Visibility, Violence, and Consent"[10]

"The symbolism of sexual intercourse runs like a thread through the law of sex and violence and with it the symbolism of the penis/phallus. In the 1888 case of *Clarence*, still a precedent for the limitations to consent induced by fraud, the defendant knowingly inserted a diseased penis into his wife. *She* did not know that he was suffering from venereal disease and he duly infected her. This was held to be no more of an assault than the communication of any contagious disease by or not by direct physical contact. Further, the court stated, the real intention of the defendant (implied to be the satiation of sexual desire) 'could not have been grievous bodily harm or indeed any harm on his wife'. Mrs Clarence's consent was held not to have been fraudulently obtained because there was no fraud as to the nature of the act. It was sexual intercourse in its pure symbolic construction.

It was clear that the act of intercourse was defined purely in terms of the physical act from the point of view of the male subject. From the point of view of the female other, the act did not end with the ending of intercourse. It was not circumscribed by a simple act of intercourse. As a result of the intercourse, a continuing battery took place resulting in grievous bodily harm and the defendant was aware that there existed the (strong) risk of such harm — further, that which was introduced into her physical space was not a penis but a diseased penis. However, the law defines the nature of the act as no different from the one consented to by the complainant. Mrs Clarence is thereby constructed as other, as having consented to what her husband knew he was doing, not what she believed him to be doing and, thereby violating her, unprotected."

7.2.ii *Consent*

It is not only the physical act of sexual violation involved in rape which is problematic. The mental element involved requires it to be shown that the man knows the woman is not consenting to intercourse, or is reckless as to whether she is consenting or not. The question has arisen of whether an honest, but mistaken, belief in consent is sufficient to negate the criminal liability of the defendant.

In *D.P.P. v. Morgan*,[11] the defendant, Morgan, invited the three other defendants, McDonald, McLarty and Parker, to his house where he proceeded to invite them to have intercourse with his wife. He told them that if she resisted this was mere pretence on her part. The men had intercourse with

---

[9]   *R. v. Clarence* (1882) 22 Q.B.D. 23. This case is discussed again below with regard to its implications for the law on rape within marriage.
[10]   (1995) 22 *Journal of Law and Society* 326 at 336.
[11]   *D.P.P. v. Morgan* [1976] A.C. 182.

Mrs Morgan despite her protests. They were charged with rape and, together with Morgan, with aiding and abetting rape. Mrs Morgan argued throughout that she did not consent. McDonald, McLarty and Parker gave evidence that Mrs Morgan had resisted at first, but later actively co-operated. At first instance the trial judge directed the jury that if it concluded that Mrs Morgan had not consented, but that the defendants believed, or might have believed, that she did, then the defendants should be convicted if the jury found there were not reasonable grounds for that belief. Accordingly the defendants were convicted and their appeals were dismissed. The defendants appealed to the House of Lords. A majority of 3:2 held that a defendant's honest belief in a woman's consent to intercourse meant that the defendant could not be convicted of rape, even if the jury found that there were no reasonable grounds for this belief.[12] The judges in the majority clearly demonstrate the centrality of a masculine perspective in the interpretation of the act of intercourse. Of more concern is the way in which this interpretation is articulated as giving rape its "ordinary" meaning and as resulting from "inexorable logic":

D.P.P. v. Morgan
[1976] A.C. 182 at 203, *per* Lord Cross

"Rape is not a word in the use of which lawyers have a monopoly and the first question to be answered in this case, as I see it, is whether according to the ordinary use of the English language a man can be said to have committed rape if he believed that the woman was consenting to the intercourse and would not have attempted to have it but for this belief, whatever his grounds for so believing. I do not think that he can ... [T]o the question whether a man, who has intercourse with a woman believing that she is consenting to it, though she is not, commits rape, I think that he would reply 'No. If he was grossly careless then he may deserve to be punished but not for rape.' That being my view as to the meaning of the word 'rape' in ordinary parlance, I next ask myself whether the law gives it a different meaning. There is very little English authority on the point but what there is — namely, the reported directions of several common law judges in the early and the middle years of the last century — accords with what I take to be the ordinary meaning of the word."

D.P.P. v. Morgan
[1976] A.C. 182 at 214, 215, *per* Lord Hailsham

"Once one has accepted, what seems to me abundantly clear, that the prohibited act in rape is non-consensual sexual intercourse, and that the guilty state of mind is an intention to commit it, it seems to me to follow as a matter of inexorable logic that there is no room either for a 'defence' of honest belief or mistake, or of a defence of

---

[12] The trial judge had consequently misdirected the jury. Despite this finding, however, the defendants' appeals were dismissed. The proviso to section 2(1) of the Criminal Appeal Act 1968 was applied, it being clear that the jury rejected the defendants' allegations of Mrs Morgan's co-operation. A different verdict would not have been returned even if the jury had been properly directed.

honest and reasonable belief or mistake. Either the prosecution proves that the accused had the requisite intent, or it does not. In the former case it succeeds, and in the latter it fails. Since honest belief clearly negatives intent, the reasonableness or otherwise of that belief can only be evidence for or against the view that the belief and therefore the intent was actually held . . .

I am content to rest my view of the instant case on the crime of rape by saying that it is my opinion that the prohibited act is and always has been intercourse without the consent of the victim and the mental element is and always has been the intention to commit that act, or the equivalent intention of having intercourse willy-nilly not caring whether the victim consents or no. A failure to prove this involves an acquittal because the intent, an essential ingredient is lacking. It matters not why it is lacking if only it is not there, and in particular it matters not that the intention is lacking only because of a belief not based on reasonable grounds."

D.P.P. v. Morgan
[1976] A.C. 182 at 237, *per* Lord Fraser

"It seems to me that the meaning of the direction and of the earlier dicta is that the mens rea of rape is an intention to have intercourse with a non-consenting woman or to have non-consensual intercourse. If that is so, then the logical difficulty of requiring a belief in the woman's consent to be based on reasonable grounds arises sharply. If the effect of the evidence as a whole is that the defendant believed, or may have believed, that the woman was consenting, then the Crown has not discharged the onus of proving commission of the offence as fully defined and, as it seems to me, no question can arise as to whether the belief was reasonable or not. Of course, the reasonableness or otherwise of the belief will be important as evidence tending to show whether it was really held by the defendant, but that is all."

The decision in *Morgan* has since been given a statutory footing. Section 1(2) of the Sexual Offences (Amendment) Act 1976 confirms that:

1. — (2) It is hereby declared that if at a trial for a rape offence the jury has to consider whether a man believed that a woman [or man] was consenting to sexual intercourse, the presence or absence of reasonable grounds for such a belief is a matter to which the jury is entitled to have regard, in conjunction with any other relevant matters, in considering whether he so believed.

The focus upon male belief in the existence of consent has to be considered in the context of beliefs about female sexuality in a phallocentric culture:

C. SMART
Feminism and the Power of Law[13]

"PATHOLOGIZING FEMALE SEXUALITY IN A PHALLOCENTRIC CULTURE

It might be useful to consider some examples of this pathologization to which all women are vulnerable, most especially as this 'incomprehension' is imported wholesale

---

[13] (London: Routledge, 1989), pp. 28–32.

into the rape trial. The following quotations come from a survey of men's 'sex lives' carried out by the magazine *Woman*. In this book the men are said to speak for themselves about aspects of their sexual relationships, their satisfactions and dissatisfactions. What is clear is that they speak volumes on phallocentrism. In fact these men do not simply speak for themselves since the author of the book adds the necessary framework to ensure that these men's comments are understood 'correctly'. In case we fail to take the message from the men themselves [the author] informs us that women are too reserved and guilty to enjoy sex and satisfy their husbands. In other words the comments are contextualized into the phallocentric framework — as if this were really necessary. Unfortunately it does not occur to the author that there could be another interpretation of these men's comments.

> 'My wife is very conventional when it comes to sex. These days she will not let me give her oral sex ... and she has never given oral sex to me. She tried it once but she didn't like the taste of it. I have offered to put some sort of different flavour on my penis but she still won't try.
>
> I have bought her sexy underwear and offered to buy some for me, but she is not interested. She will not wear suspender belt and stockings for sex as she thinks it is kinky.
>
> I would like my wife to be much keener on sex than she is now. Her lack of interest bothers us both but we are trying to adjust to it.
>
> I would like to try anything in bed but to have to persuade her a little at a time. This has to be a slow process as nothing destroys an intimate atmosphere quicker than realising she is 'closing her eyes and thinking of England.' She *must* enjoy it as well.' (emphasis added)

These quotations are so familiar that they might be a script that is rehearsed over and over again. Basically the complaint is that wives do not 'come across' enough. What is implicit is the view that women possess something they are not prepared to share. This sharing is seen as a simple thing which could be easily achieved and which would make men very happy. This view is given substance by the often stated 'fact' that these wives used to provide the right kind of sex, either before marriage or during the early years. This recollection is presented as 'proof' that women can do it, can enjoy a particular form of sexual relationship, and confirms the belief that women are either selfish and unloving, or that their libido deteriorates, hence demonstrating the problematic nature of female sexuality (which contrasts with the virile straightforwardness of male sexuality).

The commonsense accounts provided by the men in the quotations are, of course, real experiences. The point is not to deny their reality, nor indeed the frustrations of these men, but to try to understand how male and female sexuality has been constructed and why this discourse, which pathologizes female sexuality, has so much currency. It must be stressed that there is no simple biological imperative underlying these understandings of sexual desire and frustration. The construction of sexuality and desire results from a complex interplay between culture (language), the psyche, and the body and it is precisely the deconstruction of sex-as-natural that feminists, historians, psychoanalysts, and philosophers have managed to achieve. Hollway, for example, has challenged the conceptualization of sex-as-natural and has argued that the discourse of the insatiable male sex drive empowers men and constructs women as the passive objects of desire. She goes further, however, to reveal that part of this discourse entails the belief that women are potentially powerful and dangerous, and that they can 'swallow up' men who show weakness. Hence men's desire is constructed as omnipotent yet vulnerable to the wiles of women who, although appearing passive, will castrate them emotionally if they can. Men must therefore resist women on an emotional level, whilst exploiting them fully on a sexual level. The ideal therefore becomes the unemotional but highly proficient (hetero)sexual stud.

We need to consider how this widely disseminated discourse and its relationship to the everyday experiences of men (and women) relate to rape. It would follow that if all women are seen as having the thing that men most need, if they are also seen as grudging with it, or as so out of touch with their 'real' sexual feelings that they deny it to themselves and to men, then the problem for men is how to gain control of women's sexuality in spite of women themselves. This is as much a scenario for 'seduction' as for rape, but rape also serves to avoid the potential 'trap' of emotionality. As with prostitution, the raped woman cannot assert her 'misconceived' power by trapping the man into commitment or love.

In this formulation women's sexuality is constructed as separate from women themselves. Figuratively speaking women are seen as having charge of something which is of greater value to men than to women themselves. At the same time women can enjoy sex 'in spite of themselves'. So this sexuality of which they have charge is construed as an essence which can by-pass consciousness or which has a will of its own. This in turn allows for the construction of women's consciousness simply as a one-dimensional prudery, an inappropriate moral standard imposed by mothers on daughters. It is not regarded as an expression of a woman's will but rather the mouthing of a convention which defeats the woman's own potential for sexual satisfaction. In other words if women say 'no' they do not *really* mean it. This view is articulated clearly in *The Woman Report on Men*:

> 'Marriage may have made it officially OK for a woman to be sexual, but the parental prohibitions are still there in her head . . . "Mother" is still in there, making her tense when her husband approaches her sexually, blocking her from making a pass when she feels sexy.'

Not only do Mothers wreck things for their husbands, it seems they can spoil things for the next generation of men too.

It is these accounts which also form the basis of many accounts of rape. From the judge to the convicted rapist there is a common understanding that female sexuality is problematic and that women's sexual responsiveness is whimsical or capricious. As women do not know their own sexual responsiveness and enjoyment, it is held that it could occur in the most unlikely circumstances. It is held to occur even when a woman is in fear of her life or being gang raped. Yet by the same token it can simultaneously be maintained that it does not matter if she enjoys it or not. As men cannot 'really know' when they give pleasure to women, they can really only hope to please themselves. Men therefore do not have to trouble themselves with the mystery of women's pleasure. The following statements from convicted rapists reveal the continuity of this heterosexist discourse:

> 'Rape is a man's right. If a women [sic] doesn't want to give it, the man should take it. Women have no right to say no. Women are made to have

sex. It's all they are good for. Some women would rather take a beating but they always give in; it's what they are for.

I think I was really pissed off at her because it didn't go as planned. I could have been with someone else. She led me on but wouldn't deliver . . . I have a male ego that must be fed.

Rape gave me the power to do what I wanted to do without feeling I had to please a partner or respond to a partner. I felt in control, dominant. Rape was the ability to have sex without caring about the woman's response. I was totally dominant.'

Clearly there are themes here that resonate with the articulations of men who would not define themselves as rapists. For example, 'I feel my wife has the upper hand all the time. My sex life is what my wife will allow me to have and not what I would like'. The resentment felt by this man is clear, he would much rather be able to control his wife's sexual responsiveness and he sees her as too powerful because she can say 'no' and he does not want to risk taking other partners in case his wife divorces him. From where he stands she has failed to meet the contractual exchange of security and commitment for freely available sex. In his terms he has 'reason' to be angry and it is not hard to see that this resentment can extend to a generalized misogyny. The point is, however, that this contract represents the material and psychic oppression of women. Little wonder that so many women try to find a way out of such contracts. Yet women who do are the focus of abuse, and *all* women may be regarded as potential renegades and hence contemptible.

It is clear that in saying 'no' to sex, women are also challenging (even if unwittingly) the extensive power of men which goes beyond sex. The 'no' is understood as a challenge to manhood (or phallocentrism) which, in a way, it is. It is a form of resistance which goes beyond the site of individual relationships. . . .

This 'no' is the very core of the rape trial . . . The question is how can women say 'no' in law when their subjective 'no' is objectively overlaid with contradictory meanings. What anger does her 'no' inevitably tap, not simply in the mind of the rapist but in the minds of the judge, the jury, the barristers, the police (not all of whom are men)?"

Not surprisingly it is the issue of consent which has provided the focus of much feminist criticism. Consent is constructed from a male perspective in that it demands consideration of the event as the man (honestly) believed it to be. Carol Smart, for example, states that "[i]n practice it would seem that consent is assumed and the raped woman must prove non-consent".[14] The inferences of the *Morgan* decision are discussed in the following extract by Sheila Duncan in which she analyses, from a theoretical perspective, the legal text of the case. Duncan raises a series of questions:

[14]   C. Smart, *ibid.*, p. 33.

S. DUNCAN
"Law as Literature: Deconstructing the Legal Text"[15]

"What is this discourse that is law as it is expressed in the legal text? How is this discourse constructed? What are its 'truths'? What does it exclude in constructing those truths? Who is the subject of this discourse? What are its defining concepts? What is the relationship between legal discourse and justice? How can this discourse and its defining concepts of reason, consent, intention and honest belief be deconstructed in the context of the case of *Morgan*?"

Duncan sets out the "primary drama" of the scenario presented in *Morgan*[16] before seeking answers to these questions in the deconstruction of the legal text of the case:

S. DUNCAN
"Law as Literature: Deconstructing the Legal Text"[17]

"Issues at the Level of the Legal Text
In their original decision, unaffected by any potentially defective ruling by the judge, the jury accepted that Mrs Morgan did not consent. It is clear that the House of Lords also accepted that. The issue is *not* her consent but whether the defendants needed, as the judge at the original trial had said, to have reasonable grounds for their belief that she did consent.

There are four sets of actors in this secondary drama — the appeal to the House of Lords: counsel for the appellants; counsel for the D.P.P., the three judges in the majority judgment: Lords Cross, Hailsham and Fraser and the two judges in the minority judgment: Lords Simon and Edmund-Davies.

At the level of the text of the law the issues are these: reason, honest belief, intention and consent.

Reason
It is necessary to analyse how the law's primary tool 'reason' is used and not used to construct the male as subject. 'Reason' appears here in many masks: the reasonable man, the reasonable jury, the reasonable belief.

First, counsel for the three younger defendants addresses the court:

'The young men on the basis of what the husband told them had been led to expect some resistance. The judgment of a reasonable man is not a reliable guide to the beliefs of these young men who had drunk a lot and who were expecting something to happen by way of resistance.'

The reasonable man is not relevant in arbitrating in these circumstances on desire, the desire of the subject, the defendant. Indeed, there is a suggestion that reason and honest

---

[15]   (1994) 5 *Law and Critique* 3.
[16]   S. Duncan, *ibid.*, at 18–20.
[17]   S. Duncan, *ibid.*, at 21–29.

belief lie in opposite directions, that reason could not even be a factor in the determination of honest belief.

Although reason is discounted by the defence in arbitrating on the defendant's desire, it is to rules and paradoxically to reason that they appeal in asking for the defendants acquittal, asking the Court not to exercise their proviso even if they decide in favour of the appellants on the point of law.

The appellant's counsel goes on to argue that the Court must address the following question: Could a *reasonable* jury, properly directed, have failed to convict? A reasonable jury on a direction of honest not reasonable belief would, it is intimated by the Defence, not have convicted the defendants. Reason would have operated in the absence of reason to ensure acquittal. The reason is closure. The reasonable application of non-reason. Reason allows the space for the male speaking subject.

It is counsel for the Prosecution who uses the notion of reason to set an external standard, to remove the issue from the exclusive preserve of the interpretation of the defendants.

> 'In practice, the mental element in the crime is that the act was deliberate. Belief that the woman was not consenting or not caring whether she consented or not is the state of mind which must be proved. But this must rest on reasonable grounds. Otherwise an accused might successfully raise as a defence such a belief based on his drunkenness or his vanity i.e. his confidence that his charms were irresistible. The defendant can only raise mistake as a defence if he gives his reasons, because it is such an easy defence to raise, as for example in the case of assault where the accused raises the defence that he believed he was going to be attacked.'

The appeal to reason in this context is an appeal based on the victim's response (whether or not she consented) and what the defendant may have deduced of that response outside of those things which are entirely within and of him and operate not simply *not* to pick up the victim's response but operate to exclude it.

For the judges in the majority judgment who will decide that the defendant's belief does *not* have to be reasonable, it is necessary that they find strategies for the avoidance of reason.

Such is the power of notions of reasonableness in the law that each of these majority judges must in some way leave it untarnished and hallowed while finding his way round it. Lord Cross summarises the noble history of the notion of a mistaken belief being reasonable. He says:

> 'there is nothing unreasonable in the law requiring a citizen to take reasonable care to ascertain the facts relevant to his avoiding doing a prohibited act'

and in respect of intercourse between unmarried partners he argues:

> 'It is only fair to the woman and not least unfair to the man that he should be under a duty to take reasonable care to ascertain that she is consenting to the intercourse and be at the risk of a prosecution if he fails to take such care.'

Lord Cross's route round reason is the concept of 'rape'. If the Sexual Offences Act

1956 had made it an offence to have intercourse with a woman who does not consent to it, he would have accepted the notion that mistaken belief must be reasonable but the Act does not say this. The Act says 'that a man who *rapes* a woman commits an offence.'

So what is rape? Leaving reasonableness intact, Lord Cross steps outside legal discourse to consider the 'ordinary' use of the word 'rape':

> 'Rape is not a word in the use of which lawyers have a monopoly and the first question to be asked in this case, as I see it, is whether according to the ordinary use of the English language a man can be said to have committed rape if he believed that the woman was consenting to the intercourse and would not have attempted to have it but for this belief, whatever his grounds for so believing. I do not think that he can. Rape to my mind imports at least indifference as to the woman's consent.'

Lord Cross has moved here from legal discourse to popular discourse on rape.

> '. . . to the question whether a man who has intercourse with a woman believing that she is consenting to it though she is not, commits rape, I think that he would reply 'No'. If he was grossly careless then he may deserve to be punished but not for rape.'

The woman's absence of consent does not constitute rape, it is that absence, in conjunction with the belief of the male subject as to that consent which constitutes it. The law looks outside the discourse of its own rules to the ordinary use of the English language — not to the *reasonable* man but to the ordinary use by the ordinary man.

The law's reason is indeed a flexible and mercurial concept, prayed in aid by both prosecution and defence. As one of law's 'truths' it is powerful and purports to create an objective standard. But the space for the sexual violence and desire of the male subject, requires that the law's truth 'reason' does not arbitrate on reason's others.

Honest Belief and Consent

What must be deconstructed here is the notion of belief. What sort of belief? What are the grounds for this belief? Who is the believing subject? In the context of which truth production does he believe? Lord Cross sets up a straw man of the man only requiring the intention to have intercourse with a woman who does not consent even though he believes she is consenting. The issue is on what basis does he believe it and what are the implications of this belief for the victim. If this belief is not reasonable, does not appeal to any standards outside the individual male subject, where is the space for the consent of the female other?

Indeed the judges in both the minority and majority work their way through a variety of existing law to establish that their own text does, in other matters, hold that mistaken belief, however honest, must be reasonable. These cases are different claim the majority judges, they are not dealing with rape.

In the absence of theorised sexual difference, what is the space for consent? There is no space for the female subject's consent, no space for the female subject. In the absence of subjectivity, she cannot consent, she cannot desire, she can only mirror — mirror his unreasonable beliefs, whatever her actions or her words, he can sustain that belief. Here we are in the realm not of whether the woman consented, for it is assumed that she did not. But the realm of her non-consent and his belief and in that area of

physical intimacy, with her non-consenting, he is *not* required to appeal to any standard external to that belief in its support.

Reason is neatly sidestepped by saying that if there is a requirement of reasonableness, there will be no space for the male subject to believe in the consent of the
unconsenting woman and arguably there is no space, so in *Morgan* the law *creates*
one.

A space has been created for these defendants but are they able to stand in it? The
court has determined on the evidence that Mrs Morgan was not consenting, they argue
that the jury determined that and indeed the jury had to be satisfied on this point to
find the defendants guilty. But the issue has now become honest, not reasonable belief
as far as the defendants were concerned and, arguably the jury could have acquitted
them if given this direction. They found no reason but could they have found honest
belief? Given that Mrs Morgan was not, in fact, consenting the court are only prepared
to accept honest belief if the defendants retain their story that Mrs Morgan's protests
were understood in the context of her husband's assurance that they were part of her
sexual excitement.

> 'If the appellants when they came to give evidence had said that what Mrs
> Morgan said was perfectly true, that she had never at any stage given any
> sign that she was consenting to — let alone enjoying — the intercourse, but
> that they were so much influenced by what her husband had told them that
> they believed throughout that her manifestations were only play acting, then
> it is conceivable that a jury on a proper direction, might have acquitted them
> ... But the appellants chose — most unwisely — to challenge the truth of
> Mrs Morgan's evidence and to assert that although to start with she mani-
> fested some unwillingness, when it came to the point she co-operated in the
> proceedings with evident relish.'

Their honest belief can only be sustained if it accords with Mrs Morgan's proven
honesty that she struggled, screamed, did not consent because they honestly believed
what her husband denied saying to them — that her resistance was part of her sexual
enjoyment. And even in their own account, Morgan talked about apparent resistance
and play acting. If the Law Lords believed Mrs Morgan's testimony of on-going determined resistance, how, even on Lord Cross's suggestion, could there have been an
honest belief?

Inscribed in the disputed words of the male subject are the foundings of honest belief
not undermined by the on-going resistance and horrifying domestic context of Mrs
Morgan.

Intention and Consent

For Lord Hailsham, the issue is simple. He first sidesteps and then jettisons reason by
focusing on intention. The defendant had to *intend* to commit non-consensual intercourse. In other words he must know/believe that the woman is not consenting:

> 'Either the Prosecution proves that the accused had the requisite intent, or it
> does not ... Since honest belief clearly negatives intent, the reasonableness
> or otherwise of that belief can only be evidence for or against the view that
> the belief and therefore the intent was actually held ... the insertion of the
> word reasonable can only have the effect of saying a man intends something
> which he does not.'

He does extend intention to cover 'the equivalent intention of having intercourse willy-nilly not caring whether the victim consents or not':

> 'It matters not why it [the intention] is lacking if only it is not there, and in *particular* it matters not that the intention is lacking only because of a belief not based on reasonable grounds.'

However, to intend to have intercourse with a woman who does not consent implies that the male subject has considered whether or not she is consenting — the stage before knowledge, belief or not caring. Intention is closure, facilitating the closure round the space of desire.

Lord Fraser who concurs with Lord Hailsham on the matter of intention, similarly argues:

> 'If the defendant believed (even on unreasonable grounds) that the woman was consenting to intercourse then he cannot have been carrying out an intention to have intercourse without her consent.'

By defining these parameters, the legal text is not enforcing a prohibition but creating a permission. The responsibility falls to the Prosecution to prove that the defendant *intended* to have non-consensual intercourse. But how does the prosecution prove there was no honest belief? The reasonableness of that belief is only evidence for or against it. Further, any attempt to enshrine reason will be falsely constructing non-existent reason. This illusive honesty is now a problem for the prosecution and not for the defence and the relationship between the defendant's belief and the non-consent of the victim is further and further removed.

Mrs Morgan said 'no' in every way open to her and the jury and the court of appeal accepted that. At the level of the subject's narrative/space this creation of honesty, becomes harder and harder to disprove; it is an expansive space in which the male subject determines what constitutes consent, the victim, the female Other, dissolves as rape is defined in these terms and non-consensual sex is legalised. Who is protected in this crime? What is protected? The space of the male subject is both protected and further constructed.

Justice
The legal text has created a powerful web of notions in its construction of the power of the male subject. One of the minority judges, Lord Simon, appeals outside this discourse to the discourse of justice. In doing so he moves into a space which acknowledges that the law's discourse must sometimes look beyond the specific 'mechanisms of power,' of the legal text, to another discourse — policy and beyond that to the discourse of justice:

> 'The policy of the law in this regard could well derive from its concern to hold a fair balance between victim and accused. It would hardly seem fair just to fob off a victim of a savage assault with such comfort as he could derive from knowing that his injury was caused by a belief, however absurd, that he was about to attack the accused. A respectable woman who has been ravished would hardly feel that she was vindicated by being told that her assailant must go unpunished because he believed, quite unreasonably, that she was consenting to sexual intercourse with him.'

What is remarkable about this approach is its need to get out of the discourse of the legal text in order to obtain any perspective which gives credence to the victim and through credence, justice. It is interesting here to consider Foucault's point in *The Order of Discourse*:

> 'It is always possible that one might speak the truth in the space of a wild exteriority, but one is "in the true" only by obeying the rules of a discursive "policing".'

It does seem extreme to talk of Lord Simon's space which is in the discourse of justice as the space of 'a wild exteriority' but exterior it most certainly is to the discourse of the judgment and arguably the discourse of the law. He is not 'in the true' not in the realm of the rules of 'discursive policing', not in the concepts of reason, consent, intention and honest belief.

Lord Simon, albeit only by example and analogy, at that level acknowledges that rape ought to be the same as a non-sexual physical assault and in doing so, acknowledges that it is not. He distinguishes also between the male victim of an assault who is defined only in terms of his victimisation and the female victim (and of course the victim of rape . . . [at the time of the decision in *Morgan* could] only be female) who has a right to justice not as a victim but as a *respectable female* victim. Lord Simon does not give an example of the man who is assaulted with his assailant expressing honest belief in *consent* because in respect of physical assault on a male, the law wishes to contract rather than expand the space for consent. In rape, the legal text extends it.

Conclusion: Violence and Desire

The legal text of *Morgan* has compounded the sexual violence of its primary drama with its own violence. The violence of its exclusion of the woman as subject, the violence of its own hierarchy which constructs space for the male subject's desire by its dismissal of its own 'truth' — reason — and its provision of the space for legitimated sexual violence and desire — discarding reason to give space to reason's others.

This legal text fails to symbolise sexual difference. The woman is condemned to be other of the Same, mirroring the desire of the male subject. In its construction of consent, it creates complicity between the other and her own ontological degradation because the unavoidable part of consent is *his* construction of it. This too is part of the textual violence of Morgan. This violence will be repeated extra-textually in each rape trial where consent is an issue.

While consent lies within his honest belief, the realm of his desire, *her* desire remains unsymbolised, unrepresented. Subjectivity denied, she is granted no desire. If she had subjectivity, the legal text would not test for her consent but for her desire. While the law purports to forbid rape, it creates a permission in the mirror which reflects the male subject and his desire — not the rational male subject but the sexual, embodied, desiring male subject. The law's logos fails to theorise sexual difference, providing space for the male subject and in its violence and licence to sexual violence, disciplining the female body. Rape is preserved as the legitimate fantasy of the legal logos.

This legal text has used and abused its own 'truths' in preserving the space for its underside. The law has used its cold, unclouded concepts not to arbitrate on the primary drama of *Morgan* but to permit it. It has appealed to the popular discourse of rape and suggested how even on these facts, a defendant could have been acquitted. It has discarded the discourse of justice and ignored its own discourse of reasonableness in honest belief. It is a document of desire — the desire of the male subject, its will to truth bound to violence and to power."

7.3   Consent and "real" rape

Popular perceptions of rape incidents often centre upon the "stranger" rape scenario. Dark nights, unlit paths, ferocious struggles and bruised and bleeding victims spring to mind. Of course it is rare that actual events reflect popular cultural representations. But the lack of correspondence between "fact" and "fiction" may exacerbate the difficulties that a woman has in showing in court that she has been raped. Particularly a woman's difficulty may depend upon her inability to show a lack of consent.

Much debate has occurred recently around instances of so-called "date" rape. In these cases there is a degree of acquaintance between the alleged victim and her assailant. The lack of correspondence between this type of incident and that of the classic "stranger" rape scenario may suggest that the woman consented to a sexual encounter or that the accused honestly believed given their previous acquaintance that she had consented and thus the woman has not undergone a "real" rape ordeal. As such, her suffering may be viewed as of less depth than that of the "real" rape victim. This may translate into a defendant receiving more lenient treatment in the courts.

A further instance of the non-stranger rape scenario is that of a woman who is actually married to her assailant. She too may find it extremely difficult to prove that she did not consent to her violation and that what happened to her fulfils the legal requirements to establish a conviction for rape.

7.3.i   *"Date" rape*
The issue of date rape raises once again concerns about the legal and social construction of female sexuality. MacKinnon concedes that, while men may sometimes appreciate that the women with whom they have intercourse are not consenting, "women are also violated every day by men who have no idea of the meaning of their acts to women. To them it is sex. Therefore to the law, it is sex."[18] This perspective appears to be borne out in the interpretation of the sexual act engaged in by Austen Donnellan and a fellow student following a Christmas party, resulting in his acquittal on a charge of rape.

The Times, October 20, 1993

"Austen Donnellan staked his future and freedom on a gamble to prove his innocence against the accusations of a woman who cried rape after a night of heavy drinking and sex. University authorities wanted to keep the affair quiet. They put pressure on him to admit to a lesser offence, apologise to his 'victim' and leave to continue his studies elsewhere.

Mr Donnellan said no. He was so sure that a jury would acknowledge his innocence that he went to the police and asked them to charge him with rape.

---

[18]   C. A. MacKinnon, *supra*, n. 7 at 652–653.

His accuser claimed that he took advantage of her when she was drunk and incapable of rejecting him. She then reported him to the disciplinary committee of King's College London, where the two students, both aged 21, were studying.

Miss X admitted at the Old Bailey trial that she kissed Mr Donnellan passionately before they had sex. But she added that 'a kiss is just a kiss' not an invitation to something more.

Mr Donnellan told the jury that he had once loved the girl who so nearly ruined his life. His feelings for her cooled only when she rejected all attempts to build a permanent relationship.

Miss X told the jury that she had rejected Mr Donnellan's suggestion that she become his girl friend. But she cherished him as a friend, confiding in him and telling him about her experiences of loveless one-night stands. When she had too much to drink, which happened frequently, she would kiss him passionately but always regret it in the sober light of morning.

While admitting that he fell for her, sending Valentine's day flowers and a fluffy toy for her birthday, Mr Donnellan said that by the time of the Christmas party his feelings had changed. She had boasted to him about her drunken and passionate one-night stands with various men, he said. He thought her attitude to sex was a 'defence mechanism' because she had been so hurt when her first real love affair ended disastrously.

Events after an end-of-term Christmas party in the Penthouse Club at King's College last year were central to the case. 'The Penthouse is a fairly rowdy and wild establishment,' Mr Donnellan told the court. 'It was regarded as a good pulling joint.'

On the night of the party the club was 'awash with booze', the jury was told. Mr Donnellan, Miss X and several college friends were all the worse for drink by midnight. Miss X was seen to drink three pints of strong cider, two vodkas and two Drambuies. She might have had even more to drink, it was alleged. In any event she appeared very drunk. She admitted in court that she had given Mr Donnellan and others French kisses that night.

Mr Donnellan said that she dragged him on to the dance-floor at the club then fell over in his arms, kissing him repeatedly. Even when they went outside to get some fresh air she continued to kiss him passionately. He said that when Miss X's legs finally gave way he picked her up and carried her to her room in the college hall of residence.

Miss X said that it was there that he raped her. She told the jury she fell asleep but woke to find, to her horror, that she was naked and that a man was having sex with her.

She had no recollection of what had happened earlier that night because of the amount of alcohol she had drunk. She ran from the room and later reported the incident to the college disciplinary tribunal.

Mr Donnellan's version of events was rather different. He told the jury that although he was no longer in love with Miss X, he had become aroused by her because of her passionate eagerness to have sex with him. He told the court that she lay in his arms 'murmuring and making noises of sexual pleasure'. He added: 'She was very energetic and active.'

Twice during their hour-long sex session, he asked if she was sure she wanted to go ahead. Miss X made it very clear she did. He said that friends from the party interrupted their love-making to see if Miss X was all right. They came into the room and chatted for about 20 minutes. Not long afterwards Miss X leapt out of bed, and ran from the room saying something like: 'I cannot believe you tried to screw me.' Her reaction left him confused.

When Mr Donnellan returned to college after the Christmas vacation he was summoned to see Brian Salter, the university's deputy registrar. He was told that Miss X was accusing him of 'having sex with her without her knowledge or consent'.

At that stage he did not take the accusation seriously, he said. But after carrying out Mr Salter's request to write down his version of events he realised the disciplinary committee wanted to 'paper over' the whole embarrassing episode, with him as a scapegoat.

Mr Salter told him the committee wanted him to admit to a 'lesser charge', apologise to Miss X and leave the university.

'I was not going to allow that to happen,' Mr Donnellan said. He was innocent 'of any sort of wrong-doing' and, to try to clear his name, he went to the police. Miss X was said to have been furious at his action.

Among those to give evidence for Mr Donellan was Dr Robin Moffat, 66, a senior Metropolitan police forensic examiner since 1958. He told the jury that Miss X must have known exactly what was happening. She was certainly not in a coma and unable to prevent herself from being raped. 'She was capable of saying yea or nay at all times.'

Katherine Philp, a friend of Mr Donnellan, told the court that she knew Miss X well and that when he had taken another girl friend she had shown an interest that went beyond that of a platonic friend. 'It was akin to jealousy,' she said.

But perhaps most important of all was the evidence of another defence witness, Madelaine Allen, a former girl friend of Mr Donnellan. She described having gone to bed with him at the end of a drunken evening. When she told him that she did not want sex, however, he respected her wish. 'At no time did he behave other than as a gentleman,' she said.

After the verdict, Lord Russell, Mr Donnellan's history tutor, said: 'It's a victory for British justice. I'm not surprised, but for the expected thing to happen is always a surprise. It was what should always have happened and I'm very relieved that it did. You have to remember, he is an innocent man accused of something he has not done.' "

The construction of the behaviour of the protagonists in this scenario is striking. Donnellan sent Valentine's day flowers and a fluffy toy. A former girlfriend testified to his gentlemanly conduct. Miss X, on the other hand, had a stream of "loveless one-night stands", drank too much and fell over at parties. One might infer that her conduct was anything other than lady-like. Viewed in this light, what did she expect?

Another widely-publicised encounter with a drunken woman led to Angus Diggle's conviction in 1993 for attempted rape. Diggle was initially sentenced to three years imprisonment, but this was reduced to two years on appeal.

R. v. Diggle
(1995) 16 Cr. App. R. (S) 163 at 164–168

"The jury accepted the complainant's account of what had occurred and they rejected the appellant's. I therefore take this summary from her evidence. She and the appellant had met at a conference (they are both solicitors) about six weeks before the relevant date. It was a short meeting, about one hour, in the course of an evening function at which they were both present. They talked and discovered a mutual interest in dancing, including Highland dancing, and the appellant suggested that she might like to accompany him to the Grosvenor House Hotel in London for the St Andrew's Night Ball, which was about six weeks hence. The ball on November 30 was held on a Monday evening and it involved a special journey to London for both of them. They had about half-a-dozen telephone conversations during the intervening period. She decided to make a weekend of it in London and to stay at a friend's flat near Earls Court. The friend and the friend's boyfriend, who lived there together, were away from the flat for the weekend but they came back on the Monday afternoon.

The appellant had expected to stay at accommodation in Wandsworth. The complainant was not familiar with London and thought of Wandsworth as being a little way from the centre of London where the ball was being held. The ball was due to last until after 3.30 a.m.

Both of them were planning to catch early trains back to Manchester and Edinburgh respectively at some time which might have been as early as 7.00 a.m. or 8.00 a.m. the following morning. It follows there was some talk of him being able to spend the few hours which would remain of the night at her friend's flat where she was staying.

On the Saturday she sprained her ankle. She telephoned the appellant and said that she thought she could still manage the dance. He said: 'We'll still have a good time'. In the event, her ankle mended sufficiently for them to go.

They met at the Grosvenor House Hotel at about 7.30 p.m. It has to be said straightaway that the evening was not a great success. He was put out to find that she was not familiar with all the reels and Scottish dances that were in the programme. They danced only two or three times and she danced another threesome without him. Unfortunately, as it turned out, they both drank a great deal. They were both drunk in the sense that they were under the influence of alcohol when they left the hotel some time before 4.00 a.m. She had realised early on that no sort of intimate relationship was going to develop between them, although she said in evidence that she thought or hoped they might remain friends. There was scarcely any physical contact between them except for one quite vigorous Hamilton House reel when she allowed him to put his arm around her waist and to kiss her once, she said, on her cheek.

They took a taxi together back to the Earls Court flat. Because of the short time which he would have until he had to catch his train, she had agreed, and maybe even suggested, that he should not have to go to Wandsworth and then back to the station in central London and that he should come back to the flat, and there was some talk of them having coffee and a snooze there. In the taxi he was, according to her description, fairly amorous. That involved putting his arm around her. There was no suggestion of any form of intimacy, or that they talked about sleeping together or that sexual intercourse might take place.

When they got back to the flat, they both realised they were quite drunk. They made quite a lot of noise and she told him to be quiet so as not to disturb the friend and boyfriend whose flat it was. Nevertheless, they managed to wake those two, who were sleeping in the bedroom of the flat. In the sitting room was a single bed and a sofa. The complainant showed the appellant the kitchen and how to make coffee and then all she wanted to do was to go to sleep.

Her account was this. She took off her dress, her tights and shoes with her back to him. Wearing only her knickers, she got into bed, curled up facing the wall under the duvet and went to sleep. The next thing she knew, apart from hearing a rustling noise, was that she was being forced on to her back, the appellant was on top of her, his legs were forcing hers apart and she realised that his penis was erect and wearing a condom. That was the reason, no doubt, for the rustling sound which she had vaguely heard. As she described it, his penis was coming into contact with her vagina. She screamed and she said that she struggled for what was about 10 to 15 seconds, although it seemed longer, and eventually she pushed him off and on to the floor. She also grabbed the telephone but she was not sure why. Then she rushed into the bedroom where her friend and the boyfriend had been woken again by the screams, of which there were as many as six. She was described as being in a hysterical state. She lay on the friend's bed. She was covered with the duvet because she was naked, her knickers having come off, and then the friend and the boyfriend went into the sitting room where they found the appellant naked, lying on his back, his penis being what was described as semi-erect and wearing a condom. Those two had some conversation with him which they found distinctly odd. A little later but not immediately the police were called.

The police arrived and the appellant was arrested and taken to the police station in a police car.

(The Court dismissed the appeal against conviction.) We turn to the question of sentence.

It was suggested in the notice of appeal, although this has not been pursued by Mr Ferguson, that this is the kind of case to which the sentencing guidelines set out in *Billam* do not apply, or where the guidelines themselves should be modified. We do not agree. As has been said many times before, guidelines are guidelines, and no more. They are not a rigid formula or a straitjacket which must be forced onto every case. The fact that they are guidelines means that they leave room for the exceptional, perhaps even for the unusual case. They are flexible enough to include all cases. They do not fix absolute maximum or absolute minimum sentences and there is no such thing as an automatic result. Moreover, it cannot be said in our judgment that the present case is at the furthest extreme from the kind of violent rape by a stranger to which *Billam* undoubtedly does apply. These were not two persons who had lived together or had had consensual intercourse together before. They had met only once. This was the first evening they spent in each other's company. There was no suggestion or promises of sexual intercourse at any stage of the evening before the incident occurred. The girl did not say yes and then change her mind. She did not even suggest that she might say yes and then think better of it. The appellant himself appears to have recognised this. He says that he remembered being surprised and pleased when, as he thought, the girl indicated her willingness to him. The jury has rejected his evidence that she did act in that way, but it remains clear on his own evidence that before the incident itself she was not giving him any reasons to hope that sexual intercourse might take place. What she did was get undressed and get into bed and then immediately fall asleep with her back to him. If he had not had so much to drink he would not have reacted as he did, but the alcohol released the inhibitions which otherwise would have held him in check, and what was, on any view, an indecent assault was taken as far as attempted rape. The rape falls between the two extremes of violent rape or attempted rape between strangers and intercourse without the girl's consent on a particular occasion after she had consented previously or indicated that she might consent. We agree with Mr Ferguson's submission. We have no hesitation in holding that the *Billam* guidelines do apply when deciding what is the appropriate sentence for this offender and this offence.

With regard to the appellant, the learned judge had the benefit of two thorough and helpful reports from the probation officer, Mr Peter Graham, and from Dr Eastman of St George's Hospital Medical School. He described a person remarkably similar to the picture which emerges from the evidence the jury accepted of what happened that night. The appellant is not without sexual experience but he is sexually naive and his attitude towards women, and in some respects towards society generally, is unconventional and somewhat disturbing. This does not prevent him from being a congenial and lively companion for women as well as men, but when his inhibitions are loosened by alcohol his domineering attitude towards them can result in anti-social behaviour. He is also described as arrogant, and consistently with this he has shown no remorse for this offence. He regards himself as the victim and we have no indication that his attitude has changed. The most striking phrase in the reports which was quoted to the judge is that 'he is likely not to be good at picking up social cues from women'. As the judge said:

'Your attitude to women leaves a great deal to be desired.'

As Mr Ferguson put it, he is not the norm in that respect. The fact is that on the evening in question he was out of his depth, and probably he knew it. The restraint which normally he exercised was overcome by alcohol. This offence was the result.

The learned judge dealt with the matter of sentence as follows. He referred first to the trust which the complainant had placed in the appellant by agreeing to go to the dance in the company of a comparative stranger. He said that he was quite satisfied that when the complainant asked the appellant back to the flat, no kind of sexual encounter was in her mind and he said that the appellant had subjected her to what was undoubtedly a terrifying and degrading ordeal. He added that the appellant had shown no remorse. He had not pleaded guilty, which was not a matter of aggravation but which meant that no mitigation was available to him on that ground. He said this with regard to the complainant giving evidence:

'And that was, as I saw for myself, an experience she found quite visibly distressing . . . I have come to the conclusion that your attitude to women leaves a great deal to be desired. However, I have concluded that this is a case which is so serious that only a custodial sentence can be justified.'

Having said that there were no aggravating features, he mentioned four mitigating features. First, that the appellant, having met with resistance and being thrown off the bed, had not returned to the attack. Secondly, his naivete in sexual matters. Thirdly, the publicity which had caused him anxiety and distress before and during and after the trial. Finally, some letters which the appellant had written to the judge and of which we have seen copies.

In the notice of appeal further grounds have been added. First, the short duration of the incident which, even on the girl's evidence, was no more than about 10 to 15 seconds. Secondly, the minimal amount of force or violence used. Thirdly, it is submitted that the assault was not planned or premeditated and as the victim herself said, it was more a case of indecent assault. Last, but by no means least, the appellant's ruined career.

We think it right to take account, in considering the whole of the circumstances of what might be called the whole build up in the course of the evening to the situation in which they found themselves together in the flat in the early hours of the morning, as they did.

Mr Ferguson, taking his lead from the case of *Taylor* where a non-custodial sentence was imposed in an exceptional case of rape, where the rape was of a mentally defective girl and was described as being more like an indecent assault, submitted first that the present case was similar, in the sense that it too was properly described as more like a case of indecent assault.

The girl herself, when she was spoken to by the police officers shortly afterwards said this:

'Q: Has he raped you, penetrated you?
A: He tried but I stopped him.
Q: So he attempted to rape you?
A: Well, yes, but I am a solicitor and I would not want him to get into trouble for rape. It is more an indecent assault.'

Indeed, the offence initially for that reason was charged as such.

Secondly, Mr Ferguson submits that in sexual matters the defendant is 'not the norm' and, as Mr Ferguson put it, he was less understanding, due perhaps to a personality defect, of the consequences which his actions would have. Thirdly, Mr Ferguson submits that fortunately on the evidence the girl seems to have suffered no long-term adverse effects. Whilst making that submission Mr Ferguson emphasises that he is not seeking in any way to minimise the offence or its consequences for the complainant.

Finally, Mr Ferguson has stressed the personal, social and professional devastation and ruin which has resulted for the appellant.

We have borne these matters well in mind, but the fact is that the appellant was found guilty of attempted rape when an alternative verdict of indecent assault was expressly left to the jury. In these circumstances we cannot bypass the court's duty to pass sentence in accordance with the jury's verdict.

What does remain as a strong mitigating factor is that the appellant desisted from committing the full offence of rape when he met the resistance which he did. Secondly, his personal characteristics and the limited effect of the offence upon the complainant can properly be taken into account, but we have to bear in mind that the jury and the judge clearly were impressed by her evidence. He described it as a terrifying and degrading ordeal for her. There was also evidence from the friend, whose flat it was, and the boyfriend, that she screamed out hysterically and was in a state of great shock. The girl's evidence was quoted as follows:

'She was shaking as if she was in shock. She was in a dreadful state emotionally.'

In our judgment, the learned judge was correct to hold that a non-custodial sentence could not be justified. He was also correct in applying the guidelines in *Billam*'s case and in doing so to start with a notional sentence which clearly was somewhat in excess of three years' imprisonment.

The question is whether he reduced it sufficiently to reflect the mitigating factors to which we have referred as regards first the offence itself: secondly, the circumstances in which it was committed, and thirdly, the consequences for the complainant. What is not available to the appellant in this case is the further mitigation, often described as the best mitigation of all, made available by a guilty plea. The fact that the appellant pleaded not guilty, as he was perfectly entitled to do, meant that the girl had to give her evidence not once but twice. This is one, but only one, aspect of the question of remorse. Even after conviction and even whilst still maintaining that he was and is innocent, the appellant could have some regard to her feelings and could express his remorse to her and to the court. He has not done so.

Notwithstanding that factor, we have to come to the conclusion that the learned judge could properly have made some greater reduction in the sentence than he did. Alternatively, it can be said in our view the sentence of three years did not reflect fully the matters which have been placed before us.

In our judgment, the period should be reduced to two years, but not reduced further, bearing in mind that first, there was no plea of guilty, and, secondly, the learned judge was clearly impressed by the complainant's evidence.

For these reasons, the appeal against conviction will be dismissed. The appeal against sentence will be allowed to the extent of substituting a period of two years' imprisonment."

Much of the debate surrounding acquaintance rape has focused on the extent of the harm caused to the victim, the assumption being that the degree of harm is less where the woman and man are acquainted. A study carried out by Ian Bownes, Ethna O'Gorman and Angela Sayers compared twenty-one rape attacks in which the victim knew her attacker with thirty attacks in which the man was a stranger.[19] The study investigated three key elements of the assaults: the "contextual nature" of the rape encounter, the "assault characteristics" (*i.e.* force, injuries, nature of sexual activity) and the "post-rape behaviour".[20] The results of the study were as follows:

I. T. BOWNES, E. C. O'GORMAN & A. SAYERS
"Rape — A Comparison of Stranger and Acquaintance Assaults"[21]

"Contextual Nature of Encounter with Rapist
[T]here were significant differences between the stranger and acquaintance rapes with respect to the context of the initial encounter with the assailant prior to the initiation of the assault. Contact with the assailant within a social setting took place immediately prior to the assault in significantly more of the acquaintance rapes (67 per cent as opposed to 27 per cent). The majority of the victims of stranger rape initially encountered their assailant in an outdoor setting. This was significantly higher than in the acquaintance rape group (60 per cent as opposed to 19 per cent). The proportion of assaults initiated by the assailant breaking into/forcing his way into the victim's home were the same for stranger and acquaintance rape groups and were the least common (14 per cent).

Assailant-Victim Relationship
[I]n the majority (57 per cent) of cases where the victim knew the assailant, the relationship was fairly 'close', *i.e.* the assailant was a friend, neighbour, relative or former/current boyfriend of the victim.

---

[19]   I. T. Bownes, E. C. O'Gorman & A. Sayers, "Rape — A Comparison of Stranger and Acquaintance Assaults" (1991) 31 Med. Sci. Law 102.
[20]   I. T. Bownes, E. C. O'Gorman & A. Sayers, *ibid.*, at 102.
[21]   I. T. Bownes, E. C. O'Gorman & A. Sayers, *ibid.*, at 104–107.

Use of Alcohol

In both stranger and acquaintance attacks a proportion of the victims admitted to having had two or more alcoholic drinks prior to the assault. The incidence of this was higher in the stranger rape group (40 per cent as opposed to 19 per cent), this was not statistically significant. The overall incidence of alcohol use by victims was 31 per cent.

With respect to use of alcohol by the assailant, significantly more of the acquaintance rape victims reported their attackers as having 'smelled of drink' at the time of the assault (29 per cent as opposed to 0 per cent).

Setting and Duration of Assaults . . .

[S]ignificantly more of the acquaintance rapes took place indoors (52 per cent as opposed to 19 per cent). The most common setting for rapes by strangers was outdoors (47 per cent as opposed to 38 per cent NS). The incidence of rapes which took place in cars was significantly higher for the stranger group (34 per cent as opposed to 10 per cent). There was no statistical difference between the two groups with respect to rapes which took place in the victim's own home and with respect to duration of assault.

Coercion and injuries . . .

[V]erbal threats alone were successful in significantly more of the victims of acquaintance [rape] (38 per cent as opposed to 13 per cent). The majority of victims in both groups were subjected to some form of physical aggression and there were no significant differences in this respect. However, significantly more of the attacks by strangers involved the display of a weapon (24 per cent as opposed to 0 per cent). The weapons involved included guns (43 per cent) knives (43 per cent) and broken bottles (14 per cent).

With respect to victim resistance, all of the women reported having made verbal protests and 80 per cent reported having struggled at some point during the assault. They universally reported an escalation in threats/physical aggression in response to their efforts at resistance. Only two women reported having 'put up a fierce fight' — the assailants in both cases were strangers. One of these women had severe injuries requiring hospital admission.

With respect to injuries, the majority of the victims of acquaintance rape escaped without any visible injuries (52 per cent as opposed to 27 per cent).

Similar percentages of both groups had minor injuries (37 per cent overall). Proportionately more of the stranger rape victims had serious injuries (33 per cent as opposed to 14 per cent), this was not statistically significant.

Actual/attempted Sexual Activities

[T]he range of sexual acts attempted or demanded by assailants was not markedly different between the two groups. There was proportionately more coercive reciprocation of sexual activity reported by the victims of strangers. The incidence of fellatio being demanded was statistically significant (23 per cent of stranger rapes as opposed to 6 per cent of acquaintance rapes). The reported incidence of the rapist kissing the victim was significantly higher in the acquaintance group (33 per cent as opposed to 7 per cent).

Significantly more of the victims of acquaintance rape reported having been verbally abused by their attackers throughout the assault (38 per cent as opposed to 13 per cent).

A proportion of the victims in both groups reported that the rapist appeared to have experienced sexual dysfunction at some point during the assault. The victims of stranger rape reported a higher incidence of erectile insufficiency having occurred (27 per cent as opposed to 0 per cent). A similar percentage of both groups reported that the rapist experienced retarded ejaculation (22 per cent overall). Some victims reported that sexual dysfunction in the rapist was associated with demands for other sexual activities.

Post-rape Interaction
[T]here was a marked difference between the two groups with respect to the assailant's behaviour after the overt sexual part of the assault. Significantly more of the assailants who were acquaintances threatened the victim and/or warned her not to tell anyone about the attack (48 per cent as opposed to 3 per cent). An almost equal proportion of assailants in this group showed non-threatening or conciliatory behaviour post-rape and this was significantly higher than in the stranger rape group (43 per cent as opposed to 7 per cent). The proportion of assailants who robbed their victims after the rape was similar in both groups and the overall incidence of this was 6 per cent.

Intervention by a third party curtailed the attack in 13 per cent of rapes carried out by strangers, but none of the rapes by acquaintances were interrupted by a third party. Equal proportions of victims in both groups succeeded in escaping from their attacker (25 per cent overall), and in 67 per cent of the attacks in both groups the attacker abandoned the victim."

The study concludes that there was, indeed, a substantial degree of difference between the factual circumstances (contextual, force used and post-rape behaviour) of the two sets of attacks:

I. T. Bownes, E. C. O'Gorman & A. Sayers
"Rape — A Comparison of Stranger and Acquaintance Assaults"[22]

"Discussion
The results of this study showed significant differences between stranger and acquaintance rape with respect to a number of elements of the assault. However this study, like all studies of rape victims, is vulnerable to sample bias. All the victims studied were litigants, and previous research has shown that victims of acquaintance rapes are less likely to report the attack to the police. In addition, factors relating both to the victim, such as prior victimization, and to the characteristics of the attack, such as degree of force used, have been shown to influence reporting of both stranger and acquaintance rapes. It is likely therefore that with respect to all rape attacks, the proportion of acquaintance rape reported in this study is under-representative and that the proportion of rapes involving significant force and injuries may be over-representative. However, we feel that useful conclusions can still be drawn on the basis of the differences between the two groups studied.

The results demonstrate that acquaintance and stranger rapes differ significantly in

[22]   I. T. Bownes, E. C. O'Gorman & A. Sayers, *ibid.*, at 107–109.

the contextual nature of the first encounter of the victim with the assailant and in the setting of the actual assault. When the rape was carried out by an acquaintance a degree of social interaction between victim and assailant was more likely to have occurred immediately prior to initiation of the assault. Where the rape was carried out by a stranger, no antecedent social interaction between rapist and victim was attempted in the majority of cases. In addition the first encounter was more likely to have been a chance meeting in an outdoor setting. This was the most common setting for the actual rape attack in this group and significantly more of the rapes carried out by strangers took place in vehicles. This may reflect the type of predatory behaviour which has been described by many researchers as being characteristic of a significant proportion of rapists.

Stranger and acquaintance rapes differed significantly with respect to the display of weapons by the assailant. This was significantly higher in the stranger group. Guns and knives were encountered in equal proportions in contrast to a previous British study where knives were the most common weapon. It is not known whether this is a reflection of the availability of fire-arms among certain sections of the community in Northern Ireland. Only one assailant (2 per cent) actually used his knife. The possession of weapons amongst the stranger group may imply a greater degree of premeditation among these assailants with respect to the intent to commit rape. However, among the acquaintance rapists, knowledge of the victim may have conferred advantages in planning an assault especially with respect to selection of victim, setting and circumstances so that a weapon was not deemed necessary.

There were marked differences between stranger and acquaintance rapes with respect to verbal aggression. This played a much more prominant role in the acquaintance rapes. In this group verbal threats alone were effective in gaining victim compliance in significantly more cases; significantly more of the victims reported that the rapist continued to verbally abuse them throughout the rape and after compliance had been achieved, and significantly more of the assailants verbally threatened or abused their victims after the assault had been completed. There were striking differences in the way the victims reported the form and content of the verbalizations. Victims of strangers tended to report abuse or threats in a rather non-specific manner, *e.g.* 'he swore at me', 'he called me names'. In contrast, victims of acquaintances tended to report verbatim large portions of the verbal interaction: 'He said I'd been asking for it all night', 'he said I was a slut and everyone knew it'. This perhaps reflected the psychological impact this aspect of the assailant's behaviour had on the victims in this group and the increased effectiveness of this form of coercion where the assailant was able to draw on a knowledge of the victim's past and present life-style and personal circumstances.

Aggressive verbalization has been implicated in many facets of rape attacks. The role of anger in deviant sexual arousal has been well documented and aggressive verbalizations may serve both to display and enhance anger for the rapist. Establishing dominance over his victim using verbal threats is thought to be a means of asserting identity, potency and virility in a significant proportion of rapists. Verbally aggressive reactions to rejection behaviour on the part of the acquaintance victim progressing to rape have been documented by Barbaree *et al.* and Kanin.

There were significant differences between the two groups with respect to the degree and form of interaction between assailant and victim after the overtly sexual part of the assault had ended. With respect to the stranger rapist, 63 per cent of assaults ended with the attacker abandoning the victim immediately after sexual activity ceased. A small proportion (13 per cent) of attacks were curtailed when a third party intervened — this did not happen at all in the acquaintance rape group perhaps reflecting the greater proportion of these attacks taking place indoors. The absence of any significant attempts to interact with the victim post-rape among the stranger rapists may be a reflection of the setting of these attacks — the majority occurred outdoors or in cars where discovery was a possibility.

In contrast, women who were raped by acquaintances almost universally (95 per cent) reported some attempt on the part of the assailant to interact with her after the rape. Two distinct types of behaviour were reported in almost equal proportions. A large proportion of the assailants (43 per cent) displayed non-threatening or conciliatory behaviour which included falling asleep beside the victim, helping her to get dressed and offering to 'see her home'. This behaviour could be viewed as a distorted affirmation of a person-orientated relationship with the victim and evidence of cognitive errors which are frequently encountered among sexual offenders in justifying and minimalizing their actions. Threatening behaviour was displayed by a slightly larger proportion of the assailants (48 per cent). This included warnings about the consequences to the victim or her family of the attack being reported and threats of further violence or repeated attack. This obviously has implications for the reporting of and possible convictions for sexual attacks where the assailant and victim are acquainted.

In conclusion, we believe that examination and analysis of the assault's behavioural dimensions allows stranger and acquaintance rape to be clearly differentiated."

The study by Bownes, O'Gorman and Sayers focuses upon the external circumstances of the rape to compare "stranger" and "acquaintance" rape. What their study does not attempt to compare is the effect upon the victim and it is in this respect that some feminists have argued that "acquaintance" rape should not be viewed as less traumatic for its victims than stranger rape. Catharine MacKinnon argues that "women feel as much, if not more, traumatized by being raped by someone we have known or trusted, someone we have shared at least an illusion of mutuality with, than by some stranger. In whose interest is it to believe that it is not so bad to be raped by someone who has fucked you before than by someone who has not?"[23]

7.3.ii   *"Marital" rape*

Until 1991 non-consensual intercourse between man and wife was not "unlawful" (being understood in this context to mean "outside of marriage") sexual intercourse which fell within the definition of that act contained in section 1(1) of the Sexual Offences (Amendment) Act 1976 (now itself amended). The story of the marital rape exemption is detailed in the following extract:

J. L. BARTON
"The Story of Marital Rape"[24]

"In the twenty-second disputation of the second book of his *Disputationes de Martimonio*, the learned Sanchez puts a question. A woman has married. Her marriage is

---

[23]   C. A. MacKinnon, *supra*, n. 7 at 649.
[24]   (1992) 108 L.Q.R. 260 at 260–262.

not yet consummated. She wishes to leave her husband and enter religion. Within the term (ordinarily two months) which the ecclesiastical judge has allowed her for deliberation her husband has sexual intercourse with her by force. Is the marriage consummated, and if it is, does the ordinary consequence follow, that she cannot enter religion? Sanchez holds that the marriage is consummated, and indissoluble, but it is the more probable opinion that the wife may none the less enter religion. If she might not, the husband would benefit by his own wrong, and the wife would be deprived of her right without fault upon her part. It was not the only opinion. Hostiensis, in the thirteenth century, Archidiaconus and Baldus in the fourteenth, and Covarruvias in the sixteenth had held that if the marriage were consummated, whether rightfully or wrongfully, the wife could not be professed in religion.

Sanchez put the question in these terms because if the wife had not entered religion when her term of deliberation expired, and her husband *then* resorted to force, there was no room for doubt. The marriage was consummated, and neither party could enter religion. The husband who compelled his wife to submit to sexual intercourse by force or fear committed no sin, for he was exercising his right, though Sanchez agreed with those who held that he might sin in his manner of exercising it, should he resort to force without first trying the effect of persuasion, as would an owner who forcibly retook property which he might have retaken peaceably. He did not agree with Antonius de Butrio that the wife of a husband who habitually resorted to force might demand a divorce from bed and board for ill-usage. The wife would have suffered no violence had she rendered her husband his due of her own accord. If she would not, her husband had the right to compel her. If there were some excess in the manner, it was not very great, and the wife might avoid it by rendering her husband his due without compulsion, as she was bound to do.

For the canonist one, and not the least important of the reasons for which matrimony was ordained was that it was better that those incapable of continence should marry than that they should burn. If one spouse might refuse the other, this end of matrimony would be defeated, for if the frustrated spouse were unable to contain, his case would be worse than before. He would fall into the sin not merely of fornication, but of adultery. The sexual obligations of matrimony were worked out with a logical rigour and in a degree of detail which makes much of Sanchez's ninth book, *De Debito Conjugali*, rather odd reading today. 'As dirty as Sanchez' was a phrase which passed into proverb in anticlerical circles in eighteenth century France: not altogether justly, for the questions which he raises are traditional questions, and few of his answers are new.

The *debitum conjugale* was one of those obligations of matrimony which could be neither excluded nor modified by agreement, but it was not unqualified. Simple distaste, however extreme, would not entitle one spouse to refuse the other, nor would a toothache, or a headache without fever. Sickness, on the other hand, would justify a refusal, as would the after effects of childbirth, in the case of a wife, and a spouse whose health would be notably damaged would be not merely entitled to refuse the *debitum* to the other, but obliged in conscience to do so.

It has been widely asserted that Sir Matthew Hale was the first English lawyer to hold that a husband who has sexual intercourse with his wife by force cannot be convicted of rape. He may have been the first text writer to mention the point, but we may doubt whether he were the first to hold this opinion, for in medieval England, as elsewhere in Europe, the obligations of matrimony were governed by the law of the church. When, in 1436, the unfortunate Isabella Butler was abducted, forcibly married, and ravished, she successfully petitioned Parliament that she might be permitted to prosecute her abductor for rape. As the law was taken then, and indeed much later, a woman forcibly married was a wife *de facto* until the marriage was pronounced void by the sentence of an ecclesiastical court. The secular court had no jurisdiction to determine whether a marriage *de facto* were a good marriage in law. To judge from the narrative upon the Parliament Roll, it was not very probable that the threat of excommunication, or indeed actual excommunication, would be sufficient to bring Isabella's ravisher to answer before the ordinary. Her advisers seem to have taken it to follow that if she wished to proceed against him for rape, she must obtain a private Act of Parliament. Sir Matthew Hale had so little respect for the husband's ancient right of marital correction that he was prepared to hold, in defiance of sound latinity, that the saving for the husband's right of *castigatio* in the wife's writ for surety of the peace must be taken to refer to admonition and not to beating. The principle which he states in his *History of the Pleas of the Crown*, that a husband can commit no rape upon his wife because

> '... by their mutual matrimonial consent and contract the wife hath given
> up herself in this kind unto her husband, which she cannot retract'

would hardly have seemed novel to a contemporary ecclesiastical lawyer, and we may doubt whether it would have seemed novel to a common lawyer. It is improbable, at least, that he invented it from simple misogyny.

Whether he were of opinion that the wife's duty to submit was more extensive than the husband's right to exact the *debitum* is not a question which can now be answered. A general proposition in a statute cannot legitimately be held to be subject to any exception which is not expressly stated, but this is not necessarily true of a general proposition in an elementary text-book. Unfortunately this question is not considered in the printed reports until *R. v. Clarence*, in which those judges who expressed opinions upon it adopted between them every opinion logically possible."

The case of *R. v. Clarence*,[25] has already been mentioned above in relation to the primacy it accords to the phallus in its construction of the act of intercourse. But the case is also instructive in its contribution to the legal discourse upon marital rape. To summarise, Clarence, knowing that he suffered from venereal disease, passed on this disease to his wife during intercourse. He was charged with unlawfully inflicting grievous bodily harm and with assault occasioning actual bodily harm contrary to sections 20 and 47 of the Offences Against the Person Act 1861. His initial conviction was later quashed by a majority of nine to four in the Court for Crown Cases Reserved.[26] While forming part of the majority, Wills J. commented that he was not prepared to assent to the proposition that "as between married persons rape is impossible."[27] In the minority Field J. decided that "[t]here may, I think, be many cases in which a wife may lawfully refuse intercourse, and in which, if the husband imposed it by violence, he might be guilty of a crime."[28] Conversely, Hawkins J., also in the minority, argued that "[b]y the marriage contract a wife no doubt confers upon her husband an irrevocable privilege to have

---

[25]   *R. v. Clarence, supra*, n. 9.
[26]   See J. L. Barton, "The Story of Marital Rape", *supra*, n. 24 at 262–265.
[27]   *R. v. Clarence, supra*, n. 9 at 33.
[28]   *R. v. Clarence, ibid.*, at 57.

sexual intercourse with her during such time as the ordinary relations created by such contract subsist between them. For this reason it is that a husband cannot be convicted of a rape committed by him upon the person of his wife. . . . Rape consists in a man having sexual intercourse with a woman without her consent, and the marital privilege being equivalent to consent given once for all at the time of marriage, it follows that the *mere act of sexual communion is lawful*".[29]

Suffice to say that the clarity of the law in this area left something to be desired. Clarity began to emerge with some concrete exceptions being introduced to the marital rape exemption where it could be shown that the wife intended to revoke her implied consent to intercourse.[30] Clarity was finally achieved first in Scotland where the exemption was abolished in the case of *S v. H.M. Advocate*.[31] Shortly afterwards the House of Lords followed suit in its decision in *R. v. R*[32]:

R. v. R
[1991] 4 All E.R. 481 at 482–483, *per* Lord Keith

"My Lords, in this appeal to the House with leave of the Court of Appeal, Criminal Division that court has certified the following point of law of general public importance as being involved in its decision, namely: 'Is a husband criminally liable for raping his wife?'

The appeal arises out of the appellant's conviction in the Crown Court at Leicester on 30 July, 1990, upon his pleas of guilty, of attempted rape and of assault occasioning actual bodily harm. The alleged victim in respect of each offence was the appellant's wife. The circumstances of the case were these. The appellant married his wife in August 1984 and they had one son born in 1985. On 11 November, 1987 the couple separated for about two weeks but resumed cohabitation at the end of that period. On 21 October, 1989 the wife left the matrimonial home with the son and went to live with her parents. She had previously consulted solicitors about matrimonial problems, and she left at the matrimonial home a letter for the appellant informing him that she intended to petition for divorce. On 23, October 1989 the appellant spoke to his wife on the telephone indicating that it was his intention also to see about a divorce. No divorce proceedings had, however, been instituted before the events which gave rise to the charges against the appellant. About 9 pm on 12 November, 1989 the appellant forced his way into the house of his wife's parents, who were out at the time, and attempted to have sexual intercourse with her against her will. In the course of doing so he assaulted her by squeezing her neck with both hands. The appellant

---

[29] *R. v. Clarence, ibid.*, at 51. Hawkins J. went on to mark his dissent from the majority view, however, by adding that "there is a wide difference between a simple act of communion which *is lawful*, and an act of communion combined with infectious contagion endangering health and causing harm, which is unlawful" (*R. v. Clarence, ibid.*).

[30] See *R. v. Clarke* [1949] 2 All E.R. 448; *R. v. Miller* [1954] 2 Q.B. 282; *R. v. O'Brien* [1974] 3 All E.R. 663; *R. v. Steele* (1976) 65 Cr. App. R. 22; *R. v. Roberts* [1986] Crim.L.R. 188; *R. v. Kowalski* (1987) 86 Cr. App. Rep. 339. For further discussion see J. L. Barton, *supra*, n. 26 at 265–267 and the judgment of Lord Keith in *R. v. R* [1991] 4 All E.R. 481.

[31] *S v. H. M. Advocate* 1989 S.L.T. 469.

[32] *R. v. R, supra*, n. 30.

was arrested and interviewed by police officers. He admitted responsibility for what had happened. On 3 May, 1990 a decree nisi of divorce was made absolute.

The appellant was charged on an indictment containing two counts, the first being rape and the second being assault occasioning actual bodily harm. When he appeared before Owen J. in the Crown Court at Leicester on 30 July, 1990 it was submitted to the judge on his behalf that a husband could not in law be guilty as a principal of the offence of raping his own wife (see [1991] 1 All E.R. 747). Owen J. rejected that proposition as being capable of exonerating the appellant in the circumstances of the case. His ground for doing so was that, assuming an implicit general consent to sexual intercourse by a wife on marriage to her husband, that consent was capable of being withdrawn by agreement of the parties or by the wife unilaterally removing herself from cohabitation and clearly indicating that consent to sexual intercourse had been terminated. On the facts appearing from the depositions either the first or the second of these sets of circumstances prevailed. Following the judge's ruling the appellant pleaded guilty to attempted rape and to the assault charged. He was sentenced to three years' imprisonment on the former count and to 18 months' imprisonment on the latter.

The appellant appealed to the Court of Appeal, Criminal Division on the ground that Owen J.:

> 'made a wrong decision in law in ruling that a man may rape his wife when the consent to intercourse which his wife gives in entering the contract of marriage has been revoked neither by order of a Court nor by agreement between the parties.'

On 14 March, 1990 that court (Lord Lane C.J., Sir Stephen Brown P., Watkins, Neill and Russell L.JJ. [1991] 2 All E.R. 257; [1991] 2 W.L.R. 1065) delivered a reserved judgment dismissing the appeal but certifying the question of general public importance set out above and granting leave to appeal to your Lordships' House, which the appellant now does."

Following a review of the history of the marital rape exemption Lord Keith considered the meaning given to "unlawful" as used in section 1(1) of the Sexual Offences (Amendment) Act 1976:

R. v. R
[1991] 4 All E.R. 481 at 488–490, *per* Lord Keith

"The position then is that that part of Hale's proposition which asserts that a wife cannot retract the consent to sexual intercourse which she gives on marriage has been departed from in a series of decided cases. On grounds of principle there is no good reason why the whole proposition should not be held inapplicable in modern times. The only question is whether s. 1(1) of the 1976 Act presents an insuperable obstacle to that sensible course. The argument is that 'unlawful' in the subsection means outside the bond of marriage. That is not the most natural meaning of the word, which normally describes something which is contrary to some law or enactment or is done without lawful justification or excuse. Certainly in modern times sexual intercourse outside marriage would not ordinarily be described as unlawful. If the subsection proceeds on the basis that a woman on marriage gives a general consent to sexual intercourse, there can never be any question of intercourse with her by her husband being without her consent. There would thus be no point in enacting that only intercourse without consent outside marriage is to constitute rape.

R. v. Chapman [1958] 3 All E.R. 143; [1959] 1 Q.B. 100 is founded on in support of the favoured construction. That was a case under s. 19 of the Sexual Offences Act 1956, which provides:

> '(1) It is an offence, subject to the exception mentioned in this section, for a person to take an unmarried girl under the age of eighteen out of the possession of her parent or guardian against his will, if she is so taken with the intention that she shall have unlawful sexual intercourse with men or with a particular man.
>
> (2) A person is not guilty of an offence under this section because he takes such a girl out of the possession of her parent or guardian as mentioned above, if he believes her to be of the age of eighteen or over and has reasonable cause for the belief . . .'

It was argued for the defendant that 'unlawful' in that section connoted either intercourse contrary to some positive enactment or intercourse in a brothel or something of that kind. Donovan J, giving the judgment of the Court of Criminal Appeal, rejected both interpretations and continued ([1958] 3 All E.R. 143 at 145; [1959] 1 Q.B. 100 at 105):

> 'If the two interpretations suggested for the appellant are rejected, as we think they must be, then the word "unlawful" in s. 19 is either surplusage or means "illicit". We do not think it is surplusage, because otherwise a man who took such a girl out of her parents' possession against their will with the honest and bona fide intention of marrying her might have no defence, even if he carried out that intention. In our view the word simply means "illicit", *i.e.*, outside the bond of marriage. In other words, we taken [*sic*] the same view as the trial judge. We think this interpretation accords with the common sense of the matter, and with what we think was the obvious intention of Parliament. It is also reinforced by the alternatives specifically mentioned in s. 17 and s. 18 of the Act of 1956, *i.e.*, "with the intention that she shall marry or have unlawful intercourse . . .".'

In that case there was a context to the word 'unlawful' which by cogent reasoning led the court to the conclusion that it meant outside the bond of marriage. However, even though it is appropriate to read the 1976 Act along with that of 1956, so that the provisions of the latter Act form part of the context of the former, there is another important context to s. 1(1) of the 1976 Act, namely the existence of the exceptions to the marital exemption contained in the decided cases. Sexual intercourse in any of the cases covered by the exceptions still takes place within the bond of marriage. So if 'unlawful' in the subsection means 'outside the bond of marriage' it follows that sexual intercourse in a case which falls within the exceptions is not covered by the definition of rape, notwithstanding that it is not consented to by the wife. That involves that the exceptions have been impliedly abolished. If the intention of Parliament was to abolish the exceptions it would have been expected to do so expressly, and it is in fact inconceivable that Parliament should have had such an intention. In order that the exceptions might be preserved, it would be necessary to construe 'unlawfully' as meaning 'outside marriage or within marriage in a situation covered by one of the exceptions to the marital exemption'. Some slight support for that construction is perhaps to be gathered from the presence of the words 'who at the time of the intercourse does not consent to it', considering that a woman in a case covered by one of the exceptions is treated as having withdrawn the general consent to intercourse given on marriage but may nevertheless have given her consent to it on the particular occasion. However, the gloss which the suggested construction would place on the word 'unlawfully' would give it a meaning unique to this particular subsection, and if the mind of the draftsman had been directed to the existence of the exceptions he would surely have dealt with them specifically and not in such an oblique fashion. In *R. v. Chapman* [1958] 3 All E.R. 143 at 144; [1959] 1 Q.B. 100 at 102 Donovan J. accepted that the word 'unlawfully in relation to carnal knowledge had in many early statutes not been used with any degree of precision, and he referred to a number of enactments making it a felony unlawfully and carnally to know any woman-child under the age of 10. He said ([1958] 3 All E.R. 143 at 144; [1959] 1 Q.B. 100 at 103): 'One would think that all intercourse with a child under ten would be unlawful; and on that footing the word would be mere surplusage.' The fact is that it is clearly unlawful to have sexual intercourse with any woman without her consent, and that the use of the word in the subsection adds nothing. In my opinion there are no rational grounds for putting the suggested gloss on the word, and it should be treated as being mere surplusage in this enactment, as it clearly fell to be in those referred to by Donovan J. That was the view taken of it by this House in *McMonagle v. Westminster City Council* [1990] 1 All E.R. 993; [1990] 2 A.C. 716 in relation to para. 3A of Sch 3 to the Local Government (Miscellaneous Provisions) Act 1982.

I am therefore of the opinion that s. 1(1) of the 1976 Act presents no obstacle to this House declaring that in modern times the supposed marital exception in rape forms no part of the law of England. The Court of Appeal, Criminal Division took a similar view. Towards the end of the judgment of that court Lord Lane C.J. said ([1991] 2 All E.R. 257 at 266; [1991] 2 W.L.R. 1065 at 1074):

> 'The remaining and no less difficult question is whether, despite that view, this is an area where the court should step aside to leave the matter to the parliamentary process. This is not the creation of a new offence, it is the removal of a common law fiction which has become anachronistic and offensive and we consider that it is our duty having reached that conclusion to act upon it.'

I respectfully agree.

My Lords, for these reasons I would dismiss this appeal, and answer the certified question in the affirmative."

The removal of the word "unlawful" from the statutory definition of rape by the Criminal Justice and Public Order Act 1994 has confirmed this approach. One might find it hard to disagree with Barton's conclusion that "[t]he recent history of the doctrine of marital exemption is an excellent example of the manner in which a principle may be transformed when the original reason for it is forgotten, and the blame for its faults transferred to our ancestors".[33]

---

[33] J. L. Barton *supra*, n. 24 at 269–270.

Indeed, whilst he accepted that the common law had been correctly stated in *R. v. Clarence* (as seen above), Lord Keith expressed the view that removal of the marital rape exemption was appropriate in the light of the changed status of women.

R. v. R
[1991] 4 All E.R. 481 at 483–484, *per* Lord Keith

"The common law is, however, capable of evolving in the light of changing social, economic and cultural developments. Hale's proposition reflected the state of affairs in these respects at the time it was enunciated. Since then the status of women, particularly of married women, has changed out of all recognition in various ways which are very familiar and upon which it is unnecessary to go into detail. Apart from property matters and the availability of matrimonial remedies, one of the most important changes is that marriage is in modern times regarded as a partnership of equals, and no longer one in which the wife must be the subservient chattel of the husband."

The statutory amendment, however, does not mark the end of the marital rape story. The issue raised in *R. v. R* was subsequently addressed at a European level. Following his conviction for the attempted rape of his wife, CR applied to the European Commission of Human Rights claiming that his conviction amounted to a violation of Art. 7 of the European Convention on Human Rights. Art. 7(1) provides that:

"No one shall be held guilty of any criminal offence on account of any act or omission which did not constitute a criminal offence under national or international law at the time when it was committed . . .".

The Commission expressed the view that there was no violation and referred the case to the European Court of Human Rights. The Court unanimously agreed with this assessment:

CR v. The United Kingdom & SW v. The United Kingdom
(Case Nos 48/1994/495/577; 47/1994/494/576)
[1996] 1 F.L.R. 434 at 446, 448–449

"However clearly drafted a legal provision may be, in any system of law, including criminal law, there is an inevitable element of judicial interpretation. There will always be a need for elucidation of doubtful points and for adaptation to changing circumstances. Indeed, in the United Kingdom, as in the other Convention States, the progressive development of the criminal law through judicial law-making is a well-entrenched and necessary part of legal tradition. Article 7 of the Convention cannot be read as outlawing the gradual clarification of the rules of criminal liability through judicial interpretation from case to case, provided that the resultant development is consistent with the essence of the offence and could reasonably be foreseen . . .

The decisions of the Court of Appeal and then the House of Lords did no more than continue a perceptible line of case-law development dismantling the immunity of a husband from prosecution for rape upon his wife . . . There was no doubt under the law as it stood on 12 November, 1989 that a husband who forcibly had sexual intercourse with his wife could, in various circumstances, be found guilty of rape. Moreover, there was an evident evolution, which was consistent with the very essence of the offence, of the criminal law through judicial interpretation towards treating such conduct generally as within the scope of the offence of rape. This evolution had reached a stage where judicial recognition of the absence of immunity had become a reasonably foreseeable development of the law . . .

The essentially debasing character of rape is so manifest that the result of the decisions of the Court of Appeal and the House of Lords — that the applicant could be convicted of attempted rape, irrespective of his relationship with the victim — cannot be said to be at variance with the object and purpose of Article 7 of the Convention, namely to ensure that no one should be subjected to arbitrary prosecution, conviction or punishment . . . What is more, the abandonment of the unacceptable idea of a husband being immune against prosecution for rape of his wife was in conformity not only with a civilised concept of marriage but also, and above all, with the fundamental objectives of the Convention, the very essence of which is respect for human dignity and human freedom."

The contextualisation by the European Court of Human Rights of the issue of marital rape within the larger picture of the respect for human freedom and dignity is an important and welcome move. The Court did not simply find for the government on a technical interpretation of Art. 7, as well it might have done. The positive statement contained within the final sentence cited above demonstrates a commitment to placing issues of harm to women in the context of the larger dimension of the protection of fundamental rights.[34] It also recognises that this is a civilised (progressive) approach to invasions of the individual female body, uncoupling this body from that of the male to which in the past it has been so intimately wedded.

7.4 The rape trial

It is not only the text of the law on rape which has been found problematic by feminists. It is also the procedures which surround the implementation of the text. Particularly the rape trial is identified as raising difficulties for the victims of rape, often leading to it being described as a second rape ordeal or as judicial rape.[35] This may occur as a result of many factors which construct

---

[34] Some feminists have, however, contended that human rights law may be impervious to claims of violations of women's rights. See further Chap. 7.5 below. For an in-depth analysis of this decision see S. Palmer, "Rape in Marriage and the European Convention on Human Rights: *CR v. U.K., SW v. U.K.*" (1997) 5 *Feminist Legal Studies* 91.

[35] This has been widely recognised following the case of *R. v. Edwards* (1996) in which the accused questioned the complainant over a six-day period during his trial at the Old Bailey. Michael Howard, then Home Secretary, subsequently announced proposals to enable the judiciary to prevent defendants who represent themselves in rape trials from cross-examining the complainant. The proposals were described as "designed to eliminate the harrowing ordeal which rape victims can suffer" (*The Guardian*, March 15, 1997). Whilst being questioned about the

the rape victim and her experience in a problematic fashion. We examine three particular aspects of this. The first is the sexual overtone of the trial which comes to be recast as a pornographic spectacle; the second is the admission and scrutiny of the sexual history of the complainant. Thirdly, we consider the contribution of the sentencing stage of the trial to the construction of the "ideal" rape victim.

7.4.i   *A sexualised spectacle*

Feminists have sought to expose the quasi-pornographic genre of the rape trial which, in requiring the victim to speak about her violation in intimate detail, may take on a titillating and offensive mantle. Two such perspectives are considered below. On the one hand, the rape trial is described by Carol Smart as a "specific mode of sexualization of a woman's body".[36] Secondly, Sue Lees, too, identifies the pornographic spectacle constituted by the trial scenario.

C. SMART
"Law's Power, the Sexed Body, and Feminist Discourse"[37]

". . . We know that a woman's account of her abuse is always filtered through a mesh of legal relevances about, for example, consent, intention, corroboration, and so on. Her story is reconstructed into a standard form of sexual fantasy or even pornography in which she becomes the slut who turns men on and indicates her availability through every fibre of her clothing and demeanour. The only difference between the rape story and the standard fantasy is that in the former she complains. With this turn of events her story is then transcribed into another account which has considerable currency. She becomes the spiteful, avenging harpie. She is no longer just the slut, but she takes on the mantle of the 'woman scorned'. It has been stated over and over again by feminists and by women who have been raped that it is the victim who becomes the prime suspect.

The process of the rape trial can be described as a specific mode of sexualization of a woman's body — a body which has already been sexualized within the codes of a phallocentric culture. Her body becomes literally saturated with sex. She is required to speak sex, and figuratively to re-enact sex: her body and its responses become the stuff of evidence. As she occupies the metaphorical sexual space which is allocated to her during the trial, she simultaneously invokes woman as a sex; the biological woman. The natural sexed woman is always already known to be more emotional, less rational, more subjective, more mendacious, and less reliable than man. The utterances of judges constantly reaffirm this.

Almost every rape trial tells the same story; it is like the Original Story being re-enacted on a daily basis. It confirms what is known about women by women and men. In other words, women's sexual subjectivity has already been framed by the language

---

alleged rape by the rapist will undoubtedly exacerbate the woman's situation, removing the right of the accused to do so will not "eliminate" the ordeal of the rape trial. The ordeal will remain a "second violation" even when the questioning is undertaken by a barrister.

[36]   C. Smart, "Law's Power, the Sexed Body, and Feminist Discourse", *supra*, n. 8 at 205.
[37]   C. Smart, *ibid.*, at 205–206.

of rape. Women 'know' they are to blame for rape. (Rape crisis centres routinely report that women blame themselves and that their task is to try to reduce or eliminate this blaming.) The rape trial also confirms what we already 'know' about (hetero)sex, namely that men have uncontrollable urges and natural desires and that women may only passively consent.

Against the story that is constructed in the legal context of court proceedings, police interrogation, legal rules, and the adversarial system, feminists have posed women's experience. The personal accounts of what women and children have endured remain deeply shocking, no matter how familiar they become. The aim of this strategy has been to reveal the truth of rape and how it is treated and thus to challenge the myths and lies of law. But law's deployment of power is not in fact reduced by this strategy; indeed it might be argued that it is extended. This extension is achieved by silencing all but one account of rape, an account which in turn produces the rapable (biological, sexed) woman of legal discourse. It is necessary to formulate this argument carefully.

The story of rape which is told is of a humiliating, degrading, depersonalizing, and terrifying ordeal. The trial is virtually the same ordeal but with witnesses. This account eclipses all others in feminist discourse (although I have heard others). The question to pose, therefore, is how and why has this become the dominant account? The 'why' is not difficult to answer. This is the language many women use. Looking at it one way this language merely 'gives voice' to the experience. From a deconstructionist position, however, the experience is already constructed in language, a language which is part of the formation of the subjectivity of womanhood. It is a language that wins moral support and empowers the speaker. It is the language of the moral crusades of the nineteenth century which constructed women and children as the victims of the lusts of debauched and unrestrained men. It is therefore an account that has a specific history and culture."

S. Lees
Ruling Passions: Sexual Violence, Reputation and the Law[38]

"In rape trials as in pornography, the female body is publicly portrayed and debated. It is her body, not his, that is put on trial. Her body's secretions and underclothing are scrutinized, her photographed injuries distributed as exhibits, her body's level of sexual arousal debated without regard to her testimony. She is objectified in similar fashion to her objectification in rape itself. This is the meaning of the term 'judicial rape' . . .

Judges frequently direct complainants to 'speak up' in the lofty setting of most Victorian court chambers. For a woman unused to speaking in public it can be shattering. The paradox is that the very use of such language, referring to private sexual parts of the anatomy, is sufficient to render a woman unrespectable. Many women never say such words even in the privacy of their homes, let alone to strangers in open court. Giving evidence about rape can be seen as a process of 'shaming' the complainant by forcing her to describe in open court the details of the assault. According to Anna Clark, in the eighteenth century to even admit to being raped was so shaming that women tended to use euphemisms to describe what happened to them, with such terms as 'ill used'. Clark describes how male judges and lawyers were obsessed with the

[38] (Buckingham: Open University Press, 1997), pp. 78–79.

explicit details of rape and would question her as to 'how her assailant could stop her mouth, hold down her hands, pull up her petticoats and pull down her breeches all at the same time'. Clark recounts how women often faced laughter from the gallery and transcripts of rape trials were sold as titillating literature. The curiosity about the details of the rape is also derived from patriarchal concern with chastity. Even today, what matters is whether penetration of the penis has taken place, which carries the implication that the victim's value as sexual property is damaged. The effect of such a stigma is the suppression of women's speech about sex.

Only in pornography would the kind of details of sexual activity — where the man put his hands, who removed her knickers, her tampon if she had a period, and other pieces of clothing — be described in public. It is for this reason perhaps that so many women find being cross-examined such a nightmare."

Lees goes on to demonstrate that one aspect of the representation of the sexual body in the rape trial is the focus on the functioning of the woman's sexual body parts. One particular feature of this is the relevance of menstruation. Lees comments:

S. LEES
Ruling Passions: Sexual Violence, Reputation and the Law[39]

"*Rape trials as defiling the victim*
Various themes relating to the female body emerge with regularity in rape trials. The frequent portrayal of the female body as bloody or slightly disgusting is combined with its portrayal as dangerous, enticing and brimming with uncontrolled sexuality, incitement to male lust, implicitly a danger to the moral order. Comments made by defence counsels in cross-examination are often fused with a sire and repugnance, disgust and fascination . . .

The emphasis on menstruation and handing round used panties in rape trials can be understood as a . . . process of defilement. Menstruation, even today, is regarded with ambivalence. In some communities women have been confined to menstrual huts and menstruating women have been seen as contaminated and banned from the worship of God. They are defiled. Disordered menstruation, gynaecologists argued in the nineteenth century, could lead to injury to the nervous system and thus to mental illness. The menstrual taboo is also evident in rape trials. The defence counsel's disgust is often blatantly expressed. In one trial heard in August 1993 the judge intervened in the defence counsel's (DC) cross-examination of the complainant (C):

DC: Let me put it to you that in fact you were just coming off, finishing your period at the time of having sexual intercourse with Mr Jones. Do you agree with that?

C: I was on for another couple of days.

DC: Another what?

C: Two days. I was on for another two days after that.

DC: This is the early hours of Wednesday, so do you mean until the Friday, or when?

[39] S. Lees, *ibid.*, pp. 80–81.

>C: I can't remember. What has my period got to do with that?
>
>DC: Just answer the questions please.
>
>C: I don't know.
>
>DC: You see, let me tell you what I'm driving at. I am putting it to you that you were a willing partner in having sex with Jones.
>
>C: No, I wasn't. It's not right. I wouldn't go near him with a barge pole.
>
>DC: These questions may not be very tasteful, but I have got to put them to you. In order for him to insert his penis, he has to cope then with the debris of your period and the tampon, is that right?
>
>Judge: Well, she can't answer what he would or wouldn't find easy.
>
>DC: The point is — I am sorry to have to put it to you — that the channel was obstructed.
>
>Judge: I think you're making a comment.
>
>DC: Am I? All right."

7.4.ii *Sexual history*

The criticisms made of the way in which the rape trial is conducted extend beyond those related to the demands made of the woman concerned to explain her body parts to those relating to the exposure of her life-style to public view. While a woman may not normally be questioned on her previous sexual history during the course of the trial, she may nevertheless by questioned about her sexual past with the defendant. Section 2 of the Sexual Offences (Amendment) Act 1976 provides:

> **2.** — (1) If at a trial any person is for the time being charged with a rape offence to which he pleads not guilty, then, except with the leave of the judge, no evidence and no question in cross-examination shall be adduced or asked at the trial, by or on behalf of any defendant at the trial, about any sexual experience of a complainant with a person other than the defendant.
>
> (2) The judge shall not give leave in pursuance of the preceding subsection for any evidence or question except on an application made to him in the absence of the jury by or on behalf of a defendant; and on such an application the judge shall give leave if and only if he is satisfied that it would be unfair to that defendant to refuse to allow the evidence to be adduced or the question to be asked.

In order for a conviction to be assured the victim has to present herself as a credible witness. Sue Lees carried out a study of jury trials in rape cases conducted at the Old Bailey in 1988–89, part of which focused upon the relevance of questioning about previous sexual experience as one of the criterion used to establish the credibility of the rape victim:

S. Lees
Ruling Passions: Sexual Violence, Reputation and the Law[40]

"The question of whether a woman has had sexual experience outside marriage is frequently raised as a criterion of her credibility. The Sexual Offences (Amendment)

---

[40] S. Lees, *ibid.,* pp. 64–66.

Act (1976) precluded such questioning about the sexual past of the victims, except at the discretion of the judge. In two cases in my research, the judge used his discretion to allow the defence to focus on the woman's past sexual history. Over and above this, one judge himself questioned the woman about her sexual experience in the absence of any application from the defence; and defence counsel on one occasion conducted what clearly amounted to improper cross-examination without intervention from the trial judge. A woman who has been a drug addict in the past, or who smokes cannabis, is particularly at risk of having her credibility undermined. One woman, who had broken with heroin two years previously, was continually asked if she had been taking drugs, and the defence suggested that she was stoned and had been drinking when the defendant arrived at her flat. This was in spite of police evidence that she was sober. Another woman was asked about having had an abortion and having sex with her boyfriend, neither of which was the least bit relevant to the alleged rape.

> Q: With regard to your stomach hurting, you said this was because you had had a termination and you weren't supposed to have sex? When had you previously had sex?
> C: I think it was Saturday.
> Q: So you were able to have sex?
> C: Having sex with your boyfriend is different to someone raping you.

Being homeless and on social security came up in one case and was used to imply that the complainant had 'asked for it'.

> DC: You didn't have anywhere to live, did you?
> C: I've got friends, that's where I went.
> DC: I suggest you asked him if you could stay at his flat.
> C: No I didn't. He suggested it.

Lack of marital status was emphasized in another case:

> DC: Being a single mother must be hard?
> C: Not really.
> DC: Were you keen to have a relationship?
> C: Not really.
> DC: Were you keen to have a man around?
> C: Not really.

Lack of contact with her children's father was used as evidence for her 'being embittered towards men'.

> DC: As far as your two children are concerned, you don't have contact with either of the fathers?
> C: No.
> DC: You don't know where they live?
> C: I do know. They have got nothing to do with this case.
> DC: They don't support you in any way?
> C: No.

The importance of reputation based on allegations rather than evidence was underlined in a case where the defendant pleaded guilty. Judge Richardson, in his summing up, commented:

> 'She is not a promiscuous person. She is a sober, sensitive and religious young lady who will bear the mental scars for a very long time to come. Did she 'provoke' the incident by the clothes she wore, the amount she had drunk, by dancing provocatively, going to the defendant's flat, being out late at night, asking the defendant back, taking drugs or soliciting?'

Any indication of autonomous behaviour or taking an active rather than a passive role was argued by the defence as implying consent. For example, since the defendant alleged that she had insisted on coming back to her flat (in the afternoon) the defence counsel argued:

> 'She is not a young innocent girl straight off the boat from Ireland. She has worked around public houses. The sort of young woman who is well able to look after herself. She is not delicate and retiring in her appearance. Not a small girl. Why did she invite him back to her flat?'

In another case the defence counsel asked:

> DC: In your account, he asked you to go back to your place for a drink. Why did you ask him to come?
> C: To accompany me.
> DC: When you left the pub, was it not that you said 'Let's go get some more drink and come to my place?'
> C: No.
> DC: He asked to go back several times. What did you expect?
> C: I didn't expect it to happen."

Women may face difficulties in establishing their credibility because of popular perceptions that they fabricate stories of rape possibly out of feelings of guilt or shame, to explain an unwanted pregnancy or to get back at a man who has scorned them. Aileen McColgan analyses this problem in relation to the rules on corroboration of the evidence of the rape victim.

A. McColgan
"Common Law and the Relevance of Sexual History Evidence"[41]

"There is no evidence that women lie about sexual assault any more than people generally lie about other offences. Nevertheless, mistrust about such allegations pervades the handling of rape complaints throughout the criminal justice system. Chambers and Millar's Scottish study, conducted in 1980–1, found '(a)n underlying assumption . . . held by many criminal justice agents . . . that women, in particular those who are promiscuous, are prone to untruthfulness and are unreliable witnesses'. Examples of

---

[41] (1996) 16 O.J.L.S. 275 at 276–277.

the mistrust with which such allegations are treated by the courts is to be found in the 'recent complaint' doctrine and in the (until recently) mandatory judicial warning about the dangers of convicting, in respect of sexual offences, on the uncorroborated evidence of the alleged victim. (This warning had to be given even where corroboration was present.) The former rule allows a sexual offences complainant to introduce evidence of a previous consistent statement to show consistency in relation to her complaint. This, at odds as it is with the more general rule excluding evidence of previous consistent statements, appears on its face to give sexual offence complainants an advantage over other witnesses. But the previous statement is not admissible, in the case of sexual offences, as evidence of its truth. On the contrary, it is useful 'to rebut the adverse inference that might otherwise be drawn from the victim's failure to complain of the attack upon her'—the rape complainant does not benefit from the presumption of truthfulness which exists in respect of witnesses to other crimes. Equally, the requirement that judges issue corroboration warnings stemmed from the conviction that, to quote some of the versions of that warning, 'women in particular and small boys are liable to be untruthful and invent stories', that 'in sex cases women sometimes imagine things which various ingredients in their make up tend to make them imagine'.

The mandatory requirement for a corroboration warning has been removed by the Criminal Justice and Public Order Act 1994. This step is to be welcomed. But the 1994 Act does not prevent judges from issuing corroboration warnings and, in Canada, such was the persistence of some judges in issuing warnings as a matter of course after the mandatory requirement was removed that subsequent legislation expressly forbade corroboration warnings. It is too early, as yet, to determine what impact the 1994 Act has had on judicial summings-up in sexual offences cases – the one appellate decision reported thus far does little more than to confirm that judges are free to exercise their discretion not to issue a warning if they see fit."

A further aspect of the problem of evidence admitted in the rape trial is the importance of denying that the woman experienced pleasure in the sexual encounter. Where a clear lack of pleasure cannot be demonstrated a woman's consent may be inferred.

C. Smart
Feminism and the Power of Law[42]

"Consent is recognized as the central pivot of the rape trial, but the question of pleasure is equally important even if it is less obvious. In practice this means that a woman must show, beyond all reasonable doubt, that she was unwilling to have intercourse *and* that she could not possibly have enjoyed it. The denial of enjoyment is vital because if there is any suggestion that she might have taken pleasure, then lack of consent becomes immaterial. No matter what violence might have been used to achieve submission, the slightest possibility of pleasure erases any responsibility for the preceding behaviour on the part of the man ... But how do juries know whether women enjoy particular sexual experiences? I have argued ... that women's sexual pleasure remains opaque in a phallocentric culture. Men can never be sure, so it is deemed that women have no pleasure (are frigid) or take pleasure from acts defined as pleasurable

[42] C. Smart, *supra*, n. 13 at pp. 36–38.

by men. The latter can, in turn, become a double jeopardy for women. Not only is it asserted that women must enjoy penetration (because men do) but even where women may not enjoy the physical sensations of penetration, it is not infrequently argued that our pleasure is derived from being the vehicle of men's pleasure. So as long as men are enjoying themselves, women cannot deny pleasure; it is inevitably altruistic if it is not egoistic.

That women deny pleasure is unimportant in a legal forum. Their denials will usually carry weight only where class or racial difference is so great that the idea of pleasure is inconceivable. But even racial difference or social distance are no guarantee that a woman will be believed because they can be transformed into sexual preferences or perversions. Hence the racist presumption that a white woman would only have a sexual relationship with a black man if she was forced, becomes transformed into the equally racist idea that it is a kind of perversion that white women practice in choosing to have these sexual relationships. In both of these formulations the woman has no voice of her own. The black woman is also in this double bind. Racist stereotypes of black women as sexually voracious and constantly available fit black women much more readily than white women into the category of the woman who takes pleasure from promiscuous encounters or forced sexual contacts. In these circumstances, where all rapes can be deemed pleasurable, how can the jury ever be certain that a woman did not feel some pleasure? And if she felt pleasure can it be rape?"

7.4.iii *Sentencing: the relevance of the construct of Woman*
On conviction the defendant will be sentenced. Before launching into an investigation of feminist perspectives upon sentencing practices, a comprehensive legal perspective can be found in the English case of *R. v. Billam*.[43] The appellant, together with sixteen other appellants and applicants, appealed or sought leave to appeal against sentences imposed for offences of rape, attempted raped and associated offences. Lord Lane C.J. felt it an opportune moment to set out guidelines on appropriate sentences in such cases.

R. v. Billam
[1986] 1 W.L.R. 349 at 350–352, *per* Lord Lane C.J.

"In the unhappy experience of this court, whether or not the number of convictions for rape has increased over the years, the nastiness of the cases has certainly increased, and what would 10 years ago have been considered incredible perversions have now become commonplace. This is no occasion to explore the reasons for that phenomenon, however obvious they may be . . .

Judges of the Crown Court need no reminder of the necessity for custodial sentences in cases of rape. The criminal statistics for 1984 show that 95 per cent. of all defendants who were sentenced in the Crown Court for offences of rape received immediate custodial sentences in one form or another. But the same statistics also suggest that judges may need reminding about what length of sentence is appropriate . . .

The variable factors in cases of rape are so numerous that it is difficult to lay down guidelines as to the proper length of sentence in terms of years. That aspect of the

---

[43] *R. v. Billam* [1986] 1 W.L.R. 349.

problem was not considered in *R. v. Roberts (Hugh)* [1982] 1 W.L.R. 133. There are however many reported decisions of the court which give an indication of what current practice ought to be and it may be useful to summarise their general effect.

For rape committed by an adult without any aggravating or mitigating features, a figure of five years should be taken as the starting point in a contested case. Where a rape is committed by two or more men acting together, or by a man who has broken into or otherwise gained access to a place where the victim is living, or by a person who is in a position of responsibility towards the victim, or by a person who abducts the victim and holds her captive, the starting point should be eight years.

At the top of the scale comes the defendant who has carried out what might be described as a campaign of rape, committing the crime upon a number of different women or girls. He represents a more than ordinary danger and a sentence of 15 years or more may be appropriate.

Where the defendant's behaviour has manifested perverted or psychopathic tendencies or gross personality disorder, and where he is likely, if at large, to remain a danger to women for an indefinite time, a life sentence will not be inappropriate.

The crime should in any event be treated as aggravated by any of the following factors: (1) violence is used over and above the force necessary to commit the rape; (2) a weapon is used to frighten or wound the victim; (3) the rape is repeated; (4) the rape has been carefully planned; (5) the defendant has previous convictions for rape or other serious offences of a violent or sexual kind; (6) the victim is subjected to further sexual indignities or perversions; (7) the victim is either very old or very young; (8) the effect upon the victim, whether physical or mental, is of special seriousness. Where any one or more of these aggravating features are present, the sentence should be substantially higher than the figure suggested as the starting point.

The extra distress which giving evidence can cause to a victim means that a plea of guilty, perhaps more so than in other cases, should normally result in some reduction from what would otherwise be the appropriate sentence. The amount of such reduction will of course depend on all the circumstances, including the likelihood of a finding of not guilty had the matter been contested.

The fact that the victim may be considered to have exposed herself to danger by acting imprudently (as for instance by accepting a lift in a car from a stranger) is not a mitigating factor; and the victim's previous sexual experience is equally irrelevant. But if the victim has behaved in a manner which was calculated to lead the defendant to believe that she would consent to sexual intercourse, then there should be some mitigation of the sentence. Previous good character is of only minor relevance.

The starting point for attempted rape should normally be less than for the completed offence, especially if it is desisted at a comparatively early stage. But, as is illustrated by one of the cases now before the court, attempted rape may be made by aggravating features into an offence even more serious than some examples of the full offence."

It has, nevertheless, been suspected by some feminists that sentences may be accorded differently depending upon the construction placed upon the female victim. It has already been noted above that in the case of *R. v. Diggle* the sentence of the accused was reduced on appeal, it being thought that the original sentence was unduly harsh given the nature of the offence and the mitigating factors. In an analysis of the sentencing of sexual assault cases in Scotland Susan Moody identifies "the striking contrast between the image of woman which colours the progress and outcome of sexual assaults before conviction and the female stereotypes which appear to be significant at the stage of sentencing".[44] Moody, in her study, analysed a sample of Scottish appeal cases (1982–1993) and cases reported in Scottish newspapers (January 1992–June 1993) in order to ascertain the images of women revealed at the sentencing stage in sexual assault cases. She found that:

> "[I]egal discourse itself polarises and creates false opposites, 'binary divisions' of male and female, guilty and not guilty. The images of women portrayed in the sentencing of sex offenders reflect this binary division, producing at best oversimplistic generalisations and at worst crude caricatures of women's experiences of sexual assault."[45]

In particular Moody identifies four "images" of women which emerge: the "wronged woman", the "wounded woman", the "weak woman" and the "wifely woman".

S. MOODY
"Images of Women: Sentencing in Sexual Assault Cases in Scotland"[46]

"1. The wronged woman
Traditionally in sexual assault cases sentences have reflected the prevailing attitude among the judiciary towards acceptable behaviour in heterosexual relationships and also their assessment of the impact of the sexual assault on the woman. Yet increasingly reported incidents of rape involve acquaintances or even intimates. The 'commonsense view' that rape by strangers is more painful to women is not universally supported by research findings. Indeed some studies consider that the more intimately acquainted the victim is with the offender the more painful the impact. According to Home Office studies, the closer the relationship between offender and victim the shorter the sentence. Research in Scotland supports this. The sample of 1992 cases broadly reflects this with longer sentences being imposed in cases involving strangers. However, some interesting variations from this pattern emerge which suggest that changes in the status of women may have had an impact on judicial attitudes.

First the image of women within marriage appears to have changed dramatically over the last ten years. The traditional notion that a married woman could not be raped by her husband, which has held sway in most Western jurisdictions for centuries, was overturned in Scotland ... However, the impact of such a relationship on the sentence was not tested in any of those cases because the outcome was either a not guilty or a not proven verdict. Indeed one of the High Court judges was at pains to point out that a wife could still forgive her husband and that that should have an effect both on culpability and on sentence.

'Our decision does not deprive a wife of the right to forgive or to tolerate or

---

[44]   S. Moody, "Images of Women: Sentencing in Sexual Assault Cases in Scotland" in J. Bridgeman & S. Millns (eds), *Law and Body Politics: Regulating the Female Body* (Aldershot: Dartmouth, 1995), p. 214.
[45]   S. Moody, *ibid.*, pp. 222–223.
[46]   In J. Bridgeman & S. Millns, *ibid.* pp. 223–225, 227, 228–229.

to change her mind. If a wife does change her mind after complaining of rape to the criminal authorities there is little doubt that a prosecution of her husband would not be insisted upon.'

The sample of cases analysed in this chapter included four instances of sexual assault either within marriage or where a couple was cohabiting. Four years was held to be the appropriate sentence for rape by a former cohabitant on the mother of his daughter, even though she did not wish to bring the case to court. Lord Prosser indicated that, while it was right to take the victim's view into account, the offender's behaviour had been 'vicious' and involved serious non-sexual assault also. The case of *X v. H.M. Advocate* involved an estranged husband, the father of the victim's children. The 'normal' sentence for rape, five years, was not considered excessive by the Appeal Court, which supported the trial judge's obiter remarks that 'no man can rape a woman with impunity no matter what relationship exists between them'. In *Campbell* several charges of rape against cohabitants resulted in a sentence of nine years, in spite of the fact that the cohabitants resumed living with the offender after each had been raped. The Appeal Court clearly did not take the view in these cases that either forgiveness or resumption of cohabitation after the crime merited a lighter sentence. In *S v. H.M. Advocate* the court went even further. Here a sentence of two years six months for assault with intent to rape was appealed on the grounds that the offender had desisted when requested by his wife to do so and that the relationship was continuing. While the trial judge considered 'on reflection' that the sentence was unduly severe this view was not shared by the Appeal Court bench which upheld the sentence.

While these cases are important it would be wrong to assume that they reflect an acceptance on the part of the judiciary that non-consensual sexual intercourse between husband and wife or cohabitants is equivalent to the crime of rape. In each the court was quick to point out that the incidents showed extreme physical violence. The issue was not so much the right of a wife or cohabitant to refuse intercourse, rather a reinterpretation of the offending behaviour as a serious assault which happened to be perpetrated as part of a sexual encounter. This desexualising of rape provides a useful way of bringing an otherwise ambiguous area into safe waters, equating the criminal behaviour with the numerous physical assaults committed by males on males. This is not to deny that the wife and the cohabitant have both benefited from this development but to advise against unreserved enthusiasm. In effect, the raped wife or cohabitant is replaced by the male victim of assault and the uncomfortable connotations of sexuality and male-female exploitation are thereby lost. It remains to be seen whether 'normal' sexual intercourse will be viewed in the same light.

Some developments can also be seen in other relationships between rape victims and offenders outside cohabitation. The court seem to have acknowledged that a prior relationship between the parties is not automatically a mitigating factor in sentencing. Thus in *Stewart* where a divorcee was raped after she accepted a lift from a man she met at a casino a sentence of five years was imposed. (It should be noted, however, that the offence was accompanied by extreme extraneous violence and that the victim had thirteen injuries when medically examined, including a black eye and internal bleeding.) Where a young man raped an eighteen year-old at a birthday party after asking her outside four years in prison was regarded as the appropriate sentence even though the offender was under twenty-one and had no previous convictions.

Cases which the defence portray as 'ambiguous' may nevertheless be regarded by the court as matters meriting a custodial sentence. For instance, where the victim had had sex willingly with another party in the offender's flat and the offender then raped her anything less than five years was seen as inadequate. The offender's plea of 'no real injury' was rejected. However, the court was at pains to note that the victim had not encouraged or contributed to the offence. In *MacKinnon* the victim had been staying with the offender but they had had no prior sexual relationship. She got into bed with him to keep warm and was then subjected to attempted rape. Twelve months was held not to be excessive. In none of these cases did the court accept that there had been any previous sexual connection between the parties. The women were viewed as 'wronged' and therefore deserving of the court's protection.

The final area which appears to have been opened up by recent cases is sexual assault at work. The case of *Caring*, for instance, where an employer was prosecuted for a series of indecent assaults against his female employees over several months, resulted in a custodial conviction of nine months even though the accused had no previous convictions.

2. The wounded woman

... Within the sample cases, those attracting longer sentences frequently involved acts of physical violence in addition to the sexual assault itself, including threats to use, or the use of, a weapon, usually a knife. In one case the indictment describes how the accused jumped on the victim and seized her by the throat, threatening to kill her if she did not do as he wished. His appeal against an eight year sentence for rape was dismissed. In another case a sentence of ten years imprisonment for attempted rape was upheld where the offender had threatened the victim with violence and 'place[d] her in such a state of fear and alarm for her safety that she was unable to resist'. The offender's appeal against a five year sentence was dismissed where he had induced the victim at knife-point to accompany him into woods and had then committed an indecent assault on her. Eighteen months was not regarded as an excessive sentence in a case of indecent assault where the offender had torn the victim's blouse, causing bruising and lacerations.

Conversely in several cases the defence sought to rely on the absence of physical injury, the fact that no weapon was used or that the victim suffered no serious physical damage as mitigating factors. With a few notable exceptions no attempt was made by either the prosecutor or the judge to explore the victim's understanding of violent behaviour. Instead physical violence was seen as particularly malign and damaging, in line with Scots legal tradition and their own male perceptions.

3. The weak woman

... It is clear from the sample that the courts are particularly keen to protect the elderly, the young and the respectable from the depredations of men. Assaults on defenceless old ladies, innocent young women and respectable wives and mothers tend to attract the more severe sentences. The courts also consider that men occupying positions of 'trust', on whom women must depend, such as taxi-drivers and doctors, should be punished more severely. Contrary to all the statistical evidence which suggests that women are most likely to be assaulted by acquaintances or intimates in their own homes, judges seek to shield women from attacks in public places or after forced entry to the victim's home. Two cases which illustrate these points and which were featured many times in press coverage of sexual assaults merit further consideration.

Judy, a mother of three and an active campaigner for the Scottish Conservative Party was attacked and robbed in her home by a man who posed as a priest. He struck her with a poker, punched her repeatedly and committed a series of sexual assaults on her. The trial judge imposed a sentence of life imprisonment for the protection of the public but this was overturned on appeal and replaced by a six year custodial sentence on the grounds that the accused was not a danger to the public. Nevertheless, the court had in fact imposed a longer sentence than the average of five years which might have been expected. Lord Cowie noted that the court was influenced, *inter alia*, by the 'nature and circumstances of the indecent assault'. Here was a woman who represented many other women deserving of the law's protection. 'Judy', the victim, courageously expressed her concern about several aspects of the case through the media. In one newspaper article she reflects back to the judges the image of the woman in need of protection by asking whether 'these three judges [would] be happy to leave their wives and daughters in a room with Cronin'.

The other victim of sexual assault who figured prominently in media coverage over the period of the research was a sixteen year-old girl who was raped by a man almost twice her age whom she did not know. She had been a virgin and the assault had been discovered when her mother read her diary. Her parents reported the matter to the police and the accused, a well-known local restauranteur, was convicted. His Counsel sought to influence the sentence by claiming that this 'prepossessing young woman showed all the signs of being able to put this behind her and lead a life without the kind of mark that certain other victims of rape might suffer'. Both the trial judge and the Appeal Court refused to accept that submission and jailed the accused for five years. Lord Milligan, the trial judge, noted particularly the age of the girl and implicitly suggested that the sentence would have been longer had it not been for the fact that the accused had no previous convictions.

4. The wifely woman

An interesting and somewhat paradoxical image of woman which is introduced by the defence in many pleas in mitigation and in appeals against sentence generally is the supporting, controlling influence which 'good' wives, cohabitants or mothers may exert on wayward men. This is a particularly powerful image in sexual assault cases presenting women as the rescuers of men from themselves, providing women with a redeeming role in taming male sexuality. For example, in *Martin* the fact that the accused had been living with a woman for three years was noted as a factor which should be set against the sentence of ten years for rape which had been imposed at first instance. Again in *Doherty* the defence noted that the accused was married and the father of a child. In an unusual twist, the defence in *Townsley* referred to the appellant's family circumstances, emphasising that a baby would be shortly born to his wife following artificial insemination and that she was 'looking forward to setting up a family unit with the appellant again many years hence in spite of all he [had] done in the past'. Where the female partner had at first reacted unfavourably to the accused's conduct but they were subsequently reconciled the defence considered that this should be brought to the court's attention. Conversely, in several cases the defence appeared to suggest that the failure of a wife to play her wifely role contributed to the commission of the indecent assault since the couples had been temporarily separated at the time."

Moody identifies the problem which the creation of these stereotypical images may present for women in the presentation of their experiences in sexual assault cases. She asserts that these images:

"are not simply of academic interest. They help to inform and shape decisions made by judges about sentencing in sexual assault cases. They also obscure, distort and replace the descriptions which individual women themselves might otherwise present of their experiences. Such powerful stereotypes may exacerbate the difficulties which women already have in making their own assessment, in trusting their own being. Within the court many groups have problems in articulating their experience because of the hierarchy of discourses which elevates one discourse and disqualifies others. Women are likely to be doubly disadvantaged in this situation."[47]

Moody's point is that women lack a voice in the articulation of their experiences in the court room and legal process. The degree of harm they perceive as having been perpetrated on their sexual being is not necessarily reflected in the judge's perception of that harm as revealed in the sentence passed. Moody concludes that:

"[t]he ways in which women might be permitted to present these descriptions [of harm], whether directly to the court, through their own Counsel, as a written report or in a standard form, are central to qualifying those discourses as authentic and also legitimate . . . [T]he idea seems to offer a significant, if limited opportunity to challenge the absence of female discourse in law."[48]

7.5   Sex/violence/war

7.5.i   *Sex/violence*
The experience of the rape victim (and the lack of voice given to this experience in the discourse on rape) is also central to the thesis of the radical feminist Catharine MacKinnon. MacKinnon's critique of the law of rape is based upon its interpretation as a crime of violence rather than sex, and hence its exclusion of female experience of violation. Having identified the liberal view-point as that which "comprehends rape as a displacement of power based on physical force",[49] MacKinnon argues:

C. A. MacKinnon
"Feminism, Marxism, Method and the State: Toward Feminist Jurisprudence"[50]

"The more feminist view to me, one which derives from victims' experiences, sees sexuality as a social sphere of male power of which forced sex is paradigmatic. Rape

---

[47]   S. Moody, *ibid.*, p. 229.
[48]   S. Moody, *ibid.*, p. 231.
[49]   C. A. MacKinnon, *supra*, n. 7 at 646. MacKinnon identifies this approach in the work of Susan Brownmiller who, in the introduction to her comprehensive study of rape, *Against Our Will*, writes that "[m]an's discovery that his genitalia could serve as a weapon to generate fear must rank as one of the most important discoveries of prehistoric times, along with those of fire and the first crude stone axe. From prehistoric times to the present, I believe, rape has played a critical function. It is nothing more or less than a conscious process of intimidation by which *all* men keep *all* women in a state of fear" (*Against Our Will* (London: Secker & Warburg, 1975), pp. 14–15).
[50]   C. A. MacKinnon, *ibid.*, at 646–647.

is not less sexual for being violent; to the extent that coercion has become integral to male sexuality rape may be sexual to the degree that, and because, it is violent.

The point of defining rape as 'violence not sex' or 'violence against women' has been to separate sexuality from gender in order to affirm sex (heterosexuality) while rejecting violence (rape). The problem remains what it has always been: telling the difference. The convergence of sexuality with violence, long used at law to deny the reality of women's violation, is recognized by rape survivors, with a difference: where the legal system has seen the intercourse in rape, victims see the rape in intercourse. The uncoerced context for sexual expression becomes as elusive as the physical acts come to feel indistinguishable. Instead of asking, what is the violation of rape, explain what is right about sex. If this, in turn, is difficult, the difficulty is as instructive as the difficulty men have in telling the difference when women see one. Perhaps the wrong of rape has proven so difficult to articulate because the unquestionable starting point has been that rape is definable as distinct from intercourse, when for women it is difficult to distinguish them under conditions of male dominance."

One consequence of defining rape in terms of violence rather than sex is, according to MacKinnon, that it may make it more difficult for allegations of rape to be proven where violence is not used upon the victim:

C. A. MacKinnon
"Feminism, Marxism, Method and the State: Toward Feminist Jurisprudence"[51]

"Having defined rape in male sexual terms, the law's problem, which becomes the victim's problem, is distinguishing rape from sex in specific cases. The law does this by adjudicating the level of acceptable force starting just above the level set by what is seen as normal male sexual behaviour, rather than at the victim's or woman's point of violation. Rape cases finding insufficient force reveal that acceptable sex, in the legal perspective, can entail a lot of force. This is not only because of the way the injury itself is defined as illegal. Rape is a sex crime that is not a crime when it looks like sex. To seek to define rape as violent, not sexual, is understandable in this context, and often seems strategic. But assault that is consented to is still assault; rape consented to is intercourse. The substantive reference point implicit in existing legal standards is the sexually normative level of force. Until this norm is confronted as such, no distinction between violence and sexuality will prohibit more instances of women's experienced violation than does the existing definition. The question is what is *seen as* force, hence as violence, in the sexual arena. Most rapes, as women live them, will not be seen to violate women until sex and violence are confronted as mutually definitive. It is not only men convicted of rape who believe that the thing they did different from what men do all the time is get caught."

MacKinnon may have over-stated the case here. In England and Wales, the case of *R. v. Olugboja*,[52] has established that neither violence nor the threat of violence is a necessary element of rape.

---

[51] C. A. MacKinnon, *ibid.*, at 649–650.
[52] (1981) 73 Cr. App. R. 344.

R. v. Olugboja
(1981) 73 Cr. App. Rep. 344 at 350–351

"It is not necessary for the prosecution to prove that what might otherwise appear to have been consent was in reality merely submission induced by force, fear or fraud, although one or more of these factors will no doubt be present in the majority of cases of rape. . .

Although 'consent' is an equally common word [as 'dishonest'] it covers a wide range of states of mind in the context of intercourse between a man and a woman, ranging from actual desire on the one hand to reluctant acquiescence on the other. We do not think that the issue of consent should be left to a jury without some further direction. What this should be will depend on the circumstances of each case. The jury will have been reminded of the burden and standard of proof required to establish each ingredient, including lack of consent, of the offence. They should be directed that consent or the absence of it, is to be given its ordinary meaning and if need be, by way of example, that there is a difference between consent and submission; every consent involves a submission, but it by no means follows that a mere submission involves consent. . . . In the majority of cases, where the allegation is that the intercourse was had by force or the fear of force, such a direction coupled with specific references to and comments on the evidence relevant to the absence of real consent will clearly suffice. In the less common type of case where intercourse takes place after threats not involving violence or the fear of it, . . . we think that an appropriate direction to a jury will have to be fuller. They should be directed to concentrate on the state of mind of the victim immediately before the act of sexual intercourse, having regard to all the relevant circumstances, and in particular the events leading up to the act, and her reaction to them showing their impact on her mind. Apparent acquiescence after penetration does not necessarily involve consent, which must have occurred before the act takes place. In addition to the general direction about consent which we have outlined the jury will probably be helped in such cases by being reminded that in this context consent does comprehend the wide spectrum of states of mind to which we earlier referred, and that the dividing line in such circumstances between real consent on the one hand and mere submission on the other may not be easy to draw. Where it is to be drawn in a given case is for the jury to decide applying their combined good sense, experience and knowledge of human nature and modern behaviour to all the relevant facts of that case."

However, whilst neither violence nor threats of violence are a necessary element of the offence of rape, signs of violence will provide evidence of lack of consent to sexual intercourse. In a phallocentric culture in which female sexuality is understood as capricious and women believed to lie to avoid the stigma of sexual activity, absence of any signs of force will make the task of establishing lack of consent all the more difficult.

7.5.ii *Sex/war*
MacKinnon has gone on to locate the lack of expression given to female experience in a further area of the discourse on rape. She has sought to apply the sex/violence distinction in an international context, locating it within a human rights framework. Specifically, in the course of giving one of the 1993

Oxford Amnesty Lectures, she located her critique at the point of the strategic use of rape as an instrument of war, taking as her example the conflict in the former Yugoslavia.[53] Before setting out her argument in relation to the issue of rape in time of war, it is necessary to contextualise her argument within the domain of human rights law.

C. A. MacKinnon
"Crimes of War, Crimes of Peace"[54]

"Behind all law is someone's story — someone whose blood, if you read closely, leaks through the lines. Text does not beget text; life does. The question — a question of politics and history and therefore law — is whose experience grounds what law.

Human rights principles are based on experience, but not that of women. It is not that women's human rights have not been violated. When women are violated like men who are otherwise like them — when women's arms and legs bleed when severed, when women are shot in pits and gassed in vans, when women's bodies are hidden at the bottom of abandoned mines, when women's skulls are sent from Auschwitz to Strasbourg for experiments — this is not recorded as the history of human rights atrocities to women. They are Argentinian or Honduran or Jewish. When things happen to women that also happen to men, like being beaten and disappeared and tortured to death, the fact that they happened to women is not counted in, or marked as, human suffering . . . What happens to women is either too particular to be universal or too universal to be particular, meaning either too human to be female or too female to be human."

MacKinnon argues, therefore, that the current formulation of human rights law does not recognise harms done to women as violations of their human rights. This is particularly apparent in the context of war.

C. A. MacKinnon
"Crimes of War, Crimes of Peace"[55]

"For a compressed illustration of some current realities that are at once a hair's breadth and a gendered light-year away from the atrocities that ground human rights principles and fill the factual reports of Amnesty International, consider this communication from an American researcher of Bosnian and Croatian descent gathering information in Croatia and Bosnia-Herzegovina:

'Serbian forces have exterminated over 200,000 Croatians and Muslims thus far in an operation they've coined "ethnic cleansing." In this genocide, in Bosnia-Herzegovina alone over 30,000 Muslim and Croatian girls and

---

[53] C. A. MacKinnon, "Crimes of War, Crimes of Peace" in S. Shute & S. Hurley (eds), *On Human Rights: The Oxford Amnesty Lectures 1993* (New York: Basic Books, 1993), p. 83.
[54] In S. Shute & S. Hurley (eds), *ibid.*, pp. 84–85.
[55] C. A. MacKinnon, *ibid.*, pp. 86–90.

women are pregnant from mass rape. Of the 100 Serbian-run concentration camps, about 20 are solely rape/death camps for Muslim and Croatian women and children . . . [There are] news reports and pictures here of Serbian tanks plastered with pornography . . . [and reports that those who] catch the eye of the men looking at the pornography are killed . . . Some massacres in villages as well as rapes and/or executions in camps are being videotaped as they're happening. One Croatian woman described being tortured by electric-shocks and gang-raped in a camp by Serbian men dressed in Croatian uniforms who filmed the rapes and forced her to "confess" on film that Croatians raped her. In the streets of Zagreb, UN troops often ask local women how much they cost . . . There are reports of refugee women being forced to sexually service them to receive aid . . . Tomorrow I talk to two survivors of mass rape, thirty men per day for over three months . . . The UN passed a resolution to collect evidence, a first step for a war crimes trial, but it is said there is no precedent for trying sexual atrocities.' . . .

The war against Croatia and Bosnia-Herzegovina exemplifies how existing approaches to human rights can work to cover up and confuse who is doing what to whom and effectively condone atrocities. All state parties are apparently covered by most of the relevant international human rights guarantees and laws of war, certainly by customary international law. But nothing has yet been invoked to stop the abuses described in the communication or to hold the perpetrators accountable. What is the problem? The fact of Serbian aggression is beyond question, just as the fact of male aggression against women is beyond question, here and everywhere. 'Ethnic cleansing' is a Serbian policy of extermination of non-Serbs with the goal of 'all Serbs in one nation' a 'Greater Serbia' encompassing what was called Yugoslavia. 'Ethnic cleansing' is a euphemism for genocide. Yet this genocidal war of aggression has repeatedly been construed as bilateral, a civil war or an ethnic conflict, to the accompaniment of much international wonderment that people cannot get along and pious clucking at the behavior of 'all sides' in a manner reminiscent of blaming women for getting themselves raped by men they know. To call this a civil war is like calling the Holocaust a civil war between German Aryans and German Jews.

One result of this equalization of aggressor with aggressed-against is that these rapes are not grasped either as a strategy in genocide or as a practice of misogyny, far less as both at once, continuous at once with *this* ethnic war of aggression and with *the* gendered war of aggression of everyday life. This war is to everyday rape what the Holocaust was to everyday anti-Semitism. Muslim and Croatian women and girls are raped, then murdered, by Serbian military men, regulars and irregulars, in their homes, in rape/death camps, on hillsides, everywhere. Their corpses are often raped as well. When this is noticed, it is either as genocide or as rape, or as femicide but not genocide, but not as rape as a form of genocide directed specifically at women. It is seen either as part of a campaign of Serbia against non-Serbia or an onslaught by combatants against civilians, but not an attack by men against women. Or, in the feminist white-wash, it becomes just another instance of aggression by all men against all women all the time, rather than what it is, which is rape by certain men against certain women. The point seems to be to obscure, by any means available, exactly who is doing what to whom and why.

When the women survive, the rapes tend to be regarded as an inevitability of armed conflict, part of the war of all against all, or as a continuation of the hostilities of civil life, of all men against all women. Rape *does* occur in war among and between all sides; rape is a daily act by men against women and is always an act of domination by men over women. But the fact that these rapes are part of an ethnic war of extermination, being misrepresented as a civil war among equal aggressors, means that Muslim and Croatian women are facing twice as many rapists with twice as many excuses, two layers of men on top of them rather than one, and two layers of impunity serving to justify the rapes: just war and just life.

Like all rapes, these rapes are particular as well as generic, and the particularity matters. This is ethnic rape as an official policy of war: not only a policy of the pleasure of male power unleashed; not only a policy to defile, torture, humiliate, degrade, and demoralize the other side; not only a policy of men posturing to gain advantage and ground over other men. It is rape under orders: not out of control, under control. It is rape unto death, rape as massacre, rape to kill or make the victims wish they were dead. It is rape as an instrument of forced exile, to make you leave your home and never come back. It is rape to be seen and heard by others, rape as spectacle. It is rape to shatter a people, to drive a wedge through a community. It is the rape of misogyny liberated by xenophobia and unleashed by official command.

It is rape made sexy for the perpetrators by the defenselessness and youth of many of the victims and the rapists' absolute power to select victims at will. It is rape made more arousing by ethnic hostility against a designated enemy — 'For Serbia' — and made to seem right by lies about the behavior of that enemy. It is rape made exciting by knowing that there are no limits on what can be done, that the women *can* be raped to death. Most of all, it is rape made sexually irresistible by the fact that the women *are* about to be sacrificed, by the ultimate power of reducing a person to a corpse, by the powerlessness of the women and children in the face of their imminent murder at the hands of their rapist. It is murder as the ultimate sexual act. Do not say it is not sex for the men. When the men are told to take the women away and not bring them back, they rape them, *then* kill them, then sometimes rape them again, cut off their breasts, and rip out their wombs. One woman was allowed to live so long as she kept her Serbian captor hard all night orally, night after night after night.

This is rape as torture and rape as extermination. Some women who are not killed speak of wanting to take their own lives. It is at once mass rape and serial rape indistinguishable from prostitution. It is concentration camp as brothel: women impounded to be passed around by men among men. It is also rape as a policy of ethnic uniformity and ethnic conquest, annexation and expansion, acquisition by one nation of others, colonization of women's bodies as colonization of the culture they symbolize and embody as well as of the territory they occupy. It is rape because a Serb wants your apartment. Most distinctively, it is rape for reproduction *as* ethnic liquidation: Croatian and Muslim women are raped to help make a Serbian state by making Serbian babies.

This is ethnic rape. If this were racial rape, it would be pure pollution, the children regarded as dirty and contaminated: their mothers' babies, as in the American South under slavery, Black babies. Because it is ethnic rape, the children are regarded as clean and purified: their fathers' babies, Serbian babies, as clean as anyone with a woman's blood in them and on them can be. The idea seems to be to create a fifth column within Croatian and Muslim society, children (all sons?) who will rise up and join their fathers. Much Serbian ideology and practice takes a page from the Nazi book. Combining with it the archaic view that the sperm carries all the genetic material, the Serbs have achieved the ultimate racialization of culture, the (one hopes) final conclusion of Nazism: now culture is genetic."

MacKinnon's style as well as the substance of her argument has not gone unchallenged. Suzanne Gibson has responded to MacKinnon's rhetoric and argument in the following terms:

S. GIBSON
"The Discourse of Sex/War: Thoughts on Catharine MacKinnon's 1993 Oxford Amnesty Lecture"[56]

"Catharine MacKinnon has a formidable reputation as a public speaker, her performance on the lecture circuit having variously been described as persuasive, powerful, passionate, and irresistible. Most British feminists have relied upon her prose for their sense of the woman and her work: its hallmark the way it swoops and swirls through strings of binaries, its structure of thesis and anti-thesis, metaphor, metonymy and synecdoche; how it operates as persuasive, unanswerable rhetoric. As she writes, so too does MacKinnon speak, although what appears lush, expansive and profuse in written form is too complex, too compact, when it is spoken. Just as the listener is about to catch the giddying drift of the language it spirals off again, onto a fresh comparison, another simile, a new metaphor, another analogy. At first, as the dichotomous world is turned upside down (or, to use the fashionable term, deconstructed) the effect is unsettling. Then, dissatisfaction with the neat juxtapositions begins to grow and the beguiling oppositions begin to look unconvincing, too symmetrical, too simple . . .

When feminists intervene in the discourse upon rape in the Balkan conflict, (in any conflict) I think we must be clear about exactly what is at stake. How is rape being *represented* in this (or any) war? If we forget to address this question we risk ending up in the same position as those white women in the southern USA whose ideologized bodies became a tool of white (male) domination. This served neither the generality of women's interests nor, obviously, those of African-Americans.

So what happens to rape in war-time?

It has been said that truth is the first casualty of war, and the very reasons which make fact-finding and truth-telling in war so difficult are the very reasons which render it essential. Successful propaganda and tenacious rumour rest upon the lowest common denominators of social prejudice (racial hatred, sexual rivalry, religious bigotry). But if the precise content of untruth in war-time derives from familiar, if hitherto furtive, prejudice, so too do the acts of atrocity themselves. Propaganda and rumour are thus doubly plausible, based as they are both upon what has long been feared in times of peace and what horrors might, not unreasonably, be expected when conflict erupts. The descent into atrocity is a descent into the symbols of human hatred; if feminism bears any relation of truth to the world, we should expect rape to emerge as one of the most potent of signifiers in the representation of war.

The linkage between notions of national identity, racial purity, and female continence has been a constant theme of twentieth century political discourse, and on any account it is a linkage which has been problematic for women. The U.S. Supreme Court, by way of example, justified the eugenic sterilization of women in 1927 by analogizing it to the sacrifice of the lives of American men in the First World War. When we examine what happens to representations of rape in war, we find the same linkage between national identity, the national interest and the violation of women.

---

[56] (1993) 1 *Feminist Legal Studies* 179 at 179, 186–188.

In an elegant and detailed historical study, Ruth Harris has explored the way in which an iconography of rape emerged in France during World War I. She describes how women's own narratives of rape were appropriated by men, and how women's experience of sexual violence thence became transformed into a representation of France as an innocent female nation assaulted by a barbaric and brutishly male Germany. She suggests that while stories of rape and pillage were nothing new, the prominence they were given in the early years of World War I requires explanation. Her account identifies concern for French national identity as the crucially important context in which the specific representation of rape emerged.

In a similar vein, when conscription was first introduced in 1916 British military recruiters are supposed to have dealt with conscientious objectors by asking them what they would do were they to encounter 'the Hun' in the act of violating their sisters. The meaning of this question is readily apparent: that a man could restrain himself in the face of almost any depravity but that one.

These two examples return us to the point that rape has not, throughout most of recorded history, been a crime against women. It has, significantly however, been a heinous crime against men: a humiliation inflicted upon a nation, an affront to a man's pride as guardian of his women, a desecration of all that man holds dear. War rape has been an outrage, and it has been condemned as a violation. But not of women, or women's rights.

If the experience of France and Britain exemplifies the manner in which women's pain is appropriated by male forces and distorted in the pursuit of masculine interests, there is a very stark warning here for feminists. It is this: that to respond to war rape with outrage or anger is not enough. We must make absolutely clear the terms in which we object to these atrocities. Our objections must be unambiguously founded upon women's right to physical autonomy. We must vigorously reject arguments which seem to be derived from discourses around the interests of the nation state, the chastity of Muslim women, the sanctity of the Islamic family, the humiliation of Bosnian men, or anything remotely similar. We must object to the war rape of women on the grounds not that there is anything about rape which requires especial condemnation; not that there is anything about rape which is worse or different, more piquant or more thrilling than what routinely happens to men: but on the grounds that rape is a violation of a basic right of bodily integrity.

Such a stance seems to me to be precisely the stance of the liberal humanist discourse of human rights. Almost unmodified."

Gibson raises the possibility of viewing rape as a violation of the right to "bodily integrity" in order to clearly identify the harm perpetrated upon women by rape. The potential utility of such a right in addressing issues of harm to women is debated by Fiona Beveridge and Siobhan Mullally. The arguments are persuasive, suggesting that one might conclude that the benefits of such a right outweigh its possible disadvantages.

F. BEVERIDGE & S. MULLALLY
"International Human Rights and Body Politics"[57]

"It is immensely difficult to cast such a right [to bodily integrity] so that it can be of use to women seeking to assert control and choice over their bodies in the wide

---

[57] In J. Bridgeman & S. Millns (eds), *supra*, n. 44 at pp. 263–265.

variety of cultural settings in which such struggles can be imagined. The right must be specific enough to make its meaning and its subject evident to those who will be charged with implementing or overseeing the application of the instrument in question, since experience has shown that gender neutral language and general formulations of rights are liable to be interpreted so as to exclude that which is the concern primarily of women. Yet it must be general enough to accommodate the wide range of body politics struggles which feminists would seek to assist. Specificity is to be avoided if it entails taking a narrow and unquestioning cultural perspective of 'women' and 'women's bodies' but this is not to say that no moral judgments should be made over the practices common in cultures other than one's own. Specificity is also to be avoided if its effect is to freeze meanings of what it is to be female. Law, for this purpose at least, should be regarded as process rather than as a static set of normative statements. And it is to assist in the shaping of that process in a variety of settings that the 'right to bodily integrity' must be proposed.

From the analysis above it can be concluded that 'privatising' rights should be avoided where possible in favour of a positive statement of the right to bodily integrity against specified harms. Moreover a specific effort should be made to ensure that international law's own version of the public/private divide is overcome. This would entail placing States under a firm positive obligation to promote and maintain the conditions under which bodily integrity can be realised and to provide effective means of redress where bodily integrity is infringed. Most importantly, the State must be obliged to protect bodily integrity from interference by private individuals. A model for this can be seen in the General Assembly Resolution on Violence Against Women. There is no reason why this obligation — to protect against violations by 'private' individuals — should not be incorporated into the definition of the right to bodily integrity.

On a more general note, consideration should be given as to whether the specific content of the 'right to bodily integrity' should be gender neutral or not. There are dangers in any course which involves recognising explicitly that women are especially vulnerable to particular forms of harm. This would be regarded by many feminists as sending out undesirable signals about women's vulnerability, perpetuating images of women as victims. However, there are other ways to ensure that a 'right to bodily integrity' reflects the experiences of women: the right might incorporate specific references to areas of body politics with which women have been concerned: reproduction, domestic violence, rape, female circumcision, to mention a few. Consideration ought to be given as to whether attention should be drawn specifically to these or other areas of concern as a means to ensure that the right cannot be 'confined' in its interpretation or application, so as to exclude the concerns of women. Of course, there is a difficulty in this, that the more the specific content of the right is detailed, the less likely it is to avoid the charge of cultural relativism and the less flexible it will be as a tool for adoption in future struggles.

An alternative approach, perhaps less attractive, might be to focus on procedural rather than substantive aspects of the right to bodily integrity. Under this approach, aspects such as access to advice and information, education and questions such as consent and choice might be addressed. Many feminist critics of rights strategies would dismiss this as inadequate to empower women in any real sense. Catharine MacKinnon, for example, attacks the focus on consent in the law of rape, arguing that it is impossible for consent to be 'freely' given in a society where sex discrimination is all-pervasive. Alan Gewirth, however, in outlining his theory of rights, suggests that the test of consent could be a strong one. An individual could not be said to be 'freely' consenting where that individual is starting from a economically or socially disadvantaged position. States would therefore be placed under a duty to take positive action to correct past discrimination. While this might seem to lend itself more to 'progressive implementation' than to immediate judicial enforcement, it should not be dismissed solely for this reason — State reporting mechanisms under existing human rights instruments provide opportunities for State delegates to be questioned about the allocation of resources to 'positive action' and/or 'affirmative action' programmes.

Would anything be achieved by the 'writing in' of a 'right to bodily integrity' to existing human rights documents? At minimum, it is suggested, its inclusion would signify, to governments and to the international public at least, that a value is placed on the human body within the value system which those documents represent. It would indicate that the body is a subject of protection from interference of some sorts. If the right is cast as an *individual* right, it would go some way to prevent practices affecting women being subsumed into group or collective rights, such as the right to family or freedom of religion, or at least provide some element of balance.

The further that it was found to be acceptable to proceed in specifying the content of the 'right to bodily integrity', the more it could be made apparent what the types of harm were to be tackled — hence, the more it would become apparent that *women's* bodies are valued and that *women* are to be protected from the harms from which *women* suffer. As can be seen from the discussion of rape in the humanitarian law context above, this would not guarantee any improvement in the condition of women; however, it would provide a tool for those seeking to ensure that such improvement does materialise.

It is not possible to foresee to any degree the fate which might befall such a right once it became embedded in mainstream human rights documents. At the jurisprudential level, the interpretation and application of existing rights has at times followed unforeseen paths. One particular feature of human rights law which should be mentioned here is the interplay in jurisprudential discourse between different rights. A right to bodily integrity might, for instance, have some impact on the interpretation of the existing right to equal treatment under the law. Constant vigilance would be required on the part of feminists to ensure that maximum capital was made of any opportunities thus presented. Constant vigilance would also be required to ensure that the bodies charged with the supervision and implementation of the human rights instruments in question, in their dialogue with States Parties on the 'right to bodily integrity', addressed the harms suffered by women."

Having considered sexual violence as a part of the wider picture of abuses of women's rights on an international scale, we move in the next chapter to a more localised, and some might argue a seemingly more trivial, instance of violation of the female sexual body, that of sexual harassment. Whereas the recognition of (at least some forms of) rape as harm against women has a substantial historical past, the legal recognition of sexual harassment as a form of harm is a comparatively recent phenomenon.

CHAPTER 8

SEXUAL HARASSMENT

John: "You vicious little bitch. You think you can come in here with your political correctness and destroy my life?

(He knocks her to the floor.)

After how I treated you . . .? You should be . . . *Rape you* . . .? Are you kidding me . . .?"[1]

Fiction and fact, violation of women's bodies may extend beyond the brutal instance of rape, to other aspects of men's conduct towards women. Unlike rape, however, it is only comparatively recently that such conduct has been hauled from its closet and has come to be viewed publicly as generating legally redressible harms. Catharine MacKinnon states that "[s]exual harassment, the event is not new to women. It is the law of injuries that it is new to. . . . This was apparently such a startling way of proceeding that sexual harassment was protested as a feminist invention."[2]

Sexual harassment is not a "feminist invention", nor is its chastisement "political correctness". Its uncovering does, however, represent an area in which feminist lawyers have been particularly interested and also rather uncharacteristically optimistic about the potential for legal success. Yet, while recognising that harassment does exist[3] and does cause injury to women,[4] it

---

[1] D. Mamet, *Oleanna* (London: Royal Court Writers Series, 1993), p. 79.

[2] C. A. MacKinnon, *Feminism Unmodified: Discourses on Life and Law* (Massachusetts: Harvard University Press, 1987), p. 103.

[3] Sexual harassment may take a multitude of forms including: "comments about appearance/body/clothes; leering and staring at a person's body; abusive, degrading, patronising or belittling remarks or behaviour, sexist remarks or jokes; unwelcomed sexual invitations or pressure; promise or threats concerning employment conditions in exchange for sexual favours; display of sexually explicit material; touching, caressing, hugging, even indecent assault or rape" (Women against Sexual Harassment, campaign leaflet, WaSH and UNISON South East Region Women's Group, Surrey).

[4] Injuries include: "anxiety/tension/anger; ill-health, depression, insomnia, headaches, digestive problems; loss of confidence and motivation, inability to concentrate, decline in work performance; absenteeism; breakdown of relationships" (Women against Sexual Harassment, *ibid.*). Injury might also include stress, in which case an action may now lie against an employer in negligence. This follows from the first successful claim in an English court for psychiatric damage arising from occupational stress in *Walker v. Northumberland County Council* [1995] I.R.L.R. 35 (see A. Sprince, "Recovering Damages for Occupational Stress: *Walker v. Northumberland County Council*" (1995) 17 *Liverpool Law Review* 189).

is quite another thing to identify in *legal* terms exactly where that injury should be situated in law in order to provide adequate redress. Given this difficulty, sexual harassment may materialise in a variety of legal guises: as sex discrimination, as a tort and even as a crime.

8.1   Sexual harassment as sex discrimination

It is in the public sphere of employment that sexual harassment has most often risen its legal head. The banter and conduct of male colleagues, which women may have endured in the past as part and parcel of their job, may, nevertheless, be tackled as sex discrimination. Before delving into the law on discrimination, it is worth pointing out that the credentials of members of the legal profession (which is, after all, engaged in promoting the application of the law) are not immune from suspicion. Barbara Hewson, elected Chairwoman of the Association of Women Barristers in 1995, investigated her profession:

B. Hewson
"Sexual Harassment at the Bar: A recent problem?"[5]

"The bad news is that sexual harassment is still unacceptably prevalent in our profession (though I have no reason to think we are worse than other professions). The recently published Shapland Report surveyed 822 Bar students on the 1989–90 Bar Finals course through pupillage and into practice. It discovered that 40 per cent of the women surveyed had experienced sexual harassment; 10 per cent of an extremely serious nature.

Another report by an internal working party of the Bar Council chaired by Julian Malins Q.C., on pupillage and training, found alarming instances of harassment by pupil-masters. The working party issued a questionnaire to those finishing their pupillage in 1994: it had not sought information on experiences of discrimination at all, but on experiences of pupillage generally. The survey of 805 young barristers received an unusually high response rate — almost 50 per cent. The information on harassment which emerged was volunteered by respondents.

This key report (which is internal and will not be published) denounced certain graphic and disturbing accounts of harassment as 'disgraceful'. It noted that the pupil/pupil-master relationship was one where pupils were especially vulnerable. It concluded that some Heads of Chambers were plainly not taking their existing responsibilities seriously.

This reinforces some of the disturbing stories I have heard, for example:

- an indecent assault on a pupil by a member of Chambers (not her pupil-master). The Head of Chambers decided to take no action;
- a woman pupil who had to move Chambers because of persistent and unwanted overtures by her pupil-master. Complaints to the Head of Chambers had proved futile;

---

[5]   (1995) 145 New L.J. 626 at 626–627.

- a woman scorned by other women in her Chambers when she raised a grievance about the unwanted attentions of a male colleague;
- a number of CLE students promised pupillages in return for sexual favours.

I have no doubt that many Heads of Chambers are at fault, in failing to implement the Bar's Equality Code for Chambers, which they received in May 1993, and in failing to set proper standards of behaviour. This Code explains in painstaking detail how discrimination can occur, and recommends good working practices (including complaints procedures) to avoid or minimise discrimination and victimisation.

Dirty tricks?

Nevertheless, most Heads are still wedded to the idea that they, and they alone, should determine grievances in Chambers. Anti-harassment policies and procedures are regarded as unnecessary because 'we don't discriminate'. Left to their own devices, though, Heads tend to react to complaints of harassment or discrimination by putting pressure on the women concerned to drop the complaint or leave Chambers. These are some of their tactics:

- tell the complainant that if she doesn't like the position in Chambers, she can always move elsewhere (a variant is: 'someone as radical as you is perhaps not suited to this really rather conservative set of Chambers');
- suggest that the complainant is falsely accusing someone of monstrous behaviour;
- suggest that the complainant is at fault ('you are being difficult/abrasive/subjective/oversensitive etc');
- suggest that the real cause of the complainant's problem is her own lack of ability;
- tell the complainant that the matter has been fully investigated, but *take no action*;
- tell the complainant that there is *nothing the Head can do in the circumstances*;
- tell the complainant that, unless she retracts the complaint, and/or apologises, a Chambers meeting will be called (the threat of expulsion is clearly implicit, if not made explicit);
- tell the complainant that she is only a probationer and will not have her tenancy confirmed;
- tell the complainant to go quietly or she will not get a good reference.

It is not surprising that women are currently deterred by the prospect of complaining about harassment. Those who have experienced these sorts of tactics suffer a massive loss of self-confidence, severe stress, and an understandable reluctance to contemplate further action.

But Heads of Chambers cannot expect to duck their responsibilities — to put in place effective anti-harassment policies and procedures — for very much longer. The mounting chorus of criticism, in the Malins report, and at the recent 'Woman Lawyer' Conference, is impossible to ignore. Our profession is on a learning curve. The Association of Women Barristers, Inns' student officers, the Bar's Equal Opportunities Officers, and CLE student officers, met in November 1993 to discuss harassment. In the summer of 1994, the Bar's Professional Conduct Committee ('PCC') received race and gender awareness training. In autumn 1994, the Bar's Young Barristers' Committee held a meeting on sexual and racial harassment addressed by the Chairman of the Bar. In January 1995, a Q.C. was suspended for sexual and racial harassment of lay and professional clients. A revised Equality Code, with a new section on sexual harassment, will go before the Bar Council in July.

The gulf between those barristers who take the problem seriously, and those who see harassment as a phantasm of 'political correctness', still exists. It is instructive to recall that when the PCC first received complaints of sexual and racial harassment against the Q.C. in question, it declined to identify these as discrimination issues, maintaining that 'it had never received any complaint of discrimination'; and it declined to press charges under para. 204 of the Code of Conduct, which prohibits discrimination, on the basis that 'conduct unbecoming' (whatever that means) was the *more serious* charge! Perhaps, given what we now know about the scale of the problem, the PCC should call a spade a spade, instead of indulging in gentlemanly euphemisms."

Calling a spade a spade is not the *forte* of the legislation dealing with discrimination. The Sex Discrimination Act 1975 does not make reference to the term "sexual harassment". The difficulty of fitting harassment into the sex discrimination paradigm is discussed by Catharine MacKinnon who notes that "[s]ex discrimination law had to adjust a bit to accommodate the realities of sexual harassment. Like many other injuries of gender, it wasn't written for this."[6] In the U.K. conduct amounting to harassment, has, however, been held to amount to direct sex discrimination contrary to the 1975 Act. Section 1(1) provides that:

> A person discriminates against a woman in any circumstances relevant for the purposes of any provision of this Act if —
> (a)   on the ground of her sex he treats her less favourably than he treats or would treat a man . . .

The 1975 Act has received reinforcement at the level of the European Union following the adoption by the European Commission of a Recommendation on the Protection of the Dignity of Men and Women at Work, together with an accompanying *Code of Practice*.[7] Art. 1 of the Recommendation states that:

> "It is recommended that the Member States take action to promote awareness that conduct of a sexual nature, or other conduct based on sex affecting the dignity of women and men at work, including conduct of superiors and colleagues, is unacceptable if:
> (a)   such conduct is unwanted, unreasonable and offensive to the recipient;
> (b)   a person's rejection of, or submission to, such conduct on the part of employers or workers (including superiors or colleagues) is used explicitly or implicitly as a basis for a decision which affects that person's access to vocational training, access to employment, continued employment, promotion, salary or any other employment decisions; and/or
> (c)   such conduct creates an intimidating, hostile or humiliating work environment for the recipient;

---

[6]   C. A. MacKinnon, *supra*, n.2 at p. 107.
[7]   Recommendation 92/C 27/04. See M. Rubenstein, "Sexual Harassment: European Commission Recommendation and Code of Practice" (1992) 21 *Industrial Law Journal* 70.

and that such conduct may, in certain circumstances be contrary to the principle of equal treatment within the meaning of Articles 3, 4 and 5 of Directive 76/207/EEC.

The explicit recognition that sexual assaults upon women may constitute an interference with their human dignity is welcome. It echoes the decision of the European Court of Human Rights in *CR v. The United Kingdom & SW v. The United Kingdom*,[8] which viewed the abandonment of the marital rape exemption as in conformity with the European Convention on Human Rights "the very essence of which is respect for human dignity and human freedom".[9] The integrity of the female body which is prioritised in this construction is an important recognition of the harm which sexual harassment can cause.

Despite the European initiative being frequently cited in cases dealing with sexual harassment, the human rights perspective upon harm arising from harassment is still not the dominant legal perspective. The primary construction of harassment remains one of direct sex discrimination. This was introduced in the case of *Strathclyde Regional Council v. Porcelli*,[10] which resolved one of the key problems facing the construction of harassment as discrimination. The difficulty centred upon the fact that sex discrimination law only recognises discrimination where something happens to one sex and not the other. This left it open for a claim to be made that, where a man would be treated in a similar fashion, there could be no discrimination.

Mrs Porcelli was employed as a school laboratory technician. Two male colleagues, Coles and Reid, engaged in offensive conduct towards her in an attempt to induce her to leave her job. The conduct involved making suggestive remarks, deliberately brushing against her, throwing out some of her belongings and putting equipment in a high cupboard so that Mrs Porcelli needed a ladder to reach it. In order to found a valid claim under the Sex Discrimination Act 1975 it has to be shown that a person of the opposite sex would have been treated in a different manner from the complainant. It was argued that a male colleague would have been subjected to similar abuse and therefore the conduct was not engaged in on the grounds of sex. This was rejected, it being felt that the abuse to which Mrs Porcelli was subjected took a specific sexual form because she was female. A man who was similarly disliked would not have been treated in the same way. Lord Emslie held:

Strathclyde Regional Council v. Porcelli
[1986] I.R.L.R. 134, Court of Session[11]

"Section 1(1)(a) is concerned with 'treatment' and not with the motive or objective of the person responsible for it. Although in some cases it will be obvious that there is a

---

[8] *CR v. The United Kingdom & SW v. The United Kingdom* (Case Nos 48/1994/495/577; 47/1994/494/576) [1996] 1 F.L.R. 434.
[9] *CR v. The United Kingdom & SW v. The United Kingdom*, ibid., at 449.
[10] *Strathclyde Regional Council v. Porcelli* [1986] I.R.L.R. 134.
[11] Strathclyde Regional Council was party to the proceedings because, as the employer of the men involved in the incidents of harassment, it was vicariously liable for their acts of discrimina-

sex related purpose in the mind of a person who indulges in unwanted and objectionable sexual overtures to a woman or exposes her to offensive sexual jokes or observations that is not this case. But it does not follow that because the campaign pursued
against Mrs Porcelli as a whole had no sex related motive or objective, the treatment
of Mrs Porcelli by Coles, which was of the nature of 'sexual harassment' is not to be
regarded as having been 'on the ground of her sex' within the meaning of s. 1(1)(a).
In my opinion this particular part of the campaign was plainly adopted against Mrs
Porcelli because she was a woman. It was a particular kind of weapon, based upon
the sex of the victim, which, as the industrial tribunal recognised would not have been
used against an equally disliked man . . .

The industrial tribunal reached their decision by finding that Cole's and Reid's treatment of an equally disliked male colleague would have been just as unpleasant. Where
they went wrong, however, was in failing to notice that a material part of the campaign
against Mrs Porcelli consisted of 'sexual harassment', a particularly degrading and
unacceptable form of treatment which it must be taken to have been the intention of
Parliament to restrain. From their reasons it is to be understood that they were satisfied
that this form of treatment — sexual harassment in any form — would not have
figured in a campaign by Coles and Reid directed against a man. In this situation the
treatment of Mrs Porcelli fell to be seen as very different in a material respect from
that which would have been inflicted on a male colleague, regardless of equality of
overall unpleasantness, and that being so it appears to me that upon a proper application of s. 1(1)(a) the industrial tribunal ought to have asked themselves whether in
that respect Mrs Porcelli had been treated by Coles (on the ground of her sex) 'less
favourably' than he would have treated a man with whom her position fell to be
compared. Had they asked themselves that question it is impossible to believe that
they would not have answered it in the affirmative. In the result it has not been shown
that the Employment Appeal Tribunal were not entitled to substitute their own
decision in Mrs Porcelli's favour for that of the industrial tribunal and I am of the
opinion that the appeal by Strathclyde Regional Council should be refused."

The violation of the female body perpetrated by acts of sexual harassment
does not have to be at the level of harm to the *physical* body. The harm may
be caused by verbal insult and occur at a *mental* level, for example, where
injury to feelings can be shown. It may be more appropriate in this respect to
view harassment as a form of psychological bullying. In *Insitu Cleaning Co.
Ltd v. Heads*,[12] Doreen Heads had been greeted by the son of two of the

---

tion carried out during the course of their employment (Sex Discrimination Act 1975, s. 41).
Under section 41 an employer may evade liability where it can be shown that he acted as a
reasonable employer taking all reasonable steps to prevent the discrimination. "Reasonable" steps
may involve, for example, the establishment of an equal opportunities policy and the investigation
of allegations of discrimination. It need not involve the employer taking action against the person
allegedly engaging in the acts of harassment (*Balgobin v. Tower Hamlets L.B.C.* [1987] I.R.L.R.
401). This leads Anne Morris and Susan Nott to suggest that "the standard required of an
employer in these circumstances is very low indeed. As long as there is some attempt at supervision this may be deemed adequate" (A. E. Morris & S. M. Nott, *Working Women and the Law:
Equality and Discrimination in Theory and Practice* (London: Routledge, 1991), p. 92). Morris
and Nott conclude that "the Employment Appeal Tribunal seemed to indicate in Balgobin's case
that sexual harassment might be well-nigh impossible for an employer to control" (p. 92)).
[12] *Insitu Cleaning Co. Ltd v. Heads* [1995] I.R.L.R. 4.

company's directors by the words "Hiya, big tits", a remark which she found embarrassing and distressing.[13] The Employment Appeal Tribunal held that:

"For the bosses' son to make a sexual remark to a female employee nearly twice his age was calculated to and did cause distress which no doubt was a mixture of rage, humiliation and genuine embarrassment. This is a form of bullying and is not acceptable in the workplace in any circumstances."[14]

The harassment does not have to be cumulative, but may take the form of one single incident, provided that it is sufficiently serious.[15] The contrary argument is again given short shrift in the case of Doreen Heads. The EAT found that:

"Whether a single act of verbal sexual harassment is sufficient to found a complaint is also a question of fact and degree. It seems to be that because the Code [of Practice, issued by the European Commission] refers to 'unwanted conduct' it cannot be said that a single act can ever amount to harassment because until done and rejected it cannot be said that the conduct is 'unwanted'. We regard this argument as specious. If it were correct it would mean that a man was always entitled to argue that every act of harassment was different from the first and that he was testing to see if it was unwanted: in other words it would amount to a licence for harassment."[16]

It is also not necessary that the conduct be specifically directed at the woman. Lewd behaviour may amount to harassment where it continues despite the woman's objections.[17] Nevertheless, where it is the work environment itself which is problematic, for example, because of the display of sexually-suggestive materials such as pin-ups, this has been held not to constitute sexual harassment.[18] In *Stewart v. Cleveland Guest (Engineering) Ltd*[19] the Employment Appeal Tribunal did not consider that an environment in which pictures of nude or partially-clad women were on display amounted to sex discrimination. Rather, it approved the view of the industrial tribunal, that "a man might well find this sort of display as offensive as the applicant did".[20] This decision is, however, open to challenge. In her response to a similar point made in a U.S. case, Catharine MacKinnon counters that the woman "did not

---

[13] As in *Porcelli* it was argued by the appellants that a similar remark to a man (in this case in relation to his balding head or beard) might have been made and therefore the remark could not amount to direct discrimination. Morison J. responded to this argument with the contempt it deserves: "A remark by a man about a woman's breasts cannot sensibly be equated with a remark by a woman about a bald head or a beard. One is sexual, the other is not." (*Insitu Cleaning Co. Ltd v. Heads, ibid.*, at 5.)

[14] *Insitu Cleaning Co. Ltd v. Heads, ibid.*, at 5.

[15] *Bracebridge Engineering Ltd v. Darby* [1990] I.R.L.R. 3.

[16] *Insitu Cleaning Co. Ltd v. Heads, supra*, n. 12 at 5.

[17] *Johnstone v. Fenton Barns (Scotland) Ltd* (1990) Case No. S/1688/89.

[18] Pin-ups equally do not fall within the remit of obscenity legislation. See the discussion in the following chapter of Clare Short MP's unsuccessful legislative attempt to ban "page 3" pin-ups.

[19] *Stewart v. Cleveland Guest (Engineering) Ltd* [1994] I.R.L.R. 440.

[20] *Stewart v. Cleveland Guest (Engineering) Ltd, ibid.*, at 442.

say she was offended, she said she was discriminated against based on her sex."[21] This is not necessarily the same thing. It may well be the case that the attitude of women to pin-ups is different from that of their male counterparts and, therefore, a man would not be affected to the same extent by their presence in the workplace as would a woman. In this respect women are treated differently on the grounds of their sex, regardless of whether or not they take offence at the material. Michael Rubenstein asserts that:

> "it is beyond doubt that a great many women identify with pin-ups and regard them as degrading. Men, however, don't always understand this. Pin-ups present a classic instance of the differences in perception between women and men about what is appropriate. Sometimes this may be because men do not, at any rate consciously, make the link themselves between the picture of the naked woman with her legs spread apart on the factory wall and Miss Jones from accounts."[22]

Rubenstein goes on to identify the way in which pin-ups have the effect of sexualising the working environment to the disadvantage of women.

> "From an empirical standpoint, women are right to be disturbed by pin-ups because there is considerable objective evidence that they sexualise the work environment to women's detriment, thereby creating 'an intimidating, hostile or humiliating working environment'. The picture of the nude woman posted on the factory wall says that women are for sex, not for work colleagues.
>
> This may stem from resentment of working with women. The TUC sexual harassment guidelines explain that: 'Among work colleagues sexual harassment can be about territorial rights — dirty jokes and obscene pictures send the message "this is our space — you are not welcome" — a common problem for women working in male-dominated environments.' Or it may reflect the stereotyping of women as sex objects . . .
>
> Men are not routinely treated as sex objects, and the position of those with less power cannot be equated with the position of those with more power."[23]

Evidence of the "stereotyping" of women which results from a sexualised working ambience has been admitted in sexual harassment cases in the United States.

M. RUBENSTEIN
"Pin-ups and sexual harassment"[24]

"[In the case of] *Robinson v. Jacksonville Shipyards Inc.* (D.C. Fla. 1991 57 FEP Cases 971), . . . the District Court ruled that 'the sexualisation of the workplace

---

[21]   *Rabidue v. Osceola Refining* 584 F. Supp. 419, 435 (E. D. Mich. 1984) cited in C. A. MacKinnon, *supra*, n. 2 at p. 115. It was, nonetheless clear that Mrs Stewart *did* find the pictures both offensive and discriminatory.
[22]   M. Rubenstein, "Pin-ups and sexual harassment" (September/October 1994) 57 E.O.R. 24.
[23]   M. Rubenstein, *ibid.*, at 25, 26.
[24]   M. Rubenstein, *ibid.*, at 25.

imposes burdens on women that are not borne by men' because it tends to make men view their female co-workers as sex objects. When women are viewed in this manner, Judge Howell Melton reasoned, they are in effect treated differently because of their sex. On the face of it, the facts of this case bear a marked similarity to those in *Stewart v. Cleveland Guest (Engineering) Ltd.* The Court found that 'pictures of nude and partially-nude women appear throughout the JSI workplace in the form of magazines, plaques on the wall, photographs torn from magazines and affixed to the wall or attached to calendars supplied by advertising tool supply companies.'

The Court heard expert psychological evidence from Dr Susan Fiske that this led to 'stereotyping', two of the preconditions for which are 'priming' and 'workplace ambience'. 'Priming' is a process in which specific stimuli in the work environment 'prime certain categories for the application of stereotypical thinking'. Dr Fiske testified that the priming impact created by the availability of photographs of nude and partially-nude women in the JSI workplace 'may encourage a significant proportion of the male population in the work-force to view and interact with women co-workers as if those women are sex objects.' As for the ambience of the work environment, the Court noted that, according to Dr Fiske, 'studies show that the tolerance of non-professional conduct promotes the stereotyping of women in terms of their sex object status. For instance, when profanity is evident, women are three times more likely to be treated as sex objects than in a workplace where profanity is not tolerated. When sexual joking is common in a work environment, stereotyping of women in terms of their sex object status is three to seven times more likely to occur ... Non-professional ambience imposes much harsher effects on women than on men. The general principle, as stated by Dr Fiske, is "when sex comes into the workplace, women are profoundly affected in their ability to do their jobs without being bothered by it".'

Upholding the complaint, Judge Melton concluded that: 'The expert testimony of Dr Fiske provides solid evidence that the presence of the pictures, even if not directed at offending a particular female employee, sexualises the work environment to the detriment of all female employees' and that 'the sexualisation of the workplace imposes burdens on women that are not borne by men. Women must constantly monitor their behaviour to determine whether they are eliciting sexual attention ... Dr Fiske's testimony provided a sound, credible theoretical framework from which to conclude that the presence of pictures of nude and partially nude women, sexual comments, sexual joking ... creates and contributes to a sexually hostile work environment. Moreover, this framework provides an evidentiary basis for concluding that a sexualised working environment is abusive to a woman because of her sex.'

A major effect of sex stereotyping is 'sexual spillover'. In *Jenson v. Eveleth Taconite Co.* (D.C. Minn. 1993 61 FEP Cases 1252), this was defined by Dr Eugene Borgida, who gave expert psychological testimony, as the idea that 'the sexual dimension that characterises male-female relationships outside of a work environment spills over ... into the work environment, and ... becomes part of the working environment. Sexual spillover creates a sexualised work environment.' "

Yet, following *Stewart* the harm caused as a result of working within a sexualised environment remains unrecognised in Britain. Leo Flynn examines the decision uncovering its alleged neutrality, and yet its apparent partiality:

L. FLYNN
"Interpretation and Disrupted Accounts in Sexual Harassment Cases: *Stewart v. Cleveland Guest (Engineering) Ltd*"[25]

"Neutrality is a theme which recurs in *Stewart* on two, distinct levels — the neutrality of the images on display, and the neutrality of the EAT and the Industrial Tribunal as they arrive at their decisions, as they look dispassionately at the situation of Annette Stewart and the other workers in the engineering plant. The pictures on display in the factory were found by the Industrial Tribunal to be 'neutral' in relation to the sexes; to the extent to which their presence constituted a detriment it was one which had an impact on employees without distinction of sex. This finding was not challenged by the EAT, and it can be said that the tribunals put the issue of pornography in perspective. Perspective places a rationalized three-dimensional world upon a two-dimensional surface following well-established transformational rules which reflect the scene depicted onto the viewing eye. This use of a perspectival gaze requires the diminution of the viewer's emotional entanglement with the objects depicted, and it operates within a scientific model which treats that depicted not as an integral part of a larger whole but as a component of a predictable and potentially masterable order which can only be properly observed by a neutral and dispassionate researcher. This model postulates a static, unwavering eye located at a single point in front of the scene under observation. And, ultimately, it relies on the ability of the observer to confidently yoke what is seen and what it means in a stable and direct relationship . . .

The problem in *Stewart* is that there is an assumption that a single stance from which to view pornography exists. By equating the distress of Annette Stewart who feels demeaned by the images on display and a non-existent man whose moral sensibility would be disturbed by the same pictures, the tribunals do not allow for a variety of standpoints related to the actual positions of women and men in a hierarchical and gendered society . . .

Although the presence of pornographic images in a male-oriented environment of the type which prevailed on the employer's premises constitutes a paradigmatic instance of hostile environment sexual harassment, the refusal of the Tribunal to see the images as Annette Stewart saw them might be seen as a manifestation of its impartiality between the parties, its proper neutrality. This neutrality is carried over to the EAT, and is manifested in the contrasting styles employed at different points in the conclusion of the judgment. Aside from its formulation of the facts of the case, the judgment is dominated by a brief discussion of the law on when the decision of a tribunal may be overturned. The EAT emphasises that this may only be done where the decision is irrational or plainly wrong. This attention to rationality is in counterpoint to later comments of Mummery J. where he makes it clear that Ms. Stewart does have a legitimate grievance that should be listened to. '[C]omplaints of [this] kind are not [to be] treated as trivial. They should be taken up, investigated and dealt with in a sympathetic and sensible fashion'. The movement from the voice of a distanced rationality to one of a more engaged sensitivity to the applicant is of no help to Annette Stewart, but it does indicate the possibility that the case could be seen differently.

The paradigm in law for the acquisition of knowledge and a basis for authoritative claims to be made requires the removal of the decision maker from the immediate context of those who are under review. In particular, the perspective adopted by the

[25] (1996) 4 *Feminist Legal Studies* 109 at 119–122.

EAT requires that the situation in the engineering firm be moved from its initial context and that the relations between the individuals involved be examined in isolation from each other and from their daily experience outside those premises . . .

[I]t can be seen that the decision of the EAT and the Industrial Tribunal in *Stewart* are partial in the views they adopt. There is an apparent sensitivity to the possibility that different perspectives can be brought to bear on events or images whose contents are not contested. However, this recognition of difference is immediately swallowed up by the assertion that the real distress of the applicant is the same as the hypothetical distaste of a hypothetical male fellow employee. This supposedly sidesteps sex discrimination because of the postulated parity of detriment. However, that analysis is blind to the context which forms the way in which we view the world. Annette Stewart is differently positioned from that hypothetical male employee because, irrespective of the effects of pornography on male consumers' behaviour to real women, many women experience pornography as a direct assault on their self-worth, on their identity as women. To compare this with the distaste of the devoutly religious hypothetical male invoked by the tribunal is to equate a personal aesthetic with personal integrity. It is only by taking seriously what applicants claim to see, . . ., and by embracing the assumption which underlies that model, that how we see the world is a function of where we stand in the world, that the error made in *Stewart* can be corrected."

The partiality of the tribunal's perspective, as evidenced in *Stewart*, reflects only one difficulty which a female complainant may encounter when alleging harassment. A further problem is that she must demonstrate that she has suffered "detriment" as a result of her treatment, in accordance with section 6(2)(b) of the Sex Discrimination Act 1975.[26] One reason for the difficulty in showing detriment is that women who allege that they have been harassed may be accused of being over-sensitive and of over-reacting. As MacKinnon notes "[s]uch a harm would be based not on sex but on individual hysteria."[27] Fault is then located within the individual woman who may be viewed as insufficiently mature to deal with "normal" male behaviour and a "normal" working environment.

In *De Souza v. Automobile Association*,[28] it was decided that detriment would occur where it could be shown that "the putative reasonable employee could justifiably complain about his or her working conditions or environment".[29] The employee may, however, not be deemed to have suffered detriment to the same degree as would a reasonable employee, where she engages in conduct which is not viewed as appropriate in a woman. Hence, the attitude of the complainant to sexual matters is relevant in assessing the extent of her detriment. This certainly leads to stereotypical expectations of women's (conservative) attitudes to, and engagement in, sexual conduct as evidenced in the two following cases:

---

[26] Popplewell J. in *Wileman v. Minilec Engineering Ltd* [1988] I.R.L.R. 144 at 147, discussing the nature of the detriment, held that " 'Sexual Harassment' is legal shorthand for activity which is easily recognisable as 'subjecting [the woman] to any other detriment'."
[27] C. A. MacKinnon, *supra*, n. 2 at p. 108.
[28] *De Souza v. Automobile Association* [1986] I.R.L.R. 103.
[29] *De Souza v. Automobile Association*, *ibid.*, at 107.

Snowball v. Gardner Merchant Ltd
[1987] I.R.L.R. 397 at 399–400

Mrs Snowball, a catering manager, made an allegation of sexual harassment against her district manager to the effect that he had suggested that they make love on the office table, had sent her suggestive underwear and sex magazines and pestered her with telephone calls. Snowball was cross-examined about her own sexual activities and attitudes, it being suggested that she had described her bed to colleagues as a "play-pen" and talked of her black satin sheets. Mrs Snowball appealed against the ruling of the Industrial Tribunal that such evidence was admissible and relevant in showing the degree of injury to her feelings. Sir Ralph Kilner-Brown held:

"The basic principle, which is well-known, is that all evidence which is relevant is admissible. To this proposition there are four exceptions. The first exception is that as a general rule hearsay is excluded. The second is that, save for an expert giving evidence involving his own expertise, no witness may express an opinion in relation to the facts to which he deposes. The third exception is that evidence as to character or disposition is generally excluded and the fourth relates to conduct on other occasions which is generally excluded on the basis that it is not probative of a particular allegation to establish that the act or something similar occurred on a previous occasion. The most important principle, in so far as the present case is concerned, is that in cross-examination on matters which are collateral to the main question the answers given by a witness have to be regarded as final and may not be contradicted by other evidence. It is said that the reason for this is that it is desirable to avoid a multiplicity of issues. This case involves the question as to whether the matter is truly collateral and has no connection with the issue under determination. The other principle on which the respondents strongly rely is that it has always been possible to give evidence to the effect that the witness cannot be believed. This is relevant to the credibility of the witness and as the House of Lords laid down in *Toohey v. Metropolitan Police Commissioner* [1965] A.C. 595, anything which goes to affect the credibility of a witness is relevant to the issue before the court and is not to be disregarded as a side issue.

The matter which led to argument between counsel and to the ruling which is the subject of this appeal arose during the cross-examination of the applicant as to her complaint of sexual harassment. Without going into the details which might titillate the salacious minded, the general tenor of the questioning was to the effect that she had not suffered any injury to her feelings because she talked freely to her fellow employees about 'a play-pen', black satin sheets and her attitude to sexual matters. The applicant denied the various suggestions. If the matter had been left there, there would have been no problem for the Industrial Tribunal to resolve. However, counsel for the applicant became aware of his opponent's intentions to call witnesses to establish the truth of the allegations which had been put in cross-examination and gave notice to the Tribunal that he would object if counsel tried to do that. His objection would be that the cross-examination was final. The Chairman of the Industrial Tribunal at first tried sensibly to avoid any immediate ruling and suggested that Mr Popplewell got on with his case by calling the gentleman who was accused of the sexual harassment. Mr Popplewell, perhaps overlooking the wide procedural powers vested in an Industrial Tribunal, objected that he did not want to be told how to direct the case. In our opinion the Chairman would have been well within his rights if he had insisted upon Mr Popplewell calling the accused gentleman first. However he did not do so and understandably thought that the whole question should be passed to the Employment Appeal Tribunal. That is why we have been privileged to listen for two whole days to counsel of great experience expatiating on the law of evidence and referring us to cases which go back in time to the year 1811 and in space from England to California and Florida.

We hope that neither counsel will in any way be discomfited if we deal with the argument on each side quite shortly. Mr Hendy for the appellant properly submitted that cases where a woman alleges sexual harassment involve a sensitive subject and require an Industrial Tribunal to exercise a tight control over the area of investigation. So far Mr Tabachnik was in agreement, but he advanced the well-known proposition that in sexual matters it is easy to accuse and difficult to refute: and that there is no burden on a person accused to establish innocence. Therefore an Industrial Tribunal ought not overly to protect a complainant but give to the person accused a fair opportunity to test the truth of the allegations. On the other hand, Mr Hendy made the equally obvious point that in the process of so doing the complainant must not be subject to an attack by the calling of evidence as to her general character and her attitude to sexual matters. Up to this point these are generalities of which any reasonable Industrial Tribunal would be aware. We have every confidence that Industrial Tribunals always have been and always will be very careful in their conduct of cases involving allegations of sexual harassment.

In order to persuade us to prohibit the calling of the proffered evidence Mr Hendy has to establish that, either on strict grounds of admissibility or on grounds of public policy, no Industrial Tribunal should exercise its discretion to permit the calling of the sort of evidence which is proposed in this case. He sought to do so primarily on the ground that the proposed evidence did not concern the gentleman accused of sexual harassment and therefore was not relevant and consequently was inadmissible. The argument that the evidence would contradict her denials in cross-examination and therefore went to credibility was, he submitted, fallacious, because the credibility or otherwise of her denials in cross-examination had nothing to do with her claim. This submission led naturally to the further point that talking about sexual matters was a collateral issue and therefore answers given in cross-examination must be regarded as final; positive evidence to negative those answers should not be admitted. In this case, he submitted, the response on behalf of the respondent was not that she suffered no detriment, but that all her allegations were untrue. It follows therefore that evidence about her opinions on sexual behaviour do not affect the truth or otherwise of her allegations one way or the other. In consequence, whichever way it is tested the proffered evidence is irrelevant or concerns a collateral issue and no positive evidence should be admitted. On the aspect of public policy Mr Hendy repeated his general observations and said that it was not the function of an Industrial Tribunal to investigate the morals of an applicant alleging sexual harassment which is something which either had occurred or had not. There is no room in this sort of enquiry for an attack on the complainant's character. It is unfair and prejudicial, even if true, to inhibit an applicant from bringing a genuine case, if afraid of public criticism for a somewhat permissive attitude in conversation about sexual matters. A complainant attacked in this way is even less able to defend herself than a man may be who is alleged to have directed acts of sexual harassment at her.

On behalf of the respondent Mr Tabnachnik reminded us that regulation 8(1) specifically provides for a free and unfettered discretion as to the admission of evidence.

The only basis for interfering with the exercise of discretion would be if it could be shown that no reasonable Tribunal would admit evidence of this nature. In any event the evidence is doubly relevant and therefore admissible. Firstly, in order to challenge the alleged detriment and hurt to feelings, it is pertinent to enquire whether the complainant is either unduly sensitive, or as in this case, if the proposed evidence is right, is unlikely to be very upset by a degree of familiarity with a sexual connotation. This approach is a perfectly proper introduction to a testing of credibility in relation to her denials in cross-examination. Credibility, it is said, is an issue which lies at the heart of the case. The complainant's allegations are either true or false and there is no room for possible misunderstanding. He added that under the regulation an Industrial Tribunal has power to admit evidence which in strict law is inadmissible, but does not have the power to exclude evidence which is admissible. In support of this contention reference was made to the case of *Rosedale Mouldings Ltd v. Sibley* [1980] I.R.L.R. 387. We have doubts about the validity of this proposition, because as we have said earlier in this judgment, our opinion is that the power extends in some cases to the exclusion of evidence which strictly may be admissible. In *Rosedale Mouldings* the wrongly excluded evidence was highly probative and there was no room for balancing prejudice against probative value. However we do not need to resolve this possible difficulty because we accept the main argument put forward by Mr Tabachnik. There is one final matter which we should mention which flows from our view of the double-ended power. It may well be that some of the details of the proffered evidence may seem to the Industrial Tribunal to have little or no relevance but merely create an atmosphere of prejudice. We have in mind, for example, the suggested attractiveness of black satin sheets. It would be open to the Industrial Tribunal to pay no attention to this whatsoever and perhaps for the Chairman to do some editing on his own before his colleagues were troubled with some of the matters.

For the reasons set out we have unanimously reached a decision which we expressed in the form of an order and which is now hereinafter repeated: 'The Tribunal orders that the appeal be dismissed ...'

Leave to appeal refused."

Wileman v. Minilec Engineering Ltd
[1988] I.R.L.R. 144 at 147–148

Miss Wileman complained that she had suffered verbal and physical sexual harassment by Mr Atthill, a company director, over a period of four and a half years. The Industrial Tribunal upheld her complaint but awarded only £50 compensation for injury to feelings because it found that Wileman was not upset by the harassment, that her detriment was only that of minor irritation and because the clothes which she had worn to work were "scanty and provocative". Wileman appealed against the award of compensation. During the hearing before the EAT the employers wished to introduce new evidence to the effect that Wileman had posed for a national newspaper in a "flimsy costume" subsequent to the Industrial Tribunal hearing. While this was not allowed (for the reasons given below by Popplewell J.), the nominal award for compensation to feelings was upheld:

"[With regard to the admission of new evidence] we apply the test, which is the test for appeals to the Court of Appeal, and we ask ourselves, in the light of what we know about this case, has it been shown to us that the evidence is relevant and probative, and likely to have an important influence on the result of the case?

Quite clearly, the picture itself cannot affect, in any way, the question of physical harassment. Secondly, its probative value in relation to the comments made by the director seem to us to be almost minimal. A person may be quite happy to accept the remarks of A or B in a sexual context, and wholly upset by similar remarks made by C; the fact that she was upset to the extent which the Tribunal have found at the remarks made by the director are not in our judgment vitiated in any way by the fact that she was perfectly willing to pose for the national newspaper.

That she may have been upset by the remarks about going topless, and then appears in a national newspaper in the way that she did, are not necessarily inconsistent. In our judgment, if there is any relevance, as to which we have some doubt, and if there is any probative value, as to which we have much doubt, it is not, in our judgment, going to have any important influence on the result of the case.

The Tribunal clearly took a view as to the extent of the detriment in this case; it is quite clear that it is impossible to say there was no detriment, even if she were perfectly willing to have posed in this way for a national paper.

For those reasons, we do not propose to allow the introduction of this fresh evidence . . .

Against those findings [of the IT], Mr Jack [for the appellant], has made a number of criticisms. First is that the reference to her wearing clothes which were scanty and provocative on occasion was, firstly, not borne out by the evidence; and secondly, in the context of this case, should really have not been given either any weight or very little weight.

She [Miss Wileman] gave evidence saying that she did not wear, in effect, scanty clothes. Mr Atthill gave some evidence and said that he did not notice her clothes much though she did wear rather outlandish clothes. There was evidence given by Mr Horn that in the summer she wore clothes which were not practical for work — 'it was very scanty on some occasions' — said Mr Horn, and — 'once she only had paper towelling around the upper part of her body'. That was supported by Mr Baston, who said 'Miss Wileman is okay; her clothes sometimes were outrageous; she had low tops, sometimes I have had to look twice'.

There was therefore material upon which the Industrial Tribunal could say that on occasion her clothes were scanty and provocative. They have not taken it as the major factor why they have awarded a figure, which at first sight seems very small. They have said, in effect, it was a factor to take into account.

Mr Jack challenges that it has any relevance on the basis that she had the right to wear provocative clothes; that if that was causing difficulty at work, it was in Mr Atthill's power to prevent her from doing it.

We think that the Industrial Tribunal were entitled to take into account as an element — not a decisive element but an element — in deciding whether the harassment to which she was subjected really did constitute a detriment.

Leaving aside this case, if a girl on the shop floor goes around wearing provocative clothes and flaunting herself, it is not unlikely that other work people — particularly the men — will make remarks about it; it is an inevitable part of working life on the shop floor. If she then complains that she suffered a detriment, the Tribunal is entitled to look at the circumstances in which the remarks are made which are said to constitute that detriment. That is all the Industrial Tribunal were saying. In our judgment, they were perfectly entitled so to say."

Such an argument comes offensively close to suggesting that women who wear "provocative" clothing and "flaunt" themselves should not be surprised if their colleagues are induced to harass them. They are asking for it. Just as the construction of an ideal rape victim (one who did not wear a short skirt, drink too much or actively engage in sexual behaviour) has emerged in law, we now have the emergence of the ideal victim of harassment, one who does not challenge the dominant constructions of expected female behavioural patterns. Anne Morris and Susan Nott comment upon this pernicious interpretation of the assessment of detriment:

> "a woman who behaves in a familiar or flirtatious fashion with some of her colleagues or dresses 'provocatively' may have to tolerate unwanted advances from a colleague on the basis that she can expect little else because of her own behaviour. The fallacy here is to fail to distinguish between how a woman may choose to behave outside work with a partner of her own choice and the right she must have at work (or elsewhere) to reject unlooked for advances. The question of how she dresses or behaves is in any event irrelevant where she has made it plain that the conduct complained of is unwelcome."[30]

There are other similarities which manifest themselves between the treatment of those who allege rape and those who allege sexual harassment. One of these is the sexualisation of the hearing, which reconstructs the act of harassment and requires the victim to relive her ordeal. Catharine MacKinnon writes that:

> "[a] major part of the harm of sexual harassment is the public and private sexualization of a woman against her will. Forcing her to speak about her sexuality is a common part of this process, subjection to which leads women to seek relief through the courts. Victims who choose to complain know they will have to endure repeated verbalizations of the specific sexual abuse they complain about. They undertake this even though most experience it as an exacerbation, however unavoidable, of the original abuse. For others, the necessity to repeat over and over the verbal insults, innuendoes, and propositions to which they have been subjected leads them to decide that justice is not worth such indignity."[31]

A further problem associated with approaching sexual harassment as discrimination and seeking its resolution in the tribunal forum is that the remedies available may prove less than satisfactory to the woman concerned. Given that it is employers who are the respondents in any action, being vicariously

---

[30]   A. E. Morris & S. M. Nott, *supra*, n.11 at p. 91.
[31]   C. A. MacKinnon, *supra*, n.2 at p. 114.

liable for the acts of their employees, attention may be diverted away from any condemnation of the person carrying out the harassment.

I. MACKAY & J. EARNSHAW
"Skirting around sexual harassment"[32]

"The vast majority of women who take claims of sexual harassment to tribunals do so because they want the harasser to be punished for his behaviour and to prevent him subjecting others to the same behaviour. Unfortunately the extent to which tribunals are in a position to enable successful applicants to achieve this aim is extremely limited. Apart from a declaration, the remedies available under the Sex Discrimination Act are, first, a recommendation that the employer takes action to obviate or reduce the effects of the discrimination on the applicant, and secondly, compensation. In theory the ability to recommend that, for example, the harasser be sacked, or moved away from the victim has considerable appeal, but in practice it rarely happens. This is because around 75 per cent of applicants are no longer working for the original employer by the time of the tribunal hearing. The normal remedy is therefore compensation, yet this is not in general what victims want, especially if it is to come out of the employer's pocket as opposed to the harasser's."

In addition, there appears to be considerable disparity in the awards of compensation made by Industrial Tribunals. Alice Leonard reviewed the 97 sexual harassment cases which were decided in the five year period following the ground-breaking decision in *Porcelli*.[33] She found as follows:

A. LEONARD
"Remedies for sexual harassment"[34]

"The awards of compensation by tribunals are known in 49 of the 53 successful cases. The awards were analysed by comparing the lowest, highest, average and median awards for each year, with all awards converted to 1990 prices. The distribution of awards over the five-year period was also reviewed.

These figures suggest that the average and median awards have generally risen over the years. However, there were still very low awards and very high awards each year. In part, the differences in awards simply reflect the difference in compensation for loss of wages, which can vary greatly depending upon the applicant's level of earnings. But it is also true of part of the award made specifically for injury to feelings, which varied from £150 (1987) to £6,295 (1990). It is notable that one-quarter of all the awards were for less than £600 (1990 prices).

Injury to feeling
Damages in respect of an unlawful act of discrimination may include compensation

---

[32] (1995) 145 New L.J. 338.
[33] A. Leonard, "Remedies for sexual harassment" (1991) New L.J. 1514. The complainant was successful in 53 of these cases.
[34] A. Leonard, *ibid.*, at 1514–1516.

for injury to feelings, whether or not they include compensation under any other head, (Sex Discrimination Act 1975, s. 66(4)) and tribunals frequently award damages for injury to feelings in sex discrimination cases. In sexual harassment cases, the level of compensation awarded seems to have changed in 1989. Before then, there were a number of cases in which tribunals made very low awards — for example, *Miss Aldridge v. Masshouse Supersave*, where there was no repetition of unsolicited amorous advances after the applicant objected (£100 compensation); *Miss Julie Ackers v. Mr Samir Al Zalam* (1987), where the applicant was dismissed after her objection to harassment, but the harassment involved only a single incident, followed by victimisation (loss of earnings together with injury to feelings: £200); *Mrs Cooper v. Tibbett and Britten* (1988), where the applicant refused to enter into a sexual relationship and the harasser became hostile and unco-operative, but the tribunal found that a minimal amount of sexual harassment had occurred (injury to feelings: £400); *Miss Metcalfe v. R & M Charnley* (1988), where the applicant left her job following the harassment but the tribunal found that there was no prolonged period of harassment and that throughout the difficulties, the applicant had the support of her fiancé and her mother (total compensation for sexual harassment: £250); *Miss Potter v. Mr Yakub Vallie* (1988), where offending comments were harassment and lasted for some time, the tribunal found they were trivial and had not upset the applicant to any material extent (compensation for the harassment: £100); *Mrs Freakly v. Tamlight Lighting and Mr Vaughan* (1989), where the applicant left a job which she otherwise would have kept because of the harassment, but the incidents occurred over a very short space of time (compensation: £300).

In 1989, the level of awards for injury to feelings was definitely increasing. This was no doubt in part a result of the Court of Appeal's decision in *Alexander v. the Home Office* [1988] I.R.L.R. 190, a case concerning the level of compensation where racial discrimination has occurred. The Court refused to accept that damages for injury to feelings should reflect the mere fact of discrimination and said, rather, that damages should reflect compensation for the *consequences* for [*sic*] the discrimination just like any other tort. The Court also stated that compensation for discrimination 'should not be minimal because this would tend to trivialise or diminish respect for the public policy to which the Act gives effect'. The Court made it clear that aggravated damages could be awarded if appropriate. Several tribunals made awards of £1,000 or more — for example, *Ms Holmes v. Tudorgrade Limited* (1989) where harassment of the young female applicant made her ill and she could not face returning to work, after only two months in employment (injury to feelings: £1,000); *Mrs J Fergus v. Lawson Fisher Limited* (1989), where a period of harassment was followed by a period of victimisation and the applicant was dismissed, (injury to feelings: £3,000); *Miss Longmore v. Doctor Bernard Kei Kam Lee* (1989), where persistent sexual harassment made the applicant very ill and she required counselling (for injury to applicant's health and injury to feelings caused by doctor's persistence in the face of applicant's refusals: £3,000) . . .

Substantial awards have continued. In one 1991 case, where the harassment was particularly severe and the applicant became ill to the point of needing psychiatric help, a tribunal awarded the statutory maximum for injury to feelings alone. Emphasising the lack of intervention by the employer, the tribunal said:

> 'This is an appalling case and we may be criticised for using intemperate language, but we consider it is necessary in this case because of the attitude of an employer that prides itself on being an equal opportunities employer on

the one hand but yet in practice maintains, among its workforce, traditional attitudes, and has, by its conduct, perpetuated those attitudes which have led to one of its female employees having her health seriously injured and, furthermore, that the employer still, to this date and throughout this tribunal, has chosen to attack that employee and to continue against her the discriminatory behaviour. The way the case has been dealt with from beginning to end can only have perpetuated and exacerbated the injury to her feelings and therefore the tribunal feels moved to make a maximum award against the respondents. The award for injured feelings is £8,925.' *Mrs S P Wagstaff v. Elida Gibbs Limited & Another* (Leeds 1991)."

Having identified these problems with the resolution of sexual harassment claims within the discrimination framework, it should be stressed that the very introduction of sexual harassment onto the legal agenda does mark a considerable advance for women. MacKinnon locates this achievement as an important step towards the construction of feminist jurisprudence, which, it will be remembered, she identifies as being a new relationship between life and law:[35]

"For feminist jurisprudence, the sexual harassment attempt suggests that if a legal initiative is set up right from the beginning meaning if it is designed from women's real experience of violation, it can make some difference. To a degree women's experience can be written into law, even in some tension with the current doctrinal framework. Women who want to resist their victimization with legal terms that imagine it is not inevitable can be given some chance, which is more than they had before. Law is not everything in this respect, but it is not nothing either. Perhaps the most important lesson is that the mountain can be moved. When we started, there was absolutely no judicial precedent for allowing a sex discrimination suit for sexual harassment. Sometimes even the law does something for the first time."[36]

MacKinnon's optimism, particularly her preference for situating sexual harassment within the domain of sex discrimination law, is not shared by all. J. P. Minson asks "[i]f sexual harassment is the manifestation of an all-pervasive and deeply embedded system of male dominance, then under what conditions can it be appropriate for women to seek for redress to *law*, which according to many feminist theorists has traditionally provided one of the most powerful instruments and conduits of this system?"[37] Minson accuses Catharine MacKinnon of "[a] failure to think strategically about the possibilities of 'infra-legal' regulation".[38] Responding to the "second ordeal" critique of the hearings into allegations of sexual harassment, Minson asks:

---

[35] See Chap. 3 above.
[36] C. A. MacKinnon, *supra*, n. 2 at p. 116.
[37] J. P. Minson "Social Theory and Legal Argument: Catharine MacKinnon on sexual harassment" (1991) 19 *International Journal of the Sociology of Law* 355 at 359.
[38] J. P. Minson, *ibid.*, at 371.

J. P. MINSON
"Social Theory and Legal Argument: Catharine MacKinnon on sexual harassment"[39]

"is this a case of masculinist rituals of adjudication failing to do justice to, indeed exacerbating, women's experience of injury? Or are these problems an unintended consequence of an adversary system of legal process which, among other things, normally requires that all the relevant facts of a case be publicly read into the record? If the pornographic effect of testimony is the result of its public ceremonial character then that might be one reason to look to alternative judicial or semi-judicial processes. For instance, in the public tribunal hearings at which sexual harassment complaints may be heard under Australian Sex Discrimination law, where the plaintiff is likely to be seriously embarrassed by verbally rehearsing the details of the harassment, the proceedings at that point may be conducted in camera. The conciliation phase which proceeds (and typically precludes the need for) the tribunal is of course confidential.

The point of adverting to this 'Australian way' of addressing the problem of personal testimony is not to offer a specific alternative (from a very different legal culture, moreover) but simply to draw attention to MacKinnon's silence concerning any alternative form of dispute resolution. What seems to be lacking is any sense that limits to the law's potential might reflect anything other than the entrenchment of structurally reinforced male interests. There are surely quite legitimate reasons to doubt whether law can or should be (re-)made to bear the radical weight of responsibility which in her vision of equality she wishes to place upon it: namely that of serving as the fulcrum of radical social and personal transformation.

This vision of radical social transformation, it could be urged, leads her to place an exaggerated trust in the commanding status of law and concomitantly in the consciousness-raising impact of legal publicity. It is as if, once the law can be remade so as to embody a feminist structural understanding of what gives rise to sexual harassment; to approximate women's experience of the injury it imposes; and to foreshadow a radical alternative set of relations between the sexes, its traditional majesty could then be invoked in order to provide an Archimedian point of transformation. No wonder MacKinnon has no time for privately conducted alternative dispute resolution procedures. Well-publicised legal cases have an undoubted impact. However, it is unlikely that any impact they might have can be sustained if the significance of sexual harassment law is conceived solely in terms of the exercise of a legal *sovereignty* over sexist conduct . . .

In addition to a code of conduct accompanied by a complaints procedure and a range of sanctions and preventative measures, a management policy on sexual harassment may also offer encouragement, training and advice aimed at encouraging employees in some circumstances to confront it personally and informally. With or without that assistance, where women employees, individually or as a body, take matters into their own hands, this too may be seen as part of the subjection of sexual harassment to a kind of policing or government. This is so even on occasions when direct action may conflict with procedural avenues.

MacKinnon's assumption that in targeting inequitable and gross manners, attempts to modify the *ethos* of the workplace would *necessarily* have no effects on the balance of power (*vis à vis* those relations between the sexes which encourage the practice of

---

[39]   J. P. Minson, *ibid.*, at 371–372.

sexual harassment) is certainly not based upon anything like an examination of the range of measures involved in such attempts."

Despite the advice to look to non-legal strategies, it is apt to investigate alternative legal approaches to sexual harassment outside of its construction as sex discrimination. One area in which much recent debate has been focused, and indeed encouraging glimpses of judicial creativity gleaned, is that of the law of torts.

8.2 "[T]here is no tort of harassment"[40] — is there?

Sexual harassment may not merely occur within the public sphere of employment. Beyond this, however, any redress would fall outside of the ambit of the Sex Discrimination Act 1975. Even within the sphere of employment, it might be argued that some of the problems identified above which result from the harassment-as-discrimination configuration might be better solved by reference to an alternative form of legal action, such as one in tort. If so, which is the most appropriate tort upon which to found a claim, indeed might one countenance the creation of a new tort of harassment?[41]

J. CONAGHAN
"Harassment and the Law of Torts: *Khorasandjian v. Bush*"[42]

"Sexual harassment is behaviour which most women find offensive and intolerable. Yet traditionally, the law of torts has been slow to characterise such behaviour as a legal wrong absent offensive physical contact (battery) or the immediate threat of it (assault). Persistent harassment in the form of offensive sexual comments, solicitations and insults, even threats of physical violence not properly described as 'immediate' (for example because they are communicated over the telephone), are generally regarded as giving rise to no legal claim . . ."

Using the analogy of defamation, Joanne Conaghan explores why tort law in its traditional guise has been able to turn a blind eye to the harm caused by sexual harassment:

J. CONAGHAN
"Gendered Harms and the Law of Tort: Remedying (Sexual) Harassment"[43]

"It is the contention of many feminist legal scholars writing about tort law that it has traditionally ignored injuries commonly suffered by women, while protecting those

---

[40] *Patel v. Patel* [1988] 2 F.L.R. 179, *per* Waterhouse L.J. at 182.
[41] For an in-depth review of the application of tort law to claims of sexual harassment see J. Conaghan, "Gendered Harms and the Law of Tort: Remedying (Sexual) Harassment" (1996) 16 O.J.L.S. 407.
[42] (1993) 1 *Feminist Legal Studies* 189 at 189–190.
[43] J. Conaghan, *supra*, n. 41 at 428–429.

interests valued by, and associated with, men. For example, while the law routinely denies the existence of a tort of harassment, despite the violation of physical and emotional integrity which it entails, it recognizes through the well-established law of defamation, the serious social wrong involved in false imputations affecting the reputation and standing of an individual. Although both defamation and sexual harassment may be characterized as wrongs which offend the *dignity* of the individual, while a good reputation is highly prized, the right to freedom from unwanted harassment is barely regarded.

It might be argued that such a comparison is unfair in that the two wrongs can be readily distinguished. Thus, it might be said that while defamation is often accompanied by perceptible financial loss (for example, lost business associations or weakened commercial or professional standing), sexual harassment too often results in only the intangible harms of hurt feelings or mental distress. However, where, as is often the case, a woman's livelihood or physical health is affected, sexual harassment takes a tangible financial form also. It might also be argued that while defamation usually involves some malevolent intention to injure, sexual harassment can often be the product of benign and harmless motives. But again, this distinction is groundless: the tort of defamation does not generally require any malevolent motive in order to render it actionable, and, in any case, the law of tort has hitherto had no difficulty in imposing liability for trespass to the person despite the presence of a benign or even laudable purpose.

Finally it may be contended that the injury which results from defamation is objective, in the sense that it can be recognized and condemned by good-thinking people generally while the injury which flows from sexual harassment is far more subjective — what offends one person may even please another. In such circumstances the law could have great difficulty defining the boundaries of such a wrong. However, the perception of sexual harassment as a 'subjective' harm, if true, might merely underline the importance of achieving its legal recognition. It may be precisely because *the law* recognizes the 'wrong' inherent in defamation that it is socially perceived; it may be because the law *denies* a remedy for many of the acts which constitute sexual harassment that it is too often socially denied. In other words harm is socially constructed and legally constituted; unless a harm is recognized as such by society and by law, it is not *experienced* as such. That is why for years many women have put up with sexual harassment without complaint: the social and legal failure to recognize the injury entailed has led women simply to *endure* it, repressing their feelings of violation, incipient outrage, the sense that a *wrong* had been perpetrated."

Legal recognition of the injury caused by harassment has, however, begun. In *Thomas v. National Union of Miners*,[44] Scott J. held that "[t]he law has long recognised that unreasonable interference with the rights of others is actionable in tort".[45] Set within the context of the 1984/5 Miners' Strike the case upheld the right of working miners to use the public highway without being subjected to "unreasonable harassment" by those on strike. This leads Joanne Conaghan to suggest that:

---

[44] *Thomas v. National Union of Miners* [1986] Ch. 20.
[45] *Thomas v. National Union of Miners*, *ibid.*, *per* Scott J. at 64.

"as the decision in *Thomas* shows, the common law is not so inflexible as to preclude the possibility of development in this field. If Scott J. can bend it to promote the claims of harassed strike-breakers, then surely feminist lawyers can direct it in defence of harassed women."[46]

The possibility for doing so was strengthened in the case of *Khorasandjian v. Bush*.[47] Khorasandjian and Bush had been friends for several months until their friendship broke down. Khorasandjian, the complainant, told Bush that she wanted nothing further to do with him. He could not come to terms with this and engaged in a series of activities designed to plague the plaintiff such as pestering her with telephone calls, scratching the paintwork on her car and threatening her with violence. This led to criminal proceedings. The defendant continued to engage in a campaign of harassment by making telephone calls to the plaintiff (for which he was fined under the Telecommunications Act 1984). The behaviour persisted and the plaintiff was granted an interlocutory injunction by the county court judge, Stockdale J., restraining the defendant from "using violence to, harassing, pestering or communicating with the plaintiff in any way . . ." The defendant appealed against this injunction on the grounds that this type of conduct did not fall within the recognised boundaries of tortious liability. The court considered whether the conduct amounted to the tort of indirect and intentional infliction of physical harm[48] or private nuisance. Private nuisance comprises an unlawful interference with another's use and enjoyment of land, and may take a wide variety of forms including an interference with the complainant's comfort or convenience.[49] However, ordinarily the complainant would have to demonstrate a legal interest in the land affected in order to succeed.

Khorasandjian v. Bush
[1993] 3 All E.R. 669 at 675–676, *per* Dillon J.

"To my mind, it is ridiculous if in this present age the law is that the making of deliberately harassing and pestering telephone calls to a person is only actionable in the civil courts if the recipient of the calls happens to have the freehold or a leasehold proprietary interest in the premises in which he or she has received the calls . . .

I apprehend that it is correct, historically, that the tort of private nuisance, which originated as an action on the case, was developed in the beginning to protect private property or rights of property, in relation to the use or enjoyment of land. It is stated in *Clerk & Lindsell on Torts* (16th edn, 1989) para. 24–01 that 'the essence of nuisance is a condition or activity which unduly interferes with the use or enjoyment of land'.

---

[46] J. Conaghan, "Harassment and the Law of Torts: *Khorasandjian v. Bush*" *supra*, n. 42 at 190.
[47] *Khorasandjian v. Bush* [1993] 3 All E.R. 669. Detailed commentary upon this case is to be found in J. Bridgeman & M. Jones, "Harassing conduct and outrageous acts: a cause of action for intentionally inflicted mental distress?" (1994) 14 *Legal Studies* 180.
[48] *Wilkinson v. Downton* [1897] 2 Q.B. 57.
[49] M. Jones, *Textbook on Torts* (London: Blackstone Press, 4th ed., 1996), pp. 213–239.

That a legal owner of property can obtain an injunction, on the grounds of private nuisance, to restrain persistent harassment by unwanted telephone calls to his home was decided by the Appellate Division of the Alberta Supreme Court in *Motherwell v. Motherwell* (1976) 73 D.L.R. (3d) 62. The court there rejected, by reference to English authority, a submission (at 67) —

'that the common law does not have within itself the resources to recognise invasion of privacy as either included in an existing category or as a new category of nuisance, and that it has lost its original power, by which indeed it created itself, to note new ills arising in a growing and changing society and pragmatically to establish a principle to meet the need for control and remedy; and then by categories to develop the principle as the interests of justice make themselves sufficiently apparent.'

Consequently, notwithstanding *Malone v. Laskey* the court held that the wife of the owner had also the right to restrain harassing telephone calls to the matrimonial home. Clement JA who delivered the judgement of the court said (at 78):

'Here we have a wife harassed in the matrimonial home. She has a status, a right to live there with her husband and children. I find it absurd to say that her occupancy of the matrimonial home is insufficient to found an action in nuisance. In my opinion, she is entitled to the same relief as is her husband, the brother.'

I respectfully agree, and in my judgment this court is entitled to adopt the same approach. The court has at times to reconsider earlier decisions in the light of changed social conditions; in this court we saw an example of that, only the day before the hearing of this appeal began, when we were referred to *Dyson Holdings Ltd v. Fox* [1975] 3 All E.R. 1030; [1976] Q.B. 503. If the wife of the owner is entitled to sue in respect of harassing telephone calls, then I do not see why that should not also apply to a child living at home with her parents.

Damage is, in the relevant category, a necessary ingredient in the tort of private nuisance, and I shall have to refer further to that later. So far as the harassing telephone calls are concerned, however, the inconvenience and annoyance to the occupier caused by such calls, and the interference thereby with the ordinary and reasonable use of the property are sufficient damage. The harassment is the persistent making of the unwanted telephone calls, even apart from their content; if the content is itself as here threatening and objectionable, the harassment is the greater.

In relation to harassment by telephone calls, there is also the decision of this court (Arnold P. and Sir Roualeyn Cumming-Bruce) in *Burnett v. George* decided on 6 March, 1986 but only recently reported in [1992] 1 F.L.R. 525. There, in a context in which, as in the present case, s. 1 of the Domestic Violence and Matrimonial Proceedings Act 1976 was not applicable, it was held that an injunction to restrain harassment by telephone calls should only be granted if there was evidence that the health of the plaintiff was being impaired by molestation or interference calculated to cause such impairment, in which case the relief should be granted to the extent necessary to avoid the impairment of health.

It is to be observed that in that case the attention of the court was not directed to the cases concerned with interference with the ordinary and reasonable enjoyment of property as being a nuisance. It was directed instead to a different line of authority (see *Wilkinson v. Downton* [1897] 2 Q.B. 57; [1895–9] All E.R. Rep. 267 and *Janvier v. Sweeney* [1919] 2 K.B. 316; [1918–19] All E.R. Rep. 1056) which establishes that false words or verbal threats calculated to cause, and uttered with the knowledge that they are likely to cause and actually causing physical injury to the person to whom they are uttered are actionable: see the judgment of Wright J. in *Wilkinson v. Downton* [1897] 2 Q.B. 57 at 59; [1895–9] All E.R. Rep. 267 at 269 cited by Bankes L.J. in *Janvier v. Sweeney* [1919] 2 K.B. 316 at 321–322; [1918–19] All E.R. Rep. 1056 at 1059. There was a wilful false statement, or unfounded threat, which was in law malicious, and which was likely to cause and did in fact cause physical injury, viz illness of the nature of nervous shock.

From this two points follow.

Firstly, in my judgment, the decision in *Burnett v. George* does not preclude this court from taking a wider view of the telephone harassment under the heading of private nuisance in the light of the interference with the ordinary and reasonable enjoyment of property since that was not considered at all in *Burnett v. George*.

Secondly, *Janvier v. Sweeney* is authority that verbal threats made orally to a person are actionable if they cause illness. This is of somewhat the less importance in the present case since the actual threats (as opposed to other acts of pestering in addition to the telephone calls) were threats to assault and it is not in doubt that, even without consequent illness, such threats can be restrained by injunction, because they are threats to commit a tort."

Joanne Conaghan comments that:

J. Conaghan
"Harassment and the Law of Torts: *Khorasandjian v. Bush*"[50]

"where the application of traditional common law principles produces a 'ridiculous' result, Dillon L. J., like Scott J. in *Thomas*, is happy to eschew such principles in order to achieve a result more consonant with his own perception of what constitutes justice and common sense. And yet, what is plainly ridiculous is that a person in the plaintiff's position should have to rely on the tort of private nuisance, associated as it is with the protection of private property rights, to protect her from what is in fact an invasion of her physical integrity. The real issue of interest in *Khorasandjian* is to what extent it paves the way for the recognition of an independent tort of harassment."

Khorasandjian v. Bush
[1993] 3 All E.R. 669 at 677–680, *per* Dillon J.

"We have also been referred to the unreported decision of this court in *Pidduck v. Molloy* [1992] C.A. Transcript 155. That was a case in which Lord Donaldson M.R., in giving the leading judgment, with which Stocker and Farquharson L.JJ. agreed, said of the defendant's conduct: 'No one denies that there was ample practical justification for the making of an order in the widest terms which the law permits.' That observation is, in my judgment, equally applicable in the present case.

[50] J. Conaghan, *supra*, n. 42 at 192–193.

The actual issue in *Pidduck v. Molloy* was that it was argued for the appellant that injunctions which a judge had granted against him by way of replacement of earlier wider injunctions were still too wide. The replacement injunctions were:

'1. The defendant do not assault the petitioner; 2. The defendant do not speak to the plaintiff; and 3. The defendant do not visit or enter the curtilage of the plaintiff's home.'

In relation to the attack on the second of these, Lord Donaldson M.R. said:

'[Counsel] did submit that speaking to the plaintiff was not of itself a tort, nor was it of itself a crime, and in that he is quite correct. But it is the fact that the past conduct of the defendant has suggested that, if he does speak to her, it is usually for the purpose of intimidating, threatening or abusing her, all of which are capable of amounting to crimes or torts, and in the circumstances I would modify the second part of the injunction to read "not to speak to the plaintiff in an intimidatory threatening or abusive manner".'

In *Pidduck v. Molloy* the plaintiff and the defendant had at one time cohabited, although the 1976 [Domestic Violence and Matrimonial Proceedings] Act did not apply, and they had had a child. There was therefore a topic on which there might have been a need for him to speak to her. In the present case there is no such topic, and a modification of the injunction in Lord Donaldson M.R.'s form would not, in my judgment, be adequate because the parts of his letters to her which are not directly intimidatory, threatening or abusive are concerned to press his unwanted suit on her as part of his campaign of harassment.

Subject to that comment, *Pidduck v. Molloy* is in point as a decision of this court that intimidating or abusive conduct by a man towards a woman can be restrained.

I come now to *Patel v. Patel* [1988] 2 F.L.R. 179 decided by a division of this court consisting of May L.J. and Waterhouse J. This was a dispute between a father-in-law, the plaintiff, and his son-in-law, the defendant. There had been an injunction against the defendant restraining him from assaulting, molesting, or otherwise interfering with the plaintiff or communicating with the plaintiff otherwise than through solicitors and from trespassing upon the plaintiff's property or from approaching within 50 yards of it. A judge had discharged that injunction and substituted an injunction to the effect that the defendant should not assault or molest the plaintiff or trespass on his property. The plaintiff appealed; apart from an issue as to costs, which is irrelevant to the present case, he sought (1) to reinstate the order restraining the defendant from approaching within 50 yards of the plaintiff's property and (2) to have a fine of £25 which the judge had imposed on the defendant for minor acts of molestation increased.

May L.J. rejected both grounds of appeal. As to (1) he said that unless an actual trespass was committed or was more than likely to be committed, it did not seem to him that merely to approach to within 50 yards of a person's house gave a cause of action which might be restrained by an injunction in those terms. As to (2) he drew attention to the very minor acts of molestation which the judge had found proved, and to the fact that many more serious allegations had not been accepted by the judge. That judgment of May L.J., while good warrant for Judge Stockdale's curtailment of the earlier injunction granted by the Barnet County Court in the present case, does not, in my judgment, affect the present appeal in the circumstances of the present case.

Waterhouse J. agreed with May L.J. and indorsed the approach adopted by the judge in reformulating the injunctions. He added, however:

> 'The essence of the appellant's complaint is that he has been the victim of repeated harassment since May 1985, but in the present state of the law there is no tort of harassment. The judge was right, in my judgment, in limiting the scope of the injunctions in the way that he did.'

I find it difficult to give much weight to that general dictum that there is no tort of harassment, when the reformulated injunctions which Waterhouse J. approved included an injunction restraining the defendant from molesting the plaintiff.

I should next refer to the decision of Scott J. in *Thomas v. National Union of Mine-workers (South Wales Area)* [1985] 2 All E.R. 1; [1986] Ch. 20, to which we were referred. That case arose out of the miners' strike of 1984. In the course of a fairly long and careful reserved judgment, Scott J. held that miners who wanted to return to work were entitled to use the public highway to enter the colliery where they worked without unreasonable harassment and in particular without having abuse shouted at them by some 50 to 70 striking miners who were picketing the colliery. The actions of the striking miners were therefore actionable in nuisance. The relevant part of the judgment of Scott J. was criticised in argument in *News Group Newspapers Ltd v. Society of Graphical and Allied Trades 1982 (No 2)* [1987] I.C.R. 181, a case about another industrial dispute which came before Stuart-Smith J. The criticism, in which Stuart-Smith J. saw force (at 206) seems to have been to the effect that mere interference with a person's right to use the public highway could not per se be a new tort, when an action by an individual for obstruction of the public highway as a nuisance only lay on proof of special damage: see *Clerk & Lindsell* para. 24–68. I do not find it necessary for the determination of this appeal to examine the correctness of the decision of Scott J.

For reasons I have endeavoured to indicate, I regard the injunction granted by Judge Stockdale as in principle justified in law as an interlocutory injunction on the facts of this case as they were before him. I turn to consider the question of the choice of words, and the wording of any continuing injunction.

The word 'molest' is well known to, and well understood by, lawyers in its context in s. 1 of the 1976 Act and, therefore, the enforcement of an injunction against 'molestation' under that Act presents little difficulty. It was said by Ormrod L.J. in *Horner v. Horner* [1982] 2 All E.R. 495 at 497; [1982] Fam. 90 at 93 that the word molesting in s. 1 of the 1976 Act —

> 'does not imply necessarily either violence or threats of violence. It applies to any conduct which can properly be regarded as such a degree of harassment as to call for the intervention of the court.'

In *Johnson v. Walton* [1990] 1 F.L.R. 350 at 352 Lord Donaldson M.R. held, with the concurrence of the other members of the court, that the word 'molestation' has that meaning whenever it is used, regardless of whether the particular proceedings are or are not brought under the 1976 Act.

It follows, in my judgment, that in the circumstances of the present case there could have been no objection if Judge Stockdale had granted an injunction to restrain the defendant from 'molesting' the plaintiff.

There are, obviously, certain advantages from the point of view of enforcement proceedings, if an injunction is granted in terms which are well known to lawyers and have, to lawyers, a well-understood meaning. On the other hand, Judge Stockdale could reasonably have thought that though the word 'molesting' is well understood by lawyers, its full implications might not have been readily apparent to a person in the position of the defendant. It is desirable that an injunction should be expressed in words which the person restrained can readily understand, particularly if the person restrained is not present in court, with his or her legal advisers, at the time when the injunction was granted. Therefore Judge Stockdale was entitled, at his discretion, to drop the word 'molesting' and express the injunction in the words he used, as being words which the defendant would be readily able to understand. On the facts of this case the alternative words he chose are appropriate; if they differ at all in their effect from the injunction against 'molestation' I cannot regard the difference as so significant that it goes beyond the scope of any injunction which the judge had jurisdiction to grant.

Since, therefore, the choice of words was a matter of the judge's discretion, I would respect his choice without variation or qualification and consequently, for the reasons I have given, I would dismiss this appeal.

I have had the advantage of reading in draft the judgment of Peter Gibson J. I note that he would qualify the injunction by adding words such as 'by doing acts calculated to cause the [plaintiff] harm'.

I regard such a qualification as undesirable, because it would complicate enforcement of the injunction pending trial of the action; the defendant would assert that any act of pestering or harassment of which complaint was made was not by itself calculated to cause the plaintiff harm.

I also regard the qualification as unnecessary because (i) the campaign of harassment has to be regarded as a whole without consideration of each ingredient in isolation, and viewed as a whole it is plainly calculated to cause the plaintiff harm, and can be restrained quia timet because of the danger to her health from a continuation of the stress to which she has been subjected (ii) threats of violence can be restrained per se, whether or not the threat, without the subsequent violence, is calculated to cause the plaintiff harm and (iii) telephone harassment is, in my judgment, as indicated above, an actionable interference with her ordinary and reasonable use and enjoyment of property where she is lawfully present, and thus, on the past history, can be restrained quia timet without further proof or damage."

Joanne Conaghan responded to the development of the case of *Wilkinson v. Downton* in *Khorasandjian v. Bush* in an optimistic manner:

J. Conaghan
"Harassment and the Law of Torts: *Khorasandjian v. Bush*"[51]

"Its cautious application in *Burnett* and *Khorasandjian* belies the fact that the *principle*, namely that an action lies for the wilful commission of acts calculated to cause harm, is extremely broad in scope. In the United States, courts have sought to limit its application by the imposition of particular conditions, such as that the act in question must be 'outrageous' and that the emotional distress which results must be 'severe'.

---

[51]   J. Conaghan, *supra*, n. 42 at 196.

No doubt English courts will soon be embarking upon a similar endeavour. It is important that feminist lawyers, engaged in sexual harassment litigation, make full use of the emerging principle and contribute actively to its shape and future development.

Thus, *Khorasandjian* is a case brimming with potential. It offers a litigatory approach to those suffering from harassment, both sexually and more generally. It illustrates the creative application of old, forgotten authorities such as *Wilkinson* and new, highly controversial decisions such as *Thomas*. While it is undoubtedly the case that the common law is, by tradition, insensitive to the particular wrongs suffered by women, its essentially dynamic and indeterminate nature render it accessible to the strategems of the creative lawyer. Although ideologically steeped in the politics of the individual, tort law *can* be responsive to the politics of gender."

Tort law has, however, not been quite as responsive as hoped and anticipated. In *Burris v. Azadani*,[52] martial arts instructor Mr Azadani endeavoured unsuccessfully to engage his former pupil Ms Burris in a closer relationship. Burris was then subjected to a campaign of telephone calls, threats, unwanted communications and assault on her property, whereupon she sought an injunction restraining Azadani from harassing her. The terms of the injunction granted prohibited Azadani from "harassing, threatening, pestering or otherwise interfering with the plaintiff" or "making any communication to the plaintiff ... whether in writing or orally, whether by telephone or otherwise" and restrained him "from coming or remaining with[in] 250 yards of the plaintiff's home". The defendant unsuccessfully contested the injunction arguing that the exclusion order was beyond the jurisdiction of the county court because it sought to restrain conduct which did not necessarily amount to an unlawful act. Sir Thomas Bingham M.R. in the Court of Appeal held that the county court did have the requisite jurisdiction to restrain conduct of this type:

> "It would not seem to me to be a valid objection to the making of an exclusion zone order that the conduct to be restrained is not in itself tortious or otherwise unlawful, if such an order is reasonably regarded as necessary for the protection of a plaintiff's legitimate interest."[53]

Sir Thomas Bingham M.R. did, however, go on to recognise that the decision to grant an order would have to reflect a careful balance between the rights of the harasser and those of the harassee:

Burris v. Azadani
[1995] 4 All E.R. 802 at 810–811

"Neither statute nor authority in my view precludes the making of an exclusion zone order. But that does not mean that such orders should be made at all readily, or

---

[52] *Burris v. Azadani* [1995] 4 All E.R. 802.
[53] *Burris v. Azadani*, *ibid.*, at 807–808.

without very good reason. There are two interests to be reconciled. One is that of the defendant. His liberty must be respected up to the point at which his conduct infringes, or threatens to infringe, the rights of the plaintiff. No restraint should be placed on him which is not judged to be necessary to protect the rights of the plaintiff. But the plaintiff has an interest which the court must be astute to protect. The rule of law requires that those whose rights are infringed should seek the aid of the court, and respect for the legal process can only suffer if those who need protection fail to get it. That, in part at least, is why disobedience to orders of the court has always earned severe punishment. Respect for the freedom of the aggressor should never lead the court to deny necessary protection to the victim.

Ordinarily, the victim will be adequately protected by an injunction which restrains the tort which has been or is likely to be committed, whether trespass to the person, or to land, interference with goods, harassment, intimidation or as the case may be. But it may be clear on the facts that if the defendant approaches the vicinity of the plaintiff's home he will succumb to the temptation to enter it, or to abuse or harass the plaintiff; or that he may loiter outside the house, watching and besetting it, in a manner which might be highly stressful and disturbing to a plaintiff. In such a situation the court may properly judge that in the plaintiff's interest — and also, but indirectly, the defendant's — a wider measure of restraint is called for."

This decision represents a rather curious development:

J. CONAGHAN
"Equity rushes in where tort fears to tread: The Court of Appeal decision in *Burris v. Azadani*"[54]

"In the light of *Khorasandjian*, the decision in *Burris* is curious, to say the least. In *Khorasanjian*, Dillon L.J. went to considerable lengths to find a wrong upon which to hang Ms Khorasandjian's claim and thereby grant her relief. In *Burris*, the court appear to have dispensed with the need to identify a wrong in the first place. While it is true that the actual words conferring a power on the courts to grant an injunction *are* very wide, it is, at the same time, 'well understood' that such a power 'presupposes the existence of an action, actual or potential . . .' Thus, in the context of proceedings relating to alleged torts, it is generally assumed that there is no jurisdiction to restrain or prohibit conduct which is not in itself tortious.

The decision in *Burris* highlights a degree of uncertainty in equity as to the scope of the court's inherent jurisdiction to grant injunctive relief. On the one hand, it has been judicially asserted that:

> 'It is a fundamental rule that the court will only grant an injunction at the suit of a private individual to support a legal right.'

On the other hand, it has also been argued that such a rule no longer applies in the light of legislative changes in the Supreme Court Act 1981. More commonly, uncertainty emerges as to what constitutes a 'right' for purposes of founding a claim and in a number of decisions a 'right' has been identified by the courts for purposes of

---

[54]   (1996) 4 *Feminist Legal Studies* 221 at 226–228.

injunctive relief, although not specifically founded upon a recognised cause of action.

This uncertainty is reflected in the Court of Appeal's decision in *Burris*. On the one hand Sir Thomas Bingham acknowledges that:

'It is of course quite clear that the court cannot properly grant an injunction unless the plaintiff can show at least an arguable cause of action . . .'

Yet, almost in the same breath he asserts that the court's power to grant an injunction is not limited to situations where the conduct restrained is 'tortious or otherwise unlawful'.

It seems then that Sir Thomas Bingham's concept of 'an arguable cause of action' is tentative indeed. He relies instead upon the rather elusive notion of 'a plaintiff's legitimate interest', although no effort to define 'interest' for these purposes is made. Does he mean a *legal* interest? Is he invoking the idea of a recognised 'right', commonly assumed to underlie the granting of injunctive relief? It is true that *Burris* involves a situation where many of the plaintiff's legal rights have been invaded. Does this then justify prohibiting the defendant from engaging in conduct which does *not* infringe upon her legal rights? Sir Thomas Bingham clearly thinks so:

'It would not seem to me to be a valid objection to the making of an exclusion zone order that the conduct to be restrained is not in itself tortious or otherwise unlawful, if such an order is reasonably regarded as necessary for the protection of the plaintiff's legitimate interest.'

But then again maybe not? Perhaps the Master of the Rolls is simply relying on a rather loose application of the *quia timet* principle. Just as Dillon L. J. in *Khorasandjian* was empowered to grant an injunction *quia timet* to prevent the commission of a wrong before it has in fact occurred, so also can the court in *Burris* restrain conduct which is not in itself tortious but which will place the defendant in the plaintiff's vicinity where he may 'succumb to the temptation to enter it, or to abuse or harass the plaintiff'.

However, with respect, this seems quite a long way from the power to grant an injunction *quia timet* where the plaintiff is generally required to show a very strong probability of a future infringement of a legally recognised right and the likelihood of damage of a most serious nature. While the evidence presented indicates that the plaintiff was enormously distressed by the behaviour of the defendant, there is no discussion, except in the broadest possible terms of what rights or 'interests' of the plaintiff might be infringed by the defendant's mere presence in the neighbourhood nor of the degree of likelihood required to justify this form of injunctive relief. The fact is that the court at no time addresses with any degree of specificity the nature of the alleged wrongs committed by Mr Azadani. Moreover, while the case may recognize a broader inherent jurisdiction to restrain harassing conduct than was previously generally acknowledged, it does not clarify the questions raised by *Khorasandjian* as to the nature and (potential) scope of the cause of action under *Wilkinson v. Downton*. In fact, *Wilkinson v. Downton* is not cited anywhere in the judgement. While Sir Thomas Bingham clearly disagrees with Waterhouse J.'s pronouncement in *Patel* that no tort of harassment exists, he fails to give any further guidance as to the status of this tort, its content or its application.

Thus, in the aftermath of *Burris*, most of the questions raised by *Khorasandjian* remain unsolved. While *Burris* does raise serious questions about the court's inherent jurisdiction to grant injunctive relief, it does not assist a claimant seeking substantive relief (in the form of damages) against acts of harassment nor does it necessarily advance the interests of those seeking to restrain harassing conduct by providing a precedent which is both uncertain in scope and, as things stand, probably contrary to the weight of existing authority. One is left with the feeling that an important opportunity has been lost. There is no doubt that the perceived legal significance of *Khorasandjian* lay in the fledgling tort it put to flight. After *Burris*, the bird remains aloft but, regrettably, alone."

It should not be assumed that a new formulation of sexual harassment as either a tort or crime would necessarily be unproblematic. In what remains a persuasive article suggesting a move away from the harassment-as-discrimination perspective, Janet Dine and Bob Watt identify some of the difficulties of such a move:

J. DINE & B. WATT
"Sexual Harassment: Moving Away From Discrimination"[55]

"There are at least two possible legal solutions which may be adopted to deal with sexual overtures made in the context of a workplace. One is to outlaw overt sexual activity within the bounds of the employment relationship, i.e. to create a 'sex-free' zone with geographical and temporal limits. This will not prevent sexual signals operating between members of the workforce, but the law would seek to find an acceptable definition of overt sexual activity and outlaw it. Finding this definition must be problematic and we suggest that this is an unduly restrictive approach in view of the number of partners who first meet at their place of employment. How is a first approach ever to be made?

In the United States and at European Community level, the alternative course has been adopted of classifying sexual advances as harassment only where the behaviour is 'unwanted' or 'unwelcome.' This raises a number of issues: (i) Is unwanted behaviour the same as non-consensual behaviour? (ii) What role must the 'victim' play in signalling lack of consent and unwantedness? (iii) Should there be an objective standard to determine when behaviour should be regarded as acceptable behaviour? And (iv) what role should the concept of hostility play?

(a) Unwantedness and consent
The concept of 'unwelcomeness' is used in the United States cases. The same concept appears in the European Commission's Code of Practice in the word 'unwanted.' The choice of this word has the effect of importing the United States distinction between consensual behaviour and 'unwanted' conduct. The relationship between the latter concepts was addressed in the *Meritor* case. Rehnquist J. stated:

'the fact that the sex-related conduct was "voluntary," in the sense that the complainant was not forced to participate against her will, is not a defence

[55]   (1995) 58 M.L.R. 343 at 355–362.

to a sexual harassment suit brought under Title VII. The gravamen of any sexual harassment is that the alleged sexual advances were "unwelcome' . . . The correct inquiry is whether the respondent by her conduct indicated that the alleged sexual advances were unwelcome, not whether her actual parti- cipation in sexual intercourse was voluntary.'

Rehnquist J.'s approach is broadly to be welcomed, for it takes account of the fact that, from time to time, people participate in activities which they would prefer to eschew. However, his approach does not do full justice to an analysis of the concepts of 'voluntariness' and 'welcomeness.'

It is useful to draw a distinction between activities which are intrinsically desired and those which are extrinsically desired. An action is intrinsically desired when a participant wants to join that activity in and for itself, and not for any further reason, whilst an extrinsically desired action is one in which the participant joins because he or she desires the consequence rather than the action for its sake. Similarly, a particip- ant can intrinsically consent to, for example, a love affair — because he or she wishes to enter a relationship with another; alternatively, he or she may extrinsically consent because he or she wishes to avoid, for example, dismissal. It is suggested that an action for sexual harassment should succeed where the complainant is able to show that he or she only consented extrinsically to the activity.

There are a number of objections to this proposal. Firstly, there is the evidential point — how may a person show that he or she only consented extrinsically? It is suggested that there are a number of indicia which can go to show that the relationship was not desired for itself but was entered for some other motive. Primary indicia include a difference in institutional power between the parties and the threat of some substantial sanction or the promise of some substantial reward predicated upon entry into the relationship. Secondary indicia include such factors as might distinguish the relationship from an everyday norm: a wide age difference, the adulterous nature of the proposed relationship, a homosexual relationship where one of the parties had previously been heterosexual or vice versa, the secret nature of the relationship and so on. Clearly, none of these secondary indicia suffice on their own.

A particularly useful measure of whether the actions of the harasser were consented to derives from the nature of the behaviour. It is plain that any behaviour may be perceived as having two dimensions; it has a character (*e.g.* sexual) and it has a gravity or degree of seriousness. The character and gravity of the behaviour are relevant both to the matter of consent and to a consideration of whether the behaviour was hostile. Clearly a person may consent to behaviour of an explicitly sexual character, even where it occurs in the workplace. However, the more intimate the sexual activity, the more necessary it is for a clear and positive consent to be given. In situations of sexual intimacy in the workplace, there is a need for clarity about the nature of the consent given. A convenient division between grave behaviour (which should be actionable) and trivial behaviour (which should not) may be drawn at the level of the distinction between a threat to the occurrent autonomy and a threat to the dispositional autonomy of the victim. The distinction between the two types of autonomy is well made by Robert Young. A person's occurrent autonomy is restricted in those cases where she is prevented from acting autonomously in a particular and limited situation. On the other hand, a person's dispositional autonomy is restricted where she is prevented from making a choice concerning the overall course of her life. Clearly, expected stand- ards of autonomy will differ from culture to culture and person to person, and the role of an objective standard is discussed below.

It is plain that people sometimes participate in sexual intercourse within fully consensual, indeed loving, relationships for extrinsic reasons when they would prefer intrinsically to abstain on that occasion. This situation may be distinguished from sexual harassment by a comparison of the social settings or circumstances. It is likely that the context and content of sexual harassment is limited to sexual relations and necessary workplace collaboration, whilst a true relationship has more varied and richer dimensions.

It is arguable that sexual congress with the forced consent of the victim is ultimately more damaging to her than cases in which the harassee is simply physically assaulted against her will. This is because the formation of limited, or bogus, relationships is likely to present a real threat to the dispositional autonomy of a victim because it may prevent the harassee from forming real relationships and thus result in a stunting of personality.

(b) Role of the victim

The concept of unwanted behaviour adopted in the European Commission's Code of Practice appears to place a duty on the recipient of sexual attentions to indicate whether such attentions are unwelcome. Failure to so indicate may prevent such attention from being classified as harassment. According to the Code:

> 'The essential characteristic of sexual harassment is that it is unwanted by the recipient, that it is for each individual to determine what behaviour is acceptable to them and what they regarded as offensive. Sexual attention becomes sexual harassment if it is persisted in once it has been made clear that it is regarded by the recipient as offensive, although one incident of harassment may constitute sexual harassment if sufficiently serious. It is the unwanted nature of the conduct which distinguishes sexual harassment from friendly behaviour, which is welcome and mutual.'

Several comments are appropriate. First, the statement appears to equate sexual attention with friendly behaviour, an extraordinary assumption which would certainly defeat any attempt to establish 'sex-free' zones. Secondly, the burden of indicating the unwantedness of the behaviour is placed on the victim. This may leave open the problem of intimidation of a victim who is frightened to indicate that the attentions are unwelcome. There are also practical problems; for example, what signals must the victim send in order to make 'clear' that the attentions are unwelcome? Must an official complaint be made? Must the communication be in writing? Is there an objective standard so that a communication, which would have been understood by a reasonable person (gender specific?), will be sufficient? Is some behaviour so inappropriate to the workplace that it cannot be 'welcomed' there?

(c) An objective standard?

The next question is whether an objective element is part of the definition of welcomeness . . .

On the one hand, it seems invidious to impose liability on employers for conduct which reasonable people would accept and use of the notion of the gender specific reasonable person may prevent the objective standard from perpetuating the status quo, normally male domination of a workplace. However, 'any reasonable person' is not an easy character with whom to deal. In sexual harassment cases, issues regarding age, culture and religious beliefs could well be relevant to the offensiveness of the conduct. Should they be imported into the objective definition? If so, it diminishes the objectivity of the viewpoint. Certainly, views may legitimately differ as to the normal degree to which touching one another should be part of a workplace relationship, and views will certainly differ (and change) across the European Union.

The authors' view is that an objective standard is necessary to prevent a form of 'reverse harassment' by those of extreme or unreasonable sensitivity, but that the formulation of a standard can best be done in every individual workplace by using an approach analogous to sex-free zones, while recognising that no 'zone' can be completely free of sexual interaction. A court's task would be greatly simplified if the behaviour is in breach of a code accepted by the employees in a particular workplace . . .

When adjudicating on cases where no code or no acceptable code exists, the authors believe that courts should start from the position that there should be a presumption against overt sexual advances in the workplace. The presumption that any such advances constitute harassment would be rebutted only where there is clear evidence of intrinsic consent. In determining whether behaviour amounts to harassment, the relevant factors should be (i) whether the actions are unacceptable from the viewpoint of the victim; and (ii) whether the actions would be unacceptable from the viewpoint of a reasonable person sharing the victim's characteristics of gender, race and ethnic origin, and sexual orientation.

(d) The concept and role of hostility

All three members of the Court of Session in *Porcelli* made the point that it was not the motive of the offender which was relevant in assessing whether less favourable treatment had been administered, but the nature of the treatment itself . . .

It is plain that Mrs Porcelli was subjected to hostile action by the two harassers. Furthermore, both the harassers and Mrs Porcelli would agree in categorising the action as hostile. Yet it is not necessarily the case that all forms of hostile action are, or ought to be, sufficient to found an action. It is plain that an action can rightly be said to be hostile when, without the consent of the victim, the actor invades his or her bodily integrity and such actions should attract criminal or tortious liability. Furthermore, there is no reason to think that there is any difference in principle between those cases in which there is an 'indecent battery' — that is to say, at least in the simple cases, an actual touching of the sexual organs — and those in which the victim is exposed to indecent material in the form of pictures, although clearly the former is much more serious.

There are also forms of sexual harassment in which the harasser would not join with the victim in classing the action as hostile; the harasser would claim to be motivated by affection or by frolic. This situation, which is much more difficult to characterise, may arise where the harasser annoys the victim by persistent sexual importuning which may be accompanied by unwanted gifts, social invitations and the like. At a certain point, the effect of the action, or the action as perceived, changes from friendly to hostile. It is at this stage, and not before, that we suggest that tortious or criminal liability should be triggered. We identify this as the point at which the threat perceived by the unwilling recipient changes from a threat to her occurrent autonomy to a threat to her dispositional autonomy. We think it plain that criminal sanctions should not be invoked against a person who, by acts that he considers friendly, causes another to refrain from, for example, sitting at a particular table for lunch. However, where a person acts in such a way and the effect is to cause another to resign his or her employment, it is suggested that either a criminal sanction or exemplary tortious damages are appropriate."

For other feminists, the whole concept of using tort as a mechanism for providing a remedy to sexual harassment is unsatisfactory. Catharine MacKinnon, particularly, has been critical of the potential of tort law in this area. She has argued that the focus in tort law upon the *individual* nature of *moral* injury obscures the fact that sexual harassment is a *group* and *social* injury.[56] J. P. Minson responds strongly to this argument:

J. P. MINSON
"Social Theory and Legal Argument: Catharine MacKinnon on sexual harassment"[57]

"MacKinnon's main caveats against tort law remedies, it will be recalled, went to the difficulty of registering sexual harassment as a 'social' injury and as an *employment-*related issue. Tort law construes it, by contrast, as a 'moral' injury, in the liberal sense. Liberalism is here of course identified with a philosophy or ideology of individual (negative) liberty which furnishes a justification for demarcating certain areas of life as private zones of personal discretion, moral (or immoral) choice, etc. and which are *ipso facto* not open to state intervention. It follows that to characterise sexual harassment as a 'moral problem' in this sense is to assume that it is essentially a private issue of personal morality and individual responsibility. In making this assumption, tort law 'rips . . . injuries to women's sexuality out of the context of women's social circumstances as a whole'. In order to capture the 'social injury' of sexual harassment this 'moral' assumption must be written out of its legal definition. The progressive possibilities of Anti-Discrimination law are seen as a simple function of the extent to which it transfers the problem (at the level of legal and social forms of perception, definition, etc.) from 'the' private to 'the' public sphere.

This line of argument suffers from a tendency to repeat rather than to challenge simplistic 'liberal' philosophical or ideological suppositions of a single neat division between private and public realms of human existence. True, this categorisation is assigned to the realm of ideology — 'women's place . . .' does not reflect any 'natural' abilities or dispositions of sexes; 'private' relationships do in reality have 'political' dimensions and repercussions, etc. However, for MacKinnon, to categorise an activity or domain as private is to imply that it is non-social and not subject to regulation; and that if a space can be shown to be crossed by regulation, power-relationships, resistance, etc., then this signifies that 'really' it has no private dimension at all. 'The private is the public for those for whom the personal is the political. In this sense *there is no private*, either normatively or empirically. Feminism confronts the fact that women have no privacy to lose or to guarantee'.

It hardly needs stating that this breathtaking MacKinnonesque generalisation flies in the face of a substantial corpus of arguments and evidence (from both feminist and non-feminist sources) of a considerable diversity in the forms, purposes and above all

---

[56] C. A. MacKinnon, *Sexual Harassment of Working Women* (New Haven: Yale University Press, 1979), pp. 164–174.
[57] (1991) 19 *International Journal of the Sociology of Law* 355 at 366–367.

impacts on women of public-private differentiations. To dichotomise 'the private' and 'the social' is to ignore the extent to which, especially in a liberal style of *government*, as distinct from the simplistic *ideology* with which MacKinnon identifies liberal moral- ity, arenas, agents or relationships are designated as private for some purposes but not others. They may also function as both effects and instruments of public regulation, ranging from state regulation, through a series of intermediate bodies, to self- regulation. There is therefore no *necessary* incompatibility between construing sexual harassment as a 'social' problem whilst simultaneously regarding its regulation, to a great or lesser degree, as the responsibility of some 'private' body, such as the manage- ment of a corporation. The one construction does not cancel out the other."

In contrast, Adrian Howe argues that it is the categorisation of harassment as a social injury which is the strength of Catharine MacKinnon's analysis:

A. Howe
"The Problem of Privatized Injuries: Feminist Strategies for Litigation"[58]

"The creation of a legal cause of action for the injury of sexual harassment has brought a new awareness of [the] 'social reality' which 'urges the priority of defining women's injuries as women perceive them'. Such an awareness has obvious ramifications for the theorization of social injury.

[W]e need note . . . two crucial and interrelated themes: her [MacKinnon's] prioritiz- ing women's 'lived-through experience' and of the '*social* reality of women as a sex' (my emphasis). This social dimension of women's lives is not only one of the most persistent themes of *The Sexual Harassment of Working Women*, it is central to an understanding of the 'inequality' approach in which the 'social position' of women has a special place. Indeed, one of her focal concerns is 'the *social* context' of women's lives — the 'level of communality that makes sexual harassment a women's experi- ence'; its 'social impact'; the '*social* dynamics' of women's suffering which are not reflected in the law, especially tort law which fails to redress injuries to 'public and shared *social* existence' such as sex in employment. Similarly, she is concerned with tort theory's failure to 'capture the broadly *social* sexuality/employment nexus that comprises the injury of sexual harassment'; its failure to treat these incidents as integral to women's '*social* status' and its failure to analyze the *relevant* dimensions of the problem — namely, the '*socially* determinate character' of gender. Furthermore, sex discrimination for MacKinnon consists of 'the systematic disadvantage of *social* groups' (or the 'systematic depravation of one sex because of sex'), and the main point of reference for anti-discrimination law should be 'the *social* situation and experience of women' — the '*social* experience' of battering, rape and other assaults (My emphasis).

As MacKinnon's analysis develops, it becomes apparent that this social dimension of women's experience is as intrinsic to her understanding of the 'systematic damage done women' through their regulation to 'secondary *social* status' as it is to her critique of tort law. Tort's inadequacy as a remedy for sexual harassment is that it personalizes

[58] In M. A. Fineman & N. S. Thomadsen, *At the Boundaries of Law: Feminism and Legal Theory* (New York: Routledge, 1991), pp. 159–160.

what is, in effect, a social injury — one which has a psychological impact on women's 'socialized sense of self-worth'. More bluntly:

> '. . . tort is conceptually inadequate to the problem of sexual harassment to the extent it rips injuries to women's sexuality out of the context of women's social circumstances as a whole.'

In short, tort law 'omits the social dynamics' of women's subordinate position: it considers individual and compensable something which is fundamentally social. Crucially, MacKinnon's point here is not that sexual harassment is not a personal injury, but rather that it is 'a social wrong and a *social injury* that occurs on a personal level' (My emphasis).

In the final analysis then, MacKinnon actually names sexual harassment as a 'social injury.' Indeed, all her analysis has lead, logically, to this outcome. Furthermore, in the process of elaborating her conceptualization of women's injuries as socially-based, she has done well phenomenologically: she has helped immensely to clarify the nature of our injuries to insure that they become legally recognized. She has described 'the pain, isolation, and thingification of women' and their pacification into 'nonpersonhood'; she has defined the damage to our sexuality as 'the absence of life, of the ability to live in security or wholeness'. And, equally important, she has empowered women to speak out publicly about how what she calls 'our real injuries,' such as pornography, have hurt them. In effect, by politicizing their injuries she has given them standing to speak."

8.3   Sexual harassment and criminal law

For those who remain unpersuaded by the merits of employing tort law or discrimination law in order to redress the harm caused by sexual harassment, a further possibility lies in the use of the criminal law. This suggestion can be applied to harassment which occurs in both the public sphere of employment and the private sphere

Section 154 of the Criminal Justice and Public Order Act 1994 inserts a new section 4A into the Public Order Act 1986. This provision closely resembles that under section 5 of the same Act:

4A.-(1)   A person is guilty of an offence if, with intent to cause a person harassment, alarm or distress, he-
    (a)   uses threatening, abusive or insulting words or behaviour, or disorderly behaviour or
    (b)   displays any writing, sign or other visible representation which is threatening, abusive or insulting, thereby causing that or another person harassment, alarm or distress.

5.-(1)   A person is guilty of an offence if he-
    (a)   uses threatening, abusive or insulting words or behaviour, or disorderly behaviour, or

(b) displays any writing, sign or other visible representation which is threatening, abusive or insulting, within the hearing or sight of a person likely to be caused harassment, alarm or distress thereby.

These provisions are designed primarily to deal with incidents of racial violence and racial harassment.[59] Their utility in dealing with sexual harassment is, therefore, circumspect. Irene Mackay and Jill Earnshaw argue that section 5:

"was not designed to assist victims of sexual harassment, but to outlaw, in a place other than a dwelling, behaviour which amounts to more than mere annoyance or disturbance. Arguably this section could be used to frame a charge against the perpetrator of sexual harassment although its use falls outside the spirit of the Public Order Act 1986 and is at the lowest end of summary offences and so does not reflect the effect which harassment can have on the victim."[60]

Janet Dine and Bob Watt are, however, slightly more optimistic about the possibility of using section 5:

J. DINE & B. WATT
"Sexual Harassment: Moving Away From Discrimination"[61]

"The House of Lords established in *Brutus v. Cozens* that the words 'threatening, abusive or insulting' carry their everyday meanings and that the quality of the behaviour was a matter of fact to be determined by the court at first instance. However, the word 'insulting' has been construed more widely by Glidewell L.J. in *Masterson v. Holden*, and it may be that this wider meaning is especially helpful to victims of sexual harassment. Glidewell L.J. said that a person may be insulted by the suggestion being made that they would themselves find reprehensible conduct acceptable. It may be argued that a sexual invitation in a workplace would insult the recipient by suggesting that they would find, for example, adulterous or promiscuous conduct acceptable. It is plain that the element of insult is subjective with respect to the hearer and, further, that the harassee's voluntary attendance does not negate the offence.

The mental state of the harasser appears to be widely defined by the Public Order Act 1986, s. 6(4) of which provides for two alternative mental states: intention (to threaten, abuse or insult) or awareness (that the words or behaviour may be threatening, abusive or insulting). The latter state appears sufficiently wide as to encompass both subjective and objective recklessness. The defence of reasonable conduct is available to a defendant under s. 5(3)(c) of the Act and it seems that this defence would be particularly useful to anyone who is threatened with action by an exceptionally sensitive individual."

---

[59] M. Wasik & R. Taylor, *Blackstone's Guide to the Criminal Justice & Public Order Act 1994* (London: Blackstone Press, 1995), pp. 98–100.

[60] I. Mackay & J. Earnshaw, "Skirting around sexual harassment" (1995) 145 New L.J. 338 at 340.

[61] J. Dine & B. Watt, *supra*, n. 55 at 354–355.

The new, and more serious, offence of intentional harassment, which was created by section 154 of the Criminal Justice and Public Order Act 1994, may yet prove of more utility to those who are subjected to sexual harassment. Despite being primarily aimed at combating abuse on the grounds of race, its statutory construction is not exclusive in this respect. A complainant of sexual harassment would have to prove that the accused had the requisite intention to cause harassment, which may be slightly problematic, but this new crime does at least mark an acknowledgement that the criminal law has a role to play in censoring conduct designed to harass the victim.

Finally, a more innovative construction of the harassment-as-crime configuration has occurred through use being made of the Offences Against the Person Act 1861. Section 20 of this Act makes it an offence to "unlawfully and maliciously wound or inflict any grievous bodily harm". Irene Mackay and Jill Earnshaw take up the story:

I. Mackay & J. Earnshaw
"Skirting around sexual harassment"[62]

"Recently harassment has been brought to the attention of the court in a robust and novel way in the unreported case of *R. v. Gelder*. It was an attempt to reflect the serious effect of the harasser's behaviour upon his victim and surprisingly it succeeded at first instance. The harassment was by way of obscene telephone calls, made anonymously by the defendant, a bank employee, to a female customer at her home. The calls were persistent and threatening. The complainant suffered fear, anxiety, personality changes and at times physical sickness. She required medication in the form of tranquillisers. The defendant was charged on indictment with inflicting grievous bodily harm, contrary to s. 20 of the Offences Against the Person Act 1861 and was sentenced to 18 months' imprisonment. This case shows the gravity of the matter in the eyes of those prosecuting and the sentence indicates clearly the attitude of the court to the campaign of harassment to which she was subjected. Nevertheless once again it amounts to shoe-horning harassment into existing legal machinery where it does not fit.

Two major issues haunt this case. The first is whether the harm suffered by this victim can be said to constitute grievous bodily harm on a proper interpretation of s. 20 of the Offences against the Person Act 1861. The Court of Appeal in *R. v. Chan-Fook* decided that actual bodily harm could include psychiatric injury but does not include mere emotions such as fear, distress, panic or an hysterical or nervous condition, nor does it include states of mind that were not themselves evidence of some identifiable clinical condition. In *R. v. Gelder* the Crown took this judgment a stage further by successfully alleging that the harm suffered by the victim amounted to grievous bodily harm. We believe that this use of s. 20 is questionable.

The second issue surrounds the word 'inflict' which is required by s. 20. Can one inflict grievous bodily harm by means of persistent, unwanted and obscene telephone calls? Although it has been established that there can be infliction of grievous bodily harm without an assault, the word 'inflict' is narrower than 'cause'. Therefore in the

---

[62]　I. Mackay & J. Earnshaw, *supra*, n. 60 at 340.

absence of an assault, it must be proved that the defendant was responsible for the complainant's really serious bodily harm in a way which goes beyond merely causing it. It must amount to the defendant doing something intentionally, which results in force being applied violently to the body of the victim, and this was not the case with Gelder's victim.

This was one of the grounds upon which Gelder's recent appeal against conviction was founded but it was not considered by the Court of Appeal who allowed the appeal on a completely separate issue of a misdirection by the judge. At present, where the sexual harasser's conduct falls short of assault occasioning actual bodily harm, there is no regulation of the behaviour under the criminal law which reflects its seriousness. Existing criminal law, properly interpreted, will not tolerate being stretched as it was in *Gelder*. Although replacement of the unsatisfactory Offences against the Person Act 1861 would help, harassment must find a place of its own, which will reflect the seriousness and unacceptability of such conduct."

Section 20 has been applied more recently in *R. v. Burstow*,[63] a classic case of "stalking". Although not specifically articulated in terms of sexual harassment, it is clear that the conduct engaged in in this case would fall within the remit of lay usage of the term. It is equally clear that the gender dimension of the relationship between harasser and victim was not unimportant. Mr Burstow was a petty officer in the navy. He became acquainted with Mrs Sant, a civilian employee at the naval base at which he was stationed and a friendship developed between them. When Mrs Sant decided to put an end to the relationship Burstow could not accept this. He started to follow her, pestered her with telephone calls, letters and photographs, and frequently visited her home. Mrs Sant complained to the police and Burstow was arrested and sentenced to several terms of imprisonment for his behaviour. There was no dispute as to the injury which Mrs Sant had suffered which was regarded as a grievous harm of a psychiatric nature, comprising endogenous depression with marked features of anxiety. Burstow's appeal against conviction under section 20 of the Offences Against the Person Act 1861 was, therefore, based on the question of whether or not the requirement to "inflict" grievous bodily harm under section 20 meant that physical force had to be applied directly or indirectly to the body of the victim.

When heard before the House of Lords the case was joined with a case of a similar nature, *R. v. Ireland*,[64] which also raised issues regarding the application of the Offences Against The Person Act 1861. In the *Ireland* case, however, it was section 47 of the Act, concerning "assault occasioning actual bodily harm", which was invoked in response to conduct of the appellant consisting of making a series of unwanted, silent telephone calls to three women. Each of the women was examined by a psychiatrist who found evidence of a range of psychological symptoms in the women. Ireland appealed against his conviction under section 47 on the grounds that a telephone call, followed by silence, did not constitute an "assault".

---

[63] *R. v. Burstow* [1997] 3 W.L.R. 534.
[64] *R. v. Ireland* [1997] 3 W.L.R. 534.

While the two cases of *Burstow* and *Ireland* each raised a distinct issue with respect to section 20 and section 47 of the 1861 Act, there was nonetheless a common element which united the two cases—the question of whether or not psychiatric illness fell within the phrase "bodily harm" as used in sections 20 and 47 of the 1861 Act. Dismissing unanimously the appeals of the two men, and recognising the significance of the harm which a campaign of harassment might entail for female victims, the House of Lords responded to the three separate issues raised in the following manner:

R. v. Ireland; R. v. Burstow
[1997] 3 W.L.R. 534 at 537–538, 541–547, *per* Lord Steyn

"My Lords, it is easy to understand the terrifying effect of a campaign of telephone calls at night by a silent caller to a woman living on her own. It would be natural for the victim to regard the calls as menacing. What may heighten her fear is that she will not know what the caller may do next. The spectre of the caller arriving at her door-step bent on inflicting personal violence on her may come to dominate her thinking. After all, as a matter of common sense, what else would she be terrified about? The victim may suffer psychiatric illness such as anxiety neurosis or acute depression. Harassment of women by repeated silent telephone calls, accompanied on occasions by heavy breathing, is apparently a significant social problem. That the criminal law should be able to deal with this problem, and so far as is practicable, afford effective protection to victims is self-evident.

From the point of view, however, of the general policy of our law towards the imposition of criminal responsibility, three specific features of the problem must be faced squarely. First, the medium used by the caller is the telephone: arguably it differs qualitatively from a face to face offer of violence to a sufficient extent to make a difference. Secondly, *ex hypothesi* the caller remains silent: arguably a caller may avoid the reach of the criminal law by remaining silent however menacing the context may be. Thirdly, it is arguable that the criminal law does not take into account 'mere' psychiatric illnesses.

At first glance it may seem that the legislature has satisfactorily dealt with such objections by section 43(1) of the Telecommunications Act 1984 which makes it an offence persistently to make use of a public telecommunications system for the purpose of causing annoyance, inconvenience or needless anxiety to another. The maximum custodial penalty is six months imprisonment. This penalty may be inadequate to reflect a culpability of a persistent offender who causes serious psychiatric illness to another. For the future there will be for consideration the provisions of sections 1 and 2 of the Protection from Harassment Act 1997, not yet in force, which creates the offence of pursuing a course of conduct which amounts to harassment of another and which he knows or ought to know amounts to harassment of the other. The maximum custodial penalty is six months imprisonment. This penalty may also be inadequate to deal with persisent offenders who cause serious psychiatric injury to victims. Section 4(1) of the Act of 1997 which creates the offence of putting people in fear of violence seems more appropriate. It provides for maximum custodial penalty upon conviction on indictment of five years imprisonment. On the other hand, section 4 only applies when as a result of a course of conduct the victim has cause to fear, on at least two occasions, that violence *will* be used against her. It may be difficult to secure a conviction in respect of a silent caller: the victim in such cases may have cause to fear that violence *may* be used against her but no more. In my view, therefore, the provisions of these two statutes are not ideally suited to deal with the significant problem which I have described. One must therefore look elsewhere.

It is to the provisions of the Offences against the Person Act 1861 that one must turn to examine whether our law provides effective criminal sanctions for this type of case . . .

The common question: Can psychiatric illness amount to bodily harm?
It will now be convenient to consider the question which is common to the two appeals, namely, whether psychiatric illness is capable of amounting to bodily harm in terms of sections 18, 20 and 47 of the Act of 1861. The answer must be the same for the three sections.

The only abiding thing about the processes of the human mind, and the causes of its disorders and disturbances, is that there will never be a complete explanation. Psychiatry is and will always remain an imperfectly understood branch of medical science. This idea is explained by Vallar's psychiatrist in Iris Murdoch's *The Message to the Planet*:

> Our knowledge of the soul, if I may use that unclinical but essential word, encounters certain seemingly impassable limits, set there perhaps by the gods, if I may refer to them, in order to preserve their privacy, and beyond which it maybe not only futile but lethal to attempt to pass and though it is our duty to seek for knowledge, it is also incumbent on us to realise when it is denied us, and not to prefer a fake solution to no solution at all.'

But there has been progress since 1861. And courts of law can only act on the best scientific understanding of the day. Some elementary distinctions can be made. The appeals under consideration do not involve structural injuries to the brain such as might require the intervention of a neurologist. One is also not considering either psychotic illness or personality disorders. The victims in the two appeals suffered from no such conditions. As a result of the behaviour of the appellants they did not develop psychotic or psychoneurotic conditions. The case was that they developed mental disturbances of a lesser order, namely neurotic disorders. For present purposes the relevant forms of neurosis are anxiety disorders and depressive disorders. Neuroses must be distinguished from simple states of fear, or problems in coping with every day life. Where the line is to be drawn must be a matter of psychiatric judgment. But for present purposes it is important to note that modern psychiatry treats neuroses as recognisable psychiatric illnesses: see "Liability for Psychiatric Injury," Law Commission Consultation paper No. 137 (1995) Part III (The Medical Background); *Mullany and Hanford, Tort Liability for Psychiatric Damages* (1993), discussion on "The Medical Perspective," at pp. 24–42, and particularly at p. 30, footnote 88. Moreover, it is essential to bear in mind that neurotic illnesses affect the central nervous system of the body, because emotions such as fear and anxiety are brain functions.

The civil law has for a long time taken account of the fact that there is no rigid distinction between body and mind. In *Bourhill v. Young* [1943] A.C. 92 at 103 Lord Macmillan said:

> 'The crude view that the law should take cognisance only of physical injury resulting from actual impact has been discarded, and it is now well recognised

that an action will lie for injury by shock sustained through the medium of the eye or the ear without direct contact. The distinction between mental shock and bodily injury was never a scientific one.'

This idea underlies the subsequent decisions of the House of Lords regarding post-traumatic stress disorder in *McLoughlin v. O'Brian* [1983] 1 A.C. 410, 418, *per* Lord Wilberforce; and *Page v. Smith* [1996] A.C. 155, 181A–D, *per* Lord Browne-Wilkinson. So far as such cases are concerned with the precise boundaries of tort liability they are not relevant. But so far as those decisions are based on the principle that the claimant must be able to prove that he suffered a recognisable psychiatric illness or condition they are by analogy relevant. The decisions of the House of Lords on post-traumatic stress disorder hold that where the line is to be drawn is a matter for expert psychiatric evidence. By analogy those decisions suggest a possible principled approach to the question whether psychiatric injury may amount to bodily harm in terms of the Act of 1861.

The criminal law has been slow to follow this path. But in *R. v. Chan-Fook* [1994] 1 W.L.R. 689 the Court of Appeal squarely addressed the question whether psychiatric injury may amount to bodily harm under section 47 of the Act of 1861. The issue arose in a case where the defendant had aggressively questioned and locked in a suspected thief. There was a dispute as to whether the defendant had physically assaulted the victim. But the prosecution also alleged that even if the victim had suffered no physical injury, he had been reduced to a mental state which amounted to actual bodily harm under section 47. No psychiatric evidence was given. The judge directed the jury that an assault which caused an hysterical and nervous condition was an assault occasioning actual bodily harm. The defendant was convicted. Upon appeal the conviction was quashed on the ground of misdirections in the summing up and the absence of psychiatric evidence to support the prosecution's alternative case. The interest of the decision lies in the reasoning on psychiatric injury in the context of section 47. In a detailed and careful judgment given on behalf of the court Hobhouse L.J. said, at p. 695:

'The first question on the present appeal is whether the inclusion of the word 'bodily' in the phrase "actual bodily harm" limits harm to harm to the skin, flesh and bones of the victim . . . The body of the victim includes all parts of his body, including his organs, his nervous system and his brain. Bodily injury therefore may include injury to any of those parts of his body responsible for his mental and other faculties.'

In concluding that 'actual bodily harm' is capable of including psychiatric injury Hobhouse L.J. emphasised, at p. 696:

'it does not include mere emotions such as fear or distress nor panic nor does it include, as such, states of mind that are not themselves evidence of some identifiable clinical condition.'

He observed that in the absence of psychiatric evidence a question whether or not an assault occasioned psychiatric injury should not be left to the jury.

The Court of Appeal, as differently constituted in *R. v. Ireland* and *R. v. Burstow*, was bound by the decision in *R. v. Chan-Fook*. The House is not so bound. Counsel for the appellants in both appeals submitted that bodily harm in Victorian legislation cannot include psychiatric injury. For this reason they argued that *R. v. Chan-Fook* was wrongly decided. They relied on the following observation of Lord Bingham of Cornhill C.J. in *R. v. Burstow* [1997] 1 Cr.App.R. 144, 148–149:

> 'Were the question free from authority, we should entertain some doubt whether the Victorian draftsman of the 1861 Act intended to embrace psychiatric injury within the expressions "grievous bodily harm" and "actual bodily harm".'

Nevertheless, Lord Bingham C.J. observed that it is now accepted that in the relevant context the distinction between physical and mental injury is by no means clear cut. He welcomed the ruling in *R. v. Chan-Fook*: at p. 149B. I respectfully agree. But I would go further and point out that, although out of considerations of piety we frequently refer to the actual intention of the draftsman, the correct approach is simply to consider whether the words of the Act of 1861 considered in the light of contemporary knowledge cover a recognisable psychiatric injury. It is undoubtedly true that there are statutes where the correct approach is to construe the legislation 'as if one were interpreting it the day after it was passed:' *The Longford* (1889) 14 P.D. 34. Thus in *The Longford* the word 'action' in a statute was held not to be apt to cover an Admiralty action in rem since when it was passed the Admiralty Court 'was not one of His Majesty's Courts of Law:' see pp. 37, 38. Bearing in mind that statutes are usually intended to operate for many years it would be most inconvenient if courts could never rely in difficult cases on the current meaning of statutes. Recognising the problem Lord Thring, the great Victorian draftsman of the second half of the last century, exhorted draftsmen to draft so that 'An Act of Parliament should be deemed to be always speaking:' *Practical Legislation* (1902), p. 83; see also *Cross, Statutory Interpretation*, 3rd ed. (1995), p. 51; *Pearce and Geddes, Statutory Interpretation in Australia*, 4th ed. (1996), pp. 90–93. In cases where the problem arises it is a matter of intepretation whether a court must search for the historical or original meaning of a statute or whether it is free to apply the current meaning of the statute to present day conditions. Statutes dealing with a particular grievance or problem may sometimes require to be historically interpreted. But the drafting technique of Lord Thring and his successors have brought about the situation that statutes will generally be found to be of the 'always speaking' variety: see *Royal College of Nursing of the United Kingdom v. Department of Health and Social Security* [1981] A.C. 800 for an example of an 'always speaking' construction in the House of Lords.

The proposition that the Victorian legislator when enacting sections 18, 20 and 47 of the Act 1861, would not have had in mind psychiatric illness is no doubt correct. Psychiatry was in its infancy in 1861. But the subjective intention of the draftsman is immaterial. The only relevant inquiry is as to the sense of the words in the context in which they are used. Moreover the Act of 1861 is a statute of the 'always speaking' type: the statute must be interpreted in the light of the best current scientific appreciation of the link between the body and psychiatric injury.

For these reasons I would, therefore, reject the challenge to the correctness of *R. v. Chan-Fook* [1994] 1 W.L.R. 689. In my view the ruling in that case was based on principled and cogent reasoning and it marked a sound and essential clarification of the law. I would hold that 'bodily harm' in sections 18, 20 and 47 must be interpreted so as to include recognisable psychiatric illness.

R. v. Burstow: the meaning of 'inflict' in section 20

The decision in R. v. Chan-Fook opened up the possibility of applying sections 18, 20 and 47 in new circumstances. The appeal of Burstow lies in respect of his conviction under section 20. It was conceded that in principle the wording of section 18, and in particular the words 'cause any grievous bodily harm to any person' do not preclude a prosecution in cases where the actus reus is the causing of psychiatric injury. But counsel laid stress on the difference between 'causing' grievous bodily harm in section 18 and 'inflicting' grievous bodily harm in section 20. Counsel argued that the difference in wording reveals a difference in legislative intent: inflict is a narrower concept than cause. This argument loses sight of the genesis of sections 18 and 20. In his commentary on the Act of 1861 Greaves, the draftsman, explained the position: *The Criminal Law Consolidation and Amendment Acts* (1861). He said, at pp. 3–4:

'If any question should arise in which any comparison may be instituted between different sections of any one or several of these Acts, it must be carefully borne in mind in what manner these Acts were framed. None of them was rewritten; on the contrary, each contains enactments taken from different Acts passed at different times and with different views, and frequently varying from each other in phraseology, and ... these enactments, for the most part, stand in these Acts with little or no variation in their phraseology, and, consequently, their differences in that respect will be found generally to remain in these Acts. It follows, therefore, from hence, that any argument as to a difference in the intention of the legislature, which may be drawn from a difference in the terms of one clause from those in another, will be entitled to no weight in the construction of such clauses; for that argument can only apply with force where an Act is framed from beginning to end with one and the same view, and with the intention of making it thoroughly consistent throughout.'

The difference in language is therefore not a significant factor.

Counsel for Burstow then advanced a sustained argument that an assault is an ingredient of an offence under section 20. He referred your Lordships to cases which in my judgment simply do not yield what he sought to extract from them. In any event, the tour of the cases revealed conflicting dicta, no authority binding on the House of Lords, and no settled practice holding expressly that assault was an ingredient of section 20. And, needless to say, none of the cases focused on the infliction of psychiatric injury. In these circumstances I do not propose to embark on a general review of the cases cited: compare the review in *Smith and Hogan, Criminal Law*, 8th ed. (1996), pp. 440–441. Instead I turn to the words of the section. Counsel's argument can only prevail if one may supplement the section by reading it as providing 'inflict *by assault* any grievous bodily harm.' Such an implication is, however, not necessary. On the contrary, section 20, like section 18, works perfectly satisfactorily without such an implication. I would reject this part of counsel's argument.

But counsel had a stronger argument when he submitted that it is inherent in the word 'inflict' that there must be a direct or indirect application of force to the body. Counsel cited the speech of Lord Roskill in R. v. Wilson (Clarence) [1984] A.C. 242, 259E–260H, in which Lord Roskill quoted with approval from the judgment of the full court of the Supreme Court of Victoria in R. v. Salisbury [1976] V.R. 452. There are passages that give assistance to counsel's argument. But Lord Roskill expressly stated, at p. 260H, that he was:

'content to accept, as did the [court in *Salisbury*] that there can be the infliction of grievous bodily harm contrary to section 20 without an assault being
committed.'

In the result the effect of the decisions in *R. v. Wilson* and *R. v. Salisbury* is neutral
in respect of the issue as to the meaning of "inflict." Moreover, in *R. v. Burstow*
[1997] 1 Cr.App.R. 144, 149, Lord Bingham of Cornhill C.J. pointed out that in *R.
v. Mandair* [1995] 1 A.C. 208, 215, Lord Mackay of Clashfern L.C. observed with
the agreement of the majority of the House of Lords: 'In my opinion . . . the word
"cause" is wider or at least not narrower than the word "inflict."' Like Lord Bingham
C.J. I regard this observation as making clear that in the context of the Act of 1861
there is no radical divergence between the meaning of the two words.

That leaves the troublesome authority of the Court for Crown Cases Reserved in *R.
v. Clarence* (1888) 22 Q.B.D. 23. At a time when the defendant knew that he was
suffering from a veneral disease, and his wife was ignorant of his condition, he had
sexual intercourse with her. He communicated the disease to her. The defendant was
charged and convicted of inflicting grievous bodily harm under section 20. There was
an appeal. By a majority of nine to four the court quashed the conviction. The case
was complicated by an issue of consent. But it must be accepted that in a case where
there was direct physical contact the majority ruled that the requirement of infliction
was not satisfied. This decision has never been overruled. It assists counsel's argument.
But it seems to me that what detracts from the weight to be given to the dicta in *R. v.
Clarence* is that none of the judges in that case had before them the possibility of the
inflicting, or causing, of psychiatric injury. The criminal law has moved on in the light
of a developing understanding of the link between the body and psychiatric injury. In
my judgment *R. v. Clarence* no longer assists.

The problem is one of construction. The question is whether as a matter of current
usage the contextual interpretation of 'inflict' can embrace the idea of one person
inflicting psychiatric injury on another. One can without straining the language in any
way answer that question in the affirmative. I am not saying that the words cause and
inflict are exactly synonymous. They are not. What I am saying is that in the context
of the Act of 1861 one can nowadays quite naturally speak of inflicting psychiatric
injury. Moreover, there is internal contextual support in the statute for this view. It
would be absurd to differentiate between sections 18 and 20 in the way argued on
behalf of Burstow. As Lord Bingham C.J. observed in *R. v. Burstow* [1997] 1
Cr.App.R. 144, 149, this should be a very practical area of the law. The interpretation
and approach should, so far as possible be adopted which treats the ladder of offences
as a coherent body of law. Once the decision in *R. v. Chan-Fook* [1994] 1 W.L.R.
689 is accepted the realistic possibility is opened up of prosecuting under section 20
in cases of the type which I described in the introduction to this judgment.

For the reasons I have given I would answer the certified question in *R. v. Burstow*
in the affirmative.

R. v. Ireland: was there an assault?

It is now necessary to consider whether the making of silent telephone calls causing
psychiatric injury is capable of constituting an assault under section 47. The Court of
Appeal, as constituted in *R. v. Ireland* case, answered that question in the affirmative.
There has been substantial academic criticism of the conclusion and reasoning in *R. v.
Ireland*: see *Archbold News*, Issue 6, 12 July 1996; *Archbold's Criminal Pleading,
Evidence & Practice*, Supplement No. 4 (1996), pp. 345–347; *Smith and Hogan, Crim-*

inal Law, 8th ed. (1996), 413; 'Assault by Telephone' by Jonathan Herring [1997] C.L.J. 11; 'Assault' [1997] Crim.L.R. 434, 435–436. Counsel's arguments, broadly speaking, challenged the decision in *R. v. Ireland* on very similar lines. Having carefully considered the literature and counsel's arguments, I have come to the conclusion that the appeal ought to be dismissed.

The starting point must be that an assault is an ingredient of the offence under section 47. It is necessary to consider the two forms which an assault may take. The first is battery, which involves the unlawful application of force by the defendant upon the victim. Usually, section 47 is used to prosecute in cases of this kind. The second form of assault is an act causing the victim to apprehend an imminent application of force upon her: see *Fagan v. Metropolitan Police Commissioner* [1969] 1 Q.B. 439–444D–E.

One point can be disposed of, quite briefly. The Court of Appeal was not asked to consider whether silent telephone calls resulting in psychiatric injury is capable of constituting a battery. But encouraged by some academic comment it was raised before your Lordships' House. Counsel for Ireland was most economical in his argument on the point. I will try to match his economy of words. In my view it is not feasible to enlarge the generally accepted legal meaning of what is a battery to include the circumstances of a silent caller who causes psychiatric injury.

It is to assault in the form of an act causing the victim to fear an immediate application of force to her that I must turn. Counsel argued that as a matter of law an assault can never be committed by words alone and therefore it cannot be committed by silence. The premise depends on the slenderest authority, namely, an observation by Holroyd J. to a jury that 'no words or singing are equivalent to an assault:' *R. v. Meade and Belt* (1823) 1 Lew. 184. The proposition that a gesture may amount to an assault, but that words can never suffice, is unrealistic and indefensible. A thing said is also a thing done. There is no reason why something said should be incapable of causing an apprehension of immediate personal violence, *e.g.* a man accosting a woman in a dark alley saying, 'Come with me or I will stab you.' I would, therefore, reject the proposition that an assault can never be committed by words.

That brings me to the critical question whether a silent caller may be guilty of an assault. The answer to this question seems to me to be 'Yes, depending on the facts.' It involves questions of fact within the province of the jury. After all, there is no reason why a telephone caller who says to a woman in a menacing way 'I will be at your door in a minute or two' may not be guilty of an assault if he causes his victim to apprehend immediate personal violence. Take now the case of the silent caller. He intends by his silence to cause fear and he is so understood. The victim is assailed by uncertainty about his intentions. Fear may dominate her emotions, and it may be the fear that the caller's arrival at her door may be imminent. She may fear the *possibility* of immediate personal violence. As a matter of law the caller may be guilty of an assault: whether he is or not will depend on the circumstance and in particular on the impact of the caller's potentially menacing call or calls on the victim. Such a prosecution case under section 47 may be fit to leave to the jury. And a trial judge may, depending on the circumstances, put a common sense consideration before jury, namely what, if not the possibility of imminent personal violence, was the victim terrified about? I conclude that an assault may be committed to the particular factual circumstances which I have envisaged. For this reason I reject the submission that as a matter of law a silent telephone caller cannot ever be guilty of an offence under section 47. In these circumstances no useful purpose would be served by answering the vague certified question in *R. v. Ireland*.

Having concluded that the legal arguments advanced on behalf of Ireland on section

47 must fail, I nevertheless accept that the concept of an assault involving immediate personal violence as an ingredient of the section 47 offence is a considerable complicating factor in bringing prosecutions under it in respect of silent telephone callers and stalkers. That the least serious of the ladder of offences is difficult to apply in such cases is unfortunate. At the hearing of the appeal of *R. v. Ireland* attention was drawn to the Bill which is annexed to Law Commission report, 'Legislating the Criminal Code: Offences Against the Person and General Principles.' (Law Com. No. 218) (1993) (Cm. 2370). Clause 4 of that Bill is intended to replace section 47. Clause 4 provides that 'A person is guilty of an offence if he intentionally or recklessly causes injury to another.' This simple and readily comprehensible provision would eliminate the problems inherent in section 47. In expressing this view I do not, however, wish to comment on the appropriateness of the definition of 'injury' in clause 18 of the Bill, and in particular the provision that 'injury' means 'impairment of a person's mental health.'

The disposal of the appeals
The legal arguments advanced on behalf of Burstow have failed. The appeal must be dismissed.

The legal arguments advanced on behalf of Ireland have also failed. But counsel for the appellant submitted that the appeal should be allowed because on an examination of the statements there was no prima facie case against him. I reject this submission. The prosecution case was never fully deployed because Ireland pleaded guilty. The fact of his plea demonstrated his *mens rea*. It was said, however, that the ingredient of psychiatric injury was not established on the statements. It is true that the statement from the psychiatrist is vague. But I would not accept that read in context it was insufficient to allow the case to go before a jury. It would be an exceptional course, in the face of an unequivocal and deliberate plea of guilty, to entertain an appeal directed exclusively to the sufficiency of evidence. Such a course is not warranted in the present case. I would therefore dismiss the appeal of Ireland."

To conclude that harassment must "find a place of its own" (as do Mackay and Earnshaw, above) or to treat as self-evident the fact that the *criminal* law should be capable of dealing with the "apparently [. . .] significant social problem" of harassment of women by a campaign of silent telephone calls (as *per* Lord Steyn above), should not, at the end of the day, amount to an exclusive choice. Absent the specific creation by Parliament of a new legal forum in which to locate sexual harassment (such as a statutory tort or crime) a woman complainant must review and select from amongst the various legal avenues open to her. Indeed, she may decide to pursue a combination of options depending upon the nature of the harassment and the sort of injury sustained. This approach is advocated by Dine and Watt who respond to the question "tort or crime?" as follows:

J. DINE & BATT
"Sexual harassment: Moving Away From Discrimination"[65]

"Views as to the point at which behaviour should become criminalised vary according to different perceptions of the purposes of the criminal law. A moral judgment of the

[65] J. Dine & B. Watt, *supra*, n. 55 at 362–363.

seriousness of the behaviour also affects the place at which it is believed the line should be drawn. A number of writers have suggested criteria for determining whether a criminal sanction is appropriate for a particular type of behaviour. Packer advances a 'benchmark for the optimal use of the criminal sanction' and suggests a number of criteria which should be satisfied before criminality is judged to be appropriate. The first criterion is that the offending conduct 'is prominent in most people's view of socially threatening behaviour and is not condoned by any significant section of society.'

We would argue that sexual harassment, indeed harassment more generally, fulfils this condition provided that it presents a significant threat to personal autonomy in the ways we have outlined. We suggest that, following prosecution of the harasser, victims should proceed in a civil action against the tortfeasor. This is not unprecedented. In a very recent case, the victim of harassment took the necessary steps to initiate a prosecution and then used the industrial tribunal system to secure redress.

The case involved an unnamed woman who won an award of £34,160. One Jeffrey Tucker, the woman's employer, 'fondled' her and then exposed his penis before he pushed her against a wall, masturbated and ejaculated over her. Clearly these actions constituted a serious criminal assault and the woman complained to the police. Whilst Mr Tucker was on bail for the assault, he dimissed the woman from her job and refused to give her any pay owed to her. The woman, apart from suffering the indignity of these assaults, proved to the tribunal that she subsequently suffered from anxiety, insomnia, a stress-related stomach ulcer and psychological disorders, including self-mutilation. Mr Tucker was jailed for 18 months for the assaults and ordered to pay the woman £11,000 for the harassment. The balance of the award comprised £12,960 for back-pay and lost wages, £5,200 for future loss of earnings and £5,000 for the 'added insult' of being dismissed."

By way of conclusion to this chapter, what, nevertheless, seems crucial for feminists in addressing sexual harassment is that a *legal* response is articulated and rigorously pursued. Given the present climate, which appears reasonably responsive to the situation of sexual harassment on the political agenda, the time is ripe for action. The opportunity should not go unseized.

J. CONAGHAN
"Gendered Harms and the Law of Tort: Remedying (Sexual) Harassment"[66]

"[T]he need to engage with law derives not just from the current absence of remedies for many individual women who sustain harm; feminists must engage with law because law is an important and unavoidable site of political struggle. Law's constitutive power in relation to the recognition of harm is of crucial importance in the struggle to ensure that women's voices are heard and understood. If, as Catharine MacKinnon suggests, 'law sees and treats women the way men see and treat women', then women *must* challenge that view. It is simply not open to feminists to eschew law on grounds of its gendered content. The struggle must take place both within law and outside it, both through it and beyond it. Legal change is neither the starting point nor the end result of the feminist project but, as an inevitable part of that project, it must be addressed."

[66]   J. Conaghan, *supra*, n. 41 at 431.

CHAPTER 9

IMAGES OF THE BODY

The first difficulty encountered in discussing images of the body is one of defining the subject matter. What does it mean to speak of images? A second, and related, question may then be posed, that is, what do these images have to do with law? To address the first issue one might start with the perhaps obvious point that images of the female body are pervasive. They are disseminated through many media. To the "older" forms of media such as film and terrestrial television, magazines and newspapers, can now be added the "newer" forms of satellite television and the internet. What this has to do with law is that the law is employed to regulate such imagery and identify the boundaries of permissible depictions. Feminist interest in the law lies with investigation into where the boundary lines are drawn. An assessment of the boundaries will indicate the extent to which images of the female body are judged inoffensive and, by implication, the cause of no harm. Feminists may seek to challenge this delineation and its implications for the construction of the female sexual body.

The legal regulation of images of the female body is under scrutiny here in two particular areas. The first is the regulation governing pornography (or obscenity). The second is that governing advertising images.

9.1 Pornography

9.1.i *Ways of seeing*
To speak of "pornography" is to speak of something which escapes definition, both in a legal and an extra-legal context. Its meaning depends very much on the perspective of the person attempting to articulate the definition. In keeping with the theme of this book, the perspective which we adopt here is concerned with the legal regulation of imagery of the *female* body, our expectation being that the limits of regulation may reveal something of legal and cultural perceptions of that body. Nevertheless, this does not mean that we propose to articulate a definition of pornography based solely upon harmful depictions of women, which would certainly be to misrepresent the issue. The problem of definition is much more complex, as Emily Jackson notes:

E. JACKSON
"The problem with pornography: A critical survey of the current debate"[1]

"Much of the discourse appears to plunge into discussion about what should be done about pornography without first attempting to elucidate precisely what it is. Pornography is not a self-defining concept; indeed its connection with sexual arousal means that it is, probably, an inherently subjective notion. I am troubled by the possibility that pornography's meaning may be too fluid to serve as an adequate foundation for the layers of argument which rest upon some assumed definitional solidity. For example, does the intention of the consumer or the producer of the image have any impact upon what is categorised as pornography? Our instinct may be to deny emphatically any such suggestion, but there are difficulties with this. First, paedophiles are often attracted to images of children which might in other contexts be wholly innocent. If a paedophile ring traffics in 'holiday snaps' of children, do these images acquire illegitimacy through the purpose to which they are put? Can it become an offence to sell pictures of naked children, when most parents have drawers full of such photos? Second, some feminists write about experiences of sexual abuse and exploitation in a way that might seem to mirror descriptions of such acts in pornographic magazines. For example, in Andrea Dworkin's novel *Mercy*, the heroine is repeatedly humiliated, sexually assaulted and tortured: is this then pornography? It might be argued that Dworkin's heroine does not appear to get pleasure from her abuse; but much hard-core pornography also shows women distressed by the sexual violence used against them. It might then be suggested that it should not be seen as pornography because we can be sure that was not what the author intended. Yet, if 'intention to exploit' becomes a necessary ingredient of the pornographic, we would have a readily manipulable defence which would effectively nullify attempts at regulation.

Furthermore, there are dangers in disallowing any expression which addresses sexual degradation. The paintings of Rene Magritte feature dehumanized images of women; in one picture, Le Viol, a woman's face is replaced with a torso: her breasts become her eyes, and her pubic hair becomes a beard. Perhaps this shows women to be reducible to their sexual parts. But is it comment on a society that does this to women, or is it pornography?

It seems clear that any definition of pornography rests upon background assumptions about what, if anything, is wrong with it. If sexual explicitness is the central concern, lesbian erotica is undoubtedly pornography. If, on the other hand, the harm of pornography is perceived to be the exploitation of women, such imagery is relatively unproblematic. So the term 'pornography' would then seem easily manipulable."

The hazardous exercise of defining pornography has not prevented some feminists from attempting this feat. Looking at the literal meaning of pornography the radical feminist Andrea Dworkin states that:

"The word *pornography*, derived from the ancient Greek *pornē* and *graphos*, means 'writing about whores.' *Pornē* means 'whore', specifically and exclusively the lowest class of whore, which in ancient Greece was the brothel slut available to all male citizens. The *pornē* was the cheapest (in the literal sense), least regarded, least protected of all women, including slaves. She was, simply

---

[1]   (1995) 3 *Feminist Legal Studies* 49 at 50–51.

and clearly and absolutely, a sexual slave. *Graphos* means 'writing, etching, or drawing.'

The word *pornography* does not mean 'writing about sex' or 'depictions of the erotic' or 'depictions of sexual acts' or 'depictions of nude bodies' or 'sexual representations' or any other such euphemism. It means the graphic depiction of women as vile whores.[2]

Catharine MacKinnon defines the "feminist" (one might add "unmodified") view of pornography as follows:

"Pornography, in the feminist view, is a form of forced sex, a practice of sexual politics, an institution of gender inequality. In this perspective, pornography is not harmless fantasy or a corrupt and confused misrepresentation of an otherwise natural and healthy sexuality. Along with rape and prostitution in which it participates, pornography institutionalizes the sexuality of male supremacy, which fuses the eroticization of dominance and submission with the social construction of male and female. Gender is sexual. Pornography constitutes the meaning of that sexuality. Men treat women as who they see women as being. Pornography constructs who that is. Men's power over women means that the way men see women defines who women can be. Pornography is that way.[3]

This perspective upon pornography is identified by Carol Smart as the "pornography-as-violence" position.[4] It concentrates on the explicitness and the coercive nature of pornographic material, a focus which is not in itself unproblematic. Smart comments:

C. SMART
Feminism and the Power of Law[5]

"It is the sexual content of the degradation which moves pornography to the top of the political agenda, not the degradation itself. This argument is both the strength and the weakness of this position. Its strength lies in the way it challenges the naturalistic and liberal view that if a thing is sexual it cannot be coercive because sex is taken as natural, springing from desire not culture. In the liberal view the sexual meaning 'overrides' the coerciveness which is central to the representation. From this arises the argument that what is important in pornography is the way in which the sexual 'neutralizes' domination. Presumably for these feminists representations of non-sexualized dominance are not a problem because their meaning is (arguably) clear and unobscured. This is an important point, yet it is the transformation of this insight into a legally enforceable definition which raises political problems for feminism and reveals

[2] A. Dworkin, *Pornography: Men possessing women* (London: The Women's Press, 1981), pp. 199–200.
[3] C. A. MacKinnon, *Feminism Unmodified: Discourses on Life and Law* (London: Harvard University Press, 1987), p. 148.
[4] C. Smart, *Feminism and the Power of Law* (London: Routledge, 1989), p. 120.
[5] (C. Smart, *ibid.*, p. 121.

the weakness of this position. Not only does it lead to a narrowing of feminist definitions of pornography, but it also leads to an underestimation of economic forms of
dominance (amongst others) which are not sexual. Indeed it goes further, since this
perspective has the tendency to reduce all forms of domination to the sexual, seeing
this as the mainspring of all forms of power."

The "violence" perspective upon pornography may be contrasted with what
Smart has identified as the "pornography-as-representation" position.

C. Smart
Feminism and the Power of Law[6]

"Pornography-as-representation stresses the distinction between sexual relationships
and representations of sex, and attempts to shift the emphasis away from concepts of
explicitness to the idea of pornography as a way of seeing. Perhaps the clearest exposition of this perspective is provided by Ros Coward[7] in which she develops the argument that pornography is a regime of representations . . . The basic point here is that
nothing is intrinsically pornographic, no image or word has an intrinsic meaning which
is immutable. But, in addition to this, this basic starting point alerts us to the fact that
we bring various and different 'interpretations' to images and words . . . Notwithstanding this, there are regimes of representation. This means that there are codes of interpretation which we learn and apply when representations comply with certain modes
of signification."

The failure to recognise the problematic aspect of wider representations of
women has led to claims of fundamentalism.

E. Wilson
"Feminist fundamentalism: The shifting politics of sex and censorship"[8]

"We need to unpick the whole concept of pornography, recognizing that it makes
more sense to speak in general terms of forms of cultural production of which some
are sexually explicit. Some we may like and some we may criticize; however, only if
we·view the sexually explicit in the context of the whole range of visual and written
texts will we challenge the dominant sexual ideology of our society, which does indeed
want 'the sexual' to be cordoned off and separated from the rest of life . . .
    Feminists do, however, need an analysis of imagery, and of representations gener-
ally. Such an analysis ought to enable women to express anger and rejection, while at
the same time it must recognize that the discourse of sex in Western culture is not
monolithic but contradictory and often ambiguous . . .
    The anti-porn campaigns constitute a form of secular fundamentalism. By funda-

---

[6] C. Smart, *ibid.*, p. 125.
[7] R. Coward, "Sexual violence and sexuality" in Feminist Review (ed.), *Sexuality: A Reader*
(London: Virago, 1987).
[8] In L. Segal and M. McIntosh, *Sex Exposed: Sexuality and the Pornography Debate* (London:
Virago, 1992), pp. 24, 26–28.

mentalism I mean here a way of life, or a world-view or philosophy of life, which insists that the individual lives by narrowly prescribed rules and rituals: a faith that offers certainty . . .

A truly feminist agenda on sex, sexuality and representation would emphasize the need for sex education for children; it would attack sexism as a representation of male power, rather than attacking sexual material as a representation of male sexuality; it would challenge the monopoly or quasi-monopoly ownership of the mass media, political censorship and the erosion of civil liberties. Feminists must — and do — attack the sexual abuse of children and the exploitation of women: these are central issues. But these issues are linked as much to ideologies of the family and employment as they are to pornography — indeed much more so. To have made pornography both the main cause of women's oppression and its main form of expression is to have wiped out almost the whole of the feminist agenda, and to have created a new moral purity movement for our new (authoritarian) times."

The regimes of representation which link images of women disseminated through pornography to other depictions of women disseminated through other media, such as advertising, are brought out in the second half of this chapter. Suffice to say, at this stage, that the law regulating pornography has been rather more concerned with the explicit nature of material and its effect on the viewer, rather than with the more pervasive dissemination of cultural perceptions of women.

9.1.ii *Pornography through the eyes of the criminal law*

Pornography is regulated in Britain through the criminal law on obscenity. This means that it is viewed as a moral issue, as opposed to a political issue or one of harm to women. The degree of overlap between what is deemed "obscene" and what is pornographic has been a habitual source of inquiry (and dissatisfaction) for feminists and will be delved into following a brief exposition of the current law on obscenity.[9]

The law on obscenity is governed by the Obscene Publications Acts 1959 and 1964. Obscenity is defined in section 1(1) of the 1959 Act:

> **1.-(1)** For the purposes of this Act an article shall be deemed to be obscene if its effect or (where the article comprises two or more distinct items) the effect of any one of its items is, if taken as a whole, such as to tend to deprave and corrupt persons who are likely, having regard to all relevant circumstances, to read, see or hear the matter contained or embodied in it.

This statutory definition retained the common law "deprave and corrupt" test for obscenity laid down by Cockburn C.J. in *R. v. Hicklin*:[10]

> . . . I think the test of obscenity is this, whether the tendency of the matter charged as obscenity is to deprave and corrupt those whose minds are open

---

[9] A more detailed account of the law can be found in D. Feldman, *Civil Liberties and Human Rights in England and Wales* (Oxford: OUP, 1993), pp. 698–732.

[10] *R. v. Hicklin* (1868) Q.B. 360.

to such immoral influences, and into whose hands a publication of this sort
may fall."

It is of no import that the person into whose hands the publication may fall
may already be corrupted. In *D.P.P. v. Whyte* Lord Wilberforce stated that:

> ". . . the Act is not merely concerned with the once for all corruption of the
> wholly innocent, it equally protects the less innocent from further corruption,
> the addict from feeding or increasing his addiction."[11]

Under the Obscene Publications Act 1959, s. 2(1) (as amended by the 1964
Act, s. 1(1)) an offence is committed where a person "whether for gain or not,
publishes an obscene article or has an obscene article for publication or gain
(whether gain to himself or gain to another)." For these purposes an "article"
is described as "any description of article containing or embodying matter to
be read or looked at or both, any sound record, and any film or other record
of a picture or pictures" (Obscene Publications Act 1959, s. 1(2)). This definition is sufficient to include computer pornography and videos. The 1959 Act
does, however, provide a defence of public good. Section 4(1) states that there
will no conviction ". . . if it is proved that publication of the article in question
is justified as being for the public good on the grounds that it is in the interests
of science, literature, art or learning or of other objects of general concern."

The relationship between pornography and obscenity is not particularly
easy to gauge from the above legislation. As a broad measure, the law appears
to differentiate between hard-core and soft-core pornography, deeming the
former and not the latter obscene — although there is no legal basis for this
distinction. Feminists on both sides of the Atlantic have argued that the match
between pornography and obscenity is misconstrued:

S. EASTON
"A plea for censorship"[12]

"The trouble with the OPA and other indecency legislation is that it is drafted largely
with the object of regulating matters of morality, sexuality and prurient and lascivious
conduct, and not with the object of regulating the graphic depiction of extreme violence and torture. The 'deprave and corrupt' test envisaged was one which would be
capable of drawing a distinction between a work of literary merit and works of
smut, . . .

[T]he Metropolitan Police's obscene publications squad does what it can to stem the
incoming tide of hatred and violence and has referred these cases to the CPS for prosecution. It is a matter for the CPS to assess whether the criteria for prosecution are
satisfied. Is there a reasonable prospect of conviction; is there a sufficiency of evidence
and is it in the public interest to prosecute? Is the reasonable prospect of conviction

---

[11] *D.P.P. v. Whyte* [1972] 3 All E.R. 12.
[12] (1991) 141 New L.J. 1478 at 1480.

the first or paramount consideration to which the CPS will turn, and if so, what precisely will it be evaluating — the legislation itself or the likely opinion of jurors of the material? On the other hand, if public interest is considered, whose interest is of paramount importance — will it be the interests of women and children who become defined by and in this material, or is the interest of those who argue that they should be free to decide what they read? Lord Wilberforce predicted in *Whyte*: 'I have serious doubts whether the Act will continue to be workable in this way, or whether it will produce tolerable results.' "

C. A. MacKinnon
"Not a moral issue"[13]

"Obscenity law is concerned with morality, specifically morals from the male point of view, meaning the standpoint of male dominance. The feminist critique of pornography is a politics, specifically politics from women's point of view, meaning the standpoint of the subordination of women to men. Morality here means good and evil; politics means power and powerlessness. Obscenity is a moral idea; pornography is a political practice. Obscenity is abstract; pornography is concrete. The two concepts represent two entirely different things. Nudity, explicitness, excess of candor, arousal or excitement, prurience, unnaturalness — these qualities bother obscenity law when sex is depicted or portrayed ... Sex forced on real women so that it can be sold at a profit to be forced on other real women; women's bodies trussed and maimed and raped and made into things to be hurt and obtained and accessed, and this presented as the nature of women; the coercion that is visible and the coercion that has become invisible — this and more bothers feminists about pornography. Obscenity as such probably does little harm, pornography causes attitudes and behaviours of violence and discrimination that define the treatment and status of half of the population."

The issue of power which is revealed here forms an important part of MacKinnon's inquiry into, and critique of, the obscenity standard, which is ultimately revealed in its male guise:

C. A. MacKinnon
"Not a moral issue"[14]

"This inquiry is part of a larger project that attempts to account for gender inequality in the socially constructed relationship between power — the political — on the one hand and the knowledge of truth and reality — the epistemological — on the other. For example, the candid description Justice Stewart once offered of his obscenity standard, 'I know it when I see it,'[15] becomes even more revealing than it is usually understood to be if taken as a statement that connects epistemology with power. If I ask, from the point of view of women's experience, does he know what I know when I see what I see, I find that I doubt it, given what's on the newsstands. How does his point of

---

[13] In C. A. MacKinnon, *supra*, n. 3 at p. 147.
[14] C.A. MacKinnon, *ibid.*, pp. 147–148.
[15] *Jacobellis v. Ohio* 378 U.S. 184, 197 (1964) (Stewart J., concurring).

view keep what is there, there? To liberal critics, his admission exposed the obscenity standard's relativity, its partiality, its insufficient abstractness. Not to be emptily universal, to leave your concreteness showing, is a sin among men. Their problem with Justice Stewart's formulation is that it implies that anything, capriciously, could be suppressed. They are only right by half. My problem is more the other half: the meaning of what his view permits, which as it turns out, is anything but capricious. In fact, it is entirely systematic and determinate. To me, his statement is precisely descriptively accurate; its candor is why it has drawn so much criticism. Justice Stewart got in so much trouble because he said out loud what is actually done all the time; in so doing, he both *did it* — and gave it the stature of doctrine, even if only dictum. That is, the obscenity standard — in this it is not unique — *is* built on what the male standpoint sees. My point is: *so is pornography.*"

Adrian Howe argues that the value of Catharine MacKinnon's approach is her recognition of pornography as a social injury rather than as a moral harm.

A. Howe
"The Problem of Privatized Injuries: Feminist Strategies for Litigation"[16]

"Let us first consider her interpretation of the harm of pornography. While that interpretation is controversial, and while Robin West, for one, has condemned it for abandoning 'feminist practice' and for failing to take account of the 'felt subjective desire' of many women for 'eroticised submission', it is, nevertheless, a theoretically significant one. First, it takes as its starting point women's experience of pornography and their testimony about the pain it has caused them. Second, it does analytically privilege the notion of injury to women in ways which anticipate the development of the conceptualization of women's injuries as *social* injuries which I believe is crucial for the advancement of feminist legal theory, and consequently, of women. Her contribution is seen clearly in the way in which she distinguishes her view of the pain of pornography from traditional versions. Thus, pornography is not a 'moral harm': indeed, to define the pornographic as obscenity is to misconstrue its harm. Rather, 'its harm is the harm of male supremacy made difficult to see because of its pervasiveness . . .' Indeed, the issue for MacKinnon is not what the harm of pornography is, but how to make it visible. This she sees as a huge problem insofar as pornography's invisibility — and this is critical — is a measure of its 'success in constructing *social* reality' (my emphasis). Furthermore, it is a harm difficult to grasp by those following legal reasoning such as 'First Amendment logic' because it is not 'linearly caused in the "John hit Mary" sense.' MacKinnon rejects such a positivistic (that is — 'individuated, atomistic, linear, isolated "tort-like"') conception of injury because the harm of pornography 'does not work like this.' Further, it privitizes the injury and fails to take account of its group-basis. Most significantly, pornography hurts women 'as members of the group "women"'.

Critically too, MacKinnon argues that the liberal critique of pornography as 'dehumanizing' is also inadequate. While the condemnation of pornography as 'dehumanizing' is 'an attempt to articulate its harm,' this misses the specificity of the harm to

---

[16] In M. A. Fineman & N. S. Thomadsen, *At the Boundaries of Law: Feminism and Legal Theory* (New York: Routledge, 1991), pp. 158–159, 160.

women. From her feminist perspective, pornography dehumanizes women 'in a culturally specific and empirically descriptive — not liberal moral — sense ...'. Her ordinance, then, was designed to get at this specificity by naming the harm done to women — 'our damage, our pain, our enforced inferiority.' Accordingly, it defined pornography as 'a systematic practice of exploitation and subordination based on sex which differentially harms women.' This differential impact is crucial to MacKinnon's meaning: for 'as a *social* group, men are not hurt by pornography the way women as a *social* group are' (my emphasis). In this way, MacKinnon moved away from a moral concept of harm to a concept of a group-based-social harm ...

My conclusion from all this is that MacKinnon's naming strategy — her naming of our pains as socially-based injury — has been vitally important in winning them public and legal recognition. But it needs to be extended. Just as she developed our understanding of discrimination theory by showing how 'the best attempt at grasping women's situation in order to change it by law' — the analyzing of sex and race — 'gets a lot' but also 'misses a lot,' so her 'inequality' approach to discrimination gets a lot (including the all-important social dimension of women's pain), but falls short of elaborating a theory of that pain as social injury. My suggestion is simply that we keep MacKinnon's focus on women's experience but that we shift our focus from inequality to social injury by superimposing a social injury framework on her inequality framework.''

If the obscenity standard is perceived to be the problem of the inability of law to address female subordination through the dissemination of pornographic imagery, it becomes expedient to reflect upon alternatives. Two possibilities are countenanced below. The first concerns an attempt at increased censorship and the second the creation of an offence of incitement to sexual hatred.

9.1.ii.a An attempt at censorship: page 3. While hard-core pornography may fall within the obscenity test, other images of the female body will fall without. Page 3 is one example of this. In March 1986, under the 10 Minute Rule Bills procedure, the Labour MP Clare Short introduced her Indecent Displays (Newspapers) Bill into the House of Commons. The Bill read as follows:

A BILL

To make illegal the display of pictures of naked or partially naked women in sexually provocative poses in newspapers.

BE IT ENACTED by the Queen's most Excellent Majesty, by and with the advice and consent of the Lords Spiritual and Temporal, and Commons, in this present Parliament assembled, and by the authority of the same, as follows: —

   1. It shall be an offence to publish in newspapers pictures of naked or partially naked women in sexually provocative poses.
   2.–(1) A person found guilty of an offence under section 1 above, shall be liable on summary conviction or on conviction on indictment to a fine not exceeding one pence for each copy of the newspaper published.

(2)   A person found guilty on two or more occasions of an offence under this Act shall be liable to a fine not exceeding two pence for each copy of the newspaper published.

3.   For the purposes of the Act the word "newspaper" shall mean any paper containing public news and published daily or on Sunday.

C. Short
Dear Clare . . . this is what women feel about page 3[17]

House of Commons Debates
Vol. 93, pp. 937–939, March 12, 1986

"MS CLARE SHORT (Birmingham, Ladywood): I beg to move, that leave be given to bring in a Bill to make illegal the display of pictures of naked or partially naked women in sexually provocative poses in newspapers.

This is a simple but important measure. I stress that I should like the rule to apply to newspapers and only newspapers. If some men need or want such pictures, they should be free to buy appropriate magazines, but they have no right to foist them on the rest of us.

It is said that we are free not to buy such newspapers, but things are not as simple as that. I have received several letters from women whose husbands buy such newspapers. Those women object strongly to those newspapers and object to them being left lying around the house for their children to see.

I have also talked to teachers, including my brother. He asks children to bring newspapers to school for use in discussing current affairs or for making papier mâché, and so on. Both he and the children are embarrassed by the children's reaction to the Page 3 pictures.

A precedent for my Bill can be found in the Indecent Displays (Control) Act, which provides that public hoardings cannot show such pictures, although they are not illegal when they appear in magazines or when they are seen in private. The same reasoning applies: we should not all be forcibly exposed to them. The argument and precedent are exactly the same.

During the debate on the private Member's Bill introduced by the hon Member for Davyhulme (Mr Churchill), I said that I intended to introduce a Bill such as this. Since then I have received about 150 letters from all over the country. About one third of them are from men — [*Interruption*] — the vast majority of whom agree with me. Of course, I received some obscene letters from men, and Mr Murdoch and those Conservative Members who keep shouting out now should know that such people support and defend Page 3.

The letters came predominantly from women, particularly young women. They stressed time and again that they did not consider themselves to be prudes but objected very strongly to such pictures. One letter came from a young woman who worked in an office. She was writing on behalf of quite a few young women. They considered

---

[17]   C. Short, *Dear Clare . . . this is what women feel about page 3* (London: Radius, 1991), Preface.

themselves to be young and attractive, but every day they were subjected to men reading such newspapers in the office, and to them tittering and laughing and, making rude remarks such as, 'Show us your Page 3s then'. Such women feel strongly that this Bill should be enacted. [*Laughter*]. Conservative Members display their attitudes for everyone to see, and will be judged accordingly.

Many of the letters that I received came from mothers with small children who said that they felt that page 3 undermined their efforts to instil decent attitudes in their children. Many of them commented time and again on the front-page stories of nasty newspapers such as *The Sun* — [*Interruption*]. It is the nastiest. Such stories deplore some brutal rape or attack on a child. The reader then turns to Page 3 to see the usual offering.

I agree with the women who think that there is some connection between the rising tide of sexual crime and Page 3. Obviously, that is unprovable, but the constant mass circulation of such pictures so that they are widely seen by children must influence sexual attitudes and the climate towards sexuality in our society. Those pictures portray women as objects of lust to be sniggered over and grabbed at, and do not portray sex as something that is tender and private.

When future generations read that in our day about 10 million newspapers carried such pictures every day to be left around and seen by children and by lots of women who did not want to see them, they will see those pictures as symbolic of our decadent society. That is why we should take action to make them illegal.

MR ROBERT ADLEY: (Christchurch): *rose* —

MR SPEAKER: Does the hon Gentleman seek to oppose the Bill?

MR ADLEY: Yes, Mr Speaker. The hon Member for Birmingham, Ladywood (Ms Short) is a prominent supporter of women's rights and her speech was a titillating mixture of politics, prejudice and prurience. It is barely credible that she should come before the House today with such a proposal. Why is she proposing that only pictures of women should be outlawed? Should we not outlaw cheesecake pictures of men? The hon Lady is clearly proposing to introduce a very sexist measure. Where are we supposed to draw the line?

Writing about her Bill in *The House Magazine*, the hon Lady refers to 'partially naked women in sexually provocative poses in *newspapers*'. The italics are hers, I imagine. It is fascinating to consider who will decide whether a woman is or is not partially naked, and whether her pose is or is not sexually provocative.

The hon Lady referred to *The Sun* and to Mr Murdoch. I noticed that she did not refer — it happened by sheer chance, I am sure — to *The Daily Mirror*. To make sure that I did my job properly in opposing the Bill, I had a look at *The Sun* and *The Daily Mirror* today. I am not sure which of these newspapers would fall foul of the hon Lady's strictures. Perhaps it is only newspapers owned by Australians, or perhaps by ex-Labour Members of Parliament who are now capitalists.

The hon Lady does less than justice to her fellow citizens. She would have our newspapers resembling *Pravda*. That would be more in keeping with some of her own political views. Where do we go from here? When the hon Lady has dealt with the newspapers and expunged from them everything that she finds objectionable, perhaps she and Mr Livingstone will go round the parks of London doing away with all the statues that she thinks might deprave people. There are a few pleasures left to us today. One that I enjoy is sitting in an underground train watching the faces of the people who are pretending not to be looking at Page 3 of the newspapers. If the hon Lady has her way, we will be deprived of that pleasure.

MR TONY MARLOW (Northampton, North): I believe that my hon Friend should treat this matter seriously, if only because I imagine that neither of us has ever seen the Press Gallery so full.

MR SPEAKER: Order. The hon Member must not interrupt. He knows perfectly well that there can be no interruptions of the debate on a Ten Minute Bill, and that, in any case, he must not refer to those who are not in the Chamber.

MR MARLOW: I apologise profusely, Mr Speaker.

MR ADLEY: The trouble with the hon Lady, and those who think like she does, is that she tends to mix only with those who share her views. To suggest seriously, as she does, that these pictures are offensive to the overwhelming majority of women is inaccurate. I suggest that they are offensive to the overwhelming majority of those with whom the hon Lady is in touch, which is not the same thing at all.

This is a ridiculous proposal. I propose to divide the House so that every Opposition Member can stand up and be counted. I suggested that, of all the measures that have been proposed to the House during this session, this Bill deserves the booby prize."

The Bill was approved by 97 votes to 56. It failed to achieve a second reading, however, as it was continuously objected to by a succession of anonymous MPs. The Bill was introduced for a second time on April 13, 1988 with the addition of a clause to the effect that the display of pornography in the work-place would be unlawful. Again, although the vote was won (163:48), the Bill, like the majority of Ten Minute Rule Bills, failed to progress. Clare Short in taking this stand was vilified in the press. She describes her experiences:

C. SHORT
Dear Clare ... this is what women feel about page 3[18]

"*The Sun* newspaper took a particularly virulent line in their attacks on me. They branded me 'Crazy Clare', 'Killjoy Clare', and assembled a number of unflattering photographs and printed them daily inviting their readers to write in Freepost to 'Stop Crazy Clare'. They also produced a car sticker and invited readers to send for one. I've only ever met one person who has seen the sticker, Jeremy Corbyn, Labour MP for Islington North. When a number of journalists later enquired how many readers had written in, *The Sun* refused to answer. They also refused to say how many car stickers had been distributed.

[18] C. Short, *ibid.*, pp. 6–7.

Shortly after my Bill was introduced, *The Sun* approached a number of MPs who had voted against me asking them to appear on Page 3 with their favourite 'lovely'. Four or five did this, including Peter Bruinvels, then Tory MP for Leicester East, and a member of the Church of England Synod. I received another letter from the chair of one of their Conservative Associations saying that she had demanded an apology from her MP, Geoffrey Dickens, who hadn't been present to vote but had agreed to appear on Page 3. The apology was duly given. Another interesting example of women's power.

The Sun did cause me one panic attack. I didn't, of course, read the paper and didn't bother to look at it properly when their hate campaign was on. But one evening I received a phone call from one of my sisters who lives in Brighton. She had met a friend in her local pub who told her he'd seen a copy of *The Sun* at work. There was a piece entitled 'Twenty Things You Never Knew About Crazy Clare'. It was impossible for me to see a copy of the paper until I went to the House of Commons library the next day; I thought and worried about all the things I had ever done in my life in which *The Sun* might be interested. When I finally saw the piece, I laughed with relief. They listed such 'horrifying' accusations as that I had once appeared at the despatch box in tight black trousers and a long pink jacket; that I was supposed to be left wing but right wingers in the Labour Party said they liked me; and that I had been a Civil Servant . . . *The Sun* continued its campaign for years. During the 1987 election, they printed a completely blank Page 3 with a little box saying this is how their paper could be if 'Killjoy Clare's' party won the election."

Quite clearly what Clare Short felt to be offensive about page 3 fell outside the legal definition of obscene materials. It is insufficiently violent, explicit or offensive to the viewer and, perhaps, by virtue of their pervasiveness, the images have become accepted. As a regime of representation, however, its effects may be equally, some might argue more, pernicious in their pervasive dissemination of a particular depiction of the female body which comes to be taken for granted as a cultural norm. The debate highlighted the problem of determining what images were included within any definition of pornographic material and the question whether further censorship is an appropriate solution.

9.1.ii.b An attempt at redefinition: inciting sexual hatred. A different legal approach to the issue of pornography might be to view it as an incitement to sexual hatred. This approach is constructed along similar lines to the offence of incitement to racial hatred.[19] Susan Easton advocates this development after a careful consideration of the advantages and disadvantages which such a construction entails:

---

[19] In an article which responds to the arguments for an analogy between pornography and racist speech in an attempt to secure equality (as contained in Catharine MacKinnon's book *Only Words* (Cambridge, MA: Harvard University Press, 1993)) Wojciech Sadurski addresses the problematic assimilation of sex and race in this area (W. Sadurski, "On 'Seeing Speech Through an Equality Lens': A Critique of Egalitarian Arguments for Suppression of Hate Speech and Pornography" (1996) 16 O.J.L.S. 713).

S. EASTON
"Pornography as Incitement to Sexual Hatred"[20]

"The law on racial incitement was reconsidered in the 1980s as part of a general review of public order law and consolidated in Part III of the 1986 Public Order Act. Under section 18[1]:

(1) A person who uses threatening, abusive or insulting words or behaviour or displays any written material which is threatening, abusive or insulting, is guilty of an offence if:
  (a) he intends thereby to stir up racial hatred, or
  (b) having regard to all the circumstances racial hatred is likely to be stirred up thereby.

(2) An offence under this section may be committed in a public or private place, except that no offence is committed where the words or behaviour are used, or the written material is displayed, by a person inside a dwelling and are not heard or seen except by other persons in that or another dwelling.

The legislation regulating incitement to racial hatred was framed in the light of free speech concerns similar to those found in the pornography and censorship debate. Its scope was limited to satisfy the protection of free speech interests. In retrospect, the free speech arguments were voiced with far less intensity than those employed by libertarians in the United States or Britain when resisting proposals for the regulation of pornography.

If incitement to racial hatred legislation is to be considered as a model for the regulation of pornography, then its effectiveness as a remedy for racial hatred needs to be reviewed, as well as the problems which may arise in applying it to sexual hatred."

Easton summarises the problems with the offence of racial incitement. These include a move towards propaganda which is less blatantly racist and therefore of a more rational and harmless appearance; the fact that the legislation has rarely been used, (indeed the number of prosecutions since 1986 has fallen) and that it is necessary to obtain the consent of the Attorney-General to undertake a prosecution; that it may be difficult to prove that behaviour was intended to incite racial hatred and that the wording of the Act may be insufficient to encompass all forms of racism. Easton continues:

S. EASTON
"Pornography as Incitement to Sexual Hatred"[21]

"The major objections raised to an incitement to sexual hatred offence are as follows; first, that the above problems which have been encountered in the case of incitement to racial hatred suggest that a similar offence covering sexual hatred is unlikely to succeed. Second, there has been a general reluctance on the part of some liberals and

[20] (1995) 3 *Feminist Legal Studies* 89 at 91.
[21] S. Easton, *ibid.*, at 95–104.

feminists to pursue such legislation, even when they have accepted the validity of the incitement to racial hatred offence. Generally we find a stronger defence of free speech concerns in relation to sexual hatred than in relation to racial hatred. The value of the analogy of sexual hatred with racial hatred *per se* also has been questioned, irrespective of the issue of effectiveness.

(i) *The Limits of the Law*

Given the experience of the incitement to racial hatred offence, would an incitement to sexual hatred offence be more successful? The incitement to racial hatred provision is rarely used, but would a law aimed at incitement to sexual hatred be more frequently used by women. If physical assaults on women are under-reported, are women more likely to proceed on the basis of 'rape-speech'?

There are also fears that the problems encountered with the incitement to racial hatred legislation would recur if it were used as the basis for a sexual hatred offence. Similar concerns regarding vexatious litigants have been voiced in relation to the regulation of pornography and one way of dealing with these fears would be to require the Attorney-General's consent to prosecute, although clearly this might limit its effectiveness. As few prosecutions have succeeded under the POA and RRA [Race Relations Act 1976], one might argue that the success rate is unlikely to be greater for a sexual hatred offence and that education rather than legal measures should be used to change attitudes towards pornography. But equally one could argue that when in place such legislation might be used more frequently than the Public Order Act provisions. Already the Sex Discrimination legislation is used more frequently and more successfully than the Race Relations Act. There are also substantially more prosecutions under the Obscene Publications Act than under section 18 of the Public Order Act. So it is possible that the offence of incitement to sexual hatred would yield a higher number of prosecutions and convictions . . .

(ii) *The Desirability of the Law*

While many liberals and some feminists have been reluctant to countenance the regulation of pornography, they have, nonetheless, acknowledged the legitimacy of the legal regulation of racist material. Many of the discussions of censorship and pornography have dwelt at great length on the implications of regulation for free speech rights, on whether the law will be abused by over-zealous prosecutors and complainants. Similar fears were expressed in the earlier debates on incitement to racial hatred but were not found to be justified. When the incitement to racial hatred legislation was enacted, although the free speech issue was raised, the question of censorship did not figure so prominently as it has in the pornography debate. While the weakness of the racial incitement legislation in part reflects attempts to reconcile speech controls with freedom of speech, there has been far less concern over the free speech question in the courts, academic writings and the media on the issue of racism than in relation to the regulation of pornography.

Fears of a heckler's veto have been expressed in relation to a sexual hatred offence. But if one hypothesises that feminist objectors might challenge the showing of a pornographic film, raising public order considerations, the quixotic nature of these fears become apparent. Official statistics, self-report and victimisation studies show that women as a social group are more likely to be targets than perpetrators of violent acts and are far less likely to engage in violent confrontations . . .

The fact that limitations on racist speech may be countenanced shows that in certain cases the commitment to free speech is not paramount. The underlying justifications of prohibitions on speech likely to cause racial violence include the desire to maintain social order which has been given more weight than the desire to protect the feelings of a minority group. Yet in many cases the issue may not be one of immediate risk of disorder, as defined by the clear and present danger test in *Shenck v. United States* 249 U.S. 47 (1919) although this could apply in some instances. If racist speech is permitted to flourish, then the long-term effect is likely to be a hardening of racist attitudes and the creation of a climate in which disorder becomes more likely, as exemplified by the link between racism and disorder in the Los Angeles riots of 1992. The popular counter-argument, of course, is that the repression of racist or patriarchal attitudes drives them underground and if anxieties are not freely discussed, tensions may intensify, leading to attacks on ethnic minorities or women. This is a form of the 'bad speech should be challenged by more speech' cathartic argument.

Defenders of free speech have argued that the best way to deal with hate speech, whether in the form of racist remarks or rape speech, is for the offended groups to respond with more speech to put forward their own viewpoints, instead of imposing constraints on speech . . .

But it may be difficult for a weak group to gain access to the means of communication. Racist speech is difficult to combat because there is no objective rational terrain on which the attacker's view may be challenged. Although feminist arguments for the regulation of pornography do not rely solely on 'mere offensiveness', it could certainly be argued that if injury to feelings is sufficient to protect victims of racist speech, then women's feelings demand equal consideration and respect . . .

(iii) *The Problems with the Racial and Sexual Hatred Analogy*
While some have ignored the racial-sexual hatred analogy, others have explicitly rejected it. Criticism has emanated from quite distinct sources: first, defenders of the free market in pornography, and second, from some feminists and political activists.

It might be argued that while racist speech is motivated by hatred and has no merits or public benefits, the prime purpose of pornography is the exploration of sexuality albeit within a commercial context. Racist speech and pornography should therefore be distinguished. The benefits of pornography have been extolled by defenders of pornography and focus on sexual liberation . . . This denial of hatred as a defining feature of pornography is hard to reconcile with the persuasiveness of denigratory and hostile views of women in pornography, for example, of bound and gagged women enjoying rape and domination.

Some feminist writers also find the analogy of racial and sexual hatred as unsatisfactory, albeit on quite different grounds. The fundamental differences between the position of ethnic minorities and women, it is argued, render the use of the analogy inappropriate and over-simplistic. The position of ethnic minorities within Europe and the United States has to be understood in the context of distinct historical experiences including black slavery, genocide and persecution, which do not compare to white European women's experiences. Feminism is divided on the validity of this analogy depending on the primacy given to gender and ethnicity as the source of oppression . . .

In view of these problems how viable is the incitement to racial hatred offence as a model for a sexual hatred offence? Would there be problems in using the notion of 'hatred' when considering the contents of pornographic material? It is not difficult to infer hatred from the contents of 'hard' pornography, of rape, abuse, mutilation and denigration. The focus on hatred would also provide a potential way of distinguishing pornography and erotica, if the latter is seen as based on desire and on a positive rather than a negative view of sexuality, celebrating and enhancing rather than brutalising sexual relationships. Proving intent might be problematic but could be avoided by including a 'likelihood' clause, that he intends thereby to stir up sexual hatred or having regard to all the circumstances sexual hatred is likely to be stirred up thereby, based on section 18 of the 1986 Public Order Act.

The enactment of a law marks the beginning rather than the end of change. The purpose of the criminal law is to express society's moral position on appropriate behaviour and to include racism and sexism within its compass would be a significant step forward. Racist and patriarchal attitudes may not be changed immediately by legal interventions, but in the long-term they can have an impact. Furthermore, legislation, even if not uniformly enforced, puts the racist on the defensive while its absence endows racism with tacit legitimacy. Notwithstanding the shortcomings of the Race Relations Acts, there have been some changes in the development of affirmative action programmes, the ethnic composition of the labour force and the implementation of equal opportunities policies.

A law to regulate pornography would by itself be insufficient to combat the oppression of women, just as it has failed to combat racism. But those involved in the critique of pornography would not see this as the only strategy or solution but as part of a wider campaign against patriarchy. Constructing the debate in terms of the free speech versus censorship divide, as pornographers and some civil libertarians have attempted, fails to take account of the fact that already inroads into free speech have been made and that these are, in many cases, accepted as morally legitimate. The feminist campaign against pornography is not an isolated assault on free speech rights but could be seen as a recognition of the difficulty and undesirability of absolutism in a pluralist society."

9.1.iii *Seeing pornography through the eyes of E.U. law*
It is not only U.K. domestic law which has had to confront and regulate the availability of pornographic material. The issue has also arisen in the context of the European Union. In this respect it has been necessary to consider the implications of E.U. law with regard to the freedoms contained within the Treaty of Rome.[22] Leo Flynn, in his insightful analysis of "The Body Politic(s) of E.C. Law"[23] notes the "dominance of a market paradigm" in E.C. Law[24] and considers the possible incorporation of the female body within this paradigm.

L. FLYNN
"The Body Politic(s) of E.C. Law"[25]

"The E.C. institutions have, for the most part, maintained that any activity and any object can be assimilated to the market. A wide definition of the objects and subjects

---

[22] *I.e.* the free movement of goods, of persons, of capital and freedom of establishment.
[23] L. Flynn, "The Body Politic(s) of E.C. Law" in T. D. Hervey & D. O'Keeffe (eds), *Sex Equality Law in the European Union* (Chichester: John Wiley, 1996), p. 301. Other "body politics" issues are raised by the freedoms conferred by European Law. For example, see the discussion in Chap. 4.1 on new reproductive technologies and in Chap. 5.3 on abortion in the context of the right to receive medical treatments in another member state and also the discussion in the final chapter dealing with the free movement of prostitutes as workers.
[24] L. Flynn, *ibid.*, p. 310.
[25] L. Flynn, *ibid.*, pp. 310–311.

incorporated into the internal market's legal order is evident in a Commission's statement that, 'contrary to what is widely imagined, the EEC Treaty applies not only to
economic activities but, as a rule, to all activities carried out for remuneration, regardless of whether they take place in the economic, social, cultural (including in particular
information, creative or artistic endeavours and entertainment), sporting or any other
sphere.'

The Court of Justice also has a broad view of the market, as seen in its jurisprudence
on what constitute 'goods' for the free movement rules contained in the Treaty. This
approach does not flow automatically from any internal rationale of E.C. law, found
within the norms and the jurisprudence of E.C. law; rather it is a question of bringing
transactions, administrative actions and individuals within the jurisdiction of the Commission and the Court. What emerges from a critical consideration of its case law is
that the Court defines the market, it does not discover it. It gives pre-eminence to a
market paradigm, disregarding critics who assert, regarding free movement of goods,
that, 'the central problem is that the EEC fails to differentiate between different kinds
of goods. One should look to the nature of the good because all goods are *not* the
same. After all, some commercial transactions have a negative environmental impact'.
This critique of the Court's inability to differentiate products based on their effects on
the environment treats this as a local anomaly. Once the masculine nature of E.C. law
is identified, a systemic failure can be recognised. A basic feature of E.C. law is its
powerful impulse towards market deference. The primacy of market access as a value
in E.C. law often subordinates other core legal values such as consistency. That failure
cannot be addressed until E.C. law adopts other values, of connection and solidarity,
and a different epistemology, embracing 'masculine' assumptions of atomistic, decon-
textualised objects and individuals as well as a 'feminine', holistic vision. Until such a
shift occurs then human bodies, including female bodies, will be considered primarily
as market objects in E.C. law, and there is no reason to suppose that the impact of
this apparently neutral market order will have the same impact or allocate similar
burdens between the sexes."

The regulation of the female body within the paradigm of the internal market
has implications for the circulation of pornographic materials, in that it raises
questions about the free movement of goods and the extent to which this may
be restricted upon grounds of public policy. Art. 30 of the Treaty of Rome
provides that:

> "Quantitative restrictions on imports and all measures having equivalent
> effect shall, without prejudice to the following ·provisions, be prohibited
> between Member States."

Art. 34 similarly prohibits restrictions on exports. Art. 36 goes on to state,
however, that:

> "The provisions of Articles 30 to 34 shall not preclude prohibitions or restric-
> tions on imports, exports or goods in transit justified on grounds of public
> morality, public policy or public security; the protection of health and life of
> humans, animals or plants; the protection of national treasures possessing
> artistic, historic or archaeological value; or the protection of industrial and
> commercial property. Such prohibitions or restrictions shall not, however,

constitute a means of arbitrary discrimination or a disguised restriction on trade between Member States."

The extent to which Art. 36 may be used to prevent the distribution of pornography was discussed by the European Court of Justice in *R. v. Henn and Darby*.[26] In this case the defendants had shipped pornographic films and magazines (depicting acts of rape, abduction of a woman, buggery involving humans and animals and gross indecency with children) into the U.K. from the Netherlands. They were convicted of "being knowingly concerned in the fraudulent evasion of the prohibition of the importation of indecent or obscene articles" in contravention of section 42 of the Customs Consolidation Act 1876 and section 304 of the Customs and Excise Act 1952. They appealed against their conviction on the basis that this amounted to a restriction upon the free circulation of goods within the European Community.[27] The European Court of Justice delivered the following judgment as to the applicability of Art. 30 and the effect of Art. 36:

R. v. Henn and Darby
(Case 34/79) [1981] A.C. 850, paras 11–22

"11. The first question asks whether a law of a member state which prohibits the import into that state of pornographic articles is a measure having equivalent effect to a quantitative restriction on imports within the meaning of article 30 of the Treaty.

12. That article provides that "quantitative restrictions on imports and all measures having equivalent effect" shall be prohibited between member states. It is clear that this provision includes a prohibition on imports inasmuch as this is the most extreme form of restriction. The expression used in article 30 must therefore be understood as being the equivalent of the expression "prohibitions or restrictions on imports" occurring in article 36.

13. The answer to the first question is therefore that a law such as that referred to in this case constitutes a quantitative restriction on imports within the meaning of article 30 of the Treaty.

Second and third questions

14. The second and third questions are framed in the following terms:

'2. If the answer to question 1 is in the affirmative, does the first sentence of article 36 upon its true construction mean that a member state may lawfully impose prohibitions on the importation of goods from another member state which are of an indecent or obscene character as understood by the laws of that member state?

'3. In particular: (i) is the member state entitled to maintain such prohibitions in order to prevent, to guard against or to reduce the likelihood of

---

[26] *R. v. Henn and Darby* (Case 34/79) [1981] A.C. 850.
[27] The conviction was upheld because the trade of the goods in question was equally restricted in the U.K.

breaches of the domestic law of all constituent parts of the customs territory of the state? (ii) is the member state entitled to maintain such prohibitions having regard to the national standards and characteristics of that state as demonstrated by the domestic laws of the constituent parts of the customs territory of that state including the law imposing the prohibition, notwithstanding variations between the laws of the constituent parts?'

It is convenient to consider these questions together.

15. Under the terms of article 36 of the Treaty the provisions relating to the free movement of goods within the Community are not to preclude prohibitions on imports which are justified, *inter alia,* 'on grounds of public morality.' In principle, it is for each member state to determine in accordance with its own scale of values and in the form selected by it the requirements of public morality in its territory. In any event, it cannot be disputed that the statutory provisions applied by the United Kingdom in regard to the importation of articles having an indecent or obscene character come within the powers reserved to the member states by the first sentence of article 36.

16. Each member state is entitled to impose prohibitions on imports justified on grounds of public morality for the whole of its territory, as defined in article 227 of the Treaty, whatever the structure of its constitution may be and however the powers of legislating in regard to the subject in question may be distributed. The fact that certain differences exist between the laws enforced in the different constituent parts of a member state does not thereby prevent that state from applying a unitary concept in regard to prohibitions on imports imposed, on grounds of public morality, on trade with other member states.

17. The answer to the second and third questions must therefore be that the first sentence of article 36 upon its true construction means that a member state may, in principle, lawfully impose prohibitions on the importation from any other member state of articles which are of an indecent or obscene character as understood by its domestic laws and that such prohibitions may lawfully be applied to the whole of its national territory even if, in regard to the field in question, variations exist between the laws in force in the different constituent parts of the member state concerned.

Fourth, fifth and sixth questions

18. The fourth, fifth and sixth questions are framed in the following terms:

'4. If a prohibition on the importation of goods is justifiable on grounds of public morality or public policy, and imposed with that purpose, can that prohibition nevertheless amount to a means of arbitrary discrimination or a disguised restriction on trade contrary to article 36?

'5. If the answer to question 4 is in the affirmative, does the fact that the prohibition imposed on the importation of such goods is different in scope from that imposed by the criminal law upon the possession and publication of such goods within the member state or any part of it necessarily constitute a means of arbitrary discrimination or a disguised restriction on trade between member states so as to conflict with the requirements of the second sentence of article 36?

'6. If it be the fact that the prohibition imposed upon importation is, and a prohibition such as is imposed upon possession and publication is not, capable as a matter of administration of being applied by customs officials responsible for examining goods at the point of importation, would that fact have any bearing upon the answer to question 5?'

19. In these questions the House of Lords takes account of the appellants' submissions based upon certain differences between, on the one hand, the prohibition on importing the goods in question, which is absolute, and, on the other, the laws in force in the various constituent parts of the United Kingdom, which appear to be less strict in the sense that the mere possession of obscene articles for non-commercial purposes does not constitute a criminal offence anywhere in the United Kingdom and that, even if it is generally forbidden, trade in such articles is subject to certain exceptions, notably those in favour of articles having scientific, literary, artistic or educational interest. Having regard to those differences, the question has been raised whether the prohibition on imports might not come within the second sentence of article 36.

20. According to the second sentence of article 36 the restrictions on imports referred to in the first sentence may not 'constitute a means of arbitrary discrimination or a disguised restriction on trade between member states.'

21. In order to answer the questions which have been referred to the court it is appropriate to have regard to the function of this provision, which is designed to prevent restrictions on trade based on the grounds mentioned in the first sentence of article 36 from being diverted from their proper purpose and used in such a way as either to create discrimination in respect of goods originating in other member states or indirectly to protect certain national products. That is not the purport of a prohibition, such as that in force in the United Kingdom, on the importation of articles which are of an indecent or obscene character. Whatever may be the differences between the laws on this subject in force in the different constituent parts of the United Kingdom, and notwithstanding the fact that they contain certain exceptions of limited scope, these laws, taken as a whole, have as their purpose the prohibition, or at least the restraining, of the manufacture and marketing of publications or articles of an indecent or obscene character. In these circumstances it is permissible to conclude, on a comprehensive view, that there is no lawful trade in such goods in the United Kingdom. A prohibition on imports which may in certain respects be more strict than some of the laws applied within the United Kingdom cannot therefore be regarded as amounting to a measure designed to give indirect protection to some national product or aimed at creating arbitrary discrimination between goods of this type depending on whether they are produced within the national territory or another member state.

22. The answer to the fourth question must therefore be that if a prohibition on the importation of goods is justifiable on grounds of public morality and if it is imposed with that purpose the enforcement of that prohibition cannot, in the absence within the member state concerned of a lawful trade in the same goods, constitute a means of arbitrary discrimination or a disguised restriction on trade contrary to article 36.

23. In these circumstances it is not necessary to answer the fifth and sixth questions."

A similar issue arose in a subsequent case involving the legality of the seizure of inflatable life-size rubber dolls (variously described as "Love, Love" dolls, "Miss World Specials", "Rubber Ladies" and "Sexy Vacuum Flasks") imported from Germany. The difference between this case and *Henn and Darby*, however, being that the sale of these goods was not prohibited in Britain. The ban on the importation was, therefore, held to be unlawful. The grounds of public morality contained within Art. 36 could not be relied upon in order to prohibit importation of goods on the basis that they were obscene or indecent, where the same goods could be made and sold freely within the Member State.

Conegate Ltd v. Customs and Excise Commissioners
(Case 121/85) [1987] Q.B. 254, paras 13–21

"13. The court would observe that the first question raises, in the first place, the general problem of whether a prohibition on the importation of certain goods may be justified on grounds of public morality where the legislation of the member state concerned contains no prohibition on the manufacture or marketing of the same products within the national territory.

14. So far as that problem is concerned, it must be borne in mind that according to article 36 of the EEC Treaty the provisions relating to the free movement of goods within the Community do not preclude prohibitions on imports justified 'on grounds of public morality.' As the court held in *R. v. Henn* (Case 34/79) [1981] A.C. 850, in principle it is for each member state to determine in accordance with its own scale of values and in the form selected by it the requirements of public morality in its territory.

15. However, although Community law leaves the member states free to make their own assessments of the indecent or obscene character of certain articles, it must be pointed out that the fact that goods cause offence cannot be regarded as sufficiently serious to justify restrictions on the free movement of goods where the member state concerned does not adopt, with respect to the same goods manufactured or marketed within its territory, penal measures or other serious and effective measures intended to prevent the distribution of such goods in its territory.

16. It follows that a member state may not rely on grounds of public morality in order to prohibit the importation of goods from other member states when its legislation contains no prohibition on the manufacture or marketing of the same goods on its territory.

17. It is not for the court, within the framework of the powers conferred upon it by article 177 of the EEC Treaty, to consider whether, and to what extent, the United Kingdom legislation contains such a prohibition. However, the question whether or not such a prohibition exists in a state comprised of different constituent parts which have their own internal legislation, can be resolved only by taking into consideration all the relevant legislation. Although it is not necessary, for the purposes of the application of the above-mentioned rule, that the manufacture and marketing of the products the importation of which has been prohibited should be prohibited in the territory of all the constituent parts, it must at least be possible to conclude from the applicable rules, taken as a whole, that their purpose is, in substance, to prohibit the manufacture and marketing of those products.

18. In this instance, in the actual wording of its first question the High Court took care to define the substance of the national legislation the compatibility of which with Community law is a question which it proposes to determine. Thus it refers to rules in the importing member state under which the goods in question may be manufactured freely and marketed subject only to certain restrictions, which it sets out explicitly, namely, an absolute prohibition on the transmission of such goods by post, a restriction on their public display and, in certain areas of the member state concerned, a system of licensing of premises for the sale of those goods to customers aged 18 years

and over. Such restrictions cannot, however, be regarded as equivalent in substance to a prohibition on manufacture and marketing.

19. At the hearing, the United Kingdom again stressed the fact that at present no articles comparable to those imported by Conegate are manufactured on United Kingdom territory, but that fact, which does not exclude the possibility of manufacturing such articles and which, moreover, was not referred to by the High Court, is not such as to lead to a different assessment of the situation.

20. In reply to the first question it must therefore be stated that a member state may not rely on grounds of public morality within the meaning of article 36 of the Treaty in order to prohibit the importation of certain goods on the grounds that they are indecent or obscene, where the same goods may be manufactured freely on its territory and marketed on its territory subject only to an absolute prohibition on their transmission by post, a restriction on their public display and, in certain regions, a system of licensing of premises for the sale of those goods to customers aged 18 and over.

21. That conclusion does not preclude the authorities of the member state concerned from applying to those goods, once imported, the same restrictions on marketing which are applied to similar products manufactured and marketed within the country."

Leo Flynn, in his critique of *Henn and Darby* (which might be applied also to *Conegate*) demonstrates the ECJ's abject failure to address the issue of harm caused to women by the circulation of pornographic material.

L. FLYNN
"The Body Politic(s) of E.C. Law"[28]

"The Court of Justice has been concerned with representations of the female body in a number of its cases arising out of Member States' control on the free movement of goods. In *R. v. Henn and Darby* the Court of Justice had to consider the meaning of the public morality element of Article 36 of the Treaty (the derogation to the free movement of goods principle) following a preliminary reference from the House of Lords.

The case concerned an appeal by two individuals against their criminal convictions for importing indecent or obscene articles into the United Kingdom, and of being knowingly concerned in the fraudulent evasion of that prohibition on the importation of indecent or obscene articles. The materials were Danish in origin and consisted of films and magazines showing activities, including rape, abduction of a woman, buggery (involving humans and animals), indecent assault and acts of gross indecency towards children under 14 years of age, which were contrary to United Kingdom criminal law.

The appellants argued that the legislation under which they had been convicted was incompatible with Articles 9 and 30 of the Treaty.

The Court of Justice took the view that Article 36 allows a Member State lawfully to impose prohibitions on the import of articles that are indecent or obscene under its domestic laws. It also held that the Member State may apply such prohibitions throughout all of its territory, even if there are regional variations in its different constituent parts as to the laws in force about the matter in question.

[28] L. Flynn, *supra*, n. 23 at 316–317.

Neither the Court of Justice, nor the Advocate General, nor the Member States who intervened in the case, considered the nature of the harm that is constituted by pornography. All the aforementioned accepted that pornography is legitimately regulated under standards which rest on obscenity and indecency, or as the Court accepted, in relation 'to a single idea, that of offending against recognised standards of propriety'. The Court did not examine this concept in any detail. It may have agreed with the observations of the United Kingdom in the case that public morality, unlike public policy, is comparatively self-defining. There is no indication in the case that the political economy of pornography was considered or that the application of the public policy derogation to free movement of goods was considered a more appropriate basis for regulation of these goods.

The work done by feminists dealing with pornography has undermined the traditional liberal/conservative lines of debate on pornography that frame the Court's analysis.

The harm of pornography, the reason that best justifies control of its production, distribution and consumption, relates to the damage that it does to women and not the offence it causes when exposed to the public gaze. The complex debate on the appropriate legal regulation of pornography will not be reopened here. However, the Court does not indicate that there is any need to discuss such issues; the only questions that arise are whether materials are obscene or indecent and whether the Member State has developed a single standard for domestic and imported goods.

The test endorsed by the Court is based on pornography's disruption of public space, because of the offence it engenders when placed in the public gaze.

The result is that the Court compounds the adverse effect that pornography has on women. It does not hint that pornography has a role to play in the persistent political and economic inequalities of women. The gendering strategy evident in this case is one silencing women, rendering the female figure a silent and acquiescent one. The Court in *Henn and Darby* finds women as a set of two dimensional figures to be seen and not heard, and it leaves them in that position as well . . ."

In short, the harm of pornography is even less visible through the eyes of E.U. law than it is through those of the criminal law. Might the civil law, instead, hold the key to revealing what has so far proved invisible?

9.1.iv   *Seeing pornography through the eyes of the Civil law*
Feminists who have felt that the obscenity standard for determining the pornographic draws the line in favour of a male perspective on offensive and damaging material have looked elsewhere for a legal solution. Catharine MacKinnon's solution formulates pornography as a civil rights issue, more specifically one of sex equality.[29] This formulation perceives pornography as a cause of harm against women. In this view pornography is seen as a form of degradation of women in that it turns sex into a commodity and turns women into sexual objects. It is also viewed as a form of violence against women as evidenced in the slogan that "pornography is the theory, rape is the practice." MacKinnon takes up her story:

---

[29]   For a detailed account of the history of the anti-pornography ordinance drafted by MacKinnon and Dworkin see S. Colombo, "The Legal Battle for the City: Anti-Pornography Municipal Ordinances and Radical Feminism" (1994) 2 *Feminist Legal Studies* 29.

C. A. MacKinnon
"Francis Biddle's Sister: Pornography, Civil Rights, and Speech"[30]

"At the request of the city of Minneapolis, Andrea Dworkin and I conceived and designed a local human rights ordinance in accordance with our approach to the pornography issue. We define pornography as a practice of sex discrimination, a violation of women's civil rights, the opposite of sexual equality. Its point is to hold those who profit from the benefit from that injury accountable to those who are injured. It means that women's injury — our damage, our pain, our enforced inferiority — should outweigh their pleasure and their profits, or sex equality is meaningless."

The ordinance defined pornography in the following terms:

1. "Pornography" means the graphic sexually explicit subordination of women through pictures and/or words that also includes one or more of the following:

   (a) women are presented as dehumanized as sexual objects, things, or commodities; or
   (b) women are presented as sexual objects who enjoy humiliation or pain; or
   (c) women are presented as sexual objects experiencing sexual pleasure in rape, incest or other sexual assault; or
   (d) women are presented as sexual objects tied up or cut up or mutilated or bruised or physically hurt; or
   (e) women are presented in postures or positions of sexual submission, servility or display; or
   (f) women's body parts — including but not limited to vaginas, breasts, or buttocks — are exhibited such that women are reduced to those parts; or
   (g) women are presented being penetrated by objects or animals; or
   (h) women are presented in scenarios of degradation, humiliation, injury, torture, shown as filth or inferior, bleeding, bruised or hurt in a context that makes these conditions sexual.

2. The use of men, children or transsexuals in the place of women in [1] of this definition is also pornography for purposes of this law.

The definition presented in the ordinance is striking in its explicitness. MacKinnon explains why:

C. A. MacKinnon
"Francis Biddle's Sister: Pornography, Civil Rights, and Speech"[31]

"To define pornography as a practice of sex discrimination combines a mode of portrayal that has a legal history — the sexually explicit — with an active term that is central to the inequality of the sexes — subordination. Among other things, subordination means to be in a position of inferiority or loss of power, or to be demeaned or

---

[30] In C. A. MacKinnon, *supra*, n. 3 at p. 175.
[31] C. A. MacKinnon, *ibid.*, pp. 176–177.

denigrated. To be someone's subordinate is the opposite of being their equal. The definition does not include all sexually explicit depictions of the subordination of women. That is not what it says. It says, this which *does* that: the sexually explicit that subordinates women. To these active terms to capture what the pornography *does*, the definition adds a list of what it must also contain. This list, from our analysis, is an exhaustive description of what must be in the pornography for it to do what it does behaviourally. Each item in the definition is supported by experimental, testimonial, social, and clinical evidence. We made a legislative choice to be exhaustive and specific and concrete rather than conceptual and general, to minimize problems of chilling effect, making it hard to guess wrong, thus making self-censorship less likely, but encouraging (to use a phrase from discrimination law) voluntary compliance, knowing that if something turns up that is not on the list, the law will not be expansively interpreted."

The ordinance proposed a series of civil causes of action leading to awards of damages and/or injunctions. These actions would be open to those who were coerced into performing for pornography, those who had pornography forced upon them in any place of employment or education, home, or any public place, those who were assaulted or physically attacked due to pornography, those whose name, and/or recognisable personal likeness was defamed through pornography and those who suffered harm as a result of any trafficking (*i.e.* production, sale, exhibition or distribution) of pornography. Nicola Lacey comments upon the merits of the ordinance:

N. LACEY
"Theory into Practice? Pornography and the Public/Private Dichotomy"[32]

"In many respects, the ordinance represented an inspired piece of feminist legal politics. First, the conceptualization of pornography as sex discrimination placed at the heart of the legislation a feminist view of pornography. Moreover, by pitching one constitutional standard (free expression) against another (equal protection) it in effect forced the courts in the United States of America into a position where, if they were to hold the ordinance unconstitutional, they had to do so in terms which were easily interpreted as valuing an at best dubiously worthwhile form of expression over and above the removal of sex discrimination, and as valuing men's expression over the worth or even possibility of women's."

In fact this is just what the United States Supreme Court proceeded to do. The ordinance was challenged as constituting a violation of the free speech guarantee contained within the First Amendment of the U.S. Constitution[33] and in *American Booksellers Assoc. Inc. v. Hudnut* it was declared unconstitutional.[34] The Supreme Court affirmed the Court of Appeal decision that "[a]ny

[32] In A. Bottomley and J. Conaghan (eds), *Feminist Theory and Legal Strategy* (Oxford: Blackwell Publishers, 1993), p. 105.
[33] "Congress shall make no law . . . abridging the freedom of speech, or of the press, or the right of the people peaceably to assemble, and to petition the Government for a redress of grievances."
[34] *American Booksellers Assoc. Inc. v. Hudnut* 475 US 1132 (1986).

other answer leaves the government in control of all of the institutions of culture, the great censor and director of which thoughts are good for us." Despite this legal failure, the ordinance did represent a success on other counts. Nicola Lacey continues:

N. LACEY
"Theory into Practice? Pornography and the Public/Private Dichotomy"[35]

"Secondly, the reform process itself was a model of feminist political practice. The hearings gave a public voice to women whose suffering had been hidden and silenced; indeed, they constituted precisely the kind of civic forum which illustrates the inadequacy of the traditional public/private distinction and its focus on the state. Thirdly, the important choice of civil over criminal enforcement helped to some extent to defuse the accusation that the ordinance amounted to censorship. More significantly, the process of giving individual women rights of action was symbolically apt. It sought to empower women to use a legal process whose terms are generally constructed in ways which are inattentive or even hostile to the interests and needs which many women may wish to defend legally. Finally, by defining pornography *as* sex discrimination, causal links between pornography and harms to women were taken as already established. Hence the legal process was relieved from having to deal with intractable questions about the relationship between pornography and sexual violence: these would only arise legally in the specific cases where this was what the cause of action alleged."

The presumed causal connection between imagery and harm which is inherent in the view of pornography as sex discrimination has proved problematic. The harm might be identified as that perpetrated on women who are involved in the making of pornography, those involved in assaults which may arise out of male usage of pornography and harm perpetrated on women generally as a result of the widespread dissemination of imagery which debases women as a group. Catharine MacKinnon tackles the causality issue by pointing to individual instances in which it has been acknowledged to her that women have experienced harm resulting from men's use of pornography.

C. A. MACKINNON
"Francis Biddle's Sister: Pornography, Civil Rights, and Speech"[36]

"Under the obscenity rubric, much legal and psychological scholarship has centered on a search for the elusive link between harm and pornography defined as obscenity. Although they were not very clear on what obscenity was, it was its harm they truly could not find. They looked high and low — in the mind of the male consumer, in society or in its 'moral fabric,' in correlations between variations in levels of antisocial acts and liberalization of obscenity laws. The only harm they have found has been harm to 'the social interest in order and morality.' Until recently, no one looked very

---

[35] N. Lacey, *supra*, n. 32 at p. 106.
[36] C. A. MacKinnon, *supra*, n. 3 at pp. 186–189.

persistently for harm to women, particularly harm to women through men. The rather obvious fact that the sexes *relate* has been overlooked in the inquiry into the male consumer and his mind. The pornography doesn't just drop out of the sky, go into his head, and stop there. Specifically, men rape, batter, prostitute, molest, and sexually harass women. Under conditions of inequality, they also hire, fire, promote, and grade women, decide how much or whether we are worth paying and for what, define and approve and disapprove of women in ways that count, that determine our lives.

If women are not just born to be sexually used, the fact that we are seen and treated as though that is what we are born for becomes something in need of explanation. If we see that men relate to women in a pattern of who they see women as being, and that forms a pattern of inequality, it becomes important to ask where that view came from or, minimally, how it is perpetuated or escalated. Asking this requires asking different questions about pornography than the ones obscenity law made salient.

Now I'm going to talk about causality in its narrowest sense. Recent experimental research on pornography shows that the materials covered by our definition cause measurable harm to women through increasing men's attitudes and behaviors of discrimination in both violent and nonviolent forms. Exposure to some of the pornography in our definition increases the immediately subsequent willingness of normal men to aggress against women under laboratory conditions. It makes normal men more closely resemble convicted rapists attitudinally, although as a group they don't look all that different from them to start with. Exposure to pornography also significantly increases attitudinal measures known to correlate with rape and self-reports of aggressive acts, measures such as hostility toward women, propensity to rape, condoning rape, and predicting that one would rape or force sex on a woman if one knew one would not get caught. On this latter measure, by the way, about a third of all men predict that they would rape, and half would force sex on a woman.

As to that pornography covered by our definition in which normal research subjects seldom perceive violence, long-term exposure still makes them see women as more worthless, trivial, nonhuman, and objectlike, that is, the way those who are discriminated against are seen by those who discriminate against them. Crucially, all pornography by our definition acts dynamically over time to diminish the consumer's ability to distinguish sex from violence. The materials work behaviorally to diminish the capacity of men (but not women) to perceive that an account of a rape is an account of a rape. The so-called sex-only materials, those in which subjects perceive no force, also increase perceptions that a rape victim is worthless and decrease the perception that she was harmed. The overall direction of current research suggests that the more expressly violent materials accomplish with less exposure what the less overtly violent — that is, the so-called sex-only materials — accomplish over the longer term. Women are rendered fit for use and targeted for abuse. The only thing that the research cannot document is which individual women will be next on the list. (This cannot be documented experimentally because of ethics constraints on the researchers — constraints that do not operate in life.) Although the targeting is systematic on the basis of sex, for individuals it is random. They are selected on a roulette basis. Pornography can no longer be said to be just a mirror. It does not just reflect the world or some people's perceptions. It *moves* them. It increases attitudes that are lived out, circumscribing the status of half the population.

What the experimental data predict will happen actually does happen in women's real lives. You know, it's fairly frustrating that women have known for sometime that these things do happen. As Ed Donnerstein, an experimental researcher in this area, often puts it, 'We just quantify the obvious.' It is women, primarily, to whom the research results have been the obvious, because we live them. But not until a laboratory study predicts that these things *will* happen do people begin to believe you when you say they *did* happen to you. There is no — *not any* — inconsistency between the patterns the laboratory studies predict and the data on what actually happens to real women. Show me an abuse of women in society, I'll show it to you made sex in the pornography. If you want to know who is being hurt in this society, go see what is being done and to whom in pornography and then go look for them other places in the world. You will find them being hurt in just that way. We did in our hearings.

In our hearings women spoke, to my knowledge for the first time in history in public, about the damage pornography does to them. We learned that pornography is used to break women, to train women to sexual submission, to season women, to terrorize women, and to silence their dissent. It is this that has previously been termed 'having no effect.' The way men inflict on women the sex they experience through the pornography gives women no choice about seeing the pornography or doing the sex. Asked if anyone ever tried to inflict unwanted sex acts on them that they knew came from pornography, 10 per cent of women in a recent random study said yes. Among married women, 24 per cent said yes. That is a lot of women. A lot more don't know. Some of those who do testified in Minneapolis. One wife said of her ex-husband, 'He would read from the pornography like a textbook, like a journal. In fact when he asked me to be bound, when he finally convinced me to do it, he read in the magazine how to tie the knots.' Another woman said of her boyfriend, '[H]e went to this party, saw pornography, got an erection, got me . . . to inflict his erection on . . . There is a direct causal relationship there.' One woman, who said her husband had rape and bondage magazines all over the house, discovered two suitcases full of Barbie dolls with rope tied on their arms and legs and with tape across their mouths. Now think about the silence of women. She said, 'He used to tie me up and he tried those things on me.' A therapist in private practice reported:

> 'Presently or recently I have worked with clients who have been sodomized by broom handles, forced to have sex with over 20 dogs in the back seat of their car, tied up and then electrocuted on their genitals. These are children, [all] in the ages of 14 to 18, all of whom [have been directly affected by pornography,] [e]ither where the perpetrator has read the manuals and manuscripts at night and used these as recipe books by day or had the pornography present at the time of the sexual violence.'

One woman, testifying that all the women in a group of ex-prostitutes were brought into prostitution as children through pornography, characterized their collective experience: '[I]n my experience there was not one situation where a client was not using pornography while he was using me or that he had not just watched pornography or that it was verbally referred to and directed me to pornography.' 'Men,' she continued, 'witness the abuse of women in pornography constantly and if they can't engage in that behavior with their wives, girl friends or children, they force a whore to do it.' "

MacKinnon's concentration upon graphic instances of harm which she views as paramount examples of the subordination of women's bodies is not immune from challenge. Having outlined the merits of the ordinance, Nicola Lacey goes on to reveal its weaknesses:

N. Lacey
"Theory into Practice? Pornography and the Public/Private Dichotomy"[37]

"As is well known, however, the ordinance also raised some very difficult questions for feminist politics, and generated a bitter controversy within the women's movement. At its heart, this controversy had to do with the basic shape of the feminist analysis on which the ordinance rested: in short, the claim that pornography is a *central* means of perpetuating women's oppression. Many feminists see pornography and sexual violence as epiphenomenal rather than as central: as the product of economic and other material means of subordination. For the purposes of this discussion, I shall make an intermediate assumption: that is, that pornography in the forms which predominate in our culture, whilst not being a root cause of women's oppression, is a practice which does contribute to sex discrimination, not just in the sense of sexual violence but also in the sense of contributing to the low esteem in which women are held by men and, all too often, in which we hold ourselves. Pornography is by no means the only or even the most important means of degrading objectification to which women (and indeed men) are subjected in our society, but as one such form, it is of political relevance and concern. To this extent, bringing the *issue* of pornography into public debate, and the recognition of the interdependence between privately consumed pornography and the public status of women, is entirely progressive.

However, reflection on the instrumental and symbolic implications of legislation against pornography of the kind embodied in the ordinance gives serious pause for thought about how the public/private critique is to be realized in political practice. Such a legislative strategy exhibits two features which I have already suggested are among the failings of the feminist development of the critique. First, it participates in an over-concentration on the public/private *spheres* aspect of the critique at the expense of its ideological or discursive aspects. It recognizes the discursive power of pornography, but adopts a strategy which, though it has short-term attractions because of its concreteness, is likely to be discursively counter-productive in the medium term. The price of this way of constructing pornography as a public wrong is that it has to be fitted into the conceptual straitjacket of an already legally recognized harm: in the case of the ordinance, sex discrimination. But it is unlikely that all the important aspects of the feminist critique of pornography can be captured in terms of the individualized and relatively tangible harms to which both criminal and civil law have tended to address themselves and which the idea of sex discrimination evokes. Secondly and relatedly, a legislative strategy risks falling back into the assumptions made by the public/private dichotomy itself about the importance of the state as the main source of political/regulatory power. If the power which has kept in place the negative aspects of public/private thinking inheres in a wide variety of institutions and discursive practices, the resort to state/legal reform as a means of undermining public/private divisions looks less promising than the proponents of the legislative strategy have assumed."

In terms of its implications for the regulation of pornographic material in the U.K., the adoption of a scheme along the lines of the ordinance would raise somewhat similar problems.

---

[37] N. Lacey, *supra*, n. 32 at pp. 106–107.

N. LACEY
"Theory into Practice? Pornography and the Public/Private Dichotomy"[38]

"The virtually absolute constitutional protection of free speech in the United States of America presented Dworkin and MacKinnon with a very constraining legal and political framework. Conversely, the greater salience of litigation strategies as part of political life in the United States of America means that the gains to be expected of such a strategy may well have been greater than in the United Kingdom. Some of the most important problems presented by a legal reform strategy against pornography, however, would arise in most jurisdictions. For example, how many women could gather the resources, financial and otherwise, to bring cases against pornography? The experience in Britain and elsewhere of individual-initiated sex discrimination litigation is not encouraging. Even in the few cases where the best legal representation is available, and even where litigants have a very firm political commitment to their cause and a great deal of emotional and material support, research suggests that they may find it a disempowering experience rather than the reverse. Strategic litigation funded by pressure groups may be a more realistic possibility, but the knock-on effects of local cases such as could have been brought under the ordinance can easily be overestimated, whilst the resources which would have to be devoted to litigation strategies, as some women's groups in Canada can attest as a result of their experience under the Charter of Rights and Freedoms, are enormous. Conversely, we have to consider who might use the law in question. Given the breadth of the ordinance's definition, it cannot be doubted that such a law might be exploited by right-wing litigants to attack a wide range of sexually explicit art and literature including that evoking or expressing lesbian sexuality. These, of course, are forms which radical feminists would not see as coming within the ambit of the definition because of the background equality which may be argued to be possible in principle in homosexual but not heterosexual relations. It seems unlikely that judges would confine themselves to such an interpretation. A feminist conception of pornography, already moulded to fit a legal framework, could be further distorted in the interpretive process so as to push it towards a conservative conception inimical to the direction of feminist analysis.

Nor can we assume that a reasonable proportion of cases challenging pornographic material would succeed. Problems of proof — particularly of requirements such as being 'coerced' into pornography, 'forcing' pornography on a person, an attack or injury being 'directly caused by specific pornography' — give strong reason to think that cases would be fraught with practical difficulties, and that the success rate, as in other sex discrimination cases, would be low. In any event, would the remedies envisaged by the ordinance be instrumentally effective? What level of awards of damages could be realistically expected in cases where the harm involved is intangible? How often would courts be willing to award injunctions, and how effectively would or could these be policed? If injunctions were to be awarded and enforced, the argument that the law is not a form of censorship would be hard to sustain. More importantly, what would be the impact on the working conditions in the pornography production industry? The ordinance focused on victims at the production stage only in so far as they have been coerced into performing. Such a law would have no bite against the social conditions which put women into the position where they are able to be so

[38] N. Lacey, *ibid.*, pp. 107–109.

coerced, particularly where their performance for pornography is a rational way of making a living because of the poverty of their other options. It seems unlikely that a broad interpretation of coercion such as would cohere with a feminist analysis of this issue would gain a secure foothold in legal practice.

A supporter of the legislative strategy against pornography could justly object that I have been assuming that legal reform intervenes only at a concrete, material level, underplaying the discursive aspects of law and exaggerating the difference between the discursive and the material. If power inheres to an important extent in discourses, as I have argued, then influential discourses such as law *are* material in constituting social relations, and legal interventions can deploy discursive power in seeking to change the world, as well as operating at the level of the concrete. We need, then, to look also at what are sometimes called the 'symbolic' aspects of this kind of law reform. Here again, several considerations suggest that a law such as the ordinance might be counter-productive. In the first place, if the instrumental arguments just rehearsed are correct, a symbolic message follows from them: the political meaning of having an unenforceable or unenforced law on the statute books is, at best, ambiguous and, at worst, suggests that legal policy is being used as a sop to political sentiment and as a way of avoiding the need for more effective political action. An interesting analogue here is the British (criminal) law on incitement to racial hatred — an offence which is sometimes suggested as a model for anti-pornography legislation. The number of successful prosecutions since this offence was first introduced has been miniscule, and the law is widely regarded as a costless (for government) sop to concern about racism which merely serves to legitimate government's relative inaction in other more potentially fruitful areas. In addition, each unsuccessful prosecution implies the *legitimacy* of the racist conduct thereby condoned. A second symbolic worry about this sort of anti-pornography law lies in its openness to use by litigants motivated by other than feminist concerns, and indeed in the need (realized in the political process in Indianapolis) to build political alliances with those on the (evangelical) right in order to enact and sustain the legislation. In certain quarters the pornography debate in the United States of America has increased the image of feminism as moralistic and potentially repressive. Doubtless this is to some extent inevitable: the charge of moralism is one way of trying to marginalize a view with which one disagrees. But the feminist position has been made more vulnerable because of the quick inference from the theoretical reconstruction of pornography as public to the idea that *some* instrumental regulatory strategy must be appropriate, and hence by a failure to engage in a sufficient debate about not just the efficacy but also the ethics of legal control. At a discursive level, the implications of the legislative strategy seem at best, uncertain and at worst, damaging."

9.1.v   *Taking off the reformist rose-tinted spectacles*

In the light of the various critiques of ways of seeing pornography through the eyes of the criminal law, European law and civil law, it might be thought that feminists are engaging in an elusive exercise in seeking out a legal "solution" to the pornography "problem". Given that the problem appears to escape definition, any solution must necessarily be viewed circumspectly. If we discard our rose-tinted (law reform-seeking) spectacles and take a step outside the legal frameworks on offer, might not a space be created in which feminist strategy may be viewed from a fresh perspective?

N. LACEY
"Theory into Practice? Pornography and the Public/Private Dichotomy"[39]

"In short, the inference from the reconstruction of pornography as a political issue to the strategy of legislating against it seems to me to be unjustified. First, it takes an unduly narrow view of the power and role of feminist critique conceived as a form of political practice. Secondly, it falls into the trap of thinking that as feminist lawyers we have to be lawyers first and feminists second — in other words, that we have to find legal solutions to all the problems identified by feminist critique. As a general assumption this is dangerous, for questions about law reform are essentially strategic and have to be assessed carefully in the context of particular reform possibilities. At least in the United Kingdom, such an assessment in the case of pornography leads . . . to the conclusion that legal reform of the kind attempted in Minneapolis is likely to be a counter-productive feminist strategy. Finally, the history of the pornography debate illustrates the importance of distinguishing between different aspects of the public/ private dichotomy and its deconstruction in feminist theory. The critique of public/ private divisions in social, political, and legal thought cannot of itself recommend particular political strategies. What it can do, properly differentiated, is to give us a broader conception of the political and a sense of the questions we have to confront. In their work on not only pornography but also a range of other issues — abortion, sexual harassment, rape, and so on — radical feminist lawyers have made an invaluable contribution to feminist politics, irrespective of their activities around law reform. To regard legislative reform as the invariable core of feminist legal politics is to exaggerate the power of such reform and to undervalue the power of legal critique."

9.2 Advertising images

The sexual violation of women and the production, use and display of pornography are glaring examples of the violence perpetrated upon, and objectification of, the bodies of women in the western world in the late twentieth century. To focus upon these examples, however, belies the everyday exposure of women to images which dehumanise us and portray us as objects. The final part of this chapter widens the focus from the portrayal of women's bodies as sex objects in pornography to a consideration of images of women in advertising.[40] It is suggested that representations of women in the media — representations to which we are constantly exposed — may have profound consequences upon the way that we as women feel about ourselves, our appropriate role and what is expected of us (as well as for the way we are viewed by men). Hence, the present regulation of advertising is under consideration. This prompts the question of whether the law has a role to play in securing a more diverse representation of women in advertising images.

---

[39] N. Lacey, *ibid.*, pp. 110–111.

[40] Advertising is merely one form of media imagery which affects women in numerous and diverse ways. It is selected here as an example through which to explore the role which the law may play in the regulation of media images. As Valverde suggests, "[e]ven if violent porn is what angers women most, it is not necessarily the cultural form most dangerous to our own emotional and sexual development" (M. Valverde, *Sex, Power and Pleasure* (Toronto: The Women's Press, 1985), p. 133, cited in C. Smart, *supra*, n. 4 at 136).

9.2.i *Images of the ideal*
Women, or idealised images of Woman, are displayed in advertising (on television, billboards, in magazines), in television soap operas, cinema films, novels,
magazines and newspapers.[41] The development of technology has facilitated
the growth of a mass communications industry which is instrumental in the
presentation and formation of ideas. The difficulty in establishing a causal
relationship between, for example, violent images and subsequent violent
behaviour or pornographic images and degrading treatment of women has
been mentioned above. It is similarly problematic to establish a causal relationship between "sexist" images of women (images which limit women to
narrowly defined roles as mother, wife and lover) and male and female attitudes towards women. The impact of images cannot be measured given their
dissemination within a shifting cultural context and within the shifting meanings attributed to the image by the viewer. The lack of distinction between
pornographic and other representations of women is clearly identified in the
following extract by Emily Jackson. Starting with an exposition of the radical
feminist critique of pornography, she moves to a wider consideration of the
disempowering effects of cultural representations of the female body.

E. JACKSON
**"The Problem with Pornography: A Critical Survey of the Current
Debate"**[42]

"The substantive reason for focusing on pornography is . . . part of the feminist claim
that the cultural construction of sexuality is of central importance. Feminists like
Dworkin and MacKinnon have claimed that pornography damages all women by
equating their sexuality with their abuse.

This last claim requires further investigation. Feminists often start from the supposition that women are harmed by pornography. There is a wealth of scientific evidence
which suggests that exposure to pornography increases the likelihood that the average
man will force sex on a woman. And there are interminable debates about whether
this research documents a mere correlation, or a causal relationship between pornography and rape. Of course there are scientific reports which appear to show the opposite: that relaxation of censorship in Scandinavian countries is associated with a
decrease in sexual violence. The latest piece of research in the U.K. found that it was
not possible to prove that pornography *caused* sexual violence, but that neither was it
proven that pornography had any beneficial effects in creating outlets for male aggression.

I think it unhelpful to become entrenched in an unproductive series of claims and
counterclaims. Deborah Cameron and Elizabeth Frazer persuasively argue that causal

---

[41] It is suggested that media representations of women construct the ideal Woman. This raises
questions about the wider context of, and the role of the law in relation to, harms perpetuated
upon women in their pursuit of that ideal. The issue is taken up further in the next chapter looking
at anorexia, cosmetic surgery and female genital surgeries. For a more extensive exploration see
S. Bordo, *Unbearable Weight: Feminism, Western Culture and the Body* (Berkeley: University of
California Press, 1993).
[42] E. Jackson, *supra*, n. 1 at 60–63.

explanations of human action are completely inappropriate. When a man sees a pornographic movie his response to it is not analogous to the behaviour of a heavy object dropped from a great height. Human behaviour is not susceptible to precise causal rules comparable to the laws of gravity. Reaction to pornography is not dictated by natural instinct, instead it consists in the interpretation of images. The meaning pornography has for its consumers is not self-constituting, it is one part of the cultural landscape, and its impact does not exist in isolation from broader experiences of sexuality.

Although we should clearly be concerned about evidence suggesting that men who are violent towards women often use pornography before or during that abuse, the problem with pornography should not be limited to the question of whether any single image is capable of creating an instant rapist.

Indeed, Catharine MacKinnon, a staunch believer that "porn is the theory, rape is the practice", does also suggest that pornography has an impact beyond that on its direct consumers and victims. In her view it does not simply present distorted images of sex to those who choose to consume it. Instead, it damages all women because it inescapably sets the groundrules for all sexual relations. She argues that pornography has made sex into an unequal encounter between a man who dominates and a woman who submits. This image is reproduced so many times that it becomes inculcated into our consciousness as the way things are. MacKinnon argues that the resulting cultural hegemony is sustained by other media which affirm the values of pornography: the male is the possessor and the woman the possessed.

So pornography is one mechanism in the continuing process of gender definition. Pornography is one example, among many, from a cultural tradition that appears to devalue women. There is patently some connection between representations of sex and the sexual values of a community. But the relationship between the two is complicated. It is undeniable that pornography exists as one cultural medium in the ongoing social construction of reality. The gender hierarchy which dictates rigid and debilitating sexual identities is culturally constructed. Pornography presents particularly crude and polarised images of women and men, but it does not, on its own, create sexual inequality.

Women can only think about their sexuality and articulate their desires through the filter of a deeply internalized set of patriarchal norms. It may then be true that feminine sexuality outside of its confining cultural representation has, historically, been profoundly silenced. We cannot easily articulate alternative sexual identities because our experiences do not transcend our gendered culture. Feminism must struggle against the imposition of rigid sexual norms. This is, nevertheless, a vast project, and its success depends upon recognising the prevalence of pornography as but one link in the chain.

Indeed the fact that pornography is extreme may, according to some women, mean that it has less influence than other, more widely available material. In the U.K. Clare Short, a Labour M.P., introduced a piece of draft legislation which, if implemented, would have prevented the most popular daily newspaper printing a provocative photograph of a topless model on its page 3. The inclusion or not of this sort of image under the rubric "pornography" is controversial. But in being widely available, cheap, and published in the relatively privileged arena of the news media, it could be argued that these images have a profound effect on perceptions of women's sexuality. Not least because each morning *The Sun* will publish a new picture, and yesterday's copy is discarded. This disposability may amplify the objectification process.

Naomi Wolf has argued that images of women in 'legitimate' contexts such as women's magazines, Hollywood movies and pop videos have joined more traditional pornographic formats as means of disseminating dangerous images of women. 'Beauty pornography' involves the use of perfected women's bodies in poses borrowed from soft and hard core pornography to sell products to women. Women are told that the way to be sexy, desirable and to have self respect is to be beautiful, skinny, and, increasingly, tied up and submissive. Movies portraying sexual exploitation and abuse have proliferated. Promotional pop videos have featured stylised images of women in danger. The mainstream cliché is thus one of stylish objectification and sadomasochism. Wolf is then not surprised that this has produced a generation that honestly believes that violence against women is sexual. The impact is not just on men, women's attitudes toward themselves are affected; Wolf finds it axiomatic that studies have found that 50 per cent of women have submissive sexual fantasies. Wolf may then be close to MacKinnon in arguing that this has become the reality of sex.

It is irrefutable that current cultural representations of sexuality frequently articulate disempowering stereotype sex roles. Yet outlawing pornography, without altering its current definition would not even begin to deal with images that have become cloaked in respectability. Perhaps more fundamentally, pornography just reinforces sexual identities which are simultaneously created and sustained in other ways.

If pornography is then simply one facet of an infinitely broader process, its legal proscription would not fatally undermine current sexual norms. Indeed, it could be argued that the preoccupation with law reform may, in fact, be seriously obstructive."

It is not possible to establish a causal link between images of women, the way women feel about ourselves when continually confronted with the media ideal and the resort to methods of body modification considered in the next chapter. However, the increase in eating disorders, the extent to which dieting dominates the lives of women, the time spent on exercise programmes (in the gym or at home with books and videos), the investment in beauty regimes and cosmetic surgery all have to be considered in the context of a society in which we are continually exposed to images of the ideal Woman. Susie Orbach argues that these practices may be considered as methods employed to "mediate the harrowing effects of culturally induced body insecurity".[43] Susan Bordo suggests that through media images we learn how to behave and what is expected of us.[44] Women have gained access to education, to employment, to roles in the public life of administration, government and business and are freed from the inevitability of repeated motherhood through contraception (whatever its obvious limitations might be). Still, the assumption that a woman's basic, and most valuable, role is in the home tending children and catering for the needs of her husband by providing him with food, clean clothes, and sex is a durable one. As Susie Orbach explains in *Hunger Strike*,[45] the movement of women into the public world has not been a comfortable transition. Whilst the successes of feminism have secured for women access to the "public" world of men, women have had to fit into that world on existing

[43] S. Orbach, *Hunger Strike: The Anorectic's Struggle as a Metaphor for our Age* (Harmondsworth: Penguin, 1993), p. 3.
[44] S. Bordo, *supra*, n. 41 at 169.
[45] S. Orbach, *supra*, n. 43 at pp. 3–10.

terms. The result is female participation in an environment which feels alien. The successful woman in media imagery is one who has taken on the role of career woman in addition to the existing roles as glamorous wife and loving mother. As women have ventured into the public world, we have been increasingly exposed to images of the ideal Woman, and are under pressure, whilst participating in that public world, to retain our femininity and attain the feminine ideal.

S. Orbach
Hunger Strike: The Anorectic's Struggle as a Metaphor for our Age[46]

"[W]omen today are presented with an apparently bewildering number of social role options. One only has to choose what one wishes and the world is open . . .

Participation in the modern world involves the pursuit of success for its own sake and as defined by our culture rather than an evaluation of the basis of this world. In spite of the rhetoric of women's equality, feminine values have not been assimilated outside the domestic sphere. Women entering the world beyond the home do so as guests and not as principals; the necessary shifts, adjustments and negotiations are contingent on women making them. Women are required to accommodate themselves to the public sphere much as they accommodate others in private. Even if they are no longer relegated to the role of mere midwives to the activities of others, they must nevertheless ensure that their presence is quasi-unobtrusive. They must conform to prevailing masculinist values and accept entry on that basis.

The late twentieth century has failed to bring about a substantially new role relationship between men and women. To be sure, women's work is now more visible and discrimination on job training and job entry is couched in apologetic terms. Reformist struggles taken up by the second wave of feminism have made for dramatic improvements and changes in the lives of many, many women. However, American women still live in a society in which the Equal Rights Amendment remains unratified, while the legal equality granted to English women has been found to be inadequately legislated and enforced. These manifestations of women's continued inequality are reflected in both subtle and crude ways in the family, education, the health system and the world of work. Equality has little chance of being consolidated if society is not, even in principle, committed to it. Even with legal protection, if equality is to enter the hearts, experience and day-to-day reality of contemporary men and women, it requires a concerted struggle at every level — a questioning of our most basic assumptions and society's commitment to change. No such move has been initiated at a state level. No commitment to the examination and change of male and female roles has been undertaken. In this context the woman of today faces contradictory pulls. She is culturally and psychologically prepared for a life in which she should continue to service the needs of others, while at the same time she is teased with the possibility of living a life for herself. These themes enter directly into current child-rearing practices where children observe and experience upbringing in a predominantly female ambience while receiving the 'new' message that the world outside of the home is the domain of all. Femininity is inextricably linked with the home and with mothering. The new feminin-

---

[46] S. Orbach, *ibid.*, pp. 7–9.

ity outside the home depends upon the assuming of masculine values or the extension of the feminine role into the work force in the form of service work.

Today women from every generation experience themselves being pushed and pulled in opposing directions. While individual women can find a way to balance new possibilities and pressures, all women live with a tension about their place in the world."

The media image is an ideal, albeit unobtainable, against which we constantly assess ourselves and which we strive to obtain. Advertising in particular, because it is about selling goods, employs this image of the unobtainable ideal (where the advertised product offers the promise of securing for the purchaser the ideal).

Models photographed for advertising do not represent the norm of women generally. They are slim (thin), white, young and attractive. It is very rare for images to be of older women or larger women or women of ethnic minorities — unless the product being sold is aimed at them. But the message of success is pervasive and effective as women strive for the unobtainable by using the techniques offered by the diet, cosmetic and fashion industries, and in doing so reproduce cultural concepts of beauty.

Beauty, as represented by the current ideal, has not, as Kathy Davis explains, historically (and is not contemporarily in other cultures), been solely the concern of women. Davis notes how, in the late eighteenth century, beauty became "women's concern" and in the twentieth century, with mass production, the concern of all women: "By the twentieth century, the cultivation of appearance had become a central concern for women of different classes, regions, and ethnic groups, simultaneously uniting them in their desire for beautification, and setting up standards to differentiate them according to class and race."[47] She explains that the consistent force within a constantly changing ideal[48] was "that beauty was worth spending time, money, pain, and perhaps life itself. Beauty hurts, and it appeared that modern women were willing to go to extreme lengths to improve and transform their bodies to meet cultural requirements of femininity."[49] Kathy Davis describes the different analyses of beauty as either a form of oppression or as a cultural discourse:

K. DAVIS
Reshaping the Female Body: The Dilemma of Cosmetic Surgery[50]

"Within feminist scholarship, women's preoccupation with their appearance is invariably explained as an artefact of femininity in a context of power hierarchies between

---

[47] K. Davis, *Reshaping the Female Body: The Dilemma of Cosmetic Surgery* (London: Routledge, 1995), p. 40.

[48] Changes occur because what is considered beautiful is culturally and historically specific. This stands in opposition to the ideology of the "beauty myth", that, "[t]he quality called 'beauty' objectively and universally exists" masking that it is a "culturally imposed physical standard" (N. Wolf, *The Beauty Myth* (London: Vintage, 1990), p. 12).

[49] K. Davis, *supra*, n. 47 at 41.

[50] (London: Routledge, 1995), pp. 49–52.

the sexes and among women of different social and cultural backgrounds. Feminists have tended to cast a critical eye on women's quest for beauty, which is described in terms of suffering and oppression. Women are presented as the victims both of beauty and of the ideologies of feminine inferiority which produce and maintain practices of body maintenance and improvement. Originally, the culprit was sought in what was described as a system of cultural beauty norms. These norms demanded eternal youth and impossible beauty from women: slender but voluptuous shapes, faces unmarked by the passage of time, and, most of all, an appearance in keeping with the conventions of upper-class, Western femininity. By linking the beauty practices of individual women to the structural constraints of the beauty system, a convincing case was made for treating beauty as an essential ingredient of the social subordination of women. Beauty was seen as an ideal way to keep women in line by lulling them into believing that they could gain control over their lives through continued vigilance over their bodies.

In recent years, feminist scholarship on beauty as oppression has begun to make way for a more postmodern approach which deals with beauty in terms of cultural discourses. In this framework, routine beauty practices belong to the disciplinary and normalizing regime of body improvement and transformation, part and parcel of the production of 'docile bodies' . The focus is on the multiplicity of meanings attributed to the female body as well as the insidious workings of power in and through cultural discourses on beauty and femininity. The body remains a central concern, this time, however, as a text upon which culture writes its meanings. Following Foucault, the female body is portrayed as an imaginary site, always available to be inscribed. It is here that femininity in all her diversity can be constructed — through scientific discourses, medical technologies, the popular media, and everyday common sense.

Although the theoretical perspectives for understanding women's beauty practices differ in their emphasis on beauty as oppression or as cultural discourse, the focus remains on how these practices work to control or discipline women. In the first perspective, femininity is defined in terms of women's shared experiences of which the most central is oppression. Power is primarily a matter of male domination and female subordination. In the second perspective, the unified category 'woman' is abandoned in favor of a diversity of femininities. Femininity is regarded as a (discursive) construction with power implicated in its construction. Power is no longer a matter of top-down repression or coercion, but the vehicle through which femininity is constituted at all levels of social life. In both perspectives, women's preoccupation with their appearance is viewed as part of a complex system of structured social practices, variously referred to as the politics of appearance, the technologies of body management, the beauty system, the aesthetic scaling of bodies, the fashion-beauty complex, or the beauty backlash. This system includes the myriad procedures, technologies, and rituals drawn upon by individual women in their everyday lives, the cosmetic industry, the advertising business, and the cultural discourses on femininity and beauty. Beauty is central to femininity, whereby Woman as sex is idealized as the incarnation of physical beauty, while most ordinary women are rendered 'drab, ugly, loathsome or fearful bodies'. This ambivalence concerning the female body is implicated in the reproduction of unequal power relations between the sexes. It aids the channelling of women's energies in the hopeless race for a perfect body. As Bartky has noted, the 'fashion-beauty complex,' like the military-industrial complex, is a 'major articulation of capitalist patriarchy'.

The beauty system also articulates social hierarchies based on class, race, and ethnicity. In Western culture, dominant discourses of the body enable privileged groups —

notably, white, bourgeois, professional men — to transcend their own material bodies and take on a god's eye view as disembodied subjects. They become the ones who set the standards and judge, rather than the ones who are judged against standards they can never hope to meet. Subordinate groups are defined by their bodies and are defined according to norms which diminish or degrade them. Those designated by the dominant culture as Other (old, homosexual, disabled, fat, and/or female) become imprisoned in their bodies.

Beauty standards set up dichotomies of Otherness and power hierarchies between women.

> 'Blue-eyed, blonde, thin white women could not be considered beautiful without the Other — Black women with classical African features of dark skin, broad noses, full lips, and kinky hair.'

White, Western women are trapped by the promise that they are special, which gives them a vested interest in maintaining the beauty system. The norms which equate the light-skinned, Western look with beauty permeate relations between white women and women of color, as well as between women and men of color. Women of color are bombarded with cultural messages which not only link whiteness to feminine beauty, but, more importantly, to 'gentility, female domesticity, protection from labor, the exacting standards of the elite, and Anglo-Saxon superiority' — in short, to power."

Davis argues that the problem with these approaches is that they portray women as "cultural dopes" blindly pursuing the attainment of the ideal body image. In doing so they fail to acknowledge the extent to which women know the risks and limitations of body modification. Susan Bordo comments:

S. BORDO
Unbearable Weight: Feminism, Western Culture and the Body[51]

"Recognizing that normalizing cultural forms exist does not entail, as some writers have argued, the view that women are 'cultural dopes,' blindly submitting to oppressive regimes of beauty. Although many people *are* mystified (insisting, for example, that the current fitness craze is only about health or that plastic surgery to 'correct' a 'Jewish' or 'black' nose is just an individual preference), often there will be a high degree of consciousness involved in the decision to diet or to have cosmetic surgery. People *know* the routes to success in this culture — they are advertised widely enough — and they are not 'dopes' to pursue them. Often, given the racism, sexism, and narcissism of the culture, their personal happiness and economic security may depend on it."

9.2.ii *Regulation of Advertising Images*
The law places some limits upon the images which may be displayed through the law on obscenity. In addition to the criminal offences relating to obscene publications, mechanisms exist for the regulation of film, television and

---

[51] S. Bordo, *supra.*, n. 41 at p. 30.

advertising broadcasting. The British Board of Film Classification (BBFC) assesses films and videos and provides certificates of suitability. The certificate has no legal force in relation to films for public showing.[52] The Cinemas Act 1985 limits the public showing of films to licensed premises. Licences are granted by district councils and London Boroughs which usually accept the assessments of the BBFC. This means that a condition frequently imposed by the licence is that films exhibited either have a BBFC certificate or are shown with the permission of the licensing authority.[53] Whilst the classification of films for showing in cinemas is voluntary, under the Video Recordings Act 1984 all videos must be submitted for consideration by the Board for certification as appropriate for home viewing.[54] The Independent Television Commission established by the Broadcasting Act 1990 licenses and regulates television services (other than the BBC) and is required to ensure that a "wide range of television services is available throughout the U.K., and that the programmes (taken as a whole) are of high quality and cater for a variety of tastes and interests".[55]

Advertising images are presently subject to a system of self-regulation. The Advertising Standards Authority (ASA) supervises the *British Code of Advertising Practice* (BCAP), drawn up by the Committee of Advertising Practice ensuring that the industry abides by its terms. The *Code of Practice* applies to advertisements in newspapers, magazines and other printed publications, posters, cinema and video cassette commercials, brochures and leaflets. The ASA does not initiate investigations but responds to complaints from the public about particular advertisements.

In challenging advertisements on the grounds of oppressive representations of women it is usually the paragraphs on decency which are addressed:

BRITISH CODE OF ADVERTISING PRACTICE (para. 5.1)
January 1995

"Advertisements should contain nothing that is likely to cause grave or widespread offence. Particular care should be taken to avoid causing offence on the grounds of race, religion, sex, sexual orientation or disability. Compliance with the Codes will be judged on the context, medium, audience, product and prevailing standards of decency."

Following investigation in response to complaints by members of the public, the ASA may consider that an advert contravenes the Code, in which case the

---

[52] *Halsbury's Laws*, Vol. 45 (1985), para. 980.
[53] S. H. Bailey, D. J. Harris & B. L. Jones, *Civil Liberties: Cases and Materials* (London: Butterworths, 1995), pp. 323–334.
[54] This is with the exception of educational, sporting, musical or religious videos (see G. Robertson, *Freedom, the Individual and the Law* (Harmondsworth: Penguin Books, 1989), p. 224).
[55] S. H. Bailey, D. J. Harris & B. L. Jones, *supra*, n. 53 at p. 335. The Broadcasting Standards Council monitors television programmes and adjudicates on complaints relating to "sex, violence, taste and decency" (S. H. Bailey, D. J. Harris & B. L. Jones, *ibid.*, p. 335).

advertiser will be asked to withdraw or amend it. A Report is produced by the ASA which is available to those in the industry providing information regarding the decisions of the ASA. Further publication of adverts upon which the ASA has recommended alteration is thereby prevented until the alterations have been made.[56] In short, therefore, the regulation of advertising is carried out by informal means being based primarily upon the co-operation of those engaged in the industry.[57]

Section 9 of the Broadcasting Act 1990 imposes a statutory duty on the Independent Television Commission (ITC) to draw up and enforce a code governing standards and practice in television advertising. The ITC draws up the Code, advises broadcasters on interpretation, monitors compliance and investigates complaints. The relevant paragraph, which a sexist advertisement may offend is:

ITC CODE OF ADVERTISING STANDARDS AND PRACTICE, (para. 13) May 1993

"No advertisement may offend against good taste or decency or be offensive to public feeling and no advertisement should prejudice respect for human dignity."

The notes accompanying this section state that on matters of taste individual reactions can differ and the Commission expects licensees to exercise responsible judgments "and to take account of the sensitivities of all sections of their audience when deciding on the acceptability or scheduling of advertisements. Particular care should be taken to avoid treatments which, through the unthinking use of stereotyped imagery, could be hurtful to certain sections of the audience."

The regulation of advertisements under the *British Code of Advertising Practice* and the ITC *Code of Practice* may perpetuate attitudes because advertisements are judged according to whether they offend current standards in society. This is explicitly so under the BCAP under which continued presentation of sexist images of women may provide a consistency which reinforces their acceptability. If the current regulation of advertising images perpetuates representations of the unobtainable ideal which have a harmful effect upon the bodies and lives of women, is it possible, or appropriate, to seek to

---

[56] The decisions of the Advertising Standards Authority are subject to judicial review (*R. v. Advertising Standards Authority, ex p. The Insurance Service* (1989) S.J. 1545). See R. Lawson, "Regulating the Advertising Regulators" (1993) 137 S.J. 366.

[57] Under the Control of Misleading Advertisements Regulations 1988, should the advertiser seek to publish despite an adverse ruling by the ASA, the Director General of Fair Trading can seek an injunction to prevent publication. An advertisement is defined as misleading if "in any way, including its presentation, it deceives or is likely to deceive the persons to whom it is addressed or whom it reaches and if, by reason of its deceptive nature, it is likely to affect their economic behaviour or, for those reasons, injures or is likely to injure a competitor of the person whose interests the advertisement seeks to promote." (See H. Johnson, "A Legal Campaign: Advertising Freedom and Legal Controls" (1990) 32 *Managerial Law* 1 at 5–9).

use the law to ensure the creation of more diverse and positive images of women? It is difficult to perceive of a legal mechanism which would be able to achieve this. The problems of introducing a civil ordinance, as proposed by Catharine MacKinnon and Andrea Dworkin, and objections to censorship have been raised in relation to pornography and are equally as applicable to non-pornographic images. As a strategy by which to improve the position of women in society, feminists have identified the reasons why women should be cautious about recourse to the law. As with pornography, the regulation of advertising images may be one area where, despite an existing system of regulation which perpetuates images of women as an unobtainable ideal, we should not advocate greater legal regulation.

C. Smart
Feminism and the Power of Law[58]

"It may be that representations of women in advertising, in soap operas, and in romantic novels carry a much more pervasive influence [than pornography]. It is also the case that if we direct ourselves to the problem of the extension of the pornographic genre rather than pornographic material as such, then the law as a possible remedy appears less and less useful. It is vital to remember that the meanings of representations is not immutable or unitary, although there may be dominant forms of interpretation. The benefit of the strategy of using civil law was that it allowed for a new interpretation of pornographic representation, its deficit was that it seriously attempted to use law to enforce this definition. Pornography is an issue which clearly reveals the limits of law in terms of feminist strategy. It reveals that there are major problems in transforming any feminist analysis of women's oppression into a legal practice, as if law were merely an instrument to be utilized by feminist lawyers with the legal skills to draw up the statutes."

The source of this difficulty may be in identifying precisely the nature of the injury caused to women by sex-stereotyped images. However, "naming" the injury (identifying the harm as a social injury) may engender a feeling that there are legitimate grounds for a remedy. Identification of the injury, based on female experience, may enable an appropriate legal strategy to be pursued:

A. Howe
"The Problem of Privatized Injuries: Feminist Strategies for Litigation"[59]

"I must face the danger that social injury will go the way of all feminist legal initiatives: that however we theorize our claims, they will become transmogrified into legal categories which mask the nature of women's socially-based oppression. Undoubtedly, this constitutes our biggest challenge: to be or not to be involved in and committed to

[58] C. Smart, *supra*, n. 4 at pp. 136–137.
[59] In M. A. Fineman & N. S. Thomadsen , *At the Boundaries of Law: Feminism and Legal Theory* (New York: Routledge, 1991), pp. 165–166.

restructuring law for women. For some, 'harm by discrimination' — is not actionable at law and as far as women are concerned, law has not proved to be the useful 'form of social criticism' nor the deliverer of 'at least some of the goods' which David Trubek claimed it to be. Others are less pessimistic. While they recognize that anti-discrimination laws fit the model of 'conformative institutions' which 'contain, incorporate and moderate' conflict within capitalist societies, they insist that these institutions also have 'an ambiguous character' — one which 'creates new opportunities for pressing demands'. They also warn against the dangers of abstentionism from law reform, such as perpetrating women's exclusion and disempowerment.

On one side then, are those who maintain that concern with law reform diverts 'the energy of the women's liberation movement into a narrow focus on legally articulate claims' or who insist that 'the use of law in women's struggle for emancipation is a problematic tactic for feminists' insofar as male legal and judicial hegemony means that for the foreseeable future 'the conception and execution' of legal change is going to be 'masculine'. On the other side are those such as Elizabeth Kingdom who reminds us that while in the past law has been 'dismissed by sections of the left and feminists as being irredeemably reactionary and hence politically impenetrable,' legal practices have been 'a site of feminist intervention'. Similarly, Carol Smart has argued that our legal 'disappointments' notwithstanding, we need to continue engaging with law. In particular, she has suggested that 'the willingness of courts to be influenced by non-legal criteria is a sign that yet other considerations can be brought into the legal forum'. Social injury, I suggest, is a strong candidate. Further, she has offered her concept of 'the uneven development of law' — which recognizes that law both facilitates and obstructs change — in the hope that it will open the possibility of seeing law as 'a means of "liberation" '.

In the wake of feminist disenchantment with law and with the concept of rights in particular as a means of pressing feminist claims in law, Smart and Julia Brophy have suggested a new starting point — women's experience, not 'abstract notions of law, justice or equity'. In this way, they give expression to a growing recognition that our theorizing must 'escape imprisonment within the dominant discourse' and become experientially-grounded in women's lives. Similarly, Scandinavian feminists have insisted that we must privilege women's lives, not legal definitions. For Dahl, for example, the project of building women's law involves prompting 'dignity, integrity and self-realization as basic needs of women today.' From the social injury perspective, it is significant that her notion of integrity is 'especially connected to the right to be left in peace, both physically and psychologically', for it is the physical and psychological damage caused by women's social injuries which we need to highlight in our fight to maintain our integrity. On the one hand, then, feminist legal scholars are condemning legal liberalism for having no language to adequately conceptualize our oppression; on the other hand, they are calling for innovative discursive practices grounded in women's lives. At yet another level altogether, they are deciding that there may be no single response to women's legal issues: the approach we take is simply a question of strategy. In the still inchoate state of feminist legal theorizing, I offer my social injury strategy as an affirmation of my faith in the progressive possibilities of feminist interventions in law."

CHAPTER 10

BODY IMAGE

The issues considered within this chapter — the treatment of anorexics without their consent, cosmetic surgery and female genital mutilation — can all be considered as harm inflicted upon women by other individuals or as a consequence of cultural pressures operating within society.[1] However, central to all three is the choice of the woman herself to pursue slenderness to the extreme, to submit to an operation to surgically alter her body for cosmetic reasons, or to respond to cultural pressures and choose to undergo female genital surgery. In this way, women can also be considered to be harming themselves. These activities highlight both the importance placed upon the female body at the end of the twentieth century and women's dissatisfaction with their own image:

"The whole focus is on our bodies. Our bodies are there for men's pleasure, not ours, and they never measure up. And women are supposed to pluck their eyebrows, shave their legs, slim themselves, wear high heels. It doesn't seem to me to be a very large step from the woman who sits there, you know, bashing her thighs with her fists, saying, 'I'm so fat, I shouldn't have eaten that cream cake' to a woman cutting herself."[2]

As Ann Lloyd comments, "it's a continuum with societal encouragement at one end, and condemnation at the other"[3] — "normal" practices of modifying and beautifying the body are encouraged, only to be labelled as pathological behaviour when perceived to have been taken to the extreme. This chapter seeks to present an understanding of the pervasive nature of the objectification

---

[1] It is our view that law colludes in the perpetuation of this harm. The issues covered in this chapter are not exclusive in that respect. Another instance of the law harming women is considered by Michael Thomson in his study of foetal protection policies. These policies cause economic harm by excluding women from some industries. Also, in focusing upon damage to the *female* reproductive system, harm which may occur to *men*, and through them to a subsequent pregnancy or to the environment, is ignored. The policies construct all women as potential mothers (in one example given by Thomson women between the ages of 5 and 63 are included in the remit of the policy). Furthermore, the policies perpetuate the understanding of women as unable to make informed decisions and thus as representing a threat to the potential foetus (M. Thomson, "Employing the Body: The Reproductive Body and Employment Exclusion" (1996) 5 *Social & Legal Studies* 243 at 258–9).
[2] L. Arnold, Bristol Crisis Service for Women, interview in A. Lloyd, *Doubly Deviant, Doubly Damned: Society's Treatment of Violent Women* (Harmondsworth: Penguin, 1995), p. 180.
[3] A. Lloyd, *ibid.*, p. 180.

and violation of women within society (beyond the examples considered earlier of sexual violence and pornography) against which women constantly fight and survive. This chapter, therefore, follows from the consideration in the previous chapter of contemporary representations of the ideal Woman within western society. Through an examination of the treatment of anorexics without their consent, laws concerning cosmetic surgery and the prohibition of female circumcision, this chapter considers the ways in which the law, when engaging with the female body, reinforces societal expectations of the nature of women and our appropriate gender role.

10.1   The law's engagement with the Anorexic

There are a number of different explanations for the development of anorexia:

R. Dresser

"Article and Commentary on *Anorexia Nervosa*: Feeding the Hunger Artists: Legal Issues in Treating *Anorexia Nervosa*"[4]

"What lies behind the anorexic's desperate pursuit to become thin? Many clinicians believe that the anorexic resorts to her behavior out of a need for control over her life. The typical anorexic is a 'good little girl' who has spent her life endeavoring to please her elders by successfully performing every task they have given her. She is especially considerate and submissive until, usually during adolescence, she stops eating normally. She becomes defiant and stubborn; the struggle with others over her failure to eat begins. Hilde Bruch, a physician and recognized authority on *anorexia nervosa*, believes anorexics are making a bid for autonomy. According to Bruch, anorexics are unequipped to exercise control over their lives in more positive ways because they grew up responding to the demands of others, instead of their own needs. At the onset of puberty and adolescence, these girls are unprepared to cope with the accompanying physical, psychological and social changes signalling independence and adulthood. They seek to gain control over their lives by dominating their own bodies, rather than by directing their energies toward the outside world. For the anorexic, each pound lost adds to the power that gives her 'another kind of "weight," the right to be an individual.' From this perspective, anorexia constitutes a response to the adolescent challenge of identity formation.

Some commentators believe the anorexic maintains her behavior for other reasons as well. A well known British clinician and researcher on anorexia, A. H. Crisp, sees a parallel between the anorexic and the religious ascetic who seeks purification by denial of physical needs. Like the ascetic, the anorexic seeks an ideal through discipline and concentration. And like the ascetic, the anorexic may report heightened perception and ecstatic feelings during her fast. 'They will speak of the world as gloriously, or unbearably, vivid, or say that all their senses are keener.'

Weight loss also gives the anorexic respite from the stresses of puberty, adolescence and young adulthood. Physically, she returns to her pre-pubescent state. With the cessation of menstruation, sexual feelings diminish. Her body literally returns to child-

---

[4]   [1984] Wis. L. Rev. 297 at 302–306.

hood, and she no longer must confront the disturbing developmental changes in her body. Bruch calls the anorexic's conduct an 'effort to make time stand still.'

Anorexic behavior may receive additional social reinforcement. Besides the triumph over her own physical needs, the anorexic discovers a means of exercising power and control over others, particularly her parents. Commentators commonly assert that the condition is closely linked with family attitudes and interaction patterns. Indeed, family therapists provide one of the major theoretical perspectives on anorexia. The American spokesperson for this approach, Salvador Minuchin, has coined the phrase 'psychosomatic families' to describe families in which anorexia is likely to develop. Anorexia thus becomes a 'diagnosis of the family system,' a condition 'defined not only by the behavior of one family member, but also by the interrelationship of all family members.'

Family therapists describe the anorexic's family as a system in which overt conflict and independence are not tolerated. Hence, the anorexic cannot openly rebel to establish her individuality. She mimics the family's conflict avoidance strategy by undertaking a passive method of expressing her defiance. At some point, however, she can no longer be ignored. The family is provoked into controversy by the 'stark evidence of the *anorexia nervosa*,' and the power struggle between parent and child is clarified. As one anorexic triumphantly declared, 'They can force me to do anything they want, . . . but they can't make me swallow even a single mouthful more!' Family therapists also note the anorexic's adoption of the family habit of denial. When observers encourage her to seek help for her condition, the anorexic stubbornly insists that she is 'fine.' This attitude, combined with her passive resistance strategy, creates a resolve that therapists agree is among the most steadfast they encounter.

Anorexia may have roots in social forces beyond the family. Commentators agree that anorexia's overwhelmingly disproportionate gender distribution is probably attributable to sociocultural factors. As Bruch notes, '[t]o weigh less than is comfortable is an all-American preoccupation.' Cultural attitudes foster the notion that slimness will bring happiness and respect to the dissatisfied individual, and the young woman is a special target for this message. Fashion magazines, beauty pageants, the diet industry and the dance world all declare that 'the best women are rich and thin.' Given this environment, commentators ask, is it at all surprising that the anorexic expects to find salvation through her starvation?

Yet the phenomenon may be more complex than a mere wish to be fashionable. While the anorexic represents a caricature of the ethereal feminine ideal, her appearance also communicates a rejection of conventional expectations for women in our culture. Her act of physical regression has been interpreted as a refusal to assume the perceived burdens accompanying mature womanhood. Anorexic girls may be responding to mixed cultural commands concerning the broader issue of a woman's role in today's developed world. Intelligent and attractive adolescent females experience pressure to achieve dual, yet often contradictory, goals. They are encouraged to attain such traditional feminine ends as beauty, marriage and children, while at the same time they learn the importance of establishing themselves in a world of work that tends to measure achievement quite differently. The anorexic who belongs to a social class in which competition and goal attainment are stressed may be especially motivated to achieve a status that earns for her the admiration of others."

Rebecca Dresser continues by suggesting that only the socio-cultural model, whilst not being an exhaustive explanation, addresses the increased incidence of anorexia amongst women over recent years (thus providing a gendered analysis). Anorexia is not exclusively, but is principally, suffered by females, with some studies concluding that 90–95 per cent of sufferers are women.[5] The message of the images of slim beautiful models to which we are constantly exposed is that success depends upon achieving the same. Dieting, weight loss programmes and exercise regimes are normal practices for women who understand the standard by which we are measured and through that how to attain success. As Susie Orbach points out, the thin body of the anorexic is both femininity at its most exaggerated and a rejection of femininity as the female body loses its sexual characteristics.[6] The feminist socio-cultural model asserts that anorexia and bulimia arise out of normal feminine practices taken to their extreme:

S. ORBACH
Hunger Strike: The Anorectic's Struggle as a Metaphor for our Age[7]

"The anorectic woman, or rather the woman who finds an anorectic response, is in a sense echoing or proclaiming in an extreme form the actions, the fears, concerns, desires, hopes and wishes of women in general. The anorectic's attempts to change her body are in essence an exaggeration of the activities of all woman who must enter a society in which they are told that not only is their role specifically delineated, but success in that role relates in large part to the physical image they can create and project."[8]

The socio-cultural model rejects the medical explanation for anorexia and bulimia as representing a distinct pathology. Whilst dieting (and the see-sawing of denial and indulgence which accompanies it) may certainly be unhealthy, taken to its extreme "disordered eating" can cause permanent damage. Studies testify to the extent of dieting amongst women in Britain today, and the distorted image women have of our bodies, and by extension, ourselves which, at the extreme, takes the form of an "eating disorder". Susan Bordo explains that Body Image Distortion Syndrome (BIDS) has been considered clinically to be a symptom of anorexia but refers to studies which show that a "distorted" view of the size of our bodies is widespread amongst women. Susan Bordo argues that the ideal body is a fatless body and suggests that the anorexic is not seeing a distorted image of her body, but is seeing her body in comparison with the fatless ideal.

[5]   R. Dresser, "Article and Commentary on *Anorexia Nervosa*: Feeding the Hunger Artists: Legal Issues in Treating *Anorexia Nervosa*", *ibid.*, at 301.
[6]   S. Orbach, *Hunger Strike: The Anorectic's Struggle as a Metaphor for our Age* (Harmondsworth: Penguin, 1993), p. 66.
[7]   S. Orbach, *ibid.*, p. 85.
[8]   Susie Orbach's analysis of anorexia incorporates socio-cultural factors and psychoanalytic theory on the development of the self as a separate individual (thereby raising questions about the relationship between mothers and daughters).

S. Bordo
Unbearable Weight: Feminism, Western Culture and the Body[9]

"The feminist perspective on eating disorders, despite significant differences among individual writers, has in general been distinguished by a prima facie commitment both to taking the perceptions of women seriously and to the necessity of systemic social analysis. These regulatory assumptions have predisposed feminists to explore the so-called perceptual disturbances and cognitive distortions of eating disorders as windows opening onto problems in the social world, rather than as the patient's 'idiosyncratic' and 'idiopathic . . . distortions of data from the outside world.' From the latter perspective, when a patient complains that her breasts are too large and insists that the only way to succeed in our culture is to be thin because, as one woman described it, 'people . . . think that someone thin is automatically smarter and better,' it is described as flawed reasoning, a misperception of reality that the therapist must work to correct. From a feminist/cultural perspective, this approach ignores the fact that for most people in our culture, slenderness is indeed equated with competence, self-control, and intelligence, and feminine curvaceousness (in particular, large breasts) with wide-eyed, giggly vapidity.

Virtually every proposed hallmark of 'underlying psychopathology' in eating disorders has been deconstructed to reveal a more widespread *cultural* disorder. A dramatic example is the case of BIDS, or Body Image Distortion Syndrome, . . . BIDS has functioned to emphasise a discontinuity between anorexic and 'normal' attitudes toward weight and body image . . .

In 1984, however, a study conducted by *Glamour* magazine and analyzed by Susan Wooley and Wayne Wooley revealed that 75 per cent of the 53,000 women surveyed considered themselves 'too fat,' despite the fact that only one-quarter were deemed overweight by standard weight tables, and 30 per cent were actually *under-weight* . . . A study by Kevin Thompson, found that out of 100 women 'free of eating-disorder symptoms' more than 95 per cent overestimated their body size — on average one-fourth larger than they really were. Such findings, of course, made the postulation of strictly perceptual defect problematic — unless it was supposed that most American women were suffering from perceptual malfunction.

The clinical response to these studies was to transfer the site of 'distortion' from perceptual mechanism to affective/cognitive coloration: the contribution to perception of the mind's eye. According to this model, it is not that women actually *see* themselves as fat; rather, they evaluate what they see by painfully self-critical standards. Lack of self-esteem now became the cause of women's body-image problems: 'The better people feel about themselves,' as Thompson concluded, 'the less they tend to overestimate their size.' But women, as study after study has shown, do *not* feel very good about their bodies. Most women in our culture, then, are 'disordered' when it comes to issues of self-worth, self-entitlement, self-nourishment, and comfort with their own bodies; eating disorders, far from being 'bizarre' and anomalous, are utterly continuous with a dominant element of the experience of being female in this culture."

Susan Bordo considers BIDS as a paradigmatic example of the continuity between the beliefs held widely by women about their bodies and those of the anorexic. She gives other examples of "distorted beliefs" which she argues

[9] (Berkeley: University of California Press, 1993), pp. 54–57.

represent the reality for dieting women such as the power of forbidden foods, the need for complete control to maintain a diet and a dislike of being seen eating.[10]

Recently the courts have been forced to consider the legal position of the anorexic woman following referral by the medical profession of cases where the woman is refusing her consent to proposed treatment. The legal issues in these cases are different depending upon whether the anorexic is an adult or below the age of majority (18) as a consequence of the distinctions concerning the ability of adults and children to give and refuse their consent to medical treatment. The courts, whether considering the treatment of an adult or a minor, have accepted the medical model of anorexia. The legal process has provided no room for acknowledgement of socio-cultural factors.

10.1.i   *The law can make you eat*
The facts of *Re W (A Minor) (Medical Treatment: Court's Jurisdiction)*, the first occasion upon which the courts were asked to consider the legality of treatment in the light of the anorexic's refusal to eat, are given in the judgment of Lord Donaldson M.R.:

Re W (A Minor) (Medical Treatment: Court's Jurisdiction)
[1992] 4 All E.R. 627 at 629–630, CA, *per* Lord Donaldson M.R.

"Fate has dealt harshly with W. She is now aged 16, having been born on 31 March, 1976. She has an older sister, now aged 18, and a younger brother, now aged 13. In November 1981, when she was 5, her father died of a brain tumour and in September 1984, when she was 8, her mother died of cancer.

An aunt had been named as the testamentary guardian of the children but, through no fault of hers, was unable to care for them and they were received into the care of the local authority. That authority arranged for them to be temporarily fostered by a local doctor and three months later, in December 1984, they were moved to the home of their first permanent foster parents. Again W was singularly unlucky. She was bullied by an older child of the foster family and did not receive the protection from the foster parents which she deserved. As a result, in November 1987, she had to be referred to a family consultation clinic suffering from depression and a nervous tic.

In August 1988, when W was 12, it was appreciated that this fostering arrangement could not continue and she and the other children were moved to new foster parents. True to form, fate struck again when in December 1989 the new foster mother had to undergo surgery for breast cancer. This was followed in February 1990, when W was almost 14, by the death of her grandfather, to whom she was greatly attached. Indeed it may be that this was 'the last straw' for W.

Anorexia nervosa, which is W's current problem, first manifested itself in June 1990 when W became obsessive about her schoolwork, wanted to leave school and began losing weight. It should be stressed that anorexia nervosa is an illness which is not the fault of the sufferer. In this it is no different from pneumonia or appendicitis. It is, however, much more difficult to treat and cure, not least because one of its clinical

---

[10]   S. Bordo, *Unbearable Weight: Feminism, Western Culture and the Body, ibid.,* pp. 54–60.

manifestations, which is part and parcel of the disease, is a firm wish not to be cured, or at least not to be cured unless and until the sufferer wishes to cure herself. In this sense it is an addictive illness although, unlike other addictions such as drug taking, the sufferer is not to be blamed for having allowed herself to become addicted.

In September 1990 W was referred back to the clinic which had seen her three years before and began sessions with a clinical psychologist. Unfortunately this did not resolve the problem and in January 1991, when W was coming up towards her 15th birthday, it was necessary to resort to in-patient treatment. For this purpose she was admitted to a specialist residential unit for children and adolescents under the care of Dr M, a consultant psychiatrist whom she had first met when she had been referred to the family consultation clinic in 1987. Treatment was continued by the clinical psychologist who had previously been treating W. Whilst at this unit W displayed violence towards the staff and began injuring herself by picking her skin. This again is a symptomatic consequence of suffering from anorexia nervosa.

To add to W's problems, as if she had not enough already, the clinical psychologist treating W left the area in March 1991, W then being nearly 15, and was not replaced for five months.

By August 1991 W's condition had deteriorated to the point at which for a short time she had to be fed by nasogastric tube and have her arms encased in plaster. Although this was undoubtedly artificial feeding, contrary to some newspaper reports it was not 'forced feeding', because W consented to the insertion and use of such a tube. Again, contrary to those reports, W's arms were not encased in plaster without her consent. It was done to prevent her giving way to a compulsive wish to injure herself by picking at her skin.

W's chapter of misfortunes continued when, in September 1991, Dr M suffered a heart attack and contact between him and W was necessarily severed for some three months. Furthermore W's foster parents indicated at about this time that if W were discharged they could not continue to offer her a home. It is not wholly surprising, and is certainly not W's fault, that she remained in the grip of the disease, gradually losing weight or that on one occasion she used violence towards a member of the staff in circumstances which led to the police being called."

The local authority applied to the court under section 100 of the Children Act 1989 for an order that it could place W in a hospital and provide her with treatment if necessary without her consent. At that time the local authority did not have any specific treatment in mind but considered that "it was clearly possible that W might at any time refuse consent to some form of treatment, . . . because one of the symptoms of anorexia nervosa is a desire by the sufferer to 'be in control' and such a refusal would be an obvious way of demonstrating this".[11] Leave was granted and by the time of the hearing the local authority had identified a centre where they wished W to receive treatment if necessary without her consent. At first instance before the Family Division of the High Court, Thorpe J. held that he had the jurisdiction to make the orders sought and authorised her move and subsequent treatment.

The legal issues considered by the Court of Appeal were: first, whether the court could override W's refusal to consent to the proposed treatment (W

---

[11] *Re W (A Minor) (Medical Treatment: Court's Jurisdiction)* [1992] 4 All E.R. 627, at 630j–631a, *per* Lord Donaldson M.R.

wished to continue with her present course of treatment); secondly, if it could, what could it authorise? On the first question, Lord Donaldson M.R. was in no doubt that, whilst section 8 of the Family Law Reform Act 1969 provided a presumption that minors aged 16 and 17 were competent to give their consent to "surgical, medical and dental treatment", in those cases where a competent minor (17 or under) refused consent the court could give consent as could (obiter) anyone with parental authority (such as a parent, guardian or local authority). This has the effect of protecting the doctor from legal liability.[12] On the second issue, both of the alternatives considered by the court — leaving W where she was or transferring her to a specialist clinic in London — were supported by a responsible body of medical opinion. Lord Donaldson M.R. accepted the finding of Thorpe J. that W was competent, that she understood the nature and consequences of the proposed treatment (continuing with the present treatment or moving to a different centre) and of the implications of her refusal. However, his Lordship upheld the decision of Thorpe J. that W should be transferred to the London clinic. The decision of Lord Donaldson M.R. can be criticised as paternalistic in that it overrides W's fundamental right to self-determination.

J. BRIDGEMAN
"Old Enough to Know Best?"[13]

"Although their Lordships gave reasoned judgments, they are very much predicated upon the (understandable) wish to act on behalf of another whom they perceive to be in difficulty. This denies that other the right to exercise self-determination. The judgement shows the court taking a paternalistic approach, based on the assumption that treatment recommended by the medical profession must always be in the patient's best interests. The decision is disturbing in the extent to which it allows others to control the lives of teenagers when it would have been possible to reach a decision which gives young people greater control; and suggests that a re-appraisal of the relationship between the generations is required. The law has to be re-assessed to give young adults the self-determination which they deserve . . .

In reaching his conclusion in *Gillick*, Lord Scarman expressed the opinion that, 'the law relating to parent and child is concerned with the problems of growth and maturity of the human personality.' Despite echoing these sentiments, it seems to be this very process of growth and development that the conclusion reached in *Re W* ignored. The facts of the case itself, where a young woman was suffering from *anorexia*, illustrate this point. This illness is often suffered by young women who feel that there are great expectations placed upon them. One way for her to achieve, in a body image-conscious

---

[12]   Much has been written on the issues raised by this case with regard to parental rights and responsibilities and the participation of minors in decisions about their medical treatment. See, for example, J. Eekelaar, "White Coats or Flak Jackets? Doctors, Children and the Courts — Again?" (1993) 109 *Law Quarterly Review* 182; R. Thornton, "Minors and Medical Treatment — Who Decides?" [1993] *Cambridge Law Journal* 34; J. Bridgeman, "Old Enough to Know Best?" (1993) 13 *Legal Studies* 69.
[13]   J. Bridgeman, *ibid.*, at 69, 79.

society, is by denying herself food, taking the quest for a desired body shape further than everyone else, taking it to damaging extremes. Forcing treatment upon a young sufferer of *anorexia* merely reinforces her lack of self-confidence by taking this decision out of her control, and denies her the capacity for self-directed action which must be developed if she is to recover from this illness. W was suffering from *anorexia* as a result of circumstances which seem to be entirely different; as a result of a series of sad and unfortunate events which, in the words of Dr G, a consultant psychiatrist specialising in *anorexia nervosa*, resulted in what he considered to be an understandable condition of, '. . . fear of losing control of her eating and thus developing into an adult woman, which makes her fight against her ever-present hunger . . .' As Lord Donaldson said, 'Fate has dealt harshly with W'. *Anorexia* can be caused by a number of different factors but W, like the young women described above, wanted some degree of self-determination and control over her own life. She emphasised that she wished to stay in the adolescent psychiatric unit and decide for herself when she would eat. The law should have respected this. Hilda Bruch makes the point that control over their selves is important to anorexics,

> 'Though anorexic patients may die from their condition it is not death they are after but the urgent need to be in control of their own lives and have a sense of identity.'

It must seem to W that the legal system, in taking this control from her, dealt harshly with her."

Margaret Brazier and Caroline Bridge consider *Re W* to be one example of a number of cases in which the judiciary has overridden what the court had concluded to be autonomous choices in order to facilitate treatment.[14] They argue that the decision in *Re W* amounted to giving doctors the power to determine the competence of minors on the basis of outcome, which may come down to "whether or not others approve the outcome of that decision"[15] — which, in W's case they did not. They suggest that the cases concerning the treatment of anorexics raise fundamental questions about adolescent autonomy and suggest that an essential aspect of autonomy is making a true choice. Drawing upon the arguments of John Harris in *The Value of Life*,[16] Brazier and Bridge provide an analysis of adolescent autonomy which may enable a reappraisal of *Re W* but which certainly demonstrates the criticisms which can be levelled at the reasoning of the Court of Appeal. John Harris, they explain, argues that fully autonomous choice is an ideal, frequently not attained. However, only if that choice is defective through "defects in control, defects in reasoning, defects in information and defects in stability" should it not be respected.

---

[14] M. Brazier & C. Bridge, "Coercion or Caring: analysing adolescent autonomy" (1996) 16 *Legal Studies* 84.
[15] M. Brazier & C. Bridge, *ibid.*, at 90.
[16] J. Harris, *The Value of Life* (London: Routledge, 1985).

M. Brazier & C. Bridge
"Coercion or Caring: analysing adolescent autonomy"[17]

"What constitutes autonomous choice? . . . The moral philosopher, John Harris suggests that fully autonomous choice is largely an ideal. Control of destiny is in practical terms often beyond our power. The best we can manage is a maximally autonomous choice. In determining whether a particular individual choice demands respect we should look to see whether that choice is undermined by any irremediable defect in the autonomy of the choice in question. Harris identifies *four* different kinds of defect, defects in control, defects in reasoning, defects in information and defects in stability. A defect in control arises most obviously in cases where an individual suffers from some recognised mental disorder . . . Harris, . . ., stress[es] that the presence of mental disability does not itself indicate a defect in control, an incapacity to choose. The disability must be such as to affect the particular decision in question by depriving the patient of insight into her condition, or imposing a compulsion which negates choice. Harris however would not limit the impact of defects in control to persons affected by mental disability. Addiction to drugs or food or drink may be such as to prevent the sufferer breaking free of addiction however much he may desire to do so. A 'current preference' destroys the person's ability to promote her true choices.

Defects in control can affect adults as much as minors. But minors may be susceptible to pressures less likely to affect the older person. The 15-year-old is likely to be more heavily influenced by parental wishes than the 25-year-old. An apparent choice based on conscience may more readily be perceived as subject to parental control. Yet totally arbitrary age limits lack rationality. The 19-year-old who has never left home, has been brought up in a strict environment and 'protected' from external influence, may have infinitely less control over her choices than many 15-year-olds growing up in more liberal homes.

Defects in reasoning, according to Harris, may also vitiate, or partially vitiate, an apparent choice. Harris gives an example of someone who declares that she smokes because 'there's no harm in it'. The premise on which she bases her choice is manifestly wrong and no true choice exists. This does not mean to say an autonomous choice must be an objectively rational choice. A Jehovah's Witness who refuses blood because of his belief that the Bible prohibits transfusion may be viewed as irrational by other Christians who dispute his interpretation of the texts, or by atheists who regard belief in God as irrational. There is no defect in his reasoning. He advances a cogent explanation for his choice of faith above the consequences of refusing blood.

As with defects in control, defects in reasoning are by no means the preserve of minors. They may be more likely in youth. Impetuosity may cause the younger person to defy reason. A 15-year-old girl might declare that all this rubbish about cervical cancer and early sexual intercourse is invented by 'oldies' to destroy her pleasure and found her choice to go on the Pill on that basis. Conversely she might adhere to the myth that pregnancy is not possible if sexual intercourse takes place standing up. In both cases a defect in reasoning undermines the validity of her choice. The problem then becomes in what circumstances the defect is so significant as to destroy the validity of the choice altogether. Harris acknowledges we all on occasion act on caprice and recognises caprice as a valid element of choice. The difference lies between the individual who recognises and chooses her caprice, and her sister who truly but mistakenly believes that she has good reason for her choice.

---

[17] M. Brazier & C. Bridge, *supra*, n. 14 at 91–93.

Defects in control and reasoning can, Harris suggests, negate an apparently autonomous choice, and justify paternalistic intervention. The final two categories of defects in autonomy, in information and stability pose greater problems. A choice based on false or incomplete information is not a true choice. But the remedy is self-evident. The defect in information must be corrected. That may justify short-term paternalistic action. If a patient exercises a choice to operate at a time when she will not be competent, for example, when she will be anaesthetised or in a coma, and that choice is based on erroneous information, action may have to be taken at a time when it is impossible to remedy the defect in information. So if a patient refusing blood . . . has been given incomplete information about the efficacy of substitutes for blood, a gamble must be taken. How would she have chosen on the basis of complete and adequately explained information? If she is allowed to die, no one will ever know. If she receives a transfusion and recovers the blood cannot be removed from her. The law, whether with adults or minors, has to decide where to place the benefit of the doubt.

Defects in information may well be especially relevant in cases involving younger patients. Lack of experience may result in inadequate information, communication between older professionals and child patients may be perceived as poor, and in particular instances the individual child's own circumstances may have deprived her of the opportunity to be fully informed on the matter now demanding choice. Acknowledging the reality of defects in information should not however lead to an automatic judgment to overrule a minor's choice. Steps must rather be taken to ensure that both on a general and an individual level young people are better informed about health care choices. Accurate information is just as crucial to valid choice where the teenager is consenting to treatment as when she rejects treatment.

Harris's final category of defect in autonomy concerns defects in stability which may be seen as peculiarly pertinent to younger patients. Values and preferences change over time. Judgments of all kinds made in youth may be regretted at 40. Harris rejects any argument that a defect in stability should be allowed to justify others to overrule an autonomous choice. He argues:

> 'Autonomy is the running of one's own life according to one's lights. The fact that these lights change colour and intensity over time is no evidence at all that the later lights are either better or more "one's own" than the earlier ones. They're just different. To be autonomous, self-determined, just is to be able to do as one wishes-not to be able to do as one will wish at some future time.'

He adds two other cogent arguments. If defects in stability are generally considered sufficient to undermine autonomous choice, only the choice of the very old can be considered maximally autonomous. The authors may regret choices made by them at 18 now both have reached middle age. Who is to say we will not equally regret choices made in our forties when we reach pensionable age? Harris cites Mill. The capacity to make choices like all 'human faculties of perception, discriminative feeling, mental activity and even moral choice are exercised only in making a choice'. Autonomy has to be learned through experience. Lord Scarman's concept of evolving autonomy receives powerful backing.

Defects in stability *per se* then should not undermine autonomous choice and justify paternalist intervention. The logic of the argument advanced by Harris is impeccable. Parental feeling may provoke dissent. Teenage choices are notoriously unstable. Where a choice has irreversible consequences the temptation to take some account of defects in stability in nigh on irresistible. At least two considerations should be taken into account in an attempt to resist that temptation. First, in individual cases apparent defects in stability should be analysed fully. Is the apparent defect in stability in reality a much more fundamental defect in information and/or experience? A teenager who has never experienced a loving, stable home, who has never found psychological peace with himself, lacks information on which to make certain choices. He suffers from more than the usual fickleness of youth. Second, if all that is at stake is 'youthful impetuosity or caprice' before acting on that defect in stability in cases relating to medical treatment, the law should review its attitude to age and other choices. Marriage is permitted at 16. Heterosexual teenagers can legally consent to sexual intercourse at 16. At 16 the law permits the purchase of cigarettes, a lethal substance. Criminal responsibility is imposed at 10 providing that the child is found capable of knowing right from wrong. The law affirms several choices made at a time of perceived instability. Is patient autonomy so totally different in nature?"

In this analysis the decision of W may be seen not to be an autonomous decision because of a defect in control or a defect in reasoning. As such her decision could be overridden without infringing her rights.

The Court of Appeal perceived W to be a competent individual making an autonomous choice, but to respect her decision as that of an autonomous individual would have left W where she was, continuing to receive what seemed to be unsuccessful treatment. Determining that consent could be obtained from anyone with parental responsibility enabled Lord Donaldson M.R. to give effect to the wishes of the medical profession as to what in its opinion was in W's "best interests". In their analysis of *Re W*, Nigel Lowe and Satvinder Juss also accord primacy to the medical view of what was best:

N. LOWE & S. JUSS
"Medical Treatment — Pragmatism and the Search for Principle"[18]

"Can it humanely be argued, in these circumstances, that the court ought not to have intervened? We agree with Ward J. (in *Re E (A Minor)* (1990) 9 B.M.L.R. 1) that a court should be slow to let a child martyr himself. To those who question how a child can be held able to give a valid consent yet be unable to exercise a power of veto, we would reply that there *is* a rational distinction to be made between giving consent and withholding it. We must start with the assumption that a doctor will act in the best interests of his patient. Hence, if the doctor believes that a particular treatment is necessary for his patient, it is perfectly rational for the law to facilitate this as easily as possible and hence allow a '*Gillick* competent' child to give a valid consent, and also to protect the child against parents opposed to what is professionally considered to be in its best medical interests. In contrast, it is surely right for the law to be reluctant to allow a *child* of whatever age to be able to veto treatment designed for his or her benefit, particularly if a refusal would lead to the child's death or permanent damage."

---

[18]   (1993) 56 *Modern Law Review* 865 at 871–872.

Lowe and Juss also ask, "[i]s autonomy meaningful if it is irrational?"[19] given that, in the words of Lord Donaldson M.R., "it is a feature of anorexia nervosa that it is capable of destroying the ability to make an informed choice. It creates a compulsion to refuse treatment or only to accept treatment which is likely to be ineffective. This attitude is part and parcel of the disease and the more advanced the illness, the more compelling it may become."[20]

Maureen Mulholland points out that W's refusal was not completely irrational:

M. MULHOLLAND
"Re W (A Minor): autonomy, consent and the anorexic teenager"[21]

"Here the treatment proposed for W was a different sort of treatment from that which she had been receiving, involving different carers and a different location. Her objections to this move were based on not entirely irrational arguments. She had become attached to the clinic and the staff there and felt that she still had some control over her own condition — a control which would be denied or threatened if, against her will, she were to be transferred to the eating disorders unit."

Judith Masson criticises the unquestioning acceptance of the views of the experts[22]:

J. MASSON
"Re W: appealing from the golden cage"[23]

"The court heard evidence from Dr M, a consultant psychiatrist who was treating J, Dr G, the consultant in charge of the proposed London hospital unit, and Dr D, a consultant psychiatrist with special experience in the field of anorexia nervosa. Initially, Dr D supported J's remaining under Dr M's care but subsequently changed his mind. The court was influenced by the failure of Dr M to make progress with J's treatment and the lack of control the unit appeared to have over her. There is no evidence that it weighed other elements of the respective treatments, their theoretical basis or their success rates. The decision may have been a vote of confidence in Dr M or acceptance of Dr D's advice based on his discussions about (but not with) J.

J was not refusing all treatment although there were clear doubts about her true willingness to comply with the requirements of her current placement. Her weight had fallen to an extremely low level and she was refusing all solid food. Something clearly needed to be done. However, it was not clear that a compulsory move to the London

---

[19] N. Lowe & S. Juss, "Medical Treatment — Pragmatism and the Search for Principle", *ibid.*, at 871.
[20] *Re W (A Minor) (Medical Treatment: Court's Jurisdiction)*, *supra*, n. 11 at 637e, *per* Lord Donaldson M.R. at 637e.
[21] (1993) 9 *Professional Negligence* 21 at 23.
[22] In this extract "W" is referred to as "J" which was the initial by which she was referred to in the first newspaper reports of this case.
[23] (1993) 5 J.C.L. 37 at 38–39.

unit would necessarily improve her condition. Palmer comments that there is a lack of good comparative data on different treatments but suggests that a positive outcome may depend less on the details of the regime than on the extent to which it is enthusiastically and thoroughly carried out. J did not want to go to the new unit and felt she had a good relationship with her current therapist. She might, therefore, be even less co-operative there than where she was currently placed. There is no clear evidence that success rates are improved for anorexic patients treated compulsorily. Furthermore, maintaining links with her home area would be difficult while she was in London, conversely it would be a considerable burden on her future foster parents to attend outpatient clinics in London after she left the hospital. The decision to support her transfer looks more like a decision of last resort than an objective assessment of what was in J's best interests. Indeed, if any weight is to be given to a child's wishes it would seem appropriate to do so here because the advantages of two alternatives are unquantified.

If courts, doctors, parents or local authorities are going to claim the power to override a child's decision it would seem reasonable to expect them objectively to demonstrate that their decision is likely to produce an objectively better outcome for the child. They might do this by comparing the likely outcomes of their proposed solution and indicating their decision-making experience showing their past judgmental successes. Their fears about the possible consequences of a child's choice should not be determinative unless they can show objectively (or statistically) that the outcome of the child's choice is demonstrably worse. In the case of anorexic patients the least that might be expected on this basis is that the patient's choice was more likely to result in death or permanent physical harm and less likely to result in a long-term cure than that of the doctor. Applying this test, it would be hard (on the evidence before the court) to justify any decision other than the child's in this case. The court's (and the local authority's) reliance on the doctors seems misplaced without information about their judgment and treatment successes in the past, particularly given the complete change of views of one of the experts. The court's failure to explain logically the legal basis on which it sought to override J's wishes and its rather uncritical approach to the medical opinions might suggest that its decision, though clearly paternalistic, was no more likely than J's to promote her welfare."

Lord Donaldson explained why he considered that an alternative legal response—use of the Mental Health Act 1983—should be avoided:

Re W (A Minor) (Medical Treatment: Court's Jurisdiction)
[1992] 4 All E.R. 627 at 639d–e, *per* Lord Donaldson M.R.

"The provisions of the Mental Health Acts were not considered in any detail in the course of the argument. Suffice it to say that in some circumstances they authorise treatment despite the objections of the patient, whether minor or adult. Probably they would have had no application to W, but even where they are applicable it may be in the long-term interests of the minor that if the same treatment can be secured upon some other basis this shall be done. Although mental illness should not be regarded as any different from physical illness, it is not always so viewed by the uninformed and the fact that in later life it might become known that a minor had been treated under the Acts might redound to his or her disadvantage."

Margaret Brazier and Caroline Bridge argue that, in an effort to avoid using the provisions of the Mental Health Act 1983, the Court of Appeal made inappropriate use of the principles of the common law to achieve its desired outcome[24]:

M. BRAZIER & C. BRIDGE
"Coercion or Caring: analysing adolescent autonomy"[25]

"The Mental Health Act provides for hospital admission for assessment and treatment for mental disorder without the consent of the patient and there is no statutory bar to the civil commitment of a minor. Thus under the Act a child can be provided with prompt treatment in an appropriate setting, removing the burden of responsibility, (temporarily) away from the child and her family, yet providing the safeguards of the Act, including the Mental Health Act Commission and the mental health review tribunal, safeguards against inappropriate psychiatric treatment not present under procedures initiated under the Children Act. Age alone is a strange criterion for determining how to treat mental disorder. Brenda Hoggett predicted that, after the Children Act, 'it may be necessary to invoke the Mental Health Act procedures a little more frequently than has previously been thought.' Her prediction has failed to materialise because of judicial fear of stigmatisation of young people treated under that legislation. Yet stigmatisation is a self-fulfilling prophecy. Judges resorting to that argument to invoke child law procedures to deal with mental disorder implicitly endorse the stigma. If treatment is not successful fairly swiftly, at 18 the teenage patient will have either to confront the 'stigma' or go untreated. And the principles developed by the courts to assist the disturbed child equally undermine the autonomy of his 'normal' sibling. Yet the courts continue to prefer child welfare means of securing the welfare of the mentally ill teenager . . .

The judicial retreat from *Gillick* and the consequent attack on adolescent autonomy was motivated by diverse concerns. Misunderstanding of what constitutes maximally autonomous choice resulted in judges apparently overruling 'competent' choices which analysis shows to be in no real sense autonomous choice. Anxiety about the impact of invoking Mental Health Act procedures to protect minors caused judges to seek means to attain that Act's ends by different means. Many difficult cases relating to minors could be properly resolved once the law comprehends more fully the concept of autonomy and overcomes fears of stigmatisation in relation to mental illness. One problem however defies any neat solution. If an adolescent has made an autonomous choice, if he suffers from no mental disability, can society bring itself to endorse an outcome the vast majority of the community reject? Eekelaar offers a model of dynamic self-

---

[24]   A further worrying legal development has arisen in the case of C (aged 16), in which Wall J. in the High Court gave consent to detain C against her will in a treatment centre to provide her with feeding treatment and to the use of reasonable force to detain her there (*Re C* (1997) 5 Med. L. Rev. 227). The judge, Wall J., is reported to have said that he had "no doubt" as to his powers not only to authorise detention, but also to authorise the use of reasonable force to keep C at the clinic (*The Independent*, March 13, 1997). His Lordship stated that the court also had the power to authorise the use of force in the provision of treatment, although it was not appropriate to do so in the case before him. The same issue—how to carry out the treatment if the "patient" does not wish to comply—has arisen in relation to court-ordered caesarian sections, discussed in Chap. 6.

[25]   M. Brazier & C. Bridge, *supra*, n. 14 at 97, 109.

determinism which reconciles best interests and autonomy in many, many instances. He imposes a final *caveat*. An apparently autonomous choice by a minor may be overridden where such a choice threatens the child's *self-interest*. His proposition begs the question of who defines that self-interest . . . If society is not prepared to allow adolescents to court unfavourable outcomes in judgments relating to medical treatment, we should say so openly. The law should not pretend to apply a 'functional' test of autonomy to every patient when younger patients are in fact subjected to an 'outcome' test."

When the treatment of adults is at issue, the Mental Health Act has been the very instrument employed to enable the medical profession to treat a refusing anorexic. Thus, Margaret Brazier and Caroline Bridge rightly point out that the lengths to which Lord Donaldson M.R. went in *Re W* in order to avoid using the Mental Health Act 1983 may have been in vain given that that this is the mechanism employed in order to facilitate the treatment of a competent, but refusing, adult patient. Cases in which this situation has arisen will be considered before turning to the ways in which a feminist socio-cultural account can inform our understanding of the law's engagement with the anorexic.

10.1.ii *Food for body and mind*

Competent adult patients have an absolute right to give or refuse their consent to treatment. In a different context, Lord Donaldson M.R. in *Re T*,[26] affirmed what he referred to as the "absolute right" of a competent patient to determine the medical treatment received:

Re T (An Adult) (Consent to Medical Treatment)
[1992] 3 W.L.R. 782 at 786H, *per* Lord Donaldson M.R.

"An adult patient who, like Miss T, suffers from no mental incapacity, has an absolute right to choose whether to consent to medical treatment, to refuse it or to choose one rather than another of the treatments being offered . . . This right of choice is not limited to decisions which others might regard as sensible. It exists notwithstanding that the reasons for making the choice are rational, irrational, unknown or even non-existent."

Likewise, the House of Lords in *Airedale N.H.S. Trust v. Bland*,[27] confirmed that a competent adult patient is at liberty to give or refuse their consent to medical treatment, even if a refusal may result in adverse consequences or even death. Lord Keith went as far as to say that:

---

[26] *Re T (An Adult) (Consent to Medical Treatment)* [1992] 3 W.L.R. 782.
[27] *Airedale NHS Trust v. Bland* [1993] 3 W.L.R. 316.

Airedale NHS Trust v. Bland
[1993] 3 W.L.R. 316 at 360H, *per* Lord Keith

". . . it is unlawful, so as to constitute both a tort and the crime of battery, to administer medical treatment to an adult, who is conscious and of sound mind, without his consent: *In Re F (Mental Patient: Sterilisation)* [1990] 2 A.C. 1. Such a person is *completely* at liberty to decline treatment, even if the result of his doing so will be that he will die." (emphasis added)

However, where the patient is detained under the Mental Health Act 1983, her consent may, in certain circumstances, be unnecessary. In *Riverside Mental Health NHS Trust v. Fox*,[28] the question was whether a 37 year-old woman, Caroline Fox, could be force-fed despite her refusal. The Court of Appeal quashed the declaration of the High Court that it would be lawful, on a technicality. This was because it was effectively an "interim" declaration (a declaration for the time being, given until all parties could be heard), made pending a determination of the matter at a full hearing, and there is no possibility of such a declaration in law. Caroline Fox was detained under section 3 of the Mental Health Act 1983. The declaration sought, and granted, by the Family Division of the High Court contained a number of alternative propositions to the effect that feeding Caroline Fox without her consent was medical treatment for her mental disorder under section 63 of the Mental Health Act 1983 and was, consequently, lawful.[29] Margaret Brazier explains the requirements for admission for treatment under section 3 and for compulsory treatment under section 63. For section 3 to apply anorexia must be a mental illness. Mental illness is not defined in the Act (although anorexia is classified as a mental illness by the World Health Organisation) and whether anorexia is a mental illness is a matter of clinical judgment. It is important to note Brazier's view that these provisions will ordinarily only authorise the compulsory treatment of a very few people and yet they seem now, with the sanction of the Court of Appeal, to be widely used in the treatment of anorexics.

---

[28] *Riverside Mental Health NHS Trust v. Fox* [1994] 1 F.L.R. 614.
[29] Wall J., in the Family Division, held that, although the court did not have the power to make an interim declaration, the declaration was a final declaration made *ex parte* and that, following the case of *Re S*, the court did have the jurisdiction to make a final declaration *ex parte* "where matters of life and death are concerned". Gillian Douglas in her commentary in *Family Law* states that "[t]he effect of the court's judgment is therefore to require that, except in cases of urgent necessity, such as *Re S (Adult: Surgical Treatment)*, there should be an *inter partes* hearing to deal properly with the substantive question and then a final declaration made, if appropriate" (1994) 24 *Family Law* 321). This demonstrates the impact which one case (such as *Re S*, discussed in Chap. 6) may have upon the development of the law.

M. BRAZIER
Medicine, Patients and the Law[30]

"*Mental Health Act 1983*
Part II of the Act makes provision for the detention in hospital of certain mentally disordered patients. Only a tiny minority of patients with mental disorder are in fact detained in hospital under the Act. An application for admission for assessment (observation and tests) must be based on the written recommendations of two medical practitioners who testify that the patient (1) is suffering from mental disorder of a nature warranting his detention in hospital, at least for a limited period, and (2) ought to be so detained in the interests of his own health or safety, or to protect others. Admission for the assessment authorises the patient's detention for twenty-eight days. If he is to be detained longer an application for admission for treatment must be made. Such an application made under section 3 of the Act must be founded on grounds that the patient:

(a) ... is suffering from mental illness, severe mental impairment, psychopathic disorder or mental impairment and his mental disorder is of a nature or degree which makes it appropriate for him to receive treatment in a mental hospital; *and*

(b) in the case of psychopathic disorder or mental impairment, such treatment is likely to alleviate or prevent a deterioration in his condition; *and*

(c) it is necessary for the health and safety of the patient or for the protection of other persons that he should receive such treatment and it cannot be provided unless he is detained under this section.

'Severe mental impairment' is defined as 'a state of arrested or incomplete development of mind which includes severe impairment of intelligence and social functioning'. 'Mental impairment' is similarly defined, save that impairment need not be severe. Where the grounds for detention are based either on degree of mental impairment or on psychopathic disorder there must additionally be evidence of 'abnormally aggressive or seriously irresponsible conduct'.

The number of mentally handicapped individuals eligible to be detained under the Act is thus small ... Only the most dangerously disordered and profoundly handicapped patients will be detained in hospital under the Act ...

Part IV of the Mental Health Act provides for the compulsory treatment of that minority of patients detained under the Act ... Section 63 provides that:

'The consent of a patient shall not be required for any medical treatment given to him for the mental disorder from which he is suffering, not being treatment given within section 57 or 58 [of the Act].'

Section 63 applies to detained patients only. It cannot be used on voluntary patients, or on an out-patient basis. ... Section 63 could be used to dispense with a patient's consent to treatment only where that patient actually needed to be detained in hospital. If he did not need to be so detained, the conditions laid down in section 3 for admission

---

[30] (Harmondsworth: Penguin, 1992), pp. 104–106.

for treatment were not met, and the use of section 3 to enforce treatment was an unlawful fiction.

Section 63 thus authorises routine psychiatric treatment. As I said earlier, it cannot be used to authorise treatment for physical illness; it applies only to treatment for mental disorder."

The Court of Appeal in *Fox* set aside the order on the grounds that the court did not have the jurisdiction to make an interim order, but nevertheless approved of the use of court declarations in such circumstances by expressly stating that, should Fox's condition not improve, a further application should be made by the health authority.

Riverside Mental Health NHS Trust v. Fox
[1994] 1 F.L.R. 614 at 621, *per* Sir Stephen Brown P.

"A case of this nature raises difficult and sensitive considerations. This court appreciates, as do all the Divisions of the High Court, that the position of doctors treating patients in certain circumstances is exceptionally difficult. The dilemmas which confront them are very real. They are aware of the fact that there are legal restraints in relation to certain aspects of possible treatment. They, therefore, seek on occasions to avail themselves of the declaratory jurisdiction of the High Court. As will be recalled, Lord Bridge of Harwich in the case of *Re F (Mental Patient: Sterilisation)* [1990] 2 A.C. 52; [1989] 2 F.L.R. 376 indicated the very real dilemma which confronts doctors in these difficult situations. However, situations vary. Happily we have been told by counsel for the Health Trust in this case that the condition of this patient has not, in fact, required the forcible feeding which had been contemplated and that she has, in fact, put on some weight. That fortunately removes some of the stress from this present appeal. But this court is left to decide the question as to whether the judge, Stuart-White J., had jurisdiction to make the order which he purported to make. I have to say that both counsel have agreed that there is no such concept known to the law as an interim declaration. It is clear to me that the judge did, in effect, seek to make an interim declaration. It cannot be regarded as a final declaration . . .

In my judgment, the order should have been set aside by Wall J. The appeal should therefore be allowed and the order set aside. Having said that, it should be borne in mind that it may be necessary, in case the condition of this patient does not continue to improve, for the Health Trust to consider making a further application *inter partes*."

The judgment does not tell us why Caroline Fox started to eat but her decision to do so raises questions about the power of the law in cases such as hers. It also raises the possibility that being told by medical carers that if consent is not given they will use the provisions within the Mental Health Act 1983 or obtain a declaration of the court, might be a very persuasive way of securing the co-operation of the patient in the proposed treatment. Andrew Grubb, in his commentary upon the case, notes that the declaration explicitly sanctioned force by stating that, in the circumstances, forced-feeding would be lawful. Grubb states that "[i]t seems an anathema to speak of medical treatment that is forced upon the patient. How can this be consistent with the well-recognised fact that treatment is a co-operative process between doctor and patient? However, the use of force must logically be 'part and parcel' of a court order that supports treatment without the patient's consent."[31]

The subsequent case of *South West Hertfordshire Health Authority v. KB*[32] concerned 18½ year-old K Brady who had had anorexia since she was 14. At the time of the application she, like Caroline Fox, was detained under section 3 of the Mental Health Act 1983. A declaration of the court was sought to the effect that feeding her by naso-gastric tube without her consent would be lawful. The health authority argued (i) that feeding by nasogastric tube was medical treatment for her mental disorder which could be carried out without her consent under section 63 of the Mental Health Act 1983; and (ii) under common law K lacked the capacity to give or refuse her consent to treatment.

South West Hertfordshire Health Authority v. KB
[1994] 2 F.C.R. 1051 at 1053, *per* Ewbank J.

"There are two approaches made by the health authority. The first is the statutory approach and the other is the common law approach. Section 63 of the Mental Health Act 1983, it is submitted, is the section which applies to this case. This reads:

> 'The consent of a patient shall not be required for any medical treatment given to him for a mental disorder from which he is suffering if the treatment is given by or under the direction of a responsible medical officer.'

Medical treatment is interpreted in s.145 of the Act as including nursing, care, habilitation and rehabilitation under medical supervision. Habilitation is defined in the Shorter Oxford Dictionary as the action of enabling or endowing with ability or fitness, capacitation, qualification.

It is agreed that feeding by naso-gastric tube is medical treatment and was so held to be in the case of *Airedale NHS Trust v. Bland* [1994] 1 F.C.R. 485. It is said by the health authority that the feeding by tube is given to K for the mental disorder from which she is suffering. On behalf of K it is said that that is not so. The feeding is for physical symptoms, not for mental illness. The feeding is to increase her weight and is not being given for the mental disorder as required under the Act.

On behalf of the health authority it is pointed out that the mental disorder from which she suffers is anorexia nervosa which is an eating disorder and relieving symptoms is just as much a part of treatment as relieving the underlying cause. If the symptoms are exacerbated by the patient's refusal to eat and drink, the mental disorder becomes progressively more and more difficult to treat and so the treatment by nasogastric tube is an integral part of the treatment of the mental disorder itself. It is also said that the treatment is necessary in order to make psychiatric treatment of the underlying cause possible at all.

This argument, in my judgment, is correct and makes it clear that feeding by naso-

---

[31] A. Grubb, Commentary on *Riverside Mental Health NHS Trust v. Fox* (1994) 2 Med. L. Rev. 97 at 99.
[32] *South West Hertfordshire Authority v. KB* [1994] 2 F.C.R. 1051.

gastric tube in the circumstances of this type of case is treatment envisaged under s.63 and does not require the consent of the patient."

Although Ewbank J. thought that K lacked the capacity to refuse consent, he based his decision upon the first point which was sufficient for the purposes of securing the forced feeding sought within the application. The *Brady* decision, therefore, provides the answer to the problem originally raised in *Fox*, extending the treatment which can be lawfully provided under the Mental Health Act 1983 from treatment for mental illness itself to treatment of the symptoms of the mental illness and to treatment necessary before treatment for the mental illness can be effectively given.

A. GRUBB
(1994) 2 Med. L. Rev. 208 at 209–210

"This case confirms that a patient suffering from anorexia nervosa may be force fed without her consent under the provisions of the Mental Health Act 1983. Ewbank J. confirmed the view of the trial judge and the assumption of the Court of Appeal in *Riverside Mental Health NHS Trust v. Fox* [1994] 1 F.L.R. 614 and (1994) 2 Med. L. Rev. 95 that force feeding is 'medical treatment given to [the patient] for a mental disorder' under s.63 of the 1983 Act . . .

The upshot is, therefore, that an anorectic patient may be comprehensively treated under the Mental Health Act even if competent. However, there is a well-taken argument that such patients may lack competence if their decision to refuse food is based upon a compulsive will or a delusion of their physical condition or prognosis . . . And, as if to find solace in the patient's incompetence, Ewbank J. decided that the patient was, in fact, not competent to refuse treatment relying on the evidence of the consultant psychiatrist. She stated that 'the patient did not understand her true position: the patient thought she was fat (which was plainly wrong); she saw death as a long term or theoretical prospect' when it had been explained to her she would die within 14–21 days. On this basis the judge was, perhaps, justified in his conclusion . . . [However, the] point Ewbank J. seems to have in his mind is the old one that the mentally ill are *ipso facto* incompetent to consent or (more importantly) refuse consent to treatment for their mental disorder. This is wrong, has long been shown (and accepted) to be so, and is inconsistent with the consent provisions in Part IV of the Mental Health Act 1983. The patient in *Brady* may have been incompetent to refuse consent but it was not simply because she was suffering from a mental disorder which needed treatment. It was because of her lack of understanding. Anyway, treatment for her mental disorder was justified regardless of this fact under the 1983 Act as a special case where competence is irrelevant."

As implied in this commentary, there is every possibility that the use of the Mental Health Act 1983 will (wrongly) lead to the view that the anorexic not only has a mental illness but, because of that mental illness, is incompetent to make decisions regarding her treatment. In his commentary on *Brady*, Andrew Grubb argues that the interpretation given to "medical treatment . . . for mental disorder" in section 63 of the Mental Health Act 1983 to include forced-feeding of an anorexic is "eminently sensible".[33] This was the interpretation required to give effect to the treatment proposed by the medical profession.[34]

10.1.iii *The limits of care*

Facilitating the forced-feeding of women with anorexia may achieve the goal of weight increase but may also increase the woman's feelings of lack of control which could be at the heart of her condition. Forced-feeding is brutal and invasive. It constitutes a violent infringement of the bodily integrity of a competent adult and must surely result in a loss of trust in her medical carers. The anorexic prompts a strong emotional response in those with whom she comes into contact. We understand her pursuit of thinness, for we also live in the culture where a fatless body is the ideal. However, the extent to which she is able to deny herself food suggests that there is something very different about her. As Susie Orbach explains, our response to this person who has taken her denial of food to such extremes is to force food upon her and, faced with her determined rejection, to seek to overcome her refusal:

S. ORBACH

Hunger Strike: The Anorectic's Struggle as a Metaphor for our Age[35]

"Anorexia is a spectacular and dramatic symptom. To encounter an anorectic woman is to be confronted with turbulent and confusing feelings. These feelings can be so uncomfortable that one is inclined to try to distance oneself from the experience by various means. Unknowingly one moves into the role of the spectator. A sense of bewilderment, linked with a desire to understand, shortly turns to discomfort. One begins to look upon the anorectic and the anorexia uncomprehendingly. Compassion turns to fear and a wish for distance; a need to disassociate oneself from the painful sight. The anorectic is rarely engaged with, especially not about her experience of anorexia. Turning anorexia into an exotic state, with the attendant labelling and judging, substitutes for engagement. By these means a distance is created between oneself and the anorectic.

---

[33] A. Grubb, (1994) 2 Med. L. Rev. 208 at 209. In *Tameside and Glossop Acute Services Trust v. CH* (1996) 4 Med. L. Rev. 193, CH was suffering from paranoid schizophrenia and detained under section 3. In the thirty-first week of her pregnancy there was evidence that the foetus was not growing normally and her obstetrician believed that unless a caesarian section was performed the foetus would die. Her medication had been interrupted as a consequence of her pregnancy and her doctors feared that she might resist surgical intervention should it, in their opinion, become necessary. This view was taken as a result of her resistance to the monitoring of her pregnancy because of delusions that the medical professionals were attempting to harm her foetus. Wall J. held that a caesarian could be performed under section 63 as "medical treatment for mental disorder" upon the evidence that birth of a healthy child would improve her condition whilst its death would prove detrimental to her. This case develops from the wide interpretation given to the statutory provisions in *Brady*.

[34] In comparison, the doctors caring for the anorexic woman Nikki Hughes respected her refusal of consent to feeding as a competent refusal. They also felt that they could not use the Mental Health Act. She subsequently died (*The Guardian*, January 4, 1996).

[35] S. Orbach, *supra*, n. 6 at pp 78–80.

This distance is sought because in reality, there is a painful continuity between most women's daily experience and that of the anorectic woman. Nearly all women feel the necessity to restrain their appetites and diminish their size. The original compassion stirred in us when encountering an anorectic woman is about this continuity of experience. But equally, there is a substantial and qualitative difference between anorectic experience and the daily experiences of other women. For although both experiences contain the same attempt at restraint, the anorectic relation to eating and not eating takes on a life of its own. While many a woman may unthinkingly envy the anorectic her will-power and ability to withstand the temptation of food, may even desire to catch a small dose, she can scarcely comprehend how involuntary this food refusal has become. So in a sense, we can understand the labelling of the anorectic's experience as an acknowledgement of this distance . . .

Let us take on the straightforward, albeit enormously painful, realisation that to *encounter an anorectic woman is to encounter a woman who is starving herself.* Before judgement, distance, or indeed perceptive analysis cause us to retreat from that realisation, the starkness of this fact should not be allowed to escape us.

As we let this realization enter us, we are chilled. Our body reverberates with a 'No'. We feel impelled to reject the idea, to make the starvation into something different, something less. We wish to deny what we see; to mute our response. We wish to change the behaviour of the woman. We are horrified if we seriously contemplate the actuality of the starvation. But we must confront and accept this aspect of the anorexia if we are to understand its meaning.

Linked to the impulse to repress what we see, is the desire to change it. We feel an urge to act; to take over the feeding of the person, to stuff her full of food, to control the behaviour which is causing us so much stress. We can only cope with what we see if we can act. But we must look full face at the fact that many many hundreds, indeed many thousands of women in the United States, the United Kingdom and Western Europe are caught in a process in which they are starving their bodies of needed nourishment, not because they cannot afford to eat, but because in their view, *they do not have the right to eat.* . . .

It is extremely hard to come to grips with the fact of this food refusal. But by taking account of our feelings towards her and imagining ourselves in her shoes, the rebellion the anorectic woman is expressing reverberates and we can feel the strength that is bound up in the refusal and rejection of food. There is a force propelling that refusal, a force that one wishes to overpower, a resilience which calls forth an equally belligerent response — a desire on the part of the observer to control. The extent to which one wishes to intervene and press food on the anorectic, is a measure of the strength of her refusal.

The next thing we may feel is a kind of coldness emanating from the anorectic. A frigid shield creates an almost physical boundary that we dare not, or know not how to, penetrate. It is as though she is wearing a placard saying 'Keep Off'. We are deterred in our effort to make a connection and we catch a sense of brittleness; as though all connections are continually being broken or in some kind of jeopardy."

As evidenced in the cases discussed, the courts, when faced with requests for declarations in respect of the treatment of anorexic women, accept the medical model advanced by the profession. The limits of the legal system do not enable the courts to situate the behaviour of anorexics in the context of the position of women in western society in the late twentieth century. Anorexia is accepted as a pathological condition and thus one that can be solved by medical intervention alone. The medical profession have successfully resorted to the mechanisms of the law to ensure that what it sees as being in the best interests of the woman concerned is lawfully carried out — whether that is forced-feeding or exposing her to a different treatment regime. The anorexic betrays the notion of liberal political theory and the legal tradition which perceives individuals as isolated atomistic individuals. The cases concerned with the treatment refusals of anorexics demand that we, the medical profession and the legal profession acknowledge our connection with another person. They require that we acknowledge our will for her to live. The response of the medical profession in these cases is portrayed as the rational response of the man of reason. However, the profession's search for means to facilitate treatment demonstrates both its connection with the anorexic and its inability as a profession trained in healing and the saving of life to stand by and do nothing when it feels there is something to be done to help.

R. DRESSER
"Article and Commentary on *Anorexia Nervosa:* Feeding the Hunger Artists: Legal Issues in Treating *Anorexia Nervosa*"[36]

'[T]he clinician attempting to treat the anorexic confronts the phenomenon of treatment refusal in its most obstinate form. Unlike patient consent to other medical interventions, an anorexia patient's express acceptance of treatment is no guarantee of future, or even present, compliance. To the contrary, the literature suggests that in a substantial number of cases such agreement is meaningless. Moreover, efforts to treat this condition, without the anorexic's true co-operation, can produce harmful consequences. The clinician occupies an unenviable position, which Crisp openly acknowledges:

> 'How does the would-be therapist, intent on "getting her better" through what can easily come to be seen as an imposed treatment programme, escape the paradox that he thereby becomes yet one more person denying her the right to exercise and develop her own "self"?'

This situation has prompted several clinicians to warn against resorting too easily to coercive treatment methods. The anorexic's overriding fear of losing control suggests to term that she will accept treatment only if she feels she has some degree of control over the process. Because of her need for control and her ability to defeat unwanted treatment, efforts by health professionals to win the anorexic's trust and to secure her cooperation are crucial to the success of any treatment program . . .

If so many commentators agree that coercive treatment is ineffective and damaging, why have anorexics so frequently been forced to undergo painful and at times punitive treatment for their condition? Even clinicians who view preserving life and health as

---

[36] R. Dresser, *supra*, n. 4 at 321–326.

legitimate reasons for forcible intervention write of numerous cases in which their patients were exposed by other clinicians to cruel or unnecessary coercive procedures designed to produce weight gain. Those who denounce these practices believe they can be attributed partially to a lack of knowledge about anorexia's psychological features among clinicians with little experience in treating the condition. Other commentators, however, blame some coercive treatment on the disturbing reactions the anorexic can evoke in her observers.

A common response is anger aroused by the anorexic's defiance of efforts to make her eat. One physician believes the anorexic's disobedience stimulates aggression and even 'sadistic tendencies' in others, which may lead them to impose such needlessly severe forms of treatment as total confinement, tube feeding and electroconvulsive therapy. The sight of the anorexic's extreme emaciation and her seemingly fragile grip on life reminds observers of their own mortality as well as hers. To dispel this discomfort, parents and others may be eager to remove the anorexic from their presence and to admit her to a hospital for forcible feeding so that her unsettling appearance will be changed as soon as possible. In addition, the clinician may become discouraged by the frequent setbacks and lengthy recovery periods characterizing anorexia treatment. Successful therapy demands 'almost superhuman' patience; clinicians who cannot endure the frustration may too easily interrupt long term therapy to obtain the speedier but potentially harmful results of forced renourishment. There is a danger, then, that decisions to impose treatment on anorexics may be influenced more by these emotional reactions than by a detached medical and psychological evaluation.

Anorexia may produce another complex set of emotions: 'Fear of hunger is so universal that undergoing it voluntarily often arouses admiration, awe, and curiosity in others . . .' In addition, the cultural ideal of slimness rewards the anorexic for her behavior. Anorexics who detect these positive responses are encouraged to maintain their behavior despite treatment efforts. A former anorexic recounts a past conversation between another anorexic and herself: '[T]hey're in awe of us. It sounds insane, but maybe it's something like [being a] celebrity. Everybody wants to be thin after all. Right? Including the doctors, our mothers, and our friends. We've achieved what they can't. They're jealous. They want to take it away from us?'

Each of these responses to *anorexia nervosa* and its treatment provides a vivid example of the emotional content of medical treatment choices. Robert Burt has masterfully challenged the notion that the legal process can inject pure objectivity into medical decisionmaking by giving one party complete control over the treatment outcome. He argues for legal recognition of the emotional and interactive qualities of such decisionmaking and for a legal system that stimulates and prolongs the negotiations he believes are necessary to optimal resolution of conflicts between doctors and patients. Burt's critique seems especially relevant to the treatment of *anorexia nervosa*."

However, the limitations of the medical model are further revealed if the influence of culture and the position in society of women with eating disorders is acknowledged. Removal to a different unit or forced-feeding may deal with the immediate problem but medicine alone cannot address the culturally transmitted messages about success in modern society and the forced treatment will not present any "cure" for this condition. Recognition of the social and cultural context in which anorexia occurs militates against forced treatment:

R. DRESSER

"Article and Commentary on *Anorexia Nervosa*: Feeding the Hunger
Artists: Legal Issues in Treating *Anorexia Nervosa*"[37]

It seems appropriate to ask whether the essential irrationality of anorexic behavior lies
in the culture, rather than the individual. The increasing prevalence of *anorexia nervosa* suggests that many cases are strongly influenced by sociocultural factors. While
some individuals might become anorexic in the absence of the cultural ideal of thinness, a substantial number would never become anorexic if they were not subjected to
the constant message that thinness paves the way to successful womanhood in our
society. From another sociocultural perspective, anorexia is a form of rebellion against
cultural restrictions upon women. According to this view, the anorexic rejects others'
expectations that she fulfill the traditional female role. Because of her submissive personality, she adopts an indirect means of protest. The apparently self-destructive anorexic behavior is, according to this view, a method of communicating to society the
dread with which certain adolescent females contemplate becoming adult women.
Some commentators believe this anxiety is only exacerbated in certain girls by new
career expectations and economic demands upon women. Some adolescent girls may
be intimidated by the high level of performance they perceive society now demands of
them. They see frustration and compromise in the traditional adulthood of their
mothers, and anxiety and stress in contemporary, career-oriented female adulthood. A
culture that encourages young girls to achieve in school and career, yet still promotes
a passive feminine ideal and fails to provide actual equality of opportunity in the world
of work, might well contribute to the adolescent female's confusion and protest.

In summary, sociocultural explanations of *anorexia nervosa* challenge the notion
that the condition is a mental illness attributable solely to sources within the individual. A legal approach adopting the socio-cultural perspective would be reluctant to
define anorexia as a mental disorder invariably justifying involuntary treatment and
confinement. Such an approach would again support reserving civil commitment for
anorexics with the most extreme mental impairment. It would place the burden on
other social institutions to address the condition, for this perspective suggests that
changes in the social systems, which currently encourage and reward the anorexic
appearance, would reduce the incidence of *anorexia nervosa* more effectively than
coercive treatment . . .

We live in a society that reflects inconsistency and ambivalence about the extremely
thin feminine form. Sometimes the shape is revered, but if it represents severe *anorexia
nervosa*, it is viewed with horror. Our culture is also highly competitive, expecting
certain of its young women to achieve not only the ideal appearance, but to perform
well at work and at home. Some individuals intimidated by these demands of modern
womanhood develop symptoms of anorexia. The specter of *anorexia nervosa* evokes
uneasiness in its observers. The legal system should be reluctant to ease this discomfort
by broadly sanctioning forcible treatment that may temporarily remove the condition's
obvious symptoms, but too often ignores the needs of the individual who suffers from
them. Strict legal limits on the involuntary treatment of anorexics could encourage a
more widespread examination of the cultural context of *anorexia nervosa*. Because
available evidence indicates that unrestricted forcible treatment confers little or no long
term benefits upon anorexics, but instead can reduce their chances for full recovery,

---

[37]   R. Dresser, *ibid.*, at 337–338, 374.

anorexics quite possibly would be better off if their audience were forced more frequently to confront their disturbing appearance. Perhaps their presence among us would constitute a compelling challenge to the social forces shaping the strange phenomenon of *anorexia nervosa*."

Rebecca Dresser concludes that involuntary treatment should only be given to anorexics who are in imminent danger of death and whose refusal should no longer be respected because of impaired mental functioning, or to those who are incapable of understanding information relevant to the treatment decision. She argues that limiting court-ordered treatment will have the effect of forcing those treating and caring for anorexics to engage with the cultural context and to further efforts to secure the co-operation of the anorexic in her treatment. This approach, Dresser suggests, will not only be more sympathetic to the context in which anorexia develops and to the relationships between the anorexic and her family but will be more successful.[38]

10.1.iv   Hunger-Strike

An interesting comparison with the above cases is *Secretary of State for the Home Office v. Robb*,[39] which concerned the application of the Home Office for a declaration that it was lawful to respect the decision of Robb, at the time in prison, to refuse to eat whilst he was competent to make that refusal. Robb had a "disordered personality" but in the view of the professionals who examined him he was competent. Thorpe J. in the High Court held that the Home Office would be acting lawfully and in doing so invoked the "fundamental principles" of personal integrity ("that every person's body is inviolate and proof against any form of physical molestation") and self-determination ("that respect must be given to the wishes of the patient").[40] Thorpe J. acknowledged the obiter comment of Lord Keith in *Airedale NHS Trust v. Bland*,[41] that the principle of sanctity of life was not absolute and therefore did not authorise the "forcible feeding of prisoners on hunger strike". He then went on to consider the approach taken in other jurisdictions:

> ### Secretary of State for the Home Office v. Robb
> [1995] 1 All E.R. 677 at 681–683, *per* Thorpe J.

"There have been much fuller developments in other common law jurisdictions, particularly in the United States, and all counsel have drawn attention to and relied upon a number of decisions, all of which consider the right of the individual to refuse nutrition in differing circumstances. I will refer only to recent decision[s] in the United States that [are] directly concerned with adult prisoners on hunger strike. The most

---

[38]   This conclusion has many similarities with the ethic of care approach to decisions relating to the sterilisation of women with learning difficulties discussed in Chap. 5.4.

[39]   *Secretary of State for the Home Office v. Robb* [1995] 1 All E.R. 677.

[40]   Presented in the skeleton argument by Counsel for the Home Office.

[41]   *Airedale NHS Trust v. Bland* [1993] A.C. 789 at 859, *per* Lord Keith.

recent, and for me the most helpful, is the decision of the Supreme Court of California, *Thor v. Superior Court* (1993) 5 Cal. 4th 725. That authority upheld a decision at first instance that the prison authorities failed in their application for an order authorising force feeding of a quadriplegic prison inmate who had determined to refuse food and medical treatment necessary to maintain his life. The conclusion of the court was that the right of self-determination prevailed but the court recognised that the right of self-determination was not absolute and that there were four specific state interests that might countervail. They were specifically (i) preserving life, (ii) preventing suicide, (iii) maintaining the integrity of the medical profession, and (iv) protecting innocent third parties.

The other United States case which is relevant to these arguments is the case of *Re Caulk* (1984) 125 N.H. 226. There, the Supreme Court of New Hampshire identified a very similar balancing exercise but found that the balance tipped against the right of self-determination. It seems that that decision was not specifically considered in the judgments given in the later case of *Thor*, and I have to say that I find more persuasive the dissenting judgment of Douglas J. than the judgment of the majority given by Bachelder J.

These decisions are obviously relevant and helpful in reaching a decision as to how the law stands in this jurisdiction. I consider specifically the four countervailing state interests that were set against the individual's right of self-determination.

The first, namely the interest that the state holds in preserving life, seems to me to be but part and parcel of the balance that must be struck in determining and declaring the right of self-determination. The principle of the sanctity of human life in this jurisdiction is seen to yield to the principle of self-determination. It is within that balance that the consideration of the preservation of life is reflected.

The second countervailing state interest, preventing suicide, is recognisable but seems to me to be of no application in cases such as this where the refusal of nutrition and medical treatment in the exercise of the right of self-determination does not constitute an act of suicide.

The third consideration of maintaining the integrity of the medical profession is one that I find hard to recognise as a distinct consideration. Medical ethical decisions can be acutely difficult and it is when they are at their most acute that applications for declaratory relief are made to the High Court. I cannot myself see that this is a distinct consideration that requires to be set against the right of self-determination of the individual.

The fourth consideration of protecting innocent third parties is one that is undoubtedly recognised in this jurisdiction, as is evidenced by the decision of Sir Stephen Brown P. in *Re S (adult: refusal of medical treatment)* [1992] 4 All E.R. 671; [1993] Fam. 123. Also recognised within this jurisdiction is a consideration that was given weight in the decision of *Re Caulk*, namely the need to preserve the internal order, discipline and security within the confines of the jail. But neither of these considerations arise in the present case.

It seems to me that within this jurisdiction there is perhaps a stronger emphasis on the right of the individual's self-determination when balance comes to be struck between that right and any countervailing interests of the state. So this decision is not a borderline one: this is a plain case for declaratory relief. The right of the defendant to determine his future is plain. That right is not diminished by his status as a detained prisoner ... Against the specific right of self-determination held by the defendant throughout his sentence there seems to me in this case to be no countervailing state interest to be set in the balance. I have no hesitation in making the declarations in the form ultimately agreed between counsel."

The reasoning of Thorpe J., following *Thor*, is based upon an assessment of whether the rights of the prisoner to self-determination should override the competing interests of the State. This reasoning presents a very different framework for deciding the case from that taken in the anorexic cases. Should not the right to self-determination of a legally competent anorexic likewise prevail over the State's interest in the preservation of life? It could be argued that forced medical treatment is a violation of the anorexic's right to bodily integrity. Failure to address the rights of the anorexic who has refused medical treatment may be compared with the sterilisation of women with learning difficulties without their consent. Lord Hailsham in *Re B* suggested that B did not possess the right to reproduce because she was not capable of exercising that right,[42] presumably meaning that she could not purposively set out to exercise that right. Is it also the case that anorexics do not possess the right to self-determination because their condition is viewed as preventing them from a meaningful exercise of that right (it being remembered that the Court of Appeal in *Re W* accepted the view that an anorexic may refuse treatment in order to remain in control)?

In *Robb*, Thorpe J. dismissed the case of *Leigh v. Gladstone*,[43] in which a suffragette sought damages for assault after having been force-fed whilst in prison, and in which Lord Alverstone C.J. in his summing up told the jury that "[i]t was the duty of the officials to preserve the health and lives of the prisoners, who were in the custody of the Crown".[44] Thorpe J. considered that this case had no modern application and should be "consigned to the archives of legal history". In *Leigh* the jury, which had to decide whether feeding was necessary and whether it had been undertaken in a proper manner without undue violence, found in favour of the Home Office. Susie Orbach in *Hunger Strike*, compares the anorexic's refusal of food with the use of food refusal by suffragettes as a political tool, arguing that this perspective enables us to comprehend the anorexic's actions as a deliberate response to the conditions in which she is living:

S. ORBACH
Hunger Strike: The Anorectic's Struggle as a Metaphor for our Age[45]

"A woman who overrides her hunger and systematically refuses to eat is in effect on hunger strike. Like the hunger striker, the anorectic is starving, she is longing to eat, she is desperate for food. Like the hunger striker, she is in protest at her conditions. Like the hunger striker, she has taken as her weapon a refusal to eat. Like the suffra-

---

[42] *Re B (A Minor) (Wardship: Sterilisation)* [1987] 2 W.L.R. 1213 at 1216E, *per* Lord Hailsham.
[43] *Leigh v. Gladstone* (1909) 26 T.L.R. 139.
[44] *Leigh v. Gladstone, ibid.*, at 142.
[45] S. Orbach, *supra*, n. 6 at pp. 82–83, 88, 96.

gettes at the turn of the century in the United Kingdom or the political prisoners of the contemporary world, she is giving urgent voice to her protest. The hunger strike becomes the means of protest to draw attention to the illegitimacy of the jailer, the moral righteousness of the cause, or in her case, the necessity for action. She is driven to act in a dramatic and seemingly self-punishing way through the conviction that she jeopardizes her cause if she eats, just like the explicitly political prisoner. But unlike her fellow hunger strikers, she may not be able to articulate the basis of her cause. The hunger strike may be her only form of protest.

To situate the act of not eating in the realm of the political is to shed a new light on both the activity and the plight of the anorectic woman. We begin to see the anorexia as an attempt at empowering, and the food refusal as the action of one whose cause has been derogated, dismissed or denied. There is an urgency and a strength in the refusal to eat. This is no mere passing whim but the action of someone either desperate, fearless or both. To subject one's body to the rigours of starvation — to keep it fed only to the absolute minimum required to ensure survival — is an act of extraordinary desperation and courage.

To see the anorectic's food refusal as a hunger strike is to begin the process of humanizing her actions. If we do not yet fully comprehend her cause, we nevertheless open ourselves up to the possibility of understanding that there is a cause she is fighting for. We can move away from our initial recoil, envy or disdain and try to enter into an understanding of her actions at a quite different level. While she may not be able to talk directly about her cause, we can begin to decipher her language. The text we read is the transformation of her body and her action of food refusal. A seemingly incoherent set of actions and activities begins to display the outlines of something quite purposeful. She expresses with her body what she is unable to tell us with words . . .

Her cause is no less imperative than that of the overtly political hunger striker. The resolve of her commitment is equally intense. The political prisoner who embarks upon a hunger strike does so to draw attention to the injustice of her or his incarceration and the righteousness of her or his cause. The anorectic woman on hunger strike echoes these themes. Her self-denial is in effect a protest against the rules that circumscribe a woman's life, a demand that she has an absolute right to exist . . .

The angular and skinny woman with the large bulging eyes whom we have wished to avoid soon becomes an understandable and approachable human being. Her struggle for survival, her hunger strike, the cause she has taken on become increasingly apparent as we allow ourselves to engage with her actions. The universe she inhabits is that same universe given to all women. Her response is an inchoate political protest, her *gestalt* the indictment of a world which squanders that richest of all resources — the capacities, passions and nobility of both sexes."

10.2 Cosmetic surgery

Elective cosmetic surgery, that is, surgical operations undertaken for aesthetic reasons, should be distinguished from plastic surgery which involves reconstruction or other techniques employed to restore features after an accident. If resort to cosmetic surgery arises out of the same belief system as the practices of dieting, exercise programmes and "making-up", consideration here of the law relating to cosmetic surgery is appropriate. Industries have developed around the pursuit of beauty (dieting products, make-up, face creams, health farms) which depend upon women's perceptions of ourselves as failing to measure up to the ideal of beauty transmitted in a particular culture at a particular time. Cosmetic surgery can be included as one of the practices available to enable women to attain a body that conforms to dominant perceptions of beauty. While this may suggest that women who resort to cosmetic surgery (like their sisters who diet to excess) are another set of "cultural dopes", blindly pursuing beauty,[46] Kathy Davis argues for a feminist analysis that acknowledges the active role of women in seeking out cosmetic surgery. As such, cosmetic surgery may be viewed as a solution to a problem, the limitations of which women fully appreciate:

K. DAVIS
Reshaping the Female Body: The Dilemma of Cosmetic Surgery[47]

"[W]hile contemporary feminist scholarship has made a strong case for linking beauty to an analysis of femininity and power, it has been less successful in finding ways to understand women's lived experience with their bodies, how they actually decide to have cosmetic surgery, and how they access their actions after the fact. Thus, my brief foray into feminist scholarship on beauty leaves me with a problem. While I am now armed with a critical perspective on cosmetic surgery, I am left empty-handed in terms of how to take women who have cosmetic surgery seriously. In order to avoid relegating women who have cosmetic surgery to the position of cultural dopes, I would need to be able to explore their lived relationship to their bodies, to recast them as agents, and to analyze the contradictions in how they justify their decision to have cosmetic surgery . . .

The political theorist Iris Marion Young provides a theoretical framework for understanding how women negotiate a sense of self in relation to their bodies. Drawing upon phenomenological theories of embodiment, she explores the typical tensions of feminine embodiment as women attempt to become embodied subjects rather than 'mere bodies.' On the one hand, women participate in a gendered social order where they are continually defined through their bodies. The female body is the perennial object of the intentions and manipulations of others. Women often adopt this attitude themselves, viewing their own bodies at a distance through the critical eyes of others. It is easy for women to feel 'mired in materiality,' to experience their own body as a thing or as an encumbrance to their projects. On the other hand, women, like men, experience their bodies as vehicles for enacting their desires or reaching out in the world. Whereas they do not transcend their bodies as men presumably can, as subjects women can never be entirely satisfied with a rendition of themselves as nothing but a body. This tension accounts for the unease many women experience with their bodies and, through their bodies, with themselves . . .

Young's notion of feminine embodiment enables me to situate women's experience of their bodies as potential objects for surgical manipulation in a broader context of

---

[46] K. Davis, "Remaking the She-Devil: A Critical Look at Feminist Approaches to Beauty" (1991) 6 *Hypatia* 21. See Chap. 9.2 for discussion of Kathy Davis's "oppression model" (siting beauty as an element in the oppression of women) and "discourse model" (explaining social institutions as constructive of the norms of feminine beauty), and the denial by Susan Bordo that the latter positions women as "cultural dopes".

[47] (London: Routledge, 1995), pp. 58–64.

the tensions of feminine embodiment in Western culture. I can explore cosmetic surgery as symptomatic of a culture where it is possible to view one's body as separate
from who one is or would like to become and as site, particularly for women, to
negotiate their identities in a context of structured hierarchies of power. Cosmetic
surgery becomes both an expression of the objectification of the female body and of
women's struggles to become embodied subjects rather than mere bodies.

The sociologist Dorothy Smith is concerned with femininity as an active and know-
ledgeable accomplishment of the female agent. Like Chapkis, Smith situates women's
dissatisfaction with their appearance as well as their involvement in the beauty system
in the context of patriarchal and capitalist relations of ruling. Women's energies and
activities are channeled into the all-consuming business of creating an acceptable feminine appearance, while, at the same time, waiting passively and with apprehension
for the male stamp of approval. Smith rejects the notion, however, that women blindly
internalize the dictates of femininity. On the contrary, women are always agents —
agents who, as she puts it, 'give power to the relations that "over-power" them' . . .

Women relate to their bodies as objects — not as sex objects for others — but rather
as objects of work, as something to be improved, fixed, or transformed. While women
cultivate the appearance of beauty without effort and adopt a passive attitude of waiting until the masculine subject finds them attractive, such appearances are deceiving.
In reality, women are agents, albeit secret ones.

> 'There is a secret agent behind the subject in the gendered discourse of femin-
> inity; she has been at work to produce the feminine subject-in-discourse
> whose appearance when read by the doctrines of femininity transfers agency
> to the man'.

Smith's notion of agency allows me to tackle several issues concerning women's
involvement in cosmetic surgery which are obscured by a cultural-dope approach to
beauty. I can explore women's decisions to alter their bodies surgically in the context
of their having to 'do femininity.' I can begin to look at how they actively and know-
ledgeably transform the texts of femininity into a desire for cosmetic surgery. Cosmetic
surgery becomes viewable as a possible remedy — a way for women to do something
about their dissatisfaction. And, finally, I can explore the decision to have cosmetic
surgery as a way for women to take action — paradoxically, perhaps, to become
female agents.

The feminist philosopher Sandra Bartky has offered a penetrating analysis of how
women actually grapple with femininity as moral actors rather than the victims of false
consciousness. Like Smith, she regards agency and the sense of mastery which accompany women's involvement in the beauty system as essential to femininity. And, like
Young, she draws upon phenomenological frameworks to explore how women's
struggles with femininity might actually feel. Unlike Smith and Young, however,
Bartky is particularly concerned with how women become embroiled in the moral
contradictions posed by practices which are both desirable and denigrating, seductive
and disempowering. Taking the prototypical experiences of masochism, narcissim, and
shame as objects for her analysis, she shows how women's everyday struggles to make
sense of needs which are in conflict with their (feminist) principles can be a resource
for a critical intervention in the oppressive practices of femininity.

Her analysis of shame is a case in point. Shame is one of the most profoundly
disempowering features of feminine experience. It is the gut-level sense of being flawed
or at fault which structures a woman's image of her body, her perception of who she

is, her interactions with others, and her capacity to move about freely in the world. It can be read in women's bodily demeanor: their hunched shoulders, bowed heads, hollowed chests, or flushed faces. Without being linked to a specific act or a negative reaction, it evokes silence, hiding, evasion, and the 'confused and divided consciousness' which sabotages women's intentions and politics. In short, shame is the feminine emotion par excellence.

In view of this pervasive sense of bodily deficiency, it is not surprising that women become committed to the rituals and practices of body improvement: the 'sacraments' which provide 'the closest thing to a state of grace'. Femininity is a need which is no less real for being repressive. Despite the 'repressive satisfactions' of femininity and the 'fashion-beauty complex,' women would feel lost and abandoned without them.

The experience of having to make sense of needs which are both heartfelt and harmful is morally unsettling, however. The contradictory lures and oppressions of femininity can be experienced as 'ontological shocks' — that is, disjunctures between a woman's values and beliefs and her practical or lived consciousness of being-in-the world, between how she thinks she *should* feel and how she, in fact, *does* feel.

Bartky is critical of attempts to resolve these troublesome ontological contradictions discursively — for example, by propagating the freedom of the individual to 'do her own thing' without concern for the structural constraints of femininity or by providing a radical code of ethics for feminist behavior 'which divides women within the movement and alienates those outside of it'. Both solutions are inadequate for coming to terms with women's struggles as moral actors to make sense of the troubling or painful dimensions of their experiences. She proposes instead an approach which takes women's 'ambiguous ethical situation' as an opportunity for reflection and, ultimately, for 'exorcising one's own demons.' Although Bartky's approach might be seen as pessimistic and non-utopian, it offers a program for feminist analysis which is grounded in women's everyday moral experience in a gendered social order.

In conclusion, Bartky's work is useful for uncovering women's ambivalence concerning cosmetic surgery. It can help me pinpoint the ways that a woman's gut-level sense of bodily deficiency might sabotage her reservations about cosmetic surgery as well as her critical stance toward the feminine beauty system in general, enabling me to understand what makes cosmetic surgery both desirable and morally problematic for the recipients themselves. I can treat women's ongoing struggles to justify a contradictory practice like cosmetic surgery as a resource for developing a feminist response which speaks to women's experiences rather than simply reiterating the correct line on women's involvement in the beauty system.

Taken together, the work of Young, Smith, and Bartky provide the theoretical tools necessary for a feminist analysis of cosmetic surgery which avoids viewing recipients as the duped and passive victims of the feminine beauty system. They show that embodiment, agency, and moral contradictions are central to understanding women's problems with their appearance as well as their decisions to have their bodies altered surgically."

Davis's argument is that it is important to understand the decisions of women to undergo cosmetic surgery as active choices taken in order to solve a particular problem in full awareness of the risks involved. Davis suggests that this "embodied agent" approach avoids portraying women who undergo cosmetic surgery as "cultural dopes" who unquestioningly subject their bodies to mutilating surgery in pursuit of the culturally-dictated ideal. She argues that, in order to understand the decisions of women who resort to cosmetic surgery, it is important to listen to the justifications which women themselves give for making this choice. These accounts are explored in her book, *Reshaping the Female Body: The Dilemma of Cosmetic Surgery.*[48] Whilst presenting the decision of women to undergo cosmetic surgery as one taken to address a specific problem, in the knowledge of the risks of surgery, and in response to the pressures upon women to conform to a dominant ideal of beauty, Davis's analysis fails to really grapple with a key issue — that is the pressures under which women actively seek painful, risky and not always successful surgery in order to look more like the ideal Woman. Women should not have to look a certain way — young, slim, Caucasian, free of wrinkles and stretch marks — in order to feel good about themselves. Cosmetic surgery does offer women the possibility of altering their bodies in personal and idiosyncratic ways, but is primarily used to modify the body in accordance with the ideal, to remove the effects of pregnancy or eradicate the signs of ageing. Cosmetic surgery perpetuates the dominant view of beauty and further provides women who do not meet the ideal with the means to alter their appearance.

Kathryn Pauly Morgan confesses to "genuine epistemic and political bewilderment when I, as an ageing (like most mortals) feminist philosopher/woman, try to reflect critically on contemporary practices and individual choices in the area of elective cosmetic surgery."[49] She explores rights discourse in application to cosmetic surgery only to find it limited in the extent to which it confronts the moral and political issues surrounding the practice. Consequently, she suggests an alternative framework which locates cosmetic surgery within the increasing technological modification of areas of human life previously considered natural, given and unalterable. Decisions to undergo cosmetic surgery, apparently paradigm examples of the exercise of free choice, have to be considered in the context of the cultural and personal pressures exerted upon individuals. She further emphasises that the body altered by cosmetic surgery is usually female. In the following extract Kathryn Pauly Morgan explores why it is that women choose to undergo cosmetic surgery:

K. P. MORGAN
"Gender Rites and Rights: The Biopolitics of Beauty and Fertility"[50]

"Virtually every culture has a set of categories, symbols, and ritualized practices associated with Nature. Often they carry with them gendered and racialized associations. Some cultures regard the domain of the Natural as a limit to be preserved with respect, kinship, affiliation. Other cultures operate with a view of the domain of the Natural as primitive, open for exploration and domination, something to be tamed and

---

[48]   K. Davis, *ibid.*

[49]   K. P. Morgan, 'Gender Rites and Rights: The Biopolitics of Beauty and Fertility' in L. W. Sumner and J. Boyle (eds), *Philosophical Perspectives on Bioethics* (Toronto: University of Toronto Press, 1996), p. 214.

[50]   K. P. Morgan, *ibid.*, pp. 223–225.

exploited. In western cultures women's oppression has been 'justified' by assimilating Woman to Nature, to the domain of the Natural, where the 'natural' is set up in binary opposition to 'culture', to the 'fully human.' To give credibility to theories of the naturalized inferiority of women, western European and North American scientific traditions have often sought to demonstrate empirically how women, and women's bodies in particular, are essentially pathological approximations to men and the bodies of men. As a result, the assimilation of Woman to the Natural coupled with empirical demonstrations of natural pathology have led to oppressive misogynous structures of material, social, and political control by men. Male physicians have played a prominent role in this oppression.

In the latter cultures what is designated the 'natural' functions primarily as a 'frontier' rather than as a 'limit' or 'barrier.' While genetic identity, human sexuality, fertility, reproductive outcome, and longevity previously were regarded as open to variation primarily in evolutionary terms, biotechnological cultures see them as domains for creation and control. Often the role assigned to technology is that of transcendence, transformation, control, exploitation, or destruction; correlatively, the technologized object or process is conceptualized as inferior or primitive, in need of perfecting transformation in the name of some 'higher' purpose or end, or as deserving of eradication because it is seen as harmful or evil. Cosmetic surgeons, for example, see human bodies as a carnal site of challenge. As one plastic surgeon remarks, 'patients sometimes misunderstand the nature of cosmetic surgery. It's not a short cut for diet or exercise. *It's a way to override the genetic code*' (emphasis added).

Given the oppressive consequences of associating women with the Natural in capitalist, racist, patriarchal cultures, it is not surprising that women themselves should envision access to technological control as a way of severing this connection. Modifying the original quotation from Mary Wollstonecraft, we now need to ask whether still being taught from infancy that youth, beauty, fertility, and heterosexual affiliation are women's sceptre, women's bodies are coming to shape themselves to women's minds. We also need to ask whether, with this inversion, women's artefactual bodies serve as new kinds of cages, new kinds of horizons — or both. As more and more experts and technicians administer to and transform women's bodies in terms of appearance and child-bearing, we need to ask whether RoboBeauty and RoboFertility do represent a genuine advance for women or whether new forms of oppression are entering our lives.

How do these remarks regarding technology and women apply to particular women, and why? Full social approval for many women in many cultures is dependent upon their acting within — and resisting within — interlocking norms of compulsion: compulsory attractiveness, compulsory fertility and social nurturance, and compulsory heterosexuality. These patterns of compulsion determine, for many women, the 'legitimate' limits of attraction, motherhood, and commitment. In these cultural contexts women's attractiveness is defined as attractive-to-men; women's eroticism is defined as non-existent, pathological, deviant, or peripheral when it is not directed to phallic goals; and legitimate motherhood is defined in terms of legally sanctioned and constrained reproductive service to particular men and to particular institutions, such as the nation, the race, the owner, and the class, institutions that are, themselves, more often than not male dominated. Now biotechnology is making beauty, the appearance of youthfulness, fertility, and the appearance of heterosexuality through trans-sexual surgery accessible to virtually all women who can afford them — and increasingly large numbers of women are making other sacrifices in their lives in order to buy access to the technical expertise.

Why? Why do women's hearts and imaginations resonate with the question posed by Snow White's stepmother — and by the participants and observers in the many Beauty Contests in Life: 'Who is the fairest of all?' What does the public affirmation of beauty, of fertility, bring to women in many cultures? What is frequently the fate of women who are classified among the plain, the ugly, the aged, and the barren in those cultures that prize women's beauty and fertility?

Speaking about their choices in relation to elective cosmetic surgery, the voices and the narratives of the women themselves are seductive. They speak of gaining access to transcendence, achievement, liberation, and power, and we must acknowledge the lived reality of that discourse. Electing to undergo cosmetic surgery not only appears to but often does in reality give a woman a sense of identity that to some extent she has chosen herself. Second, it offers her the possibility of raising her status both socially and economically through increasing her opportunities for heterosexual affiliation (especially with white and/or powerful men). Third, by committing herself to the pursuit of beauty, a woman can give a kind of integrity to her life. This pursuit involves a consistent set of values and choices that she knows will bring her widespread approval and consequently contribute to a more positive sense of herself. Finally, the technologically based pursuit of beauty gives rise to a large range of individuals who will care for that woman and care directly for her body in a way that is often lacking [in] the day-to-day lives of many women in cultures in which direct bodily nurturance and caring between women is devalued or prohibited. In short, the choice to pursue beauty through biotechnological means is directly linked with experience of self-creation, self-fulfilment, self-esteem, and being cared for."

Whilst recognising the positive effects of cosmetic surgery, Kathryn Pauly Morgan identifies what she describes as "Three Paradoxes of Choice":

K. P. MORGAN
"Gender Rites and Rights: The Biopolitics of Beauty and Fertility"[51]

"Paradox 1: The Choice of Conformity: Aspiring to be Number '10' ...
While the technologies of cosmetic surgery, ... clearly could be used to create and celebrate idiosyncrasy, eccentricity, and uniqueness, it is clear that they are not at present being used in this way. In the area of cosmetic surgery, surgeons report that legions of women appear in the offices demanding to have 'Bo Derek' breasts (or those of whoever happens to be the most recent mammary goddess of choice in Hollywood). Jewish girls and women appear in their offices demanding reductions of their noses so as to be able to 'pass' as one of their Aryan sisters, who form the dominant ethnic group. Affluent girls and young women in South Korea standardly have their noses lifted, their eyes widened, and their cheekbones shaved in order to 'go Anglo,' despite the conservative naturalism built into the traditions of Confucianism. Asian girls and women in other countries bring in pictures of Elizabeth Taylor and of Japanese movie actresses demanding the 'westernizing' of their faces in hopes of improved employment and marital prospects. What is being created in these instances is often white or light, westernized, Anglo-Saxon bodies in cultures that are racist, anti-Semitic, and increasingly ageist in their norms and practices. Affluence and class privilege are being vis-

---

[51]   K. P. Morgan, *ibid.*, pp. 226–233.

cerally inscribed in the visible physiognomy of a woman's skin, facial features, silhouette, and curvature through the needles, the knives, the cannulas, and the implants. 'Designer Labels' of the famous cosmetic surgeons are being stitched, literally, into women's flesh.

Prior to the rise of cosmetic biotechnology, a woman's degree and kind of makeup, her dress, gestures, degree and definition of feminine cleanliness, degree of muscularity, odours, degree of hirsuteness, voice, vocabulary, patterns of silence, hands, feet, skin, hair ... often have been evaluated, regulated, and disciplined in the light of often dominant males and male viewers present in the assessing gaze of other women. Now women can gain the appreciation and approval of other men through demonstrations of achieved femininity by submitting to more invasive procedures of incisions, stitches, staples, anaesthesias, artificial implants, cellular suction and reimplantation, and scar tissue ...

[T]he first serious paradox I see is this: that what look like optimal situations of deliberation, maximized choice, and self-determination often simultaneously signal the production of conformity.

Paradox 2: Choosing Dependence in the Name of Autonomy

A woman's desire to create a permanently beautiful and youthful appearance not vulnerable to the threats of externally applied cosmetic artifice or to the ageing processes of the body must be understood as a deeply existential project. So, too, must a woman's desire to choose, to control, and to shape her own fertility and her child be so understood. In both cases these desires deliberately involve a shift from a submission to what is contingent and uncertain in human existence to a posture of rational human control, prediction, and security in some of the most intimately experienced domains of human embodiment — the body as beautiful, the body as fertile. Biotechnology is accessed in the name of transcendence: transcendence of hereditary predestination, of lived time, of one's given 'limitations,' of control over the uncertainties of conception, maternity, and birth. This involves an important metaphysical shift that is important to track: what comes to have primary significance is not the real, given, existing woman but the potentially beautiful, fertile woman. Her present state of embodiment increasingly is viewed as a 'primitive entity' seen only in terms of its (her?) potential, as a kind of raw material or set of fertility functions to be bioechnologically transformed in the name of beauty, fertility, eroticism, and nurturance.

As Foucault and others have noted, practices of coercion and domination often are effectively hidden behind practical rhetoric and supporting theories that claim to be benevolent, therapeutic, and protective of individual choice. I believe that in the areas of cosmetic surgery and reproductive biotechnology precisely this kind of camouflage is practised. In the past, material, psychological, and social colonizing was often done in the name of bringing 'civilization' to 'primitive, barbaric people.' Contemporary colonizers mask their exploitation of 'raw materials and human labour' in the name of 'development.' But who is colonizing here? Often it is a particular man or a variety of men. The woman who wanted to undergo a facelift, a tummy tuck, and liposuction all in one week to win heterosexual approval *from a man she had not seen in twenty-eight years* and whose individual preference she could not possibly know experiences the power involved in heterosexual approval almost in the abstract. Actual men — sons, brothers, fathers, male lovers, male beauty 'experts,' male employers, male colleagues — and hypothetical men, such as 'future husbands,' live in the imaginations and hearts of women. They are present, too, as male engineering students who taunt and harass women and in the form of male cosmetic surgeons who offer 'free advice' in social gatherings to women whose 'deformities' and 'severe problems' could be cured through their healing needles and knives. Their presence is immediate. Some girls and women know, all too well, how their violation of the norms of feminine perfectibility can result in violence, abuse, or abandonment by those men, regardless of class. Or they live more ghostly powerful lives — sometimes as the desired prince who will rescue those girls and women from the violence and the oppressiveness of poverty. But live there they do as a critical locus of coercive power.

In electing to undergo cosmetic surgery, women appear to be protesting against the constraints of the 'given' in their embodied lives and to be seeking liberation from those constraints. Nevertheless, I believe women are, in fact, in danger of becoming more vulnerable, more dependent upon male assessment and the services of those experts who promised to render them liberated, independent, and beautiful. The beauty culture is coming to be dominated by a variety of experts, and consumers of youth and beauty will find themselves increasingly dependent not only on cosmetic surgeons but on anaesthetists, nurses, aestheticians, nail technicians, manicurists, dieticians, hairstylists, cosmetologists, trainers, pedicurists, electrolysists, pharmacologists, and dermatologists. Again, it is a public sign of affluence and privilege to have both the leisure and the income to be able to afford these continuing forms of expert dependence . . .

Here then is the second serious paradox: that in choosing to become involved in the biotechnologies in the areas of elective cosmetic surgery and reproduction, women become involved in processes that undermine the integrity-preserving preconditions for full womanly autonomy and lead to greater dependence on experts who are, for the most part, men.

Paradox 3: Coerced Voluntariness and the Technological Imperative

Initially, women who choose to become involved in the biotechnologies of cosmetic surgery . . . often seem to represent a kind of paradigm case of a rational chooser. They are coming from an increasingly wide range of economic groups (a rate of participation accelerated by inclusion of these biotechnologies in public health plans) and clearly make a choice, often at significant cost to the rest of their life, to participate in the technologies. They often are highly critical consumers of these services and expect consultation, information with respect to risks and benefits, and professional guarantees of expertise. Unlike most other recipients of health care services, generally they are young and in good health and are not afflicted with any trauma, sickness, or chronic condition that might impair their capacity to make choices. One might even say that they epitomize relatively invulnerable, free, rational agents making a decision under virtually optimal conditions . . .

Many women are under enormous pressure to be beautiful and now to achieve perfection through the use of cosmetic biotechnologies. This pressure is on the increase. Cosmetic surgeons report on the wide range of clients who buy their services. They pitch their advertising to a large audience through the use of the media and parade their 'successes' in front of television cameras. They use rhetoric that encourages women to think in terms of seemingly trivial 'nips' and 'tucks' that will transform their lives — or of recycling the 'raw material' of their fat cells from an ugly site to one of beauty such as the lips or breasts. The cosmetic 'success stories' can be seen as more permanent forms of the already normalized 'make overs' that dominate women's media and, like the 'success stories' of the fertility technologies, the cosmetic 'success stories' are displayed on talk shows along with their makers, while surgically transformed women win the Miss America beauty pageants.

[W]e can see a Technological Imperative take hold through this normalization. Increasingly, women who refuse to submit to the knives and the needles, to the anaesthetics and the bandages are seen as deviant in one way or another. Women who refuse to use these technologies are already becoming stigmatized as 'unliberated,' as 'not caring about their appearance,' as 'refusing to be all that you could be,' or as (the ultimate label of scorn!) 'granola heads.' Not caring about one's appearance as a woman is already taken by patriarchal psychologists, social workers, and psychiatrists as a sign of disturbed gender identity and pathologically low self-esteem. Serious consequences for a woman often can result when she is in the 'care' and control of such professionals.

When greater access to power comes to those women who do 'care about themselves' via cosmetic technologies, more coercive dimensions enter the scene. In the past only those women who were perceived to be *naturally* beautiful (or rendered beautiful through relatively superficial artifice) had access to power, and economic social mobility closed off to women regarded as plain or ugly or old (if there were no overriding factors such as privileged family connections and/or wealth). Now, however, womanly beauty is becoming transformed into a technological commodity for which each and every woman can, in principle, sacrifice and purchase if she wants to succeed in a culture that defines and commodifies womanly beauty and describes these sacrifices as liberation. In such cultures technology is making obligatory the appearance of youth and the reality of 'beauty.' Natural diversity of appearance is being supplanted by biotechnologically produced norms of beauty, which exercise an increasingly coercive effect in the lives and choices of girls and women.

Here too, I argue that we find the dynamic of the double-pathologizing of the normal with respect to women's embodiment. What until recently had been described in both technical and popular literature as normal variations of female bodily shapes or described in the relatively innocuous language of 'problem areas,' are now being described as 'deformities,' 'ugly protrusions,' 'unsightly concentrations of fat cells,' and 'acutely ptotic breasts' — a litany of phrases designed to intensify feelings of disgust and shame and to promise relief at the possibility of technological cures. Cosmetic surgery promises more and more women the creation of beautiful, youthful-appearing bodies. As a consequence, many more women will become labelled 'ugly' and 'old' in relation to this more select population of surgically created beautiful faces and bodies that have been contoured and augmented, lifted and tucked to a state of achieved feminine perfection. We are witnessing a pathological shift here: the naturally 'given' is coming to be seen as the technologically 'primitive' — this is the first stage of pathologizing. The second stage enters in because it will no longer be sufficient to remedy this normal pathology of women's unadorned appearance through artifice; now even the artifice and makeup will be seen as a pathological substitute when women are given the opportunity to achieve status as a beautiful artefact through the surgical technology.

This is the third paradox: that the Technological Beauty ... Imperative and the pathological double-inversion of the naturally given are coercing increasing numbers of women to 'choose' cosmetic ... technologies; hence the description of Coerced Voluntariness."

Our legal system is predicated upon the goal of maximising the choices of the rational autonomous individual. To what extent does the law place limits upon the performance of cosmetic surgery?

10.2.i   *The incision of the surgeon's knife and the criminal law*
A surgeon who makes an incision into the skin of a patient would commit (in the absence of a defence) an offence contrary to section 47 or section 20 of the Offences Against the Person Act 1861:

Offences Against the Person Act 1861, s. 47
(c. 100)

"Whosoever shall be convicted upon an indictment of any assault occasioning actual bodily harm shall be liable . . . to be kept in penal servitude . . ."

Offences Against the Person Act 1861, s. 20
(c. 100)

"Whosoever shall unlawfully and maliciously wound or inflict any grievous bodily harm upon any other person, either with or without any weapon or instrument, shall be guilty of a misdemeanor, and being convicted thereof shall be liable . . . to be kept in penal servitude . . ."

The section 47 offence, assault occasioning actual bodily harm, is committed when the harm caused is "more than merely transient or trifling", although it does not need to be permanent.[52] The section 20 offence, to unlawfully and maliciously wound or inflict grievous bodily harm upon any other person, is a more serious offence than assault occasioning actual bodily harm and, for a wound, requires that the whole of the skin and not just the outer layer be broken.[53] The surgeon will inflict upon the patient the harm prohibited under both sections 47 and 20. Both offences also require the *mens rea* of intentionally or recklessly committing the prohibited harm. A surgeon who cuts his patient will intend to make an incision in the sense that it will be the purpose of the act of cutting to do so.[54] Whether the surgeon commits an offence will depend upon whether the patient has given a valid consent. In *R. v. Brown (Anthony), R. v. Lucas, R. v. Jaggard, R. v. Laskey, R. v. Carter,*[55] the House of Lords considered an appeal against convictions for offences contrary to the 1861 Act by men who had willingly participated in homosexual sado-masochistic activities involving the consensual infliction of harm (none of which was permanent or required hospital treatment) upon a passive partner. The House of Lords confirmed that there are limits placed upon the harm to which individuals can give a valid consent. First, the law limits the amount of

[52]   *R. v. Donovan* [1934] 2 K.B. 498, *per* Swift J.
[53]   *J.J.C. (A Minor) v. Eisenhower* [1983] 3 All E.R. 230.
[54]   *R. v. Mohan* [1976] Q.B. 1 (intention here meaning "a decision to bring about, insofar as it lies within the accused's power, [a particular consequence], no matter whether the accused desired the consequence of his act or not". This might otherwise be described as an "aim").
[55]   *R. v. Brown (Anthony), R. v. Lucas, R. v. Jaggard, R. v. Laskey, R. v. Carter* [1993] 2 W.L.R. 556.

harm to which a valid consent can be given at the point at which the activity does, or is intended to, cause actual bodily harm. However, there are certain circumstances in which causing such harm is justified in the public interest. In these situations, a valid consent will mean that no criminal offence is committed by the perpetrator.

R. v. Brown (Anthony), R. v. Lucas, R. v. Jaggard, R. v. Laskey,
R. v. Carter
[1993] 2 W.L.R. 556 at 560e–f, *per* Lord Templeman

"In some circumstances violence is not punishable under the criminal law. When no actual bodily harm is caused, the consent of the person affected precludes him from complaining. There can be no conviction for the summary offence of common assault if the victim has consented to the assault. Even when violence is intentionally inflicted and results in actual bodily harm, wounding or serious bodily harm the accused is entitled to be acquitted if the injury was a foreseeable incident of a lawful activity in which the person injured was participating. Surgery involves intentional violence resulting in actual or sometimes serious bodily harm but surgery is a lawful activity. Other activities carried on with consent by or on behalf of the injured person have been accepted as lawful notwithstanding that they involve actual bodily harm or may cause serious bodily harm. Ritual circumcision, tattooing, ear-piercing and violent sports including boxing are lawful activities."

Lord Mustill referred to "proper medical treatment," which he explained as being in a "category of its own".[56] In the earlier case of *Attorney-General's Reference (No. 6 of 1980),*[57] Lord Lane C.J., in the Court of Appeal had expressly affirmed the legality of "reasonable surgical interference" which, he explained, although causing actual bodily harm, was justified in the public interest. These cases leave unanswered the question of what is meant by "proper medical treatment" or "reasonable surgical interference".

L. Bibbings & P. Alldridge
"Sexual Expression, Body Alteration, and the Defence of Consent"[58]

"[I]t is usually the status of the person performing the alteration which is most significant. For instance, cosmetic surgery is apparently permitted where it is carried out by a qualified or registered practitioner. This includes a wide range of techniques which are possibly analogous to less conventional forms of body alteration. Male circumcision is considered to be lawful when performed by a medical practitioner or religious actor as part of a ritual. Face-lifts involve the cutting of facial tissue although the object is that no scarring should be visible. In contrast, it would appear that branding, scarification, and cutting for the purpose of body decoration when performed by a

---

[56]   *R. v. Brown, ibid.,* at 593F.
[57]   *Attorney-General's Reference (No. 6 of 1980)* [1981] Q.B. 715.
[58]   (1993) 20 *Journal of Law and Society* 356 at 361.

third party who is not a doctor constitutes a criminal act. In *Adesanya* (*The Times*, July 16/17, 1974) a mother was convicted of assault occasioning actual bodily harm when she cut the cheeks of her sons, aged nine and fourteen, in accordance with tribal custom and with (so far as they were able to give consent) their consent. She was given an absolute discharge."

The Law Commission, in its consideration of consent (carried out as part of its project of codification of the criminal law) found no case in which an English court had considered the legality of an operation performed for purely cosmetic reasons.[59]

LAW COMMISSION
Consent in the Criminal Law[60]

"[I]t would not be possible to identify a therapeutic benefit in every case, and it may be that this is a field in which English law unconsciously recognises that the criminal law has no acceptable place in controlling operations performed by qualified practitioners upon adults of sound mind with their consent."

This conclusion amounts to an understanding that cosmetic surgery is not presently within the realm of lawful operations, at least those for which there is no therapeutic benefit.[61] However, because of the trust which can be placed in qualified medical practitioners, the performance of cosmetic operations is of no concern to the law but remains a private matter between doctor and patient.

10.2.ii   *Full, informed and free consent*

The law does not permit individuals to consent to the commission of a crime upon the self. Consequently, the criminal law sets the parameters of the civil law which provides damages for direct and intentional infliction of unlawful personal contact. A doctor who performs a surgical operation upon a competent adult patient without a valid consent will commit a civil battery and be liable for damages. To be valid, consent must be "full, informed and freely given".

---

[59]   The Law Commission proposes that legislation should make it clear that no offence is committed, whatever the seriousness of the injury caused, if injury occurs during the course of proper medical treatment. Furthermore, the proper medical treatment must be carried out by or under the direction of a qualified medical practitioner. This would include "surgical operations performed for cosmetic purposes" (Law Commission, *Consent in the Criminal Law*, Law Commission Consultation Paper No. 139, (1995), para. 8.30).

[60]   Law Commission, *ibid.*, para. 8.30.

[61]   The distinction between cosmetic operations which are purely aesthetic and those in which there is a therapeutic benefit is difficult to draw. The distinction between therapeutic and non-therapeutic procedures has been rejected in other fields of medical law (see Chap. 5.4).

R. F. V. Heuston & R. A. Buckley
Salmond & Heuston on the Law of Torts[62]

"A man cannot be said to be 'willing' unless he is in a position to choose freely; and freedom of choice predicates the absence from his mind of any feeling of constraint interfering with his will."

The focus of free consent is upon individuals who have the ability to make free choices and ensures the choice made is not coerced.

Re T (Adult: Refusal of Medical Treatment)
[1992] 3 W.L.R. 782 at 797c–d, *per* Lord Donaldson M.R.

". . . [T]he doctors have to consider whether the decision is really that of the patient. It is wholly acceptable that the patient should have been persuaded by others of the merits of such a decision and have decided accordingly. It matters not how strong the persuasion was, so long as it did not overbear the independence of the patient's decision. The real question in each such case is 'Does the patient really mean what he says or is he merely saying it for a quiet life, to satisfy someone else or because the advice and persuasion to which he has been subjected is such that he can no longer think and decide for himself?' In other words 'Is it a decision expressed in form only, not in reality?' "

The concern is that the rational legal subject is not coerced by external factors so that the expressed choice is a real choice. Doubts are raised in the above extract from Kathryn Pauly Morgan as to whether the woman deciding to undergo cosmetic surgery makes a free choice because of the influence upon her of social, cultural and personal pressures. The notion of free or voluntary consent seeks to ensure that the will of the patient is not overborne. It does not acknowledge that wider pressures may fetter choice.

The decision to consent to surgery can only be made if information is provided.[63] In the context of medically necessary treatment this includes information as to the nature and inherent risks of the treatment, advice upon the condition, the risks of foregoing treatment, alternative methods of treatment, and the benefits and consequences of the contemplated treatment. *Sidaway* established that the duty upon the medical profession when providing advice to patients was to "act in accordance with a competent body of professional opinion". However, the risks of cosmetic surgery, about which surgeons may, as a matter of common practice, inform women, may exclude risks which women themselves may consider to be important. The primary concern of the profession will be "medical" risks. Cosmetic surgeons may not, for example, warn women of the risk of loss of sensation in the breast as a result of surgery. In this respect, the questions to be raised about whether

---

[62] (London: Sweet & Maxwell, 21st ed., 1996), p. 478.
[63] *Sidaway v. Bethlam Royal Hospital Governors* [1985] 1 All E.R. 643, HL.

women give informed consent to cosmetic surgery are much the same as those relating to information concerning contraception.[64] A further matter of concern is the extent to which cosmetic surgery poses risks to health. This does not simply mean the risks involved in undergoing a surgical procedure under anaesthetic, but also the harm which may be caused by the use of any "products" (such as the silicone or saline implants deployed in breast augmentation).[65]

Is cosmetic surgery a matter of individual choice, liberating and an opportunity to "make the most of yourself"? Alternatively does it amount to the transformation of the individual in accordance with the demands of dominant culture such that the lack of legal regulation permits the infliction of harm upon the bodies of women? The approach taken by the law to cosmetic surgery is that, if it is performed by responsible and skilled professionals upon competent adults who freely and autonomously choose to undergo the surgery, it is not the law's concern. Individuals are free to choose to undergo surgery which, in theory, maximises their choice. But individuals are not isolated, autonomous beings taking decisions unhindered by societal, cultural and personal pressures.

Kathryn Pauly Morgan suggests that it is necessary to challenge the norms of beauty, to remove the power which surgeons have attained by altering the bodies of women and to explore the actual and potential diversity of our physical differences.[66] This demands an understanding of the present practice of cosmetic surgery, as with the normal feminine practices of diet, exercise and body alteration and the extremes of anorexia within the contemporary cultural context of western society as we approach the twenty-first century. The importance of cultural context is addressed in the next section on female genital surgeries. Like the practices already described, these practices require that feminists engage with the question of how, through law or other means, the social and cultural pressures to which women respond by modifying their bodies, may be changed.

10.3   Female genital surgeries

The final part of this chapter explores the harm inflicted upon the female body by the practice of female genital mutilation. It examines the legal approach adopted towards the practice in Britain and whether alternative regulation to the criminalisation of those performing female genital surgeries would be more appropriate. The positioning in this chapter of the discussion of female genital mutilation directly following that of cosmetic surgery is adopted in order to offer a further example of the alteration of the bodies of women in accordance with the dictates of self-perpetuating cultural norms.

---

[64]   Considered above in Chap. 5.1.

[65]   Also considered in relation to contraception in Chap. 5.1.

[66]   K. P. Morgan, *supra*, n. 49 at p. 234. See also an earlier article by K. P. Morgan, "Women and the Knife: Cosmetic Surgery and the Colonization of Women's Bodies" (1991) *Hypatia* 25, in which she explores the strategy of appropriation involving the resort to cosmetic surgery in the pursuit of ugliness and the opening of "Body Beautiful Boutiques."

There is deep division even amongst African women in the U.K. as to the appropriate description of, and thus legal response to, these practices. Brent councillor Poline Nyaga, has described female circumcision as "a spiritual act which divides childhood from adulthood" and, as such, she advocates that it should not only be lawful within the U.K., but available on the NHS. Efua Dorkenoo, director of Forward International, holding the contrary view, describes the practices as child abuse and recognised by "[i]nformed African opinion" as "a harmful and obsolete practice which has no place in modern society".[67] To avoid prejudging the issues by the terminology employed, the different practices which are frequently referred to collectively as "female genital mutilation" will here be included under the description, "female genital surgeries".

As a consequence of the migration of peoples amongst whom female genital surgery is a current traditional practice, countries where, in the late twentieth century, these operations are not normally performed, as in the United Kingdom, have been forced to address their legality. As with women who undergo cosmetic surgery, we may find it difficult to understand why women choose to submit to such surgeries or why mothers choose them for their daughters. But we must listen to the women themselves and seek to understand.

Female genital surgeries are performed in parts of Asia, Australia, Europe, the former Soviet Union, twenty African countries, Oman, South Yemen, United Arab Emirates, Indonesia, Malaysia, India and Pakistan and throughout the world as a consequence of the movement of people from these countries.[68] Female genital surgeries encompass a number of different operations. In a circumcision or "sunna" operation the prepuce or hood of the clitoris is removed. An excision involves removal of the clitoris and all or part of the labia minora. In an infibulation or pharaonic circumcision, the clitoris, labia minora and a large proportion or all of the medial part of the labia majora are removed. The two sides of the vulva are then joined together by silk or catgut sutures or with thorns, apart from a very small opening which is preserved by the insertion of a tiny piece of wood or a reed. The girl is kept immobile until the wound heals.

The age at which genital surgeries are performed differs according to local tradition, ranging from the eighth day after birth, to puberty, to a woman's wedding night or after the birth of her first child. In the majority of countries it is carried out between the ages of three and eight. The surgeries, especially the more extensive form of infibulation, have adverse health effects including infection, incontinence, painful menstruation, pain experienced during intercourse and childbirth, and in some cases even death.[69]

---

[67] Both cited in A. Boulton, "Calls for circumcision on NHS sparks storm", *The Observer*, March 14, 1993.
[68] E. Dorkenoo & S. Elworthy, *Female Genital Mutliation: Proposals for Change* (London: Minority Rights Group, 1992), p. 11.
[69] The different forms of the surgeries, the ages at which they are performed and the health consequences are discussed in L. Bibbings, "Female Circumcision: Mutilation or Modification?" in J. Bridgeman & S. Millns (eds), *Law and Body Politics: Regulating the Female Body*, (Aldershot: Dartmouth, 1995), pp. 151–156; E. Dorkenoo & S. Elworthy, *ibid.*; O. Koso-

Isabelle Gunning identifies the problems experienced by western feminists analysing female genital surgeries. First, is it appropriate to examine the practices of an entirely different culture? Secondly, in the light of that different culture, is the law an appropriate tool to be employed in the eradication of these practices?[70] Gunning suggests a three-stage "world-travelling" method which might enable western feminists to analyse the practice of female genital surgeries and to acknowledge both the "independence" and "interconnectedness" of others.

10.3.i *Take a look back to our own past*

The first task of the "world-travelling" method is to examine the incidence of what can be described as "culturally-challenging practices" within the historical context of our own culture:

I. GUNNING
"Arrogant Perception, World-travelling, and Multicultural Feminism: The Case of Female Genital Surgeries"[71]

"The most interesting aspect of seeing oneself (meaning Westerner) in historical context is exploring a fact that is often omitted, if not actually denied, in discussions of genital surgeries in other countries. This is the fact that genital surgeries have been performed in Western countries as well. Ben Barker-Benfield's . . . article *Sexual Surgery in Late-Nineteenth-Century America* is a fascinating article because he places genital surgeries — both clitoridectomies and female castration — firmly within their historical and social contexts. His article not only documents the existence of clitoridectomies and other related surgeries, but unearths the same kinds of rationales that are currently expounded where the practices continue to flourish.

Barker-Benfield sets the stage for the rise of female genital surgeries in the United States by identifying a number of social concerns that confronted white men after the civil war. First is an increasing concern with the alleged propensity of women to fall into hysteria or madness which was traced to their sexuality. Second are 'disorderly women,' whom one doctor identified as every woman from women's rightists, bloomerwearers to midwives. Included too were lesbians, anyone suspected of lesbian inclinations and those with 'an aversion to men;' and women who, as described in 1871 by the American Medical Association President, 'seek to rival men in manly sports and occupations.' Third is the sense of America 'as a beleaguered island of WASP righteousness surrounded by an encroaching flood of dirty prolific immigrants,' hence the need for racial purity.

Within this social context arose a new medical specialty (predominated by men): gynecology to cure women's condition, 'precisely as they discovered women generally were deteriorating.' The new gynecologists operated under the same social constructs

---

Thomas, *The Circumcision of Women: A Strategy for Eradication* (London: Zed Books Ltd, 1987); E. Dorkenoo, *Cutting the Rose, Female Genital Mutilation: The Practice and its Prevention* (London: Minority Rights Publication, 1994), Chaps 1 & 2.

[70] I. Gunning, "Arrogant Perception, World-travelling, and Multicultural Feminism: The Case of Female Genital Surgeries" (1991–2) 23 *Columbia Human Rights Law Review* 189.

[71] I. Gunning, *ibid.*, at 205–207.

and suppositions of the other men of their time and so equated female mental disorders, not with any social injustice in the role assigned to women, but to their sexual organs. Surgery then was the logical answer, and it created a trend that Barker-Benfield describes as 'characterized by flamboyant, drastic, risky and instant use of the knife.'

Barker-Benfield notes that clitoridectomy was the first cure for female mental disorder. It was invented by an English gynecologist, Dr Isac Baker Brown, who was considered one of the ablest and most innovative surgeons in England. Reports of the number of surgeries Brown performed range from several hundred to several thousand. Brown's concern was to 'solve' women's mental health problems: '. . . the main culprit was masturbation . . . The treatment was clitoridectomy.' Brown's 'cures' were repudiated as quackery by the British medical establishment in 1867 and he was expelled from the Obstetrical Society."

In this extract, Isabelle Gunning refers to the clitoridectomy operations performed by the English practitioner Baker Brown in the 1860s. He offered the operations to cure women of "female nervous diseases", claiming the operation presented a cure for masturbation, depression, marital dissatisfaction and nymphomania:

E. SHOWALTER
Sexual Anarchy: Gender and Culture at the Fin de Siècle[72]

"Baker Brown performed clitoridectomies in his busy London clinic on scores of clients, including five women whose 'madness' consisted of wanting divorces; in each case the woman returned to her husband subdued. He believed that the operation was particularly effective in cases of nymphomania, because he never saw a recurrence of such unbridled female passion after the surgery."

The practices of Baker Brown were eventually challenged by the British Medical Association and he was struck-off. Isabelle Gunning suggests that the reasons given in the nineteenth century for the performance of these operations upon women are still in evidence today. These reasons constructed surgical intervention as a method by which women could be controlled and were carried out in the belief that, because men and women possessed distinct natures and hence were suited to different roles, surgery offered a corrective to women who demonstrated "manly" characteristics.

There have been more recent examples of the surgeries being performed in the western world. In December 1988, Dr James Burt was charged by the Ohio State Medical Board with gross unprofessional conduct. He performed surgery which he claimed would reconstruct the female body which is, in his view, structurally unsuited to intercourse. In addition to suffering adverse health consequences from the surgery the women upon whom he had operated had to undergo corrective surgery. He left medical practice in January 1989.[73]

---

[72] (London: Virago, 1990), p. 130.
[73] E. Showalter, *Sexual Anarchy: Gender and Culture at the Fin de Siècle*, ibid., pp. 141–2.

In November 1993, Harley Street consultant, Farouk Hayder Siddique, appeared before the General Medical Council (GMC) charged with performing "female circumcision" knowing the operation to be contrary to the law. He was struck-off by the GMC for serious professional misconduct. Siddique, however, denied the allegations that he had agreed to perform a circumcision for a fee of £500 upon a journalist who claimed that she was getting married and that her future husband wanted her to have the operation.[74]

10.3.ii *Take a look at your own culture now*
Having situated female genital surgeries in their historical context, Gunning's second stage in the "world-travelling" method is to make comparisons with practices within our own cultures, to raise awareness of our own traditional practices which control women and perpetuate norms about female nature and appropriate feminine roles.

I. GUNNING
"Arrogant Perception, World-travelling, and Multicultural Feminism: The Case of Female Genital Surgeries"[75]

"This involves appreciating the fact that just as a Westerner may view the surgeries as a cultural challenge, the street runs two ways: non-Westerners too can view Western practices as culturally challenging. One good example . . . is the American practice of cosmetic breast surgery, but there are others.

Self-starvation techniques, anorexia and bulimia, have been identified largely in women as a part of the current cultural struggle over female identity, both of perceptions of our own beauty as well as our uncertainties about controlling our lives. In societies where not just malnutrition (which is an embarassing American phenomenon as well) but starvation and dire poverty are aspects of everyday life, the thought of women refusing food for cosmetic purposes (as opposed to providing for their families' nutritional needs) or wasting food by eating it and then regurgitating it must be close to sacrilege.

Looking at ourselves as others might see us ultimately deepens our view of ourselves. In addition to the caution and care that the legacy of imperialism requires Western feminists to take in appreciating and participating in truly egalitarian relationships with women in non-Western cultures, the general air of superiority and self-righteousness must wither away upon reviewing where we have come from and how far we still have to go within our own cultures."

Lois Bibbings compares female genital surgeries with non-essential practices in Western cultures, and body modification within western subcultures:

---

[74] H. Davidson & A. Alderson, " 'Mutilation' doctor banned", *The Sunday Times*, November 28, 1993.
[75] I. Gunning, *supra*, n. 70 at 212–213.

L. BIBBINGS
"Female Circumcision: Mutilation or Modification?"[76]

"FEMALE GENITAL ALTERATION AND OTHER BODY MODIFICATION PRACTICES

[T]hese practices are isolated from the context of other permanent body modification techniques. This is symptomatic of a general tendency to conceal, over simplify or generalise when considering issues related to FC/FGM [Female Circumcision/Female Genital Mutilation] . . . Reconceptualising FC/FGM practices as fragmented forms of body modification allows for a more accurate and less culturally specific view to be adopted. This will allow parallels to be drawn between the ways in which FC/FGM, cosmetic surgery and other forms of permanent body modification are perceived.

Body modification can be defined as either the permanent (irreversible) or temporary alteration or adornment of the body. Such procedures are often described as being *elective* as they are operations which are performed for aesthetic reasons or are non-essential. Those which can be described as permanent include cosmetic surgery, body and facial piercings (any loose flesh on any part of the body can potentially be pierced, including the ears, nose, tongue, cheeks, lip, eyebrows, nipples, navels and male and female genitals), scarification (the making of marks on the flesh by burning or cutting) and tattoos. Some of these procedures, like ear piercing and tattooing, are reasonably acceptable (although not uncontroversial) in the West whilst others can be described as being nonmainstream . . .

Cosmetic surgery is becoming increasingly popular in the West amongst women and men. Whilst some proponents of human rights have not perceived cosmetic surgery as a major concern, the practice has not gone unchallenged. Feminist commentators on women's cosmetic surgery often perceive it as an example of body fascism; as a facet of patriarchal oppression which portrays the female form as imperfect and perpetuates norms of feminine beauty and the need for conformity. Thus the 'choice' to be operated upon is often dismissed as the result of 'false consciousness'. There are clear parallels here to the manner in which some feminist or rights-based critics of traditional practices have denied the validity of the Exotic Other Female's choice to be 'mutilated'. In such accounts of FC/FGM and cosmetic surgery the women who choose to undergo the procedures themselves, perform them on others or cause them to be performed on others, are frequently undermined and belittled. Kathy Davis presents a challenge to the conventional feminist view of cosmetic surgery. She argues that '[c]osmetic surgery may be, first and foremost, about being ordinary, taking one's life in one's hands, and determining how much suffering is fair' and that a woman who chooses cosmetic surgery may have realistically balanced the suffering caused by her present situation against that which the solution offered by cosmetic surgery would entail. 'When viewed against this backdrop, the decision could conceivably become a moment of triumph — a moment when a women turns the tables and does something to help herself.' Thus, in this model, the decision to be operated upon could itself conceivably be perceived as being liberating or empowering . . .

Similarly advocates of the various forms of body alteration in the West have argued that body modification can be viewed as a means of empowerment which allows an individual to redefine or recreate her/himself. This argument is particularly common amongst those who practice forms of nonmainstream body modification in the West.

[76]   In J. Bridgeman & S. Millns (eds), *supra*, n. 69 at pp. 160–163.

For example, women in particular view such practices as empowering or as a means of reclaiming their bodies after breast-feeding or even sexual abuse. Such alterations can also serve as a form of initiation into a group or subculture. Alternatively modifications may be chosen for aesthetic reasons and viewed as a means of beautification (by making a person's body conform to a conventional image of beauty or making their appearance more distinctive and individual). Similarly in some parts of Africa FC/FGM is considered equally fashionable. In this view body modification is a means of bodily self-determination. Thus, here again, there are parallels with the justifications for FC/FGM . . .

The majority of nonmainstream practices (which often have Third World or 'tribal' origins) are viewed as primitive, deviant, repulsive or barbaric by Westerners when practised in the West . . . It would, perhaps, be interesting to learn the response of Third World populations upon discovering that in the West some women have fat sucked from their bodies (liposuction), lumps of silicon placed in their breasts, their skin stretched or chemically scraped and their tummies tucked for aesthetic reasons, suffering considerable pain and discomfort in the process and risking unforeseen health complications or indeed the complete lack of success of the operation."

The principal differences identified by Lois Bibbings between practices such as cosmetic surgery or body piercing and genital surgery when "voluntarily" entered into by an adult, are that greater pressure may be applied to women to undergo genital surgery than that applied to western women to induce them to modify their bodies. Also the different circumstances under which the operations are performed may mean that the health risks are greater in the case of genital surgery. In an earlier article, written in conjunction with Peter Alldridge, Lois Bibbings suggests that the purpose of the procedures is different. Cosmetic surgery and body piercing are decorative whilst "[f]emale circumcision is not for decoration. Instead, many argue that its purpose lies in the control and oppression of women and the suppression of female sexuality . . ."[77] The lack of free choice under which women elect to undergo genital surgeries is discussed in the following extract:

A. T. SLACK
"Female Circumcision: A Critical Appraisal"[78]

"People in most societies are generally free to treat their bodies as they please, even if this means compromising their own health and well-being . . .

People who 'voluntarily' engage in potentially harmful practices, however, may not be entirely aware of the possible consequences of their decisions. It is conceivable that if the consequences of some potentially dangerous cultural operations were known in advance, the decision of a person to proceed might well be reversed. The initial

---

[77] L. Bibbings & P. Alldridge, "Sexual Expression, Body Alteration, and the Defence of Consent", *supra*, n. 58 at 362. The question whether women who undergo cosmetic surgery do so as a matter of free choice is considered above in Chap. 10.2.
[78] (1988) 10 *Human Rights Quarterly* 437 at 470–472.

decision, therefore, to become engaged in a potentially harmful practice should only be considered truly voluntary if it is made with full awareness of the possible outcomes.

This consideration can be aptly applied to the issue of female circumcision. Those who support the practice state that most of the women or older girls who are circumcised have made the decision to do so themselves. It is not clear, however, that the women are actually aware of the extent to which they may be harmed or deformed by the practice. Many of the arguments in defense of the practice are based on false information (for example, myths and religious requirements). Can the argument for personal choice be legitimate if the reasons for choosing are unfounded? If women understood that a normal clitoris does not grow to the size of a man's penis, they might well refuse to have themselves excised. If women knew that infibulation might risk their lives, or the lives of their children, they might be less inclined to comply with tradition.

Unfortunately, the level of education, especially for women, is low in most of the countries where female circumcision is routinely practiced. Accordingly, there is little access to information that might shed light on the subject. Little about the health hazards of circumcision is available in print, but even if the information were more available, the illiteracy rate is so high that dissemination would still be difficult.

Social pressure also influences the degree to which behaviour can be considered voluntary. Underlying the importance of tradition to a culture is the fear of the consequences that might result from disregarding the traditions. 'It is believed that any attempt to abandon such customs would be met by the disapproval of society manifested in ostracism and insults.'

The same qualities of a tradition that serve to bind a society together in a positive way, can also serve to intimidate members of that society into conforming to its mandates. It would appear, therefore, that inherent in the justification of female circumcision on the grounds of tradition, especially in poor rural communities with ancient customs, is 'the fear that any deviation from tradition means being disapproved of or ostracized by society.' Can the decision to be circumcised even when all the facts and risks are known, be considered truly voluntary when the only alternative is to be ostracized for such aberration? 'Faced with this societal mandate that circumcision improves their feminine anatomy and morality, women 'consent' to be circumcised.'
. . .

In addition to cultural pressures, economic and social concerns may compel women to consent 'voluntarily' to these operations. In most of the countries where female circumcision is still practiced, marriage is the only hope that women have for social and economic survival: poverty, illiteracy and low status of women are combined with hunger, ill-health, overwork, and lack of clean water, and an uncircumcised wom[a]n is stigmatized and not sought in marriage. It is, therefore, understandable that the victims of the practice are also its strongest proponents. A woman who questions tradition loses the support of the community that is necessary for her survival."

10.3.iii *Consider the cultural context of the other*
The third element in Isabelle Gunning's "world-travelling" method to genital surgeries is to consider the practices within the cultural context in which they occur. Isabelle Gunning suggests that it is easier for western women to understand the complex forces resulting in the decision to undergo cosmetic surgery and to place the issue raised within the wider context of issues affecting women, than it is to understand culturally-challenging practices:

I. Gunning
"Arrogant Perception, World-travelling, and Multicultural Feminism: The Case of Female Genital Surgeries"[79]

"The easy part of understanding female genital surgeries in their own organic social environment, for the Western feminist, is understanding them as part of a complex system of male domination of women. Not unlike Western societies, women in cultures where genital surgeries are performed find 'their social status and economic security [derive] from their roles as wives and mothers.' . . . Marriage in these societies, beyond the satisfaction of emotional and psychological needs, is an essential career move . . .

Being a virgin is largely the way that a woman maintains her own reputation and marriageability as well as the reputation of her family members. As in many Western societies the purity of the 'family' or male lineage is of great importance. Female sexuality or 'hypersexuality' must be reined in. Rather than relying on 'mere' moral suasion to ensure chastity, circumcision, arguably, will physically require it . . .

[T]hese economic pressures are, of course, intertwined with social pressures. Preserving one's chastity and giving sexual pleasure to one's husband are related to the emotional needs to acquire and keep a husband and family. If one is not 'properly' circumcised and resutured after childbirth, one risks losing him as he resorts to prostitutes, additional wives, or even divorce. Not only are such social pressures emotionally frightening, but the fear of divorce has an economic aspect as well.

Aside from the bad (often 'economic') consequences that will likely befall one if one remains uncircumcised, one would be essentially bad or unclean . . .

Finally, . . . the surgeries are widely believed to have health benefits similar to the benefits doctors in Nineteenth Century America claimed for such surgeries. Perhaps their key health benefits are those associated with increasing fertility. This is the key health benefit because bearing children is one of the few resources that women can control, and any procedure believed to enhance a woman's production of healthy children is likely to be embraced firmly . . .

For the African feminists who clearly agree that the surgeries must be abolished, the practice is viewed as only one of a number of problems besetting women, including poverty, scarce water and land, heat and dust storms, and generally bad health care. The surgeries do not head the list of wrongs that need to be righted to improve the status of women . . .

When one sees that 'other' within her own context, one sees women making a number of choices within the context of their complex social fabric. To be sure, there is the coercive aspect of patriarchal control in terms of physical violence as well as economic and social pressures . . .

The three-pronged world-travelling approach, in balancing the similarities we share as women with the differences we most respect as different women, underscores the need to be particularly attuned to the requirement of according different cultures the same respect for their complexity and holistic, organic nature that one can easily identify in one's own culture. Western women have confronted the same problem of female genital surgeries that African women face today, albeit in our own cultural context."

Morayo Atoki explains the cultural understanding underpinning female gential surgeries in African socieities where they are performed:

---

[79] I. Gunning, *supra*, n. 70 at 215–218, 225–226.

M. ATOKI
"Should Female Circumcision Continue to be Banned?"[80]

"Why a practice is carried out in a particular society and not in another, is often connected with its jurisprudential nature. The practice of female circumcision has its foundation in African jurisprudence, where the female genitalia is perceived as a symbolic organ that connotes purity and fecundity. Indeed it is on the female genitalia that two important concepts in African jurisprudence, 'virginity' and 'fertility' are based. Contracts of marriage and family patterns in many African societies are structured entirely on these two concepts.

In these traditional societies a good marriage is one contracted with a virgin bride. The virginal state of the bride is based on her genitalia and has both symbolic significance of purity and economic value. Virginity signifies purity and determines the value of the dowry given by the bridegroom. It is the standard upon which the marriage is contracted and any hint of blemish in the bride diminishes the value of her dowry, and also reduces her chances to marry. The female genitalia is thus an important element in the negotiation of marriage contracts and an undefiled one carries the highest value.

It is therefore not surprising that in some of these societies there is much preoccupation with the appearance of the female genitalia. The genitalia had to be re-created in a form that indicated purity of the organ. Excision of parts was the procedure adopted to remove those areas of the female genitalia considered inimical to purity and this eventually evolved as a cultural practice. Female circumcision is in essence genital aesthetics and this is the reason why many practise it.

It is interesting to note, that in many societies where the practice is carried out, female circumcision is done on pubertal girls and only then are they eligible for marriage. In contrast, where female circumcision is not practised, girls are often married before they attain puberty. Child betrothal, or marriage before the onset of menstruation, being a way of ensuring purity of the bride."

It is important, when analysing female genital surgeries, to understand the important link between marriage as fundamental to the economic survival of women, virginity as a prerequisite to marriage and surgery as evidence of virginity. The approach suggested by Isabelle Gunning shows how, as women living under the pressures to conform with the dominant Western norm of beauty, we may understand why women undergo cosmetic surgery whilst being shocked at female genital surgery. Looking to the social context in which the surgeries are performed enables greater understanding and demonstrates the similarities between female genital surgeries and practices within our own culture which extend male control over the female body. Likewise, by focusing upon context, we may gain greater insight into the concerns of women who inhabit other cultures, whose main priorities may be poverty, inadequate food and polluted water rather than genital modification.

The three stage approach suggested by Isabelle Gunning focuses upon a consideration of the practices of genital surgeries within the countries in which they are currently traditionally performed, leading the author to an exploration of whether international law is an appropriate tool for eradication. How-

[80]   (1995) 3 *Feminist Legal Studies* 223 at 225–226.

ever, Gunning's approach can be applied to reach an understanding of the performance of the operations in the West as a result of the movement of people from cultures where the practice is indigenous. In these cases, understanding the "Other" in her cultural context demands acknowledging the complexities of the Other's adaptation to a different culture whilst keeping her own traditions alive. This involves a search which, rather than seeing the surgeries as abominations imposed upon women in other cultures, locates genital surgeries as one example of a practice which exposes women to health risks and involves the imposition of control over women. In addressing the response of English law to the surgeries, it also involves identifying the boundaries between the "tolerable, the problematic, and the criminal", that is, between the "legal, the questionable, and the illegal".[81] This may lead to a better understanding of the approach taken by English law and also its shortcomings.

Before addressing the appropriate legal response, however, it is necessary to attempt to understand the reasons for the different forms of operations, which is an aspect of the third step of the approach advocated by Isabelle Gunning. A variety of explanations and justifications are given including any combination of the following: custom; religion (although surgery is not a requirement of any faiths); family honour; cleanliness (although it is commonly agreed that surgery does not have any effect in ensuring hygiene and that infibulation, in particular, has the opposite effect by inhibiting urination and menstruation); initiation into womanhood (although this may no longer be the case as the operations are increasingly performed at a younger age); prevention of female promiscuity;[82] and, as mentioned above, insurance of virginity at marriage. The operations are usually performed by women at the instigation of female relatives.

M. DALY
Gyn/Ecology: The Metaethics of Radical Feminism[83]

"The use of women as token torturers is horribly illustrated in this ritual. At the International Tribunal on Crimes Against Women the testimony of a woman from Guinea was brought by a group of French women. The witness described seeing 'the savage mutilation called excision that is inflicted on the women of my country between the ages of 10 and 12.' . . .

It is men who demand this female castration, and possession in marriage is required in *their* society for survival. The apparently 'active' role of the women, themselves mutilated, is in fact a passive, instrumental role. It hides the real castrators of women. Mentally castrated, these women participate in the destruction of their own kind —

---

[81] L. Bibbings & P. Alldridge, *supra*, n. 58 at 356.
[82] Female sexual desire is viewed as beyond the individual female's control. The focus of this desire is recognised to be the clitoris, so excising protects the woman from temptation whilst preserving her chastity.
[83] (London: The Women's Press, 1991), pp. 163–165.

of womankind — and in the destruction of strength and bonding among women. The screaming token torturers are silencing not only the victim, but their own victimized Selves. Their screams are the 'sounds of silence' imposed upon women in sado-ritual . . .

The fact that 'women did it — and still do it — to women' must be seen in this context. The idea that such procedures, or any part of them, could be woman-originated is only thinkable in the mind-set of phallocracy, for it is, in fact, unthinkable. The use of women to do the dirty work can make it appear thinkable only to those who do not wish to see. Yet this use of women does effectively blunt the power of sisterhood, having first blocked the power of the Self.

Most horrifying is the fact that mothers insist that this mutilation be done to their own daughters. Frequently it is the mother who performs the brutal operation. Among the Somalis, for example, the mother does the excising, slicing, and final infibulation according to the time-honored rules. She does this in such a way as to leave the tiniest opening possible. Her 'honor' depends upon making this as small as possible, because the smaller this artificial aperture is, the higher the value of the girl."

Where a woman's future depends upon marriage, where she is marriageable only if she is a virgin and only if she has been operated upon providing to her future husband external evidence of virginity, a mother who arranges for her daughter to have surgery is ensuring the best possible future for her daughter. A "normal" woman is one who has been operated upon.[84]

10.3.iv *Prohibition of female circumcision*

There was some doubt expressed both in the House of Commons and the House of Lords in the debates on the Prohibition of Female Circumcision Bill as to whether specific legislation was necessary given that the practice of female genital surgery was already contrary to the criminal law, amounting to an assault occasioning actual bodily harm or unlawful wounding contrary to section 47 and section 20 of the Offences Against the Person Act 1861.[85] If the operation were performed on a child under the age of 16 a prosecution could also be brought under section 1 of the Children and Young Persons Act 1933 which makes it an offence for a person over the age of 16 to "wilfully assault[], ill-treat[], neglect[], abandon[], or expose[]" or to cause or procure another to do so to a child "in a manner likely to cause him unnecessary suffering or injury to health".[86] As Susan Akers explains, there was legislation in existence in 1985 contrary to which those performing the operations and the family members who sought the operations could be prosecuted.[87] How-

---

[84] M. Daly in *Gyn/Ecology: The Metaethics of Radical Feminism*, *ibid.*, notes (p. 167) that "[o]nly a mutilated woman is considered 100 per cent feminine".

[85] Sections 47 and 20 of the Offences Against the Person Act 1861 are set out in Chap. 10.2 above.

[86] This chapter does not address the child protection policies which may be invoked to prevent young girls from being operated upon either as a result of their family paying for a circumcision practitioner to travel to this country in order to operate or taking their daughters to visit relatives overseas and operating upon them whilst they are there. Child protection mechanisms are discussed in S. Akers, "Female genital mutilation — cultural or criminal?" (1994) 6 *Journal of Child Law* 27; E Dorkenoo, *supra*, n.69, Chap. 6.

[87] S. Akers, *ibid.*, at 27.

ever, the Prohibition of Female Circumcision Act 1985 specifically addressed the issue of genital surgeries, making the illegality of such operations entirely beyond doubt.

HOUSE OF COMMONS DEBATES
Vol. 77 at 583, April 19, 1985, Mrs Marion Roe

"The purpose of the Bill is to make it clear beyond doubt that the practice of female circumcision should be illegal in Britain. Although, as the law stands, it might be argued that to perform such an operation constituted an act of actual bodily harm, there is no precedent detailing this. The degree of abhorrence of these procedures felt by all can leave no room for uncertainty. The Bill, though short, is both concise and exact and achieves that purpose."

HOUSE OF LORDS DEBATES
Vol. 463 at 1241, May 15, 1985, Baroness Trumpington

"The main objective of this course . . . is to put beyond any shadow of doubt that the practice of female circumcision is illegal in this country. It may be of course that female circumcision as such, which can consist of severe mutilation, is already against the criminal law. Certainly, if any cases were referred to the Department of Health we would pass the information to the Director of Public Prosecutions for him to consider criminal proceedings. However . . . I am not aware that this point has ever been tested by the courts, and there could be no certainty until that were done."

The Bill, which was eventually enacted in 1985, was the third to be introduced to Parliament on the issue.[88] The first, introduced by Lord Kennet in 1983 fell with the dissolution of Parliament prior to the General Election. Baroness Trumpington, during debate in the House of Lords upon what was to become the 1985 Act, stated that any legislation must serve three purposes. First, it should clarify the law. Secondly, it should prohibit female circumcision and, thirdly, it should not prohibit "legitimate forms of surgery".[89] The second attempt at legislation had fallen down on Trumpington's third criterion. This issue was similarly contentious in the parliamentary debates upon the Bill which eventually became law, focusing upon the terms of section 2 which exempts from the ambit of the Act any necessary surgical operations.

[88] For a description of the Parliamentary process leading to the passage of the Prohibition of Female Circumcision Act 1985 see E. A. Sochart, "Agenda Setting, The Role of Groups and the Legislative Process: The Prohibition of Female Circumcision in Britain" (1988) 41 *Parliamentary Affairs* 508.
[89] H. L. Debs, Vol. 463 at 1241, May 15, 1985, Baroness Trumpington.

Prohibition of Female Circumcision Act 1985
(c. 38)

Prohibition of female circumcision

1.—(1) Subject to section 2 below, it shall be an offence for any person —
- (a) to excise, infibulate or otherwise mutilate the whole or any part of the labia majoria or labia minora or clitoris of another person; or
- (b) to aid, abet, counsel or procure the performance by another person of any of those acts on that other person's own body.

(2) . . .

Saving for necessary surgical operations

2.—(1) Subsection 1(a) of section 1 shall not render unlawful the performance of a surgical operation if that operation —
- (a) is necessary for the physical or mental health of the person upon whom it is performed and is performed by a registered medical practitioner; or
- (b) is performed on a person who is in any stage of labour or who has just given birth and is so performed for purposes connected with that labour or birth by —
  - (i) a registered medical practitioner or registered midwife; or
  - (ii) a person undergoing a course of training with a view to becoming a registered medical practitioner or registered midwife.

(2) In determining for the purpose of this section whether an operation is necessary for the mental health of a person, no account shall be taken of the effect on that person of any belief on the part of that or any other person that the operation is required as a matter of custom or ritual.

Section 1 makes it a criminal offence to perform or participate in the performance of excision, infibulation or mutilation of another. Section 2 provides the exemption for "necessary" surgical operations, ensuring that no offence is committed by a midwife or medical practitioner who carries out an episiotomy or stitching after childbirth, or the reinfibulation of infibulated mothers. What was controversial in the parliamentary debates was the saving in section 2(1)(a) which enables an operation necessary in the interests of the physical *or mental* health of the woman thereby condoning "cosmetic" operations. However, section 2(2) provides that in deciding whether an operation is necessary in the interests of the mental health of the woman, the effect of custom or ritual should not be taken into consideration. The Commission for Racial Equality was of the view that this was racially discriminatory:

"The 1985 version of the Bill unfortunately uses a form of words in clause 2(2) which the Commission has already described as likely to be discriminatory in effect and undesirable in principle ... The reason for concern is as follows: a doctor, when assessing mental health as justifying the performance of an otherwise prohibited operation, will normally base his judgment on the patient's state of mind as he finds it. To suggest that some reasons for that state of mind may be acceptable and others, broadly confined to those which might affect persons of African origin or descent, are not, is in the Commission's view discriminatory and therefore to be avoided."

Alternative proposed wordings had sought to make it clear that "cosmetic" operations, to "change the size or shape to an acceptable appearance" were acceptable; in that "[s]uch operations to the external genitalia of women should be permitted just as freely as they are permitted to the external genitalia of men, or, come to that, to noses or chins".[90]

No prosecution has been brought under the 1985 Act which provides no preventative powers but was designed to act as a deterrent. The Act imposes criminal penalties without giving consideration to the cultural traditions in which genital surgery is performed. Adherents to such traditions may justifiably feel the victims of cultural imperialism. Lois Bibbings discusses the initial ignorance of, and subsequent attempts at understanding, the cultural differences which have to be respected if eradication is not to be resisted by those who participate in the practice of genital surgery:

L. BIBBINGS
"Female Circumcision: Mutilation or Modification?"[91]

"The collection of practices which are referred to as FC/FGM have become a relatively frequent subject of discussion and media campaigns (including both television documentaries and broadsheets), amongst women and within feminist, human rights and/or academic circles. Such debates now take place in countries which have no long-term and on-going tradition of excision (predominantly States in the West), within those where FC/FGM has been practised for hundreds or thousands of years (most often Third World States) and at an international level.

Those contributions which emanate from within non-practising countries are relatively recent in origin. Until the late 1970s the only discussions tended to be within anthropological, sociological and psychological accounts of 'primitive' or 'native' practices and these do not represent attempts to alter or eradicate the practices. However, the earliest attempts to end FC/FGM were instigated by British colonial governments and Christian missionaries. Not surprisingly such efforts were largely unsuccessful. For

---

[90] H. L. Debs, Vol. 464, p. 572, June 3, 1985, Lord Kennet.
[91] In J. Bridgeman & S. Millns (eds), *supra*, n. 69 at pp. 156–160.

instance, attempts in the 1940s by the British government in Sudan to outlaw infibulation took no account of local culture. As a result such procedures were merely driven underground and their continuance became a symbol of resistance to foreign influences. Thus such episodes arguably incited resistance to change.

In countries within which forms of FC/FGM are traditionally practised some have also spoken out against the practices. African women began to publicise their concerns during the late 1970s. By the early 1980s a sizable opposition to FC/FGM had developed in Africa.

Notwithstanding the comparative youth of the debates, many of the reactions have been vehement. However, commentators and campaigners have not been united in their responses. Indeed various splits have emerged between, for example, Western and Third World feminists, and between those who argue for FGM to be recognised as an abuse of human (or more specifically women's) rights and those who maintain that some respect for different cultures must, at the very least, be iterated if not maintained. These various positions are, of course, not mutually exclusive . . .

Westerners from traditionally non-practising States have tended to be highly critical of FC/FGM, viewing it as a violation of rights or, for some feminists, as an example of patriarchal oppression. Western feminists in particular have tended to attack such customs and call for their eradication . . .

Such overtly critical comments by Westerners are one reason for Third World objections to Western involvement in the development and implementation of policy in relation to FC/FGM. Those from cultures which have a tradition of genital alteration view outsiders who condemn such procedures as standing in judgment upon their culture and their people. In addition, practising societies reject the imposition of Western norms upon their very different cultures . . .

[S]ome Third World critics of Western feminism have, despite their own rejection of such practices, challenged the latter's attitudes to FC/FGM. For example, Marie Angelique Savane, President of the Association of African Women, published an article criticising the cultural insensitivity of Westerners. Such objections are, in part, one facet of a wider debate which centres around calls for Western feminists to reconsider their conceptions of women, women's oppression and women's needs in the light of cultural difference. The suggestion here is that both feminism as a discourse and women-centred approaches are culturally specific. Thus Third World women wish to deny the monolithic and essentialist view of women which many Western feminists perpetuate . . .

Vehement Western feminist anti-FC/FGM statements also tend to anger those from the Third World because sometimes they are viewed as being patronising and as revealing latent racism. There is particular resentment of those who refer to customs as 'barbaric'.

Those who respond either to Western rights-based or feminist arguments tend to stress that Third World women (and men) have very different conceptions not only of rights but also of exploitation, oppression and needs. Thus it has been argued that calls for the abolition of the various forms of excision are less important than basic economic and material requirements including sufficient supplies of food and clean water. In addition, the Western focus upon FC/FGM means that the role of multinational corporations, (often Western in origin), and their exploitation of labour, is either ignored or granted a lower priority.

More specifically, there has been criticism of some Western feminists' tendency to sexualise issues; to use sexualism as a 'lens' by which to measure women in other cultures. In relation to FC/FGM this has involved a tendency to focus upon the clitoris and clitoridectomy whilst marginalising historical and political aspects of the practice. Chandra Talpade Mohanty has noted that Fran Hosken, in writing about human rights and FGM, bases her whole discussion upon the premise that the purpose of the practice is to mutilate the sexual pleasure and satisfaction of women, and T. Patterson observed at the 1982 African Studies Association meeting that many objected to Hosken's focus upon clitoridectomy as the major form of women's oppression in Africa and the Middle East.

Thus several common factors are discernible in many of the Western approaches to FC/FGM. Generally, non-practising States look down from above upon (practising) Third World peoples and their cultures and attempt to argue or imply that the Western way is best ... Such responses ... objectify women from practising cultures rather than recognising them as subjects. Thus, for example, some feminist approaches to FC/FGM have either ignored or dismissed Third World women's arguments supporting the practices (by implication as a form of 'false consciousness') or have offered maternalistically to change the mind of what Karen Engle has described as the 'Exotic Other Female'. Engle concludes that both human and women's rights-based approaches tend (albeit to varying degrees) to imagine, rather than engage, the 'Exotic Other Female' ...

Third World reactions to Western criticisms of FC/FGM have, however, had a clear effect upon Western and international responses and initiatives. The perceived cultural sensitivity of the discussion of FC/FGM as a human rights issue arguably led the WHO to delay consideration of the practices. Also there has been some recognition that a new approach must be adopted if international initiatives are to be successful in their attempts to lessen the frequency of, or eradicate, FC/FGM. Thus Westerners have tended to step back and allow those from practising cultures to formulate policy and guide actions. For example, Western members of the UN Sub-Commission on the Prevention of Discrimination and the Protection of Minorities which considered FC/FGM did not, for the most part, participate in discussions. Thus, more recently, Western and international efforts tend to take a supporting role and Westerners are generally more aware of cultural issues."

The criminal law was perceived, in Parliament, to be the appropriate means by which to clearly mark the disapproval of the performance of female genital surgeries in the U.K. This is backed by the longer term project of education with the aim of eventually eradicating the practice. Campaigners against the practice may identify it as an infringement of the liberty of the person, a form of torture, slavery or a violation of a woman's right to health and thus contrary to rights protected under international law.[92] Alternatively, to prohibit the surgeries may amount to an infringement of the right to self-determination so that a regulatory approach which scrutinises the practices to ensure that

---

[92] I. Gunning, *supra*, n. 70 at 231–248. Alison Slack argues for recognition that involuntary operations which threaten life infringe the fundamental right to health (A. T. Slack, "Female Circumcision: A Critical Appraisal", *supra*, n. 78). The limitations of existing mechanisms of international law in protecting the bodies of women, including against female genital surgeries, together with a possible strategy for protection via the adoption of a right to bodily integrity, is considered by F. Beveridge & S. Mullally in "International Human Rights and Body Politics" in J. Bridgeman & S. Millns (eds), *ibid.*, p. 240. The right to bodily integrity is discussed above in Chap. 7 in the context of mass rape.

surgery is only performed upon informed, freely consenting adults, may be more appropriate:

M. ATOKI
"Should Female Circumcision Continue to be Banned?"[93]

"Law is a social phenomenon and its primary function is to create order in society. In traditional societies, conventions and culture are essential for preserving the established society and are often embodied in the law. As society evolves, the law adapts to the interests and needs of the population. Modifying the law balances the demands of various groups within the population and strives at a just compromise between competing groups.

Any law enacted in respect of female circumcision must, on the one hand, prevent the infringement of the rights of the individual to cultural determination. It must protect those who wish to freely exercise their right to be circumcised and ensure that the practice is carried out within the law. Such a law must, on the other hand, expressly guard the rights of the child against abuse, protect the freedom of those who elect not to be circumcised and guarantee the right to proper information concerning circumcision. The law should limit the performance of the operation to trained practitioners and require the surgery to be performed only in approved settings. The services should be provided only to clients who have given their informed and expressed consent. One suggestion is that clients should be at least sixteen years of age, as this is the age of majority in many African countries.

A law in this form, would be more efficacious than one which bans female circumcision in its entirety. Banning the practice will not eradicate it; it will only succeed in driving it underground. In countries where there have been prosecutions the police have largely depended on the goodwill of persons to report the circumcision. It is for this reason several anti-circumcision laws are ineffective."

"Medicalisation", that is, requiring the surgery to be performed in hygienic conditions by a medically qualified practitioner may eliminate some of the health risks of surgery. But, like legal regulation, it does nothing to address the assumptions about female nature and women's appropriate role. The view of the female body as dirty, the perception of the female as promiscuous and the propagation of the belief that her only option in life is marriage (which depends upon evidence of virginity provided by surgery alone) can only be challenged through education. Education was acknowledged within the parliamentary debates upon the Prohibition of Female Circumcision Act 1985 as a fundamental prerequisite for the elimination of the practices, although there it was understood as being a necessary accompaniment to the conveyance of the message that the surgeries are inherently unacceptable, as evidenced by their criminalisation. Whilst criminalisation of the operations by the 1985 Act may be detrimental in giving the impression that traditions of minority cultures are not to be respected, and may result in the entrenchment of those customs in a defence against imperialism, it is acknowledged that education

---

[93] M. Atoki, *supra*, n. 80 at 234–235.

alone will not suffice. For female genital surgeries to be eradicated within Britain it is also necessary to challenge assumptions about the nature and appropriate role of women and to effect a change in the circumstances in which surgery is demanded such that society no longer requires that the female body be altered in order to secure women's economic and social survival.

SECTION FOUR

OFFENSIVE BODIES

INTRODUCTION

THE CONSTRUCTION OF THE FEMALE OFFENDER

Understandings of how women are expected to behave and about how their minds and bodies work affect the way in which women are treated throughout the criminal justice system, from decisions to prosecute and grant bail, through to mitigation of sentences and ultimately imprisonment.[1] Criminological theories, which search for explanations for criminal behaviour, are, in general, presented as gender neutral, equally applicable to male and female criminals. Until feminist criminology started to specifically consider the causes of female criminality, however, these theories were based upon the male subject and failed to explain why women commit crime.[2] Carol Smart argues that the reasons for the failure to study female criminality are that women commit less crime than men (with the exceptions of shoplifting and soliciting) and that, once convicted of an offence, women are less likely to reoffend. Thus, she suggests, women present less of a threat to social order.[3] In the following extract, Frances Heidensohn discusses the extent of offending by women and the type of crimes committed:

F. HEIDENSOHN
Women And Crime[4]

"*The female share of crime*
    [T]he one thing most people know about women and crime is that women's contri-

---

[1]   S. Edwards, *Women on Trial* (Manchester: Manchester University Press, 1984).

[2]   N. Naffine, *Female Crime: The Construction of Women in Criminology* (Sydney: Allen and Unwin, 1987). Ngaire Naffine and Faye Gale argue that female criminals may experience poverty and employment differently and have different relationships to their family and dependants from their male counterparts upon whom studies have traditionally been based (N. Naffine & F. Gale, "Testing the Nexus: Crime, Gender and Unemployment" (1989) 29 *Brit. J. Criminology* 144).

[3]   C. Smart, *Law, Crime and Sexuality: Essays in Feminism* (London: Sage, 1995), p. 16.

[4]   (London: Macmillan, 1985), pp. 5–11. Although the statistics used in this extract date from the early 1980s, the points which they serve to illustrate remain equally as valid today.

bution to total criminality is modest. Indeed this is an area of public achievement where women hardly compete with men.

In the analysis in this section I have used ... data for England and Wales. This data provides a reasonable example and has the advantage of coming from a single jurisdiction with a reasonably standard system of reporting and recording ... This presentation is therefore intended to be merely an example; while there are recent changes and local variations the patterns we shall find in recent British experience have a remarkable robustness and stability.

If we take the most recent year for which figures are available, 1982 (all the figures in this paragraph are from Home Office, 1983) some 2 million offenders were found guilty by all courts in England and Wales. More than 1 million were found guilty of summary motoring offences. Of all those found guilty 1 in 9 was female (11 per cent). For indictable offences (that is, broadly, more serious offences) 1 in 7 was female (14 per cent). However, when figures of cautions are included — that is, where a formal warning was given and recorded by the police — the picture changes somewhat, as females are more likely to be cautioned. Thus in 1982 as in previous years a higher proportion of female offenders — 34 per cent of females but only 17 per cent of male offenders were cautioned for indictable offences. Therefore 83 per cent of those found guilty of, or cautioned for, indictable offences were male and 17 per cent female ...

Females contribute to the officially recorded tariffs of all known offences. Even where there are legal requirements, as with rape, which women cannot fulfil, they may be charged as accomplices to a crime. Certain offences relate only to women: it is only mothers who can be charged with infanticide and offences by prostitutes involve soliciting and similar actions by females. Male homosexual relations are still much more heavily restricted by criminal sanction. But the overwhelming majority of offenders are charged with motoring offences or theft, relatively few with those where there is a discriminatory factor in the law. It is therefore interesting to note that women's participation in different offence categories does vary considerably. Thus in England and Wales for every year from 1972 to 1982 some 200 women were convicted or cautioned for robbery while the numbers of men rose over the same period from 3,500 to 4,300 while for shoplifting in 1982 there were over 48,000 convictions of males and just over 32,000 for females. Shoplifting is in practice the only major category of crime to which women make a significant contribution. Even so, the rate of convictions in relation to population at risk has been higher in recent years for men than women and in an earlier study Gibbens and Prince suggested that men stole more expensive items. Mayhew has suggested that shoplifting is one activity in which women's opportunities to commit crime are greater than any other since shopping is a legitimate and indeed essential public activity for women. She quotes three surveys from the USA and Ireland which recorded similar rates of observed shoplifting in male and female shoppers. However, her analysis is not borne out by a more recent and methodologically much more exacting British study. In observing a sample of shoppers who entered a small department store, Buckle and Farrington found that 'men are proportionally twice as likely to shoplift as women'. Moreover, men stole about five times as many items as did women and these were items of considerably greater value.

... In Britain and the USA more women have been participating in the past decade, with their age-related rates growing slightly faster than those for males (2–3 per cent) while for females they averaged 3–4 per cent between 1971 and 1981. But this shift, while it increased the numbers of women going to prison, did not result in women taking a noticeably larger role in recorded criminality.

While official data is not very helpful on this, it does seem that women commit fewer serious crimes and are rather less likely to be recidivists. Men predominate in homicide — 176 : 8 in 1982 — and the infanticide figures hardly change the picture (three cases in 1982). Studies of cautioning and sentencing procedures suggest, for the UK at least, that the lesser showing of women is due to the more trivial nature of their offences and their comparative lack of 'form' . . .

If we were to try to draw a portrait of a 'typical' female offender at this stage she would be a young girl, a first offender charged with shoplifting, and her likely destiny would be a caution or a non-custodial sentence. There are, of course, small groups of women who deviate from this: the regular drunk with a string of convictions, or the prostitute regularly fined for soliciting, as well as a sprinkling of women convicted of serious crimes such as murder, and offences associated with terrorism. However, while a very few female offenders have attracted unusual popular attention the picture is not on the whole an exciting one. 'Monster' murderers or big-time gangsters are scarcely found amongst the ranks of women offenders."

Carol Smart expresses the concern that the lack of studies into female criminality has meant that a number of questionable studies form the basis of understandings and treatment of female offenders. She explains the theory of Lombroso and Ferrero who, in *The Female Offender*, located the causes of female criminality in women's primitive state of development, believing that all females were at a lesser stage of development than males.[5] They argued that women were by their nature passive and generally were not inclined towards criminal behaviour. A woman who committed a crime was, therefore, either by nature deviant or pathological as she departed from the true nature of Woman. Biology is, on this view, the principal explanation for female crime. As all women could be considered to be inherently unlikely to commit crime, the management of criminal behaviour was predicated upon an understanding of the pathology located within the individual, rather than upon a view of crime as the result of conscious deliberation within the context of particular social circumstances. The appropriate response to female criminality, it followed, was treatment for a woman's disordered mind. A further view presented in the work of Lombroso is that, because of female biology, women are less sensitive to pain. Hence, as criminals, women are more evil.

Carol Smart also outlines the work Otto Pollak who, writing in 1950, argued, in *The Criminality of Women*, that women commit crime to the same extent as men but that the type of crimes committed and female social roles mean that their crimes are not detected.[6] Pollak argued that women are more deceitful than men. He explained this by the fact that women developed the ability to mask emotion (illustrated by the ability of the female body to participate in sex despite a lack of orgasm) and that social expectations encourage deceit in requiring women to hide the fact that they are menstruating.[7] Com-

---

[5] C. Lombroso & W. Ferrero, *The Female Offender* (London: Fisher and Unwin, 1895) discussed in C. Smart, *supra*, n.3, Chap. 2.

[6] O. Pollak, *The Criminality of Women* (Pennsylvania: Pennsylvania Press, 1950) discussed in C. Smart, *ibid.*

[7] Discussed in C. Smart, *ibid.*, pp. 23–24.

bined with the opportunities provided by their social position, women were, in Pollak's view, better at hiding their crimes than men.

C. DOCHERTY
"Female Offenders"[8]

"[S]ome of these theories suggest that certain women have deviant psychological or biological traits, and may, therefore, have a predisposition or tendency to commit crimes, another theory, currently popular, suggests that all women are slaves to their biology, and may commit crimes — particularly violent ones — as a result of a natural and uniform female biological process. Pollak, for example, emphasised the influence of the generative phases of pregnancy, menstruation and the menopause in female crime, suggesting that it was a:

> 'generally known and recognized fact that these generative phases are fre-
> quently accompanied by psychological disturbances, which may upset the
> need and satisfaction balance of the individual, or weaken her internal inhibi-
> tion, and thus become causative factors in female crime.'

Hormonal imbalance in women of all ages has long been considered to be implicated in female crime by various sections of the medical profession, and this continues to be the most persistent of those theories which suggest that there is a direct link between female physiology and crime. However, whilst it is one thing to say that one's biological make-up has a general effect on one's behaviour, it is quite a different thing to suggest that a certain biological process can be related directly with certain specific forms of behaviour . . .

Feminists and others have consistently attacked this reliance on . . . hormonal conditions as extenuating, or contributory, factors, since the suggestion that women are controlled and determined by their biology, denies women the characteristics of free, autonomous beings, and offers a 'justification' for unequal treatment. Thus, from the perspective of the hormonal theory of crime, a woman is subject to what may be termed 'hormonal imbalance' from the onset of menstruation to the time of her menopause. She would, therefore, be theoretically predisposed to commit crime for most of her natural life . . .

The belief that female crime is a consequence of biological or physiological processes results in women being seen as constrained and confined by hormones, and leads to the courts ignoring socio-economic and historical factors. Moreover, all women are subject to the same processes, however mild their symptoms may be. Thus, all women are stigmatised by their natural bodily functions."

In contrast to theories of biological determinism stand socialisation theories which assert that women are taught to be more passive, conformist and law-abiding than men. Hence women are socialised to conform to laws rather than to break them as do aggressive, active, peer-pressured males.

---

[8] In S. McLean & N. Burrows (eds), *The Legal Relevance of Gender: Some Aspects of Sex-Based Discrimination* (London: Macmillan Press, 1988), pp. 172, 174, 175.

C. DOCHERTY
"Female Offenders"[9]

"[S]ubsequently, several writers attempted to account for the pattern and volume of female crime, not in terms of psychological or physiological variables, but in terms of the different role expectations, and methods of socialisation, to which males and females are subject, as well as to their differential access to opportunity structures. Whereas, for example, boys are encouraged to be aggressive and adventurous, girls are taught to be non-violent, passive and cooperative, and, according to Cohen, whilst males tend to see success in educational or employment terms, girls are typically encouraged to see child-rearing and marriage as the most desirable ambition. Since ambition, in male terms, is not something routinely encouraged amongst girls, Cloward and Ohlin argued that female delinquency was less likely to occur, as females were correspondingly less likely to suffer from the same type of thwarted ambition . . .

Role theory was one of the more significant sociological contributions to the debate on women and crime, shifting the focus from the idea of individual pathology to an examination of social forces. However, whilst it offered an important new perspective, this theory was limited by the fact that it failed to address itself to the social and cultural origins of gender roles — to why, despite being socialised to conform, a small but significant number of women choose to engage in crime. The most fundamental criticism of role theory is that it continues to see women as regulated, albeit not by physiology, but by gender roles, and denies women the same free will, independent from biological or social factors, which is accorded to men . . .

[I]t is also often suggested that the difference between male and female crime rates is exaggerated — a consequence of much female crime going unreported, a lower detection rate for female offenders and chivalrous attitudes by the police and the courts, which result in women being treated more leniently. Whilst Pollak correctly highlighted the limitations of official statistics as a means of accurately measuring the incidence of crime, his view that the 'hidden' figure for women is larger than for men, as a consequence of females being more able to disguise the extent of their criminality, is largely speculative. It is generally accepted that those offenders who are eventually convicted in court, and who appear in the official statistics, represent a small proportion of those who actually commit offences."

A further explanation for the lower numbers of women appearing before the courts, identified in the above extract, is the "chivalry hypothesis" which asserts that a "gentlemanly" attitude prevails towards women so that those in authority are reluctant to see women appear in court. Women are given ways out of the criminal justice system so that only the worst offenders make it as far as court. Further, it is argued, when women do appear before the courts they are treated more leniently than comparable men. Whilst the statistics might give this impression, once it is recognised that women commit less serious crimes, and are more likely to be appearing before the courts for the first time, this argument becomes unsustainable:

[9]   C. Docherty, *ibid.*, pp. 176, 179.

C. DOCHERTY
"Female Offenders"[10]

"[T]he law, it has been suggested, treats men and women, who have been charged with the same crime, differently. The decision whether or not to charge and prosecute a person involves the use of discretion, as does the nature of the sentence which a court imposes upon an offender. Pollak argued that females received preferential treatment from the authorities, purely as a consequence of their sex, suggesting that: 'Men hate to accuse women and thus indirectly to send them to their punishment, police officers dislike to arrest them, district attorneys to prosecute them, judges and juries to find them guilty.' A number of other writers however, have questioned this premise and have suggested that women are in fact discriminated *against* by the criminal justice system. Hindelang, for example, discovered that, whereas a lesser proportion of women were reported to the police, this apparent bias vanished when the seriousness of the offence was controlled for. Several studies looking at the willingness of store detectives and customers to report shoplifters, have concluded that, although male shoplifters were more likely to be reported to the police, this was largely accounted for by the fact that males tended to steal more expensive goods than females. Further evidence comes from Robin, who noted that, whilst shops prosecuted 75 per cent of those who stole goods worth more than 30 dollars, they only referred 30 per cent of those who stole items worth less than this to the police. These studies were unable to find evidence to support the view that women were treated more leniently as regards being reported to the police, and in fact suggest that, in the case of serious crimes, women were marginally more likely to be reported to the authorities than men.

Moreover, it has been asserted that a female offender is more likely to receive a caution than a male offender. Walker, for example, compared the number of males and females cautioned, as a percentage of those cautioned or found guilty in court, to support this assertion. Official statistics do appear to indicate that a woman is more likely to receive a caution than a man. However, the statistics fail to account for several factors — principally that female offenders tend to commit less serious crimes than males, irrespective of the category. This, rather than the sex of the offender, may account for a significant number of female offenders being cautioned.

This is not to say, however, that the sex of the offender is completely unconnected with their treatment, however irrelevant it may be in fact. For example, there are indications that, in the pre-trial stage, women receive harsher treatment than men at the hands of the authorities, in certain cases. Edwards, for example, noted that the proportion of women who are refused bail, and who are eventually found not guilty or receive a non-custodial sentence, is much higher than that for men. The response of the authorities may largely relate to the extent to which the woman's behaviour conforms to role expectations, and it has been claimed that women tend to be remanded in custody when the crime they are charged with is a non-typical one. Similarly, it has been noted that courts tended to remand more women than men in custody for psychiatric or medical reports. These are important findings, given that being remanded in custody can adversely affect a person's ability to prepare an effective defence, and that those remanded in custody are more likely to plead guilty or be convicted.

The greater eagerness of the courts to call for social and medical reports on female

---

[10]   C. Docherty, *ibid.*, pp. 182–185.

offenders, particularly where the offence is 'unnatural' or violent, underlines the 'sickness' model of female criminality. This model is clearly not confined to physical illness, since it has already been noted that there is frequently an assumption that female offenders are psychologically or psychiatrically ill, particularly in the case of violent crimes.

Many of those who argue that women are the beneficiaries of chivalrous attitudes in the criminal justice system focus on what they see as a reluctance amongst the judiciary to sentence female offenders harshly. Official statistics do appear to indicate that women receive preferential treatment at the sentencing stage; male offenders are more likely to receive an immediate custodial sentence. Whilst females are less likely, in general, to be imprisoned, none the less certain women receive more severe disposals than men, particularly when their offence steps over the boundaries of sex-role expectations. Edwards, for example, has suggested that:

> 'women, whether as suspects, defendants or offenders are dealt with, in part,
> in accordance with the degree to which their criminal behaviour deviates
> from what is expected of them in their appropriate gender role.'

Several factors, apart from seriousness of the crime, have been proposed as an explanation for the apparent leniency of court disposals in the case of female offenders. Previous record may be important, as may the nature of the offence. In fact, women and men seem to be equally likely to receive a custodial sentence once previous criminal record and nature of the offence have been controlled for. Another factor which may have an effect on the likelihood of a woman receiving a custodial sentence is the impact such a sentence would have on the family, particularly on the children, rather than on the woman herself. As Smith suggested, '[any] special consideration given to a woman is given not because she is a woman but because she is a mother, wife or maintaining an elderly relative.'

Indeed, any apparent equality becomes less obviously real when it is noted that, although fewer women are imprisoned by the criminal courts, they tend to be imprisoned for less serious crimes, and frequently serve longer periods in prison for similar offences."

The view that women are treated more leniently throughout the criminal justice process ignores the extent to which women "are punished for breaching not only the criminal law but also sex role expectations".[11] At trial, and after conviction, a woman is dealt with by the criminal justice system according to the extent to which her crime deviates from the norms of appropriate female behaviour. She may go to prison not only because of the seriousness of her crime, but because of stereotypical views which discriminate against certain types of women. In recent years a greater number of women have received custodial sentences: a 40 per cent increase in the two years to 1995:[12]

---

[11] A. Morris, "Sex and Sentencing" [1988] Crim.L.R. 163.
[12] H. Fletcher, "The Unacceptable Face of Sentencing" (1995) 9 *The Lawyer* 12.

H. Fletcher
"The Unacceptable Face of Sentencing"[13]

"Last year [1994] 32 per cent of all women were jailed for less than 12 months and 33 per cent of all receptions into custody last year were for fine default. Evidence from probation staff indicates that a majority of those jailed for theft and fraud committed the offences either to feed themselves and their children or to sustain a drug or alcohol habit. Virtually all of this group are on benefit, in multiple debt and half of all women currently inside have dependent children. An analysis of the data shows that there are acute differences in the way in which male and female offenders are dealt with by the courts. Forty-six per cent of men were jailed last year for offences of violence compared to 29 per cent of women. Conversely, just 11 per cent of men were jailed for theft, compared with 23 per cent of women. In addition 35 per cent of women in jail have no previous convictions compared to 12 per cent of men. Finally of those received into custody, a quarter of the women were eventually jailed, compared to 42 per cent of the men."

Consistent with the view that women who commit crime break both the law and gender constructs is the fact that, whilst in prison, the rehabilitation of women is focused upon resocialisation into traditional female roles or upon treatment of mental illness which provides the explanation for some female criminal behaviour.

The bare facts concerning the imprisonment of women do more than raise questions about current penal policy, that is, the aims of the penal system and the extent to which the imprisonment of women who have committed minor offences against property meets those aims. They raise questions about the impact upon female offenders of legal constructions of Woman. Allison Morris explains how women, in comparison with men, rarely appear before the criminal justice system. Hence, different explanations are found for their appearance and, as a consequence, the way in which they are treated differs. Women who commit crime may be considered to lack responsibility for their actions, either because they are "social casualties" or because they are mentally ill. Allison Morris concludes that, when it comes to sentencing, the ways in which real women depart from the ideal of Woman (or, where they have children, from the ideal of Mother) are taken into account:

"provided a woman acted her part — modest, humble, remorseful — and references could be made to her previous good character, domestic pressures or competence in the home, she was not seen as 'criminal'. She was a 'proper' woman".[14]

Where a woman does not conform, she is punished for departing from the behaviour expected of the ideal Woman/Mother.

This said, we do not propose in this section to investigate the work of

---

[13] H. Fletcher, *ibid.*, at 12.
[14] A. Morris, *supra*, n. 11 at 166.

criminologists searching for explanations for female offending or that of peno-
logists considering the penalties imposed upon women who commit crimes.
Instead we propose to consider the application of a selection of substantive
laws to female criminals. It will become evident that, in the application of
laws, as in explanations for criminal behaviour, assumptions about the nature
of Woman and the workings of her mind and body are evident.

It is necessary, however, to start with some fundamental principles of the
criminal law. Premised upon the principles of liberal political philosophy, the
foundational aim of the criminal law is to do justice to individuals.

H. L. A. HART
Punishment and Responsibility[15]

"[T]he principle that punishment should be restricted to those who have *voluntarily*
broken the law . . . incorporates the idea that each individual person is to be protected
against the claim of the rest for the highest possible measure of security, happiness or
welfare which could be got at his expense by condemning him for a breach of rules
and punishing him. For this a moral licence is required in the form of proof that the
person punished broke the law by an action which was the outcome of *his free choice*."

Norrie argues, in *Crime, Reason and History*, that the criminal law can only
be understood by considering it within the context of its historical origins and
the contradictions which existed at that moment in time.[16] He argues that
the criminal law has its origins in the period of the enlightenment and the
understanding of the person as a self-interested individual exercising freedom
of choice. Rather than impose a harsh penal code, utilitarian theory applied
to the criminal law suggested that individuals would work out the benefits to
be gained from the crime against the cost to themselves of punishment and,
on the basis of that assessment, determine whether to commit the crime. If
the punishment outweighed the benefits (and it should do but only by a very
small degree) the rational individual would conclude that it was not worth
committing the criminal act. Norrie, however, suggests that the abstract individual upon which the criminal law was premised was misconceived:

A. NORRIE
Crime, Reason and History[17]

"In place of real individuals belonging to particular social classes, possessing the infi-
nite differences that constitute genuine individuality, the reformers proposed an ideal
individual living in an ideal world. 'Economic man' or 'juridical man' were abstrac-

---

[15] (Oxford: Clarendon, 1968) p. 22, cited in A. Norrie, *Crime, Reason and History* (London:
Weidenfeld and Nicolson, 1993), p. 12.
[16] A. Norrie, *ibid.*
[17] A. Norrie, *ibid.*, p. 23.

tions from real people emphasising one side of human life — the ability to reason and calculate — at the expense of every social circumstance that actually brings individuals to reason and calculate in particular ways. Crime was a social problem. It arose out of particular social conditions and was brought into being in the midst of struggles between social classes over definitions of right and wrong."

As Norrie emphasises, people commit crimes for a wide variety of reasons more complex than a cost/benefit (*i.e.* punishment/gains) analysis. It is only by considering individuals within their social and historical context that the reasons for committing crime can begin to be understood.

Norrie argues that the criminal law, based upon this abstract individual, has to identify the social factors influencing an individual's behaviour in order to discard them as irrelevant:

> ". . . [I]f criminal law deals with individuals and the responsibilities of individuals, how does it meet the claim, that might be raised by those who gain least from the prevailing social order, that they were not responsible for what they did because of circumstances which excuse, permit or justify their actions?"[18]

Norrie argues that the need to retain a notion of individual responsibility has determined the development of legal principles. He demonstrates that the abstract individual upon whom the law is premised is moulded in the image of the economically powerful middle-class. Further, Ngaire Naffine argues that the legal subject is a "middle-class man whose masculinity assumes a middle-class form".[19] The criminal law is presented as equally applicable to all individuals, punishing individuals only for freely chosen criminal acts. The familiar myth is one of legal neutrality — that sex differences are irrelevant to the criminal law. However, the reality is that the criminal legal subject is premised upon male values and modes of behaviour. The conduct of all is judged against these standards. For relief from criminal liability to be granted or for responsibility to be reduced through the application of criminal law defences, women have to fit their conduct within male modes of behaviour. The law is not, as the myth would have it, gender-neutral. Instead it excludes the experiences of women. This point is articulated by Katherine O'Donovan in the context of the issue considered in Chapter 11.1 below, that is the defences available to battered women who kill:

K. O'DONOVAN
"Defences for Battered Women Who Kill"[20]

"Recent articles on legal theory suggest that the concepts 'standpoint' and 'perspective' may be useful in probing certain issues. The idea is to recognize a pluralism of views,

---

[18]   A. Norrie, *ibid.*, p. 26.
[19]   N. Naffine, *Law and the Sexes: Explorations in Feminist Jurisprudence* (London: Allen & Unwin, 1990), p. 115.
[20]   (1991) 18 *Journal of Law and Society* 219 at 219–220.

values, interests, and experiences which affect what we know about law. This involves questioning the Archimedian position, that of the detached neutral observer who sits on Olympus and decides what is right or fair in judgement, law-making or indeed academic writing. Instead an experiential approach to law is put forward. For example, it is argued that the perspectives and experiences of many groups have been ignored in the past, and that these must be considered in law making and application. Changes in many aspects of law, including legislation, case-law, practice, and procedure, might follow.

This paper represents an effort to apply the experiential approach to an area of law where it seems particularly appropriate: the case of the victim of aggression who kills the assailant. If we are 'to shape the definitions to make law fit women's experience', the problem of the battered woman who kills provides a site of investigation. For it is often alleged that the current form of law ignores women's experiences and that the defences of self-defence and provocation which justify or partially excuse homicide are limited to male definitions and behavioural practices. What is being suggested is that long experience of being a victim of violence may lead a woman to kill, only to find that the law condemns her.

There is a burgeoning literature on this topic in North American law journals, but discussion in Britain is just beginning. This paper focuses not only on the charge of lack of even-handedness which has been levelled against law, but also on the methodological problems involved in incorporating pluralism of experiences in law-making . . . It is common, in papers such as this, to start with the statistics on homicide. Whether the evidence is taken from England and Wales, or the United States of America, the following conclusions emerge: about a quarter of all homicides are domestic; women are more likely to be the victims of homicide than the perpetrators; when female homicide victims are grouped, domestic killing forms the largest category, that is, the killing of wives or cohabitants.

The purpose of looking to statistical evidence is to paint the background to the picture. What we see are patterns of behaviour which colour conceptions of violence and fear. Men are the majority of killers and the killed; killing tends to be a male act. Gender role is a relevant aspect of investigations of killing: women rarely kill by comparison with men. But women do fear male violence. This leads Taylor to draw the conclusion: '[F]emale homicide is so different from male homicide that women and men may be said to live in two different cultures, each with its own "subculture of violence".'

The cultural argument can be taken further, not only in relation to homicide but also in relation to domestic violence. Much of the modern literature argues that the context of killing and of the law that surrounds it includes gender factors, whether the killing is done by a man or a woman. Violence and fear have a relationship to gender. When these matters come to court other cultural factors enter in through the law. Definitions of defences are informed by the past history of homicide and its character as primarily a male act. The gender aspects are rarely articulated. Laws are made by judges and legislators who are mainly drawn from one gender and whose experience is limited. When women do kill after experiencing violence they enter an alien culture which lacks an understanding of the context of their act. They encounter legal categories that do not accommodate their behaviour and are 'tried and sentenced by courts that ignore or misunderstand their actions and motivations'."

Law's "alien culture" does not recognise or accommodate the real life experiences of women. Consequently, the behaviour of women under the scrutiny of the criminal justice system is judged against the behaviour of Man. But it is also judged against the behaviour expected from the ideal of Woman. Ann Lloyd explores the thesis that women are punished both for the crimes they commit and for the extent to which they fail to conform to stereotypical notions of femininity — as passive, caring, domesticated and wifely: "Such a woman is 'doubly deviant' ".[21] This is the case for a determination of guilt as much as for the punishment given following conviction. Because the ideal Woman does not commit crime, the behaviour of a woman accused of a crime is explained either in terms of her mental state (and lack of reason, as expected from Man) or in terms of her extreme evilness (and lack of compliance with the ideal Woman).

Women are unusual participants in the criminal justice system. Statistics show that when women do offend, crimes of violence are rare[22] as are those which cause death. More usually offences are minor and are committed against property rather than people. Thus, to focus in this section upon the female offenders that we do, *i.e.* upon women who kill (either another adult who has been violent or a new-born child) and upon female prostitutes, may be considered a distortion of reality. However, the selective attention is, in our view, justified. First, "battered women who kill" is one area in which the criminal behaviour of women has received much publicity in recent years and may be considered to be a paradigmatic example of the failure of the substantive criminal law to achieve justice in its application to women. Secondly, infanticide, whilst again a rarely committed offence, demonstrates clearly the tendency of the law to seek explanations for female offending within the bodily processes of the individual female. The female prostitute, who is the subject of the second chapter in this section, is punished for using her body in a way which is seen to depart from that normally expected of Woman. Notable is the extent to which the acts of female prostitutes are criminalised whilst those of their male clients are not. The law, however, does not prohibit prostitution entirely but attempts to confine it outside the public view. Access to the sexual services of women are secured, as long as those services are not publicly touted.

Thus, the criminal woman brings sharply into focus the perception of the influence of the bodies of women over our minds and our actions. The rational thinking of Man, at the root of liberal political philosophy, is placed in opposition to the irrationality of Woman.

C. DOCHERTY
"Female Offenders"[23]

"[T]here is no doubt that the criminal justice system does discriminate on the grounds of sex, and often in line with received wisdom about appropriate gender roles.

---

[21] A. Lloyd, *Doubly Deviant, Doubly Damned: Society's Treatment of Violent Women*, (Harmondsworth: Penguin, 1995), p. 36.
[22] This is illustrated by the conclusions drawn from available statistics by Katherine O'Donovan in the above extract.
[23] C. Docherty, *supra*, n. 8 at p. 185.

Discrimination is at its most overt when the female is involved in offences which challenge traditional stereotypes of acceptable female behaviour . . . Even in offences which are not related to sexual activity, the predominance of assumptions about the female sex-role is reflected in the assertion that women who commit 'female' offences may be treated differently, that the woman's role as homemaker may influence sentencing policy, or that females in general, and offenders in particular, are conditioned by their emotional or physiological processes. In other words, although the sex of an offender is irrelevant to the insult felt by the community as a result of the offence, attitudes to women as a group, and to the sub-group of offenders, are formulated as much to protect the male concept of female behaviour, as they are seriously to explain criminality."

CHAPTER 11

WOMEN WHO KILL

11.1 Battered women who kill

Legal interaction with, and governance of, female behaviour and the female body operates in a myriad of ways. Law "disseminates" ideas of what it is to be Woman. It "reinforces" constructs of Woman by rewarding those real women who fulfil the ideal and punishing those who do not. Law also performs an "educative" function by informing women how they should behave.[1] These methods are shown particularly clearly in the regulation of female offenders.

Popular perceptions of female traits such as passivity, irrationality and irresponsibility are woven through the legal discourse on women offenders. For example, Hilary Allen's examination of psychiatric and probation reports demonstrates how, after having been found guilty of serious violent crimes, the explanations given for the behaviour of women are such as to deny women's responsibility for their crimes. The reports focus upon the psychological state of the woman to suggest that at the time of the crime she was not acting consciously or voluntarily, but rather was passively caught up in events:

H. ALLEN
"Rendering them Harmless: The Professional Portrayal of Women Charged with Serious Violent Crimes"[2]

"[T]he psychologisation of the case allows the question of the criminal intentions of the female offender ... to be reinvoked at the point of sentencing — and to be reinvoked in terms which both displace the material significance of the offence and attenuate the offender's moral responsibility for it.

The manoeuvre depends upon undercutting the formal acknowledgement of the offender's actions with the assertion that at the moment of the deed she was acting without conscious volition, without comprehension or without meaning. In a few cases ... sophisticated medical explanations are given for this curious state of mind. More commonly, however, no such explication seems to be regarded as necessary; instead,

---

[1] D. Nicolson, "Telling Tales: Gender Discrimination, Gender Construction and Battered Women who Kill" (1995) 3 *Feminist Legal Studies* 185 at 186.
[2] In P. Carlen & A. Worrall, *Gender, Crime and Justice* (Oxford: Oxford University Press, 1987), pp. 84, 85.

there is a simple denial of the woman's mental engagement with her behaviour, as if an unreasoning and unreasonable condition were a quite natural state of womanhood, for which no exceptional cause need be sought . . .

The initial psychologisation of female behaviour thus provides the conditions for a further characteristic manoeuvre — that of the *naturalisation* of the crime. Through the suppression or denial of criminal intention, the violent deed which provides the occasion for judgment is progressively erased or redefined. Having first been displaced from a domain of *culpable* human actions, for which the subject can be held morally responsible, the crime may then, by extension, come to be displaced from the domain of human actions altogether. Instead, it is rewritten as a mere event in nature, a natural disaster in whose devastation the offender has simply been swept away, without either volition or responsibility. Conspicuously, this naturalisation of female crime will have the effect of blunting whatever moral discredit would otherwise attach to its author, and will thereby reduce the apparent need for any punitive sanction against her. And in the more extreme cases, it may even allow the offence to enter the moral calculus paradoxically. Instead of counting *against* the offender, as a morally reprehensible action for which she must be punished, the 'tragic event' of the crime may actually come to be added to the sum of her involuntary and undeserved troubles, for which, if anything, she deserves public compensation."

Allen argues that the discursive construction of woman is as a passive, mentally unstable individual to whom events happen rather than as an individual who is actively responsible for occurrences in her life. It is also presumed that returning this woman to the domestic sphere better enables her to abide by the law.

H. ALLEN
"Rendering them Harmless: The Professional Portrayal of Women Charged with Serious Violent Crimes"[3]

"Throughout, the credibility and the coherence of these documents [psychiatric and probation reports] depends on their resonance with certain taken-for-granted images of female lives and subjectivity. In the insistence on the domestic statuses of these women, this appeal to the familiar and the 'normal' is relatively unambiguous. What my discussion may have obscured, however, is the degree of normalisation that is also involved in the other manoeuvres of these reports. In my attempt to expose these manoeuvres, I sought to construct a sense of their 'strangeness' — the strangeness of presenting their crimes as impersonal misfortunes rather than personal misdeeds; of claiming that even at the decisive moment of their crimes, these adult and averagely intelligent individuals were behaving without volition, intention, understanding or consciousness. But this sense of strangeness is exterior to the texts themselves. Within the texts, these portrayals are treated unproblematically, as if reflecting a taken-for-granted and uncontentious perspective on the everyday reality of female existence.

Thus the 'absence of agency' that characterises the description of women's crimes is not presented in these texts as any sudden or aberrant departure from their female normality: instead, it appears continuous with even the most unremarkable moments

---

[3] H. Allen, *ibid.*, pp. 90–91.

of their existence. In the brief biographies that routinely form part of these texts, it is not simply in relation to *crimes* that there appears a reluctance to describe these subjects as intentional or active: there appears a striking paucity of references to these women doing anything intentional *at all*. The lives of *male* offenders are regularly described in simple statements in the active voice, detailing the succession of things that the offender has 'done' in his life. By contrast, the description of women's lives is everywhere hedged about with circumlocutions and grammatical inversions that constantly obscure the subjects' active responsibility and agency. There is a conspicuous concern with the women's emotional responses to the material events of their lives, but little expectation that they will normally be the active authors of these events – and every readiness to conclude that they are *not* . . .

The image of the female sex as passive, ineffectual, unstable and irresponsible is a familiar target for criticism by feminists, as indeed is the expectation that women's social and legal existence will be governed by the restraints of domesticity and the family. Feminist analyses of the law have long recognised that the privileges and exemptions that such conceptions may allow are bought at the expense of making legal invalids of women, of excluding them from their full status as legal subjects, and of perpetuating their social and legal subordination. And in the specific field of criminal justice, feminist authors have been uniformly suspicious of the judicial 'lenience' towards female offenders which such conceptions of female incapacity can help to sustain.

On one hand, this judicial lenience can be theorised as merely compounding the initial invalidation of women's action and responsibility. The imposition of a modest or nugatory sentence, as is common in cases of violence by women, carries the public implication that the crime itself need not be taken particularly seriously. From this perspective, the lenient sentencing of violent women can be interpreted as a more or less calculated tactic of patriarchal oppression, whereby the potential power of women's action can be censored from public recognition, and the politically sedative myth of women's compliance and harmlessness can be conveniently preserved. On the other hand, the accompanying preference for 'rehabilitation' of deviant women routinely involves the reinforcement of conventional sexist expectations about the 'proper' domains of feminine activity often implies no more than the women's supervised attachment or reattachment to the informal controls of the family. From a radical perspective, any apparent gains of this approach may be dismissed as illusory: they are won only by exchanging overt coercion for a 'privileged' and 'voluntary' submission to patriarchal authority, which neither relieves women from the normal constraints of sexual oppression, nor removes the threat of explicitly coercive sanctions in the event of further dissidence."

Women who kill act in a way which is contrary to that expected of Woman, who is constructed primarily as a law-abiding individual. The response of the law reinforces the construct of Woman as non-criminal by locating the explanation for female crime within the disordered mind of the individual woman (*i.e.* within her female biology) or within her unusually excessive evil nature. Both explanations enable the construct of Woman to be maintained. The former locates disorder within the female bodily processes of the individual and thereby reveals an underlying current of danger lurking within the bodies of all women. The latter demands that the individual be exposed to the full impact of legal regulation and sanction.

11.1.i   *Killing in defence of the self*

Celia Wells argues that, given the small number of women who are convicted of the murder of an abusive partner (about three or four each year), the increase in literature on "Women who Kill" is disproportionate and that the real significance of the focus upon these cases is their "metaphorical role as witness to the social reality of the abuse of women".[4] Statistics support the view that women rarely kill. In 1994, thirty-four women were indicted for murder or manslaughter. Six were acquitted, seven were found guilty of murder, six of manslaughter by reason of diminished responsibility, twelve of manslaughter on other grounds and two of infanticide.[5] Of those killed, eighteen were the spouse, former spouse or cohabitant of the woman who killed.[6] Sue Bandalli analysed the statistics relied upon by the Home Office in 1991 in its written answer to a Parliamentary question on the defences available to, and the treatment by the courts of, men and women in cases of domestic killing. The statistics had been interpreted as supporting the view that women who kill were treated more favourably. Sue Bandalli argues that statistics do not present the complete picture:

S. BANDALLI
"Provocation from the Home Office"[7]

"On October 17, 1991 Sir John Wheeler M.P. asked the Home Secretary at that time, Kenneth Baker, for statistical information on the 'acceptance of defences' to murder raised by women and men in cases of domestic homicide and their treatment by the courts. The written answer to this Parliamentary question was presented by Home Office Minister, Mr John Patten and consisted of a compilation of statistics held by the Home Office . . .

[B]etween 1982 and 1989, 164 women were indicted for murder, 13 for manslaughter. For men the figures were 753 and 32 respectively. The percentages of manslaughter indictments in the total of homicide charges are therefore 7 per cent for women and 4 per cent. for men. Home Office conclusion: 'women are nearly twice as likely as men to be indicted for manslaughter rather than murder.' There are however alternative conclusions which can be drawn from the same set of figures:

   (a)   nearly two and a half times as many men (32) as women (13) receive the
         initial act of leniency in the prosecution process of being indicted for man-

---

[4]   C. Wells, "Battered woman syndrome and defences to homicide: where now?" (1994) 14 *Legal Studies* 266. Christine Bell and Marie Fox point out that feminist attention has focused upon "battered women who kill" failing to confront the difficult questions posed for feminists by women who kill an innocent party such as Susan Christie, found guilty of the manslaughter of Penny McAllister, her lover's wife, or Rosemary West: C. Bell & M. Fox, "Telling Stories of Women Who Kill" (1996) 5 *Social and Legal Studies* 471.
[5]   *Criminal Statistics: England and Wales, 1994*, Cm. 3010 (1995) (London: HMSO), Table 4.8, pp. 86–87.
[6]   *Criminal Statistics: England and Wales, 1994, ibid.*, pp. 80–81.
[7]   [1992] Crim.L.R. 716 at 716–717, 719–720.

slaughter rather than murder. The use of percentages when the numbers involved diverge so dramatically is clearly misleading.

(b) for both men and women the great majority (93 per cent. women and 96 per cent. men) who are charged with homicide are indicted for murder rather than manslaughter . . .

Home Office conclusion: 'Women are more likely than men to be finally convicted of manslaughter rather than murder.'

This is true: manslaughter convictions as a percentage of murder and manslaughter convictions were 80 per cent. for women and 63 per cent. for men. In actual numbers this means 106 women were found guilty of manslaughter and only 27 of murder: 464 men were found guilty of manslaughter and 278 of murder. Percentages are once again concealing the true picture and implying either leniency or legal 'partial defence' success which is not there numerically . . .

[Home Office conclusion] 'Around half of the homicide convictions for women were for "other manslaugter" on the grounds of provocation, compared with 30% men.'

Fifty-three per cent. of women (70) as opposed to 30 per cent. of men (225) were convicted of 'other manslaughter,' a category including all manslaughters except diminished responsibility (Homicide Act 1957, s.2) and stated in the written answer to be 'mostly on the grounds of provocation.'

There is no support for this statement.

(i) Manslaughter verdicts will be returned in cases where no intention to cause grievous bodily harm or to kill is found. The Home Office categorises all manslaughter which is not section 2 (diminished responsibility) as 'other manslaughter' but obtains and provides no independent information as to whether this is the result of lack of intent or provocation.

(ii) The statistics do not differentiate between those manslaughter convictions which result from accepted guilty pleas and those which result from trial. If a plea of guilty to manslaughter is accepted there is no record kept of the reason, whether lack of intent or general doubts about the evidence, or fear that a jury would sympathise and acquit, or prejudgment of the issue of provocation. The Home Office receives and keeps no record of whether manslaughter is the result of trial or plea, nor of whether the issue of provocation was raised in either case.

A review of the cases involving battered women who kill their husbands suggests that whenever the issue of provocation becomes a tried issue (where the doctrine may be enforced more strictly) the woman in question will generally not succeed because the pressures on her and her subsequent behaviour are not within those recognised as relevant in the gendered legal concept of provocation. The cases where provocation does succeed in trials seem to have distinct elements of self-defence. If the Home Office is seeking to maintain that wom[e]n succeed in tried issues of provocation, and that as a result there is no need to review the law in this area, then this should be substantiated with hard evidence.

4. 'When convicted (of) manslaughter, men were more likely to receive a prison sentence and it was likely to be longer.'

As far as this cursory implication in the written answer of sentencing leniency is concerned, it would be as well to note the inadvisability of making sweeping statements about sentences. In order to judge the leniency or otherwise of a sentence, it is necessary to have some data on seriousness and other legally and socially relevant factors. To suggest that the only factor which can explain an apparently more lenient sentence is sex is a gross simplifications and misrepresentation. There is well documented research which indicates that the sentencing equation for women is a very much more complicated one than 'biology equals leniency.' "

Lorraine Radford likewise emphasises the importance of considering the social context of crime. She argues that the reality of the discriminatory effect of the law can only be understood if the circumstances in which the offences occur and the success rate of the various defences pleaded are acknowledged:

L. RADFORD
"Pleading for Time: Justice for Battered Women who Kill"[8]

"The Home Office findings do not, however, counter the claims of injustice made by abused women and their sympathizers. Statistics can cover a variety of untruths and encourage inappropriate conclusions. Statistics do not show the different experiences of men and women, rich and poor, black and white. One could conclude that the innocent get a good deal as fewer of them end up in prison than do the guilty. There is no way of learning from the *figures* the circumstances underlying men's and women's claims of diminished responsibility and provocation. We would need to know the circumstances leading up to the pleas of provocation and diminished responsibility to make conclusive empirical claims about discriminatory practice. Reported cases of provocation and diminished responsibility currently show that when the circumstances leading up to homicidal acts are examined, justice for battered women who kill is at the very best inconsistent. In December 1991 at Plymouth Crown Court, Pamela Sainsbury was put on probation for two years for killing the man described in court as 'a violent, jealous psychopath'. Sainsbury successfully argued a case based upon her diminished responsibility for a sudden, impulsive act of homicide. Sara Thornton's plea of diminished responsibility, however, was rejected at her original trial. Men such as Joseph McGrail and Rajinder Bisla defended themselves from murder charges by arguing either provocation or diminished responsibility due to women's interminable 'nagging'. Yet a few moments' gap between a woman's response to an act of violence from a habitually aggressive man is taken as proof of her desire for revenge.

The Home Office may have leapt too readily from the finding that women are able to argue provocation successfully to the conclusion that this defence is relevant and accessible to the circumstances of *abuse victims*."

Research suggests that a far wider problem than women who kill their abusive partner is the extent of personal violence taking place within the home to which, when it is exposed, the responses of the police, prosecuting authorities and criminal and civil remedies are found wanting.[9] The extent of violence occurring within the home means that the resources presently available to deal with it are inadequate. Despite increased awareness and changing practices, "domestic" violence is still not responded to in a way which is appropriate to the serious crime that it is. This is perpetuated by the use of terminology

---

[8]   In H. Birch (ed.), *Moving Targets: Women, Murder and Representation* (London: Virago, 1993) pp. 184–185.
[9]   S. M. Edwards & A. Halpern, "Protection for the Victim of Domestic Violence: Time for Radical Revision?" [1991] *Journal of Social Welfare and Family Law* 94.

which refers to the repeated infliction of physical and mental violence as "a domestic".[10] A common question asked of women who kill their abusive partners is why do they not simply leave? This reveals a lack of understanding of the position of women who are abused and of the effectiveness of policing and legal mechanisms in protecting them from their abusers. The questions of why the abuser was violent towards his partner or why she was not provided with the help she sought to enable her to escape from his violence, are not asked.[11] Beldam L.J. in the Court of Appeal in *R. v. Thornton* quoted the trial judge, Judge J. who said:

> "There are . . . many unhappy, indeed miserable, husbands and wives. It is a fact of life. It has to be faced, members of the jury. But on the whole it is hardly reasonable, you may think, to stab them fatally when there are other alternatives available, like walking out or going upstairs."[12]

Kiranjit Ahluwalia, imprisoned after her trial for the murder of her husband, has explained the family and cultural pressures placed upon her to remain with her husband. The success of their marriage was her responsibility and the family honour depended upon it:

K. AHLUWALIA
(1991) 20 *Trouble & Strife* at 20–21

"Dear ladies and gentlemen . . . My heart is full of things to say, but it is difficult to decide how and where to start telling my story. My culture is like my blood coursing through every vein of my body. It is the culture into which I was born and where I grew up which sees the woman as the honour of the house. In order to uphold this false 'honour' and 'glory', she is taught to endure many kinds of oppression and pain, in silence. In addition, religion also teaches her that her husband is her God and fulfilling his every desire is her religious duty. A woman who does not follow this path in our society, has no respect or place in it. She suffers from all kinds of slanders against her character. And she has to face all sorts of attacks and hurt entirely alone. She is responsible not only for her husband but also his entire family's happiness.

For ten years, I tried wholeheartedly to fulfil the duties endorsed by religion. I don't

---

[10]   S. Wright, "Domestic violence and the role of the police" in R. E. Dobash, R. P. Dobash & L. Noakes (eds), *Gender and Crime* (Cardiff: University of Wales Press, 1995). Kathryn McCann in "Battered Women and the Law: the limits of the legislation" in J. Brophy & C. Smart (eds), *Women-in-Law: Explorations in Law, Family and Sexuality*, (London: Routledge & Kegan Paul, 1985) suggests that the ideology of the sanctity of the privacy of the home has undermined the effectiveness of the Domestic Violence and Matrimonial Proceedings Act 1976 and Domestic Violence and Magistrates' Court Act 1978 which were premised upon the need to invade the privacy of the home in order to provide protection. She asserts (at p. 94) that "ideals of family privacy can be invoked as a rationale for non-intervention in cases of domestic violence, but here this privacy only serves to protect those who are already powerful within the family structure, namely the violent man."

[11]   M. Fox, "Legal Responses to Battered Women who Kill" in J. Bridgeman & S. Millns (eds), *Law and Body Politics: Regulating the Female Body* (Aldershot: Dartmouth, 1995), p. 189.

[12]   *R. v. Thornton* [1992] 1 All E.R. 306 at 312, *per* Beldam L.J. quoting Judge J. at first instance.

wish to compliment myself but I was a very good daughter-in-law, wife and mother. I tried to make my husband and in-laws happy in every way possible. I put up with everything. But, I also tried several times to escape from the trap of my anguished married life. But each time, my husband and family put pressure on me, in the name of upholding their 'izzat', their honour. The desire to keep up appearances also stopped me leaving. The result — at my age I am undergoing imprisonment in jail; far from my children. Were they at fault that they should have their mother's love snatched from them? Not only have they lost their father's love but their mother's as well.

I didn't even want to become a mother, because I was so unhappy in my marriage. For five years I managed to avoid it. I didn't want my children to have to suffer as well as me. But my mother-in-law's insults and my husband's beatings made me a mother twice over. In my culture, if a woman doesn't have a baby soon after marriage then she has to endure constant taunts. Today, writing all this down, I realise that first marriage was forced on me, then a denial of divorce was forced on me and then motherhood was forced on me. What combination of force and helplessness was it that kept me in a ten year sentence; and now sentences me legally to punish me for who knows how long?

After my marriage I forgot how to laugh. I could not eat or drink when I wanted to; I could not make friends with whoever I wanted to; I could not see my family and other relatives too often — I didn't have permission to. Small things were always flaring up into big fights. It wasn't only me but my small children who suffered as well. They were always scared and cowed down. But even though I tried to compromise as much as I could, I was made use of in every way possible. I could not make either my in-laws or my husband happy.

Today, I have come out of my husband's jail and entered the jail of the law. But I have found a new life, in this legal jail. It's in this cage that I have found a kind of freedom. I have been given love by the officers; love which I never found outside. Meeting others, I had the freedom to talk to them — which when I was free, I never had. I have met many different kinds of people, experienced their environment, and learnt many things. But I am sad that I am not getting a proper education here. This is a world apart from my world. My world was just my home, and my children. That's all.

My greatest sorrow, the punishment inflicted on me, is that I have been separated from my children. I think about them all the time. I cannot eat properly, or sleep properly. They need me and I need them. They are still very little, so I cannot explain things to them. Every time they come here they say, 'Mummy, come home'. How can I tell them where Mummy is? Or where home is? I have lost everything. I never thought in my wildest dreams that my mistake would have this result. That night, I had lost the strength to reason or think. I never thought that I would be wounded for life. A wound that would never heal.

For ten years, I lived a life of beatings and degradation and no-one noticed. Now the law has decreed that I should serve a sentence for life. *Why?*

No-one asked *why* all this had happened. Though I had two little children, I worked without rest for 50 or 60 hours a week in order to build up my home. *Why would I set fire to that house? Why did everyone use me as they chose?* Up to the point that though I was the mother of two children I couldn't take any decision on my own. I could not even name my children as I chose. This is the essence of my culture, society, religion. Where a woman is a toy, a plaything — she can be stuck together at will, broken at will. Everybody did what they wanted with me. No-one ever bothered to find out what kind of life I was leading after I was married . . . one of physical and mental torture.

Now at least, I am grateful that everyone has tried to understand my pain, to share in it and to continue doing that. From all sides, my friends and relatives are helping me. Even if this meeting does not result in any specific help for me I will not be disappointed. I would never want any sister or friend to ever undergo such suffering. There are countless women who have been subjected to such oppression — there is only one thing that prevents them from challenging or being freed from this kind of married life. That is my society, religion and culture. I will never let this religion and culture influence my children. I will never let them be stifled by the bondage of arranged marriages. I will give them the right to live their own lives . . .

Thank you
Yours faithfully,
Kiranjit Ahluwalia"

Not only may women who do leave an abusive relationship find themselves pursued by their abuser, without the means to support themselves and in fear of losing their children, but, as Katherine O'Donovan argues, "women's own accounts reveal emotional ties to the abuser which increase the difficulty of leaving."[13] Recognition of this fact may require a new legal perspective. O'Donovan continues:

> "If the legal process is to come to terms with this it will have to accept that for many women connection to others is important. In other words, women's ways of looking at relationships will have to be valued equally with those of men."[14]

L. RADFORD
"Pleading for Time: Justice for Battered Women Who Kill"[15]

"Why don't battered women leave their abusers? Why are they abused so many times? And why, when they kill, do they suddenly strike back with fatal effect? These are the three key questions asked in the courts of battered women who kill. Anyone who has the slightest experience of a divorce should be well aware that it is not easy to 'just walk out' of a relationship. Poor welfare provision and limited economic opportunities for women compound the difficulties of leaving violent men. Breaking free from a possessive man, like Deepak Ahluwalia, who musters up relatives' support to enforce ties to hearth, home or family honour is infinitely more difficult. To ask why battered women don't leave is to ask the wrong question; instead, we should ask what and who prevents them from doing so.

A vast amount of research, much based upon survivors' accounts, has shown beyond doubt that battered women do try to leave time and again. Many succeed and become survivors, while others find themselves forced back into an abusive relationship by fear

---

[13] K. O'Donovan, "Defences for Battered Women Who Kill" (1991) 18 *Journal of Law and Society* 219 at 235.
[14] K. O'Donovan, *ibid.*, at 235.
[15] L. Radford, *supra*, n.8 at pp. 177–179.

of losing their children, lack of alternatives (usually accommodation), or inadequate protection, . . .

The question 'Why don't battered women leave?' also rests upon the naive assumption that leaving will end the violence. Research into survivors' experiences shows that up to a third of the women who leave violent men suffer abuse after the separation. In theory, women who suffer domestic violence should receive equal protection from the criminal law of assault and from a variety of legal sanctions and injunctions, some specifically devised for the protection of battered women. Special provisions for battered women — as in the Domestic Violence and Matrimonial Proceedings Act 1976 and the Domestic Proceedings and Magistrates' Court Act 1978 — are, however, of little use if they are not enforced by the police or the courts. Even within the much-publicised Domestic Violence Units, battered women are not guaranteed protection from abuse. In May 1991 Jayanti Patel killed his second wife Vanda whilst being 'conciliated' within a domestic violence unit at Stoke Newington Police Station. Patel had also previously been convicted of violent assaults and stabbing his former wife . . .

Domestic homicides committed by women tend to be defensive and victim-precipitated. Typically, battered women who kill do so in response to an attack or following a threat from the abuser to harm another, usually a child. Some kill whilst the abuser sleeps after an attack, convinced that it will continue when he awakens. They kill because they feel there is simply no other way out. After previous failed attempts, they lose hope of escaping. The violence, tension and fear reach a point where death seems inevitable: a choice between suicide and homicide. Housing departments, social welfare agencies and law enforcers who adopt policies of non-intervention and return women to violent relationships thereby give abusers implicit support. If they refuse to become involved, both the woman and the abuser may believe that it is impossible for a victim of abuse to break free from a violent relationship. There is nothing to stop an abuser, armed with this realization, from stepping up the level of violence or repeating the violence in another relationship."

The cases addressed in this section have wider relevance beyond the very important issue of the liberty of the individual concerned. Their selection (despite their statistical rarity) is justified as it offers the means through which to explore questions about the position of women in the criminal justice system. Given that women are more frequently the victims of unlawful killing than the instigators, women who kill find themselves confronted with definitions of criminal offences and with defences which have developed in response to male standards of behaviour. The cases illustrate how, both in the way the substantive laws are defined and in their application, the experiences of women are not accommodated.

As has been explained above, where women do appear before the criminal justice system, their behaviour is judged against the social and legal construct of Woman.[16] Woman, by nature, is portrayed as inherently unlikely to commit offences. A woman who kills fall into one of the two categories of criminal women. She is either an "evil" woman who accepts responsibility for her actions or an "irresponsible" woman whose actions may be attributed to her individual pathology. As a consequence of women who kill being categorised

---

[16] D. Nicolson, *supra*, n. 1 at 186.

into one of either of these two types, the reasons for their actions are not explored. The female killer is labelled either "bad" or "mad".

Whilst explanations for female offending mean that female defendants are treated distinctly from male defendants, each woman is tried according to the extent to which she departs from the ideal of Woman. The application of the defences available to battered women who kill, that is provocation, diminished responsibility and self-defence, results in a "haphazard quality of justice".[17] It is towards a consideration of each of these defences that we now turn before going on to demonstrate how they influence legal constructions of female killers and appropriate female behaviour.

11.1.ii *Provocation*

The defence of provocation was developed at common law, but is now given statutory force in section 3 of the Homicide Act 1957. Recourse must, nevertheless, be made to the common law in order to apply the statutory provision. Section 3 states:

> Where on a charge of murder there is evidence on which the jury can find that the person charged was provoked (whether by things done or by things said or by both together) to lose his self-control, the question whether the provocation was enough to make a reasonable man do as he did shall be left to be determined by the jury; and in determining that question the jury shall take into account everything both done and said according to the effect which, in their opinion, it would have on a reasonable man.

There are two conditions which have to be satisfied in order for the defendant to successfully rely upon provocation reducing the crime from one of murder to manslaughter[18]:

(i)   The provocation must be such as to actually cause in the accused a sudden and temporary loss of self-control as a result of which the accused killed the deceased, and

(ii) the provocation must be such as to cause a reasonable person to suffer a loss of self-control and to act in the manner of the accused.

11.1.ii.a Loss of self-control. In relation to the first condition, the accused must have been provoked to lose self-control and must have responded to the provocation by killing when out of control, that is in the heat of the moment. The defence is not available, even in response to horrific provocation, if the accused responds in a manner which suggests deliberation. This was made clear in the case of *R. v. Duffy*,[19] in which the Court of Appeal approved of

---

[17]   A. McColgan, "In Defence of Battered Women who Kill" (1993) 13 O.J.L.S. 508 at 509.
[18]   This enables discretion in sentencing which is not available following a murder conviction. For example, leniency may be exercised to the extent that a non-custodial sentence is passed. See J. Horder, "Sex, Violence, and Sentencing in Domestic Provocation Cases" [1989] Crim.L.R. 546.
[19]   *R. v. Duffy* [1949] 1 All E.R. 932.

the direction given by Devlin J., a direction which has subsequently been approved as equally applicable to cases occurring after the 1957 Act was passed.

R. v. Duffy
[1949] 1 All E.R. 932 at 932–933, *per* Lord Goddard
[delivering the judgment of the court]

"The only possible defence that could be set up was that the appellant acted under such provocation as to reduce the crime to manslaughter, and on this point the summing-up of the learned judge, in the opinion of this court, was impeccable. I am going to read a passage from his summing-up, because I think it deserves to be remembered as as clear and accurate a charge to a jury when provocation is pleaded as can well be made. He said:

> 'Provocation is some act, or series of acts, done by the dead man to the accused which would cause in any reasonable person, and actually causes in the accused, a sudden and temporary loss of self-control, rendering the accused so subject to passion as to make him or her for the moment not master of his mind. Let me distinguish for you some of the things which provocation in law is not. Circumstances which merely predispose to a violent act are not enough. Severe nervous exasperation or a long course of conduct causing suffering and anxiety are not by themselves sufficient to constitute provocation in law. Indeed, the further removed an incident is from the crime, the less it counts. A long course of cruel conduct may be more blameworthy than a sudden act provoking retaliation, but you are not concerned with blame here — the blame attaching to the dead man. You are not standing in judgment on him. He has not been heard in this court. He cannot now ever be heard. He has no defender here to argue for him. It does not matter how cruel he was, how much or how little he was to blame, except in so far as it resulted in the final act of the appellant. What matters is whether this girl had the time to say: 'Whatever I have suffered, whatever I have endured, I know that Thou shalt not kill.' That is what matters. Similarly, as counsel for the prosecution has told you, circumstances which induce a desire for revenge, or a sudden passion of anger, are not enough. Indeed, circumstances which induce a desire for revenge are inconsistent with provocation, since the conscious formulation of a desire for revenge means that a person has had time to think, to reflect, and that would negative a sudden temporary loss of self-control which is of the essence of provocation ... Provocation being, therefore, as I have defined it, there are two things, in considering it, to which the law attaches great importance. The first of them is whether there was what is sometimes called time for cooling, that is, for passion to cool and for reason to regain dominion over the mind. That is why most acts of provocation are cases of sudden quarrels, sudden blows inflicted with an implement already in the hand, perhaps being used, or being picked up, where there has been no time for reflection. Secondly, in considering whether provocation has or has not been made out, you must consider the retaliation in provocation — that is to say, whether the mode of resentment bears some proper and reasonable relationship to the sort of provocation that has been

given. (Fists might be answered with fists, but not with a deadly weapon, and that is a factor you have to bear in mind when you are considering the question of provocation.)'

That is as good a definition of the doctrine of provocation as it has ever been my lot to read, and I think it might well stand as a classic direction given to a jury in a case in which the sympathy of everyone would be with the accused person and against the dead man and it was essential that the judge should see that the jury had an opportunity of vindicating the law, whatever the consequences might be. That the appellant was properly convicted of murder according to law there can be no doubt, and, therefore, this appeal fails."

The consideration of the defence of provocation in *Duffy* arose as a result of Mrs Duffy killing her husband who had for a long time been violent towards her. There had been violence during the evening following her attempts to leave him and she killed him whilst he slept. As she had killed him whilst he was asleep, and not immediately in response to his threats and violence, the defence of provocation was not available to her. Despite the abuse which she had suffered at his hands she did not respond with a "sudden temporary loss of self-control".[20] The Court, applying the supposedly gender-neutral law, looked to the male response in such a situation, expecting someone who was provoked to respond immediately. In so doing the court ignored the effect which the husband's abuse might have upon his wife, and the difference in physical size between them. The lapse of time was, in the view of the court, time during which Mrs Duffy formulated a plan of revenge.

The subjective condition, requiring that the defendant kill in a sudden and temporary loss of self-control was considered in both *R. v. Thornton* and *R. v. Ahluwalia*.[21]

R. v. Thornton
[1992] 1 All E.R. 306 at 308–310, 313–314, *per* Beldam L.J.

"The appellant was born in Nuneaton, Warwickshire. Her parents were in comfortable circumstances and the appellant went to a public school in Somerset. Whilst at school she began to suffer from a personality disorder. At 16 she was asked to leave. After several relationships with young men which did not work out she met her first hus-

---

[20] This requirement remains despite the absence of any reference to "sudden and temporary" in section 3.

[21] Both of these cases are discussed in detail below. By way of résumé, Sara Thornton was convicted of murder in 1990. Her appeal in 1991 (*R. v. Thornton* [1992] 1 All E.R. 306) was dismissed. In 1995 the Home Secretary referred her case back to the Court of Appeal on the basis of further medical evidence being available. Upon this second appeal (*R. v. Thornton (No.2)* [1996] 2 All E.R. 1023) her conviction was quashed and a retrial ordered at which Thornton was found guilty of manslaughter on the grounds of diminished responsibility. Kiranjit Ahluwalia, at her initial hearing, was also convicted of murder. On appeal in 1992 (*R. v. Ahluwalia* [1992] 4 All E.R. 889) fresh evidence was produced to show that at the time of the killing her mental responsibility was diminished. The appeal was allowed and a retrial ordered, as a result of which she was convicted of manslaughter on the grounds of diminished responsibility.

band. She was then 23. She gave birth to a daughter the following year and initially the marriage was happy. However, when her husband's business took him abroad and she later joined him, she found that he had begun to drink heavily. He was violent towards her, so she left him and returned to England with her daughter and went to live in Coventry with her grandparents. On several occasions she attempted suicide, but it is questionable whether she actually intended to take her own life. After a particularly stressful period of her life in 1981 she was admitted to Walsgrave Hospital, Coventry as a patient under the Mental Health Act 1959 but was discharged after a short time.

She met the deceased, Malcolm Thornton, in a public house in May 1987. He was an ex-policeman, who was working as a security officer at the time. From the start she realised he was a heavy drinker and was jealous and possessive. That autumn she and her daughter moved in to live with the deceased in his home in Atherstone. By December the following year he was obviously suffering from alcoholism, and he was admitted to a clinic for treatment. The treatment appeared to be successful and in August 1988 the appellant and the deceased were married. At first the marriage was successful but by the following Christmas the deceased had resumed his drinking and on occasions was violent in the home, breaking furniture and assaulting the appellant. Early in 1989 he lost his driving licence and his job and in May, after an argument, he committed a serious assault on the appellant. She complained to the police, who eventually charged him.

After this incident she went to stay with her father and stepmother in Devon for several days. While she was there the deceased's son by his former marriage, Martin, returned to live with his father at Atherstone. On 26 May, the appellant returned home and, according to her, for the next fortnight the deceased made a real effort to give up drink. On 9 June, he asked the appellant if she would withdraw the charges which he faced and which were due to be heard on 21 June.

On the weekend of 10–11 June, the appellant attended a sales conference at the De Vere Hotel, Coventry, organised by her employers. A fellow employee attending this conference, Mrs Thomas, said that the appellant seemed to be enjoying herself but that there was an incident following a telephone call to the deceased. After the telephone call Mrs Thomas told the appellant that she had to sort the matter out and, according to her, the appellant replied: 'I am going to kill him.'

But for subsequent events Mrs Thomas might well have dismissed this as no more than an expression of exasperation. Mrs Thomas accompanied the appellant home the following morning. The deceased had clearly been drinking and had a hangover. The appellant became very frustrated and showed it. After Mrs Thomas had gone at about lunch-time there was a row, which was witnessed by the deceased's son, Martin. Martin was a witness who was realistic about his father's shortcomings and accepted many of the criticisms made of him. According to him, in the course of the row the deceased picked up a guitar and threatened the appellant with it. The appellant for her part picked up a knife, held it in front of her pointing towards the deceased and said: 'You touch my daughter, you bastard, and I'll kill you.'

Martin intervened and made her put the knife down. Later that day, when the row had died down, the appellant gave the deceased two Mogadon tablets and later introduced four more into his food. She telephoned the doctor saying that the deceased had taken an overdose of Mogadon and that he was suicidal. She later explained her actions by saying that she wanted to get the deceased committed to hospital. An ambulance and the police arrived, but the deceased revived and refused to accompany them to hospital. When they had gone he was incensed by what the appellant had done and he threw a chair through the glass window of the kitchen door, breaking the glass.

On the following day, Monday, the appellant telephoned Mrs Thomas telling her she had found drink concealed in the house. She talked about the difficulties of divorce as they had only been married a short time and she spoke of the difficulty of financial settlements. The deceased went out drinking. He came home and was sick, caused a burn hole in the arm of a chair and spent the night sleeping on the couch downstairs.

On Tuesday there was a further row in the home. The deceased was drunk but not helpless, and when he arrived home an argument developed with the appellant. During the row the deceased abused her and told her to get out of the house and that she must leave. The appellant arranged for her daughter to leave and shortly afterwards she spoke on the telephone to Mrs Thomas, saying: 'I am going to have to do what I said I would do', which Mrs Thomas understood to be a reference to the threat to kill the deceased made the previous weekend.

That evening the appellant went out for a drink to the local public house with the deceased's son, Martin. Before leaving she wrote on her bedroom mirror in lipstick: 'Bastard Thornton. I hate you.' When they left the house the deceased was sleeping on the couch. Martin returned home first. The deceased was still sound asleep on the couch. The appellant returned later in a taxi. The taxi driver described the appellant as 'quarrelsome and arrogant'.

By the time she arrived home Martin was in bed but was not asleep, though not fully conscious. The appellant went up to her bedroom and changed into her night-clothes. She then went down, according to her, to try to persuade the deceased to come to bed. He refused, called her 'a whore' and said she had been selling her body: she was not going to get any money from him and he would kill her if she had been out with other men. She said that she had only been trying to raise money for their business. She was hurt and wounded by his remarks but recalled advice she had been given by Alcoholics Anonymous that she should go and try to calm down. She went into the kitchen and looked in the drawer for a truncheon, which the deceased kept there, so that she had some protection if he attacked her. Not finding it, she saw a knife. It was a long carving knife and according to a subsequent statement she made to the police, she sharpened it. She then returned to the sitting room, where the deceased was lying on the sofa. She again asked him to come up to bed but he refused and again made wounding remarks to her saying that he would kill her when she was asleep. She then sat on the edge of the couch by his chest and said: 'Come to bed.'

He made no move, so she stood up in front of him holding the knife in her clenched hand over his stomach. She then brought it down towards him thinking he would ward it off. He did not do so and the knife entered his stomach. She did not mean to kill him or harm him in any way. Her object in having the knife was merely to frighten him. She only brought the knife down slowly, not quickly. Martin upstairs had heard no sound of raised voices but he heard a scream from his father. He went downstairs and was met by the appellant, who said: 'Martin, I've killed your father.' . . .

[Counsel for the defence] Lord Gifford suggested that the legal concept of provocation did not require loss of self-control to be sudden, and that such a requirement had been incorporated into the law by a too literal adoption of the words used by Devlin J. in his summing up to the jury in *R. v. Duffy* [1949] 1 All E.R. 932, which was emphatically approved by Lord Goddard C.J. on appeal. . .

The words 'sudden and temporary loss of self-control' have ever since been regarded as appropriate to convey to a jury the legal concept of provocation first expressed by

Tindal C.J. in *R. v. Hayward* (1833) 6 C & P 157 at 159, 172 E.R. 1188 at 1189 in mitigation of the rigour of the law for acts committed —

> 'while smarting under a provocation so recent and so strong, that the prisoner might not be considered at the moment the master of his own understanding ...'

Lord Gifford argued that Devlin J.'s words are no longer appropriate in the case of reaction by a person subjected to a long course of provocative conduct, including domestic violence, which may sap the resilience and resolve to retain self-control when the final confrontation erupts. In such circumstances it is misleading, he says, to talk of a sudden loss of control. He points to the words of s. 3 of the Homicide Act 1957, which require the jury, in determining whether the provocation was sufficient to make a reasonable man do as the accused did, to take into account everything both done and said according to the effect it would have on a reasonable man. Lord Gifford also referred us to passages in the judgment in *D.P.P. v. Camplin* [1978] 2 All E.R. 168 esp. at 177; [1978] A.C. 705 esp. at 721, where Lord Morris said:

> 'It seems to me that as a result of the changes effected by s. 3 of the 1957 Act a jury is fully entitled to consider whether an accused person, placed as he was, only acted as even a reasonable man might have acted if he had been in the accused's situation.'

The changes in the law of provocation made by s. 3 of the Homicide Act 1957 and the reasons for them are well known. It has never, so far as we are aware, been suggested that the distinction drawn by Devlin J. between a person who has time to think and reflect and regain self-control and a sudden temporary loss of self-control is no longer of significance. On the contrary, the distinction drawn by Devlin J. is just as, if not more, important in the kind of case to which Lord Gifford referred. It is within the experience of each member of the court that in cases of domestic violence which culminate in the death of a partner there is frequently evidence given of provocative acts committed by the deceased in the past, for it is in that context that the jury have to consider the accused's reaction. In every such case the question for the jury is whether at the moment the fatal blow was struck the accused had been deprived for that moment of the self-control which previously he or she had been able to exercise. The epithet 'sudden and temporary' is one a jury are well able to understand and to recognise as expressing precisely the distinction drawn by Devlin J. We reject the suggestion that in using the phrase 'sudden and temporary loss of control' there was any misdirection of the jury."

The argument of Counsel that, because section 3 made no reference to "sudden and temporary" the loss of self-control was no longer to be limited in this way but had to be considered in the light of all the circumstances (including the fact that someone who had experienced repeated violence might react differently to that violence) was rejected. Whilst cumulative provocation is relevant to the question of whether or not the defendant was provoked, so that an accumulation of events over a period of time makes comprehensible the loss of self-control in response to an apparently minor incident, the defence is only available if the defendant reacts, even to a small incident, by losing self-control and, in such a state, killing.[22] The defence is not available if the defendant does not react immediately to provocative treatment but reacts after enough time has passed to suggest that there was an element of deliberation. There is no recognition of the effects of acts which amount to cumulative provocation in terms of the way that this cumulation might affect the way a person reacts.[23] This was again raised in *R. v. Ahluwalia* where Counsel argued that the requirement for a "heat of the moment" reaction is based upon a male orientated view of behaviour and that there are other ways of reacting to violence particularly where there is a history of repeated violence. In such cases a "slow-burn" of fear, despair and anger may cumulate erupting in the killing of the abuser, not immediately but later, when he cannot strike back because he is, for example, asleep or drunk.

R v. Ahluwalia
[1992] 4 All E.R. 889 at 891–893, 894–896, *per* Lord Taylor C.J.

"This is a tragic case which has aroused much public attention.

On 9 May, 1989 the appellant, after enduring many years of violence and humiliation from her husband, threw petrol in his bedroom and set it alight. Her husband sustained terrible burns from which, after lingering painfully for six days, he died on 15 May.

The appellant was indicted for murder. Her trial started on 29 November, 1989 in the Crown Court at Lewes and on 7 December she was convicted of murder by a majority of ten to two. The learned judge then imposed upon her the mandatory sentence of life imprisonment.

She now appeals against that conviction by leave of the single judge granted only on 12 September, 1991, well out of time.

The appellant is now 36. She was born in India into a middle class family. She completed an arts degree and then began a law course, but came under pressure from her family to marry. The deceased came from a family of Kenyan Asians who had emigrated in 1971. The appellant went to Canada to stay with her brother and sister-in-law. A marriage was arranged between her and the deceased. They had not previously met. The marriage took place in Canada. They then came to England and settled in Crawley. Both had jobs. Two boys were born to them, one in July 1984 and one in January 1986.

The appellant had suffered violence and abuse from the deceased from the outset of the marriage. He was a big man; she is slight. Her complaints of violence were supported by entries in her doctor's notes. Thus, in October 1981, there is a record of her being hit three or four times on the head with a telephone and thrown to the ground.

---

[22] M. Wasik suggests that cumulative provocation may result in either a more lenient or a more harsh sentence; the former because the accused may be seen as a victim, the latter because of the belief that there were other options available to her (M. Wasik, "Cumulative Provocation and Domestic Killings" [1982] Crim.L.R. 29).

[23] In Australia, experience suggests that removal of the suddenness requirement does not result in a dramatic increase in murder acquittals. Under Australian law the accused seeking to rely on provocation must, *inter alia*, establish that she had lost self-control when she killed, but this does not need to follow immediately from the provoking incident (S. Yeo, "Provocation Down Under" (1991) 141 New. L.J. 1200).

In September 1983, a note states she was 'pushed' by her husband whilst pregnant and sustained a bruised hand. The next month she had a broken finger due to another argument. She made attempts at suicide in 1983 and again in 1986. The Croydon County Court granted her an injunction to restrain the deceased from hitting her in 1983. In 1986 the deceased abused the appellant and tried to run her down at a family wedding. She obtained her second injunction from the court after the deceased had held her throat and threatened her with a knife. He threatened to kill her and threw a mug of hot tea over her. Despite the court order, the deceased continued his violence, which intensified after January 1989.

The appellant's doctor made a statement which was read at the trial. He confirmed that he found bruising to her face and wrist on 18 April, and fresh bruising on the left cheek, temple and arm on 24 April. At Easter 1989 the deceased knocked the appellant unconscious. She suffered a broken tooth, swollen lips and was off work for five days. Her work supervisor gave evidence that she lost weight and showed signs of nervousness and distress. Other evidence to like effect was given by a workmate, by her Canadian sister-in-law who came to stay and even by the deceased's brother, who spoke to the deceased about it on 7 May. On the evidence at the trial there was, therefore, no doubt that the appellant had been treated very badly over a long period. In addition, she discovered in March 1989 that the deceased was having an affair with a woman who worked with him at the Post Office. He taunted the appellant with this relationship. Despite all of this, the appellant wished to hold the marriage together, partly because of her sense of duty as a wife and partly for the sake of the children.

The state of humiliation and loss of self-esteem to which the deceased's behaviour over the ten years of the marriage had reduced her is evidenced by a letter she wrote him after he left her for three days about April 1989. It is a letter on which Mr Robertson Q.C. strongly relies. In the course of begging him to come back to her and to grant her ten minutes to talk it over, she made a number of self-denying promises of the most abject kind:

> 'Deepak, if you come back I promise you — I won't touch black coffee again, I won't go town every week, I won't eat green chilli, I ready to leave Chandikah and all my friends, I won't go near Der Goodie Mohan's house again. Even I am not going to attend Bully's wedding, I eat too much or all the time so I can get fat, I won't laugh if you don't like, I won't dye my hair even, I don't go to my neighbour's house, I won't ask you for any help.'

Events of 8–9 May
The appellant visited her mother-in-law on the afternoon of 8 May. She then returned home with her younger son, who was unwell. The deceased spoke to his girlfriend from his work place telling her that the appellant was going to pack and leave that evening. He arrived home about 10.15 pm. What happened thereafter was described by the appellant in police interviews, although she has not been wholly consistent. It seems she put her son to bed and gave the deceased his dinner. He then tried to mend the television set. The appellant tried to talk to him about their relationship, but he refused indicating that it was over. He demanded money from her to pay a telephone bill and, according to her, threatened to beat her if she did not give him £200 the next morning. He then began to iron some clothes and threatened to burn the appellant's face with the hot iron if she did not leave him alone.

The appellant went to bed about midnight. She was unable to sleep and brooded upon the deceased's refusal to speak to her and his threat to beat her the next morning.

She had bought some caustic soda a few days earlier with a view to using it upon the deceased. She had also bought a can of petrol and put it in the lean-to outside the house. Her mind turned to these substances and some time after 2.30 am she got up, went downstairs, poured about two pints of the petrol into a bucket (to make it easier to throw), lit a candle on the gas cooker and carried these things upstairs. She also took an oven glove for self-protection and a stick. She went to the deceased's bedroom, threw in some petrol, lit the stick from the candle and threw it into the room. She then went to dress her son.

The deceased, on fire, ran to immerse himself in the bath and then ran outside screaming, 'I'll kill you,' and shouting for help. He was assisted by neighbours.

Other neighbours rushed to the house. They found the door locked and saw the appellant standing at a ground-floor window clutching her son, just staring and looking calm. They shouted to her to get out of the house. She opened a window and said, 'I am waiting for my husband,' and closed the window again. She was prevailed upon to hand the child out and later emerged herself. She stood staring at the blazing window with a glazed expression.

Fire officers came and extinguished the flames. They found a bucket still smelling of petrol on the landing outside the bedroom, also a saucepan in the bathroom basin with caustic soda in the bottom. Later, the effects of caustic soda were found on the bathroom floor.

The deceased suffered severe burns. He responded to treatment for a while but deteriorated and died on 15 May.

On 12 May he made a declaration before a magistrate. In fairness to him he was in no condition to give his account of the whole course of the marriage and the factual background given in this judgment is necessarily based on the evidence given at trial. In his declaration he denied having a girlfriend, asserted the appellant had thrown caustic soda over him in the bedroom rather than petrol, and had thrown something else over him in the bath. He admitted telling her he did not wish to spend his life with her. He had gone to bed after telling her to leave.

The appellant was arrested. She wrote to her mother-in-law from prison saying, amongst other things, that the deceased had committed so many sins, 'so I gave him a fire bath to wash away his sins'. However, in the course of interview she repeated a number of times that she did not intend to kill the deceased, but only to give him pain . . .

Sudden and temporary loss of self-control

The classic definition of provocation in law is that given by Devlin J. which was approved by this court in *R. v. Duffy* [1949] 1 All E.R. 932 . . .

In the present case the learned judge followed that direction faithfully. He repeated it almost verbatim when he first directed the jury on provocation. Later he said:

'Bear in mind it is a sudden and temporary loss of self-control for which you are looking, not a thought-out plan how to punish him for his wickedness.'

Towards the end of the summing up he reminded the jury to look at the evidence to see whether 'there might have been a sudden and temporary loss of self-control'. His final direction read:

'Sudden loss of self-control. That is what you have to consider and consider in the context of the facts as described by the defendant herself.'

[Counsel for the defence] Mr Robertson boldly argues that the *Duffy* direction followed by the judge is wrong. Whatever the position may have been prior to the Homicide Act 1957, he submits that a *Duffy* direction is based on a failure to comprehend the true meaning and impact of s.3 of that Act as explained by the House of Lords in *D.P.P. v. Camplin* [1978] 2 All E.R. 168, [1978] A.C. 705. . .

In a passage in his speech in *D.P.P. v. Camplin* [1978] 2 All E.R. 168 at 173; [1978] A.C. 705 at 716, Lord Diplock referred to that section [section 3 of the Homicide Act 1957] abolishing all previous rules of law as to what can or cannot amount to provocation. But he did not, it should be noted, redefine provocation itself.

Even if there were no authority to the contrary, we consider Mr Robertson's argument is misconceived. Section 3 of the Homicide Act 1957 did not provide a general or fresh definition of provocation which remains a common law not a statutory defence. The changes effected by the 1957 Act are conveniently summarised in Smith and Hogan *Criminal Law* (6th ed., 1988) p. 337:

> '(i) It made it clear that "things said" alone may be sufficient provocation if the jury should be of the opinion that they would have provoked a reasonable man . . . (ii) It took away the power of the judge to withdraw the defence from the jury on the ground that there was no evidence on which the jury could find that a reasonable man would have been provoked to do as [the defendant] did . . . (iii) It took away the power of the judge to dictate to the jury what were the characteristics of the reasonable man . . .'

In *D.P.P. v. Camplin* the House of Lords was concerned with the objective element in provocation, the 'reasonable man' limb of the defence. It was to this aspect of the defence that Lord Diplock was giving attention. Although *R. v. Duffy* [1949] 1 All E.R. 932 was cited, neither Lord Diplock nor any of the other Law Lords suggested it was wrong, nor has any decision since so suggested. On the contrary, there has been a consistent line of binding authority approving the use of the phrase 'sudden and temporary loss of self-control'. For example, in *R. v. Ibrams* (1981) 74 Cr. App. R. 154 at 159–160 Lawton L.J. referred favourably to the direction in *R. v. Duffy*, noting that it had been approved by this court in *R. v. Whitfield* (1976) 63 Cr. App. R. 39 at 42.

In *R. v. Thornton* [1992] 1 All E.R. 306 a similar argument to that advanced by Mr Robertson was considered and rejected. Beldam L.J. giving the judgment of the court said (at 313–314):

> 'The words "sudden and temporary loss of self-control" have ever since been regarded as appropriate to convey to a jury the legal concept of provocation first expressed by Tindal C.J. in *R. v. Hayward* (1833) 6 C. & P. 157 at 159; 172 E.R. 1188 at 1189 in mitigation of the rigour of the law for acts committed — "while smarting under a provocation so recent and so strong, that the prisoner might not be considered at the moment the master of his own understanding . . ." . . . The changes in the law of provocation made by s. 3 of the Homicide Act 1957 and the reasons for them are well known. It has never, so far as we are aware, been suggested that the distinction drawn by Devlin J. between a person who has time to think and reflect and regain self-control and a sudden temporary loss of self-control is no longer of significance . . . The epithet "sudden and temporary" is one a jury are well able

to understand and to recognise as expressing precisely the distinction drawn by Devlin J.'

The phrase 'sudden and temporary loss of self-control' encapsulates an essential ingredient of the defence of provocation in a clear and readily understandable phrase. It serves to underline that the defence is concerned with the actions of an individual who is not, at the moment when he or she acts violently, master of his or her own mind. Mr Robertson suggested that the phrase might lead the jury to think provocation could not arise for consideration unless the defendant's act followed immediately upon the acts or words which constituted the alleged provocation. He submits a direction to this effect would have been inappropriate and inconsistent with a number of authorities (see, for example, *R. v. Hall* (1928) 21 Cr. App. R. 48; *Lee Chun-Cheun v. R.* [1963] 1 All E.R. 73; [1963] A.C. 220 and *Parker v. R.* [1964] 2 All E.R. 641, [1964] A.C. 1369).

Nevertheless, it is open to the judge, when deciding whether there is any evidence of provocation to be left to the jury and open to the jury when considering such evidence, to take account of the interval between the provocative conduct and the reaction of the defendant to it. Time for reflection may show that after the provocative conduct made its impact on the mind of the defendant, he or she kept or regained self-control. The passage of time following the provocation may also show that the subsequent attack was planned or based on motives, such as revenge or punishment, inconsistent with the loss of self-control and therefore with the defence of provocation. In some cases, such an interval may wholly undermine the defence of provocation; that, however, depends entirely on the facts of the individual case and is not a principle of law.

Mr Robertson referred to the phrase 'cooling off period' which has sometimes been applied to an interval of time between the provocation relied upon and the fatal act. He suggests that although in many cases such an interval may indeed be a time for cooling and regaining self-control so as to forfeit the protection of the defence, in others the time lapse has an opposite effect. He submits, relying on expert evidence not before the trial judge, that women who have been subjected frequently over a period to violent treatment may react to the final act or words by what he calls a 'slow-burn' reaction rather than by an immediate loss of self-control.

We accept that the subjective element in the defence of provocation would not as a matter of law be negatived simply because of the delayed reaction in such cases, provided that there was at the time of the killing a 'sudden and temporary loss of self-control' caused by the alleged provocation. However, the longer the delay and the stronger the evidence of deliberation on the part of the defendant, the more likely it will be that the prosecution will negative provocation.

In the present case, despite the delay after the last provocative act or words by the deceased, and despite the appellant's apparent deliberation in seeking and lighting the petrol, the trial judge nevertheless left the issue of provocation to the jury. His references to 'sudden and temporary loss of self-control' were correct in law. He did not suggest to the jury that they should or might reject the defence of provocation because the last provocative act or word of the deceased was not followed immediately by the appellant's fatal acts."

The Court of Appeal made it clear that a time delay was not a legal bar to provocation but simply evidence on which to assess whether self-control was in fact lost.[24] Jeremy Horder, writing after Sara Thornton's first appeal, criticised that judgment and the direction of Devlin J. in *R. v. Duffy*, arguing that the common law had never required the loss of self-control to be sudden.

J. HORDER
"Provocation and Loss of Self-Control"[25]

"[T]he suddenness requirement anomalously rewards with the possibility of mitigation those for whom it was natural to respond immediately with fatal violence, whilst seeming to deny it to those who may have made efforts to control their anger, but who boil over when they find that they cannot."

11.1.ii.b   The reasonable reaction. In addition to the requirement that the accused did lose her self-control is the objective condition that a reasonable man may have reacted in the same way as the accused to the acts or words of provocation. Prior to the 1957 Act, the reasonable man against whom the reaction of the accused was judged had no idiosyncrasies or peculiar characteristics.[26] This was reconsidered by the House of Lords in *R. v. Camplin*.[27] Lord Diplock in the House of Lords stressed that the reasonable man is an ordinary person of either sex:

> "As I have already pointed out, for the purposes of the law of provocation the 'reasonable man' has never been confined to the adult male. It means an ordinary person of either sex, not exceptionally excitable or pugnacious, but possessed of such powers of self-control as everyone is entitled to expect his fellow citizens will exercise in society as it is today."[28]

Further, the reasonable man is an ordinary person of the age and sex of the accused, sharing the characteristics of the accused which would affect the impact of the provocation upon the accused.

R. v. Camplin
[1978] 2 All E.R. 168 at 175c, *per* Lord Diplock

"The judge should state what the question is, using the very terms of the section. He should then explain to them that the reasonable man referred to in the question is a person having the power of self-control of an ordinary person of the sex and age of the accused, but in other respects sharing such of the accused's characteristics as they

---

[24]   D. Nicolson & R. Sanghvi in "Battered Women and Provocation: The Implications of *R. v Ahluwalia*" [1993] Crim.L.R. 728 at 730, suggest that this may be the most important aspect of the decision.
[25]   (1992) 108 L.Q.R. 191 at 193.
[26]   *Bedder v. D.P.P.* [1954] 1 W.L.R. 1119.
[27]   *R. v. Camplin* [1978] 2 All E.R. 168.
[28]   *R. v. Camplin, ibid.*, at 173j; *per* Lord Diplock.

think would affect the gravity of the provocation to him, and that the question is not merely whether such a person would in like circumstances be provoked to lose his self-control but also would react to the provocation as the accused did."[29]

The endowment of the reasonable person with the permanent personal characteristics of the accused (at least as far as they had an impact upon the severity of the provocation to her) allows account to be taken of women's experiences. It may be asked, would the reasonable woman have done as the accused did? The court must look to the ordinary person, and then consider whether the characteristics of the accused to which the provocation related meant that the provocation would have had a different effect upon the accused than it would have had upon the ordinary person.

The objective condition was one of the grounds for appeal in *Ahluwalia*. The trial judge had directed the jury that the relevant characteristics were that she was an Asian woman, married to an Asian man and living in Britain. The judge also directed that the jury may consider that the fact that she was an educated woman with a university degree was a relevant characteristic. Counsel argued that the jury had not been directed to consider the relevance of "battered woman syndrome".[30]

R. v. Ahluwalia
[1992] 4 All E.R. 889 at 896–898, *per* Lord Taylor C.J.

"The defendant's characteristics
Mr Robertson's second ground of appeal is based upon another aspect of the learned judge's direction on provocation. It concerns the way the learned judge dealt with the appellant's 'characteristics' in seeking to follow the model direction set out by Lord Diplock in *D.P.P. v. Camplin* [1978] 2 All E.R. 168 at 175; [1978] A.C. 705 at 718...

In the present case the judge's direction to the jury contained this passage:

'The only characteristics of the defendant about which you know specifically that might be relevant are that she is an Asian woman, married, incidentally to an Asian man, the deceased living in this country. You may think she is an educated woman, she has a university degree. If you find these characteristics relevant to your considerations, of course you will bear that in mind.'

That direction is criticised on two grounds, first, because the learned judge did not refer specifically to a particular characteristic which will be mentioned below and,

---

[29] *R. v. Camplin, ibid.*, at 175c.
[30] Why these were relevant characteristics is difficult to see. Can, for example the fact that she was educated to university level be described as a physical or mental characteristic? Further, the provocation was not directed at her race, arranged marriage or education. To suggest that the provocation was connected to these characteristics widens consideration of the circumstances far beyond the limits to which the criminal law is usually taken. See below at 11.1.ii.c for discussion of the (de)merits of introducing evidence of battered woman syndrome.

secondly, because he closed the list of characteristics instead of leaving it open to the jury to find others which they might think might affect the gravity of the provocation.

As to the second of these grounds, Mr Robertson conceded that if the judge had left the list open, there was only one characteristic he could suggest which the jury might properly have taken into account.

This ground of appeal therefore turns upon the one characteristic which it is complained the learned judge ignored. Mr Robertson submits that this appellant was suffering from a 'battered woman syndrome', such that it had become a characteristic within the meaning of Lord Diplock's formulation. He says that not only had the appellant suffered violence, abuse and humiliation over some ten years and thereby undergone a dreadful ordeal. That course of ill-treatment had affected her personality so as to produce a state of 'learnt helplessness', a phrase used by experts who have identified this condition. Accordingly, submits Mr Robertson, the learned judge ought to have referred to this characteristic in his direction to the jury. Alternatively, he ought at the very least to have left the list open so that the jury could have latched on to this characteristic even if he had not.

The use of the word 'characteristics' in *D.P.P. v. Camplin* seems, it is argued, to derive from the statutory language used in New Zealand. Section 169 of the New Zealand Crimes Act 1961 expressly referred to 'a person having the power of self-control of an ordinary person, but otherwise having the characteristics of the offender . . .'

In *R. v. Newell* (1980) 71 Cr. App. R. 331 this court adopted as correct the statement of principle by North J. in *R. v. McGregor* [1962] N.Z.L.R. 1069. Part of his judgment reads (at 1081–1082):

> 'The offender must be presumed to possess in general the power of self-control of the ordinary man, save insofar as his power of self-control is weakened because of some particular characteristic possessed by him. It is not every trait or disposition of the offender that can be invoked to modify the concept of the ordinary man. The characteristic must be something definite and of sufficient significance to make the offender a different person from the ordinary run of mankind, and have also a sufficient degree of permanence to warrant its being regarded as something constituting part of the individual's character or personality . . . it must be such that it can fairly be said that the offender is thereby marked off or distinguished from the ordinary man of the community. Moreover, it is to be equally emphasised that there must be some real connection between the nature of the provocation and the particular characteristic of the offender by which it is sought to modify the ordinary man test . . . Special difficulties, however, arise when it becomes necessary to consider what purely mental peculiarities may be allowed as characteristics.'

English cases concerned with the 'reasonable man' element of provocation, and examples given by judges, have tended to focus on physical characteristics. Thus age, sex, colour, race and any physical abnormality have been considered. However, the indorsement of the New Zealand authority in *R. v. Newell* shows that characteristics relating to the mental state or personality of an individual can also be taken into account by the jury, providing they have the necessary degree of permanence.

Examples from New Zealand case law are *R. v. Taaka* [1982] 2 N.Z.L.R. 198 and *R. v. Leilua* [1986] N.Z. Recent Law 118. In *R. v. Taaka* the Court of Appeal held that psychiatric evidence was admissible to show the appellant suffered from a pathological condition making him an 'obsessively compulsive personality'. In *R. v. Leilua* the same court admitted evidence from a psychiatrist suggesting that the appellant suffered from chronic post-traumatic stress disorder, a condition recognised in medical science.

Those decisions serve to underline the nature of the evidence which would normally be anticipated when special characteristics relating to mental state or personality of a defendant are put forward as matters for the jury to consider.

In the present case, there was no medical or other evidence before the judge and jury, and none even from the appellant, to suggest that she suffered from a post-traumatic stress disorder, or 'battered women syndrome' or any other specific condition which could amount to a 'characteristic' as defined in *R. v. McGregor* [1962] N.Z.L.R. 1969. True, there was much evidence that the appellant had suffered grievous ill-treatment; but nothing to suggest that the effect of it was to make her 'a different person from the ordinary run of [women]', or to show that she was 'marked off or distinguished from the ordinary [woman] of the community'."

The Court of Appeal admitted that battered woman syndrome *may* be a relevant characteristic (relevant characteristics not being limited to physical, but including mental characteristics)[31] but that there was no evidence that Kiranjit Ahluwalia was suffering from the syndrome. In the earlier case of *R. v. Newell*,[32] the Court of Appeal had accepted that mental characteristics would be relevant if they were permanent and if there was a direct connection between the mental characteristic and the provocation. This could mean either that the defendant must have been provoked by a taunt directed at the mental characteristic and which affected the gravity of the provocation to the defendant, or that the characteristic must be connected to the loss of self-control by making the defendant a different person from the ordinary person. The Court of Appeal in *Ahluwalia* accepted that battered woman syndrome may be a relevant characteristic without considering the need for the taunt to be connected to the characteristic. If the taunt must be so connected, this would necessarily limit the relevance of the syndrome.

The appeal of Emma Humphreys succeeded on the grounds that the jury had been instructed not to consider traits of immaturity and attention-seeking as relevant characteristics:

R. v. Humphreys
[1995] 4 All E.R. 1008 at 1011–1012, 1021–1022, *per* Hirst L.J.

"The main facts as to the appellant's earlier life, and the events leading up to the killing, were contained in her interview which she confirmed on oath in her brief and unchallenged evidence in court.

She has a very unhappy family background. When she was about five years old her mother and father separated, her mother remarried and the appellant went to live with her and her stepfather in Canada until December 1983. Both her mother and her

---

[31] This was *obiter*.
[32] *R. v. Newell* (1980) 71 Cr. App. R. 331.

stepfather were alcoholics. From early adolescence she herself took drugs, drank too much alcohol, and was sexually promiscuous. She returned to England in December 1983 and went to live with her father and his second wife, and subsequently with her grandmother. However, on 30 August, 1984, aged 16, she left home and went to work as a prostitute.

Shortly thereafter she was picked up by the victim, Trevor Armitage. He had a predilection for girls much younger than himself, had previous convictions for violence, was a drug addict and was known to the vice squad as somebody who was seen most evenings driving round the vice area.

Trevor Armitage took the appellant to live with him at his house in Turnbury Road, Bulwell. He was jealous and possessive, although he did not object to her continuing to work as a prostitute and, indeed, lived in part on her earnings. Their relationship began as a sexual one, but shortly after they first met he beat her up on a number of occasions and this caused her to lose interest in him.

Over Christmas and the New Year 1984–1985 she appeared before the criminal courts as a result of two incidents and for some weeks she was on remand at Risley, until 21 February, 1985, when she was conditionally discharged. While she was away Trevor Armitage took in another young girl.

This miserable history from August 1984 onwards was the prelude to the critical events of 24 to 26 February, 1985. Before reciting them, however, it is important to record another very important and unhappy aspect of her personal history, namely that she had a strong tendency to seek attention, exemplified in her case by frequent attempts, dating back to her residence in Canada, to cut her wrists, leaving marks and scars which were plainly visible; these were described by a doctor who examined her shortly after the killing, and who found three recent cuts to her right wrist, fifteen well-healed scars to her right forearm, nine recent cuts running across her left wrist with fresh, dry blood over them, and seven well-healed vertical scars running up her left forearm.

On 24 February, 1985 a Mrs Whitehead, who was a witness at the trial, saw the appellant in a bar and described her as very lonely, depressed and desolate. The following day two friends met up with Trevor Armitage and his son Stephen, aged 16, in a bar, where the appellant was also present. They left the bar with the appellant and Trevor Armitage told her that 'we'll be all right for a gang bang tonight'.

The group then went on to another public house and finally to Trevor Armitage's house where he arrived drunk. The appellant went upstairs and turned on the radio. Shortly afterwards Trevor Armitage left to drive his son home.

After they had left she went down to the kitchen and took two knives from a drawer, fearing that there might be trouble when he came back and that he might give her another beating. At this juncture she cut both her wrists with one of the knives.

When Trevor Armitage returned she was sitting on the landing, listening to music with one of the knives in her hand. He came up and went past her into the bedroom, where he undressed and then came and sat near her on the landing with only his shirt on. She said she got the feeling that he wanted sex while she did not and that she was fearful that he might force himself upon her.

At this critical juncture there occurred the event which was relied upon as triggering her loss of self-control, when Trevor Armitage taunted her that she had not made a very good job of her wrist slashing.

She reached across him as he lay on his back and stabbed him with a blow from one of the knives which penetrated his heart and went through into his liver, in a manner which expert evidence stated required a moderate degree of force . . .

[Counsel for the defence] Mrs Grindrod, while accepting that the 'explosive' trait would not in itself qualify as an eligible characteristic (since it connoted no more than that the appellant lacked normal powers of self-control), submitted that the other two abnormal characteristics, namely attention seeking through wrist slashing and immaturity, were eligible characteristics, particularly in the light of *Dryden*, where she said the relevant mental characteristics were closely comparable. In her argument she stressed the attention-seeking trait, but she submitted that immaturity was also relevant, particularly in the light of *Camplin*.

It followed, she argued, that the judge's direction to ignore all three of these characteristics was fundamentally flawed.

For the Crown, Mr Milmo Q.C. supported the judge's direction and submitted that both the characteristics relied upon by Mrs Grindrod were, on a correct application of the law, ineligible and not properly to be attributed to the reasonable man or woman.

The crux of his argument was that any characteristic is ineligible for attribution to the reasonable man or woman if it is wholly inconsistent with or repugnant to the general concept of an ordinary reasonable person — an approach which he submitted was fully in line with the reasoning of this court in *Morhall*. It followed, he contended, that attention seeking by wrist cutting, which was the abnormality principally relied upon by Mrs Grindrod, was ineligible, seeing that it should be regarded as wholly inconsistent with or repugnant to such a concept.

Mr Milmo realistically recognised that *Dryden* presented formidable difficulties to his submission. But he argued that *Dryden* could not stand with *R. v. Morhall* since the abnormal characteristics relied upon in the former should also have been regarded as repugnant and wholly inconsistent with the concept of the reasonable and ordinary person. He therefore boldly suggested that in this case we should overthrow *Dryden* as having been decided per incuriam and follow *Morhall*, which, he suggested, may have been overlooked by the court in *Dryden*.

Alternatively, he invited us to distinguish *Dryden* on the footing that in the present case one of the three characteristics (explosiveness) was plainly ineligible.

We say at once that we are unable to accede to this last invitation. Although accepting as we do that explosiveness, in isolation, is ineligible, that in no way affects the eligibility of the other two characteristics, if they could properly be relied upon and left to the jury.

So far as the *Dryden* case is concerned, we think it inconceivable that *Morhall* could have been overlooked, since barely seven months separated the two decisions and in both cases the court was presided over by the Lord Taylor of Gosforth C.J. Nor do we accept that the characteristics relied upon in *Dryden* are repugnant to or wholly inconsistent with the concept of the reasonable man or woman, or comparable with self-induced glue sniffing, which would seem to fall outside the *McGregor* test on a number of counts, not least because it may be regarded as 'a self-induced transitory state'.

Mr Milmo accepted and, indeed, suggested that, for example, dyslexia and anorexia would qualify as eligible characteristics. We think there is much force in Mrs Grindrod's submission in her reply that the appellant's tendency to attention seeking by wrist slashing is closely comparable to the latter and like the latter can, in truth, be regarded as a psychological illness or disorder which is in no way repugnant to or wholly inconsistent with the concept of the reasonable person. It is also a permanent condition which, as Dr Tarsh stated, was abnormal and therefore set the appellant apart.

Furthermore, it was clearly open to the jury to conclude that the provocative taunt relied upon as the trigger inevitably hit directly at this very abnormality and was calculated to strike a very raw nerve.

Immaturity is clearly in no way repugnant; indeed, it suggests that the appellant was unduly young for her comparatively young age and thus brings the case, on this ground, into close comparison with *Camplin*.

We therefore consider that the judge should have left for the jury's deliberation these two relevant characteristics as eligible for attribution to the reasonable woman, it being for them to decide what, if any, weight should be given to them in all the circumstances. This is in full conformity with the requirement of s. 3 of the 1957 Act, that it is for the jury and not the judge to determine this issue."

Donald Nicolson and Rohit Sanghvi suggest that the judgment in the case of Emma Humphreys is consistent with recent cases demonstrating greater appreciation of the position of women who have been abused:

D. NICOLSON & R. SANGHVI
"More justice for battered women"[33]

"Her appeal succeeded on two grounds. The first criticised the judge's direction to the jury to consider only the deceased's taunts about her wrist-slashing in deciding whether she had been provoked and whether her reaction was reasonable. It was argued that the whole history of their relationship was relevant. His violence towards her, his taking in another girl, the reference to a 'gang-bang' and his sitting next to her dressed only in a shirt should have been treated as part of the provocative conduct, not merely as background to the taunt. In upholding this argument, the Court of Appeal has, it is hoped, resolved a conflict in the cases as to whether juries may consider a period of cumulative provocation culminating in a loss of self-control or only the immediately-preceding provocative conduct. This decision will be extremely useful to battered defendants, given that their reaction to some final, perhaps trivial, act of provocation may only make sense against the background of often years of repeated violence and mental abuse.

Moreover, the Court of Appeal's specific criticism of the jury direction seems to require trial judges in summing up not merely to leave evidence of cumulative provocation to the jury, but to carefully analyse each of its various strands. Accordingly, future juries may well give greater prominence to the effect of domestic violence on battered defendants, especially if, following *Ahluwalia*, expert evidence is allowed as to battered woman syndrome or more generally as to the effects of domestic violence. Indeed, in the light of both decisions, the exclusion of psychiatric and other expert evidence on how battered defendants can be expected to respond to provocation may prove to constitute a ground of appeal.

The appellant's second ground of appeal alleged that the trial judge had wrongly omitted to direct the jury to consider her characteristics of attention-seeking and immaturity. This was upheld on the grounds that neither characteristic was repugnant or wholly inconsistent with the concept of the reasonable person. Furthermore, in the case of attention-seeking, it was both a sufficiently permanent condition and directly

---

[33]   (1995) 145 New L.J. 1122.

relevant to the deceased's taunts. To the extent that these requirements of non-repugnancy, permanence and relevance are required by existing authority, the decision in *Humphreys* (unlike that in *Ahluwalia*) is consistent with authority. Nevertheless, a less sympathetic court could well have decided that in fact the characteristic of attention-seeking failed to accord with these requirements.

In conclusion, the *Humphreys* decision evidences no dramatic legal changes, merely a continuation of the appellate judiciary's greater understanding of battered women who kill, which had commenced in *Ahluwalia*. The approach now seems to be to allow battered defendants great latitude in putting forward circumstances and characteristics relevant to their provocation defences. At trial level it has become common for murder charges to fail or not even to be attempted in the case of battered defendants."

The majority of the Privy Council in *Luc Thiet Thuan v. The Queen*,[34] however, held that mental characteristics of the accused were not relevant to the standard of the reasonable man. Lord Steyn, dissenting, advocated the second interpretation above, namely that mental characteristics may be the reason that the defendant was less able to exercise self-control than the reasonable man. He supported this perspective by giving examples of situations in which women kill, thereby showing the importance of woman-centred dramas upon the development of legal reasoning in the area of provocation:

Luc Thiet Thuan v. The Queen
[1996] 3 W.L.R. 45 at 60b, *per* Lord Steyn

"Let me imagine the case where a woman shortly after giving birth to a child stabs and kills her husband during an argument. She wishes to put to the jury as part of her defence of provocation that she was suffering from postnatal depression which rendered her more prone to loss of self-control. A second example is the case where there is evidence that a woman, as a result of ill treatment by her husband, suffers from 'battered woman syndrome.' When taunted by her lover she stabs and kills him. She wants to rely on evidence of battered woman syndrome as part of her defence of provocation. The third example is a woman who suffered from a personality disorder which makes her more prone to loss of self-control. During a quarrel she stabs and kills her husband. She wants to rely on the personality disorder as a part of her defence of provocation. A common feature of the three examples is that in none of them can the woman in any way be said at fault in inducing her condition. None of the cases can be explained away on the broad view of the provocative conduct of the husband or lover, *i.e.* the 'last straw' argument. In all three cases the merits or demerits of the woman's argument cannot be determined on a *priori* grounds: in the context of provocation it is a matter of fact for exploration in evidence. But in all three cases the particular characteristic of the defendant is potentially relevant only in as much as it affects the degree of self-control of the defendant."

---

[34] *Luc Thiet Thuan v. The Queen* [1996] 3 W.L.R. 45. As a Privy Council decision this case is not binding.

Approving of *Ahluwalia*, *Humphreys* and *Thornton (No. 2)*, Lord Steyn argued that mental characteristics of the accused should be relevant to modification of the reasonable man standard.

The acceptance of the experiences of (battered) women as relevant to the standard by which the conduct is judged as reasonable is of limited assistance to women who kill given the overarching requirement that their behaviour coincide with standards set by male experiences, particularly that it constitutes a sudden and temporary loss of self control. This was acknowledged in the judgment given on Sara Thornton's second appeal in which it was held:

R. v. Thornton (No. 2)
[1996] 2 All E.R. 1023 at 1030, *per* Lord Taylor C.J.

"[S]ince reliance *is* placed upon the appellant's suffering from a 'battered woman syndrome', we think it right to reaffirm the principle. A defendant, even if suffering from that syndrome, cannot succeed in relying on provocation unless the jury consider she suffered or may have suffered a sudden and temporary loss of self-control at the time of the killing.

That is not to say that a battered woman syndrome has no relevance to the defence of provocation. The severity of such a syndrome and the extent to which it may have affected a particular defendant will no doubt vary and is for the jury to consider. But it may be relevant in two ways. First, it may form an important background to whatever triggered the actus reus. A jury may more readily find there was a sudden loss of control triggered by even a minor incident, if the defendant has endured abuse over a period, on the 'last straw' basis. Secondly, depending on the medical evidence, the syndrome may have affected the defendant's personality so as to constitute a significant characteristic relevant (as we shall indicate) to the second question the jury has to consider in regard to provocation."

The limitations of the reference to particular gender characteristics are clearly spelt out in an article by Katherine O'Donovan from which the following extract is taken:

K. O'DONOVAN
"Defences for Battered Women Who Kill"[35]

"The barrier posed by the definition of provocation in *Duffy* as 'a sudden and temporary loss of self-control' and the opposition thereto of 'revenge killing' means that the issue of provocation will not be put to the jury in most cases of the killing of a batterer where delay occurs. Yet, should the jury become seized of the issue, there is in the case-law language which permits a taking into account of the battered wife context. An example is the *Camplin* case.

In *Camplin* it was reaffirmed that provocation in homicide cases can reduce an offence to manslaughter. The question concerned the wording of s.3 of the 1957 Hom-

---

[35]   K. O' Donovan, *supra*, n. 13 at 225–229.

icide Act, which provides that 'the question whether the provocation was enough to make a reasonable man do as he did shall be left to be determined by the jury'. The accused was a fifteen year old youth who had killed a middle-aged man. His defence was that the deceased had first buggered him and then laughed at him. In the House of Lords an attempt was made to broaden concepts of provocation to encompass differences of age, ethnicity, and sex from the adult, white, male traditional model. Lord Diplock made clear his view that provocation is a relative concept — relative to characteristics of the defendant and to social standards of the day. So he said:

> 'When Hale was writing in the seventeenth century, pulling a man's nose was thought to justify retaliation with a sword; when *Mancini v. D.P.P.* (1942) was decided by this House, a blow with a fist would not justify retaliation with a deadly weapon ... But now that the law has been changed so as to permit of words being treated as provocation even though unaccompanied by any other acts, the gravity of verbal provocation may well depend upon the particular characteristics or circumstances of the person to whom a taunt or insult is addressed.'

Thus social standards of the time, and particular characteristics or circumstances are relevant when considering whether actions or words are provocative or retaliation reasonable. This has the effect of reducing the concept from absolute to relative. Age at the time of killing is relevant for it 'is a characteristic which may have its effects on temperament as well as physique'. Of course this does not answer the problem that the response to provocation must be 'in the heat of the moment', but it does suggest a possible line of development.

On gender, Lord Diplock stated that 'for the purposes of the laws of provocation the "reasonable man" has never been confined to the adult male. It means an ordinary member of either sex . . .' Lord Morris took the same line, saying that the term 'reasonable man' included a reasonable woman:

> 'If words of grievous insult were addressed to a woman, words perhaps reflecting on her chastity or way of life, a consideration of the way in which she reacted would have to take account of how other women being reasonable women would or might in like circumstances have reacted.'

Lord Simon took a similar view thinking that 'a jury could arguably ... take the sex of the accused into account in assessing what might reasonably cause her to lose her self-control.' From this we may conclude that, provided the issue of provocation is put to the jury, the emergence of a woman's standpoint is possible. But this does require a definition of provocation which itself takes account of women's experiences. At present the definition of provocation is still limited by the *Duffy* decision. So although there may be relativity on the question of reasonableness of response which is open to the jury, this is a question which does not go to the jury if the court decides that what happened does not fit the definition of provocation. In the *Ibrams* case which was subsequent to *Camplin* the jury was prevented from considering the defence of provocation because a delay was involved. To some extent provocation as a concept remains within an overly-narrow framework of analysis. It is tempting to conclude that the judiciary has been willing to broaden the standard of reasonableness, but has retained a male-oriented view of provocative behaviour.

The analysis of notions of provocative behaviour as stemming from a narrow perspective can be illustrated by the speeches in *Camplin*. Although their Lordships were attempting to broaden the standard of the 'reasonable man' to cover issues of ethnicity, gender, age, and particular characteristics, their language nevertheless reveals their difficulties in abandoning tradition. Thus Lord Morris's example of an insult to a woman concerned imputations against her chastity. Two points may be made concerning this. First, that a woman's 'unchastity' may be of more concern to her male partner than it is to her. Many heat-of-passion killings of women by men concern the victim's sexuality. Criminal law has traditionally been sympathetic to men who killed their wives or their wives' lovers *in flagrante delicto*, that is, upon discovering them in an act of adultery. And in those rare cases where the Slander of Women Act 1891 is invoked to vindicate a woman's chastity, concern seems to be directed towards 'her prospects in the marriage market', that is, towards a future husband's standpoint on female sexuality. Secondly, Taylor points out that while the law:

> 'sympathised with the jealous rage of men, it assumed that wives did not experience similar rage. In 1946, 274 years after a court first announced the defence of provocation, an English court finally stated that wives who killed their husbands or their husbands' lovers could also avail themselves of the defence.'

The investigation of double standards can now be taken further. The double standard, whether on adultery or provocation, contains three elements: definition, from a particular perspective, containing assumptions about 'the other'. Even when the double standard is abandoned 'the other' may be expected to conform to a standard based on a particular perspective. In relation to provocation Taylor's comment is pithy:

> 'Although the defence of provocation upon the discovery of adultery now applies to women as well as to men, it is a shallow concession to equality that bears little legitimacy or meaning. Cases and social studies show that women rarely react to their husband's infidelity with deadly violence . . .
> Female homicide defendants may be exceptional because they are rare, but they may not be exceptional women; they may be ordinary women pushed to extremes. Yet the law has never incorporated these "ordinary" women into its standards for assessing the degree of criminality in homicide, as it has done with "ordinary" men.'

What is being argued here is that allowing women to claim provocation in cases of male infidelity is a small concession. Considering violence and fear would have more meaning.

It might seem that the broadened standard of reasonableness put forward in *Camplin* is a progressive standard, covering gender, ethnicity, and age. But can it deal with the question of what is provocative to a particular temperament? Without an experiential element which takes account of participant standpoint, the 'other' will remain defined from an ethno- or phallo-centric perspective. The standpoint of the accused must be permitted to emerge. Temperament is both relevant and relative according to Lord Diplock.

This is an important point and it may again be illustrated by language from Lord Morris who said that the racial and ethnic origins of the accused are relevant in considering whether things said are provocative, and the reaction to such words. 'The question would be whether the accused, if he was provoked, only reacted as even any reasonable man *in his situation* would or might have reacted.' This language is suggestive of a standard of reasonableness which takes account of certain characteristics, but which is not entirely subjective. In other words it is an attempt to find a standard which is neither exclusive to the adult, white, male, nor is subjective to the accused. This is to be welcomed as a recognition of pluralism. The difficulties of expression of such a standard should not be underestimated. Seeing from another perspective is not easy.

Yet Lord Simon's speech in *Camplin* may be taken to illustrate one of the difficulties involved. In an effort to explain how reasonableness is relative to situation Lord Simon expanded in hypothetical terms on gender. Having said that the sex of [the] accused was relevant to a determination of what might reasonably cause her to lose her self-control, he added in parenthesis:

'(A "reasonable woman" with her sex eliminated is altogether too abstract a notion for my comprehension or, I am confident, for that of any jury. In any case it hardly makes sense to say that an impotent man must be notionally endowed with virility before he ranks within the law of provocation as a reasonable man, yet that a normal woman must be notionally stripped of her femininity before she qualifies as a reasonable woman.) If so, this is already some qualification on the "reasonable person" as a pure abstraction devoid of any personal characteristics, even if such a concept were of any value to the law. This qualification might be crucial: take the insult "whore" addressed respectively to a reasonable man and a reasonable woman.'

This speech by Lord Simon has been taken as evidence of judicial prejudice against women: that he considers femininity and reason to be opposed qualities. Yet an alternative reading is that this is a clumsy way of disposing of the case of *Bedder* in which the jury was directed to disregard the defendant's characteristic of sexual impotence in applying the test of reasonability. Lord Simon described the *Bedder* decision as having implications which 'constitute affronts to common sense and any sense of justice'. In other words, his discussion of gender is intended to establish its relevance as a characteristic in applying the reasonableness test. His unfortunate choice of words indicates how difficult it is for judicial members of the House of Lords to come to terms with the challenges of feminism. Thus the statement about notionally stripping a woman of her femininity before she qualifies as reasonable may be read either as a blatant example of sexism, or as an argument for situational ethics. The latter interpretation offers greater scope to those attempting to broaden the approach of the English judiciary to gender issues. This does not gainsay Lord Simon's confirmation of his inarticulate premise: that the abstract reasonable person is the normal, potent, male.

Some academic commentators on the reasonable man test do suggest that, in its origins and application, the test is for a person opposed to the feminine gender. But perhaps a better analysis is that provided by Allen:

'Legal discourse constructs for itself a standard human subject, endowed with consciousness, reason, foresight, intentionality, an awareness of right and wrong and a knowledge of the law of the land. These are the reasonable attributes which provide the grounds for legal culpability.'

Pleas of self-defence or provocation represent an acknowledgement by the law that, under certain circumstances, necessity or loss of self-control may overcome that intentionality and consciousness which the law elevates as the standard. 'The "reasonable man" test allows this "frailty of the normal" to be acknowledged and taken into account.'

Cases of battered women who kill tend to follow a pattern. The woman waits until the batterer is quiet, in bed or asleep. Then she attacks. For example, in *Ahluwalia*, having been beaten and burned, the defendant poured petrol over her husband when he was asleep and set him alight. The delay led to a conviction for murder. Yet similar cases where diminished responsibility is pleaded may lead to two years' probation.

Delay is viewed as leading either to revenge or to calming down. In either case legal discourse constructs a person who is rational and calculating with legal responsibility. The idea of cumulative rage, the slow burn, has not been accepted in English law, although it has some purchase in California. Perhaps cumulative rage might be posited as a response to cumulative violence.

Taking account of the characteristics of the provoked person, such as gender or age, is limited by case-law to situations where there was a 'real' connection between the nature of the provocation and the characteristic in question. Whether the courts might be willing to see cumulative fear and rage as a gender characteristic is doubtful. Yet it is fear which leads to a delay in responding immediately to violence.

New South Wales has amended its law relating to provocation in order to reflect an increased awareness of domestic violence. The Crimes (Homicide) Amendment Act 1982 allows any past conduct of the deceased towards the defendant to be the basis of provocation. The events immediately prior to the killing are de-emphasized. However, encouraging pleas of provocation in such cases may have certain drawbacks. Arguments which blame the victim may also be encouraged. Attention, which should focus on cumulative violence and the appropriate response thereto by the law, the police, the community, may shift onto the victim.

Arguments about gender characteristics have to be handled with care. The traditional reasonable man, based on an idealized male subject, appears to have been replaced by a standard relative to age, ethnicity, and gender. The law lords have abandoned the notion of the neutral legal subject. The instatement in *Camplin* of gender as central to conceptions of reasonableness has not been universally approved. Allen points out that legal agents such as police, psychiatrists, and physicians are strongly influenced by assumptions about gender, whilst upholding legal notions of neutrality. These assumptions about gender in the interpretation of a subject's actions and behaviour lead to divergences in the treatment of male and female offenders. These disparities may be offensive to a sense of justice."

In a later article, Katherine O'Donovan argues that the concept of the "reasonable man" used in the objective test of provocation presents a view of the behaviour of the ordinary man as the common experience of all people. This masks the fact that the behaviour expected of the "reasonable man" is based upon the experiences and reactions of the *male* subject.

K. O'DONOVAN
"Law's Knowledge: The Judge, The Expert, The Battered Woman, and her Syndrome"[36]

"In the courtroom of legal reason, a person on a homicide charge has limited choices in the presentation of a defence. In my previous paper I presented three options for

---

[36] (1993) 20 *Journal of Law and Society* 427 at 428–429.

the abused woman accused of killing the abuser: self-defence which is a complete justification; provocation; or diminished responsibility. These latter two defences, if successful, reduce the charge to manslaughter. Cases subsequent to my first paper confirm my observations in so far as new ideas have had to be fitted into existing defences and it is on those defences identified above that debate has centred.

New ideas about the justifying or excusing of killings in particular circumstances are policed by definitions and rules from existing legal doctrine. For a woman who kills, after having experienced cumulative violence, this means fitting herself into existing paradigms. Her actions must be accommodated within the text of the law; the context may be treated by rules of evidence, or by definitional language, as irrelevant. Thus, the failure to respond to violence with immediate violence can lead to the conclusion that, when action was taken, it was premeditated. Displacing this assumption has proved well-nigh impossible in English law. Thus, the Lord Chief Justice, in a recent appeal, reiterated the binding nature of previous decisions 'unless we are convinced that they were wholly wrong'. Responsibility for change is ascribed to the legislature:

'There are important considerations of public policy which would be involved should provocation be redefined so as possibly to blur the distinction between sudden loss of self-control and deliberate retaliation.'

Resorting to expert evidence in order to support pleas based on women's experiences of abuse requests a judge to admit such evidence. This has happened in common law jurisdictions elsewhere, but not in England and Wales. That resistance illuminates a broad area of inquiry of which the present investigation is a small part. What is happening is a contest over knowledge between women's groups and a largely male judiciary with male definitions and understandings of human behaviour, which are claimed as universal. This contest over knowledge can be chronicled as a precursor of future legal battles.

The judge's power over knowledge is revealed when we consider the construction of the 'reasonable man' in the legal discourse of defences to homicide. This construct possesses the ability to respond immediately to physical threat or verbal attack with violence. He can assess the degree of violence necessary to repel an invader of his bodily integrity, or to vindicate an insult to his masculinity. He can remain reasonable whilst losing mastery of his mind under provocation. In short, in his physical ability, in action and response, he is embodied as a male. He feels powerful enough to defend himself or to lose his temper. This construct is built into the law as a definition of the defences to homicide and of reason. His existence does not have to be justified by expert evidence. He is taken to be part of the common sense experience of us all.

The reasonable man's claims to universality are under siege. The contest comes from those whose experiences are other than his. The problem for them is how to effect a point of entry into the legal discourse of common sense and reasonableness. That discourse, taken as belonging to everyone, is exclusive to those with power over knowledge. So the problem is epistemological: how to alter ways of seeing, understanding, and defining the normalcy of the reasonable man. The object of so doing is not only to point out exclusivity, but also to enter in, to be included, to create an understanding of epistemologies and ontologies of 'others'. But it is not so easy for women. As Genevieve Lloyd points out, 'the maleness of the Man of Reason ... is no superficial linguistic bias'. Her argument is that reason is conceptually linked to masculinity, truth, and the intellect, and raises discursive barriers to femininity to which it defines itself in opposition. It is not just that femininity, emotion, and disorder are associated but that the constructed differences are in a hierarchy of deference of emotion to reason.'

Katherine O'Donovan considers the challenge to stereotypes about women and the introduction of the experiences of women into the legal process through the admission of expert evidence. Whilst being aware that reliance upon experts may lead to the view that women who are abused can be treated as a homogenous group (which then excludes those whose experiences do not fit into the official behavioural explanations of the experts) Katherine O'Donovan suggests that the introduction of such evidence may be necessary in order to challenge the universality of the "reasonable man" and to permit the introduction of women's differential experiences:

K. O'Donovan
"Law's Knowledge: The Judge, The Expert, The Battered Woman, and her Syndrome"[37]

"Notwithstanding my argument about strategy and effecting a point of entry for women into legal discourse, certain misgivings and doubts remain. Some of these centre on the 'syndrome'; others on the medicalization implicit in the calling of experts to testify. In my earlier paper I expressed doubts about scientific claims of objectivity about human behaviour based on limited and dated psychological research on dogs in cages. In particular, the idea of 'learned helplessness', pivotal to battered woman syndrome, does not fully explain how the accused comes to act, with fatal results for the abuser. The position of expert is also open to question. The expert makes a claim to positive knowledge; knowledge of how women as a group respond when in a battering relationship. Not only may the reader be sceptical about the expert, scientific method, the syndrome, and its applicability to human beings, but also scepticism may arise as to generalizations about women as a group based on material from particular studies. Christine Littleton argues that expert evidence labels women as 'unreasonable, incompetent, suffering from psychological impairment or just plain crazy' and that the effect is to shift the focus from 'the intolerable conditions under which these women live'.

The objection based on medicalization has been answered in Australia by calling on non-medical experts such as criminologists and proposing the use of social workers and women's refuge workers. But this does not answer the questions about scientific positivism and claims to specialist knowledge of human behaviour. The objection to generalization from particular women's experiences to 'what would be expected of women generally' can be met by pointing to legal method's construction of the ordinary person as a standard. But what this achieves is a shift of the objection away from one aspect of legal discourse to another. Furthermore, the universality of the 'ordinary person' is doubtful. The objection to the description of experiences within the range of the ordinary person as a syndrome (that is, women are 'just plain crazy') has already been answered with the idea of a strategy whereby some women's experiences can enter criminal defences. But the overall explanation to meet these objections calls on recent work interrogating legal method and how law makes its claims to knowledge . . .

The challenges to law's claims to universality, generality, and neutrality, from feminist legal theorists, and others, have yet to meet a response in English law. In so far as

---

[37]   K. O'Donovan, *ibid*, at 431, 433–435.

law's empire is built on limited cognition, rigid procedure for admission of knowledge, and a claim to universality, it may be impossible for a shift to pluralism to take place. The trial and its process are reductive. But the bunker of positivism and coercion is under assault. I see two major problems for law in its efforts to retain its legitimacy.

First, there is the universality question. This takes a variety forms of which my criticisms of the legal subject of the laws of provocation and self-defence as an embodied male are a part. Ngaire Naffine has pointed to the 'man of law' as a white, middle-class male, produced and reproduced in a myriad of legal practices. If there is a 'woman of law' it is likely that she is, as Judy Grbich suggests, a legal self produced by male imaginings as a projection of their views about women. Where she cannot be accommodated to a male legal subject, then it is easier to put her into the 'diminished responsibility' category, thus confining the disordering of classifications that she creates.

Feminist theory proposes a strategic answer to legal subjectivity with plural legal subjects. It is for those with experiences of embodied womanhood to inscribe women in law. Whilst knowing that we are not all the same, that there are differences within and among us female subjects, nevertheless, we recognize that there are 'differences between all of us and the male subject'. The inscription of our experiences should not have to be done via 'experts'. It should not have to rely on doubtful claims of scientific experiments on animals, transposed to women. The requirement of the objectification of women's experiences by science is an indication of women's lack of legal subjectivity. However, if this is the only way that such experiences can gain legal cognition, then the strategy of objectification may be temporarily necessary. Battered woman syndrome and its theory of 'learned helplessness' are metaphors for the suffering of abused women, and it is as metaphors that we should accept these terms.

The second problem for law in its contests with women over knowledge is the claim to neutrality from which the rule of law derives legitimacy. To some extent the failure to instate women as legal subjects, and the reinstatement of imaginary women by powerful males, is an aspect of lack of neutrality. But bias goes further, and infects applications, decisions, sentences, reports, legal education, the myriad legal practices of daily life. Some jurisdictions cognize this bias and are attempting conversations about it. Others persist in their habits of denial. Denial means never having to say that you are sorry, and that you do not have to change. Yet, failure to change carries its own risks to legitimacy.

Even if the powerful persons who run law were to read and recognize the above, would it be possible for women's knowledge to enter the machinery? The answer must depend on the reader's legal theory. Grounded and specific studies of legal methodology by feminists raise detailed questions about law's adaptability to women's experiences. It is no longer adequate or sufficient for the male subject 'to conjugate his being in the universalistic logocentric mode', claiming to represent all of us in himself. But can he find his way out of the system of law which he has created? As a cultural artifact law is male; yet it aspires to represent us all. If it is to do so it will have to change its practice. It will have to know, to have knowledge of, to acknowledge, difference."

11.1.ii.c Battered Woman Syndrome. Battered woman syndrome has been used with self-defence in the U.S. to explain the reaction of the woman as reasonable in the circumstances. The Court of Appeal in *R. v. Ahluwalia* accepted that it may be a relevant characteristic to modify the standard of the reasonable person in the objective test of provocation. The origins of battered woman syndrome are explained by Donald Nicolson and Rohit Sanghvi:

D. NICOLSON & R. SANGHVI
"Battered Women and Provocation: The Implications of *R. v. Ahluwalia*"[38]

"BWS was developed by the American psychologist Lenore Walker in order to dispel myths and misconceptions about domestic violence and to help establish the reasonableness of homicide by battered women. It consists of two elements. The 'cycle theory' postulates that male violence against women partners typically follows a three-phase pattern. The first involves a period of heightening tension caused by the man's argumentativeness, during which the woman attempts various unsuccessful pacifying strategies. This 'tension-building' phase ends when the man erupts into a rage at some small trigger and acutely batters the woman. This is followed by the 'loving-contrite' or 'honeymoon' phase, in which the guilt-ridden batterer pleads for forgiveness, is affectionate and swears off violence. But he breaks his promise and the cycle is repeated.

The second element of BWS involves the theory of 'learned helplessness,' derived from experiments in which dogs were tortured with electric shocks. After repeated unsuccessful attempts at escape, they became increasingly passive and 'learned' helplessness so that they later spurned proffered chances to escape. According to Walker, the randomness and apparent unavoidability of their beatings produce similar reactions in battered women. They also develop a number of common characteristics, such as low self-esteem, self-blame for the violence, anxiety, depression, fear, general suspiciousness, and the belief that only they can change their predicament."

Nicolson and Sanghvi suggest a number of problems with battered woman syndrome which may recommend caution in introducing expert evidence of the syndrome into the courtroom.[39] Expert evidence on battered woman syndrome permits the voices of experts to be heard, rather than obliging the court to listen to women themselves. Not only does this construct the experiences of battered women as unified, it reinforces the stereotype of female passivity. It locates the reasons for female criminal behaviour within the individual rather than locating her behaviour within the context of male violence to women and society's condonation of that violence. The woman who kills is measured against the socially constructed image of femininity. She is punished not only for her crime but for the extent to which she fails to measure up to the ideal[40]:

---

[38] D. Nicolson & R. Sanghvi, *supra*, n. 24 at 733.

[39] In other jurisdictions, battered woman syndrome has been invoked as a mental state which normal people may experience. See S. Yeo, "Battered woman syndrome in Australia" (1993) 143 New L.J. 13.

[40] These factors are also discussed in C. Wells, *supra*, n.4 at 273–275; K. O'Donovan, *supra*, n.13 at 230–232; M. Fox, *supra*, n.11 at pp. 181–185.

D. Nicolson & R. Sanghvi
"Battered Women and Provocation: The Implications of *R. v. Ahluwalia*"[41]

"Walker's methodology and conclusions have been persuasively criticised. BWS is presented as typical for all battered women, yet Walker's own data and other research show that not all women experience the entire cycle of violence or display all characteristics of learned helplessness. Where this happens, experts and juries might be unwilling to accept the existence of BWS and the defendant would be expected to have exercised the same degree of self-control as the reasonable woman. Instead of paying due regard to the reality of a battered woman's experience, the issue could become one of consulting a check list.

A major problem with the syndrome has become apparent from its use in the United States. Although expert evidence on BWS was accepted in *Ahluwalia* as relevant to the objective condition of provocation, once admitted, such evidence would also presumably be taken into consideration by juries in deciding that, despite the existence of a time lag between provocation and killing, the subjective condition is satisfied. Unfortunately, however, whether due to Walker's theory itself or the way in which it tends to be used, it fails to address the relevant legal and moral issues raised by the provocation defence. Undoubtedly, it will prove useful in explaining features of a defendant's case which might otherwise be regarded as inconsistent with the defence, thus supporting her credibility. Expert witnesses could testify as to why many battered women fail to leave their batterers, why many appear calm rather than enraged during and after killing, etc. But, whereas BWS is useful in explaining the reasonableness of the general behaviour of battered women, it is not well-suited (at least as presently developed and applied) to establishing the reasonableness of her killing in provocation, nor that it took place during a sudden loss of self-control. The syndrome is associated with despair, anxiety and fear, yet provocation requires evidence of anger and loss of self-control. Moreover, reliance on learned helplessness involves a logical inconsistency: if battered women are helpless, how do they come to kill?

But even if BWS is developed to address the pertinent issues, it will always actively shift the emphasis from the reasonableness of the defendant's actions to her personality in a way which confirms existing gender stereotypes, silences battered women and conceals society's complicity in domestic violence. While not a justification like self-defence, nor is provocation an excuse like insanity or diminished responsibility, which are solely based on the individual's ability to conform their behaviour to legal standards. However, not least because of its designation as a 'syndrome,' BWS suggests reliance on personal incapacity. This might lead not only to battered defendants being treated as mentally abnormal, but also to the therapeutisation of domestic violence.

There has long been a tendency both here and in the United States to see domestic violence in terms of the personality defects of victims as well as batterers. Both parties have been commonly regarded as being incapable of avoiding violence because of personality disorders or individual upbringing. The highpoint was reached with the 'women who love too much' (thesis) which portrayed women as seeking out, triggering and even enjoying male violence. Walker's work was specifically aimed at and is obviously an improvement on such dangerous ideas in that the syndrome is regarded as flowing from the man's violence, rather than the woman's inherent personality disorders. Nevertheless, it is likely to move the issue of killing by battered women from

[41]   D. Nicolson & R. Sanghvi, *supra*, n. 24 at 733–736.

the legal and moral into the medical arena. The testimony of psychologists and psychiatrists is likely to become crucial. Cases may become battles of the experts and a question of who has more degrees and publications. Experts will supplant, rather than supplement, the voice of battered defendants.

This will add to a problem already inherent in the syndrome: the fact that it resonates with familiar sexist stereotyping. Battered women who kill are survivors. Yet the syndrome portrays them as passive victims, as incapacitated and as sufferers of yet another 'women's condition.' It reaffirms the view that when problems arise, women develop headaches, become depressed, take pills and dissolve into nervous wrecks. BWS replaces one stereotype with another. The rugged man who instinctively lashes out to defend his honour is replaced with the passive women who can only be helped by doctors and psychiatrists. BWS will help make successful defences by battered women dependent upon their conforming to a socially constructed image of femininity, continuing the tendency whereby the character of women killers, rather than their actions, are placed on trial. Unless they act like the paradigmatically violent man, battered women will need to show that they fit law's image of women: a faithful wife, a devoted mother, someone who tries to keep her family together at all costs and who reacts meekly and pathologically to violence. Otherwise, they might face life imprisonment.

BWS also helps reinforce gender differences in a more subtle way. By focusing on the defendant's personality, attention is diverted from society's complicity in the killing and the situation which helped precipitate it. Contemporary society both fosters and condones a culture of male power and violence. It is this society, not battered women, which is responsible for domestic violence. Battered women do not ask for, nor consent to, violence. On the contrary, they frequently seek help in escaping it. And the response from state institutions in particular tends to be woefully inadequate. Furthermore, it is socialisation and the lack of socio-economic alternatives for women, rather than 'learned helplessness,' which makes leaving violent men so difficult. All of this is pushed under the carpet by the syndrome, which focuses on the personality and problems of individual defendants, thereby suggesting that the solution lies with therapy rather than social change. To paraphrase another commentor, BWS might help individual defendants escape the mandatory life sentence, but it does nothing for battered women as a group."

The introduction of expert evidence on battered woman syndrome may perpetuate the view of women being driven to commit crime because of their psychiatric instability, reinforcing explanations for female criminality as located within the individual rather than within the social situation of women. To avoid such a conclusion Donald Nicolson and Rohit Sanghvi advocate that the reasonableness of the reactions of the accused be assessed in the context of the abuse to which she was subjected:

D. NICOLSON & R. SANGHVI

"Battered Women and Provocation: The Implications of *R. v. Ahluwalia*"[42]

"Instead of expecting jury members to consider how reasonable syndrome sufferers would have reacted to provocation — itself absurdly unrealistic — judges can be asked

---

[42]   D. Nicolson & R. Sanghvi, *ibid*, at 738.

to direct juries to simply consider how a reasonable person in the shoes of the defendant, having suffered the same level of violence and abuse, might have been expected to act. And to help juries understand the context of domestic violence, without medicalising and stereotyping battered women, lawyers need to press for expert evidence, not just from the 'psy' professions, but preferably also from those who work with battered women and if possible from battered women themselves. Such evidence would be directed not at BWS, but at explaining the whole context in which battered women kill: the typical slow-burn reaction of many battered women, their outwardly calm appearance and how their killing can be regarded as a reasonable reaction in the circumstances. Obtaining admission of such evidence is likely to be an uphill struggle given the opinion evidence rule, and law's traditional privileging of scientific over feminist and experimental discourses. But it is one worth waging given the potential for assisting battered defendants without compromising the aims of the feminist movement." ·

The invocation of battered woman syndrome as a feminist strategy which may force recognition of the context of the actions of the woman is considered by Sheila Noonan with respect to its potential for exposing the social context of female criminality and the agency of the woman who offends[43]:

S. NOONAN
"Battered Woman Syndrome: Shifting the Parameters of Criminal Law Defences (or (Re) inscribing the Familiar?)"[44]

"Subjectivity which seeks acceptance within the domain of the social relies upon the violent expulsion and destruction of those aspects of 'self' submerged in fear and horror. Kristeva's concept of abjection defines the socially configured boundaries of the clean and proper body. Those cases before the courts which succeed on the basis of BWS rely upon fixing the woman in the position of victim, or the abject.

The strategy of pleading BWS is appealing precisely because the results may be auspicious: acquittal; reduction of sentence; and, in some instances, release from incarceration. However, reinscribing woman as victim constrains not only our understanding of female criminality, but it encodes woman as subjectless within law.

> 'It could be argued that, pragmatically, evidence as to 'battered woman's syndrome' represents a compromise made by defence lawyers in order to minimise the sentences their clients may suffer. This may indeed be a compromise, but it is one in the manner of the Faustian bargain, in which the bargainer loses at every turn.'

In a highly sophisticated piece, Alison Young argues (at least implicitly) that because of the sacrificial nature of the marriage contract, invocation of BWS as a strategy

---

[43] This extract on the utility of battered woman syndrome as a feminist strategy has been selected because of the centrality within Noonan's analysis of feminist debates about engagement with law. It should be noted, however, that the content of this extract does not represent the main focus of Noonan's argument which is upon the position of women of colour who kill and the impact of race in constructions of criminality.

[44] In A. Bottomley (ed.), *Feminist Perspectives on the Foundational Subjects of Law* (London: Cavendish, 1996), pp. 216–219.

should be eschewed. Reliance on BWS in the context of either exonerating or mitigating sentence acts to 're-sacrilise her as victim', thereby positioning woman as subjectless.

The trade-off between theory and practice is starkly posed; in it, feminism finds itself at something of an impasse in the debates around legal engagement. Rhetorical styles have altered (anti-legal engagement in particular is now infused with insights from post-structuralism) but fundamentally the divisions parallel and replicate familiar positions.

On the one hand there are theorists, sometimes located 'outside' law who stress that, at least predominately, law's power to regulate daily life should be resisted, and de-centred. Thus, Carol Smart characterises law quintessentially 'as a mechanism for fixing gender differences and constructing femininity and masculinity in oppositional modes'.

Within feminist legal theory, few would dispute Smart's claim that law *does* this. And yet, it must be stressed that legal discourse cannot be situated as foundational. To attribute the fixing of gendered differences solely (or even predominately) to law is to consign legal discourse to the realm of metaphysical; in this respect Smart over draws the 'power of law' in the very move calculated to de-centre it ...

On the other hand, there are those for whom engagement within law carries the potential to wield (at least) small, concrete gains for particular women. Anne Bottomley and Joanne Conaghan argue that law provides space for argument, engagement and resistance. In their view law is general, is neither so uni-dimensional or undifferentiated as Smart's (re)presentation would suggest. They thus conclude:

> 'The operation of law involves a continual use of strategies, in which one is constantly balancing the possibilities against the probabilities. Again, let us be clear in general, it is a more than uneven fight. As law is constituted in a society which still privileges sections of that society in terms of gender, race, class, and socially defined standards of ability, so it is by no means a "free space" for equal engagement. But neither is it closed space which we must continually struggle against rather than within. When Smart states that "the entry of feminists into law has turned law into a site of struggle rather than being taken only as a tool of struggle" we would agree, but we would add that it is [a] site within which we find tools; it was never a tool because it was not a single entity or practice.'

Sheila McIntyre argues that, '[a]bandoning law altogether is a luxury of theory and/or privilege from the perspective of those long abandoned by reformers and reformism'.

... Though ultimately less than successful on its own terms, that is in assisting in understanding how the cumulative effects of violence may impinge on subjective assessments relevant to substantive criminal defences, BWS evidence could perhaps legitimately be regarded as an incursion. Within the parameters of criminal law discourse, the re-conceptualisations occasioned by virtue of the introduction BWS evidence may yet be significant.

By virtue of its effort, though rarely fully realised in practice, to contextualise action against the backdrop of coercive relationships, the door is opened to what has heretofore remained almost invisible. In particular, the recognition of BWS carries the potential for social locatedness to inform assessments of agency and moral culpability. These cases thus challenge criminal law's penchant for the separating of context from agency. It is, therefore, unsurprising that BWS evidence has most frequently been used at the time of sentencing, where traditionally broader questions in relation to factors leading to individual culpability have been permitted. In other words, it may be because BWS is so potentially *subversive* to the containment of social context that the courts have been reluctant to permit it to more fully infiltrate substantive criminal defences. Thus, the potential for the door to be opened to more contingent and contextualised assessments of culpability is precisely what makes these cases so significant both at the level of practice and theory.

Practically, BWS cases have opened the door to more nuanced discussions of moral (and legal) culpability. This is evidenced by the heightened scrutiny of juridical sentencing practices. Particularly in England (but also in Australia) the imposition of lengthy periods of incarceration has attracted the attention of women's groups, and the public at large. The media have played an important role in highlighting glaring examples of morally unacceptable sentencing practices. Thus, a number of women who have initially been convicted of murder have had their sentences reduced on appeal . . .

In general, it appears that women are currently receiving shorter sentences where self-preservation is at issue. Mandatory life sentences for murder where an abusive partner has been killed are now the exception rather than the rule.

Theoretically, the dividing line between 'criminal women' and 'women' in general is arguably increasingly difficult for the courts to sustain. Thus, at one level the juridical failure of incomplete or inadequate contextualisation of action may speak to the very instability of the category victim/agent itself. Rather it may suggest unease about the ability of either the tropes of victimisation or unreason to ultimately safely contain female criminality."

By way of summarising and concluding the discussion of the (de)merits of the provocation defence, the work of Marie Fox identifies four aspects of the application of the defence which demonstrate that the judiciary does not understand the position of women. The four elements are: the failure to acknowledge the physical differences between men and women; the construction of a "provocative" event; the understanding of provocation as a reaction in anger rather than fear; and the failure to comprehend the lack of alternatives available to women who have been abused.

M. Fox
"Legal Responses to Battered Women Who Kill"[45]

"Certainly, an examination of British case-law produces numerous dicta to support the view that judges think in terms which are paradigmatically male. In at least four separate ways they have demonstrated their incomprehension of the battered woman's situation. The first misunderstanding relates to the general physical differences in female and male bodies. This is exemplified by the cases of *Thornton* and *Ahluwalia*. In waiting until their violent husbands were asleep and employing weapons against them, their cases fitted a pattern of domestic killings by women who have been subjected to cumulative violence. However, rather than acknowledging this, the courts abstracted each woman from her social situation and construed her actions as deliber-

---

[45] In J. Bridgeman & S. Millns (eds), *supra*, n. 11 at pp. 174–176.

ate and premeditated. Thus, the individualisation introduced by *Camplin* does not avail women like Sara Thornton or Kiranjit Ahluwalia whose reactions were not the instantaneous and hot-blooded ones of some males . . .

[I]t is clear that the paradigmatic case of provocation for a judge is a sudden fight between two males of approximately equal strength — a model which effectively excludes most women from the ambit of the defence. Similar assumptions underpin comparable dicta in cases like *R. v. Phillips* and *R. v. Mancini*. These betray a failure to recognise the relative disparity in physical strength between women and men which deny most women the opportunity of striking a simple blow, which would only be likely to precipitate greater wrath. For as long as judges fail to take on board such considerations female reactions to male violence will be classified as revenge and thus murder . . .

Secondly, judges take an unduly restrictive view of what constitutes a provocative event, limiting this to certain situations and incidents — those to which men are particularly likely to react violently. As Taylor contends, what law really deems provocative is women who assert their sexual independence. Thus, women who refuse sex with their partners, leave or threaten to leave them, or commit adultery will be characterised as having provoked their partners to understandable violence. To effect meaningful reform for women the judiciary must recognise that women respond in different ways and situations from men — usually resorting to violence, not in the case of infidelity, but where their personal safety or that of their children is at stake. Thus, as currently constituted, law appears to place a greater premium on a man's sexual pride than on a woman's personal safety. Furthermore, the statutory definition of provocation which extends the defence to cover verbal abuse appears to equate such abuse with violent physical assault. Again this entails that men are more likely to benefit from the defence, given their propensity to react to weaker stimuli than women.

Thirdly, judges also fail to grasp the complexity and diversity of possible emotional responses to which those circumstances give rise. Although they acknowledge the *rage* resulting in loss of self-control which men feel in provocative situations; the *fear* or *despair* which cumulative violence may engender in women is not so readily accepted by the judiciary as causing female defendants to use weapons in order to retaliate or defend themselves. As Douzinas and Warrington have proposed: '[i]n the idiom of cognition, fear is either reasonable and can be understood by the judge or is unreasonable and therefore non-existent.' Moreover, where a woman displays anger (and her response is likely to be a complex amalgam of the two emotions), she is characterised as 'unfeminine' and threatening. By definition an angry woman who breaks the law commits a double transgression — she is seen as offending both the tenets of the criminal law and the dictates of nature. Whereas for men violence per se is not unacceptable — it becomes so only when they go too far — for women displays of violence are always deemed unacceptable and unnatural.

Judges also fail to appreciate the effect on a woman of living with the constant threat of abuse. In stressing that juries should focus upon the blameworthy conduct of the defendant, and not that of the victim, law colludes in downplaying the violence to which the woman's body has been subjected. Yet, the essence of provocation entails blameworthy conduct by the victim, and as Edwards argues, '[w]hen a male defendant stands trial . . . all too frequently the blame attaching to the dead woman becomes a crucial part of the defence of provocation . . .'. To fully assess the responsibility of a woman for her actions we surely need to have available a broader picture of the context of her actions which will include the assessment of responsibility for the final violent act.

Fourthly, judges have demonstrated a wholly unrealistic appreciation of the options available to battered women . . . [J]udges lack awareness of the effect of cultural conditioning on women not to react aggressively, even in situations where they are under threat. They are denied the opportunities open to boys to learn how to defend themselves in threatening situations. This entails that they are typically no match for men in hand-to-hand combat and can only repel a male assailant by resorting to deadly weapons."

In the light of the limitations of the provocation defence identified by Marie Fox, feminists have found it worthwhile to investigate the further possibility of the defence of self-defence as an aid to battered women who kill. This defence too is problematic in its failure to contextualise the behaviour of female offenders.

11.1.iii *Self-defence*

Force causing personal injury, damage to property or even death may be justified because the force was reasonably used in the defence of public or private interests. Force may be used to effect an arrest and in the prevention of crime, in defence of the person or in defence of property. Section 3 of the Criminal Law Act 1967 provides:

(1) A person may use such force as is reasonable in the circumstances in the prevention of crime, or in effecting or assisting in the lawful arrest of offenders or suspected offenders or of persons unlawfully at large.
(2) Subsection (1) above shall replace the rules of the common law on the question when force used for a purpose mentioned in the subsection is justified by that purpose.

Section 3 replaces the rules of the common law on the use of force in the prevention of crime. It does not provide a statutory defence of self-defence. However, the principles of the common law right to use force in defence of oneself or another against an unjustifiable attack are the same as those governing the operation of the statutory provision. There are two elements to both the statutory and the common law defences:

(i) the force used must be *necessary* (in the circumstances which the defendant believed to exist), and
(ii) the defendant must use the amount of force reasonably required (again according to the circumstances as the defendant believed them to be).

11.1.iii.a Pre-emptive force: the hostage analogy. The requirement that the use of force be necessary means that a person who acts in self-defence is usually under attack. Reliance upon the defence is not, however, precluded where a pre-emptive strike is made to prevent an apprehended attack. A woman who has been exposed to repeated violence may anticipate, because of her past experiences of the pattern of abuse, that she is shortly to be

exposed to a further bout of violence. Fearing what she is shortly to be subjected to she may kill her abuser whilst he is asleep or drunk. There is no
British case in which a woman has successfully pleaded self-defence after
having killed using pre-emptive force against an apprehended attack. Using
the example of someone being held hostage by terrorists, Aileen McColgan
illustrates her argument for the inclusion of pre-emptive force within the limits
of self-defence:

A. McColgan
"In Defence of Battered Women who Kill"[46]

"Where the defendant uses force in response to a perceived, rather than an actual
attack, she may still be entitled to plead self-defence. Lord Griffiths stated in *Beckford
v. R* that 'a man about to be attacked does not have to wait for his assailant to strike
the first blow or fire the first shot; circumstances may justify a pre-emptive strike'. In
order to render a pre-emptive strike necessary, however, the defendant must, in the
words of the Lord Justice General Lord Normand in the Scottish case of *Owens v.
H.M. Advocate* have 'believed that he was in imminent danger', . . . The so-called
imminence requirement might appear to deny self-defence to a woman who uses force
other than in expectation of an attack which she believes is just about to occur, and
is perhaps why many such killings are not readily perceived as being by way of self-
defence. In the leading case of *Palmer v. R*, however, Lord Morris laid down no inflexible rules about imminence but simply stated that '[I]f the moment is one of crisis for
someone in imminent danger he may have to avert the danger by some instant reaction.
If the attack is all over and no sort of peril remains then the employment of force may
be by way of revenge or punishment or by way of paying off an old score or may be
pure aggression. There may no longer be any link with a necessity of defence'. This
passage, far from requiring that the defendant be under threat of immediate force
before being allowed to use force in self-defence, makes it clear that the proximity of
the expected attack is merely a factor to be considered in determining whether the
defendant's use of force was necessary, or whether it was 'by way of revenge'.

Where the defendant killed in the context of a one-time adversarial encounter, a
strict view of imminence is appropriate as, unless the attack is actually under way or
is almost immediately threatened, the defendant will have alternatives to the use of
force. He may flee or contact the police or others for assistance, in which case the use
of force would generally be unnecessary and therefore unreasonable. There are other
cases, however, where the use of force by the defendant may be manifestly reasonable
despite the absence of an immediate physical threat. Where, for example, someone is
held hostage by terrorists who let him know, expressly or by implication, that he is to
be seriously injured or killed within the next few days, it is unlikely that the courts
would require him to wait until a weapon was actually raised to him before they
allowed him to use violence against his captors. The danger which could be seen as
imminent here, if imminence is required, is the second-order danger of the hostage
finding himself in a position where the threat of later violence will become inescapable,
rather than the first-order danger of physical violence itself. He cannot be entirely sure
that his captors will carry out their threat to kill him, but neither can he reasonably

---

[46]   A. McColgan, *supra*, n. 17 at 517–519.

be expected to postpone his use of force until a time when he will most probably not be able to defend himself, given the numerical superiority of his captors or the fact that they are armed and he is not. His only feasible method of escape from the threatened danger might be to seize an opportunity to attack while his captor is asleep or otherwise vulnerable. The fact that his captors have put him in the situation where he has to make unpalatable decisions to avert what he considers to be the threat to his life or safety must mean that the role of the imminence requirement (to exclude, so far as possible, the use of force against an attack which may never occur, or from which non-violent methods of escape might become available) is outweighed by the unavailability to him of any realistic options besides submission and resistance. The more commonly available alternatives of flight and seeking out assistance have been denied him by the actions of his prospective attacker. To allow the attacker to profit from their unavailability by having his captive forced to wait obligingly until he is attacked or just about to be attacked before himself engaging in physical resistance, would be Kafkaesque.

A strict view of 'imminence', then, should not, on the authority of *Palmer*, cause an otherwise arguable plea of self-defence to be jettisoned where there is no realistic alternative open to the person threatened. The lack of immediate physical peril would not prevent a hostage's use of force from being necessary and therefore potentially reasonable, although the requirement of proportionality would still have to be satisfied. The same is true of a battered woman who believes that an attack will (or may) occur before she is able to effectively escape, and that she must therefore strike while her prospective attacker is made vulnerable by sleep or alcohol. She, like the hostage, is caught within a potentially life-threatening situation. Just as the hostage might take the view that a desperate bid for freedom might result in his death rather than his freedom, so too might the battered woman believe, and believe reasonably, that any attempt to escape would carry with it the risk of death rather than the promise of freedom. The possibilities of seeking police protection or of simple flight may not constitute adequate alternatives to the use of force as she may know from experience that either measure is simply a temporary one. Many abusive men use the threat of even greater violence to prevent their partners leaving the abuse, and one recognized aspect of continued abuse is the perception it creates in the abused person of the abuser as all-powerful, inescapable."

11.1.iii.b   Walk away. The requirement that the use of force be necessary also raises the question of whether or not the defendant could have left, and whether there is a "duty to retreat". Celia Wells puts the question in the following terms: "Should she [the long-term battered wife] be required to go on retreating for ever?":

C. Wells
"Domestic violence and self-defence"[47]

"An image underlying all discussions of self-defence is that these are one-off occurrences which can be responded to or repelled. Although the duty to retreat is not strict it is not premised on persistent, systematic, relational violence. So we need to consider

[47]   (1990) 140 New L.J. 127.

more closely how far the duty to retreat should apply to the long-term battered wife. She will probably have retreated time and time again. Should she be required to go on retreating forever? Should we not take into account on the one occasion that she does not retreat that she has indeed retreated before?

One way in which the duty to retreat could be more favourably applied to the victim of domestic violence would be to recall the right of the property owner to repel an intruder. The right to 'stand fast' in defending one's home is itself a qualification of the duty to retreat. By analogy should not a woman be able to defend her right to occupy her home without fear of attack? This is not to advocate a general licence to take the law into her own hands. Merely to suggest that when she eventually does retaliate we should take into account that it is not just her physical integrity which has been threatened by the violence but also her right to peaceful occupation of her home.

Another strategy would be to adopt the approach of the Court of Appeal in *Field*. This was a case in which the court rejected the argument that a victim had to avoid places where she knew, because of experience of previous threats, that she might be attacked. Although we might share Ashworth's caution about this and require a prima facie duty to inform the police, it might nonetheless be appropriately invoked by a battered woman. She may have attempted to invoke police help in the past. Even if she hadn't, she could hardly be blamed for having absorbed so well the social message that this is really a private matter. In any case, the place we are asking her to avoid is her own home. We could combine the right to remain on one's own property with the *Field* principle to give her more chance of showing that the force she was driven eventually to use was necessary in all the circumstances."

11.1.iii.c   A sense of proportion. Whether or not the force used was reasonable in the circumstances as the defendant supposed them to be is a question to be answered by the jury. It formulates the defence according to an *objective* test. However, given the nature of the defence (the use of force in defence of the *self*) the jury should not ignore the state of mind of the defendant altogether. A direction should be given along the lines of Lord Morris in *Palmer v. R*:

Palmer v. R
[1971] 1 All E.R. 1077 at 1088f-g, *per* Lord Morris

"If there has been attack so that defence is reasonably necessary it will be recognised that a person defending himself cannot weigh to a nicety the exact measure of his necessary defensive action. If a jury thought that in a moment of unexpected anguish a person attacked had only done what he honestly and instinctly thought was necessary that would be most potent evidence that only reasonable defensive action had been taken. A jury will be told that the defence of self-defence, where the evidence makes its raising possible, will only fail if the prosecution show beyond doubt that what the accused did was not by way of self-defence."

Inherent in this formulation, and as a result of the historical development of the defence, is the concept of proportionality. Traditionally this has meant, for example, that a weapon could not be used in response to an attack by a fist. Celia Wells explains that this requirement seeks to ensure a balance between "the right to life and physical security of both attacker and victim":

> "[W]hat we are talking about is the use of lethal force to prevent persistent, but not lethal, physical bullying and violence. Where should the balance lie?"[48]

The balance lies against the female defendant because the concept of reasonableness is weighted against her. The small number of female killers has resulted in a defence framed by the experiences and reactions of men which are incompatible with stereotypical femininity so that, even when women kill in the course of a violent attack, defence lawyers and the court do not consider the defence of self-defence.[49] Aileen McColgan cites the example of Janet Gardner[50]:

A. McCOLGAN
"In Defence of Battered Women Who Kill"[51]

"Janet Gardner. . . killed her abusive partner in the midst of a violent attack by him. He had his hands around her neck and was beating her head against the kitchen doorway when she grabbed a knife from the wall and fatally stabbed him. He had regularly beaten, kicked and punched her over a period of five years, and had on one occasion attempted to slit her throat. She had tried to escape him on many occasions but her will had been broken on each of these occasions by his persistence in tracking her down and renewing his attacks upon her. The Court of Appeal, in replacing her five-year sentence for manslaughter on the ground of provocation with a two-year probation order on the basis of psychiatric evidence that she was suffering from severe depressive illness triggered by years of abuse, warned that there were 'exceptional circumstances' in the case and opined that the year she had already spent in jail was sufficient to 'expiate in some measure the guilt she must feel for the rest of her life'."

McColgan goes on to argue that there is nothing in the principles of self-defence to prevent it being used appropriately when "use of force is reasonable in the circumstances properly considered".[52] Celia Wells also proposes that it is not the principles which deny women the defence but the stereotypical image of the circumstances in which self-defence is available:

C. WELLS
"Battered woman syndrome and defences to homicide: where now?"[53]

"It is often suggested that the definition of self-defence precludes its application to women who kill since they typically do so when their assailants are asleep or have

---

48 C. Wells, *ibid*, at 128.
49 A. McColgan, *supra*, n. 17 at 515.
50 *R. v. Gardner, The Independent*, October 30, 1992.
51 A. McColgan, *supra*, n. 17 at 515.
52 A. McColgan, *ibid.*, at 516.
53 C. Wells, *supra*, n. 4 at 272.

their backs to them. Self-defence assumes that the killing was necessary in order to resist immediate and deadly violence from the victim. Yet it can be seen that it is not so much the definition as the construction of this defence which prevents its use by women. Behind it lies an image, a stereotype, of isolated, one-to-one (man to man) violence. Domestic violence is outwith this paradigm. Where it occurs it is chronic, cyclical, and often inescapable. The idea that women can leave and seek help is demonstrably untrue. Common law has always allowed a person to use force to protect their own property without having to flee. The same leniency should extend to women who are being beaten in their own home.

There is a danger that the public images of male, street violence, will be allowed to cloud our reception of her story and lead to the inappropriate inference that because she had survived the regime of violence thus far, it must mean that she was not in danger. Not only do the statistics demonstrate all too well that spousal violence does put women in mortal danger, but self-defence doctrine shows tolerance to the defendant who is mistaken in his assessment of the danger he is in, or who fails precisely to gauge his retaliation proportionately with the attack."

There is no reason why women who kill in response to violence should not be able to rely upon the defence of self-defence if it were better contextualised by defence lawyers and the courts to reflect the experiences of battered women. Presently, it is not.

A. McColgan
"In Defence of Battered Women who Kill"[54]

"The application of self-defence to many battered women who kill does not involve any alteration or extension of the defence, rather a rethinking of the way in which the requirement that the defendant's use of force be reasonable is applied to cases other than those involving the traditional model of a one-off adversarial meeting between strangers. Self-defence is frequently regarded as a justificatory defence, and it is this aspect of it perhaps which underlies the unease which is expressed about its application in cases other than those in which it has traditionally been accepted. One judge felt obliged to warn, while directing the acquittal of a woman who killed her rapist while defending herself from further attack, that his ruling was 'not to be regarded in any way as a charter for . . . rape victims, to kill their assailants' . . . To acquit a defendant who has killed, however, is not, in the words of Lord Edmund-Davies in *Lynch*, 'to express approval of the action of the accused but only to declare that it does not merit condemnation and punishment'. Even if self-defence were properly categorized as a justification, a resulting acquittal amounts to an admission by the court that the defendant's use of force was the lesser of two evils. In *Lavallee* Wilson J. expressed the view that the defendant had had to choose between using force against her partner when he was vulnerable or accepting 'murder by installment' by postponing any use of force until an attack upon her was already under way. 'Society gains nothing' from requiring such a delay 'except perhaps the additional risk that the battered woman will herself be killed'.

In any case, the acceptance by the Privy Council in *Beckford* that the threat to the

---

[54]   A. McColgan, *supra*, n. 17 at 527–529.

defendant, and the reasonableness of her reaction to it, must be judged on the facts as she saw them makes impossible any analysis of self-defence purely in terms of justification. Further, as Marianne Giles points out, even where the defendant's perception of the facts is correct, the approach of the Privy Council in *Palmer*, and of the Court of Appeal in *Shannon* and *White*, have so emphasized her honest and instinctive belief in the necessity for the use of force and in the level of force required as to render the test of reasonableness almost subjective. The House of Lords established in *Camplin* that the reasonableness of a defendant's reaction to provocation could not be determined without consideration of her characteristics, and in *Ahluwalia* Lord Taylor C.J. stated that the reasonableness of the defendant's reactions fell to be considered in the light of the 'history of [her] . . . marriage, the misconduct and ill-treatment of the appellant by her husband'. So, too, in the context of self-defence, the reasonableness of the defendant's conduct cannot be assessed in a vacuum. The jury's assessment of whether she believed that she was under threat of attack and of the seriousness of an anticipated attack will clearly be influenced by evidence of the abuser's past conduct. Many women experience abuse as a cyclical occurrence where a period of increasing tension is followed by physical abuse which is in turn followed by remorse on the part of the abuser. A battered woman might anticipate an impending attack from signals which have in the past marked the transition from the period of tension-building to the battering phase. Under such circumstances, evidence of the cyclical pattern as it has affected the defendant herself, rather than generalized expert evidence about the nature of woman's battering, can enable the jury to appreciate her apprehension of danger even where no threat is apparent to an onlooker. Equally, abuse often escalates in seriousness between one battering episode and the next, and many women who kill do so when they fear that they will be unable to survive the next episode. Again, it is vital that jurors are made aware of the history in order that they may understand the nature of the threat which the defendant feared. Even where a woman kills a sleeping partner, evidence of her circumstances may allow a jury to appreciate the absence of alternatives open to her, so that they may consider the reasonableness of her actions as they might those of a hostage who sees no alternative to the proactive use of force against a threat which may be rendered insurmountable if he waits to be attacked.

Self-defence exists in order to allow citizens to take steps to protect themselves where circumstances render it necessary for them so to do. Many battered women are faced with no realistic alternative to the use of force against abusive partners. The construction of the family as private and the resulting societal blindness to violence within it, the power inequalities which result from men's greater earning potential and the resulting economic dependency of many women, the isolation of many women within their homes and their subsequent alienation from formal and informal support structures, the unavailability of decent alternative accommodation for women who leave their abusers, the fear of pursuit and greater injury or death; these factors render many women hostages of domestic violence and make invisible any escape from that violence except by the use of force. The way to prevent battered women killing is to provide them with adequate alternative means of escape from violence, and perhaps then to condemn those who choose to use violence instead. Such a course of action would have the effect of saving the lives of battered women as well as those of their abusers. It is however a long-term solution, and one which requires the commitment of Government rather than the law alone. In the meantime, society's failure to protect women from violence within their homes must be brought to the fore by defence lawyers and taken into account by those whose task it is to allocate blame."

11.1.iv   *Diminished responsibility*

Diminished responsibility, like provocation, is a statutory defence which reduces a charge of murder to manslaughter. Section 2(1) of the Homicide Act 1957 provides:

> (1) Where a person kills or is party to the killing of another, he shall not be convicted of murder if he was suffering from such abnormality of mind (whether arising from a condition of arrested or retarded development of mind or any inherent causes or induced by disease or injury) as substantially impaired his mental responsibility for his acts and omissions in doing or being a party to the killing.

Accordingly, the defence of diminished responsibility is available to a defendant who was "suffering from such abnormality of mind" which was caused by "a condition of arrested or retarded development of mind or any inherent causes or induced by disease or injury" so as to affect her "mental responsibility". An abnormality of mind is, in the words of Lord Parker C.J. in *R. v. Byrne*[55]:

> "a state of mind so different from that of ordinary human beings that the reasonable man would term it abnormal. It appears to us to be wide enough to cover the mind's activities in all its aspects, not only the perception of physical acts and matters, and the ability to form a rational judgement as to whether an act is right or wrong, but also the ability to exercise will-power to control physical acts in accordance with that rational judgement."

The abnormality of the mind, resulting from a condition of arrested or retarded development of mind or any inherent causes or induced by disease or injury must be considered to have impaired the accused's "mental responsibility" for the killing. Again one may look to the judgment of Lord Parker C.J. in *Byrne* for guidance:

> "The expression 'mental responsibility for his acts' points to a consideration of the extent to which the accused's mind is answerable for his physical acts which must include a consideration of the extent of his ability to control his physical acts."[56]

Whether the abnormality of the mind substantially impaired the accused's responsibility for the killing is a question to be considered by the jury.

The appeal of Kiranjit Ahluwalia was allowed on the grounds of diminished responsibility. This had not been raised at the original trial, but the Court of Appeal considered that there was medical evidence suggesting that the appellant was suffering from a "major depressive disorder at the material time". Thus, Ahluwalia's case was submitted to retrial and her conviction of murder

---

[55]   *R. v. Byrne* [1960] 2 Q.B. 396 at 403.
[56]   *R. v. Byrne, ibid.*, at 403.

substituted for one of manslaughter on the grounds of diminished responsibility. The defence of diminished responsibility amounts to an acknowledgement that the acts of the killer resulted from an abnormal state of mind, without requiring a consideration of the wider context in which the killing occurred. As such its use in cases of battered women who kill is consistent with the tendency to locate female criminality within the bodily processes of the female offender enabling the social context and, specifically, the violence of the (eventual) victim to be ignored. As Donald Nicolson and Rohit Sanghvi suggest:

> "[m]any defendants, like Mrs Ahluwalia herself, might not care as much about their categorisation as about their liberty. But some will undoubtedly perceive it to be deeply insulting to be told that, unless they accept a label of psychological abnormality, they run the risk of escaping the prison of domestic violence only to spend a long time in a less metaphorical prison."[57]

11.i.v *Constructions of female killers*
The defences available to women who kill are defined according to male standards of behaviour which exclude women's experiences and behaviour patterns.[58] Paradigmatic examples of provocation are given below. The first is of a male who finds his wife in bed with another:

The Times
May 10, 1995

"A Chinese chef who 'chopped up' a man with an ornamental samurai sword after finding him in bed with his wife was jailed for four years for manslaughter yesterday. Toi King Chiu, 30, rained almost 40 blows on Terry Cheung. Toi's wife Vicki, 21, was also struck during the attack and her wrist was nearly severed, Manchester Crown Court was told.

Toi, of Fallowfield, Manchester, had denied murder but pleaded guilty to manslaughter on the ground of provocation . . .

He seized the 11in ceremonial sword and launched a 'frenzied attack' on Mr Cheung. Toi then dialled 999 and said: 'I have just chopped my wife up and somebody else. I caught her in bed with somebody else.' Mr Cheung died later in hospital.

Mr Goldstone said: 'It is difficult to imagine a more instantly provocative situation. It was the ultimate provocation, particularly perhaps for a man such as the defendant who was born in a community where the issues of pride and honour are of paramount importance.' "

The second example is of a man taunted about his sexual prowess:

---

[57] D. Nicolson & R. Sanghvi, *supra*, n. 24 at 737.
[58] K. O'Donovan, *supra*, n. 13.

The Times
February 22, 1994

"A man who stabbed his wife to death after she taunted him about his sexual prowess and threatened to remove his testicles with a kitchen knife walked free from court yesterday after the judge told him: 'If there is an exceptional case, this is it.' . . .

Roy Greech, 58, of Littleborough, Greater Manchester, pleaded guilty at Manchester Crown Court to the manslaughter of his wife, Sandra, 49, after she had taunted him and admitted having an affair. After stabbing her 23 times, he called the police.

Judge Rhys Davies, Q.C. gave Greech, a Youth Training Scheme instructor, a two-year suspended jail sentence."

A third scenario is that of the man who snaps in response to nagging:

The Times
January 30, 1992

"A man who strangled his wife in front of their three children to stop her incessant nagging walked free from the Central Criminal Court in London yesterday after a jury had cleared him of murder.

Judge Denison gave Bisla Rajinder Singh, aged 44, of Erith, Kent, a suspended sentence for manslaughter in order that he could maintain a family life with his children, who would suffer if their father went to jail. Rajinder Singh, a shopkeeper, had denied murdering his wife, Abnash, also 44, at their home last May, but admitted manslaughter on the grounds of provocation. He was sentenced to 18 months in prison, suspended for a year.

The judge told him: 'You have suffered through no fault of your own a terrible existence for a very long time. You bore it better probably than most people would have done until, finally, your self-control snapped and you did what you always admitted doing . . .'

Michael Stuart-Moore, Q.C., for the prosecution, told the court that the couple had an arranged marriage in 1973 and it had been unhappy from the start. For years, Abnash Singh terrorised her family with insults and bullying, he said: 'She was, in truth, a very domineering lady who rather wanted to rule the roost over the family and to lay down the law at home. In doing so, she had a sharp and persistent tongue.'

Rajinder Singh had strangled his wife after she shouted and swore at him for two hours. He first grasped her around the neck with his hands and then used a cord . . ."

Killing after provocation may be the reaction of an angry husband originating, as Sue Bandalli argues, in the protection of property in his wife. She cites Lord Holt in *R. v. Mawgridge*[59]:

"When a man is taken in adultery with another man's wife, if the husband shall stab the adulterer, or knock out his brains, this is bare-manslaughter;

---

[59] *R. v. Mawgridge* [1707] Kel. 119.

for jealousy is the rage of a man, and adultery is the highest invasion of property."[60]

Women who do not respond immediately to a provocative event or to one act of provocation having been subjected to such acts for years, may not be able to rely upon the defences of provocation or self-defence, having instead to explain their actions as the result of diminished responsibility. A comparison of the facts of the above cases with that of Sandra Fleming below demonstrates this point:

The Times
January 14, 1993

"A woman who killed her partner after he subjected her to ten years of torture was given probation yesterday.

Sandra Fleming, 26, admitted at Liverpool Crown Court killing Christopher Porter with his own gun at their home in April last year. The mother-of-three denied murder on the ground of diminished responsibility, but pleaded guilty to manslaughter.

She had suffered a decade of torture at the hands of Porter, who mutilated her, sexually abused her and threatened to kill her. Judge Wickham put her on probation for three years after hearing evidence in what he described as a 'wholly exceptional' case. But he said: 'No woman should get the idea that if she has been ill-treated by her partner she has the right to shoot him.'

He said of the night that Fleming shot Porter: 'It was a terrible thing to do but the doctors say you were suffering from an 'abnormality of mind'. Fleming was committing herself to a 'life of horror' at the age of 15 when she met Porter, the judge added.

David Harris, Q.C., for the defence, told how Fleming had been sexually assaulted, humiliated and tortured by Porter during their relationship. She had had a tattoo so her body could be recognised if she was killed and cut up as Porter had threatened. He removed the tattoo with a heated knife.

Mr Harris also told the court how Porter, a drug dealer and loan shark, had a pathological fear of doctors examining Fleming. That led Porter to deliver their second child at home without medical help by cutting Fleming with a razor and putting surgical spirit on her wounds.

Fleming had taken a cocktail of drugs and alcohol to dull the pain of a particularly gruesome ordeal at Porter's hands. When he was asleep, she fetched a gun Porter had hidden underneath floorboards in their children's bedroom and shot him at their home in Bootle, Merseyside."

The circumstances which led to Pamela Sainsbury killing her partner provide a similar testimonial:

---

[60] S. Bandalli, "Provocation — A Cautionary Note" (1995) 22 *Journal of Law and Society* 398 at 399.

The Times
December 14, 1991

"A woman who strangled the man she was living with, sawed up the body and dumped the remains in a field, was placed on probation for two years yesterday. Pamela Sainsbury, aged 30, was treated like a dog, Plymouth crown court was told.

Mr Justice Auld said that she attacked Paul Sainsbury after receiving a prolonged and particularly severe beating. 'You killed him in a sudden and impulsive act, driven as much by fear and hopelessness as anger.'

Sainsbury, a mother of two, of Sidmouth, Devon, denied murder but admitted manslaughter on the grounds of diminished responsibility. She also pleaded guilty to concealing a body . . .

Mr Justice Auld told her: 'All the evidence shows for many years you suffered regular and increasing violence and other forms of extreme sadism and sexual degradation at his hands. His domination of you mentally and physically was such you lost even the nerve to run away from him.'

Earlier, the degradation and violence Sainsbury suffered was detailed by Helena Kennedy, Q.C., for the defence. During years of 'tyrannical abuse', he had made her eat from a bowl on the floor like an animal; put a collar and leash round her neck; whipped her with a cane; made her perform degrading sex acts; took degrading photographs of her; and kept her a prisoner in their council home. 'There can be few cases as bad as this in documenting one human being's abuse to another,' Miss Kennedy said.

Sainsbury, described by her counsel as gentle and intelligent, strangled Paul Sainsbury, aged 35, with a nylon cord as he slept after he had subjected her to two hours of punching and kicking, Miss Kennedy said. 'It was like eight years of anger coming out in an instant. She did not want to kill him but could not stop pulling. She was on automatic pilot.'

Mr Sainsbury, the jury was told, had been before the courts for many offences of violence, one involving a woman. But Pamela Sainsbury did not leave him because she 'was in total fear for her life'. He would beat her if she used 'too educated' a word. As a result, she became virtually monosyllabic. Dr Patrick Gallwey, a psychiatrist, said she was virtually a hostage and required the same sort of help and treatment."

Wilson J. in the Canadian Supreme Court recognised that the textbook self-defence case is a "one-time barroom brawl between two men of equal size and strength" so that the "definition of what is reasonable must be adapted to circumstances which are, by and large, foreign to the world inhabited by the hypothetical 'reasonable man'."[61] The partial defence of provocation and the defence of self-defence depend upon the use of force to meet threatened harm in an angry, aggressive and immediate way. This requirement demands conduct which is different from that of many women. The circumstances in which the defences may be relied upon are narrowly circumscribed around the behaviour of the rational legal male subject. Susan Edwards criticises the interpretation limiting provocation to a sudden outburst of anger which is then controlled, as a "legal fiction" in which the "over rigid legal conceptualis-

---

[61] *R. v. Lavallee* (1990) 1 S.C.R. 852 at 874, cited in K. O'Donovan, *supra*, n. 36 at 429.

ation of heat of the moment suggests only one psychological and/or physiological possibility or reaction."[62] Whilst men react in legally relevant ways, the experiences of women are "legally irrelevant"[63]:

S. EDWARDS
"Battered Women Who Kill"[64]

"Given the singularity of the development of case law on provocation regarding sexual matters, it is difficult for the battered wife to advance a defence which accommodates or even begins to do justice to her predicament. On the one hand where men have been betrayed or taunted, the 'reasonable man' has been invested with the notional 'physical characteristics of the accused', but where battered women are defendants this reasoning has not been applied for two reasons. One is that the courts and jurors are not cognisant of the effects of perpetual victimization and associative fear and are therefore unable to assess what impact such circumstances may have on the battered woman's assessment of his threats and future behaviour. Second, heat of the moment as an essential prerequisite of a provocation defence means that women who delay in their fatal action, thereby fall outside its legal strictures and are denied provocation as a defence."

Invoking the defences of self-defence and provocation amounts to a claim that the actions of the accused were "reasonable" (normal) in the circumstances. Given that Woman is not disposed to criminal activity and Woman does not kill, and that real women who do commit crime are not "normal" but have killed due to their unstable biology, it is unsurprising that the defence of diminished responsibility is more readily accepted to provide an explanation for female criminal behaviour:

H. ALLEN
Justice Unbalanced: Gender, Psychiatry and Judicial Decisions[65]

"The defence of provocation rests on a notion of the *normality* of the mental response that underlies the offence. The defendant is excused because any reasonable subject might have responded in this way, and what is explicitly excluded is recourse to the defence by anyone whose response falls *outside* this norm. In the diminished responsibility provisions, by contrast, a precisely inverted logic is applied. What is invoked is a kind of reverse 'reasonable man' test, in which it is the *abnormality* of the response that grounds the exculpation: the defendant is to be excused in precisely those cases where no reasonable person would have responded in such a way."

---

[62] S. Edwards, "Battered Women who Kill" (1990) 140 New L.J. 1380 at 1381.
[63] S. Bandalli, "Battered Wives and Provocation" (1992) 142 New L.J. 212.
[64] S. Edwards, *supra*, n. 62 at 1381.
[65] (Milton Keynes: OUP, 1987), p. 26 (emphasis in original).

By forcing women who kill to rely upon diminished responsibility the abnormality of their actions is emphasised:

K. O'Donovan
"Defences for Battered Women Who Kill"[66]

"[Diminished responsibility] avoids placing the issue of justification before the court. If the accused wishes to vindicate her conduct, a plea of diminished responsibility alienates her from a claim to have acted justly. Instead of proposing herself as a legal subject responsible for her actions, she denies this and proposes abnormality of mind. This prevents attention being given to cumulative violence and appropriate responses. Instead the focus is on her mental state at the time of what is acknowledged as a crime. Her personality, characteristics and problems are on trial."

In comparison, the defence of provocation introduces recognition that the accused acted in response to the conduct of another:

K. O'Donovan
"Defences for Battered Women Who Kill"[67]

"The defence of provocation recognizes the killing which occurred as wrongful behaviour. Were it not for the excuse the defendant would be held accountable. Excused behaviour is personal to the actor and involves an inquiry into the circumstances and character of the defendant. There is an acknowledgement by the defendant that her conduct was wrong. She asks to be excused. But there is also a partial element of justification in provocation which relates to the conduct of the deceased victim — did the victim ask for it?"

The woman who kills may successfully plead diminished responsibility which reduces her charge of murder to manslaughter. In the process, however, her own "mental responsibility" is denied. The cause of her actions is identified in the imbalance of her mind. Her actions can thus be explained and the threat which she presents to society and indeed to the social and legal construction of the archetypal Woman are removed. Whilst provocation and self-defence enable the actions of the accused to be partially excused or justified because of the circumstances in which they occurred, this depends upon the woman acting in accordance with male standards. Consequently, the explanations for female criminality are that either the individual woman was, as a result of her hormonal imbalance, in some way "mad" or that she is just plain evil, that is "bad", and an aberration from Woman.

This is not to say that women may never successfully plead provocation. Susan Edwards gives some examples of women who have successfully done

---

[66] K. O'Donovan, *supra*, n. 13 at 229.
[67] K. O'Donovan, *ibid.*, at 225.

so.[68] For example, Celia Ripley shot her husband who had been physically violent towards her and threatened that he would force her to take part in sexual acts and shoot her. Her plea of guilty of manslaughter on the grounds of both provocation and diminished responsibility was accepted.[69] Mary Bernard's plea of guilty of manslaughter by reason of provocation was accepted after she had killed a man by pouring paraffin over him and setting it alight whilst he slept.[70] Rosina Ratcliffe's plea of provocation was accepted even though she killed her husband six days after his last provocative act.[71]

The subtleties involved in entering a successful plea should not be underestimated. It may depend rather more upon how the individual woman on trial accords with notions surrounding female criminality and the explanations given for female offending than upon an equal application of legal principles. Helena Kennedy (who, in her book *Eve Was Framed*,[72] gives many more examples of the inconsistent application of these defences) argues that the success of a defence has much to do with the perception of the defendant held by the judge:

H. KENNEDY
Eve Was Framed[73]

"Justice is likely to remain a lottery whilst so much depends on the woman's fulfilment of society's expectations. One of the factors which undoubtedly affects the outcome of murder trials is, as always, the persona of the woman in the dock. It is my view that this is what really determines the outcome. Women who conform to the conventional image of the cowed victim fare better than those who come to trial angry that they are being blamed for what ultimately took place."

This may provide the explanation for the convictions of Gillian Philpott and Elizabeth Line for manslaughter on the grounds of provocation:

The Times
January 8, 1991

"A former bank cashier who strangled her husband when her marriage broke down after his affair with her twin sister and tried to make his death look like suicide was jailed for two years yesterday. Gillian Philpott, aged 28, killed her husband Graham, a bank manager, on New Year's eve 1989 when she could [no longer] cope with the love triangle, the jury at the Central Criminal Court was told. She then tried to take a drug overdose. When that failed she drove to Beachy Head, intending to drive her car

---

[68] S. Edwards, *supra*, n.62 at 1381.
[69] *The Guardian*, November 1, 1983.
[70] *The Express*, June 17, 1982.
[71] *The Times*, May 13, 1980.
[72] H. Kennedy, *Eve Was Framed* (London: Chatto & Windus Ltd, 1992).
[73] H. Kennedy, *ibid.*, p. 225.

over the cliff, but was found slumped over the wheel. Philpott, of Orpington, Kent, denied murder but her plea of manslaughter on the ground of provocation was accepted. Judge Denison told Philpott that her greatest punishment would be having to live the rest of her life with the knowledge of what she had done. No one could fail to have sympathy with her but she had deprived two children of a father and had made what happened seem like suicide . . .

Philpott strangled her husband in his bedroom with a pink dressing gown cord after they returned from a party in the early hours. She dragged his body down the stairs to a half-landing where she tied another dressing gown cord round a banister 'to indicate he committed suicide' . . . She then took 30 painkillers with some alcohol but was sick. She drove to Beachy Head and wrote a note which she hoped would persuade people that she and her husband had committed suicide. It said: 'We could not live separately. We wanted to die together. Please keep us together, I beg of you. We loved one another so much.' A passer-by found her slumped in the driver's seat of the car. Mr Nutting said police broke into the couple's home and found Mr Philpott's body. There was no tension on the cord joining him to the banister and it was clear that he had been placed there. Philpott was arrested on January 2 and in police interviews denied killing her husband, saying he was alive when she left home . . . Asked by police if she thought he intended her serious harm, she replied: 'I don't know, but from the look on his face I think he wanted to. I begged him to love me. I tried everything possible to make the marriage work. I loved him so much. He said he didn't want me. I just didn't know what I was doing. All I could see was Graham standing there shouting at me,' she said. Alan Suckling, Q.C., for the defence, told the judge that it became plain that Mr Philpott was hopelessly infatuated with her sister. His wife was provoked by his conduct. Mr Suckling said: 'Surely there can be nothing more provoking than for the man you have married to fall in love with and have an affair with your sister. She did everything she could to patch up the marriage. Any reasonable woman in her position may have acted in the way she did.' "

The Independent
February 4, 1992

"A former nun who killed her drunken and bullying husband by stabbing him 17 times with a kitchen knife was yesterday given a suspended jail sentence. Elizabeth Line, 29, wept at Southwark Crown Court, south London, after she was convicted of manslaughter and sentenced to 18 months' imprisonment, suspended for two years. Judge Gerald Butler, Q.C. said Mrs Line had been subjected to months of violence and sexual abuse of the worst kind, had been in prison for more than seven months awaiting trial, and had suffered enough . . .

Polish-born Mrs Line, who was found not guilty of murder, had told the court that she came from a strict Catholic background. She entered a convent at 17, staying for three years before becoming a nurse. She married her husband, Ronald, four years after coming to Britain in 1986. The marriage was happy at first but he was soon regularly beating and raping her.

Stephen Leslie, for the defence, said: 'She would wait for him to come to bed at three or four in the morning to be assaulted, to be buggered, to be raped. She endured having her kitten killed. She was pushed over the limit by a man who no doubt when sober was a loving and caring husband but when [drunk] was rather like Jekyll and Hyde.'

Michael Corkery, Q.C., for the prosecution, said Mr Line was stabbed at the couple's home in White City, west London, last June. His wife had burst in on a neighbour's children's party and said: 'Call the police. I have just stabbed my husband.' "

Judicial perceptions of the female accused in the more notorious cases of Sara Thornton and Kiranjit Ahluwalia have not escaped feminist investigation. Donald Nicolson analyses the judgments of the Court of Appeal in the cases of Sara Thornton[74] and Kiranjit Ahluwalia, arguing that the sympathy shown towards the appellants and the arguments on the points of law made on their behalf were influenced by the judiciary's view of the appellants as women and their conformity with the ideal of Woman.[75] He explains how the judgments carefully draw upon "facts" to support the Court of Appeal's interpretation of events and justify its conclusion that, whilst Ahluwalia should be accorded sympathy for what happened to her as a passive and irrational woman, Thornton deserved punishment for her agency in the killing of her husband.

D. NICOLSON
"Telling Tales: Gender Discrimination, Gender Construction and Battered Women who Kill"[76]

"The tone of the two stories are clearly set by their opening sentences. The detached listing of Sara Thornton's personal details anticipates the court's lack of sympathy for her. Throughout the judgment, Beldam L.J. distanced himself from the emotive aspects of the case, baldly relating the 'facts' without comment and concentrating on action rather than understanding. This attempt at objectivity is markedly absent in the *Ahluwalia* judgement. Its opening words 'This is a tragic case . . .' portend the sympathy for Kiranjit which pervades the judgment. But whereas Lord Taylor C.J. openly stated his opinions, those of Beldam L.J. are apparent from his description of Sara.

By commencing with a reference to her 'comfortable' upbringing and public school education, Beldam L.J. provides a basis with which to contrast her downward spiral, through 'expulsion' from school, broken marriage, remarriage to an alcoholic and eventual conviction as a murderer. The intimation that Sara ungratefully threw away a promising start to life is expanded into the more damning suggestion that she was responsible for her battered experience. Thus we are told that her previous husband drank and was violent, and that '[f]rom the start she realised that [Malcolm] was a heavy drinker and was jealous and possessive.' This echoes both the idea that sexual offence victims 'ask for it' and the equally absurd 'women who love too much' thesis, which portrays battered women as pathologically needing and even enjoying male violence.

Sara's characterisation as the pathological Other is more obvious in the references to her suffering a 'personality disorder' at school and being admitted to hospital as a mental patient '[a]fter a particularly stressful part of her life'. But her pathological

---

[74] *R. v. Thornton* [1992] 1 All E.R. 306, *i.e.* Thornton's first appeal.
[75] D. Nicolson, *supra*, n.1.
[76] D. Nicolson, *ibid.*, at 191–200.

Otherness was not linked to passivity. Instead, she was portrayed as fickle. Like Kiranjit Ahluwalia, Sara had attempted suicide, but in her case Beldam L.J. commented: 'it is questionable whether she actually intended to take her own life'.

Only the more negative characteristics of appropriate femininity were attributed to Sara. By fatuously commenting that Sara had 'several relationships with young men which did not work' and noting that she had moved in with Malcolm shortly after meeting him in a pub, Beldam L.J. subtly suggests that Sara is promiscuous. Later he paraphrased Sara's reply to Malcolm's allegations that she had been selling her body as saying that 'she had only been trying to raise money for their business', thus leaving open the possibility that his allegations were true.

Sara was also portrayed as having rejected a woman's allotted domestic role. Her strenuous efforts to help Malcolm combat his alcoholism and to keep him alive were ignored. Instead we learn that while Malcolm was unemployed, Sara continued to work and attended a weekend conference where she 'seemed to be enjoying herself'. Her relationship with her daughter was left undeveloped and, when mentioned, was portrayed negatively. The information that Sara 'and her daughter' moved in with Malcolm contains the implication that Sara subjected Luise to her own suspect sexual mores. Although Sara was described as threatening to kill Malcolm if he touched Luise, by omitting to give reasons for the threat Beldam L.J. was able to insinuate unjustified aggression and 'typical female hysteria', rather than maternal concern.

The most striking and significant aspect of the judgment is that it drastically downplayed the single most important feature of the case: Sara's experience as a battered woman. Whereas, a total of 161 lines were devoted to describing 'the facts which led to the deceased's death', only five dealt directly with his violence and abusive behaviour. Moreover, their tone is so impassive as to completely understate Sara's pain and misery and their influence over her actions.

Thus, unlike in *Ahluwalia*, no mention was made of the size difference between Malcolm and Sara. Repeated and increasingly frequent violence over almost two years were reduced to describing Malcolm as being 'on occasions . . . violent in the home, breaking furniture and assaulting the appellant'. Only one specific incidence of 'serious assault' was mentioned. We learn that Malcolm was an alcoholic, but despite the leading of relevant expert evidence, not how this would have affected Sara. . .

By contrast, 41 out of 100 lines describing Kiranjit Ahluwalia's story were devoted to her 'many years of violence and humiliation.' Moreover, their description clearly indicates where Taylor L.J.'s sympathies lay. Deepak was described as 'a big man', Kiranjit as 'slight'. Her injuries and maltreatment were recounted in detail. She was described as being reduced to a 'state of humiliation and loss of self-esteem'. So affected was Lord Taylor C.J. by Kiranjit's ordeal that he quoted from a letter in which she begged Deepak to return from his lover and made 'a number of self-denying promises of the most abject kind'.

However, this letter is also important because it illustrates Kiranjit's conformity with the attributes of passive femininity. From the judgment she appears as meek, obedient and submissive. Until the night she killed him, Kiranjit is shown as reacting passively and pathologically to Deepak's violence, losing weight, showing 'signs of nervousness and distress' and twice attempting suicide.

The opening line of the judgment may have depicted Kiranjit's story as tragedy, but unlike Sara Thornton's it was not told in the classical dramaturgic tradition, in terms of which the tragedy stems from the protagonist's own character flaws. Kiranjit's tragedy was presented as that of a passive victim of harsh fate. Thus, although we learn of her comfortable, middle class background, her biography was not traversed for signs of complicity in her own downfall. Instead, by noting that Kiranjit's studies were aborted due to being pressurised into an arranged marriage, Lord Taylor C.J. implicitly traced the tragedy back to her culture rather than personal choice and reinforced the image of Kiranjit as passive victim.

Throughout the judgment the focus is on what was done to Kiranjit rather than on her own actions: her marriage was arranged, she suffered violence, etc. Even when she did act, her actions were described in the passive. Thus her marriage 'took place in Canada', her two sons 'were born' to her, 'The Croydon County Court granted her an injunction'.

The characteristic of passivity also emerges from the focus on Kiranjit's submissive role as mother and wife. Having detailed Deepak's violence and adultery, Lord Taylor C.J. commented: 'Despite all of this, the appellant wished to hold the marriage together, partly because of her sense of duty as a wife and partly for the sake of the children.' In the description of the night of the killing Kiranjit frequently appears in her maternal role. For example, we learn that Kiranjit returned home from visiting Deepak's mother with her son, 'who was unwell'. The caring mother theme was most effectively used by immediately following the description of the killing with the sentence: 'She then went to dress her son'. The picture of passive femininity disrupted by Kiranjit's violence is thus partly restored by an image of domesticity and nurturing. . .

The marginalisation of Sara Thornton's status as 'victim' of conjugal violence and the converse accentuation of Kiranjit Ahluwalia's was reinforced by the Court of Appeal's treatment of Malcolm and Deepak. Technically both were victims. Yet only Malcolm was cast as such. This was done by giving him an identity, and by de-personalising Deepak.

Thus in the paragraph describing Sara's battering experience we are told almost as much about Malcolm as a person as his violence. By contrast, apart from his birthplace and employment status, all we learn of Deepak relates to his treatment of Kiranjit. Whereas Malcolm appears as a rather sorry character, Deepak remains the shadowy figure of faceless violence. Indeed, we only learn of his name from Kiranjit's letter. This erasure of Deepak as a person left the stage empty for Kiranjit to play the part of the victim.

A similar process occurred in relation to the children affected by the killings. In *Thornton*, Beldam L.J. unnecessarily related that Malcolm's son was near to the killing, 'not asleep, though not fully conscious' and the first sentence to follow the description of the stabbing was: 'Martin upstairs had heard no sound of raised voices but he heard a scream from his father.' We thus see Sara not just killing Malcolm, but also depriving a son of his father. In *Ahluwalia*, a similar theme was eschewed by the narrative tying the children to Kiranjit rather than Deepak. . . .

Lord Taylor C.J.'s willingness to reserve the role of victim for Kiranjit is most striking in his cursory, two line treatment of evidence suggesting premeditation. A few days before setting alight Deepak, Kiranjit had bought petrol and caustic soda. Although she only used the former, only her intention to use the latter was mentioned. Regarding the petrol, the judge said: 'She had also bought a can of petrol . . .', thus rendering its purchase both innocent and subordinate to that of the caustic soda.

The suggestion of premeditation is further reduced by the story's narrative sequence. A chronological sequence, with conjugal violence being followed by the purchases, the provocation and then the killing would have suggested that, notwithstanding provocation, the killing flowed from a subsisting intention to take revenge. Instead, the purchases were mentioned in the form of a flashback during the description of Kiranjit's actions after Deepak's provocative action. Thus while brooding about her treatment, '[h]er mind turned to these substances'. The only relevance of the earlier purchases to this narrative is that it provided Kiranjit with the means to execute an intention formed in response to provocation.

The description of events also implies diminished responsibility. It was not Kiranjit who remembered the substances, it was her mind which turned to them. This divorce of Kiranjit from her mind subtly suggests a breakdown in mental responsibility. Although the court's reform of the law and its disposal of the appeal did not require a finding that killing had resulted from provocation or diminished responsibility, nevertheless neither course of action was compatible with strong evidence of the rational execution of a preconceived plan.

Whereas in *Ahluwalia* potentially strong evidence of agency and rational planning was swept under the carpet, in *Thornton* the opposite occurred. Thus almost a quarter of the description of the facts covered the four days preceding the killing, and in particular a series of 'rows' between the Thorntons. The recounting of these 'rows' served three narrative functions.

First, their description suggested that Sara could give as good as she got. For example, when Malcolm threatened her with a guitar, she 'for her part' pointed a knife at him, called him a 'bastard' and threatened to kill him. The impression conveyed of two equal protagonists — eloquently conveyed by the phrase 'for her part' — is reinforced by the constant characterisation of Malcolm's threats and her responses as mere 'rows'.

Secondly, in recounting these 'rows' Beldam L.J. was able to augment his picture of a woman who has rejected appropriate femininity by portraying Sara as uppity, rebellious and aggressive. Sara did not meekly crumple under Malcolm's threats; she armed herself, and retaliated with threats and bad language. After the penultimate 'row' with Malcolm, Sara is described as arranging for Luise to leave the marital home, going out drinking with Martin and returning after him in a 'quarrelsome and arrogant' mood.

The judicial portrait of a woman who lacks demure femininity and maternal responsibility is completed by the information that she wrote 'on her bedroom mirror in lipstick: 'Bastard Thornton. I hate you.' As Alison Young has commented, this symbolises 'Sara Thornton's increasing inversion of the norms of femininity: she uses her lipstick, not to rouge her mouth (in the gestures of conventional femininity), but to inscribe a message of violence to her husband.' Moreover, the action takes place at the bedroom mirror, traditionally a feminine domestic locus, surrounded by those accoutrements used to make women attractive to men.

Finally, the concentration on the 'rows' was used to hint at a premeditated killing. Stripped of the context of marital violence, the tension built up by a narrative sequence in which 'row' follows 'row' and then climaxes with the killing carries with it the implication that the 'rows' were the cause of Sara's actions, not simply the last straw.

The narrative tension and the suggestion of premeditation are also embedded in the other focus of this part of the story: a series of conversations between Sara and Mrs Thomas, a work colleague. The first occurred on the weekend before Malcolm's death. Upset by a telephone conversation with Malcolm, Sara was reported to say: 'I am going to kill him.' Many people make similar threats without intending to carry them through. Yet, not only did Beldam L.J. fail to mention Sara's denial of the alleged threat, he gave it the following gloss (made more dramatic by appearing in a new paragraph): 'But for subsequent events Mrs Thomas might well have dismissed this as no more than an expression of exasperation.'

The narrative style recalls the genre of radio and television thrillers, where the narrator heightens the tension by warning us of the drama to come. By alluding to known future events, Beldam L.J.'s comment also masterfully turned ambiguity into certainty. As Sara did kill Malcolm, we are encouraged to infer that Mrs Thomas did not dismiss Sara's threat as mere exasperation; nor in fact was it such.

Two days later the two women discussed Malcolm's continuing drinking problem and the difficulties facing Sara in obtaining a divorce and financial settlement from him. Then following another fight on the morning of the killing, Sara said: 'I am going to have to do what I said I would do'. Again this threat was highly ambiguous. As Sara alleged at trial, it could have referred to the divorce previously discussed. Nevertheless, by stating that Mrs Thomas understood it to refer to Sara's earlier threat, Beldam L.J. reconstructed an ambiguous reference to an ambiguous threat into a narrative in which Sara expressed an intention to kill Malcolm on the weekend and repeated it hours before murdering him. . .

The appellant's agency in killing could not be denied. Nor could the jury findings that they intended to kill be challenged. What was relevant on appeal was whether they had acted rationally and in cold-blood (murder) or irrationally due to a sudden and temporary loss of self-control (provocation) or to impaired mental responsibility (diminished responsibility).

Thus far, by focusing on Sara Thornton's actions and intention prior to stabbing Malcolm, rather than on his violence and its effect on her, Beldam L.J. has created the impression that, far from being reduced to mental abnormality or the end of her tether, Sara was angry and aggressive, but nevertheless in control. Indeed, she had decided to kill Malcolm. In comparison, by emphasising Deepak's violence and its effect on Kiranjit and by de-emphasising evidence of premeditation, Lord Taylor C.J. has depicted her as passively borne along by events over which she had no control. These differing themes were subtly reinforced by the narrative style in which the two killings were recounted.

In *Ahluwalia*, the action was described in long, disjointed sentences containing a number of short clauses.

> 'Her mind turned to [the petrol and caustic soda] and some time after 2.30 a.m. she got up, went downstairs, poured about two pints of the petrol into a bucket (to make it easier to throw), lit a candle on the gas cooker and carried these things upstairs. She also took an oven glove for self-protection and a stick. She went to the deceased's bedroom, threw in some petrol, lit the stick from the candle and threw it into the room.'

The impression created is of the action running headlong like a runaway train out of the control of its driver.

By contrast in *Thornton*, the description of the equivalent sequence of events was twice as long, largely due to its more deliberative pace. Quotations are preceded by colons rather than commas and qualifying phrases appear between commas rather than in brackets. Sentences are shorter and contain no more than two separate actions. Sentences and clauses are linked with conjunctives. The pace of the narrative is further slowed by ideas being spelt out in full and by the provision of the sort of detail omitted in *Ahluwalia*. For example, whereas Kiranjit 'took an oven-glove for self-protection', Sara 'went into the kitchen and looked in the drawer for a truncheon, which the deceased kept there, so that she had some protection if he attacked her.' The differing narrative pace in the two judgments is best appreciated by contrasting the following passage with the above quotation from *Ahluwalia*.

'[S]he stood up in front of him holding the knife in her clenched hand over his stomach. She then brought it down towards him thinking he would ward it off. He did not do so and the knife entered his stomach. She did not mean to kill him or harm him in any way. Her object in having the knife was merely to frighten him. She only brought the knife down slowly not quickly.'

The narrative's slow motion quality implies a calm control, incompatible with provocation and not particularly supportive of diminished responsibility either. . .

The calm and deliberate narrative pace continues in the description of the events which immediately followed.

'Martin . . . was met by the appellant, who said: 'Martin, I've killed your father.'
   She then telephoned for the ambulance and for the police. The police and the ambulance arrived. The appellant told the police officer that she had stabbed the deceased with a carving knife. He asked her: 'Have you tried to kill him?' She replied: 'I wanted to kill him.'

The lack of emotion attributed to Sara is compatible with the shocked reaction of a battered woman who has finally snapped and killed her batterer. However, by de-emphasising Sara's battering and by contrasting her calmness with her admission of murderous intent, Beldam L.J. depicts a callous woman, unconcerned, if not pleased by her actions; a woman who knew exactly what she had done and was doing.

   The picture of Kiranjit Ahluwalia after she set Deepak alight is also one of calmness, a calmness accentuated by contrasting it with the frenzy of Deepak who 'on fire, ran to immerse himself in the bath and then ran outside screaming, "I'll kill you", and shouting for help' and the neighbours who 'rushed' to the fire. However the calmness is not that of someone in control of their actions, but of an automaton. Kiranjit was described as 'just staring and looking calm' and as 'staring at the blazing window with a glazed expression'. While the house burnt she remained inside 'clutching her son'. When neighbours shouted for her to leave, she replied 'I am waiting for my husband' and closed the window, as if they were about to embark on an outing. By recounting Kiranjit's bizarre behaviour, Lord Taylor C.J. clearly indicates that she was not acting normally or rationally.

   By contrast, evidence of Sara Thornton's equally bizarre behaviour following the killing was ignored by Beldam L.J. According to the police, she cooked a meal, asked for her guitar and pinched an officer's bottom. Such evidence would have augmented the picture of Sara as heartless and immoral, but it would also have suggested irrationality, mental abnormality and hence diminished responsibility. Accordingly, the focus was kept firmly on Sara's state of mind when she killed rather than on her background mental condition.

   Unlike in *Ahluwalia* where the issue of Kiranjit's intention was submerged, in *Thornton* various statements made by Sara concerning her state of mind were discussed at length. From her quoted and paraphrased words, she is shown to have admitted an intention to kill immediately afterwards, but in later interviews to have changed her story to one of accident. This narrative sequence suggests that the accident theory was fabricated after Sara had time to reflect, a suspicion strengthened by the reference to an intervening telephone conversation with her solicitor. As we also know that Sara later relied on marital abuse, provocation and personality disorders, the theme introduced is that of the calculating female Other: the woman who, having thrown off her femininity and murdered her husband, came to court and brazenly played the role of passive victim of male violence and inherent female pathology. So rhetorically powerful is this theme that it overshadows the incompatibility between the fact that, for the purposes of casting Sara as a revengeful, scheming killer, Beldam L.J. strongly hinted that he was unconvinced that she killed accidentally, whereas for the purpose of suggesting that Sara had maintained her self-control despite provocation, he accepted the accident theory at face value."

The Court of Appeal, which eventually allowed Sara Thornton's appeal against her conviction for murder, ordering a retrial, painted a rather different picture of the "facts" from that presented in her first appeal:

R. v. Thornton (No. 2)
[1996] 2 All E.R. 1023 at 1025–1027, per Lord Taylor C.J.

"Sara Thornton appeals against her conviction of murdering her husband, Malcolm Thornton. The case has been referred to the court by the Secretary of State pursuant to s.17 of the Criminal Appeal Act 1968. The appellant was convicted on 23 February 1990 in the Crown Court at Birmingham after a nine-day trial. There was an appeal, which was dismissed by a different constitution of this court on 29 July, 1991 (see [1992] 1 All E.R. 306). Subsequently, representations were made to the Secretary of State on the appellant's behalf. They were based primarily upon further medical evidence and its impact on the defence of provocation, a defence which was not relied upon by the appellant at her trial, although it was left to the jury by the judge.

In August 1993 the Secretary of State decided not to refer the case back to this court. Further representations followed and on 12 May, 1995 the present reference was made.

The appellant comes from a comfortable background, but from childhood onwards her life was punctuated by problems and unhappy incidents. She was asked to leave her boarding school. She twice had pregnancies which were terminated before meeting her first husband by whom she had her one child, Luisa. She went abroad with that husband but left him in Venezuela because of his drinking and there was a divorce. She made a number of attempts at suicide by cutting her wrists, by cutting her throat and by overdose of drugs. In March 1981 she was admitted to a hospital for a period under the Mental Health Act 1959. She had a third abortion in 1983. It was common ground that this history was attributable to the fact that the appellant suffered and continues to suffer from a personality disorder, although after 1981 there appeared generally to be some improvement in her mental state.

She met the deceased, her second husband, in May 1987. Like her, he had been married before and he had a son, Martin, aged 18. The appellant and the deceased began living together in the autumn of 1987 and were married in August 1988. Even before the marriage, it was clear that the deceased had a serious drink problem. He underwent treatment for alcoholism but his condition and behaviour deteriorated in 1989. As a result the marriage was stormy. There were angry arguments when the deceased was drunk and he used violence to the appellant. In her evidence she described a number of assaults. It is unnecessary to specify all the incidents prior to the final weekend, but on about 20 May the appellant left the house (which was in their joint names) after the deceased had punched her in the face and knocked her out.

She reported that incident to the police and the deceased was charged with assault. The case was pending at the time of his death. After the appellant left, the deceased's son, Martin, came to stay at the house. On 26 May, the appellant and her daughter returned.

Matters came to a head between Saturday, 10 and Tuesday, 13 June. On the Saturday, the appellant was attending a conference in Coventry in connection with her work. According to her, she learnt by telephone that the deceased had either assaulted Luisa or otherwise driven her from the home, so that she was in night-clothes at a taxi rank. Mrs Thomas, a friend and fellow employee of the appellant, gave evidence that the appellant said after the phone call 'I am going to kill him', adding that she was not prepared to lose everything. The appellant, in evidence, denied saying these things.

On 11 June, she returned home accompanied by Mrs Thomas. The deceased had been drinking and there was an angry altercation. It continued after Mrs Thomas left. The deceased picked up a guitar and threatened to hit the appellant with it. She had a kitchen knife in her hand. According to Martin, she said 'You touch my daughter, you bastard, and I'll kill you', pointing the knife at the deceased and holding it in both hands. Martin claimed he had to take the knife from her. The appellant's account was that she had the knife in the normal course of preparing lunch, that she made no threat to kill the deceased and was not disarmed by Martin. On the same day, when the deceased was in the bath, the appellant gave him Mogadon tablets. Martin saw her administer two, but she crushed four more and concealed them amongst pieces of chicken she fed to the deceased. She then telephoned the doctor saying he had taken an overdose and was suicidal, which, as she admitted in evidence, was a deliberate lie. An ambulance and the police were called but the deceased refused to go to hospital. After they left there was an angry scene. The deceased threw a chair, which broke the glass in the kitchen door. The police were called again.

Still later on that day, the appellant spoke to Mrs Thomas on the telephone. According to the latter, the appellant talked of divorce, said she was not prepared to give everything up for the deceased and that she would set about forging some cheques. In evidence the appellant denied that account of the conversation.

Next day, 12 June, according to the appellant, the deceased said he wanted her and her daughter out of the house. He then went drinking. On his return, he was sick in the kitchen, he later burnt a hole in the armchair and he spent the night on the couch.

Tuesday, 13 June, brought the fatal dénouement. The deceased was again drunk. When he arrived home he noticed the appellant was not wearing her wedding ring. She said they did not have much of a marriage. He then threw his wedding ring into the garden. He abused the appellant, telling her to get out and take Luisa. Clothes were thrown out of the window. Luisa left. The appellant spoke to Mrs Thomas on the telephone, saying: 'I'm going to have to do what I said I'd do.' The appellant said in evidence that meant merely that she going to leave. She wrote in lipstick on her bedroom mirror: 'Bastard Thornton, I hate you.' Later, she and Martin went out leaving the deceased dozing on the couch. Martin returned home first and went upstairs. The appellant got a taxi home. The taxi driver said she was arrogant and quarrelsome, which she denies.

Her account in evidence of what happened after that was that she found the deceased still lying inert on the couch. She went upstairs, changed into her night-clothes and came down again to persuade the deceased to come to bed. He insulted her, calling her a whore and alleging she had been selling her body. He wanted her out of the house and threatened to kill her. She went to the kitchen to calm down. She decided to try again to persuade him to come to bed, but looked for a truncheon retained from when he had been a policeman so as to protect herself if he became violent. Not finding the truncheon, she picked up a large kitchen knife. She returned to the deceased, who again threatened to kill her and called her a whore. She stood beside him, lifted the knife and then brought it down slowly. A post-mortem examination showed the single stab had entered just below the ribs and penetrated deeply through to the back of the ribcage. In evidence the appellant said she did not stab the deceased deliberately. She denied she did it because she was provoked or because she was mentally upset. Asked in cross-examination if it was an accident, she repeatedly said Yes.

Martin, who was upstairs when the appellant came home, had heard no quarrel or raised voices. What he did hear was the rattling of cutlery in the drawer, followed by a scream from his father. He went downstairs. The appellant said in a cold matter-of-fact tone: 'I've killed your father.' She telephoned for an ambulance and said: 'I've just killed my husband. I've stuck a six-inch carving knife in his belly on the left-hand side.' The ambulance and police came. To a police officer the appellant said: 'I've stabbed him with this carving knife.' Asked 'Have you tried to kill him?' she said: 'I wanted to kill him.' When the emergency service were making efforts to save him the appellant said: 'I don't know why you are bothering, let him die.' Martin heard her say: 'Let the bastard die.' The police officer asked: 'Do you understand what you are saying?' She replied: 'Yes, I know exactly what I am saying. I sharpened up the knife so I could kill him. Do you know what he has done to me in the past?' Asked 'When did you sharpen the bread-knife?' she replied:

'After I went to see him in there. I said are you coming to bed love and he told me to fuck off out and fuck some blokes to get some money, so I just walked into the kitchen, got the knife, sharpened it up and stuck it in his belly.
Q: Did he beat you up tonight? A: No.
Q: Did he threaten to? A: He would have.'

Later, the appellant said to the police: 'I nearly did it on Sunday you know.' Whilst the police were at the house, the appellant behaved in a surprising, Mr Mansfield, Q.C. says bizarre, manner. She began to use the floor-mop, she talked about the washing, a meal, and wanting to tune the guitar. She wanted to take photographs of her husband and telephone the taxi for her handbag and cigarettes. She pinched a police officer's bottom, telling him he had 'a lovely bum'."

With new medical evidence presented of Thornton's personality disorder, and "battered woman syndrome" admitted as a characteristic relevant to whether a reasonable person in Thornton's position would have reacted as she did, the Court of Appeal ordered a retrial. Thornton was subsequently found guilty of manslaughter on the grounds of diminished responsibility and released.[77]

Rosina Rossiter killed her husband by stabbing him with a knife following an argument. He had inflicted violence upon her including attacking her with a rolling pin and made as if to strangle her with his hands and with a tea-towel. He was about to hit her when she stabbed him. Rosina Rossiter was

[77] W. Bennett, "Sara Thornton is cleared of murder: Killer walks free but verdict fails to resolve legal issues over domestic violence" *The Independent*, May 30, 1996.

convicted of murder, her defence of self-defence being unsuccessful. The Court of Appeal accepted that provocation should have been left to the jury. The facts clearly show that the Court could have reached no other conclusion (except for raising the question of why self-defence was not accepted at trial). Despite allowing her appeal, the judge took a very unfavourable view of her conduct:

R. v. Rossiter
[1994] 2 All E. R. 752 at 753–754, *per* Russell L.J.
[giving the judgment of the court]

". . . The case arises out of matrimonial discord and, before we deal with it in any detail, perhaps some preliminary observations would not be out of place. Matrimonial disharmony does not in itself and cannot entirely excuse, let alone justify, extreme violence. The other observation we make relates to this particular case. The members of this court have all read transcripts of the evidence given by this appellant as well as a transcript of the summing up. The impression we have all gained is that the appellant was a very unsatisfactory witness and, making all allowances for the stress of her predicament, her various versions of events, as given first to the police and later to the court, led to a confused and confusing picture. It created enormous difficulties for those charged with the responsibility of defending Mrs Rossiter and it also created problems for the judge.

Counsel had to follow their client's instructions and at no stage did she concede that she had deliberately inflicted injury upon her husband who was the victim of the charge. Her case was that the death of her husband at her hands was a ghastly accident. Alternatively, as she suggested during the course of the hearing, she had been defending herself, though let it be plainly understood not defending herself when striking the fatal blows.

The absence of any concession by the appellant to a deliberate stabbing of her husband inhibited the defence in the way of running before the jury the defence that it is suggested should have been left for the jury's consideration, namely provocation . . ."

Feminist commentators have focused upon the fact that, whilst offering the possibility of avoiding the mandatory life sentence, the defence of diminished responsibility does not demand a consideration of the context in which the killing occurs. What is masked by this defence, and which may be revealed by provocation and self defence, is the extent of violence occurring within the family, a locus usually portrayed as a secure and safe haven from the dangers to women in the public sphere. The wider social context of violence, the inadequate response of the legal system in dealing with men who are repeatedly violent to their partners and the failure to assist women who wish to leave a violent relationship are thereby ignored.

11.1.vi *"Tinkering with legal definitions"*?[78]
Much of the feminist attention to the cases discussed in this chapter has been devoted to the ways in which the law could be reformed so as to accommodate

[78] C. Wells, *supra*, n. 4 at 275.

the experiences of women who kill. Possible reforms include the removal of the requirement of a "sudden" loss of self-control[79] and the reconceptualisation of self-defence to acknowledge the threat to the self caused by repeated systematic violence.[80] A third possibility, the introduction of a new defence of self-preservation, is considered in the following extract:

J. RADFORD & L. KELLY

"Change the Law (2)"[81]

"[I]t would be an important victory to have the unequal position of women and children in families/households recognised in law — such that the very fact of having to endure a history of sexual/physical abuse is the basis of the defence. Whilst not worded in gender-specific ways, the reality is that the vast majority of cases would involve women and children abused by male members of the household.

Our starting point in thinking about a new defence is all the research on, and personal testimony by, women who have killed abusive men. The common theme which emerges is reaching a point where they feel it's his life or theirs. Both the history of the violence and the many attempts they have made to avoid/escape it result in a sense of hopelessness and despair.

Although this amendment, like all law, needs to be universal in its application, we feel it should also acknowledge the ways in which differences in women's cultural background specifically shape their situation and perception of courses of action open to them. For example we are aware of how the 'izzat' code of honour was one of the several circumstantial factors which served to trap Kiranjit in her marriage. However we do not want law to problematise minority ethnic cultural groups in ways which could feed into racist stereotypes. Further we are aware that other women can be trapped and isolated by dominant ideologies or beliefs of their communities. For example we have learned how women from Christian fundamentalist groups may be punished by their communities for leaving violent relationships — for example ROW [Rights of Women] has been contacted by women from faiths like Jehovah's Witnesses who have lost custody of their children and been forced out of their community when they left violent husbands. Knowledge of the power of community response can be part of the complex web of factors binding women in dangerous situations.

While we need the assistance of lawyers in the drafting of this defence, we see it as containing the following elements:

- [I]t is a defence open to a person who kills a partner or someone in a familial or intimate relationship who
- has subjected them to continuing sexual and/or physical abuse and intimidation combined with psychological abuse to the extent that they
- have an honest belief that there was no alternative available.

We would include subsections to allow for the following situations:

- a person acting in the protection of a child being subjected to abuse;
- a child or adolescent acting in the protection of a parent or sibling being abused;

---

[79] Considered in C. Wells, *ibid.*
[80] K. O'Donovan, *supra*, n. 13 at 232–233.
[81] (1991) 22 *Trouble & Strife* 12 at 14.

- in the case of a child or young person victimised by sexual abuse acting to prevent the abuse being carried on to a sibling;
- household or family members acting together against a household/family member who is abusing all of them.

The defence would require the woman to provide evidence to demonstrate the history of violence and abuse. This would take the form of the woman's/child's own testimony with or without other corroboration, which might take the form of testimony from, for example, other members of the household, including children, friends, family, neighbours, doctor's or police reports, legal statements, court orders or evidence from other agencies."

Given the deeply entrenched assumptions amongst the judiciary about femininity and the nature of the female offender, it is questionable whether legal reform will bring about effective change for the treatment of women who kill.[82] Celia Wells points out that that "tinkering with legal definitions" will not provide a solution given that "[t]hese cases tell us not just that women have different lives, but that they live on a different emotional, and possibly moral, planet."[83] She argues that it is necessary to consider the actions of women who kill within the context of violence within society towards women, of "entrenched images of good/bad wives," of the "underlying empathy with the reasons which might excuse men who abuse their wives", and of the " 'normalisaton' of male authority in women's everyday lives".[84] It is suggested by Marie Fox that, in order to achieve justice for both battered women who kill, and for women generally, it is necessary to avoid the tendency to construct women who kill as different, as oppositional to women. Instead we should seek to understand the battered woman's response as the action of a woman exposed to heterosexual violence of an extreme form but nonetheless violence commonly perpetuated on women by men.[85] Fox points out the danger of constructing the battered woman who kills as exceptional and thereby masking the commonality of her experience in the context of a society in which male aggression towards women is widespread. Given that violence against women is endemic within society, focusing upon reform of the defences available to women who kill their abuser enables the extent of that violence to be shrouded by the depiction of the actions of these women as extraordinary. Hence, she suggests the focus should not be upon the specific definitions of the defences available. Instead it ought to rest upon with the behaviour of the abuser in a society which condones male aggression towards women, and upon the means by which to eliminate the violence to which a very few women react by killing:[86]

---

[82]   M. Fox, *supra*, n. 11 at p. 180.
[83]   C. Wells, *supra*, n. 4 at 275.
[84]   C. Wells, *ibid.*, at 275.
[85]   M. Fox, *supra*, n. 11 at 171.
[86]   M. Fox, *ibid.*, at 172.

M. Fox
"Legal Responses to Battered Women Who Kill"[87]

"As the debate is currently constructed, it seems that the media, academic lawyers and the legal system are colluding in avoiding the tougher question of how, and indeed whether it is possible, to do justice to the individual battered woman without cost to women as a class. To act justly we must broaden the issue beyond what happens in the trial court, where the law is applied, or at appellate level where it may be reformed. Although I continue to believe that reform of criminal law is important, I think that its role in securing justice for women is limited. To effect the changes necessary to do justice to battered women we need to adopt a position outside of law.

What this might entail in practice, at a minimum, is to require that society devote adequate resources to the funding of refuges, to advertising their existence, and to emphasising the widespread nature of domestic violence, thus decreasing the stigma which still attaches to it. The necessity for such measures is illustrated by the caselaw. Both Thornton and Ahluwalia had approached numerous groups and agencies for help to no avail. As we have seen judges (and probably juries) tend to assume wrongly that other options are available. We cannot rest content with pointing out the lack of such options (and turning again to law reform); but must insist that resources be made available to enable women to leave violent relationships. However, inevitably such measures are an exercise in damage limitation. Moreover, it is important to address the fact that the dependency of many women upon violent men is emotional as well as physical, economic and social, which makes the problem much more intractable. Although feelings of emotional dependency may actually stem from a culturally created lack of self-esteem, this does not make them any less real, and women have encountered problems because courts, even when they do perceive fear as a reason for not leaving the relationship, do not regard love as an equally valid reason. Change therefore will require more than simply providing resources which would help empower women to leave.

In the longer term, more intractable problems need to be tackled such as that of sex-stereotyping. Dealing with this issue requires knowledge of attitudes held by actual and potential jurors. The many murder convictions of battered women who have killed suggest a lack of understanding of their plight. If empirical research were to confirm this, it would be necessary to formulate strategies to combat this . . .

Another practical, albeit more difficult, way of effecting meaningful change would be to articulate a language to enable battered women to convey their experiences to society. This raises a general problem of *whose* truth gets to count — that of the lawyer or layperson. Minow has argued that there may be more fundamental problems than legal or evidential ones when it comes to a woman articulating her experience of violence, as the words simply do not exist to enable her to convey the reality of her life. She identifies the need for a different language which reflects the experiences of those abused by domestic violence and which does not trivialise or distance us from the horrific reality of it as much judicial discourse does. Thus, language has a vital part to play in rendering domestic violence visible and helping us re-shape our perceptions of battered women. We have to use language to promote a new understanding of violence against women which recognises the power and control at play in violent relationships. Only when women can articulate their experiences and render visible to

---

[87] In J. Bridgeman & S. Millns (eds), *ibid.*, pp. 187–190.

society and juries the extreme physical and emotional abuse to women's bodies which the oxymoronic term 'domestic violence' obscures, can we begin to formulate a more effective strategy for legal intervention which really protects women and prevents men from inflicting such violence . . .

However, the task is an enormous and perhaps ultimately a utopian one. Law is implicated in the current plight of battered women especially if they kill their abusers. It can be used to effect change but its role is inevitably limited. While we should continue to strive for ways to ameliorate the position of the battered woman who kills, by seeking to educate judges and jurors, and questioning the existence of defences like provocation, law can most effectively be used in an attempt to prevent the situation ever arising where the woman feels compelled to fight back with lethal force. Before that point it must intervene to remove the male perpetrator of abuse. As Eber contends, given the ineffectiveness of the available legislation and remedies, the legal system has thus far evaded its responsibility to treat this critical problem as a crime against society. Various options have been canvassed, such as criminal statutes to deal specifically with domestic violence, although, as Eber argues, there is a need for very clear definitions in any proposed statutes, as well as an awareness that they could lead to such violence being deemed of a different, and less serious order, than 'real' violence occurring in the public sphere. Whatever measures are taken to deal with domestic violence must reflect its gravity and criminality. Such interventions are also essentially short-term, and limited to curtailing the extreme manifestations of woman abuse. In the longer term our concern must be to prevent such violence from ever occurring. This will involve locating the particularity of the battered woman's experience in the context of the generality of inequality and power imbalance that currently seems integral to intimate relationships and seeking to change that inequality."

11.2   Infanticide

In terms of its incidence, infanticide may be considered to be a crime more of historical interest than a contemporary social problem. In 1994, two women were convicted of infanticide and six of manslaughter by reason of diminished responsibility (as the cases outlined later demonstrate this category is not limited to but may include, women who killed a child in its first year of life).[88] There is no doubt that infanticide was widely practised in the past through "overlaying" of "neonates, bastards, and/or infants thought to be defective in some manner".[89] Robert Weir explains that the motivations for infanticide were economic deprivation, social attitudes and abnormality of the child.[90] He argues that infanticide as a twentieth century phenomenon primarily occurs in the form of selective non-treatment of neonates. This chapter does not consider whether the withdrawal of medical treatment from new-borns — "a rational response to the failure of a baby to fit the appropriate culturally determined criteria"[91] — is a legitimate form of infanticide in western demo-

---

[88]   *Criminal Statistics: England and Wales, 1994, supra,* n. 5 at pp. 86–87, Table 4.8.
[89]   R. Weir, *Selective Nontreatment of Handicapped Newborns* (Oxford: Oxford University Press, 1984), p. 13.
[90]   R. Weir, *ibid.,* Chap. 1.
[91]   C. Wells, "Whose Baby is it?" (1988) 15 *Journal of Law and Society* 323 at 325.

cracies at the end of the twentieth century.[92] The focus of this chapter is the legal regulation of infanticide as "an irrational act on the part of a mother disturbed by childbirth".[93] In her consideration of the non-treatment of neonates, Celia Wells notes the dominant perception of violent crime as occurring in a public place between two strangers against which the home is considered a "safe haven". The wider context of the personal violence inflicted upon "battered" women who kill (discussed immediately above), and the sexual violation of women by men who are known to them (discussed in Chapter 7), exposes the hidden nature of violence which occurs in private, as well as the reluctance of authorities to respond to this violence in the same manner as to violence inflicted by a stranger in a public place. Infanticide, a crime committed by a woman arising out of her role as mother, and perpetrated against her own child, raises many of the same questions concerning dominant constructions of Woman as cases of battered women who kill their abuser. It also exposes once more the failure of the legal system to recognise the social context in which women commit crimes by virtue of its "pathologisation" of the female criminal.[94]

Motherhood is idealised as Woman's primary and most valued role, the occupation which gives her total fulfilment. Where a mother kills her newborn child, her treatment within the criminal justice system depends upon the explanations given for her behaviour, and how those explanations may be

---

[92] The non treatment of new-born babies is discussed by I. Kennedy & A. Grubb, *Medical Law: text with materials* (2nd ed., London: Butterworths, 1994), pp. 1238–1263.

[93] C. Wells, *supra*, n. 91 at 325.

[94] A further example of the tendency to explain the behaviour of women which is contrary to societal expectations as the effect of female biology is the raising of pre-menstrual tension (PMT) as a partial defence or in mitigation of sentence (see J. M. Stoppard, "A Suitable case for Treatment? Premenstrual Syndrome and the Medicalisation of Women's Bodies" in D. H. Currie & V. Raoul, *Anatomy of Gender: Women's Struggle for the Body* (Ottowa: Carleton University Press, 1992)). Whilst PMT may be an explanation for the crimes of some women, the lack of definition as to what is PMT, and the tendency to class all women together as sufferers, failing to distinguish between the cyclical changes that all women experience and the particular extremes which have a profound influence upon the emotions or actions of a woman, has led to claims that PMT may enable all women to evade responsibility for their criminal actions. The relationship between menstruation and unsocial or criminal behaviour is not a new inquiry to the English criminal justice system (see, for example, P. Vanezis, "Women, Violent Crime and the Menstrual Cycle: a review" (1991) 31 Med. Sci. Law 11). PMT has been included as a relevant factor at the sentencing stage when women have committed serious crimes (*R. v. Morris* [1988] Crim.L.R. 257, CA). If a woman is suffering from PMT at the time she killed, the courts have been willing to interpret that as suffering from abnormality of the mind induced by disease which was such as to substantially impair her mental responsibility for the killing, providing a partial defence of diminished responsibility, reducing liability to manslaughter (*R. v. Reynolds* [1988] Crim.L.R. 678). However, the Court of Appeal has rejected the argument that PMT should amount to a complete defence, either on the basis of automatism, or as a denial of moral responsibility. Explaining the criminal behaviour of women as a result of a pathological condition linked to cyclical changes that all women experience denies or lessens the significance of the social origins and political meanings of women's deviance and perputates the notion that women do not react to their environment with anger or violence but rather that female criminality can be fully explained by female biology. See further H. Allen, "At the Mercy of her Hormones: premenstrual tension and the law" [1984] *m/f* 19; and S. Edwards, "Mad, bad or premenstrual?" (1988) 138 New L.J. 456.

consistent with understandings of the nature of Woman, despite the fact that she has killed and killed her own child.

A. Morris & A. Wilczynski
"Rocking the Cradle: Mothers who Kill their Children"[95]

"Not all mothers who kill their children are perceived sympathetically. At least some are given prison sentences, and a few are convicted of murder. Ania Wilczynski examined twenty-two English cases (collected from a variety of sources) of women who had killed their children. In these, it was clear that distinctions were drawn between 'good' and 'bad' women and, more particularly, between 'good' and 'bad' mothers.

Fourteen women were identified as essentially 'good' women and 'good' mothers for whom something had gone tragically wrong. They were given probation or hospital orders. Sara, for example, allegedly suffocated her eleven-month-old child whilst she was acutely depressed, then tried to commit suicide. She denied manslaughter, arguing that the death was a cot death, but was convicted of manslaughter on the grounds of diminished responsibility. At Sara's trial, it was stated that her child had been healthy and happy and that all who knew her regarded her as a loving and caring mother. The judge seemed to agree and gave Sara a three-year probation order, saying: 'You are in need of help and not of punishment'.

Eight women in Wilczynski's sample, however, were given prison sentences. These women tended to be viewed as having acted in ways inconsistent with traditional conceptions of women's behaviour. That is to say, they were viewed as 'bad' women and 'bad' mothers — selfish, cold, neglectful, uncaring and sexually active.

In 1988, Susan Poole and her common-law spouse Frederick Scott were convicted of the manslaughter by starvation of their ten-month-old son and the wilful neglect of their two-year-old son. They were given seven years' and ten years' imprisonment respectively. Susan Poole was described by the popular press as 'evil', 'callous' and 'vile', and was said to have referred to her child as 'it'. The jury were told that she sometimes left the children alone while she accompanied Frederick Scott to the pub which was a hundred yards down the road, that she had severely neglected the housework, and that although she was grossly overweight, her son had starved to death. My Justice Owen, at the trial in the Central Criminal Court in London, commented that she must have seen the pleading look in her son's eyes:

> 'When one thinks of the extraordinary maternal sacrifice and care shown by lower animals, one has to wonder at her apparent selfishness.'

Yvonne Roberts, a journalist who interviewed Susan Poole after her conviction, presents her in a very different light from the popular perceptions of her. She describes her as a young, immature woman from a chaotic, abused and neglected background who in the two months before her son's death became increasingly despondent and depressed because of her deteriorating relationship with her violent and unsupportive partner, her social isolation and her feelings of being unable to cope with the care of her children. According to Roberts, when Susan Poole did go to the pub with Frederick

---

[95] In H. Birch (ed.), *Moving Targets: Women, Murder and Representation* (London: Virago, 1993), pp. 212–214.

Scott, she rarely drank more than half a lager. Susan Poole is reported as saying: 'I'd go because I was so lonely. I was on my own all day with the children, I felt I was going mad.'

At the trial, the evidence of four psychiatrists and one doctor was presented. They all believed that the combination of Susan Poole's immaturity, personality disorder and severe depressive illness would have been sufficient to impair her responsibility for her actions in at least the two months before her child's death. Although Mr Justice Owen accepted Susan Poole's plea of guilty to manslaughter on the basis of her diminished responsibility, he also seems to have regarded her as fully culpable and as, in essence, a 'bad' mother. He said: 'When all is said and done, you killed your one son and you failed properly to care for the other.'

The seven-year sentence given to Poole appears to have been more a reflection of the negative image created of Susan Poole as a mother than of the medical evidence presented. On appeal, the period of imprisonment was only reduced to five years, as was her common-law husband's. Despite clear evidence of depression in Susan Poole's case, infanticide seems never to have been considered ... It is difficult to avoid the conclusion that it was the negative portrayal of her as a *woman* and as a *mother* which was the determining factor in her treatment within the criminal justice system."

The study by Ania Wilczynski examined the explanations given by parents who killed their children:

A. WILCZYNSKI
"Child-killing by parents: Social, legal and gender issues"[96]

"Filicides were classified into eleven categories of motive: 'retaliating' killings; jealousy of, or rejection by, the victim; the unwanted child; discipline; altruistic; psychosis in the parent; Munchausen Syndrome by Proxy; self-defence; killings secondary to sexual or organised abuse on the victim or another person; no intent to kill or injure; and cases where the motive is unknown. The classification took account both of the sample cases, and other types of cases reported in the literature not represented in the sample. Emphasis was placed on the suspects' explanations for their behaviour immediately after the offence and in police interview. Since filicide cases often involve more than one motivation, cases were classified according to both their 'primary' (major or predominant) and 'secondary' (apparently less significant) motives. In cases which appeared to involve two major motivations, 'psychosis' was always classified as a primary motivation, and 'discipline' was always classified as a secondary motivation (since it was the more immediate and transitory reason for the killing).

It should be noted, however, that whilst a 'motive' in cases of filicide can often be identified, most of the killings in the sample, as in other studies, were not instrumental or premeditated — they were usually sudden and impulsive. Thus care must be taken not to 'over-determine' motives.

In *retaliating killings*, anger towards another person — typically the person's partner — is displaced on to the child. Men were more likely than women to commit these killings. A common hallmark of these cases was a history of severe marital conflict, often involving physical violence by one or both partners.

[96]   In R. E. Dobash, R. P. Dobash & L. Noaks, *supra*, n. 10 at pp. 168–172.

The male 'retaliating' filicides were often characterised by possessiveness, sexual jealousy and the exertion of power within the marital relationship . . .

Conversely, the female 'retaliating' cases were rather different. In these the female perpetrator tended to be motivated by resentment at her *lack* of power. For example one woman was angry at always being told what to do by her husband, whilst another resented her second husband's constant emotional abuse and harsh physical discipline of her mentally retarded teenage son.

Jealousy of, or rejection by, the victim was an exclusively male category, apart from one case in which both the man and the woman had abused and killed the child. The reasons for the perpetrators' resentment included: suspicion or knowledge that they were not the child's biological parents; resentment of the attention the child received from the mother; or 'rejecting' behaviour by the child due to illness or prior abuse.

Unwanted child filicides usually involve female perpetrators. These cases were classified according to the age of the victim (neonates or older) and also the stage at which the child became unwanted. Most of the unwanted victims were *children unplanned and unwanted from the time of conception*. These cases usually involve *neonaticide*, the killing of new-born babies within twenty-four hours of birth, usually by somewhat passive and immature young single women who deny and conceal their unplanned pregnancies. Less commonly, the victims are *older than one day*, such as one boy whose teenage mother was pressured by her parents to keep him rather than let him be adopted as she had wanted. The one victim who was *wanted by the parent at conception but not after the birth* was unwanted because of her characteristics after birth. The baby girl was completely rejected by her father because she had Down's Syndrome.

Discipline killings occur as a result of attempts to discipline a child for behaviour regarded as annoying or disobedient. Although both men and women killed during the course of discipline, it was more common amongst the male offenders. For example Alan shook his three-year-old son and banged his head against a wall in a fit of temper. The child, who was frequently disobedient, had fallen down the stairs. As is typically said by parents who kill during the course of discipline, Alan said that he hadn't meant to harm the child seriously.

In *altruistic* filicide, the parent (usually the mother) perceives the killing as being in the child's best interests. *'Primary' altruistic killings* are what have been termed 'mercy-killings', in which there is a real degree of suffering in the victim (for example mental or physical handicap or disease) and an absence of secondary gain for the parent. There was one of these cases in the sample. The much more common *'secondary' altruistic killings* involve no real degree of suffering in the child. In these cases the parent, virtually always the mother, is suffering from depression. These women expressed acute feelings of failure to measure up to society's standards of 'good' mothers or wives. For instance, one woman regarded herself as a bad mother and wife, worried that the child was abnormal in some way, and felt that she did everything but it was never enough.

Psychotic parents include those diagnosed as psychotic at the time of the killing. There were both men and women in this category, but more women than men. In some cases the killing was committed directly under the influence of delusions, such as a schizophrenic man who repeatedly stabbed his daughter because he believed she was possessed by the devil. In other cases the killing was in some way altruistic: either the parent delusionally believed the child was suffering in some way (such as one mother who believed her children had venereal disease and had therefore stopped growing), or their psychotic illness led them to want to commit suicide and the child was killed secondarily to this primary suicidal urge.

In *Munchausen Syndrome by Proxy* (MSBP), the parent fakes or induces illnesses in a child, and presents them — often repeatedly — for medical assessment and care. Smothering to induce seizures or fits is the most common method. Some children die from the abuse . . .

The following three categories were not represented amongst the sample cases.

Some filicides are *secondary to sexual or ritual (or organised) abuse*, either on the child or another person. There were no sample cases of this type, and there were no suspected cases of sexual assault. However, sexual abuse is particularly difficult to detect, and at the time of the sample cases (1984) there was not the current level of professional awareness of this type of abuse. Where filicides involving sexual abuse do occur, the child may be killed inadvertently during the course of the sexual assault, or else deliberately killed in order to prevent disclosure of the abuse. . . .

In some filicides there is *no intent to kill or injure* the child at all. This excludes cases in which there was *any* intention to harm the child (for example cases typically classified as 'battering' in some prior classifications, where there is at least an intent to injure, if not to kill). This category includes many cases where children die from neglect. These deaths are usually due to ignorance of the food and health requirements of the baby, compounded by the stresses of social disadvantage and personal inadequacies . . .

Overall, the most common categories of filicide motivation were retaliating, discipline, the unwanted child (both neonaticides and older children), secondary altruism, psychosis and jealousy. This was true both of primary motivations alone and when analysed together with the secondary motivations. It is also clear that men and women tend to kill their children for very different reasons. Men's motives tend to be associated with retaliation, discipline, or jealousy of or rejection by the victim. Women tend to kill because they are psychotic, or the child is unwanted (typically a neonate killed by a passive and immature young woman), or for altruistic reasons. This sex difference reflects an extreme version of traditional gender roles, in which men are socialized to be aggressive, dominant and sexually possessive, and women are taught to internalize stress and anger, and be passive, nurturing and self-sacrificing. Although the use of select samples and differences in classification in previous studies makes direct comparison difficult, the literature reports comparable results on both these findings."

Wilczynski suggests that the differing explanations given by men and women may, to a certain extent, explain the more lenient treatment of mothers who kill:

A. WILCZYNSKI
"Child-Killing by parents: Social, legal and gender issues"[97]

"Turning to the legal treatment of filicidal parents, it is clear that men and women who kill their children are perceived and treated in very different ways by the criminal justice system. This is in accordance with the view that 'men are bad and normal, women are mad and abnormal'. Generally men are treated in accordance with the

---

[97] A. Wilczynski, *ibid.*, pp. 174, 178.

'legal/punishment' model of child abuse, and women in accordance with the 'welfare/
treatment' model . . .

Whilst men and women are clearly treated very differently by the criminal justice
system, the interpretation of this difference is by no means clear. An examination of
the sample cases indicated that there are certainly some differences in the circumstances
in which men and women kill their children, which could be used to justify women's
more lenient treatment. This could be on traditional tariff criteria — for example
women are less likely to have prior convictions or to have abused the child on a
previous occasion. Their typical categories of motivation are also those which tend
to be regarded as less morally reprehensible than those in which men predominate.
Alternatively, women's more lenient treatment could be justified on the grounds of
women's social role and responsibilities, since women still retain primary responsibility
for child-rearing with little support. Nonetheless, it would still appear that the differences which do exist between male and female filicide are exaggerated by the criminal
justice system, and that such dramatically different treatment cannot be justified. It is
also apparent that more informal means of social control can have a greater impact
on the legal processing of women than men — for example to justify the imposition
of a non-custodial sentence. These informal means of control were found to include
psychiatry, social work, the family, being perceived as a 'good parent', and self-
punishment through remorse."

The Infanticide Act 1938, s.1(1), constructs the woman who kills her own
child as suffering from a pathological condition such that her mind and her
actions are affected by the changes to her hormones due to "the effect of
giving birth to the child or by reason of the effect of lactation consequent
upon the birth of the child". The Infanticide Act 1938 creates the offence of
infanticide, and provides a defence to murder:

Infanticide Act 1938, s. 1(1)
(c. 36)

"Where a woman by any unlawful act or omission causes the death of her child being
a child under the age of twelve months, but at the time of the act or omission the
balance of her mind was disturbed by reason of her not having fully recovered from
the effect of giving birth to the child or by reason of the effect of lactation consequent
upon the birth of the child, then, notwithstanding that the circumstances were such
that but for this Act the offence would have amounted to murder she shall be guilty
of felony, to wit of infanticide, and may for such offence be dealt with and punished
as if she had been guilty of the offence of manslaughter of the child."

Infanticide is a unique offence in that it is a gender-specific crime. There is no
similar provision for fathers who kill. This might be explained by the presumptions about the effects of pregnancy and childbirth which underpin the
Infanticide Act. The Act recognises that women are different from men in that
men's bodies are not affected by the birth of their child in such a way as to
affect their rational thought processes and their culpability for criminal acts.
Women, who may be so affected, are accordingly entitled to different (special)

legal treatment. Consistent with the presumptions surrounding female criminality, the Infanticide Act is also unique in creating an offence for which mental abnormality is a positive precondition for conviction.[98] This has not always been the case. The offence of Infanticide was originally introduced with the aim of influencing moral attitudes and social behaviour by imposing severe penalties upon unmarried mothers whose babies died:

K. O' DONOVAN
"The Medicalisation of Infanticide"[99]

"The first statute to create a crime of infanticide was passed in 1623. It was a sex-specific crime committed by women and confined to bastard children as victims. The offence involved was concealment of death rather than death itself, but the concealment operated as a presumption of guilt of murder. To rebut the presumption a witness had to be produced to give evidence that the child was born dead. Given the secrecy of the pregnancy and birth in most cases, this was difficult. By contrast, the suspected murder of children born in wedlock was treated as any other crime of homicide until 1922. The burden of proof was on the prosecution to show that the child had been born alive and had completely severed its connection with its mother's body . . .

The statute of 1623 was considered harsh. Blackstone said it 'savours pretty strongly of severity'. Public attitudes to infanticide by unmarried mothers were punitive, yet for single women in certain forms of employment there was considerable risk of pregnancy. It has been suggested that, in the eighteenth century half the unmarried women under the age of 26 were living-in servants, vulnerable to seduction and rape. Because their good 'character' was of economic and social value to them, pregnancy for these women was a catastrophe. Travelling and abandoning the child was not an available option, so concealment and infanticide were likely to follow pregnancy. Even where the child was born dead, producing a witness to the court was probably difficult because of the secrecy of the affair. According to Blackstone the severity of the statute was mitigated in practice with the burden of proof shifting to the prosecution.

Cases of child murder within wedlock were treated with less harshness. As Blackstone stated: 'to kill a child in its mother's womb is now no murder, but a great misprision.' The reasons why married parents might not wish to accept a new child into the family could have been economic, or related to some physical problem the child had.

Langer argues that 'infanticide has from time immemorial been the accepted procedure for disposing not only of deformed or sickly infants but of all such new borns as might strain the resources of the individual family or the larger community.' Opportunities for disposing of the child through overlaying, accident, sickness or infanticidal nursing were far greater than those available to single women. Writers on medieval coroner rolls suggest that the absence of records on infanticide may be due to the public attitude, that such matters were insignificant.

In 1803 Lord Ellenborough's Act was passed, repealing the Act of 1623, and placing infanticide trials on the same footing as homicide trials. This change has been inter-

---

[98] See further H. Allen, *Justice Unbalanced: Gender, Psychiatry and Judicial Decisions, supra,* n. 65.
[99] [1984] Crim.L.R. 259 at 259–262.

preted as meaning that infanticide could be committed with impunity: 'even the police seemed to think no more of finding a dead child than of finding a dead dog or cat.' Throughout the nineteenth century there were scandals over burial clubs and baby-farming. The law was seen to be in disarray. There were numerous acquittals for lack of proof that the child had been born alive. The 1803 Act contained a proviso whereby the jury could in acquiting the defendant of murder, make a finding of concealment of birth which had a maximum two year sentence . . .

In the twentieth century a new legal approach to child murder was inaugurated by the Infanticide Act 1922. The Act reduced the offence from murder to manslaughter where a woman caused the death of her newly-born child by any wilful act or omission, 'but at the time of the act or omission she had not fully recovered from the effect of giving birth to such child, but by reason thereof the balance of her mind was then disturbed.' It has been convincingly argued that the Act was the product, not of nineteenth century medical theory about the effects of child-birth, but of judicial effort to avoid passing death sentences which were not going to be executed. But medical theory provided a convenient reason for changing the law. Judicial evidence to the Commission on Capital Punishment was that juries would not convict for infanticide, and that the judiciary were concerned not to have to go through the 'solemn mockery' involved in a murder trial . . .

The Infanticide Act 1938 reformed the 1922 Act in two directions. It altered the definition of the victims of infanticide from 'newly born' to 'under the age of 12 months,' and it extended the medicalisation of the crime through the addition of language about 'the effect of lactation.' The cases which brought about the fixing of the age at 12 months illustrate the tension between the socio-economic model of the crime, which informed the statute of 1623, and the medical model which informed the 1922 and 1938 Acts. In *O'Donoghue* the defendant who had killed her 35 day old child was sentenced to death and duly reprieved. The admitted facts, on which her counsel based his argument on appeal, were that the mother 'was in great distress at the time of the birth for some weeks from poverty and malnutrition, and had only just obtained employment when she killed the child.' In an unsuccessful effort to persuade the court that the trial judge was wrong in holding that a 35 day old child was not newly born, counsel also argued that 'there was between insanity and sanity a degree of mental derangement which the medical authorities called "puerperal".' Thus, a mixture of socio-economic causes and medical theory was used in argument. *Hale* was a case in which the mother killed her second child when it was three weeks old and inflicted injuries on herself. The medical evidence was that at the birth of her first child the mother had symptoms bordering on puerperal insanity. The trial judge, claiming himself bound by *O'Donoghue*, directed the jury to find the defendant 'guilty but insane.' "

A woman who kills her child not only departs from the traditional expectations of her as Woman, but also those of her as Mother, as one who is loving, self-sacrificial and finds ultimate fulfilment in caring for her child. Her actions are explained by the inherent instability of Woman located within the female hormones which are particularly unpredictable following childbirth. This view of the effect of female hormones upon the actions of women permits women to receive more lenient treatment in law. The infanticide provisions enable a woman to avoid the mandatory life sentence for murder, although she may receive a psychiatric disposition or probation contingent upon receipt of psychiatric treatment rather than imprisonment.[1]

There are many parallels between the crime of infanticide and the defence of diminished responsibility. As the cases outlined below demonstrate, this defence may be called upon by women who kill their children (and by fathers who cannot rely upon the Infanticide Act 1938). The Butler Committee, reporting in 1975, noted that the woman who killed her new-born child when the balance of her mind was disturbed by the effects of childbirth would be able to rely upon the defence of diminished responsibility.[2] However, the Report continued to identify the advantage of the infanticide provisions in that they enabled the prosecution, by laying a charge of infanticide rather than murder, to relieve the woman of having to establish that her mind was affected by childbirth. Hence, in the absence of a specific defence, a woman who kills her new-born child may be charged with murder and would have to establish that her responsibility was diminished following the birth of her child.[3]

As with a successful plea of diminished responsibility for a woman who kills her abuser, the Infanticide Act locates the explanation for the criminal behaviour of the woman within her body, rather than forcing acknowledgement of the social, cultural and historical circumstances in which the crime is committed. The Infanticide Act and the offence/defence provided therein proceed on the assumption that the physical processes of childbirth and lactation upon the body of the woman influence her behaviour in such a way as to reduce criminal responsibility when she kills the child to whom she has just given birth.[4] Whilst some, but not all, women who kill their infant children may be suffering from puerperal psychosis or psychotic depression,[5] the terminology of disturbed balance of mind labels all women as inherently unstable and explains the conduct of women who kill their children by identifying internal causes rather than external ones, such as unwanted pregnancy, poverty, poor housing, lack of social support or the fact that their experience of

---

[1] A. Wilczynski & A. Morris, "Parents who kill their Children" [1993] Crim.L.R. 31. In 1994, the two women found guilty of infanticide were both put on probation. Of the six women found guilty of manslaughter by reason of diminished responsibility (which may include women who killed a new-born child), two received custodial sentences of less than four years, two a hospital order with restrictions, one a hospital order and one probation (*Criminal Statistics: England and Wales, 1994 supra*, n. 5 at Table 4.8).

[2] The Butler Committee, *Report of the Committee on Mentally Abnormal Offenders*, Cmnd. 6244 (1975), (London: HMSO), para. 19.22. The study by R. D. Mackay, "The Consequences of Killing Very Young Children" [1993] Crim.L.R. 21 at 29, suggests that "the criteria within the 1938 Act were being used primarily as a legal device for avoiding the mandatory penalty and thus ensure that leniency could be shown in appropriate cases". The suggestion is, therefore, that there were cases of infanticide which would not have come within section 2 of the Homicide Act 1957.

[3] *Report of the Committee on Mentally Abnormal Offenders*, ibid., para. 19.26.

[4] The Act does not apply, however, if the woman kills older siblings or the father of the child.

[5] D. Maier-Katkin & R. Ogle, "A Rationale for Infanticide Laws" [1993] Crim.L.R. 903 at 908.

motherhood is very different from the ideal portrayed. The Butler Committee noted the lack of support for the medical basis of the Infanticide Act 1938:

THE BUTLER COMMITTEE
Report of the Committee on Mentally Abnormal Offenders[6]

"The medical principles on which the Infanticide Act is based may no longer be relevant. The theory behind the Act was that childbirth produced a hormonal disorder which caused mental illness. But puerperal psychoses are now regarded as no different from others, childbirth being only a precipitating factor. Minor forms of mental illness following childbirth are common, but psychoses, which usually occur in the first month, are much less so (between 1 and 2 per 1,000 deliveries). The danger to the infant in the acute stages is well recognised and guarded against in the provisions made for the care of such cases. Mental illness is probably no longer a significant cause of infanticide. Dr D. J. West, who studied cases where married women had killed their children, found no particular association with this period. The operative factors in child killing are often the stress of having to care for the infant, who may be unwanted or difficult, and personality problems; to some extent these affect the father as well as the mother and are not restricted to a year after the birth.

Perhaps the most impressive evidence we have had on the subject of infanticide is from the Governor and Staff of Holloway Prison, which is worth quoting at length:

'The disturbance of the "balance of mind" that the Act requires can rarely be said to arise directly from incomplete recovery from the effects of childbirth, and even less so from the effects of lactation. Infanticide due to puepperal psychotic illness is rare. The type of infanticide where the child is killed immediately after birth and which is usually associated with illegitimate concealed pregnancies is also very uncommon. Most cases of child murder dealt with by the courts as infanticide are examples of the battered child syndrome in which the assault has had fatal consequences and the child is aged under 12 months. A combination of environmental stress and personality disorder with low frustration tolerance are the usual aetiological factors in such cases, and the relationship to "incomplete recovery from the effects of childbirth or lactation" specified in the Infanticide Act is often somewhat remote. The Act is nevertheless nearly always invoked in cases of maternal filicide when the victim is aged under 12 months, in order to reduce the charge from murder to manslaughter. The illogical operation of the Act is illustrated by the fact that an exactly similar type of case where the victim happens to be over the age of 12 months can no longer be dealt with as infanticide ... We consider that the repeal of the mandatory penalty for murder would make the Infanticide Act unnecessary.' "

The Criminal Law Revision Committee subsequently recommended that the 1938 Act be amended to incorporate the wider societal causes of infanticide. Thus it would extend the offence to a woman whose balance of mind at the

---

[6] *Supra*, n. 2 at paras 19.23–19.24.

time of killing was "disturbed by reason of the effect of giving birth to the child *or circumstances consequent upon that birth*"[7]:

CRIMINAL LAW REVISION COMMITTEE (14TH REPORT)
Offences Against the Person[8]

"Between 1938 and the early 1960s, the cases of baby-killing dealt with by the courts commonly were of two types. The more common was that of the young, unmarried woman who had kept the fact of her pregnancy from her family and those around her and had given birth to the child, whom soon afterwards she had killed. At the trial in this type of case there was usually a plea of guilty to infanticide and no issue was raised by anyone about the balance of the woman's mind being disturbed by birth or lactation. The other type of case was that of the mother who had given birth to a grossly deformed or disabled child. These cases also were likely to be dealt with on pleas of guilty to infanticide and without contested medical issues. In the last two or three decades the Courts have had to deal, all too frequently, with the so-called 'battered baby' cases. Before then, these had often been undetected because doctors had tended to accept the explanations of accident given by the parents. They do not do so as readily nowadays, because knowledge of the so-called 'baby battering syndrome' is widespread amongst doctors, nurses and social workers. If the child dies and is under the age of 12 months, the mother may be charged with infanticide; if over 12 months, with either murder or manslaughter but usually the latter. During the past two decades the judges have acquired much experience of these cases and the social conditions and pressures which bring them about. They vary greatly. There are those in which the mother finds her child an obstacle to the kind of life she wants to lead. In this type of case the appropriate charge, when death results, would be, and should continue to be, either murder or manslaughter depending on the evidence. In contrast are the tragic cases in which the social and emotional pressures on the mother consequent on the birth are so heavy that her balance of mind is disturbed and she gives way under them, either killing the child intentionally or battering him to death. We think it humane that in these cases a conviction for an offence other than murder should result. But we are not, with respect to the Butler Committee, satisfied that the offence of manslaughter by diminished responsibility could cover all such cases as does infanticide at present ... There would be the possibility, if the offence of infanticide were abolished, that in a case where a conviction for infanticide would today result, the defendant would be convicted of murder. Naturally in such a case counsel and medical witnesses would strain the interpretation of the law on diminished responsibility to ensure that a verdict of manslaughter was returned, but we would not wish to make a recommendation that puts too great a strain upon the professional consciences of expert witnesses. We therefore recommend that the offence of infanticide should be retained ...

Under the present law infanticide is committed when at the time of the act or omission 'the balance of [the woman's] mind was disturbed by reason of her not having fully recovered from the effect of giving birth to the child or by reason of the effect of

---

[7] Criminal Law Revision Committee, Fourteenth Report, *Offences Against the Person*, Cmnd. 7844 (1980), (London: HMSO), para. 106 (emphasis added).

[8] *Ibid.*, paras 102, 105.

lactation consequent upon the birth of the child'. As we mentioned above, the medical principles underlying the Infanticide Act are, it seems, not proven. For example, the medical basis for the reference in the Act of 1938 to 'the effect of lactation' was that lactation might be associated with mental illness (known in the early part of the century as 'lactational insanity'). The medical experts say now, however, that there is little or no evidence to support this. In view of this we unanimously recommend that the reference to the effect of lactation should be removed from the definition of the offence. Furthermore, it is now thought that mental disturbance following childbirth is not confined exclusively to the effects of giving birth. The Royal College of Psychiatrists described to us four types of circumstances any of which may lead to a disturbed balance of mind and which they suggest justify and should continue to justify an infanticide verdict but would not come within section 4 of the Mental Health Act 1959. They are the following: '(1) overwhelming stress from the social environment being highlighted by the birth of a baby, with the emphasis on the unsuitability of the accommodation etc; (2) overwhelming stress from an additional member to a household struggling with poverty; (3) psychological injury, and pressures and stress from a husband or other member of a family from the mother's incapacity to arrange the demands of the extra member of the family; (4) failure of bonding between mother and child through illness or disability which impairs the development of the mother's capacity to care for the infant.' Whether or not those examples fall within the present definition if it is applied strictly, we agree that they are types of situations which are at present being dealt with by the courts as cases of infanticide and which should continue to fall within the ambit of the offence. Each one of them rests on a mental disturbance resulting in a real sense from childbirth but not all can be proved to arise 'by reason of [the mother] not having fully recovered from the effect of giving birth'. That phrase we consider to be unduly restrictive. We think that the statute would more accurately reflect the existing practice of the courts if it specified the offence as being committed when, at the time of the act or omission, the balance of the woman's mind was disturbed by reason of the effect of giving birth or circumstances consequent upon that birth. In cases now dealt with as infanticide it is a matter of human experience that the mental disturbance is connected with the fact of the birth and the hormonal and other bodily changes produced by it, even where it is related primarily to environmental or other stresses consequent upon the birth; but we think that the connection, where it is indirect in this sense, might be difficult to establish by medical evidence if expressed in a modern statute as a direct consequence of the birth."

Cases show that the Infanticide Act 1938 has enabled the courts to treat women who kill their children leniently and, importantly, to avoid the mandatory life sentence for murder. But the explanations for the behaviour of these women are located within "psychiatrically unsound" criteria which are based upon an understanding of a link between female biology and instability.[9] Puerperal psychosis is a severe mental disorder which affects one or two women in every 1,000 deliveries. Yet about a third of women suffer post-natal depression and up to 95 per cent experience periods of fear and depression.[10] The courts have allowed a verdict of infanticide where there is no evidence of

[9]　R. D. Mackay, *supra*, n.2 at 30.
[10]　A. Oakley, *Women Confined: Towards a Sociology of Childbirth* (Oxford: Martin Robertson, 1980).

psychosis but upon evidence that the woman was suffering from post-natal depression:

The Times
May 7, 1994[11]

"A teenage mother was recorded on a hospital surveillance camera trying to smother her baby, six weeks after killing her stepdaughter, a court was told yesterday.

She was filmed holding her hand over the eight-month-old boy's mouth. 'Substantial post-natal depression' had led her to suffocate the girl in the same way.

Yesterday a judge sentenced the mother, who was 18 at the time and cannot be named for legal reasons, to five years' detention to reflect 'public concern and repugnance for what she did'.

She admitted manslaughter on the grounds of diminished responsibility and attempted grievous bodily harm with intent.

Bristol Crown Court was told that she could not cope with three stepchildren after the birth of her son.

Within weeks of the infant's birth in June 1992, the woman's one-year-old stepdaughter suffered breathing problems. She was taken to hospital near the family home in Cheltenham, Gloucestershire, on a dozen occasions, 'floppy and blue'.

Arrangements were made for her to see a specialist but on the day of the appointment she was found dead in bed.

Doctors became concerned when her half-brother began suffering the same attacks and it was decided to keep the mother and the child under video surveillance.

Neil Butterfield Q.C., for the prosecution, said that the attack on the boy 'was extremely dangerous'. The baby needed resuscitation."

The Independent
September 1, 1995[12]

"A woman who killed her baby by swinging him by his feet into the stairs was allowed to walk free from the Old Bailey yesterday.

Suzanne Oatley was suffering from post-natal depression when she killed 11-day-old Alexander in what Judge Gerald Gordon called a tragic case. He imposed a two-year probation order on condition that Oatley receives medical treatment.

Oatley, 37, of Manor Drive, Hinchley Wood, Surrey, had admitted infanticide. A secretary and linguist who has worked in South America and the Middle East, she was unable to cope when her son was born.

Richard Horwell, for the prosecution, said Oatley told medical staff: 'Perhaps we should have him adopted. I wish it was just the two of us again,' referring to her lover Alan Lewis.

During her unplanned pregnancy Oatley had sought an abortion, telling doctors Mr Lewis did not want the baby. But she later changed her mind and told her GP he was

---

[11] Headline: "Mother tried to smother baby."
[12] Headline: "Woman who killed baby is free."

being very supportive. In fact, said Andrew Trollop, for the defence, Mr Lewis had been supportive throughout the pregnancy.

Just 11 days after Alexander was born Mr Lewis went out for a quick drink after caring for the baby all day. When he returned he found Oatley and the baby lying at the bottom of the steps. Alexander died soon afterwards in hospital from head injuries.

At first Oatley claimed the fall had been an accident, but later admitted swinging him by his legs into the stairs in what she described as 'a nightmare, a black fog'.

She told police she was afraid to confess because she feared the reaction of her parents and Mr Lewis. But, said Mr Trollop, he and her parents stood by her and now she hoped to start again with Mr Lewis.

After Alexander was born, she found it difficult to cope with motherhood. A doctor recorded: 'I have been in practice for 10 years and have never seen a mother so depressed at such an early stage'. She was prescribed anti-depressants after assuring the doctor she would never hurt Alexander. The next day she killed him.

Describing her as 'a vulnerable and emotionally fragile lady', Mr Trollop said: 'There is nothing she regrets more than killing her baby but she was plainly very ill indeed.' "

The Times
January 3, 1997[13]

"A mother who shook her $2\frac{1}{2}$-month-old daughter to death while suffering from post-natal depression walked free from court yesterday.

The death of Wendy Preer's baby in February 1995 was at first put down to natural causes, but the file was reopened when doctors were called to treat injuries to her twin brother two months later, Leeds Crown Court was told.

The girl's body was exhumed and a post-mortem examination carried out. It revealed that she had suffered fractured ribs twice while being violently shaken, and the second time had also received a fatal brain injury. Brian Walsh, Q.C., the Recorder of Leeds, said no useful purpose would be served by sending Preer, 23, to jail. Sentencing her to three years' probation on condition that she underwent psychiatric treatment, he said: 'For a mother to behave in the way you did is a terrible thing indeed, but it is clear on the whole of the evidence that at the time you were ill.'

Preer admitted infanticide while the balance of her mind was disturbed and causing grievous bodily harm to her son.

Robert Smith, Q.C., for the prosecution, said that Preer lived in a one-bedroomed flat in Leeds with her boyfriend and the twins. The girl was admitted to Leeds General Infirmary after apparently having breathing problems. She was put on a life-support machine but it was switched off two days later.

Michael Harrison, Q.C., for Preer, said that she had endured a difficult pregnancy and that her home circumstances were poor. There was no evidence of persistent acts of cruelty.

Peter Wood, an independent psychiatrist, said she had developed a psychiatric illness and had suffered from sleep deprivation. The surviving child is living with his parental grandmother."

---

[13] Headline: "Depressed mother who shook daughter to death walks free."

As noted by the Criminal Law Revision Committee (cited above), the medical view of birth precipitating mental disturbance has received much criticism. The view that may now be said to predominate is that it is the fact of birth, and the stresses consequent upon it, which are of greater significance. The wider circumstances which surround the killing by women of new-born children are apparent from the facts outlined in the above newspaper reports. However, they are even more apparent in those cases in which there is *no* consideration given of the state of the woman's mind at the time of the killing. In such cases, the fact that a woman has killed her new-born child (and thereby transgressed expectations of "normal" maternal behaviour) seems to be sufficient evidence of her mental disturbance.

The Times
August 24, 1993[14]

"A teenager wept yesterday as she admitted throwing her new-born daughter from a bedroom window because she was frightened that her mother would discover the birth.

The $6\frac{1}{2}$lb infant died from head injuries and exposure, Ann Curnow Q.C., for the prosecution, told the Old Bailey.

The 16-year-old mother, who gave birth during the night in the bedroom that she shared with her younger sister, who slept throughout, admitted infanticide. Judge Steel ordered that the unmarried girl from Willesden, northwest London, should not be identified and she was bailed until next month for reports.

The slightly built girl had repeatedly denied being pregnant when questioned by her mother, saying her stomach was growing because of over-eating. She went into labour in April. Afterwards, she woke her mother who, suspecting that she had had a baby, took her to hospital.

After the birth, the girl admitted that she had thrown the baby out of the window because she was frightened of being sent back to Jamaica. The court was told that she now lived with an aunt."

The Times
December 21, 1996[15]

"The daughter of a retired chief executive of the Rank Organisation who killed her newborn son after giving birth alone and in secret in her Kensington flat was put on probation yesterday after pleading guilty to infanticide.

'In a situation such as this the law does not wish to punish,' Sir Lawrence Verney, the Recorder of London, told Emma Gifford, 22, at the Central Criminal Court. The law wished to help because help was still required.

'The circumstances of this birth could not have been more lonely for you and what occurred immediately afterwards, although it must cause you great remorse, is not something which should be allowed to cloud your life for the whole of the future.'

---

[14]   Headline: "Mother, 16, threw baby to its death."
[15]   Headline: "Baby Killer gets probation".

William Boyce, for the prosecution, said Gifford, from Ashford, Kent, admitted to police that she had given birth at between 2am and 3am last April 6 and had agonised over her future until 5pm the next day when she was expected at work. Mr Boyce said: 'She felt as though she had no option. She didn't know what to do. So she placed a flannel, which she had used to clean the child, over his face.' Gifford had suffered from depression since the age of 13.

Rebecca Poulet, Q.C., for the defence, said: 'Her mother is an alcoholic and as a result her childhood, adolescence and later teens were extremely disturbed. She was persistently abused and developed an obedient and pleasing personality to assuage trouble.'

Gifford pleaded not guilty to a second charge of trying to conceal the birth, and agreed to a course of treatment as a condition of her probation."

The facts of reported cases likewise raise questions about the hidden causes of infanticide. The appellant in *R. v. Sainsbury*,[16] was fifteen years old when she became pregnant. She did not tell anyone but gave birth without medical assistance in the bathroom of her boyfriend's flat. The baby was wrapped in a blanket and put in the river. The body was found some months later. The appellant pleaded guilty to infanticide and was sentenced to twelve months in a young offenders institution. On appeal the sentence was reduced to proba-tion. The trial judge in passing sentence said that the balance of the young woman's mind was disturbed by the effect of giving birth and that she was immature, but that these factors did not remove responsibility, and regard to the welfare of society meant that a custodial sentence was appropriate. On appeal, the court noted that there had been no custodial sentence for infanti-cide between 1979 and 1988. The court did not think that there was anything to make this case any different from the previous ones and hence reduced the sentence accordingly.

Rather than the balance of Sainsbury's mind being disturbed by childbirth, would not a more likely explanation for her acts (the concealment of her pregnancy, giving birth in a bathroom and placing the baby in the river) be that, at aged fifteen, she wished to conceal an unplanned child? Rather than being precipitated to criminal conduct by hormones unleashed by pregnancy, the facts suggest, for example, that she may have been motivated by an inabil-ity to support the child, financially or emotionally, and by a knowledge of societal attitudes to unwed teenage mothers. The questions raised by a case such as this must go beyond medical explanations of the effect of giving birth upon rational thought towards a consideration of sex education, economic reality and popular reactions to teenage pregnancy.

Similar issues are raised in the case of *R. v. Lewis*.[17] The appellant was twenty when she became pregnant. She did not tell anyone and gave birth, without medical assistance, in the bathroom of her half-sister's house. She put the baby into two plastic bags, believing it to be stillborn. However, there were signs of movement so she stabbed the baby several times through the

---

[16]   *R. v. Sainsbury* [1990] Crim.L.R. 348.
[17]   *R. v. Lewis* [1990] Crim.L.R. 348.

plastic bags with a pair of scissors and hid the baby in a shed. She admitted what had happened when taken to hospital for the removal of the placenta. She pleaded guilty to manslaughter on the grounds of diminished responsibility. In sentencing Lewis to twelve months imprisonment, the judge claimed that he had to have regard to the needs of society as well as those of the woman concerned, and that her actions were a "denial of the cardinal obligation to protect human life". On appeal, the sentence was varied to a probation order with requirements relating to residence and submission to psychiatric treatment, acknowledging that this was not a case where a custodial sentence was required in order to mark public revulsion or effect deterrence on potential offenders. Once more, the verdict puts into question the state of the woman's mind without properly addressing the real pressures leading to the killing.

A final example is the (unreported) case of Victoria Pay,[18] aged twenty-one, who was put on probation for two years after the prosecution accepted her plea of guilty to a charge of infanticide. Victoria Pay concealed her pregnancy and the existence of the baby once it was born. She gave birth in the staff lavatory at the hotel where she lived and worked, put the baby in a dustbin liner and threw it in a nearby lake where it died. The judge told her: "[i]t's clear that you were not at that time entirely responsible for what you did", and ordered that she undergo twelve months psychiatric treatment. The fact that two years earlier she had given birth in the lavatory at her mother's home, the baby being later adopted, and the previous year had had an abortion, suggest that her responsibility for her actions cannot be considered in isolation from a lack of sex education and an inability to cope with motherhood at that point in her life.

Katherine O'Donovan argues that presenting the infanticidal mother as pathologically deviant enables her to be treated sympathetically by the courts without forcing the law to acknowledge that social and economic circumstances may be influential in prompting this crime.

K. O'DONOVAN
"The Medicalisation of Infanticide"[19]

"From its inception as a sex-specific crime in 1623 infanticide has been concerned with theories about women. The initial object of the law was to punish single women for becoming pregnant and for refusing to live with their sin. Thus the crime was created to affect moral and social behaviour. In the nineteenth century the discourse changed. Symptoms of temporary madness were discerned including catatonia, hallucinations, delirium and depression. These were labelled lactational insanity, puerperal psychosis, or exhaustion psychosis. In the twentieth century, in order to mitigate the severity of the crime this discourse was utilised by the law. It is only in the past 20 years that

---

[18] *The Independent*, October 15, 1992 (unrep.).
[19] K. O'Donovan, *supra*, n. 99 at 264.

explanations for infanticide related to the mother's social and economic environment have been resurrected.

Proposals for reform have vacillated between the two models of the crime. It is not hard to understand why. To admit that social and economic circumstances, or motherhood, may cause crime is to open a hitherto tightly closed box. To deny recognition of infanticide as a separate, lesser crime is to invite juries to refuse to convict for murder. So the solution has been to fudge the issue by retaining discredited medical theory."

The medical basis of infanticide is no longer accepted, such that mental illness may not be a major cause of infanticide (which is not to deny that it may be the explanation, or a contributing factor, in some cases). Of more relevance than medical explanations may be the social pressures consequent upon the arrival of a new child, including financial demands, unsuitable housing, the effects on existing family relationships, a lack of support and isolation (all of which arise in the context of the attainment of society's idealised goal of motherhood).

The infanticide provisions follow the path of describing female deviancy as pathological. Labelling the woman who kills her new-born child as abnormal enables her conduct to be explained as the result of hormonal changes occurring within her body after childbirth:

A. WILCZYNSKI & A. MORRIS
"Parents who kill their Children"[20]

"[I]t may be that women who kill their children, far from being penalised for breaches of traditional expectations, benefit from them. Women are assumed to be inherently passive, gentle, and tolerant; and mothers are assumed to be nurturing, caring and altruistic. It is an easy step, therefore, to assume that a 'normal' woman could surely not have acted in such a way. She must have been 'mad' to kill her own child."

However, as a consequence there is no acknowledgement of the need to address the social circumstances in which women kill their new-born children. Furthermore, all women, because of the explanation of the behaviour of infanticidal women as the result of hormonal changes occurring after childbirth, are potentially disordered in this fashion. All women have potentially offensive bodies.

[20] A. Wilczynski & A. Morris, *supra*, n. 1 at 35–36.

CHAPTER 12

FEMALE PROSTITUTES

This chapter looks at the criminalisation of female prostitutes, that is those women who make use of their bodies in order to earn money. Like the woman who kills, the prostitute offends against expectations of Woman: "female prostitutes — breaking out of the passive role traditionally allocated to women in sexual matters — may be seen as deviant."[1] We examine the offences which the female prostitute and those who come into contact with her may commit. The context for this consideration is the meanings attributed to, and the legal constructions placed upon, the body and behaviour of the prostitute. The material covered draws together some of the key themes encountered throughout this book: the issue of conduct in the public and private spheres, the liaison between sex and (sexual) violence and the extent of female autonomy.

12.1 Historical feminist perspectives

Prostitution is not a recent phenomenon.[2] Nor have feminists been united in their assessment of the problems which prostitution raises and the solutions to these problems. Some early feminists such as Josephine Butler (together with her Ladies National Association) organised their campaign around demands for the repeal of the Contagious Diseases Acts (1864, 1866, and 1869). These Acts allowed plain-clothes policemen in military towns to identify a woman as a "common prostitute". The woman could then be forcibly examined for venereal disease and, where this was found, confined to a lock hospital. Men were not subjected to similar treatment. The Contagious Diseases Acts involved the surveillance of women engaged in prostitution to ensure that the demand for women to provide sexual services would be met by women who would not "contaminate" their clients. In the following

---

[1]   C. Docherty, "Female Offenders" in S. McLean & N. Burrows (eds), *The Legal Relevance of Gender: Some Aspects of Sex-Based Discrimination*, (London: Macmillan Press, 1988) p. 181.
[2]   C. Pateman, in *The Sexual Contract* (Cambridge: Polity Press, 1988), p. 195, argues that prostitution has been taken to include disparate activities such as "temple prostitution in ancient Babylonia, the sale of their bodies by destitute women for food for themselves and their children, 'white slavery', the provision of field brothels for troops, the proffering of women to white explorers, *maisons d'abattages* or *malaya* prostitution in Nairobi". These may, however, have little to do with the form of prostitution which has developed in Western countries since the turn of the nineteenth century.

extract Linda Mahood explains in more detail the provisions and implications of the legislation:

L. MAHOOD
The Magdalenes: Prostitution in the nineteenth-century[3]

"The Contagious Diseases (Women) Act was given Royal Assent by 21 July 1864. It was intended to be an 'exceptional' piece of legislation designed for the military and navy in an effort to increase the efficiency of the armed forces by decreasing the cost of treating venereal diseases among the bachelor troops. In other words, the Act, which was enforced in Portsmouth, Plymouth, Woolwich, Chatham, Sheerness, Aldershot, Colchester, Shorncliffe, the Curragh, Cork, and Queenstown, was a special piece of legislation which provided for the registration or licencing of 'prostitutes' in these districts.

A special branch of the Metropolitan Police, entirely outside the jurisdiction of the local authorities and answerable only to the Admiralty and War Offices was established. Special plain-clothes constables were stationed in subjected districts and assigned the task of identifying the women and forcing their submission to a medical examination. The Act also provided for the establishment of state-run lock hospitals for the treatment of women with venereal disease. No provision was made for infected men, or their wives and families. The Act was directed only at the women, who were charged as 'common prostitutes'. This term, however, was never properly defined. Consequently the authorities had broad discretionary powers. According to the Act, any woman could be charged with prostitution upon the testimony of a police inspector, superintendent, or medical examiner before a magistrate. At the trial the burden was on the woman to prove that she was not a 'prostitute'. If a woman failed to prove her 'virtue' she was forced to undergo a vaginal examination by an army surgeon. If she was found to be infected, she was sentenced to three months detention and treatment in a lock hospital. Failure to comply with the conditions of the Act meant imprisonment for one month for the first offence and two months for every subsequent offence. The initial suggestion that the examination of enlisted men be included under the Act in order to discourage soliciting by both sexes was quickly ruled out because the Act was based on the premise that women and not men were responsible for the spread of disease and that while men would be degraded if subjected to genital examination, the women who satisfied male sexual urges were already so degraded that further indignities scarcely mattered. Protection for men was supposed to be assured by the inspection of women. Hence, by not imposing periodic inspection upon male clientele, the architects of the Act obliterated from the start whatever effectiveness they might have had as a sanitary measure.

The first C.D. Act passed through Parliament without debate at any reading in either House. Although originally intended to be restricted to the policing of 'prostitutes' in sixteen garrison towns and naval ports, a campaign for its extension quickly arose and the Act was amended in 1866. The amended Act, which included the town of Windsor, was a more comprehensive version of the first. Under the amended Act, known 'prostitutes' were forced to undergo an examination every three months, again on the evidence of one appointed official before a magistrate. Suspected women within a ten mile

---

[3]   (London: Routledge, 1990), pp. 138–141.

radius of the protected area could avoid a court appearance if they agreed to submit to a medical examination every three months. This draft of the Act proved equally ineffective because many women avoided the police simply by moving out of the area and commuting to town each night. The Act was amended for the final time in 1869 when a report by the Association for the Extension of the C.D. Acts revealed that the legislation was not succeeding. The resulting and most thorough piece of legislation extended the Act to six more towns: Canterbury, Dover, Gravesend, Maidstone, Winchester, and Southampton, making eighteen in all. The protected area was extended to a fifteen-mile radius of the towns, thus making commuting expensive and inconvenient. Other loop-holes were avoided by a clause which provided for a five-day compulsory incarceration of women before their examination, without trial or provision for release by habeas corpus.

The membership of the Association for Promoting the Extension of the C.D. Acts can be divided into three groups from the higher social strata: the military, the medical profession, and the civilian élite, including aristocrats, politicians, and intellectuals. The military had initiated the legislation to decrease the cost of treating diseased soldiers on the grounds that this would further the military interests of the nation by increasing the efficiency of the troops. Consequently, the military did not push for extension as long as the Acts continued to be enforced in the garrison towns. Therefore, it was really the medical profession and the civilian élite who were responsible for the C.D. Acts' change from a limited sanitary measure to a far-reaching piece of social legislation.

The members of the medical profession who supported the Acts did so largely in the name of science. This reflects the implementation of the belief that strict scientific laws of social improvement were discoverable and applicable to the masses ... Although the C.D. Acts split the medical profession into two opposing camps, physicians like Acton, who supported them, argued on medical grounds that just as the state made provision for controlling other contagious diseases, it should also endeavour to control syphilis and other venereal diseases. Sanitary arguments like this were complemented by the civilian élite who had the power and political clout to get the Acts passed and extended. The civilian push for extension, however, was just as ideological as the military and medical spheres. For many 'regulationists', as these groups were called, the C.D. Acts were another phase of progressive legislation in Victorian public-health policy which reflected the new interventionist approach to social problems. The mid-century sanitary movement perceived public order as synonymous with public health. The registration of 'prostitutes', however, was seen as more than just a vehicle for controlling venereal disease; it was also a system for controlling prostitution and a means of containing street disorder and intervening in the lives of the 'unrespectable' poor. Finally, for those who supported the Acts because of the double standard, prostitution was regarded as an inevitable and necessary consequence of social life. The Acts were seen as central to the maintenance of the chastity and virginity of higher-class females. They therefore defended sexual access to working-class women as a 'time-honoured prerogative of gentlemen'."

It was certainly not the case, however, that all women viewed the Contagious Diseases Acts as pernicious in their effect upon women and their construction of female sexuality. Indeed, in campaigning for an end to the Acts,[4] Josephine

---

[4] The Acts were suspended in 1883 and repealed in 1886.

Butler was required to remove herself from other aspects of the women's movement at that time. Other feminists did not regard prostitution as a feminist cause and thought any association with prostitutes may damage the credibility of their own movement.[5]

C. SMART & J. BROPHY
"Locating law: a discussion of the place of law in feminist politics"[6]

"The early feminist involvement with what we would now call the politics of sexuality and reproduction raised questions and dilemmas that are still not resolved. Perhaps the most difficult area then was prostitution because it appeared to be the very antithesis of female sexuality. During the nineteenth century many feminists held the view that women were superior to men with regard to sexual morality. It was therefore extremely difficult for those feminists to embrace a campaign such as that launched by Josephine Butler and the Ladies National Association (LNA), which actually supported and sided with women who were commonly regarded as lax in moral standards. Moreover, Butler's campaign was a radical one. The LNA was fundamentally a separatist organisation which promoted women's political autonomy, although it did make useful strategic alliances with working-class men to further its cause. In addition, the LNA refused on occasion to follow the constitutional line. For example, it declined to give evidence to the Royal Commission of 1871 which had been charged with investigating the operation of the Contagious Diseases Acts. This was because Butler maintained that it was not the LNA's job to make the Acts work more efficiently, but to work to abolish them.

A further reason why the campaign against the Contagious Diseases Acts was unpopular amongst other feminists (*e.g.* Millicent Fawcett) was because it attracted a great deal of notoriety. Campaigns over education and the Married Women's Property Acts may have provoked ridicule or disdain, but in the 1870s Josephine Butler provoked outrage and even violence. Her campaign was a double one: it was against repressive legislation, but also against a repressive cultural norm which would not allow women to be critical of the sexual division of labour. Defending prostitutes against unremitting exploitation (by men) and harassment (by the state) was a real threat to Victorian patriarchy. In fact, merely to talk of sexual acts in public was akin to heresy for a woman."[7]

---

[5]   C. Smart & J. Brophy, "Locating law: a discussion of the place of law in feminist politics" in C. Smart & J. Brophy (eds), *Women in Law: Explorations in Law, Family and Sexuality* (London, Routledge & Kegan Paul, 1985), p. 5. For further discussion of Butler's campaign see L. Bland, "Feminist vigilantes of late-Victorian England" in C. Smart (ed.), *Regulating Womanhood: Historical Essays on Marriage, Motherhood and Sexuality* (London: Routledge, 1992), pp. 35–38. In Chap. 5.1, the same attitudes are discussed in relation to the provision of contraception such that the association of contraception with prostitution and, hence, promiscuity and disintegration of the nuclear family, had to be overcome before contraception was supplied by the State.

[6]   In C. Smart & J. Brophy (eds), *ibid.* pp. 13–14.

[7]   The double standards of Victorian sexuality in which the public front of high moral standards (for the wives of middle and upper-class men) hid male access to the services of prostitutes, was also reflected in the attitudes towards women alleging rape. As Carol Smart explains, "the mere fact that a woman could talk of rape disqualified her as the sort of woman who deserved to be protected by a law against rape" (C. Smart, "Law's Truth/women's experience" in R. Graycar

The view of female sexuality which underpinned the Contagious Diseases Acts did not, however, disappear at the end of the nineteenth century following their repeal. A similar perspective was very much evident in the policing of female prostitutes during the First World War. Given the context of war, and the fervent desire to defend the realm, prostitutes were seen as posing a threat to national security and to the health of the nation. Such a view is permeated with unhelpful representations of female sexuality, both that of the traditional prostitute and that of the new breed of war-time harpy:

L. BLAND
"In the name of protection: the policing of women in the First World War"[8]

"War had barely started yet already there were moves to introduce oppressive restrictions on women — In the name of 'protection' of 'our' troops. From numerous sources came claims that multitudes of young women were *infesting* military camps, *preying* upon soldiers, *spreading* nasty diseases. Infesting, preying, haunting harpies became the war's stock terms for young women who visited the military camps stationed in their neighbourhood. The 'amateur prostitute', or simply 'amateur', was the other key term. Such a woman was not, however, a prostitute at all. The term seems to have reflected a difficulty with understanding the possibility of active female sexuality outside the institution of prostitution. Yet it was precisely her distinction *from* the professional prostitute which was of such concern. She appeared to be much younger than the professional and to seek and 'give' sex 'for free'. Unlike the professional (assumed to be working class), she was thought to be drawn from all social classes, and of greatest concern, she was believed to be the key transmitter of venereal disease . . . Indeed the very *definition* of VD in many texts, including medical texts, put the blame for the disease squarely on women. VD was 'the contagious disease that men are apt to catch by dealing with infected women' . . ."

Thus, while providing 'comfort' to the troops, female prostitutes were also viewed as undermining the health of the military and the nation. This provided justification enough for restricting their rights.[9] Lucy Bland cites an example of the measures taken against female prostitutes in order to protect the military from sexually transmitted disease, while not restricting men's rights:

(ed.), *Dissenting Opinions: Feminist Explorations in Law and Society* (Sydney: Allen & Unwin, 1990), p. 17.

[8] In C. Smart & J. Brophy (eds), *Women in law: Explorations in law, Family and Sexuality* (London: Routledge and Kegan Paul, 1985), p. 28.

[9] This was not only the case in Britain. Across the Channel in France it was held in the case of *Dames Dol et Laurent* (*Conseil d'Etat*, February 28, 1919) that the exceptional circumstances of the First World War were sufficient to justify an interference in the rights to commerce and to free movement of certain "*filles publiques*"' who were prevented from entering and working in bars and soliciting in the area near to the military camp at Toulon (M. Long *et al.*, *Les grands arrêts de la jurisprudence administrative* (Paris: Sirey, 1993), p. 195).

L. Bland
"In the name of protection: the policing of women in the First World War"[10]

"In December 1914 the commanding officer of Cardiff, Colonel East, invoked DORA [the Defence of the Realm Act] and imposed a curfew on women 'of a certain class' between the hours of 7 pm and 8 am. When asked by a deputation of protesting feminists for his justification, he replied that his concern was not immorality, but protection from disease. *Votes for Women* (the paper of the United Suffragists) sarcastically retorted:

> 'It does not seem to have occurred to the military rulers of Cardiff that in protecting the troops from the women they have failed to protect the women from the troops, or that they might have accomplished both ends by closing the streets to soldiers instead of to the prostitutes.'

Almost immediately after the introduction of Easts's order, five women were arrested during the curfew hours and committed by a military court martial to sixty-two days of imprisonment. Possibly in an attempt to deal in some way with the 'amateur', Colonel East also took it upon himself to ban all women from pubs in Cardiff between the hours of 7 pm and 6 am ...

The military had not reckoned on the extent of feminist opposition. On hearing of the Cardiff regulations, Sylvia Pankhurst's East London Federation of Suffragettes (ELFS) immediately organised a deputation to the War Office. The War office denied all responsibility: Cardiff was under martial law and that was apparently explanation enough. The ELFS then wrote in protest to Lord Kitchener, arguing that the orders represented 'a grave infringement to the liberties of women', and that the army's business was to control the troops not the civilians. Further, the ELFS argued, the orders were next to useless in the military's *own* terms since 'To merely lock prostitutes in their homes will not prevent soldiers ... from following them to those homes'."

It was, however, not just *men* who were involved in the policing of prostitution during the First World War. The role of *women* in this task is discussed by Bland, who notes that one reason for the involvement of women police and patrols was as a result of women's campaigns to end the "white slave trade" which was in operation just prior to the outbreak of war and involved the enforced prostitution of girls and women, often entailing their shipment abroad.[11] In addition it was thought that policewomen would be better guardians of morality and have a better preventive moral presence than their male counterparts.[12] Women might also be persuaded into undertaking this activity through their concern to protect other women. Bland explains the consequences as follows:

[10] L. Bland, *supra*, n. 8 at p. 28.
[11] L. Bland, *ibid.*, p. 24.
[12] L. Bland, *ibid.*

L. BLAND
"In the name of protection: the policing of women in the First World War"[13]

"To employ women to dissuade other women from promiscuous behaviour with soldiers and sailors in many ways appeared a most attractive and efficient way of dealing with the 'amateur', and thus also, so it was believed, with the VD problem. While women police and patrols thought of themselves as protecting *women* sexually and morally, they were viewed by the authorities as an ideal means of protecting *men:* men's physical protection from VD through the 'protection'/control of women."

As will become apparent below, this formulation of the "problem" of prostitution in terms of a concern to protect moral welfare and to secure the interests of men (in obtaining access to the sexual services of women) while paying small heed to those of prostitute women, has changed little to the present day.

12.2 Prostitution and criminal offences

The Wolfenden Report[14] which considered prostitution and homosexuality has been highly influential in the formulation of the law on prostitution in its present guise. The view expressed in the Report in relation to both issues was one of distinguishing issues of private morality, which were not the law's business, from matters of public concern. As far as prostitution is concerned this translates into a desire to keep prostitution off the streets and out of public view without regard for prostitute women themselves and the difficulties they may face. At the same time, the law is constructed primarily in terms of criminalising the activity of female prostitutes, rather than their male clients.

12.2.i *The female offender and her offensive sexual body*
The most usual offence with which a woman who engages in prostitution may be charged is that of soliciting contrary to section 1(1) of the Street Offences Act 1959.[15] Section 1(1) provides that "[i]t shall be an offence for a common prostitute to loiter or solicit in a street or public place for the purpose of prostitution." The nature of this offence raises several questions, primarily that of defining a "common prostitute".

12.2.i.a Who is a "common prostitute"? A woman may be labelled a "common prostitute" after having been cautioned twice for loitering or solicit-

---

[13] L. Bland, *ibid.*, p. 31.
[14] Wolfenden Report, *Homosexual Offences and Prostitution* Cmnd. 247 (1957), (London: HMSO).
[15] In 1994, 7,039 women were prosecuted under section 1(1) of the 1959 Act (*Criminal Statistics England and Wales, Supplementary Tables,* Vol. 1, Cm. 3012 (1994), (London: HMSO). A woman may also be charged with brothel-keeping (Sexual Offences Act 1956, s. 33) or with being "a common prostitute behaving in a riotous manner in a public place" (Vagrancy Act 1824, ss. 3 & 4).

ing and being found to be doing so on a third occasion. The term "common prostitute" is, by law, only applicable to women. The sex-specific construction of the label was upheld in *D.P.P. v Bull*.[16] In this case the respondent, a *male* prostitute, was charged under section 1(1) of the Street Offences Act 1959. The magistrates' court dismissed the case on the basis that there was no case to answer, given that section 1(1) applied only to female prostitutes. The D.P.P. appealed by way of case stated:

D.P.P. v. Bull
[1994] 4 All E.R. 411 at 413, 414–416, *per* Mann L.J.

"There is before the court an appeal by way of case stated. The appellant is the Director of Public Prosecutions and the respondent is Andrew John Bull. The case has been stated by Mr Ian Michael Baker, Metropolitan Stipendiary Magistrate for the Inner London Commission Area, in respect of his adjudication as a magistrates' court sitting at Wells Street Magistrates' Court, London W1, on 27 April, 1993. On that day Mr Baker had before him a charge against the respondent to the effect that on 4 December, 1992 he, being a common prostitute, did loiter in a street or public place for the purpose of prostitution contrary to s. 1(1) of the Street Offences Act 1959. At the conclusion of the prosecution case, counsel for the respondent submitted that there was no case to answer on the basis that s. 1(1) applies only to female prostitutes. This submission was upheld by the magistrate, who has now posed this question for the opinion of the court:

'Whether I was correct in construing s. 1(1) of the Street Offences Act 1959, so as to limit it to the activities of female prostitutes and to exclude from its scope the activities of male prostitutes.' . . .

The submission for the appellant was that s. 1(1) of the 1959 Act is unambiguous and is not gender specific. Our attention was drawn to the following six factors which were relied upon. (i) The phrase in s. 1(1) 'a common prostitute' was linguistically capable of including a male person. The *Oxford English Dictionary* (2nd edn, 1989), vol XII, p 637 includes within the possibilities for 'prostitute', 'a man who undertakes male homosexual acts for payment'. (ii) Lord Taylor C.J. has recently said in *R. v. McFarlane* [1994] 2 All E.R. 283 at 288; [1994] Q.B. 419 at 424.

'. . . both the dictionary definitions and the cases show that the crucial feature in defining prostitution is the making of an offer of sexual services for reward.'

I do not regard this factor as of significance. Lord Taylor C.J. was speaking in a case which concerned a woman who had been clipping. (iii) Section 1(2) and (3) of the 1959 Act refer respectively to 'a person' and 'anyone'. (iv) In contrast s. 2(1) refers specifically to 'a woman'. The reason for this is conjectured by Mr Carter-Manning to be that until the Sexual Offences Act 1967 homosexual acts between men were crim-

---

[16] *D.P.P. v. Bull* [1994] 4 All E.R. 411.

inal offences and thus cautioning was inappropriate. (v) Since 1967 male prostitution has been in certain circumstances not unlawful and accordingly in the new environment it is open to the court to interpret s. 1(1) of the 1959 Act as being applicable to prostitutes who are male, 'even if this was not the original intent of the provision'. This in my opinion is a bold submission. It was based upon observations by Lord Bridge of Harwich in *Wicks v. Firth (Inspector of Taxes)* [1983] 1 All E.R. 151 at 154; [1983] 2 A.C. 214 at 230, but Lord Bridge was dealing with a situation where an enactment has been *re-enacted* in a new context. (vi) Where Parliament intends to deal with gender specific prostitution it uses specifically the word 'woman', 'girl' or 'her' as in ss. 22, 28, 29, 30 and 31 of the Sexual Offences Act 1956. See also s. 5 of the Sexual Offences Act 1967 as regards a 'woman' living on male prostitution.

It is to be observed, for completeness, that Mr Carter-Manning recognised he could obtain no assistance from the gender provisions of s 6 of the Interpretation Act 1978, because the provision that words importing the feminine gender (as does ordinarily the phrase 'common prostitute') include the masculine is inapplicable to enactments such as the 1959 Act (see Sched. 2, Pt. I).

Mr Adrian Fulford who appeared for the respondent submitted that the phrase 'common prostitute' was for many years before 1959 (and is now) regarded as a term of art which had the meaning formulated by Darling J. when delivering the judgment of the Court of Criminal Appeal in *R v. De Munck* [1918] 1 K.B. 635 at 637–638; [1918–19] All E.R. Rep. 499 at 500. He said:

'The Court is of opinion that the term "common prostitute" in the statute is not limited so as to mean only one who permits acts of lewdness with all and sundry, or with such as hire her, when such acts are in the nature of ordinary sexual connection. We are of opinion that prostitution is proved if it be shown that a woman offers her body commonly for lewdness for payment in return.'

The statute referred to was s. 2(2) of the Criminal Law Amendment Act 1885 which however was gender specific for it spoke of 'women or girls'. Although the decision was in that context, I believe there to be great force in Mr Fulford's submission that 'common prostitute' is ordinarily regarded as signifying a woman. The statute was referring to a common law concept. Mr Fulford drew our attention to the only text which appears to deal with the problem. It is Rook and Ward, *Sexual Offences*, para. 8.12, where the authors state:

'The better view is that the offence under section 1(1) may be committed as principal only by a woman.'

However, Mr Fulford's main submission was that the court should avail itself of the report which led to the 1959 Act and of the Parliamentary debate upon the Bill for the Act (see *Pepper (Inspector of Taxes) v. Hart* [1993] 1 All E.R. 42; [1993] A.C. 593). The availability of a report which led to an Act as an aid to interpretation is discussed in Bennion, *Statutory Interpretation* (2nd edn, 1992) p 450. He cites *Fothergill v. Monarch Airlines Ltd* [1980] 2 All E.R. 696 at 706; [1981] A.C. 251 at 281, where Lord Diplock said:

'Where the Act has been preceded by a report of some official commission or committee that has been laid before Parliament and the legislation is introduced in consequence of that report, the report itself may be looked at by the court for the limited purpose of identifying the "mischief" that the Act was intended to remedy, and for such assistance as is derivable from this knowledge in giving the right purposive construction to the Act.'

Section 1(1) of the Act was a result of a recommendation in the *Report of the Committee on Homosexual Offences and Prostitution* (Cmnd. 247) (the Wolfenden Committee) para. 256. The relevant chapters of the report are chs VIII and IX and a perusal of them leaves me in no doubt that the committee was concerned only with the female prostitute. Thus, and for example:

> '223. It would have taken us beyond our terms of reference to investigate in detail the prevalence of prostitution or the reasons which lead women to adopt this manner of life . . .
>
> 261. . . . The problem of the prostitute is, in terms of numbers, far greater than that of the male importuner and, for that matter, far more of a public nuisance. In any event, we think it would be too easy to evade the formula by a game of 'general post' in which an individual prostitute would not loiter in a particular place though the number of prostitutes in that place at a given time might be constant.
>
> 262. Our second difficulty related to the criteria which would enable the police to infer that a person was loitering 'for the purposes of prostitution.' We have in mind the possibility that any woman might, from ignorance or indiscretion, put herself in a position in which she might said to be loitering, and by conduct which was quite innocent give rise to a suspicion in the mind of an observant policeman that she was loitering for the purposes of prostitution.'

It is plain that the 'mischief' that the Act was intended to remedy was a mischief created by women.

The assistance which I derive from the report confirms my strong impression that notwithstanding the use of 'a person' and 'anyone' in sub ss. (2) and (3), s. 1(1) of the 1959 Act is confined to women. The term 'common prostitute' is ordinarily regarded as applying to a woman and, importantly, it seems improbable that Parliament intended to create a new male offence which was but subtly different from the extant s. 32 of the Sexual Offences Act 1956. Accordingly, I would dismiss this appeal and answer the magistrate's question in the affirmative."

The actual activities which constitute the role of the "common prostitute" are discussed in the cases of *R. v. de Munck*[17] (referred to in the extract from *D.P.P. v. Bull*, above), *R. v. Webb*[18] and *R. v. McFarlane*.[19]

In *R. v. de Munck* the appellant was charged *inter alia* with attempting to procure her fourteen year-old daughter to become a common prostitute contrary to section 2(2) of the Criminal Law Amendment Act 1885. Medical evidence given at the date of the trial showed that the girl was *virgo intacta*.

[17]   *R. v. de Munck* [1918] 1 K.B. 635.
[18]   *R. v. Webb* [1964] 1 Q.B. 357.
[19]   *R. v. McFarlane* [1994] 2 All E.R. 283.

The jury was directed by the learned commissioner who tried the case that the term "prostitute" was not necessarily confined to a woman who for gain offered her body for natural sexual intercourse, and that a finding of guilt would be justified where the jury concluded that de Munck had procured her daughter to offer her body for gain for the gratification of the sexual passions of any man by any unnatural and abnormal act of indecency. The jury convicted.

The judgment of the Court was delivered by Darling J.:

R. v. de Munck
[1918] 1 K.B. 635 at 637–638, *per* Darling J.

"In this case the appellant was convicted under an indictment containing twelve counts framed under three different Acts of Parliament, but the only question which the Court has to determine is whether that which the appellant did, or attempted to procure her daughter to do, amounts to procuring or attempting to procure her daughter to become a common prostitute. The evidence shows that during a period of some months the appellant permitted her daughter to bring men to the appellant's house and to be in private with them in circumstances which would lead to the inference that she had repeatedly had sexual intercourse with them; but it was conclusively proved that the girl was virgo intacta in the limited sense that she had never had ordinary sexual intercourse with any man.

We have to decide what is a prostitute or what is prostitution. The argument advanced on behalf of the appellant practically was that the offering by a woman of her body for the gratification of the sexual passions of men, even if it is done as a regular trade, indiscriminately and for gain, is not prostitution unless the men's passions are gratified by the act of sexual connection and not otherwise. We have come to the conclusion that that contention is not well founded. It was advanced before the learned commissioner at the Central Criminal Court and he laid down the law practically as we are now going to lay it down, and we, therefore, uphold his decision. The Court is of opinion that the term 'common prostitute' in the statute is not limited so as to mean only one who permits acts of lewdness with all and sundry, or with such as hire her, when such acts are in the nature of ordinary sexual connection. We are of opinion that prostitution is proved if it be shown that a woman offers her body commonly for lewdness for payment in return. There was ample evidence that this girl did that, and that the appellant knew what she was doing and procured her for this particular conduct.

The appeal will therefore be dismissed."

In *R. v. Webb* the defendant sought to draw a distinction between "active" and "passive" acts of intercourse (such as masturbation) suggesting that the latter were not sufficient as to amount to an act of common prostitution.

R. v. Webb
[1964] 1 Q.B. 357 at 363–364, *per* Lord Parker C.J.

"The defendant was convicted at the Central Criminal Court on four counts of an indictment. The first two counts charged him with attempting to procure a woman to become a common prostitute, the third count with procuring a woman to become a common prostitute, and the fourth with living on the earnings of prostitution. The defendant was sentenced in all to two years' imprisonment and he now appeals against his conviction only.

The short facts were these. As regards count 1, a girl of 19 answered an advertisement for a female assistant for a masseur which stated 'No previous experience required.' According to her evidence, she was shown how to massage clients who came to the defendant's premises and she complained to him that some of the men had the wrong idea, and that, indeed, one of the men had invited her to masturbate him. According to her, the defendant said: 'If you want to earn tips, you do it. Also you could get them through faster that way.' At any rate, her evidence was that the defendant had conveyed to her that it was part of her job to do this.

Count 2 dealt with the procuring of another young girl, aged 17, and her evidence again was that she understood from the defendant that she was to do what the client asked her to do. Count 3 concerned a third girl of 19 who gave evidence that, on her very first day, another girl had told her, in the defendant's presence, that sometimes men would become physically excited and that it was then her job to masturbate them, and this she had done.

Count 4 dealt with living on the immoral earnings of prostitution. In that connection, evidence was given by the police that, on a number of days, men and girls had been seen on the premises in dubious positions and that a tape recorder and microphone were found connected to one of the rooms where massage was given.

The defence was that, at this establishment, the defendant carried on a legitimate business for providing a relaxing type of massage and that, if any of the girls had done what was suggested, they had done so of their own accord and without any encouragement from him. It is quite clear that the jury felt themselves unable to accept the defendant's evidence and found the case for the prosecution proved. The sole question here is whether these facts, which the jury by their verdict must have found proved, in fact constituted the offences charged. This in turn depends upon the proper meaning to be given to the words 'common prostitute' in the procuring charges and to the word 'prostitution' in the fourth charge dealing with living on immoral earnings.

The judge, in directing the jury on this matter, said: 'Now we come to the term "common prostitute." That is not limited to meaning a woman who commonly permits actual sexual intercourse for money. It has been held by an appeal court that prostitution is proved if it be shown that a woman offers her body commonly for lewdness in return for payment. Now, as far as the facts of this case are concerned, if the girl or woman did in fact masturbate any men who having chanced to see the advertisement came to seek that particular form of sexual gratification and paid for it, that constitutes acting as a common prostitute.' It is that direction which is challenged in this court, and it is said that, on the facts as they must have been found by the jury, there was no prostitution nor any procuring of the girls nor any attempts to procure them to become common prostitutes.

As long ago as 1918, in *R. v. De Munck*, it was sought by counsel for the defendant to confine the meaning of 'prostitute' to a woman who offered her body to men for the gratification of normal sexual appetite, namely, for sexual intercourse. It was stressed that, although the word 'prostitute' was capable of having a wide meaning, yet in a penal statute it should be confined to the meaning of the word as ordinarily understood."

Lord Parker C.J. outlined the facts and judgment of Darling J. in *R. v. de Munck* and continued:

R. v. Webb
[1964] 1 Q.B. 357 at 365–367, *per* Lord Parker C.J.

"The words used by Darling J. . . . . namely, that 'prostitution' means 'the offering by a woman of her body commonly for lewdness for payment' may well have been taken from the dictionary meaning. Indeed, in the Shorter Oxford English Dictionary under 'prostitution,' the first meaning given is: 'The offering of the body to indiscriminate lewdness for hire.' The court in *R. v. De Munck* were clearly treating lewdness in the expression they used as not confined to the gratification of normal sexual appetite.

It appears from cases to which we have been referred that in the United States it has been held that while 'lewdness' may include obscene acts, 'prostitution' is confined to the exposure by a woman of her body for sexual intercourse. So far as this court is concerned, however, we see no reason to depart in any way from the decision of this court in *R. v. De Munck*. While this court does not treat itself as bound by its previous decisions with the same strictness as other courts and would be prepared to depart from a previous decision if they felt it was clearly wrong, the court can see nothing wrong whatever in the decision in *R. v. De Munck*, and, accordingly, will treat themselves as bound by it.

It is, nevertheless, argued by Mr Lincoln, on behalf of the defendant, that even so the definition given by Darling J. should be read as confined to cases where the woman offers her body for lewdness in what one might call a passive way or where she submits to something being done to her; and he contends that the whole conception of a prostitute and prostitution is inapt to embrace active acts of indecency by the woman herself. It must be remembered, of course that the words used by Darling J. are not the words of the Sexual Offences Act, 1956; they are merely his definition for the purposes of that case of circumstances in which prostitution may be said to have been proved. The Sexual Offences Act, 1956 — and we are dealing here with a comparatively recent statute — refers to 'common prostitute' and 'purposes of prostitution' in section 22 and to 'the earnings of prostitution' in section 30. We can see no reason why the meanings of those words should be confined in the way suggested by Mr Lincoln. From a purely practical point of view, it would be artificial, to say the least, to draw a distinction between the case of a woman who takes a passive role and one in which she takes an active role. Indeed, it can be said with some force that some activity on her part is of the very essence of prostitution. It cannot matter whether she whips the man or the man whips her; it cannot matter whether he masturbates himself on her or she masturbates him. In our judgment, the expression used by Darling J., 'a woman offers her body commonly for lewdness,' means no more and was intended to mean no more than 'offers herself,' and it includes, at any rate, such a case as this where a woman offers herself as a participant in physical acts of indecency for the sexual gratification of men.

In these circumstances, this court can see nothing wrong in the direction given by the judge who tried the case and, accordingly, the appeal is dismissed."

Thirdly, the case of *R. v. McFarlane* deals with the distinction between the activities of a "clipper" and a prostitute. The appellant was charged with living on the earnings of prostitution (contrary to the Sexual Offences Act 1956, s.30(1)). He did indeed live with the woman concerned. But it was denied that this woman was in fact a prostitute. Rather, it was contended that she was a "clipper", *i.e.* that she offered sexual favours for reward and took the money without intending to provide the favours. At first instance it was found that the woman was a dishonest prostitute and there was no difference between a prostitute and a clipper. The appellant was convicted. On appeal, Lord Taylor of Gosforth C.J. found as follows:

R. v. McFarlane
[1994] 2 All E.R. 283 at 285–286, *per* Lord Taylor of Gosforth C.J.

"A submission was made to the learned judge that acting as a clipper did not amount to acting as a prostitute. Although at that stage counsel both for the prosecution and the defence supported that view, the learned judge rejected it. When the appeal came on before another constitution of this court, counsel then appearing for the Crown (not counsel who has appeared for the Crown today) again supported the appellant's submission that the learned judge's ruling was wrong. However, the court itself took the view that the matter should be fully argued, saying:

'There was a substantial argument in favour of the view taken by the trial judge.'

It is most convenient therefore to deal first with what the learned judge said both in giving his ruling and in directing the jury. In his ruling he said:

'The question of whether someone offering themselves, but intending — and it has to be intending — firmly never, ever to make good that offer — it has to go that far — it has never, so far as I can see, been adjudicated upon. My view is that the indications in the textbooks — and I have looked at *Blackstone's Criminal Practice* and it is not so obvious, but again it speaks of offering — the dictionary, and decided cases say that as soon as you are offering yourself for lewdness for reward, you are indulging in prostitution and that is how I propose to direct the jury.'

When it came to the summing up, the learned judge said this to the jury:

'She has told you she is not a prostitute, she is a clipper. But, a prostitute is a person who offers her body for lewdness for reward. Put in slightly more "with it" words, such as Sarah Tuckey [that is the sister] used, 'offers sexual services'. I am bound to say that I prefer the directness of the old Anglo-Saxon, but there it is. Miss Josephs said, "Yes, I do offer sexual services, but I do not mean to make that offer good." And she suggests to you that for that reason she is not a prostitute. But, members of the jury, she has made the offer. It is at that point that she is a prostitute. The fact that the offer is bogus, rather than genuine, if it was, is neither here nor there. There are not two categories — a clipper and a prostitute. There are prostitutes who are honest and prostitutes who are dishonest. Miss Josephs tells you that she is a dishonest prostitute. But she is a prostitute, members of the jury.'

The issue on this appeal is whether, as a matter of law, the judge was correct to rule and direct the jury that a woman who offers herself for sexual services, takes the money and fails to provide the services, is engaging in prostitution within the meaning of s. 30 of the Sexual Offences Act 1956. Section 30, so far as is relevant, provides as follows:

'(1) It is an offence for a man knowingly to live wholly or in part on the earnings of prostitution . . .'

Mr Carne for the appellant submits that to be a prostitute a woman must not only offer sexual services, but must provide them, or be prepared to do so. For the Crown, Mr Carter-Manning Q.C. submits the essence of the offence is the offer of the sexual services in return for reward.

The words 'prostitute' and 'prostitution' are not defined in any statute. Our attention was drawn to dictionary definitions and to three decided cases. *The Concise Oxford Dictionary* defines a prostitute as:

'A woman who offers her body to promiscuous sexual intercourse esp. for payment . . .'

The Shorter Oxford English Dictionary defines a prostitute as:

'A woman who is devoted, or (usu.) [who] offers her body to indiscriminate sexual intercourse, esp. for hire; a common harlot . . .'

Mr Carne points to the definition of 'offer' in *The Shorter Oxford English Dictionary*, and to one meaning given there:

'To give, make presentation of . . . To tender for acceptance or refusal . . .'

However, another meaning within the same dictionary is:

'To make the proposal, suggest . . . To propose, or express one's willingness (to do something), conditionally on the assent of the person addressed.' "

Following a résumé of the reasoning in *R. v de Munck* and *R. v Webb*, Lord Taylor continued:

R. v. McFarlane
[1994] 2 All E.R. 283 at 287–288, *per* Lord Taylor of Gosforth C.J.

"The third authority to which we were referred was *R v. Morris Lowe* [1985] 1 All E.R. 400; [1985] 1 W.L.R. 29. There, the issue was whether it was sufficient to constitute a woman a 'common prostitute' if she indulged in sexual activity for reward with one man on one occasion. That is again a totally different issue from that which faces this court. Lord Lane C.J. said ([1985] 1 All E.R. 400 at 402; [1985] 1 W.L.R. 29 at 32):

'A common prostitute is any woman who offers herself commonly for lewdness for reward. This appellant on his own version plainly attempted to persuade the woman in each case to offer herself for lewdness for reward. What about the word 'common' or its adverbial form? Is it a meaningless word which adds nothing to the word 'prostitute', or does it have some effect? That really is the only point in this appeal. It is clear to us that the word is not mere surplusage. We do not pause to consider whether the performance by a woman of a single act of lewdness with a man on one occasion for reward constitutes the woman a prostitute. But we are of the view that it does not make her a woman who offers herself commonly for lewdness. That must be someone who is prepared for reward to engage in acts of lewdness with all and sundry, or with anyone who may hire her for that purpose.'

Again in that passage Mr Carne seeks to pick out one sentence, the final sentence, to support his argument. However, the court did not have in contemplation in that case the instance of a woman making an offer she did not intend to fulfil. To read the last sentence of the passage quoted as support for the appellant's argument here would be in conflict with the first sentence of the passage where Lord Lane C.J. defined 'common prostitute' as 'any woman who offers herself commonly for lewdness for reward'.

In our judgment both the dictionary definitions and the cases show that the crucial feature in defining prostitution is the making of an offer of sexual services for reward. Mr Carne submits that the true offence here was not one of living off immoral earnings, and that the woman in question, Miss Josephs, was not acting by way of prostitution. She was acting dishonestly and she could have been proceeded against, he submits, for obtaining money by false pretences. It may be that the appellant could have been proceeded against for conspiring with her to do so, or for aiding and abetting her. But it is submitted that the offence of living off immoral earnings is not made out. Mr Carne also submits that the mischief against which s. 30 of the Sexual Offences Act 1956 is directed is the exploitation of women. Here, the appellant was not exploiting Miss Josephs sexually, only dishonestly. However, if Mr Carne's argument were right, the mischief aimed at in other statutes requiring proof of prostitution would not be defeated. There have been a number of statutes, from the Vagrancy Act 1824 through the Town Police Clauses Act 1847, up to and including the Street Offences Act 1959, whose object has been to prevent the nuisance of women soliciting and offering sexual favours in public places. If it were a defence to soliciting for prostitution under s. 1 of the 1959 Act that the accused woman was acting as a 'clipper' and not as a 'hooker', proof of such offences would be extremely difficult. It would be necessary to prove not merely the offer of sexual services in a public place, but that the services were actually provided, or were at the time of the offering intended to be provided. The mischief being simply the harassment and nuisance to members of the public on the streets, the distinction between 'clippers' and 'hookers' is immaterial.

We have no doubt that the ruling of the learned judge was both robust and correct (to adopt the phrase used by Mr Carter-Manning in his submission). For a man to live off the earnings of a woman who offers sexual services, takes the money and then reneges on the offer, if she does, is in our view to live off the earnings of prostitution, or, as it used to be termed, immoral earnings. Indeed, most people would consider such earnings doubly immoral. This appeal is dismissed."

A further feature of the offence created under section 1(1) of the Street Offences Act 1959 is that it requires that the act of loitering or soliciting take place in a "street or public place". This requirement is very much in line with the interpretation of the "problem" of prostitution as articulated in the Wolfenden Report and with what Lord Taylor referred to as "[t]he mischief [of prostitution] being ... the harassment and nuisance to members of the public on the streets", in that it is the public touting of the prostitute's body and its potential for creating a public nuisance which are perceived as most damaging. Consequently, there has been a proliferation of "private sphere" prostitution, taking place off the streets. This type of prostitution does, however, depend quite heavily upon advertising in order to attract clients. The obscenity created by such advertisements is clearly spelt out in the decision of the House of Lords in *Shaw v. D.P.P.*[20] in which it was found that the publication of a booklet, "The Ladies Directory", the object of which was to advertise the services of prostitutes (listing names, addresses, telephone numbers, photographs and abbreviations indicating the type of "perverse practices" on offer) amounted to the newly created common law offence of conspiring to corrupt public morals.

Shaw v. D.P.P.
[1961] 2 All E.R. 446 at 451–453, HL, *per* Viscount Simonds

"My Lords, as I have already said, the first count in the indictment is 'Conspiracy to corrupt public morals', and the particulars of offence will have sufficiently appeared. I am concerned only to assert what was vigorously denied by counsel for the appellant, that such an offence is known to the common law and that it was open to the jury to find on the facts of this case that the appellant was guilty of such an offence. I must say categorically that, if it were not so, Her Majesty's courts would strangely have failed in their duty as servants and guardians of the common law. Need I say, my Lords, that I am no advocate of the right of the judges to create new criminal offences? I will repeat well-known words:

> 'Amongst many other points of happiness and freedom which your Majesty's subjects have enjoyed there is none which they have accounted more dear and precious than this, to be guided and governed by certain rules of law which giveth both to the head and members that which of right belongeth to them and not by any arbitrary or uncertain form of government.'

These words are as true today as they were in the seventeenth century and command the allegiance of us all. But I am at a loss to understand how it can be said either that the law does not recognise a conspiracy to corrupt public morals or that, though there may not be an exact precedent for such a conspiracy as this case reveals, it does not fall fairly within the general words by which it is described. I do not propose to examine all the relevant authorities. That will be done by my noble and learned friend. The fallacy in the argument that was addressed to us lay in the attempt to exclude from the scope of general words acts well calculated to corrupt public morals just because they had not been committed or had not been brought to the notice of the court before. It is not thus that the common law has developed. We are, perhaps, more accustomed to

[20] *Shaw* v. *D.P.P.* [1961] 2 All E.R. 446.

hear this matter discussed on the question whether such and such a transaction is contrary to public policy. At once the controversy arises. On the one hand it is said that it is not possible in the twentieth century for the court to create a new head of public policy, on the other it is said that this is but a new example of a well-established head. In the sphere of criminal law, I entertain no doubt that there remains in the courts of law a residual power to enforce the supreme and fundamental purpose of the law, to conserve not only the safety and order but also the moral welfare of the state, and that it is their duty to guard it against attacks which may be the more insidious because they are novel and unprepared for. That is the broad head (call it public policy if you wish) within which the present indictment falls. It matters little what label is given to the offending act. To one of your Lordships it may appear an affront to public decency, to another, considering that it may succeed in its obvious intention of provoking libidinous desires, it will seem a corruption of public morals. Yet others may deem it aptly described as the creation of a public mischief or the undermining of moral conduct. The same act will not in all ages be regarded in the same way. The law must be related to the changing standards of life, not yielding to every shifting impulse of the popular will but having regard to fundamental assessments of human values and the purposes of society. Today a denial of the fundamental Christian doctrine, which in past centuries would have been regarded by the ecclesiastical courts as heresy and by the common law as blasphemy, will no longer be an offence if the decencies of controversy are observed. When Lord Mansfield, speaking long after the Star Chamber had been abolished, said that the Court of King's Bench was the custos morum of the people and had the superintendency of offences contra bonos mores, he was asserting, as I now assert, that there is in that court a residual power, where no statute has yet intervened to supersede the common law, to superintend those offences which are prejudicial to the public welfare. Such occasions will be rare, for Parliament has not been slow to legislate when attention has been sufficiently aroused. But gaps remain and will always remain since no one can foresee every way in which the wickedness of man may disrupt the order of society. Let me take a single instance to which my noble and learned friend, Lord Tucker, refers. Let it be supposed that, at some future, perhaps, early, date homosexual practices between adult consenting males are no longer a crime. Would it not be an offence if, even without obscenity, such practices were publicly advocated and encouraged by pamphlet and advertisement? Or must we wait until Parliament finds time to deal with such conduct? I say, my Lords, that, if the common law is powerless in such an event, then we should no longer do her reverence."

Whether it be through the common law or through statute law, the focus upon the public display of the Prostitute and the sex-specific interpretation of her activity, serve to reinforce sexual stereotypes and conventional wisdom about prostitution. They also enable a distinction to be drawn between the criminality and legal interpretation of the sexual acts of women and those of men. In short, Carol Smart argues that the construction of the offence of soliciting quite clearly constitutes an act of discrimination against women:

"Our current laws on soliciting and loitering (1959 Street Offences Act) is a prime example of straightforward legal sexual discrimination because only women can be defined as common prostitutes and so only women become subject to the particularly repressive regime of regulation that follows from this definition."[21]

12.2.i.b   The prostitute's offensive sexual body. It is not merely the fact that the offence of soliciting can only be perpetrated by women which is a cause for concern. Both Carol Smart and Sheila Duncan analyse the relationship between laws on prostitution and constructions of female sexuality to show that the harmful effects of the law governing prostitution may have more to do with the way in which female sexuality is viewed within the framework of the law than with the simple fact that the Street Offences Act 1959 applies only to women.

Smart argues that the Street Offences Act 1959 identifies:

> "a special class of women as specific 'legal subjects' with fewer rights than other citizens, I would also wish to argue that it is legislation and legal practice informed by specific ideologies of female sexuality which serves to construct prostitute women as mere 'sexual objects'. In turn this sexual objectification of prostitute women reinforces their special status as denigrated legal subjects and helps to preserve legislation which, by most standards, must be regarded as unusually harsh and repressive."[22]

In 1981 Smart conducted a series of interviews with twenty-five randomly selected magistrates (fourteen men and eleven women) in Sheffield. From these interviews she identifies the connection between the Prostitute as female offender and judicial perceptions of female sexuality:

C. SMART
"Legal subjects and sexual objects: ideology, law and female sexuality"[23]

"When discussing women's sexuality it is important to recognise that it is extremely difficult to avoid talking at the same time about marriage, love, the family and children. Although feminist work on sexuality attempts to produce an analysis of it which does not impart ideas on how female sexuality can *only* be fulfilled inside a monogamous, heterosexual, legally sanctioned union, this is the common-sense view of women's sexuality. Women and girls who have sex outside marriage are still regarded as promiscuous or more colloquially as slags and sluts; ... [M]ost discussions of prostitution also invoke the cultural ideals of heterosexual love, monogamous marriage and the sanctity of the family ...

[With regard to the Sheffield magistrates] prostitution was always discussed in a context which idealised marriage or monogamous relationships. Marriage always remained the point of comparison and departure. What the magistrates had to say about female sexuality outside the regulated and authorised boundaries of the legal

---

[21]   C. Smart, "Legal subjects and sexual objects: ideology, law and female sexuality" in C. Smart & J. Brophy (ed), *supra*, n. 5 at 50.

[22]   C. Smart, *ibid.*, at 51.

[23]   C. Smart, *ibid.*, at 52–55.

contract of marriage therefore also spoke volumes about what may constitute 'acceptable' forms of female sexuality. Hence, although magistrates were speaking only about
prostitute women, the content of their statements has ideological significance for all
women. Consider the following statements:

> 'Well I think that detectives in the vice squad are so very familiar with this
> sort of problem that they would never put that sort of a handle on a woman
> who was *anything near decent*' (my emphasis)
>
> 'I think one would be reluctant to send a girl to prison when she had
> children. I'm told by probation officers that *some of them make very good
> mothers.*' (my emphasis)
>
> 'Even though they are *undesirable ladies* they are not bad mothers.' (my
> emphasis)
>
> 'No *decent* man will have anything to do with them afterwards. They can't
> get boy friends.' (my emphasis)

The theme running through these comments, and many more which littered the speech
of almost all the magistrates, is that prostitute women are quite beyond the pale. They
may have some redeeming features but these are cause for remark and, not infrequently, even astonishment that they may still have some 'human qualities'. Yet *all*
prostitute women have done is to offend a sexual taboo. Surprisingly, the magistrates
were not talking about serious criminals but about women who earn a living with
their sexuality. Moreover, the dividing line (allowing for the sake of argument that
such a division exists) between prostitute women and other women is extremely
narrow. It would take very little for any woman to slip beyond the pale into the almost
non-human species referred to by the magistrates. It may simply hang on a police*man*'s
ability to distinguish between the category of 'indecent' women and '*near decent*'
women or, equally, some probation officer's remarks on the capacity for child care.
So when magistrates (or indeed any persons) speak so disparagingly of prostitute
women, their remarks are, in some form, meant for all women. Either they constitute
a coded warning (to remain decent, monogamous or married) or they reflect a simple
misogyny which does not in any case distinguish between women."

Smart used the information gained from her interviews with the Sheffield
magistrates to identify three predominant discourses on prostitution and
female sexuality. These correspond to three separate ways of viewing the
"problem" of prostitution:

C. SMART
"Legal subjects and sexual objects: ideology, law and female sexuality"[24]

"These discourses I have identified as liberal/permissive (the largest category), puritan/
authoritarian (the second largest) and welfarist . . .

a) *The liberal/permissive discourse*
This discourse was probably most clearly articulated in the Wolfenden Report (1957)

---

[24] C. Smart, *ibid.*, at 55–60.

which argued that what consenting adults did in private should not be the concern of the criminal law. The magistrates who adopted this view also felt that what adults did in private was their affair and, like Wolfenden, argued that prostitution was only a matter for the criminal law when it became visible on the streets. The solution, they tended to argue, was a pragmatic recognition of the need for licensed brothels where people could get on with it without causing a nuisance . . .

b) The puritan/authoritarian discourse

This category of magistrates were concerned to control not just prostitution but also prostitutes; the tended to be in favour of imprisoning women, felt the police 'did a good job' and saw no reason to reform the laws on soliciting. They were the group which displayed most overt hostility towards prostitute women, . . .

The puritan/authoritarian discourse relied significantly upon three main axes: a Christian morality which sees prostitution as immoral and undermining of the value of family and social life; a puritan ethic which condemns prostitution because it is assumed (mistakenly) to be a way of making easy money without really working for it; and an exaggerated concern over disease . . .

c) The welfarist discourse

The third discourse articulated by the magistrates is based on vague psychoanalytic theories of child development which are much influenced by a melange of welfare concerns and a good deal of 'common sense'. This constituted the smallest category and was made up almost exclusively of women magistrates. Basically this position held or presumed that there was something psychologically amiss with prostitute women and this was frequently explained in terms of childhood development. Prostitution was not usually seen as resulting directly from economic need or greed as with the two previous categories. Rather it was perceived of as the result of some unresolved personality problem . . .

[Smart concludes]

Although it was only within the puritan/authoritarian discourse that prostitutes were constituted as completely undesirable and as social parasites, all the magistrates, even those with a welfare orientation, located prostitutes in a distinct social category which was at some distance to 'normal' or 'respectable' people. The magistrates continually referred to *these* people or *these* women thus constructing a special category of persons . . . This legal category in turn lends some rigidity to the conventional wisdom on prostitutes and permits the development of further methods and measures which can be justified because they deal exclusively with this legally and common-sensically identified group of errant women. In other words, the magistrates' views on prostitute women are legitimated and sustained by the legislation which is in turn deeply rooted in a conventional (misogynist) morality."

Sheila Duncan analyses the relationship between law, sexuality and the construction of the "Female Other" in the laws of rape, incest and prostitution.[25]

---

[25] S. Duncan, " 'Disrupting the Surface of Order and Innocence': Towards a Theory of Sexuality and the Law" (1994) 2 *Feminist Legal Studies* 3. See Chap. 3 above for location of this article in a theoretical context.

Duncan argues that, while in the two examples of rape and incest the woman takes the "dubious cover" of the label of victim, she does not even have this in relation to prostitution. Instead she is perpetrator.[26] Yet, even, as perpetrator she is still viewed as external to law's domain:

S. DUNCAN
" 'Disrupting the Surface of Order and Innocence': Towards a Theory of Sexuality and the Law"[27]

"The defining characteristic of the prostitute's construction is exclusion. Prostitution per se is not illegal but the law creates potential offences in respect of every aspect of the Prostitute's life. What is particular to this exclusion is that it is not so much her truth and her individuality which is undermined by the law — although they certainly are — but that the bulk of the offences create her exclusion by raising the spectre of an offence for almost everyone who comes into contact with her and upon whom she depends for her survival. She is, therefore, constructed as pariah — a legal leper who may infect all she meets."

Sheila Duncan argues that through the label of "common prostitute":

'the dominant male discourse, constructs the Prostitute as separate from other women as object beneath contempt, undermining even her basic civil right to pass and re-pass on the highway and ensuring that any legal protection she may seek from violence towards her will be undermined by the Court's awareness of her status as common prostitute.'[28]

The American academic Mary Joe Frug offers a not dissimilar picture of the construction of the female body by laws governing prostitution. Frug argues first that "legal rules — like other cultural mechanisms — encode the female body with meanings".[29] She then gives prostitution as her prime example of this, arguing that the law operates as a form of "terrorization", "sexualization" and "maternalization" of women.

M. J. FRUG
"A Postmodern Feminist Legal Manifesto (An Unfinished Draft)"[30]

"Since most anti-prostitution rules are gender neutral, let me explain, before going any further, how I can argue that they have a particular impact on the meaning of the

---

[26] S. Duncan, *ibid.*, at 22.
[27] S. Duncan, *ibid.*, at 22.
[28] S. Duncan, *ibid.*, at 23.
[29] M. J. Frug, "A Postmodern Feminist Legal Manifesto (An Unfinished Draft)" (1992) 105 *Harvard Law Review* 1045 at 1049. For consideration of the theoretical perspectives raised in this article see Chap. 3 above.
[30] M.J. Frug, *ibid.*, at 1052–1056.

female body. Like other rules regulating sexual conduct, anti-prostitution rules sexualize male as well as female bodies; they indicate that sex — unlike, say, laughing, sneezing, or making eye contact — is legally regulated. Regardless of whether one is male or female, the pleasures and the virtue of sex are produced, at least in part, by legal rules. The gendered lopsidedness of this meaning system — which I describe below — occurs, quite simply, because most sex workers are women. Thus, even though anti-prostitution rules could, in theory, generate parallel meanings for male and female bodies, in practice they just don't. At least they don't right now.

The legal definition of prostitution as the unlawful sale of sex occurs in statutes that criminalize specific commercial sex practices and in decisional law, such as contract cases that hold that agreements for the sale of sexual services are legally unenforceable. By characterizing certain sexual practices as illegal, these rules sexualize the female body. They invite a sexual interrogation of every female body: is it for or against prostitution?

This sexualization of the female body explains an experience many women have: an insistent concern that this outfit, this pose, this gesture may send the wrong signal — a fear of looking like a whore. Sexy talking, sexy walking, sexy dressing seem sexy, at least in part, because they are the telltale signs of a sex worker plying her trade. This sexualization also explains the shadow many women feel when having sex for unromantic reasons — to comfort themselves, to avoid a confrontation over some domestic issue, or to secure a favor — a fear of acting like a whore.

This reading of the relationship between prostitution rules and the female body is aligned with but somewhat different from the radical feminist description of the relationship between prostitution and female subjectivity. Catharine MacKinnon's 1982 *Signs* piece describes the relationship this way:

> [Feminist] investigations reveal . . . [that] prostitution [is] not primarily [an] abuse[] of physical force, violence, authority, or economics. [It is an] abuse[] of sex. [It] need not and do[es] not rely for [its] coerciveness upon forms of enforcement other than the sexual. . . .
>
>   . . .
>   . . . If women are socially defined such that female sexuality cannot be lived or spoken or felt or even somatically sensed apart from its enforced definition, so that it *is* its own lack, then there is no such thing as a woman as such, there are only walking embodiments of men's projected needs.'

MacKinnon's description of the impact of prostitution on women suggests that the sexual experience of all women may be, like sex work, the experience of having sex solely at the command of and for the pleasure of an other. This is a more extreme interpretation of the sexualized female body than mine and not one all women share.

> 'The feminists' point of view? Well, I would like to point out that they're missing a couple of things, because, you know, I may be dressing like the typical bimbo, whatever, but I'm in charge. You know. I'm in charge of my fantasies. I put myself in these situations with men, you know . . . [A]ren't I in charge of my life?' [Interview with Madonna (ABC Television Broadcast, December 3, 1990)].

Although I believe Madonna's claim about herself, there are probably a number of people who don't. Anyone who looks as much like a sex worker as she does couldn't possibly be in charge of herself, they are likely to say; she is an example of exactly what MacKinnon means by a 'walking embodiment[] of men's projected needs.' Without going further into the cottage industry of Madonna interpretation, it seems indisputable that Madonna's version of the female sexualized body is radically more autonomous and self-serving than MacKinnon's interpretation, and significantly less troubled and doubled than mine.

Because sex differences are semiotic — because the female body is produced and interpreted through a system of signs — all three of these interpretations of the sexualized female body may be accurate. The truth of any particular meaning would depend on the circumstances in which it was asserted. Thus, the sexualized female body that is produced and sustained by the legal regulation of prostitution may have multiple meanings. Moreover, the meaning of the sexualized female body for an individual woman is also affected by other feminine images that the legal regulation of prostitution produces.

Anti-prostitution rules terrorize the female body. The regulation of prostitution is accomplished not only by rules that expressly repress or prohibit commercialized sex. Prostitution regulation also occurs through a network of cultural practices that endanger sex workers' lives and make their work terrifying. These practices include the random, demeaning, and sometimes brutal character of anti-prostitution law enforcement. They also include the symbiotic relationship between the illegal drug industry and sex work, the use of prostitutes in the production of certain forms of pornography, hotel compliance with sex work, inadequate police protection for crimes against sex workers, and unregulated bias against prostitutes and their children in housing, education, the health care system, and in domestic relations law. Legal rules support and facilitate these practices.

The legal terrorization of prostitutes forces many sex workers to rely on pimps for protection and security, an arrangement which in most cases is also terrorizing. Pimps control when sex workers work, what kind of sex they do for money, and how much they make for doing it; they often use sexual seduction and physical abuse to "manage" the women who work for them. The terrorization of sex workers affects women who are not sex workers by encouraging them to do whatever they can to avoid being asked if they are 'for' illegal sex. Indeed, marriage can function as one of these avoidance mechanisms, in that, conventionally, marriage signals that a woman has chosen legal sex over illegal sex.

One might argue that the terrorized female body is not that much different from the sexualized female body. Both experiences of femininity often — some might say always — entail being dominated by a man. Regardless of whether a woman is terrorized or sexualized, there are social incentives to reduce the hardships of her position, either by marrying or by aligning herself with a pimp. In both cases she typically becomes emotionally, financially, physically, and sexually dependent on and subordinate to a man.

If the terrorized and sexualized female bodies can be conflated and reduced to a dominated female body, then Madonna's claim that she's in charge, like the claims other women make that they experience sexual pleasure or autonomy in their relations with men, is suspect — perhaps, even, the product of false consciousness. But I argue that the dominated female body does not fully capture the impact of antiprostitution rules on women. This is because anti-prostitution rules also maternalize the female body, by virtue of the interrelationship between anti-prostitution rules and legal rules that encourage women to bear and rear children. The maternalized female body triangulates the relationship between law and the meanings of the female body. It proposes a choice of roles for women.

The maternalization of the female body can be explained through the operation of the first and second postmodern 'principles.' That is, because we construct our identities in language and because the meaning of language is contextual and contingent, the relationship between anti-prostitution rules and the meaning of the female body is also affected by other legal rules and their relationship to the female body. The legal rules that criminalize prostitution are located in a legal system in which other legal rules legalize sex — rules, for example, that establish marriage as the legal site of sex and that link marital sex to reproduction by, for example, legitimating children born in marriage. As a result of this conjuncture, anti-prostitution rules maternalize the female body. They not only interrogate women with the question of whether they are for or against prostitution; they also raise the question of whether a woman is for illegal sex or whether she is for legal, maternalized sex.

The legal system maintains a shaky line between sex workers and other women. Anti-prostitution laws are erratically enforced; eager customers and obliging hotel services collaborate in the 'crime' prostitutes commit with relative impunity, and the legal, systemic devaluation of 'women's work' sometimes makes prostitution more lucrative for women than legitimate wage labor. Anti-prostitution rules formally preserve the distinction between legal and illegal sexual activity. By preventing the line between sex workers and 'mothers' from disappearing altogether, anti-prostitution rules reinforce the maternalized female body that other legal rules more directly support.

The legal discourse of anti-prostitution law explicitly deploys the image of maternalized femininity in order to contrast sex workers with women who are not sex workers. This can be observed in defamation cases involving women who are incorrectly identified or depicted as whores. In authorizing compensation for such women, courts typically appeal to maternal imagery to describe the woman who has been wrongly described; they justify their decisions by contrasting the images of two female bodies against each other, the virgin and the whore — madonna and bimbo. The discourse of these decisions maternalizes the female body. The maternalized female body is responsible for her children. Madonna's bambino puts her in charge.

The conjunction and displacement of these alternative meanings of the female body are rationalized in legal discourse, where they are presented as both 'natural' but also necessary . . ."

12.2.i.c Offended sexual bodies.

The privatised nature of prostitution ensuring that the activities of prostitutes are performed out of public view creates the conditions wherein the prostitute is constantly at danger from sexual violence. One particular feature of the legal "exclusion" of the Prostitute is the way in which she may be silenced when she is the victim, rather than the perpetrator of a criminal offence. The radical feminist Catharine MacKinnon locates prostitution as being another form of sexual violence against women: "[r]ape, battery, sexual harassment, sexual abuse of children, prostitution, and pornography, . . . form a distinctive pattern: the power of men over women in society."[31]

The link between prostitution and sexual violence against women is high-

---

[31] C. A. MacKinnon, *Feminism Unmodified: Discourses on Life and Law* (Cambridge MA: Harvard University Press, 1987), p. 5.

lighted by the treatment which prostitutes receive at the hands of the legal system when making allegations of abuse. It has already been noted above by Sheila Duncan, that the protection of prostitutes against physical and sexual violence is not assured. The body of the female Prostitute may be viewed as less deserving of legal protection, than that of other women. Consequently it may be more difficult to sustain accusations of physical and sexual violence or rape. Mary Joe Frug gives an American example of this:

M. J. FRUG
"A Postmodern Feminist Legal Manifesto (An Unfinished Draft)"[32]

"Sometime after three o'clock in the morning on a December night in Malden Square, a police cruiser entered a parking lot where police officers had heard screams. 'Seeing the headlights of an approaching car,' Judge Liacos wrote for the Supreme Judicial Court, a woman 'naked and bleeding around the mouth, jumped from the defendant's car and ran toward [the police cruiser] screaming and waving her arms.' She claimed that she had been raped, that the defendant had forced her to perform oral sex and to engage in intercourse twice. After the defendant was convicted on charges of rape and commission of an unnatural and lascivious act, he appealed. He claimed that he had wrongfully been denied the opportunity to inform the jury that the complainant had twice been charged with prostitution. He argued that the complainant's allegation of rape, which he denied, 'may have been motivated by her desire to avoid further prosecution.'

The trial court had prohibited the defendant from mentioning the complainant's arrests to the jury because of the Massachusetts rapeshield statute, a rule that prohibits the admission of reputation evidence or of specific instances of a victim's sexual conduct in a rape trial. The purpose of the rule is to encourage victims to report rapes, to eliminate victim harassment at trial, and to support the assumption that reputation evidence is 'only marginally, if at all, probative of consent.' Reasoning that a defendant's right to argue bias 'may be the last refuge of an innocent defendant,' the Supreme Judicial Court lifted the shield.

> 'We emphasize that we do not depart from the long held view that prostitution is not relevant to credibility.... Nor do we depart from the policy of the statute in viewing prostitution or the lack of chastity as inadmissible on the issue of consent. Where, however, such facts are relevant to a showing of bias or motive to lie, the general evidentiary rule of exclusion must give way to the constitutionally based right of effective cross-examination.'

This interpretation of the rape-shield statute, broadly applied, denies sex workers who dare to complain of sexual violence the presumption of innocence. Because prostitution is unlawful, this ruling simultaneously terrorizes, sexualizes, and de-maternalizes sex workers. This triple whammy is accomplished by an appeal to fairness:

> '[T]he defendant is entitled to present his own theory of the encounter to the jury.... The relevancy of testimony depends on whether it has a 'rational

---

[32] M. J. Frug, *ibid.*, at 1056–1057.

tendency to prove an issue in the case.' ... Under the defendant's theory he
and the complainant, previously strangers to each other, were in a car late at
night parked in a vacant parking lot. Having just engaged in sexual acts, they
were both naked. A police car was approaching. The defendant intended to
show that the complainant, having been found in a similar situation on two
prior occasions, had been arrested on each occasion and charged with prostitution. We cannot say that this evidence has no rational tendency to prove
that the complainant was motivated falsely to accuse the defendant of rape
by a desire to avoid further prosecution.'

Seems perfectly reasonable. Fair. If a guy can't explain a gal's reasons for misrepres-
enting a situation, that bleeding mouth might compromise *his* credibility."

12.2.ii   *Other offences and the prostitute "pariah"*

The predominant legal construction of prostitution around the art of soliciting
does not mean that others involved in the prostitution of women do not
commit offences (even though they may be less likely to be prosecuted for
doing so).[33] The Sexual Offences Act 1956 creates a range of offences which
may be committed by others whose lives touch that of the Prostitute. It is an
offence to procure a woman to become a common prostitute (s.22(1)), to
procure a girl under the age of twenty-one to have unlawful sexual intercourse
(s.23), to detain a woman in a brothel or other premises (s.24), to permit a
girl under thirteen to use premises for intercourse (s.25), to permit a girl
between thirteen and sixteen to use premises for intercourse (s.26), to permit
a defective to use premises for intercourse (s.27(1)), to cause or encourage the
prostitution of, intercourse with, or indecent assault upon a girl under sixteen
(s.28(1)) and to cause or encourage the prostitution of a defective (s.29(1)).

In addition, it is an offence for a man to knowingly live on the earnings of
prostitution (s.30(1)). Under this section "a man who lives with or is habitually in the company of a prostitute, or who exercises control, direction or
influence over a prostitute's movements in a way which shows he is aiding,
abetting or compelling her prostitution with others, shall be presumed to be
knowingly living on the earnings of prostitution, unless he proves the contrary" (s.30(2)). It is also an offence "for a woman for purpose of gain to
exercise control, direction or influence over a prostitute's movements in a way
which shows she is aiding, abetting or compelling her prostitution" (s.31).

Further offences within the Sexual Offences Act 1956 aim to suppress the
keeping of brothels. Section 33 provides that "[i]t is an offence for a person
to keep a brothel, or to manage, or act or assist in the management of, a
brothel", and section 34 that "[i]t is an offence for the lessor or landlord of
any premises or his agent to let the whole or part of the premises with the
knowledge that it is to be used, in whole or in part, as a brothel, or, where

---

[33] While in 1994 7,039 women were prosecuted for loitering and soliciting under the Street
Offences Act 1959, only 1,185 men were charged with kerb crawling contrary to the Sexual
Offences Act 1985 (*Criminal Statistics England and Wales, Supplementary Tables, supra,* n. 15.

the whole or part of the premises is used as a brothel, to be wilfully a party to that use continuing". Furthermore, section 35(1) makes it an offence for the "tenant or occupier, or person in charge, of any premises" to permit the premises to be used as a brothel and section 36 for the tenant or occupier to permit premises to be used for prostitution.

The term "brothel" is broadly construed, being premises in which two or more prostitutes work. Duncan comments on the pernicious aspect of these provisions for the prostitute:

> "Not only is the Prostitute precluded from obtaining customers by street walking, she is also forbidden to work from or in a premises frequented by any other prostitute. It is clear that the criminalisation of brothels isolates the prostitute at work, leaves her without the physical protection that the presence of other women could provide and deprives her of any collective means of organising her working environment."[34]

The application of these provisions has negative implications also for the Prostitute's home life and personal relationships:

> "The criminalisation of brothels ensure that she [the Prostitute] cannot share her home with another woman. Further, it was held in *Donovan v. Gavin* [1965] 2 Q.B. 648 that even separately let rooms may constitute a brothel if they are close enough together to create 'a nest of prostitutes.' The premises offences also ensure that she will have difficulty in securing and retaining accommodation. Even the legitimate landlord knowingly letting out to one prostitute can fall foul of s.30 which technically creates the offence of a man living off the earnings of prostitution but which extends to cover the landlord who over-charges the prostitute, knowing that she is a prostitute.
>
> In her personal relationships, the prostitute is legally circumscribed by her inability to live with another woman without incurring the possibility of this arrangement being construed as a brothel or an offence under s.31 of the 1956 Act, namely a woman exercising control over a prostitute.
>
> Section 30 creates the virtual certainty that a man living with a prostitute who is husband, lover or even friend can be convicted of the offence of living on the earnings of prostitution.
>
> That same section as developed by case law also circumscribes the small space for the prostitute's uncertain survival, creating the possibility of convictions for those making exorbitant charges for the prostitute's goods and services where they will further prostitution in some way even though they may not be exclusively referable to it.
>
> The law constructs the prostitute as pariah. When she touches the lives of landlords, tenants, other prostitutes, the people who live with her, even shop keepers, there arises, as a result of that connection, the possibility of conviction, however infrequently enforced these offences may be. She is provided with just enough space to ensure that the speaking male subject can buy her sexual services."[35]

---

[34] S. Duncan, *supra*, n. 25 at 24.
[35] S. Duncan, *ibid.*, at 24–6.

In a move away from the legal focus on the woman prostitute, legislation enacted in 1985 creates new offences in relation to the activities of male clients. Section 1 of the Sexual Offences Act 1985 creates the offence of kerb crawling and section 2 that of persistently soliciting women for the purpose of prostitution:

> 1.-(1) A man commits an offence if he solicits a woman (or different women) for the purpose of prostitution —
>> (a) from a motor vehicle while it is in a street or public place; or
>> (b) in a street or public place while in the immediate vicinity of a motor vehicle that he has just got out of or off,
>
> persistently or in such manner or in such circumstances as to be likely to cause annoyance to the woman (or any of the women) solicited, or nuisance to other persons in the neighbourhood.

> 2.-(1) A man commits an offence if in a street or public place he persistently solicits a woman (or different women) for the purpose of prostitution.

The inclusion of offences committed by the male client, does not, however, challenge the dominant legal constructions of the Prostitute as female offender. The present legal regulation, Sheila Duncan argues, provides space in which the male subject may continue to have access to the services of prostitutes, while failing to alter the legal position of the Prostitute herself:

> "The male subject is constructed through a law which provides only enough space to ensure that he may buy sexual services while controlling and creating as pariah the woman who provides them. The legal possibility of this purchase with the simultaneous branding as outlaw and legal leper of the Other purchased, underwrites the subjectivity of the male subject. This construction is at the level of the speaking male subject, it is not confined to the client, for the client could be any male speaking subject and this construction is part of the power of the male subject at the highest level of generality. It also constructs the power of the male subject in the prostitution encounter."[36]

Duncan goes on to investigate the position of male subjects other than the client in the prostitution encounter, notably the pimp:

S. DUNCAN
" 'Disrupting the Surface of Order and Innocence': Towards a Theory of Sexuality and the Law"[37]

"[T]he law also constructs one specific male subject who is related to and whose power flows from the construction of the Prostitute Other — the male pimp. He is constructed

[36] S. Duncan, *ibid.*, at 27.
[37] S. Duncan, *ibid.*, at 27–28.

in a legal space which excludes the prostitute Other. He is constructed by her exclusion and by the criminalisation of brothels.

The legal workspace of the Prostitute is so constrained by the laws against soliciting and the criminalisation of brothels while prostitution *per se* is legal, that it constructs the power of the male pimp, creating its own necessary intermediary of and for the male subject. She cannot live and work with other prostitutes, she falls foul of soliciting legislation on the streets, so this male intermediary, finds her clients, controls her life and lives off her earnings. He may well have procured the woman to work for him as a prostitute in the first instance but . . . he is very unlikely to have been charged to this effect.

It is true that s.30 Sexual Offences Act 1956 creates the offence of 'a man living on the earnings of prostitution.' If he does not live with the Prostitute or provide her with premises of which he is either landlord or tenant, the possibility of his being charged is tiny . . .

The law, therefore, constructs the male pimp with both power and freedom. The Prostitute is silenced in respect of his sexual violence: she sells her consent, she will not be believed in a rape trial. She is effectively silenced in the face of any physical violence he may use against her. Perhaps in the encounter between the Prostitute Other and the male pimp as speaking subject, it is possible to see the most extreme forms of the law's construction of the male subject and the female Other . . ."

12.2.iii   *Sentencing*

The appropriate sentence for someone involved in prostitution is a further matter of contention. If fines are imposed, this may lead the Prostitute (or any other person charged) to engage in further acts of prostitution in order to meet the payment. Alternatively, a prison sentence, while having a possible deterrent effect on others, may seem an excessive deprivation of liberty for an offence of this nature. This dilemma is discussed in the case of *R. v. Payne*[38] and in Professor Brian Hogan's commentary upon the case[39]:

R. v. Payne
[1980] Crim. L.R. 595

"Lawton L.J., Michael Davies and Balcombe JJ.: May 15, 1980. The appellant, a woman, pleaded guilty to one count of keeping a disorderly house and three of exercising control over a prostitute. She was sentenced to 18 months' imprisonment for keeping the disorderly house, fined a total of £1,950 on the other counts, and ordered to pay the prosecution's costs not exceeding £2,000. The disorderly house was a brothel organised in a large suburban house. Over the period of observation, a total of 249 men and 50 women were seen to visit the house, and when it was raided the police found 53 men and 13 women. The premises were equipped and arranged to cater for various sexual tastes; pornographic films were shown and exhibitions of sexual intercourse took place. The appellant had four previous convictions for keeping a brothel, and there was evidence that the appellant had indicated the intention to resume brothel keeping as soon as possible after the conclusion of the present proceed-

---

[38] [1980] Crim.L.R. 595.
[39] B. Hogan, "Mrs Payne's Punishment" [1980] Crim.L.R. 400–401.

ings. *Decision*: keeping a brothel in the form of a disorderly house had been an offence at common law for centuries, and had been the subject of legislation from time to time. A summary offence had been included in the Sexual Offences Act 1956, punishable with six months' imprisonment on a second conviction, but in the present case the prosecution had elected to proceed for the common law offence, which was not subject to any maximum penalty. The Court was not concerned with the argument that brothels should be legalised. The offences of exercising control over prostitutes were incidental to the keeping of the brothel, and although the offence was punishable with seven years' imprisonment, the present case was nowhere near the kind of case — involving gangs controlling prostitutes — which Parliament had in mind in providing that maximum penalty. The Court would approach the case as a bad case of brothel keeping. The appellant had been fined on previous occasions, and as fines had proved ineffectual, there was no alternative to a custodial sentence. As Parliament had relatively recently decided that the maximum penalty for brothel keeping should be six months, the Court found it difficult to see why a longer term should be imposed in the present case. The sentence would be reduced to six months, with the fines unaffected."

B. HOGAN
"Mrs Payne's Punishment"[40]

"So there it is. Now we can all sleep safe in our beds. Mrs Cynthia Payne, brothel-keeper extraordinary, is behind bars for six months — four if she keeps her nose clean — and the Great British Public can breathe a collective sigh of relief.

And that is not the only good news. Those of us, momentarily stunned by the report that professional colleagues were eagerly awaiting their turn on the staircase of the house in darkest Streatham's Ambleside Avenue, have had our faith restored in their integrity. Personally, I was from the outset less than fully convinced that barristers and solicitors were ever involved. Age, ache, penury might drive some of us to bringing sandwiches to work or even cause us to revictual at the local soup-kitchen, but there is surely nothing that could turn us to the use of pre-paid meal tickets. No self-respecting lawyer would wish to be found dead in possession of one of these.

Thus the prisons, stretched to the very limits of their capacity, must open their doors to squeeze in Mrs Payne. Am I the only one left wondering what good this will do for Mrs Payne and for the public? The Court of Appeal (according to the report in *The Times*) appeared to be moved by three aspects of her case. The first was the nuisance aspect. Although no evidence was given of *any* complaint being lodged by *any* of Mrs Payne's neighbours, the Court boldly concluded that 'it did not follow that those living there did not know about it and were not outraged.' Indeed, 'it must have given great offence to those living near by.' But it does seem, with respect, surprising that those neighbours who knew and cared should not have troubled to make a call to the local police station, and, according to a wireless report, at least some of Mrs Payne's neighbours thought highly of her. Has it never occurred to anyone that having a brothel next door might cause no more nuisance than living close by a public house, a boys' club, or — come to that — a police station?

Second was the profit aspect. No doubt Mrs Payne did tolerably well from her business, but there was no evidence of any improper, still less illegal, pressure brought by her to bear harshly on the prostitutes; and the customers, even without the light refreshments thrown in, seem — to coin a phrase — to have had a fair crack of the whip. No doubt to fine Mrs Payne was a fair response if only because purely practical considerations make it difficult for the Inland Revenue to catch up with her.

But, and this was the third and probably dominant aspect, Mrs Payne had been fined and fined again all to no avail and thus 'the law had to deprive her of her liberty.' But was there any 'had to' about it? What harm did Mrs Payne do which rendered her incarceration imperative? The prostitutes were not overreached, the customers did not complain of the charges, and every one of them was a consenting adult. Strip away the moral disapproval, stronger in some than others, of the conduct involved and what have you got? What is left is the possibility of a nuisance which, if neighbours so regard it, they are entitled to have terminated. Since nuisances of many other kinds can be terminated without sending the originator to prison, or even bringing a criminal charge, why should this nuisance be so exceptionally treated?

Quite why the taxpayer should house, clothe and feed Mrs Payne for the next four to six months is beyond me to explain. It is a classic case of throwing good money after bad and I am unimpressed by the argument that we throw so much good money after so much bad that a few bob wasted on Mrs Payne won't be missed."

Changes in sentencing practice for activities involving prostitution have been brought about following the introduction of the Criminal Justice Act 1991. These changes and their effects are discussed in the following extract:

R. LENG
"Imprisonment for Prostitutes"[41]

"One of the major objectives of the Criminal Justice Act 1991 is to reduce the prison population and to ensure that prison is reserved for those who present real danger. This aim is primarily effected by s. 1 which places restrictions on custody and requires the sentencer to distinguish between the serious offender, and the serious nuisance who repeatedly commits minor offences. However, it seems likely that the unit fine scheme introduced by s. 18 will also indirectly operate to reduce the prison population. When brought into operation in October this should dramatically cut the pointless and wasteful practice of imprisonment for fine default by forcing magistrates to take seriously their duty to fine according to the defendant's means. Among the first beneficiaries of this change in the law are likely to be prostitutes convicted of loitering or soliciting who presently find themselves in prison for non-payment of fines.

A recurring nightmare for law-makers and courts is how to punish offences which are not only marginal in terms of perceived seriousness and public tolerance but also serve a profitable market. The difficulty in finding a sentence which is an effective deterrent, not disproportionately expensive for society and fair to the offender is well illustrated by the recent history of the offence of loitering or soliciting for prostitution.

Prior to 1959, the maximum penalty of a £2 fine reflected a view of the offence as a minor public nuisance. That approach was swept aside by the Street Offences Act 1959, which implemented the proposals of the Wolfenden Committee, for whom the primary consideration was effectiveness in clearing the streets. Under the 1959 Act,

[41] (1992) 142 New L.J. 270–272.

imprisonment was introduced as a penalty for a third or subsequent conviction. It is implicit that imprisonment was not viewed as commensurate with the seriousness of the offence. Rather it was hoped that the mere threat of prison, coupled with the cautions and fines which necessarily preceded it, would be sufficient to deter a woman from pursuing her trade on the street.

In terms of effectiveness the Act was judged a success, with convictions for loitering or soliciting dropping from 19,536 in 1958 to 2,733 in 1960. However, if it was hoped that imprisonment would be a sanction which would never be used, the Act must be judged a failure. Between 1960 and 1983 large numbers of women experienced imprisonment as a direct sentence for prostitution. The explanation for the failure is that the theory of deterrence appeals to the rationality of the potential law breaker. But for some women, street prostitution is a rational choice. The need to work the streets may be compelling because of lack of money or lack of opportunity, and the stigma of prison means little to a person already branded a common prostitute. Thus, the cost of effective general deterrence was largely borne by those women who were not personally deterred and who ended up in prison as a result.

By 1982 the fact that women were being imprisoned for little more than smiling at passers by, had become a national scandal. The campaign to abolish imprisonment was supported in many different quarters. It was pointed out by prostitutes' organisations that imprisonment generated problems in terms of debt, homes lost and children taken into care, which impacted not only on the prostitute and her family but also on the caring agencies. NACRO pointed to the proved ineffectiveness of imprisonment as a deterrent while the Prison Officers' Association expressed concern about the influence of prostitutes on other young women in prison and the practical difficulties involved in dealing with a constantly shifting prison population of women serving short sentences. Imprisonment as a direct sentence for loitering or soliciting was finally abolished by means of a private member's amendment which became s. 71 of the Criminal Justice Act 1982.

Following this reform, two things soon became apparent. The first was that many in the legal establishment were unhappy with losing the sanction of prison. The second was that in practice the imprisonment of prostitutes never ceased . . .

By mid 1983 concern was voiced by probation officers' organisations and in Parliament that some benches were pursuing a deliberate policy of imposing substantial fines beyond women's means with periods of imprisonment as automatic alternatives. In other areas prostitutes would be bound over in substantial sums, with prison as the expected consequences of breach.

Despite these early criticisms, the practice of imprisoning women for loitering and soliciting continues to the present day. The Home Office does not publish precise figures; however, in 1989 some 505 women fine defaulters were imprisoned for offences other than violence, dishonesty, motoring and drunkenness. It is reckoned that a large proportion of this group were convicted prostitutes. For all female fine defaulters, the average time spent in prison in 1989 was six days. This period has reduced significantly following the implementation of s. 60 Criminal Justice Act 1988 which halved periods of imprisonment for default on most levels of fine.

The continued presence in prison of women convicted for soliciting is attributable to two factors. First, it is alleged that some benches set fines high, in the anticipation that the women will default and experience prison. Secondly, some courts subscribe to a particular approach to sentencing in cases where there is a profit motive in the offending behaviour. The theory underlying this is that where the offender stands to profit from the crime, a low fine will be treated simply as a tax on the offending conduct rather than as a real deterrent. Thus, it is necessary to increase the fine to a level at which the trade becomes unprofitable, for it is only at this point that deterrence strikes. In relation to prostitution, imprisonment is not the only unpalatable consequence of this sentencing principle. Since the fine is set in anticipation of future profits, the prostitute must renew her efforts to meet it. Although a cliché, the charge that the State is the biggest pimp of all is difficult to resist.

The original version of the Criminal Justice Bill provided for fines to be increased in order to take account of any profit made by the offender. This would have preserved the power of the court to impose fines beyond a prostitute woman's lawful means. However, the provision was dropped during the passage of the Act and replaced by specific provisions preventing an offender profiting by evading a road traffic fixed penalty or by not buying a television licence. Thus, except in these two specific cases, the courts will no longer be able to award fines on the basis of depriving the offender of the profits of crime.

What then are the implications of the unit fine scheme for sentencing prostitutes? Under s. 1(2) Street Offences Act 1959 loitering or soliciting for the purposes of prostitution is punishable by a level 2 fine, or a level 3 fine for second and subsequent convictions. Under s. 17(1) Criminal Justice Act 1991, maximum fines will be raised to £500 for level 2 and £1,000 for level 3. Fines will be calculated initially in units rather than in financial terms.

The number of units should reflect the court's view of the seriousness of the offence. A maximum of five units can be imposed for a level 2 offence, and a maximum of 10 units for a level 3 offence. The actual fine to be paid by an offender will be calculated by multiplying the number of units awarded by a figure, determined by the court as the appropriate unit for the particular defendant. This will normally be the offender's disposable weekly income, but subject to a minimum of £4 and a maximum of £100. Lower limits will apply to women under 18 for whom the minimum unit will be 80 pence and the maximum £20. The offender's disposable weekly income will be assessed by the court under rules to be made by the Lord Chancellor which are anticipated in April 1992.

Thus, from October, fine assessment will be firmly tied to the offender's means. The key issue will be whether, under the rules to be issued, the court will be permitted to take account of earnings from prostitution. This has clearly been the practice of some courts in the past. However, it is doubted whether it could ever be acceptable to consider anticipated earnings of prostitution in the context of a public assessment of means, under statutory guidelines, for the purpose of setting a fine. To do so would be to acknowledge that the woman is expected to pay the fine out of the profits of prostitution, and in reality this would mean further street offences. If fines are to be calculated on a woman's earnings, other than those from prostitution, the value of unit will often be low: in many cases the minimum £4. On this basis the maximum fine for a second or subsequent offence would be £40. Although the periods of imprisonment for default will be calculated in terms of units rather than in financial terms (under s. 22 CJA 1991), with lower fines the likelihood of default and consequent imprisonment will be considerably reduced. Further, where the woman receives income support, the fine may be deducted at source, thereby removing the possibility of default (s. 24).

If this analysis is correct, the Criminal Justice Act will virtually end the practice of the unjustified imprisonment of women guilty of soliciting for the instrumental purpose of deterring the others.''

12.2.iv *Legalisation*

In the light of the above critique of the current legal response to prostitution, legitimisation of the activities of prostitutes appears a potentially attractive proposition. One advantage of legalisation is that it effects a move away from the negative and punitive criminalisation of the activities of prostitutes. In legitimising prostitution the stigmatisation of prostitutes may be removed. Legalisation may also counter the current social exclusion of prostitutes and ameliorate the conditions in which they work. It may mean that prostitutes would be entitled to welfare benefits and might extend unemployment rights to them also.

There are, nonetheless, some possible disadvantages of legalisation. It may simply enable the State to exercise greater control over the lives of prostitutes. It may increase surveillance and regulation of their activities. It may require that they submit themselves to health checks and screening. The motivation behind legalisation may have less to do with improving the material conditions of prostitutes, than with "cleaning up" the streets. Carol Smart, following her interviews with magistrates in Sheffield, notes their lack of enthusiasm for current legal provisions and found that 76 per cent of her sample were in favour of the introduction of legalised brothels. However, she concludes:

C. SMART
"Legal subjects and sexual objects: ideology, law and female sexuality"[42]

"This predominant view in favour of legalised brothels did not stem from a concern for prostitute women. The considerations which motivated the magistrates tended to be a concern for the tone of residential areas of the city (one magistrate suggested that the brothel could be located outside the city limits in the Derbyshire countryside), a concern for clients to meet prostitutes without causing a nuisance, and a belief that women working in the brothels could be more closely regulated . . .

The men magistrates (71 per cent of them) were much more concerned about controlling disease than the women (36 per cent), but their concern was in almost all cases extremely naive and displayed a fundamental ignorance about VD. Such medical checks could have little value unless they were carried out after every sexual encounter or on every man prior to intercourse (which is unlikely in practice). In effect, such checks would simply be a further enforced harassment of women. They also raise the question of what would happen if women refused to submit to the compulsory medical examination. Would it, for example, lead to a revival of the nineteenth-century Contagious Diseases Acts in which women could be held in detention in lock hospitals? Or would such women be forced back into the unlicensed market on the streets where they would face much harsher penalties than exist under current legislation? The legalised brothel may appear to be the rational, permissive, sanitised answer to what is perceived as the problem of prostitution, but it imports many more repressive measures than those currently employed."

---

[42] In C. Smart & J. Brophy (eds), *supra*, n. 5 at pp. 63–64.

In a different mode from some of her later work (in which she warns feminists to "avoid the siren call of law"),[43] Carol Smart identifies the possibilities of law reform in this area:

C. SMART
"Legal subjects and sexual objects: ideology, law and female sexuality"[44]

"The laws on soliciting, which are so concrete in their effects on prostitute women, also carry an ideological message to all women and so create an unavoidable issue for the women's movement. But they also make it impossible for the women's movement to absorb prostitution into the wider campaigns on women's poverty, equal pay, day care facilities and so on because the criminal law makes prostitute women into a special category which constantly calls for the attention of a single issue campaign (*i.e.* to end imprisonment, to decriminalise, to resist brothels) . . .

Working in any area of law reform raises the possibility of perpetuating the cause of the problem by ameliorating its symptoms. But we have to recognise that working for reforms is not always an attempt to ameliorate a static situation, but is frequently an attempt to stop a situation deteriorating further. In this respect there is little option for feminists but to confront the law, even though working on specific campaigns around prostitution sustains the very distinction between prostitute women and non-prostitute women which is so divisive. Arguably, a major priority must be to remove the legal category of common prostitute which, as we have seen, lends support to conventional wisdom about divisions between moral classes of women. If the law ceased to be able to define the issues around which the women's movement should organise it would be far easier to concentrate on the issues that unite rather than those that have always successfully divided women."

Examples from other countries suggest that legalisation may not be unproblematic. In the U.S. State of Nevada prostitution is no longer legally prohibited:

J. KELLY
"Nevada Vice"[45]

"Nevada Revised Statutes 201.354 provides: 'It is unlawful for any person to engage in prostitution or solicitation . . . except in a licensed house of prostitution.' This statute must be read with NRS 244.345, which prohibits brothels in any county with 400,000 or more people, which effectively only bans prostitution in Las Vegas. The Nevada Supreme Court in *Nye County v. Plankinton*, 94 Nev 739 (1978), concluded that the above statutory scheme repealed the common law prohibition of prostitution as a nuisance *per se* since it allowed local regulation. A minority of the 17 Nevada counties have legalised prostitution. Some counties have not issued any ordinances on

---

[43] C. Smart, *Feminism and the Power of Law* (London: Routledge, 1989), p. 160.
[44] C. Smart, *supra*, n. 5 at pp. 68–69.
[45] (1993) 143 New L.J. 948 at 950.

the subject; and several small towns have, therefore, allowed regulated brothels. If a Nevada county does legalise brothels, they cannot be located within 400 yards of a church or school.

Nevada state regulations require pre-employment testing for VD and HIV, and subsequent weekly and monthly testing of prostitutes. State regulations also require all patrons to use condoms. If a prostitute leaves the brothel for more than 24 hours, she must be re-tested for HIV and VD.

The most famous brothel is the Mustang Ranch in Storey County. It employs the services of 60 to 90 prostitutes who work for three weeks and then have 7 to 10 days off. According to its controversial former owner/manager, Joe Conforte, the only qualifications for employment are that prostitutes must not be on drugs nor be 'too young or too ugly'. Initially he hoped the Mustang would become a publicly-traded corporation and thus raise $10 million through stock offerings. Conforte earlier had to seek exile in Brazil because of legal problems, and was only allowed to return to Nevada after agreeing to testify against a federal judge accused of corruption. After he resumed operation of the Mustang Ranch, Conforte again ran into serious difficulties with the Internal Revenue Service.

In September 1990, the Mustang Ranch was forced to seek relief in a federal bankruptcy court for an alleged debt of $13 million to the IRS. The bankruptcy court-appointed trustee attempted to entice the 45 prostitutes back to work by promising that: 'the house will take less and you girls will take more'. The ladies feared their independent contractor status (they split their earnings 50–50) might be changed to that of a federal employee, requiring them to pay social security and income tax on their salary and tips. In operating what would be the 'nation's largest legal whorehouse', television stations began to joke about the brothel's 'federally operated Orgy Room'. When the property was finally auctioned off by the IRS, it was purchased for $1.49 million and re-opened by Mustang Properties Inc, a corporation whose only disclosed officer was Conforte's long-time lawyer.

This naturally allowed Conforte to return to managing the Mustang Ranch where he was able to resume his yearly 'donation of 1,000 turkeys to the poor' as well as offering free brothel passes to groups such as Desert Storm veterans. As Conforte explained:

> 'We had 800 Desert Storm guys show up. At $1,000 a day, splitting that 50–50 with the girls like I always do, I figure that cost me $400,000. I'm very patriotic.'"

12.3 Sex work and the sexual contract

12.3.i *Prostitution and wage labour*
The case for legalisation of prostitution operates at the level of introducing sex work into the legitimate realm of the labour market. The consequences of this might be for prostitutes to benefit from employment rights, from greater control over the organisation of their industry and from membership of trade unions. The exploitation of prostitutes might consequently be curtailed.

Carol Pateman locates prostitution as one aspect of the "sexual contract". She argues that "[p]rostitution is an integral part of capitalism . . . Like other forms of capitalist enterprise, prostitution is seen as private enterprise, and the contract between client and prostitute is seen as a private arrangement between a buyer and a seller."[46] She explains:

> "Contractarians argue that a prostitute contracts out a certain form of labour power for a given period in exchange for money. There is a free exchange between prostitute and customer, and the prostitution contract is exactly like — or is one example of — the employment contract. From the standpoint of contract, the prostitute is an owner of property in her person who contracts out part of that property in the market. A prostitute . . . contracts out use of *sexual services*."[47]

Thus it is sexual services which are on offer in the market place. Everyone is free to enter this market place to sell their wares or buy the services of others. Not surprisingly, English law rejects the construction of prostitution as a form of contractual agreement for the provision of services.

Yet, although prostitution is viewed as an immoral activity, this has not stopped the Inland Revenue seeking the payment of taxes upon earnings gained in the course of prostitution. In *Inland Revenue Commissioners v. Aken*[48] it was held that since prostitution itself is not an illegal activity (although activities associated with it quite clearly are), the earnings of Ms Aken (otherwise known as Lindi St Claire) were taxable. Parker L.J. stated that:

> "[Prostitution] is not a criminal offence; it is not subject to criminal sanctions. It is not even an activity which may be lawfully carried on subject to penalties. It is a lawful activity, in the course of which offences may or may not be committed. Should they be so committed, the prostitute may no doubt be convicted and sentenced according to law, but as is accepted, prostitution itself is not unlawful. What the prostitute will be doing in such cases is simply committing offences in the course of carrying on an unprohibited and thus lawful, albeit immoral, trade. As with a bookmaker, she cannot enforce her bargains, but in my judgment she, like the bookmaker, is trading and is taxable. The Revenue will not, by taxing her, be seeking to share the profits of a criminal or prohibited act."[49]

If the words "double standard" do not yet spring to mind, then they may do so after consideration of the following case in which the efforts of Lindi St Claire to register her company Lindi St Claire (Personal Services) Ltd were thwarted. The High Court allowed an application for judicial review of the decision of the Registrar of Companies to incorporate and register the company and ordered the decision to be quashed:

[46] C. Pateman, *supra*, n.2 at p. 189.
[47] C. Pateman, *ibid.*, p. 191.
[48] *Inland Revenue Commissioners v. Aken* [1990] 1 W.L.R. 1374.
[49] *Inland Revenue Commissioners v. Aken, ibid.*, at 1384–1385, *per* Parker L.J.

R. v. Registrar of Companies, ex parte Attorney-General
[1991] B.C.L.C. 476 at 476–479, *per* Ackner L.J.

This application has many of the indicia that one might expect to find in a student's end of term moot. It appears indirectly to have been stimulated by the action of the Policy Division of the Inland Revenue.

The Attorney General applies to quash the incorporation and registration by the Registrar of Companies nearly a year ago, that is on December 18, 1979, of Lindi St Claire (Personal Services) Ltd as a limited company under the provisions of the Companies Acts 1948 to 1976.

The grounds of the application, to state them quite briefly, are these. In certifying the incorporation of a company and in registering the same the Registrar of Companies acted *ultra vires* or misdirected himself or otherwise erred in law, in particular as to the proper construction and application of s.1(1) of the Companies Act 1948 in that the company was not formed for any lawful purpose but, on the contrary, was formed expressly with the primary object of carrying on the business of prostitution, such being an unlawful purpose involving the commission of acts which are immoral and contrary to public policy.

The first point to consider is the validity of the procedure which has been adopted in this case, that is by way of application for judicial review, such application being made by the Attorney General.

Section 15 of the Companies Act 1948 provides:

'(1) A certificate of incorporation given by the registrar in respect of any association shall be conclusive evidence that all the requirements of this Act in respect of registration and of matters precedent and incidental thereto have been complied with, and that the association is a company authorised to be registered and duly registered under this Act . . .'

That on the face of it would appear to be a difficulty in the way of this application, but the matter was dealt with in the case of *Bowman v. Secular Society Ltd* [1917] A.C. 406; [1916–17] All E.R. Rep. 1. In that case the Secular Society was registered as a company limited by guarantee under the Companies Acts 1862 to 1893. The question which there had to be considered was whether its objects were legal, criminal or otherwise such that the company should not be registered.

The matter of procedure was dealt with by Lord Parker in his speech in these terms ([1917] A.C. 406 at 439; [1916–17] All E.R. Rep. 1 at 17):

'My Lords, some stress was laid on the public danger, or at any rate the anomaly, of the Courts recognising the corporate existence of a company all of whose objects, as specified in its memorandum of association, are transparently illegal. Such a case is not likely to occur, for the registrar fulfils a quasi-judicial function, and his duty is to determine whether an association applying for registration is authorised to be registered under the Acts. Only by misconduct or great carelessness on the part of the registrar could a company with objects wholly illegal obtain registration. If such a case did occur it would be open to the Court to stay its hand until an opportunity had been given for taking the appropriate steps for the cancellation of the certificate of registration. It should be observed that neither s.1 of the Companies Act, 1900, nor the corresponding section of the Companies (Consolidation) Act, 1908, is so expressed as to bind the Crown, and the Attorney-General, on behalf of the Crown, could institute proceedings by way of certiorari to cancel a registration which the registrar in affected discharge of his quasi-judicial duties had improperly or erroneously allowed.'

Then he deals with the instant case.

That view was expressly accepted in his speech by Lord Dunedin and was referred to by Lord Buckmaster in shorter terms at the conclusion of his speech (see [1917] A.C. 406 at 478; [1916–17] All E.R. Rep. 1 at 38). So clearly the Attorney General is entitled to bring these proceedings.

Now as to the facts, these come within a very short compass and they amount to the following. A firm of certified accountants, Gilson Clipp & Co., on August 16, 1979 wrote to the Registrar of Companies at Companies House, Crown Way, Maindy, Cardiff pointing out that they had received a letter from the Inland Revenue Policy Division, who stated that they considered prostitution to be a trade which is fully taxable, and that they, the certified accountants, saw no reason why their client should not be able to organise her business by way of a limited company. They asked whether the name 'Prostitute Ltd' was available for registration as a limited company, pointing out the main object of the company would be that of organising the services of a prostitute.

The registrar did not like that name and did not accept it, nor did he accept another name 'Hookers Ltd' which was offered. But subsequently two further names were offered, 'Lindi St Claire (Personal Services) Ltd' and 'Lindi St Claire (French Lessons) Ltd', and it was the former which he registered.

The memorandum of association said in terms that the first of the objects of the company was 'To carry on the business of prostitution'.

The only director of the company is Lindi St Claire, Miss St Claire describing herself specifically as 'Prostitute'. The other person who owns also one share is a Miss Duggan, who is referred to as 'the cashier'.

Leave having been obtained to apply for judicial review, Miss St Claire wrote in these terms:

> 'I would like to say that prostitution is not at all unlawful, as you have stated, and I feel it is most unfair of you to take this view, especially when I am paying income tax on my earnings from prostitution to the government Inland Revenue.
>
> Furthermore, I feel it is most unfair of you to imply that I have acted wrongly, as I was most explicit to all concerned about the sole trade of the company to be that of prostitution and nothing more. If my company should not be deemed valid, then it should have not been granted in the first place by the Board of Trade. It is most unfair of the government to allow me to go ahead with my company one moment, then quash it the next.'

In regard to that paragraph Miss St Claire is perfectly right that she was most explicit to all concerned as to the trade of the company, and in that paragraph she confirms that it was the sole trade of the company. Mr Simon Brown on behalf of the Attorney General, concedes that, if the company should not be deemed valid, then it should not have been registered in the first place by the Board of Trade, and therefore the issue with which we are concerned is the validity of the registration.

That takes us to s.1(1) of the Companies Act 1948, and I need only read that subsection:

> 'Any seven or more persons, or, where the company to be formed will be a private company, any two or more persons, associated for any lawful purpose may, by subscribing their names to a memorandum of association and otherwise complying with the requirements of this Act in respect of registration, form an incorporated company, with or without limited liability.'

It is well settled that a contract which is made upon a sexually immoral consideration or for a sexually immoral purpose is against public policy and is illegal and unenforceable. The fact that it does not involve or may not involve the commission of a criminal offence in no way prevents the contract being illegal, being against public policy and therefore being unenforceable. Here, as the documents clearly indicate, the association is for the purpose of carrying on a trade which involves illegal contracts because the purpose is a sexually immoral purpose and as such against public policy.

Mr Simon Brown submits that if that is the position, as indeed it clearly is on the authorities, then the association of the two or more persons cannot be for 'any lawful purpose'.

To my mind this must follow. It is implicit in the speeches in the *Bowman* case to which I have just made reference. In my judgment, the contention of the Attorney General is a valid one and I would order that the registration be therefore quashed."

12.3.ii *Prostitution and European Union law*

While the construction of prostitution as a sexual service and employment activity may not be one favoured in English law, it does have implications in the field of European Union Law in that it raises questions at the level of the freedoms contained in the Treaty of Rome.[50] Particularly of interest, in the context of prostitution is the free movement of workers. It has been noted above (in the context of pornography and the free movement of goods) that E.U. Law is constructed upon the "dominance of a market paradigm"[51] which, Leo Flynn argues, is resistant to the incorporation of the female body (and particularly, for present purposes, the issue of prostitution) within its remit.

Flynn considers the regulation of the female body within the market paradigm via an analysis of the case of *Adoui and Cornuaille*[52] The case concerns the principle of the free movement of workers guaranteed under Art. 48 of the Treaty of Rome and derogations from that principle, which may be entered "on grounds of public policy, public security or public health" (Art. 48(3)). Ms Adoui and Ms Cornuaille were French nationals who had been refused permission to reside in Belgium on public policy grounds, being

---

[50] *I.e.* the free movement of goods, of persons, of capital and freedom of establishment.
[51] L. Flynn, "The Body Politic(s) of E.C. Law" in T. K. Hervey & D. O'Keeffe (eds), *Sex Equality Law in the European Union* (Chichester: John Wiley, 1996), p. 301 at 310.
[52] Joined Cases 115 and 116/81 [1982] E.C.R. 1665.

allegedly engaged in acts of prostitution.[53] Repressive measures were not taken to combat similar conduct when carried out by Belgian nationals. The European Court of Justice was called upon to consider the scope of the public policy derogation contained in Art. 48(3):

Adoui and Cornuaille
(Joined Cases 115 and 116/81) [1982] E.C.R. 1665, paras 7–9

"7. The reservations contained in Articles 48 and 56 of the EEC Treaty permit Member States to adopt, with respect to the nationals of other Member States and on the grounds specified in those provisions, in particular grounds justified by the requirements of public policy, measures which they cannot apply to their own nationals, inasmuch as they have no authority to expel the latter from the national territory or to deny them access thereto. Although that difference of treatment, which bears upon the nature of the measures available, must therefore be allowed, it must nevertheless be stressed that, in a Member State, the authority empowered to adopt such measures must not base the exercise of its powers on assessments of certain conduct which would have the effect of applying an arbitrary distinction to the detriment of nationals of other Member States.

8. It should be noted in that regard that reliance by a national authority upon the concept of public policy presupposes, as the Court held in its judgment of 27 October 1977, in Case 30/77 *Bouchereau* [1977] E.C.R. 1999, the existence of 'a genuine and sufficiently serious threat affecting one of the fundamental interests of society'. Although Community law does not impose upon the Member States a uniform scale of values as regards the assessment of conduct which may be considered as contrary to public policy, it should nevertheless be stated that conduct may not be considered as being of a sufficiently serious nature to justify restrictions on the admission to or residence within the territory of a Member State of a national of another Member State in a case where the former Member State does not adopt with respect to the same conduct on the part of its own nationals repressive measures or other genuine and effective measures intended to combat such conduct.

9. The answer to Questions 1 to 9, 11 and 12 should therefore be that a Member State may not, by virtue of the reservation relating to public policy contained in Articles 48 and 56 of the Treaty, expel a national of another Member State from its territory or refuse him access to its territory by reason of conduct which, when attributable to the former State's own nationals does not give rise to repressive measures or other genuine and effective measures intended to combat such conduct."

Flynn comments upon the application of this doctrine to the issue of prostitution:

---

[53] Or, to use the more delicate terminology of the judgment, the allegation being that "the conduct of Ms Adoui and Ms Cornuaille was considered to be contrary to public policy by virtue of the fact that they were waitresses in a bar which was suspect from the point of view of morals."

L. FLYNN
"The Body Politic(s) of E.C. Law"[54]

"In essence, therefore, the Court of Justice considered the extent to which Member States retain their discretion to order public space as they see fit. E.C. law does not, according to the Court, impose a normative system of its own. It is, in a word, neutral. Its only demand is that the State act consistently and not turn a blind eye to those of its own nationals engaging in prostitution while acting against aliens who do so.

The Court did not directly address the issue of prostitution in its judgment. The decision of the Court focuses on the issue of constitutional significance raised in the case, the powers of Member States under Article 48(3), and ignores the fact that it also directly affects how sex workers' lives are regulated through a linked set of threats; the removal of their co-workers from the State, in the case of national sex workers; and deportation, in the case of sex workers, from other Member States. However, the issue of prostitution was discussed to some extent in the Opinion of Advocate General Capotorti and in the observations supplied by several Member States and the Commission.

The national court had asked the ECJ, *inter alia*, whether the exercise of a trade that is not prohibited (but on the contrary is protected from exploitation and is lawfully taxable), may constitute a serious threat to a fundamental interest of society. Advocate General Capotorti observes in his Opinion on this matter that Member States may legitimately take action against aliens of either sex who have entered into the territory to carry on prostitution. None of the other parties or decision makers in the case make any such comment as to the sex of sex workers. This single remark of the Advocate General purports to underline the sex neutral nature of the prohibition in national law. However, placed as it is in parentheses in his Opinion, it highlights that prostitution is an activity that is predominantly, though not exclusively, carried out by women. This remark also returns our attention to the point where the impact of the Court's judgment will ultimately be most acutely felt — on women, and how they use (and are forced to use) their bodies.

The referring national court also asked whether Member States are entitled to take into account the private life of the persons concerned in deciding to refuse or withdraw residence permits. In its decision, the Court did not respond directly to this question, submerging it in the issue of the disparity between the measures taken against national, as opposed to foreign, sex workers. However, this question provoked widely differing responses from those Member States that submitted observations to the Court. The Commission's observations are the most interesting and insightful in the case because it noted the malleability of this category of private life. It stated that 'there are various types of conduct, of the sexual and other kinds, which are purely private, and which are viewed very differently as between one Member State and another and even, within a single Member State, from one period to another'. While the Court of Justice did not express any view on this point, it would not have had to compare the treatment of nationals and non-nationals from other Member States unless it concluded that public policy issues were raised in the case. Therefore, it must either have accepted that the acts (and/or the consequences of those acts) were in the public domain, or that the Member States are free to draw the scope of the public as they [see] fit.

---

[54] L. Flynn, *supra*, n. 51 at pp. 312–314.

The latter conclusion is difficult to reconcile with other elements of the Court's jurisprudence on public policy that limit, without eliminating, the Member States' discretion to identify what is a fundamental interest of society and, as a consequence, a public matter. As a result, it seems most likely that the court accepted that sex workers' activities come within the public gaze and are therefore appropriate objects of regulation. This positioning of sex workers reinforces the gendering strategies of domestic laws which place women in transgressive roles in the public sphere and penalises them for their presence there."

12.3.iii *Commodification of the female body*

The objection to viewing prostitution as a form of wage labour is that prostitution commodifies the female body which, in the sexual contract, becomes an object for sale. In this view it is not *sexual services* which are on offer in the sexual market place. Rather it is the prostitute herself, more specifically it is her sexual body parts.

The commodification inherent in the sex work contract, radical feminists argue, does nothing to change the sexual subordination of women to men. In fact it may serve only to reinforce it. Other feminists, adopting a more liberal perspective, see the sexual contract as offering the possibility of female sexual autonomy. But, they, in turn, object to the *kind* of sexual autonomy on offer, that is one which perpetuates the objectification of women's bodies. Having outlined the above positions, Mary Joe Frug goes on to set out the "postmodern position" which, she argues, offers the possibility of a new construction of sex work by removing its reproductive overtones (maternalization) and its permissive violence (terrorization):

M. J. FRUG
"A Postmodern Feminist Legal Manifesto (An Unfinished Draft)"[55]

"Sex workers themselves — who inspire the postmodern position as I develop it here — want legal support for sex that is severed from its reproduction function and from romance, affection, and long-term relationships. Because 'legal' sexual autonomy is conventionally extended to women only by rules that locate sexuality in marriage or by rules that allow women decisional autonomy regarding reproductive issues, arguments in support of law reforms that would legalize sex work conflict with the language of the maternalized female body. The arguments that sex workers are making to assimilate their work into the wage market appeal to a sexualized femininity that is something other than a choice between criminalized and maternalized sex or a choice between terrorized and maternalized sex. This appeal to a fresh image of the female body is based on a reorganization of the three images of femininity I described earlier; it arises within the play of these three images. Its originality suggests, to me, resistance to the dominant images."

Even if prostitution is constructed as the sale of a woman's *sexual body* as

---

[55] M.J. Frug, *supra*, n. 29 at 1058–1059.

opposed to her *sexual services*, the question might be asked, so what? Why should women not decide to use their bodies in order to make money should they so desire? The perception of the prostitute as offending against norms of behaviour for women, and thereby constructed as deviant, may encourage a perception of her decision to engage in prostitution as a consequence of unrestrained sexuality explicable by unbalanced hormones or an unfortunate past, rather than a rational decision to engage in an activity which pays better than other employment opportunities for women.[56] The arguments which support an exercise of female autonomy in this area are similar to those discussed earlier to justify commercial surrogacy arrangements.[57] Like the surrogate who uses her reproductive capacity to earn her living a woman might use her sexual capacity in a similar fashion. The economic incentive to do so is framed by Catharine MacKinnon as follows:

> "[I]t is instructive to ask: What is woman's best economic option? In 1981, the average street walker in Manhattan earned between $500 and $1,000 a week. Aside from modeling (with which it has much in common), hooking is the only job for which women as a group are paid more than men. Check that out in terms of what we are valued for. A recent study shows that the only difference between hookers and other women with similar class background is that the prostitutes earn twice as much."[58]

One of the dangers of this approach is pointed out later by MacKinnon. It may not in fact be the women prostitutes who actually benefit from their activity. MacKinnon argues that "most prostitutes may never get the money; pimps do".[59] Carol Pateman makes a similar point, stating that "prostitution developed into a major industry within patriarchal capitalism, with the same structure as other capitalist industries; prostitutes work in an occupation that is controlled by men."[60] As a consequence Pateman locates the problem of the sexual contract as ultimately one of politics rather than sexual morality. She states that "[t]o try to answer the question of what is wrong with prostitution is to engage in argument about political right in the form of patriarchal right, or the law of male sex-right . . . [U]nless masters are overthrown, unless subordinates engage in political action, no amount of critical reflection will end the subjection and bring them freedom."[61] In this view, giving legitimacy to a woman's right to trade in her own flesh goes nowhere near resolving the more deep-seated problem of patriarchy and wage-labour exploitation.

A similarly negative view is expressed by Andrea Dworkin whose "brothel model" explains the way in which women are sexually dominated by men.[62]

---

[56] C. Docherty, *supra*, n. 1 at p. 182.
[57] See Chap. 4 above. The connection is discussed in detail by Carol Pateman, *supra*, n. 2 at pp. 209–218.
[58] C. A. MacKinnon, *supra*, n. 31 at pp. 24–25.
[59] C. A. MacKinnon, *ibid.*, p. 52.
[60] C. Pateman, *supra*, n. 2 at p. 197.
[61] C. Pateman, *ibid.*, p. 205.
[62] A. Dworkin, *Right-wing Women* (London: The Women's Press, 1983), p. 174. This "model" is discussed in Chap. 4 above in the context of new reproductive technologies.

Women under this model are constructed as being used by men for sex and only for sex: "Women are defined strictly with reference to sex and they are defined unfailingly without reference to personality or individuality or human potential."[63] Such a construction allows women no space from which to freely exercise choice in pursuing a career in prostitution.

12.3.iv   *Male power and the international traffic in women*

The commodification of the bodies of women has particular resonance in the context of the increasing international trade in female flesh and the increase in the phenomenon of "sex tourism".[64] Here the lack of women's "choice" in engaging in this economic activity is made particularly clear.

The international dimension to the trade in female flesh is explored by Susanne Kappeler.[65] Kappeler identifies the "male agency" factor which, she argues, underpins all aspects of the international sex trade:

S. KAPPELER
"The International Slave Trade in Women, or, Procurers, Pimps and Punters"[66]

"What appears as a diversity of sub-categories — the white slave trade, the international traffic in women, child prostitution, and the prostitution of boys, etc. — obscures what is the one consistent and unifying factor: the adult male agent of slavery, trafficking and prostitution .... The categorising of practices according to objects screens procurers, pimps — and one should add, punters: the male agents of traffic, slavery and prostitution ...

Slavery, possession and trade are intrinsic to male power (the power of adult males): it is *sexual* slavery not by virtue of the sexual object, but by virtue of the sexual subject: the gendering of power as specifically male, because it is adult men who inhabit that power and because that power defines adult masculinity. It is therefore impossible to separate sexual from non-sexual power and exploitation: powerlessness itself and the object of power and exploitation become gendered female as a result of the gendering of power as male."

This international racket, Kappeler argues, is about much more than the provision of sexual services to tourists. It extends to the recruitment of women from all over the world who are co-opted into sex work and domestic work

---

[63]   A. Dworkin, *ibid.*, p. 177.

[64]   As noted at the beginning of this chapter, the world-wide trade in female flesh is not a purely recent phenomenon. The "white slave trade" was an early form of procuring women for the provision of sexual services overseas. Recent steps have been taken, however, to tackle the increase in trafficking. To this end Art. 6 of the Convention on the Elimination of All Forms of Discrimination Against Women 1979, adopted by the United Nations General Assembly, provides that "State parties shall take all appropriate measures, including legislation, to suppress all forms of traffic in women and exploitation of prostitution of women."

[65]   S. Kappeler, "The International Slave Trade in Women, or, Procurers, Pimps and Punters" (1990) 1 *Law and Critique* 219.

[66]   S. Kappeler, *ibid.*, at 219–220, 224.

"under conditions of unlimited exploitation: bonded marriage and bonded labour — forms of sexual slavery".[67]

S. KAPPELER
"The International Slave Trade in Women, or, Procurers, Pimps and Punters"[68]

"The men in the business of trafficking in women are at least more open than are legislators and ideologues about the continuities of different forms of sexual slavery, from prostitution to marriage: 'Women in Bangkok you have to pay for — for one night, for one week or for your whole life.' You pay for them, but you don't pay them, you pay another man for them. Sex tourism is just another variant of the introduction agency, where the buyers bestir themselves to the market instead of ordering from a mail order catalogue; and they, too, don't really distinguish between the whore for a night and the whore for life. A delighted sex tourist reports from his holiday in the pornographic magazine *Forum*:

> 'The bar-girls were just as enchanting as I had been led to believe. To call them "prostitutes" is to flatter the European practitioners of that trade — really, a new word is needed. What they give is far more than sex — it includes friendship, tenderness, warmth — everything one might hope for from a 'girlfriend', even a rather idealized girlfriend . . .' "

The power of the male agents emphasised in this viewpoint presents a complete picture of female commodification and subordination through the trade in flesh. Kappeler concludes that:

> "the men of East and West, North and South, First and Third World, are bonding harmoniously to build a multinational traffic in women and ensure, by force, economic superiority and through law, the transnational global dominance of men. So that men will be Men and women will be Women, and gendered inequality continue to rule the world."[69]

12.4 Concluding remarks

It may seem unduly pessimistic to end this book with the above quotation. Or so it would be if we were to concede the implications that it contains, *i.e.* that women are powerless in the face of male domination and incapable of resistance. The quotation offers a challenge, a challenge to which this book is a response. Legal constructions of Woman are not automatically premised upon women's status as victims. Women may certainly engage with the legal system in this subject position at some point in their lives, yet this is not likely to be their only interaction with law. Women may be perpetrators of crime

---

[67] S. Kappeler, *ibid.*, at 233.
[68] S. Kappeler, *ibid.*, at 219–220, 233.
[69] S. Kappeler, *ibid.*, at 235.

and interact with the criminal justice system. They may, alternatively, seek legal intervention in order to secure access to services such as medical treatments. They may interact with law in order to avoid medical treatment.

This book, has, we hope, demonstrated that women's engagement with law does not occur in a uniform fashion. Women come to law as mothers (potential and actual) as survivors of sexual and physical violence, and as criminal offenders. They offer up for the scrutiny of the legal system their reproductive bodies, their sexual bodies and their offensive bodies. If this book has offered the possibility of glimpsing pockets of resistance at the juncture of this moment of scrutiny — that is, resistance to male power and agency, to legal discourse and to predominant constructions of women, their bodies and their behaviour — it will have gone some way towards achieving its aim.

INDEX